THE
CAMBRIDGE EDITI[ON]
THE LETTERS AND WORKS [OF]
D. H. LAWRENCE

THE WORKS OF D. H. LAWRENCE

EDITORIAL BOARD

The opening of 'The Fight for Barbara' (1912) in manuscript (Roberts E130a). By courtesy of the Harry Ransom Humanities Research Center, The University of Texas at Austin.

THE PLAYS

D. H. LAWRENCE

EDITED BY
HANS-WILHELM SCHWARZE
AND
JOHN WORTHEN

CAMBRIDGE
UNIVERSITY PRESS

CAMBRIDGE UNIVERSITY PRESS
Cambridge, New York, Melbourne, Madrid, Cape Town,
Singapore, São Paulo, Delhi, Mexico City

Cambridge University Press
The Edinburgh Building, Cambridge CB2 8RU, UK

Published in the United States of America by Cambridge University Press, New York

www.cambridge.org
Information on this title: www.cambridge.org/9780521242776

This, the Cambridge Edition of the text of *The Plays* is established from the
original sources and first published in 1999, © the Estate of Frieda Lawrence
Ravagli 1999. Introduction and notes © Cambridge University Press 1999.
Permission to reproduce this text entire or in part, or to quote from it, can be
granted only by the Literary Executor of the Estate, Laurence Pollinger Ltd,
18 Maddox Street, Mayfair, London WIR OEU. Permission to reproduce the
introduction and notes entire or in part should be requested from Cambridge
University Press. Acknowledgement is made to William Heinemann Ltd in
the UK and the Viking Press in the USA, who hold the exclusive book publication rights for the plays as published (copyright 1914, 1920, 1926, 1936,
1965) in their respective territories, for the authorisation granted to Cambridge
University Press through the Frieda Lawrence Ravagli Estate for use of the
work as published in preparing the new scholarly text.

First published 1999

A catalogue record for this publication is available from the British Library

ISBN 978-0-521-24277-6 Hardback
ISBN 978-0-521-00704-7 Paperback

Cambridge University Press has no responsibility for the persistence or
accuracy of URLs for external or third-party internet websites referred to in
this publication, and does not guarantee that any content on such websites is,
or will remain, accurate or appropriate.

CONTENTS

GENERAL EDITOR'S PREFACE

D. H. Lawrence is one of the great writers of the twentieth century – yet the texts of his writings, whether published during his lifetime or since, are, for the most part, textually corrupt. The extent of the corruption is remarkable; it can derive from every stage of composition and publication. We know from study of his MSS that Lawrence was a careful writer, though not rigidly consistent in matters of minor convention. We know also that he revised at every possible stage. Yet he rarely if ever compared one stage with the previous one, and overlooked the errors of typists or copyists. He was forced to accept, as most authors are, the often stringent house-styling of his printers, which overrode his punctuation and even his sentence-structure and paragraphing. He sometimes overlooked plausible printing errors. More important, as a professional author living by his pen, he had to accept, with more or less good will, stringent editing by a publisher's reader in his early days, and at all times the results of his publishers' timidity. So the fear of Grundyish disapproval, or actual legal action, led to bowdlerisation or censorship from the very beginning of his career. Threats of libel suits produced other changes. Sometimes a publisher made more changes than he admitted to Lawrence. On a number of occasions in dealing with American and British publishers Lawrence produced texts for both which were not identical. Then there were extraordinary lapses like the occasion when a typist turned over two pages of MS at once, and the result happened to make sense. This whole story can be reconstructed from the introductions to the volumes in this edition; cumulatively they will form a history of Lawrence's writing career.

The Cambridge edition aims to provide texts which are as close as can now be determined to those he would have wished to see printed. They have been established by a rigorous collation of extant manuscripts and typescripts, proofs and early printed versions; they restore the words, sentences, even whole pages omitted or falsified by editors or compositors; they are freed from printing-house conventions which were imposed on Lawrence's style; and interference on the part of frightened publishers has been eliminated. Far from doing violence to the texts Lawrence would have wished to see published, editorial intervention is essential to recover them.

Though we have to accept that some cannot now be recovered in their entirety because early states have not survived, we must be glad that so much evidence remains. Paradoxical as it may seem, the outcome of this recension will be texts which differ, often radically and certainly frequently, from those seen by the author himself.

Editors have adopted the principle that the most authoritative form of the text is to be followed, even if this leads sometimes to a 'spoken' or a 'manuscript' rather than a 'printed' style. We have not wanted to strip off one house-styling in order to impose another. Editorial discretion has been allowed in order to regularise Lawrence's sometimes wayward spelling and punctuation in accordance with his most frequent practice in a particular text. A detailed record of these and other decisions on textual matters, together with the evidence on which they are based, will be found in the textual apparatus which records variant readings in manuscripts, typescripts and proofs; and printed variants in forms of the text published in Lawrence's lifetime. We do not record posthumous corruptions, except where first publication was posthumous. Significant MS readings may be found in the occasional explanatory note.

In each volume, the editor's introduction relates the contents to Lawrence's life and to his other writings; it gives the history of composition of the text in some detail, for its intrinsic interest, and because this history is essential to the statement of editorial principles followed. It provides an account of publication and reception which will be found to contain a good deal of hitherto unknown information. Where appropriate, appendixes make available extended draft manuscript readings of significance, or important material, sometimes unpublished, associated with a particular work.

Though Lawrence is a twentieth-century writer and in many respects remains our contemporary, the idiom of his day is not invariably intelligible now, especially to the many readers who are not native speakers of British English. His use of dialect is another difficulty, and further barriers to full understanding are created by now obscure literary, historical, political or other references and allusions. On these occasions explanatory notes are supplied by the editor; it is assumed that the reader has access to a good general dictionary and that the editor need not gloss words or expressions that may be found in it. Where Lawrence's letters are quoted in editorial matter, the reader should assume that his manuscript is alone the source of eccentricities of phrase or spelling.

ACKNOWLEDGEMENTS

We are especially grateful to Michael Black, Andrew Brown and James T. Boulton for their help, comments, criticisms and suggestions. We are enormously indebted to the work which Lindeth Vasey put into this volume over many years. Linda Bree and other staff of Cambridge University Press have been extraordinarily helpful. Bethan Jones kindly allowed us to use her transcriptions of Lawrence's music for *David* as the basis for the music texts printed in this volume. We would also like to thank those who have helped us in the preparation of this edition: those who have given us hospitality, shown great patience in answering queries and offered untiring co-operation: Carl† and Helen Baron, Moina and Tom† Brown, W. H. Clarke, Macdonald Daly, Sam Dawson, Ellen Dunlap, Lothar Fietz, Joan Forrest†, David Garnett†, Andor Gomme†, George and Christopher Harvie, Cathy Henderson, Hilary Hillier, Dorothy Johnston and the staff of the Department of Manuscripts at the University of Nottingham, Dorothy and Norman Karasick, Joan King, Brandon Kinton, Hans-Werner Ludwig, Michael Marland, Katie Mitchell, Frank Muir†, Margaret Needham, David Norton, Denis Pearson, Peter and Barbara Preston, Estelle Rebec, Ian Robinson, Lisa Smith, Russell Stephens, John Turner, Ian Weekley, W. J. West, Elizabeth Worthen, F. M.† and D. G. Worthen, Peter Worthen.

We also wish to record our gratitude to the late George Lazarus for his hospitality and for access to his manuscript collection over many years. We would like to thank Gerald J. Pollinger, and also Bob† and Eileen Forster for advice and assistance; and we are grateful to the following libraries and institutions (together with their librarians and archivists) for making available materials for this edition: Altrincham Garrick Society, the British Library, Nottingham City and County Libraries, the Berg Collection at New York Public Library, Cheshire County Newspapers of Altrincham, Cambridge University Library, the Turnbull Library in Wellington, the Bancroft Library of the University of California at Berkeley, the Library of Dartmouth College, the Library of the University of Nottingham, the Library of the University of New Mexico at Albuquerque, the Library of the University of Salford, the Harry Ransom Humanities Research Center of the University of Texas at Austin, the Library of the University of Tulsa, the Alderman Library of the University of Virginia.

We are grateful to the Universities of Nottingham, Swansea and Tübingen (Vereinigung der Freunde der Universität Tübingen) for support and study leave, and for financial assistance.

Our greatest debt, for their love and help, is to our families: to Gitte Schwarze-Hahn and Cornelia Rumpf-Worthen.

We would, finally, like to acknowledge our own collaboration, which has endured many years of hard work, consultation and shared experience, and has brought to us a renewed fascination with Lawrence's work. H.-W. S. had the responsibility for the texts, Introduction, Explanatory notes, Textual apparatus and Appendixes for *A Collier's Friday Night*, *The Widowing of Mrs. Holroyd*, *The Merry-go-Round*, *The Married Man* and *The Fight for Barbara*; J. W. for the texts, Introduction, Explanatory notes, Textual apparatus and Appendixes for *The Daughter-in-Law*, Preface to *Touch and Go*, *Touch and Go*, *Altitude*, *Noah's Flood* and *David*.

December 1997   H.-W. S. & J. W.

CHRONOLOGY

Note Only stage, radio and television premières, productions in DHL's lifetime and other particularly significant productions are included.

11 September 1885	Born in Eastwood, Nottinghamshire
September 1898–July 1901	Pupil at Nottingham High School
October 1902–1908	Pupil teacher; student at University College, Nottingham
7 December 1907	First publication: 'A Prelude', in *Nottinghamshire Guardian*
October 1908	Appointed as teacher at Davidson Road School, Croydon
November 1909	Publishes five poems in Ford Madox Hueffer's *English Review*
by November 1909	*A Collier's Friday Night* written
by November 1910	*The Widowing of Mrs. Holroyd* written; sent to Violet Hunt and Hueffer
3 December 1910	Engagement to Louie Burrows; broken off on 4 February 1912
November 1910–January 1911	*The Merry-go-Round* written
9 December 1910	Death of his mother, Lydia Lawrence
19 January 1911	*The White Peacock* published (New York); 20 January in London
July 1911	Sends *A Collier's Friday Night* and *The Merry-go-Round* to Hueffer, who sends *The Widowing of Mrs. Holroyd* to Harley Granville-Barker (returned to DHL in August)
4 October 1911	Meets Edward Garnett; sends him *The Widowing of Mrs. Holroyd*
19 November 1911	Ill with pneumonia; resigns his teaching post on 28 February 1912

early March 1912	Meets Frieda Weekley; they leave for Germany on 3 May
25–31 March 1912	Visits George Henry Neville in Bradnop, Staffs.
early April 1912	Hueffer returns *A Collier's Friday Night* and *The Merry-go-Round*; DHL sends them to Garnett
by 23 April 1912	*The Married Man* written
23 May 1912	*The Trespasser* (London)
1 June–5 August 1912	With Frieda Weekley in Icking, near Munich
9 June 1912	Sends 'Paul Morel' to Heinemann
4 July 1912	Sends 'Paul Morel' to Garnett at his request
18 July 1912	Refers to a 'comedy', perhaps first idea for *The Fight for Barbara*
4 August 1912	Has decided to rewrite 'Paul Morel', later *Sons and Lovers*
5 August–*c.* 5 September 1912	On foot and by bus and train to Riva, Italy
17 September 1912– 30 March 1913	At Villa di Gargnano, Lago di Garda, Italy
28–30 October 1912	Writes *The Fight for Barbara*
18 November 1912	Sends *Sons and Lovers* to Duckworth
by mid-January 1913	*The Daughter-in-Law* written and sent to Garnett
by 1 February 1913	*The Merry-go-Round*, *The Married Man* and *The Fight for Barbara* returned to DHL by Garnett
February 1913	*Love Poems and Others* (London)
25 February 1913	Garnett offers *The Widowing of Mrs. Holroyd* to Mitchell Kennerley (accepted in April)
29 May 1913	*Sons and Lovers* (London)
19 June–6 August 1913	In England
7 August 1913–June 1914	In Germany, Switzerland and Italy
August–November 1913	Revises *The Widowing of Mrs. Holroyd* for Kennerley
1 April 1914	*The Widowing of Mrs. Holroyd* (New York); 17 April in London
July 1914–December 1915	In London, Bucks. and Sussex
13 July 1914	Marries Frieda Weekley in London

26 November 1914	*The Prussian Officer and Other Stories* (London)
30 September 1915	*The Rainbow* (London); suppressed by court order on 13 November
30 December 1915– 15 October 1917	In Cornwall
1 June 1916	*Twilight in Italy* (London)
July 1916	*Amores* (London)
26–31 December 1916	Stage première of *The Widowing of Mrs. Holroyd* in Los Angeles
15 October 1917	DHL ordered to leave Cornwall by military authorities
October 1917–May 1918	In London and Hermitage (Berks.)
26 November 1917	*Look! We Have Come Through!* (London)
May 1918–April 1919	Based in Mountain Cottage, Middleton-by-Wirksworth, Derbyshire, with visits to London and Hermitage
22–28 October 1918	Writes *Touch and Go* in Hermitage
October 1918	*New Poems* (London)
April–November 1919	In Hermitage, Newbury and Pangbourne
July 1919	Revises *Touch and Go* in Hermitage; writes 'Preface'
November 1919– February 1922	To Italy, then Capri and Sicily
20 November 1919	*Bay* (London)
9–13 March 1920	*The Widowing of Mrs. Holroyd* staged in Altrincham, near Manchester
May 1920	*Touch and Go* (London); 5 June in New York
9 November 1920	Private publication of *Women in Love* (New York)
25 November 1920	*The Lost Girl* (London)
10 May 1921	*Psychoanalysis and the Unconscious* (New York)
12 December 1921	*Sea and Sardinia* (New York)
March–August 1922	In Ceylon and Australia
14 April 1922	*Aaron's Rod* (New York)
September 1922– March 1923	In New Mexico
23 October 1922	*Fantasia of the Unconscious* (New York)
24 October 1922	*England, My England* (New York)

by 22 March 1923   *The Ladybird, The Fox, The Captain's Doll* (London)

March–November 1923   In Mexico and USA

27 August 1923   *Studies in Classic American Literature* (New York)

13 September 1923   *Kangaroo* (London)

9 October 1923   *Birds, Beasts and Flowers* (New York)

December 1923–March 1924   In England, France and Germany

March 1924–September 1925   In New Mexico and Mexico

19–23 June 1924   In Taos: *Altitude* written

28 August 1924   *The Boy in the Bush* with Mollie Skinner (London)

10 September 1924   Death of his father, John Arthur Lawrence

October 1924   Discusses play project with Ida Rauh

3 March 1925   Sends Ida Rauh outline of *Noah's Flood*

mid-March 1925   *Noah's Flood* started, quickly abandoned

by 25 March 1925   Probably starts to write *David*

29 March–1 April 1925   In Santa Fe, discusses plays with Ida Rauh

6–14 April 1925   Completes scenes I–V of *David*

by 1 May 1925   *David* 'well on: $\frac{2}{3}$ done'

7 May 1925   *David* finished

14 May 1925   *St. Mawr together with The Princess* (London)

17–18 May 1925   DHL reads *David* aloud to Ida Rauh, Frieda and Dorothy Brett

by 18 June 1925   Dorothy Brett finishes typing *David*: copies sent to Curtis Brown to send to theatre managements

July 1925   Frieda starts to translate *David* into German (finished February–March 1926, opening typed by Elsa Weekley)

September 1925–June 1928   In England and, mainly, in Italy

7 December 1925   *Reflections on the Death of a Porcupine* (Philadelphia)

December 1925–January 1926   Revises *David* in first and second proof

21 January 1926   *The Plumed Serpent* (London)

25 March 1926   *David* (London); 23 April in New York

?March 1926–Summer 1927   *Noah's Flood* revised and new text created, then abandoned

May–June 1926   Completes typing and translation of *David* into German

12, 13, 19 December 1926   *The Widowing of Mrs. Holroyd* staged (London)

22, 23 May 1927   Stage première of *David* in London (two scenes cut)

June 1927   *Mornings in Mexico* (London)

24 May 1928   *The Woman Who Rode Away and Other Stories* (London)

June 1928–March 1930   In Switzerland and, principally, in France

June 1928   *Lady Chatterley's Lover* privately published (Florence)

September 1928   *Collected Poems* (London)

July 1929   Exhibition of paintings in London raided by police; *Pansies* (London) manuscript earlier seized in the mail

September 1929   *The Escaped Cock* (Paris)

2 March 1930   Dies at Vence, Alpes Maritimes, France

April–May 1933   Exhibition of manuscripts, typescripts and first editions at the London bookshop of J. and E. Bumpus (including manuscripts of *The Merry-go-Round*, *The Married Man*, *Altitude* and *David*)

July 1933   *The Plays of D. H. Lawrence* (London)

23–28 October 1933   *David* staged in Cambridge (one scene cut)

December 1933   Abridged text of *The Fight for Barbara* (as *Keeping Barbara*) in *Argosy* (London)

June 1934   *A Collier's Friday Night* (London)

26 May 1936   Modified text of *The Daughter-in-Law* (as *My Son's My Son*) staged in London and on tour

October 1936   *Phoenix*, including second version of *Noah's Flood* (London)

Summer 1938   *Altitude* in the *Laughing Horse* (Taos, New Mexico)

22, 25 March 1939   Stage première of *A Collier's Friday Night* in Morley, Yorks.

Autumn 1940   *The Married Man* in *Virginia Quarterly Review*

Winter 1940–1	*The Merry-go-Round* in *Virginia Quarterly Review*
14 September 1953	Radio première of *The Widowing of Mrs. Holroyd* by BBC Home Service
4–6 February 1958	*David* staged in Cambridge (complete text)
23 March 1961	Television première of *The Widowing of Mrs. Holroyd* (shortened text) by ITA
8, 15 August 1965	*A Collier's Friday Night* staged in London
December 1965	*Complete Plays* (London), including *The Daughter-in-Law* and Scene II of *Altitude* (1966 in New York)
14–25 June 1966	*The Widowing of Mrs. Holroyd* staged in Leicester
17 January 1967	Stage première of *The Daughter-in-Law* in Edinburgh (later in London and Sheffield)
31 March 1967	Radio première of *The Daughter-in-Law* by BBC Third Programme
9 August 1967	Stage première of *The Fight for Barbara* (shortened text) in London (New York in 1978)
29 February–4 May 1968	London season of three 'colliery plays', *A Collier's Friday Night*, *The Daughter-in-Law*, *The Widowing of Mrs. Holroyd*
16 August 1971	Radio première of *A Collier's Friday Night* by BBC Radio 4
6 October 1973	Stage première of *Touch and Go* in Ealing, near London
7 November 1973	Stage première of *The Merry-go-Round* in London (until 9 December)
8 May 1974	*The Widowing of Mrs. Holroyd* televised by PBS (USA)
30 September 1976	Television première of *A Collier's Friday Night* (BBC 1) (Part I, 30 September; Part II, 7 October)
5–7, 10–11 November 1979	*Touch and Go* staged in Oxford and London
25 August 1985	Television première of *The Daughter-in-Law* by BBC 1
16 December 1991	Radio première of *The Fight for Barbara* (shortened text) by BBC Radio 4

CUE-TITLES

A. Manuscript locations

BL	British Library
NCL	Nottingham County Libraries
NYPL	New York Public Library
NZNL	National Library of New Zealand
UCB	University of California at Berkeley
UN	University of Nottingham
UNM	University of New Mexico
USal	University of Salford
UT	University of Texas at Austin
UTul	University of Tulsa
UV	University of Virginia

B. Printed works

(The place of publication, here and throughout, is London unless otherwise stated.)

Complete Plays	D. H. Lawrence. *The Complete Plays of D. H. Lawrence*. Heinemann, 1965.
Early Years	John Worthen. *D. H. Lawrence: The Early Years 1885–1912*. Cambridge: Cambridge University Press, 1991.
E.T.	E. T. [Jessie Chambers]. *D. H. Lawrence: A Personal Record*. Cape, 1935.
Hardy	D. H. Lawrence. *Study of Thomas Hardy and Other Essays*. Ed. Bruce Steele. Cambridge: Cambridge University Press, 1985.
KJB	*The Holy Bible Containing the Old and New Testaments (Authorised King James Version)*.
Letters, i.	James T. Boulton, ed. *The Letters of D. H. Lawrence*. Volume I. Cambridge: Cambridge University Press, 1979.

Letters, ii.	George J. Zytaruk and James T. Boulton, eds. *The Letters of D. H. Lawrence.* Volume II. Cambridge: Cambridge University Press, 1981.
Letters, iii.	James T. Boulton and Andrew Robertson, eds. *The Letters of D. H. Lawrence.* Volume III. Cambridge: Cambridge University Press, 1984.
Letters, iv.	Warren Roberts, James T. Boulton and Elizabeth Mansfield, eds. *The Letters of D. H. Lawrence.* Volume IV. Cambridge: Cambridge University Press, 1987.
Letters, v.	James T. Boulton and Lindeth Vasey, eds. *The Letters of D. H. Lawrence.* Volume V. Cambridge: Cambridge University Press, 1989.
Letters, vi.	James T. Boulton and Margaret H. Boulton, with Gerald M. Lacy, eds. *The Letters of D. H. Lawrence.* Volume VI. Cambridge: Cambridge University Press, 1991.
Letters, vii.	Keith Sagar and James T. Boulton, eds. *The Letters of D. H. Lawrence.* Volume VII. Cambridge: Cambridge University Press, 1993.
Memoirs	*Frieda Lawrence: Memoirs and Correspondence.* Ed. E. W. Tedlock. Heinemann, 1961.
Nehls	Edward Nehls, ed. *D. H. Lawrence: A Composite Biography.* 3 volumes. Madison: University of Wisconsin Press, 1957–9.
"Not I, But the Wind ..."	Frieda Lawrence. *"Not I, But the Wind ..."* Santa Fe: Rydal Press, 1934.
OED2	*The Oxford English Dictionary.* 2nd edn. Prepared by J. A. Simpson and E. S. C. Weiner. 10 volumes. Oxford: Clarendon Press, 1989.
Plays	D. H. Lawrence. *The Plays of D. H. Lawrence.* Martin Secker, 1933.
Roberts	Warren Roberts. *A Bibliography of D. H. Lawrence.* 2nd edn. Cambridge: Cambridge University Press, 1982.
Sagar	Keith Sagar, ed. *A D. H. Lawrence Handbook.* Manchester: Manchester University Press, 1982.

Storer | Ronald W. Storer. *Some Aspects of Brinsley Colliery and the Lawrence Connection*. Selston, 1985.

Tedlock | E. W. Tedlock. *The Frieda Lawrence Collection of D. H. Lawrence Manuscripts: A Descriptive Bibliography*. Albuquerque: University of New Mexico Press, 1948.

WL | D. H. Lawrence. *Women in Love*. Ed. David Farmer, Lindeth Vasey and John Worthen. Cambridge: Cambridge University Press, 1987.

INTRODUCTION

INTRODUCTION

D. H. Lawrence the playwright

D. H. Lawrence began writing plays early in his career, and finished six of them (*A Collier's Friday Night, The Widowing of Mrs. Holroyd, The Merry-go-Round, The Married Man, The Fight for Barbara, The Daughter-in-Law*) between late 1909 and early 1913 – the period when he was establishing himself as a writer. He then did not create a play for five years, when he wrote *Touch and Go*; then there was a gap of five years before he tried again. By 1926 he had completed another play (*David*) and had two play fragments (*Altitude, Noah's Flood*) on his hands; but no more than three of his eight full-length plays were even published in his lifetime, and only two were performed (both of them in amateur or small-scale professional productions). He never saw a play of his own on the stage.[1]

He recognised early on, however, that getting his work performed depended as much on the theatre's readiness to accept the kind of plays he was writing as on finding a company willing to stage them. At the start of his career, as an inexperienced dramatist with no knowledge of theatre

---

[1] The plays, the dates of their composition, first performance and first single and collected or reprinted publication, are as follows:

A Collier's Friday Night (written 1909; perf. 1939): published 1934, repr. *Complete Plays*

The Widowing of Mrs. Holroyd (written 1910, revised 1913; perf. 1916): published 1914, repr. *Plays* and *Complete Plays*

The Merry-go-Round (written 1910–11; perf. 1973): published 1941 (*Virginia Quarterly Review*), repr. *Complete Plays*

The Married Man (written 1912; unperf.): published 1940 (*Virginia Quarterly Review*), repr. *Complete Plays*

The Fight for Barbara (written 1912; perf. 1967): published 1933 as *Keeping Barbara* (*Argosy*), repr. *Complete Plays* (both in a shortened version)

The Daughter-in-Law (written 1913; perf. 1967): published *Complete Plays*

Touch and Go (written 1918, revised 1919; perf. 1973): published 1920, repr. *Plays* and *Complete Plays*

Altitude (fragment, written 1924; unperf.): Scene I published 1938 (*Laughing Horse*), Scenes I and II published *Complete Plays*

Noah's Flood (fragment, written 1925, revised 1926–7; unperf.): published *Phoenix: The Posthumous Papers of D. H. Lawrence*, ed. Edward D. McDonald (New York, 1936), repr. *Complete Plays*

David (written 1925; perf. 1927): published 1926, repr. *Plays* and *Complete Plays*

practice, he regularly expressed his willingness to revise his work to suit a prospective producer or company. Early in 1913 he remarked, rather more aggressively: 'I believe that, just as an audience was found in Russia for Tchekhov, so an audience might be found in England for some of my stuff, if there were a man to whip 'em in. It's the producer that is lacking, not the audience.'[2] But few producers who read his work were inclined to accept it; the book publication of his plays did little to promote their performance; and this situation did not essentially change until the 1960s. Interest in Lawrence from the 1930s onwards concentrated on the better-known prose works, his letters and his life as reflected in biographies and memoirs, while literary historians and critics generally disregarded his plays. Ignorance of his dramatic work was not helped by what is arguably his best play, *The Daughter-in-Law*, remaining unpublished until 1965 in the first complete edition of his plays.

Public awareness of Lawrence's plays began with productions for radio, television and the theatre in Britain during the 1960s. The renaissance of interest in his writings during the late 1940s and 1950s had established him as a major modern author; and his early plays, in particular, turned out to fit the changed – and increasingly naturalistic – environment of stage and television provoked by the British theatrical revival of the 1950s and 1960s. Ordinary people – especially the working class – were increasingly being shown in day-to-day situations; and Lawrence's plays have a richness of expression in dialogue and are characterised by a lively vernacular which can, if necessary, sustain silences in which words unspoken can be 'heard'.

In 1953, *The Widowing of Mrs. Holroyd* was Lawrence's first play to be broadcast on British radio (it aroused little interest in the one critic known to have reviewed it); but in 1961, heavily cut, it was the first Lawrence play on television.[3] Interest was beginning to stir; in the summer of 1965, two Sunday-night performances of *A Collier's Friday Night* on the London stage received favourable attention from critics and directors,[4] and at the end of the year all Lawrence's plays were finally published in *Complete Plays*.[5]

---

[2] *Letters*, i. 509. (Subsequent references to *Letters* volumes are given in brackets in the text.)

[3] 14 September 1953, BBC Home Service; Granada Television production, 23 March 1961.

[4] The English Stage Society at the Royal Court Theatre, London, in a production without décor, directed by Peter Gill, 8 and 15 August 1965: see below, pp. c–ci.

[5] *Complete Plays* stated that 'In several cases alternative drafts of the plays in this volume exist in manuscript form, but the versions here printed are regarded as being the most complete' (p. [6]). However, the heavily cut 1933 version of *The Fight for Barbara* was printed. The volume also contained erroneous information about the dates of writing or revision of four of the ten plays (*The Merry-go-Round, The Married Man, The Daughter-in-Law, Touch and Go*).

Ironically, television returned to his work as a source of drama in 1966 and 1967, but not to his plays: thirteen short stories were adapted into eleven one-hour plays, and were enthusiastically acclaimed by audiences and critics alike for the realism of their dialogue and their naturally dramatic form.[6] The time for the discovery of his stage work had finally come. *The Daughter-in-Law* and *The Fight for Barbara* were staged for the first time in 1967, and in 1968 the London season of *A Collier's Friday Night*, *The Daughter-in-Law* and *The Widowing of Mrs. Holroyd* left him with an established reputation as a playwright.[7] Cheap editions of these last three helped create a new and growing reading public, and the late 1960s also saw the start of critical discussion of all the plays. *A Collier's Friday Night*, *The Daughter-in-Law* and *The Widowing of Mrs. Holroyd* have since established themselves as part of the theatre's repertory, and a television production can now draw an audience counted in millions, even outside Britain.[8]

Writing, publication, performance and reception 1909–27

1909–12. *A Collier's Friday Night*, *The Widowing of Mrs. Holroyd*, *The Merry-go-Round* and *The Married Man* written

The extant autograph manuscript of Lawrence's first play, *A Collier's Friday Night*,[9] most probably dates from November 1909, when (with the encouragement of Ford Madox Hueffer[10]) he was using the setting of a Midlands colliery family for the first time in his work; he wrote, for example, the first drafts of the short story 'Odour of Chrysanthemums' that same autumn. Lawrence showed the play to his friend Jessie Chambers when she visited him in Croydon on 27 November 1909; she remembered 'a play that was about his home on a Friday night. Sitting there in the tiny suburban room, it troubled me deeply to see his home put before me in his vivid phrases.' 'It's very true', she remembered saying of

---

[6] Granada Television productions, broadcast in January and February 1966 and in June 1967. An advertisement claimed that DHL 'wrote television plays before television was invented ... some of his short stories are perfect television material' (*The Times*, 7 June 1967, p. 8).

[7] The three plays were in repertory at the Royal Court Theatre from February to May, in Peter Gill's productions: see below, pp. cv–cvii.

[8] The BBC's *The Daughter-in-Law* in 1985 attracted about 6 million viewers, while a German ZDF television broadcast of the play in 1974 reached about 8 million.

[9] Roberts numbers and locations of manuscripts, typescripts, etc. of the plays in this volume are given in the section 'Texts', pp. cxi–cxxiv.

[10] Later Ford Madox Ford, novelist and editor (1873–1939), edited the *English Review* from December 1908; responsible for DHL's first poems in print (1909) and gave him a great deal of advice about writing and publishing. See *Letters* i. 137–8, and *Early Years* 214–18.

it.[11] She took the manuscript home and probably returned it to Lawrence during the Christmas holidays.

However, as some details draw upon events dating from November 1906, it has been argued that he may have composed a version before 1909.[12] For example, the character close to Lawrence himself, Ernest Lambert, is twenty-one and at college, exactly as Lawrence was in 1906, and a note pencilled in at the top of the first page of the manuscript (probably added in April 1912) announces: 'This was written when I was twenty-one + almost before I'd done anything. It's most horribly green. DHL'. But, thinking of the play as apprentice work, Lawrence had every inclination to push its composition back in time. There is no reference to the play in his correspondence or the memoirs of others before 1909, while Jessie Chambers stated that 'He certainly wrote it that autumn',[13] and the manuscript contains evidence also dating it to 1909. There are references to Lawrence's poem 'A Life History in Harmonies and Discords' written late in 1909, to the death of Swinburne in April 1909 and to the imminent first Christmas for Lawrence's niece, Margaret King, born 9 February 1909.[14] The manuscript as we now have it was certainly written in 1909, with the play drawing on events dating from 1906 and 1909.[15]

There is no evidence that Lawrence ever worked on *A Collier's Friday Night* again; he left the manuscript (together with others) with his friend and mentor, Edward Garnett, when he went abroad in May 1912.[16] He had, however, returned to the setting and some of the issues of the play while writing his third novel, 'Paul Morel' (which eventually became *Sons and Lovers*). Almost half of chapter VIII of the draft written between

---

[11] E.T. 166. Jessie Chambers (1887–1944) was DHL's intimate friend until 1912.

[12] See, e.g., Keith Sagar, *D. H. Lawrence: A Calendar of his Works* (Manchester, 1979), p. 5.

[13] See 'The Collected Letters of Jessie Chambers', ed. George J. Zytaruk, *D. H. Lawrence Review*, xii (1979), 105.

[14] See Explanatory notes on 29:32, 18:2 and 25:23. For what survives of 'A Life History', see *Early Years* 495–9. It is almost certain that DHL also showed Helen Corke (1882–1978) *A Collier's Friday Night* in the autumn of 1909. She was a fellow teacher in Croydon. Her own autobiographical play, 'The Way of Silence' (UTul), was written during the winter of 1909–10; it is close to DHL's work in setting, stage directions, characters and dialogue; one of its characters is based on DHL, and its action runs from early March 1909 to a week before Christmas 1909.

[15] Cf. Jessie Chambers's comment on the bread-burning scene which features in both *A Collier's Friday Night* and *Sons and Lovers*: 'an interesting example of the way Lawrence would take several incidents happening at different times and even with different people and compress them into one scene of greatly heightened significance' ('The Collected Letters of Jessie Chambers', ed. Zytaruk, p. 74).

[16] Critic, essayist and playwright (1868–1937), reader for the firm of Duckworth; from August 1911 to mid 1914 he advised and helped DHL.

February and March 1912 ('Strife in Love' in the published version) deals with similar incidents on a Friday night in the Morel family; there are also similarities with the play's dialogue, though it seems extremely unlikely that Lawrence actually referred to the manuscript of the play.[17] His radically new use of the material early in 1912, however, helps explain why, a month or so later, he might have considered the play 'most horribly green'.

The writing of Lawrence's second play, *The Widowing of Mrs. Holroyd*, also falls into the period 1909–10; it was finished by 9 November 1910, when he offered to send it to a friend to read,[18] but may well have been completed by October, before he started the first version of 'Paul Morel'. The play's closeness in subject matter, selection of characters and atmosphere to 'Odour of Chrysanthemums' is, however, so striking that the play's origins may be directly linked to the first version of the story, which Lawrence sent to Hueffer on 9 December 1909 and which he had extensively revised by March 1910.[19] The play was yet another of those works about the Midlands which Hueffer had been encouraging Lawrence to write; not surprisingly, Hueffer had first access to it, in November 1910.

We know when and where Lawrence began his third play, *The Merry-go-Round*: 'in the interminable watches of the bedroom' during late November and early December 1910, when his mother was fatally ill and he had gone back to Eastwood to be with her (i. 200, 189). She died on 9 December. The play was still under way four days later (i. 200); it may have been finished early in 1911.[20] When Lawrence wrote it, he was determined that

---

[17] See *Sons and Lovers* ed. Helen Baron and Carl Baron (Cambridge, 1992), 234:22–254:20; originally pp. 272–81 in the Spring 1912 version (surviving in Roberts E373e, pp. 295–304). The section was identified by Helen Baron in her article '*Sons and Lovers*: The Surviving Manuscripts from Three Drafts Dated by Paper Analysis', *Studies in Bibliography*, xxxviii (1985), 302–3.

[18] *Letters*, i. 186, 188 and n. 1, 199 and n. 3. Grace Lovat Fraser (née Crawford), a London friend, saw one of DHL's plays and wrongly remembered him sending her *A Collier's Friday Night* (in her memoir *In the Days of My Youth*, 1970, p. 150); it is clear from *Letters*, i. 199–200, that the play DHL had sent her in November 1910 was *The Widowing of Mrs. Holroyd*. It is also possible that the poem 'Nils Lykke Dead' (later 'A Man Who Died'), which DHL added to his poetry notebook sometime in the autumn of 1910 (Roberts E320.1: see *Early Years* 486), coincided with the writing of the play: it takes the form of a dramatic monologue spoken by a woman over the dead body of her husband.

[19] *Letters*, i. 147 and n. 2. DHL made the plot more conventionally dramatic in the play: the short story has no lover for the wife, or female acquaintances for the husband, and the husband appears only when dead. See too Explanatory note on 61:12; *Letters*, i. 199 and v. 593; and *The Prussian Officer and Other Stories*, ed. John Worthen (Cambridge, 1983), p. 272, Explanatory note on 181:1.

[20] See Explanatory notes on 111:18, 116:25 and *Letters* i. 252, 269, 242 and n. 2, 245, 247, 259.

it '*shall* be playable. It is high comedy. When things get too intolerably tragic one flies to comedy, or at least romance – and is cured, I hope, of heavy heroics and Jeremiahishness' (i. 200).

The main problem for Lawrence as a young playwright was what to do with his plays once they were written. He had – after all – still seen very little of his writing in print. Violet Hunt (Hueffer's companion of many years) – and probably Hueffer – read *The Widowing of Mrs. Holroyd* in November 1910,[21] and Lawrence sent Hueffer *A Collier's Friday Night* and *The Merry-go-Round* shortly before the end of July 1911 (i. 309). By then, Lawrence was making every possible effort to establish himself as a full-time writer, so that he could give up school-teaching; he clearly hoped to remind Hueffer of the one play he already had, and to get him to use his contacts with the theatrical world. The ploy succeeded; Hueffer sent *The Widowing of Mrs. Holroyd* to Harley Granville-Barker.[22] There could hardly have been a more exciting development for Lawrence as a dramatist. But by the end of August, he had 'had back the play that Hueffer had sent to Granville-Barker – with a "read it with much interest but afraid I don't want it" note' (i. 298); nothing further is known about Granville-Barker's opinion.

Lawrence then tried to develop his dramatic career in other directions. He decided to try for publication, and in October 1911 sent *The Widowing of Mrs. Holroyd* to Garnett (i. 309), who was just starting to help get Lawrence's work into print. Garnett – a published and performed playwright (he gave Lawrence his own two published plays, *The Breaking Point* and *The Feud*) – was impressed enough to suggest the possibility of a volume of plays, just as he suggested a volume of poems (i. 309–10, 316). Unfortunately, Hueffer had mislaid the other two plays and could not find them for many months (i. 309, 311, 317, 323) – something which left Lawrence particularly anxious, as they existed only in manuscript. There could be no further discussion of a volume while they remained lost.

The literary career towards which Lawrence had been slowly working during 1911 was both disrupted and transformed between September 1911 and March 1912. Edward Garnett had done more than anyone else to convince Lawrence not just that he was a good writer, but that he should

---

[21] *Letters*, i. 199. In her memoirs, Violet Hunt (1866–1942), biographer and novelist, wrongly recollected that, in the autumn of 1910, DHL sent her three plays: see *The Flurried Years* (1926), pp. 150–1. In fact he sent only *The Widowing of Mrs. Holroyd* in November 1910 (*Letters*, i. 199).

[22] Playwright, producer and theatrical authority (1877–1946): see too footnote 35.

devote himself to his writing. Then came Lawrence's serious illness of November 1911, which meant that he had to abandon school-teaching more abruptly than he had intended. Finally, some time early in March 1912, he met Frieda Weekley, married to the Professor of Modern Languages at University College, Nottingham, and mother of three children.[23] Very shortly afterwards, Lawrence and Frieda started the affair which led to their going away together to Germany at the beginning of May. At just the same time, however, Lawrence heard that George Henry Neville – 'my very old friend, the Don Juanish fellow' – had clandestinely married in November 1911 and that his wife had recently had a son (i. 373 and n. 4). Neville, one of Lawrence's closest male friends during their adolescence and College years,[24] was now a head-teacher in North Staffordshire, while his wife and child stayed in Stourbridge. Lawrence went to visit Neville in Bradnop from 25 to 31 March 1912 (i. 377, 379). Soon after returning home he combined elements of his own and of Neville's current situation into *The Married Man*, a play containing fictional portrayals of himself, Neville and Frieda Weekley.[25] He finished it by 23 April, and referred to it as 'a comedy – middling good' (i. 386).

This sudden creation of a new play was probably also influenced by a development for which Garnett was responsible. Ten days before going away to see Neville, Lawrence had heard that his missing plays had turned up – 'The things were at the Authors' club all the while' (i. 376) – and Violet Hunt forwarded them to Eastwood on 5 April (i. 381). Lawrence re-addressed them to Garnett the same day, probably adding the pencilled note on the first page of *A Collier's Friday Night*. Garnett read them immediately, was impressed and sent one of them to Ben Iden Payne.[26] We cannot be certain which play was sent, but probably not *The Merry-go-Round*: Lawrence's subsequent reference to 'the little play' (i. 386) suggests that it may have been *A Collier's Friday Night*, or – given what we know about Garnett's later admiration for it – the relatively short *Widowing of Mrs. Holroyd*. Lawrence was thoroughly enthusiastic about the idea, which he heard of before 17 April: Payne was not only the country's foremost

---

[23] See Explanatory note on 237:9 and *Early Years* 562–3.

[24] See Neville's *A Memoir of D. H. Lawrence (The Betrayal)*, ed. Carl Baron (Cambridge, 1981), pp. 26–31; see too Explanatory note on 191:14.

[25] Sometime between 1912 and 1933, the manuscript lost its first five pages (including the title-page); see pp. cxiii–cxiv below. DHL returned to Neville and his amatory exploits in part 1 of *Mr Noon*: see *Mr Noon*, ed. Lindeth Vasey (Cambridge, 1984), Explanatory note on 7:18.

[26] Actor, producer and director (1881–1976): he moulded the first true British repertory theatre in Manchester at Miss Horniman's Gaiety Theatre (1907–11).

exponent of the Manchester School of theatrical realism, but had produced
Garnett's play *The Feud* in Manchester, and he and Garnett were currently
planning the production of Garnett's adaptation of Fernando de Rojas's *La
Celestina* (1499), which would be staged as *The Spanish Lovers* at London's
Little Theatre on 22 May 1912. Lawrence wrote to Garnett:

> It is huge to think of Iden Payne acting me on the stage: you are like a genius of
> Arabian Nights, to get me through. Of course I will alter and improve whatever I
> can, and Mr Payne has fullest liberty to do entirely as he pleases with the play –
> you know that. And of course I don't expect to get money by it. But it's ripping to
> think of my being acted.   (i. 384)

It was in this expectant mood that he wrote his comedy, *The Married Man*;
there was some point in writing plays if productions of them might result.
On 9 April, too, he had been given a copy of Chekhov's plays *The Seagull*
and *The Cherry Orchard* (i. 382, 385 and n. 3) – which he read at once –
and they would have helped focus his mind upon the theatre.

A meeting with Payne in London was arranged for 25 April but, two
days before they met, Lawrence wrote to Garnett: 'I should think it
wouldn't matter, would it, if I weren't in London when the little play was
performed? And I wanted to see it, but as things are, I want to go to
Germany more'.[27] Going away with Frieda Weekley was more important. A
production was not, anyway, as likely a prospect as he believed. He met the
producer at the Managers' Club in Wardour Street (i. 386–7), but Payne –
rather than discussing a production – offered to mark up the manuscript
with suggestions for changes. A week later Payne returned the play without
any specific suggestions: 'He rather amuses me – He was going to show me
what he wanted altering, but now says I know what wants doing without his
troubling. So I do' (i. 389). The manuscripts of *A Collier's Friday Night* and
The Merry-go-Round show no sign of the kinds of revision Lawrence might
have been expected to make in response to Payne's suggestions, however,
while the manuscript of *The Widowing of Mrs. Holroyd* has been lost. It
seems likely that Payne had not been encouraging enough about the play's
chances to make it seem worth Lawrence's while to start work on it again –
particularly when he had more pressing things on his mind.

Garnett's relationship with Payne might have launched Lawrence as a
playwright, just as Hueffer's relationship with Granville-Barker might
have done. But Payne, although interested in new plays, was turning away

---

[27] *Letters*, i. 386. DHL did not apparently express much more interest when, during his last
meeting with Jessie Chambers (on 21 April), 'he spoke of a play that was perhaps going to
be produced in London' (E.T. 215).

from the realism of the Manchester school. He would soon be invited to America and would consequently dissolve his acting companies.[28] Lawrence's work had come to his attention too late. As it was, Lawrence simply left the manuscripts of his four plays – like all the other manuscripts he had no immediate prospect of publishing – in Garnett's keeping; and went to Germany with Frieda on 3 May 1912.[29]

1912–16. *The Fight for Barbara* and *The Daughter-in-Law* written; *The Widowing of Mrs. Holroyd* published and performed

Lawrence and Frieda lived in Bavaria from the end of May to the start of August 1912; it was there that he finished the third version of 'Paul Morel', and (in June) sent the manuscript to the publisher Heinemann, who rejected it. Garnett, however, once again came to the rescue: he read it, for Duckworth, and returned it to Lawrence with comments so that the latter could write it 'over again' that summer and autumn (i. 427, 431). Lawrence first mentioned his next play ('I am amusing myself writing a comedy', i. 427 and n. 1) to Garnett on 18 July, just as the latter was returning the manuscript of 'Paul Morel'. As Lawrence had left his other four plays with Garnett, he must have been working on a new play altogether – if he was indeed writing drama rather than fiction. But 'Paul Morel', which would earn him the kind of money he badly needed to support Frieda and himself, took priority; he seems to have abandoned the 'comedy' immediately.

We can, however, guess what may have been in it, because in October a 'comedy' which he did write, *The Fight for Barbara*, recreated his early relationship with Frieda and her relatives; the work started in July may well have used similar material. In the interim, Lawrence and Frieda had crossed the Alps on foot and in September had settled in Italy beside the Lago di Garda, at Villa di Gargnano, in a house called the Villa Igea;[30] and *The Fight for Barbara* draws upon incidents which had happened in Bavaria at the end of July and the start of August, and in Italy during September and October. It also used the Villa Igea as its setting. If any of his comedy sketch had actually survived from July, it would have had to have been completely rewritten, or at least substantially added to.

[28] B. I. Payne, *A Life in a Wooden O: Memoirs of the Theatre* (New Haven, Conn., 1977), pp. 114–16.

[29] Garnett's son, David, donated the manuscript of *A Collier's Friday Night* to UNM to help raise money for their DHL Fellowship Fund; by April 1960 it had been purchased by UT.

[30] They lived in a flat there from 18 September 1912 to 30 March 1913; see *Letters*, i. 453, 456–8, 535. See, too, Explanatory note on 239:6.

The *Fight for Barbara* manuscript was written between 28 and 30 October, in a break from revising 'Paul Morel'. Lawrence wrote it very fast indeed (i. 466) but he still had time to make some extensive interlinear revisions to the manuscript in the early parts.[31] Full of enthusiasm, he sent it to Garnett at once:

> I've written the Comedy I send you by this post in the last three days, as a sort of interlude to Paul Morel ... This comedy will amuse you fearfully – much of it is word for word true – it will interest you. I think it's good. Frieda makes me send it you straight away. She says I have gilded myself beyond recognition, and put her in rags. I leave it to the world and to you to judge.   (i. 466)

Frieda, too, contributed to that letter, as she regularly did (she had also added a few words to the manuscript of the play). It was the autobiographical quality which she, too, stressed:

> I hope you will like the play, it's all of it really lived, Ernst's very words and me, though I dont like myself; L[awrence] makes himself out the strong, silent man, it is'nt fair, authors can have it all their own way; he is'nt half so nice or steady or easy, but I must say he is like the English in the bull-dog quality of hanging on ... (i. 467)

As she told another friend,

> I was cross with L[awrence] about the play, he makes himself the 'strong, silent man', the *wretch*, he *did* hang on to me, but not quite so unflinchingly and I did *not* wobble [Lawrence adds: (?)] so; he wrote the play when he was in a rage with me! [Lawrence interjects: (No no!!)] So there, but I think it *is* a good play!   (i. 476)

The details of her life with Lawrence which had provided so much of the play's raw material remained clear in her mind more than twenty years later, when she noted:

> The 'Fight for Barbara' was written in the winter of 1912 at the Villa [Igea] ... The setting is the setting of the villa, the kitchen with its copperpans is the kitchen of the Villa Igea, the postman at the door, the pretty girl with the milk and the butcher are real. But of course some of the characters are not real people – My sister found the play at her house in the Isartal after Lawrence's death ... I cannot see it detachedly enough to be able to judge its value as a work of art, to me it is a record of those vivid hours with Lawrence full of hope and gaiety on the Lago di Garda in 1912 –[32]

By 19 November, Lawrence had, however, heard from Garnett that he did not think much of it. Lawrence reacted with a certain deference – he

---

[31] Originally, Barbara had been unmarried, having left her fiancé a week before the wedding (see Explanatory note on 245:1), but in the revisions she has been married for three years before she elopes.

[32] Frieda Lawrence to Nancy Pearn, undated [?1933], from Kiowa Ranch, New Mexico (UN). Annie ('Nancy') Ross Pearn (1892–1950) was manager of the Magazine Department of Curtis Brown (London) and later worked at the Laurence Pollinger literary agency in

had just sent Garnett the manuscript of *Sons and Lovers* (as 'Paul Morel' had now become) and badly needed Garnett's approval. 'As for the "Fight for Barbara" – I don't know much about plays. If ever you have time, you might tell me where you find fault with the "Fight for Barbara" ... You think it couldn't be any use for the stage?' Lawrence also asked Garnett to return *The Married Man* and *The Merry-go-Round* so that he might start 'recasting and re-forming them' (i. 477). 'Re-forming' was a word especially directed at Garnett: it referred to a long-standing disagreement between them. Lawrence had insisted earlier in the same letter, even before Garnett had criticised the novel, that *Sons and Lovers* 'has got form – *form*' (i. 476). He obviously suspected that 'form' was what Garnett had found lacking in his plays, too; but he still had faith in his own ability to write them.

He showed this faith – and his undiminished fascination with the theatre – only ten weeks after finishing *The Fight for Barbara*. It had been an exceptional year, even for a regular play-goer like himself. He and Frieda had seen Shaw's *Man and Superman* in Nottingham in April 1912, a passion-play in Bavaria at the end of May (i. 411) and Ibsen's *Ghosts* in Munich during the summer of 1912. They had probably gone to the theatre in Bad Tölz during their journey from Bavaria to Italy; and late in November or early in December they had seen Verdi's *Rigoletto* in Saló, at the southern end of the Lago di Garda. Then, to crown it all, in December the Compagnia Drammatica Italiana Adelia Di Giacomo Tadini – a touring troupe of actors – had come to the theatre in Gargnano with a whole repertoire of plays. On 28 December, Lawrence saw their version of *Ghosts* (very different from that in Munich), D'Annunzio's play *The Light under the Bushel* on 6 January and Silvio Zambaldi's comedy *The Wife of the Doctor* on the 9th – and almost certainly wrote his sixth play, *The Daughter-in-Law*, during the first twelve days of January 1913. Four days after finishing his own play, he would see *Hamlet* – as *Amleto*.[33] The concentrated experiences of theatre during the year must have helped him focus his new work theatrically. His single reference to it in his surviving correspondence came on 12 January 1913, when he told Garnett:

I am going to send you a new play I have written. It is neither a comedy nor a tragedy – just ordinary. It is quite objective, as far as that term goes, and though no

London; the letter was probably written in mid-1933 during negotiations to get the play published. Frieda's sister was Else Jaffe (1874–1973): see below, p. xci, for another account by Frieda, placing the play's discovery in Munich.

[33] *Twilight in Italy and other Essays*, ed. Paul Eggert (Cambridge, 1994), pp. xxv–xxvi and 74:36 – 80:23; *Mr Noon*, ed. Vasey, 241:5–6; *Early Years* 458.

doubt, like most of my stuff, it wants weeding out a bit, yet I think the whole thing is there, laid out properly, planned and progressive. If you don't think so, I am disappointed.

I enjoy so much writing my plays – they come so quick and exciting from the pen – that you mustn't growl at me if you think them waste of time. At any rate, they'll be stuff for shaping later on, when I'm more of a workman. And I look at the future, and it behoves me to keep on trying to earn money somehow. (i. 500–1)

The context in which that letter was written helps explain Lawrence's caution. Garnett's reaction to *Sons and Lovers* – just as Lawrence feared – had been that it was still far too long and shapeless, and that it would have to be cut. He had undertaken the job himself. Lawrence had been dismayed at Garnett's reaction to the novel: 'I sit in sadness and grief after your letter. I daren't say anything. All right, take out what you think necessary' (i. 481). He was now being very careful about the play.

The other context significant for Lawrence's writing of *The Daughter-in-Law* was his precarious financial situation. What he earned by his writing was all that he and Frieda had to live on, one of the reasons why speedy publication of *Sons and Lovers* was so important. Garnett's revisions would, however, delay the novel until 29 May 1913 – and Lawrence knew that 'it behoves me to keep on trying to earn money somehow'. Even in a place as inexpensive as Villa di Gargnano (Italy's cheapness had been the original motive he and Frieda had had for going there), he remained scared – as he went on in his letter of 12 January to Garnett – 'of having no money at all ... I must see to the money part. I *do* think this play might have a chance on the stage' (i. 501). The last two remarks are connected; Lawrence was not the only writer of his period to be attracted by the idea of the money which a successful play could earn.

He must have sent the manuscript of *The Daughter-in-Law* to Garnett shortly after writing this letter. His next surviving letter to Garnett, of 1 February,[34] begins by thanking him for sending *The Merry-go-Round* and *The Married Man*, together with *The Fight for Barbara*, all of which he had asked to be returned back in November, for possible revision and reworking. We therefore do not know what Garnett's reaction to *The Daughter-in-Law* had been.[35] In his letter of 1 February, however,

---

[34] Any other letters he may have written to Garnett during the previous fortnight are lost: there exists only a postcard of 20 January.

[35] DHL's 20 January remark – 'I am glad you think my prospects so good' (i. 507) – cannot relate to Garnett's reaction to the play (which he would not have had time to read) but to *Sons and Lovers*. DHL did not ask for *A Collier's Friday Night* or *The Widowing of Mrs. Holroyd*; he believed either that he could do no more with them, or (more likely) that –

Lawrence made one of his very rare statements about contemporary British theatre, and how his work might fit into it.

I'm sure we are sick of the rather bony, bloodless drama we get nowadays – it is time for a reaction against Shaw and Galsworthy and [Granville-]Barker and Irishy (except Synge) people – the rule and measure mathematical folk. But you are of them and your sympathies are with your own generation, not with mine. I think it is inevitable. You are about the only man who is willing to let a new generation come in. It will seem a bit rough to me, when I am 45, and must see myself and my tradition supplanted. I shall bear it very badly. Damn my impudence, but don't dislike me. But I don't want to write like Galsworthy nor Ibsen, nor Strindberg nor any of them, *not* even if I could. We have to hate our immediate predecessors, to get free from their authority. (i. 509)

Those remarks almost certainly refer to *The Daughter-in-Law*: a naturalistic dialect play, combining psychological and class insight, which was very different from the work of most contemporary British and European dramatists. Lawrence was freeing himself from authority in many forms during 1912–14 – and would end by freeing himself from Garnett's authority, too. Even Garnett, more favourable than anybody else to his writing, sympathised (Lawrence knew) with his 'own generation'.

Furthermore, if Garnett had actually thought highly of any of Lawrence's early plays – and it appears that the only one he cared much for was *The Widowing of Mrs. Holroyd* – he would also have been aware (for he was a dramatist himself) that if producers like Granville-Barker and Payne did not want the plays, trying to stage any of them in England was fairly pointless. The dialect in many of Lawrence's plays, for a start – and this was especially true of *The Daughter-in-Law* – would have been impossible for many actors to speak and most audiences to understand; while the unashamedly working-class concerns of some, the stark realism of others, and their general refusal to create what would then have been thought of as typically 'dramatic' confrontations, would have ruled them out for most commercial theatres. More than twenty years later, *The Daughter-in-Law* would still be regarded by theatrical managements as unacceptable unless rewritten by a professional dramatist.[36] At some stage – perhaps in February 1913, but more likely rather later – Garnett presumably returned the manuscript of *The Daughter-in-Law* to Lawrence. There was nothing

after Granville-Barker's and Iden Payne's comments – nothing he could do would significantly improve their chances. They were also both serious plays, and he may well have decided to try and concentrate on his comedies for the moment.

[36] See below, pp. xciii–xciv.

he could do with it.[37] And in spite of Lawrence's hopes of using his plays as material for 'shaping' later on, so far as is known he neither looked at, nor referred to, any of his early plays again – with the exception of *The Widowing of Mrs. Holroyd.*

The latter was different because Garnett apparently thought it was sufficiently 'dramatic' in a conventional sense to have some chance. He retained its manuscript and on 25 February 1913 he offered both Lawrence's first book of poems and the play to the American publisher, Mitchell Kennerley, who had published Lawrence's second novel *The Trespasser* and who had paid handsomely for Lawrence's story 'The Soiled Rose' for his magazine, *Forum*. Kennerley declared that he was looking 'forward to reading the manuscript of the play', and suggested that it might fit into his 'Modern Drama Series'; he also offered to provide printed sheets for an English edition to be published by Duckworth (i. 542 n. 2).

As the term 'manuscript' was still being used by printers and publishers of the period – and also by Lawrence – to mean 'autograph manuscript' or 'typescript',[38] it is difficult when reconstructing the publishing history of this play to determine exactly what state of the text is being referred to in the correspondence. The puzzle is complicated because neither the manuscript nor any typescripts or proofs of the play have survived.

In March or April 1913, Kennerley was sent an unrevised version of the play, very likely a typescript copy Garnett had had made after his decision to offer the play for publication,[39] rather than the manuscript. In April, Garnett told Lawrence he had accepted, on Lawrence's behalf, Kennerley's offer to publish the poems and the play (i. 542). Lawrence was very happy with the arrangement, telling Garnett on 21 April: 'You know you can accept things for me without my knowing, if you think them good. Anyhow I am very glad of Kennerley's offer, and accept gratefully' (i. 542).

---

[37] The manuscripts of *The Merry-go-Round*, *The Married Man* and *The Fight for Barbara*, which had gone back earlier, remained in the possession of Frieda's sister, Else Jaffe, until 1931: DHL probably left them with her either in May 1913, when he and Frieda returned to England after spending six weeks in Bavaria, or in September 1913, when they went back to Italy. The history of the manuscript of *The Daughter-in-Law* is unknown: it surfaced again only in 1933.

[38] The term 'typescript' did not come into general use until the second decade of the twentieth century; the first English citation in *OED2* is dated 1907. 'Manuscript', abbreviated to MS, went on being used in printing and publishing alongside 'typescript' (TS), and is still used to mean 'author's copy'.

[39] Garnett would have used his typist nephew, Douglas Clayton; for a discussion of Clayton's typing for DHL 1912–13, see *The Prussian Officer*, ed. Worthen, p. xxxvi and n. 80.

The Widowing of Mrs. Holroyd would be the only play by an English author in Kennerley's series, which included Henrik Ibsen, Leonid Andreyev and Arthur Schnitzler, as well as American writers.

In England between June and August, Lawrence recovered his play – almost certainly the manuscript – from Garnett and took it back to Germany. In Irschenhausen, in mid-August 1913, unaware of how far Kennerley's publication plans had advanced, Lawrence started revising it. He reported that he had been 'very busy reading the play to Frieda', and though he found it 'a jolly fine play', he was sure that 'It wants *a lot* of altering. I have made it heaps better.' In the same letter he told Garnett: 'You must by no means let the MS. go to the printer before I have it – neither here nor in America' – for he was determined to have his revisions included (ii. 58). Two months later, he gave details of what he had done: 'I saw how it needed altering – refining. Particularly I hated it in the last act, where the man and woman wrangled rather shallowly across the dead body of the husband. And it seemed nasty that they should make love where he lay drunk' (ii. 71). He also noted that 'There is one speech in it ... the keystone of the play, and I *will* have it in.'[40] In August, he remarked that he was waiting for a 'typed copy ... so I may alter it' (ii. 58): that is, transfer to it the revisions he had made in the manuscript, and thus prevent the printer setting the old, unrevised text.

Revision probably took Lawrence about two weeks. When he sent the revised text to Kennerley on 24 August – 'It is pretty much altered, and much improved' (ii. 65) – he must have sent either the manuscript or the typed copy he had asked for, with the revisions inserted in it. It is probable, however, that the typescript had not arrived in time (only eleven days elapsed between Lawrence asking for it and his despatch of his revised text), so that he would have to have sent the much-revised manuscript. He wrote to Kennerley: 'The MS. forwarded you by Mr Duckworth, revised by me, looks rather messy, but I am sure is perfectly easy for a printer to decipher – He can correct from that copy. There is not, after all, such a great amount of alteration' (ii. 71). At this stage Lawrence still wished to see proofs containing his revised text (ii. 65, 78) – unless that would delay publication. Only the title still worried him: 'Must I find another title? *The Widowing of Mrs Holroyd* describes it, but doesn't sound very well' (ii. 58). Garnett did not approve of the title, and Lawrence suggested

---

[40] *Letters*, ii. 78. DHL was probably referring to Mrs Holroyd's speech over the dead body of her husband (108:13–27); the equivalent speech in 'Odour of Chrysanthemums' was revised several times during the process of composition and revision (see *The Prussian Officer*, ed. Worthen, p. li).

'"Afterdamp"' on his revised text: 'It would do exceedingly well, in idea, but I don't like the word. I wish it were the German: "Schlagender Wetter"' (ii. 72).[41] However, he could not find anything better.

It was a shock for Lawrence to find, early in September, that Kennerley had already had the play set up in type from his unrevised text. Lawrence now realised that he had 'caused trouble by coming in so late with my revision of the play'. Almost as an afterthought he added in his letter to Kennerley: 'if it is very late for you, your own proof-reader might do the corrections' (ii. 72). On 19 September Kennerley informed Lawrence (who received the letter on 5 October), and on 22 September wrote to Garnett, that that would indeed be the procedure: 'I am now making all the changes and corrections he desires, and shall shortly send him a revised proof' (ii. 80; ii. 72 n.1). Kennerley had had a clean typescript made of the heavily revised manuscript which Lawrence had sent him, for the proof-corrector to work from; it was apparently the editor of the 'Modern Drama Series', Edwin A. Björkman, who did the job and who also wrote a biographical and critical introduction to the volume.[42]

It is, however, very unlikely that 'the proofs' which Lawrence received in Fiascherino on 4 October (ii. 79) were the 'revised' proofs Kennerley mentioned in his letter of 22 September, and Lawrence was puzzled about what he ought to do with them. He was more puzzled still to receive, some time later, a clean typescript of his own revised text (probably a carbon copy of the typescript which Kennerley had made for the proof-correction to be done from): on 19 November, he told Kennerley that he had received it 'a little while back, and let lie, not knowing you wanted me to go over it'. He eventually appears to have revised it and returned it to Kennerley, describing his new changes, however, as 'not important': 'If the proofs of the play have gone in [to the printer] before this corrected MS [typescript] arrives [in New York], then no matter. What alterations there are, are not important. But they go to improving the surface. One can feel so much better when one can go straight forward over a plain typed copy – as over proofs.' He also commented that 'The play seems to me pretty complete now, as it stands. I am sorry that it is a play of unbelief – a bit cynical in conception. One has no right to be cynical'.[43] At some stage he must have

---

[41] *Letters*, ii. 58, 72. The correct German – for firedamp – is 'schlagende Wetter'; see Explanatory note on 104:4. It is possible that Granville-Barker's play *The Marrying of Ann Leete* (1902; published 1907) had influenced DHL's original title.

[42] See Appendix II. In 1920, Thomas Seltzer would also make a clean typescript of a heavily revised text which DHL had submitted; see *WL* xlv and n. 62.

[43] The Rendells Catalogue 166, 1983, Item 59.

received, too, a set of the proofs containing his revisions, but probably too late to do anything useful with them. The publisher's contract was signed on 25 November 1913.

More than ten years later he remembered 'how, in a cottage, by the sea, in Italy, I re-wrote almost entirely that play, *The Widowing of Mrs. Holroyd*, right on the proofs which Mitchell Kennerley had sent me. And he nobly forbore with me'.[44] However, his memory deceived him. If he was thinking of the original, unrevised 'proofs' which arrived on 4 October, it is clear that he only worked briefly to try and recreate his revised text on them: he described later how he had 'wrestled with them', but had then 'given them up to await the arrival of the MS' (ii. 80). If he meant the revised proofs or the clean typescript, which came rather later, then he apparently did very little with them: he called the changes he made to the text at this later stage 'not important'. What Kennerley had been noble enough to tolerate was an author sending in a heavily revised text after his unrevised text had already been set up in type.

At this stage, early January 1914 was being envisaged as the American publishing date. We cannot be sure whether those final authorial revisions from November 1913 were ever incorporated; but as the American edition did not actually appear until April, there would appear to have been time for them to be added. We have, however, no way of distinguishing between the revisions which Lawrence made in August, October or November on manuscript, typescript and either set of proofs, because all the evidence has been lost: the only text to survive is Kennerley's first edition.

In February 1914, Lawrence was eagerly waiting for the play to be published and the first copies to arrive. He wished the event to coincide with the publication of an article about him (including a photograph) in the *Bookman* and with the publication of poems and short stories in the *English Review*. Such a concerted action might further his 'reputation' which he thought was 'new-born and wants skilful handling' (ii. 135). Lawrence again thanked Kennerley for correcting the text for him: 'Don't you think it is rather a beautiful play, as it stands? . . . I am very grateful to you for setting up the play at all that expense you took: I should have felt so hollow-hearted about it had it come out in its first bad form. Now I am pretty sure of it' (ii. 144–5). Lawrence received his first copy early in March 1914 (ii. 152). Mitchell Kennerley published *The Widowing of Mrs. Holroyd* on 1 April 1914, in an edition of 500 copies, probably at $1.50

[44] 'The Bad Side of Books', in Edward D. McDonald, *A Bibliography of the Writings of D. H. Lawrence* (Philadelphia, 1925), p. 11 (reprinted in *Phoenix*, ed. McDonald, p. 233).

each.[45] Duckworth followed on 17 April with an English edition of 500 copies (costing 3s 6d), from sheets supplied by Kennerley.

Lawrence had originally remarked, of Björkman's 'Introduction': 'Of course I take unto myself all the beautiful and laudatory things he says about me in the preface: they seem to me very just. I never did read Freud [whom Björkman mentioned], but I have heard about him since I was in Germany' (ii. 80). However, it had what he diplomatically called a 'strong flavour' (ii. 144), and in May 1914 he would slangily (and unfairly) dismiss it as a 'filthy little notice' (ii. 174).

The Widowing of Mrs. Holroyd became his first play to be staged, and the one for which directors would in future regularly lay plans. For the author of the revolutionary 1914 version of _The Rainbow_, however, the publication of a play closer in style and content to _Sons and Lovers_ and the even earlier 'Odour of Chrysanthemums' remained an ambivalent subject. Lawrence sent copies to Edward Marsh, Henry Savage, Arthur McLeod and John Middleton Murry – yet though he had told the latter in August 1913 that 'I am going to have a play published. It's a good one. You must look out for it, and say nice things about it to people', he now commented: 'The play – well, it's not bad. I don't set great store by it. I will send you a copy ... It isn't worth 3/6 of your money, at any rate'.[46]

The reviews appearing in America and England were in general very favourable, but Lawrence nevertheless echoed Garnett's doubts: 'I suppose, as you say, plays never sell. The notices were very good' (ii. 174). The _New York Times Book Review_ characterised Lawrence – 'practically unknown to the American public' – as a young author who had 'suddenly sprung before playgoing London as the author of a most terrific bit of realism'; it described the play as 'mere photography, but it is the excellence

---

[45] Roberts A5; no. 5 in the 'Modern Drama Series'; 1,000 copies printed, 500 of which were sold to Duckworth as sheets. The price printed on the dust-jacket spine was $1 but all known copies have this altered to $1.50. The American dust-jacket announced:

> This is first of all what a play should be to achieve suspense: a conflict of human wills. But it constitutes also a striking exposition of the difference between the male and the female attitude toward such a conflict and all it involves. The author must be reckoned one of the most promising of the younger writers now making a place for themselves in England.

In 1921, Thomas Seltzer reissued the play in New York; Mark Schorer published an edition in 1956 in San Francisco. It was the first play in _Plays_ and _Complete Plays_, and appeared in the play selections _The Daughter-in-Law and Other Plays_, ed. Michael Marland (London, 1968) and _Three Plays_, ed. Raymond Williams (Harmondsworth, 1969).

[46] Unpublished letter to Murry, 30 August 1913; _Letters_ ii. 171. Edward Marsh (1872–1953), writer, civil servant and editor of _Georgian Poetry_; Henry Savage (b. 1881?), free-lance journalist and essayist; Arthur McLeod (1885–1956), schoolteacher (at Croydon) and headmaster; John Middleton Murry (1889–1957), editor and critic.

of the lens which makes it a good play'.[47] It was 'terrifying to read; how it could be presented seems almost inconceivable; its sordidness is too intolerable, its truth too overwhelming'. In London, too, *The Times* enthusiastically commended the play's 'qualities of finished craftsmanship. It is extraordinarily "lean"; there is not an ounce of superfluous flesh on it. The language is utterly plain ... the dialogue is packed with significance and suggestion ... As to the form ... it is finely built and perfectly shaped'. Lawrence could be seen as 'one of the writers who carry on a work practically begun by Mr. Hardy – the revelation of the shades and complexities and depths in "simple" natures'.[48] The *Nation* (London) compared the play favourably with the work of other modern dramatists; the 'flatness and dryness', 'dramatic schemes and conventional attitudes' of other plays stood in sharp contrast to Lawrence's 'essential power of ennobling life'; their 'play of intellectual subtleties' omitted 'life's realities' as apparent in Lawrence's work. The reviewer went on: 'I know nothing on the modern stage quite comparable with such work as "The Widowing of Mrs. Holroyd," and I should like to see the Stage Society attempt it.'[49]

Such a plan had already been proposed. Back in the winter of 1913, the novelist and playwright Arnold Bennett – who had been deeply impressed by *Sons and Lovers*, and who may well have heard in advance from Garnett about *The Widowing of Mrs. Holroyd* – had advised the prestigious Stage Society (founded 1899) that if ever they could get hold of a play by Lawrence, they should stage it. The Society had written to Lawrence in December 1913, and he – after worrying about the legibility of the text of the play he had in his possession (either the old, revised original manuscript or the partly corrected proofs from October 1913) which he feared might be 'in such a state they could not read it' – had felt obliged to ask them to wait for the appearance of the American edition promised by Kennerley for January 1914 (ii. 127, 136). However, he eventually sent them a set of proofs (ii. 152); Kennerley may have at last despatched the revised proofs which – in September 1913 – he had originally planned to send (ii. 72 n.1), or Lawrence may have sent them his own old set of partly corrected proofs.

Lawrence's new friend Edward Marsh – who knew many people in the

---

[47] 4 October 1914, p. 416.
[48] 24 April 1914, p. 4; reprinted in *The Times Literary Supplement*, 30 April 1914, p. 209.
[49] 'Mr. Lawrence's Tragedy', 2 May 1914, pp. 176–7. Further reviews: *Independent* (New York), 25 May 1914, p. 324; *New Statesman*, 6 June 1914, pp. 281–2; *Nation* (New York), 23 July 1914, p. 112; *Dial* (Chicago), 16 January 1915, p. 48; *Yale Review*, iv (April 1915), 622–4.

theatrical world, including Beerbohm Tree,[50] Tree's stage manager Basil
Dean and Granville-Barker – had also asked to see a copy of the play,
which he would pass to a 'friend' who could 'put the thing on the stage'
(ii. 152), and Lawrence forwarded the first copy of Kennerley's edition he
received, early in March. And then, back in London himself in June and
July 1914 (he and Frieda would get married on 13 July), Lawrence followed
up contacts with two actor–managers, Harold V. Neilson of the Vaudeville
Theatre and Lena Ashwell of the Kingsway Theatre (ii. 17, 187 and n. 3,
201 and n. 1). Later, Lena Ashwell recalled how 'he wanted me to act in a
very tragic play of his ... It was terribly tragic, and I felt if I acted in it I
would make the part unbearable for even the toughest audience.'[51]
Nothing further came of the plans, however; the Stage Society rejected the
play 'after long consideration' on the grounds that 'you could not
satisfactorily conclude an evening's entertainment with the laying out of a
dead body and twenty minutes of weeping, wailing, and washing'.[52] In
August 1915, Esmé Percy, who had been an actor at the Gaiety Theatre in
Manchester, suggested staging the play in repertory theatres outside
London (ii. 17, 382, 384 and n. 4). This plan too came to nothing, but
Percy remained loyal to the play: in 1926 he would direct its first
professional production in England, with the Stage Society.

But where Britain had failed, America succeeded. The first performance
of a Lawrence play took place in the Little Theater, Los Angeles, 26–31
December 1916; Aline Barnsdall staged *The Widowing of Mrs. Holroyd* in a
professional production with her Players Producing Company.[53] There is
no reference in Lawrence's surviving correspondence to the event; we do
not know if Kennerley (with whom by then he had a long-running financial
dispute) acted as go-between, and we cannot even be sure that Lawrence
knew about the production. The play was, however, a critical success and
played to capacity houses. Grace Kingsley in the *Los Angeles Times* commented that the 'greatest qualities of the play are its manifestations of two
souls trembling on the verge of a mighty passion, but held back by

---

[50] DHL had actually seen the actor–manager Tree in 1908 when he visited Davidson Road
School, Croydon (i. 97 and n).

[51] Nehls, i. 598 n. 537. She made no mention of either DHL or the play in her autobiography
Myself a Player (1936).

[52] *Sunday Times*, 19 December 1926, p. 4. The 1926 reviewer recalled the rejection by 'the
older society some time ago' and commented: 'I do not even begin to agree'.

[53] Aline Barnsdall (1882–1946), theatre producer, political consultant and advertising genius:
see Norman and Dorothy Karasick, *The Oilman's Daughter: A Biography of Aline Barnsdall*
(Encino, Calif., 1993).

deadening circumstances'. But the play's 'startling' realism – 'Poignant, gripping and vivid' – shocked its audience; and it was felt that, 'almost repellently gruesome' – 'Its bleak human misery has not been surpassed on the stage' – it had hardly been a good choice for the festive season. It was compared unfavourably with John Galsworthy's work – presumably his famous and successful colliery play, *Strife* – which was thought to illuminate 'painful, sordid realism . . . with some big significance'.[54]

1918–20. *Touch and Go* written and published; *The Widowing of Mrs. Holroyd* performed

After finishing *The Daughter-in-Law* early in 1913 and revising *The Widowing of Mrs. Holroyd* later in the year, Lawrence wrote no play for five years. Living in England again during the First World War, he was reduced to poverty by his inability to publish: *The Rainbow* was banned in 1915, and no publisher would take *Women in Love* (first finished in 1916) for four years. To help him in his financial distress during the last year of the war, his sister Ada Clarke rented a cottage for him and Frieda in Middleton-by-Wirksworth, a few miles from her own house in Ripley, in May 1918: the Lawrences were based there for almost a year, until April 1919. As a result, Lawrence saw more of the region in which he had grown up than he had for many years; he visited his home-town more than once, seeing old Eastwood friends like Sallie and Willie Hopkin and their daughter Enid. The Hopkins also came to Middleton in May 1918, and stayed there for a weekend in June, while Lawrence saw Willie Hopkin again in late September or early October.[55]

Lawrence became especially aware, during the last six months of 1918, of the tensions in the mining industry (exacerbated by soaring food prices). Disputes, strikes and stoppages were becoming common, and would grow still more frequent with the end of the war in November.[56] Joseph Birkin, a checkweighman at Moorgreen colliery in Eastwood, influential in (and later Vice-President of) the Nottinghamshire Miners' Association, was the Eastwood miners' leader in their negotiations with Barber Walker & Co., the local colliery company.[57] Lawrence doubtless heard a good deal about him and the Eastwood collieries from Hopkin, who must have known Birkin, and who was himself an indefatigable socialist, commentator in the

---

[54] 28 December 1916, section 2, p. 3. For *Strife*, see p. xlvi and footnote 59.
[55] *Letters*, iii. 292. For Hopkin, see Explanatory note on 369:6. DHL apparently saw him shortly before going to London on 7 October 1918 (iii. 292).
[56] See Explanatory note on 373:17.
[57] See G. C. H. Whitelock, *200 Years in Coal* (n.p., n.d. [1957]), pp. 57, 60.

local newspaper and public speaker. Lawrence was showing a greatly increased interest in politics and politicians, after years of alienation from them: having, in Autumn 1917, discussed a campaign of industrial action in the north of England to bring the war to an end,[58] he now declared (in September 1918) that he wanted to get to know people like Robert Smillie, Philip Snowdon and Margaret Bondfield, some of the foremost figures in the Independent Labour Party (ILP): 'It is no good, one cannot wait for things to happen' (iii. 284).

With the prospects for peace growing during October 1918, Lawrence found himself hoping that 'the world yet might get a turn for the better, if it but had a little shove that way' (iii. 293). He probably started to write *Touch and Go*, his seventh play, during a visit to Hermitage in Berkshire, where he and Frieda arrived on the 22nd. By the 28th (iii. 293), the play was finished: Lawrence wanted it to produce just such 'a little shove' – 'I believe the last I am capable of' (iii. 293). Like John Galsworthy's famous and successful play, *Strife*, a decade earlier (which Lawrence had hoped to see on stage in 1909 but had missed, and which he would refer to in his Preface), *Touch and Go* would attempt to make clear the problems of human conflict in the industrial age.[59] He immediately wrote to his friend Lady Cynthia Asquith, who worked as private secretary to the playwright J. M. Barrie and who had many friends in the literary and theatrical world:

I've written a play – very nice – which *might* be acted. Shall I send it you, and you can ask [Charles] Whibley about it, perhaps. I will remain anonymous – my name is like red pepper in people's noses. – Of course we are thrilled – one must be thrilled. I see myself a second Sir Jas [James Barrie], with a secretary. – But no, truly, I am ashamed in daylight to confess it, I have written a play out of my deep and earnest self, fired up my last sparks of hope in the world, as it were, and cried out like a Balaams ass.[60]   (iii. 293)

---

[58] The musician Cecil Gray recalled how, during 1917, DHL

> more than once expressed to me – and to others, no doubt – his intention of initiating a disruptive, pacifist and nihilist campaign in the industrial North, with a view to bringing about a speedy end to the War. I remember vividly an occasion in his cottage at Tregerthen before the eviction [October 1917], when he declared that he had definitely determined on this course of action . . .   (Nehls, i. 430)

Gray was not a reliable memoirist and almost certainly exaggerated the extent of DHL's commitment to the idea, but doubtless DHL discussed it with him.

[59] The manuscript of *Touch and Go* shows some irregularities perhaps deriving from the haste of its composition: pp. 26, 27 and 28 are followed by three further pages also numbered 26, 27 and 28 (in this edition the latter pages are referred to as 26a, 27a and 28a). For *Strife* (1909), see *Letters*, i. 138, 140, E.T. 109 and the Preface, 365:26–7.

[60] Lady Cynthia Asquith (1887–1960), née Charteris, daughter of the Earl of Wemyss, daughter-in-law of H. H. Asquith (Prime Minister, 1908–16, and Earl of Oxford and Asquith, 1925); Sir J. M. Barrie (1860–1937), famous author of *Peter Pan* (1904). DHL

The play begins with Willie Houghton – a recreation of Willie Hopkin – addressing a group of miners in a mining village market-place one Sunday morning; Hopkin regularly addressed Sunday-morning ILP meetings in Eastwood market-place, and Lawrence had once told him that 'unless I stopped speaking at Socialist meetings he would one day "take me off"'.[61] The play also includes versions of Joseph Birkin (as the miners' leader Job Arthur Freer) and of members of the Barber family, directors of Barber Walker & Co.;[62] Lawrence was thus using his own knowledge of the Eastwood colliery district and its social and political divisions to focus upon larger problems of the industrial age. The play, Lawrence boasted to his old American friend, the poet Amy Lowell, was 'one of my unspotted "sagesses"', but 'not wicked but too good is probably the sigil of its doom' (iii. 296).

Cynthia Asquith seems, however, to have told him not to send her the manuscript just yet: she probably wanted to take soundings among her theatrical friends. Accordingly, Lawrence sent the play to Katherine Mansfield, who wrote to Lady Ottoline Morrell: 'Lawrence has sent me today a new play of his – very long – just written – I must read it. I have glanced inside and it looks *black* with miners – the frenzied miners that he felt on his spine so in the Midlands – Poor dear man! I do wish he could come up [*sic*] out of the Pit for ever – But he wont – '[63] What she wrote to him about it, we don't know. Early in November she passed the manuscript on to Lawrence's friend, the writer Catherine Carswell, whom he told that he was 'rather thrilled' by his play: but it was her opinion as an ex-drama critic he particularly wanted: 'I remember you once did theatres.'[64] After she had returned it – she had not much liked it (iii. 469) – on 23 November Lawrence rather apologetically sent it to J. B. Pinker, his agent since June 1914: 'I know I ought to write something saleable –

---

had met her friend and admirer Charles Whibley (1859–1930), critic, editor and journalist, in November 1917 (*Letters*, iii. 187 and n. 1). For Balaam's ass (a favourite DHL reference), see Numbers xxii. 21–35. The ass can see the divine messenger which Balaam cannot.

[61] Note on title-page of Hopkin's copy of *Touch and Go*; when DHL sent it to Hopkin, he also inscribed the title-page 'Here you are Willie! D. H. L.' (NCL). The Sunday-morning meetings witnessed, e.g., the first singing of 'The Red Flag' in Eastwood (*Eastwood and Kimberley Advertiser*, 18 June 1909, p. 2).

[62] See Explanatory notes on 369:2, 5 and 6.

[63] Letter of 4 November 1918 (*The Collected Letters of Katherine Mansfield*, ed. Vincent O'Sullivan and Margaret Scott, Oxford, 1987, ii. 287). Katherine Mansfield (1888–1923), New Zealand short-story writer and first wife of John Middleton Murry; Lady Ottoline Morrell (1873–1938), society hostess and patroness of artists and writers.

[64] *Letters*, iii. 297. Catherine Carswell (1879–1946), critic, biographer of Burns and DHL (*The Savage Pilgrimage*, 1932) and novelist, had worked as reviewer and drama critic for the *Glasgow Herald*, 1907–11; in 1915, m. Donald Carswell (1882–1940).

but this is rather a wonderful play, and I wanted to do it. You will see what you think of it. One day it will be acted' (iii. 299–300). The fact that at some stage he supplied on the verso of the cover page a list of characters divided (as convention required, but uniquely in his play manuscripts) into male and female roles shows how much he hoped that *Touch and Go* would be published and staged.

But less than a fortnight later, having heard from Cynthia Asquith that she might be able to get the play into the hands of Mrs Patrick Campbell – one of the best-known actresses of the day[65] – Lawrence asked Pinker for the manuscript back: 'I would like to show it to a friend' (iii. 301). This demonstrated his greater faith in such theatrical contacts, for an essentially topical piece of work, than in his agent's ability to do anything with it. On 6 December he sent the manuscript to Cynthia Asquith: 'Read it, and tell me what you think of it. And if you like, show it to Mrs Patrick Campbell – but just as you think fit. I'm afraid no manager would look at it at the moment. Later, however, it is possible' (iii. 305). Cynthia Asquith had, he believed, 'some part in some new theatrical concern' (iii. 315). Nearly three months later, however, she sent the manuscript back: she had, after all, not been able to help. 'Don't bother a bit about the play,' Lawrence reassured her, 'the hour isn't ripe. I don't bother' (iii. 333).

Accordingly, in mid-March 1919, he returned the manuscript to Pinker: 'Some time it might be useful' (iii. 338). It was probably at this stage that Pinker had the manuscript typed, in a single copy (iii. 396 n. 3): if he had had it typed back in the winter, Lawrence would probably not have felt it necessary to post the manuscript to him in March. The fact that Pinker made only one copy is, however, significant. It reveals that he only intended sending the play round theatrical managements and publishers in England, believing there was no chance for it in the North American market. Pinker's decision was characteristic of his pessimistic attitude towards Lawrence's work at this stage. All that Lawrence could do was continue showing the play to friends. He wrote to Pinker on 20 May – by which time he had left Mountain Cottage in Middleton and was living again in Hermitage in Berkshire – asking for the manuscript back: 'I should like to look at it again, and a friend wants to criticise it' (iii. 360). The friend may have been Barbara Low,[66] who was about to visit the Lawrences. Catherine Carswell, who also visited them in Hermitage at

---

[65] Mrs Beatrice Stella Cornwallis-West (1865–1940), generally known by the name of her first husband, Captain Patrick Campbell (d. 1900). The part of Eliza Doolittle in George Bernard Shaw's *Pygmalion* (1913) had been written especially for her.

[66] Psychoanalyst and writer (1877–1955).

Whitsun 1919 (5–9 June), later wrongly stated that Lawrence had written the play that spring,[67] but may thus inadvertently have recorded the fact that she saw Lawrence making some revisions after recovering the manuscript from Pinker. She may also have seen the address ('Hermitage / nr. Newbury / Berks.') which he cannot have added to the title-page before May–June 1919.

However, around 8 July, Lawrence heard from an acquaintance, Douglas Goldring,[68] that he had recently started the 'People's Theatre Society' for the production of contemporary left-wing and revolutionary plays, and had persuaded the publisher C. W. Daniel to publish them under the series title 'Plays for a People's Theatre' (iii. 371–2). This series – which, over the years 1920–4, would expand to twenty-seven volumes – had grown out of Goldring's own pamphlet play, *The Fight for Freedom*, which (he later explained) 'I had submitted to him [Daniel] for publication. This I had provided with a preface detailing my scheme for an "all-red" theatre of the kind that was beginning to spring up in various parts of Europe.'[69] Only a couple of years younger than Lawrence, Goldring had admired his work greatly for years. He would later assert that he had founded the 'People's Theatre Society' specifically 'to secure the production of one of Lawrence's plays' (iii. 371 n. 4), but this conflicts with his earlier account of the Society's origins among the English supporters of the so-called 'Clarté' movement, something inherently more likely.[70]

Best of all, Goldring was specifically interested in *Touch and Go*, which he had probably heard about from Barbara Low.[71] The play sounded admirably suited for publication by Daniel (Lawrence understood that it would indeed inaugurate the series); and Goldring also thought it might be performed. There was a possibility that the manager of London's Royal Court Theatre, James B. Fagan, would be putting on a 'People's Theatre Society' series; in which case Lawrence's play could (Goldring suggested) be staged first (iii. 374). The whole idea of the People's Theatre

---

[67] *The Savage Pilgrimage*, p. 111. She had actually known about the play early in November 1918 (*Letters*, iii. 297).

[68] Novelist, playwright, anti-war propagandist, international socialist, left-wing activist, editor and journalist (1887–1960). See Nehls, i. 493–6, ii. 36–8, for Goldring's own account of *Touch and Go*.

[69] Nehls, ii. 36; Goldring's preface as published, however, was probably not part of the original submission as it is dated 'August 1919'.

[70] Nehls, i. 493: 'Clarté' was an international socialist movement founded by Henri Barbusse (1873–1935).

[71] Goldring was introduced to DHL by the latter's long-time friend, the Russian translator S. S. Koteliansky (1880–1955), but he associated Barbara Low with the acquaintance: see Nehls, i. 491.

enormously appealed to Lawrence: 'I should love to be in it' (iii. 372). He had, after all, a play on his hands not only which Pinker was unable to place but which Lawrence was certain would work on the stage, and he hoped that Goldring could come to some agreement with Fagan: 'a little understanding, even about the play itself', because 'I want it to be the first production, and I want it to be a success' (iii. 374–5).

But although Daniel's series of plays was clearly successful, Goldring proved too sanguine in his hopes for their production at the Royal Court. Pinker sent his typescript of *Touch and Go* to Fagan, but the latter returned it at the end of October 1919, commenting 'It is well written but I am afraid in my opinion it would not succeed on the stage'.[72] And *Touch and Go* was certainly one of the more stageable of the plays.

In his immediate enthusiasm for Goldring's series in July, however, Lawrence set to work and created a special Preface for *Touch and Go* as the inaugural play which (perhaps to link with the date of revising the play in Hermitage) he predated to 'Hermitage. June 1919'. His immediate problem, however, was that he was bound by his arrangement with Pinker for the latter to arrange for the publication and production of his work: 'I am under Pinker ... I must settle with him' (iii. 372). Lawrence however was growing increasingly disillusioned with what Pinker was able to do for him: it would shortly become clear that Pinker had never even sent a copy of *Women in Love* to Benjamin Huebsch, who was now Lawrence's major American publisher (iii. 466). *Touch and Go* was another case in point. Lawrence himself had made the contact with Goldring which was likely to lead to the play's publication (and perhaps to its production), while Pinker had done nothing. He would, however, take his usual 10 per cent. A few months earlier Lawrence had asked Pinker whether he really wanted to go on acting as his agent (iii. 296); and he made *Touch and Go* the occasion for his first break with Pinker's control of his work. Having decided to go ahead with Goldring and Daniel, Lawrence wrote to Pinker on 10 July 1919, 'I wish you would let me go ahead and do as I like with this play – on my own', though he did later promise Pinker to 'tell Douglas Goldring to arrange with you in a little while' (iii. 374). But, without waiting for Pinker's reply, he told Goldring the same day: 'You may announce it in your series of plays, too' (iii. 374). The literary and theatrical agent, Walter Peacock, who was acting as agent for the 'People's Theatre' venture – Goldring must have told Lawrence about him – proved willing to take on

---

[72] *Letters*, iii. 374 n. 2. As Fagan returned the typescript to Pinker, it must have been the Pinker typescript which he had received; for the play's other three typescripts, see below, p. cxvii.

Touch and Go. After, perhaps, making some final corrections in pencil, Lawrence sent the manuscript to Peacock, who had it typed as a theatrical typescript in a ribbon and two carbon copies.[73] The second carbon copy (which survives) went to Daniel to use as setting-copy, Peacock presumably using the two clearer copies to try and interest theatres and theatrical managers.

Pinker was considerably annoyed when he found out what Lawrence had done; and a month later, on 23 August, Lawrence disingenuously apologised to him: 'I'm sorry, Douglas Goldring and Walter Peacock were arranging it before I really knew' (iii. 385). In fact, he had known exactly what was going on: and six days later he signed his contract with Daniel.[74] Pinker was still complaining in September, and Lawrence was still back-pedalling: 'I think I explained to you that owing to circumstances I had to settle *Touch and Go* with the People's Theatre agent, Walter Peacock' (iii. 396). To make matters worse, Daniel apparently wrote to Pinker asking for another typescript copy of the play to send to a potential American publisher (probably Thomas Seltzer). Pinker's annoyance would have been exacerbated on being approached by a publisher with whom he had not made any agreement. The fact that Lawrence then complained to Pinker about his failure to send copies out – insisting that 'You have copies of the play. You had *two* type-written copies made' (iii. 396) – would have made things rather worse. It had been Peacock who had made the multiple copies, not Pinker.

Working without Pinker, however, led to problems. On Goldring's advice, Lawrence allowed Daniel to arrange the American publication of the play with Seltzer, who was also publishing Goldring's play *The Fight for Freedom* (Goldring was currently working as Seltzer's English agent). This naturally annoyed Lawrence's established American publisher Huebsch, however, who was – after the *Women in Love* debacle – particularly sensitive when not consulted about Lawrence's work (iii. 427). In addition, not only did Fagan turn down *Touch and Go*, but Goldring was after all unable to persuade his own 'People's Theatre Society' committee to agree to its staging: 'The theatrical experts, of whom I was not one, pronounced it impossible of production.'[75] To cap everything, it

---

[73] A number of pages in the manuscript (e.g. 25, 30, 32, 33, 66, 69, 71) show pencil corrections: see Explanatory notes on 392:19, 399:4, 400:33, 401:5, 19, 23, 425:38, 428:32, 429:4 and 431:13. On the front cover of the manuscript is inscribed, in very faint pencil, presumably by Peacock or his typist, '3 Copies'. The carbon copy (marked '2nd carbon') is stamped with Peacock's name.

[74] 'Memorandum of Agreement' (UN).

[75] Nehls, i. 495, ii. 37.

turned out that *Touch and Go* would not after all be the first play in
Daniel's series. *The Fight for Freedom* came out as no. 1, in November
1919, while *Touch and Go* appeared as no. 2 in the first week of May 1920.
Goldring later insisted that this was Daniel's decision: 'Mr Daniel not
unnaturally published the plays in the order in which he received them'.[76]
But as Lawrence's Preface was written in July 1919 especially for Goldring,
and was clearly designed to inaugurate the series, while Goldring's Preface
is dated 'August 1919', Lawrence's play and Preface had probably been
ready as early as Goldring's. What may well have happened is that
Goldring – when he read Lawrence's Preface – decided that he did not
after all want it to launch the series: it would certainly have struck him as
lacking political commitment. As originator of the series, too, he may well
have wanted his own play to be no. 1. Anyway, he ensured that Daniel
brought out *The Fight for Freedom* well before *Touch and Go*. At least one
reviewer, however, reading Lawrence's Preface, naturally assumed that
Touch and Go was the first of the series.[77]

Lawrence was furious: 'That will be another fiasco', he wrote to
Catherine Carswell on 4 February 1920, thinking of his own specially
written Preface. What made matters worse was that he hated *The Fight for
Freedom*:

a pamphlet play with a detestable and inartistic motive. Goldring got *Touch and Go*
out of me, saying it *Touch and Go* would be the first of the 'Plays for a Peoples
Theatre'. Then the sly journalist went and put this offensive *Fight for Freedom* as
the first play – and for sure has damned and doubly damned the lot. I don't *want* to
be associated with the *Fight for Freedom* and it's knavish preface. And there is
Touch and Go, with a preface written specially. Curse the sly mongrel world.
Fortunately the *Fight for Freedom* has been utterly ignored – so that, publicly at
least, *Touch and Go* escapes much connection. I know you don't like the play – but
anyhow it's not *base*.   (iii. 469)

Goldring's belief in 'the spirit of revolutionary idealism and ardent
aspiration towards that new day which must dawn', and his faith in a
future 'when that red dawn really breaks', were inimical to Lawrence:
while the play's closing moments (showing the two main characters quietly
singing 'The Red Flag' together) were by any standards 'inartistic'.[78] The
review which *The Fight for Freedom* received in the *Athenaeum* – for, in
spite of Lawrence's hopes, Goldring's play would by no means be ignored

---

[76] Nehls, ii. 37.
[77] 'Tarn' [Amabel Williams-Ellis], *Spectator*, 28 August 1920, p. 279.
[78] *The Fight for Freedom* (1919), pp. 10, 7, 96.

– shrewdly remarked that in it 'there is more speechifying than dialogue'.[79] The speeches, however, were what Goldring wanted his play and his series to proclaim.

Goldring's behaviour did not matter very much, however: to judge by their subsequent correspondence, Lawrence soon forgave him. There is no surviving record of Daniel sending Lawrence proofs or of Lawrence correcting them, but neither is there extant any correspondence between them, where such arrangements would have been made. Proofs would probably have been ready shortly after Lawrence left England for Italy in November 1919, but Italian postal strikes were making it very difficult to get proofs and manuscripts to and from England.[80] There are small changes in the first edition for which Lawrence was probably not responsible, but he certainly made the single major revision between the setting-copy and the published play – the song employed by the miners in the last scene.[81] He received his copies of Daniel's edition by 10 May 1920.[82]

Touch and Go received rather few reviews. It was Lawrence's first prose work for four years (he had published a volume of poems annually from 1916 to 1919), but it was short, issued by a small publisher, not widely advertised and unlikely to bring him much public recognition. A number of newspapers and magazines which might have been expected to review a new Lawrence book ignored it. Nothing appeared in the *Manchester Guardian*, for example, a steadfast reviewer of him before the war: and this in spite of reviews (on 17 May) of Secker's edition of the translation of Leo Shestov (*All Things Are Possible*) which Lawrence had turned into English and supplied with a Foreword, and (on 20 July) of the third play in Daniel's series, *The Power and the Glory*, by the well-known journalist and writer Hamilton Fyfe. *The Times Literary Supplement* (ignorant, of course, of the parallel existence of some of the characters in the still unpublished *Women in Love*), in a 'Brief Notice' on 13 May noted 'an obscure plot' and 'an

---

[79] 'New Books', 5 March 1920, p. 321.
[80] See *The Lost Girl*, ed. John Worthen (Cambridge, 1981), p. xxvii.
[81] At 426:40: see 'Texts', p. cxvii.
[82] Roberts A14; no. 2 in the 'Plays for a People's Theatre' series, price 3/6, number of copies unknown. DHL still had no copy on 28 April but sent one to Compton Mackenzie on 10 May (*Letters*, iii. 510, 522): it was probably published in the week 3–8 May. Seltzer's American edition was published on 5 June 1920, DHL receiving six copies on 10 July – 'Amusing it looks' (ibid., 565) – and he apparently used them for presents in the autumn: his uncle Fritz Krenkow inscribed his copy of the Seltzer edition 'F. Krenkow Oct 26, 1920, Present from author' (Deighton Bell, Cambridge, Catalogue 253, 1990, p. 20), while DHL sent a copy (probably Seltzer's edition) to the German publisher of the Insel Verlag, Dr Anton Kippenberg, on 4 November (*Letters*, iii. 618). It was the second play in *Plays* and the sixth in *Complete Plays*.

enigmatic love affair' between Gerald and Anabel, 'whose changing desires and repulsions are in a high degree perplexing'. The review suggested, however, that the play's strength lay 'in its picture of colliery life': the owners and labour leaders 'make a strong impression of reality'. It singled out the last scene for its 'excellent piece of crowd psychology which should prove even more effective in the theatre than in the printed page' (p. 304). The only other favourable review appeared in the *Daily Mail* on 14 May, written by Fyfe; his praise for Lawrence's work was as politic (given his own contribution to the series) as it was uninformed: he claimed that 'When Mr. D. H. Lawrence began to write he was at work in or about a mine.' Yet Fyfe did observe the remarkable way in which Lawrence refused to take sides in the drama: 'He does not plead or excuse. He neither attacks employer nor champions the employee. He holds his mirror up to nature with detached and impartial interest in getting a complete reflection ...' (p. 10). Amabel Williams-Ellis, daughter of the *Spectator*'s editor John St Loe Strachey, and perhaps influenced by Daniel's advertisement announcing Lawrence's play as 'A play with a "Labour" interest',[83] however, attacked Lawrence savagely on 28 August for writing an 'extensive slab of propaganda':

His dramatic style is as yet very different from his poetic style, and he has in the present instance shown himself to be possessed of an extraordinarily heavy hand ... it is a sort of performance (I will not say entertainment) through which none but the Earnest could sit ... Mr. Lawrence does not make this mistake of open didacticism when he writes poetry. Why, oh! why, does he write drama like this?

(pp. 279–80)

The only part of the book she approved of was the Preface – 'entertaining enough' (p. 279). The *Nation* chose the book in its weekly selection of five new books 'which we commend to the notice of our readers', but did not give it a review.[84] The anonymous reviewer in the *New Age*, however, was simply scathing about the series, the 'People's Theatre', Lawrence's play and its introduction:

The People's Theatre does not exist, and these plays are suitable for production in it. Mr. Lawrence has even less sense of the theatre than Mr. Goldring, and his rambling preface is repeated in his rambling play ... If Mr. Lawrence would try the simple experiment of reading his play aloud, he would discover that he knows nothing of dramatic speech, while his characters are drawn from the dustbin.[85]

---

[83] See the *Nation* (Supplement), 15 May 1920, p. 235, and 'Tarn', *Spectator*, 11 September 1920, p. 342. The book was also reviewed by T[homas] M[oult], 'Mr. D. H. Lawrence and the "People" ', *Athenaeum*, 11 June 1920, p. 777.

[84] 'The World of Books', 8 May 1920, p. 176.

[85] Vol. xxvi, no. 11 (15 July 1920), 175.

The book's reception in America – where Seltzer brought it out on 5 June – was rather better; at least Amy Lowell, writing for the *New York Times Book Review*, recognised the play's attempt to strike a balance between its protagonists ('Mr. Lawrence has been fair in making his mine-owner almost as pig-headed a brute as any of his men ... Mr. Lawrence has courageously uttered a truth which will be popular with neither side'), though she too was rather more impressed by the Preface ('a fine little masterpiece of eight pages') than by the play.[86] A review by Ludwig Lewisohn in the New York *Nation* of the plays by Goldring and Lawrence was full of praise for the venture they were spearheading and – to a lesser extent – for the plays themselves: 'Neither Mr. Lawrence's ideas nor his dramaturgic methods are as firm and clarified as Mr. Goldring's. The reason is that he is on the edge of even fresher perceptions and subtler cognitions ...' Lewisohn thought, however, that a conversation in Act II of *Touch and Go* recalled 'Schnitzler in its ... quiet penetration to the true character of human contacts'; and though 'Neither play is a great play', yet 'To us, at this hour in the development of our theater and of the society it is to serve and express, both are important and, indeed, precious'.[87]

Fagan and the 'People's Theatre' group had both turned the play down, so, late in 1919, Lawrence sold the dramatic rights for £15 to Norman Macdermott, director and producer of the Everyman Theatre in Hampstead (iii. 440); but no production resulted. A suggestion by Compton Mackenzie in the spring of 1920 that his mother – who was proposing to turn the Grand Theatre Nottingham into a repertory theatre – should put on both *Touch and Go* and *The Widowing of Mrs. Holroyd* (iii. 509 n. 5) came to nothing;[88] it did, though, provoke a characteristic mock-furious reaction from Lawrence:

Nottingham! Cursed, cursed Nottingham, gutsless, spineless, brainless Not-

---

[86] 22 August 1920, Section 3, p. 7; reprinted in *Poetry and Poets* (Cambridge, Mass., 1930), pp. 175–86.

[87] Cxi (11 September 1920), 306. The comparison with the Austrian dramatist and novelist, Arthur Schnitzler (1862–1931), suggests the play's psychological insight, especially in sexual matters.

The following also reviewed the play in 1920: B. L., *Survey*, xliv (20 August), 592; Gilbert Seldes, *Dial*, lxix (August), 215; J. Ranken Towse, *New York Evening Post Literary Review*, 27 November, Section 3, p. 3; Dorothy Grafley, *Springfield Republican*, 5 September, p. 11a; Elva de Pue, *Freeman*, ii (15 December), 332.

[88] DHL had known the novelist Sir Edward Montague Compton Mackenzie (1883–1972) since 1914, but had recently re-established contact with him in Italy. Mackenzie came from a family of well-known actors and actresses; his father, Edward Compton, had run his own touring company, and his mother, Mrs Edward Compton, ran the Theatre Girls' Club in Soho for many years. Her Nottingham venture, however, proved a catastrophic failure.

tingham, how I hate thee! But if my two plays could be thrown so hard into thy teeth as to knock thy teeth out, why then, good enough ... I confess that the very thought of the plays coming in Nottingham gives me such a fright I almost feel like deserting my own identity.   (iii. 509–10)

Touch and Go did not reach the stage for another fifty-three years.

The Widowing of Mrs. Holroyd, however, remained a more attractive proposition, and the Altrincham Garrick Society, an amateur company based near Manchester, presented it from 9 to 13 March 1920: the first production of a Lawrence play in England.[89] The *Altrincham Guardian* roundly criticised the first-night audience for its reaction to the moment when Holroyd's dead body was carried on at the end: 'the bulk of the audience accepted the situation as funny and utterly destroyed the work of author and players'. But the reviewer, disappointed in his expectation of a 'well-made play', considered Lawrence's work 'badly constructed', 'the act endings being weak and the finale inconclusive' – something which cannot have been helped by the audience's laughter. The review stressed, however, the obvious merits of the play: 'Mr. Lawrence makes great tragedy of a sordid theme – the dismalness of life in a small colliery town, where work and drink provide the occupations of the people. Here is a picture that presents an unpleasant commentary on our civilisation.' It also praised the cast, the staging and the ambition of those who had chosen the play, insisting that they deserved a 'far better and more understanding audience'.[90]

Lawrence, now living in Sicily, was unable to go and see the production. Again thinking of Catherine Carswell in her old role as a drama critic, he asked her if she could go and, if possible, 'write a notice of it for some paper'. Although not well off himself, he sent her the money for the train fare (iii. 477). In the event, however, she obtained a commission from *The Times* and did not need his £5; but she obviously watched a later performance than that seen by the local reviewer, as she recalled in 1932 that 'To do justice to the Altrincham players and the Altrincham audience, no sniggering was elicited by the scene where the dead miner's body is washed by his women.' Her review was too long, however, and *The Times* only published it in a cut version: 'all my warmest commendations were omitted', she remarked ruefully.[91] The review was still full of praise: 'Here

---

[89] Staged in the Unitarian Schools, Altrincham, Cheshire. Information kindly provided by Cheshire County Newspapers, Altrincham, and the Altrincham Garrick Society. See also *Letters*, iii. 428, 430.

[90] 12 March 1920, p. 7; reprinted Sagar 286–7.

[91] Carswell, *The Savage Pilgrimage*, pp. 130, 135, 137.

we have an every-day situation stripped, as only a master can strip it, of all inessentials, developing and coming to a crisis of clear statement by means only of every-day action and every-day speech, yet in its simplicity making an intense impression on the mind and the emotions'.[92] Her main criticism was of the lack of any real sense of Holroyd's feelings for his wife in the early days of their marriage, and the printed review ended with a sensible criticism she may nevertheless have blushed for: 'It is a pity that the author ... could not for himself have seen a performance showing so clearly ... what alterations are demanded by the action of his fine and stimulating play' (p. 14). Twelve years later she described the production as 'creditable if no more', but also declared herself convinced that 'a body-washing scene was theatrically unacceptable'. What was powerful on the printed page could not work on stage:

Either it must be done 'off' with only the voices and the footsteps of the women to give it reality, or the stage must be darkened to a firelight glow and the whole production lifted into a plane beyond realism with movements that were classically simplified. To read, the scene is simple and tragic. Outside the Irish People's Plays I reckon we can hardly match it in English with any other scene of dramatic dialogue having working folk as the protagonists. And the play holds its own against the Irish plays.

She concluded that 'the theatre itself was antipathetic to Lawrence' and that his plays 'are not truly adapted to the mechanics of our stage ... He was not interested in "problems," effective situations, or any of the sophisticated trickery of the modern theatre.'[93]

Lawrence was 'disappointed by the general lack of notice'[94] of the Altrincham production and rightly deduced that Catherine Carswell had found it 'altogether a bit of a bore, and that you were miserable' (iii. 495); but he remained grateful to her for going. The production had, after all, been a significant moment, though it had also sharpened his sense of himself as an author who had an extremely ambivalent relationship with his public. On the one hand, he desired to have a significant impact upon them – on the other hand, he did not want to feel himself confined by any need to write for them.

A few weeks after the Altrincham production, he wrote to Mackenzie that

My idea of a play is that any decent actor should have the liberty to alter as much as he likes – the author only gives the leading suggestion. Verbatim reproduction seems to me nonsense. – I should like to see the things done, and done properly.

---

[92] *The Times*, 12 March 1920, p. 14; reprinted Sagar 285–6.
[93] Carswell, *The Savage Pilgrimage*, pp. 135–6.
[94] Ibid., p. 137.

Oh, if there were *actors*! I'd like to be there to *beat* the actors into acting. What
terrifying thrills ahead!   (iii. 510)

Some days later he added, however, that 'I *can't* be *very* interested in plays,
even my own. I somehow have no belief in the public . . . ' (iii. 522).

The Altrincham production may, however, have helped Goldring persuade
the management committee of the 'People's Theatre Society' (currently
joining forces with the politically committed Curtain Group) to stage *The
Widowing of Mrs. Holroyd*; and that might conceivably have put Lawrence
on the map in theatrical London. Lawrence had discussed the play with
Goldring in the summer of 1919, and had suggested that Goldring's Irish
actress wife, Betty, should play the part of Mrs Holroyd: 'I'd like to see her
act'.[95] Goldring too had been to see the Altrincham production, 'was
greatly impressed and hurried back to London, in triumph, to report to
my colleagues . . . If a company of amateurs could put on the play
successfully in the provinces, surely, with all the professional talent at our
command, we could do the same in London.'[96] During the week of 19–26
March 1920, the 'People's Theatre' production was announced, and, on 27
March, Goldring and Harold Scott (the joint Hon. Secretaries) gave
further details. However, Goldring faced the opposition of the Curtain
Group and remembered that: 'No sooner had I won over dear Harold, by
hours of argument, to my views, than they fell upon him and won him
back again!' In spite of all his efforts, 'I was, to my despair, outvoted on the
Lawrence issue, and resigned from the society . . . My many months of toil
on Lawrence's behalf were thus completely wasted.'[97] It would be another
six years before the play was staged in London.

1924–6. *David* considered, *Altitude* and *Noah's Flood* written

Four years later, Lawrence turned to thinking about plays again. He and

[95] Nehls, i. 491; *Letters*, iii. 380.

[96] Nehls, i. 495.

[97] Ibid., i. 496. During an interval in an evening of one-act plays by the Curtain Group at the
Lyric Opera-House, Hammersmith, in March 1920, 'an outline was given of the immediate
intentions of the People's Theatre Society, into which the Curtain Group is to be merged
forthwith. Among the plays announced for early production were . . . Mr. D. H. Lawrence's
"The Widowing of Mrs. Holroyd" ' (*Athenaeum*, 26 March 1920, p. 423); Nehls, ii. 36. On
27 March, Goldring and Scott confirmed that the production of *The Widowing of Mrs.
Holroyd* was 'in active preparation, and the date of performance will be announced in due
course' (*Athenaeum*, 2 April 1920, p. 458). After Goldring's resignation, the Society staged
Srĝan Tučić's *The Liberators* (tr. Fannie S. Copeland, 1918) – see *Observer*, 20 June 1920,
p. 7 – 'and promptly died of it, in debt' (Nehls, i. 496).

Frieda were on their second visit to America – this time accompanied by the artist Dorothy Brett – and they were all living in Taos, New Mexico, in houses owned by Mabel Dodge Luhan.[98] It had been Mabel Luhan who had originally invited him to New Mexico in 1921; and although relations between her, the Lawrences and her Indian husband, Tony, were often strained, they continued to see each other – and each other's visitors – during the spring and summer of 1924. In the spring of 1924 Mabel had visits from Santa Fe – 'half a day's trip then each way' – from her friend the one-time actress Ida Rauh: Ida and her new partner, the painter Andrew Dasburg, would occupy one of the numerous houses on Mabel's estate.[99] On 7 April, Lawrence described Ida as 'very nice' and was thinking of her in a most friendly way a month later (v. 28, 42). According to Brett, Ida Rauh was

a small, lithe woman with a mass of dark, curly hair like a great mop on her head. Level, narrow, beautifully formed eyebrows over bright, intelligent eyes, behind large tortoise shell spectacles. A big, well-shaped, curved nose; finely cut lips. She is burnt a dark brown and bears an amazing resemblance to Sarah Bernhardt.[100]

She and Lawrence would almost certainly have talked about theatre when they met (he had met very few actors, even retired ones, in the course of his career); and it was with her, her son Daniel Eastman and Dasburg that the Lawrences took part in games of acting and charades during April. Even when they had gone back to Santa Fe, the Lawrences continued to see them; a whole party from Taos including the Lawrences and Brett stayed (probably with Ida Rauh and Dasburg) in Santa Fe for a few days at the end of April. Dasburg recalled of Lawrence how 'No one enjoyed himself more playing charades than he'; Brett remembered how 'You [Lawrence] and Ida are the stars ... How *real* it all is to you ... Ida, acting with you, is helpless from laughing. Often and often we act Charades ...' Mabel Luhan, too, had happy memories of playing charades during those

---

[98] The Hon. Dorothy Brett (1883–1977), painter, daughter of 2nd Viscount Esher; studied at Slade School of Art, London; went to New Mexico with DHL and Frieda in 1924 and made it her home until her death; wrote *Lawrence and Brett: A Friendship* (Philadelphia, 1933). For Mabel and Tony Luhan, see Explanatory note on 539:12.

[99] Witter Bynner, *Journey with Genius* (New York, 1953), p. 249; see Explanatory notes on 539:12 and 547:19. When she divorced her husband, Max Eastman, in 1922, and went to live in Santa Fe with Dasburg, she gave up her theatre career for painting and sculpture. At some stage she made a clay bust of DHL, a photograph of which appeared as the frontispiece to *Laughing Horse*, no. 13 (April 1926).

[100] *Lawrence and Brett*, p. 49. There is a photograph of Ida Rauh in *Letters*, v.

'boisterous evenings with Ida and Dasburg': Lawrence 'was so gay and witty when he was playing! He could imitate anything or anybody.'[101]

In this context of a new interest in theatre and acting, it was apparently Frieda who originally gave her husband the idea for a play drawn from the Bible. According to her own account, she 'had been reading the old testament again in German and the puzzling figure of "David" with his so personal relationship to the Lord would send me to Lawrence asking him "How was it?" '[102] Some time during April 1924, Lawrence, Frieda, Brett, Mabel Luhan and Ida Rauh were returning to Taos after bathing in the nearby Manby Hot Springs when, according to Brett, Lawrence suddenly asked Ida:

'Ida, what kind of a play do you like best?' Ida, surprised, replies:
'Oh, I like stories from the Bible best.'
You [Lawrence] say: 'Do you know the story of David's wife, Michel?'
'No,' says Ida.
'After David came back from the wars, Michel said, "I'll never live with you again," and she never did. Do you like that story, Ida?'
Ida says, laughing: 'Yes, I think it's perfect.'
And you reply with a laugh, saying, 'I'll write a play about it for you.' And that was the beginning of your play, *David*.[103]

In detail, this must be an unreliable account: Lawrence knew his Bible too well to get it so palpably wrong.[104] But Frieda had apparently got him thinking about the David story, and, since he did eventually write *David*

---

[101] Nehls, ii. 197; Brett, *Lawrence and Brett*, p. 52; Mabel Luhan, *Lorenzo in Taos* (New York, 1932), p. 68.

[102] Letter from Frieda Lawrence to Kathryn Herbig, 26 April 1938 (*D. H. Lawrence's Manuscripts*, ed. Michael Squires, 1991, pp. 173–4). There is an obvious link between Frieda's initial interest in David and her subsequent determination to translate DHL's play into German (see Appendix v iii).

[103] *Lawrence and Brett*, p. 60. The fact that Ida Rauh was Jewish would perhaps have confirmed DHL in such a plan.

[104] Michal (Brett's spelling is wrong), quite late in the story of David, sees David 'girded with a linen ephod . . . leaping and dancing before the Lord', and 'despised him in her heart', remarking 'How glorious was the King of Israel to day, who uncovered himself to day in the eyes of the handmaids of his servants . . . Therefore Michal the daughter of Saul had no child unto the day of her death' (2 Samuel vi. 14–23, *KJB*). It seems unlikely that DHL could have turned this episode into the one in Brett's anecdote (the play as finished used no significant material after 1 Samuel xx), though he knew it well (see *The Rainbow*, ed. Mark Kinkead-Weekes, Cambridge, 1989, 170:9–12) and may have considered using it; David is given the word 'leaps' at 449:17. See too note on 499:2. After finishing the play, he revised his essay, 'The Crown', during July 1925 and incorporated yet another reading of the Bible story: 'And David never went in unto Michal any more, because she jeered at him. So that she was barren all her life' (*Reflections on the Death of a Porcupine and Other Essays*, ed. Michael Herbert, Cambridge, 1988, 268:32–4).

for Ida, he very probably discussed the Bible story with her before he, Frieda and Brett moved out of Taos, at the start of May. They went up to Lobo Ranch (which Mabel Luhan had given to Frieda, and which from August 1924 onwards they called Kiowa Ranch) eighteen miles away, where they spent most of the summer.

David was not the play Lawrence first wrote, however. On 19 June 1924, he, Frieda and Brett came down from the ranch to begin what turned out to be a five-day visit to Mabel and Tony Luhan in Taos,[105] when they also saw Elizabeth – Mabel's seventeen-year-old adopted daughter – and a number of Mabel's guests, including Clarence Thompson, an artist, and Alice Sprague (from New York) who was staying in Mabel's 'Pink House'.[106] With the acting, charades and his knowledge of Ida Rauh's old career, and impressed by the strikingly varied group of friends and acquaintances who came and went as Mabel Luhan's guests, staying in the houses she owned, it was natural that sometime during or (perhaps) shortly after the visit Lawrence should again have turned his hand to writing a play (which he called *Altitude*). He had planned to do the same kind of thing back in 1916 with the group of friends he was then living with: 'We are going to write, all of us together, a comedy for the stage, about Heseltine and his Puma and so on. It will be jolly'.[107] That idea had come to nothing; but in 1924 Lawrence at least started his play. The Taos guests' practice was to sleep in the houses allocated them and to gather at Mabel Luhan's house for breakfast; according to Brett, one morning 'there is no Amelia [Mabel's Mexican cook], so you and I [Lawrence and Brett], finding ourselves the first up, cook the breakfast. The others come in one by one, and each one, to your polite, amused enquiry as to how they feel, say: "Fine – oh, fine!" On this theme you start, later, to write a play.'[108] Mabel Luhan gave a very similar account of the play's origins, though she set the events earlier in the spring, while Ida Rauh was still in Taos and Mary Austin was a visitor: it is possible that she was actually influenced by her memories of the play when she wrote her account.

---

[105] DHL and Frieda were at Lobo Ranch on Wednesday 18 June (*Letters*, v. 57), in Taos on Thursday 19th (v. 58), and – though they had planned to return to Lobo on Saturday 21st (v. 59) – they only went back on Monday 23rd (v. 60).

[106] See Explanatory note on 539:12.

[107] Philip Heseltine (1894–1930), then staying with DHL and Frieda in Cornwall, and his mistress Minnie Lucy Channing (b. 1894), known as 'Puma' (ii. 501). DHL drew on them both in writing *Women in Love* a few months later, when he also incorporated a scene of impromptu ballet and mime. See *WL* 536, note on 62:22, and 91:5 – 92:4.

[108] *Lawrence and Brett*, p. 108; Brett places the occasion early in the summer of 1924.

He laid the opening scene in the morning in our house, with the usual anomalous mixture of people. The guests straggle into the big kitchen, one by one, to breakfast, and Mary Austin is keeping her promise to make us waffles.

'Oh, good morning, Mrs. Austin. How are *you* this morning?'

'Fine.'

'Hello, Mabel. How is everything?'

'Fine.'

Ida strolls in, looking tragic.

'Hello, Ida. How do you feel today?'

'Fine.' ...

A tap at the door, and a smiling Indian face peering in.

'Oh, it's Juan. How are you, Juan?'

'Fine.'

'Fine – fine – fine! That's all Americans have to say about themselves!' Lorenzo had scolded one day. 'I'll show them.' And he started to write it.[109]

Willard ('Spud') Johnson,[110] a friend who was a regular visitor but not actually there in mid-June, offered a rather different version of the play's origins which suggests the joint production ('all of us together') planned in 1916:

[Lawrence] scribbled the opening lines on the back of a candy box one evening in Mabel Luhan's living room, with several friends present offering suggestions as to who the characters should be and what they should do and say. It was an amusing game, and few of those who played it knew until many years later that the next day Lawrence finished this first scene and began a second.[111]

It seems likely that the fun of *Altitude* depended upon the persons in it recognising themselves and their characteristics, and it may very well have started as the kind of group production Johnson describes. Although some of the text may originally have been scribbled down as he claims, Lawrence's surviving pencil manuscript is inscribed on the first fourteen leaves of an otherwise empty small school composition book signed 'D. H. Lawrence / Taos': it is a strikingly clean text for such an apparently spontaneous production, suggesting that it may well have been preceded by a rough draft. The fact that the notebook is marked 'Taos' is evidence that the manuscript may have been started during an actual stay in Taos. Johnson is, however, misleading about the second scene, which was not unfinished, but complete.[112] The play unfortunately stops at that point –

[109] *Lorenzo in Taos*, p. 177.

[110] See Explanatory note on 539:12.

[111] *Laughing Horse*, no. 20 (Summer 1938), 12. DHL wrote to Johnson on 21 June (*Letters*, v. 59–60), evidence that Johnson was not in Taos during that particular visit.

[112] This may well have been because he was only printing Scene 1 in the *Laughing Horse*.

'Too bad', commented Mabel Luhan – but it is a significant and witty memorial to a 'group of more or less remarkable people, in a remarkable place, at a remarkable altitude'.[113] The two surviving scenes demonstrate Lawrence's acute ear for the nuances of people's speech, and his sharp eye for their characteristic poses. But the piece (printed in Appendix III) was strictly a *jeu d'esprit*, belonging wholly to the time and circumstances of its composition; there is no evidence that Lawrence ever thought of it again or tried to complete it.

After spending the rest of the summer of 1924 at the ranch, the Lawrences and Brett probably next saw Ida Rauh in mid-October, when they spent a couple of days in Santa Fe on their way to Mexico, eventually to the town of Oaxaca: Lawrence had decided to rewrite his Mexican novel 'Quetzal-coatl' (which became *The Plumed Serpent*).[114] While in Santa Fe, Lawrence and Ida again discussed the idea of a play; after the Lawrence party had left, Ida (never one to lose an opportunity of putting Mabel Luhan down) immediately told her about the plan. Mabel, always jealous of Lawrence and his talents, seems to have been annoyed. She wrote to Lawrence about it, only to have him reply tactfully, in a letter written on 29 October: 'Don't talk to me about plays – the very word makes me swear. At the minute there's not a play-word in me, and I'd rather be in New Mexico ... If I can sit still in Oaxaca, I shall probably pull off a play. But quien sabe!' (v. 158). The following day, writing to Dasburg, Lawrence was far more positive: 'Tell Ida the play is not dead, but sleeping' (v. 160). He had almost certainly not yet started it. A fortnight later, he wrote to Ida herself from Oaxaca:

In two days F[rieda] and I are going into a house, and then I shall really sit down to the play: and make it either Aztec or Jewish – King David or Moses: or else Montezuma. But I want it to be as *little* of a costume play as possible: only the *people*, not the so-called romance. I hope I'll be able to do it ... I'll really have a shot at the play. But don't count on it very much. I may not manage it, and if I do, probably no-one will like it. However – never say die.   (v. 174)

This suggests that Ida remained interested in the idea, and had reminded him of his promise in a letter which does not survive; but what most interested her may have been the idea of a play which she (with her continuing theatrical contacts) would get produced, rather than one in which she would herself necessarily make an appearance – though the

[113] *Lorenzo in Taos*, p. 177; see 548:39 – 549:1.
[114] See *The Plumed Serpent*, ed. L. D. Clark (Cambridge, 1987), pp. xxviii–xxxii.

thought of a major contemporary writer creating a play especially for her was not one any actress would have passed over lightly. Lawrence had, however, committed himself to writing his final version of 'Quetzalcoatl' (he needed the income which a novel would generate); and apart from a few essays and four sketches of life in Oaxaca, collected in *Mornings in Mexico*, he wrote very little besides the novel between November 1924 and the start of February 1925.

On 16 January 1925, however, he wrote to Ida, telling her how hard he had been working on the novel, and how 'I could take a wonderful and terrible play out of it, if I dared'. He was probably not yet in a position to do that, and simply promised her 'I shall not forget that play. It's rankling somewhere' (v. 199). However, the day he finished his novel – probably 1 February – he 'went down, as if shot in the intestines' (v. 230): he almost died of a combination of tuberculosis, influenza, malaria and typhoid. He and Frieda struggled back to Mexico City on 25 February (Brett had already returned to New Mexico at the end of January), but Lawrence had a relapse and had to stay in Mexico City for another four weeks before he was able to leave. In spite of being ill, almost the first thing he did was sketch out to Ida, on 3 March 1925, what he thought would be a 'very attractive scheme'. He was now planning to bring together the Atlantis myth with the Old Testament story of Noah:

Noah, and his three sons, his wife and sons' wives, in the decadent world: then he begins to build the ark: and the drama of the sons, Shem, Ham, Japhet, – in my idea they still belong to the old demi-god order – and their wives – faced with the world and the end of the world: and the jeering-jazzing sort of people of the world, and the sort of democracy of decadence in it: the contrast of the demi-gods adhering to a greater order: and the wives wavering between the two: and the ark gradually rising among the jeering.   (v. 217–18)

Clearly he had already done some serious thinking about *Noah's Flood*. He explained that he would be creating the part of the wife of Japhet especially for Ida, but still felt obliged to 'wonder if I'll feel enough strength to do it! But oh, what about the actors!' (v. 218).

He probably started writing some time in mid-March; and in one sense he did exactly what he had suggested in January, and took the play 'out of' the novel. In the penultimate chapter of *The Plumed Serpent*, his heroine Kate Leslie has a vision of the 'old pre-Flood world' and its 'old mode of consciousness':

She had a strange feeling, in Mexico, of the old prehistoric humanity, the dark-eyed humanity of the days, perhaps, before the glacial period. When the world was colder, and the seas emptier, and all the land-formation was different. When the waters of the world were piled in stupendous glaciers on the high places, and high, high upon the poles ... Then there was a mysterious, hot-blooded, soft-footed humanity with a strange civilisation of its own.[115]

Lawrence had been attracted to ideas of Atlantis and pre-history since 1917, by which time he knew Madame Blavatsky's *The Secret Doctrine* (1888) (iii. 150) – which linked the biblical Noah story to the Atlantis myth. By 1921 he had also read Thomas Belt's *The Naturalist in Nicaragua* (1874), with its references to Atlantis, while some of the reading he had done in Mexico while working on *The Plumed Serpent* had made him consider once again the myth of 'the way of the world before the Flood, before the mental-spiritual world came into being'.[116] There are other connections too between the novel and the play; the colour symbolism of red, yellow, blue, white and black used in the Huitzilopochtli scenes (chap. XXIII) corresponds directly with the colours of the robes worn by Shem, Ham, Japhet and Noah in *Noah's Flood*.[117] If we compare this new writing with the way he had written about Noah and the Flood at the start of 1924,[118] it is clear that early in 1925 he was creating a whole new context of meaning around Noah.

The manuscript of the unfinished first version of *Noah's Flood*, a pencil fragment only eleven pages long, survives in a notebook Lawrence used in Mexico; its text is inscribed immediately after the essay fragment 'Man is essentially a soul', also in pencil, which was written after 10 January 1925 and probably not until mid-March.[119] The text of *Noah's Flood* was

---

[115] Ed. Clark, 415:1, 3–4; 414:22–7, 30–2.

[116] Ibid., 415:4–5, 9–11. DHL's 'Foreword' to *Fantasia of the Unconscious* (1922) shows how seriously he took the myth of Atlantis and of Lemuria, a sunken Pacific continent: he refers there specifically to Belt's arguments, which hypothesise that a vast volume of the earth's water was once trapped in glaciers and that mean sea level was as much as 1,000 feet lower than it is today. DHL also probably knew Lewis Spence's *The Problem of Atlantis* (1924).

[117] See 564:39–40; see too *The Plumed Serpent*, ed. Clark, 378:32–4, and 'The Woman Who Rode Away', *The Woman Who Rode Away and Other Stories*, ed. Dieter Mehl and Christa Jansohn (Cambridge, 1995), 61:4–5, 8–12.

[118] See 'Books', *Reflections on the Death of a Porcupine*, ed. Herbert, 199:3–9, 200:14–17.

[119] The play is on pp. 133–43 (stamped numbering), the essay fragment on pp. 130–3. See too *Reflections on the Death of a Porcupine*, ed. Herbert, pp. liii and 389–90. *Noah's Flood* was also probably written soon after the unfinished novel *The Flying-Fish*, the first nine pages of which DHL – too ill to write – had had to dictate to Frieda, and notes for which had appeared in the same notebook as *Noah's Flood*, in ink, on pp. 129–30; these may well have been inscribed as early as January. (*The Flying-Fish* itself was written in another notebook.) The arguments for dating *The Flying-Fish* to 11–19 March 1925 advanced in *St. Mawr and Other Stories*, ed. Brian Finney (Cambridge, 1983), p. xxxiv, on the grounds of DHL's inability to write are, however, not conclusive: DHL was able to write a letter on 16 March (see *Letters*, v. 224). It seems certain, however, that the order of writing was (a)

originally prefaced by six-and-a-half lines of pencil summary or introduction which Lawrence almost completely deleted, perhaps when he
wrote out the character descriptions of Shem, Kanah, Ham, Shelah, etc.,
immediately below the deleted lines. The character of Noah may originally
have been set against 'modern humanists' (one of the few phrases still
legible).[120] The play develops the idea of an old-world, pre-Flood and
religious society opposed to a modern, unbelieving and democratic society;
it belongs to the same habit of thought as the passage in *The Plumed
Serpent*. Gethin Day, in *The Flying-Fish*, too, probably written late in
February or early in March, just before *Noah's Flood*, refers specifically to
'the presence of those handsome, dangerous, wide-eyed men left over from
the ages before the flood in Mexico'.[121]

It is fortunate that the letter to Ida Rauh of 3 March 1925 quoted above
survives, to give us some idea of the direction in which *Noah's Flood* was
headed: the extant manuscript fragment hardly makes it clear. On 19
March, Lawrence told Ida that he was at last actually engaged in writing
the play, and that he thought it would 'poco a poco ... come to what I
want: and you want' (v. 226). As he gave no sign of its being anything
other than the play he had so recently and so enthusiastically outlined to
her, he was almost certainly still engaged with *Noah's Flood*. The surviving
eleven-page fragment of the play, however (printed in Appendix IV) would
not have taken him long to write, even if he had been writing in bed, as the
pencil suggests. It is, however, possible that, before leaving Mexico City six
days later, he put *Noah's Flood* aside to experiment with another play
altogether.

The Lawrences started their journey back to the ranch on 25 March,
but were held up at the American border at El Paso for two days. They
finally got through, reached Santa Fe on the afternoon of 29 March and

the notes for *The Flying-Fish*, (b) *The Flying-Fish*, (c) 'Man is essentially a soul', (d)
Noah's Flood. The first was perhaps written in January 1925 and the second at the end of
February or the start of March, while the last two were probably written towards the end
of the time DHL spent in Mexico City (27 February–25 March).

[120] All that can now be read of the Introduction on p. 133 is:
Noah's Flood: Noah
the
modern humanists. He holds the old
his
own va   in men's   . One son
i   is materialistic &
                    Noah a rather faint-
hearted
                    his spiritual son

[121] See footnote 119 above and *St. Mawr*, ed. Finney, 209:30–1.

stayed there a couple of days.[122] Lawrence would have taken the chance of discussing his play with Ida Rauh, and – whatever was said – it sealed the fate of *Noah's Flood*. The next time we hear of the play Lawrence is writing, he had reverted to his original idea about David; and that project he would (as we shall see) carry through to completion.

Some time in the following two years, however, Lawrence began to rewrite *Noah's Flood*; the text he created then appears in a notebook bought at the Cartoleria L'Ancora in Florence, and is therefore unlikely to have been started before the end of March 1926, when he was in Florence for some days on his first visit since 1921. The notebook is even more likely to have been bought at some date after May 1926, when the Lawrences moved to their new home in the Villa Mirenda, just outside the city.[123] The first few pages of this second version show remarkably few variations from the first version, though it then becomes more seriously revised; but for some reason he stopped copying and revising when just over half-way through the first version.[124] Though working on it would have allowed him to continue to develop ideas he had begun to explore in his play *David* – and which did indeed get into the essays he started in June 1927 for his travel book *Sketches of Etruscan Places*[125] – the reception of *David* in London in May 1927 would probably have convinced him that a Bible play was not a good medium for the development of such ideas. This might suggest a rather earlier period of revision – perhaps as early as May–June 1926, provoked by his revision of *David* when re-working Frieda's German translation (see Appendix v iii). Whenever he went back to *Noah's Flood*, however, it would have reminded him of his illness of February–March 1925, while its themes would have been linked in his mind with *The Plumed Serpent*, with which he was feeling increasingly disillusioned (the writing of the first *Lady Chatterley's Lover* in the autumn of 1927 was in part a response to that). Some time between the late spring of 1926 and the summer of 1927, and probably in the first half of that period, he abandoned *Noah's Flood* for good.

---

[122] Nehls, ii. 398.

[123] The Mexican notebook would not have been suitable to continue the play, as by then it only had seven blank leaves following the play fragment. Some jottings concerning the sale of *Lady Chatterley's Lover* in 1928 appear on the Italian notebook's back cover, but provide no evidence of the second version's date; they indicate that, by the middle of 1928, DHL was using his notebook for other things.

[124] For the revisions, see the Textual apparatus to Appendix iv.

[125] Published as *Etruscan Places* by Martin Secker in 1932; *Sketches of Etruscan Places and Other Italian Essays*, ed. Simonetta de Filippis (Cambridge, 1992).

1925–6. *David* written and published

On 1 April 1925, Ida Rauh and Dasburg drove Frieda and Lawrence – still a very sick man – from Santa Fe over to Taos and then up to the Del Monte Ranch, home of Lawrence's friends the Hawk family,[126] where Brett had already settled herself in the orchard cabin; and on 5 April, Lawrence and Frieda travelled the two miles further up to Kiowa (v. 228, 230). In his first certain reference to *David*, Lawrence wrote to Ida on the 6th that 'I'll go on with the play when the spirit moves me; I hope soon. Anyhow it's a real thing to me, in a world of unrealities' (v. 233). The words 'go on' probably indicate that something was on paper, which in turn would suggest that he had started to write it either in Mexico City or (just possibly) in Santa Fe. The manuscript shows that, after completing the third scene, he inserted the heading 'Scene IV', in readiness for a new start, but did not begin the scene itself until later; it is possible that this marks the point he had reached before discussing the play with Ida, and the place where he took the play up again at Kiowa.

He was still too ill to do much, however, especially after the journey up from Mexico. In 1938 Frieda remembered how 'it was spring, and he lay on a canvas bed on the small porch outside the cabin and slowly, day by day his strength came back, he could hardly believe it. It seemed a miracle … The poignancy of "David" is partly a result of Lawrence's own escape from the valley of death.'[127] By 14 April, the manuscript was 'six scenes' long (v. 236): around 11,000 words, occupying 54 notebook pages, and written in pencil – which may suggest a man writing in bed, with his notebook propped up on his knees, and so not using his fountain-pen. At his usual rate of composition, Lawrence could have written that much in three or four days; but he was working slowly – Frieda remarked that he was 'sleeping quite a lot of the time' (v. 233) – and the next 10,000–11,000 words would take him about a fortnight. It seems sensible to assume that he had written something (perhaps the first 3 scenes) in Mexico City or Santa Fe, had shown what he had done to Ida, and then written the next 3 scenes between 6 and 14 April.

When he reported his progress to Ida, one of the interesting things was that it had decisively changed from being a play primarily for *her* to take the starring role in:

Myself I like it very much. But it's nearly all *men*. You may not like Michal, but I

---

[126] William (1891–1975) and his wife Rachel Woodman Hawk (b. 1898) ran a small dairy farm on his parents' ranch, near Kiowa.

[127] *D. H. Lawrence's Manuscripts*, ed. Squires, pp. 173–4.

think she'll interest you. Today I shall give the MS so far to Brett, she will begin typing, and when she's ready, I'll send you a copy – even though it's only six scenes – and you can see what you think of it: also I shall be very glad of Andrew's opinion. But don't say anything to anybody else. When it's a bit further on, you and Andrew must come up, and we'll talk everything over. (No acts – only about 12 scenes, one after the other.) (v. 236–7)

David eventually grew to seventeen scenes, and was then cut back to sixteen. Lawrence was still a long way from being restored to health – as he told his sister Emily King on 21 April, 'I don't work yet' (v. 244) – and he took what was for him quite a long time to finish the play. But by 1 May it was 'well on: $\frac{2}{3}$ done, easily. Brett is slowly typing' (v. 248). He had finished perhaps twelve of the seventeen scenes he then planned, which would have meant that he was up to p. 131 in his notebook. However, a major revision to the ending had delayed the play's completion for a few days: this involved him writing and then deleting two complete scenes, a false start and then a completely new final scene.[128] He finally announced on 7 May that he had finished (v. 250).

David was unlike anything else he had ever written. Extensive as was his own biblical knowledge, it is inconceivable that he could have quoted so accurately without at times referring to a Bible, and he was a long way from books and libraries. He might have been obliged to use the *American Standard Version* (first published in 1901) or the *Revised Version* (1881–5), or even the German Bible which had given Frieda her initial interest in the character. But the text he produced shows that he must have had a copy of the *King James Bible* of 1611.[129] Around the quotations, Lawrence wove prose so often endowed with the cadences and language of *KJB* that it is sometimes impossible – without checking – to tell precisely where quotation stops and pastiche begins.[130]

Although the play is in one sense heavily dependent upon a Bible story, and upon the language of *KJB*,[131] Lawrence's work was that of a writer

---

[128] The progress of DHL's revision can be reconstructed from the manuscript: see Appendix v i. He numbered the fifteenth scene 'XIV', which affected all subsequent numbers.

[129] Cf. 438:38–9 ('the chief of the things which should have been utterly destroyed') with 1 Samuel xv. 21 ('the chief of the things which should have been utterly destroyed', *KJB*; 'the chief of the devoted things', *ASV* and *RV*). The Bible was probably Mabel Luhan's; Frieda referred in the summer of 1924 to the fact that, at the ranch, 'we have no books, except your bible!' (*Lorenzo in Taos*, p. 250).

[130] In *David*, DHL often confined himself (even when using modern words) to a relatively simple vocabulary: so that in scene 1, e.g., words like 'jackal', 'sand-storm' and 'tinkle' (435:14, 15, 30) stand out as both non-*KJB*, and subsequent to 1611.

[131] It was written in a decade which saw at least one other major dramatic treatment of the story of David: the oratorio *Le Roi David* (1921) by the French composer Arthur

appropriating the Bible for his own purposes: and those purposes remained those which had informed his thinking about *Noah's Flood*. They included the definition of a God who was certainly not the Jewish God, and of a religion that was most certainly not that of the Judeo-Christian tradition, but of an older, animist and cosmic kind. We can see Lawrence in *Noah's Flood* creating a myth about civilisation's movement away from its older, religious origins; the myth is fleshed out in *David* and finally clarified in the essays he wrote for *Sketches of Etruscan Places*. In some ways, those essays are clearer than either of the plays: it is as if the plays had been work in progress, and - having made another abortive stab at *Noah's Flood* after finishing *David* – Lawrence had been able to reap the rewards of clarity and understanding in the travel book. The latter would claim that

> The old idea of the vitality of the universe was evolved long before history begins, and elaborated into a vast religion … we see evidence of one underlying religious idea: the conception of the vitality of the cosmos … and man, amid all the glowing welter, adventuring, struggling, striving for one thing, life, vitality, more vitality: to get into himself more and more of the gleaming vitality of the cosmos.[132]

As if to confirm that this was something he had learned from the play, Lawrence then drew a direct comparison with David: 'This was the idea at the back of all the great old civilisations. It was even, half-transmuted, at the back of David's mind, and voiced in the Psalms. But with David the living cosmos became merely a personal god.'[133] That was an insight to which the play had led Lawrence, and one of the reasons why the figure of Saul would become increasingly important to him.[134] The play creates Saul as the last of the old civilisation, as one of the believers in the old relationship between man and the cosmos, whereas David is by comparison modern man, living through his wits and his intelligence, and believing in a personal relationship with a personal God, which is all that his intelligence permits him.

Such a distinction between an older, heroic, mythic Saul, living instinctively, and a younger, cleverer, more self-conscious David, was itself the culmination of a distinction which had been growing clearer not only in Lawrence's thinking during the early months of 1925, but in many of

---

Honegger (1892–1955) – libretto by René Morax (1873–1963), Swiss dramatist – was performed in a revised version in London on 17 March 1927, two months before the first performance of DHL's *David*. No one appears, however, to have commented on the coincidence.

[132] *Sketches of Etruscan Places*, ed. de Filippis, 57:30–9.
[133] Ibid., 58:8–11.
[134] At some point, he considered re-naming the play *Saul*: see Explanatory note on 435:1.

his references to David over the years.[135] It also accounts for the play's deliberate (and, in first proof revision, frequent) replacement of the Judaic 'Lord' or 'Lord God' with the name of a cosmic principle, such as 'Thunder', 'Wave', 'Fire' or 'Deep', who is far closer – both in conception and in the language in which such a being is described – to the animist religions of the North American Indians by which Lawrence was fascinated.[136] Consequently, the play became (paradoxically) both Lawrence's most Bible-influenced work, and an attempt to get behind the Bible story completely: something similar to his thinking when he wrote *Apocalypse* in the winter of 1929. In both works he would develop his thinking about cultural and religious change – something which he would probably have claimed to be implicit in the Bible account, but which was primarily part of his own developing myth about change, his own attempt to understand how modern man came to be as he was.

In the early summer of 1925, however, upon finishing *David*, Lawrence's immediate thoughts were about its potential in the theatre; and for that reason he very much wanted Dasburg and Ida Rauh – who had both been concerned with the play during its long period of gestation – 'to see it and say what you think'. She was currently his only real contact with the theatre world, while he also hoped that Dasburg would 'make stage sketches' (v. 248).[137] Brett remembered this part of the work: 'You are writing the play for Ida – *David* – and I am once more typing. I have done a great deal. I have plenty of time in my cabin in the orchard.'[138] Having finished it on 7 May, Lawrence wrote to Ida Rauh that they would be pleased to see her as soon as she could come – they hoped for the following weekend, 9–10 May – and that Brett would put her up in her cabin at Del Monte Ranch: 'Do hope you'll like the play'. Frieda added a postscript saying 'I like the play very much' and that 'I think Mical is a good role and for you!' (v. 250). Three days later, a little concerned at not having heard from Ida Rauh – she had been ill – Lawrence wrote again: 'the play is

---

[135] See *Hardy* 61:27–62:16, 74:2–5; 'The Reality of Peace', 'The Crown', *Reflections on the Death of a Porcupine*, ed. Herbert, 48:30, 257:38, 268:25 – 269:5; 'The Theatre', *Twilight in Italy*, ed. Eggert, 146:25–6; and the essay 'David', *Sketches of Etruscan Places*, ed. de Filippis, 185–9. In the 1915 version of 'The Crown', however, David turns to Jonathan as one 'given up to the flux of corruption ... *This* is the reason of homosexuality ... the higher, more developed type seeking to revert to the lower' (*Reflections on the Death of a Porcupine*, ed. Herbert, 472).

[136] See, e.g., Explanatory notes for 439:30 and 454:27.

[137] Six surviving pencil sketches of sets for *David* (UTul) may originate with Dasburg: they follow an (ink) list of scenes requiring sets.

[138] *Lawrence and Brett*, p. 217.

finished, and a good deal is typed out. We might have some fun with it, when you come ... it will be amusing to read, amongst us' (v. 252).

Around 15 May, plans were being made for her imminent arrival, and a letter Lawrence wrote to her on 18 June describes things on the ranch – together with changes which had happened since mid-May – which would probably only have made sense if she had already visited them (v. 268). Brett remembered that Ida's visit took place shortly before Frieda's nephew, Friedel Jaffe, came to stay, and he arrived on 19 May. It seems most probable that Ida Rauh arrived around 16 May and – as planned – stayed with Brett at Del Monte Ranch.[139] The night she arrived, Lawrence went down to meet her, and the three of them (according to Brett) sat 'a little while after supper talking about ... *David* and the part of Michal you have written for her to act in, when it is produced'.[140] Whether Ida was so committed to acting in it was another matter.

In spite of Lawrence's original plan of reading the play 'amongst us', the manuscript was still the only complete copy available (Brett's typing had been very slow). So Lawrence read the whole of it out loud, at Kiowa Ranch over the next two days:

in the slightly shy, bashful way you have; and you sing in a soft voice the little songs you have invented for the play. You live every part. In some subtle way you change and change about, as the characters alter from men to women, from young to old. You read till evening, with pauses for tea; then suddenly you stop in the very middle of one of the songs and say:

'I feel so embarrassed. You all embarrass me. I cannot go on.' But my enthusiasm for the play urges you on again; I am so keen for Ida to hear it. She, though, is strangely silent. What can be the matter with her?

But there is no time to finish it: you are too tired by now, your voice is getting hoarse; so we leave and arrange to come up again tomorrow.[141]

The reading seems to have taken place inside the cabin on the first day; but Brett photographed Lawrence sitting at a table on the porch with Ida and Frieda, perhaps in the act of reading it the following day.[142] When he reached the end – 'you are sitting at the table and Ida is also sitting at the

---

[139] Although DHL would tell Idella Purnell on 5 June that they had not yet 'seen anybody from Santa Fe ... since we are here' (*Letters*, v. 261), he almost certainly meant that they had not seen her friends Witter Bynner or Spud Johnson. Idella Purnell (1901–82) was a poet and former student (1918–19) at the University of California of the poet Witter Bynner (1881–1968), who now lived in Santa Fe, and for whom Johnson worked as secretary for a time.

[140] *Lawrence and Brett*, p. 217.

[141] Ibid., p. 219.

[142] Ibid. The photograph is reproduced in *D. H. Lawrence and New Mexico*, ed. Keith Sagar (Salt Lake City, 1982), p. 48.

table leaning her head on her hand, her thick dark curly hair like a bush shading her face' – Ida remained silent.

She shows no enthusiasm; yet I know she feels the beauty of the play. You look at her and she looks up at you, strangely, and says in a flat, tired voice:

"I am too old, Lorenzo; too old to play the part of Michal – so young, so radiant a creature!"[143]

Brett felt that everyone was 'appalled': the thought that Ida might be too old for the part (she was forty-eight) 'had never entered our heads'. The fact that she subsequently read the play in manuscript suggests that her immediate reaction was not final, and that she was willing to reconsider. In mid-July, Lawrence was still writing to her in the hope that 'you'll tackle Michal' (v. 277): 'I understand your feelings about the play, but don't approve of them: that is, I don't approve of your feeling old. It is only when one *lets go* that one feels old: or is old. You're not old' (v. 282). However, as Brett's account of the reading suggests, Ida's objections may not have been simply about the age of the character. She apparently told Lawrence that what she really wanted was a play 'about a woman', something he remembered three years later, when he criticised her for 'hysteria' and 'nagging about intimate companionship' and '*talk* about herself and personalities' (vii. 24). After she had read *David*, in July 1925, Lawrence told her that he felt 'you weren't very much interested: and that you'd have much preferred a more personal play, about a woman. Probably you would – and naturally. But I myself am a bit tired of personal plays, "about a woman." Time we all sank our personalities a bit, in something bigger' (v. 276). It is, however, perfectly possible that Ida – an extremely experienced actress and highly independent woman – had originally placed such a stress on the age of the character in order to disguise other and more profound objections to the play, and to the idea of her taking part in a production of it; but she had not chosen a good way of convincing a man who, four years earlier, had remarked that 'Our stage is all wrong, so boring in its personality.'[144]

In spite of Ida's reaction, however, Lawrence did not give up the idea of having *David* staged. On 26 May he told his English agent Curtis Brown[145] about the play, and that he would send it on when it was typed: 'But I don't care about having it published' (v. 257). Brett was making both

---

[143] *Lawrence and Brett*, pp. 219–20.
[144] *Sea and Sardinia*, ed. Mara Kalnins (Cambridge, 1997), 189:37–8.
[145] Albert Curtis Brown (1866–1945) had become DHL's agent in April 1921.

a ribbon and a carbon copy, of which the ribbon copy survives; during
May or June, Lawrence revised both typescripts, heavily in places but – as
usual when he had multiple typescripts of a work – slightly differently
from each other. On 18 June, Lawrence was able to send Ida 'the last of the
play' – that is, the last part of the manuscript: Brett had at last finished the
typing. Lawrence was then able to despatch 'my other two MSS.' – i.e. the
typescript and the carbon copy – to the New York branch of Curtis Brown:
'one for London' (v. 268). As he had let Ida have the whole of the
manuscript, Lawrence thus left himself without a copy of the play; and a
fortnight later, he had to ask her to send it back, as Frieda wanted to
embark on a German translation of the text (v. 275) – which she started
that month, and finished early in 1926.[146]

Lawrence insisted to Curtis Brown on 23 June that 'It is a good play,
and for the theatre. Someone ought to do it' (v. 270), and he made the
same point to his current American publisher, Alfred Knopf, a week later,
in spite of having already heard Curtis Brown's doubts about its chances
on the stage. 'I don't want it published, unless it is produced' (v. 274), he
told Knopf, who by now had a typescript in his possession: from the start
Lawrence had been thinking of it as a play for the stage, as well as for a
particular actress.

Curtis Brown thinks it would be better if it appeared first as 'literature.' Myself, I
am a bit tired of plays that are only literature. If a man is writing 'literature,' why
choose the form of a play? And if he's writing a play, he surely intends it for the
theatre. Anyhow I wrote this play for the theatre, and I want the theatre people to
see it first. (v. 274)

Curtis Brown in England, who had been sent the carbon-copy typescript,
objected to the 'long speeches that call for a whole company of Forbes-
Robertsons', meaning actors like Sir Johnston Forbes-Robertson, of old-
fashioned histrionic power and stage presence; but Lawrence insisted that
'There might be a whole company of even better men', and revealed how
he was now thinking of its staging:

I believe there might be found Jews or Italians or Spaniards or Celts to do the thing
properly: not Teutons or Scandinavians or Nordics: it's not in their blood – as a
rule. And if the speeches are too long – well, they can be made shorter if necessary.

[146] She had assisted with the translation into German of W. B. Yeats's play *The Land of
Heart's Desire* in 1911: see *Early Years* 377 and n. 23. She had thought of translating *The
Widowing of Mrs. Holroyd* in August 1914: DHL had asked his friend Koteliansky to bring
a copy when he came to visit, as 'my wife wants to amuse herself by translating it' (*Letters*,
ii. 210), but so far as is known she did not do so. For her work on *David*, see Appendix v
iii.

But my God, there's many a *nigger* would play Saul better than Forbes-Robertson could do it. And I'd prefer the nigger. Or men and women from that Jewish theatre.[147]

Back in January 1925 he had rather cynically remarked that 'As for the stage – on it or off it, it's the same old show' (v. 199); and he was well aware how different *David* was from conventional theatre. It was the only one of his full-length plays not to have either three or five acts, but to be constructed as a series of scenes, like contemporary expressionist plays. It was also less about individuals and more concerned to convey a religious experience, as the Greek theatre had been and as *The Plumed Serpent* was. And yet he wanted it staged: 'Playgoing', he insisted, 'isn't the same as reading. Reading in itself is highbrow. But give the "populace" in the theatre something with a bit of sincere good-feeling in it, and they'll respond' (v. 274). He still hoped that he had written something which that 'populace' could respond to; he would have liked his play to appeal to just that audience which he knew his fiction could never reach.[148]

Ida Rauh had written a helpful letter earlier in the summer to Philip Moeller, one of the founders and directors of the New York Theatre Guild, founded in 1918 to produce contemporary and uncommercial work; in April 1925 they had come into the possession of a new building. The important thing was to get *David* into their hands; Lawrence asked Ida to write to them again towards the end of July, to explain that a copy would soon be arriving. It seems clear, however, that Curtis Brown (New York) regarded volume publication as both more important and more likely than stage performance, and was in no particular hurry to send the theatre a copy. However, after some delays the agency sent them the copy Knopf had had (v. 281). The Theatre Guild made up their minds remarkably quickly; they decided against it during September, while Lawrence was himself in New York, though they did not tell him before he left – 'damn them' (v. 303). He had anyway, found them 'damned week-endy' (v. 308) when he had gone to see them. Thus ended, however, Lawrence's best chance of having one of his plays performed by the kind of group which might have done it well.

---

[147] *Letters*, v. 274; the 'Jewish Theatre' was the New York Theatre Guild (see below).
[148] It is impossible to tell how far DHL realised that he would almost certainly not have been able to see his play on the public stage in Britain; the Lord Chamberlain, at that date, would have been most unlikely to license it for public exhibition, given its extensive use of (and quotation from) the Bible. It could only be staged in theatre clubs or in amateur performances.

Lawrence had been pressing for stage performance in England, too; having got the manuscript back from Ida Rauh for Frieda, only a fortnight later (on 31 July) he despatched it to England,[149] to give Curtis Brown (London) a second copy of the play to show theatre managements: something obviously considerably more important to him than Frieda's translation (or the fact that the manuscript lacked the extensive revisions of the typescripts). He also made it clear on 13 August that although his English publisher, Martin Secker, was ready to publish the play in the autumn: 'I don't want it published yet. I want to try the theatres first. I want Curtis Brown's to try the theatres in London, *quite seriously*' (v. 285). He told the agency the following day that 'I don't want the play *published* until it has been considered by any possible *producer* ... I wish you would try in London for a chance of *production*, before there is any thought of publication' (v. 286). Lawrence and his agent clearly had different priorities.

When he finally got back to England late in September 1925, however, and found that there was still no one interested in a stage production, he allowed Secker to proceed with publication. A 2-guinea limited edition of 250 copies was originally planned (v. 333), though Secker finally decided on an edition (hereafter E1) of 500 large-paper copies costing 15s each. Both plans show that Secker was aiming at the specialist market for limited editions of finely produced books: even 15s was more than four times the cost of *Touch and Go*. Secker sent his carbon copy of the play to the printers, the Riverside Press of Edinburgh, for setting-copy.

The Lawrences left England at the end of October 1925, went to Baden-Baden to see Frieda's mother and ended up in mid-November in Spotorno, on the Italian Riviera – a place recommended to them by Secker, whose wife's family lived there. Lawrence saw a 'Nice proof of *David*' just as he was leaving Baden-Baden on 12 November, and he returned Secker's publication agreement four days later (v. 336), but he did no proof correction, as he would certainly have done if he had seen a set of proofs – even galley proofs; and we know that the first page proofs arrived only in December. He had most likely seen a specimen page, despatched to show him the handsome type and large page format. He had a settled address in Spotorno by 18 November, but on the 30th was complaining that he was

---

[149] DHL's remark to Curtis Brown (London) of 31 July – 'To-day I sent off the third copy of the play' (which can only have been MS: he had sent off his two typescripts the previous month) – puzzled the editors of the Cambridge *Letters*, who noted 'This contradicts Letter 3452' (v. 283 and n. 2). Letter 3452 – written on 24 July – informed Ida Rauh that Curtis Brown (New York) had 'just received my third copy of *David*' (ibid., 281); but that 'third copy' was undoubtedly the typescript which Curtis Brown had recovered from Knopf (who had had it for a month) to pass on to the Theatre Guild.

still awaiting proofs (v. 346). He started to get his two sets of the first page proofs around 8 to 12 December; the surviving, partially corrected set marked '1st proofs' (hereafter PPI) bears date-stamps from the Edinburgh printer indicating 4, 8, 14 and 17 December for signatures A–B, C–D, E–F and G–H respectively. Secker himself came to Spotorno on 12 December to spend Christmas with his wife's family, and it is conceivable (though not likely) that he brought some signatures with him. The last two signatures from Edinburgh would probably have arrived in Spotorno between 18 and 21 December. The fully corrected set of first proofs, which was returned to the printer, was last seen around 1949, when it was described as having 'On nearly every page ... numerous alterations and corrections in the text, on the vers[o] and title page are notes for the publisher and on one blank page the list of characters.'[150] Lawrence also included a character list in PPI.[151]

Lawrence worked on the proofs immediately, for he despatched the fully corrected set to the Riverside Press in time for them to pull a revised set dated '31.12.25.' and marked '2nd Proof'. Two sets of these, again, arrived in Spotorno, probably all at one time (the individual signatures are not date-stamped) early in January: the almost uncorrected duplicate set (hereafter PPII) still survives.[152] On 6 January, Lawrence remarked in a letter that he was 'correcting final proofs of *David*, and find it good' (v. 370).

There is no indication of when Lawrence returned his corrected set of second proofs; but given his haste with the marked set of first proofs, the second proofs were probably back in Edinburgh at the latest by the middle of January. It is just possible that Secker took the corrected set back with him on 18 January when he returned to London, to protect Lawrence and his proofs against the uncertainties of the Italian postal system.

Lawrence, however, wrote to Secker less than a fortnight after his publisher had left, asking 'Why don't you defer the play a bit – perhaps even till autumn? That would do' (v. 388). The suggestion seems to have

---

[150] *A Catalogue of Valuable Books by D. H. Lawrence* (Melvin Rare Books, Edinburgh, n.d. [1948–9]), p. 14. The inclusion of the character list in DHL's hand shows them to have been first proofs: the second proofs had a printed list. See also next footnote.

[151] He presented PPI to his American bibliographer Edward McDonald on 11 January 1926 (v. 376). The fully corrected set of first proofs was returned to DHL (presumably with the second proofs) and in April 1928 he had it bound in Florence (*Letters*, vi. 348 n. 5) by his bookseller friend Giuseppe Orioli: its multi-coloured binding – 'black, grey and white decorated boards' – was characteristic of bindings Orioli supplied (see, e.g., the bindings on Roberts E351a, E412a, E362.6, E397a and E87.1a).

[152] See footnote 326 below. DHL gave them to his Florence friend, Arthur Wilkinson, at Christmas 1926. The now missing fully corrected set of second proofs would have gone back to the Riverside Press, and is unlikely to have been returned to DHL.

been made because Secker wanted an autumn book from Lawrence, and
Lawrence was increasingly afraid he might have nothing else to offer.
Nevertheless, Secker did not deviate and brought out E1 on 25 March
1926.[153] Lawrence liked its appearance – it was a handsome royal octavo,
measuring 9 × 6 inches, with uncut fore and bottom edges and wide
margins round the text – and told Secker it looked 'very nice' (v. 413); but
he was also shocked at its price, remarking to his agent 'fifteen bob for that
bit of a book!' (v. 415): it was only 128 pages long.[154] The English edition
sold out within a few days of publication; although, by the end of June,
Secker was discussing a smaller, cheaper edition, even that was planned as
a relatively expensive book; to Lawrence, once again, 'six shillings seems
dear for a plain *David* play' (v. 481). In the event, it was decided to
postpone the cheaper edition until a London stage production, first
proposed in June, had taken place.

Knopf had at first not wanted *David* at all, which was probably why he
had given up his typescript to Curtis Brown for the Theatre Guild; nor was
he attracted by the idea of a limited edition (Lawrence believed that Knopf
regarded such things as 'a bit of a swindle' – v. 415). Having agreed to go
ahead with publication, however, Knopf decided not to buy sheets from
Secker; Lawrence was pleased to find that 'Knopf sets up the *David* play
over there' (v. 460). He was less pleased, however, to hear nothing at all
about its publication: he commented in February 1927 that 'I hear Knopf
published *David* last September, and I never heard a word nor saw a sign'
(v. 638): he had obviously not seen proofs. The American edition (hereafter
A1) had actually appeared on 23 April 1926, selling for $2, Knopf's usual
price for a short Lawrence book. Knopf must have been sent either an
advance copy of E1 or (just possibly) a very carefully corrected set of
second proofs; A1 incorporated every detail of E1's regularisation of the
text and was (apart from its own compositors' regularisations and errors[155])
wholly derived from E1.

David was greeted in print in 1926 with both respect and admiration.

[153] Roberts A34; price 15s, first edition 'limited to Five Hundred copies' (p. [2]): see
advertisement in *Times Literary Supplement*, 25 March 1926, p. 229. Secker reprinted it at
6s in an edition of 1,500 copies on 3 February 1927: see advertisement in *Times Literary
Supplement*, 3 February 1927, p. 69. It became the third play in *Plays* and the second in
Complete Plays.
[154] Author's copies went to his sisters Ada Clarke and Emily King, to Brett, Ida Rauh and
Barbara Low; DHL retained the sixth and last copy himself, though he had given it away
by 8 June and had to ask Secker for another (v. 472). He also sent a copy to his Australian
collaborator on *The Boy in the Bush*, Mollie Skinner (v. 420).
[155] E.g. A1 reads 'thou are' (p. 22) where E1 (p. 26) correctly reads 'thou art' (449:29).

Edward Shanks in the *Saturday Review* on 1 May (a review headed 'Mr. Lawrence's Philosophy') called it 'This beautiful play' and – in sharp contrast with his savage criticisms of *The Plumed Serpent* in the *London Mercury* in March (pp. 549–51) – described *David* as 'certainly one of the most nearly perfect of Mr. Lawrence's productions' (p. 574). Edward Sackville-West, in the *New Statesman* of 10 July, praised the 'deliberate and well-managed archaism of its diction', its 'clarity of thought and beauty of detail': he thought the last two scenes 'superbly moving' and 'of great emotional solemnity' (pp. 360–1). Bonamy Dobrée, in an equally adulatory review in the *Nation and Athenaeum* on 24 April, found Lawrence's phrasing 'superb and varied: his play is full of poetry': 'the whole play in idea, phrasing and diction is a gloriously sustained piece of work ... the language is never excessive, but it burns like a great smokeless flame' (p. 104).[156] Both Dobrée and Sackville-West, however, expressed serious doubts about the play's possibilities on stage: 'the whole play would need relentless pruning for stage production', said Dobrée, while Sackville-West found he could 'scarcely imagine' it 'on the stage'.

1926–7. *David* and *The Widowing of Mrs. Holroyd* performed

As Lawrence had probably hoped, *David*'s appearance in print in the spring of 1926 provoked theatrical interest; and by early June 1926 he had heard that the prestigious Stage Society 'are playing *David* in Sept. in London, just one performance' (v. 470). His decision to go to England in August that year was almost certainly made in the belief that he would be able 'to see after those people who are going to give a performance of *David*' (v. 474): 'If they're rehearsing, I must keep an eye on them' (v. 475). By 8 June he had forgotten the name of the group intending to do it, but asked Secker if he knew anything about them: 'I wish you'd ask them if they keep the date fixed for the performance – if they fixed it – and tell them I shall be in London in August, and if they will be rehearsing then. I should like to have a finger in that particular pie' (v. 472). The Stage Society had expressed an interest in *The Widowing of Mrs. Holroyd* in the winter of 1913–14. Now with Geoffrey Whitworth as guiding spirit, for their production of *David* the Stage Society was planning to join with the smaller '300 Club', which had originally been inspired by Mrs Phyllis Whitworth 'in an attempt to assist young authors'.[157]

---

[156] Other reviews were: A. S. M. McDowell, 'Mr. Lawrence's "David"', *Times Literary Supplement*, 25 March 1926, p. 232; John Cournos, *Literary Digest*, November 1926.
[157] Allardyce Nicoll, *English Drama 1900–1930: The Beginnings of the Modern Period* (Cam-

But, more than a month later, Lawrence had heard nothing further, telling Catherine Carswell: 'I don't know the dates of the play, nor anything about it, and feel a bit tepid. God knows what these private societies are like!' (v. 498). Not apparently, until he and Frieda got to London on 30 July did he hear anything more; and his scepticism was confirmed by the news that rehearsals were after all not going to start until the end of August, while the play – just a 'couple of performances' – would probably not be put on before October or November (v. 506, 510). He still hoped, however, 'to see the first rehearsals, anyhow' at the end of the month and 'see if I can do anything about *David*. If I can, I shall have to stay a bit' (v. 510, 509). But he was also beginning to hope that he would not have to stay (v. 512).

What made the difference to the Lawrences' plans was their rather unexpected discovery towards the end of August of a congenial place to live, on the Lincolnshire coast. Lawrence decided not to return to Italy until he had seen at least the play's first rehearsals and had made 'what suggestions I can' (v. 517); but he only planned to go to London when 'they write to me that they are beginning' (v. 516). He wrote to Phyllis Whitworth on 2 September; but another extended silence from London left him 'annoyed and bored': 'thought I should have had some word by now. How long are they going to be, before they get a move on?' (v. 526, 522). On 8 September he had still heard nothing, 'damn them' (v. 526, 529). Frieda – in spite of feeling that 'we wont chase them – If they care so little, then they'd better be left' – tried to move things along by suggesting to Martin Secker that he might contact the Whitworths and Robert Atkins, the distinguished and experienced director who was going to take charge of the play.[158] In a postscript to her letter, however, Lawrence added 'Dont bother with anybody – Aikens or Whitworths' (v. 529); the misspelling of the director's name suggesting how little he knew either of the London theatre or of what (in this case) was going on.

A letter from Phyllis Whitworth came on 11 September, and Lawrence arranged to see her and Atkins when he and Frieda arrived in London a few days later: 'I am to see the people of the play as soon as I am in town', Lawrence remarked (v. 532). He arrived on the 16th (v. 536) but heard

---

bridge, 1973), p. 88. Phyllis Whitworth, née Bell (1884–1964), theatrical producer; m. 1910 Geoffrey Whitworth (1883–1951), critic, dramatist and founder of the British Drama League.

[158] Also producer and actor (1886–1972), who had once worked with Forbes-Robertson, Atkins had staged every Shakespeare play in the Folio while director of the Old Vic Theatre between 1920 and 1925: 'a man of almost Napoleonic drive' (Margaret Lamb, *'Antony and Cleopatra' on the English Stage*, London and Toronto, 1980, p. 106).

nothing; and by the 21st he had still not seen anyone to do with the play, though he had heard that they were 'still slowly assembling the cast' (v. 538). Letters had gone to the wrong address; and Phyllis Whitworth had still not got a copy of the play (v. 556). Finally, on 27 September – the day before the Lawrences left England – Lawrence met her and Atkins for lunch. After all his misgivings, Lawrence was impressed: 'I believe they'll do it pretty well' he told his mother-in-law, Anna von Richthofen (v. 544). But, he learned, 'they are putting off the actual performance till second week in December – to have time'. He promised both Phyllis Whitworth and Atkins 'to come back for the later rehearsals and the play' (v. 543). The plan for a December performance also gave Secker a new provisional publication date for his cheap edition, but Lawrence suggested (probably on Atkins's advice) that 'it would be better not to publish the cheap edition until after the play has actually been performed. So will you please hold it back until such time' (v. 556).

A fortnight later, back in the warmth of Italy, he was feeling distinctly uncertain about returning to England in mid-winter: 'I'm not *very* sure if I shall do so', he told his sister-in-law, Else Jaffe (v. 555). He continued to think about the production, however, telling Atkins on 16 October how 'I hope I can come to London and help, later, if you think it really worth while. If only one can get that feeling of primitive religious passion across to a London audience. If not, it's no good. I'm wondering what sort of cast you are planning' (v. 557). Probably as a result of his earlier discussion with Atkins, Lawrence also enclosed the music he had composed for *David* in the summer of 1925 and part of which he had inserted into Brett's typescripts: none of it, however, had got into print. He now carefully worked it out again: Lily Gair Wilkinson, the Lawrences' neighbour, recorded in her diary on 13 October that Lawrence came over 'to borrow the use of the piano and sat for more than an hour very happily composing a chant for his play of David'. On the following day, 'Lawrence came in with the manuscript score for the Psalm in his David, and we were able to find a good many mistakes ... He went off very happy to have his M.S ready for the post'. The music 'is very simple, needs only a pipe, tambourines, and a tom-tom drum. I hope it will do.'[159] Lawrence told Koteliansky that the music drew upon the Hebrew musical version of Psalm xxxiii – music which Koteliansky had taught him back in 1914 (ii. 252 n. 3): 'Wonder if you'll recognise the prophets singing Ranané Sadíkim. But it won't sound the same.' He was not at all sure 'if

---

[159] Communication from Mrs Lisa Smith; *Letters*, v. 557; see Appendix V ii.

they'll make anything of the play, anyhow. I don't feel very sanguine' (v. 557).

The production of *David* was yet again postponed, however, until the following March. To make up for it, the combined 300 Club and Stage Society decided to put on his earlier play, *The Widowing of Mrs. Holroyd*, in December instead. Lawrence only heard the news in mid-November, rather unfairly commenting that 'That Robert Atkins funked *David*': 'found it a bit heavy for him, I suppose ... though he is a nice man and I liked him I doubt very much if he's subtle enough for *David*'.[160] But he was also pleased about the postponement, 'because I needn't go to England now till end February, at least' (v. 576). He did not feel that his earlier play – 'my first play, that I wrote when I was still in Croydon' (v. 582), he remembered, slightly inaccurately – required his presence at rehearsals, especially in mid-winter; this was unlike *David*, which being 'a much more difficult play to put on, I must go and help' (v. 613). The only real problem with the postponement was with Secker's much-delayed cheap edition. 'All things considered,' Lawrence wrote to Secker on 23 November, 'it seems to me much fairer to hold *David* until the end of February. Then the limited edition buyers won't feel swindled, and there will be an easy excuse for bringing it out cheaper' (v. 581). And Secker yet again postponed it.

The December 1926 production of *The Widowing of Mrs. Holroyd* – still his only play to have been performed – was the play's third time on stage. It was directed by Esmé Percy in fulfilment of his long-standing desire to put it on, and was given performances at the Kingsway Theatre in London on Sunday 12, Monday 13 and Sunday 19 December, with a debate about it on the evening of the 21st.[161] Phyllis Whitworth, the play's producer, sent Lawrence press-cuttings and photographs after the first two performances. Rolf Gardiner, acquainted with Lawrence since August 1926, saw it at the Monday matinée – 'a very good performance', he thought it – though another friend (probably Catherine Carswell) thought 'the grandmother whined too much'.[162] Gardiner quoted Bernard Shaw, who also

---

[160] Unpublished letter to Phyllis Whitworth, 15 November 1926 (to be included in *Letters*, viii.).

[161] The director's prompt copy – a copy of the Duckworth edition of 1914 – contains lighting directions, notes about the positioning of characters and stage business; a few words are added to the spoken text in red and black pencil and about 100 lines are cut (UN). The debate was noted on the programme.

[162] *Letters*, v. 604. Rolf Gardiner (1902–71), farmer and forester, organiser of Land Service camps; in a letter of 13 December 1926 (Nehls, iii. 121 and n. 143).

saw the Monday performance, saying that 'the dialogue was the most magnificent he had ever heard, and his own stuff was "The Barber of Fleet Street" in comparison'. Percy later quoted the remark as 'Compared with that, my prose is machine-made lace. You can hear the typewriter in it' (v. 605 n. 1). Shaw himself recalled the occasion 'when I saw a play by him which rushed through in such a torrent of profuse yet vividly effective dialogue, making my own seem archaic in comparison'.[163]

Catherine Carswell, however, thought that the 1926 production was not as good as the Altrincham production of 1920;[164] and the reviews were not encouraging. Horace Shipp of the *English Review* for January 1927 recognised that Lawrence's play stood 'outside the ordinary traffic of Shaftesbury Avenue'; it was 'constructionally and dramatically a great piece of work in its bareness, its bleakness and desperate life-likeness' (pp. 120–1). *The Times*, however, found it difficult to come to terms with Lawrence's seemingly 'deliberately flat' drawing of the characters and his 'economy in the use of dialogue'.[165] Watching the performance was like watching 'a frieze' rather than living characters; the play seemed rigid, stagnant and tormenting, lying 'like a burden on the mind': while Ivor Brown thought the play set up 'a good situation, from which the dramatist has bolted in a way disastrous to his piece'. Although reviewers in the *New Statesman* and *Outlook* wrote approvingly, stressing the play's intense and richly charged dialogue, they both thought that the washing of Holroyd's body at the end was too drawn out.[166]

Lawrence discussed some of these points in a letter to Percy. He remarked that 'I have to confess it's years since I read the play myself. I wrote it fifteen years ago, when I was raw'. He thought that the audience and critics were probably right

---

[163] *Time and Tide* (London), 6 August 1932, p. 863. 'The Barber of Fleet Street' refers to plays in the melodramatic, posturing Sweeney Todd genre, e.g., Frederick Hazelton's *Sweeney Todd: The Barber of Fleet Street: Or The String of Pearls* (1862). Frieda reported that DHL was 'vastly pleased' by Shaw's comment and remarked: 'He ought to know about dialogue, it's very generous of him' ('Lunch with Mr and Mrs Bernard Shaw', *Memoirs* 147).

[164] Carswell, *The Savage Pilgrimage*, p. 135.

[165] 14 December 1926, p. 12; reprinted Sagar 289–90.

[166] Ivor Brown, *Saturday Review*, cxlii (18 December 1926), 767–8; Desmond MacCarthy, *New Statesman*, 18 December 1926, p. 310; *Outlook*, 24 December 1926, p. 629. Further reviews in 1926: *Era*, 15 December, p. 5; *Stage*, 16 December, p. 19; *Nation and Athenaeum*, 18 December p. 422; *Observer*, 19 December, p. 13; *Sunday Times*, 19 December, p. 4; *Graphic* (London), 25 December, p. 1093; and J. T. Grein, *Illustrated London News*, 4 June 1927, p. 1010.

when they say that the last act is too much taken up with washing the dead, instead of getting on a bit with life. I bet that would be my present opinion. If you've a moment to spare, tell me, will you, what you think – and what Miss Vanne [acting Mrs Holroyd] thinks. – And then, if ever the play were to be done again, I'd re-model the end. I feel I should want to. (v. 604)

He made the same point to an old Eastwood friend – 'I believe most of the people found it too gloomy. I think, if it were being done again, I should alter the end, and make it more cheerful. Myself, I hate miserable endings, now. But it's so long since I wrote that play' (v. 610) – and also to Phyllis Whitworth, whom however he also told 'I'm glad it was so well done, and very grateful to you for giving it a show ... I do hope you weren't disappointed in the reception ... It seems hard lines, after such noble hard work. But you have my gratitude, really'.[167] The play was not produced again during his lifetime.

There was, however, still the problem of Secker's cheap edition. April, Lawrence commented to him on 12 January, 'seems late for the book ... if you like, then bring it out as soon as you wish' (v. 623). Secker delayed no further; he published his 6s *David* (an uncorrected reprint of E1) on 3 February 1927.[168]

As early as the end of December, Lawrence was starting to wonder whether he would really have to risk his increasingly precarious health to attend rehearsals of *David* in England in February (v. 616). News early in the New Year that the play would be staged in April, not March, therefore pleased him: 'I'd much rather stay *here* till the sun warms up a bit in the north' (v. 621). As time went on, Lawrence became more and more reluctant to attend the rehearsals: 'perhaps I shan't go', he remarked on 6 February: 'I feel an infinite disgust at the idea of having to be there while the fools mimble-pimble at the dialogue' (v. 637). Three weeks later he was still more reluctant: he had been ill. 'I don't think I shall go ... Curse them, let them produce *David* as they like. Why should I mix myself up with them personally! I hate the very thought of them all' (v. 648). And ten days later, he finally made up his mind: 'I simply wont go, to have my life spoilt by those people. They can maul and muck the play about as much as

---

[167] Unpublished letter to Phyllis Whitworth, 20 December 1926 (to be included in *Letters*, viii.).

[168] See footnote 153. The reprint was on smaller paper but used standing type from E1, as is demonstrated by some errors where type was disturbed during the process of reprinting. Commas fell out on pp. 13, 36 and 97 and a serious error occurred on p. 76: where E1 read 'is there no other' the reprint reads 'here ts oi outher' (the 'u' an upside down 'n'). All these errors were carried over into Secker's 3s 6d New Adelphi Library reprint of 1930.

they like. They'd do it anyhow. Why should they suck my life into the bargain?' (v. 651).

He still felt obliged to see a performance; but with the play itself postponed one final time, to May – with good reason he remarked 'It feels forever so uncertain' – he also had a new reason for being reluctant to go: 'There is something very antipathetic to me about going to London, and especially in fuddling with theatrical people ... Even *David* itself is quite out of my mood at present – I feel I don't want to see it or hear it or even think about it' (vi. 50). This was not, however, what he said to Phyllis Whitworth: at the end of April he was still telling her that he would try to be in London the following week, 'And then we must do what we can about that play'.[169] He had recently completed the second version of *Lady Chatterley's Lover*, however; the mood and meaning of *The Plumed Serpent*, in which *David* had been conceived, was now far behind him. His Mexican novel had been published in January 1926, and it has been argued that 'Lawrence's near silence after publication ... was perhaps a sign that his belief in its importance was diminishing', while *David*'s association with his illness at the start of 1925 was also something he wanted to forget; Frieda would later comment that 'Later on he did not care so much for the play, maybe it had cost him too much.'[170] Further illness at the start of May 1927 settled the matter; he felt quite unable to go to London, 'in spite of a guilty Conscience and lamenting letters' (vi. 56), at least one of the latter from Phyllis Whitworth saying 'they want my help' (vi. 46). Catherine Carswell confirmed that Lawrence's failure to attend rehearsals 'caused some natural resentment in London, where much hard voluntary work and a considerable sum of money was being expended on the production, and it was felt that Lawrence ought to make every effort to encourage and direct the enterprise'. The final cost was apparently some £400.[171]

He did, however, write a lengthy letter to Phyllis Whitworth apologising again and answering some questions from its producer Ernest Milton about cuts and costumes.

I am more sorry than I can say about my not coming to *David*. This infernal cold got mixed up with a return of malaria ... If only the journey weren't so long, I'd risk it. But I would hate to arrive and have to go to bed and be a nuisance to somebody. As it is, I'm deaf as a lump of wood, with quinine. Really no luck!

[169] Unpublished letter to Phyllis Whitworth, 30 April 1927 (to be included in *Letters*, viii.).
[170] *The Plumed Serpent*, ed. Clark, p. xlvi; *D. H. Lawrence's Manuscripts*, ed. Squires, p. 174.
[171] *The Savage Pilgrimage*, p. 253: unpublished letter to Phyllis Whitworth, *c.* 27 May 1927 (to be included in *Letters*, viii.).

Tell Mr Milton to cut as he thinks best: perhaps the whole of Scene III – a good deal of Saul's long speech – and then anything that makes the movement drag. I wish I'd been there, to see if the long speeches, especially Samuel's, I mean not only his prayer, those towards the end too – if they dragged. If they really go over, I'd be glad if they weren't cut – because I didn't want the effect of the play to be snappy, rather slow and archaic-religious. But if that doesn't really succeed, then cut the longish mouthfuls and spit it out quick and sharp. Anything rather than let it be long-drawn-out and a nuisance ... As for clothes, there is very little in it: for the men, a short sleeveless shirt, to the knee: over that, on occasion, a longish loose-sleeved coat in cotton or wool, may be coloured, tied in at the waist – then, on occasion, a burnous mantle. For the women, a long sleeveless coat, loose or tied, and sometimes a shorter, wide-sleeved coloured coat.[172]

The play, minus two scenes,[173] was staged at the Regent Theatre in London in a performance at 7.30 p.m. on Sunday 22 May and a matinée on Monday 23rd. Although a number of people Lawrence knew in London – Koteliansky, Nancy Pearn, Millicent Beveridge[174] – wrote to him saying they had liked it, and although Milton thanked the audience at the end of the Sunday night performance for their 'enthusiastic reception' – and expressed regret that Lawrence's health had prevented him from attending (vi. 66 n. 1) – the production got the most dreadful reviews. The reviewer ('Omicron') of the *Nation and Athenaeum* (28 May 1927) thought it

of such an uninspired nature that one hesitates to blame the author entirely for the resultant fiasco, though the fact that the play lacked all dramatic movement no doubt made it very hard to produce ... What on earth is the good of a twentieth-century writer striving to imitate the style of the early seventeenth. The result can only be a tedious Wardour Street diction, frequently interlarded with quotations from the most well-known book in English.   (p. 261)

Richard Jennings in the *Spectator* (28 May 1927) thought the play quite undramatic, and was not at all inclined to blame the actors. The play reminded him of the film of *Ben Hur*: 'it is a series of chromolithographic "views" of scriptural scenes and persons, expressed in an idiom which can only diverge from the Authorised Version for the worse, and resembling the cinema in that it concentrates upon such "features" as make for tableaux ...' (p. 939). *The Times* (24 May 1927), too, found it 'wearisome', 'neither drama nor poetry' and 'a difficult piece to act': it singled out for praise Angela Baddeley as Michal, but particularly criticised Peter Cress-

---

[172] Unpublished letter to Phyllis Whitworth, 13 May 1927 (to be included in *Letters*, viii.).

[173] A note in the programme (p. [v]) explained: 'In order to bring the Play within the time limit of a single performance, the Producer has, to his regret, been obliged to omit the whole of scenes iii and x' (UN).

[174] Anne Millicent Beveridge (1871–1955), Scottish painter.

well as Saul: 'we missed many shades of meaning in his performance'.[175]
The account of the Sunday night performance given by Lawrence's old
friend, Edward Marsh, reveals why Cresswell was so bad; Marsh displayed
a very sharp eye and ear:

The fun began with a rather tactlessly worded announcement in the programme
that 'owing to unavoidable circumstances the part of Saul would be taken at short
notice by Mr. A,' as if they had strained every nerve to prevent him from acting
but had failed. This would have been believable, for he was extremely bad. Perhaps
the funniest scene was when Saul went mad and Jonathan brought David in to see
what he could do about it. Saul was raving on a throne at the back of the stage and
David sat down on a settee near the footlights and began singing one of his own
psalms to the tune we all know so well from Morning Prayer, which seems a very
unlikely cure for the jimjams. Saul took no notice, and went on with a rigmarole,
the point of which seemed to be (as far as I could hear through the psalm-singing)
that God was really an enormous Beetle who had laid the Earth as an egg and a bad
one at that. Every now and then he made David jump by throwing a javelin at him,
which rattled him a good deal, so that he sang things like 'Thou hast given him
dominion over the works of thy Feet, and put all things under his Hands'. Another
good bit was near the end, when Saul again went mad on the top of Mt. Gilboa or
wherever it was and began abusing David. 'David,' he said, 'is like a – like a – (to
Prompter) what?' (*Prompter* – 'A weasel') Saul: 'Oh yes, a weasel, a virgin weasel
which cannot bring forth her young.' I should have thought that if there *was* a line
that it would be hardly possible to forget it was the one about the Virgin Weasel.

Goliath was killed 'off' after a partly-audible slanging match with David in the
wings, which was a pity, as I should like to have seen the fight. When David
returned in triumph Saul's daughters and their handmaidens rushed to and fro
with their tambourines saying *Tootleoo*, they sang it so often and so distinctly that I
can't have been mistaken. I didn't know the expression came from so far back.[176]

All kinds of things went wrong on the Sunday night: not only did
Cresswell forget his words more than once, but he was also inaudible at
moments – 'his monologue directed against David ... was not heard at all'
– while 'For one cruel moment during the play a young man in evening
dress became, by mistake, visible on the stage to the audience.'[177]

---

[175] P. 14. Further reviews: *Stage*, 26 May 1927, p. 16; *Era*, 25 May 1927, p. 5.
[176] Christopher Hassall, *Edward Marsh: Patron of the Arts* (1959), p. 547. The programme
note (p. [v]) ran: 'Owing to unavoidable circumstances, Mr Peter Cresswell has taken up
the part of Saul at very short notice'. The 'beetle of the beginning' is at 489:38; David
sings Psalm 8 from 490:23, and verse 6 should run: 'Thou madest him to have dominion
over the works of thy hands; thou hast put all things under his feet' (*KJB*). Javelin
episodes occur at 491:7–8 and 18, and the 'weasel that is a virgin' at 520:15. Saul's
daughters and handmaidens sing variations of 'Lu-lu-a-li-lu-lu-lu' in scenes 9 and 10:
'tootleoo' was contemporary slang for 'goodbye'.
[177] S. S. Koteliansky to Sydney Waterlow, 21 June 1927 (NZNL): *Nation and Athenaeum*, 28
May 1927, p. 261.

Things were no better on Monday, when the distinguished drama critic James Agate attended the 2.00 matinée:

There one sat in the cavernous gloom of the Regent Theatre, unable to see if one had a neighbour, uncertain whether one ought to be ashamed of single *ennui*, without the support of community boredom ... Mr. Harcourt Williams [playing Samuel], looking like Noah and Methuselah put together, and with a beard which touched the floor and curled up again like Turkish slippers, piled lament upon dirge, coronach upon threnody. What this speech [scene II] may be like to read I do not know. What I do know is that in the theatre it sounded longer and duller than the famous 'Récit de Thérainène' [Théramène], and that outside the theatre it was May, the sun was shining, and at Lord's Middlesex were heading the New Zealanders' score. But the intellectual, when once he has got you in his grip, is notoriously without mercy.[178]

He noted that two scenes of the play had been cut – 'But two from sixteen still leaves fourteen, and for fourteen scenes we shook a few sad last grey hairs and, as the poet says, sat and heard each other groan.' He praised the producer for 'giving us a number of pretty pictures and a convincing display of costume', but noted the disadvantage of that approach: 'It is in my mind that the East, though picturesque, has always been an untidy, sandy place, whereas everything about this production was as neat as a new pin.' He thought Angela Baddeley, as Michal, 'some thousand of years too modern'; and, like others, he thought that Frank Vosper as Jonathan gave the production's only good performance. The Irish playwright St John Ervine, in the *Observer* of 29 May, was much ruder: 'Scarcely any of the fine dialogue that we heard in "The Widowing of Mrs Holroyd" was heard in this play, which, as it meandered on through its three hours, reduced the audience to an appalling state of lassitude and limpness. We were bored, bored, bored.' The fault, he reckoned, was partly Lawrence's and partly that of the production: 'A play of such length and variety of scene as this is needs more rehearsal than the Three Hundred Club, even in conjunction with the Stage Society, can give it ... [Milton] needed better actors and actresses than were in the cast, and at least a month of incessant and serious rehearsals' (p. 15). Nancy Pearn made the same point to Lawrence about 'the limited opportunities for rehearsals' (vi. 70 n. 1).

Koteliansky and the artist Mark Gertler saw the Sunday night performance, and the former wrote to Lawrence about it:

The chief fault was in the fact that Saul (by Peter Creswell – I don't know who that actor is) acted very badly; that he misunderstood your Saul completely, and made

---

[178] *Sunday Times*, 29 May 1927, p. 6; in *Phèdre* (1677), by Jean Racine (1639–98), Théramène reports at length on how Hippolyte was killed.

of him a rather stagey, very common thing. It is a wonder that his acting did not kill the play. David was not bad, but neither was he good. (Robert Haries) I don't know who the actor is; but I don't think he is English. Judging by his voice, which was not pleasant, and its poor modulations, he is either a Jew or a Welshman. Yet he tried to act 'David' according to your text, but without a real intimate understanding of the character. The best, I think, was Jonathan (Frank Vosper). He not only acted quite well, but he seemed to me to understand and interpret your Jonathan correctly. Michal (Angela Baddeley) acted very, very well. She was your Michal, remarkably well realised. She and Vosper, I believe, saved the play from Saul's bad and cheap acting.   (vi. 66 n. 1)

Koteliansky insisted that 'in the hands of a first rate producer, with real good actors of Saul and David, the play could be extremely good'; he felt sure that it would be taken up by someone else, 'not only for the sake of its artistic value, but because it can be made a great financial success'. This was not just the opinion of a loyal friend: that hard-headed man Curtis Brown went on believing in *David* until the middle 1930s: 'If only it were not for the absurd prejudice against sacred subjects, reverently treated, *David* would, indeed, have made not only a fine play, but a notable film. Perhaps it will yet.'[179] It never succeeded as a play, however; and it was never filmed.

Lawrence got Koteliansky's letter on 27 May: 'It seems to me just as well I wasn't there', he commented: 'you can't make a silk purse out of a sow's ear ... Actors haven't enough *inside* to them' (vi. 66). He was annoyed by the 'impudent' response he was getting: 'They say it was just dull. I say they are eunuchs, and have no balls' (vi. 72). The Council of Management of the Incorporated Stage Society organised – as they usually did – 'an informal Debate' about the play, on the Monday evening after the matinée, in a room at the Central Hall, Westminster,[180] and Koteliansky and Millicent Beveridge attended (vi. 82), but no information survives about what was said. Lawrence still hoped to come to England at some stage and enjoy the production party Phyllis Whitworth had promised him – especially if she could 'assemble if possible David and Saul and Michal and all, for us. That would be great fun'.[181] But he never went to England again.

---

[179] *Contacts* (1935), p. 73.
[180] Programme, p. [iii]. The same had been organised after the 1926 *Widowing of Mrs. Holroyd* production: see above (p. lxxxii).
[181] Unpublished letter to Phyllis Whitworth, *c.* 27 May 1927 (to be included in *Letters*, viii.). He did give her a copy of *Mornings in Mexico* with the inscription 'Mrs Whitworth / from D. H. Lawrence / remembering *David* / May 1927' (Bloomsbury Book Auctions Sale, 19 June 1997, Catalogue 304, Item 294).

Publication, performance and reception 1932–64

1932–41. *The Plays of D. H. Lawrence* **published and** *The Fight for Barbara* **published as** *Keeping Barbara*; *David* **performed;** *The Daughter-in-Law* **performed as** *My Son's My Son*; *A Collier's Friday Night* **published and performed;** *Noah's Flood, Altitude, The Merry-go-Round* **and** *The Married Man* **published**

Lawrence died in Vence in March 1930. In March 1932, Frieda Lawrence and George Arthur Lawrence (Lawrence's surviving elder brother), sharing the administration of his estate at the time, signed an agreement with Secker – who was doing his best to keep new Lawrence books coming out – for a collected volume of plays. This was planned to include the three published plays (*The Widowing of Mrs. Holroyd*, *Touch and Go* and *David*) and the unpublished fragment *Altitude*, though the latter was dropped.[182] There had been no discussion about including any of the other five full-length plays, as Curtis Brown did not yet know anything about them. The manuscript of *A Collier's Friday Night* was still in the possession of Edward Garnett, and that of *The Merry-go-Round* was not rediscovered until 1933. The manuscripts of *The Daughter-in-Law*, *The Married Man* and *The Fight for Barbara*, had all been found by Else Jaffe in May 1931, and Frieda certainly knew about them shortly after they were found (she referred to *The Fight for Barbara* in 1931 as a play that 'I love very much, it's when we were first together').[183] She seems, however, to have preferred to keep these three new plays unpublished – probably so that a second volume of plays could be brought out later: in 1934 Secker and Curtis Brown did indeed discuss the publication of a volume to include *The Fight for Barbara*, *The Merry-go-Round*, *The Married Man* and *Altitude* (*A Collier's Friday Night* had already been published in a volume by itself). *The Daughter-in-Law* was left out probably because it was by then in the hands of a theatrical agent; no one seems to have thought of including *Noah's Flood*. In July 1933, Secker's *The Plays of D. H. Lawrence* came out, consisting simply of the three published plays,[184] but in that way

---

[182] 8 March 1932, Curtis Brown files (UT).

[183] *Frieda Lawrence and her Circle: Letters from, to and about Frieda Lawrence*, ed. H. T. Moore and D. B. Montague (1981), p. 32.

[184] Roberts A65, published July 1933, price 7s 6d; the first printing was 2,000 copies. Reissued February 1938 by Heinemann. See *The Times Literary Supplement*, 20 July 1933, p. 497 and D. G. Bridson, 'Lawrence as Dramatist', *New English Weekly*, 17 August 1933, pp. 425–6.

matching Secker's publication of *The Tales of D. H. Lawrence* (1934), which also excluded all unpublished and recently discovered work.

In March 1933, Frieda publicly announced the discovery of the manuscripts of *The Daughter-in-Law*, *The Married Man* and *The Fight for Barbara*: she had had 'no idea that the plays existed ... until the manuscripts were discovered in my sister's house in Munich. One is a light, gay comedy called "Fight for Barbara" ... These will be published, and, I hope, performed. "Fight for Barbara" is what is described as thoroughly commercial.'[185] The Curtis Brown agency, however, was still locating and copying all the unpublished Lawrence manuscripts it could find. An exhibition at the London bookshop, Bumpus, in April and May 1933, of Lawrence's *Original Manuscripts, Corrected Typescripts, Sketches, etc.* (the manuscripts of *The Merry-go-Round* and *The Married Man* – with the first five pages missing – as well as those of *David* and *Altitude* were included)[186] also triggered off the recovery of previously unknown materials: Edward Garnett, for example, sent his manuscript of *A Collier's Friday Night* to the exhibition after it opened, and in May 1933, before it was returned, Curtis Brown had a typescript made. The fact that Curtis Brown carbon-copy typescripts survive of all five newly discovered plays shows that the agency hoped all five were publishable or capable of being produced. The first to be considered was probably *A Collier's Friday Night*; it was offered to T. S. Eliot's magazine *Criterion* (published by Faber) in the summer of 1933, in the hope that it might be serialised. It was turned down by the magazine, but Faber offered to publish it as a Christmas gift book. Martin Secker, however, who held the publication rights, did not agree, and published it himself the following year. Late in 1933 or early in 1934, the Stage Society considered a production of the play to coincide with Secker's publication, but nothing came of the idea. Almost as quickly, in the summer of 1933, Curtis Brown sold *The Fight for Barbara* to the magazine *Argosy*, which published it under the title *Keeping Barbara* in December 1933, in a heavily cut and altered version: there is no indication as to who authorised the cutting of almost a quarter of the autograph text. *Argosy* advertised the play as a 'literary discovery' and introduced it as 'D. H. LAWRENCE'S Brilliant Comedy / A new play by the author of "Sons and Lovers" and "Lady Chatterley's Lover," recently discovered among his manuscripts and now appearing exclusively in the "Argosy" '.[187]

The publication in July 1933 of *The Plays of D. H. Lawrence*, along with

[185] *Daily Telegraph*, 24 March 1933, p. 15.
[186] J. and E. Bumpus, Ltd (1933).
[187] Roberts C213, *Argosy*, xiv, 68–90. It was the fifth play in *Complete Plays*.

the continuing publicity about Lawrence's life and work, may have helped encourage a second production of *David* in the autumn: it was staged at the Cambridge Festival Theatre on 23–28 October. The producer, Joseph Gordon MacLeod, had written to Frieda Lawrence (now back in New Mexico) about the production, and she had replied: 'I wish I could be at the performance – but I am here – I hope it will be a great success. I always loved that play – Thank you for thinking of me – I wish Lawrence could know this!'[188] MacLeod's production was shorter and sparer than Milton's had been in 1927; it lasted only about $2\frac{1}{2}$ hours, with a setting 'practical, satisfactory and well lit'. MacLeod, however, had also cut the play heavily; and rather astonishingly, he omitted Scene xv completely 'on the grounds that it could not be adequately represented on the stage'. As one reviewer pointed out, this deprived the play of 'the scene which we should imagine Lawrence intended as the play's climax'.[189] The Cambridge staging received generally better notices than the London production had: 'It is not a great play, but I am thankful for it. It has moments of surprising beauty and passages of magnificent, though highly mannered prose' wrote the reviewer of the *Gownsman*. But the basic criticisms remained the same as those voiced in London: the *Cambridge Chronicle and University Journal* commended the company for striving 'valiantly to get across an undramatic play' while criticising Lawrence for 'metaphorical floweriness' and noting that 'there would be considerable improvement if the play were cut down, especially in the late scenes'.[190] To be fair to Lawrence, he himself knew that this was necessary; in 1927 he had written to Max Mohr – who was trying to set up a production in Berlin of the Lawrences' own German translation – that 'of course the whole play is too literary, too many words'. He thought that 'perhaps they – and you – could cut it into shape' (vi. 204). So far as is known, however, *David* has not been professionally performed since 1933.[191]

Of the five typescripts made by Curtis Brown in 1933, three got into the hands of theatrical impresarios, but only one production resulted. Between

---

[188] Frieda to MacLeod, 5 October 1933, Festival Theatre Programme, p. 2: MacLeod (1903–84), actor, director, author and broadcaster, ran the Festival Theatre from 1933 to 1936.

[189] *Gownsman*, 28 October 1933, p. 19. See advertisement in *Cambridge Daily News*, 24 October 1933, p. 6.

[190] 28 October 1933, p. 19; 25 October 1933, p. 2.

[191] An American student production took place at Occidental College in Los Angeles on 12 May 1938, directed by Kurt Baer von Weisslingen and staged in the outdoor Hillside theatre. Frieda Lawrence and Aldous Huxley both attended the performance; their reaction is not known (*D. H. Lawrence's Manuscripts*, ed. Squires, p. 174 and n. 1).

28 December 1933 and 19 February 1934, the London manager Melchior
Lengyel was given *The Merry-go-Round* and *The Married Man* to evaluate.
He admired Lawrence and thought the plays interesting, suggesting that in
a 'proper adaptation' they might succeed on the English stage, though they
would be unsuitable for continental audiences.[192] The best prospects, however, seemed those of *The Daughter-in-Law*: this may well be why there
were no plans to include it in the proposed 1934 volume of unpublished
plays. Either the ribbon copy or a second carbon of the surviving carbon
typescript (hereafter TCCI) was sent to the theatrical impresario, actor–
manager and producer Leon M. Lion (who ran the Playhouse Theatre at
Charing Cross), in October 1933.[193] Lion did not think the play suitable
for the London stage as it stood, but commissioned the writer Richard
Hughes to work on it. Frieda could not understand why the play needed
adapting, but Laurence Pollinger (now handling the affairs of the Lawrence
Estate at Curtis Brown) assured her that 'it was necessary that the play
should be revised in certain places if it were ever to be produced'.[194]
Hughes had the play for more than eighteen months, but failed to do the
job; and in April 1936 Lion handed it over to the writer Walter Greenwood.[195] The play was hastily revised by Greenwood, typed and retitled
My Son's My Son, and staged at Lion's Playhouse Theatre on 26 May
1936; later it went on tour. It was advertised – exactly as its contract
demanded – as 'an unrevised play by D. H. Lawrence completed by Walter
Greenwood'.[196] In fact, all that Greenwood did was to 'complete' the play in
the sense of making additions clarifying the fate of characters like Mrs
Purdy, her daughter Bertha and Joe Gascoyne.[197] The contract had specified
that 'Mr. Greenwood will keep as close as possible to the spirit and intention

---

[192] Notes in the Curtis Brown files (UT).
[193] For an account of Lion as a professional man of the theatre not long before the mid-1930s,
see chap. XI of Ethel Mannin's *Confessions and Impressions* (1936).
[194] Correspondence (*c.* 1936) in the Curtis Brown files (UT). Hughes (1900–76) was best
known as a playwright and for his novel *A High Wind in Jamaica* (1929).
[195] Greenwood (1903–74) was author of the well-known novel of working-class life, *Love on
the Dole* (1933), which had proved extremely successful in a 1934 stage adaptation done by
Ronald Gow: 'By the end of 1935 a million people had seen the play on the stage' (Ray
Speakman, 'Introduction' to Ronald Gow and Walter Greenwood, *Love on the Dole*, 1986).
Greenwood was in some sympathy with DHL: a quotation from Huxley's edition of
DHL's *Letters* (1932) had prefaced his novel.
[196] '*AGREEMENT / Re: "DAUGHTER IN LAW"*' between '*MRS. FRIEDA LAWR-
ENCE* and LEON M. LION Esqre.', 15 May 1936, clause (8) (UN).
[197] In Greenwood's version the Purdies get paid the £40 they want: the money is provided by
Mrs Gascoyne, proud of her unborn grandchild. Joe's fate in Greenwood's version is also
made explicit: crippled by the riot at the end of the play, he is – apparently in accordance
with notes provided by Lion – consigned to his mother's care.

of the original manuscript making any changes reasonably considered by the Licensee to be necessary for the success of the said play'.[198] Greenwood's melodramatic ending was presumably what Lion wanted.

Apart from making those additions to the end of Act II and towards the end of the final scene, Greenwood did surprisingly little with Lawrence's text, as is clear from the surviving typescript prompt copy. He made some small cuts, to shorten the action and dialogue slightly, and made a few modifications to the dialect (the word 'stall', for example, vanishes). The process of simplification was continued in rehearsal: the prompt copy shows, for example, that where Greenwood had originally left unaltered the phrase 'scrape your tabs' (meaning 'search your ears'), it was normalised into 'scrape your breeches'. Reviewers believed, however, that what they were seeing was Lawrence's play 'completed' – that is, with its last act – by Greenwood, and they responded accordingly. One remarked that 'the play rambled too much from one theme to another, and it was an obvious mistake to keep Mrs Gascoigne off the stage throughout the second act'; the *Evening Standard* on 27 May stated that:

> The play reflects D. H. Lawrence in every line of the first two acts and Walter Greenwood, who has more of the theatre in one of his little fingers than Lawrence could muster from a whole life's suppressed eructation [belching], has contrived to make of the third act a living, breathing thing. A drama in one act with an introduction by D. H. Lawrence.

In fact, Greenwood contributed only eight pages to a last act which otherwise consisted of forty pages of pure (if slightly cut) Lawrence.[199]

In spite of Greenwood's modifications, the actors still had considerable problems with the dialect, which remained largely unaltered: the reviewer in the *Evening Standard* remarked that 'no-one could miss the passages of pure Kensington which crept persistently in, and into which Miss Sara Erskine, as Luther's wife, at last frankly lapsed' (p. 10). Although the play was revived at the Golders Green Hippodrome in August 1936 and at the Palace Theatre in Manchester in November, it was not much of a success at either venue.[200]

During the protracted negotiations over *The Daughter-in-Law, A*

---

[198] As note 196, clause (9). Some of the material discussed by Sagar 298–300 (including Lion's notes), once in the possession of USal, is now missing.

[199] *My Son's My Son*, prompt copy (USal), 1.6; D. B., *Evening Standard*, 27 May 1936, p. 10. Other reviews in 1936: *The Times*, 27 May, p. 14; James Agate, *Sunday Times*, 31 May, p. 6; H. H., *Observer*, 31 May, p. 13; A. V. Cookman, *London Mercury*, xxxiv (July), 249–50. See too G[eorge]. W. B[ishop], *Sunday Times*, 24 May 1936, p. 6.

[200] See Sagar 300. Greenwood's text was performed in Swedish as *Min son är min* [*My Son is Mine*], première at the Blancheteatren in Stockholm, 31 March 1937; it toured Swedish

Collier's Friday Night had got into print from Curtis Brown's copy. Discussion of its publication by Secker had started in January 1934, and the contract was signed by Frieda Lawrence (from December 1932 the sole beneficiary of the Lawrence estate) on 8 February 1934.[201] Secker's publication was also planned to coincide with a production of the play by the Stage Society which, however, failed to materialise. The play was also offered to magazines, but without success. Two months before publication in June 1934,[202] Edward Garnett wrote an introduction for it (printed in Appendix 1); he drew attention to 'the sureness of touch and penetrating directness of this dramatic chronicle of family life' and admired the powerful opening and closing scenes, but in general found the play 'a bit too artless and diffuse, too lacking in concentration and surprise'.

The first review of *A Collier's Friday Night*, by the Irish playwright Sean O'Casey, appeared in the *New Statesman*. He succinctly summarised the play's qualities of atmosphere, feeling, vividness, drawing of character, humour and poetry; for him its weaknesses were its lack of dramatic action, softness and pathos. All the same, he was deeply impressed by it as a play 'with the touch and go of life', 'the sweat of life' in it. It was certainly not a play, he observed, 'that the English managers would rush out to meet', and his appreciation of the play turned into an attack on contemporary British theatre.

Here is a play that was worth production when it was first written, and it is worth production now. Had Lawrence got the encouragement the play called for and deserved, England might have had a great dramatist. It's no use saying that the play was hid, and no-one knew about it; the point is that even had everyone known about it the play would not have been produced, for the play is too good in essence to ensure a shower of gold into a manager's lap. Life has vanished, and art has vanished off the English stage.[203]

O'Casey's lament culminated in the words: 'He came into the theatre, and the theatre received him not.' A short review by Osbert Burdett in the August *London Mercury*, too, was generally approving and argued that the play had certainly been written to be acted and not to be read, and that Lawrence's dramatic ability was obvious. But Burdett thought that the

provincial theatres and was staged over seventy times by April 1938 (Marko Modiano, 'An Early Swedish Stage Production of D. H. Lawrence's *The Daughter-in-Law*', *D. H. Lawrence Review*, xvii, Spring 1984, 49–59).

[201] UT.

[202] Roberts A69; published at 5s, the first printing consisted of 1,500 copies. It was the seventh play in *Complete Plays*.

[203] 28 July 1934, p. 124; reprinted in *Blasts and Benedictions: Articles and Stories by Sean O'Casey*, ed. Ronald Ayling (1967), pp. 222–5.

autobiographical features were too prominent and that Lawrence's inexperience was apparent in the way that 'the play is not dramatic in the sense of having arresting "curtains" or tense situations, though there is such a situation in the third act'; 'the story ... misses unity and a climax of interest' (p. 376).

The next two of Lawrence's plays to be published were the fragments, *Noah's Flood* and *Altitude*. The text of the second version of *Noah's Flood* was printed in the collection of Lawrence's posthumous work, *Phoenix*, which Viking and Heinemann brought out in 1936.[204] No reviews of *Phoenix*, however, paid particular attention to *Noah's Flood*; and the longer text of the first version remained unpublished. Most of the first scene of *Altitude* was published for the first time in 1938 in the magazine *Laughing Horse* by Spud Johnson.[205]

The decade ended, however, with another first performance: the première of *A Collier's Friday Night* in Morley, Yorkshire, by an amateur group, the Morley Adult School Players, on 22 and 25 March 1939;[206] the play was their entry in the annual British Drama League Festival. The reviewer in the *Morley Observer* believed that the play represented a faithful transcript of Lawrence's own experience; apart from the third act, it had not 'the slightest dramatic quality', and could be seen as an extreme example of 'the school of photographic realism': 'if the reader knows what a collier's Friday night is like, then he knows what this play is about'.[207] The actor who played Ernest Lambert remembered that there was 'quite a sensation when we performed the play and crowded houses were the result. Four telegrams were received, from Bernard Shaw, Ashley Dukes, Sir Barry Jackson and the last one came from Frieda Lawrence who was then in Hollywood.'[208]

The only two plays which Curtis Brown had not been able to place were *The Merry-go-Round* and *The Married Man*; and although their texts were typed in 1933 and again in 1934, with copies being sent to the New York branch,[209] in the mid-1930s Pollinger seems to have given up hope of

---

[204] Roberts A76, pp. 811–16. It was the tenth play in *Complete Plays*.
[205] Roberts C222; no. 20 (Summer 1938), 12–35; see above, p. lxii. It was the ninth play in *Complete Plays*.
[206] Produced by John T. Kirk. A folder containing a typescript of the play (TCCI), located at UCB, contains a letter from Kirk, a programme and press cuttings relating to this production.
[207] 'Adult School Presents "World Premiere" ', 24 March 1939, p. 4; cf. *Yorkshire Evening News*, 23 March 1939, p. 3.
[208] George W. Atkinson, letter to eds., 1986.
[209] Memorandum in the Curtis Brown files (UT).

selling them. Frieda took the manuscripts of the two plays back with her to the ranch in New Mexico, along with that of *The Fight for Barbara*.[210] The manuscript of *The Married Man* was not complete: its first five pages had been missing when Curtis Brown had first made copies in 1933, and all surviving texts of the play lack the start of the opening scene. In Autumn 1939, Frieda approached the editor of the *Virginia Quarterly Review*, Lawrence Lee, about the possibility of the magazine printing some unpublished manuscript material;[211] in October 1939 he was offered a short story ('Delilah and Mr. Bircumshaw') and the three plays. Lee asked to see all four items; Frieda was, however, naturally reluctant to send Lee the original manuscripts because she had 'only one copy each'. It may have been at this stage that she started to make her own handwritten copy of one of the items.[212] She was however urged to have typed copies made for the magazine, and a cheque for $15 was sent to her to cover the cost of typing. She had told Lee about the plays: 'I daresay Lawrence would have rewritten them if he had seen them again later in his lifetime. One is called: "The Fight for Barbara" another the Merry-go-Round and the third one begins at page 6 and has lost its title – Perhaps I can remember ... Also the typing is not so easy here. Taos is a small place, but I hope to find somebody soon'. She found two typists; receipts for payments to them are dated 3 January 1940.[213]

The *Virginia Quarterly Review* prided itself on printing only unpublished work, so set out to find if any of the four items had previously appeared anywhere else. Lee also proposed contacting publishers in New York about a volume to contain all four items; he further suggested enquiring into the plays' chances of being produced. Lawrence's bibliographer, Edward McDonald, however, explained that *The Fight for Barbara* had been published before.[214] Lee offered Frieda $275 to publish the other three items, and a title ('With a Little Love') was suggested for the play with the missing title-page. Frieda consented to this, but when the play was published it appeared under its correct title, *The Married Man*: either

---

[210] L. C. Powell's *the manuscripts of d. h. lawrence: A Descriptive Catalogue* (Los Angeles, 1937) provides information (not altogether reliable) about manuscripts in Frieda's possession at that date.

[211] Letters at UV.

[212] See footnote 288.

[213] Letters at UT; one typist was paid $9.20 for *The Fight for Barbara* (92 pages), the other $17 for 178 pages of the two other plays; Frieda received another $12. The three plays were typed on identical paper watermarked 'EMCO'.

[214] McDonald to Lee, 19 January 1940 (UT). McDonald thought *The Fight for Barbara* a 'really light and amusing' comedy, 'of course, essentially autobiographical'.

she had remembered the title Lawrence had once mentioned in a letter (i. 509) or someone had noticed the reference to the play in Aldous Huxley's edition of Lawrence's letters.[215] *The Married Man* and *The Merry-go-Round* were retyped by the *Virginia Quarterly Review*, and these new typescripts used as setting-copy. *The Married Man* was published in the Autumn 1940 number, *The Merry-go-Round* as a supplement to the Christmas number, Winter 1941.[216]

1941–64. Neglect

All Lawrence's writings, not just his plays, were widely neglected during the 1940s, and many of them went out of print (paper was in short supply during the War and reprinting became difficult). Among the few who commented on him as a playwright was the drama critic, Eric Bentley. He remarked – purely on the strength of *The Plays of D. H. Lawrence* – that Lawrence 'wrote three plays, none of them without interest', but that it 'will be agreed that many great artists have written for the modern theater without producing great dramas. Indeed there is hardly an important modern writer – not Auden, nor Joyce, nor Lawrence, nor Henry James – who has not fancied himself as a dramatist with largely unhappy consequences.'[217] Assessing Lawrence's plays in 1950, Richard Aldington wrote:

> Except for *David* I am bound to say I think Lawrence's plays almost negligible. I don't think he had any real 'theatre' in him. The play was not his form. The matter of *A Collier's Friday Night* surely appears to better advantage in *Sons and Lovers*; and the theme of the rather better *Widowing of Mrs Holroyd* comes out more dramatically in the short story, *Odour of Chrysanthemums*.[218]

There appears to have been just a single performance of a Lawrence play: BBC Radio's Home Service presented *The Widowing of Mrs. Holroyd* on 14 September 1953. J. C. Trewin in the *Listener* was dismissive. Although the play had been 'acted and produced with determination', he found it 'dolorous' and singled out 'the chat over (I believe) the laying-out'.[219]

[215] *The Letters of D. H. Lawrence*, ed. Aldous Huxley (1932), p. 103.

[216] Roberts C226, *Virginia Quarterly Review*, xvi, 523–47; Roberts C227, *Virginia Quarterly Review*, xvii, Supplement, 1–44. They were the third and seventh plays respectively in *Complete Plays*. *The Merry-go-Round* was also separately published as a privately produced off-print, dated 1940. No reviews have been found.

[217] *The Playwright as Thinker: A Study of Drama in Modern Times* (1946; New York, 1967), pp. 280, 76.

[218] *D. H. Lawrence: An Appreciation* (Harmondsworth, 1950), p. 30.

[219] 'Drama: Talking Points', 24 September 1953, p. 520. Trewin also compared the play with the 'much more impressive' anti-fascist play about the early Christians in Rome, *As It Was In the Beginning*, by Naomi Mitchison and L. E. Gielgud (1939), broadcast the same week.

References to Lawrence's plays otherwise continued to be sporadic, and often suffered from lack of precise information. Uncertainty continued about the number of plays and about the order of their writing. Harry T. Moore's pioneering book, *The Life and Works of D. H. Lawrence*, gave the first survey; he listed six plays and a fragment and offered short summaries.[220] Mark Schorer had *The Widowing of Mrs. Holroyd* reprinted in America in 1956 with the aim of recovering an almost totally forgotten play, yet declared that it was 'certainly' not a great play.[221] Also in America, *David* appeared in an anthology of *Religious Drama* edited by Marvin Halverson, who declared the play 'poetic and ecstatically religious', although he insisted that Lawrence 'stands outside the modern movement of religious drama'.[222] The British stage of the 1940s and early 1950s was predominantly concerned with verse drama and classic revivals; plays in a realist mode dating from the early years of the century were forgotten.[223]

An extensive though still not yet comprehensive or reliable academic essay on Lawrence's plays was finally published in 1960. A. E. Waterman, however, laid stress on ideas, themes and parallels between the plays and Lawrence's prose fiction, rather than on the dramatic features of the plays themselves. Lawrence's own attitude to his plays was misrepresented: 'Lawrence didn't take his dramatic work very seriously.' And what – in spite of the frequently good reviews the published plays had received – had become a critical cliché about Lawrence's plays was repeated: 'For the most part critics have ignored Lawrence's plays. They are justified in that none of them is very good drama and contains nothing new in dramatic technique.'[224]

From the mid-1950s, however, a dramatic revival in Britain steadily gathered force, creating new interest in plays in the realist tradition, many of them about working-class life (the often-abused 'kitchen-sink drama').

---

[220] (New York, 1951), pp. 330–1: *The Fight for Barbara* and *Noah's Flood* were ignored, and *The Daughter-in-Law* only included as an unnamed 'unfinished play'.

[221] *A Play by D. H. Lawrence. 'The Widowing of Mrs Holroyd'* (San Francisco, 1956), p. 3; Schorer described it as the earliest of what he estimated were DHL's five plays and five play fragments.

[222] *Religious Drama I* (New York, 1957), pp. 165–266: for quotation, see p. 7.

[223] The only recorded staging of a DHL play in this period was an amateur production, 4–6 February 1958, of *David* at Gonville and Caius College, Cambridge, by the College Dramatic Society under the direction of Andor Gomme, an enthusiast for DHL, with David Pass as Saul, Jim Hunter as David and Susan Koechlin as Michal. For the first time it was performed uncut.

[224] 'The Plays of D. H. Lawrence', *Modern Drama*, ii (1960), 349; the essay, significantly, gained wide currency from being reprinted in *D. H. Lawrence: A Collection of Critical Essays*, ed. Mark Spilka (Englewood Cliffs, N.J., 1963), pp. 140–9.

In addition, television drama was reaching a steadily increasing audience, and it too employed predominantly naturalistic means. By the early 1960s, radio, television and the theatre had begun to prepare the way for the reception of a writer such as Lawrence as a significant twentieth-century dramatist, while the trial of *Lady Chatterley's Lover* in November 1960 brought his name and work to the attention of the public in a way unparalleled since his death.

In 1961, *The Widowing of Mrs. Holroyd* became the first Lawrence play to be produced for television.[225] Introductory material in the *TV Times* – reproducing the point of view of a number of the defence submissions in the *Lady Chatterley* trial – described the play as 'a moral work, written by a man who all his life was a highly moral writer. It is rooted in the Nottingham mining community into which Lawrence was born, and in which he evolved his interpretation of the dignity he wished to see in man.'[226] The adaptation – which reduced the play to 'one hour minus commercials' – was very well received. The *Daily Telegraph* linked it directly with contemporary theatre, describing it as ' "Kitchen Sink" D. H. Lawrence'; *The Times* characterised it as 'typical Lawrence of the *Sons and Lovers* period' with 'crisp, spare and genuinely dramatic' dialogue; the *Observer* admired dialogue 'with that whirlpool quality suggesting undertones that is Lawrence's speciality'.[227] *David* also received its first lengthy academic discussion in George A. Panichas's article in *Modern Drama* in 1963;[228] but that was very much of a side issue in Lawrence's rehabilitation as a dramatist. As yet there had been no revival of his plays in the theatre itself.

Revival 1965–95

1965–6. *A Collier's Friday Night* performed; *The Complete Plays*, including *The Daughter-in-Law*, published; short stories dramatised on television

What made the crucial difference to Lawrence's reputation as a dramatist was a momentous first professional performance of *A Collier's Friday Night*

---

[225] Granada TV (ITA), 23 March 1961, adapted by Ken Taylor for the Television Playhouse series, directed by Claude Whatham.

[226] 18–25 March 1961, pp. 1, 13, 33.

[227] 24 March, p. 16; 24 March, p. 18; 26 March, p. 26. See too Sagar 300–1.

[228] 'D. H. Lawrence's Biblical Play *David*', vi, 164–76. An amateur production of *David* was staged by the Peninsula Religious Drama Guild at Palo Alto, California, in August 1965.

in August 1965. Peter Gill, an assistant director at the Royal Court Theatre, had heard 'astonished reports' of the 1961 television version of *The Widowing of Mrs. Holroyd*, and had tentatively planned a Sunday night production of it without décor (the English Stage Company's usual practice for trying out, in a single performance, new work not deemed commercial). Gill sent for a copy of the text; but what came back, by mistake, was a copy of *A Collier's Friday Night* – which so impressed him that he decided to do it instead. It proved so successful, on Sunday 8 August, that it was repeated the following Sunday.[229] *The Times*'s reviewer criticised the construction of the play as naïve – 'simply a representation of an evening in the lives of people Lawrence knew from long experience' – but admitted that it made 'inventive use of common domestic incident to provide shape and suspense', and stressed the 'fair-mindedness' with which Lawrence treated all his characters. Eric Shorter in the *Daily Telegraph* praised the way in which the play was 'humming with authentic observation of scene' and recognised 'its hold on the house' as 'showing a remarkable dramatic insight'; he also noted a 'true feeling for the stage and for dialogue that encourages acting'. Two years later, *The Times* would claim that the production had 'exploded the idea that Lawrence the dramatist could safely be ignored'.[230]

This influential stage production was, by a fortunate coincidence, followed four months later by the publication of all eight of Lawrence's full-length plays and the two fragments in Heinemann's edition of the *Complete Plays*. This could hardly have come at a better moment.[231] *The Daughter-in-Law* was published at last, the three full-length plays which had only appeared in magazines now became widely available, and the other four plays came back into print.[232] The Heinemann edition was also widely reviewed and the plays generally received with enthusiasm, in a

---

[229] Sagar 301. See also Hugh Hebert, 'The Whipper-in', *Guardian*, 7 November 1973, p. 12.

[230] 'The Economics of Affection', *The Times*, 9 August 1965, p. 5 (reprinted in part, Sagar 302–3); 'Lawrence's First Play Well Acted', *Daily Telegraph*, 9 August 1965, p. 14; *The Times*, 28 January 1967, p. 13. Terry Coleman astutely suggested in the *Guardian*: 'If I were a television producer who wanted to be thought enterprising I should get hold of the scripts of those other … plays. I have a feeling, there is someone's reputation to be made out of them' (9 August 1965, p. 5).

[231] Roberts A105; London, Heinemann, 1965, costing 63s; the first printing was of 3,000 copies, reprinted in 1970 in an edition of 1,250 copies. Viking Press published it in New York in 1966, with minor corrections. In 1969, Heron Books (London) published a reprint of *Complete Plays* under the title *Plays*, introduction by Malcolm Elwin.

[232] *The Daughter-in-Law* was the fourth play in *Complete Plays*, pp. [203]–267. Early in 1965, James G. Hepburn had provided a complete listing of DHL's plays; he also engaged in speculation about lost plays which proved to be non-existent (*Book Collector*, xiv, 78–81).

climate of interest which could have been calculated to promote the performance of his plays in the theatre. Irving Wardle of the *Observer* noted that Lawrence wrote 'fine and truthful dialogue' and that the plays contained some 'superb scenes of domestic conflict and domestic peace'; he criticised some of the plays because of their 'poverty of form' and thought Lawrence had not been able to free himself from the conventions of the theatre he despised. However, he also claimed that Lawrence 'was born at the right time for the regional drama revival, but the wrong place: a few miles farther north and he would have been swept into the Manchester repertory movement'.[233] (Lawrence's abortive meeting with Payne in 1912 had shown how untrue that was.) Tony Tanner's review in the *Spectator* (7 January 1966) singled out 'moments of vivid immediacy and compelling authenticity', the display of a 'delicate, attentive and penetrating ... sense of people and environment'; but he insisted that the early plays were very different from the later *David*, a 'fascinating, impossible piece of writing' in 'incantatory rhetoric' (p. 16). Anaïs Nin, in the *New York Times Book Review* (10 April 1966), compared the plays with the novels; in the plays Lawrence respected the need for action, dialogue and a 'faithfulness to what is manifested on the surface and directly expressed' – and consequently had to steer clear of the deep exploration and revelation of emotions and the unconscious so characteristic of his prose fiction: 'he is content to present a lifelike portrait of instants. He makes no attempt to break with conventions of the theater, as he did with those of the novel'.[234] These judgements were shortly to be tested by audiences' experiences in the theatre; while just at the right moment to help the long-delayed revival of interest in him as a dramatist, Granada Television transmitted thirteen of his short stories as television plays between January 1966 and June 1967. The stories turned out to lend themselves extremely well to dramatisation and filming; Lawrence's dramatic gift quickly became known to a very wide audience.[235]

---

[233] 'Lawrence on Stage', 12 December 1965, p. 26.

[234] Pp. 4, 33. Further reviews in 1966: Alan Rudrum, 'Stage Sons, Stage Lovers', *Listener*, 10 February, pp. 214–15; 'Out of the Closet', *Time*, 1 April, p. 60; David J. Gordon, *Nation* (New York), 6 June, pp. 686–7; V. S. Pritchett, 'Lawrence's Laughter', *New Statesman*, 1 July, pp. 18–19; Andor Gomme, 'Writing the Play', *Times Literary Supplement*, 17 November, p. 1041.

[235] Ken Taylor wrote about his adaptation of *The Widowing of Mrs. Holroyd* and of several of DHL's short stories:

I ... took the unfashionable view that the dialogue was true and naturalistic and should be used wherever possible. I also advocated that the sub-text should not be rewritten extensively as dialogue, but that we should expect the actors to convey the thoughts and

1966–8. *The Widowing of Mrs. Holroyd,* **The Daughter-in-Law,** *A Collier's Friday Night* **and** *The Fight for Barbara* **performed**

Riding on the tide of interest created in 1965, Clive Perry directed *The Widowing of Mrs. Holroyd* at the Phoenix Theatre in Leicester from 14 to 25 June 1966. R. P. Draper contributed a programme note which praised the language of the play for being 'different from the language of the novels. It has no great passages of poetic splendour. As a dramatist Lawrence bent himself to the realistic and prosaic demands of the early twentieth century picture-frame theatre ... The result is spare and forcefully economical domestic drama.'[236] The *Daily Telegraph* reviewer further remarked that 'Indeed, you would never think a novelist had written the play at all, such is its simple, theatrical grasp, and its capacity for detailed observation of character through dialogue alone.'[237] The final breakthrough came six months later when *The Daughter-in-Law* – which had caught the attention of several reviewers when it appeared in the *Complete Plays* – was at last given to the theatrical public. Early in 1967, the play was staged in quick succession in Edinburgh, London and Sheffield, and was also broadcast on the BBC Third Programme, as directors, actors and audience realised that this was the Lawrence play they had been looking for. It got generally good reviews; but each time the play was performed, the notices improved, even those by reviewers who had previously been hostile to Lawrence's talents as a dramatist. *The Times* review (28 January) of the Edinburgh production at the Traverse Theatre (directed by Gordon McDougall) found 'the truthfulness and warmth of its best scenes ... piercing and remarkable and make a great impact' (p. 13), though the reviewer in the *Stage* (26 January) remarked that the play 'presents a drab canvas of working-class life' and suggested it had 'no real climaxes ... it trudges through its plot too steadily for any dramatic excitement' (p. 16). In London, however, directed by Peter Gill at the Royal Court with two of the actors from *A Collier's Friday Night* in the cast, the play worked extremely well. Irving Wardle in *The Times* (17 March) noted 'the sense of incurable tension, a bond that holds the characters permanently together no matter how emotions ebb and flow' (p. 12); Ronald Bryden in the *Observer* (19 March) thought that 'it makes most of our post-war essays in working-class drama look flimsy' (p. 25);

emotions between the lines. This may not seem very revolutionary now, but at that date the work of Harold Pinter was not so highly developed nor widely imitated! (Letter to eds., 17 February 1983)

[236] Programme in NCL.

[237] 'Lawrence Piece Shows Drama Grasp', 15 June 1966, p. 19.

R. B. Marriott in the *Stage* (23 March) called it 'this passionate, penetrating, extremely moving drama' (p. 13); while Frank Marcus asked, in *Plays and Players*:

Was D. H. Lawrence a great dramatist? No, but he might have become one if he had been able to see a performance as good as this. The marital rows come blazingly to life; he could have built on that. He could have re-written the curtain lines; he could have ventured beyond strict naturalism. He knew that he was offering emotional truth: he could have learned to express it in dramatic terms ... it seems hardly credible that a play of the quality of *The Daughter-in-Law* could have remained unperformed ...[238]

During the next three years, the play was also staged in Lincoln, Harrogate, Crewe, Nottingham, Hornchurch, Farnham and Derby, as well as being seen again in London.[239]

Directors were now on the look-out for other unperformed Lawrence plays, and Robin Midgley staged *The Fight for Barbara* at the Mermaid Theatre in London, opening on 9 August 1967. The text used, of course, was the shortened one available in the *Complete Plays*, and this led to the director's major problem: the play (lasting about ninety minutes) was too short for a full evening's theatre. The problem was overcome – and the whole nature of the production altered – by staging readings from other Lawrence works about himself, Frieda and her first husband, Ernest Weekley, as the first half of the evening, under the heading 'Men and Women', with the actors who had performed the readings taking the appropriate parts in the play. The play was thus presented as pure autobiography, something confirmed by the stage design – which incorporated paintings by Lawrence (anachronistic by fifteen or more years) on its walls – and by the programme, which reproduced numerous photographs of Lawrence and Frieda and a chronological table of their lives.[240] Some reviewers asked whether these links needed to be stressed so overtly. An advance notice in *The Times*, drawing on publicity from the theatre, however, summarised the play as follows: 'Barbara, an upper-class woman ... elopes to Italy with a labourer ... In addition to echoing the Lady Chatterley theme the play is said to have a strong autobiographical element.'[241] Midgley was quoted as saying that he found 'several parallels'

---

[238] 'The Dominant Sex', xiv (May 1967), 19.
[239] The director of the production at Nottingham Playhouse (4 March 1970), Stuart Burge, acknowledged the assistance given by Jessie Chambers's brother, Professor J. D. Chambers (programme in possession of the eds.).
[240] Programme in possession of eds.; it also reproduced DHL's essay 'Making Pictures' and five of his paintings.
[241] 7 July 1967, p. 7.

between Jimmy Porter in John Osborne's famous 1956 play, *Look Back in Anger*, and Lawrence's self-portrait (as Jimmy Wesson) in *The Fight for Barbara*.[242]

Given the production's biographical stress, reviewers naturally concentrated on those features and commented upon the effect of prefacing the play with readings. Philip Hope-Wallace in the *Guardian* called the play 'stiff, sub-Strindbergian stuff, a sex feud'; he considered the readings in the first half of the evening 'much more interesting, revealing and amusing than the fictional drama'.[243] Irving Wardle in *The Times* on 10 August ('Forgotten Play shows Power of Genius') had also drawn a comparison with Strindberg: 'This latest exhumation from the forgotten archive of Lawrence's plays again shows him as the British theatre's closest relative to Strindberg . . . the play is essentially a duet for the lovers; and on these terms autobiography blazes up into art' (p. 5). The reviewer in the *Daily Telegraph* (10 August) also stressed the play's autobiographical content (its headline read 'Lawrence Play on Own Flight') and praised the scenes between the lovers, but criticised the play because Lawrence had not managed – and probably had not wished – 'to develop his minor characters . . . These people do not come to life' (p. 17). Harold Hobson in the *Sunday Times* (13 August) felt that the production did not succeed in confirming the growing impression of Lawrence as 'a considerable dramatist. But it may not be altogether Lawrence's fault.' He criticised the production for creating caricatures and remarked that the play's dialogue 'seemed to me not to be beyond the erotic resources of a child of fifteen' (p. 21). *The Fight for Barbara*, in this production, did not advance the case for Lawrence as a dramatist.

The most distinguished productions so far had undoubtedly been those by Peter Gill; and he brought his work to a climax by reviving *The Daughter-in-Law*, restaging *A Collier's Friday Night* and adding a new production of *The Widowing of Mrs. Holroyd*, in a season of Lawrence's plays at the Royal Court in the early months of 1968.[244] The programme set the tone for the productions: lovingly detailed, with an explanation of

---

[242] Sean Day-Lewis, 'D. H. Lawrence on Stage', *Daily Telegraph*, 5 August 1967, p. 11.

[243] 11 August 1967, p. 7. Further reviews on 10 August: Herbert Kretzmer, *Daily Express*, p. 5; Milton Shulman, *Evening Standard*, p. 5; B. A. Young, *Financial Times*, p. 18. Other reviews in 1967: Helen Dawson, *Observer*, 13 August, p. 15; *Stage and Television Today*, 17 August, p. 17; V. S. Pritchett, *New Statesman*, 18 August, pp. 211–12; John Russell Taylor, *Plays and Players*, xv (October), 40–1; J. W. Lambert, *Drama*, no. 87 (Winter), 24; also Ben Kimpel and T. C. Duncan Eaves, *D. H. Lawrence Review*, i (1968), 72–4. See Sagar 305–7.

[244] *A Collier's Friday Night* opened on 29 February, *The Daughter-in-Law* on 7 March, *The Widowing of Mrs. Holroyd* on 14 March; they stayed in repertory until 4 May. See Barry

mining terms and history, contemporary photographs of miners at work, and texts of one of Lawrence's essays and several dialect poems.[245] For the majority of reviewers, the meticulously crafted and slowly paced productions revealed depths of poignancy in the plays which had not been expected; audiences became thoroughly involved with the work, performed as it was 'with an exact, unobtrusive veracity'.[246] The *Stage Year Book* for 1969 would claim that the Royal Court season had 'at last established Lawrence as a classic playwright' (p. 32), and reviewer after reviewer echoed Philip French's judgement in the *New Statesman* that Lawrence 'is a major dramatist in the naturalistic tradition, unrivalled in his ear for working-class speech'. Ronald Bryden, of the *Observer*, saw the season as a 'superb enterprise' which put together 'the three plays of childhood, marriage and death in a Nottinghamshire village as one panorama of English working-class life'. He confessed that 'Individually, perhaps, none of the plays is quite a masterpiece ... But even separately they have a truth and purity which makes the theatre's normal currency ... seem vulgar, and together they add up to something magnificent'. Benedict Nightingale in *Plays and Players* also stressed their extraordinary emotional truthfulness:

where else in our early twentieth century drama do we find any comparable intelligent attempt to deal with personal relationships onstage? Shaw? Too facetious, too glibly cynical. Galsworthy, then? Thin and predictable; didactic, too. Lawrence doesn't seek to impose any preconceived meaning on his plays. Rather, they are in the fullest sense of that overworked adjective, exploratory. All his energy goes into observing human conflict, comprehending and trying to explain it, as much (you feel) for his own peace of mind as for his audience's pleasure.[247]

The reviewers' comments on *A Collier's Friday Night* concentrated on the play's naturalism: some reviewers felt that loving recreation of detail was no

Hanson, 'Royal Court Diary, Rehearsal Logbook of the Three D H Lawrence Plays in Repertoire at the Royal Court till April 20', *Plays and Players*, xv (April 1968), 47, 52–3, 74; reprinted Sagar 308–18.

[245] Programme in possession of eds.

[246] Philip French, 'A Major Miner Dramatist', *New Statesman*, xv (22 March 1968), 390.

[247] 'A Major Miner Dramatist', 390; 'Lawrence Triptych', 17 March 1968, p. 1; 'On the Coal Face', xv (May 1968), 18–21, 51. Other reviews in 1968 were: Irving Wardle, 'A Strindberg of Our Own', *The Times*, 2 March, p. 19; Herbert Kretzmer, *Daily Express*, 15 March, p. 5; Harold Hobson, *Sunday Times*, 17 March, p. 49; Simon Gray, *New Society*, xi (21 March), 423–4; Hilary Spurling, 'Old Folk at Home', *Spectator*, 22 March, pp. 378–9; Mollie Panter-Downes, *New Yorker*, xliv (11 May), 101–2; J. W. Lambert, *Drama*, lxxxix (Summer), 22–3; C. G. Sândulescu, 'Lawrence Dramaturg', *Contemporanul*, iv (4 October), 4; also Christian Moe, 'Playwright Lawrence Takes the Stage in London', *D. H. Lawrence Review*, ii (1969), 93–7, and Keith Sagar, 'D. H. Lawrence: Dramatist', *D. H. Lawrence Review*, iv (1971), 154–82.

substitute for drama. Eric Shorter in the *Daily Telegraph*, for example, remarked that 'The cinema and the kitchen sink drama, not to speak of *Coronation Street* [the television soap-opera], have accustomed us to the charms of photographic realism which evidently delight Mr. Gill. He ponders dangerously on them. And since the author himself ponders, dramatically speaking, the two hours pass very slowly.' Other reviewers, however, praised the very things that Shorter criticised: Irving Wardle in *The Times*, for example, wrote how 'one is left to discern the complex family bonds under the daily traffic of eating, washing, gossiping, and sharing out the pay packet . . . [the acting reawakens] one to what naturalism should be: the art of riveting the attention by telling the truth about ordinary life.'[248] There was more agreement about the 1968 *Daughter-in-Law*. Michael Billington in *The Times* called it a 'powerful, controlled piece of writing, full of rich dialect, quiet humour and strong emotional collision'; he praised Gill's production for its 'fidelity to the details of ordinary domestic life' and insisted that 'Lawrence certainly possessed the dramatist's most basic gift, the ability to project simultaneously into the heart and mind of two separated, contrasted individuals'.[249]

But it was the production of *The Widowing of Mrs. Holroyd* which drew most admiration. Above all, reviewers (and audiences) were spellbound by the spectacle of the actress playing Mrs Holroyd, Judy Parfitt, weeping over Holroyd's body as she and her mother-in-law washed the corpse at the end of the play; the audience felt happier with this kind of dramatic emotional realism than with the complexities of emotional collision. The play was also praised for its superior – more conventional – structure.[250] In spite of some of the reviewers' reservations about naturalism, the response to the season as a whole was overwhelmingly favourable; and the major legacy of Gill's work was the recovery of these three plays for the

---

[248] 1 March 1968, p. 19; 1 March 1968, p. 12. Further reviews, 1 March 1968: Arthur Thirkell, *Daily Mirror*, p. 18; *Guardian*, p. 8; *Sun*, p. 4; on 2 March: *Financial Times*, p. 14; on 3 March: *Observer*, p. 31; *Sunday Telegraph*, p. 12; and on 9 March: J. C. Trewin, *Illustrated London News*, pp. 32–3.

[249] 'Fine Way with a Lawrence Play', 8 March 1968, p. 12. Further reviews, 8 March 1968: Arthur Thirkell, *Daily Mirror*, p. 20; *Daily Telegraph*, p. 19; Milton Shulman, *Evening Standard*, p. 4; B. A. Young, *Financial Times*, p. 38; *Sun*, p. 7; Philip Hope Wallace, *Guardian*, p. 8; on 10 March: Ronald Bryden, *Observer*, p. 31; *Sunday Telegraph*, p. 14; Harold Hobson, *Sunday Times*, p. 50; on 16 March: *Illustrated London News*, p. 32.

[250] Reviews on 15 March 1968: *Daily Telegraph*, p. 19; *Evening Standard*, p. 4; *Guardian*, p. 8; *The Times*, p. 13; *Sun*, p. 7; on 17 March: *Observer*, p. 31; *Sunday Telegraph*, p. 14; *Sunday Times*, p. 49; on 19 March: *Financial Times*, p. 26; on 22 March: *Spectator*, ccxx, 378–9; and on 23 March: *Illustrated London News*, pp. 28–9. Selection of reviews reprinted Sagar 307–22.

standard repertory of amateur and professional companies in Britain and abroad.[251]

1968–95. *Touch and Go* and *The Merry-go-Round* performed; plays by Lawrence as part of theatre and television repertoire

Following Gill's Lawrence season in London, 'productions promptly mushroomed round the country'.[252] *The Daughter-in-Law* had, for example, three more productions in 1968, in Lincoln, Harrogate and Nottingham, while *The Widowing of Mrs. Holroyd* was rediscovered in the USA in 1973 when Arvin Brown mounted a production in New Haven (believed, wrongly but understandably, to be the play's American première).[253] Stanley Kauffman deplored the play's thinness of texture and its unclear dramatic line of action but found the dialogue, with its 'real Laurentian graininess and pith', remarkable; the play proved to him that 'as Lawrence was Britain's first significant working-class novelist, so he was also the first significant working-class dramatist'.[254] Of great importance to the revival of Lawrence as a dramatist was the republication in cheap editions in 1968 and 1969 of the plays which had made the breakthrough in the theatre. Michael Marland produced an edition of *The Widowing of Mrs. Holroyd* and *The Daughter-in-Law* in 1968, and in his introduction offered some of the first intelligent discussion of Lawrence as a playwright; he also provided a useful dialect glossary. Andor Gomme in *The Times Literary Supplement* greeted the arrival of Marland's edition by asserting that *The Daughter-in-Law* was 'easily Lawrence's best' play, and 'ought to be as well known as *Sons and Lovers* and the best Nottinghamshire stories'.[255] The Penguin edition of 1969 (entitled *Three Plays*, thus taking its cue from the Gill productions of 1968) added *A Collier's Friday Night*, together with an informative introduction by Raymond Williams which concentrated on the specific kind of naturalism within which Lawrence worked. These two editions were widely used in schools and by amateur and professional companies, and an ever-increasing public came to know Lawrence's plays through them.

---

[251] The Royal Court production of *The Daughter-in-Law* was taken on tour in continental Europe in the summer of 1968.

[252] Irving Wardle, *The Times*, 13 August 1985, p. 7, in a review of a production of *The Daughter-in-Law*.

[253] Lincoln, June 1968; Harrogate, July–August 1968; Nottingham, October 1968; Long Wharf Theater, New Haven, Connecticut, November 1973.

[254] *New Republic*, 15 December 1973, p. 22.

[255] 6 March 1969, p. 253.

A number of Lawrence's plays still awaited production, however; given the interest in Lawrence's early 'colliery' plays, it was perhaps surprising that *Touch and Go* had to wait so long. Not until 1973 did an amateur group with professional standards, the Questors, stage it in their theatre in the round, in the London suburb of Ealing. Its first professional production was not until November 1979 at the Oxford Playhouse (followed by a single performance at the Royal Court Theatre in London). Neither production, however, was received very favourably. The 1973 staging, with extra songs added by its director, Peter Whelan, was found 'slow and monotonous': the headline 'Top Acting in Boring Drama' in the local paper summed up its reception. Only the last scene – which reviewers back in 1920 had claimed would be a theatrical success – was singled out for adding 'an exciting ending to an otherwise tedious story'.[256] Lawrence's honeymoon period with reviewers was at an end: Allardyce Nicoll was no longer in a minority when he noted, in 1973, that 'except, perhaps, for *A Collier's Friday Night* ... it seems probable that, if they had not borne his [Lawrence's] name, they would never have been dug out of their dusty obscurity'.[257] That had not been the experience of audiences, critics or theatre managers in the mid-1960s. In 1979 a new production of *Touch and Go*, mistakenly billed as the play's première,[258] was in general critically received: 'There isn't a character worthy of the name ... As for the abrupt stereotyped action, this is often laughable', said Garry O'Connor in the *Financial Times*, while John Barber remarked in the *Daily Telegraph* that 'the play ... leaps absurdly from drawing-room sing-songs to love scenes in a part ... Altogether, in fact, the play is a mess'. Nicholas de Jongh in the *Guardian*, however, admitting that it was a 'play of flaws', exclaimed 'what rewards in the midst of them'.[259]

Perhaps the most interesting première of the 1970s was that of *The Merry-go-Round*, also in 1973, staged by Gill on 7 November at the Royal Court.[260] This time Gill cut and adapted the play, something he had resolutely refused to do in his other productions, where he had been a stickler for the exact words of the text. He removed the onstage goose of Act I, for example, and modified the roles of the Polish vicar and his wife. The construction of *The Merry-go-Round* nonetheless raised eyebrows, the emotional realism and dramatic tensions of the first three-quarters of the

---

[256] *Questopics*, no. 84, September 1973; J. R., *Middlesex County Times and West Middlesex Gazette*, Ealing edition, 12 October 1973, p. 15.
[257] *English Drama 1900–1930*, p. 383.
[258] See Nicholas de Jongh, *Guardian*, 18 August, p. 3; 10 November, p. 13.
[259] 8 November, p. 23; 12 November, p. 15; 10 November, p. 13.
[260] In repertory until 9 December 1973; see Sagar 324.

play – again, worked over lovingly by Gill and his troupe, which included (as Mrs Hemstock) Ann Dyson, a veteran of the 1968 season – being abruptly dispelled in the sudden and parodic *As You Like It* ending, in which three couples agree to marry. Some reviewers saw this simply as a theatrical device – Irving Wardle in *The Times* referred to the 'sense of reality' as being 'total, until the farcical wheels start accelerating at the end'. But other reviewers found it a fundamental flaw. Benedict Nightingale in the *New Statesman* complained of Lawrence's 'most uncharacteristic smirk and shrug' as 'the putative tragedy becomes a piece of romantic fluff blown in from Shaftesbury Avenue', while Russell Davies in *Plays and Players* criticised 'the rib-tickling bonhomie of the last five minutes' for being

in unacceptable contrast with the preceding couple of hours ... A stageful of splenetic brooders is turned in a trice, as if galvanised by a whopping pay-rise or a few swift pints of black-and-tan into a pack of rustics. One of the chiefest charms of drama is that it lets us in on the public gallery as moral issues are judged: *The Merry-Go-Round* abruptly settles out of court, a dastardly thing to do.[261]

Still other reviewers had problems with the dialect speech. At least one voice, however, was raised in favour of the play and its 'supreme vitality': Michael Billington in the *Guardian* remarked that the 'deeper the Royal Court ventures into D. H. Lawrence's plays, the more obvious it becomes that British Theatre has been sitting on a goldmine. No other native dramatist in the early part of the century dealt so intelligently with personal relationships; and few ... painted such a vivid picture of British provincial life.'[262] But that – apart from the professional *Touch and Go* of 1979 – was the end of the production of new Lawrence plays. *The Merry-go-Round* has not been revived, and *The Fight for Barbara* has apparently been staged only once since 1967 (and never in its full-length form),[263] while *The Married Man* has very rarely been performed at all.[264]

---

[261] 8 November 1973, p. 12; lxxxvi (16 November 1973), 748–9; xxi (January 1974), 50–1.

[262] 7 and 8 November 1973, p. 12; see also Hugh Hebert on Peter Gill in the *Guardian*, 7 November 1973, p. 12. Further reviews in 1973 – on 8 November: *Daily Telegraph*, p. 14; *Financial Times*, p. 3; *The Times*, p. 13; on 11 November: *Observer*, p. 35; *Sunday Telegraph*, p. 18; *Sunday Times*, p. 37; on 16 November: *New Statesman*, pp. 748–9; on 17 November: *Spectator*, pp. 646–7; and *Drama* (Winter), pp. 26–8. Some reviews reprinted Sagar 324–6.

[263] Nat Horne Theater, New York (27 November 1978), directed by David Macenulty. A rehearsed reading had been given in the Department of English at the University of Nottingham on 2 March 1973. A semi-staged production of *David* (preceded by a reading of *Noah's Flood*) was also given in the New Theatre, University of Nottingham, 28 February–2 March 1974 (information from John McRae).

[264] Nine performances were given by students of the Royal Academy of Dramatic Art in London, at the GBS Studio at Kennington Park, between 22 and 31 October 1997; the production was directed by Brigid Panet.

Remembering the difficulties that director, actors and audience had had with *David*, Lawrence once remarked that 'The actual technique of the stage is foreign to me' (vi. 204). His lack of experience of the theatre led to far fewer problems than might have been imagined, however, particularly in the work he produced between the years 1909 and 1913: it was striking how little Walter Greenwood felt he needed to change when he revised *The Daughter-in-Law* into *My Son's My Son* in 1936 – he was really only concerned to tie up what he regarded as loose ends in the plot, and to create a more dramatic climax. Lawrence on the stage between the 1970s and 1990s is represented by regular revivals of *A Collier's Friday Night*, *The Widowing of Mrs. Holroyd* and *The Daughter-in-Law*, which have also become standard repertory on radio and television.[265] It is a remarkable outcome for plays whose texts had such a chequered history, and for a man who – although he often went to see plays and read a great many – knew very few directors, never worked with actors, never went back-stage, never saw a play of his own performed. It confirms the truth of the critical point that much of Lawrence's work was always and essentially dramatic.

Texts

A Collier's Friday Night

Lawrence wrote the surviving manuscript (hereafter MS)[266] in the autumn of 1909 while teaching in Croydon; it was finished by 27 November 1909. The 134-page MS is in black ink; it has few deletions, corrections or substitutions and contains only minor revisions. It consists of 12 unstitched gatherings (quires) of 8 and 12 pages, written on one side; the pages are not numbered but Lawrence numbered the gatherings with Roman numerals. The paper is ruled with 21 lines per page and watermarked 'Boots/CASH STATIONERS'; Lawrence used similar paper for other manuscripts dating from 1907 to 1911.

MS was typed in May 1933 (TCCI).[267] The typist was fairly accurate, but to some degree regularised the punctuation, omitted a few lines, and altered or misinterpreted a number of words. In February 1934 further

[265] See Chronology; also the entries on DHL in *The Concise Oxford Companion to the Theatre* (1972), *The Oxford Companion to the Theatre* (1983) and *The Cambridge Guide to World Theatre* (Cambridge, 1988). See too Sylvia Sklar, *The Plays of D. H. Lawrence: A Biographical and Critical Study* (1975).
[266] Roberts E74a (UT).
[267] Roberts E74b (UCB).

copies were made, of which a carbon-copy survives (TCCII),[268] the copies being prepared from the state of the text represented by TCCI. TCCII heavily interfered with the punctuation and the dialect, so that the play underwent extensive standardisation. This state of the text was used as setting-copy for the first English edition in 1934 by Secker (E1), when still further interference by typesetters and publishers' house-styling changed the character of the text. E1 was the source of the text in *Complete Plays*;[269] some slight textual modifications (e.g. revision of stage directions and punctuation) were applied to all the plays in *Complete Plays*.

MS has been adopted as base-text. TCCI, TCCII and E1 have no textual authority; their variants have been recorded in the Textual apparatus, however, as recording the stages by which the play came into print.

The Widowing of Mrs. Holroyd

Lawrence conceived the play during the period 1909–10; the manuscript was finished by 9 November 1910. Early in 1913 Garnett had the manuscript typed and sent a text to Mitchell Kennerley, who offered to publish it. Typesetting started in America without Lawrence's knowledge; he revised the manuscript in August. His revisions arrived in America in September, and were almost certainly incorporated in the text. Lawrence saw a corrected version in October, including a clean typescript made by Kennerley, revised it further in November and may have returned it to Kennerley. It cannot exactly be determined which or how many of Lawrence's revisions and alterations made in August, October or November were finally incorporated in the text Kennerley published in 1914 (A1).[270] Neither the original manuscript, nor any typescripts or proofs have survived. The first English edition, published by Duckworth in 1914 (E1), used sheets supplied by Kennerley and is textually identical with A1. E1 was the source of the text in *Plays* and again in *Complete Plays*.[271]

The base-text is A1. It is reproduced with minimal alteration, but the layout and typography of the printed page have been standardised according to the general practice followed in his volume (see 'Conventions adopted for the printing of texts in this edition', pp. cxxv–cxxvi). There is no Textual apparatus for this play.

[268] From the Viking Press: no Roberts number (UT).
[269] [469]–530.
[270] Roberts A5.
[271] 7–79; [11]–61.

The Merry-go-Round

Lawrence began his third play in late November and early December 1910 when his mother was fatally ill. It was probably finished early in 1911. The original manuscript (MS)[272] consists of 152 pages and is in ink; it has few deletions, corrections or substitutions except for 2 passages with heavy interlinear revision. It consists of 13 unstitched gatherings, each consisting of 5 or 6 folded sheets, numbered (in Lawrence's hand) with Roman numerals. The paper is identical with that used for *A Collier's Friday Night*. The pages are numbered by Lawrence in Arabic numerals 1–148 with 4 doublings.

MS was typed in London in 1933 and 1934. A ribbon copy and two carbon copies survive,[273] most probably from the 1934 typing; they have identical features. These typescripts, however, did not influence the transmission of the text.

MS remained in Frieda Lawrence's keeping and was taken to New Mexico. It was copied in Taos in the winter of 1939–40, the ribbon copy (TSI) and one carbon copy surviving.[274] A copy was sent to the editor of the *Virginia Quarterly Review* at Charlottesville who re-typed it in a line-by-line and page-by-page manner and then marked up the new typescript as setting-copy for publication in the periodical; the corrected and marked up ribbon copy (TSII)[275] and an uncorrected carbon-copy[276] – with two pages ribbon copy – survive. The play was published in the winter of 1940–1 as a Supplement (pp. 1–44) to the periodical's Christmas number, vol. xvii (Per). Off-prints 'Privately Printed 1940' also exist, produced in a heavier grade of paper and with a different title-page.

The American copyists, editor and typesetter altered or misinterpreted Lawrence's text in quite a number of instances; his multiple punctuation and dialect words were affected most. Per was used in preparation of the first English edition in *Complete Plays* (E1).[277]

MS has been adopted as base-text. TSI, TSII, Per and E1 have no textual authority; their variants have been recorded in the Textual apparatus.

---

[272] Roberts E237a (UCB).
[273] Roberts E237b (UCB) and E237c (UT).
[274] Roberts E237d (UCB).
[275] No Roberts number (UV).
[276] Roberts E237c (UTul).
[277] [387]–467.

The Married Man

Lawrence wrote the original manuscript (MS)[278] in April 1912; it was finished by 23 April. The 67-page MS is in blue ink, but the first 5 pages are missing; the first surviving page of MS is numbered '6.' in Lawrence's hand. These pages had become separated or lost before MS was typed in London in 1933. The pagination is in Arabic numerals 6–72. MS has little interlinear revision or correction. The first surviving page also carries a note in pencil '? MARRIED MAN', probably added in 1939–40. The text is written on one side of single leaves of slightly translucent ruled paper with 26 lines per page (except for pp. 24 and 36, which are unruled), apparently torn from a writing pad gummed at the top.

MS was typed in London in June 1933 (a ribbon copy survives)[279] and again in 1934 (a ribbon copy and a carbon copy survive).[280] These typescripts, however, did not influence the transmission of the text.

MS remained in Frieda's keeping and was taken to New Mexico. It was typed in Taos in the winter of 1939–40; the ribbon copy (TSI) and one carbon copy survive.[281] A copy was sent to the *Virginia Quarterly Review* and re-typed and marked up in the same way as *The Merry-go-Round*; the corrected and marked-up copy, of mixed ribbon and carbon pages (TSII)[282] and an uncorrected mixed ribbon and carbon copy[283] survive.

The play was published in the autumn of 1940 in the *Virginia Quarterly Review*, xvi, 523–47 (Per). The copyist, editor and typesetter in Charlottesville occasionally altered or misunderstood Lawrence's text and extensively tampered with the punctuation. Per was used in preparation of the first English edition in *Complete Plays* (E1).[284]

MS has been adopted as base-text. TSI, TSII, Per and E1 have no textual authority; their variants have been recorded in the Textual apparatus.

The Fight for Barbara

Lawrence wrote the extant 56-page manuscript (MS)[285] between 28 and 30 October 1912. His reference to the play as 'a sort of interlude to Paul

---

[278] Roberts E229a (UCB).
[279] Roberts E229c (UT).
[280] Roberts E229b (UCB); from the Viking Press, no Roberts number (UT).
[281] Roberts E229d (UCB).
[282] No Roberts number (UV).
[283] Roberts E229e (UTul).
[284] [155]–201.
[285] Roberts E130a (UT).

Morel' (i. 466) is confirmed by the fact that the paper of MS is identical with that of the last pages of the manuscript of *Sons and Lovers* and with that used in letters he wrote on 30 October and 14 November 1912.[286] MS is written in black ink on one side of gatherings of ruled leaves (6-leaf, 8-leaf and 10-leaf quires) and on loose leaves probably torn from gatherings. The pagination runs 1–55, with two pages numbered '28' (the second one occurring when Lawrence started a new gathering). Extensive interlinear revision occurs four times in MS where Lawrence rewrites part of the dialogue. Four pencil interpolations in German and English occur, two of them certainly in Frieda Lawrence's handwriting. Lawrence sent MS to Edward Garnett immediately after finishing it. It is not known whether he worked on it again after he had it back from Garnett in February 1913.

MS was typed in 1933. Lawrence's agents sold the 'serial rights' to the English fiction magazine, the *Argosy*, in June 1933, and offered the publisher Martin Secker an option for subsequent publication. In December 1933 the magazine published a shortened (with almost one quarter of the text cut) and extensively house-styled version of the play as *Keeping Barbara*, pp. 68–90 (Per). The agents expressed surprise when they saw the play published under a different title; it can be assumed that the cuts had also not been agreed. Of the typescript copies made in 1933, which would certainly have represented the complete MS, none has survived. Two extant typescripts[287] reproduce the shortened and house-styled version of the play published in Per, but the punctuation of Per is closer to MS. It seems probable that the typesetters of Per were using a typescript made from MS in 1933 but no longer extant, which had the cuts and changes marked in it (most probably by the magazine's editors) but whose punctuation remained close to MS; such a marked typescript was itself the source of the extant early typescripts which tampered with the punctuation. MS was typed again during the winter of 1939–40, when Frieda probably made a handwritten copy of the play's opening.[288]

The truncated version of the play published in Per was used as copy for

---

[286] Information kindly provided by Helen and the late Carl Baron: *Letters* i. nos. 510 and 513, and in six quires of paper of various sizes used in the last part of the manuscript of *Sons and Lovers*, finished 19 November 1912.

[287] Carbon copy Roberts E130c (UT) and carbon copy (from the Viking Press) with no Roberts number (UT).

[288] This typescript (Roberts E130b, UCB) played no part in the transmission of the play: it was almost certainly prepared for the *Virginia Quarterly Review*. A manuscript of the beginning of the play (Roberts E130d, UT) is in Frieda's hand: she may have started making a copy when anxious about sending MS to the *Virginia Quarterly Review* late in

Complete Plays (E1);[289] the play's title was restored. The present edition of
The Fight for Barbara publishes the complete text for the first time.

MS has been adopted as base-text. Per and E1 have no textual authority;
their variants have been recorded in the Textual apparatus.

The Daughter-in-Law

Lawrence probably wrote the manuscript (MS)[290] during the first twelve
days of January 1913; it is inscribed in black ink on 63 numbered pages of
large Italian paper. He posted it to Edward Garnett in mid-January and
probably never saw it again. By the autumn of 1933, MS was in the
possession of Curtis Brown Ltd, who had typescripts made; the surviving
example – a carbon copy (TCCI)[291] – bears the stamp of Curtis Brown's
New York office on its cover-sheet. After Walter Greenwood had adapted
the play in 1936 as *My Son's My Son* (creating a new typescript[292]), *The
Daughter-in-Law* vanished for nearly thirty years. At some stage – probably
when plans for its publication in *Complete Plays* (E1) were being drawn up
in the early 1960s – TCCI was retyped without reference to MS; the
typing survives in a solitary ribbon copy (TSII).[293] The last of Lawrence's
plays to reach print, it first appeared in E1 in 1965.[294] The text of E1 was
taken from the state of text represented by TSII, probably from a carbon-
copy. The text of E1 had thus been subject to the regularising intentions of
a publisher as well as to the influence of two different typists, one of whom
– the typist of TCCI – had some problems understanding Lawrence's
version of the dialect of the English Midlands.

MS has been adopted as base-text. TCCI, TSII and E1 have no textual
authority; their variants have, however, been recorded in the Textual
apparatus, as recording the stages by which the play came into print. The
Greenwood typescript has not been collated.

1939 (see p. xcvii above) before it was agreed that MS should be typed. This fragment
stops in the middle of the fourth page in mid-sentence (240:28 in the present edition) and
has no textual authority.
[289] [269]–319.
[290] Roberts E84a (NYPL).
[291] Roberts E84c (UCB).
[292] Roberts E84d (USal), in the Greenwood collection.
[293] Roberts E84b (UT).
[294] [203]–267.

Touch and Go

Lawrence created the manuscript (MS),[295] of 70 incorrectly numbered pages (plus an unnumbered cover page with the cast-list on the verso) in black and blue ink, probably between 22 and 28 October 1918. The play was first typed from MS in the office of J. B. Pinker, either in the winter of 1918 or in the spring of 1919. Only a single ribbon-copy typescript was made: an annotation made in Pinker's office on a letter from Lawrence asserting that they had made two copies reads 'one' (iii. 396 n. 3), and in September 1919 – with that typescript in the hands of a theatrical management – Pinker was unable to supply a second copy. It is not known whether Lawrence ever corrected the Pinker typescript, which is not extant. At some stage, probably in June 1919, Lawrence revised MS in pencil; some of his revisions were simple clarifications of words that were difficult to read, and he also marked things such as the underlining of stage directions at the start of scenes, suggesting that he may have been preparing MS for typing. MS was typed again in the summer of 1919, by the theatrical agent Walter Peacock, in a ribbon copy and two carbons. An uncorrected carbon copy, marked '2nd Carbon.' (TCC) survives;[296] it became the setting-copy for the play's publisher, C. W. Daniel, and is marked by the compositors employed by the printers, Neill and Co., Ltd. It is almost certain that Lawrence never saw it; he certainly made no alterations to it. Before the play's English first edition was published by Daniel in May 1920 (E1), Lawrence sent a text (which he called 'the MS') to Compton Mackenzie (iii. 510); this may have been MS, the Pinker typescript or one of the Peacock typescripts,[297] but this text did not influence Daniel's publication. MS was preserved, perhaps in the possession of Pinker, and the setting-copy TCC survived at first in the possession of Daniel and then probably with Pinker. The American edition was produced from sheets supplied by Daniel, and bound in coloured cloth boards: 'Amusing it looks', commented Lawrence (iii. 565). The play was reprinted from E1 in *Plays*; that text was the source of *Complete Plays*.[298]

MS has been adopted as base-text. None of the changes made by Peacock's typist in TCC, working directly from MS, has any authority. Lawrence did not correct TCC, and it is unlikely that he saw proofs. Only one of the changes in E1 (the replacement of one song by another) has

---

[295] Roberts E401.6 (UN).
[296] No Roberts number (UN).
[297] See footnote 38 above.
[298] 91–182; [325]–386.

any obvious authorial authority, and was probably transmitted separately to Daniel.[299] On a further ten occasions, substantive changes were made in the printed text, and though it is theoretically possible that Lawrence was responsible for them in proof (at 387:26, 388:33–4, 396:6, 397:6, 401:34, 402:28, 403:16, 407:9, 421:29, and 422:2), it is hard to imagine him confining himself to eleven alterations in eighty-eight pages.[300] Eight of the changes are to single words, most of them are designed to simplify the text and none of them is particularly near to any other – whereas Lawrence's characteristic method of revision was to make clusters of changes of both words and phrases, re-thinking and re-casting as much as changing. Only the change at 426:40 has been adopted in this edition. The variants of TCC and E1 have been recorded in the Textual apparatus.

Preface to *Touch and Go*

Lawrence wrote the Preface in June 1919. The manuscript (MS),[301] on nine sheets of thin paper with twenty-one ruled lines, was not typed but used as setting-copy by Neill and Co., Ltd, Edinburgh, the printers of the first edition of the play itself (E1).[302] Compositors' names appear in pencil on p. 2 ('Gallagher') and p. 5 ('Brady'). MS probably survived in the possession of Pinker. It is unlikely that Lawrence saw proofs of E1 (see above). The Preface was reprinted from E1 in *Plays*.[303] It was omitted from Heinemann's *Complete Plays* but appeared in *Phoenix II* in 1968.[304]

MS has been adopted as base-text. The variants of E1 and two editorial emendations (at 364:14 and 365:20) have been recorded in the Textual apparatus.

Altitude

Lawrence wrote the play (possibly in a now-missing first draft) around 19–23 June 1924, and inscribed it on twenty-eight pages of a notebook (MS).[305] When Spud Johnson printed Scene 1 in the *Laughing Horse* (Per)

[299] See p. liii and Explanatory note and Textual apparatus at 426:40.
[300] In his correction of the first proofs for *The Lost Girl*, which he saw later in the same year, he made about 70 alterations in 112 pages. See *The Lost Girl*, ed. Worthen, p. xxxviii.
[301] No Roberts number (UN).
[302] *Touch and Go* (1920), pp. 5–12.
[303] 83–90.
[304] *Phoenix II: Uncollected, Unpublished and Other Prose Works by D. H. Lawrence*, ed. Warren Roberts and Harry T. Moore (1968), pp. [289]–293.
[305] Roberts E13a (UCB).

in 1938, he used a rather amateurishly typed but fairly accurate ribbon-copy typescript (TS)[306] of the whole of MS, supplied by the bookseller and collector Jake Zeitlin: the latter had had TS made (in a ribbon and at least one carbon copy) in 1937, while MS, then owned by Frieda Lawrence, was on exhibition in Los Angeles.[307] Johnson revised Scene I in TS with such changes and improvements as he thought desirable (TSC): he rewrote some stage directions, and cut the end completely. He noted that Lawrence 'finished this first scene and began a second' (Per 111), but did not print Scene II, perhaps because he believed that it was only a fragment, perhaps because he thought it less interesting than the first. His queried emendations of typing errors in TSC show that he did not have MS available to consult.

The process of revision was continued at the magazine proof stage, when numerous further alterations and modifications to the text of Scene I were made. Johnson also supplied Per with a list of characters, adding comments on each. A surviving carbon copy of the Zeitlin typescript is not corrected and is identical with the text of TS: it has not been included in the collation.[308] MS was also typed on another occasion, probably for Curtis Brown Ltd. during the 1930s; two carbon copies of this typescript survive.[309] As they played no part in the transmission of the text, they have not been included in the collation. *Complete Plays* (E1)[310] took Per as its source for Scene I; for Scene II – which was printed for the first time – one of the Zeitlin typescripts was used,[311] and MS was not consulted. Scene II's opening stage direction was modified and three speeches omitted (presumably by accident).

This edition adopts Lawrence's MS as its base-text, and therefore prints his version of Scene I for the first time, without the overlay of Johnson's modifications; Scene II has its missing speeches restored. The Textual apparatus records the variants in TS, TSC, Per and E1; suggested emendations of stage directions for performances of the play follow the text.

---

[306] *Laughing Horse*, no. 20 (Summer 1938), 12–35: Roberts E13d (UT).

[307] Zeitlin had helped put on the exhibition of Frieda's collection of DHL's manuscripts in the Los Angeles Public Library: see the catalogue for the exhibition prepared by Powell: *the manuscripts of d. h. lawrence*.

[308] Roberts E13c (UCB).

[309] Roberts E13b (UCB) and E13c (UT).

[310] [545]–548.

[311] Errors in the Zeitlin typescripts at 551:5, 552:5, 553:3 and 37 (see Textual apparatus), transmitted into E1 but not appearing in the Curtis Brown carbon-copy typescripts, show that a Zeitlin typescript was the source for E1.

Noah's Flood

There are two surviving manuscript fragments (MSI and MSII), MSI being the eleven-page manuscript Lawrence wrote early in 1925,[312] and MSII being a ten-page text he began to transcribe (altering it as he did so) in a notebook sometime between 1926 and 1927.[313] The text of MSII is even more of a fragment than that of MSI: it lacks the second half for which MSI is the sole authority.

MSII, although started in a new notebook, is a revision of MSI and not a new text. It has been used to emend the first half of MSI. The text of MSII was printed in *Phoenix* (A1),[314] from a copy of the same typing that survives in three identical carbon copies (TCC);[315] the text in *Complete Plays* was taken from A1. Apart from nineteen lines, MSI has not previously been printed.[316] MSI has been adopted as base-text, emended from MSII. The text has been collated with that of TCC and A1, whose variants are recorded in the Textual apparatus; suggested emendations of stage directions for performances of the play follow the text.

David

The manuscript (MS) was written in pencil between late March and 7 May 1925, on 172 pages originally in a notebook.[317] There are some small corrections in ink (e.g. pp. 164, 167–8). MS was typed between May and July 1925 by Dorothy Brett; this typescript originally existed in a ribbon copy (TS)[318] and a carbon copy, now missing. TS, though better typed than some of Brett's typescripts, is both inaccurate and unclear; the carbon copy, subjected to a great deal of double-striking, must have been especially difficult to read. Brett also sometimes missed out punctuation and omitted or added words and phrases, and on occasion left out whole lines and speeches. She also frequently left words incomplete on the right-hand edge of the page, where her typewriter's margin-setting refused to allow her to type further; either she or Lawrence regularly filled in the

---

[312] Roberts E273a (UT).
[313] Roberts E273b (UCB).
[314] *Phoenix*, ed. McDonald, pp. 811–16.
[315] First carbon copy, Roberts E273d (UNM); second carbon copy, Roberts E273c (UT); third carbon copy, Roberts E273c (UCB). The first bears the label of Curtis Brown, Ltd, the numbered stamp '24' and the words 'MUST AWAIT AMERICAN RELEASE DATE'.
[316] Tedlock 126.
[317] Roberts E87a (UN): see Appendix v i for details of the writing and revision of MS.
[318] Roberts E87b (UT).

missing letters in ink on TS and almost certainly did so too on the carbon copy.

Lawrence went through TS and the carbon copy making corrections, alterations and additions to create TSR, but he does not seem at any stage to have compared MS with what Brett had produced. As usual, he revised TS and the carbon copy slightly differently; he read them with an eye to developing his work, and only corrected the most obvious errors. At times, however, the alterations he made in response to Brett's mistypings developed his text to a stage from which editorially, there can be no return to the readings of MS; at other times, he patched up the mistakes Brett had made as best he could, and it is more satisfactory to return to the readings of MS. Editorial decisions of both kinds are discussed in the Explanatory notes.

Secker used the carbon copy as the setting-copy for the first proofs, of which a mostly uncorrected set (PPI) survives.[319] Lawrence corrected the proofs in the winter of 1925–6, but apparently had no access to MS, TS or the setting-copy while doing so: if the printers did send him the latter, he does not appear to have consulted it. Those of PPI's substantive differences from TS which clearly derive from Lawrence, however, preserve the substantive variants of the setting-copy.[320]

It is possible to study the nature and sequence of Lawrence's work on the proofs by comparing PPI with PPII and the first English edition (E1). In PPI, he radically cut down his references to 'God' and 'Lord' by making a large number of cosmic and animist substitutions, as mentioned above; he also made nearly all his verbal revisions and was surprisingly careful in his correction of minute details. In PPII, he appears to have made only two verbal changes, but continued to adjust the punctuation and capitalisation.[321] The printers, however, regularised Lawrence's text at every stage; a comparison of the surviving typescript and PPI shows that they regularly inserted commas where convention required them, cut out punctuation marks which seemed unnecessary, and continued this process in PPII.[322]

---

[319] Roberts E87c (UT).

[320] At 503:30, for example, PPI suggests that Lawrence, inserting into the carbon copy the word 'a' which Brett had omitted, must have misplaced it: instead of altering his text to 'a man falling', as he correctly did in TSR (p. 77), he must have produced 'man a falling', which PPI reproduced as 'man a-falling' (p. 100).

[321] The surviving set of PPII shows that, in his work on PPI, in a great many cases he had replaced 'God' and 'Lord' with words such as 'Deep', 'Might' and 'Bolt': see Explanatory note on 439:30.

[322] See pp. cxxiii–cxxiv for the strategies adopted in this edition to distinguish the printer's alterations of punctuation from what may be DHL's own proof corrections.

PPI also shows that, in the original setting, they had begun the process of capitalising pronouns in references to the God of Israel (they completed the process in PPII) and also made the remaining 'lord' and 'god' forms (when referring to the Old Testament deity) consistent by capitalising them.[323] They also engaged, at both stages of the proofing process, but particularly when turning PPII into E1, in some relineation to avoid crowded lines; they also made numerous small modifications, such as adding brackets around stage directions, to improve the appearance of the printed page still further.[324]

Although the fully corrected set of first proofs survived in Lawrence's possession for some time, it is no longer extant. Lawrence corrected second proofs early in 1926; again, the corrected set is no longer extant. The surviving set of almost uncorrected second proofs (PPII)[325] contains one sheet deriving from the set originally designed for the printer, and two authorial corrections in it (PPIIR) indicate that Lawrence was responsible for some of the corrections in the English edition (E1).[326] The text of Knopf's American edition (A1) derived wholly from E1, being taken from either a fully corrected set of PPII or (more likely) an advance copy of E1.[327] E1 was used as the source for *Plays* and the latter was the source of *Complete Plays*.[328]

Base-text for the bulk of *David* is MS; base-text for the end of Scene IV (451:3-17), written into the setting-copy typescript and into TS, is (in the absence of the setting-copy) PPI. TS is in general a textual cul-de-sac for both substantives and punctuation; the missing setting-copy was the source

---

[323] See 'Note on silent emendations'.

[324] The compositors must have been told to be especially concerned with the layout of what would be a rather short and relatively expensive book. The width of the newly introduced capitals 'H' and 'T' in 'He', 'His', 'Him', 'Thou' and 'Thee' forms often resulted in crowded lines, which were accordingly relineated; and attention was paid to avoiding wordbreaks at the ends of lines. Some of this tidying was done at the PPI stage, and some at the PPII stage: e.g. the relineation at 121:8 and 121:9 was done at the PPI stage and appears in PPII, but the relineation at 77:24 and 77:25 must have been done at the PPII stage.

[325] No Roberts number (UN).

[326] Having made two corrections on p. 13, when DHL turned over to p. 14, he must have discovered that the ends of three consecutive lines of text in the middle of the page were obscured. He ringed the damage, but then removed the whole printed sheet from the signature (its conjoint leaf being the title-page and its verso) and substituted the sheet from his duplicate set of proofs, which presumably did not have the fault. The single partly corrected sheet thus survives in the otherwise almost uncorrected duplicate set.

[327] See above, p. lxxviii.

[328] 185-312; [67]-154.

of both E1 and A1, and its readings (when they can be distinguished and recovered from the text of PPI) have been preferred to those surviving in TS.

The variant printed substantives of PPI – which normally record authorial corrections in the setting-copy – have generally been adopted: cases where this has not been done are signalled in the Textual apparatus and discussed in the Explanatory notes. PPI sometimes retains traces of the missing setting-copy which E1 obliterated: see, e.g., Textual apparatus for 503:30. The authorial emendations to substantives which Lawrence must have made in the corrected set of first proofs (appearing in PPII), and those made in the corrected set of second proofs (appearing in E1: see below) have also been adopted.

The compositors of PPI began a process of normalising Lawrence's pronouns for God. These had appeared with lower-case initial letters in MS and TS, but PPI printed a number of them with upper-case initial letters. The process of normalisation was continued and completed in the proof-correction of PPI and PPII. There is a solitary example in Scene II of the surviving duplicate copy of PPII (at 439:33) of Lawrence himself altering 'his' to 'His', but this has not been regarded as compelling evidence for following, in this edition, what was in its origins a compositor's regularisation of the text. Lawrence was responding to (and attempting to make consistent) a textual *fait accompli*: his form 'thee' had already been altered to 'Thee' one line earlier, at 439:32.

The surviving sheet of PPII bearing corrections does, however, assist an estimate as to how much of the alteration of the text in E1 might derive from Lawrence in proof. Lawrence, on p. 13 of PPII, changed 'his' to 'His' and corrected 'feardest' to 'fearest' (439:15). Two other changes, however, appeared in E1: the deletion of a comma (439:31) and the capitalisation of an 'm' (439:35). This confirms the editorial hypothesis that many of the changes in E1 were due to the Riverside Press of Edinburgh. Of the 138 changes made in E1, the majority (89) were normalisations (spellings – such as 'inquire' for 'enquire' at 465:13 – altered, commas and hyphens added or deleted, full stops turned to exclamation marks, etc.); on 13 occasions, words were capitalised or uncapitalised; on 10 occasions, 'Oh' was changed to 'O' or vice versa.

This pattern of minor changes, with very few changes of words, is unlike Lawrence's revision elsewhere. It has therefore been decided to classify the changes of E1 as non-authorial except where there is compelling evidence (as at 468:8 and 471:28) that Lawrence was responsible for them. Only 9 of the 138 changes may derive from Lawrence, and only 2 have been accepted as emendations of the text.

The punctuation of MS and of the corrections in the first proofs (PPIR) is adopted in this edition except where undoubted or arguably authorial punctuation was either inserted into the setting-copy (thus appearing in PPI), or into the corrected sets of first and second proofs. Where it is unclear whether the variant punctuation of the surviving set of PPI derives from compositors' regularisation of the missing setting-copy, or from punctuation variants inserted by Lawrence himself into the setting-copy, the punctuation of TSR has been adopted as more certainly authorial. As, however, it is clear from both proof sets that Lawrence was prepared to make the most minute corrections to his text in proof revision, much of the new punctuation appearing for the first time in PPII and E1 has been adopted.

The variant readings of TS, TSR, PPI, PPIR, PPII, PPIIR and E1 are recorded in the Textual apparatus; A1, derived directly from E1, has not been included in the collation.

CONVENTIONS ADOPTED FOR THE PRINTING OF TEXTS IN THIS EDITION

The *Plays* volume poses editorial problems unlike those in any other volume in *The Cambridge Edition of the Letters and Works of D. H. Lawrence*. When writing his plays, Lawrence generally did not think of the special conventions applied to the *printing* of play-texts. He treated them like his other prose: he did not often bother about underlining stage directions (to indicate italics); he was not consistent in how he positioned stage directions or what form he used for them; and he was not consistent in how he inscribed characters' names in speech headings.

The main editorial choice lies between following (to some extent) the conventional layout of plays in printed form, and printing – in effect – transcriptions of the manuscripts. If the editors had opted for the latter, the texts would all look very different from each other, at times would not look like plays at all, and some would be difficult to read. We have, with the approval of the Editorial Board, effected a limited standardisation. The following conventions have been applied:

1 A complete list of the full names of characters (printed in small capitals) is provided: this is in the order of the characters' appearance, except in *The Widowing of Mrs. Holroyd* (where the first edition prints a list of characters) and *Touch and Go* (where Lawrence prepared his own list, divided – as one convention of the time demanded – into male and female characters). Where the latter two have been editorially emended, the emendations appear in square brackets. Lawrence inserted a list of characters (with some brief descriptions) in the first proofs of *David*, and the list was subsequently used in the first edition: but it includes only twenty-eight of the fifty-four individual characters and groups. It has been printed following the full character list.
2 Characters' names as speech headings for the dialogue, and characters' names within stage directions, are printed in small capitals. Speech headings are followed by a colon.
3 Stage directions are printed in italics. Stage directions at the beginning of acts and scenes are printed without round brackets and end with a full stop. Stage directions (and additions to stage directions) in square

brackets have been supplied editorially. Stage directions on all other occasions are printed within round brackets. Stage directions following speech headings start in lower case and are followed by a colon outside the bracket; other stage directions start in upper case and have a full stop, within the bracket. The only exception to this rule is when – within dialogue – the stage direction indicates that a speech is being directed at a particular character. In this case, when followed by a lower-case word, the stage direction starts in lower case and no punctuation is included; when followed by an upper-case word or a name, it starts in upper case and is followed by a colon outside the bracket. Lawrence sometimes started a new line for stage directions: such stage directions are given on a new line.

4 Acts start with the indication 'Act I.', 'Act II.', etc. Scenes start with the indication 'Scene 1.', 'Scene 2.', etc. The end of acts and scenes is indicated by '*(Curtain)*'.

When states of the text which include stage directions are recorded in the Textual apparatus, however, they have been printed exactly as they stand in the surviving documents, and conventions of standardisation have not been applied.

See too 'Textual apparatus' and 'Silent emendations', pp. 715–16 below.

THE PLAYS

A COLLIER'S FRIDAY NIGHT

MOTHER, MRS LAMBERT
NELLIE LAMBERT
GERTIE COOMBER
FATHER, MR LAMBERT   5
ERNEST LAMBERT
BARKER
CARLIN
MAGGIE PEARSON
BEATRICE WYLD[☆]   10

A COLLIER'S FRIDAY NIGHT[☆]

Act I.

The kitchen or living room[☆] *of a working man's house. At the back, the
fireplace, with a large fire burning. On the left, on the oven side of the
stove, a woman of some fifty-five years sits in a wooden rocking chair,
reading. Behind her and above her, in the recess made by the fireplace,
four shelves of books, the shelf-covers being of green serge, with woollen
ball fringe, and the books being ill-assorted schoolbooks, with an edition of
Lessing,*[☆] *florid in green and gilt, but tarnished. On the left, a window
looking on a garden where the rain is dripping through the first twilight.
Under the window, a sofa, the bed covered with red chintz. By the side of
the window, on the wall near the ceiling, a quiver-clothes-horse*[☆] *is
outspread with the cotton articles, which have been ironed, hanging to air.
Under the outspread clothes*[☆] *is the door which communicates with the
scullery and with the yard. On the right side of the fireplace, in the recess
equivalent to that where the bookshelves stand, a long narrow window,
and below it, a low brown fixed cupboard, whose top forms a little
sideboard on which stand a large black-enamel box of oil-colours, and a
similar japanned box of water colours, with Reeve's silver trade mark.*[☆]
*There is also on the cupboard top a tall glass jar containing ragged pink
chrysanthemums.*[☆] *On the right is a book case upon a case of drawers.
This piece of furniture is of stained polished wood in imitation of
mahogany. The upper case is full of books, seen through the two flimsy
glass doors: a large set of the "World's Famous Literature"*[☆] *in dark
green at the top—then on the next shelf prize books in calf and gold, and
imitation soft leather poetry books, and a Nuttall's dictionary, and
Cassell's French, German and Latin dictionaries. On each side of the
book-case are prints from water colours,*[☆] *large, pleasing, and well framed
in oak. Between the little brown cupboard and the book case, an armchair, small, round, with many little staves: a comfortable chair such as is
seen in many working class kitchens; it has a red chintz cushion. There is
another Windsor chair on the other side of the book case. Over the mantel
piece, which is high, with brass candle sticks and two 'Coronation'*

5

10

15

20

25

30

5

*tumblers** in enamel, hangs a picture of Venice, from one of Stead's
Christmas Numbers,*—nevertheless satisfactory enough.*

*The woman in the rocking chair is dressed in black, and wears a black
sateen apron. She wears spectacles, and is reading the 'New Age'.* Now*
5 *and again she looks over her paper at a piece of bread which stands on a
hanging-bar before the fire, propped up by a fork, toasting. There is a
little pile of toast on a plate on the boiler hob beside a large saucepan, the
kettle and a brown teapot occupying the oven-top near the woman. The
table is laid for tea, with four large breakfast cups in dark blue willow
10 pattern, and plates similar. It is an oval mahogany table, large enough to
seat eight comfortably. The woman sees the piece of bread smoking, and
takes it from the fire. She butters it and places it on the plate on the hob,
after which she looks out of the window, then taking her paper, sits down
again in her place.*

15 *Someone passes the long narrow window, only the head being seen, then
quite close to the large window on the left. There is a noise as the outer
door opens and is shut, then the kitchen door opens and a girl enters. She
is tall and thin, and wears a long grey coat and a large blue hat, quite
plain. After glancing at the table, she crosses the room, drops her two
20 exercise books on the wooden chair by the book-case, saying:*

"Oh I am weary!"

MOTHER*: —You are late!

NELLIE LAMBERT: I know I am. It's Agatha Kerton—she is a great
gaby. There's always something wrong with her register, and old
25 Tommy* gets in such a fever, the great kid.

*(She takes off her hat, and going to the door on right, stands in the
doorway hanging it up with her coat on the pegs in the passage, just by
the doorway.)*

—And I'm sure the youngsters have been regular little demons;
30 I could have killed them.

MOTHER: I've no doubt they felt the same towards you, poor little
wretches.

NELLIE LAMBERT *(with a short laugh)*: I'll bet they did, for I
spanked one or two of 'em well.

35 MOTHER: Trust you, trust you. You'll be getting the mothers if
you're not careful.

NELLIE LAMBERT *(contemptuously)*: I had one old cat this afternoon. But I told her straight. I said: 'If your Johnny or Sammy
or whatever he is is a nuisance, he'll be smacked, and there's an
40 end of it.' She was mad, but I told her straight, I didn't care.

She can go to Tommy if she likes: I know he'll fuss her round, but I'll tell *him* too. Pah, he fusses the creatures up—!—I *would*! *(She comes towards the table, pushing up her hair with her fingers. It is heavy and brown, and has been flattened by her hat. She glances at herself in the little square mirror which hangs from a nail under the right end of the mantel piece, a mere unconscious glance which betrays no feeling and is just enough to make her negligently touch her hair again. She turns a trifle fretfully to the table.)*
Is there only potted meat? You know I can't bear it!

MOTHER *(conciliatorily)*: Why I thought you'd like it, a raw day like this—and with toast.

NELLIE LAMBERT: You know I don't. Why didn't you get some fruit?—a little tin of apricots—.

MOTHER: I thought you'd be sick of apricots—I know Ernest is.

NELLIE LAMBERT: Well I'm not—you know I'm not. Pappy potted meat—!

(She sits down on the sofa weariedly. Her MOTHER pours out two cups of tea, and replaces the pot on the hob.)

MOTHER: Won't you have some then?

NELLIE LAMBERT *(petulantly)*: No, I don't want it.

(The MOTHER stands irresolute a moment, then she goes out. NELLIE LAMBERT reaches over to the bookshelves and takes a copy of 'The Scarlet Pimpernel', which she opens on the table, and reads, sipping her tea, but not eating. In a moment or two she glances up as the MOTHER passes the window and enters the scullery. There is the sound of the opening of a tin.)*
Have you fetched some?—Oh, you are a sweetling!

(The MOTHER enters with a little glass dish of small tinned apricots. They begin tea.)

MOTHER: Polly Goddard says her young man got hurt in the pit this morning.

NELLIE LAMBERT: Oh—is it much?

(She looks up from her book.)

MOTHER: One of his feet crushed. Poor Polly's very sad. What made her tell me was Ben Goddard going by. I didn't know he was at work again, but he was just coming home, and I asked her about him, and then she went on to tell me of her young man. They're all coming home from Selson,* so I expect your father won't be long.

NELLIE LAMBERT: Goodness!—I hope he'll let us get our teas first.

MOTHER: Well, *you* were late. If he once gets seated in the Miner's Arms,* there's no telling when he comes.

5 NELLIE LAMBERT: I don't care when he does so long as he doesn't come yet.

MOTHER: Ah, it's all very well—!

(They both begin to read as they eat. After a moment another girl runs past the window and enters. She is a plump fair girl, pink and white. She
10   *has just run across from the next house.)*

GERTIE COOMBER: Hello, my duck, and how are you?

NELLIE LAMBERT *(looking up)*: Oh, all right, my bird.

GERTIE COOMBER: Friday tonight! No Eddie for you! Oh poor Nellie! Aren't *I* glad though!

15   *(She snaps her fingers quaintly. The* MOTHER *laughs.)*

NELLIE LAMBERT: Mean cat!

GERTIE COOMBER *(giggling)*: No I'm not a mean cat. But I like Friday night: we can go jinking off up town and wink at the boys. I like market night.

20 *(She puts her head on one side in a peculiar quaint simple fashion. The*
                  MOTHER *laughs.)*

NELLIE LAMBERT: *You* wink! If she so much as sees a fellow who'd speak to her, she gets behind me and stands on one foot and then another.

25 GERTIE COOMBER: I don't! No I don't, Nellie Lambert. I go like this 'Oh good evening, *how* are you. I'm sure I'm very pleased —'

(She says this in a very quaint 'prunes and prisms' manner, with her chin in the air, and her hand extended. At the end she giggles. The
30 MOTHER *with her cup in her hand, leans back and laughs.* NELLIE LAMBERT, *amused in spite of herself, smiles shortly.)*

NELLIE LAMBERT: You are a daft object! What about last week when David Thompson—

(GERTIE COOMBER puts her hand up and flips the air with affected
35   *contempt.)*

GERTIE COOMBER: —David Thompson! A bacon sawyer! Ph!

NELLIE LAMBERT: You brazen madam! He's as good as you. And then Johnny Grocock.*

GERTIE COOMBER: What a name! Not likely! Mrs Grocock! *(She*
40 *giggles.)* Oh dear no, nothing short of Mrs Carooso.*

(She holds back the skirts of her long pinafore with one hand, and affects the Gibson bend.) ☆

MOTHER *(laughing heartily)*: Caruso! Caruso! A great fat fellow— —!

GERTIE COOMBER: Besides, a collier! I'm not going to wash stinking pit-things.

NELLIE LAMBERT: You don't know what you'll do yet, my girl. I never knew such cheek! I should think you want somebody grand, you do.

GERTIE COOMBER: I do that. Somebody who'll say 'Yes dear! Oh *yes* dear! Certainly, certainly.'

(She simpers across the room, then giggles.)

NELLIE LAMBERT: You soft cat, you! But look here Gert, you'll get paid out treating Bernard Hufton as you do.

GERTIE COOMBER *(suddenly irritated)*: Oh I can't abide him. I always feel as if I could smack his face. He thinks himself so ikey. He always makes my — —

(A head passes the narrow side window.)

—Oh glory, there's Mr Lambert! I'm off!

(She draws back against the book case. A man passes the large window. The door opens, and he enters. He is a man of middling stature, a miner, black from the pit. His shoulders are pushed up because he is cold. He has a bushy, iron grey beard. He takes from his pocket a tin bottle and a knotted 'snap' bag—his food bag of dirty calico—and puts them with a bang on the table. Then he drags his heavily shod feet to the door on Right: he limps slightly, ☆ *one leg being shorter than the other. He hangs up his coat and cap in the passage, and comes back into the living room. No one speaks. He wears a grey and black neckerchief, and being coatless, his black arms are bare to the elbow, where end the loose dirty sleeves of his flannel 'singlet'. The MOTHER rises, and goes out to the scullery carrying the heavy saucepan. The man gets hold of the table and pulls it nearer the fire, away from his daughter.)*

NELLIE LAMBERT: Why can't you leave the table where it was! We don't *want* it stuck on top of the fire.

FATHER: Ah dun, if you dunna.

(He drags up his arm chair and sits down at the table, full in front of the fire.)

—'An yer got a drink for me?

(The MOTHER comes and pours out a cup of tea, then goes back to the scullery.)

—It's a nice thing as a man as comes home from th' pit parched up canna ha'e a drink got 'im.

(He speaks disagreeably.)

MOTHER: Oh, you needn't begin. I know you've been stopping
5   drinking.

FATHER: Dun yer?—well yer know too much then: you' wiser than them as knows, you are!

(There is a general silence, as if the three listeners were shrugging their shoulders in contempt and anger. The FATHER *pours out his tea into his*
10   *saucer, blows it, and sucks it up.* NELLIE LAMBERT *looks up from her book and glowers at him with ferocity.* GERTIE COOMBER *puts her hand before her mouth and giggles behind his back at the noise. He does not drink much, but sets the cup back in the saucer and lays his grimed arms wearily along the table. The* MOTHER *enters with a plate of cabbage.)*

15   MOTHER: Here, that's a clean cloth!

(She does not speak unkindly.)

FATHER *(brutally)*: You should put a dotty *(dirty)* 'un on then.

(The MOTHER *takes a newspaper and spreads it over the cloth before him. She kneels at the oven, takes out a stew-jar, and puts meat and*
20   *gravy on the plate with the cabbage, and sets it before him. He does not begin at once to eat. The* MOTHER *puts back her chair against the wall, and sits down.)*

MOTHER: Are your trousers wet?

FATHER *(as he eats)*: A bit.

25   MOTHER: Then why don't you take them off?

FATHER: Fetch my breeches an' wascoat down, Nellie. *(In a tone of brutal authority.)*

NELLIE LAMBERT *(continuing to read, her hands pushed in among her hair)*: You can ask me properly.

30   *(The* FATHER *pushes his beard forward and glares at her with futile ferocity. She reads on.* GERTIE COOMBER, *at the back, shifts from one foot to the other, then coughs behind her hand as if she had a little cold. The* MOTHER *rises and goes out by door on Right.)*

FATHER: You lazy idle bitch, you let your mother go.

35   NELLIE LAMBERT *(shrugging her shoulders)*: You can shut up. *(She speaks with cold contempt.)*

*(*GERTIE COOMBER *sighs audibly. The tension of the scene will not let her run home.* NELLIE LAMBERT *looks up, flushed, carefully avoiding her father.)*

40   NELLIE LAMBERT: Aren't you going to sit down, Gert?

GERTIE COOMBER: No, I'm off.

NELLIE LAMBERT: Wait a bit, and I'll come across with you. I
don't want to stop *here*.

(The FATHER *stirs in his chair with rage at the implication. The*
MOTHER *comes downstairs and enters with a pair of black trousers, from*   5
which the braces are trailing, and a black waistcoat lined with cream and
red lining. She drops them against her husband's chair.)

MOTHER *(kindly—trying to restore the atmosphere)*: Aren't you going
to sit down, Gertie? Go on the stool.

*(*GERTIE COOMBER *takes a small stool on the right side of the fire-place,*   10
and sits toying with the bright brass tap of the boiler. The MOTHER *goes*
out again on Right, and enters immediately with five bread tins and a
piece of lard paper. She stands on the hearth rug greasing the tins. The
FATHER *kicks off his great boots and stands warming the trousers before*
the fire, turning them and warming them thoroughly.)   15

GERTIE COOMBER: Are they cold, Mr Lambert.

FATHER: They are that! Look you, they steaming like a sweating
hoss.

MOTHER: Get away, man, the driest thing in the house would
smoke if you held it in front of the fire like that.   20

FATHER: Ah *(shortly)* I know I'm a liar. I knowed it to begin wi'.

NELLIE LAMBERT *(much irritated)*: Isn't he a nasty-tempered kid?

GERTIE COOMBER: But those front bedrooms are clammy.

FATHER *(gratified)*: They h'are, Gertie, they h'are.

GERTIE COOMBER *(turning to avoid* NELLIE LAMBERT*'s contempt,*   25
and pottering the fire): I know the things I bring down from
ours, they fair damp in a day.

FATHER: They h'are, Gertie, I know it. An' I wonder how 'er'd like
to clap 'er 'arce into wet breeches. *(He goes crambling off to door*
on Right, trailing the breeches.)   30

NELLIE LAMBERT *(fiercely)*: Father!

*(*GERTIE COOMBER *puts her face into her hands and laughs with a half*
audible laugh that shakes her body.)

NELLIE LAMBERT: I can't think what you've got to laugh at, Gert
Coomber.   35

(The MOTHER, *glancing at her irate daughter, laughs also. She moves*
aside the small wooden rocking chair, and, drawing forth a great panchion
of dough from the corner under the book shelves, begins to fill the bread
tins. She sets them on the hearth—which has no fender, the day being
Friday, when the steel fender is put away, after having been carefully   40

cleaned, to be saved for Saturday afternoon. The FATHER *enters, the braces of his trousers dangling, and drops the heavy 'mole-skin' pit-breeches in corner on Right.)*

5   NELLIE LAMBERT: I wonder why you can't put them in the scullery; the smell of them's hateful.

FATHER: You mun put up wi' it then. If you were i' th' pit, you'd niver put your nose up at them again.

(He sits down and recommences eating. The sound further irritates his daughter, who again pushes her fingers into her hair, covering her ears
10   *with her palms. Her* FATHER *notices, and his manners become coarser.*
      NELLIE LAMBERT *rises, leaving her book open on the table.)*

NELLIE LAMBERT: Come on Gert!

(She speaks with contemptuous impatience. Her FATHER *watches them go out. He lays his arms along the newspaper wearily.)*

15   FATHER: I'm too tired ter h'eat.

MOTHER *(sniffing,* * *and hardening a little)*:   I wonder why you always have to go and set her off in a tantrum as soon as you come in.

FATHER: A cheeky bitch, 'er wants a good slap at th' side o' th'
20   mouth!

MOTHER *(incensed)*: If you've no more sense than that, I don't wonder— —.

FATHER: You don't wonder, you don't wonder— —! No, I know you don't wonder. It's you as eggs 'em on against me, both on
25   'em.

MOTHER *(scornfully)*: You set them against yourself. You do your best for it, every time they come in.

FATHER: Do I, do I! I set 'em against me, do I. I'm going to stand 'em orderin' me about, an' turnin' their noses up, am I?

30   MOTHER: You shouldn't make them turn their noses up then. If you do your best for it, what do you expect.

FATHER: —A jumped-up monkey! An' it's you as 'as made 'em like it, the pair on 'em. There's neither of 'em but what treats me like a dog. I'm not daft! I'm not blind! I can see it.

35   MOTHER: If you're so clever at seeing it, I should have thought you'd have sense enough not to begin it, and carry it on as you do.

FATHER: Me begin it! When do I begin it? You niver hear me say a word to 'em, till they've snapped at me as if I was a—as if I was
40   a—. No, it's you as puts 'em on it, it's you, you blasted—!

(He bangs the table with his fist. The MOTHER *puts the bread in the oven, from which she takes a rice pudding, then she sits down to read. He glares across the table, then goes on eating. After a little while he pushes the plate from him. The* MOTHER *affects not to notice for a moment.)*

'An yer got any puddin'? 5

MOTHER: Have you finished?

(She rises, takes a plate and crouching at the hearth, gives him his pudding. She glances at the clock, and clears the tea-things from her daughter's place. She puts another piece of toast down, there remaining only two pieces on the plate.) 10

FATHER *(looking at the rice pudding)*: Is this what you'n had?

MOTHER: No, we had nothing.

FATHER: No, I'll bet you non 'ad this baby pap.

MOTHER: No, I had nothing, for a change, and Nellie took her dinner. 15

FATHER *(eating unwillingly)*: Is there no other puddin' as you could 'a made?

MOTHER: Goodness, man, are you so mightily particular about your belly? This is the first rice pudding you've had for goodness knows how long, and——! No, I couldn't make any other. In 20 the first place it's Friday, and in the second, I'd nothing to make it with.

FATHER: You wouldna ha'e, not for me. But if you'd 'a wanted——

MOTHER *(interrupting)*: You needn't say any more. The fact of the matter is, somebody's put you out at the pit, and you come 25 home to vent your spleen on us.

FATHER *(shouting)*: You're a liar, you're a liar! A man comes home after a hard day's work to folks as 'as never a word to say to 'im, as shuts up the minute 'e enters the house, as 'ates the sight of 'im as soon as 'e comes in th' room——! 30

MOTHER *(with fierceness)*: We've had quite enough, we've had quite enough! Our Ernest'll be in in a minute, and we're not going to have this row going on: him coming home all the way from Derby,* trailing from college, to a house like this, tired out with study and all this journey: we're not going to have it, I tell you. 35

(Her husband stares at her dumbly, betwixt anger and shame and sorrow; of which, an undignified rage is predominant. The MOTHER *carries out some pots to the scullery, re-enters, takes the slice of toast, and butters it.)*

FATHER: It's about time as we had a light on it. I canner see what I'm eatin'. 40

(The MOTHER *puts down the toast on the hob, and having fetched a dust-pan from the scullery, goes out on* Right *to the cellar to turn on the gas and to bring coals. She is heard coming up the steps heavily. She mends the fire, and then lights the gas at a brass pendant hanging over the table.*

5 *Directly after, there enters a young man of twenty one, tall and broad, pale, clean shaven, with the brownish hair of the 'ginger' class, which is all ruffled when he has taken off his cap, after having pulled various books from his pockets, and put them on the little cupboard top. He takes off his coat at door on* Right *as his sister has done.)*

10 ERNEST LAMBERT *(blowing slightly through pursed lips)*: Phww! It is hot in here.

FATHER *(bluntly, but amiably)*: Hot! It's non hot! I could do wi' it ten times hotter.

MOTHER: Oh you! You've got, as I've always said, a hide like a
15 hippotamus.✻ You ought to have been a salamander.

FATHER: Oh ah, I know tha'll ha'e summat ter say.

MOTHER: Is it raining now, Ernest?

ERNEST LAMBERT: Just a drizzle in the air, like a thick mist.

MOTHER: Ay, isn't it sickening! You'd better take your boots off.

20 ERNEST LAMBERT *(sitting in his sister's place on the sofa)*: Oh they're not wet.

MOTHER: They must be damp.

ERNEST LAMBERT: No they're not. There's a pavement all the way. Here, look at my rose! One of the girls in Coll. gave it me, and
25 the tan-yard girls tried to beg it. They are brazen hussies! 'Gie's thy flower, Sorry, gie's thy buttonhole'—and one of them tried to snatch it. They have a bobby down by the tanyard brook every night now. Their talk used to be awful, and it's so dark down there under the trees. Where's Nellie?

30 MOTHER: In Coomber's.

ERNEST LAMBERT: Give me a bit of my paper father. You know the leaf I want: that with the reviews of books on.

FATHER: Nay, I know nöwt about reviews o' böwks. Here t'art. Ta'e it.

35 *(He hands the newspaper to his son, who takes out two leaves and hands the rest back.)*

ERNEST LAMBERT: Here you are, I only want this.

FATHER: Nay, I non want it. I mun get me weshed. We s'll ha'e th' men here directly.

ERNEST LAMBERT: I say Mater,* another seven and six up your sleeve.

MOTHER: I'm sure! And in the middle of the term* too. What's it for *this* time?

ERNEST LAMBERT: Piers the Ploughman, that piffle, and two books of Horace: Quintus Horatius Flaccius,* dear old chap.

MOTHER: And when have you to pay for them?

ERNEST LAMBERT: Well, I've ordered them, and they'll come on Tuesday. I'm sure I don't know what we wanted that Piers Ploughman for, it's sheer rot, and old Beasley could have gassed on it without making us buy it, if he'd liked.—Yes, I did feel wild, seven and sixpence!

FATHER: I should non get 'em then. You nedna buy 'em unless you like — — dunna get 'em then.

ERNEST LAMBERT: Well, I've ordered them.

FATHER: If you 'anna got the money, you canna 'a'e 'em, whether or not.

MOTHER: Don't talk nonsense, if he has to have them, he has. But the money you have to pay for books, and they're no good when you've done with them!—I'm sure it's really sickening, it is!

ERNEST LAMBERT: Oh never mind, Little, I s'll get 'em for six shillings. Is it a worry, Mutterchen?*

MOTHER: It is, but I suppose if it has to be it has.

ERNEST LAMBERT: Old Beasley is an old chough. While he was lecturing this afternoon Arnold and Hinrich were playing nap:* and the girls always write letters, and I went fast asleep.

FATHER: So that's what you go'n to collige for, is it?

ERNEST LAMBERT (*nettled*): No it isn't. Only old Beasley's such a dry old ass, with his lectures on Burke.* He's a mumbling parson, so what do you expect.

(*The* FATHER *grunts, rises, and fetches a clean new bucket from the scullery. He hangs this on the brass tap of the boiler, and turns on the water. Then he pulls off his flannel singlet, or vest, and stands stripped to the waist, watching the hot water dribble into the bucket. The pail half-filled, he goes out to the scullery on left.*)

ERNEST LAMBERT: Do you know what Professor Staynes* said this morning, mother? He said I'd got an instinct for Latin—and you know he's one of the best fellows in England on the classics: edits Ovid and what not. An instinct for Latin, he said.

MOTHER *(smiling, gratified)*: Well, it's a funny thing to have an instinct for.

ERNEST LAMBERT: I generally get alpha plus. That's the highest, you know, Mater. Prof. Staynes generally gives me that.

5 MOTHER: Your grandfather was always fond of dry reading: economics and history. But I don't know where an instinct for Latin comes from—not from the Lamberts, that's a certainty. Your Aunt Ellen would say, from the Vernons.

(She smiles ironically, as she rises to pour him another cup of tea,
10 *taking the teapot from the hob, and standing it, empty, on the father's*
plate.)

ERNEST LAMBERT: Who are the Vernons?

MOTHER *(smiling)*: It's a wonder your Aunt Ellen or your Aunt Eunice has never told you.. . .

15 ERNEST LAMBERT: Well they haven't. What is it, Mutter?

MOTHER *(sniffing)*: A parcel of nonsense.. . .

ERNEST LAMBERT: Oh go on, Ma, you are tantalising! You hug it like any blessed girl.

MOTHER: Yes, your Aunt Ellen always said she would claim the
20 peacock and thistle for her crest if ever— —

ERNEST LAMBERT *(delighted)*: The Peacock and Thistle!—It sounds like the name of a pub— —.

MOTHER: My great-great-grandfather married a Lady Vernon:—so they say. As if it made any matter—a mere tale.

25 ERNEST LAMBERT: Is it a fact though, Matoushka? Why didn't you tell us before?

MOTHER *(sniffing)*: What should I repeat such—

FATHER *(shouting from the scullery, whence has come the noise of his washing)*: 'An yer put that towil ter dry!

30 MOTHER *(muttering)*: The towel's dry enough.

(She goes out, and is heard taking the roller towel from behind the outer door. She returns, and stands before the fire holding up the towel to dry. ERNEST LAMBERT, having frowned and shrugged his shoulders, is reading.)

35 MOTHER: I suppose you won't have that bit of rice pudding?

(Her son looks up, reaches over and takes the brown dish from the hearth. He begins to eat from the dish.)

ERNEST LAMBERT: I went to the 'Savoy' today.

MOTHER: I shouldn't go to that vegetable place. I don't believe
40 there's any substance in it.

ERNEST LAMBERT: Substance: Oh Lord! I had an asparagus omelette,—I believe they called it. It was too much for me— —! A great stodgy thing—! But I like the Savoy generally. It was — —

(Somebody comes running across the yard. NELLIE LAMBERT *enters with a rush.)*   5

NELLIE LAMBERT: Hello. Have you done.

FATHER *(shouting from scullery)*: Are you going to shut that doo-ar?

NELLIE LAMBERT *(with a quick shrug of the shoulders)*: It *is* shut. *(Brightly, to her brother)*: Who brought this rose? It'll just do for   10
me. Who gave it you—Lois?*

ERNEST LAMBERT *(flushing)*: What do you want to know for? You're always saying 'Lois'. I don't care a button about Lois.

NELLIE LAMBERT: Keep cool, dear boy, keep cool.

(She goes flying lightly round, clearing the table. Her FATHER, *dripping,*   15
bending forward almost double, comes hurrying from the scullery to the fire. NELLIE LAMBERT *whisks by him, her long pinafore rustling.)*

FATHER *(taking the towel)*: Öw *(she)* goes rushin' about, draughtin'. *(He rubs his head, sitting on his heels very close to the fire.)*

NELLIE LAMBERT *(smiling contemptuously,—to herself)*: Poor kid.   20

FATHER *(having wiped his face)*: An' there isn't another man i' th' kingdom as 'ud stan' i' that scullery stark naked. It's like standin' i' cöwd watter.

MOTHER *(calmly)*: Many a man stands in a colder.

FATHER *(shortly)*: Ah, I'll back: I'll back there is! Other men's   25
wives brings th' panchion onto th' 'arthstone, an' gets the watter for 'em, an'—.

MOTHER: Other men's wives may do: more fools them: you won't catch me.

FATHER: No, you wunna: you may back your life o' that! An' what   30
if you 'ad to?

MOTHER: Who'd make me?

FATHER *(blustering)*: Me!

MOTHER *(laughing shortly)*: Not half a dozen such.

(The FATHER *grunts.* NELLIE LAMBERT, *having cleared the table, pushes*   35
him aside a little, and lets the crumbs fall into hearth.)

FATHER: A lazy idle stinkin' trick!
(She whisks the table cloth away without speaking.)
An' tha doesna come waftin' in again when I'm weshin' me, tha remembers.   40

ERNEST LAMBERT *(to his mother, who is turning the bread)*: Fancy, Swinburne's dead!*

MOTHER: Yes, so I saw. But he was getting on.

FATHER *(to* NELLIE LAMBERT, *who has come to the boiler and is kneeling getting a lading-can full of water)*: Here Nellie, gie my back a wesh!

(She goes out and comes immediately with flannel and soap. She claps the flannel on his back.)

FATHER *(wincing)*: OOO! Tha nasty bitch!

*(*NELLIE LAMBERT *bubbles with laughter: the* MOTHER *turns aside to laugh.)*

NELLIE LAMBERT: You great baby, afraid of a cold flannel!

(She finishes washing his back and goes into the scullery to wash the pots. The FATHER *takes his flannel shirt from the book-case cupboard, and puts it on, letting it hang over his trousers. Then he takes a little blue-striped cotton bag from his pit-trousers' pocket and throws it on the table to his wife.)*

FATHER: Count it.*

(He shuffles upstairs. The MOTHER *counts the money, putting it in little piles, checking it from two white papers. She leaves it on the table.* ERNEST LAMBERT *goes into the scullery to wash his hands, and is heard talking to his sister, who is wiping the pots. A knock at the outer door.)*

ERNEST LAMBERT'S VOICE: Good Evening, Mr Barker!

A VOICE: Good Evenin', Ernest.

(A miner enters, pale, short, but well-made. He has a hard-looking head with short black hair. He lays his cap on a chair.)

Good Evenin', Missis! 'Asn't Carlin come? Mester up stairs?

MOTHER: Yes, he'll be down in a minute. I don't expect Mr Carlin will be many minutes. Sit down, Mr Barker. How's that lad of yours?

BARKER: Well, 'e seems to be goin' on nicely, thank yer. Dixon* took th' splints off last wik.

MOTHER: Oh, well that's better! He'll be all right directly. I should think he doesn't want to go in the pit again—.

BARKER: 'E doesna. 'E says 'e shall go farmin' wi' Jakes, but I shanna let 'im. It's nöwt o' a sort o' job, that.

MOTHER: No, it isn't. *(Lowering her voice.)* And how's Mrs?

BARKER *(also lowering his voice)*: Well—I don't know. I want ter get back, as soon as I'n got a few groceries an' stuff in. I sent for

Mrs Smalley afore I com'n out. An' I'n come an' forgot th' market bag—— —.

MOTHER *(going into the scullery)*: Have mine, have mine. Nay, I've got another. *(She brings him a large carpet bag with leather handles.)* 5

BARKER: Thank yer, Missis. I can bring it back next wik: you sure you wunna want it?

(Another knock. Enter another man, fair, pale, smiling: an inconsiderable man.)

CARLIN: Hgh! Tha's bested me then? Good evenin' Missis! 10

BARKER: Yes, I'n bet thee.

(Enter FATHER. He has put on a turndown collar and a black tie, and his black waistcoat is buttoned, but he wears no coat. The other men take off the large neckerchiefs, grey and white silk, in fine check, and show similar collars. The FATHER assumes a slight tone of superiority.) 15

FATHER: Well, you'n arrived then! An' 'ow's th' Missis by now, Joe?

BARKER: Well, I dun know, George. It might be any minnit.

FATHER *(sympathetically)*: Hu! We may as well set to then, an' ger it done. 20

(They sit at the table, on the side of the fire. ERNEST LAMBERT comes in, and takes an exercise book from the shelves, and begins to do algebra, using a text book. He writes with a fountain pen.)

CARLIN: They gran' things them fountain pens.

BARKER: They are that! 25

CARLIN: What's th' mek on it, Ernest?

ERNEST LAMBERT: It's an Onoto.☆

BARKER: Oh ah! An' öw *dun* yer fill it? They sayn as it hold it wi' a vackum.

ERNEST LAMBERT: It's like this—you push this down, put the nib 30 in th' ink, and then pull it out. It's a sort of a pump.

BARKER: Um! It's a canny thing that!

CARLIN: It is an' a'!

FATHER: Yes, it's a very good idea.

(He is slightly condescending.) 35

MOTHER: Look at the bread Ernest.

ERNEST: All right, Mater.

(She goes upstairs, it being tacitly understood that she shall not know how much money falls to her husband's share, as chief "butty",☆ in the weekly reckoning.) 40

BARKER: Is it counted?
FATHER: Yes. It's all right Ernest?
ERNEST *(not looking up)*: —Yes.
*(They begin to reckon, first putting aside the wages of their day men, then
the* FATHER *and* BARKER *take four and threepence, as equivalent to
Carlin's rent, which has been stopped, then the* FATHER *gives a coin each,
dividing the money in that way. It is occasionally a puzzling process, and
needs the Ready Reckoner,* from the shelf behind.)*

(Curtain)

Act II.

Scene as before: the men are just finishing reckoning. BARKER *and*
CARLIN, *talking in a low mutter, put their money in their pocket.* ERNEST
LAMBERT *is drawing a circle with a pair of compasses.* CARLIN *rises.*

CARLIN: Well, I might as well be shiftin'— —.   5
BARKER: Ay, I mun get off.
(Enter NELLIE LAMBERT, *who has finished washing the pots, drying her
hands on a small towel. She crosses to the mirror hanging at the right
extremity of the mantelpiece.)*
CARLIN: Well Nellie!   10
NELLIE LAMBERT *(very amiably, even gaily)*: Good evening Mr
    Carlin:—just off—?
CARLIN: Yes—ah mun goo.
BARKER: An' öw's th' instrument by now, Nellie?
NELLIE LAMBERT: The instrument? Oh the piano! Ours is a   15
    tinny old thing! Oh yes, you're learning. How are you getting
    on.
BARKER: Oh, we keep goin' on, like. 'Ave you got any fresh music?
FATHER: Ah, I bet 'er 'as. Öw's gerrin' some iv'ry day or töw.
NELLIE LAMBERT: I've got some Grieg*—lovely! Hard though. It   20
    is funny—ever so funny!
BARKER: An' yer iver 'eered that piece 'The Maiden's Prayer'?*
NELLIE LAMBERT *(turning aside and laughing)*: Yes, do you like it?
    It is pretty, isn't it!
BARKER: I 'ad that for my last piece.   25
NELLIE LAMBERT: Did you! Can you play it?
BARKER *(with some satisfaction)*: Yes, I can do it pretty fair. An' yer
    got th' piece.
NELLIE LAMBERT: Yes. Will you play it for us. Half a minute—!
(She finishes stroking her hair up with her side combs, and, taking the   30
    matches from the mantel-piece, leads the way to door.)
    Come on.
FATHER: Yes, step forward Joe.
*(*MR BARKER *goes out after* NELLIE LAMBERT. *Through the open door
comes the crashing sound of the miner's banging* through the 'Maiden's*   35
Prayer', on an old sharp-toned piano. CARLIN *stands listening, and
shakes his head at the* FATHER, *who smiles back, glancing at the same
time nervously at his son, who has buried his hands in his hair.)*

CARLIN: Well, are ter comin' down, George?

(He moves towards the door.)

FATHER *(lighting his pipe—between the puffs)*: In about quarter of an hour, Fred.

5   CARLIN: Good night then! Goodnight Ernest.

(He goes out. The MOTHER *is heard coming downstairs. She glances at her son, and shuts the passage door. Then she hurries to the oven and turns the bread. As she moves away again, her husband thrusts out his hand and gives her something.)*

10   FATHER *(going towards the passage door)*: I know it's a bad wik. *(He goes out.)*

MOTHER *(counts the money he has given her, gives a little rapid clicking with her tongue on the roof of her mouth, tossing her head up once)*: Twenty-eight shillings!

15   *(She counts again.)*

Twenty-eight shillings! *(To her son)*: And what was the cheque?

ERNEST LAMBERT *(looking up with a frown of irritation)*: Eight pounds, one and six, and stoppages.

20   MOTHER: And he gives me a frowsty twenty-eight ....and I've got his club to pay,* and you a pair of boots ..... twenty eight! — —I wonder if he thinks the house is kept on nothing— — — I'll take good care he gets nothing extra, I will too— — —I knew it, though, I knew he'd been running up a nice score at

25   the Tunns*— — —that's what it is. There's rent, six and six, and clubs seven shillings, besides insurance and gas and everything else. I wonder how he thinks it's done—I wonder if he thinks we live on air—!

ERNEST LAMBERT *(looking up with pain and irritation)*: Oh Mater,

30   don't bother....what's the good...if you worry for ever it won't make it any more.

MOTHER *(softened, conquering her distress)*: Oh yes, it's all very well for you— —but if I didn't worry, what would become of us, I should like to know.

35   *(*GERTIE COOMBER *runs in. She is wearing a large blue felt hat and a Norfolk costume:* she is carrying a round basket. From the parlour comes the sound of Grieg's 'Anitra's Tanz' and then 'Åse's Tod'*—played well, with real sympathy.)*

GERTIE COOMBER *(with a little shy apprehension)*: Who's in the

40   parlour?

MOTHER: It's only Mr Barker... *(Smiling slightly.)* He wanted to show Nellie how well he could play the 'Maiden's Prayer'.

(GERTIE COOMBER suddenly covers her mouth and laughs.)

GERTIE COOMBER *(still laughing)*: He He!!—I'll bet it was a thump! Pomp, Pomp! *(She makes a piano-thumping gesture.)* Did you hear it Ernest?

ERNEST LAMBERT *(not looking up)*: Infernal shindy!

(GERTIE COOMBER puts up her shoulders and giggles, looking askance at the student, who, she knows, is getting tired of interruptions.)

MOTHER: Yes, I wish he'd go ... *(almost whispering)*—and his wife is expecting to go to bed any minute.

(GERTIE COOMBER puts her lower lip between her teeth and looks serious. The music stops; BARKER and NELLIE LAMBERT are heard talking— then the FATHER. There is a click of boots on the tiled passage, and they enter.)

NELLIE LAMBERT: What did you think of Mr Barker, mother— don't you think it's good?—I think it's wonderful—don't you Ernest?

ERNEST LAMBERT *(grunting)*: Mm—it is.

(GERTIE COOMBER suddenly hides behind her friend and laughs.)

MOTHER *(to BARKER)*: Yes, I'm sure you get on wonderfully— wonderfully—considering.

BARKER: Yes—ah'n non done so bad, I think.

FATHER: Tha 'asna, Joe, tha 'asna indeed!

MOTHER: Don't forget the bag, Mr Barker—I know you'll want it.

BARKER: Oh, thank yer. Well, I mun goo. Tha'rt comin' down, George?

FATHER: Yes, I'm comin' down Joe. I'll just get my top coat on, an' then— —

(He struggles awkwardly into his overcoat. BARKER resumes his grey muffler.)

BARKER: Well, goodnight everybody: goodnight Ernest:—an' thank yer Missis!

MOTHER: I hope things will be— *(she nods significantly)* —all right.

BARKER: Ah, thank yer, I hope it will: I expect so: there's no reasons why it shouldn't: Goodnight.

ALL: Goodnight Mr Barker.

(The FATHER and he go out. Immediately NELLIE LAMBERT flings her arms round GERTIE COOMBER's neck.)

NELLIE LAMBERT: Save me Gert, save me! I thought I was done

for that time...I gave myself up...the poor piano! Mother, it'll
want tuning now, if it never did before.

MOTHER *(with slight asperity, half amused)*: —It may want at it then.

GERTIE COOMBER *(laughing)*: You're done, Nellie, you're done
brown! If it's like dropping a saucepan-lid—no—you've got to
put up with it—

NELLIE LAMBERT: I don't care, it couldn't be much worse than it
is, rotten old thing.

*(She pulls off her pinafore and hangs it over the back of a chair: then she
goes to the mirror once more to arrange her hair.)*

GERTIE COOMBER: Oh come on, Nellie, Cornell's will be
crammed.

NELLIE LAMBERT: Don't worry, my dear. What are you going to
fetch?—anything nice?

GERTIE COOMBER: No I'm not—only bacon and cheese: they send
you any stuff: cat and candles—any muck!

*(The MOTHER takes the little stool and sits down on it on the hearth rug
lacing up her boots.)*

MOTHER: I suppose you're not going out, Ernest?

ERNEST LAMBERT: No.

MOTHER: Oh—so you can look after the bread. There are two
brown loaves at the top: they'll be about half an hour: the white
one's nearly done. Put the other in as soon as they come out.
Don't go and forget them now.

ERNEST LAMBERT: —No.

MOTHER: He says 'no'.

(She shakes her head at him with indulgent, proud affection.)

NELLIE LAMBERT *(as if casually, yet at once putting tension into the
atmosphere)*: Is Mag coming down?

(He does not answer immediately.)

MOTHER: I should think not, a night like this, and all the mud there
is.

ERNEST LAMBERT: She said she'd come and do some French.—
Why?—.

NELLIE LAMBERT *(with a half-smile, off-handedly)*: Nothing...!

MOTHER: You'd never think she'd trapse through all this
mud— — —

NELLIE LAMBERT: Don't bother, she'd come if she had to have
water-wings to flop through.

(GERTIE COOMBER begins to giggle at the idea. The MOTHER sniffs.)

ERNEST LAMBERT *(satirically)*: Just as you'd flounder to your Eddie.

*(*GERTIE COOMBER *lifts her hands with a little sharp gesture, as if to say 'now the fun's begun'.)*

NELLIE LAMBERT *(turning suddenly, afire with scorn)*: Oh should I!—you'd catch me running after anybody— —

MOTHER *(rising)*: There, that'll do. Why don't you go up town, if you're going.

*(*NELLIE LAMBERT *haughtily marches off and puts on a dark coat and a blue hat.)*

NELLIE LAMBERT: Is it raining Gert?

GERTIE COOMBER: No, it's quite fine.

NELLIE LAMBERT: I'll bet it's fine...

GERTIE COOMBER: Well, you asked me. It *is* fine: it's not raining.

(The MOTHER *re-enters from the passage, bringing a bonnet and a black coat.)*

NELLIE LAMBERT: Want me to bring anything Mater?

MOTHER: I shall leave the meat for you.

NELLIE LAMBERT: All right. Come on Gert!

(They go out.)

MOTHER *(she dreads that her son is angry with her, and affecting carelessness, puts the question to him to try)*: Should we begin getting a few Christmas-tree things for little Margaret?—I expect Emma and Joe will be here for Christmas: it seems nothing but right: and it's only six weeks now.

ERNEST LAMBERT *(coldly)*: All right.

(He gets up and takes another book from the shelf without looking at her. She stands a moment suspended in the act of putting a pin through her bonnet.)

MOTHER: Well I think we ought to make a bit of Christmas for the little thing, don't you?

ERNEST LAMBERT: Ay. You gave our things to the lads, didn't you?

(He still does not look up from his books.)

MOTHER *(with a sound of failure in her voice)*: Yes. And they've kept them better than ever I thought they would. They've only broken your blue bird—the one you bought when you were quite little.

(There is a noise of footsteps and a knock at the door. The MOTHER *answers.)*

MOTHER *(trying to be affable, but diffident, her gorge having risen a little)*: Oh, is it you Maggie? Come in. How ever have you got down a night like this?—didn't you get over the ankles in mud?

(She re-enters, followed by a ruddy girl of twenty, a full-bosomed,
5   *heavily built girl, of medium stature, and handsome appearance, ruddy and black. She is wearing a crimson tam-o'-shanter and a long grey coat. She keeps her head lowered, and glancing only once splendidly at* ERNEST LAMBERT, *replies with a strange humble defiance.)*

MAGGIE PEARSON: No—Oh it's not so bad: besides I came all
10   round by the road.

MOTHER: I should think you're tired, after school.

MAGGIE PEARSON: No: it's a relief to walk in the open; and I rather like a black night, you can wrap yourself up in it. Is Nellie out?

MOTHER *(stiffly)*: Yes, she's gone up town.

15   MAGGIE PEARSON *(non-significantly)*: Ah, I thought I passed her. I wasn't sure. . .She wouldn't notice me, it *is* dark over the fields.

MOTHER: Yes, it is. I'm sure *I'm* awful at recognising people.

MAGGIE PEARSON: Yes—and so am I generally. But it's no good bothering. . .If they like to take offence, they have to. . .I can't
20   help it.

(The MOTHER *sniffs slightly. She goes into the passage and returns with a string net bag. She is ready to go out.)*

MOTHER *(still distantly)*: Won't you take your things off? *(She looks at the bread once more before going.)*

25   MAGGIE PEARSON: Ah thanks—I will.

(She takes off her hat and coat and hangs them in the passage. She is wearing a dark blue cloth 'pinafore' dress, and beneath the blue straps and shoulder-pieces a blouse of fine woollen stuff with a small intricate pattern of brown and red. She is flushed and handsome: her features are large,
30   *her eyes dark, and her hair falls in loose profusion of black tendrils about her face. The coil at the back is coming undone: it is short and not heavy. She glances supremely at* ERNEST LAMBERT, *feeling him watching her.)*

MOTHER *(at the oven)*: You hear, Ernest! This white cake will be done in about five minutes, and the brown loaves in about
35   twenty.

ERNEST LAMBERT: All right, my dear.

(This time it is she who will not look at him.)

MAGGIE PEARSON *(laughing a low, short laugh)*: My hair!—is it a sight? I have to keep my coat collar up, or it would drop right
40   down—what bit of it there is.

(She stands away from the mirror, pinning it up; but she cannot refrain from just one glance at herself. ERNEST LAMBERT *watches her, and then turns to his mother, who is pulling on a pair of shabby black kid gloves.* MRS LAMBERT, *however, keeps her eyes consciously averted: she is offended, and is a woman of fierce pride.)*

MOTHER: Well, I expect I shall see you again, Maggie.

MAGGIE PEARSON *(with a faint grave triumph)*: It depends what time you come back. I shan't have to be late.

MOTHER: Oh, you'll be here when I get back.

MAGGIE PEARSON *(submissive, but with minute irony)*: Very well.

MOTHER: And don't forget that bread, Ernest.

(She picks her bag off the table and goes out without having looked at either of them.)

ERNEST LAMBERT *(affectionately)*: No, Little, I won't.

(There is a pause for a moment. MAGGIE PEARSON *sits in the arm chair opposite him, who is on the sofa, and looks straight at him. He raises his head after a moment and smiles at her.)*

MAGGIE PEARSON: Did you expect me?

ERNEST LAMBERT *(nodding)*: I knew you'd come. You know, when you feel as certain as if you couldn't possibly be mistaken— —. But I *did* swear when I came out of coll. and found it raining.

MAGGIE PEARSON: So did I. Well, not swear, but I was mad. Hasn't it been a horrid week.

ERNEST LAMBERT: Hasn't it!—and I've been so sick of things.

MAGGIE PEARSON: Of what?

ERNEST LAMBERT: Oh—of fooling about at college,—and everything.

MAGGIE PEARSON *(grimly)*: You'd be sicker of school.

ERNEST LAMBERT: I don't know. At any rate I should be doing something real, whereas as it is—Oh, Coll's all foolery and flummery.

MAGGIE PEARSON: I wish I had a chance of going. I feel as if they'd been pulling things away from me, all week— — — like a baby that has had everything taken from it.

ERNEST LAMBERT *(laughing)*: Well, if school pulls all your playthings and pretty things away from you, College does worse: it makes them all silly and idiotic, and you hate them—and—what then— —?

MAGGIE PEARSON *(seriously)*: Why?— —how?

ERNEST LAMBERT: Oh, I don't know. You have to fool about so

much, and listen when you're not interested, and see old Professors like old dogs walking round as large as life with ancient bones they've buried and scratched up again a hundred times, and they're just as proud as ever. It's such a farce! And
5 when you see that farce, you see all the rest: all the waddling tribe of old dogs with their fossil bones—parsons and professors and councillors—wagging their tails and putting their paws on the bones and barking their important old barks—and all the puppies yelping loud applause.

10 MAGGIE PEARSON (*accepting him with earnestness*): Ay!—But are they all alike?

ERNEST LAMBERT: Pretty well. It makes you a bit sick. I used to think men in great place were great— —.

MAGGIE PEARSON (*fervently*): I know you did.

15 ERNEST LAMBERT: —And then to find they're no better than yourself—not a bit— —

MAGGIE PEARSON: Well, I don't see why they should be.

ERNEST LAMBERT (*ignoring her*): —it takes the wind out of your sails. What's the good of anything if that's a farce—?

20 MAGGIE PEARSON: What?

ERNEST LAMBERT: The folks at the top. By Jove, if you once lose your illusion of 'great men', you're pretty well disillusionised of everything, religion and everything.

(MAGGIE PEARSON *sits absorbedly, sadly biting her forefinger: an act*
25 *which irritates him.*)

ERNEST LAMBERT (*suddenly*): What time did mother go out?

MAGGIE PEARSON (*starting*): I don't know?—I never noticed the time.

ERNEST LAMBERT (*rising and going to the oven, picking up the oven*
30 *cloth from the hearth*): At any rate I should think it's five minutes.

(*He opens the oven door, and takes from the lower shelf a 'cake' loaf, baked in a dripping tin, and, turning it over, taps it with his knuckle.*)
I should think it's done— —I'll give it five minutes to soak.

35 (*He puts the bread on the oven shelf, turns the brown loaves, and shuts the oven door. Then he rises and takes a little note book from the shelf.*)
Guess what I've been doing!

MAGGIE PEARSON (*rising, dilating, reaching towards him*): —I don't know. What?

40 ERNEST LAMBERT (*smiling*): —Verses.

MAGGIE PEARSON *(putting out her hand to him, supplicating)*: Give them to me!

ERNEST LAMBERT *(still smiling)*: They're such piffle.

MAGGIE PEARSON *(betwixt supplication and command)*: Give them to me.

(He hands her the little volume and goes out to the scullery. She sits down and reads with absorption. He returns in a moment, his hands dripping with clear water, and, pulling forward the panchion from the corner, takes out the last piece of white dough, scrapes the little pieces together, and begins to work the mass into a flattish ball, passing it from hand to hand. Then he drops the dough into the dripping pan, and leaves it standing on the hearth. When he rises and turns to her, she looks up at him swiftly with wide, brown, glowing eyes, her lips parted. He stands a moment smiling down at her.)

ERNEST LAMBERT: Well do you like them?

MAGGIE PEARSON *(nodding several times, does not reply for a second)*: Yes, I do.

ERNEST LAMBERT: They're not up to much though.

MAGGIE PEARSON *(softly)*: Why not?

ERNEST LAMBERT *(slightly crestfallen at her readiness to accept him again)*: Well, are they?

MAGGIE PEARSON *(nodding again)*: Yes, they are! What makes you say they're not? I think they're splendid.

ERNEST LAMBERT *(smiling, gratified, but not thinking the same himself)*: Which do you like best?

MAGGIE PEARSON *(softly and thoughtfully)*: I don't know. I think this is so lovely, this about the almond tree.

ERNEST LAMBERT *(smiling)*: —And you under it.

(She laughs up at him a moment splendidly.)

But that's not the best.

MAGGIE PEARSON *(looking at him expectantly)*: No?

ERNEST LAMBERT: That one,—'A Life History' 's—best.⁎

MAGGIE PEARSON *(wondering)*: Yes?

ERNEST LAMBERT *(smiling)*: It is. It means more. Look how full of significance it is, when you think of it. The profs. would make a great long essay out of the idea. Then the rhythm is finer: it's more complicated.

MAGGIE PEARSON *(seizing the word to vindicate herself when no vindication is required)*: Yes, it is more complicated: it is more complicated in every way. You see, I didn't understand it at first. It is best, yes, it is.

(She reads it again. He takes the loaf from the oven and puts the fresh one in.)

5   ERNEST LAMBERT: What have *you* been doing?

MAGGIE PEARSON *(faltering, smiling)*: I? Only—only some French.

ERNEST LAMBERT: What, your diary?

MAGGIE PEARSON *(laughing, confused)*: Ah—but I don't think I want you to see it.

10 ERNEST LAMBERT: Now you know you wrote it for me! Don't you think it was a good idea, to get you to write your diary in French?* You'd never have done any French at all but for that, and you'd certainly never have told me——. You never tell me *your* side—.

15 MAGGIE PEARSON: There's nothing to tell.

ERNEST LAMBERT *(shaking his finger excitedly)*: That's just what you say, that's just what you say! As many things happen for you as for me—.

MAGGIE PEARSON: Oh, but you go to Derby every day, and you see

20 folks, and I——

ERNEST LAMBERT *(flinging his hand at her)*: Piffle! I tell you—do I tell you the train was late?—do I—

MAGGIE PEARSON *(interrupting, laughing in confusion and humility)*: —Yes you do—ah!

25 *(He has stopped suddenly with tremendous seriousness and excitement.)*

ERNEST LAMBERT: When?

MAGGIE PEARSON *(nervous, apologising, laughing)*: On Sunday— when you told me you'd have—

ERNEST LAMBERT *(flinging her words aside with excited ges-*

30 *ture)*: There you are, you're raking up a trifle to save you from the main issue! Just like a woman—! What I said was *(He becomes suddenly slow and fierce)*: You never tell me about you, and you drink me up,* get me up like a cup with both handles and drink yourself breathless—and—and there you are—you,

35 you never pour me any wine of yourself—

MAGGIE PEARSON *(watching him fascinated, and a little bit terror-struck)*: But isn't it your fault?

(He turns on her with a fierce gesture. She starts.)

ERNEST LAMBERT: How can it be when I'm always asking you—?

40 *(He scratches his head with wild exasperation.)*

MAGGIE PEARSON *(almost inaudibly)*: —Well—!
(He blazes at her so fiercely she does not continue, but drops her head and
looks at her knee, biting her finger.)
ERNEST LAMBERT *(abruptly)*: Come on—let's see what hundreds
of mistakes— 5
(She looks at him—dilates—laughs nervously, and goes to her coat,
returning with a school exercise book, doubled up. He sits on the sofa,
brings her beside him with a swift gesture. Then he looks up at the fire,
and starts away round the table. Going into the scullery and crossing the
room with the dustpan): 10
I must mend the fire. There's a book of French verse with my
books. Be looking at that while I— —.
(His voice descends to the cellar, where he is heard hammering the coal.
He returns directly. She stands at the little cupboard, with her face in a
book. She is very short sighted. He mends the fire without speaking to 15
her, and goes out to wash his hands.)
ERNEST LAMBERT *(returning)*: Well, what do you think of it? I got
it for fourpence.
MAGGIE PEARSON: I like it ever so much.
ERNEST LAMBERT: You've hardly seen it yet. Come on. *(They sit* 20
together on the sofa and read from the exercise book, she nervously.
Suddenly): Now look here—oh the poor verbs! I don't think
anybody dare treat them as you do! Look here! *(She puts her*
head closer. He jerks back his head, rubbing his nose frantically,
laughing): Your hair did tickle me. *(She turns her face to his,* 25
laughing, with open mouth: he breaks the spell): Well, have you
seen it?
MAGGIE PEARSON *(hesitating—peering across the lines)*: No—o—o!
ERNEST LAMBERT *(suddenly thrusting his finger before her)*: There! I
wonder it doesn't peck your nose off. You *are* a— *(She has* 30
discovered her mistake and draws back with a little vibrating laugh
of shame and conviction.)—You hussy, what should it have
been?
MAGGIE PEARSON *(hesitating)*: 'Eurent.'
ERNEST LAMBERT *(sitting suddenly erect and startling her up* 35
too): What! The *preterite*: the *preterite*, and you're talking about
going to school! *(She laughs at him with nervous shame: when he*
glares at her she dilates with fine terror. He—ominously): Well—?
MAGGIE PEARSON *(in the depths of laughing despair, very softly and*
timidly): I don't know. 40

ERNEST LAMBERT *(relaxing into pathetic patience)*: Verbs of motion
take être, and if you do a thing frequently, use the imperfect.*
You are—well, you're inexpressible!
(They turn to the diary, she covered with humiliation, he aggrieved.
5   *They read for awhile, he shaking his head when her light-springing hair*
                   tickles him again. He—softly):
What makes you say that?
MAGGIE PEARSON *(softly)*: What?
ERNEST LAMBERT: That you are 'un enfant de Samedi'—a Saturday
10   child?*
MAGGIE PEARSON *(mistrusting herself so soon)*: Why—it's what they
say, you know.
ERNEST LAMBERT *(gently)*: How?
MAGGIE PEARSON: Oh—when a child is serious—when it doesn't
15   play except on Saturdays, when it is quite free—.
ERNEST LAMBERT: And you mean you don't play? *(She looks at*
him seriously.)—No, you haven't got much play in you, have
you?—I fool about so much.
MAGGIE PEARSON *(nodding)*: That's it. You can forget things and
20   play-about. I always think of Francis Thompson's 'Shelley':*
you know, how he made paper boats— —.
ERNEST LAMBERT *(flattered at the comparison)*: But I don't make
paper boats. I tell you you think too much about me. I tell you I
have got nothing but a gift of coloured* words. And do I teach
25   you to play?—not to hold everything so serious and earnest?
(He is very serious. She nods at him again. He looks back at the
paper. It is finished. Then they look at one another, and laugh a
little laugh, not of amusement): Ah your poor diary! *(he speaks*
very gently, she hides her head and is confused)—I haven't marked
30   the rest of the mistakes. Never mind, we won't bother, shall we?
You'd make them again just the same. *(She laughs; they are*
silent a moment or two: it is very still.) You know *(he begins sadly,*
and she does not answer)—you think too much of me—you do,
you know. *(She looks at him with a proud, sceptical smile. He*
35   *waxes suddenly wroth)*: You are such a flat, you won't believe me!
But *I* know—if I don't, who does? It's just like a woman, always
aching to believe in somebody or other, or something or other.
(She smiles.) I say, what will you have?—Baudelaire?
MAGGIE PEARSON *(not understanding)*: What?
40   ERNEST LAMBERT: Baudelaire.

MAGGIE PEARSON *(nervous, faltering)*: But who's—?

ERNEST LAMBERT: Do you mean to say you don't know who Baudelaire is?

MAGGIE PEARSON *(defensively)*: How should I?

ERNEST LAMBERT: Why I gassed to you for half an hour about him   5
a month back—and now he might be a Maori—!

MAGGIE PEARSON: It's the names—being foreign.

ERNEST LAMBERT: Baudelaire, Baudelaire—it's no different from Pearson!

MAGGIE PEARSON *(laughing)*: It sounds a lot better.   10

ERNEST LAMBERT *(laughing also, and opening the book)*: Come on!
Here, let's have 'Maîtresse des Maîtresses': Should we?

MAGGIE PEARSON *(with gentle persuasiveness)*: Yes. You'll read it?

ERNEST LAMBERT: *You* can have a go if you like—. *(They both
laugh. He begins to read 'le Balcon',* in tolerably bad French, but   15
*with some genuine feeling. She watches him all the time. At the end
he turns to her in triumph, and she looks back in ecstasy.)* There,
isn't that fine! *(She nods repeatedly.)* That's what they can do in
France. It's so heavy and full and voluptuous: like oranges
falling and rolling a little way along a dark blue carpet, like   20
twilight outside when the lamp's lighted you get a sense of rich
heavy things, as if you smelt them, and felt them about you in
the dusk: isn't it? *(She nods again.)* Ah, let me read you the
'Albatross'! This is one of the best—anybody would say so—
you see, fine, as good as anything in the world. *(He begins to*   25
*read. There is a light quick step outside, and a light tap at the door,
which opens. They frown at each other, and he whispers)*: Damn!—
(Aloud): Hello Beat!

*(There enters a girl of twenty three or four, short, slight, pale, with dark
circles under her rather large blue eyes, and with dust-coloured hair.*   30
*She wears a large brown beaver hat and a long grey-green waterproof
coat.)*

BEATRICE WYLD: Hello Ernie, how are ter! Hello Mag! Are they all
out?

ERNEST LAMBERT *(shutting up the book and drawing away from*   35
MAGGIE PEARSON—*the action is reciprocal—while* BEATRICE
WYLD *seats herself in the arm chair opposite)*: They've gone up
town. I don't suppose Nellie will be long.

BEATRICE WYLD *(coughing—speaking demurely)*: No, she won't see
Eddie tonight.   40

ERNEST LAMBERT *(leaning back)*: Not till after ten.

BEATRICE WYLD *(rather loudly, sitting up)*: What, does he come round after they shut the shop up?

ERNEST LAMBERT *(smiling ironically)*: —Ay, if it's getting on for eleven— —!

BEATRICE WYLD *(turning in her chair)*: Good lawk!—are they that bad!—I'n't it fair sickenin'?

ERNEST LAMBERT: Ma gets a bit wild sometimes.

BEATRICE WYLD: I should think so, at that price. Shall you ever get like that, Mag?

MAGGIE PEARSON: Like what, Beatrice?

BEATRICE WYLD: Now Maggie Pearson, don't pretend to be 'ormin'. She knows as well as I do, doesn't she Ernie?

MAGGIE PEARSON: Indeed I don't. *(She is rather high and mighty, but not impressive.)*

BEATRICE WYLD: Garn! We know you, don't we Ernie? She's as bad as anybody at th' bottom, but she pretends to be mighty 'ormin'.

MAGGIE PEARSON: I'm sure you're mistaken, Beatrice.

BEATRICE WYLD: Not much of it, old girl. We're not often mistaken, are we Ernie? Get out, we're the 'dead certs', aren't we Willie?

(She laughs with mischievous exultance, her tongue between her teeth.)

MAGGIE PEARSON *(with great but ineffectual irony)*: Oh, I'm glad somebody is a 'dead cert'. I'm very glad indeed! I shall know where to find one now.

BEATRICE WYLD: You *will* Maggie!

(There is a slight dangerous pause.)

BEATRICE WYLD *(demurely)*: I met Nellie and Gertie, coming.

ERNEST LAMBERT: Ay, you would.

MAGGIE PEARSON *(bitterly)*: Oh yes!

BEATRICE WYLD *(still innocently)*: She had got a lovely rose. I wondered— —.

ERNEST LAMBERT: Yes, she thought Eddie would be peeping over the mouse traps and bird cages. I bet she examines those drowning-mouse engines every time she goes past.

BEATRICE WYLD *(with vivacity)*: Not likely, not likely. She marches by as if there was nothing but a blank in the atmosphere. You watch her. Eyes *Right*!!—but she nudges Gert to make her see if he's there.

ERNEST LAMBERT *(laughing)*: And then she turns in great surprise— —.
BEATRICE WYLD: No she doesn't. She keeps 'Eyes Front!', and
smiles like a young pup—and the blushes!—Oh, William, too
lovly f'r anyfing!*   5
ERNEST LAMBERT: I'll bet the dear boy enjoys that blush.
BEATRICE WYLD: Ra-thèr! *(Artlessly revenant à son mouton):* And
he'll have the rose and all, to rejoice the cockles of his heart this
time.
ERNEST LAMBERT *(trying to ward it off)*: Ay.—I suppose you'll see   10
him with it on Sunday...
BEATRICE WYLD *(still innocently)*: It *was* a beauty, William! Did
you bring it for her?
ERNEST LAMBERT: I got it in Derby.
BEATRICE WYLD *(unmasking)*: Did you? Who *gave* it you, Willie?   15
ERNEST LAMBERT *(evasively—pretending to laugh)*: Nay, it wouldn't
do to tell.
BEATRICE WYLD: Oh William, *do* tell us. Was the Dark, or the
athletics?
ERNEST LAMBERT: What if it was neither?   20
BEATRICE WYLD: Oh Willie, *another*! Oh it *is* shameful! Think of
the poor things, what damage you may do them.
ERNEST LAMBERT *(laughing uneasily)*: Yes, they are delicate pieces
of goods—Women. Men have to handle them gently: like a man
selling millinery.   25
BEATRICE WYLD *(hesitating, then refraining from answering this
attack fully)*: It's the hat pins, Willie dear. But *do* tell us. Was it
the Gypsy*— —let's see, you generally call it her in German,
don't you?—What's the German for 'gipsy', Maggie?—But was
it the Gypsy, or the Athletic Girl that does Botany?   30
ERNEST LAMBERT *(shaking his head)*: No! It was an Erewhonian.*
BEATRICE WYLD *(knitting her brows)*: Is that the German for
another? Don't say so William. *(She sighs heavily.)*—'Sigh no
more ladies.'* Oh William! And these two are quite fresh ones,
and all. Do you *like* being a mutton bone, William, one bitch at   35
one end and one at the other. Do *you* think he's such a juicy
bone, to squabble for, Maggie?
MAGGIE PEARSON *(red and mortified)*: I'm sure I don't think
anything at all about it, Beatrice.

BEATRICE WYLD: No, we've got more sense, we have, Maggie. We
know him too well—he's not worth it, is he?

*(MAGGIE PEARSON will not reply. BEATRICE WYLD looks at her dress,
carefully rubbing off some spot or other, then she resumes):*

5   But surely it's not another, Willie?

ERNEST LAMBERT: What does it matter who it is! Hang me, I've
not spoken to——I've hardly said ten words——you said
yourself, I've only just known them.

BEATRICE WYLD: Oh Willie, I'm sure I thought it was most

10   desperate—from what you told me. *(There is another deadly
silence.* BEATRICE *resumes innocently, quite unperturbed):* Has he
told *you*, Maggie?

MAGGIE PEARSON *(very coldly):* I'm sure I don't know.

BEATRICE WYLD *(simply):* Oh he can't have done then. You'd

15   never have forgot. There's one like a Spaniard—or was it like an
Amazon,* Willie?

ERNEST LAMBERT: Go on, either'll do.

BEATRICE WYLD: —a Spanish Amazon, Maggie,—olive coloured
—like the colour of a young clear bit of sea-weed, he said

20   —and—oh I know, 'great free gestures': a cool clear colour, not
red. Don't you think she'd be lovely?

MAGGIE PEARSON: I do indeed.

BEATRICE WYLD: Too lovly f'r anyfing!——And the other. Oh,
yes: 'You should see her run up the college stairs! She can go

25   three at time, like a hare running up-hill'—and she was top of
the Inter list for Maths and Botany. Don't you wish you were at
college Maggie?

MAGGIE PEARSON: —For some things.

BEATRICE WYLD: *I* do! We don't know what he's up to when he's

30   there, do we?

MAGGIE PEARSON: I don't know that we're so very anxious——.

BEATRICE WYLD *(convincingly):* We're not, but he thinks we are.
And I believe he makes it all up. I bet the girls just think
'Hm! Here's a ginger and white fellow, let's take a bit of the

35   conceit out of him'—and he thinks they're gone on him,
doesn't he?

MAGGIE PEARSON: Very likely.

BEATRICE WYLD: He *does*, Maggie, that's what he does. And I'll
bet if we could hear him—the things he says about us! I'll bet

40   he says there's a girl with great brown eyes—

ERNEST LAMBERT: Shut up, Beat, you little devil;—you don't know when to stop.

BEATRICE WYLD *(affecting great surprise)*: William! Maggie! Just *fancy*!!

(There is another silence, not ominous, this time, but charged with suspense.)

—What am I a devil for—? *(Half timidly.)*

ERNEST LAMBERT *(flashing up at the sound of her ill-assurance)*: Look here, you may just as well drop it. It's stale, it's flat. It makes no mark, don't flatter yourself—we're sick of it, that's all. It's a case of ennui. Vous m'agacez les nerfs. Il faut aller au diable.☆ *(He rises, half laughing, and goes for the dustpan.)*

BEATRICE WYLD *(her nose a trifle out of joint)*: Translate for us, Maggie.

(MAGGIE PEARSON shakes her head without replying. She has a slight advantage now. ERNEST LAMBERT *crosses the room to go to the coal-cellar.* BEATRICE WYLD *coughs slightly, adjusts her tone to a casual disinterested conversation, and then says, from sheer inability to conquer her spite)*: You *do* look well, Maggie. I don't think I've seen anybody with such a colour. It's fair fine.

(MAGGIE PEARSON laughs and pulls a book towards her. There is silence. ERNEST LAMBERT's *steps are heard descending to the cellar and* [he is heard] *hammering the coal. Presently he remounts. The girls are silent,* MAGGIE PEARSON *pretending to read,* BEATRICE WYLD *staring across the room, half smiling, tapping her feet.)*

ERNEST LAMBERT *(hurrying in and putting the coal on the hob)*: Begùm, what about the bread?

MAGGIE PEARSON *(starting up and dilating towards him with her old brilliance)*: Oh, what have we—?—is it?—Oh—!

(ERNEST LAMBERT has forestalled her at the oven. There issues a great puff of hot smoke. He draws back a little and MAGGIE PEARSON utters a quick, tremulous 'Oh!')

BEATRICE WYLD *(with concern)*: Hel-lo Ernest, that smells a bit thick. *(He pulls out the loaves one after another. There is one brown loaf much blackened, one in tolerable condition, and the white 'cake' very much scorched on one side.* BEATRICE WYLD *begins to laugh, in spite of her sympathy, at the dismay: he is kneeling on the hearth, the oven door open, the oven-cloth in his hand, and the burnt bread toppled out of its tins on the hearth before him;* MAGGIE PEARSON *is bending over his shoulder in great concern.* BEATRICE WYLD *splutters with more laughter.*

ERNEST LAMBERT *looks up at her, and the dismay and chagrin on his face change also to an irresistible troubled amusement at the mishap, and he laughs heartily.* MAGGIE PEARSON *joins in, strainedly at first, then with natural shaking, and all three laugh with abandonment,* BEATRICE
5   WYLD *putting her hand up over her face, and again doubling over till her head touches her knees.)*

ERNEST LAMBERT: —Ho—Ho—Won't Ma be wild though!—— What a beastly shame!—

*(*BEATRICE WYLD *breaks out afresh, and he, though grieved, bubbles*
10   *again into grudging laughter)*:
Another day the rotten fire would burn slow, but tonight it's ramped like—

BEATRICE WYLD: Hell, Ernie!

(She goes off again into a wild tossing of laughter, hesitating a moment to
15   *watch him as he lugubriously picks up the worst loaf and eyes it over.)*

ERNEST LAMBERT *(grimly)*: It's black bread now, that they talk about.

(He sniffs the loaf. BEATRICE WYLD *resumes her mad, interrupted laughter,* MAGGIE PEARSON *sits down on the sofa and laughs till the tears*
20   *come.* ERNEST LAMBERT *taps the loaf with his finger.)*

BEATRICE WYLD: Are you trying to see if it's done, William? *(From naïve irony she immediately departs into laughter.* ERNEST LAMBERT *answers, his lugubrious soul struggling with laughter, the girls laughing the while.)*

25   ERNEST LAMBERT: No! I was listening if it sounded hollow. Hark *(They listen—laughter)*: It sounds cindery——I wonder how deep it goes.

(In a spirit of curiosity he rises and fetches a knife, and pulling a newspaper over the hearth, begins to cut away the burnt crust. The bread-
30   *charcoal falls freely on the paper. He looks at the loaf)*:
Hm! By Jove, there *is* a lot! It's like a sort of fine coke. *(The girls laugh their final burst, and pant with exhaustion, their hands pressed in their sides.)* It's about done for, at any rate. *(He puts it down and takes the other brown loaf: taps it)*: This is not so bad, really, is it? *(Sadly)*: It sounds a bit desiccated though. Poor
35   Ma! *(He laughs.)* —She'll say it's your fault, Mag!

MAGGIE PEARSON *(with astonished incredulous laughter)*: Me?

BEATRICE WYLD: She will, Mag, she will! She'll say if you hadn't been here making a fuss of him———

40   MAGGIE PEARSON *(still laughing)*: I'd better go before she comes.

BEATRICE WYLD: You want to scrape that with the nutmeg grater Ernest. Where is it? Here, give it me.
(She takes the loaf and he goes out and returns with the grater. She begins to grate the loaf. MAGGIE PEARSON *takes up the white 'cake' and feels the pale side, tapping the bottom.)*

MAGGIE PEARSON *(with decision)*: This isn't done. It's no good cutting it off till it's all finished. I may as well put it in again. *(She feels the heat of the two shelves, and puts the loaf on the upper.* ERNEST LAMBERT *picks up the ruined loaf.)*

ERNEST LAMBERT: What will she say when she sees this?

MAGGIE PEARSON: Put it on the fire and have done with it. *(They look at her in some astonishment at the vandalism of the remark.)*

ERNEST LAMBERT: —But— —! *(He looks at the loaf on all sides.)*

MAGGIE PEARSON: It's no good, and it'll only grieve their poor hearts if they see it. 'What the heart doesn't— —.'*

BEATRICE WYLD: Ay, put it on, William. What's it matter! Tell 'em the cat ate it.

ERNEST LAMBERT *(hesitating)*: Should I?

BEATRICE WYLD *(nudging his elbow)*: Ay, go on.

(He puts the loaf on the fire, which is not yet mended, and they stand watching the transparent flames lick up it.)

ERNEST LAMBERT *(half sad, whimsically, repentant)*: The Staff of Life— —!*

MAGGIE PEARSON: It's a faggot now, not a staff.

ERNEST LAMBERT: Ah well! *(He slides all the cinders and Beatrice's scrapings together in the newspaper and pours them in the fire.)*

BEATRICE WYLD *(holding up her scraped loaf)*: It doesn't show, being brown. You want to wrap it in a damp cloth now. Have you got a cloth?

ERNEST LAMBERT: What?—a clean tea-towel?

BEATRICE WYLD: Ay—that'll do. Come here, let's go and wet it.

(She goes out and re-enters directly with the towel screwed up. She folds it round the loaf, the others watching. She sets the shrouded loaf on the table, and they all sit down. There is a little pause.)

BEATRICE WYLD: Have you given over coming down to Chapel now, Maggie?

MAGGIE PEARSON: N-no. I don't know that I have. Why?

BEATRICE WYLD: You don't often put in an appearance now.

MAGGIE PEARSON *(a trifle petulantly)*: Don't I? Well, I don't feel like it, I suppose.

BEATRICE WYLD: William, you have something to answer for, my
boy. *(She speaks portentously.)*

ERNEST LAMBERT: Shall I? Ne'er mind, I'll say 'adsum' every
time. Recording Angel: 'Ernest Lambert?'—'Adsum'!!

5   BEATRICE WYLD: But you don't know what the little Ma's say
about you, my lad.

ERNEST LAMBERT: The dear little Ma's, they will be gossiping
about—

BEATRICE WYLD *(springing from her chair)*: Look out, there's

10   Nellie. Take that in th' pantry William! Come out! *(She thrusts
the towelled loaf into ERNEST LAMBERT's hands and he hurries
away with it, while she hastily shoots the coal on the fire, and
putting down the dust-pan by the boiler, sits in her chair and looks
'ormin'. Enter NELLIE LAMBERT and GERTIE COOMBER, blinking.)*

15   NELLIE LAMBERT *(bending her head to shield her eyes)*: Hasn't Ma
come? I never saw her. Hello Maggie, you've *not* gone yet, you
see. *(She sniffs and goes straight to the oven.)* Goodness, what a
smell of burning!—have you been and forgotten the bread?
        (She kneels and looks in the oven.)

20   BEATRICE WYLD *(very quietly and negligently)*: Ernest forgot that
one. It's only a bit caught.

   *(NELLIE LAMBERT peeps in the panchion where the other loaves
are—those baked by the mother.)*

NELLIE LAMBERT: He generally forgets if Maggie's here.

25   *(BEATRICE WYLD bursts out laughing.)*

MAGGIE PEARSON *(rising, indignant)*: Why Nellie, when has it ever
been burnt before?

NELLIE LAMBERT *(smiling a careless smile)*: Many a time.

MAGGIE PEARSON: Not when I've been here.

30   NELLIE LAMBERT: Aren't you going to sit down a bit, Gert?

GERTIE COOMBER: No, I'm off. Our Frances'll be wanting her
ducks.

   *(She laughs, but does not go. MAGGIE PEARSON, her head hanging, goes
to put on her hat and coat. The other girls smile meaningly at one

35   another.)*

GERTIE COOMBER: Are you going then, Maggie?

MAGGIE PEARSON *(distantly)*: Yes, it's getting late. I've a long walk,
you see.

GERTIE COOMBER: You have! I'm glad I've not got it. I often wonder
how you dare go through those woods on a pitch-dark night.

BEATRICE WYLD: I daresn't. *(She laughs at herself.)*

MAGGIE PEARSON: I'd rather go through our wood than through Nottingham Road with the people—!

BEATRICE WYLD: I'm glad you would, for I wouldn't.

(ERNEST LAMBERT pulls on his over-coat and his cap. He gathers certain books. He looks at MAGGIE PEARSON and she at him.)

MAGGIE PEARSON: Well, goodnight everybody, I shall have to go. *(She hesitates, finding it difficult to break away.)*

BEATRICE WYLD AND NELLIE LAMBERT: Goodnight.

GERTIE COOMBER: Goodnight Maggie, I hope it won't be too muddy for you.

(MAGGIE PEARSON laughs slightly.)

NELLIE LAMBERT *(as the two go through the door—loudly)*: And don't be ever so late back, our Ernest! *(They do not reply. As their steps are heard passing the side window,* BEATRICE WYLD *flings up her arms and her feet in an ungraceful, exultant glee, flickering her fingers with noiseless venom.)*

BEATRICE WYLD *(in an undertone)*: I gave her beans!!

NELLIE LAMBERT *(turning with a smile and lighting up):* Did you? What did you say?

GERTIE COOMBER *(amused, giggling, but shamefaced)*: Did you!

BEATRICE WYLD *(exultant)*: Oh Lum! I'll bet her cheeks are warm— —

(Curtain)

Act III.

The same room half an hour later. BEATRICE WYLD *sits in the arm chair,
and* NELLIE LAMBERT *on the sofa, the latter doing drawn-thread work
on a white tray cloth, part of which is fixed in a ring: at this part* NELLIE
5   LAMBERT *is stitching.*

BEATRICE WYLD: Ah, it makes you grin: the way she used to talk
   before she had him—!
NELLIE LAMBERT: She did! She thought nobody was as good as her
   Arthur. She's found her mistake out.
10   BEATRICE WYLD: She *has* an' all! He wanted some chips for his
   supper the other night when I was there. 'Well' I said 'it's not
   far to Fretwell's, Arthur.' He did look mad at me. 'I'm not going
   to fetch chips' he said, a cocky little fool, and he crossed his
   little legs till I should 'a liked to have smacked his mouth. I said
15   to her 'Well Mabel, if *you* do, you're a fool.'—In her state, and
   all the men that were about! He's not a bit of consideration. You
   never saw anybody as fagged as she looks.
NELLIE LAMBERT: She does. I felt fair sorry for her when I saw her
   last Sunday but one. She doesn't look like she used.
20   BEATRICE WYLD: By Jove, she doesn't. He's brought her down a
   good many pegs. I shouldn't wonder if she wasn't quite safe,
   either. She said she had awful shooting pains up her side, and
   they last for five minutes.
NELLIE LAMBERT *(looking up)*: —Oh?
25   BEATRICE WYLD: Ay! I'm glad I'm not in her shoes. They may talk
   about getting married as they like!—Not this child!
NELLIE LAMBERT: Not to a thing like him.
BEATRICE WYLD: I asked her if she didn't feel frightened, an' she
   said she didn't care a scrap. I should care though—and I'll bet
30   she does, at the bottom.
(The latch clicks. The MOTHER *enters carrying a large net full of
purchases, and a brown paper parcel. She lets these fall heavily on the
table, and sits on the nearest chair, panting a little, with evident labour of
the heart.)*
35   MOTHER: Yes my lady——you called for that meat,—didn't you?
NELLIE LAMBERT *(rising and going to look in the parcels)*: Well my
   Duck, I looked for you down town, then when I was coming
   back I forgot all about it.
MOTHER: And I—was silly enough—to hug it myself—

NELLIE LAMBERT *(crossing to her mother, all repentant)*: Well what *did* you for?—you *knew* I could fetch it again!—you do do such ridiculous things!

(She begins to take off her mother's bonnet.)

MOTHER: Yes! We know your fetching it—again. If I hadn't met little Abel Gibson—I really don't think I should have got home.

BEATRICE WYLD *(leaning forward)*: If Nellie forgets it you should forget it, Mrs Lambert. I'm sure you ought not to go lugging all those things!

MOTHER: But I met young Abel Gibson just when I was thinking I should *have* to drop them—and I said 'Here Abel my lad, are you going home?', and he said he was, so I told him he could carry my bag. He's a nice little lad. He says his father hasn't got much work, poor fellow. I believe that woman's a bad manager. She'd let that child clean up when he got home—and he said his Dad always made the beds. She's not a nice woman, I'm sure.

(She shakes her head, and begins to unfasten her coat. NELLIE LAMBERT, seeing her mother launched into easy gossip, is at ease on her score, and returns to the bags.)

You needn't go looking, there's nothing for you.

NELLIE LAMBERT *(petulantly)*: You always used to bring us something— —.

MOTHER: Ay, I've no doubt I did... *(She sniffs and looks at BEATRICE WYLD.)*

NELLIE LAMBERT *(still looking, unconvinced)*: Hello! Have a grape Beatrice!

(She offers BEATRICE WYLD a white paper bag of very small black grapes.)

MOTHER: They want washing first, to get the sawdust out. Our Ernest likes those little grapes, and they *are* cheap: only fourpence.

BEATRICE WYLD *(looking up from the bag)*: Oh, they are cheap. No I won't have any Nellie, thanks.

NELLIE LAMBERT: I'll wash them.

MOTHER: Just let the tap run on them—and get a plate.

NELLIE LAMBERT: Well, as if I shouldn't get a plate! The little Ma thinks we're all daft.

MOTHER *(sniffing—it is her manner of winking)*: Is all the bread done?

NELLIE LAMBERT: Yes. I took the last out about a quarter of an hour ago.*

[NELLIE LAMBERT *goes into the scullery.*]

MOTHER *(to* BEATRICE WYLD*)*: Was Maggie Pearson gone when
5   you came?

BEATRICE WYLD: No—she's only been gone about three quarters of an hour.

MOTHER *(tossing her head, and lowering her tone confidentially)*: Well really, I stopped looking at a man selling curtains a lot longer
10   than I should, thinking she'd be gone.

BEATRICE WYLD: Pah—it makes you sick, don't it?

MOTHER: It does. You wouldn't think she'd want to come trailing down here in weather like this, would you?

BEATRICE WYLD: You wouldn't. I'll bet you'd not catch me!—and
15   she knows what you think, all right.

MOTHER: Of course she does.

BEATRICE WYLD: She wouldn't care if the Old Lad was here scowling at her, she'd come.

MOTHER: If that lad* was at home.

20   BEATRICE WYLD: Ay! *(Scornfully.)*

(The MOTHER *rises and goes out with her coat.* NELLIE LAMBERT *enters
with a plate of wet black grapes.)*

NELLIE LAMBERT: —Now Beat—! *(Offering the grapes.)*

BEATRICE WYLD: No Nellie, I don't think I'll have any.

25   NELLIE LAMBERT: Go on—have some!—have some, go on! *(She
speaks rather imperatively.* BEATRICE WYLD *takes a few grapes in
her hand.)* What a scroddy few! Here, have some more.

BEATRICE WYLD *(quietly)*: No Nellie, thanks, I won't have any more. I don't think they'd suit me.

30   *(NELLIE LAMBERT *sits down and begins to eat the grapes, putting the
skins on a piece of paper. The* MOTHER *re-enters. She looks very tired:
she begins carrying away the little parcels.)*

NELLIE LAMBERT: Don't you put those away, Mother, I'll do it in a minute.

35   *(The* MOTHER *continues.* NELLIE LAMBERT *rises in a moment or two,
frowning):*

You *are* a persistent little woman, why don't you wait a bit and let me do it?

MOTHER: Because your father will be in in a minute, and I don't
40   want him peeking and prying into everything, thinking I'm a

millionaire. *(She comes and sits down in her rocking chair by the oven.* NELLIE LAMBERT *continues to carry away the goods which have littered the table, looking into every parcel.)*

NELLIE LAMBERT: Hello, what are these little things?

MOTHER: Never you mind.

NELLIE LAMBERT: Now Little Woman, don't you try to hug yourself and be secretive. What are they?

MOTHER: They're pine kernels. *(Turning to* BEATRICE WYLD*)*: Our Ernest's always talking about the nut-cakes he gets at Mrs Dacre's, I thought I'd see what they were like. Put them away, don't let him see them. I shan't let him know at all if they're not up to much. I'm not going to have him saying Mother Dacre's things are better than mine.

BEATRICE WYLD: I wouldn't—for I'm sure they're not.

MOTHER: Still—I rather like the idea of nuts—! Here, give me one, I'll try it.

(They each eat a pine kernel with an air of a connoisseur in flavors.)

MOTHER *(smiling to herself)*: Um—aren't they oily!

BEATRICE WYLD: They *are*! But I rather like them.

NELLIE LAMBERT: So do I! *(She takes another.)*

MOTHER *(gratified)*: Here, put them away Miss!

*(*NELLIE LAMBERT *takes another. The* MOTHER *rises and snatches them away from her, really very pleased):*

—There won't be one left, I know, if I leave them with *her. (She puts them away.)*

NELLIE LAMBERT *(smiling and nodding her head after her mother—in a whisper)*: Isn't she fussy?

*(*BEATRICE WYLD *puts out her tongue and laughs.)*

MOTHER *(returning)*: I tried a *gelatine* sponge last week. We like it much better than corn-flour.—Mrs Dacre puts them in mince-meat, instead of suet—the pine kernels—I must try a bit.

BEATRICE WYLD: Oh! It *sounds* better.

MOTHER *(seating herself)*: It does. *(She looks down at the bread—* BEATRICE WYLD *puts up her shoulders in suspense)*: I think you let this one dry up.

NELLIE LAMBERT: No, I didn't. It was our Ernest who let it burn.

MOTHER: Trust him! And what's he done?—*(She begins to look round.* BEATRICE WYLD *pulls a very wry face, straightens it quickly and says calmly.)*

BEATRICE WYLD: Is your clock right, Mrs Lambert.

MOTHER *(looking round at the clock)*: Ten minutes—ten minutes fast. Why, what time is it?

BEATRICE WYLD *(rising suddenly)*: Good Lack, it's half past ten. Won't our Pa rave? 'Yes, my gel—it's turning-out time again.
5 We're going to have a stop put to it.' And our Mother will recite! Oh, the recitations!—there's no shutting her up when she begins—but at any rate she shuts our Pa up, and he's a nuisance when he thinks he's got just cause to be wrath. Where did I put my things?

10 MOTHER: I should think that Nellie's put hers on top. *(She looks at* NELLIE LAMBERT*)*: Don't sit there eating every one of those grapes. You know our Ernest likes them.

NELLIE LAMBERT *(suddenly incensed)*: Good Gracious! I don't believe I've had more than half a dozen of the things!

15 MOTHER *(laughing and scornful)*: Half a dozen!

NELLIE LAMBERT: Yes, half a dozen.—Beatrice, we can't have a thing in this house—everything's for our Ernest.

MOTHER: What a story! What a story!! But he *does* like those little grapes.

20 NELLIE LAMBERT: And everything else.

MOTHER *(quietly, with emphasis)*: He gets a good deal less than you.

NELLIE LAMBERT *(withdrawing from dangerous ground)*: I'll bet.

(GERTIE COOMBER runs in.)

BEATRICE WYLD: Hello Gert, haven't you seen John?

25 GERTIE COOMBER *(putting up her chin)*: No.

BEATRICE WYLD: A little nuisance—fancy!

GERTIE COOMBER: Eh, I don't care—not me.

NELLIE LAMBERT: No, it's her fault. She never does want to see him. I wonder any fellow comes to her.

30 GERTIE COOMBER *(nonchalantly)*: Um—so do I.

BEATRICE WYLD: Get out, Gert, you know you're fretting your heart out 'cause he's not come.

GERTIE COOMBER *(with great scorn)*: Am I?—Oh *am* I? Not me! If I heard him whistling this moment I wouldn't go out to him.

35 NELLIE LAMBERT: Wouldn't you?—I'd shove you out, you little cat.

GERTIE COOMBER *(with great assumption of amusing dignity)*: Oh would you indeed!

(They all laugh. BEATRICE WYLD *pins on her hat before the mirror.)*

40 GERTIE COOMBER: You haven't got Ernest to take you home

tonight, Beat. Where is he, with Maggie Pearson? Hasn't he come back yet?

MOTHER *(with some bitterness)*: He hasn't! An' he's got to go to college tomorrow. Then he reckons he can get no work done.

GERTIE COOMBER: Ha!—they're all alike when it suits them. 5

MOTHER: I should thank her not to come down here messing every Friday and Sunday.

NELLIE LAMBERT: Ah, she's always here. I should be ashamed of *myself.*

BEATRICE WYLD: Well—our Pa! I must get off. Goodnight every- 10
body—see you tomorrow Nell.

NELLIE LAMBERT: I'll just come with you across the field.

(She fetches a large white cashmere shawl and puts it over her head. She disposes it round her face at the mirror. BEATRICE *winks at the*
MOTHER.*)* 15

GERTIE COOMBER: She's going to look for Eddie.

NELLIE LAMBERT *(blushing)*: Well, what if I am! Shan't be many minutes, Ma.

MOTHER *(rather coldly)*: I should think not! I don't know what you want at all going out at this time o' night. 20

*(*NELLIE LAMBERT *shrugs her shoulders, and goes out with* BEATRICE
WYLD, *who laughs and bids another goodnight.)*

MOTHER *(when they have gone)*: A silly young hussy, gadding to look for *him.* As if she couldn't sleep without seeing him.

GERTIE COOMBER: Oh, he always says 'Come and look for me 25
about eleven.' I bet he's longing to shut that shop up.

MOTHER *(shortly)*: Ha, he's softer than she is, and I'm sure that's not necessary. I can't understand myself how folks can be such looneys. I'm sure I was never like it.

GERTIE COOMBER: And I'm sure I never should be. I often think 30
when John's coming, 'Oh hang it, I wish he'd stop away.'

MOTHER: Ah but that's too bad, Gertie. If you feel like that you'd better not keep it on any longer.—Yet I used to be about the same myself. *I* was born with too much sense for that sort of slobber. 35

GERTIE COOMBER: Yes, isn't it hateful. I often think 'Oh get off with you!' I'm sure I should never be like Nellie.—Isn't Ernest late! You'll have Mr Lambert in first.

MOTHER *(bitterly)*: He *is* late. He must have gone every bit of the way— 40

GERTIE COOMBER: Nay—I bet he's not—that.

(There is silence a moment. The MOTHER *remembers the bread.)*

MOTHER *(turning round and looking in the panchion)*: Well, there ought to be two more brown loaves! What have they done with them, now?

(She turns over the loaves, and looks about.)

GERTIE COOMBER *(laughing)*: I should think they've gone and eaten them between them.

MOTHER: That's very funny.

(She rises, and is going to look round the room. There is a whistle outside.)

GERTIE COOMBER *(turning her head sharply aside)*: Oh *hang* it!! I'm not going, I'm not!!

MOTHER: Who is it, John?

GERTIE COOMBER: It is, and I'm *not* going! *(The whistle is heard again.)* He can shut up, 'cause I'm not going!

MOTHER *(smiling)*: You'll have to just go and speak to him if he's waiting for you.

(The whistle is heard louder.)

GERTIE COOMBER: Isn't it hateful! I don't care, I'll tell him I was in bed. I should be if my father wasn't at the Ram.*

MOTHER *(sighing)*: Ay! But you may guess he's seen Nellie, and she's been saying something to him.

GERTIE COOMBER: Well she needn't, then!! *(The whistle goes again.*

GERTIE COOMBER *cannot resist the will of the other, especially as the* MOTHER *bids her go. She flings her hand, and turns with great impatience)*: He can shut up! What's he want to come at this time for? Oh *hang* him. *(She goes out slowly and unwillingly, her lips closed angrily.)*

MOTHER *(smiles, sighs, and looks sad and tired again. To herself)*: It's a very funny thing! *(She wanders round the room looking for the bread. She lights a taper and goes in the scullery. Repassing, she repeats: A* very *remarkable thing. She goes into the pantry on right, and after a moment returns with the loaf in the damp cloth, which she has unfolded. She stands looking at the loaf, repeating a sharp little sound against her palate with her tongue, quickly vibrating her head up and down. To herself)*: So this is it, is it? It's a nice thing—! And they put it down there thinking I shouldn't see it. It's a nice thing! *(She goes and looks in the oven, then says bitterly)*: I always said she was a deep one. And he thinks he'll stop out till his father comes!——And what have they done with the other?—Burnt it, I should think. That's what they've done. It's a nice thing, a nice thing!

(She sits down in the rocking chair perfectly rigid, still overdone with weariness and anger and pain. After a moment the garden gate is heard to bang back, and a heavy-step comes up the path, halting, punctuated with the scratch and thrust of a walking stick, rather jarring on the bricked yard. The FATHER *enters. He also bends his head a little from the light, peering under his hat brim. The* MOTHER *has quickly taken the withered loaf and dropped it in among the others in the panchion. The* FATHER *does not speak, but goes straight to the passage, and hangs up his hat, overcoat, and jacket, then he returns and stands very near the fire holding his hands close down into the open ruddy grate. He sways slightly when he turns, after a moment or two, and stands with his hands spread behind his back very near the fire. The* MOTHER *turns her head away from him. He remains thus for a minute or so, then he takes a step forward, and leaning heavily on the table begins to pick the grapes from the plate, spitting out the skins into his right hand and flinging them at random towards the fire behind his back, leaning all the time heavily with the left hand on the table. After awhile this irritates the* MOTHER exceedingly.)*

MOTHER: You needn't eat all those grapes. There's somebody else!

FATHER *(speaking with an exaggerated imitation of his son's English)*: 'Somebody else!' Yes, there *is* 'somebody else'! *(He pushes the plate away and the grapes roll on the table)*: I know they was not bought for me! I know it! I know it!! *(His voice is rising.)* 'Somebody else!!' Yes, there *is* somebody else. I'm not daft: I'm not a fool!

(The MOTHER *turns away her head with a gesture of contempt. The* FATHER *continues with maddening tipsy ironic snarl)*: I'm not a fool! I can see it, I can see it!! I'm not daft! There's nothing for me. Nothing's got for me. Noo—! You can get things for them—you can, but you begrudge me every bit I put in my mouth.

MOTHER *(with cold contempt)*: You put enough down your own throat. There's no need for anybody else. You take good care you have your share.

FATHER: I have my share! Yes, I do, I do!

MOTHER: Yes, you do. *(Contemptuously.)*

FATHER: Yes, I do. But I shouldn't if you could help it, you

begrudging* bitch. What did you put away when I come in, so
that I shouldn't see it? Something! Yes! Something you'd got for
them! Somebody else, Yes! *I* know you'd got it for somebody
else.

5 MOTHER *(quietly, with bitter scorn)*: As it happens, it was nothing.

FATHER *(his accent is becoming still more urban. His 'os' are 'as', so
that 'nothing' is 'nathing')*: Nathing, Nathing! You're a liar,
you're a liar. I heard the scuffle. You don't think I'm a fool, do
you, woman! *(She curls her lips in a deadly smile.)* I know, I
10 know! Do *you* have what you give me for dinner? No, you don't.
You take good care of it!*

[*Sometime during the following, the* FATHER *sits down in a chair.*]

MOTHER*: Look here, you get your good share. Don't think *you*
keep the house. Do you think I manage on the few lousy
15 shillings you give me? No, you get as much as you deserve, if
any man did. And if *you* had a rice pudding, it was because *we*
had *none*. Don't come here talking. *You* look after *yourself*,
there's no mistake.

FATHER: An' I mean to, an' I mean to.

20 MOTHER: Very well then—!

FATHER *(suddenly flaring)*: But I'm not going to be treated like a
dog in my own house! I'm *not*, so don't think it. I'm master in
this house, an' I'm *going* to be. I tell you, I'm master of this
house.

25 MOTHER: You're the only one who thinks so.

FATHER: I'll stop it, I'll put a stop to it. They can go, they can go!—!

MOTHER: You'd be on short commons if they did.

FATHER: What! What! Me! You saucy bitch, I can keep myself, an'
you as well, an' him an' all, as holds his head above me—am
30 doing—an' I'll stop it, I'll stop it—or they can go.

MOTHER: Don't make any mistake—*you* don't keep us. You hardly
keep yourself.

FATHER: Do I, do I? And who does keep 'em then.

MOTHER: I do—and the girl.

35 FATHER: You do, do you, you snappy little bitch. You do, do you.
Well, keep 'em yourself, then. Keep that lad in his idleness
yourself then.

MOTHER: Very willingly, very willingly. And that lad works ten
times as hard as you do.

40 FATHER: Does he. I should like to see him go down th' pit every

day. I should like to see him working every day in th' hole. No, he won't dirty his fingers.

MOTHER: Yes, you wanted to drag all the lads into the pit, and you only begrudge them because I wouldn't let them.

FATHER *(shouting)*: You're a liar—you're a liar. I never wanted 'em in th' pit.

MOTHER *(interrupting)*: You did your best to get the other two there, anyway.

FATHER *(still shouting)*: You're a liar. I never did anything of the sort. What other man would keep his sons doing nothing till they're twenty two? Where would you find another? Not that I begrudge it him, I don't, bless him . . .

MOTHER: Sounds like it.

FATHER: I don't, I begrudge 'em nothing. I'm willing to do everythink I can for 'em, and 'ow do they treat me. Like a dog, I say, like a dog.

MOTHER: And whose fault is it?

FATHER: Yours, you slinking hussy. It's you as makes 'em like it. They're like you. You teach 'em to hate me: You make me like dirt for 'em: you set 'em against me . . .

MOTHER: You set them yourself.

FATHER *(shouting)*: You're a liar! *(He jumps from his chair and stands bending towards her, his fist clenched and ready and threatening.)* It's you. It always 'as been you—You've done it—
(Enter ERNEST LAMBERT.*)*

ERNEST LAMBERT *(pulling off his cap and flashing with anger)*: It's a fine row you're kicking up. I should bring the neighbours in.

FATHER: I don't care a damn what I do, you sleering devil you! *(He turns to his son but remains in the same crouching threatening attitude.)*

ERNEST LAMBERT *(flaring)*: You needn't swear at me, either.

FATHER: I shall swear at who the devil I like. Who are you, you young hound, who are you, you measley little—— —.*

ERNEST LAMBERT: At any rate, I'm not a foul-mouthed drunken fool.

FATHER *(springing towards him)*: What! I'll smite you to the ground if you say it again, I will, I *will*!!

ERNEST LAMBERT: Pah!

(He turns his face aside in contempt from the fist brandished near his mouth.)

FATHER *(shouting)*: What! Say it! I'll drive my fist through you!

ERNEST LAMBERT *(suddenly tightening with rage as the fist is pushed near his face)*: Get away, you spitting old fool— — —

(His FATHER *jerks nearer and trembles his fist so near the other's nose that he draws his head back, quivering with intense passion and loathing, and lifts his hands.)*

MOTHER: Ernest, Ernest don't.

(There is a slight relaxation. The MOTHER *lamentable, pleading):* Don't say any more, Ernest!—Let him say what he likes— —. What should I do if— —

(There is a pause. ERNEST LAMBERT *continues rigidly to glare into space beyond his father. The* FATHER *turns to the* MOTHER, *with a snarling movement, which is nevertheless a movement of defeat. He withdraws, sits down in the arm chair, and begins, fumbling, to get off his collar and tie, and afterwards his boots.* ERNEST LAMBERT *has taken a book, and stands quite motionless, looking at it. There is heard only the slash of the father's bootlaces. Then he drags off the boot and it falls with a loud noise.* ERNEST LAMBERT, *very tense, puts down the book, takes off his overcoat, hangs it up, and returns to the side of the sofa nearest the door, where he sits pretending to read. There is silence for some moments, and again the whip of bootlaces. Suddenly a snarl breaks the silence.)*

FATHER: But don't think I'm going to be put down in my own house. It would take a better man than you, you white-faced jocky—or your mother either—or all the lot of you put together. *(He waits awhile.)* I'm not daft, I can see what she's driving at. *(Silence.)* I'm not a fool, if you think so. I can pay you yet, you sliving bitch. *(He sticks out his chin at his wife.* ERNEST LAMBERT *lifts his head and looks at him. He turns with renewing ferocity on his son)*: Yes, and you either. I'll stand no more of your chelp. I'll stand no *more*! Do you hear me?

MOTHER: Ernest—!

*(*ERNEST LAMBERT *looks down at his book. The* FATHER *turns to the* MOTHER.*)*

FATHER: Ernest! Ay, prompt him! Set him on—you know how to do it—you know how to do it. *(There is a persistent silence.)*—I know it, I know it.—I'm not daft, I'm not a fool.

(The other boot falls to the floor. He rises, pulling himself up with the arms of the chair, and turning round, takes a Waterbury watch* with a brass chain from the wall beside the bookcase: his pit watch that the mother hung there when she put his pit-trousers in the cupboard—and

winds it up, swaying on his feet as he does so. Then he puts it back on the nail, and a key swings at the end of the chain. Then he takes a silver watch from his pocket, and fumbling, missing the key hole, winds that up also with a key, and, swaying forward, hangs it up over the cupboard. Then he lurches round, and limping pitiably, goes off upstairs. There is a heavy silence. The Waterbury watch can be heard ticking.)

ERNEST LAMBERT: I would kill him if it weren't that I shiver at the thought of touching him.

MOTHER: Oh, you mustn't. Think how awful it would be if there were anything like that. I couldn't bear it.

ERNEST LAMBERT: He is a damned accursed fool.

(The MOTHER *sighs. He begins to read. There is a quick patter of feet and* GERTIE COOMBER *comes running in.)*

GERTIE COOMBER: Has Mr Lambert come?

MOTHER: Ay—in bed.

GERTIE COOMBER: My father hasn't come yet. Isn't it sickening?

MOTHER: It is, child. They want horsewhipping, and those that serve them, more.

GERTIE COOMBER: I'm sure we haven't a bit of peace of our lives. I'm sure when mother was alive, she used to say her life was a burden, for she never knew when he'd come home, nor how.

MOTHER: And it is, so.

GERTIE COOMBER: Did you go far, Ernest.

ERNEST LAMBERT *(not looking up)*: I don't know. Middling.

MOTHER: He must have gone about home, for he's not been back many minutes.

GERTIE COOMBER: There's our Frances shouting.

(She runs off.)

MOTHER *(quietly)*: What did you do with that other loaf?

ERNEST LAMBERT *(looking up, smiling)*: Why, we forgot it, and it got all burned.

MOTHER *(rather bitterly)*: Of course you forgot it. And where is it?

ERNEST LAMBERT: Well, it was no good keeping it. I thought it would only grieve your heart, the sight of it, so I put it on the fire.

MOTHER: Yes, I'm sure—! That was a nice thing to do, I must say ... Put a brown loaf on the fire, and dry the only other one up to a cinder—*(The smile dies from his face, and he begins to frown. She speaks bitterly)*: It's always alike, though. If Maggie Pearson's here, nobody else matters. It's only a laughing matter if the bread gets burnt to cinders and put on the fire. *(She suddenly bursts into a glow of bitterness.)* It's all very well, my son, you may talk about caring for me, but when it comes to Maggie Pearson, it's very little you care for me—or Nellie—or anybody else.

5   ERNEST LAMBERT *(dashing his fingers through his hair)*: You talk *just* like a woman! As if it makes any difference—! as if it makes the least difference!

MOTHER *(folding her hands in her lap and turning her face from him)*: Yes, it does!

10   ERNEST LAMBERT *(frowning fiercely)*: It doesn't—why should it? If I like apples, does it mean I don't like—bread. You know Ma, it doesn't make any difference.

MOTHER *(doggedly)*: *I* know it does.

ERNEST LAMBERT *(shaking his finger at her)*: But why should it, why should it? You know you wouldn't be interested in the
15   things we talk about: you know you wouldn't.

MOTHER: Why shouldn't I?

ERNEST LAMBERT: Should you, now? Look here, we talked about French poetry: should you care about that? *(No answer.)* You
20   know you wouldn't! And then we talked about those pictures at the Exhibition—about Frank Brangwyn—about Impressionism,☆ for ever such a long time. You would only be bored by that...

MOTHER: Why should I? You never tried.

25   ERNEST LAMBERT: But you wouldn't. You wouldn't care whether it's Impressionism or Pre-Raphaelitism☆— — *(Pathetically.)*

MOTHER: I don't see why I shouldn't.

ERNEST LAMBERT *(ruffling his hair in despair—after a pause)*: And besides—there are lots of things you can't talk to your own folks
30   about, that you would tell a stranger.

MOTHER *(bitterly)*: Yes, I know there are.

ERNEST LAMBERT *(wildly)*: Well, I can't help it—can I now.

MOTHER *(reluctantly)*: No—I suppose not—if you say so.

ERNEST LAMBERT: But you know— —!

35   MOTHER: *(turning aside again—with some bitterness and passion)*: I do know, my boy— —I *do* know!

ERNEST LAMBERT: But I can't help it— — *(His* MOTHER *does not reply—but sits with her face averted.)* —can I now?—can I?

MOTHER: You say not.

40   ERNEST LAMBERT *(changing the position again)*: And you wouldn't

care if it was Alice, or Lois, or Louie. You never row me if I'm a bit late when I've been with them— —It's just Maggie, because you don't like her.

MOTHER *(with emphasis)*: No, I *don't* like her—and I *can't* say I do.

ERNEST LAMBERT: But why not?—why not? She's as good as I am—and I'm sure you've nothing against her— have you now?

MOTHER *(shortly)*: No, I don't know I've anything against her.

ERNEST LAMBERT: Well then, what do you get so wild about?

MOTHER: Because I don't like her, and I never shall, so there my boy!

ERNEST LAMBERT: Because you've made up your mind not to.

MOTHER: Very well then.

ERNEST LAMBERT *(bitterly)*: And you did from the beginning, just because she happened to care for me.

MOTHER *(with coldness)*: And does nobody else care for you then, but her?

ERNEST LAMBERT *(knitting his brows and shaking his hands in despair)*: Oh, but it's not a question of that.

MOTHER *(calmly, coldly)*: But it is a question of that.

ERNEST LAMBERT *(fiercely)*: It isn't! You know it isn't! I care just as much for you as ever—you know I do.

MOTHER: It looks like it, when night after night you leave me sitting up here till nearly eleven—and gone eleven sometimes— —

ERNEST LAMBERT: Once, Mother, once—and that was when it was her birthday.

MOTHER *(turning to him with the anger of love)*: And how many times is it a quarter to eleven, and twenty to— —?

ERNEST LAMBERT: But you'd sit up just the same if I were in: you'd sit up reading, you know you would.

MOTHER: You don't come in to see.

ERNEST LAMBERT: When I am in, do you go to bed before then?

MOTHER: I do.

ERNEST LAMBERT: Did you on Wednesday night, or on Tuesday, or on Monday?

MOTHER: No, because you were working.

ERNEST LAMBERT: I was *in*.

MOTHER: I'm not going to go to bed and leave you sitting up, and I'm not going to go to bed to leave you to come in when you like. . .so there!

ERNEST LAMBERT *(beginning to unfasten his boots)*: All right—I can't help it then.

MOTHER: You mean you won't.

(There is a pause. ERNEST LAMBERT *hangs his head, forgetting to unlace his boot further.)*

ERNEST LAMBERT *(pathetically)*: You don't worry our Nellie— look, she's out now. You never row her.

MOTHER: I do! I'm always telling her.

ERNEST LAMBERT: Not like this.

MOTHER: I do! I called her all the names I could lay my tongue to last night.

ERNEST LAMBERT: But you're not nasty every time she goes out to see Eddie: and you don't forever say nasty things about *him*. . . . *(There is a moment of silence, while he waits for an answer.)* —and I always know you'll be sitting here working yourself into a state if I happen to go up to Herod's Farm.*

MOTHER: Do I?—and perhaps you would if you sat here waiting all night— —.

ERNEST LAMBERT: But Ma, you don't care if Nellie's out—.

MOTHER *(after brooding awhile—with passion)*: No, my boy, because she doesn't mean the same to me. She has never understood —she has not been—like you. And now—you seem to care nothing—you care for *anything* more than home: you tell me nothing but the little things: you used to tell me everything, you used to come to me with everything, but now—I don't *do* for you now. You have to find somebody else.

ERNEST LAMBERT: But I can't help it: I can't help it. I have to grow up—and things are different to us now.

MOTHER *(bitterly)*: Yes, things *are* different to us now. They never used to be. And you say I've never tried to care for her—I have —I've tried and tried to like her, but I can't, and it's no good.

ERNEST LAMBERT *(pathetically)*: Well, my dear, we shall have to let it be then, and things will have to go their way. *(He speaks with difficulty)*: You know, Mater—I don't care for her—really—not half as I care for you—Only just now—well I can't help it, I can't help it—but I care just the same—for you—I do.

MOTHER *(turning, with a little cry)*: But I thought you didn't!

(He takes her in his arms and she kisses him and he hides his face in her shoulder and she holds him closely for a moment. Then she kisses him and

releases him—and he kisses her. She gently draws away, saying, very
tenderly):

There—Nellie will be coming in— —.

ERNEST LAMBERT *(after a pause)*: And you do understand, don't
you Mater?

MOTHER *(with great gentleness having decided not to torment him)*:
Yes, I understand now. *(She bluffs him.)*

(ERNEST LAMBERT takes her hand and strokes it a moment. Then he
bends down and continues to unfasten his boots. It is very silent.)

I'm sure that hussy ought to be in—just look at the time.

ERNEST LAMBERT: Ay, it's scandalous.

(There are in each of their voices traces of the recent anguish, which
makes their speech utterly insignificant. Nevertheless, in thus speaking,
each reassures the other that the moment of abnormal emotion and prox-
imity is passed, and the usual position of careless intimacy is reassumed.)

MOTHER *(rising)*: I shall have to go and call her, a brazen baggage.

(There is a rattle of the yard gate, and NELLIE LAMBERT runs in,
blinking very much.)

NELLIE LAMBERT *(out of breath—but very casually)*: Hello our
Ernest, you home.

MOTHER: Yes Miss, and been home long ago. I'll not have it, My
Lady, so you needn't think it. You're not going to be down there
till this time of night: It's disgraceful. What will his mother say,
do you think, when he walks in at past eleven.

NELLIE LAMBERT: She can say what she likes: besides, she'll be in
bed.

MOTHER: She'll hear him, for all that. I'd be ashamed of myself,
that I would, standing out there slobbering till this time of
night. I don't know how anyone can be such a fool.

NELLIE LAMBERT *(smiling)*: Perhaps not, my dear.

MOTHER *(slightly stung)*: No, and I should be sorry. I don't know
what he wants running up at this time of a night.

NELLIE LAMBERT: Oh Mother, don't go on again, we've heard it a
dozen times.

MOTHER: And you'll hear it two dozen.

(ERNEST LAMBERT, having got off his shoes, begins to take off his collar
and tie. NELLIE LAMBERT sits down in the arm chair.)

NELLIE LAMBERT *(dragging up the stool and beginning to unlace her*
boots.): I could hear my father carrying-on again. Was he a
nuisance?

MOTHER: Is he ever anything else when he's like that.

NELLIE LAMBERT: He *is* a nuisance: I wish he was far enough!
Eddie could hear every word he said.

ERNEST LAMBERT: Shame! Shame!!

5   NELLIE LAMBERT *(in great disgust)*: It is! *He* never hears anything
like that. Oh I was wild. I could have killed him!

MOTHER: You should have sent him home, then he'd not have
heard it at all.

NELLIE LAMBERT: He'd only just come, so I'm sure I wasn't going
10 to send him home then.

ERNEST LAMBERT: So you heard it all, to the mild-and-bitter end.

NELLIE LAMBERT: No I didn't!—And I felt such a fool!

ERNEST LAMBERT: You should choose your spot out of earshot, not
just by the garden gate. What did you do?

15 NELLIE LAMBERT: I said 'Come on, Eddie, let's get away from this
lot.' I'm sure I shouldn't have wondered if he'd gone home and
never come near again.

MOTHER *(satirically)*: What for?

NELLIE LAMBERT: Why—when he heard that row.

20 MOTHER: I'm sure it was very bad for him, poor boy.

NELLIE LAMBERT *(fiercely)*: How should you like it?

MOTHER: I shouldn't have a fellow there at that time at all.

ERNEST LAMBERT: You thought a father-in-law that kicked up a
shindy was enough to scare him off, did you!—Well, if you
25 choose your girl, you can't choose your Pa-in-law:—you'll have
to tell him that.

*(NELLIE LAMBERT has taken off her shoes. She stands in front of the
mirror and uncoils her hair, and plaits it in a thick plait which hangs
down her back.)*

30 MOTHER: Come Ernest, you'll never want to get up in the morning.

NELLIE LAMBERT *(suddenly)*: Oh! There now, I never gave him
that rose. *(She looks down at her bosom, and lifts the head of a
rather crushed rose)*: What a nuisance!

ERNEST LAMBERT: The sad history of a rose between two hearts:

35   'Rose, red rose, that burns with a low flame,
                What has broken you?
            Hearts, two hearts caught it up in a game
                Of shuttlecock—Amen.'

NELLIE LAMBERT *(blushing)*: Go on, you soft creature. *(She looks
40 at the rose.)*

ERNEST LAMBERT: Weep over it.

NELLIE LAMBERT: Shan't!

ERNEST LAMBERT: And pickle it, like German girls do.☆

NELLIE LAMBERT: Don't be such a donkey.

ERNEST LAMBERT: Interesting item: final fate of the rose.

(NELLIE LAMBERT *goes out—returns in a moment with the rose in an* 5
egg cup in one hand, and a candle in the other. The MOTHER *rises.*)

ERNEST LAMBERT: I'll rake, mother.

(NELLIE LAMBERT *lights her candle, takes her shawl off the table, kisses*
her MOTHER *goodnight, and bids her* BROTHER *goodnight as he goes out*
to the cellar. The MOTHER *goes about taking off the heavy green table-* 10
cloth, disclosing the mahogany, and laying a doubled table-cloth half
across, she sets the table with a cup and saucer, plate, knife, sugarbasin,
brown and white teapot and tea-caddy. Then she fetches a tin bottle and a
soiled snap-bag, and lays them together on the bare half of the table. She
puts out the salt—and goes and drags the pit-trousers from the cupboard 15
and puts them near the fire. Meanwhile ERNEST LAMBERT *has come*
from the cellar with a large lump of coal, which he pushes down in the
fireplace so that it shall not lodge and go out.)

MOTHER: You'll want some small bits—and bring a few pieces for
him in the morning. 20

ERNEST LAMBERT (*returning to the cellar with the dustpan*): All
right! I'll turn the gas out now.

(*The* MOTHER *fetches another candle and lights it, and continues her*
little tasks. The gas goes suddenly down and dies slowly out. ERNEST
LAMBERT *comes up with his candlestick on a shovelful of coal. He puts* 25
the candle on the table, and puts some coal on the fire, round the 'raker'.
The rest he puts in the shovel on the hearth. Then he goes to wash his
hands. The MOTHER, *leaving her candle in the scullery, comes in with an*
old iron fire screen which she hangs on the bars of the grate, and the
ruddy light shows over and through the worn iron top. ERNEST 30
LAMBERT *is heard jerking the roller towel. He enters, and goes to his*
mother, kissing her forehead, and then her cheek, stroking her cheek with
his fingertips.)

ERNEST LAMBERT: Goodnight, my dear.

MOTHER: Goodnight!—Don't you want a candle? 35

ERNEST LAMBERT: No—blow it out.—Goodnight.

MOTHER: Goodnight. (*Very softly.*)

(*There is in their tones a dangerous gentleness—so much gentleness that*
the safe reserve of their souls is broken. ERNEST LAMBERT *goes upstairs.*
His bedroom door is heard to shut. The MOTHER *stands and looks in the* 40
fire: the room is lighted by the red glow only. Then in a moment or two

she goes into the scullery, and after a minute—during which running of water is heard—she returns with her candle, looking little and bowed and pathetic, and crosses the room, softly closing the passage door behind her.)

(Curtain)

THE WIDOWING OF MRS. HOLROYD

MRS. HOLROYD
HOLROYD
BLACKMORE
JACK HOLROYD 5
MINNIE HOLROYD
GRANDMOTHER
RIGLEY
CLARA
LAURA 10
MANAGER
TWO MINERS*

THE WIDOWING OF MRS. HOLROYD*

Act I.

Scene 1.

*The kitchen of a miner's small cottage. On the left is the fireplace, with a
deep, full red fire. At the back is a white-curtained window, and beside it*   5
*the outer door of the room. On the right, two white wooden stairs intrude
into the kitchen below the closed stair-foot door. On the left, another door.*

*The room is furnished with a chintz-backed sofa under the window, a
glass-knobbed painted dresser on the right, and in the centre, toward the
fire, a table with a red and blue check tablecloth. On one side of the hearth*   10
*is a wooden rocking-chair, on the other an armchair of round staves. An
unlighted copper-shaded lamp hangs from the raftered ceiling. It is dark
twilight, with the room full of warm fireglow. A woman enters from the
outer door. As she leaves the door open behind her, the colliery rail can be
seen not far from the threshold, and, away back, the headstocks of a pit.*   15

*The woman is tall and voluptuously built. She carries a basket heaped
full of washing, which she has just taken from the clotheslines outside.
Setting down the basket heavily, she feels among the clothes. She lifts out
a white heap of sheets and other linen, setting it on the table; then she
takes a woollen shirt in her hand.*   20

MRS. HOLROYD *(aloud, to herself)*: You know they're not dry even
    now, though it's been as fine as it has. *(She spreads the shirt on
    the back of her rocking-chair, which she turns to the fire.)*
VOICE *(calling from outside)*: Well, have you got them dry?
*(*MRS. HOLROYD *starts up, turns and flings her hand in the direction of*   25
*the open door, where appears a man in blue overalls, swarfed and greased.
He carries a dinner-basket.)*
MRS. HOLROYD: You—you—I don't know what to call you! The
    idea of shouting at me like that—like the Evil One out of the
    darkness!   30
BLACKMORE: I ought to have remembered your tender nerves.
    Shall I come in?

MRS. HOLROYD: No—not for your impudence. But you're late, aren't you?

BLACKMORE: It's only just gone six. We electricians, you know, we're the gentlemen on a mine: ours is gentlemen's work. But
5   I'll bet Charles Holroyd was home before four.

MRS. HOLROYD *(bitterly)*: Ay, and gone again before five.

BLACKMORE: But mine's a lad's job, and I do nothing!—Where's he gone?

MRS. HOLROYD *(contemptuously)*: Dunno! He'd got a game on
10   somewhere—toffed himself up to the nines, and skedaddled off as brisk as a turkey-cock. *(She smirks in front of the mirror hanging on the chimney-piece, in imitation of a man brushing his hair and moustache and admiring himself.)*

BLACKMORE: Though turkey-cocks aren't brisk as a rule. Children
15   playing?

MRS. HOLROYD *(recovering herself, coldly)*: Yes. And they ought to be in. *(She continues placing the flannel garments before the fire, on the fender and on chair-backs, till the stove is hedged in with a steaming fence; then she takes a sheet in a bundle from the table,*
20   *and going up to* BLACKMORE, *who stands watching her, says.)* Here, take hold, and help me fold it.

BLACKMORE: I shall swarf it up.

MRS. HOLROYD *(snatching back the sheet)*: Oh, you're as tiresome as everybody else.

25   BLACKMORE *(putting down his basket and moving to door on right)*: Well, I can soon wash my hands.

MRS. HOLROYD *(ceasing to flap and fold pillowcases)*: That roller-towel's ever so dirty. I'll get you another. *(She goes to a drawer in the dresser, and then back toward the scullery, where is a sound of*
30   *water.)*

BLACKMORE: Why, bless my life, I'm a lot dirtier than the towel. I don't want another.

MRS. HOLROYD *(going into the scullery)*: Here you are.

BLACKMORE *(softly, now she is near him)*: Why did you trouble
35   now? Pride, you know, pride, nothing else.

MRS. HOLROYD *(also playful)*: It's nothing but decency.

BLACKMORE *(softly)*: Pride, pride, pride!
          (A child of eight suddenly appears in the doorway.)

JACK: Oo, how dark!

MRS. HOLROYD *(hurrying agitated into the kitchen)*: Why, where have you been—what have you been doing now?

JACK *(surprised)*: Why—I've only been out to play.

MRS. HOLROYD *(still sharply)*: And where's Minnie?

                  (A little girl of six appears by the door.) 5

MINNIE: I'm here, mam, and what do you think—?

MRS. HOLROYD *(softening, as she recovers equanimity)*: Well, and what should I think?

JACK: Oh, yes, mam—you know my father—?

MRS. HOLROYD *(ironically)*: I should hope so. 10

MINNIE: We saw him dancing, mam, with a paper bonnet.

MRS. HOLROYD: What—?

JACK: There's some women at New Inn, what's come from Nottingham—

MINNIE: An' he's dancin' with the pink one. 15

JACK: Shut up our Minnie. An' they've got paper bonnets on—

MINNIE: All colors, mam!

JACK *(getting angry)*: Shut up our Minnie! An' my dad's dancing with her.

MINNIE: With the pink-bonnet one, mam. 20

JACK: Up in the club-room over the bar.

MINNIE: An' she's a lot littler than him, mam.

JACK *(piteously)*: Shut up our Minnie—An' you can see 'em go past the window, 'cause there isn't no curtains up, an' my father's got the pink-bonnet one— 25

MINNIE: An' there's a piano, mam—

JACK: An' lots of folks outside watchin', lookin' at my dad! He can dance, can't he, mam?

MRS. HOLROYD *(she has been lighting the lamp, and holds the lamp-glass)*: And who else is there? 30

MINNIE: Some more men—an' *all* the women with paper bonnets on.

JACK: There's about ten, I should think, an' they say they came in a brake from Nottingham.

(MRS. HOLROYD, *trying to replace the lamp-glass over the flame, lets it* 35
             drop on the floor with a smash.)

JACK: There, now—now we'll have to have a candle.

BLACKMORE *(appearing in the scullery doorway with the towel)*: What's that—the lamp-glass?

JACK: I never knowed Mr. Blackmore was here.

BLACKMORE *(to* MRS. HOLROYD*)*: Have you got another?

MRS. HOLROYD: No. *(There is silence for a moment.)* We can manage with a candle for to-night.

5   BLACKMORE *(stepping forward and blowing out the smoky flame)*: I'll see if I can't get you one from the pit. I shan't be a minute.

MRS. HOLROYD: Don't—don't bother—I don't want you to.

      (He, however, unscrews the burner and goes.)

MINNIE: Did Mr. Blackmore come for tea, mam?

10   MRS. HOLROYD: No; he's had no tea.

JACK: I bet he's hungry. Can I have some bread?

MRS. HOLROYD *(she stands a lighted candle on the table)*: Yes, and you can get your boots off to go to bed.

JACK: It's not seven o'clock yet.

15   MRS. HOLROYD: It doesn't matter.

MINNIE: What do they wear paper bonnets for, mam?

MRS. HOLROYD: Because they're brazen hussies.

JACK: I saw them having a glass of beer.

MRS. HOLROYD: A nice crew!

20   JACK: They say they are old pals of Mrs. Meakins. You could hear her screaming o' laughin', an' my dad says: "He-ah, missis—here—a dog's-nose* for the Dachess—hopin' it'll smell samthing"—What's a dog's-nose?

MRS. HOLROYD *(giving him a piece of bread and butter)*: Don't ask
25   me, child. How should I know?

MINNIE: Would she eat it, mam?

MRS. HOLROYD: Eat what?

MINNIE: Her in the pink bonnet—eat the dog's nose?

MRS. HOLROYD: No, of course not. How should I know what a
30   dog's-nose is?

JACK: I bet he'll never go to work to-morrow, mother—will he?

MRS. HOLROYD: Goodness knows. I'm sick of it—disgracing me. There'll be the whole place cackling *this* now. They've no sooner finished about him getting taken up for fighting than
35   they begin on this. But I'll put a stop to it some road or other. It's not going on, if I know it: it isn't.

      (She stops, hearing footsteps, and BLACKMORE *enters.)*

BLACKMORE: Here we are then—got one all right.

MINNIE: Did they give it you, Mr. Blackmore?

40   BLACKMORE: No, I took it.

(He screws on the burner and proceeds to light the lamp. He is a tall, slender, mobile man of twenty-seven, brown-haired, dressed in blue overalls. JACK HOLROYD *is a big, dark, ruddy, lusty lad.* MINNIE *is also big, but fair.)*

MINNIE: What do you wear blue trousers for, Mr. Blackmore? 5

BLACKMORE: They're to keep my other trousers from getting greasy.

MINNIE: Why don't you wear pit-breeches, like dad's?

JACK: 'Cause he's a 'lectrician. Could you make me a little injun what would make electric light? 10

BLACKMORE: I will, some day.

JACK: When?

MINNIE: Why don't you come an' live here?

BLACKMORE *(looking swiftly at* MRS. HOLROYD*)*: Nay, you've got your own dad to live here. 15

MINNIE *(plaintively)*: Well, you could come as well. Dad shouts when we've gone to bed, an' thumps the table. He wouldn't if you was here.

JACK: He dursn't—

MRS. HOLROYD: Be quiet now, be quiet. Here. Mr. Blackmore. 20
(She again gives him the sheet to fold.)

BLACKMORE: Your hands *are* cold.

MRS. HOLROYD: Are they?—I didn't know.
(Blackmore puts his hand on hers.)

MRS. HOLROYD *(confusedly, looking aside)*: You must want your tea. 25

BLACKMORE: I'm in no hurry.

MRS. HOLROYD: Selvidge to selvidge.* You'll be quite a domestic man, if you go on.

BLACKMORE: Ay.
(They fold the two sheets.) 30

BLACKMORE: They are white, your sheets!

MRS. HOLROYD: But look at the smuts on them—look! This vile hole! I'd never have come to live here, in all the thick of the pit-grime, and lonely, if it hadn't been for him, so that he shouldn't call in a public-house on his road home from work. And now he 35 slinks past on the other side of the railway, and goes down to the New Inn instead of coming in for his dinner. I might as well have stopped in Bestwood.*

BLACKMORE: Though I rather like this little place, standing by itself. 40

MRS. HOLROYD: Jack, can you go and take the stockings in for me?
They're on the line just below the pigsty. The prop's near the
apple-tree—mind it. Minnie, you take the peg-basket.

MINNIE: Will there be any rats, mam?

5 MRS. HOLROYD: Rats—no. They'll be frightened when they hear
you, if there are.

(The children go out.)

BLACKMORE: Poor little beggars!

MRS. HOLROYD: Do you know, this place is fairly alive with rats.
10 They run up that dirty vine in front of the house—I'm always
at him to cut it down—and you can hear them at night overhead
like a regiment of soldiers tramping. Really, you know, I *hate*
them.

BLACKMORE: Well—a rat is a nasty thing!

15 MRS. HOLROYD: But I s'll get used to them. I'd give anything to be
out of this place.

BLACKMORE: It *is* rotten, when you're tied to a life you don't like.
But I should miss it if you weren't here. When I'm coming
down the line to the pit in the morning—it's nearly dark at
20 seven now—I watch the fire-light in here—Sometimes I put my
hand on the wall outside where the chimney runs up to feel it
warm—There isn't much in Bestwood, is there?

MRS. HOLROYD: There's less than nothing if you can't be like the
rest of them—as common as they're made.

25 BLACKMORE: It's a fact—particularly for a woman—But this place
is cosy—God love me, I'm sick of lodgings.

MRS. HOLROYD: You'll have to get married—I'm sure there are
plenty of nice girls about.

BLACKMORE: Are there? I never see 'em *(He laughs.)*

30 MRS. HOLROYD: Oh, come, you can't say that.

BLACKMORE: I've not seen a single girl—an unmarried girl—that I
should want for more than a fortnight—not one.

MRS. HOLROYD: Perhaps you're very particular.

(She puts her two palms on the table and leans back. He draws near to
35 *her, dropping his head.)*

BLACKMORE: Look here!

(He has put his hand on the table near hers.)

MRS. HOLROYD: Yes, I know you've got nice hands—but you
needn't be vain of them.

40 BLACKMORE: No—it's not that—But don't they seem— *(He*

glances swiftly at her; she turns her head aside; he laughs ner-
vously.)—they sort of go well with one another. *(He laughs*
again.)

MRS. HOLROYD: They *do*, rather—

(They stand still, near one another, with bent heads, for a moment.   5
    Suddenly she starts up and draws her hand away.)

BLACKMORE: Why—what is it?

*(She does not answer. The children come in—*JACK *with an armful of*
    stockings, MINNIE *with the basket of pegs.)*

JACK: I believe it's freezing, mother.   10

MINNIE: Mr. Blackmore, could you shoot a rat an' hit it?

BLACKMORE *(laughing)*: Shoot the lot of 'em, like a wink.

MRS. HOLROYD: But you've had no tea. What an awful shame to
    keep you here!

BLACKMORE: Nay, I don't care. It never bothers me.   15

MRS. HOLROYD: Then you're different from most men.

BLACKMORE: All men aren't alike, you know.

MRS. HOLROYD: But do go and get some tea.

MINNIE *(plaintively)*: Can't you stop, Mr. Blackmore?

BLACKMORE: Why, Minnie?   20

MINNIE: So's we're not frightened. Yes, do. Will you?

BLACKMORE: Frightened of what?

MINNIE: 'Cause there's noises, an' rats,—an' perhaps dad'll come
    home and shout.

BLACKMORE: But he'd shout more if I was here.   25

JACK: He doesn't when my uncle John's here. So you stop, an'
    perhaps he won't.

BLACKMORE: Don't you like him to shout when you're in bed?

    (They do not answer, but look seriously at him.)

(Curtain)   30

Scene 2.

The same scene, two hours later. The clothes are folded in little piles on the table and the sofa. MRS. HOLROYD *is folding a thick flannel undervest or singlet which her husband wears in the pit and which has just*
5   *dried on the fender.*

MRS. HOLROYD *(to herself)*: Now thank goodness they're all dried.
    It's only nine o'clock, so he won't be in for another two hours,
    the nuisance. *(She sits on the sofa, letting her arms hang down in
    dejection. After a minute or two she jumps up, to begin rudely*
10   *dropping the piles of washed clothes in the basket.)* I don't care. I'm
    not going to let him have it all *his* way—no! *(She weeps a little,
    fiercely, drying her eyes on the edge of her white apron.)* Why
    should *I* put up with it all?—*He* can do what he likes. But I
    don't care, no, I don't—
15 *(She flings down the full clothes-basket, sits suddenly in the rocking-
    chair, and weeps. There is the sound of coarse, bursting laughter, in vain
    subdued, and a man's deep guffaws. Footsteps draw near. Suddenly the
    door opens, and a little, plump, pretty woman of thirty, in a close-fitting
    dress and a giddy, frilled bonnet of pink paper, stands perkily in the*
20   *doorway.* MRS. HOLROYD *springs up: her small, sensitive nose is inflamed
    with weeping, her eyes are wet and flashing. She fronts the other woman.)*
    CLARA *(with a pert smile and a jerk of the head)*: Good evenin'!
    MRS. HOLROYD: What do you want?
    CLARA *(she has a Yorkshire accent)*: Oh, we've not come beggin'—
25   this is a visit.
    *(She stuffs her handkerchief in front of her mouth in a little snorting
    burst of laughter. There is the sound of another woman behind going off
    into uncontrollable laughter, while a man guffaws.)*
    MRS. HOLROYD *(after a moment of impotence—tragically)*: What—!
30 CLARA *(faltering slightly, affecting a polite tone)*: We thought we'd
    just call—
    *(She stuffs her handkerchief in front of her explosive laughter—the other
    woman shrieks again, beginning high, and running down the scale.)*
    MRS. HOLROYD: What do you mean?—What do you want here?
35 CLARA *(she bites her lip)*: We don't want anything, thanks. We've
    just called. *(She begins to laugh again—so does the other.)* Well, I
    don't think much of the manners in this part of the country.
    (She takes a few hesitating steps into the kitchen.)

MRS. HOLROYD *(trying to shut the door upon her)*: No, you are not coming in.

CLARA *(preventing her closing the door)*: Dear me, what a to-do! *(She struggles with the door. The other woman comes up to help; a man is seen in the background.)* 5

LAURA: My word, aren't we good enough to come in?

(MRS. HOLROYD, finding herself confronted by what seems to her excitement a crowd, releases the door and draws back a little—almost in tears of anger.)

MRS. HOLROYD: You have no business here. What do you want? 10

CLARA *(putting her bonnet straight and entering in brisk defiance)*: I tell you we've only come to see you. *(She looks round the kitchen, then makes a gesture towards the armchair.)* Can I sit here? *(She plumps herself down.)* Rest for the weary.*

(A woman and a man have followed her into the room. LAURA is highly 15 *colored, stout, some forty years old, wears a blue paper bonnet, and looks like the landlady of a public-house. Both she and CLARA wear much jewellery. LAURA is well dressed in a blue cloth dress. HOLROYD is a big blond man. His cap is pushed back, and he looks rather tipsy and lawless. He has a heavy blond moustache. His jacket and trousers are black, his* 20 *vest gray, and he wears a turn-down collar with dark bow.)*

LAURA *(sitting down in a chair on right, her hand on her bosom, panting)*: I've laughed till I feel fair bad.

CLARA: 'Aven't you got a drop of nothink to offer us, mester? Come, you are slow. I should 'ave thought a gentleman like you 25 would have been out with the glasses afore we could have got breaths to ask you.

HOLROYD *(clumsily)*: I dunna believe there's owt in th' 'ouse but a bottle of stout.

CLARA *(putting her hand on her stomach)*: It feels as if th' kettle's 30 going to boil over.

(She stuffs her handkerchief in front of her mouth, throws back her head, and snorts with laughter, having now regained her confidence. LAURA laughs in the last state of exhaustion, her hand on her breast.)

HOLROYD: Shall ta ha'e it then? 35

CLARA: What do you say, Laura—are you having a drop?

LAURA *(submissively, and naturally tongue-tied)*: Well—I don't mind—I will if *you* do.

CLARA *(recklessly)*: I think we'll 'ave a drop, Charlie, an' risk it. It'll 'appen hold the rest down. 40

(There is a moment of silence, while HOLROYD *goes into the scullery.* CLARA *surveys the room and the dramatic pose of* MRS. HOLROYD *curiously.)*

HOLROYD *(suddenly)*: Heh! What, come 'ere—!

5 *(There is a smash of pots, and a rat careers out of the scullery.* LAURA, *the first to see it, utters a scream, but is fastened to her chair, unable to move.)*

CLARA *(jumps up to the table, crying)*: It's a rat—Oh, save us! *(She scrambles up, banging her head on the lamp, which swings vio-*
10 *lently.)*

MRS. HOLROYD *(who, with a little shriek, jerks her legs up on to the sofa, where she was stiffly reclining, now cries in despairing falsetto, stretching forth her arms.)* The lamp—mind, the lamp!

*(*CLARA *steadies the lamp, and holds her hand to her head.)*

15 HOLROYD *(coming from the scullery, a bottle of stout in his hand)*: Where is he?

CLARA: I believe he's gone under the sofa. My, an' he's a thumper, if you like, as big as a rabbit.

*(*HOLROYD *advances cautiously toward the sofa.)*

20 LAURA *(springing suddenly into life)*: Hi, hi, let me go—let me go— Don't touch him—Where is he? *(She flees and scrambles onto* CLARA*'s armchair, catching hold of the latter's skirts.)*

CLARA: Hang off—do you want to have a body down—Mind, I tell you.

25 MRS. HOLROYD *(bunched up on the sofa, with crossed hands holding her arms, fascinated, watches her husband as he approaches to stoop and attack the rat; she suddenly screams)*: Don't, he'll fly at you!

HOLROYD: He'll not get a chance.

MRS. HOLROYD: He will, he will—and they're poisonous! *(She*
30 *ends on a very high note. Leaning forward on the sofa as far as she dares, she stretches out her arms to keep back her husband, who is about to kneel and search under the sofa for the rat.)*

HOLROYD: Come off, I canna see him.

MRS. HOLROYD: I won't let you; he'll fly at you.

35 HOLROYD: I'll settle him—

MRS. HOLROYD: Open the door and let him go.

HOLROYD: I shonna. I'll settle him. Shut thy claver. He'll non come anigh thee.

(He kneels down and begins to creep to the sofa. With a great bound,

MRS. HOLROYD *flies to the door and flings it open. Then she rushes back to the couch.)*

CLARA: There he goes!

HOLROYD *(simultaneously)*: Hi!—Ussza! *(He flings the bottle of stout out of the door.)*

LAURA *(piteously)*: Shut the door, do.

(HOLROYD rises, dusting his trousers' knees, and closes the door. LAURA heavily descends and drops in the chair.)

CLARA: Here, come an' help us down, Charlie. Look at her; she's going off. *(Though LAURA is still purple red, she sinks back in the chair. HOLROYD goes to the table. CLARA places her hands on his shoulders and jumps lightly down. Then she pushes HOLROYD with her elbow.)* Look sharp, get a glass of water.

(She unfastens LAURA's collar and pulls off the paper bonnet. MRS. HOLROYD sits up, straightens her clothing, and tries to look cold and contemptuous. HOLROYD brings a cup of water. CLARA sprinkles her friend's face. LAURA sighs and sighs again very deeply, then draws herself up painfully.)

CLARA *(tenderly)*: Do you feel any better—shall you have a drink of water? *(LAURA mournfully shakes her head; CLARA turns sharply to HOLROYD.)* She'll 'ave a drop o' something. *(HOLROYD goes out. CLARA meanwhile fans her friend with a handkerchief. HOLROYD brings stout. She pours out the stout, smells the glass, smells the bottle—then finally the cork.)* Eh, mester, it's all of a work—it's had a foisty cork.

(At that instant the stairfoot door opens slowly, revealing the children—the girl peering over the boy's shoulder—both in white nightgowns. Everybody starts. LAURA gives a little cry, presses her hand on her bosom, and sinks back, gasping.)

CLARA *(appealing and anxious, to MRS. HOLROYD)*: You don't 'appen to 'ave a drop of brandy for her, do you, missis?

(MRS. HOLROYD rises coldly without replying, and goes to the stairfoot door where the children stand.)

MRS. HOLROYD *(sternly, to the children)*: Go to bed!

JACK: What's a matter, mother?

MRS. HOLROYD: Never you mind, go to bed!

CLARA *(appealingly)*: Be quick, missis.

(MRS. HOLROYD, glancing round, sees LAURA going purple, and runs past the children upstairs. The boy and girl sit on the lowest stair. Their

father goes out of the house, shamefaced. MRS. HOLROYD *runs downstairs
with a little brandy in a large bottle.)*

CLARA: Thanks, awfully. *(To* LAURA.*)* Come on, try an' drink a
drop, there's a dear.

5　*(They administer brandy to* LAURA. *The children sit watching, open-
eyed. The girl stands up to look.)*

MINNIE *(whispering)*: I believe it's blue bonnet.

JACK *(whispering)*: It isn't—she's in a fit.

MINNIE *(whispering)*: Well, look under th' table—*(*JACK *peers*
10　*under.)*—there's 'er bonnet. *(*JACK *creeps forward.)* Come back,
our Jack.

JACK *(returns with the bonnet)*: It's all made of paper.

MINNIE: Let's have a look—it's stuck together, not sewed.
(She tries it on. HOLROYD *enters—he looks at the child.)*

15　MRS. HOLROYD *(sharply, glancing round)*: Take that off!
*(*MINNIE *hurriedly takes the bonnet from her head. Her father snatches it
from her and puts it on the fire.)*

CLARA: There, you're coming round now, love.
*(*MRS. HOLROYD *turns away. She sees* HOLROYD*'s eyes on the brandy-*
20　*bottle, and immediately removes it, corking it up.)*

MRS. HOLROYD *(to* CLARA*)*: You will not need this any more?

CLARA: No, thanks. I'm very much obliged.

MRS. HOLROYD *(does not unbend, but speaks coldly to the children)*:
Come, this is no place for you—come back to bed.

25　MINNIE: No, mam, I don't want to.

MRS. HOLROYD *(contralto)*: Come along!

MINNIE: I'm frightened, mam.

MRS. HOLROYD: Frightened, what of?

MINNIE: Oo, there *was* a row.

30　MRS. HOLROYD *(taking* MINNIE *in her arms)*: Did they frighten
you, my pet? *(She kisses her.)*

JACK *(in a high whisper)*: Mother, it's pink bonnet and blue bonnet,
what was dancing.

MINNIE *(whimpering)*: I don't want to go to bed, mam, I'm
35　frightened.

CLARA *(who has pulled off her pink bonnet and revealed a jug-handle
coiffure)*: We're going now, duckie—you're not frightened of us,
are you?

*(*MRS. HOLROYD *takes the girl away before she can answer.* JACK *lingers*
40　*behind.)*

HOLROYD: Now then, get off after your mother.

JACK *(taking no notice of his father)*: I say, what's a dog's-nose?

(CLARA ups with her handkerchief and LAURA responds with a faint giggle.)

HOLROYD: Go thy ways upstairs. 5

CLARA: It's only a small whiskey with a spoonful of beer in it, my duck.

JACK: Oh!

CLARA: Come here, my duck, come on.

(JACK, curious, advances.) 10

CLARA: You'll tell your mother we didn't mean no harm, won't you?

JACK *(touching her earrings)*: What are they made of?

CLARA: They're only earrings. Don't you like them?

JACK: Um! *(He stands surveying her curiously. Then he touches a* 15 *bracelet made of many little mosaic brooches.)* This is pretty, isn't it?

CLARA *(pleased)*: Do you like it?

(She takes it off. Suddenly MRS. HOLROYD is heard calling, "Jack, Jack!" CLARA starts.) 20

HOLROYD: Now then, get off!

CLARA *(as JACK is reluctantly going)*: Kiss me good-night, duckie, an' give this to your sister, shall you?

(She hands JACK the mosaic bracelet. He takes it doubtfully. She kisses him. HOLROYD watches in silence.) 25

LAURA *(suddenly, pathetically)*: Aren't you going to give me a kiss, an' all?

(JACK yields her his cheek, then goes.)

CLARA *(to HOLROYD)*: Aren't they nice children?

HOLROYD: Ay. 30

CLARA *(briskly)*: Oh, dear, you're very short, all of a sudden. Don't answer if it hurts you.

LAURA: My, isn't he different?

HOLROYD *(laughing forcedly)*: I'm no different.

CLARA: Yes, you are. You shouldn't 'ave brought us if you was going 35 to turn funny over it.

HOLROYD: I'm not funny.

CLARA: No, you're not. *(She begins to laugh. LAURA joins in in spite of herself.)* You're about as solemn as a roast potato. *(She flings up her hands, claps them down on her knees, and sways up and down* 40 *as she laughs,* LAURA *joining in, hand on breast.)* Are you ready to be mashed? *(She goes off again—then suddenly wipes the laughter off her mouth and is solemn.)* But look 'ere, this'll never do. Now I'm going to be quiet. *(She prims herself.)*

5 HOLROYD: Tha'd 'appen better.

CLARA: Oh, indeed! You think I've got to pull a mug to look decent? You'd have to pull a big un, at that rate.

(She bubbles off, uncontrollably—shaking herself in exasperation meanwhile. LAURA *joins in.* HOLROYD *leans over close to her.)*

10 HOLROYD: Tha's got plenty o' fizz in thee, seemly.

CLARA *(putting her hand on his face and pushing it aside, but leaving her hand over his cheek and mouth like a caress)*: Don't, you've been drinking. *(She begins to laugh.)*

HOLROYD: Should we be goin' then?

15 CLARA: Where do you want to take us?

HOLROYD: Oh—you please yourself o' that! Come on wi' me.

CLARA *(sitting up prim)*: Oh, indeed!

HOLROYD *(catching hold of her)*: Come on, let's be movin'—*(He glances apprehensively at the stairs.)*

20 CLARA: What's your hurry?

HOLROYD *(persuasively)*: Yi, come on wi' thee.

CLARA: I don't think. *(She goes off, uncontrollably.)*

HOLROYD *(sitting on the table, just above her)*: What's use o' sittin' 'ere?

25 CLARA: I'm very comfy: I thank thee.

HOLROYD: Tha'rt a baffling little 'ussy.

CLARA *(running her hand along his thigh)*: Aren't you havin' nothing, my dear? *(Offers him her glass.)*

HOLROYD *(getting down from the table and putting his hand forcibly on

30 her shoulder)*: No. Come on, let's shift.

CLARA *(struggling)*: Hands off!

(She fetches him a sharp slap across the face. MRS. HOLROYD *is heard coming downstairs.* CLARA, *released, sits down, smoothing herself.* HOLROYD *looks evil. He goes out to the door.)*

35 CLARA *(to* MRS. HOLROYD, *penitently)*: I don't know what you think of us, I'm sure.

MRS. HOLROYD: I think nothing at all.

CLARA *(bubbling)*: So you fix your thoughts elsewhere, do you? *(Suddenly changing to seriousness.)* No, but I *have* been awful to-

40 night.

MRS. HOLROYD (*contralto, emphatic*): I don't want to know anything about you. I shall be glad when you'll go.

CLARA: Turning-out time, Laura.

LAURA (*turtling*): I'm sorry, I'm sure.

CLARA: Never mind. But as true as I'm here, missis, I should never ha' come if I'd thought. But I had a drop—it all started with your husband sayin' he wasn't a married man.

LAURA (*laughing and wiping her eyes*): I've never knowed her to go off like it—it's after the time she's had.

CLARA: You know, my husband was a brute to me—an' I was in bed three month after he died. He was a brute, he was. This is the first time I've been out; it's a'most the first laugh I've had for a year.

LAURA: It's true, what she says. We thought she'd go out of 'er mind. She never spoke a word for a fortnight.

CLARA: Though he's only been dead for two months, he was a brute to me. I was as nice a young girl as you could wish when I married him and went to the Fleece Inn—I was.

LAURA: Killed hisself drinking. An' she's that excitable, she is. We s'll 'ave an awful time with 'er to-morrow, I know.

MRS. HOLROYD (*coldly*): I don't know why I should hear all this.

CLARA: I know I must 'ave seemed awful. An' them children— aren't they nice little things, Laura?

LAURA: They are that.

HOLROYD (*entering from the door*): Hanna you about done theer?

CLARA: My word, if this is the way you treat a lady when she comes to see you. (*She rises.*)

HOLROYD: I'll see you down th' line.

CLARA: You're not coming a stride with us.

LAURA: We've got no hat, neither of us.

CLARA: We've got our own hair on our heads, at any rate. (*Drawing herself up suddenly in front of* MRS. HOLROYD.) An' I've been educated at a boarding school as good as anybody. I can behave myself either in the drawing-room or in the kitchen as is fitting and proper. But if you'd buried a husband like mine, you wouldn't feel you'd much left to be proud of—an' you might go off occasionally.

MRS. HOLROYD: I don't want to hear you.

CLARA (*bobbing a curtsy*): Sorry I spoke.

(*She goes out stiffly, followed by* LAURA.)

HOLROYD *(going forward)*: You mun mind th' points down th' line.*

CLARA'S VOICE: I thank thee, Charlie—mind thy own points.

5 *(He hesitates at the door—returns and sits down. There is silence in the room.* HOLROYD *sits with his chin in his hand.* MRS. HOLROYD *listens. The footsteps and voices of the two women die out. Then she closes the door.* HOLROYD *begins to unlace his boots.)*

HOLROYD *(ashamed yet defiant, withal anxious to apologize)*: Wheer's my slippers?

10 *(*MRS. HOLROYD *sits on the sofa with face averted and does not answer.)*

HOLROYD: Dost hear? *(He pulls off his boots, noisily, and begins to hunt under the sofa.)* I canna find the things. *(No answer.)* Humph!—then I'll do be 'out 'em. *(He stumps about in his 15 stocking feet; going into the scullery, he brings out the loaf of bread; he returns into the scullery.)* Wheer's th' cheese? *(No answer— suddenly.)* God blast it! *(He hobbles into the kitchen.)* I've trod on that brokken basin, an' cut my foot open. *(*MRS. HOLROYD *refuses to take any notice. He sits down and looks at his sole—pulls 20 off his stocking and looks again.)* It's lamed me for life. *(*MRS. HOLROYD *glances at the wound.)* Arena ter goin' ter get me öwt for it?

MRS. HOLROYD: Psh!

HOLROYD: Oh, a' right then. *(He hops to the dresser, opens a drawer, 25 and pulls out a white rag; he is about to tear it.)*

MRS. HOLROYD *(snatching it from him)*: Don't tear that!

HOLROYD *(shouting)*: Then what the deuce am I to do? *(*MRS. HOLROYD *sits stonily.)* Oh, a' right then! *(He hops back to his chair, sits down, and begins to pull on his stocking.)* A' right then— 30 a' right then. *(In a fever of rage he begins pulling on his boots.)* I'll go where I *can* find a bit o' rag.

MRS. HOLROYD: Yes, that's what you want! All you want is an excuse to be off again—"a bit of rag"!

HOLROYD *(shouting)*: An' what man 'd want to stop in wi' a woman 35 sittin' as fow as a jackass, an' canna get a word from 'er edgeways.

MRS. HOLROYD: Don't expect me to speak to you after to-night's show. How dare you bring them to my house, how dare you?

HOLROYD: They've non hurt your house, have they?

40 MRS. HOLROYD: I wonder you dare to cross the doorstep.

HOLROYD: I s'll do what the deuce I like. They're as good as you are.

MRS. HOLROYD *(stands speechless, staring at him; then low)*: Don't you come near me again—

HOLROYD *(suddenly shouting, to get his courage up)*: She's as good as you are, every bit of it.

MRS. HOLROYD *(blazing)*: Whatever I was and whatever I may be, don't you ever come near me again.

HOLROYD: What! I'll show thee. What's the hurt to you if a woman comes to the house? They're women as good as yourself, every whit of it.

MRS. HOLROYD: Say no more. *Go* with them then, and don't come back.

HOLROYD: What! Yi, I will go, an' you s'll see. What! You think you're something, since your uncle left you that money, an' Blackymore puttin' you up to it. I can see your little game. I'm not as daft as you imagine. I'm no fool, I tell you.

MRS. HOLROYD: No, you're not. You're a drunken beast, that's all you are.

HOLROYD: What, what—I'm what? I'll show you who's gaffer, though. *(He threatens her.)*

MRS. HOLROYD *(between her teeth)*: No, it's not going on. If *you* won't go, I will.

HOLROYD: Go then, for you've always been too big for your shoes, in my house—

MRS. HOLROYD: Yes—I ought never to have looked at you. Only you showed a fair face then.

HOLROYD: What! What! We'll see who's master i' this house. I tell you, I'm goin' to put a stop to it. *(He brings his fist down on the table with a bang.)* It's going to stop. *(He bangs the table again.)* I've put up with it long enough. Do you think I'm a dog in the house, an' not a man, do you—

MRS. HOLROYD: A dog would be better.

HOLROYD: Oh! Oh! Then we'll see. We'll see who's the dog and who isna. We're goin' to see. *(He bangs the table.)*

MRS. HOLROYD: Stop thumping that table! You've wakened those children once, you and your trollops.

HOLROYD: I shall do what the deuce I like!

MRS. HOLROYD: No more, you won't, no more. I've stood this long enough. Now I'm going. As for you—you've got a red face where she slapped you. Now go to her.

HOLROYD: What? What?

MRS. HOLROYD: For I'm sick of the sights and sounds of you.

HOLROYD *(bitterly)*: By God, an' I've known it a long time.

MRS. HOLROYD: You have, and it's true.

5 HOLROYD: An' I know who it is th'rt hankerin' after.

MRS. HOLROYD: I only want to be rid of you.

HOLROYD: I know it mighty well. But *I* know him!

*(*MRS. HOLROYD, *sinking down on the sofa, suddenly begins to sob half-hysterically.* HOLROYD *watches her. As suddenly, she dries her eyes.)*

10 MRS. HOLROYD: Do you think I care about what you say? *(Suddenly.)* Oh, I've had enough. I've tried, I've tried for years, for the children's sakes. Now I've had enough of your shame and disgrace.

HOLROYD: Oh, indeed!

15 MRS. HOLROYD *(her voice is dull and inflexible)*: I've had enough. Go out again after those trollops—leave me alone. I've had enough. *(*HOLROYD *stands looking at her.)* Go, I mean it, go out again. And if you never come back again, I'm glad. I've had enough. *(She keeps her face averted, will not look at him, her
20 attitude expressing thorough weariness.)*

HOLROYD: All right then!

(He hobbles, in unlaced boots, to the door. Then he turns to look at her. She turns herself still farther away, so that her back is towards him. He goes.)

25   *(Curtain)*

Act II.

The scene is the same, two hours later. The cottage is in darkness, save for the firelight. On the table is spread a newspaper. A cup and saucer, a plate, a piece of bacon in the frying tin are on the newspaper ready for the miner's breakfast. MRS. HOLROYD *has gone to bed. There is a noise of* 5 *heavy stumbling down the three steps outside.*

BLACKMORE'S VOICE: Steady, now, steady. It's all in darkness. Missis!—Has she gone to bed?
　　　(He tries the latch—shakes the door.)
HOLROYD'S VOICE *(he is drunk)*: Her's locked me out. Let me 10 smash that bloody door in. Come out—come out—ussza! *(He strikes a heavy blow on the door. There is a scuffle.)*
BLACKMORE'S VOICE: Hold on a bit—what're you doing?
HOLROYD'S VOICE: I'm smashing that blasted door in.
MRS. HOLROYD *(appearing and suddenly drawing the bolts, flinging* 15 *the door open)*: What do you think you're doing?
HOLROYD *(lurching into the room, snarling)*: What? What? Tha thought tha'd play thy monkey tricks on me, did ter? *(Shouting.)* But I'm going to show thee. *(He lurches at her threateningly; she recoils.)* 20
BLACKMORE *(seizing him by the arm)*: Here, here,—! Come and sit down and be quiet.
HOLROYD *(snarling at him)*: What?—What? An' what's thäigh got ter do wi' it? *(Shouting.)* What's thäigh got ter do wi' it?
BLACKMORE: Nothing—nothing; but it's getting late, and you want 25 your supper.
HOLROYD *(shouting)*: I want nöwt. I'm allowed nöwt in this 'ouse. *(Shouting louder.)* 'Er begrudges me ivry morsel I ha'e.
MRS. HOLROYD: Oh, what a story!
HOLROYD *(shouting)*: It's the truth, an' you know it. 30
BLACKMORE *(conciliatory)*: You'll rouse the children. You'll rouse the children, at this hour.
HOLROYD *(suddenly quiet)*: Not me—not if I know it. *I* shan't disturb 'em—bless 'em.
　　　(He staggers to his armchair and sits heavily.) 35
BLACKMORE: Shall I light the lamp?
MRS. HOLROYD: No, don't trouble. Don't stay any longer, there's no need.
BLACKMORE *(quietly)*: I'll just see it's all right.

(He proceeds in silence to light the lamp. HOLROYD *is seen dropping forward in his chair. He has a cut on his cheek.* MRS. HOLROYD *is in an old-fashioned dressing-gown.* BLACKMORE *has an overcoat buttoned up to his chin. There is a very large lump of coal on the red fire.)*

5　MRS. HOLROYD: Don't stay any longer.

BLACKMORE: I'll see it's all right.

MRS. HOLROYD: I shall be all right. He'll go to sleep now.

BLACKMORE: But he can't go like that.

MRS. HOLROYD: What has he done to his face?

10　BLACKMORE: He had a row with Jim Goodwin.

MRS. HOLROYD: What about?

BLACKMORE: I don't know.

MRS. HOLROYD: The beast!

BLACKMORE: By Jove, and isn't he a weight! He's getting fat, must

15　　be—

MRS. HOLROYD: He's big made—he has a big frame.

BLACKMORE: Whatever he is, it took me all my time to get him home. I thought I'd better keep an eye on him. I knew you'd be worrying. So I sat in the smoke-room and waited for him.

20　　Though it's a dirty hole—and dull as hell.

MRS. HOLROYD: Why did you bother?

BLACKMORE: Well, I thought you'd be upset about him. I had to drink three whiskies—had to, in all conscience—*(Smiling.)*

MRS. HOLROYD: I don't want to be the ruin of you.

25　BLACKMORE *(smiling)*: Don't you? I thought he'd pitch forward onto the lines and crack his skull.

*(*HOLROYD *has been sinking farther and farther forward in drunken sleep. He suddenly jerks too far and is awakened. He sits upright, glaring fiercely and dazedly at the two, who instantly cease talking.)*

30　HOLROYD *(to* BLACKMORE*)*: What are thäigh doin' 'ere?

BLACKMORE: Why, I came along with you.

HOLROYD: Thou'rt a liar, I'm only just come in.

MRS. HOLROYD *(coldly)*: He is no liar at all. He brought you home because you were too drunk to come yourself.

35　HOLROYD *(starting up)*: Thou'rt a liar! I niver set eyes on him this night, afore now.

MRS. HOLROYD *(with a "Pf" of contempt)*: You don't know what you *have* done to-night.

HOLROYD *(shouting)*: I s'll not have it, I tell thee.

40　MRS. HOLROYD: Psh!

HOLROYD: I s'll not ha'e it. I s'll ha'e no carryin's on i' my 'ouse—

MRS. HOLROYD *(shrugging her shoulders)*: Talk when you've got
some sense.

HOLROYD *(fiercely)*: I've as much sense as thäigh. Am I a fool?
Canna I see? What's *he* doin' here then, answer me that. 5
What—?

MRS. HOLROYD: Mr. Blackmore came to bring *you* home, because
you were *too drunk* to find your own way. And this is the thanks
he gets.

HOLROYD *(contemptuously)*: Blackymore, Blackymore. It's him tha 10
cuts thy cloth by,* is it?

MRS. HOLROYD *(hotly)*: You don't know what you're talking about,
so keep your tongue still.

HOLROYD *(bitingly)*: I don't know what I'm talking about—I don't
know what I'm talking about—don't I? An' what about him 15
standing there then, if I don't know what I'm talking about?—
What?

BLACKMORE: You've been to sleep, Charlie, an' forgotten I came in
with you, not long since.

HOLROYD: I'm not daft, I'm not a fool. I've got eyes in my head, 20
and sense. You needn't try to get over me. I know what you're
up to.

BLACKMORE *(flushing)*: It's a bit off to talk to me like that, Charlie,
I must say.

HOLROYD: I'm not good enough for 'er. She wants Mr. Blackymore. 25
He's a gentleman, he is. Now we have it all; now we understand.

MRS. HOLROYD: I wish you understood enough to keep your
tongue still.

HOLROYD: What? What? I'm to keep my tongue still, am I? An'
what about *Mr. Blackymore?* 30

MRS. HOLROYD *(fiercely)*: Stop your mouth, you—you vulgar, low-
minded brute.

HOLROYD: Am I? Am I? An' what are you? What tricks are you up
to, an' all? But that's all right—that's all right. *(Shouting.)*
That's all right, if it's *you*. 35

BLACKMORE: I think I'd better go. You seem to enjoy—er—er—
calumniating your wife.

HOLROYD *(mockingly)*: Calamniating—calamniating—I'll give you
calamniating, you mealy-mouthed jockey: I'll give you calamniating. 40

BLACKMORE: I think you've said about enough.

HOLROYD: 'Ave I, 'ave I? Yer flimsy jack—'ave I? *(In a sudden burst)* But I've not done wi' thee yet.

BLACKMORE *(ironically)*: No, and you haven't.

5 HOLROYD *(shouting—pulling himself up from the armchair)*: I'll show thee—I'll show thee.

(BLACKMORE laughs.)

HOLROYD: Yes!—yes, my young monkey. It's thäigh, is it?

BLACKMORE: Yes, it's *me*.

10 HOLROYD *(shouting)*: An' I'll ma'e thee wish it worn't, I will. What—? What—? Tha'd come slivin' round here, would ta? *(He lurches forward at BLACKMORE with clenched fist.)*

MRS. HOLROYD: Drunken, drunken fool—oh, don't.

HOLROYD *(turning to her)*: What?

15 *(She puts up her hands before her face. BLACKMORE seizes the upraised arm and swings HOLROYD round.)*

BLACKMORE *(in a towering passion)*: Mind what tha'rt doing!

HOLROYD *(turning fiercely on him—incoherent)*: Wha'—wha'—!

(He aims a heavy blow. BLACKMORE evades it, so that he is struck on
20 *the side of the chest. Suddenly he shows his teeth. He raises his fists ready to strike HOLROYD when the latter stands to advantage.)*

MRS. HOLROYD *(rushing upon BLACKMORE)*: No, no! Oh, no!

(She flies and opens the door, and goes out. BLACKMORE glances after her, then at HOLROYD, who is preparing, like a bull, for another charge.
25 *The young man's face lights up.)*

HOLROYD: Wha'—wha'—!

(As he advances, BLACKMORE quickly retreats out-of-doors. HOLROYD plunges upon him. BLACKMORE slips behind the door-jamb, puts out his foot, and trips HOLROYD with a crash upon the brick yard.)

30 MRS. HOLROYD: Oh, what has he done to himself?

BLACKMORE *(thickly)*: Tumbled over himself.

(HOLROYD is seen struggling to rise, and is heard incoherently cursing.)

MRS. HOLROYD: Aren't you going to get him up?

BLACKMORE: What for?

35 MRS. HOLROYD: But what shall we do?

BLACKMORE: Let him go to hell.

(HOLROYD, who had subsided, begins to snarl and struggle again.)

MRS. HOLROYD *(in terror)*: He's getting up.

BLACKMORE: All right, let him.

40 *(MRS. HOLROYD looks at BLACKMORE, suddenly afraid of him also.)*

HOLROYD *(in a last frenzy)*: I'll show thee—I'll—
(He raises himself up, and is just picking his balance when BLACKMORE, *with a sudden light kick, sends him sprawling again. He is seen on the edge of the light to collapse into stupor.)*
MRS. HOLROYD: He'll kill you, he'll kill you! 5
*(*BLACKMORE *laughs short.)*
MRS. HOLROYD: Would you believe it! Oh, isn't it awful! *(She begins to weep in a little hysteria;* BLACKMORE *stands with his back leaning on the doorway, grinning in a strained fashion.)* Is he hurt, do you think? 10
BLACKMORE: I don't know—I should think not.
MRS. HOLROYD: I wish he was dead; I do, with all my heart.
BLACKMORE: Do you? *(He looks at her quickly; she wavers and shrinks; he begins to smile strainedly as before.)* You don't know *what* you wish, or what you want. 15
MRS. HOLROYD *(troubled)*: Do you think I could get past him to come inside?
BLACKMORE: I should think so.
*(*MRS. HOLROYD, *silent and troubled, manœuvres in the doorway, stepping over her husband's feet, which lie on the threshold.)* 20
BLACKMORE: Why, you've got no shoes and stockings on!
MRS. HOLROYD: No. *(She enters the house and stands trembling before the fire.)*
BLACKMORE *(following her)*: Are you cold?
MRS. HOLROYD: A little—with standing on the yard. 25
BLACKMORE: What a shame!
(She, uncertain of herself, sits down. He drops on one knee, awkwardly, and takes her feet in his hands.)
MRS. HOLROYD: Don't—no, don't!
BLACKMORE: They are frightfully cold. *(He remains, with head 30 sunk, for some moments, then slowly rises.)* Damn him!
(They look at each other; then, at the same time, turn away.)
MRS. HOLROYD: We can't leave him lying there.
BLACKMORE: No—no! I'll bring him in.
MRS. HOLROYD: But—! 35
BLACKMORE: He won't wake again. The drink will have got hold of him by now. *(He hesitates.)* Could you take hold of his feet—he's so heavy.
MRS. HOLROYD: Yes.

(They go out and are seen stooping over HOLROYD.*)*

BLACKMORE: Wait, wait, till I've got him—half a minute.

*(*MRS. HOLROYD *backs in first. They carry* HOLROYD *in and lay him on the sofa.)*

5   MRS. HOLROYD: Doesn't he look awful?

BLACKMORE: It's more mark than mar.☆ It isn't much, really.

(He is busy taking off HOLROYD*'s collar and tie, unfastening the waistcoat, the braces and the waist buttons of the trousers; he then proceeds to unlace the drunken man's boots.)*

10 MRS. HOLROYD *(who has been watching closely)*: I shall never get him upstairs.

BLACKMORE: He can sleep here, with a rug or something to cover him. *You* don't want him—upstairs?

MRS. HOLROYD: Never again.

15 BLACKMORE *(after a moment or two of silence)*: He'll be all right down here. Have you got a rug?

MRS. HOLROYD: Yes.

(She goes upstairs. BLACKMORE *goes into the scullery, returning with a lading can and towel. He gets hot water from the boiler. Then, kneeling*
20 *down, he begins to wipe the drunken man's face lightly with the flannel, to remove the blood and dirt.)*

MRS. HOLROYD *(returning)*: What are you doing?

BLACKMORE: Only wiping his face to get the dirt out.

MRS. HOLROYD: I wonder if he'd do as much for you.

25 BLACKMORE: I hope not.

MRS. HOLROYD: Isn't he horrible, horrible—

BLACKMORE *(looks up at her)*: Don't look at him then.

MRS. HOLROYD: I can't take it in, it's too much.

BLACKMORE: He won't wake. I will stay with you.

30 MRS. HOLROYD *(earnestly)*: No—oh, no.

BLACKMORE: There will be the drawn sword between us.☆ *(He indicates the figure of* HOLROYD, *which lies, in effect, as a barrier between them.)*

MRS. HOLROYD *(blushing)*: Don't!

35 BLACKMORE: I'm sorry.

MRS. HOLROYD *(after watching him for a few moments lightly wiping the sleeping man's face with a towel)*: I wonder you can be so careful over him.

BLACKMORE *(quietly)*: It's only because he's helpless.

MRS. HOLROYD: But why should you love him ever so little?

BLACKMORE: I don't—only he's helpless. Five minutes since I could have killed him.

MRS. HOLROYD: Well, I don't understand you men.

BLACKMORE: Why?

MRS. HOLROYD: I don't know.

BLACKMORE: I thought as I stood in that doorway, and he was trying to get up—I wished as hard as I've ever wished anything in my life—

MRS. HOLROYD: What?

BLACKMORE: That I'd killed him. I've never wished anything so much in my life—if wishes were anything.

MRS. HOLROYD: Don't, it *does* sound awful.

BLACKMORE: I *could* have done it, too. He ought to be dead.

MRS. HOLROYD *(pleading)*: No, don't! You know you don't mean it, and you make me feel so awful.

BLACKMORE: I do mean it. It is simply true, what I say.

MRS. HOLROYD: But don't say it.

BLACKMORE: No?

MRS. HOLROYD: No, we've had enough.

BLACKMORE: Give me the rug.

(She hands it him, and he tucks HOLROYD *up.)*

MRS. HOLROYD: You only do it to play on my feelings.

BLACKMORE *(laughing shortly)*: And now give me a pillow—thanks.

(There is a pause—both look at the sleeping man.)

BLACKMORE: I suppose you're fond of him, really.

MRS. HOLROYD: No more.

BLACKMORE: You *were* fond of him?

MRS. HOLROYD: I was—yes.

BLACKMORE: What did you like in him?

MRS. HOLROYD *(uneasily)*: I don't know.

BLACKMORE: I suppose you really care about him, even now.

MRS. HOLROYD: Why are you so sure of it?

BLACKMORE: Because I think it is so.

MRS. HOLROYD: I did care for him—now he has destroyed it—

BLACKMORE: I don't believe he can destroy it.

MRS. HOLROYD *(with a short laugh)*: Don't you? When you are married you try. You'll find it isn't so hard.

BLACKMORE: But what did you like in him—because he was good-looking, and strong, and that?

MRS. HOLROYD: I liked that as well. But if a man makes a nuisance of himself, his good looks are ugly to you, and his strength loathsome. Do you think I *care* about a man because he's got big fists, when he is a coward in his real self?

5 BLACKMORE: Is he a coward?

MRS. HOLROYD: He *is*—a pettifogging, paltry one.

BLACKMORE: And so you've really done with him?

MRS. HOLROYD: I have.

BLACKMORE: And what are you going to do?

10 MRS. HOLROYD: I don't know.

BLACKMORE: I suppose nothing. You'll just go on—even if you've done with him—you'll go on with him.

(There is a long pause.)

BLACKMORE: But was there nothing else in him but his muscles
15 and his good looks to attract you to him?

MRS. HOLROYD: Why? What does it matter?

BLACKMORE: What did you *think* he was?

MRS. HOLROYD: Why must we talk about him?

BLACKMORE: Because I can never quite believe you.

20 MRS. HOLROYD: I can't help whether you believe it or not.

BLACKMORE: Are you just in a rage with him, because of to-night?

MRS. HOLROYD: I know, to-night finished it. But it was never right between us.

BLACKMORE: Never?

25 MRS. HOLROYD: Not once. And then to-night—no, it's too much; I can't stand any more of it.

BLACKMORE: I suppose he got tipsy. Then he said he wasn't a married man—vowed he wasn't, to those paper bonnets. They found out he was, and said he was frightened of his wife getting
30 to know. Then he said they should all go to supper at his house—I suppose they came out of mischief.

MRS. HOLROYD: He did it to insult me.

BLACKMORE: Oh, he was a bit tight—you can't say it was deliberate.

35 MRS. HOLROYD: No, but it shows how he feels toward me. The feeling comes out in drink.

BLACKMORE: How does he feel toward you?

MRS. HOLROYD: He wants to insult me, and humiliate me, in every moment of his life. Now I simply despise him.

BLACKMORE: You really don't care any more about him?

MRS. HOLROYD: No.

BLACKMORE *(hesitates)*: And you would leave him?

MRS. HOLROYD: I would leave him, and not care *that* about him
any more. *(She snaps her fingers.)*   5

BLACKMORE: Will you come with me?

MRS. HOLROYD *(after a reluctant pause)*: Where?

BLACKMORE: To Spain: I can any time have a job there, in a decent
part. You could take the children.

(The figure of the sleeper stirs uneasily—they watch him.)   10

BLACKMORE: Will you?

MRS. HOLROYD: When would you go?

BLACKMORE: To-morrow, if you like.

MRS. HOLROYD: But why do you want to saddle yourself with me
and the children?   15

BLACKMORE: Because I want to.

MRS. HOLROYD: But you don't love me?

BLACKMORE: Why don't I?

MRS. HOLROYD: You don't.

BLACKMORE: I don't know about that. I don't know anything about   20
love. Only I've gone on for a year now, and it's got stronger and
stronger—

MRS. HOLROYD: What has?

BLACKMORE: This—this wanting you, to live with me. I took no
notice of it for a long time. Now I can't get away from it, at no   25
hour and nohow. *(He still avoids direct contact with her.)*

MRS. HOLROYD: But you'd *like* to get away from it.

BLACKMORE: I hate a mess of any sort. But if you'll come away
with me—you and the children—

MRS. HOLROYD: But I couldn't—you don't love me—   30

BLACKMORE: I don't know what you mean by I don't love you.

MRS. HOLROYD: I can feel it.

BLACKMORE: And do you love *me*? *(A pause.)*

MRS. HOLROYD: I don't know. Everything is so—so—

(There is a long pause.)   35

BLACKMORE: How old are you?

MRS. HOLROYD: Thirty-two.

BLACKMORE: I'm twenty-seven.

MRS. HOLROYD: And have you never been in love?

BLACKMORE: I don't think so. I don't know.

MRS. HOLROYD: But you must know. I must go and shut that door
that keeps clicking.

(She rises to go upstairs, making a clatter at the stairfoot door. The noise
rouses her husband. As she goes upstairs, he moves, makes coughing
sounds, turns over, and then suddenly sits upright, gazing at BLACK-
MORE. The latter sits perfectly still on the sofa, his head dropped, hiding
his face. His hands are clasped. They remain thus for a minute.)

HOLROYD: Hello! *(He stares fixedly.)* Hello! *(His tone is undecided,*
as if he mistrusts himself.) What are—who are ter? *(*BLACKMORE
does not move; HOLROYD *stares blankly; he then turns and looks at*
the room.) Well, I dunna know.

(He staggers to his feet, clinging to the table, and goes groping to the
stairs. They creak loudly under his weight. A doorlatch is heard to click.
In a moment MRS. HOLROYD *comes quickly downstairs.)*

BLACKMORE: Has he gone to bed?

MRS. HOLROYD *(nodding)*: Lying on the bed.

BLACKMORE: Will he settle now?

MRS. HOLROYD: I don't know. He is like that sometimes. He will
have delirium tremens if he goes on.

BLACKMORE *(softly)*: You can't stay with him, you know.

MRS. HOLROYD: And the children?

BLACKMORE: We'll take them.

MRS. HOLROYD: Oh!

(Her face puckers to cry. Suddenly he starts up and puts his arms round
her, holding her protectively and gently, very caressingly. She clings to
him. They are silent for some moments.)

BLACKMORE *(struggling, in an altered voice)*: Look at me and kiss
me.

(Her sobs are heard distinctly. BLACKMORE *lays his hand on her cheek,*
caressing her always with his hand.)

BLACKMORE: My God, but I hate him! I wish either he was dead or
me. *(*MRS. HOLROYD *hides against him; her sobs cease; after a*
while he continues in the same murmuring fashion.) It can't go on
like it any more. I feel as if I should come in two. I can't keep
away from you. I simply can't. Come with me. Come with me
and leave him. If you knew what a hell it is for me to have you
here—and to see him. I can't go without you, I can't. It's been
hell every moment for six months now. You say I don't love
you. Perhaps I don't, for all I know about it. But oh, my God,

don't keep me like it any longer. Why should *he* have you—and I've never had anything.

MRS. HOLROYD: Have you never loved anybody?

BLACKMORE: No—I've tried. Kiss me of your own wish—will you?

MRS. HOLROYD: I don't know. 5

BLACKMORE *(after a pause)* : Let's break clear. Let's go right away. Do you care for me?

MRS. HOLROYD: I don't know. *(She loosens herself, rises dumbly.)*

BLACKMORE: When do you think you *will* know?

                    (She sits down helplessly.) 10

MRS. HOLROYD: I don't know.

BLACKMORE: Yes, you do know, really. If he was dead, should you marry me?

MRS. HOLROYD: Don't say it—

BLACKMORE: Why not? If wishing of mine would kill him, he'd 15 soon be out of the way.

MRS. HOLROYD: But the children!

BLACKMORE: I'm fond of them. I shall have good money.

MRS. HOLROYD: But he's their father.

BLACKMORE: What does that mean—? 20

MRS. HOLROYD: Yes, I know— *(A pause)* but—

BLACKMORE: Is it *him* that keeps you?

MRS. HOLROYD: No.

BLACKMORE: Then come with me. Will you? *(He stands waiting for her; then he turns and takes his overcoat; pulls it on, leaving the* 25 *collar turned up, ceasing to twist his cap.)* Well—will you tell me to-morrow?

(She goes forward and flings her arms round his neck. He suddenly kisses her passionately.)

MRS. HOLROYD: But I ought not. *(She draws away a little; he will* 30 *not let her go.)*

BLACKMORE: Yes, it's all right. *(He holds her close.)*

MRS. HOLROYD: Is it?

BLACKMORE: Yes, it is. It's all right.

(He kisses her again. She releases herself but holds his hand. They keep 35 *listening.)*

MRS. HOLROYD: Do you love me?

BLACKMORE: What do you ask for?

MRS. HOLROYD: Have I hurt you these months?

BLACKMORE: *You* haven't. And I don't care what it's been if you'll 40

come with me. *(There is a noise upstairs and they wait.)* You will
soon, won't you?

(She kisses him.)

MRS. HOLROYD: He's not safe. *(She disengages herself and sits on the
sofa.)*

BLACKMORE *(takes a place beside her, holding her hand in both
his)*: You should have waited for me.

MRS. HOLROYD: How wait?

BLACKMORE: And not have married him.

MRS. HOLROYD: I might never have known you—I married him to
get out of my place.

BLACKMORE: Why?

MRS. HOLROYD: I was left an orphan when I was six. My Uncle
John brought me up, in the Coach and Horses at Rainsworth.
He'd got no children. He was good to me, but he drank. I went
to Mansfield Grammar School. Then he fell out with me
because I wouldn't wait in the bar, and I went as nursery
governess to Berryman's.* And I felt I'd nowhere to go, I
belonged to nowhere, and nobody cared about me, and men
came after me, and I hated it. So to get out of it, I married the
first man that turned up.

BLACKMORE: And you never cared about him?

MRS. HOLROYD: Yes, I did. I did care about him. I wanted to be a
wife to him. But there's nothing at the bottom of him, if you
know what I mean. You can't *get* anywhere with him. There's
just his body and nothing else. Nothing that keeps him, no
anchor, no roots, nothing satisfying. It's a horrible feeling there
is about him, that nothing is safe or permanent—nothing is
anything—

BLACKMORE: And do you think you can trust *me*?

MRS. HOLROYD: I think you're different from him.

BLACKMORE: Perhaps I'm not.

MRS. HOLROYD *(warmly)*: You are.

BLACKMORE: At any rate, we'll see. You'll come on Saturday to
London?

MRS. HOLROYD: Well, you see, there's my money. I haven't got it
yet. My uncle has left me about a hundred and twenty pounds.*

BLACKMORE: Well, see the lawyer about it as soon as you can. I can
let you have some money if you want any. But don't let us wait
after Saturday.

MRS. HOLROYD: But isn't it wrong?

BLACKMORE: Why, if you don't care for him, and the children are miserable between the two of you—which they are—

MRS. HOLROYD: Yes.

BLACKMORE: Well, then I see no wrong. As for him—he would go one way, and only one way, whatever you do. Damn him, he doesn't matter.

MRS. HOLROYD: No.

BLACKMORE: Well, then—have done with it. Can't you cut clean of him? Can't you now?

MRS. HOLROYD: And then—the children—

BLACKMORE: They'll be all right with me and you—won't they?

MRS. HOLROYD: Yes—

BLACKMORE: Well, then. Now, come and have done with it. We can't keep on being ripped in two like this. We need never hear of him any more.

MRS. HOLROYD: Yes—I love you. I do love you—

BLACKMORE: Oh, my God! *(He speaks with difficulty—embracing her.)*

MRS. HOLROYD: When I look at him, and then at you—ha— *(She gives a short laugh.)*

BLACKMORE: He's had all the chance—it's only fair—Lizzie—

MRS. HOLROYD: My love.

(There is silence. He keeps his arm round her. After hesitating, he picks up his cap.)

BLACKMORE: I'll go then—at any rate. Shall you come with me?
(She follows him to the door.)

MRS. HOLROYD: I'll come on Saturday.

BLACKMORE: Not now?

(Curtain)

Act III.

Scene, the same. Time, the following evening, about seven o'clock. The table is half laid, with a large cup and saucer, plate, etc., ready for Holroyd's dinner, which, like all miners, he has when he comes home
5　*between four and five o'clock. On the other half of the table* MRS. HOLROYD *is ironing. On the hearth stands newly baked loaves of bread. The irons hang at the fire.*

　　JACK, *with a bowler hat hanging at the back of his head, parades up to the sofa, on which stands* MINNIE *engaged in dusting a picture. She has a*
10　*soiled white apron tied behind her, to make a long skirt.*

JACK: Good mornin', missis. Any scissors or knives to grind?

MINNIE *(peering down from the sofa)*: Oh, I can't be bothered to come downstairs. Call another day.

JACK: I shan't.

15　MINNIE *(keeping up her part)*: Well, I can't come down now. *(*JACK *stands irresolute.)* Go on, you have to go and steal the baby.

JACK: I'm not.

MINNIE: Well, you can steal the eggs out of the fowl-house.

JACK: I'm not.

20　MINNIE: Then I shan't play with you. *(*JACK *takes off his bowler hat and flings it on the sofa; tears come in* MINNIE's *eyes.)* Now I'm *not* friends. *(She surveys him ruefully; after a few moments of silence she clambers down and goes to her mother.)* Mam, he won't play with me.

25　MRS. HOLROYD *(crossly)*: Why don't you play with her? If you begin bothering, you must go to bed.

JACK: Well, I don't want to play.

MRS. HOLROYD: Then you must go to bed.

JACK: I don't want to.

30　MRS. HOLROYD: Then what do you want, I should like to know?

MINNIE: I wish my father'd come.

JACK: I do.

MRS. HOLROYD: I suppose he thinks he's paying me out. This is the third time this week he's slunk past the door and gone down
35　to Old Brinsley instead of coming in to his dinner. He'll be as drunk as a lord when he does come.

　　　　　(The children look at her plaintively.)

MINNIE: Isn't he a nuisance?

JACK: I hate him. I wish he'd drop down th' pit-shaft.

MRS. HOLROYD: Jack!—I never heard such a thing in my life! You mustn't say such things—it's wicked.

JACK: Well, I do.

MRS. HOLROYD *(loudly)*: I won't have it. He's your father, remember.   5

JACK *(in a high voice)*: Well, he's always comin' home an' shoutin' an' bangin' on the table. *(He is getting tearful and defiant.)*

MRS. HOLROYD: Well, you mustn't take any notice of him.

MINNIE *(wistfully)*: 'Appen if you said something nice to him, mother, he'd happen go to bed, and not shout.   10

JACK: I'd hit him in the mouth.

MRS. HOLROYD: Perhaps we'll go to another country, away from him—should we?

JACK: In a ship, mother?

MINNIE: In a ship, mam?   15

MRS. HOLROYD: Yes, in a big ship, where it's blue sky, and water and palm-trees, and—

MINNIE: An' dates—?

JACK: When should we go?

MRS. HOLROYD: Some day.   20

MINNIE: But who'd work for us? Who should we have for father?

JACK: You don't want a father. I can go to work for us.

MRS. HOLROYD: I've got a lot of money now, that your uncle left me.

MINNIE *(after a general thoughtful silence)*: An' would my father   25
stop here?

MRS. HOLROYD: Oh, he'd be all right.

MINNIE: But who would he live with?

MRS. HOLROYD: I don't know—one of his paper bonnets, if he likes.   30

MINNIE: Then she could have her old bracelet back, couldn't she?

MRS. HOLROYD: Yes—there it is on the candlestick, waiting for her.

(There is a sound of footsteps—then a knock at the door. The children start.)   35

MINNIE *(in relief)*: Here he is.

*(*MRS. HOLROYD *goes to the door.* BLACKMORE *enters.)*

BLACKMORE: It is foggy to-night—Hello, aren't you youngsters gone to bed?

MINNIE: No, my father's not come home yet.   40

BLACKMORE *(turning to* MRS. HOLROYD*)*: Did he go to work then,
  after last night?

MRS. HOLROYD: I suppose so. His pit things were gone when I got
  up. I never thought he'd go.

5 BLACKMORE: And he took his snap as usual?

MRS. HOLROYD: Yes, just as usual. I suppose he's gone to the New
  Inn. He'd say to himself he'd pay me out. That's what he always
  does say, "I'll pay thee out for that bit—I'll ma'e thee regret it."

JACK: We're going to leave him.

10 BLACKMORE: So you think he's at the New Inn?

MRS. HOLROYD: I'm sure he is—and he'll come when he's full.
  He'll have a bout now, you'll see.

MINNIE: Go and fetch him, Mr. Blackmore.

JACK: My mother says we shall go in a ship and leave him.

15 BLACKMORE *(after looking keenly at* JACK: *to* MRS. HOLROYD*)*: Shall
  I go and see if he's at the New Inn?

MRS. HOLROYD: No—perhaps you'd better not—

BLACKMORE: Oh, he shan't see me. I can easily manage that.

JACK: Fetch him, Mr. Blackmore.

20 BLACKMORE: All right, Jack. *(To* MRS. HOLROYD*)* Shall I?

MRS. HOLROYD: We're always pulling on you—But yes, do!
                    *(*BLACKMORE *goes out.)*

JACK: I wonder how long he'll be.

MRS. HOLROYD: You come and go to bed now: you'd better be out
25 of the way when he comes in.

MINNIE: And you won't say anything to him, mother, will you?

MRS. HOLROYD: What do you mean?

MINNIE: You won't begin of him—row him.

MRS. HOLROYD: Is he to have all his own way? What *would* he be
30 like, if I didn't row him?

JACK: But it doesn't matter, mother, if we're going to leave him—

MINNIE: But Mr. Blackmore'll come back, won't he, mam, and dad
  won't shout before him?

MRS. HOLROYD *(beginning to undress the children)*: Yes, he'll come
35 back.

MINNIE: Mam—could I have that bracelet to go to bed with?

MRS. HOLROYD: Come and say your prayers.
          (They kneel, muttering in their mother's apron.)

MINNIE *(suddenly lifting her head)*: Can I, mam?

MRS. HOLROYD *(trying to be stern)*: Have you finished your prayers?

MINNIE: Yes.

MRS. HOLROYD: If you want it—beastly thing! *(She reaches the bracelet down from the mantelpiece.)* Your father must have put it up there—I don't know where I left it. I suppose he'd think I was proud of it and wanted it for an ornament.

(MINNIE gloats over it. MRS. HOLROYD lights a candle and they go upstairs. After a few moments the outer door opens, and there enters an old woman. She is of middling stature and wears a large gray shawl over her head. After glancing sharply round the room, she advances to the fire, warms herself, then, taking off her shawl, sits in the rocking-chair. As she hears MRS. HOLROYD's footsteps, she folds her hands and puts on a lachrymose expression, turning down the corners of her mouth and arching her eyebrows.)

MRS. HOLROYD: Hello, mother, is it you?

GRANDMOTHER: Yes, it's me. Haven't you finished ironing?

MRS. HOLROYD: Not yet.

GRANDMOTHER: You'll have your irons red-hot.

MRS. HOLROYD: Yes, I s'll have to stand them to cool. *(She does so, and moves about at her ironing.)*

GRANDMOTHER: And you don't know what's become of Charles?

MRS. HOLROYD: Well, he's not come home from work yet. I supposed he was at the New Inn—Why?

GRANDMOTHER: That young electrician come knocking asking if I knew where he was. "Eh," I said, "I've not set eyes on him for over a week—nor his wife neither, though they pass th' garden gate every time they go out. I know nowt on 'im." I axed him what was the matter, so he said Mrs. Holroyd was anxious because he'd not come home, so I thought I'd better come and see. Is there anything up?

MRS. HOLROYD: No more than I've told you.

GRANDMOTHER: It's a rum 'un, if he's neither in the New Inn nor the Prince o' Wales. I suppose something you've done's set him off.

MRS. HOLROYD: It's nothing I've done.

GRANDMOTHER: Eh, if he's gone off and left you, whativer shall we do! Whativer 'ave you been doing?

MRS. HOLROYD: He brought a couple of bright daisies here last night—two of those trollops from Nottingham—and I said I'd not have it.

GRANDMOTHER *(sighing deeply)*: Ay, you've never been able to agree.

5   MRS. HOLROYD: We agreed well enough except when he drank like a fish and came home rolling.

GRANDMOTHER *(whining)*: Well, what can you expect of a man as 'as been shut up i' th' pit all day? He must have a bit of relaxation.

10   MRS. HOLROYD: He can have it different from that, then. At any rate, I'm sick of it.

GRANDMOTHER: Ay, you've a stiff neck, but it'll be bowed by you're my age.

MRS. HOLROYD: Will it? I'd rather it were broke.

15   GRANDMOTHER: Well—there's no telling what a jealous man will do. *(She shakes her head.)*

MRS. HOLROYD: Nay, I think it's my place to be jealous, when he brings a brazen hussy here and sits carryin' on with her.

GRANDMOTHER: He'd no business to do that. But you know,
20   Lizzie, he's got something on *his* side.

MRS. HOLROYD: What, pray?

GRANDMOTHER: Well, I don't want to make any mischief, but you're my son's wife, an' it's nothing but my duty to tell you. They've been saying a long time now as that young electrician is
25   here a bit too often.

MRS. HOLROYD: He doesn't come for my asking.

GRANDMOTHER: No, I don't suppose he wants for asking. But Charlie's not the man to put up with that sort o' work.

MRS. HOLROYD: Charlie put up with it! If he's anything to say,
30   why doesn't he say it, without going to other folks . . .?

GRANDMOTHER: Charlie's never been near me with a word—nor 'as he said a word elsewhere to my knowledge. For all that, this is going to end with trouble.

MRS. HOLROYD: In this hole, every gossiping creature thinks she's
35   got the right to cackle about you—sickening! And a parcel of lies.

GRANDMOTHER: Well, Lizzie, I've never said anything against you. Charlie's been a handful of trouble. He made my heart ache once or twice afore you had him, and he's made it ache many, many's the time since. But it's not all on his side, you know.

40   MRS. HOLROYD *(hotly)*: No, I don't know.

GRANDMOTHER: You thought yourself above him, Lizzie, an' you
know he's not the man to stand it.

MRS. HOLROYD: No, he's run away from it.

GRANDMOTHER *(venomously)*: And what man wouldn't leave a
woman that allowed him to live on sufferance in the house with   5
her, when he was bringing the money home?

MRS. HOLROYD: "Sufferance!"—Yes, there's been a lot of letting
him live on "sufferance" in the house with me. It is *I* who have
lived on sufferance, for his service and pleasure. No, what he
wanted was the drink and the public house company, and   10
because he couldn't get them here, he went out for them. That's
all.

GRANDMOTHER: You have always been very clever at hitting things
off, Lizzie. I was always sorry my youngest son married a clever
woman. He only wanted a bit of coaxing and managing, and you   15
clever women won't do it.

MRS. HOLROYD: He wanted a slave, not a wife.

GRANDMOTHER: It's a pity your stomach wasn't too high for him,
before you had him. But no, you could have eaten him ravishing
at one time.   20

MRS. HOLROYD: It's a pity you didn't tell me what he was before I
had him. But no, he was all angel. You left me to find out what
he really was.

GRANDMOTHER: Some women could have lived with him happy
enough. An' a fat lot you'd have thanked me for my telling.   25

(There is a knock at the door. MRS. HOLROYD *opens.)*

RIGLEY: They tell me, missus, as your mester's not hoom yet.

MRS. HOLROYD: No—who is it?

GRANDMOTHER: Ask him to step inside. Don't stan' there lettin'
the fog in.   30

*(*RIGLEY *steps in. He is a tall, bony, very roughly hewn collier.)*

RIGLEY: Good evenin'.

GRANDMOTHER: Oh, is it you, Mr. Rigley? *(In a querulous, spiteful
tone to* MRS. HOLROYD.*)* He butties* along with Charlie.

MRS. HOLROYD: Oh!   35

RIGLEY: An' han yer seen nowt on 'im?

MRS. HOLROYD: No—was he all right at work?

RIGLEY: Well, 'e wor nowt to mention. A bit short, like: 'adna
much to say. I canna ma'e out what 'e's done wi' 'issen. *(He is
manifestly uneasy, does not look at the two women.)*   40

GRANDMOTHER: An' did 'e come up i' th' same bantle wi' you?

RIGLEY: No—'e didna. As Ah was comin' out o' th' stall, Ah
shouted, "Art comin', Charlie? We're a' off." An' 'e said, "Ah'm
comin' in a minute." 'E wor just finishin' a stint, like, an' 'e
5   wanted ter get it set. An' 'e'd been a bit roughish in 'is temper,
like, so I thöwt 'e didna want ter walk to th' bottom wi' us. . . .

GRANDMOTHER *(wailing)*: An' what's 'e gone an' done to himself?

RIGLEY: Nay, missis, yo munna ax me that. 'E's non done owt as
Ah know on. On'y I wor thinkin', 'appen summat 'ad 'appened
10   to 'im, like, seein' as nob'dy had any knowings of 'im comin'
up.

MRS. HOLROYD: What is the matter, Mr. Rigley? Tell us it out.

RIGLEY: I canna do that, missis. It seems as if 'e niver come up th'
pit—as far as we can make out. 'Appen a bit o' stuff's fell an'
15   pinned 'im.

GRANDMOTHER *(wailing)*: An' 'ave you left 'im lying down there in
the pit, poor thing?

RIGLEY *(uneasily)*: I couldna say for certain where 'e is.

MRS. HOLROYD *(agitated)*: Oh, it's very likely not very bad,
20   mother! Don't let us run to meet trouble.

RIGLEY: We 'ave to 'ope for th' best, missis, all on us.

GRANDMOTHER *(wailing)*: Eh, they'll bring 'im 'ome, I know they
will, smashed up an' broke! An' one of my sons they've burned
down pit till the flesh dropped off 'im, an' one was shot till 'is
25   shoulder was all of a mosh, an' they brought 'em 'ome to me.
An' now there's this. . . .

MRS. HOLROYD *(shuddering)*: Oh, don't, mother. *(Appealingly to*
RIGLEY*)* You don't know that he's hurt?

RIGLEY *(shaking his head)*: I canna tell you.

30   MRS. HOLROYD *(in a high hysterical voice)*: Then what is it?

RIGLEY *(very uneasy)*: I canna tell you. But yon young electrician—Mr. Blackmore—'e rung down to the night deputy, an'
it seems as though there's been a fall or summat. . . .

GRANDMOTHER: Eh, Lizzie, you parted from him in anger. You
35   little knowed how you'd meet him again.

RIGLEY *(making an effort)*: Well, I'd 'appen best be goin' to see
what's betide. *(He goes out.)*

GRANDMOTHER: I'm sure I've had my share of bad luck, I have.
I'm sure I've brought up five lads in the pit, through accidents
40   and troubles, and now there's this. The Lord has treated me

very hard, very hard. It's a blessing, Lizzie, as you've got a bit of
money, else what would 'ave become of the children?

MRS. HOLROYD: Well, if he's badly hurt, there'll be the Union-pay,
and sick-pay*—we shall manage. And perhaps it's *not* very
much.   5

GRANDMOTHER: There's no knowin' but what they'll be carryin'
him to die i' th' hospital.

MRS. HOLROYD: Oh, don't say so, mother—it won't be so bad,
you'll see.

GRANDMOTHER: How much money have you, Lizzie, comin'?   10

MRS. HOLROYD: I don't know—not much over a hundred pounds.

GRANDMOTHER *(shaking her head)*: An' what's that, what's that?

MRS. HOLROYD *(sharply)*: Hush!

GRANDMOTHER *(crying)*: Why, what?

(MRS. HOLROYD *opens the door. In the silence can be heard the pulsing*   15
of the fan engine, then the driving engine chuffs rapidly: there is a skirr of
brakes on the rope as it descends.)*

MRS. HOLROYD: That's twice they've sent the chair down—I wish
we could see. . . . Hark!

GRANDMOTHER: What is it?   20

MRS. HOLROYD: Yes—it's stopped at the gate. It's the doctor's.

GRANDMOTHER *(coming to the door)*: What, Lizzie?

MRS. HOLROYD: The doctor's motor. *(She listens acutely.)* Dare
you stop here, mother, while I run up to the top an' see?

GRANDMOTHER: You'd better not go, Lizzie, you'd better not. A   25
woman's best away.

MRS. HOLROYD: It is unbearable to wait.

GRANDMOTHER: Come in an' shut the door—it's a cold that gets in
your bones. *(She goes in.)*

MRS. HOLROYD: Perhaps while he's in bed we shall have time to   30
change him. It's an ill wind brings no good.* He'll happen be a
better man.

GRANDMOTHER: Well, you can but try. Many a woman's thought
the same.

MRS. HOLROYD: Oh, dear, I wish somebody would come. He's   35
never been hurt since we were married.

GRANDMOTHER: No, he's never had a bad accident, all the years
he's been in the pit. He's been luckier than most. But everybody
has it, sooner or later.

MRS. HOLROYD *(shivering)*: It *is* a horrid night.   40

GRANDMOTHER *(querulous)*: Yes, come your ways in.

MRS. HOLROYD: Hark!

(There is a quick sound of footsteps. BLACKMORE *comes into the light of the doorway.)*

5   BLACKMORE: They're bringing him.

MRS. HOLROYD *(quickly putting her hand over her breast)*: What is it?

BLACKMORE: You can't tell anything's the matter with him—it's not marked him at all.

10   MRS. HOLROYD: Oh, what a blessing! And is it much?

BLACKMORE: Well—

MRS. HOLROYD: What is it?

BLACKMORE: It's the worst.

GRANDMOTHER: Who is it?—What does he say?

15   *(*MRS. HOLROYD *sinks on the nearest chair with a horrified expression.* BLACKMORE *pulls himself together and enters. He is very pale.)*

BLACKMORE: I came to tell you they're bringing him home.

GRANDMOTHER: And you said it wasn't very bad, did you?

BLACKMORE: No—I said it was—as bad as it could be.

20   MRS. HOLROYD *(rising and crossing to her mother-in-law, flings her arms round her; in a high voice)*: Oh, mother, what shall we do? What shall we do?

GRANDMOTHER: You don't mean to say he's dead?

BLACKMORE: Yes.

25   GRANDMOTHER *(staring)*: God help us, and how was it?

BLACKMORE: Some stuff fell.

GRANDMOTHER *(rocking herself and her daughter-in-law—both weeping)*: Oh, God have mercy on us! Oh, God have mercy on us! Some stuff fell on him. An' he'd not even time to cry for mercy; oh, God spare him! Oh, what shall we do for comfort? To be

30   taken straight out of his sins. Oh, Lizzie, to think he should be cut off in his wickedness! He's been a bad lad of late, he has, poor lamb. He's gone very wrong of late years, poor dear lamb, very wrong. Oh, Lizzie, think what's to become of him now! If

35   only you'd have tried to be different with him.

MRS. HOLROYD *(moaning)*: Don't, mother, don't. I can't bear it.

BLACKMORE *(cold and clear)*: Where will you have him laid? The men will be here in a moment.

MRS. HOLROYD *(starting up)*: They can carry him up to bed—

BLACKMORE: It's no good taking him upstairs. You'll have to wash him and lay him out.

MRS. HOLROYD *(startled)*: Well—

BLACKMORE: He's in his pit-dirt.

GRANDMOTHER: He is, bless him. We'd better have him down here, Lizzie, where we can handle him.

MRS. HOLROYD: Yes.

(She begins to put the tea things away, but drops the sugar out of the basin and the lumps fly broadcast.)

BLACKMORE: Never mind, I'll pick those up. You put the children's clothes away.

(MRS. HOLROYD stares witless around. The GRANDMOTHER sits rocking herself and weeping. BLACKMORE clears the table, putting the pots in the scullery. He folds the white tablecloth and pulls back the table. The door opens. MRS. HOLROYD utters a cry. RIGLEY enters.)

RIGLEY: They're bringing him now, missis.

MRS. HOLROYD: Oh!

RIGLEY *(simply)*: There must ha' been a fall directly after we left him.

MRS. HOLROYD *(frowning, horrified)*: No—no!

RIGLEY *(to BLACKMORE)*: It fell a' back of him, an' shut 'im as you might shut a loaf i' th' oven. It never touched him.

MRS. HOLROYD *(staring distractedly)*: Well, then—

RIGLEY: You see, it come on 'im as close as a trap on a mouse, an' gen him no air, an' what wi' th' gas, it smothered him. An' it wouldna be so very long about it neither.

MRS. HOLROYD *(quiet with horror)*: Oh!

GRANDMOTHER: Eh, dear—dear. Eh, dear—dear.

RIGLEY *(looking hard at her)*: I wasna to know what 'ud happen.

GRANDMOTHER *(not heeding him, but weeping all the time)*: But the Lord gave him time to repent. He'd have a few minutes to repent. Ay, I hope he did, I hope he did, else what was to become of him. The Lord cut him off in his sins, but He gave him time to repent.

(RIGLEY looks away at the wall. BLACKMORE has made a space in the middle of the floor.)

BLACKMORE: If you'll take the rocking-chair off the end of the rug, Mrs. Holroyd, I can pull it back a bit from the fire, and we can lay him on that.

GRANDMOTHER *(petulantly)*: What's the good of messing about—
(She moves.)

MRS. HOLROYD: It suffocated him?

RIGLEY *(shaking his head, briefly)*: Yes. 'Appen th' after-damp—☆

5   BLACKMORE: He'd be dead in a few minutes.

MRS. HOLROYD: No—oh, think!

BLACKMORE: You mustn't think.

RIGLEY *(suddenly)*: They commin'!

(MRS. HOLROYD stands at bay. The GRANDMOTHER half rises. RIGLEY
10 *and BLACKMORE efface themselves as much as possible. A MAN backs*
into the room, bearing the feet of the dead man, which are shod in great
pit boots. As the HEAD BEARER comes awkwardly past the table, the coat
with which the body is covered slips off, revealing HOLROYD in his pit-
dirt, naked to the waist.)

15 MANAGER *(a little stout, white-bearded man)*: Mind now, mind. Ay,
missis, what a job, indeed, it is! *(Sharply.)* Where mun they put
him?

MRS. HOLROYD *(turning her face aside from the corpse)*: Lay him on
the rug.

20 MANAGER: Steady now, do it steady.

SECOND BEARER *(rising and pressing back his shoulders)*: By Guy, but
'e 'ings heavy.

MANAGER: Yi, Joe, I'll back my life o' that.

GRANDMOTHER: Eh, Mr. Chambers, what's this affliction on my
25 old age. You kept your sons out o' the pit, but all mine's in. And
to think of the trouble I've had—to think o' the trouble that's
come out of Brinsley pit to me.

MANAGER: It has that, it 'as that, missis. You seem to have had
more'n your share; I'll admit it, you have.

30 MRS. HOLROYD *(who has been staring at the men)*: It is too much!
(BLACKMORE frowns; RIGLEY glowers at her.)

MANAGER: You never knowed such a thing in your life. Here's a
man, holin' a stint, just finishin'. *(He puts himself as if in the*
holer's position, gesticulating freely.) An' a lot o' stuff falls
35 behind him, clean as a whistle, shuts him up safe as a worm in
a nut and niver touches him—niver knowed such a thing in
your life.

MRS. HOLROYD: Ugh!

MANAGER: It niver hurt him—niver touched him.

40 MRS. HOLROYD: Yes, but—but how long would he *be (She makes a*

sweeping gesture; the MANAGER *looks at her and will not help her out.*) —how long would it take—oh—to—to kill him?

MANAGER: Nay, I canna tell ye. 'E didna seem to ha' strived much to get out—did he, Joe?

SECOND BEARER: No, not as far as Ah'n seen. 5

FIRST BEARER: You look at 'is 'ands, you'll see then. 'E'd non ha'e room to swing the pick.

(The MANAGER *goes on his knees.)*

MRS. HOLROYD *(shuddering)*: Oh, don't!

MANAGER: Ay, th' nails is broken a bit— 10

MRS. HOLROYD *(clenching her fists)*: Don't!

MANAGER: 'E'd be sure ter ma'e a bit of a fight. But th' gas 'ud soon get hold on 'im. Ay, it's an awful thing to think of, it is indeed.

MRS. HOLROYD *(her voice breaking)*: I can't bear it!

MANAGER: Eh, dear, we none on us know what's comin' next. 15

MRS. HOLROYD *(getting hysterical)*: Oh, it's too awful, it's too awful!

BLACKMORE: You'll disturb the children.

GRANDMOTHER: And you don't want *them* down here.

MANAGER: 'E'd no business to ha' been left, you know. 20

RIGLEY: An' what man, dost think, wor goin' to sit him down on his hams an' wait for a chap as wouldna say "thank yer" for his cump'ny? 'E'd bin ready to fall out wi' a flicker o' the candle, so who dost think wor goin' ter stop when we knowed 'e on'y kep on so's to get shut on us. 25

MANAGER: Tha'rt quite right, Bill, quite right. But theer you are.

RIGLEY: An' if we'd stopped, what good would it ha' done—

MANAGER: No, 'appen not, 'appen not.

RIGLEY: For, not known—

MANAGER: I'm sayin' nowt agen thee, neither one road nor t'other. 30
(There is general silence—then, to MRS. HOLROYD.*)* I should think th' inquest'll be at th' New Inn to-morrow, missis. I'll let you know.

MRS. HOLROYD: Will there have to be an inquest?

MANAGER: Yes—there'll have to be an inquest. Shall you want 35 anybody in, to stop with you to-night?

MRS. HOLROYD: No.

MANAGER: Well, then, we'd best be goin'. I'll send my missis down first thing in the morning. It's a bad job, a bad job, it is. You'll be a' right then? 40

MRS. HOLROYD: Yes.

MANAGER: Well, good-night then—good-night all.

ALL: Good-night. Good-night.

(The MANAGER, followed by the two BEARERS, goes out, closing the door.)

RIGLEY: It's like this, missis. I never should ha' gone, if he hadn't wanted us to.

MRS. HOLROYD: Yes, I know.

RIGLEY: 'E wanted to come up by 's sen.

MRS. HOLROYD *(wearily)*: I know how it was, Mr. Rigley.

RIGLEY: Yes—

BLACKMORE: Nobody could foresee.

RIGLEY *(shaking his head)*: No. If there's owt, missis, as you want—

MRS. HOLROYD: Yes—I think there isn't anything.

RIGLEY *(after a moment)*: Well—good-night—we've worked i' the same stall ower four years now—

MRS. HOLROYD: Yes.

RIGLEY: Well, good-night, missis.

MRS. HOLROYD AND BLACKMORE: Good-night.

(The GRANDMOTHER all this time has been rocking herself to and fro, moaning and murmuring beside the dead man. When RIGLEY has gone MRS. HOLROYD stands staring distractedly before her. She has not yet looked at her husband.)

GRANDMOTHER: Have you got the things ready, Lizzie?

MRS. HOLROYD: What things?

GRANDMOTHER: To lay the child out.

MRS. HOLROYD *(she shudders)*: No—what?

GRANDMOTHER: Haven't you put him by a pair o' white stockings, nor a white shirt?

MRS. HOLROYD: He's got a white cricketing shirt—but not white stockings.

GRANDMOTHER: Then he'll have to have his father's. Let me look at the shirt, Lizzie. *(MRS. HOLROYD takes one from the dresser drawer.)* This'll never do—a cold, canvas thing wi' a turndown collar. I s'll 'ave to fetch his father's. *(Suddenly.)* You don't want no other woman to touch him, to wash him and lay him out, do you?

MRS. HOLROYD *(weeping)*: No.

GRANDMOTHER: Then I'll fetch him his father's gear. We mustn't let him set, he'll be that heavy, bless him. *(She takes her shawl.)*

I shan't be more than a few minutes, an' the young fellow can
stop here till I come back.

BLACKMORE: Can't I go for you, Mrs. Holroyd?

GRANDMOTHER: No. *You* couldn't find the things. We'll wash him
as soon as I get back, Lizzie. 5

MRS. HOLROYD: All right.

*(She watches her mother-in-law go out. Then she starts, goes in the
scullery for a bowl, in which she pours warm water. She takes a flannel
and soap and towel. She stands, afraid to go any farther.)*

BLACKMORE: Well! 10

MRS. HOLROYD: This is a judgment on us.

BLACKMORE: Why?

MRS. HOLROYD: On me, it is—

BLACKMORE: How?

MRS. HOLROYD: It is. 15

*(*BLACKMORE *shakes his head.)*

MRS. HOLROYD: Yesterday you talked of murdering him.

BLACKMORE: Well!

MRS. HOLROYD: Now we've done it.

BLACKMORE: How? 20

MRS. HOLROYD: He'd have come up with the others, if he hadn't
felt—felt me murdering him.

BLACKMORE: But we can't help it.

MRS. HOLROYD: It's my fault.

BLACKMORE: Don't be like that! 25

MRS. HOLROYD *(looking at him—then indicating her husband)*: I
daren't see him.

BLACKMORE: No?

MRS. HOLROYD: I've killed him, that is all.

BLACKMORE: No, you haven't. 30

MRS. HOLROYD: Yes, I have.

BLACKMORE: *We* couldn't help it.

MRS. HOLROYD: If he hadn't felt, if he hadn't *known*, he wouldn't
have stayed, he'd have come up with the rest.

BLACKMORE: Well, and even if it was so, we can't help it now. 35

MRS. HOLROYD: But we've killed him.

BLACKMORE: Ah, I'm tired—

MRS. HOLROYD: Yes.

BLACKMORE *(after a pause)*: Shall I stay?

MRS. HOLROYD: I—I daren't be alone with him. 40

BLACKMORE *(sitting down)*: No.

MRS. HOLROYD: I don't love him. Now he's dead. I don't love him. He lies like he did yesterday.

BLACKMORE: I suppose, being dead—I don't know—

5 MRS. HOLROYD: I think you'd better go.

BLACKMORE *(rising)*: Tell me.

MRS. HOLROYD: Yes.

BLACKMORE: You want me to go.

MRS. HOLROYD: No—but *do* go. *(They look at each other.)*

10 BLACKMORE: I shall come to-morrow. *(He goes out.)*

(MRS. HOLROYD stands very stiff, as if afraid of the dead man. Then she stoops down and begins to sponge his face, talking to him.)

MRS. HOLROYD: My dear, my dear—oh, my dear! I can't bear it, my dear—you shouldn't have done it. You shouldn't have done
15 it. Oh—I can't bear it, for you. Why couldn't I do anything for you? The children's father—my dear—I wasn't good to you. But you shouldn't have done this to me. Oh, dear, oh, dear! Did it hurt you?—oh, my dear, it hurt you—oh, I can't bear it. No, things aren't fair—we went wrong, my dear. I never loved you
20 enough—I never did. What a shame for you! It was a shame. But you didn't—you didn't try. I *would* have loved you—I tried hard. What a shame for you! It was so cruel for you. You couldn't help it—my dear, my dear. You couldn't help it. And I can't do anything for you, and it hurt you so! *(She weeps bitterly,*
25 *so her tears fall on the dead man's face; suddenly she kisses him.)* My dear, my dear, what can I do for you, what can I? *(She weeps as she wipes his face gently.)*

GRANDMOTHER *(enters, puts a bundle on the table, takes off her shawl)*: You're not all by yourself?

30 MRS. HOLROYD: Yes.

GRANDMOTHER: It's a wonder you're not frightened. You've not washed his face.

MRS. HOLROYD: Why should I be afraid of him—now, mother?

GRANDMOTHER *(weeping)*: Ay, poor lamb, I can't think as ever you
35 could have had reason to be frightened of him, Lizzie.

MRS. HOLROYD: Yes—once—

GRANDMOTHER: Oh, but he went wrong. An' he was a taking lad, as iver was. *(She cries pitifully.)* And when I waked his father up and told him, he sat up in bed staring over his whiskers, and
40 said should he come up? But when I'd managed to find the

shirt and things, he was still in bed. You don't know what it is
to live with a man that has no feeling. But you've washed him,
Lizzie?

MRS. HOLROYD: I was finishing his head.

GRANDMOTHER: Let me do it, child.   5

MRS. HOLROYD: I'll finish that.

GRANDMOTHER: Poor lamb—poor dear lamb! Yet I wouldn't wish
him back, Lizzie. He must ha' died peaceful, Lizzie. He seems
to be smiling.* He always had such a rare smile on him—not
that he's smiled much of late—   10

MRS. HOLROYD: I loved him for that.

GRANDMOTHER: Ay—my poor child—my poor child.

MRS. HOLROYD: He looks nice, mother.

GRANDMOTHER: I hope he made his peace with the Lord.

MRS. HOLROYD: Yes.   15

GRANDMOTHER: If he hadn't time to make his peace with the
Lord, I've no hopes of him. Dear o' me, dear o' me. Is there
another bit of flannel anywhere?

*(MRS. HOLROYD rises and brings a piece. The GRANDMOTHER begins to
wash the breast of the dead man.)*   20

GRANDMOTHER: Well, I hope you'll be true to his children at least,
Lizzie. *(MRS. HOLROYD weeps—the old woman continues her
washing.)* Eh—and he's fair as a lily. Did you ever see a man
with a whiter skin—and flesh as fine as the driven snow. He's
beautiful, he is, the lamb. Many's the time I've looked at him,   25
and I've felt proud of him, I have. And now he lies here. And
such arms on 'im! Look at the vaccination marks, Lizzie. When
I took him to be vaccinated, he had a little pink bonnet with a
feather. *(Weeps.)* Don't cry, my girl, don't. Sit up an' wash him
a' that side, or we s'll never have him done. Oh, Lizzie!   30

MRS. HOLROYD *(sitting up, startled)*: What—what?

GRANDMOTHER: Look at his poor hand!

    (She holds up the right hand. The nails are bloody.)

MRS. HOLROYD: Oh, no! Oh, no! No!

    (Both women weep.)   35

GRANDMOTHER *(after awhile)*: We maun get on, Lizzie.

MRS. HOLROYD *(sitting up)*: I can't touch his hands.

GRANDMOTHER: But I'm his mother—there's nothing I couldn't
do for him.

MRS. HOLROYD: I don't care—I don't care.   40

GRANDMOTHER: Prithee, prithee, Lizzie, I don't want thee goin'
off, Lizzie.

MRS. HOLROYD *(moaning)*: Oh, what shall I do!

GRANDMOTHER: Why, go thee an' get his feet washed. He's setting
5   stiff, and how shall we get him laid out?

*(*MRS. HOLROYD, *sobbing, goes, kneels at the miner's feet, and begins
pulling off the great boots.)*

GRANDMOTHER: There's hardly a mark on him. Eh, what a man he
is! I've had some fine sons, Lizzie, I've had some big men of
10   sons.

MRS. HOLROYD: He was always a lot whiter than me. And he used
to chaff me.

GRANDMOTHER: But his poor hands! I used to thank God for my
children, but they're rods o' trouble,* Lizzie, they are. Unfasten
15   his belt, child. We* mun get his things off soon, or else we s'll
have such a job.

*(*MRS. HOLROYD, *having dragged off the boots, rises. She is weeping.)*

(Curtain)

THE MERRY-GO-ROUND

MRS HEMSTOCK
NURSE BROADBANKS
MR HEMSTOCK
HARRY HEMSTOCK   5
THE BARON
THE BAKER
MRS SMALLEY
DR FOULES
RACHEL WILCOX   10
THE BARONESS
MR WILCOX
FIRST MOURNER
SECOND MOURNER
THIRD MOURNER   15
FOURTH MOURNER
FIFTH MOURNER
PATTY, A GOOSE ☆

THE MERRY-GO-ROUND[☆]

Act I.
Scene 1.

The downstairs front room of a moderate-sized cottage. There is a wide
fire-place, with heaped up, ashy fire. This parlour is used as a bedroom,   5
and contains heavy old-fashioned mahogany dressing table, wash-stand,
and bedstead whose canopy is missing, so that the handsome posts stand
like ruined columns. The room is in an untidy, neglected condition,
medicine bottles and sick-room paraphernalia littered about. In the bed, a
woman between sixty and seventy, with a large-boned face, and a long   10
plait of fine dark hair. Enter the parish nurse, in uniform, but without
cloak and bonnet. She is a well-built woman of some thirty years, smooth
haired, pale, soothing in manner.

MRS HEMSTOCK: Eh Nurse, I'm glad to see thee. I *han* been
   motherless while thou's been away.   15
NURSE: Haven't they looked after you, Mrs Hemstock—?
MRS HEMSTOCK: They hanna, Nurse. Here I lie, day in, day out,
   like a beetle on my back, an' not a soul comes anigh me, saving
   th' Mester, when 'e's forced.—An' im—
     (She points to mirror of dressing table.)   20
NURSE: Who is that, Mrs Hemstock?
MRS HEMSTOCK: Canna ter see 'im? That little fat chap as stands
   there laughing at me.
NURSE: There's no little fat chap, Mrs Hemstock.
MRS HEMSTOCK: There is an' a'. He's bobbing at thee now.   25
*(*NURSE, *who has been rolling up her sleeves, showing a fine white arm,*
   throws her rolled cuffs at the mirror.)
NURSE: Then we'll send him away.
MRS HEMSTOCK: Nay, dunna thee hurt him. 'E's nowt but a little
   chap!   30
NURSE: I'll wash you, shall I?
MRS HEMSTOCK: Tha nedna but gi'e me a cat-lick. I'm as snug as a
   bug in a rug.[☆]

NURSE *(laughing)*: Very well. *(She goes into the kitchen.)*

MRS HEMSTOCK *(calling)*: Who's there in, Nurse?

NURSE: There's nobody, Mrs Hemstock.

MRS HEMSTOCK: I bet he's gallivanting off after some woman.

5 NURSE *(calling)*: Who?

MRS HEMSTOCK: Why, our Mester. 'E's a ronk 'un, I can tell you. —'As our Harry done it?

NURSE: Done what, Mrs Hemstock?

MRS HEMSTOCK: Cut 'is throat. 'E's allers threatenin'.

10 NURSE *(entering with a jug of hot water)*: What! You're not serious, Mrs Hemstock.

MRS HEMSTOCK: Aren't I? But I am. An' 'e'll do it one o' these days, if 'e's not a'ready. I 'ave-na clapped eyes on him for nine* days.

15 NURSE: How is that?

MRS HEMSTOCK: Eh, dunna ax me. 'E niver comes in if 'e can 'elp it.

NURSE: How strange! Why is it, do you think?

MRS HEMSTOCK: Summat's gen 'im mulligrubs. 'E'll non live long.

20 NURSE: What, Harry! He's quite young, and has nothing the matter, has he.

MRS HEMSTOCK: You know, Nurse, I 'ad a fish inside me. I wor like Jonah back-ards.* I used ter feel it floppin' about in my inside like a good-'un, an' nobody'd get it out—

25 NURSE: But Harry hasn't got a fish in his inside—

MRS HEMSTOCK: 'E 'asna—but I believe 'e's got a leech.

NURSE: Oh!

MRS HEMSTOCK: Dunna thee wet my 'air, Nurse—it ma'es it go grey.

30 NURSE *(smiling)*: Very well, I'll be careful.—But what makes you say Harry has a leech in his inside?

MRS HEMSTOCK: On 'is 'eart. 'Asn't ter noticed 'e gets as white-faced as a flat fish? It's that.

NURSE: Oh, and did *he* swallow it?

35 MRS HEMSTOCK: 'E didna. 'E bred it like a mackerel's head breeds maggots.

NURSE: How dreadful!

MRS HEMSTOCK: When you've owt up with you, you allers breed summat.

40 NURSE: And what was up with Mr Hemstock—

MRS HEMSTOCK: With our Mester?

NURSE: With Harry.

MRS HEMSTOCK: You knowed, didna you, as 'e'd had ructions wi' Rachel Wilcox?

NURSE: No.

MRS HEMSTOCK: Oh yes. 'E fell off 'is bike eighteen month sin', a'most into her lap, an' 'er's been sick for 'im ever sin'.

NURSE: But he didn't care for her?

MRS HEMSTOCK: I dunno. 'E went out wi' 'er for about a twelve-month—but 'e never wanted 'er.—'E's funny, an' allers 'as been.

NURSE: Rather churlish—?

MRS HEMSTOCK: No—'e wor allers one o' th' lovin' sort when 'e wor but a lad,—'d follow me about, an' 'Mammy' me.

NURSE: But he got into bad ways—

MRS HEMSTOCK: Well, I got sick of him slormin' about like a cat lookin' for her kittens, so I hustled him out. 'E begun drinkin' a bit, an' carryin' on. I thought 'e wor goin' to be like his father for women. But 'e wor allers a mother's lad—an' Rachel Wilcox cured him o' women.

NURSE: She's not a nice girl.

MRS HEMSTOCK: 'E'd only ter stick 'is 'ead out o' th' door, an' 'er'd run like a pig as 'ears the bucket. 'Er wor like a cat foriver slidin' rubbin' 'erself against him.

NURSE: How dreadful!

MRS HEMSTOCK: But I encouraged 'er. I thought 'e wor such a soft 'ae'-porth,* at 'is age, a man of thirty!

NURSE: Was he always quiet?

MRS HEMSTOCK: Eh bless you, 'e'd talk the leg off an iron pot,* once on a day. But now, it's like pottering to get a penny out of a money-box, afore you can get a word from 'im edgeways.

NURSE: And he won't come to see you.

MRS HEMSTOCK: Not him. 'E once had a rabbit what got consump-tion, an' 'e wouldn't kill it, nor let me, neither would he go near it, so it died of starvation, an' 'e throwed a hammer at me for telling him so. You see—hark! That's our Mester.

NURSE: Yes. Do I hurt you? They've let your hair get very cottered.

MRS HEMSTOCK: Get it out, Nurse—never mind me.

(Enter MR HEMSTOCK, a very white-haired old man, clean shaven, with brown eyes. There is a certain courtliness in his quiet bearing.)

MR HEMSTOCK: I'm glad to see *you* back, Nurse—very glad. *(He bows by instinct.)*

NURSE: Thank you, Mr Hemstock. I'm pleased to see you again.

MRS HEMSTOCK *(to her husband)*: Tha'rt not 'aef as glad to seen her
as I am. 'Ere I lie from hour to hour, an' niver a sound but cows
rumblin' an' cocks shoutin'—An' where dost reckon tha's been?
—tha's been slivin' somewhere like a tom-cat, ever sin' breakfast—

MR HEMSTOCK *(to NURSE)*: I've been gone ten minutes.— *(To his
wife)*: I've on'y bin for a pennorth of barm ter ma'e thee some
barm dumplings.

MRS HEMSTOCK: An' wheer's our Harry?

MR HEMSTOCK: 'E's in garden, diggin'.

MRS HEMSTOCK: What are ter out o' breath wi'?

MR HEMSTOCK: I've bin runnin' our Susy's kids. They was drivin'
our fowls again.

MRS HEMSTOCK: Tha shouldna ha' wanted ter come here, a mile
away from anybody but our Susy.

NURSE: It is rather lonely—only Mrs Smalley's farm and your
cottage. And the children *are* rather wild.

MRS HEMSTOCK: Let me live in a street. What does colliers want
livin' in country cottages, wi' nowt but fowls an' things shoutin'
at you or takin' no notice of you, as if you was not there.

MR HEMSTOCK *(to NURSE)*: We came for the garden.

NURSE: I suppose you are still on strike.☆

MR HEMSTOCK: There's a talk of settlement. I see they're opening
some of the pits. But I've done, you know.

NURSE: Of course you have—Mr Hemstock. Harry will be glad to
begin, though.

MR HEMSTOCK: I'm afraid whether 'e'll get a job. You see—

MRS HEMSTOCK: What hast got for dinner?

MR HEMSTOCK: Roast pork, rushes, barm-dumplings—

MRS HEMSTOCK: Then look slippy about gettin' it ready. I'm
clammin'. Ma'e thy heels crack—

MR HEMSTOCK *(to NURSE)*: You wouldn't think she'd been bedfast
thirteen month, would you?

MRS HEMSTOCK: Tha nedna ha'e none o' thy palaver wi' Nurse.
Nurse, ta'e no notice o' a word 'e says. *(HEMSTOCK goes out.)*

MRS HEMSTOCK: He's a good cook, and that's all you can say for
him.

NURSE: I think he's very good to you, Mrs Hemstock.

MRS HEMSTOCK: He's too busy runnin' after a parcel o' women to be good to me.

NURSE: If all men were as good—

MRS HEMSTOCK: Tha's niver had him to put up wi'. Tha's niver been married, 'as ter?

NURSE: No, Mrs Hemstock.

MRS HEMSTOCK: A man's fair enough to your face—if 'e's not as fow as a jackass; but let your back be turned, an' you no more know what's in his breeches an' waistcoat than if 'e wor another man.

NURSE: Oh Mrs Hemstock!

MRS HEMSTOCK: Yes, an' tha'll 'Oh' when tha knows.

NURSE: I'm sure you're getting tired. Won't you have your bed made.

MRS HEMSTOCK: Sin' it's gone that long, it might easy go a bit longer.

NURSE: Why, when was it made last?

MRS HEMSTOCK: How long has thee been gone away?

NURSE: Three weeks.

MRS HEMSTOCK: Then it's that long.

NURSE: Oh, what a shame! Wouldn't Mrs Smalley do it?

MRS HEMSTOCK: Our Susy! 'Er'd better not show 'er face inside that door.

NURSE: What a pity she's so quarrelsome! But you will have it made—?

MRS HEMSTOCK: I know tha'll whittle me to death if I dunna.— Does thaïgh like roast pork?

NURSE: Fairly.—Now, shall I lift you onto the couch?

MRS HEMSTOCK: No, tha wunna. I non want droppin' an' smashin' like a pot. I'm nowt but noggins o' bone, like iron bars in a paper bag. Eh, if I wor but the staunch fourteen stone* I used to be.

NURSE: You've been a big woman.

MRS HEMSTOCK: I could ha' shadowed thee an' left plenty to spare. How heavy are ter, Nurse?

NURSE: I don't know—about ten and a half stones. Will Mr Hemstock lift you, then?

MRS HEMSTOCK: I say, Nurse—just look under th' bed, atween th' bed-latts at th' bottom corner, an' see if tha can see th' will.

NURSE *(doubtful)*: What!— *(She stoops, dubious.)*

MRS HEMSTOCK: Right hand corner. I told the doctor to put it there. Canna ter see it.

NURSE: Oh yes, here it is. *(She reappears with an envelope.)*

5 MRS HEMSTOCK: That's it—it's fastened safe. It's a new will, Nurse. I made 'em do it while tha wor away—doctor and Mr Leaky.*

NURSE: Oh yes—?

MRS HEMSTOCK: An' I'm not goin' ter ha'e none on 'em gleggin' at it. I know our Susy often has a bit of a rummage, but I'm

10 sharper than 'er thinks for.

NURSE: And what shall I do with it, Mrs Hemstock.

MRS HEMSTOCK: Why, get up on th' table, an' look if there isna a hole in top o' th' bedpost, at th' head here, where a peg used ter fit in.

15 NURSE *(climbing up)*: Yes, there is.

MRS HEMSTOCK: Then roll it up, an' shove it in. On'y leave a scroddy bit out.

NURSE: That's done it, then.

MRS HEMSTOCK: Tha'll know where it is, then. Tha ought, tha's

20 been more to me than any of my own for these twelve month.

NURSE: Oh Mrs Hemstock, I hope—

MRS HEMSTOCK: Nay, tha nedna—tha'rt knowin' nowt, I tell thee.—How much dost reckon I've got, Nurse.

NURSE: I don't know, Mrs Hemstock.

25 MRS HEMSTOCK: Over five hundred, I can tell thee. I made 'em in a little shop as I had in Northrop* when the collieries hadna started long—an' I did well—an' so did our Mester—an' so 'as th' lads done—

NURSE: It is a good thing, for now they're both out of work they'd

30 have nothing.

MRS HEMSTOCK: Oh, our Harry's got a bit of his own, an' our Mester's got about a hundred. It'll keep 'em goin' for a bit, wi'out mine.

NURSE: You *are* queer, Mrs Hemstock.

35 MRS HEMSTOCK: Ha, that's what they say about th' Almighty— they canna ma'e Him out. But I'll warrant He knows His own business, as I do.

NURSE: Oh Mrs Hemstock.

MRS HEMSTOCK: Yes, an' I want my bed makin', dunna I.—Shout

40 our Harry—Harry!—Harry!

(After a moment, HARRY *enters: a man of moderate stature, rather strongly built: dark hair, heavy dark moustache, pale, rather hollow cheeks, dangerous-looking brown eyes. A certain furious shrinking from contact makes him seem young, in spite of a hangdog, heavy slouch.)*

HARRY *(to his mother—in broad dialect)*: What's want?   5

MRS HEMSTOCK: I s'd think it is 'what's want', an' I hanna set eyes
    on thee for pretty nigh a week. Tha'll happen come to lie
    thyself, my lad, an' then tha can think o' me hours an' hours by
    mysen.

HARRY: What's want—?   10

MRS HEMSTOCK: An' what art paddlin' about in thy stockin' feet
    for? Tha 'asna gumption enough ter put thy slippers on, if ter's
    been i' th' garden. Nurse, gi'e me a drop o' brandy. *(She lies
    back exhausted.* NURSE *administers.)*

NURSE: Your mother wants lifting onto the couch, Mr Hemstock.   15
    (He comes forward.) —Perhaps you will wash your hands in this
    water, will you— *(He obeys sullenly.)*

MRS HEMSTOCK: Tha'd better wesh 'em for 'im, Nurse. 'E's nowt
    but a baby.—'As 'er catched thee yet. *(He does not answer.)* —'E
    dursna go round th' corner, Nurse, for fear of a bogey—Durst   20
    ter, eh?—'E's scared to death of a wench, so 'e goes about wi' a
    goose.

(A goose comes paddling into the room, and wanders up to HARRY.*)*

NURSE: Hullo, Patty! You dear old silly.

MRS HEMSTOCK: Dost like 'er, Nurse?   25

NURSE: She's a dear old thing—

MRS HEMSTOCK: Then tha'll like *him.* He's just the same: soft,
    canna say a word, thinks a mighty lot of himself, an's scared to
    death o' nowt.

NURSE: Oh, Mrs Hemstock!   30

MRS HEMSTOCK: I canna abide a sawney.

NURSE: Are you ready, Mr Hemstock?
    (He comes forward. NURSE *wraps* MRS HEMSTOCK *in a quilt.)*

MRS HEMSTOCK: To think as I should be crippled like this!

NURSE: Yes, it is dreadful.   35
    *(*HARRY *lifts his mother—*NURSE *showing him.)*

MRS HEMSTOCK: Tha's got fingers like gre't tree-roots—

*(*NURSE *shows him how to place his hands. Then she lifts the trailing
    quilt, and follows him to the couch.)*

MRS HEMSTOCK *(rather faintly)*: I canna abide to feel a man's arms   40 shiverin' agen me. It ma'es me feel like a tallywag post hummin'.

NURSE: There, be still—you are upset. I'm sure Mr Hemstock did it gently. *(She stoops and strokes Patty, who is crouched near the bed.* 5   HARRY *moves as if to go.)* Will you fetch clean sheets and pillow slips—be quick, will you. *(*HARRY *goes out.* NURSE *begins to make the bed.)*

MRS HEMSTOCK: Isna 'e like that there goose, now.

NURSE: Well, I'm sure Patty's a very lovable creature.

10   MRS HEMSTOCK: I'm glad tha thinks so. It's not many as can find in their heart to love a gaby like that.

NURSE: Poor Patty!

MRS HEMSTOCK: An' that other hussy on'y wants him cause she canna get him.

15   NURSE: It's often the case.

MRS HEMSTOCK: It is wi' a woman who's that cunning at kissin' an' cuddlin' that a man's fair smockravelled, an' 'ud run after 'er a hundred miles for the same again.

NURSE: Is she clever, then?

20   MRS HEMSTOCK: She melts herself into a man like butter in a hot tater. She ma'es him feel like a pearl button swimmin' away in hot vinegar.—That's what I made out from 'im.

NURSE: She's not a nice girl.

MRS HEMSTOCK: An' 'e hated her cause I shoved him at her.

25   NURSE: But you don't care for her, surely.

MRS HEMSTOCK: Canna abear her. A pussy cat always rubbin' 'erself agen a man's legs—an' one o' the quiet sort.—But for all that, I should like to see him married afore I go. I dunna like, Nurse, leavin' 'im like 'e is. 'E wor my darlin'.

30   NURSE *(softly)*: Yes.

MRS HEMSTOCK: An' 'e niver wor a drunkard, but 'e's the makin's of one.

NURSE: Surely not—oh, how dreadful!

(Enter HARRY *with bedding. He helps* NURSE *shake up and make the* 35   *bed.)*

How sweet the sheets are. They were dried on the currant bushes. Did Mrs Smalley wash them?

MRS HEMSTOCK: Our Susy!—not likely. She'd never do a hand's turn. I expect our Harry there weshed 'em—an' 'is father.— 40   Dunna look so 'ormin, canna ter answer a bit of a question.

(He does not answer.)

He looks as if 'e'd swallowed a year o' foul weather.

NURSE: Hem at the top. *(She stumbles over Patty.)* Oh poor Patty —poor old bird! Come here then, you dear old thing—did I hurt you? 5

MRS HEMSTOCK: Tha's more fondness for that goose than I han, Nurse. It's too much like him. Birds of a feather flock together.

NURSE: You include me.

MRS HEMSTOCK: If tha like.

NURSE: It's not a compliment. 10

MRS HEMSTOCK: It isna. Tha'rt a lady, an' has a lady's time, an' tha'rt a fool if tha changes.

NURSE: I am not so sure—.

MRS HEMSTOCK: Tha gets a good wage,—an' th' minute tha enters a house everybody gets up to run about after thee—what more 15 dost want?

NURSE: I don't know?

MRS HEMSTOCK: No, I s'd think tha doesna.

NURSE: Sometimes I get tired, and then—I wish—I wish* I'd somebody to fad after me a bit. I nurse so many people, and—. 20

MRS HEMSTOCK: Tha'd like nursin' thysen. Eh bless you, a man's knee's a chair as is soon worn out.

NURSE: It's not that—I should like a home of my own, where I could be private. There's a lonely corner in most of us that not all the *friends* in the world can fill up— 25

MRS HEMSTOCK: And a husband only changes a lonely corner into a lonely house.

NURSE: Perhaps so.—But I should like to be able to shut my own doors, and shut all the world out, and be at home, quiet, comfortable. 30

MRS HEMSTOCK: You'd find you shut the door to stop folks hearing you crying.

NURSE *(bending down and stroking Patty)*: Perhaps so.

MRS HEMSTOCK: Tha art fond o' that bird.

NURSE *(flushing)*: I am. 35

MRS HEMSTOCK: If I wor thee, our Harry, I wouldna let Patty beat me, even.

HARRY: What dost mean?

MRS HEMSTOCK: Stroke him, Nurse—and say 'Poor old Harry.'

NURSE: Mr Hemstock will have a grudge against me if you slate him
so in my presence.

MRS HEMSTOCK: And would it grieve thee?

NURSE: I should be sorry.

5 MRS HEMSTOCK *(after a pause—vehemently)*: —Ha, if he worn't
such a slow fool!—Can thee lift me back, Nurse?

NURSE: Won't you let Mr Hemstock—?

MRS HEMSTOCK: No—thee do it. *(Exit HARRY.)* Did ter niver ha'e
a sweetheart, Nurse?

10 NURSE: Yes—when I was in hospital. He was a doctor—

MRS HEMSTOCK: An' where is he—?

NURSE: He was too good for me, his mother said, and so—.

MRS HEMSTOCK: Tha'rt well rid o' such a draggle-tail.—How long
is it since?

15 NURSE: Eight years.

MRS HEMSTOCK: Oh,—so tha'rt none heart-brokken.—We'n got a
new assistant. I like him better than th' owd doctor.—His
name's Foules.☆

NURSE: What!

20   *(Curtain)*

Act I.

Scene 2.

Time, the same.
Scene: The kitchen of Hemstock's house—A large low, old fashioned
room. Fowls are pecking on the floor. HARRY, *in a coarse apron, is* 5
washing the floor. MR HEMSTOCK, *at the table, is mixing flour in a bowl.*

MR HEMSTOCK: Who wor that scraïghtin' a bit sin'?
HARRY: Our Susy's kid.
MR HEMSTOCK: What for?
HARRY: I fetched him a wipe across th' mouth. 10
MR HEMSTOCK: There's more bother then—
HARRY: He was settin' that dog on th' fowls again.
MR HEMSTOCK: We s'll be having her round in a tear, directly, then.
HARRY: Well, I'm not— —
(There is a knock: and in the open doorway at the back a little, old, 15
withered clergyman is seen.)
THE BARON: How is the sick woman this morning?
(He speaks with a very foreign—German—accent.)
MR HEMSTOCK: I think she's middlin', thank you.
THE BARON: I will go and see her, and speak to her. 20
HARRY: We've told you a dozen times 'er non wants you.
THE BARON: It is my duty that I shall go—
HARRY *(rising from his knees)*: Tha arena—!
THE BARON: I am the vicar of this parish, I am the Baron von
Ruge,* I will do my duty— 25
HARRY *(confronting him)*: Tha'rt non goin' to bother her. Her non
wants thee.
THE BARON: Stand clear of my way, Sir—I *will* go, I will not be
barred, I will tell her, I will remind her—
HARRY *(frustrating his efforts)*: 'Er non wants thee— *(He suddenly* 30
moves: THE BARON *rushes into Patty. The goose flaps and squarks*
and attacks him. THE BARON *retreats hastily. Enter* NURSE.*)*
NURSE: Whatever is the matter?
MR HEMSTOCK: It's Patty hollin' the Baron out—
NURSE: Oh dear—how dreadful! 35
MR HEMSTOCK: 'E's bin plenty of times, an' every time our Harry
tells 'im as Missis won't be bothered wi' him—
NURSE: What a pity she won't see him. Don't you think if you let
him go— —

HARRY: Ax 'er thysen if 'er wants 'im—An' if 'er doesna want 'im, 'e's non goin'—.

NURSE: But what a pity—!

MR HEMSTOCK: You can't make heads or tails of what 'e says. I can't think what they want wi' a bit of a German Baron bein' a vicar in England—in *this* country, an' a', where there wants a bluff man.

NURSE: He's a Polish nobleman, Mr Hemstock, exiled after fighting for his country. He's a brave man, and a good gentleman. I like him very much.

MR HEMSTOCK: He treats you as if you was dirt, an' talks like a chokin' cock—

HARRY: An' 'e's non goin' pesterin' 'er when 'er doesna want 'im.

NURSE: Well of course you know best—but don't you think Mrs Hemstock ought to see a minister. I think— —

THE BAKER *(a big, stout, pale man about forty: dark moustache)*: Been havin' a shindy with the Baron?

MR HEMSTOCK: He wants to see the Missis, an' we not let him.

THE BAKER: You'd best keep th' right side of 'im. *(He swings his large basket, which he carries sack-wise on his shoulder, down to a chair.)* The strike's settled, an' th' men's goin' back on the old terms.

NURSE: Oh, I'm so glad.

THE BAKER: Fisher's a deep un. The company'll know yet as they've *got* a manager.

NURSE *(to HARRY)*: So you'll be going back to work soon, Mr Hemstock. You will be glad.

MR HEMSTOCK: Me—Oh, I s'll never work again.—An' it's doubtful as our Harry won't get on—

THE BAKER: They gave you a place before the strike, didn't they, where you had to work your inside out for about fifteen shillings a week?

HARRY: Ha. *(He goes out.)*

MR HEMSTOCK: Yes, they treated him very shably.

THE BAKER: I bet it was th' owd Baron. He's a good hand at having your eye for a word, an' your tooth for a look. I bet Harry'll get no job—.

MR HEMSTOCK: No, I'm afraid 'e wunna. The Baron will go down to Fisher—

THE BAKER: And Harry can go down to—his Godfather, eh Nurse?

NURSE: I don't understand.

THE BAKER: *Old* Harry.*

MR HEMSTOCK: I hope to goodness 'e will get something to do, else 'e'll mope himself into the cut, or the 'sylum, afore long.

THE BAKER: Oh, it's love what's upset him, isn't it? Rachel Wilcox   5
was too much for his stomach—

MR HEMSTOCK: I dunno what it is.

THE BAKER: She's a bit of a ronk un. She was his first cigar, an' it's left him sick yet. She's not half bad, you know, if you can stand 'em strong. (NURSE *goes out.*) —I've scared Nurse off.—But   10
Harry's got a bit of a thin stomach, hasn't he—Rachel's not half a bad little ha'porth.

MR HEMSTOCK: Some's got a stomach for tan-tafflins, an' some 'ud rather ha'e bread an' butter—

THE BAKER: —And Rachel's creamy—she's a cream horn of plenty   15
—eh what!

MR HEMSTOCK: A bit sickly.

THE BAKER: I dunno—it 'ud take a lot o' rich food to turn me— How many—?

MR HEMSTOCK: —One of yesterday's bakin', please.   20
(BAKER *sets the loaf on the table.*)

THE BAKER: Your Susy wasn't in—I wonder what she wants. Where is she, do you know?

MR HEMSTOCK: She'll be somewhere lookin' after th' land.

THE BAKER: I reckon she makes a rare farmer.   25

MR HEMSTOCK: Yes.

THE BAKER: Bill left the place in a bit of a mess—

MR HEMSTOCK: —A man as drinks himself to death—

THE BAKER: Ay—!—She wishes she'd had me astead of him, she says. I tell her it's never too late to mend. He's made the hole,   30
I'll be the patch.—But it's not much of a place, Smalley's farm—?

MR HEMSTOCK: It takes her all her time to manage—an' pay off Bill's debts.

THE BAKER: Debts—why, I thought from what she said—— (Enter   35
SUSY,* *a buxom ruddy bold woman of thirty five, wearing thick boots, and a dark blue milkmaid bonnet.*)

MRS SMALLEY: Wheer's our Harry?

MR HEMSTOCK: I dunno. 'E went out a bit sin'—

MRS SMALLEY: An' wheer is 'e. I'll let him know whether   40 he's—Oh, I've fun thee, have I. *(Enter* HARRY.*)* What dost reckon tha's been doin' to my lad?

HARRY: Tha nedna ha' hunted for me. I wor nobbut i' th' garden—

THE BAKER: —You should ha' looked in th' parsley bed, Susy.

5 MRS SMALLEY: —That's wheer to find *babies*˟—an' I'll baby him. What did ter hit my lad for?

HARRY: Ax thysen.

MRS SMALLEY: I'm axin' thaïgh. Tha thinks because I hanna a man to stand up for me, tha can—

10 HARRY: There's a lot o' helpless widder about thee—!˟

MRS SMALLEY: No, an' it's a good thing I'm not helpless, else I should be trod underfoot like straw, by a parcel of—

HARRY: It's thaïgh as does th' treadin'. Tha's trod your Bill a long way underfoot—six foot or more—

15 THE BAKER: It's a fat sight deeper than that afore you get to Blazes.

MRS SMALLEY: Whatever our Bill was or wasn't, 'e was not a' idle skulk livin' on two old folks, devourin' 'em—

NURSE *(entering)*: Oh, think of your mother, Mrs Smalley.

MRS SMALLEY: I s'll think of who I like—

20 THE BAKER: An' who *do* you like, Susy?

MRS SMALLEY: You keep your 'Susy' to yourself—

THE BAKER: Only too glad, when I get her—

MRS SMALLEY: An' we don't thank Nurse Broadbanks for inter-ferin'. *She* only comes carneyin' round for what she gets. Our

25 Harry an' her's matched;—a pair of mealy-mouthed creeps, deep as they make 'em. An' my father's not much better. What all of 'em's after's my mother's money.

NURSE: Oh, for shame, for shame!

HARRY: Shut thy mouth, or I'll shut it for thee.

30 MRS SMALLEY: Oh shall you. I should like to see you. It's as much as you durst do to hit a childt, you great coward, you kid.

MR HEMSTOCK: Shut it up, now, shut it up!

MRS SMALLEY: But I'll let him know, if he touches my child again; I'll give him what for. I'll thrash him myself—

35 THE BAKER: That's your brother, not your husband.

MRS SMALLEY: I will an' a'—Him an' his blessed fowls!—'E's nobbut a chuck himself, as dursn't say boh to a goose, an' as hides in th' water-butt if his girl comes to see him—

HARRY: I'll— *(He dashes forward as if to strike her.* THE BAKER

40 *interposes.)*

THE BAKER: Here, none o' that, none o' that!

MRS SMALLEY: A great coward! He thinks he'll show Nurse Broadbanks what he is, does he. I hope she'll slorm round him after
this bit.

HARRY *(in a fury)*: If tha doesn't—   5

MR HEMSTOCK: Let's have no more of it, let's have no more of it—!

THE BAKER: How much bread, Mrs Smalley?—I reckon your Bill
bettered himself when he flitted—what?—I *don't* think.—How
many loaves? I saved you a crusty one.

MR HEMSTOCK: She's crust enough on her—   10

THE BAKER: Oh, I like 'em a bit brown. Good morning, everybody.
       (He swings up his basket and follows MRS SMALLEY.)

NURSE: How shameful to make a disturbance like that!

MR HEMSTOCK: We never have a bit of peace. She won't do a
hand's turn in the house, and seems as if she can't bear herself   15
because we manage without her.

HARRY: She's after th' money.

NURSE: How dreadful! You are a strange family.

*(She goes into the parlour again, and keeps coming in and out with water
ewer and so on. MR HEMSTOCK flourishes his balls of dough. HARRY puts* 20
                       on the saucepan.)

MR HEMSTOCK: Dost think Job Arthur will marry our Susy?

HARRY: No.

MR HEMSTOCK: He seems to hang round her a good bit. Your
mother often says he lets his bread get stale stoppin' there.   25

HARRY: If 'e marries 'er, 'e'll settle her.

MR HEMSTOCK: Yes—he's all there.

HARRY: All but what he's short to pay his debts.
                       (He goes out.)

NURSE: I think I've done everything, Mr Hemstock.   30
                (She begins packing her black bag.)

MR HEMSTOCK: Could you wait half a minute while I go—to
Goddards.

NURSE: —Well—ten minutes.

(The old man takes a jar from the cupboard, and puts on his hat. At the 35
*door he meets the DOCTOR, a clean-shaven fair man rather full at the
                stomach and low at the chest.)*

DR FOULES: Good morning, Mr Hemstock—you are going out?

MR HEMSTOCK: For a second, doctor. Just to the shop—

DR FOULES: I see. Then shall I go in?   40

MR HEMSTOCK: Oh yes, doctor.

DR FOULES: Thank you. *(He enters.* NURSE *is just putting on her bonnet. The* DOCTOR *stands confused.)*

NURSE *(low and purring)*: Good-morning.

5   DR FOULES: Nurse Broadbanks—!

NURSE *(low)*: Yes—just fancy.

DR FOULES: Well, I *am* surprised. Who ever— —

NURSE: —I knew it was you. No other doctor would have been so polite about entering the house.

10   DR FOULES: Well—I can hardly find words—I am sure—

NURSE: Fancy your keeping your old shyness.

DR FOULES *(flushing)*: I don't know that I do—.

NURSE: I should have thought it would have worn off—all the experience you have had.

15   DR FOULES: Have I had so much experience?

NURSE: Eight years.

DR FOULES: Ah Nurse, we don't measure experience by years.

NURSE: Surely, you have a quotation!

DR FOULES *(smiling)*: No, I have not—for a wonder. Indeed I'm

20   growing out of touch with literature.

NURSE: I shall not know you. You used to be— —

DR FOULES: Vox, et praeterea nihil—'a voice, and nothing more.'☆

NURSE: You are yourself. But you have not had much experience, in eight years?

25   DR FOULES: Not much has happened to me.

NURSE: And you a doctor!

DR FOULES: And I a doctor!

NURSE: But you have lost your old aesthetic look—wistful, I nearly said.

30   DR FOULES: Damnosa quid non imminuit dies? 'Whom has not pernicious time impaired.'☆

NURSE: Not your stock of learning, evidently.

DR FOULES *(bowing)*: Nor your wit, Nurse. Suum Cuique.☆—You have not—?

35   NURSE: What?

DR FOULES: —You have not—married?

NURSE: Nurse *Broadbanks.*

DR FOULES: Of course—Ha Ha—how slow of me. Verbum sat sapienti.☆

40   NURSE: And you—?

DR FOULES *(bowing)*: What, Nurse—?

NURSE: Married?

DR FOULES: No, Nurse, I am not. Nor, if it is anything to your satisfaction, likely to be.

NURSE: Your *mother* is still alive? 5

DR FOULES *(bowing)*: Rem acu tetigisti.—'You have pricked the point with your needle.'*

NURSE: I beg your pardon.

DR FOULES: Do not, I beg. Do not.

NURSE: Semper idem*—I know so much Latin. 10

DR FOULES: In what am I always the same, Nurse?

NURSE: Well—your politeness.

DR FOULES: Suaviter in modo, fortiter in re.—My old motto, you remember.

NURSE: I do not know the English for it. 15

DR FOULES: 'Gentle in manner, resolute in deed.'

NURSE: In what deed, may I ask, Doctor?

DR FOULES: You may ask, Nurse—I am afraid I cannot tell you. And I, may I ask what *you* have done?

NURSE: Worked enough to be rather tired, Doctor—and found the 20 world full of friends.

DR FOULES: Non multa, sed multum. 'Not many things, but much,' Nurse. *I* could not say so much.

NURSE *(laughing)*: No?

DR FOULES: Quid rides?* 'Wherefore do you laugh?' 25

NURSE: She lives with you here?

DR FOULES: My mother?—yes.

NURSE: It will always be said of you 'He was a good son.'

DR FOULES: I hope so, Nurse.

NURSE: Yes—it is the best. 30

DR FOULES *(softly)*: You look sad.

NURSE: Not on my own behalf, Doctor.

DR FOULES: On mine, Nurse?

NURSE *(reluctantly)*: No, not quite that.

DR FOULES: Taedium vitae—all unresolved emotions and sicknesses 35 go under that 'Weariness of Life.'

NURSE: *Life*, Doctor—do we get enough *life* to be weary of it?— Work, perhaps.

DR FOULES: It may be—but—

NURSE: You don't *want* life. 40

DR FOULES *(smiling)*: Not much: I *see* too much of it to want it.

NURSE: Your mother will, I hope, live long enough to save you from experiences.

DR FOULES: I hope it is a good wish, Nurse.

5 NURSE: Do you doubt it!

DR FOULES: Will you come and see us Nurse?

NURSE: And see your mother?

DR FOULES: —And see my mother, Nurse. *(He bows.)*

NURSE *(smiling)*: Thank you—I will.

10 *(Enter* HARRY—*he stands rather confused in the doorway.)*

DR FOULES: Goodmorning, Mr Hemstock. How is Mrs Hemstock this morning?

HARRY: 'Er's pretty middlin', I believe.

(Enter MR HEMSTOCK.*)*

15 DR FOULES: I have just discovered that Nurse and I are old friends.

MR HEMSTOCK: I'm glad of that—

DR FOULES: Thank you.

NURSE: Dr Foules used to be my sweetheart.

20 MR HEMSTOCK: You don't mean it—!

DR FOULES: Is it so long ago, Nurse, that you jest about it.

NURSE: I do not jest, Doctor. You are always to be taken very seriously.

DR FOULES *(bowing)*: Thank you.

25 NURSE *(to* HARRY*)*: Where did I leave my goloshes, Mr Hemstock?

HARRY: I'll fetch 'em. *(He brings them in.)*

NURSE: How good of you to clean them for me.

(They stand watching while NURSE *pulls them on.)*

DR FOULES: 'A world full of friends,' Nurse.

30 NURSE: Mr Hemstock and I are very good friends—are we not, Mr Hemstock?

HARRY: I didna know—you know best—'appen we are.

DR FOULES: You are repudiated, Nurse.

NURSE: Twice! You shouldn't have begun it.

35 DR FOULES: I'm very sorry. It is never too late to mend.

NURSE: We've heard that before this morning.—I must go.

DR FOULES: You will come and see us—soon.

NURSE: I am at your disposal, Doctor.—Good-day everybody.

[Exit NURSE.*]*

40 ALL: Goodday, Nurse.

DR FOULES: Well, I will see how Mrs Hemstock is.
(He goes out.)
MR HEMSTOCK: He's a nice fellow.
HARRY: Hm!
MR HEMSTOCK: Fancy he used ter court Nurse!* I shouldna be 5
surprised if they got together again.
HARRY: It doesna matter to me whether 'er does or not.
MR HEMSTOCK: No, it non matters to us—on'y I should like to see
her settled wi' a decent chap. She's a good woman for any man.
If I'd a been thy age— 10
HARRY: —Wi' that other hangin' round,—an' no work to do—tha'd
ha' done wonders.
MR HEMSTOCK: T'other—tha's gen 'er the sack—an' tha can get
work elsewhere.
HARRY: Dost think 'er'd ha'e *me*! *(He laughs contemptuously.)* 'Er 15
wouldna.
MR HEMSTOCK: Tha niver knows. Tha should get a drop o' drink
in thee, an' be lively—.
(There is a noise of yelping and crying—The men stand and listen.)
It's that dog!—An' Nurse. 20
(HARRY rushes out. There is a great yelping and ki-yi-ing, a scream from
NURSE. *Immediately* NURSE *enters, carrying Patty, who flaps in a torn*
and gory state. HARRY *follows.* NURSE, *panting sets down Patty.)*
Whatever—
HARRY *(flashing, in fury)*: Has it hurt thee—did it touch thee? 25
NURSE: Me!
HARRY: I'll break its neck.
NURSE: Oh,—don't be—
HARRY: Where did it touch thee?—there's blood on thee.
NURSE: It's not me, it's Patty. 30
HARRY: 'Appen tha non knows—'appen it catched thee. Look at thy
arm—look there!
NURSE: No—I'm not hurt, I'm sure I'm not.
HARRY: I'll break its neck, the brute.
NURSE: It had got hold of poor Patty by the wing—Poor old bird. 35
HARRY: Look at thy cuffs.—I'll break its neck.
NURSE: No—oh no, don't go out—no—get me some warm water,
will you—and I'll see to Patty.
(HARRY brings a bowl of warm water, NURSE *takes bandaging from*
her bag.) 40

MR HEMSTOCK: It's been at her before—

NURSE *(to* HARRY*)*: You look after her other wing—keep her still —poor old bird— *(She proceeds to dress the wounded wing.)*

MR HEMSTOCK: She'd be all right, Nurse, without you bothering.

5   NURSE: The idea—poor old thing!

MR HEMSTOCK: We've been many a time worse hurt at pit, an' not half that attention.

NURSE: —But—you see, you're not geese.

HARRY: We're not of as much count.

10 NURSE: Hand me the scissors, please—you don't know what you are—

*(*DR FOULES *enters and stands in doorway.)*

MR HEMSTOCK: I keep telling him, if he set more stock by himself other folks 'ud think better of him.

15 NURSE: They might *know* him a little better if he'd let them.

DR FOULES: I see my help is superfluous.

NURSE: —Yes Doctor—it's one of the lower animals.

DR FOULES: Ah—

(Curtain)

Act II.

Scene 1.

Scene: The Hemstocks' kitchen; the lamp lighted.
Time: The same evening.
The BAKER *and* HARRY *sit with glasses of whisky.*

THE BAKER: An' tha doesn't want 'er?

HARRY: I heave at the sight of her.

THE BAKER: She'll ha'e a bit o' money, I reckon.

HARRY: She's got to wait till old Hezekiah cops out, first.

THE BAKER: Hm! That'll be a long time yet—if he doesn't get married again. They say he's hankerin' after Nurse.

HARRY: 'Er'll niver ha'e 'im.

THE BAKER: Too old.—But what hast got against Rachel?

HARRY: Nowt—but I heave wi' sickness at the thought of 'er.

THE BAKER: Hm! I like one as'll give as much as she takes.

HARRY: A sight more.

THE BAKER: It depends who's who.

HARRY: I can never make out why she went in service at the vicarage.

THE BAKER: Can't you?—I've had many a nice evening up there. Baron an' Baroness go to bed at nine o'clock and then—. Oh, all the girls know the advantage of being at the vicarage.

HARRY: Oh—an' does she ha'e thee up in th' kitchen?

THE BAKER: Does she not 'alf.

HARRY: I thought she wor so much struck on me—!

THE BAKER: You wait a minute. If she can't feed i' th' paddock she'll feed at th' roadside. Not but what she's all right, you know.

HARRY: I do know.

THE BAKER: She's not got the spirit of your Susy.—By Jove, *she*'s a terror. No liberties there.

HARRY: Not likely.

THE BAKER: They say Bill left 'er in debt.

HARRY: He did.

THE BAKER: Hm! She'll have a long pull, then, to get it paid off.

HARRY: She's waitin' for my mother's money.

THE BAKER: Is she likely to get much?

HARRY: Happen a couple o' hundred—happen nowt.

THE BAKER: Depends on the will?

HARRY: Yes.

THE BAKER: A couple of hundred.

HARRY: About that apiece, we should ha'e.

THE BAKER: Hm!—You've seen the will?

5 HARRY: No—my mother takes good care o' that.

THE BAKER: Then none of you know?—But you've some idea.

HARRY: We hanna. My mother's funny: there's no tellin' what 'er might do.

THE BAKER: Hm! She might leave the money away from her own

10 children?

HARRY: I shouldna be a bit surprised.

THE BAKER: Hm!—An' your Susy—

MRS SMALLEY *(entering)*: What about your Susy—?

THE BAKER: Hello!

15 MRS SMALLEY: You're stoppin' a precious long time. Where might you be bound tonight?

THE BAKER: Not far.

MRS SMALLEY: No further than th' Vicarage, an' that's two closes off.—But Rachel'll be givin' you up.

20 THE BAKER: 'Appen so.

MRS SMALLEY: Then she'll be tryin' her chances down here— —

THE BAKER: I wish her luck.

HARRY *(going out)*: I'll go an' get a bit o' bacca.

MRS SMALLEY: An' what do you call luck?

25 THE BAKER: What do you reckon is a lucky-bag, me or your Harry?

MRS SMALLEY: You're both about as good: he's only got a little bunged-up whistle, in him, an' many a hand's ferrited in you an' fetched out what's worth havin'.

THE BAKER: So I'm not worth havin'?

30 MRS SMALLEY: No, you're not, that's flat.

THE BAKER: So you wouldn't have me—?

MRS SMALLEY: You're giving yourself away, are you?

THE BAKER *(incisively)*: No, I'm not.

MRS SMALLEY: Indeed. And what's your figure, may I ask?

35 THE BAKER: A couple of hundred, to *you*. To anyone else, *more*.

MRS SMALLEY: Thank you for the offer—very kind of you, I'm sure—. And how much is it to Rachel?

THE BAKER: Two hundred an' fifty.

MRS SMALLEY: Oh! So I'm worth fifty pound to you, am I—*after*

40 I've put my two hundred down.—Ready money?

THE BAKER: Six months bill.

MRS SMALLEY: You *are* a swine.

THE BAKER: Do you accept!

MRS SMALLEY: You *are* a *pig*! You'd eat cinders if you could get
nowt else.

THE BAKER: I should.—I'd rather have you than any of the boiling;
but I must, I must, have—

MRS SMALLEY: Two hundred?

THE BAKER: Not less.

MRS SMALLEY: Six months bill.

THE BAKER: Six months bill.

MRS SMALLEY: I hope you'll get it.

THE BAKER: I intend to.

MRS SMALLEY *(after a speechless moment)*: You are a devil when
you've had a drop.

THE BAKER: Am I a dear one—?

MRS SMALLEY: Do you call yourself cheap?

THE BAKER: What do *you* think. I was always one of the 'take it or
leave it' sellers.

MRS SMALLEY: I think you imagine yourself worth a great sight
more than you are—?

THE BAKER: Hm!—I should have thought you'd have found the
figure easy.—And I've always said I'd rather it was you than
anybody.

MRS SMALLEY: You was mighty slow, then, once on a day.

THE BAKER: I was a young cock-sparrow then—common—but
would die in a cage.

MRS SMALLEY: An' what do you reckon you are now—?

THE BAKER: I'm an old duck that knows "Dilly-Dilly!"

MRS SMALLEY: —'Come and be killed.'*

THE BAKER: Scatter me a bit of golden corn—two hundred—and
you may wring my neck.

MRS SMALLEY: You must—have an empty crop.

THE BAKER: A few pebbles that'll digest *me* if I don't—

MRS SMALLEY: Debts?

THE BAKER: I said pebbles.

MRS SMALLEY: You're a positive fiend in drink.

THE BAKER: But what about— — —?

RACHEL *(a tall, pale girl, dark circles under her eyes. She has a consumed look as if her quiet pallor smothered a fire. She wears a*

servant's cap and apron, covered by a large dark shawl. She enters softly): I thought I heard you two.

MRS SMALLEY *(startled)*: You *might* knock!

RACHEL: Were you talking secrets?

5   THE BAKER: Have you come to look for me, Rachel?

RACHEL *(cuttingly)*: You think a mighty lot of yourself.

THE BAKER: Have a drop of Scotch?—No?—how's that? There's Harry's glass—drink out of that.

RACHEL: You're very clever at giving away what's not your own.

10   Give me yours.

THE BAKER: I've not finished with it—but you can drink with me.—Here!

RACHEL: No thank you.

THE BAKER *(softly—smiling)*: Why, what has offended you?

15   RACHEL: Nothing, indeed.

THE BAKER: That's all right. I don't like you to be offended.—As a sign of good luck. *(She sips.)* —Thanks.—I'm sorry I'm late.

RACHEL: You're not there yet, so you can't be late.

THE BAKER: Yea—I *am* there. What farther have I to go?

20   RACHEL *(singing)*:

> 'You've got a long way to go
> You've got a long way to go'

MRS SMALLEY *(singing in a masculine voice)*:

> 'Before you get hold of the donkey's tether
25 > You've got a long way to go.'

THE BAKER *(singing in a fine bass)*:

> 'If I had an ass and he wouldn't go,
> Would I wallop him?—Oh dear no!
> I'd give him some corn and say "Gee whoa
30 > Neddy, stand still while I mount, Oh Ho."'

MRS SMALLEY: *He*'s the donkey.

THE BAKER: Who doesn't make an ass of himself some time.

MRS SMALLEY: And *we've* got to give him some corn—

THE BAKER: For you'll never catch him to get hold of his tail—salt's

35   no good.

MRS SMALLEY: How much corn?—Tell her.

THE BAKER: Two hundred—and fifty—golden grains—no more.

RACHEL: What up with him tonight?

MRS SMALLEY: Oh, he's had a drop, an' it always sets him on edge. He's like a razor. When he's sober he lies flat, an' you can stroke him as smooth as silk. But when he's had a drop, if you stroke him you cut yourself a-two.

RACHEL: Goodness.

THE BAKER: Rachel, I'd sell my immortal soul for two hundred—and fifty—golden sovereigns.

RACHEL: I'm not buying immortal souls, thanks.

THE BAKER: With this *(He spreads out his hands.)* —this paper and string to wrap it in.

RACHEL: —An' a nice parcel of goods you are—.

THE BAKER: I'm a lucky bag, Rachel. You don't know all that's in me, yet—

RACHEL: And what is that—, pray—?

THE BAKER: I don't know myself. But you shall have leave to rummage me *(He throws open his arms.)* —Look! *(He rises from his chair, as it were, superbly. He is a fine, portly, not unhandsome man. He strikes a 'superb' attitude.)* Look Rachel. For two hundred and fifty pounds, three months bill, I am *(He bows.)* your slave. You shall *(He speaks with cynical sincerity.)* —bring down my head as low as you like. *(He bows low.)* I swear it, and I never swore a lie.

RACHEL: But what do you want £250 for?

THE BAKER: Not yet, Rachel, not yet!

HARRY *(entering)*: Has Nurse come?

THE BAKER: Not yet. Are you going to finish your glass? It has taken me all my time to stop the women sipping from it.

RACHEL: Story! You know I wouldn't—

THE BAKER: Hush! Don't be rash *now*, or you'll hate me tomorrow.

RACHEL: And should you care?

THE BAKER: I am willing to give you full rights over my immortal soul and this paper and string—

MRS SMALLEY: For two hundred down—

THE BAKER *(bowing to her—then looking to RACHEL)*: —And fifty, Mrs Smalley.

RACHEL: What do you think of it, Susy? Is it a bargain?

THE BAKER *(setting his cap on the back of his head and pulling on a large overcoat—he is well dressed)*: We have not struck hands yet.

MRS SMALLEY *(to RACHEL)*: What do *you* say.

RACHEL: Nay, I want to hear what *you* say.

MRS SMALLEY: I'm goin' to say nowt, yet awhile—

RACHEL: Well, we'll see— *(She pulls her shawl over her head to follow him.)*

5   THE BAKER: Nay—I'm going down Northrop—on business—

RACHEL: Wasn't you coming up—?

THE BAKER: To the vicarage?—I had this to tell you, that is all.

RACHEL: Well, I must say—but come up just for—

THE BAKER: Not for a moment, Rachel. I am going down Northrop.

10   MRS SMALLEY: It's no good your saying nothing, Rachel. You might as well save your breath.

THE BAKER *(smiling to RACHEL)*: You hear?—I'll see you in the morning. Goodnight all. *(Exit.)*

RACHEL *(looking after him)*: I hate him.

15   MRS SMALLEY: I'm going home. *(She hurries out.)*

(There is an awkward pause. HARRY *sits bending over the fire.)*

RACHEL: How is your mother?

HARRY: Same.

RACHEL: Who's with her?

20   HARRY: Dad.

RACHEL: Where's Patty?

HARRY: Cupboard.

RACHEL: When do you expect Nurse?

HARRY: Dunno.

25   RACHEL: Have you been drinking whisky? *(No answer.)* My word, we s'll have to chalk it up.—Are you going to leave these glasses for Nurse to see? *(No answer.)* —Are you going to let her see you drinking? *(No answer.)* —Well, I do reckon you might speak to a body. I've not spoke to you for a week—hardly seen
30   you.—I can see you in your garden from the vicarage front bedrooms.—I often watch you.—Do you want your glass?

HARRY: Gie's it here!

RACHEL: You might say thank you.—Job Arthur Bowers wants me to marry him.—And I shouldn't be surprised if I did. *(Tears.)*

35   HARRY: Well, tha nedna scraïght.

RACHEL: No—I mun only cry when I'm by myself. *(Sob)*: I'm sure I'm sobbing half the night *(Tears)*. Do you sleep bad?—You do get up early—I can see your candle at half past three—and— you don't know how it frightens me.

40   HARRY: What's it frighten thee for?

RACHEL: I don't know. I feel frightened for you. You seem so funny
    nowadays—

HARRY: 'As ter on'y just fun it out?

RACHEL: You know I've told you about it many a time.

HARRY: A sight too often.   5

RACHEL: You *are* horrid.—What have I done, tell me.

HARRY: I'm non goin' to be made shift of. Tha'rt non goin' ter ma'e
    a spittoon of me, ter spit the taste of somebody else out of thy
    mouth into.☆

RACHEL: Well, if I've been hateful, you've drove me to it—haven't   10
    you?

HARRY: I've told thee, I dunna want thee.

RACHEL: An' I went into service, so's I'd have something to do—an'
    so's I should be near—when—

HARRY: Go on—'an' so's—an' so's—an' so's'—I'm thy spittoon,   15
    tha can spit owt inter me.

RACHEL: You're right, you're full o' sawdust.

HARRY *(showing his teeth)*: What—?

RACHEL: Sawdust, like a dummy—you've no more life in you—

HARRY *(in a passion)*: What—what?   20

RACHEL: —Sawdust.

HARRY *(springing and seizing her by the shoulders)*: I'll settle thee—

RACHEL: You've been drinking.

HARRY *(shouting)*: I'll settle thee, if I hang for it—

RACHEL: You're hurting me!   25

HARRY *(quietly)*: Come here! *(He binds her in her large shawl.)*

RACHEL: Oh, what are you doing?

HARRY: I'll ha'e thee now, I will. *(He seats her in the big arm chair,*
    strapping her with a leathern belt he takes from his waist.)

RACHEL *(quietly)*: Have you gone mad?   30

HARRY: Now then—answer me.—Did ter court Bill Naylor a' th'
    time as thou wert goin' wi' me?

RACHEL: No.

HARRY *(his fist close to her eyes—loudly)*: Trewth!

RACHEL: Yes.   35

HARRY: Did ter tell him I trembled like a leaf if I wor wi' thee in th'
    dark?

RACHEL: Yes.

HARRY: Did ter tell him I used ter shout out that somebody wor
    comin' if thou wanted to kiss me—?   40

RACHEL: Yes.

HARRY: An' as I was allers swallerin' my spittle for fright—?

RACHEL: Yes—

HARRY: An' I wor like a girl, as dursn't look thee a'tween the eyes,
5   for all I was worth—

RACHEL: —Yes.

HARRY: An' dursn't I—?

RACHEL: Yes—an' don't— *(She closes her eyes.)*

HARRY: What!—An' all t'other things about me as the pit was full
10   of—?

RACHEL: Oh no—oh no—!

HARRY: Yes—tha did!

RACHEL: No, Oh no, Harry.

HARRY: An' are ter courtin' Job Arthur Bowers—?

15 RACHEL: Oh—h—

HARRY: Scream, an' I'll squeeze thy head again that chair back till it
         cracks like a nut.

RACHEL *(whimpering)*: Oh dear, Oh dear, Oh dear.

HARRY: It is 'oh dear'—an' it 'as been for me 'oh dear'. Listen 'ere,
20   tha brazend hussy. Tha keeps thy face shut when tha comes
         near me.—Dost hear?

RACHEL: Yes.

HARRY: None o' thy chelp, not another word, in future—or I'll—
         What!!

25 RACHEL: No.

HARRY: An' dunna touch me till tha'rt axed. Not so much as wi' thy
         frock. Dost hear?

RACHEL: Yes.

HARRY: What dost hear?

30 RACHEL: I mustn't touch you.

HARRY: Not till thou'rt axed. An' lu'thee here, my lady—I s'll brain
         thee if tha says a word to me.—Sithee! *(He thrusts his fist in her
         face.)*

RACHEL: Somebody will come—let me go, let me go.

35 HARRY: An' what I've said, I mean—drunk or sober: Sithee?

RACHEL: Yes, Harry! Oh, let me go.

HARRY: I'll let thee go. *(He does so, slowly.)* An' tha can go wi' who
         tha likes, an' marry who tha likes, but if tha says a word about
         me, I'll come for thee. There!

40   *(He unbinds her. She lays her hand on his sleeve.)*

No! *(He shakes her off. She rises and stands dejectedly before him.)*
I hate thee now enough to strangle thee.

RACHEL *(bursting into tears)*: Oh, you are—

HARRY: Now go—wi' who tha likes—get off.

RACHEL: You are—

HARRY: I want none on thee—go! *(She is departing.)* An' ta'e thy
shawl wi' thee. *(She, weeping, picks up her shawl.)*—An' lap it
round thee—it's a raw night. *(She does so. He speaks gently.)*
Now go. *(Exit RACHEL. HARRY pours himself another glass of
whisky. He goes to the cupboard.)* Patty! Pat! *(He takes the sleepy
bird in his arms.)* I've settled her, Pat—or I will do. *(He puts his
face caressingly among the bird's feathers.)* We'll settle her, Pat
—eh? We'll stop her gallop. Hey, Pat—! *(He tosses the bird into
the air,—wildly.)*

(Curtain)

Act II.

Scene 2.

Time: The same.

*Scene: The road just outside the Hemstocks'. Deep darkness: two cottage
lights in the back-ground: in the foreground, a large white swing-gate
leading from the farm-yard into the road. A stile beside the gate.*

MRS SMALLEY *leans against the big white gatepost. Enter* RACHEL,
drying her tears, from the background. She steps through the stile. SUSY
moves.

RACHEL: Oh! Oh! Oh Harry!

MRS SMALLEY: It's only me. Shut up.

RACHEL: Oh, you did give me a turn, Susy!

MRS SMALLEY: Whatever's up—?

RACHEL: Nothing. Who are you looking for?

MRS SMALLEY: Nobody.

RACHEL: Has Job Arthur gone?

MRS SMALLEY: You saw him go.

RACHEL: Not that *I* care.

MRS SMALLEY: I bet you don't. You carry on as if you don't care,
you do. You needn't pretend to be so mighty struck on our
Harry, you know it's all sham.

RACHEL: It's not Susy. There's no sham about it, I wish there
was.—He's got his eye on Nurse, it's my belief.

MRS SMALLEY: An' she's got her eye on my mother's money,—I
know. She's sniffing like a cat over a mouse-hole—an' cottoning
on to our Harry.

RACHEL: She's deep, she is—An' he'd be as bug as a lord—for at
the bottom he's that stuck-up he doesn't know what to do wi'
himself.

MRS SMALLEY: I believe she knows something about the will—

RACHEL: Well surely—

MRS SMALLEY: An' from summat as my mother let drop, I'd be
bound she's in it, wi' our Harry.

RACHEL: His mother always made *me* cheap in his eyes.

MRS SMALLEY: If I could get to know—

RACHEL: Doesn't your Harry know—?

MRS SMALLEY: How should I know what he knows.

RACHEL: My father's pining for Nurse—the old fool. I wish he'd
get her. *His* money might get her. I'll buck him up.

MRS SMALLEY: I'll get in her way wi' our Harry as much as I can.

RACHEL: All right. You *are* a bit gone on Job Arthur, aren't you?

MRS SMALLEY: He should ha' married me, by rights, twelve years back—

RACHEL: There's something fascinating about him—Does he really want £250?

MRS SMALLEY: Yes.

RACHEL: I believe my father would give it me—if I got married to please him.

MRS SMALLEY: All right—there's your chance then.

RACHEL: You needn't be nasty, Susy—I don't want the chance.

MRS SMALLEY: You dodge round too many corners, like a ferrit, you do.

RACHEL: At any rate, I'm not waiting for somebody to die and leave me bait to chuck to a fat fish of a fellow.

MRS SMALLEY: You'd better mind what you're saying, Rachel Wilcox.

RACHEL: I don't care about *you*—so there.

MRS SMALLEY: Doesn't ter though?—What about our Harry? I'll let him know a thing or two.

RACHEL: It's you as *has* been saying things—I know. You've been telling him about Job Arthur Bowers—

MRS SMALLEY: Oh have I?—You're mighty clever.

RACHEL: You don't need to be clever to see through you. But I'll make you pay for it, my lady—

MRS SMALLEY: What—come out here—

RACHEL: There's the Baron—an' they don't know I'm out. *(She runs into hiding—a lantern appears down the lane.* SUSY *draws after her.)*

SUSY: What's he after?

RACHEL: Lovers. They hunt 'em out every Monday night.—Shut up now. *(In a whisper)*: Does my white apron show?

BARON: We haf done good work this night.

BARONESS *(tall and spare, in an antique cloak and bonnet)*: Seven couples, Baron—and we have only been out an hour. Isn't it terrible!

BARON: These miners are not men—they are animals that prowl by night.

BARONESS: The girls are worse, with their faces of brass.* It is they who *entice* the young men into these naughty holes and crannies.

BARON: But if a man haf honor, will he not woo a maiden in her father's house, in the presence of her family—

BARONESS: This is a parish of sin, Baron—the people love sin—

BARON: Defiant in sin, they are! But I will overthrow them. I will
5   drive them before me into the pit.

BARONESS: To think of that brazen besom telling us to go home and go to bed—

BARON: And the man—ah infamous, gross insult. And coward, to revile me that I have no child—

10   BARONESS: If they had a few less—and they born of sin—the low women!—That is the house of the woman Hemstock. Have you seen her?

BARON: Not yet. I will not bury her, heathen and blasphemous woman. She shall not soil my grave yard of good dead. And
15   those her menfolk, obstreperous and enemies of God, I will bow low their necks—

BARONESS: Hush—there are some—I believe there are—behind the gate—

BARON: More—Ah misery,—more than linked worms—! Where?—
20   My dull eyes!

BARONESS: There—behind the gate-post—

BARON *(holding aloft the candle)*: —Lovers, if you be there—why do you suck at sin? Is this honour, you man?—There is no one there, Baroness.

25   BARONESS: Yes, Baron, yes. I can see her apron.—Who are you? —come out of there. You, girl, I see you—Come out, for shame. You do not know what you are doing;—or, if you do, you are the depth of wickedness. *(A titter.)*

BARON: Where is the man?—Show yourself, Sir. Let me see the
30   man.—You lurk, sir, in a hole like a rat. Ah, the disgrace of mankind!

BARONESS: What is going to become of you, girl—Go home, before it is too late—Go home and learn to do your housework.

BARON: You press into the boughs of the trees, but the boughs are
35   the little arms of God.* You hide yourselves deep in the darkness, which is but the pupil of the eye of God. Ah, like a hot spark you fret the eye of God with your lust—.

BARONESS: You will rue it this time next year, I tell you.

BARON: The face of the man is full of shame, it is afraid lest it fall

under my eye— *(He holds the lantern peering at the women. The*
BARONESS *hovers close behind.* RACHEL *pushes* SUSY *out upon the*
little man. The lantern flies away and is extinguished.)

BARONESS: Oh, Oh—Come away, Baron, come away—

BARON: Ha—Ha— *(His voice is screaming)*: It is the attack! Stand
behind me, Baroness, I defend you. *(He ends on a high note,*
flourishing a stick he carries.) I have hit him! Ha—come on.

MRS SMALLEY: You've hit me, you little swine.

BARON: Stand behind me Baroness. I defeat this man—I— *(He*
chokes with gutturals and consonants.)

MRS SMALLEY: Would you, you *little* swine.

BARON: I will thrash you—I will thrash you—low-bred knave, I
will— *(He sputters into German.)*

MRS SMALLEY: Let me get hold on thee, I'll crack thy little yed
(head) for thee.

BARONESS: Baron, Baron, they are murdering you.

BARON: Ah, my sword, my sword! Baroness, my sword! I keep him
at bay with this stick.☆

MRS SMALLEY: I'll show thee, tha little nuisance, whether tha'rt
goin' ter hit *me* on the shoulder.

BARON: I have not my strength of old. If I had my sword he were
killed.☆

BARONESS: They are murdering the Baron! Help! Help!—Oh
Baron—

RACHEL *(suddenly rushing at her)*: Shut up, you old chuck! Shoo!

BARONESS *(screaming)*: Baron—Rudolf, Rudolf! Oh—h——!

BARON *(groaning)*: Ah, Baroness! *(He turns.* SUSY *rushes through his*
guard and seizes his wrists.)

MRS SMALLEY: I'll have that stick!

BARON: The lady—the Baroness von Ruge—my wife—let me go to
her—

MRS SMALLEY: Drop that stick, tha little—!

BARON: Little!—little again! Ah, my sword to thee. Let go my
wrists, foul one, base one—fight thus—! *(He lapses into a foreign*
fizzle.)

BARONESS *(fleeing)*: Help Help Help!!!

RACHEL *(catching her by the end of her long cloak and pulling her round*
backwards): Whoa, you're goin' a bit too fast!

BARONESS: Whose voice is that?—What?—Oh—h!

NURSE *(breathless)*: Whatever is the matter?—Who is it?

MRS SMALLEY: Drop that stick, little lizard—

BARON: My wife—God, think of my wife—!

BARONESS: Baron—they're killing me—Baron!

5 NURSE: Baroness!—Oh, for shame—Oh, how dreadful! *(She runs to* RACHEL, *who flees.)*

HARRY *(rushing up)*: What's goin' off?

NURSE: The poor Baron—an old man! Oh, how dreadful!

BARONESS: Rudolf, Rudolf! Where am I—what—where?

10 BARON: I will *kill* you.

HARRY *(to his sister)*: Has ter no more sense, gre't hound.

MRS SMALLEY: What's thaïgh got ter do wi' it? *(To the* BARON*)*: Drop that stick!

BARON: I will certainly—— *(German.)*

15 HARRY: Come off! *(He wrenches loose her wrists.)*

BARON: Ha! *(In triumph)*: —Thief! *(He rushes forward.* SUSY *avoids him quickly. He attacks* HARRY, *fetching him a smart whack.)*

HARRY: Tha little wasp—

NURSE: Don't, Mr Hemstock—don't hurt him!

20 BARON: Ha! *(He rushes again.* HARRY *dodges to avoid him, stumbles, the* BARON *gets in a blow,* HARRY *goes down.)* Ha, I have smitten him—Ha!

BARONESS *(fleeing)*: Baron—Help! Help! Baron—

BARON *(pursuing)*: My wife—

25 NURSE *(to* BARONESS*)*: Come away, Baroness, come away quickly. The Baron is all right.

BARONESS: I have lost a golosher, he has lost his hat, and the lantern—Oh!

BARON: Ah Baroness, safe! God be glorified. What—Oh, only

30 Nurse. We have been ambushed by a band of ruffians.—

NURSE: You had better hurry to the vicarage, Baron. You will take cold.

BARON: Speak not to me of cold. We have narrowly escaped—are you wounded, Baroness?

35 BARONESS: Where is your hat, and the lantern, and my golosh—?

BARON: What matter—

NURSE: You had better take the Baroness home, Baron. She will be ill—

BARONESS: We can't afford to lose them—the lanthorn and your

40 hat and a pair of goloshes.

BARON: Speak not of such— *(Exeunt.)*
HARRY *(rising slowly)*: The little snipe—!
MRS SMALLEY: It sarves thee right.

(Curtain)

Act II.

Scene 3.

Time: The same.

Scene: The kitchen of the Hemstocks' house. MR HEMSTOCK *stirring a*
5   *saucepan over the fire.*

NURSE *(entering)*: I am late. Are you making the food? I'm sorry.

MR HEMSTOCK: I hardly liked leavin' her—she's funny tonight.
What's a' th' row been about?

NURSE: Somebody buffeting the Baron and Baroness. I've just seen
10   them safely on the path. Has Harry come in?

MR HEMSTOCK: No—Hark—here he is!—Whatever—! *(The door
opens—enter* HARRY, *very muddy, blood running down his cheek.)*
—Whativer 'as ter done to thysen?

HARRY: Fell down.

15   NURSE: Oh dear—how dreadful.—Come and let me look!—What a
gash!—I must bind it up. It is not serious.

MR HEMSTOCK: Tha'd better ta'e thy jacket off, afore Nurse
touches thee. *(*HARRY *does so.* MR HEMSTOCK *continues making
the food.* NURSE *sets the kettle on the fire and gets a bowl.)*

20   NURSE *(to* HARRY*)*: You feel faint—would you like to lie down?

HARRY: I'm a' right.

NURSE: Yes, you *are* all right, I think. Sit here. What a house of
calamities! However did it happen?

HARRY: The Baron hit me, and I fell over the lantern.

25   NURSE: Dear me—how dreadful!

HARRY: I feel fair dizzy, Nurse—as soft as grease.

NURSE: You are sure to do. *(Exit* MR HEMSTOCK *with basin.)*

HARRY: Drunk, like.—Tha'rt as good as a mother to me, Nurse.

NURSE: Am I?

30   HARRY: My mother worna one ter handle you very tender: 'er wor
rough, not like thee.

NURSE: You see, she hadn't my practice.

HARRY: She 'adna thy hands. 'Er's rayther bad today, Nurse. I s'll
be glad when 'er's gone. It ma'es yer feel as if you was screwed
35   in a tight jacket—as if you'd burst innerds.

NURSE: I understand—it has been so long.

HARRY: It has. I feel as if I should burst.—Tha *has* got a nice touch
wi' thee, Nurse.—'Appen 'er'll leave me a bit of money—

NURSE: Oh Mr Hemstock!

HARRY: —An' if I could get some work—Dost think I ought to get married, Nurse—?

NURSE: Certainly, when you've found the right woman—

HARRY: If I was in steady work—. Nurse, dost think I'm a kid?

NURSE: No—why?

HARRY: I want motherin', Nurse. I feel as if I could scraïght. I've been that worked-up this last eight month—

NURSE: I know, it has been dreadful for you.

HARRY: I *dunna* want huggin' an' kissin', Nurse. I want—Tha'rt a Nurse, aren't ter—?

NURSE: Yes, I'm a Nurse.

HARRY: —I s'll reckon I'm badly, an' then tha can nurse me.

NURSE: You *are* sick—

HARRY: I am Nurse—I'm heart-sick of everything.

NURSE: I know you are.

HARRY: An' after my mother's gone—what am I to do?

NURSE: What creatures you are, you men. You all live by a woman—!

HARRY: I've lived by my mother.—What am I to do, Nurse—?

NURSE: You must get married—

HARRY: If I was in steady work—

NURSE: You'll get work, I'm sure.

HARRY: And if my mother leaves me some money—

NURSE: I must tell you where the will is, for fear anything should happen.

HARRY: Then I can ax—. Is it done, Nurse?

NURSE: Just finished.

HARRY: Should I lie down?

NURSE: Let me straighten the sofa for you—Don't get up yet.—Then I must see to Mrs Hemstock—and I'll speak to you about the Baroness' things, and about the will, when I come back.—How does the head feel?

HARRY: Swimmy, like;—like a puff o' steam wafflin'.

NURSE: Come along—come and lie down.—There, I'll cover you up.

MR HEMSTOCK *(entering)*: Is he badly?

NURSE: I think he'll be fairly by tomorrow.

MR HEMSTOCK: Tha'rt cading him a bit, Nurse.

NURSE: It is what will do him good—to be spoiled awhile.

MR HEMSTOCK: 'Appen so—but it'll be a wonder.

NURSE: Why?

MR HEMSTOCK: Spoilin' 's spoilin', Nurse—especially for a man.

NURSE: Oh, I don't know. How is Mrs Hemstock.

MR HEMSTOCK: Funny. I canna ma'e heads or tails of her.

5   *(Curtain)*

Act III.

Scene 1.

Time: The morning succeeding the previous scene.
Scene: The dining-room at the vicarage, a spacious but sparsely furnished
apartment, the Baron considering himself in all circumstances a soldier. 5
The BARON, *in martial-looking smoking jacket, is seated at a desk,*
writing, saying the words aloud. The clock shows eleven. Enter
BARONESS, *in tight-sleeved paisley dressing-gown, ruched at neck and*
down the front. She wears a mob-cap.

BARON *(rising hastily and leading her to her chair)*: You are sure, 10
    Baroness, you are sufficiently recovered to do this?
BARONESS: I am only pinned together, Baron. I shall collapse if the
    least thing happens.
BARON: It shall not happen.
BARONESS: My head has threshed round like a windmill all night— 15
BARON: Did I sleep—?
BARONESS: No, Baron, no, no! How do *you* find yourself this
    morning—?
BARON: Younger, Baroness. I have heard the clash of battle—
BARONESS: I was so afraid you had felt it. 20
BARON: I———I.—But I shall fall to no sickness. I shall receive
    the thrust when I am in the pulpit, I shall hear the cry 'Rudolf
    von Ruge'. I fling up my hand, and my spirit stands at attention
    before The Commander.
BARONESS: Oh Baron, don't. I shall dread Sunday. 25
BARON: Dread it, Baroness! Ah, when it comes, what glory!
    Baroness, I have fought obscurely, I have fought the small,
    inconspicuous fight, wounded with many little wounds of
    ignominy. But then—what glory!
BARONESS: —Has Nurse come yet? 30
BARON: She has not, Baroness.
BARONESS: I wish she would.
BARON: You feel ill—hide nothing from me.
BARONESS: She promised to try and get the things—I know the hat
    will be ruined, but if we recover the golosh and the lantern, 35
    'twill be a savation.*
BARON: 'Tis nothing.
BARONESS: 'Tis, Baron, your hat, cost 15/- —and my pair of

goloshes, 3/6, and the lantern, 2/11.—What is that, Baron?—
Reckon it up.

BARON: I cannot—I have not— *(A pause)*: It is twenty one shillings
and one penny—

5   BARONESS: 15/- and 3/6—15,—16, 17, 18—that's 18/6, and 2/11
—18—19, 20— *(Conning)*[☆]: —And *five* pence, Baron. Twenty
one shillings and *five* pence.

BARON: 'Tis nothing, Baroness.

BARONESS: 'Tis a great deal, Baron.—Hark!—Who is that called?

10 BARON: I cannot hear.

BARONESS: I will go and see—

BARON: No, Baroness—*I* go.

BARONESS: To the kitchen, Baron? *(Exit.)*

(The BARON, *at the window, cries on the Lord in German.)*[☆]

15 NURSE *(at the door)*: Goodmorning.

BARONESS *(hastily turning back)*: Have you got them?

NURSE: The hat and the golosh—we couldn't find the lantern.

BARONESS: Those wicked Hemstocks have appropriated it.

NURSE: No Baroness, I think not.

20 BARONESS: Your hat is not ruined, Baron—a miracle. Put it on—it
looks as good as new. What a blessing. Just a little brushing.
—And my golosh is not hurt.—But to think those wretches
should secrete my lantern. I will show them—

BARON: Baroness!

25 BARONESS: I was going to the kitchen—I heard a man's voice.

NURSE: The Baker's cart is there.

BARONESS: Ah! *(Exit.)*

NURSE: I am very glad the Baroness is not ill this morning.

BARON: Ah Nurse, the villainy of this world. Believe that a number

30 of miners, ruffians, should ambush and attack the Baroness and
me, out of wrath at our good work. The power of evil is strong,[☆]
Nurse.

NURSE: It is, Baron—I'm sorry to say.

BARON: I think those people Hemstock instigated this, Nurse.

35 NURSE: No Baron, I am sure not.

BARON: Will you say why you are sure, Nurse?

NURSE: I saw, Baron. It was not Harry Hemstock, nor his father—

BARON: Then who, Nurse? They are criminals. It is wickedness to
cover them, to spread your cloak of mercy[☆] over their sin. Then

40 who, Nurse?

NURSE: Some people from Northrop. I cannot say whom.—You know, Baron, you are an aristocrat, and these people hate you for it.

BARON: The mob issues from its lair like a plague of rats. Shall it pull us down and devour the land—?⁕ Ah, its appetite is base, each for his several stomach—. You knew them, Nurse? 5

NURSE: No Baron.

BARON: You heard them—what they said—their voices.

NURSE: I heard one say 'Catch hold of Throttle-ha'penny'.⁕

BARON: Catch hold of 'Throttle-ha'penny'.—Throttle-ha'penny, what is that? 10

NURSE: I think it means the Baroness. They are *so* broad, these people, I can't understand them.

BARON: I will punish them. Under the sword they shall find wisdom.⁕ 15

BARONESS' VOICE: Oh shameless! Shameless!

RACHEL'S VOICE: He was looking at my brooch.

BARONESS' VOICE: Come here, Baker—come back.

BAKER'S VOICE: A stale loaf to change, Baroness?

BARONESS' VOICE: You *shall* go before the Baron this time. Go in the dining-room, Rachel. 20

BAKER'S VOICE: Me too?

(Enter RACHEL, *in cap and apron,* THE BAKER, *and the* BARONESS.)

THE BAKER *(entering)*: Thank you, Missis.—Good morning Nurse. Expect to find the Baroness in bed? I did. 25

BARONESS *(to* RACHEL*)*: Stand *there!*

BARON *(sternly, to* BAKER*)*: Stand there! Take a seat, Nurse. Pray be seated, Baroness.

THE BAKER *(seating himself in the arm-chair)*: Hope I haven't got your chair, Baron. 30

BARON: Stand, Sir.

THE BAKER *(to* NURSE, *as he rises)*: Nearly like my father⁕ said to the curate: 'They're *a'* mine.'

BARON: Baroness!

BARONESS: He was, Baron—he was— 35

RACHEL: He was bending down to look at my new brooch. *(She shows it.)*

BARONESS: With his arm—

THE BAKER: —On her apron strings—

BARONESS: He was stooping— 40

THE BAKER: To look at her new brooch.

BARON: Silence!

BARONESS: He kissed her.

BARON: Coward! Coward! Coward, *Sir*!

5 THE BAKER: Ditto to you, Mister.

BARON: What! *Sir*! Do you know— —?

THE BAKER: That you are the 'Baron von Ruge'—no, I've only your bare word for it.

NURSE: For shame, Mr Bowers.

10 THE BAKER: When a little old man, Nurse, calls a big young man a coward, he's presuming on his years and size to bully, and I say, a bully's a coward.

BARON: You contaminate my maid.

THE BAKER: I contaminate your maid?

15 BARONESS: The shameless baggage. What have I always said of her?

BARON: Baroness von Ruge! *(To* BAKER*)*: You are going to marry her?

THE BAKER: It's a question generally put to the woman.

BARON: Answer me, Sir.

20 THE BAKER: I couldn't say which she's going to marry, out of her one or two fellows.

BARONESS: Shameless! Ah, the slut!

BARON: I repeat, Sir—do you intend to marry this maid.

THE BAKER: I hadn't fully made up my mind—

25 BARON: Then, Sir, you are a villain—

THE BAKER: You've got the muscle of your years up, Mister—

BARON: You threaten me—!!

BARONESS: Baron!!!

RACHEL: I sh'd have thought you'd more about you, Job Arthur Bowers.

30 NURSE *(deprecating)*: Oh Mr Bowers—!

THE BAKER: Right you are, Nurse!

BARON: I say, Sir, a man who kisses a maid—

THE BAKER: Ought to be hanged for it—so say I.

35 BARON: Sir, your facetiousness is untimely—I say, a man who kisses a maid—

BARONESS: Baron, such people do not understand—

BARON *(kissing her hand)*: Baroness!

RACHEL *(melting)*: We're not given the chance.

40 BARON: Sir, is there no reverence in a kiss—? If you strike a match

against the box, even, you wonder at the outburst of fire. Then Sir—but do you wonder at nothing?

THE BAKER: Nothing's surprising,—but everything is comical, Baron, that's how I find it.

BARON *(puzzled and distressed)*: So! So!—Ah, but a woman *is*, according to her image in the eye of the man.

THE BAKER *(looking at the* BARONESS*)*: Some of us must have fancy eyes.

NURSE: How can you be so flippant?

BARONESS: A woman is what a man makes her.

THE BAKER: By gum, there's no tellin' what you might manufacture in time, then. It's a big job to begin of.*

RACHEL *(laughing)*: For shame, Job Arthur.

BARONESS: What have *you* to say?—you bad creature! What wonder men are as they are.

THE BAKER: When the women make them.

BARON: You are of my parish?

THE BAKER: Yes—but I'm in Northrop Church choir.

BARON: You are a chorister—?—You *wish* to marry Rachel?

THE BAKER: As I say, I haven't decided.

BARON: But—what are you doing?—What of this maid—?

BARONESS: What does he care!—Are you a married man, Baker?

THE BAKER: Not that I know to, Missis.

BARON: Sir, I am an old man, you remind me—

THE BAKER: Beg pardon, Baron.

BARON: And—a—powerless—and I *will* say it, I *will*—a 'useless'—

BARONESS: Baron!!

BARON: Sir—I shall soon be called in—and, Sir, you are of my parish, Rachel is of my house. What have I done, who am responsible?

THE BAKER: Nay Baron, I can't see as you're to fault.

BARON: My fault, Sir, is failure: and failure without honor. In three campaigns, which are my life, I have been miserably beaten.

BARONESS: No Baron, no. How are you to blame?

NURSE: No Baron, you have not failed—

BARON: In Poland, in London, and in my parish of Greenway*— Baroness, we retire to a cottage; I sit still and contain myself, under sentence—. Baroness, your pardon!

BARONESS: You shall not retire, Baron. Before God, I witness, you are no failure. Ah Rachel, see now what you've done.

RACHEL *(weeping)*: It's not me.

THE BAKER: Nay, for that matter—would you marry me, Rachel—
eh?

RACHEL: Opportunity's a fine thing, you mean.

5   THE BAKER: *Will* you marry me, Rachel?

RACHEL: I—yes, I will, Job Arthur.

BARON: She loves you, she let you kiss her. But you, Sir, do you
honor her?

THE BAKER: I do.

10   BARON: Then will you leave me—?

THE BAKER: Good morning Sir.—And thank you.

                    (Exit—and RACHEL.*)*

BARONESS: You are not ill, Baron?

BARON: No, Baroness.—Nurse, who is this man?

15   NURSE: The Baker? Oh, he's Job Arthur Bowers—a bit racketty. He
lives down Greenhills* with his old mother. She's as deaf as a
post, and a little bit crazed. But she's very fond of her son.

BARON: Ah! She is mad?—she is old.—Will Rachel be good to
her?

20   BARONESS: I very much doubt it.

NURSE: Rachel will be afraid of Job Arthur Bowers. He is too big for
her ever to get her apron strings round him.

BARON *(smiling slightly)*: I began to be afraid, Nurse—

BARONESS *(at the window)*: He is bringing my lantern.

25   NURSE: Who?—Ah, that's right.

BARONESS: Will you ring, Baron?—I will question that young man.
We must get to the bottom of last night's affair, Baron.

BARON: Those ruffians shall not go unpunished. Still I have power
for that.

30   BARONESS *(to* RACHEL*)*: Show that young man in here. Nurse, you
will help us. We must hold our own against these ungodly
creatures—Must we not, Baron?

BARON: Ah Baroness, still we fight.

RACHEL: Harry Hemstock—.

35   HARRY *(entering—his head bound up)*: I've brought this 'ere hurricane-
lamp.

BARONESS: Thank you. And where did you find it?

HARRY: Where you'd lost it.

BARONESS: What have you done to your head?

40   HARRY *(after a silence)*: —You *should* know.

BARONESS: There Baron, I was right. And you would have stolen the lantern if Nurse had not—

BARON: Leave the lantern, Baroness. Sir, who were your accomplices in this nightly attack?

HARRY: What's 'e mean, Nurse? 5

NURSE: The Baron means what men were those that attacked the Baroness and him last night. I say they were some men out of Northrop—that you could not recognise them. Mr Hemstock came to your assistance, Baron.

BARON: Is that so? 10

HARRY: I pulled 'er off 'n thee.

BARON: What is it he says, Nurse?

NURSE: He says he pulled the man away who was trying to hold you.

BARON: Ah!—Tell me, Sir—who was this ruffian? 15

HARRY: I non know no ruffian.

BARON: Who struck you that blow?—That you must know, and that must be told to me.

HARRY: Tha ought ter know thysen.

BARONESS: You are speaking to the Baron, remember. 20

HARRY: An' it wor him as gen me a crack ower th' yed.

BARON: Then you were with the enemy. Now I behold you, Sir. I will cause you, Sir, I will *make* you to confess. I will see you punished. You shall suffer this course.

NURSE: You are mistaken, Baron. 25

BARON: Nurse, I will conduct this inquiry of myself. It is not of myself. But your cowardice, yours and those others, to attack a lady, by night. There is a penalty for such. Sir, I say you are vile, and you shall name me the other villains.

HARRY: There was no other villains—without you call a couple of 30 women villains.

BARON: What mean you by a couple of women.

BARONESS: He doesn't know what he is talking about.

NURSE: There were some men, Mr Hemstock—from Northrop.

HARRY: Well, if there was, I didna see 'em. All I see'd was two 35 women draggin' at th' old Baron.

BARON: You mean to say we were attacked only by two women— Baroness?

NURSE: He must be mistaken.

BARONESS: These people would say anything.* 40

BARON: Tell me, Sir, tell me the truth at once.

HARRY: I've told you the truth.

BARON: It was some men, Baroness? At least, Baroness, one man there was—

5 BARONESS: There *was* one man—how many more I can't say.

BARON: The throat of these people is fuller of untruth than a bird's gizzard— —

HARRY: It is the truth I've told you.

BARON: Nurse—speak—was it two women?

10 NURSE: I certainly thought they were *men*, Baron.

BARON: Baroness, speak.

BARONESS: It certainly *was* men, Baron.

HARRY: Well, it certainly wasn't, an' I'm not a liar.

BARON: Then it was two women?

15 HARRY: It *was*.

BARON: And a woman has smitten your head?

HARRY: No, you did that yourself, with your thick stick, when I'd pulled our Susy off'n you. An' I fell ower your lantern and cut me.

20 BARONESS: A likely tale.

HARRY: Is it true, Nurse Broadbanks?

NURSE: I think you are mistaken, Mr Hemstock. Oh, do not be so persistent.

HARRY: I'll not be made a liar of. Wheer's Rachel?

25 BARONESS: Why Rachel?—she has nothing to do with it.

HARRY: Fetch her in then.

NURSE: She has just been in. She is engaged to Job Arthur Bowers—

HARRY: I don't care what she is.

30 BARON: I will ring.

BARONESS: Do not, Baron, do not trouble.

BARON: Sir, it was *not* two women—I defy you, Sir. You make me a silly thing—it is your spleen.

BARONESS: You had better go, you.

35 HARRY: I'm not going to be made a liar of. *(Enter* RACHEL.*)* Rachel, who was it knocked the Baron's hat off an' shook him last night?

NURSE: Do you know the names of those men from Northrop, Rachel?

RACHEL: It wasn't him, Baron, he helped you.

40 BARON: He would patch me with shame. You saw this attack—?

RACHEL: I was just slipping down to get some milk from Mrs Smalley, there was none for supper—

BARON: And what did you see—

RACHEL: I saw some men, an' I heard some shouting, and I saw somebody hit him on the head. Then I ran home, and I'd just got in when you came.

HARRY: Why, wasn't it *you* an' our Susy as was raggin' the Baron an' Baroness, an' I come up an' stopped you—?

RACHEL: Me!—Me an' your Susy—!!

HARRY: You shammer!

RACHEL: I know you went up an' stopped the men, whoever they was—

HARRY: So I'm a liar—?—so I'm a liar—?

BARONESS: Yes—and you may go—

HARRY: So I'm a liar, Nurse Broadbanks—?
(He goes out.)

BARON: God help us, we begin to believe in the spots they imagine against us. *(He looks at his hands.)* It was *not* two women, Baroness?

BARONESS: No, Baron, No.

BARON: You saw several men, Nurse?

NURSE: Yes Baron.

BARON: Rachel—but why weep! Rachel—he defended me against men?

RACHEL *(sobbing)*: Yes, Baron.

BARONESS: Rachel, leave the room. *(Exit.)*

BARON: Nurse, I am a soldier.

NURSE: You are, Baron.

BARON: I must reward that—fellow—although—

NURSE: It is good of you, Baron.

BARONESS: And you called yourself a failure, Rudolf.

BARON: I can—I must speak for him at the colliery. There I have still some influence.

NURSE: It is so good of you.

BARON: He has suffered already for his opposition. It is not good for the enemies of God to prosper. But I will write to my nephew.

NURSE: I could leave a letter, Baron—I am going past the colliery—

BARON: I will write now—then my honor is free. *(Seating himself at the desk.)*

'My dear Nephew, I am placed under an obligation to that man of whom I have spoken to you before, Henry Hemstock, of the cottage at the end of the glebe close. It is within the bounds of your generosity to relieve me of this burden of gratitude contracted to one of such order. You will, of your fulness of spirit, lap over the confine of my debt with bounty.

Your Aunt salutes you, and I reach you my right hand,
(signed) Rudolf von Ruge'

The manager of the collieries is as my own son to me, Nurse.

BARONESS: And he is a good son. He is *my* nephew.

NURSE: I will leave the letter.

(Curtain)

Act III.
Scene 2.

Time: Evening of the same day.
Scene: Nurse's room: the sitting room of a miner's cottage, comfortable,
warm, pleasant. NURSE *in the arm chair on one side of the fire,* MR
WILCOX *on the other. He is a stout, elderly miner, with grey round*
whiskers and a face like a spaniel.

MR WILCOX: No, Nurse, I've not a bit of comfort.

NURSE: Why wouldn't Rachel stay and look after you?

MR WILCOX: Nay, don't ask me—ungrateful hussy.—And I can't
seem to get a housekeeper as'll manage for me.

NURSE: It is difficult.

MR WILCOX: I've been trying this last ten year, an' I've not had a
good one yet. Either they eat you up, or waste, or drink.—What
do you think today. You know how it was raining. I got home
from pit soaked. No breeches an' waistcoat put to warm—fire
nearly out—

NURSE: Oh, it *is* too bad.

MR WILCOX: An' in the fender, a great row of roast potatoes, hard
as nag-nails—not done a bit—

NURSE: What a shame—

MR WILCOX: An' not a morsel of meat to eat to them. *She*'d ate-n
the great piece of cold mutton left from yesterday, an' then said
I hadn't left 'er no money for no meat.

NURSE: How stupid!

MR WILCOX: So it was taters—you had to chomp 'em like raw
turnip—an' drippin': an' a bit of a batter puddin' tough as whit-
leather.

NURSE: Poor man.

MR WILCOX: An' no fire—there never is when *I* come home. I
believe she sells the coal.

NURSE: Isn't it dreadful?

MR WILCOX: An' they're all alike.

NURSE: I suppose they are.

MR WILCOX: They are. You know I'm an easy man to live with,
Nurse.

NURSE: I'm sure you are.

MR WILCOX: One as gives very little trouble.—Nay, I can fettle for
myself—an' does do.

NURSE: I have seen you.

MR WILCOX: And I think I deserve a bit better treatment.

NURSE: I'm sure you do.

MR WILCOX: An' I ought to be able to get it. If I was drunken or
5   thriftless I should say nothing.

NURSE: But you're not.

MR WILCOX: No, I'm not. I've been a steady and careful man all my
         life. A chapel-going man, whereas you're church*—but that's a
         detail.

10   NURSE: It *ought* not to matter.

MR WILCOX: You know, Nurse, I've got four *good* houses—lets at
         six shillings each.

NURSE: Yes, I know you have.

MR WILCOX: Besides a tidy bit in the bank.

15   NURSE: And you have saved it all?

MR WILCOX: Every penny.

NURSE: Ha!

MR WILCOX: An' there's on'y Rachel. I'd give her a couple of
         houses straight off, an' then we should be all right *there*: nobody
20   could grumble.

NURSE: You *could* do that, of course.

MR WILCOX: Nurse?—do you know how old I am?

NURSE: No, Mr Wilcox.

MR WILCOX: I'm just fifty-eight.

25   NURSE: Hm! I should have thought you were more.

MR WILCOX: I'm not.

NURSE: It is comparatively young.

MR WILCOX: It's not *old*, is it? And though I've been a widower
         these ten years—I'm not—I'm not—good for nowt—d'yer
30   see?

NURSE: Of course you're not.

MR WILCOX: An' you know, Nurse—you're just the one for me.

NURSE *(laughing)*: Am I, Mr Wilcox?

MR WILCOX: Nurse—will you tell me your name?

35   NURSE: Broadbanks.

MR WILCOX: You know I meant your Christian name. Don't
         torment me, Nurse, I can't stand it.

NURSE: I was baptised Millicent Emily.

MR WILCOX: 'Millicent Emily'—it's like the 'Song of Soloman'.
40   Can I say it again?

NURSE: If you will say it only to yourself.

MR WILCOX: My name is James—Jim for short.

NURSE: I thought it was Hezekiah—or Ezekiel.

MR WILCOX: Hezekiah's my second name—James Hezekiah.

NURSE: I like Hezekiah better.   5

MR WILCOX: Do you—I thought you didn't—Oh, I'm glad you like it. But yours is lovely.

NURSE: I prefer Nurse.

MR WILCOX: So do I—nice and short. *(A pause.)* —Shall I sing to you, Nurse.   10

NURSE: Do you sing?

MR WILCOX: Oh yes—I used to be a great one at 'Ora pro Nobis'.※ Should I sing you 'Gentle Annie'?※ I used to sing that forty years since.

NURSE: When you were courting, Mr Wilcox?   15

MR WILCOX: Afore that. *(He hesitates—goes to the piano, and, after fumbling, begins to vamp to 'What are the Wild Waves Saying'.※ He begins to sing, 'lamentoso'.)*※

NURSE: There's someone at the door!

(Not hearing, or observing, he continues to play. She opens to DR   20
FOULES. *They stand smiling—*MR WILCOX *stops playing and wheels round.)*

DR FOULES: 'Music when soft voices die
                  vibrates in the memory.'※

NURSE: Mr Wilcox was enlivening my leisure. Do you know Mr   25
Wilcox, Dr Foules?

DR FOULES: I have not had the pleasure till now. *(He bows.)*

MR WILCOX: Good-evenin'—I wasn't aware as anybody was here.

DR FOULES: 'By rapture's blaze impelled he swelled the artless lay.'※   30

NURSE: I think Mr Wilcox sings very well indeed.—Will you finish, Mr Wilcox?

MR WILCOX: No thanks, I must be going.

DR FOULES: Pray do not let me hasten you away.

MR WILCOX: Oh, I was just going. Well—happen you'll call at our   35
house, Nurse?

NURSE: I will, Mr Wilcox. *(Exit.)*

DR FOULES: Did I interrupt you?

NURSE: You did not interrupt *me*.

DR FOULES: Then I incur no disfavour?   40

NURSE: Not for stopping poor Mr Wilcox at 'Brother I hear no singing—.'—Poor man—!

DR FOULES: You pity him?

NURSE: I do.

5   DR FOULES: Ah! Is it of the mind-melting sort—?

NURSE: I do not understand—

DR FOULES: 'For pity melts the mind to love—'*

NURSE: No—poor man. I can just imagine my mother, if I took him down to Kent. 'Well, you've done a nice thing for yourself—'

10 DR FOULES: You daren't face family criticism—?

NURSE: I daren't.

DR FOULES: Ah! Then he *does* aspire?

NURSE: Poor old fellow!

DR FOULES: I do not like your pity, Nurse—however near akin it

15   may be to something better.

NURSE: You have often incurred it, Doctor.

DR FOULES: Which of the two, Nurse?

NURSE: The pity, of course.—I have said 'poor boy'.

DR FOULES: Why?

20 NURSE: Why? *(She laughs)*: Because, I suppose, you were pitiable.

DR FOULES *(blushing)*: You mean I was to be pitied. Why?

NURSE: Because you were not like the Pears Soap baby: 'He won't be happy till he gets it'*—but you went on washing yourself without soap, good as gold.

25 DR FOULES: I cannot apply your simile.

NURSE: Perhaps not. I never was literary.

DR FOULES: You have grown brilliant—and caustic, if I may say so.

NURSE: It is the first time I have been accused of brilliance.

DR FOULES: Then perhaps I am the steel which sheds the sparks

30   from your flint—

NURSE: Oh, the sparks *may* come, but they're not noticed. Perhaps you are only the literary man who catches them on his tinder and blows them into notice. You love a phrase beyond every-thing.

35 DR FOULES: Really—I hardly recognise you, Nurse.

NURSE: And what did your mother say of me?

DR FOULES: I thank you for calling so soon.—Did she seem changed, to you?

NURSE: She looks very ill.

40 DR FOULES: Yes, I am worried.

NURSE: You are afraid it is something serious?

DR FOULES: Yes.

NURSE: I hope not. But it put me about to see her looking so frail. —She was very kind to me.

DR FOULES: You are very good, Nurse.   5

NURSE: It is my duty to be sympathetic, Doctor.

DR FOULES: And use is second nature. I will take courage, Nurse—

NURSE: Will it not be a complete disguise?

DR FOULES: Your duty does not extend to *me*, Nurse.

NURSE: No Doctor.   10

DR FOULES: You wish me to see you in *your* new guise, Nurse.— You stick daw's feathers among your dove's plumage.

NURSE *(laughing)*: What, am I a dove then?—It is a silly bird.

DR FOULES: You have had a hard time, Nurse?

NURSE: I have got over the hardness, thank you. It is all moderate,   15 now.

DR FOULES: Might it not be *more* than moderate?

NURSE: I hope it will be, some day.

DR FOULES: Could I help it, do you think?

NURSE: Everybody helps it, by being amiable—.   20

DR FOULES: But might I not help it—more particularly.—You used to—

NURSE: Say you are in love with me, Doctor—

DR FOULES: I have always been—

NURSE: Then the light has been under a bushel.*   25

DR FOULES: 'Blown to a core of ardour by the awful breath of—'* *(He smiles very confusedly.)* —I may hope then, Nurse.

NURSE *(smiling)*: Along with Mr Wilcox—

DR FOULES: Thank you for the company—

NURSE: Look here, Arthur. You have lived like a smug little candle   30 in a corner, with your mother to shelter you from every draught. Now you can get blown a bit. *I* do not feel inclined to shelter you for the rest of your life.

DR FOULES: Thank you.

NURSE: I am sorry if I am nasty. But I am angry with you—   35

DR FOULES: It is evident.

NURSE: And I will still come and see your mother, if I may.—She is a woman to respect.

DR FOULES: I do not order my mother's comings and goings. The case is the reverse, you remember.   40

NURSE: Very well.—On your high horse, you are more like the nursery than ever.

DR FOULES: Thank you.

NURSE *(mimicking)*: Thank you.

5   DR FOULES: I am surprised—

NURSE: *I* am surprised—but—was that someone at the door?

DR FOULES: I could not tell you.

NURSE: Excuse me, I will see.

DR FOULES: Let me go, first. *(Catching his hat to depart.)*

10 NURSE *(opening the door)*: *You*, Mr Hemstock. Will you come in? *(Enter HARRY.)*

DR FOULES: Good evening, Mr. Hemstock. I will make way for you.

NURSE: 'Applications considered Tuesday, between 7.0 and 9.0 p.m.' That is your meaning, Doctor?

15 DR FOULES: With your usual astuteness, you have it.

NURSE: With my *usual* astuteness, I have avoided so far the 'Matrimonial Post.'*—This is the irony of fate, Doctor. It never rains but it pours.*

DR FOULES *(bowing to NURSE and HARRY)*: The third time pays for
20 all, they say.*

NURSE *(laughing)*: I will tell you tomorrow.*

DR FOULES: It will not be too late to drop me a post card.

NURSE: I will see.—Goodnight, Dr Foules.

DR FOULES: Goodnight, Nurse Broadbanks. I wish you luck.

25 NURSE: And life-long happiness—

DR FOULES: Goodnight! *(Exit.)*

NURSE: He is very pleasant, isn't he?

HARRY: They say so.

NURSE: How is Mrs Hemstock?

30 HARRY: She's worse. She's not speakin'.

NURSE: Oh, I'm sorry to hear that. Did you want me to do anything? Poor thing, it will be a relief when she's gone.

HARRY: Th' owd doctor's bin. He told us to ax you to see her settled down—

35 NURSE: Shall I come now?

HARRY: Or in about half an hour's time—when you're ready.

NURSE: I may as well come now—when I've just tidied the room. Are you going to sit up with her?

HARRY: No—my father is, an' our Susy. I'm going to work—

NURSE: Going to work? I thought you hadn't a place.

HARRY: They sent me word as I wor to go tomorrow—buttyin' wi' Joe Birkin.

NURSE: And will it be a good place?

HARRY: Ha. It's a sight better than ever I expected.   5

NURSE: Oh, that *is* nice, isn't it.

HARRY: It's better nor mormin' about at home.

NURSE: It is. I'm so glad, Mr Hemstock. Then you'll stop at Greenway?

HARRY: I'm reckonin' so. There's nowt else, is there?   10

NURSE: No—why should there be? You'll have to begin afresh after Mrs Hemstock has gone—

HARRY: I s'll make a start o' some sort.

NURSE: You will?—Do you know, I've had old Mr Wilcox here tonight.   15

HARRY: Oh—Ah?

NURSE: He's *so* comical. He was singing to me.
                    (She laughs into her hand.)

HARRY: He must ha' wanted summat to do—

NURSE: I think so. You never heard anything like it in your life—   20

HARRY: 'E never wor but dosy-baked.

NURSE *(purring)*: What does that mean?

HARRY: Soft, batchy, sawney.

NURSE: Poor old chap. It's no use being angry with him, is it?

HARRY: What for?   25

NURSE: For thinking I would accept him.

HARRY: No, it's no good bein' mad wi' *him*.

NURSE: He looked so crestfallen.

HARRY: He'll be just as game by tomorrow.

NURSE: Of course he will. Men only pretend to be so heart broken.   30
By supper-time they've forgotten.

HARRY: An' what's a woman do?

NURSE: I don't know. You see it means more to a woman. It's her life. To a man it's only a pleasant change.

HARRY: To all appearances, you'd think it worn't such a life-an'-   35
death affair to her.

NURSE: Why?

HARRY: Women as reckoned to be pinin' for you, goes an' makes a liar an' a fool of you in front of other folks.

NURSE: You mean Rachel Wilcox.

HARRY: Ah—'appen I do.

NURSE: But, poor old Baron, it would have killed him.

HARRY: Then let him die—what good is he, here or anywhere else.

5 NURSE: Oh Mr Hemstock!

HARRY: Besides, *she* did it to spite me, because 'er wor mad wi' me.

NURSE: But she is engaged to Mr Bowers.

HARRY: 'Appen so. 'Er bites 'er nose off to spite her face.

NURSE: But poor old Baron—it would have been so cruel.

10 HARRY: Would *he* have stopped tellin' anybody else the truth?—He wouldna—

NURSE: But you can't judge in that way—

HARRY: Why canna I?—You make a liar an' a swine of *me*, an' a dam fool of him—

15 NURSE: Oh come, Mr Hemstock—

HARRY: He *is* a little fool—an' wants to boss everybody else wi' it, an' a'—

NURSE: You ought not to speak of the Baron like that.

HARRY: No, it's all palaver, an' smooth talk. I'll see anybody in
20   Hell before I'm fed wi' mealy-mouthed words like a young pigeon—

NURSE: I think you don't know what you're talking about.

HARRY: Dunna I though, but I do. I'm not going to be made a convenience of, an' then buttered up, like a trussed fowl.

25 NURSE: There is no one wants to butter you up, to my knowledge.

HARRY: All right then—then there isn't.

NURSE: And all this, I think, has been very uncalled for—and unnecessary.

HARRY: All right then—an' it has. But I'm not a kid, nor to be
30   treated like one—

NURSE: It's there you make your mistake.

HARRY: Nay, it's somebody else as has made a mistake.

NURSE: Yes—we do think the quiet vessels are the full ones. But it seems they only want shaking to rattle worse than any.

35 HARRY: All right—say what you like.

NURSE: Thank you, I don't wish to say any more—except that I pity whoever has you, for you seem to be in a state of chronic bad temper.

HARRY: All right,—I'll be going.

NURSE *(who has been tidying the room)*: I will be at your house in ten minutes.

HARRY: There's no occasions to hurry—am I to wait for you?

NURSE: No thank you—I would rather come alone.

(Curtain)

5

Act IV.

Time: The evening succeeding the last scene: third day of the play.
Scene: The kitchen at the Hemstocks.

NURSE: And what about the fire in the room?

5 MRS SMALLEY: I'll let it go out and take the ashes up by daylight.
It's falling dusk, an' I don't like being in by myself.

NURSE: Poor Mrs Hemstock—she went very quickly at the last.

MRS SMALLEY *(red eyed—sniffing)*: She did that. Eh, but wasn't
she wasted. A fair skeleton! I'm glad you laid her out, Nurse.

10 NURSE: I shall miss her. I've been coming here over a year now.

MRS SMALLEY: I hope I don't lie like that: she used to be as strong
as a horse.—But she *was* hard, you know.

NURSE: Perhaps she had enough to make her.

MRS SMALLEY: She had—wi' my father an' th' lads. She was easiest
15 wi' our Harry. He was always mother's lad.

NURSE: Yet they have been so indifferent—

MRS SMALLEY: At the bottom they haven't. She never forgave him
for going with Rachel Wilcox—an' he was always funny-tempered: would roll up like a pea-bug, at a word.

20 NURSE: I thought she favoured Rachel Wilcox.

MRS SMALLEY: No—hated her—but she used to make game of him.

NURSE: She is engaged to the Baker now.

MRS SMALLEY: Yes. He's only having her for her money—an' she'll
hate him when she's rubbed the fur off a bit. But she's one
25 would fuss round a pair of breeches on a clothesline※ rather
than have no man.

NURSE: I don't like her.

MRS SMALLEY: Not many does. She fair pines for our Harry, yet
she'd have Job Arthur for fear of getting nobody.

30 NURSE: How dreadful!— *(She goes for her cloak.)*

MRS SMALLEY: Nay, dunna go. Stop an' ha'e a cup o' tea. I durstn't
stop in by mysen. The kettle'll boil in a minute. *(She lays the
table.)*

NURSE: I really ought to go.

35 MRS SMALLEY: Don't you. I should be scar'd to death. You'll stop
five minutes, Nurse.

NURSE: A quarter of an hour.

MRS SMALLEY *(starting)*: What's that?

NURSE *(going to the door)*: It's only Patty.

MRS SMALLEY: She's been that lost a' day without our Harry.
NURSE: Poor old Patty—! *(Enter* HARRY.*)*
MRS SMALLEY: Tha'rt a bit sooner than I thought for.
HARRY *(surly)*: Am I.
MRS SMALLEY: I hanna been able to get thee no dinner.   5
HARRY: Why?
MRS SMALLEY: She on'y died at two o'clock—an' we've been busy
     ever sin' —haven't we, Nurse.
NURSE: We have, Mrs Smalley.
MRS SMALLEY: Shall ter ha'e tea wi' me an' Nurse.   10
HARRY: No.
MRS SMALLEY: What then?
HARRY: Nowt.
MRS SMALLEY: Shall ter wesh thysen?
HARRY: Ha.   15
MRS SMALLEY: Pump wor frozzen this mornin'.
HARRY: I know.
*(*MRS SMALLEY *fetches a large red panchion from outside, puts in cold*
water, brings towel and soap, setting all on a stool on hearth-rug. HARRY
sets tin bottle and knotted snap-bag on table, takes off his cap, red-wool 20
scarf, coat and waistcoat. He pours hot water from boiler into panchion,
strips off his singlet or vest—he wears no shirt—and kneels down to wash.
          NURSE *and* MRS SMALLEY *sit down to tea.)*
NURSE *(to* HARRY*)*: You must be tired today. *(No answer.)*
MRS SMALLEY: I bet his hands is sore—are they? *(No answer.)*   25
     —Best leave him alone.—They always grumble about their
     hands, first day.
HARRY: Wheer's my Dad?
MRS SMALLEY: Gone to registrar's.
NURSE: Yes, they must take some time to harden.   30
MRS SMALLEY: Shall you sit there, Nurse. I'd better light the lamp,
     you can't see.
HARRY: Tha nedna.
MRS SMALLEY: What's thaïgh to stop me for?
NURSE: No—I like the twilight—really.   35
MRS SMALLEY: There's a lot o' dirt wi' a collier—an' mess.
NURSE: Yes.
MRS SMALLEY: I allers said I'd not marry one. I'd had enough wi'
     my father an' th' lads.
NURSE: They say it's clean dirt.   40

MRS SMALLEY: Is it?—muck an' mess, to my thinkin'.
NURSE: Yes, I suppose so. I used to think it would be dreadful.
MRS SMALLEY: But you've altered—
NURSE: Well, I've thought about it—I'm afraid I should never fit in—
5   MRS SMALLEY: No—you're too much of a lady—you like a lady's ways.
NURSE: I don't know. Perhaps one *does* get a bit finicking after a
  certain time—
MRS SMALLEY *(to* HARRY*)*: Dost want thy back doin'?
(He grunts assent. She washes his back with a flannel, and wipes it as she talks.)
10 NURSE: It's the thought of it day after day, day after day—it *is*
  rather appalling—
MRS SMALLEY: The thought of any man, like that, is.
NURSE *(smiling)*: It was not the man—it was the life—the company
  one would have to keep—.
15 MRS SMALLEY: Yes.—So you wouldn't marry a collier, Nurse?
NURSE: Yes, I would—for all that—if I cared for him.
MRS SMALLEY: That makes the difference.
NURSE: It does.
MRS SMALLEY: I can't imagine you married to a collier.
20 NURSE: Sometimes it seems mad, to me: sometimes it doesn't.
MRS SMALLEY: I shouldn't ha' thought, though, Nurse, you'd ha'
  had one—
NURSE: No?—I might.
MRS SMALLEY: Not an old one?
25 NURSE: Certainly not an old one—not Mr Wilcox.
MRS SMALLEY: Ha.—Have another cup?—I wish Patty would keep
  still—she fair worrits me. I'm sure I'd like to drop your cup, she
  made me jump that much.
NURSE: I am surprised you are nervous.
30 MRS SMALLEY: We all are.—I wonder, Nurse, where my mother's
  will is?
NURSE: Oh—I meant to have told you. In the socket of the bed-post
  nearest the drawers, at the top.
MRS SMALLEY: Would you believe it!
35 NURSE: She was very quaint sometimes—poor Mrs Hemstock.
MRS SMALLEY: Do you think she was in her right mind?
NURSE: Oh yes—and Doctor does, too.
MRS SMALLEY: Well—I used to have my doubts.
NURSE: Poor Mrs Hemstock. *(A knock.)*
40 MRS SMALLEY: Oh!

RACHEL *(entering):* I thought there was nobody in, seeing no light. Is Nurse here?

NURSE: Yes.

RACHEL: The Baroness wants you to go up—she's got a pain. I've been to your place for you. 5

NURSE: Poor Baroness—what is the matter?

RACHEL: She's got a pain in her shoulder.

NURSE: Rheumatism?

RACHEL: She says she believes it's pleurisy.

NURSE *(smiling):* Poor old Baroness—she *does* fancy. 10

RACHEL: But she won't pay for a doctor, fancy or no fancy, not if she can help it. Her fancy mustn't *cost* her anything.

NURSE: She knows I can treat her.—I can go straight there—

RACHEL: Oh, an' will you go an' see what's up with my father. He's not been to work—been in bed all day—can't eat—and won't 15 have the doctor—fading away—

NURSE: That is sad! What ails him?

RACHEL: I don't know—Minnie's been up for me.—Says he feels hot inside, an' believes he's got an inflammation.

NURSE: I'll call if I have time—I must go— 20

RACHEL: He's done nothing but ask 'were his eyes bloodshot, and would Minnie be frightened if he turned delirious'. She's frit—an' *I* can't go down—

NURSE: I will call—Goodnight everybody. *(Exit.)*

MRS SMALLEY: I must light the lamp. 25

RACHEL: I didn't hear till four o'clock as she'd gone. Was she unconscious?

MRS SMALLEY: Yes—all day.

RACHEL *(to* HARRY—*who is struggling into his shirt):* And was you at work—?—Fancy, you been at home all this time, then it to 30 happen the first day you was away.—Things do happen cruel.

MRS SMALLEY: Shall you give him his tea, while I go an' see to my lad?

RACHEL: I mustn't be long. *(*MRS SMALLEY *goes out.)* What shall you have?

HARRY: Nowt. 35

RACHEL: Oh, you must 'ave somethink. Just a cup of tea, if nothing else. Come on—come an' sit here. See, it's waiting.—You must be fair sinkin' after bein' at work all day.—I've thought of you every minute, I'm sure. I've heard the driving engines* shudder-ing every time, an' I've thought of you. *(She cuts bread and toasts* 40

it): They say you're hard, but they don't know. *(Suspicion of tears)*: I used to think myself as you was a kid, a frightened bit of a rabbit—but I know different now. *(Tears)*: I know what you've had to go through—an' I've been a cat to you, I have. I
5   know what you've felt—as if you was pushed up against a wall, an' all the breath squeezed out of you—her dyin' by inches—an' I've been a cat to you.

             (She butters the toast.)

HARRY: Tha nedna do that for me.
10 RACHEL: Yes, do eat a bit—you'll be sinkin'. I've had no tea—I'll eat a bit with you, if you will. *(She sits down, drinks tea, and eats a little)*: You know I've fair hated myself—I've wished I was dead. But I needn't talk about myself.—Are your hands sore?

HARRY: A bit.
15 RACHEL: I know they must be—because you've worked like a horse, I know you have, to stop you thinking. I can see you're dog-tired. Let me look. *(She takes his hand)*: Fair raw! *(Melting into tears)*: You don't care a bit about yourself, you don't, an' it's not fair.

20 HARRY: Tha hasna bothered thysen above thy boot-tops.

RACHEL: I know I haven't.—Oh, I was jealous of your mother, 'cause I knowed you was fonder of her— *(Tears.)*

HARRY: Tha nedna— *(She weeps—he hides his face.)*

RACHEL: I s'll never forgive myself—

25 HARRY: Dunna—

(RACHEL, sobbing, goes to him, takes his head on her bosom, and rocks it.)

RACHEL: An' I've been such a cat to thee, Harry—

HARRY *(putting his arms round her waist)*: I've not seen her for two days.

30 RACHEL: Never mind, never mind. She's been wandering—never mind.

HARRY: Now 'er's gone.

RACHEL: Never mind, we s'll die ourselves some day—we shall:—I know tha loved her, better than me—tha allers would—I
35 know.—But let me be wi' thee. *(She sits down on his knee)*: Let me stop wi' thee, tha wants somebody.—An' I care for nowt but thee—tha knows I do—

HARRY: Should we go an' look at her?

RACHEL *(kissing him)*: We will. *(She kisses him again.)* Tha's been
40 like a bird on a frozzen pond, tha has. Tha's been frozzen out—

HARRY: Rachel—?

RACHEL: What—?

HARRY: Dunna kiss me yet—

RACHEL: No—I won't—I won't.

HARRY: Afterwards—

RACHEL: Yes—I know—I know. *(Silence a moment.)* —Come then, we'll go an' look at her. *(She weeps. Lighting a candle, she takes his hand. They go into the front room.)**
(Enter MRS SMALLEY.*)*

MRS SMALLEY: Where are they? I s'd think they've never carted off an' left th' 'ouse em'py. *(Calls)*: Rachel!—Oh my Goodness! —Harry!

(Enter RACHEL *and* HARRY, *both red-eyed, from the sick room.)*
—Oh, here you are.

RACHEL: Yes—did you think I'd gone?

*(*HARRY *pulls on his coat and goes out.)*

MRS SMALLEY: Yes—you said you was in a hurry.

RACHEL: I *shall* have to be goin'.

MRS SMALLEY: I wish my father would come.—Is he grumpy yet?

RACHEL: Harry?—no, he's not grumpy—no.

MRS SMALLEY: What—have you made it up?

RACHEL: There was nothing to make.

MRS SMALLEY: I'm glad to hear it—what about Job Arthur—?

RACHEL: I never did care a bit about him or anybody else—

MRS SMALLEY: No, but—

RACHEL: Well, but—

MRS SMALLEY: Has he asked you?—has he promised you?—our Harry?

RACHEL: Yes—not in words—but I know.

MRS SMALLEY: You don't. Nurse wants him, an' Nurse'll get him.

RACHEL: She won't.

MRS SMALLEY: You see.

RACHEL: Don't you fret your fat, he's not that easy to grab.

MRS SMALLEY: But he's got a fancy for Nurse. He's as proud as they make 'em, an' it would just suit him to crow over us, marryin' a lady.

RACHEL: A *Lady*!

MRS SMALLEY: Well—you know what I mean. An' I believe there's summat in the will for her. My mother harped on her an' our Harry—

RACHEL: An' does she know?

MRS SMALLEY: She's not far off o' guessin', I'll be bound. She is a deep one, Nurse is.

RACHEL: She is. Oh, she'd soon know everything if she got a
5   whifft.—An' has your father got the will?

MRS SMALLEY: No—it's in th' front room.

RACHEL: Well—you should get it, an' see what it says.—*You* should come in for something, and then—

MRS SMALLEY: Durst you come with me?

10 RACHEL: Yes, I durst come.

MRS SMALLEY: Should us then?

RACHEL: Yes—let us. You could burn it if there was owt you didn't like.

MRS SMALLEY: Durst you get it? *(She lights a candle.)*

15 RACHEL: Yes—if you'll show me.

(They go into the next room.)

MRS SMALLEY'S VOICE: Doesn't it smell cold a'ready. OO!

RACHEL'S VOICE: It does.

MRS SMALLEY'S VOICE: Look—you want to get on this table.—
20   This blessed candle does jump.

RACHEL'S VOICE: I could ha' sworn the sheet moved.

(A shriek from MRS SMALLEY—shrieks from RACHEL—a bump— shrieks—MRS SMALLEY rushes across the kitchen out of doors—in a moment HARRY appears in the outer doorway. RACHEL flies blindly into
25   *him.)*

HARRY: Whatever's up?

RACHEL: Oh Harry—Oh Harry!

HARRY: Well—what's up! What's ter got in thy hand?

RACHEL: Oh, whatever was it?—Let's go.

30 HARRY: What wor what? What!

(He starts as Patty walks mildly from the front room.)

It wor nowt but our Patty.

RACHEL: I thought I should have died.

HARRY: What wor ter doin'?

35 RACHEL: I fell off that table. Oh, and I have bruised my arm.

HARRY: What wor you doin'? what's this?

MRS SMALLEY *(entering)*: Oh Rachel—!

RACHEL: It was only Patty.

MRS SMALLEY: Did you get it?—Oh, look at our Harry opening it.

HARRY: Why, it's th' will. I sh'd ha' thought you'd have more about
you— *(He reads—)*

MRS SMALLEY: What's it say.

HARRY: Look for thysen, if tha'rt in such a mighty hurry.

MRS SMALLEY *(reading)*: Five hundred an' fifty pounds—for him   5
and Nurse Broadbanks if they marry—an' if not, to be divided
between me an' him. What did I say! Would you credit it, now?
But there's one thing, Nurse won't *have* him.

RACHEL: He doesn't want her.

HARRY: She's worth a million such as you:—cats, as wants nowt but   10
to lap at a full saucer.* You couldna let her lie quiet for five
minutes, but must be after her bit of money.

RACHEL: Indeed I didn't want the money.

MRS SMALLEY: He wants it himself, an' that's what he's been
contrivin' for all along—him an' that slivin' Nurse. There's a   15
pair of 'em.

HARRY: There's a pair of you, more like it—a couple of slitherin'
cats, nowt else. No more you think of her, than if she wor a dead
fish wi' the money in her mouth.—But you shan't have it, you
shanna, if I can scotch you.   20

RACHEL: Oh Mr Sharp-shins, you think you know everything, do
you. You're mistaken—it's not fair, it isn't. I only—

HARRY: Tha needs to tell me nowt.

NURSE *(entering)*: Oh you are here! The Baroness asked me to call
and see where you were, Rachel.   25

RACHEL: And now you've seen, you can go back an' tell her you've
been.*

HARRY: They've been after th' will: Couldna let her rest still in
her own room, but what must they do, go ferretin' for her
money—   30

MRS SMALLEY: Shut thy mouth, tha's said enough.

HARRY: That I hanna. They'd clawk the stuff out of her hand, if it
wor there—

MRS SMALLEY: Hadn't we a right to see the will.

HARRY: There's a lot of right about you. Here, come here.—Give us   35
hold of it.

MRS SMALLEY: I shan't.

HARRY: What!—Now Nurse, thee read it. We'n all read. Now thee
read it. *(NURSE reads.)* —Hast got it all?—Tha sees?

NURSE: Yes, I understand it.

HARRY: An' what dost say?

NURSE: I say nothing.

MRS SMALLEY: This is what she's been working for.

5 HARRY: Then let them as has worked be paid. What? If I say 'snip',
Nurse, will thaïgh say 'snap'. Come on—'Snap' me, Nurse,—
say 'snap'.—Snip?*

NURSE: This is hardly the occasion.

RACHEL: He doesn't love you, Nurse. This is only his temper.

10 NURSE: I think, out of respect to the dead, we ought not to go on
like this.

MRS SMALLEY: You'll be precise and proper,—all lardy-da—oh
yes——but you've got what you've been aiming at, haven't
you? You've worked it round very clever. You see what carneyin'
15 'll do for you, Rachel. If you'd ha' buttered your words, you
might ha' been all right.

RACHEL: I couldn't creep.

HARRY: No—you could slither, though.

NURSE: I'm afraid I must be going.

20 MRS SMALLEY: Yes, you can smile to yourself, and hug yourself
under your cloak in the dark. It's worth marryin' him for, five
hundred and fifty pound. *(NURSE goes out.)*

HARRY: She's a lady, she is—an' she makes you two look small.

RACHEL: Well, Harry, you can think what you like about me: and
25 you always *have* thought me as bad as you could imagine. But I
only did it to help Susy—and all I've done I've done with you
sleering at me. An' I *shan't* marry Job Arthur: I s'll go in service
in Derby.* An' you needn't sleer at me no more— because it's
your fault, even more than mine.

30 HARRY: A' right, ma'e it my fault.

RACHEL: As much as mine, I said.

HARRY: Dunna let me stop thee from ha'ein' Job Arthur.

RACHEL: Job Arthur's a man as can play his own tune on any mortal
woman, brazen as brass or cuddlin' as a fiddle—

35 HARRY: Or as ronk as an old mouth organ.

RACHEL: Or like a bagpipe as wants squeezin', or a mandoline as
wants tickling—he gets a tune out of the whole job lot, the
whole band—

HARRY: Shut up.

RACHEL: But I'll buy you a cuckoo-clock to keep you company.

HARRY: I'll buy my own.

RACHEL *(flapping her arms suddenly at him)*: Cuckoo!—Cuckoo! Cuckoo!

(Curtain) 5

Act V.

Scene 1.

Time: The Sunday following the last scene.
Place: Porch of Greenstone Church. The Hemstocks have attended the
due post-funeral service.

1ST MOURNER: Well, I niver knowed the likes—
2ND MOURNER: What?
1ST MOURNER: Nurse Broadbanks to be axed wi' old Hezekiah Wilcox, an' Job Arthur Bowers wi' Rachel Wilcox.
2ND MOURNER: An' what about it.
1ST MOURNER: Well, I never thought Nurse would have him, an' everybody said Job Arthur would never marry now.
2ND MOURNER: I'm not surprised at neither of 'em.
1ST MOURNER: I was never more taken in in my life. *(Exeunt.)*
MRS SMALLEY: —No!
3RD MOURNER: I don't call it decent—two sets of banns put up at a funeral Sunday—they might ha' waited till next week.
MRS SMALLEY: I'm going to see about this.
3RD MOURNER: Yes, th' old Baron wants telling, the old nuisance, for he's nothing else. *(Exeunt.)*
4TH MOURNER *(sighing)*: That did me good—I'm sure I've fair cried my eyes up.
5TH MOURNER: You can't make out half the old Baron says, but he makes you feel funny.
4TH MOURNER: As if you'd got ghosts in your bowels. An' when he said—what was it—?
5TH MOURNER: Was it Hezekiah Wilcox axed wi' Nurse Broadbanks—?
4TH MOURNER: Yes—fancy 'em both bein' there to hear it—what a come-down for her.
5TH MOURNER: I dunno—the old chap's tidy well off—
4TH MOURNER: But he's mushy—he slavers like a slobbering spaniel—
5TH MOURNER: Well, women like that sort. *(Exeunt.)*
MR HEMSTOCK: I allers thought 'er'd 'a worn widow's weeds for me—
HARRY: Dost wish it *mor* that road about?
MR HEMSTOCK: Nay, I non know—
HARRY: Are ter stoppin'?

MR HEMSTOCK: I want ter speak ter Nurse.

HARRY: I'm goin' then.

MR HEMSTOCK: Dunna thee—thaïgh wait a bit.

HARRY: Nay. *(Exit.)*

THE BAKER *(in very genteel black)*: Good morning Mr Hemstock.   5

MR HEMSTOCK: Good morning.

THE BAKER: We got more than we bargained for—

MR HEMSTOCK: Yes—a bit surprisin'.

THE BAKER: I'm going to strike—Nurse for a mother-in-law is too
     much of a good thing. Why bless me, you want to be careful   10
     what relatives you have—some you can't help—but a mother-
     in-law, you can.

MR HEMSTOCK: I want to speak to Nurse.

MR WILCOX *(frock coat)*: You've 'ad a big loss, Mr Hemstock—I've
     been through it myself, so I know what it is.   15

THE BAKER: Here, I say, Hezekiah—I don't mind you for a father-
     in-law—

MR WILCOX: Hello, Job Arthur! Well I never! I *ham* surprised, I can
     tell you—

THE BAKER: So'm I.   20

MR WILCOX: But it's a glad surprise—I'd rather say 'My son' to
     you, Job Arthur—

THE BAKER: Hold on a bit, Hezekiah. You've always stood me as a
     good Uncle, let's leave it at that—

MR WILCOX: I'll make you a wedding present of it, Job Arthur   25
     —that little thing—you know—

THE BAKER: I do, worse luck! I've pledged my soul and my honour
     to you, Uncle, my Uncle on the Pop-shop side, but my body's
     my ewe lamb[*]—I don't sell.—Goodmorning, Dr Foules.

DR FOULES: Goodmorning.—Er—excuse me—but Nurse Broad-   30
     banks has not gone yet?

THE BAKER: Not yet, Doctor. Here's her husband-that-is-to-be
     waiting for her.

DR FOULES: Ha!

MR WILCOX: Nurse has not gone yet, Doctor.   35

DR FOULES: Thank you.

THE BAKER: Let's have a look! *(He peeps in church.)* Oh—Oh
     Baron, may I speak to you.

     (Enter BARON, *in surplice,* BARONESS, *and* NURSE.*)*

BARON: And you, what have you to say?   40

THE BAKER: Not much. Only there's a bit of an alteration wants makin'. Rachel's given me the sack.

BARON: I do not understand, Sir.

BARONESS: He wishes to escape from his promise—he wishes to dodge Rachel—

BARON: You, Sir, have you not given your word—!

THE BAKER: And you're welcome keep it, for what it's worth. But you can't cork a woman's promise, Baroness. In short, Baron—and Mr Wilcox—Rachel has asked to be released from her engagement—hem!—with me—and I have felt it my duty to release her. *(He bows.)*

BARON: It is an indignity to the church—it is insult to the Holy Church—

BARONESS: I do not believe this man. It is his ruse to escape from a bond.

MR WILCOX: Yes, My Lady, that's what it is—my poor girl—Nurse?—Nurse?

NURSE: Let Rachel come herself.

BARONESS: She shall.

BARON *(to MR HEMSTOCK)*: Go and bring Rachel here.

MR HEMSTOCK *(shrugging)*: Where am I to go?

NURSE: Please, Mr Hemstock. *(He goes.)*

BARON: Sir, I believe you are a scoundrel.

THE BAKER: I wouldn't deny it, Baron.

MR WILCOX: No—we know him too well—he'd better not begin denyin'—had he Nurse?

NURSE: This is the man, Baron—the—the—the *Wilcox*.

BARON: What! What!

BARONESS: What do you mean, you old wicked man, insulting Nurse in this fashion?

BARON: You—*you*—you Sir! If you speak I will cut you down. The double shame, the double blasphemy!—Ah!—Leave from my sight—Go—Don't stir Sir, till you answer.

DR FOULES: May I ask, Nurse, if I am to congratulate you on your banns?

NURSE: I should think you have no need to ask. I am ready to die, I am so mortified and ashamed.

THE BAKER: Hello—I am only the mote in the eye of the church,☆ am I?—oh Uncle, uncle!

DR FOULES: Then it is a mistake?

NURSE: Worse. It is a mean, base contrivance to trap me. I knew nothing of these banns—I could have dropped. He knows I wouldn't marry him, no, not if—not if—

THE BAKER: You died in a ditch with your shoes on.⃰—I'm undone this time, curse it. Uncle, have a pound of flesh, will you, instead?—I could spare a pound and a half, cut judiciously.⃰

BARON: What do you say, Sir?

THE BAKER: I'm inviting him to have his pound of flesh, instead of his two hundred pounds of money—though it's dear meat, I own.

NURSE: What do you mean, Mr Bowers?

THE BAKER: I owe him £180, and he'll foreclose on our house in a couple of months. Then goodbye my bakery, and they cart my old mother to a lunatic asylum, though she's no more mad than I am.

BARONESS: And what have you done with the money.

THE BAKER: Paid *some* of my debts, Baroness—and some of it I have—as it were, eaten. So in a pound of flesh he'd get his money glorified.

BARON: What do you say, Sir?

MR WILCOX: I say nothing.

(Curtain)

Act V.

Scene 2.

Time: The same.

Scene: The Vicarage Garden-wall, under which runs the path. RACHEL
5 *looks over the wall. Enter* HARRY.

RACHEL: All by yourself?—Where's the others?

HARRY: Stopping.

RACHEL: Did they give my father's banns out?

HARRY: Hisn an' thine.

10 RACHEL: What!—Mine!—Why I told Job Arthur as I wouldn't have
him.

HARRY: 'Appen so.

RACHEL: I did. An' he's never told the Baron. Whatever shall I
do?

15 HARRY: What—?

RACHEL: You don't believe as I told him.

HARRY: I believe nowt.

RACHEL: But I did—an' he agreed.—And did they ask my father
and Nurse?

20 HARRY: Yes.

RACHEL: Oh—but I shan't have him—I shan't. The Baron'll give it
me—but I shan't have him. You needn't believe me, if you don't
want to.

HARRY: When did ter tell Job Arthur?

25 RACHEL: Yesterday.—An' he was glad. He doesn't really care for
me.

HARRY: Are ter having me on—?

RACHEL: May I be struck dead this minute if I am.

HARRY: An' what shall ter do?

30 RACHEL: I don't know—go to Derby. Perhaps *I'*ll learn to be a
nurse.

HARRY: She's marryin' thy *feyther.*

RACHEL *(melting into tears)*: Don't—tha's hurt me enough.
(Dashing away her tears.) Well, I must go in and see to the
35 dinner. Then I'll tell the Baron, and have my head bitten off.
(She turns to go.)

HARRY: Are ter sure tha told Job Arthur?

RACHEL: Go and ask him.

HARRY: There's no tellin' what tha does.

RACHEL: No—there isn't—for the simple reason that I've built my house on the sand.✳

HARRY: How dost mean?

RACHEL: You know right enough. Well, I'll go an' warm th' rice pudding up.   5

HARRY: Rachel—dost care for me?

RACHEL: You'll make me wild in a minute.

HARRY: Rachel—dunna go—it's that lonely.

RACHEL: I s'll have to go and put that pudding in.

HARRY: Come down here first—a minute.   10

RACHEL: Come you up here.

HARRY *(climbing up)*: Rachel.

RACHEL: What?

HARRY: It seems that quiet—like—dunna go an' leave me by mysen. I go rummagin' down i' the loose ground like a   15
moudiwarp, to look at th' coffin.

RACHEL: Do you?

HARRY: I do. I feel as if I should have to get at her an' make her speak. I canna stand this dead-o-night quiet.

RACHEL: No.   20

HARRY: Comin' out of church into this sunshine's like goin' in a cinematograph show. Things jumps about in a flare of light, an' you expect it every minute to go out an' be pitch dark. All the shoutin' an' singin', an' yet there's a sort of quiet—Rachel—?

RACHEL: Never mind;—it will be so for a bit.   25

HARRY: I canna be by myself, though—I canna.

RACHEL: There are plenty of people—

HARRY: Nay, I non want 'em.

RACHEL: Only Nurse.

HARRY: Nor her neither—never.   30

RACHEL: 'Appen so.

HARRY: Tha doesna believe me?

RACHEL: 'I believe nowt.'

HARRY: I wish I may drop dead this minute if I ever did care for her.   35

RACHEL *(smiling)*: You *thought* you did?

HARRY: 'Appen I did think so.

RACHEL: I know you did.

HARRY: But 'er knows nowt about me—like thee.

RACHEL: No.   40

HARRY: Shall ter ha'e me, Rachel?

RACHEL: You want me?

HARRY: Let us be married afore the week's out, Rachel. Dunna
leave me by mysen.

5   RACHEL: Are you in a hurry now, at the last pinch?

HARRY: Shall ter, Rachel?

RACHEL: Yes. *(He kisses her.)*

MR HEMSTOCK *(entering)*: —I should ha' thought you'd more
about you than to be kissin' there where everybody can see

10   you.— —an' today.

RACHEL: There's nobody but you.

MR HEMSTOCK: You don't know who there is.

RACHEL: And I don't care. We're going to be married directly.

MR HEMSTOCK: It'll look nice, that will—his mother buried yes-

15   terday—

HARRY: It ma'es no difference to her, does it?

MR HEMSTOCK: Tha'rt a fawce un, Rachel. Tha's contrived it, after
a'. Tha'rt a fawce un, an' no mistake. But tha's got to come to
the Baron.

20   RACHEL: What for?

MR HEMSTOCK: Nay, dunna ax *me*. Tha'd better look sharp. Ma'e
thy heels crack.

RACHEL: What's up now, I wonder.

(They go out—Curtain)

Act V.

Scene 3.

Time: The same.
Scene: The Church-porch.

BARON: Do not speak Sir. You have vilified me, you have held up   5
the Church to ridicule.

MR WILCOX: I can speak, can't I!

BARON: Do not speak, you shall not—do not speak. We will not
hear your voice. You are a blasphemer.

MR WILCOX: I can't see but what a Methodist's* as good as a   10
Church, whatever. What have I done, what have I done—?

BARONESS: What have you done—!!

MR WILCOX: Whatever anybody says, there's nobody can say I've
ever done anything as wasn't right—

BARON: What, Sir—what—   15

THE BAKER: Here's Rachel.

MRS SMALLEY: I'll bet it's her doin's. She's the deepest I ever met,
bar none.

BARON: Rachel—?

RACHEL: Yes Baron.   20

BARON: Who wrote to me the letter of the banns for—your father
and Nurse—?

MR WILCOX: I did.

BARON: Scoundrel—Imposter!

NURSE: You had not the slightest justification for it.   25

DR FOULES: Surely, Nurse, you are flattered. A woman likes a
peremptory wooing.

MR WILCOX: You accepted me on Friday night, Nurse, you know
you did.

NURSE: I did no such thing.   30

THE BAKER: Now Rachel, speak up. I say you've refused me—

RACHEL: So I have.

THE BAKER: Of course. And I forgot to take the banns back—

RACHEL: That's your look-out.

BARON: Rachel,—Ah insolent!   35

THE BAKER: Now—my case settled—did Nurse accept your father?
—Of course not.

RACHEL: She did.

MR WILCOX: There you are.

NURSE: I did not—I would not demean myself—I did not.

BARONESS: This is very funny, Nurse.

BARON: I have spoken the banns.

MR WILCOX: Come now, Nurse.

5 NURSE: You horrid, hateful old man. You know you worked yourself into a state, I thought you were delirious, and I had to promise anything.

MR WILCOX: A promise is a promise.

MRS SMALLEY: Of all the deep-uns, Rachel, you cap all.

10 RACHEL: What's it to do with me?

NURSE: You pestered and pestered and pestered me—

DR FOULES: All's fair in love and war,* Nurse.

BARON: What were the exact words?

RACHEL: 'Yes, yes, I'll marry you,—if you'll settle down now and go

15 to sleep—'

NURSE: Why! What!—You are an underhand thing.

RACHEL: What if I did happen to hear.

NURSE: You were listening!

RACHEL: I could hear—it all.

20 NURSE: How hateful, how hateful!

BARON: I do not understand—explain.

NURSE: He was shamming—

MR WILCOX: She's had me on a string—

RACHEL: She's sniffed at him for months, wondering whether or

25 not to lick him up—

DR FOULES: The debateable tit-bit—!

BARON: I will understand this matter—speak Nurse—

NURSE: He shammed fever, delirium—and to comfort him, to soothe him, I said I would marry him. I thought he was raving

30 —and I would not marry him—I'd rather beg in the streets.

MR WILCOX: Oh but, Nurse, Nurse, look here—

BARON: Silence Sir, silence. You are a base, malingering pulamiting wretch.

RACHEL: Well—she came to see him often enough, and stopped

35 long enough—

BARONESS: You cannot, Baron, blame the man for everything.

DR FOULES: A man who was delirious in fever on Friday night would hardly be disporting himself at Church on Sunday morning—

40 MR WILCOX: I'm not disporting myself.

BARONESS: I don't know. It's not much, and there *are* still miracles.

DR FOULES: Surely miracles are not wasted on—Methodists, Baroness.

BARONESS: I do not know—I do not know. Rachel, did you put the pudding to warm? 5

RACHEL: Yes'm.

BARONESS: Then it's burnt to a cinder.

THE BAKER: Crozzled up.

BARON: You, Sir, you Wilcox, are a base scoundrel.

MR WILCOX: She shall pay for this. 10

NURSE: I *must* have it contradicted—I must.

THE BAKER: I will contradict it, Nurse.

DR FOULES: And I.

MR HEMSTOCK: An' me.

HARRY: An' me. 15

BARONESS: But I'm not so sure—

BARON: Enough—enough. I am again a disgrace and a laughing stock. You, Sir, you Wilcox—

MR WILCOX: What, Baron Von Hude—?

BARON: You—you—you are a scoundrel. 20

THE BAKER: It's old news.

BARON: I withdraw and refute these double banns next Sunday—

MR WILCOX: Not with my consent—

BARON: Do not speak. And in the public paper must be a refutation— 25

NURSE: Oh, isn't it dreadful!

MRS SMALLEY: Folks shouldn't shilly-shally.

BARON: And then—I have done—

DR FOULES: Perhaps you can say there was a mistake. Substitute my name for that of Mr Wilcox. 30

THE BAKER: All's fair in love and war. Substitute Mrs Smalley's name for Rachel's.

RACHEL: A change for the better is always welcome. Substitute Harry Hemstock for Job Arthur Bowers.

BARON: This is madness and insult. 35

DR FOULES: It is deadly earnest, Baron. Nurse, will you be asked in church with me next Sunday?

THE BAKER: Susy, will you be asked in church with me next Sunday?

HARRY: Rachel, shall we be axed in church next Sunday. 40

BARON: Enough, enough. Go away, I will suffer no more of this.

BARONESS: Such wicked frivolity! Rachel, go home at once to see to that pudding.

DR FOULES: We are most deeply serious. Nurse, are we not?

5 THE BAKER: Susy, are we not?

HARRY: Rachel, are we not?

RACHEL: Chorus of ladies—'Yes!'

NURSE AND MRS SMALLEY: Chorus of ladies, 'Yes!'

DR FOULES: Millicent Broadbanks—Arthur William Foules.

10 THE BAKER: Job Arthur Bowers—Susan Smalley, née Hemstock, widow.

HARRY: Rachel Wilcox—Harry Hemstock.

BARON: Away—away—

DR FOULES: Baron, you should play Duke to our 'As You Like It'.*

15 BARON: I do not like it—I will not—

MRS SMALLEY: Then lump it.

MR WILCOX: I call it scandalous, going on like this.

RACHEL: Like it or lump it, father, like it or lump it.

DR FOULES: You accept me, Nurse?

20 NURSE: I do, Doctor. *(He kisses her hand.)*

THE BAKER: You accept me, Susan?

MRS SMALLEY: This once, Job Arthur. *(He kisses her cheek.)*

RACHEL *(after a moment)*: Come on here, Harry.

(They kiss on the mouth.)

25 BARON: Go away from here. You shall not pollute my church.

BARONESS: It is disgraceful.

MR WILCOX: They want horsewhipping, every one of them.

MR HEMSTOCK: Well—I must say—

DR FOULES: It's 'As You Like It'.

30 THE BAKER: It's 'As You *Lump* It', Hezekiah.

(Curtain)

THE MARRIED MAN

DR GEORGE GRAINGER
WILLIAM BRENTNALL
MRS PLUM
JACK MAGNEER   5
ANNIE CALLADINE
EMILY CALLADINE
ADA CALLADINE
SALLY MAGNEER
MR MAGNEER   10
ELSA SMITH
GLADYS
TOM
ETHEL, GRAINGER'S WIFE☆

THE MARRIED MAN*

Act I.

[*A bedroom in* MRS PLUM's *cottage, shared by* DR GEORGE GRAINGER *and* WILLIAM BRENTNALL. *Both men are dressing.*]

GRAINGER: Bring me some collars up.* 5
BRENTNALL: And what are you going to do?
GRAINGER: God knows.
BRENTNALL: How much money have you got.
GRAINGER: Four damn quid.
BRENTNALL: Hm!—You're well off, considering. But what *do* you 10
think of doing?
GRAINGER: I don't know.
BRENTNALL: Where do you think of going on Saturday?
GRAINGER: Hell.
BRENTNALL: Too expensive, my boy—four quid won't carry you 15
there.
GRAINGER: Oh chuck it, Billy.
BRENTNALL: What the Hanover's the good of chucking it. You're
not a blooming cock-robin, to take no thought for the morrow.
   (*Enter* MRS PLUM *with the collars.*) 20
MRS PLUM: Eee, I'm sorry I forgot 'em, Dr Grainger. I'm ever so
sorry.
GRAINGER: Don't you fret yourself about *that*, Mrs Plum. You're all
right, you are.
MRS PLUM: Eee, but I can't get it out of my head, that there what 25
you've just told me.
GRAINGER: You want to sneeze hard, Mrs Plum. That'll shift it.
MRS PLUM (*laughing*): Hee—hi—Hark you there now. And have
you got rid of it off your mind, Dr Grainger.
GRAINGER: My head's as clear as a bell o' brass, Mrs Plum. 30
Nothing ails me.
MRS PLUM: My word, it doesn't. My word, but you're looking well,

193

you're a sight better than when you come, isn't he Mr Brentnall?

BRENTNALL: He's too healthy for anything, Mrs Plum—he's so healthy, he'd walk slap into a brick wall, and never know he'd hurt himself.

MRS PLUM: Eee—I don't know.—But that there as you told me, Dr Grainger—

GRAINGER: —Here, you go and see if that's Jack Magneer, and if it is, let him come up.

MRS PLUM: You're a caution, you are that, Dr Grainger.

(Exit.)

BRENTNALL: The girl is gone on you, the kid is yours, you are a married man, and you mean to abide by your family?

GRAINGER: What the devil else is there to do?

BRENTNALL: Very well. Have you bothered about another job.

GRAINGER: No—I did when I was in Wolverhampton.※ Look what a fiendish business it is, offering yourself and being refused like a dog.

BRENTNALL: So you've taken no steps.

GRAINGER: No.

BRENTNALL: And you've absolutely no idea what you're going to do on Saturday, when you've finished here?

GRAINGER: No.

BRENTNALL: And yet you mean to stick by your wife and kid?

GRAINGER: What else can I do?

BRENTNALL: Well you're a beauty! You're just skulking, like a frightened rabbit.

GRAINGER: Am I begad?

BRENTNALL: Are you fond of the kid?

GRAINGER: I shouldn't like anything to happen to it.

BRENTNALL: Neither should I. But the feelings of your breast towards it—?

GRAINGER: Well, I'm a lot *fonder* of that youngster at my digs in Wolverhampton—you know—

BRENTNALL: Then you feel no paternal emotion.

GRAINGER: No. Don't talk rot.

BRENTNALL: How often have you been over to see your wife?

GRAINGER: Once.

BRENTNALL: Once since you were married?

GRAINGER: Yes.

BRENTNALL: And that when the baby was just born?

GRAINGER: Yes.

BRENTNALL: And you're living—which, a recluse, or a gay bachelor.*

GRAINGER: You can imagine me a recluse. 5

BRENTNALL: You're a blossom, Georgie, you're a jewel of a muddler.

GRAINGER: How could I help it! I was careful enough with the girl —I never thought, to tell you the truth, that—here's Jack!

BRENTNALL: That what? 10

GRAINGER: Shut up. Jack's a fine fellow.

BRENTNALL: Needs to be, to match you.

GRAINGER: Now Billy Brentnall, none of your sark.

JACK'S VOICE: How long are you going to be.

GRAINGER: How-do Jack! Shan't be a sec.—come up. 15

(Enter JACK*—aged 33—very big, a farmer, something of a gentleman, wears leggings and breeches, and a black bow tie.)*

JACK MAGNEER: Seem to be donning yourselves up—how are you—

GRAINGER: Mr Magneer—Mr Brentnall: Jack—Billy. 20

MAGNEER: Yes, quite so. How are you, Billy?

BRENTNALL: I'm very well. You're Miss Magneer's brother?

GRAINGER: Sally's—

MAGNEER: Yis, I am, and what of it?

BRENTNALL: Oh—only you are lucky. 25

*(*GRAINGER *whistles gaily.)*

MAGNEER: What you whistling for, George lad? Aren't I lucky?

GRAINGER: I wish Sally was *my* sister, Jack.

MAGNEER: Yis, you do, an' so do I George lad—then me an' you'd be brothers.—Oh my good God, are you goin' to be all night 30 tittivating yourselves up.

GRAINGER: Jack's in a hurry.

MAGNEER: No I'm not, but damn it all—

GRAINGER: All right Jacko, all right. I know she's a very nice girl—

BRENTNALL: Where are you taking me? 35

GRAINGER: To see some real fine girls.

MAGNEER: Not so much *fine** girls, Billy—some damn *nice* girls, *nice* girls, mind you.

GRAINGER: Quite right, Jacko. *(Seriously)*: No, but they are, Billy, real nice girls. Three sisters, orphans. 40

MAGNEER: An' the oldest of them will happen be Mrs Grainger —eh, what?

GRAINGER: Liar!

MAGNEER: You see Billy, it's like this. I'm glad you've come, because it levels us up. I believe you're a nice chap. Don't you take me wrong. I mean you're not one of these dam sods as can see nowt in a girl but—you know—

BRENTNALL: Yes.

GRAINGER: Yes, Billy knows. Most moral young man.

MAGNEER: Fooling apart, George, aren't they nice girls.

GRAINGER: *Really* nice girls, they are.

MAGNEER: But you see, there's three of 'em—an' we've never been but two of us—d'you twig?

BRENTNALL: I twig.

MAGNEER: But no fooling, mind you.

BRENTNALL: Thanks for your caution, Mr Magneer.

MAGNEER: Oh no, no, nothing of the sort: only they *are* nice girls—you see what I mean—Oh no, Billy—

GRAINGER: And three of 'em.

BRENTNALL: And the odd one falls to me. Thanks, I was born to oblige.

MAGNEER: Now Billy, no. I want you t'have a good time. You see what I mean. I'm willing to step aside. You're here only for a bit—I'm always here. So I want you— —

GRAINGER: "I want all of you t'have a good time."

MAGNEER: Yis, I do, I do that, George.

GRAINGER: That's always Jacko's cry—'I want you t'have it your own road. I'm willing any road. I want you t'have a good time.' Self-effacing chap is Jack.

BRENTNALL: Do I put on a dinner jacket.

GRAINGER: Good God no—have you brought one?

BRENTNALL: Well—I might have to dine at some people's down towards Ashbourne.

(Curtain)

Act II.

*A long, low dining room—table laid for supper—bowls of crimson and
white flowers, a large lamp—an old-fashioned room, furnished with taste.
The oldest* MISS CALLADINE—*aged 32, tall, slim, pale, dressed in black,
wearing Parma violets,*✳ *looks ladylike, but rather yearning. She walks* 5
about restlessly. Enter DR GRAINGER—*in morning coat.*

ANNIE CALLADINE: Aren't you late?

GRAINGER: A little—waiting for my friend. He's gone round to
"The George" with Jack—some arrangement about farm stock.
(He takes both her hands, which she offers him yearningly, and, 10
after glancing round, kisses her hastily, as if unwillingly.) Where's
Emily?

ANNIE CALLADINE: Emily and Ada✳ are both entertaining Mrs
Wesson in the drawing room. I hope they'll get rid of her before
Jack comes. I'm afraid we are being talked about. I'm afraid I'm 15
not doing my duty by the girls.

GRAINGER: What do you mean?

ANNIE CALLADINE: You are here so often—

GRAINGER: I'm going away directly, so you'll be safe after Saturday.

ANNIE CALLADINE: Really going away on Saturday—really—really. 20
(Puts her hands on his shoulders.)

GRAINGER: It's right—

ANNIE CALLADINE: Then people will talk more than ever. I shall be
considered loose: and what is to become of the girls—

GRAINGER: *You* considered loose—Oh Caesar! 25

ANNIE CALLADINE: Where are you going?

GRAINGER: Don't know.

ANNIE CALLADINE: Why won't you tell me?

GRAINGER: Because I don't know. I am waiting for a letter—it will
come tomorrow. Either I shall be going to Scotland, or down to 30
London—one or the other, but I don't know which.

ANNIE CALLADINE: Scotland or London—!

GRAINGER: I hope it's London.

ANNIE CALLADINE: Why do you?

GRAINGER: Well—more life, for one thing. 35

ANNIE CALLADINE: And is it 'life' you want?—that sort of life?

GRAINGER: Not that sort, exactly—but—. Oh, by the way, I told
you I was bringing my friend—

ANNIE CALLADINE: Mr Brentnall—yes.

GRAINGER: Well, don't be surprised if I seem rather different tonight, will you? Billy's very circumspect, *very* circumspect—nice, mind you, but *good*.

ANNIE CALLADINE: I see.

5   GRAINGER: You'll like him though.

ANNIE CALLADINE *(bitingly)*: In spite of his goodness.

GRAINGER: Yes, I know you like 'life' better than 'goodness'—don't you now? *(He puts his hand under her chin.)*

ANNIE CALLADINE *(drawing away)*: You seem to know a great deal
10   about me.

GRAINGER: I know what you want.

ANNIE CALLADINE: What?

GRAINGER *(glancing round to see if he is safe—taking her in his arms, pressing her close, kissing her. She submits because she can scarcely
15   help herself—there is a sound of feet and voices—he hastily releases her)*: That!

ANNIE CALLADINE *(struggling with herself)*: Indeed no, Dr Grainger.

GRAINGER: That's the ticket—keep it up, Annie.

(Enter EMILY *and* ADA CALLADINE—EMILY, *aged 27, quiet, self-
20   possessed, dressed all in black—*ADA, *aged 23—rather plump, handsome, charmingly young and wicked-looking—dressed in black and purple, with a crimson flower.)*

ANNIE CALLADINE: Has Mrs Wesson gone.

ADA CALLADINE: Not before she heard a man's voice—I told her
25   you were engaged—

GRAINGER: You what?

ADA CALLADINE *(bursting with laughter)*: I told her Annie was engaged.

ANNIE CALLADINE *(severely)*: With a caller, you mean, Ada?

30   GRAINGER: Oh, I see.

ADA CALLADINE: Yes—oh yes—oh how *funny*!

GRAINGER: Not funny at all.—Jack's doing some business round at the 'George', Emily.

EMILY CALLADINE: Is he?

35   GRAINGER *(discomfited)*: I think I'll go and hurry them up.

ADA CALLADINE: Do!

ANNIE CALLADINE: You think it is quite safe to bring your *good* friend here?

GRAINGER: Oh, quite safe, Annie—don't be alarmed. Tat-ta!
40   *(Exit.)*

(He is heard running down the stairs.)

ANNIE CALLADINE: I don't think Dr Grainger improves on acquaintance.

ADA CALLADINE: *We've* never got any further with him, so we can't say.

EMILY CALLADINE: Why do you think so, Annie?

ANNIE CALLADINE *(rather haughty)*: You would not guess what he said to me?

ADA CALLADINE: I think you've given him rather a long rope.

ANNIE CALLADINE *(with dignity)*: If I have, he's hit me across the face with it.

EMILY CALLADINE: What did he say, Annie?

ANNIE CALLADINE: He is bringing a friend—a school and college friend—in a bank in London now—rather genteel, I believe. Well, Dr Grainger said to me this evening: 'You know my friend is *very* circumspect, *very* circumspect, so you won't be surprised if my behaviour is rather different this evening.'

ADA CALLADINE: Oh indeed!

EMILY CALLADINE: You should have kept him more in his place, Annie.

ANNIE CALLADINE: I should, but I thought he was a gentleman. I don't know *how* we're going to receive them this evening.

EMILY CALLADINE: We need simply take no notice of him, and be just polite.

ANNIE CALLADINE: But we don't know what he may have told his friend about us.

EMILY CALLADINE: I never cared for him.

ADA CALLADINE: Oh what ripping fun.

ANNIE CALLADINE: Ada, be careful what you do and say.

ADA CALLADINE: It's not I who've put my foot in it. It is you if anyone.

ANNIE CALLADINE: I have been too free, perhaps: but you cannot say I have put my foot in it. I wish I had never admitted Dr Grainger at all—but he came with Jack—

EMILY CALLADINE: We shall go through all right with it. Simply despise Dr Grainger.

ANNIE CALLADINE: He is despicable.

ADA CALLADINE: He is here.

ANNIE CALLADINE: Emily, will you go downstairs and receive them. Ada, you stay here.

(*Exit* EMILY—*voices downstairs.*)

ADA CALLADINE: They are all three here—I must go also. *(Exit.)*

(ANNIE CALLADINE *straightens her hair before the mirror, rubs out her wrinkles, puts her flowers nicely, and seats herself with much composure.*

Enter GRAINGER *and* BRENTNALL, *followed by* ADA CALLADINE.*)*

GRAINGER *(stiffly)*: Miss Annie Calladine—Mr Brentnall.

BRENTNALL: What a nice smell of flowers.

ANNIE CALLADINE: It is this mezereon that Mr Magneer brought.

BRENTNALL: Did Mr Magneer bring flowers—I shouldn't have thought the idea could occur to him.

ANNIE CALLADINE: He always brings flowers from the *garden*. It would never occur to him to buy them for us.

BRENTNALL: I see—how nice of him.

GRAINGER: All country fellows cart handfuls of flowers that they've got out of their own gardens, to their girls.

ANNIE CALLADINE: Nevertheless, Mr Magneer does it nicely.

(*Enter* MAGNEER *and* EMILY.)

MAGNEER: Now we seem as if we're going to be all right. What do you say, George?

GRAINGER: I say same.

ANNIE CALLADINE: Do take a seat, all of you. Jack, you love the couch—

MAGNEER: It's a very nice couch, this is. *(Sits down.)*

BRENTNALL: I should think it would be the easiest thing in life to write a poem about a couch. I wonder if the woman was giving Cowper a gentle hint—

ADA CALLADINE *(shrieking with laughter)*: Yes—yes—yes!!

BRENTNALL: I never see a couch but my heart moves to poetry. The very buttons must be full of echoes—

MAGNEER *(bending his ear)*: Can't hear 'em, Billy.

BRENTNALL: Will none of you tune his ear?

ADA CALLADINE: Yes—yes!!

EMILY CALLADINE *(seating herself quietly beside* MAGNEER*)*: What is it you are listening for, Jack?

MAGNEER *(awkwardly)*: I've no idea.

ANNIE CALLADINE: Where will you sit, Mr Brentnall? Do choose a comfortable chair!

BRENTNALL *(seating himself beside her)*: Thanks very much.

MAGNEER: Nay-nay-nay, Billy.

BRENTNALL *(rising suddenly)*: Er—there's a broken spring in that chair, Miss Calladine. *(He crosses the hearth.)*

ANNIE CALLADINE: I'm so sorry—have a cushion in—do—do—do!

BRENTNALL: Will you allow me to sit here. 5

ADA CALLADINE: Let me give you some supper.

GRAINGER: Shall I administer the drinks?

(GRAINGER gives the women burgundy, the men whisky and soda. ADA CALLADINE hands round food. GRAINGER seats himself reluctantly beside ANNIE CALLADINE—ADA CALLADINE takes a low chair next 10 *BRENTNALL.)*

MAGNEER: Now we are all right—at least I hope so.

BRENTNALL *(to* ADA*)*: You are quite all right?

ADA CALLADINE *(laughing)*: As far as I know.

BRENTNALL *(to* EMILY*)*: I can see you are perfectly at home. 15 *(EMILY bows quietly, with a smile.)* And you, Miss Calladine?

ANNIE CALLADINE: Thank you!

BRENTNALL: Gentlemen—the ladies!

GRAINGER *(ironically)*: God Bless 'em.

MAGNEER: Amen! *(They drink.)* 20

ADA CALLADINE: Ladies—the gentlemen!

ANNIE CALLADINE: God Help Them.

EMILY CALLADINE: Amen! *(They drink.)*

BRENTNALL: Wherein must the Lord help us, Miss Calladine?

ANNIE CALLADINE: To run away,* Mr Brentnall. 25

EMILY CALLADINE: Annie!*

ADA CALLADINE: To come to the scratch, you mean.

BRENTNALL: Ha!—Gentlemen—to Marriage!

JACK: I don't think!

ANNIE CALLADINE: What is *your* comment, Dr Grainger. 30

GRAINGER: Mine!*

BRENTNALL: Dr Grainger is a confirmed misogynist.

GRAINGER: Shut up, you fool.

ANNIE CALLADINE: Oh—we've not heard so before.

MAGNEER: D'you mean George doesn't believe in marriage! Nay, 35 you're wrong there—when th' time comes—

ANNIE CALLADINE: When *does* the time come for a man to marry, Jack?

MAGNEER: When he can't help it, I s'd think.

(Silence.)

BRENTNALL: You're very quiet, George.

GRAINGER: Don't you be a fool.

ANNIE CALLADINE: Your humour is not very complimentary this
evening, Dr Grainger.

MAGNEER: There's perhaps too many of us in th' room, Eh?

ANNIE CALLADINE: Not too many for me, Jack.

ADA CALLADINE *(bursting into laughter)*: Do be complimentary,
somebody, if only to cheer us up.

MAGNEER *(putting his arm round* EMILY*'s waist)*: Yes, I will.

BRENTNALL *(putting his arm round* ADA*'s neck)*: May I kiss you, Ada.

ADA CALLADINE *(laughing)*: How *(laughs)* —how awfully nice
(laughs heartily) of you.

*(*BRENTNALL *kisses her.)*

MAGNEER: Oh my God, now we're coming on.

(He kisses EMILY *furtively.)*

BRENTNALL: Mind your own business.

(Seizes a newspaper, and screens it before him and ADA*—they put heads
together.)*

MAGNEER: I call that comin' on—eh what?

BRENTNALL *(to* ADA*—behind the newspaper)*: Your lips taste of
Burgundy.

MAGNEER *(jumping in his seat)*: Well I'll be damned!

ANNIE CALLADINE *(loudly and sarcastically)*: Do you like the
flavour, Mr Brentnall?

BRENTNALL *(from behind the paper)*: Excellent!— *(sotto voce*[*]*)*
—you are awfully jolly.

MAGNEER *(bouncing with surprise)*: Well strike me Lucky!

BRENTNALL *(throwing him another newspaper)*: Here you are then!

MAGNEER: Good God! *(He spreads the paper before him and* EMILY.*)*

GRAINGER: You dam fool, Billy Brentnall.

BRENTNALL: Dog in the manger.[*] *(Softly—to* ADA*)*: Do you think
I'm a fool?—no, you like me.

MAGNEER *(from behind his paper)*: How're you going on, Billy?

BRENTNALL: Fine—how're you going on, George?

(The four peep over their newspapers at GRAINGER *and* ANNIE.*)*

BRENTNALL: Temperature down at freezing point over there?

GRAINGER: I'll have it out of you for this, William.

ANNIE CALLADINE: Why, what has Mr Brentnall done amiss, Dr
Grainger.

BRENTNALL *(from behind his paper)*: Oh it's not I. It's Georgie's sins finding him out. Be sure your sins will find you out.

ADA CALLADINE *(softly)*: You're not a bit what I thought you would be?

BRENTNALL *(softly)*: Worse or better? 5

ADA CALLADINE *(laughing)*: Oh—better.

BRENTNALL: What did you think I should be?

ADA CALLADINE: Circumspect.

(GRAINGER sends a cushion smashing through their paper.)

MAGNEER: What the devil's up, George? 10

ANNIE CALLADINE: Oh, it annoys him to see other people enjoying themselves when he can't.

BRENTNALL *(spreading the paper for screen)*: The nail on the head, Miss—may I say Annie!

ANNIE CALLADINE: Yes, Mr Brentnall. 15

BRENTNALL: I wish I were two men, Annie.

(GRAINGER sends the cushion again smashing through the newspaper.)

MAGNEER: God help thee—George, do settle down.

BRENTNALL *(spreading the paper again)*: It's high time he did— Settle down, Georgie—it's good advice. 20

ADA CALLADINE *(softly)*: What makes him so cross tonight?

BRENTNALL *(softly)*: Don't know—unless he's shy.

ADA CALLADINE *(bursting with laughter)*: Shy!

BRENTNALL: Why, isn't he?

ADA CALLADINE: You should see the way he carries on— 25

BRENTNALL: With you?

ADA CALLADINE: Annie.

(The cushion crashes through the paper.)

MAGNEER: Damn thee George, take Annie downstairs a minute, if tha can't bide still. 30

GRAINGER: That fool there—!

BRENTNALL *(restoring the fragments of paper—softly—to ADA)*: You know there's a secret about Dr Grainger.

ADA CALLADINE: Oh *(laughs)* do tell me.

GRAINGER: Billy Brentnall! 35

BRENTNALL: I hear you calling me.

ADA CALLADINE: Do tell me the secret.

BRENTNALL: Kiss me then. *(They kiss—she laughs.)* You are awfully jolly. *(Kisses her under the ear.)*

ADA CALLADINE *(shaking with laughter)*: Don't, don't, oh don't. 40

BRENTNALL: Does my moustache tickle you—Sorry.

MAGNEER: Nation seize me, did ever you hear!

GRAINGER: Such a fool? I'll bet you never did.

ADA CALLADINE: Tell me that secret.

5 BRENTNALL: George has got another girl.

ADA CALLADINE: Who—where?

GRAINGER: Oh, cheeze it, Billy.

BRENTNALL: Sally Magneer.

GRAINGER: Damn you.

10 ADA CALLADINE: No.

BRENTNALL: Fact!—She told me herself.

MAGNEER: What's that George?

GRAINGER *(to* BRENTNALL*)*: Liar!

BRENTNALL: It's the truth—mine's pistols.

15 MAGNEER: You're a devil, George, you're a devil.

GRAINGER: I am that! *(Bitterly.)*

EMILY CALLADINE: And what is Mr Brentnall?

MAGNEER *(shaking his head)*: Nay, I'm not going to say.

(He rises heavily, draws EMILY *after him, and goes out of the room.)*

20 BRENTNALL *(rising)*: Well, this newspaper's no more good.

ADA CALLADINE: There's a fire in the drawing room—and real
    screens there.

BRENTNALL: And Jack *does* occupy *himself.* Right you are.

GRAINGER: Chuck it, Billy.

25 BRENTNALL: What?

GRAINGER: None o' that.

BRENTNALL: Well I'll go to—

GRAINGER: I've no doubt.

ANNIE CALLADINE: Dr Grainger is afraid of being left alone: he
30   must have someone to protect him.

BRENTNALL: What from?

ANNIE CALLADINE: Presumably from me— *(to* GRAINGER*)* will you
    go down with Ada to the drawing room?—Ada, do you mind?

ADA CALLADINE: Not at all. *(Exit.)*

35 GRAINGER *(bitterly)*: Very nice of you Annie, very nice of you.
    (Exit.)

                    *(*BRENTNALL *and* ANNIE *seat themselves.)*

ANNIE CALLADINE: What do you think of all this, Mr Brentnall.

BRENTNALL: Why, it's a mere lark. Jack is really courting Emily,
40   and Ada is sheer mischief, and I'm quite decent, really.

ANNIE CALLADINE: Are you really?

BRENTNALL: Judge from your own instinct.

ANNIE CALLADINE: I think you are—and is Dr Grainger?

BRENTNALL: What do you think?

ANNIE CALLADINE: There is something not nice about him. 5

BRENTNALL: Has he been courting you?

ANNIE CALLADINE *(drawing herself up)*: Well—!

BRENTNALL: You see, it's a pity—

ANNIE CALLADINE: What is a pity?

BRENTNALL: Why—shall I say just what I think—? 10

ANNIE CALLADINE: I want you to.

BRENTNALL: Well then—it's a pity that girls like you—you are over thirty?

ANNIE CALLADINE: Yes.

BRENTNALL: It's a pity that so many of the best women let their 15 youth slip by, because they don't find a man good enough—and then, when dissatisfaction becomes a torture—later on—you *are* dissatisfied with life, you *do* lack something big—?—

ANNIE CALLADINE: Yes.

BRENTNALL: When it comes to that stage, the want of a man is a 20 torture to you. And since the common men make the advances—

ANNIE CALLADINE: Yes!

BRENTNALL *(putting his arm round her and kissing her)*: You are either driven to a kind of degradation, or you go nearly, slightly 25 mad from want—

ANNIE CALLADINE: Yes.

BRENTNALL *(kissing her)*: If you want love from men like Grainger —take it for what it's worth—because we're made so that either we must have love, or starve and go slightly mad. 30

ANNIE CALLADINE: But I don't want that kind of love.

BRENTNALL: But do be honest with yourself. Don't cause a split between your conscious self and your unconscious—that is insanity. You *do* want love, almost any sort. Make up your mind what you'll accept, or what you won't, but keep your ideal 35 intact. Whatever men you take, keep the idea of man intact: let your soul wait whether your body does or not. But don't drag the first down to the second. Do you understand?

ANNIE CALLADINE: I could love you.

BRENTNALL: But I am going away in a day or two, and most 40

probably shall not be here again—and I am engaged. You see, so many women are too good for the men, that for every decent man, there are thirty decent women. And you decent women go and waste and wither away. Do think it out square, and make

5   the best of it. Virginity and all that is no good to you.

ANNIE CALLADINE: And what would you advise?

BRENTNALL: Know men, and have men, if you must. But keep your soul virgin, wait and believe in the *good* man you may never have.

10 ANNIE CALLADINE: It is not very—What made Dr Grainger so queer tonight?

BRENTNALL: Because he's married.

ANNIE CALLADINE: I *felt* it—to whom?

BRENTNALL: A girl in Wolverhampton—married last January, a son

15   in March, now it's June.

ANNIE CALLADINE: Oh, the liar!—and what sort of girl?

BRENTNALL: Decent, I believe.

ANNIE CALLADINE: Does she love him?

BRENTNALL: Yes.

20 ANNIE CALLADINE: The brute—the—

BRENTNALL: He doesn't love her, you see—

ANNIE CALLADINE: It makes it no better—and she doesn't know how he's—

BRENTNALL: Of course not.

25 ANNIE CALLADINE: I wonder if I know her—what is her name?

BRENTNALL: Marson—her people are tailors in Broad Street.

ANNIE CALLADINE: No, I don't know her!—But to think—

BRENTNALL: Don't be too ready to blame.

ANNIE CALLADINE: You men are all alike.

30 BRENTNALL: Not true—who is coming?

ANNIE CALLADINE: I don't know.

(Enter SALLY MAGNEER—*a very big, strapping farmer's daughter, evidently moderately well off.)*

SALLY MAGNEER: Good-evening!—Jack here?

35 ANNIE CALLADINE: Good evening—Yes, I believe he's in the drawing room with Dr Grainger.

SALLY MAGNEER: That's how you arrange it, is it? *(To* BRENTNALL*):* —Nice, isn't it?

BRENTNALL: Very nice.

40 SALLY MAGNEER: Who else is in the drawing room?

ANNIE CALLADINE: My sisters. I believe they're having some music.

SALLY MAGNEER: They don't make much noise over it, any way. Can I go and see?

ANNIE CALLADINE: Certainly.

(BRENTNALL opens the door for her, and whistles quickly a private call—repeats it. Grainger's whistle is heard in answer.)

SALLY MAGNEER: All right, I won't drop in on you too sudden.

(Exit.)

ANNIE CALLADINE: What impertinence!

BRENTNALL *(laughing)*: She's made a dead set at Grainger. If he weren't married, she'd get him.

ANNIE CALLADINE: How disgusting!

BRENTNALL: Maybe—but a woman who determines soon enough to get married, succeeds. Delay is fatal—and marriage is beastly, on most occasions.

ANNIE CALLADINE: I will go to the drawing room. Will you excuse me?

(Exit—BRENTNALL pours himself a drink. Enter GRAINGER.)

GRAINGER: What the Hell have you been up to?

BRENTNALL: What the Hell have you been up to?

GRAINGER: What have you been stuffing into Annie!

BRENTNALL: What have you been stuffing into Ada?

GRAINGER: Nothing, you devil.

BRENTNALL: Nothing, you devil.

GRAINGER: What's Sally after?

BRENTNALL: You.

GRAINGER: She ought to be shot.

BRENTNALL: So ought you.

(Enter MAGNEER.)

MAGNEER: What the Hell's up tonight?

BRENTNALL: My tail, and George's dander, and your—but what's Miss Magneer after?

MAGNEER: That's what I want to know. You know George here, he's a devil. He's been on wi' some little game with our Sally.

GRAINGER: You sweet liar, Jack.

MAGNEER: Now George, what is it?

GRAINGER: Nothing Jack. Sally's taken a fancy to me, an' gives me no chance. Can't you see for yourself?

MAGNEER: I can George—an' tha shanna be pestered.

GRAINGER: There's Charlie Greenhalgh won't speak to me now—
thinks I'm running him off. *I've* no desire to run Charlie off.

MAGNEER: Sally's as good as you, George.

GRAINGER: Maybe, and a thousand times better. But that doesn't
5   say as I want to marry her.

MAGNEER: No, George, no, that is so, lad.

             (Enter SALLY *and the other ladies.)*

SALLY MAGNEER: How would you arrange six folks in three
    chairs—?

10 GRAINGER: Couldn't do it.

SALLY MAGNEER: I don't think! What's your opinion, Ada?

ADA CALLADINE: Why am I asked for my opinion? *I've* never sat in
    a chair with Dr Grainger.

SALLY MAGNEER: Where have you sat then.

15 ADA CALLADINE: I may have sat on his knee while he sat in the
    chair.

SALLY MAGNEER: Here, young man, explain yourself.

GRAINGER: Well I'll be damned!

BRENTNALL: Sooner or later.

20 MAGNEER: Now look here, our Sally, we're havin' none o' this.
    Charlie Greenhalgh is your man; you stick to him, and leave
    other young fellows alone.

SALLY MAGNEER: Oh you *are* good, Jack! And what about the girl
    you took to Blackpool?

25 MAGNEER: Say no more, Sally, now say no more.

SALLY MAGNEER: No I won't. Do you want me to drive you up to
    Selson, because th' cart's at the door?

MAGNEER: No, we'll walk up.

GRAINGER: I dunno, Jack. It's getting late, and I believe Billy's
30   tired. He's a convalescent,☆ you know.

MAGNEER: Niver thought of it, lad. Sorry—sorry.

(They bid goodnight. Exit SALLY *and* GRAINGER, EMILY, JACK, *and*
               ADA.*)*

ANNIE CALLADINE: Isn't he a thing!☆

35 BRENTNALL: He's not bad—*do* be honest.

ANNIE CALLADINE: Oh *but!*

BRENTNALL: Remember what I say—don't starve yourself, and
    don't degrade the idea of man.

ANNIE CALLADINE: And shall I never see you again?

40 BRENTNALL: If I can, I will come again.

ANNIE CALLADINE: Goodbye.

(He kisses her rather sorrowfully, and departs. ANNIE CALLADINE *closes the door—drinks the last drain from his glass—weeps—dries her eyes as the girls come upstairs—there is a calling of goodbye from outside.)*

ADA CALLADINE: What's amiss?   5

ANNIE CALLADINE: Plenty.

EMILY CALLADINE: What?

ANNIE CALLADINE: Dr Grainger is only married and got a child.

ADA and EMILY: No—where—is his wife living.

ANNIE CALLADINE: His wife is at her home, in Wolverhamp-   10
ton—Broad Street.

ADA CALLADINE: I'll write to her—I will—I will.

ANNIE CALLADINE: No Ada—no.

ADA CALLADINE: I will—I will—I will. 'Dear Mrs George
Grainger, come and look after your husband. He is running the   15
rig* out here, and if you don't come quick— — —'

*(She has flung her writing case onto the table, and sits down to write.
Vain cries of 'Ada', 'Ada', from* ANNIE CALLADINE.*)*

(Curtain)

Act III.

The kitchen at Magneer's farm—SALLY MAGNEER, EMILY CALLADINE,
ADA CALLADINE—

MR MAGNEER—*farmer*—NOT *fat, but well-liking: grey hair, black*
5 *moustache, at present rather maudlin.*
JACK MAGNEER—*still in riding breeches and leggings.*
GRAINGER *and* BRENTNALL—*both in tennis flannels.*
JACK *and* EMILY *sit together on a large old couch,* GRAINGER *next them.*
SALLY *is in a chair, looking as if any moment she would take wing.*
10 BRENTNALL *is flirting with* ADA CALLADINE.

MR MAGNEER: An' so you really goin' ter leave us, Dr Grainger.
GRAINGER: That is so, Mr Magneer.
MR MAGNEER: An' when might you be goin'?
GRAINGER: Saturday.
15 MR MAGNEER: Tomorrow! My word, that's sharp.—Well, I know
one as'll be sorry you goin'.
SALLY MAGNEER: Shut up, father. *(She giggles, and twists her hand-*
kerchief. To GRAINGER*)*: We s'll be seeing you again, though?
GRAINGER: Well, I really can't say—I'm going to London.
20 SALLY MAGNEER: London? Whativer are you going there for?
BRENTNALL: Set up a wife and family.
SALLY MAGNEER: What all at once?—Give us a chance.
BRENTNALL: Not a ghost of a chance, Sally.
                    *(*ADA CALLADINE *laughs uncontrollably.)*
25 GRAINGER: Got a joke over there?
ADA CALLADINE *(laughing)*: Yes—yes—yes.
SALLY MAGNEER *(jumping up)*: Just look at your glass! *(Takes*
GRAINGER*'s tumbler and proceeds to mix him rum.)*—Why ever
didn't you speak?
30 MR MAGNEER: Yes, you must shout up when you're emp'y.
SALLY MAGNEER *(to* GRAINGER*)*: Like it sweet?
GRAINGER *(ironically)*: Not too much.
SALLY MAGNEER *(taking the glass and standing in front of him)*: How's
this for you?
35 GRAINGER *(sipping)*: Quite all right, thank you Sally.
MR MAGNEER *(laughing)*: 'Quite all right', hark ye! It's 'quite all
right.' *(He gives a great wink at* BRENTNALL. SALLY *begins to*
giggle.)
GRAINGER *(lugubriously)*: Sally's got 'em again.

JACK MAGNEER: Sit you down, Sally, an' don't look so long o' th' leg.

(SALLY *giggles half hysterically, and sinks beside* GRAINGER, *who edges away. She leans towards him—laughs uncontrollably.*)

MR MAGNEER: Now we're comin' on. What yer doin' at 'er, Doctor?

GRAINGER: Begad, I'm doing nothing, Mr Magneer. I dunno what's got her.

MR MAGNEER: He dunno, doesn't know what's got her. (*Laughs. To* BRENTNALL): We don't, do we?

BRENTNALL: Not a bit.

GRAINGER: I'll have a drop more water. (*Rises and goes to table.*)

MR MAGNEER: Come Sally, my lass, come.

(SALLY *dries her eyes, still giggles, rises.* GRAINGER *hastily takes an odd chair at the table. She stands beside him.*)

JACK MAGNEER: Are ter goin' ter sit thysen down, Sally!

SALLY MAGNEER: Am I hurtin' *you* by standin'?

JACK MAGNEER: Yis, you are.

BRENTNALL: Fill me up, Sally, there's a dear.

(SALLY *takes his glass.*)

MR MAGNEER: Sally Magneer, there's a dear. (*Rhyme.*)

GRAINGER: Isn't Charlie coming?

SALLY MAGNEER: No, did you want him?

GRAINGER: No—but I thought *you* did.

SALLY MAGNEER (*beginning to giggle*): Did you? You happen thought wrong.

BRENTNALL: Poor Charlie!

SALLY MAGNEER: What do you know about him?

BRENTNALL: Now Sally! It's best to be on with the new love, before you're off with the old.

SALLY MAGNEER (*giggling*): I don't know what you mean.

JACK MAGNEER: Art thou going to sit down.

SALLY MAGNEER: Yes. (*Retires discomfited to the couch.*)

BRENTNALL (*rising*): I'll get a light.

GRAINGER: Matches?

BRENTNALL (*going to fire*): Never mind. (*Lights his cigarette with a spill.*)

ADA CALLADINE (*laughing*): Goodbye Billy.

BRENTNALL (*blowing her kisses*): Farewell, farewell.

(*Sinks on the couch beside* SALLY.)

SALLY MAGNEER: What have you come for?

BRENTNALL: Won't you have me, Sally?

SALLY MAGNEER: I don't know.

GRAINGER *(shuffling the cards)*: A hand of crib,* Mr Magneer?

5   MR MAGNEER: I don't mind if I do. Fill up.

BRENTNALL *(taking SALLY's hand)*: Hurt your finger?

SALLY MAGNEER: My thumb!

BRENTNALL: Shame! What did you do?

SALLY MAGNEER: Chopped it.

10   BRENTNALL: How rotten. Is it getting better?

MR MAGNEER: There's a bit o' proud flesh in it.

GRAINGER: Your crib, Mr Magneer.

SALLY MAGNEER *(unwinding the bandage)*: Yes, it's going on all right now.

15   BRENTNALL *(examining it closely)*: Yes, that's healing right enough. But a nasty gash! What did Charlie say to it?

SALLY MAGNEER: Charlie!

BRENTNALL: Yes, Charlie. He's your fellow, isn't he?

SALLY MAGNEER: I don't know so much about that.

20   BRENTNALL: I heard you were as good as engaged.

SALLY MAGNEER: Oh did you—who's been telling you?

BRENTNALL: Mrs Plum.

SALLY MAGNEER: She knows so much, you see.

BRENTNALL: Let me wrap it up for you. *(Bandages her thumb.)* But

25   isn't it right?

SALLY MAGNEER: Not as *I* know of.

BRENTNALL: Oh, I'm sorry.

SALLY MAGNEER: Who are you sorry for?

BRENTNALL: Charlie, of course, poor devil.

30   SALLY MAGNEER: You needn't be sorry for him. Take your sorrow where your love lies.*

BRENTNALL: Then I s'll have to be sorry for you, Sally.

SALLY MAGNEER: I *don't* think.

BRENTNALL *(putting his arm round her waist)*: I'm sorry you've got

35   a bad finger, Sally.

SALLY MAGNEER *(beginning to giggle)*: —Are you?

BRENTNALL: You don't mind that I'm not Dr Grainger, do you, Sally?

SALLY MAGNEER: What do you mean?

40   BRENTNALL: You'd as leave have me as Dr Grainger?

SALLY MAGNEER: Yes, if you like.

BRENTNALL *(kissing her)*: That's right. *(She giggles.)*

MR MAGNEER: Whey! Whey-up! Sally, thou scawdrag!

SALLY MAGNEER *(giggling hysterically)*: What am I a scawdrag for?

MR MAGNEER: Hark-ye, hark ye?—Jack, art takin' notice over theer? 5

JACK MAGNEER: Billy's all right, Dad.

MR MAGNEER: Billy!—by gosh—Billy!!

GRAINGER: Turn, Mr Magneer.

ADA CALLADINE *(pegging)*: Two for his knobs. 10

BRENTNALL: You'd as leave have me as Dr Grainger?
    (Kisses her under the ear.)

SALLY MAGNEER *(suppressed shrieks)*: Oh—Oh, don't tickle.

GRAINGER *(turning round—with contempt)*: She'll never stop, Billy—she's got gigglomania. 15

MR MAGNEER: Gigglo-what? That's a good 'un!

BRENTNALL: Yes she will stop—take me seriously, Sally, do.
    (Squeezes her—SALLY giggles wildly. Her head rolls.)

MR MAGNEER: Hark at that—take him seriously!

SALLY MAGNEER *(exhausted)*: Don't! Don't—oh don't! 20

BRENTNALL: Sally, my dear, you are too discouraging for anything. Sit with me nicely.

SALLY MAGNEER: Oh! *(Lays her head on his shoulder.)*

BRENTNALL: Now we're coming on. *(Kisses her.)* You've not chipped with Charlie, have you? 25

SALLY MAGNEER: What d'you want to know for.

BRENTNALL: Sally, my darling.

MR MAGNEER: Gosh, it's come to 'darling'—'darling Sally!'

BRENTNALL: You haven't, have you?

SALLY MAGNEER: No. 30

BRENTNALL: Why hasn't he come tonight?

SALLY MAGNEER: Because he wasn't asked.

BRENTNALL: Has he cooled off lately.

SALLY MAGNEER: I don't care whether he has or not.

BRENTNALL: Neither do I. *(Kisses her under the ear. She squeals.)* 35

JACK MAGNEER: God love you, Sally!

ADA CALLADINE: Don't play cribbage any more, Mr Magneer.—Do play the comb-band.

MR MAGNEER *(throwing away his cards)*: No I won't—fill up—an' let's have a dance. 40

ADA CALLADINE: Yes—yes—yes.

*(The men drink—*SALLY *and* GRAINGER *push aside the table.)*

GRAINGER: Comb-band, Mr Magneer?

MR MAGNEER *(wrapping the comb in tissue paper)*: That's the very
item!

(He staggers slightly—all the men are affected by drink.)

SALLY MAGNEER *(to* GRAINGER*)*: You're going to have one with me?

GRAINGER *(awkwardly)*: —Er—I'd promised Ada.

ADA CALLADINE: That doesn't matter. Mr Brentnall will dance
with me.

MR MAGNEER *(sounding the comb)*: Now then, are you ready. Sally's
the belle of the ball, and you Doctor, it's your party—so lead
off.

GRAINGER: Polka—plain polka.

BRENTNALL: We shan't have breath to speak a word.

SALLY MAGNEER: Oh my goodness!

*(The comb-band buzzes away—they start to dance in a prancing
fashion.)*

SALLY MAGNEER: You're not going to leave me?

GRAINGER: I s'll have to.

SALLY MAGNEER: But you can't.

GRAINGER: Why not?

SALLY MAGNEER: You can't leave me now.

GRAINGER: But I've got to go to London—

JACK MAGNEER: Do you reckon you're really fond of me?

EMILY CALLADINE: I know I am—I don't reckon.

JACK MAGNEER: Not so very fond—

EMILY CALLADINE: Why not?

JACK MAGNEER: Do you reckon you've been nice to me all this
while.

EMILY CALLADINE: All what while?

JACK MAGNEER: While I've been comin' to see you.

EMILY CALLADINE: And have you been very nice to me, Jack?

JACK MAGNEER: Well, haven't I.

EMILY CALLADINE: No Jack, you haven't.

JACK MAGNEER: What do you mean?—

ADA CALLADINE: I posted her the letter yesterday.

BRENTNALL: Why, did you know the address?

ADA CALLADINE: Yes, you told Annie.

BRENTNALL: Did I?—Oh Lord, you little imp.

ADA CALLADINE: It's our turn now.

BRENTNALL: Whose turn?

ADA CALLADINE: The women's.

BRENTNALL: Don't be a vixen—

GRAINGER: Well, you won't say anything, will you? You see how   5
I'm fixed.

SALLY MAGNEER: I don't know.

GRAINGER: I'll see you tomorrow—keep it back till then.

SALLY MAGNEER: You'll see me tomorrow?

GRAINGER: Yes.—   10

JACK MAGNEER: You think I ought to get engaged to you?

EMILY CALLADINE: Or else you ought never to have come as you
have—you had the option.

JACK MAGNEER: I dunna want to get married, somehow, Emily.

EMILY CALLADINE: Is that final, Jack?   15

JACK MAGNEER: What do *you* say?

EMILY CALLADINE: You leave me nothing to say.

JACK MAGNEER: Good God, Emily, I'm not a brute.

EMILY CALLADINE: I've heard you say so often, Jack. But you
don't think it's been very happy for me—our—our friendship?   20

JACK MAGNEER: Good God, Emily—have I been—?

EMILY CALLADINE: Afraid of me, Jack. It's rather humiliating.

JACK MAGNEER: You can have me if you like—I'm not good
enough—

EMILY CALLADINE: You know I consider you good enough.   25

JACK MAGNEER: Yis—I know you do.

EMILY CALLADINE: Men lack honour nowadays.

JACK MAGNEER: Good God!

*(They dance—*SALLY *suddenly drops exhausted on a couch—*GRAINGER
moves to the other side of the room. JACK MAGNEER *flings off his coat.)*   30

JACK MAGNEER: By the Lord, it's hot work. Take your coat off
George.

*(*GRAINGER *and* BRENTNALL *take off their coats: they have on white
tennis shirts and trousers.)*

MR MAGNEER: My word, you went well. Have a drink.   35

SALLY MAGNEER: Is th' door open—set the back door open Jack.
(He goes out and returns.)

BRENTNALL: Have the next with me, Sally.

SALLY MAGNEER: I will if you like.

ADA CALLADINE: What shall it be?   40

BRENTNALL: Waltz valeta—

GRAINGER: Try a tune, Mr Magneer.

(MR MAGNEER, *having re-papered his comb tries a tune.* GRAINGER *instructs him. They start off,* SALLY *with* BRENTNALL, GRAINGER *with*

5 ADA CALLADINE.)

BRENTNALL: Why would you rather dance with Dr Grainger?

SALLY MAGNEER: I wouldn't.

BRENTNALL: Yes you would. Don't forget the two shuffle steps— *One—two*!

10 SALLY MAGNEER: I've never done that before.

BRENTNALL: Something I've taught you then. But why would you rather dance with Grainger?

SALLY MAGNEER: I *wouldn't*.

BRENTNALL: You *would*.

15 SALLY MAGNEER: I *wouldn't*.

BRENTNALL: You *would*. You're in love with him.

SALLY MAGNEER: Me! That I never am!

BRENTNALL: You are!

SALLY MAGNEER: Well I never did!

20 BRENTNALL: And you're a fool to be in love with him.

SALLY MAGNEER: Why?

BRENTNALL: For the best of all reasons.

SALLY MAGNEER: What's that?

BRENTNALL: Because he's married.

25 SALLY MAGNEER: He's not!

BRENTNALL: He is—and has got a son.

SALLY MAGNEER: Where?

BRENTNALL: In Wolverhampton, where he came from.

SALLY MAGNEER: Oh, let's sit down.

30 BRENTNALL: No, you must dance with me. Don't you like to dance with me. It's too bad, Sally.

SALLY MAGNEER: I'm getting dizzy.

BRENTNALL: You can't, not in Valeta. Besides, we'll walk the waltz steps.

35 (*He puts his arm round her.*)

SALLY MAGNEER: It's not right about Doctor Grainger, is it?

(*A lady in a motor cloak and wrap appears in the doorway. The men, slightly tipsy, bend talking to their partners, who are engrossed. No one notices the new-comer.*)

40 BRENTNALL: It is, on my honor. You believe me Sally? (*She looks*

*him earnestly in the face, as they dance the forward step. When they
come together for the waltz, he kisses her.)* You believe me?

SALLY MAGNEER *(almost in tears)*: Yes.

BRENTNALL: It is true. Poor Sally. *(Kisses her again. They begin to
laugh.)*

JACK MAGNEER: All right. I niver looked at it in that light.

EMILY CALLADINE: I know you didn't.

JACK MAGNEER: We'll count as we're engaged from now, then?

EMILY CALLADINE: What will your father say.

JACK MAGNEER: He'll be just fussy.

EMILY CALLADINE: I want him to know—I am so fond of him.

ADA CALLADINE: Oh!

GRAINGER: What?

(They break apart. MAGNEER *and* BRENTNALL *keep on dancing, the
latter kissing* SALLY. GRAINGER *goes unsteadily to the doorway.)*

ELSA SMITH: I called to see Mr Brentnall—but don't disturb him,
he looks so happy.

GRAINGER: Does—does he know you?

ELSA SMITH: A little. *(She laughs.)*

GRAINGER: Billy!—Billy!!

BRENTNALL *(looking up)*: What now? *(Sees the lady.)* No! *(Leaves
SALLY—she sways. He catches her again, takes her to a seat, draws
his fingers across her cheek caressingly, and goes to the doorway—
reels slightly.)* Quite giddy, don't you know!—space is so
small.

ELSA SMITH: Not much room for you to spread out, was there?

BRENTNALL: Was I hugging Sally?

ELSA SMITH: Sally!—how lovely, how perfectly lovely!

BRENTNALL: Did I kiss her?

ELSA SMITH: "Did I kiss her?"—no—no, you poor dear, you didn't
kiss her.

BRENTNALL: You mean I am drunk?

ELSA SMITH: Are you drunk?—no!

BRENTNALL: I am slightly tipsy, more with dancing than—drink.
Shall I come away?

ELSA SMITH: Shall he come away—oh, you dear! Why should I
decide for you!

BRENTNALL: Are you cross?

ELSA SMITH: Not in the least. Go and kiss Sally if you will.

BRENTNALL: Poor Sally—I don't want to kiss her now.

ELSA SMITH: How perfectly lovely! Do introduce me.

BRENTNALL: Mr Magneer, Sally Magneer, Emily Calladine, Ada Calladine, Jack Magneer, Dr Grainger—all of you, Elsa Smith.

ELSA SMITH: How awfully nice!—Can I come.

5 MR MAGNEER *(springing up, and bowing tipsily)*: Make yourself at 'ome, you're very welcome, Miss, you're very welcome.

ELSA SMITH: Thank you so much! I should love to dance. I've got two friends in the motor car. May I fetch them?

MR MAGNEER: Anybody you like, they're *all* welcome here, and

10 there's plenty to drink for all.

ELSA SMITH: So nice!

(Exit.)

GRAINGER: Who the devil—!

BRENTNALL: My betrothed, my fiancée, my girl.

15 CHORUS OF WOMEN: You don't mean it.

SALLY MAGNEER: Well—*men*—!

ADA CALLADINE: *Men?*

EMILY CALLADINE: Men!

MR MAGNEER: OOO—you're done this time, Billy!

20 *(Huge mirth.)*

GRAINGER: —Well *you* devil, Billy Brentnall!

JACK MAGNEER: —It's a corker, Billy, it's a winder.

EMILY CALLADINE: Are *you* any better, Jack?

JACK MAGNEER *(fiercely)*: Look here Dad, I'm engaged to Emily

25 here, fair and square.

MR MAGNEER: Come here, Em'ler, my ducky, come hither. *(EMILY goes very reluctantly. He kisses her.)* I like thee, Em'ler, I like thee. *(Kisses her again.)*

JACK MAGNEER: Cheese it, Dad.

30 MR MAGNEER: It's a winder, it is an' all.—An' aren't *you* goin' to be engaged an' all Dr Grainger.

GRAINGER: Not this time.

MR MAGNEER: Hm! 'Appen you are engaged!

GRAINGER: No I'm not.

35 MR MAGNEER: Come then, come then, come then.

(Re-enter ELSA SMITH, and two married people, lady and gentleman.)

ELSA SMITH: —All of you—Gladys and Tom: Gladys—that's Will—

MR MAGNEER: Ay—ay—Billy! Billy!! *(It amuses him highly.)*

BRENTNALL *(bowing)*: I was to come to dinner tonight. I clean forgot. Don't be angry.

TOM: Cheek, if no more.

ELSA SMITH: Oh, you don't know Will, you don't.

MR MAGNEER: An' *you* don't know Billy, Miss, it strikes me.   5
(Laughter.)

BRENTNALL: Leave me alone.—I say, Elsa, Jack *(pointing)* has just got engaged to Emily.

ELSA SMITH: How perfectly charming—I love it all so much.

BRENTNALL: What?   10

ELSA SMITH: You—this.

BRENTNALL: Take your cloak off. *(Helps her. She is a handsome woman, large, blonde, about 30—dressed for dinner.* TOM *and* GLADYS *disrobe—they are in dinner dress also.)*

TOM *(cynical)*: I suppose these are adventures.   15

GLADYS: Don't be a fool, Tom.

ELSA SMITH: This is fun.

BRENTNALL: Will you dance with me, Elsa?

ELSA SMITH: No, I won't.

BRENTNALL: Angry with me?   20

ELSA SMITH: No. I can dance with you any day.

GRAINGER: May I have the pleasure?

ELSA SMITH: No—forgive me *(very kindly)*—but I do want to dance with Jack. *(To* EMILY CALLADINE*)*: May I?

EMILY CALLADINE: Certainly. *(*JACK *pulls a face.)*   25

ELSA SMITH: He doesn't want me—but I won't let him off—no.

JACK MAGNEER: I'm shy, as a matter of fact.

ELSA SMITH: How lovely!

MR MAGNEER *(to* GLADYS*)*: Now Miss, you choose.

GLADYS: Will, you must dance with me.   30

BRENTNALL *(going to her side)*: You are shy.

MR MAGNEER: Now Ada, your turn to pick.
(ADA looks wickedly at TOM—he bows.)

TOM: Thank you.

ADA CALLADINE: Are you shy? *(She laughs wickedly.)*   35

MR MAGNEER: Now for Doctor Grainger. *(He holds out his fists to* EMILY*)*: Which of 'em? *(*EMILY *touches the right fist.)* Wrong! *(Showing a coin in his left.)* Sally gets him.

SALLY MAGNEER: Sally doesn't.

GRAINGER: Come on, Sally.

MR MAGNEER: Now then, what is it?

BRENTNALL: Waltz.

(The comb begins to buzz—the partners set off dancing—MR MAGNEER
5 *breaks the time—they laugh—he beckons EMILY, holds the comb in one*
hand, her in the other, and dances prancingly, buzzing breathlessly.)

(Curtain)

Act IV.

Scene: the bedroom in the cottage, same as Act I. It is 9.0 o'clock in the morning. GRAINGER *and* BRENTNALL *in bed.*

GRAINGER: Billy! *(No answer.)* You mean to say you're at it yet? *(No answer.)* Well I'll be damned, you're a better sleeper even than a liar. *(No answer.)* Oh strike—! *(Shies a pillow at* BRENTNALL.*)*

BRENTNALL: What the—!

GRAINGER: I should say so.

BRENTNALL: Dog in the manger! Go to sleep. I loathe the small hours—Oh—h! *(Yawns.)*

GRAINGER: Small hours begad! It's past nine o'clock.

BRENTNALL *(half asleep)*: Early, frostily early.

GRAINGER: You mean to say—! *(He shies the bolster, viciously.)*

BRENTNALL: Don't George! *(Sleeps.)*

GRAINGER: Devil! *(Shies slippers, one after the other.)*

BRENTNALL *(sitting up suddenly—furious)*: Go to blazes. *(Lies down again.)*

GRAINGER: If you go to sleep again, Billy B., I'll empty the water bottle over you—I will.

BRENTNALL: *I'm* not asleep.

GRAINGER: Billy!

BRENTNALL: What?

GRAINGER: Did you square Sally?

BRENTNALL: Eh?

GRAINGER: No, look here, Billy—

BRENTNALL *(stretching his arms)*: Georgie, you ought to be dead.

GRAINGER: I've no doubt.—Billy Brentnall.

BRENTNALL: What?

GRAINGER: Did you square Sally?

BRENTNALL: Sally—Sally—Sally—

GRAINGER: Chuck it, fool.

BRENTNALL: I don't know.

GRAINGER: What d'you mean?

BRENTNALL: I told her you were a married man with a family—and begad, you look it—

GRAINGER: That's not the point.

BRENTNALL: I apologise. I says to Sally: 'he's a married man.' Sally says to me: 'he's not.'

I say: 'he is.'
Sally says: 'I'm dizzy.'
I say: 'you might well be.'
GRAINGER: Chuck it, do chuck it.
5   BRENTNALL: It's the solemn fact. And our confab ended there.
GRAINGER: It did!
BRENTNALL: It did.
GRAINGER: Hm!
BRENTNALL: You're going to London to my rooms, aren't you?
10   GRAINGER: You say so.
BRENTNALL: Very well then—there's an end of Sally.
GRAINGER: I'm not so sure.
BRENTNALL: Why?
GRAINGER: She said she was coming round here.
15   BRENTNALL: When?
GRAINGER: This morning.
BRENTNALL: Then don't get up till this afternoon, and then bolt
for the station.
GRAINGER: I've not settled up at the Surgery.
20   BRENTNALL: Thou bungler.—Has Sally really got a case against
you?
GRAINGER: She's got a case against *some* man or other, and she'd
prefer it to be me.
BRENTNALL: But she must see *you're* quite a cold egg. And has
25   Charlie Greenhalgh really cried off?
GRAINGER: No—at least—poor old Charlie's in a bit of a mess.
BRENTNALL: How?
GRAINGER: He was secretary to the football club—and he falsified
the balance sheet, and fails to produce about fifteen quid.
30   BRENTNALL: *He's* not in a very rosy position for marriage.
However, old Magneer's not short of money?
GRAINGER: He isn't begad!
BRENTNALL: All right—let him work the oracle. Sally's no
fool—and she'll be just as well, married to Charlie. You say his
35   farm is going to the dogs. All right, she'll shoo the dogs off.
GRAINGER: Very nice.
BRENTNALL: I think so.
GRAINGER: Who's that?
BRENTNALL: Dunno—get under the bedclothes.
40   (*Sound of footsteps—enter* JACK MAGNEER.)

MAGNEER: Letting the day get well aired?

BRENTNALL: I don't believe in running risks through the chill, damp air of early morning.

MAGNEER: I s'd think you don't.

BRENTNALL: Take a seat.   5

MAGNEER: So you're going today, George?

GRAINGER: I am, Jack—and sorry to leave you.

MAGNEER: What's this our Sally's been telling me!

GRAINGER: Couldn't say, Jack.

MAGNEER: As you're married—   10

BRENTNALL: And got a kid, quite right.

MAGNEER: *Is* it, George?

GRAINGER: I believe so.

MAGNEER: Hm!

(A pause.)   15

BRENTNALL: —Well Jack, say he has your sympathy.

MAGNEER: Yis—yis—he has. But I'm not so sure— —

BRENTNALL: Eh Jack, it's a hole we might any of us slip into.

MAGNEER: Seemingly. But why didn't you tell me, George?

BRENTNALL: Don't Jack. Don't you see, I could give the whole of   20
   that recitation. 'We've been good friends, George, and you'd no
   need to keep me in the dark like that. It's a false position for
   me, as well as for you etc. etc.' That's what you want to say?

MAGNEER: Yis—and besides—

BRENTNALL: Well look here, Jack, you might have done it yourself.   25
   George was let in down at Wolverhampton—kicked out of the
   town because he owned up and married the girl—hadn't either
   a penny or a job—girl has a good home. Would *you* have wanted
   to tell the whole story to these prating fools round here.

MAGNEER: No, I can't say as I should. But then—   30

BRENTNALL: Then what?

MAGNEER: There's our Sally, and there's Annie—

BRENTNALL: What about 'em.

MAGNEER: He's courted 'em both—they're both up to the eyes in
   love with him—   35

BRENTNALL: Not Annie. On the quiet, she's rather gone on *me*. I
   showed George up in his true light to her.

GRAINGER: Rotter—rotter!

BRENTNALL: And I stepped into the lime light, and the trick was
   done.   40

MAGNEER: You're a devil, Billy.—But look here, George, our Sally—

GRAINGER: —Yes—

MAGNEER: She's,—she's gone a long way—

5 BRENTNALL *(quietly)*: How do you mean, Jack.

MAGNEER: Well, she's given up Charlie Greenhalgh—

BRENTNALL: Not quite. And you know, Jack, she really loves Charlie, at the bottom. There's something fascinating about George.

10 GRAINGER: Damn your eyes, shut up, Billy.

BRENTNALL: There's something fascinating about George. *He* can't help it. The women melt like wax before him. They're all over him. It's not his beauty, it's his manliness. He can't help it.

GRAINGER: I s'll smash you, Billy Brentnall, if you don't shut up.

15 MAGNEER: Yis, there's something in it, George.

BRENTNALL: There *is*, Jack. Well, he can't help himself, so you've got to help him. It's no good hitting him when he's down.

MAGNEER: *I*'m not hitting him.

BRENTNALL: And what you've got to do, you've got to get Charlie

20 Greenhalgh and your Sally together again.

MAGNEER: Me!—it's nowt to do with me.

BRENTNALL: Yes it has. Charlie's not been up to your place lately, has he?

MAGNEER: No.

25 BRENTNALL: And do you know why?

MAGNEER: Yis—

BRENTNALL: It's not so much because of George. Have you heard what low water he's getting into up at Newmanley?—and it appears he's fifteen quid out with the football Club.

30 MAGNEER: I've heard a whisper.

BRENTNALL: Well, you help him, Jack, for Sally's sake. She loves him, Jack, she does. And if she marries him quick, she'll pull him through, for she seems to have a business head on her, and a farming head.

35 MAGNEER: She has that.

BRENTNALL: Well you'll do what you can for poor old Charlie, won't you?

MAGNEER: I will, Billy.—And what time are you going?

BRENTNALL: 2.50 train.

MAGNEER: Well—me and you's been good pals, George. I must say I'd ha' done anything for you—

GRAINGER: I know you would, Jack.

MAGNEER: Yis, an' I would—an' I would.

BRENTNALL: —I'm going up to Blythe Hall, against Ashbourne, 5
for a day or two, Jack. Shall you come up for tennis?

MAGNEER: I hardly think so—we s'll be busy just now.

BRENTNALL: Sunday afternoon—yes you will.

MAGNEER: Goodbye, Billy.

BRENTNALL: Au revoir, Jack. 10

MAGNEER: Well—goodbye, George-lad. We've not done amiss while you've been here. I s'll miss thee.

GRAINGER: You've been all right to me, Jack.

MAGNEER: Yis—I try to do what I can for folks.

(Exit.) 15

BRENTNALL: —The atmosphere clears, George.

GRAINGER: Oh damn you, shut up.

BRENTNALL: 'Oh, what a sin is base ingratitude!'*

GRAINGER: What did you tell Annie about me?

BRENTNALL: I said you were quite manly, and couldn't help 20
yourself: all the virtues of goodnature and so on, but a bit of a libidinous goat.

GRAINGER: Thank you—very nice of you.

BRENTNALL: Add to this that you won't face a situation, but always funk it, and you understand why Annie suddenly transferred 25
her affections to me. For I showed myself, by contrast, a paragon of all virtues.

GRAINGER: You would.

BRENTNALL: I did.

GRAINGER: I shan't go to London to your rooms. 30

BRENTNALL: Now George, my dear chap—

GRAINGER: I shall not, Billy.

BRENTNALL: Then where will you go?

GRAINGER: Hell!

BRENTNALL: My dear, dear fellow, you've neither the cash nor the 35
ability—

GRAINGER: Well you're a— —

BRENTNALL: Shall we get up?

GRAINGER: I will, whether you will or not.

*(Sits on the side of the bed, whistling "On the banks of Allan Water".** Footsteps on the stairs—enter Grainger's wife, ETHEL*—Rather thin, with a light costume.)*

ETHEL: George! *(She goes forward and kisses him, not noticing*
5   BRENTNALL.) George!! *(Sinks her head on his shoulder.)* George!!!

GRAINGER: Ethel—well I'm blest! *(Kisses her.)*

ETHEL *(drawing away)*: I had to come.

GRAINGER: Yes.

10 ETHEL: Are you angry!

GRAINGER: Me angry! What should I be angry for?

ETHEL: I thought you might be.

GRAINGER: What made you come?

ETHEL: I heard you were going away—and your letters seemed so
15   constrained. Are you—?

GRAINGER: What?

ETHEL: Going away?

GRAINGER: I s'll have to—this job's done.

ETHEL: You never told me.

20 GRAINGER: What was the good?

ETHEL: Where are you going?

GRAINGER: Dunno—I don't know in the least.

ETHEL: Oh George, you must come home. Mother says you must.

GRAINGER: Hm!

25 ETHEL: Won't you?

GRAINGER: I'd rather not.

ETHEL: What will you do, then?

GRAINGER: I may—I shall probably get a job in London.

ETHEL: Oh George, don't, don't go to London.

30 GRAINGER: What else can I do?

ETHEL: Come home to mother with me.

GRAINGER: I'll be damned if I will.

ETHEL: No, you never will do anything I ask you.

GRAINGER: I shan't do that.

35 ETHEL: Don't you want to be with me?

GRAINGER: If I want ever so badly, I can't, with no money.

ETHEL: Then how are you going to live alone, with no money?

GRAINGER: I can manage for myself.

ETHEL: I know what you want, you want to run away. It is mean,
40   mean of you.

GRAINGER: What's the good of my coming to *your* place, there, where they kicked me out—?

ETHEL: And what if you've nowhere else to go?—And what are you going to do in London?

GRAINGER: Look for a job.   5

ETHEL: And what when you've got one?

GRAINGER: Save up to get some things together.

ETHEL: How much have you saved here?

GRAINGER: Not a fat lot,—but I *have* saved.

ETHEL: How much?   10

GRAINGER: Some—at any rate.

ETHEL: Have you been miserable. I know you like plenty of life. Has it made you miserable to be tied up?

GRAINGER: Not miserable—*but* it's been a bit of a devil.

ETHEL: We ought to live together.   15

GRAINGER: On what?

ETHEL: On what we can get—you ought.

GRAINGER: No thank you.

ETHEL: We might as well not be married.

GRAINGER: When?   20

ETHEL: I believe you hate me for having married you. Do you—do you?

GRAINGER: Now Ethel, drop it. Don't get excited. You know I don't feel anything of the sort.

ETHEL *(weeping)*: But you don't love me.   25

GRAINGER *(tenderly)*: Why I do, Ethel, I do.

ETHEL: I love you, George, I love you.

GRAINGER: Poor old Ethel—and I love you. And whoever says I don't, is a liar.

ETHEL: You've been true to me, George?   30

GRAINGER: What do you mean.

ETHEL: Have you been true to me.

BRENTNALL: No he hasn't.

GRAINGER *(fierce)*: Now Billy!

BRENTNALL: I am your husband's old friend, Brentnall, and *your*   35
friend, Mrs Grainger.*

(*Gets out of bed, shakes hands with* ETHEL.)

ETHEL: I didn't know you were there.

BRENTNALL: Never mind. *(Puts on a dressing gown.)*

ETHEL: Do you say George hasn't been true to me.   40

BRENTNALL: I do. Do you really love him.

ETHEL: He is my husband.

BRENTNALL: You do love him, I can see. Then, look here, *keep* him. You can do it, I should think. *Keep* him. And you, George, be
5   decent.

GRAINGER: Be decent yourself.

BRENTNALL: I am. *(Lights a cigarette.)* You don't mind if I smoke.

ETHEL: No. George, oh George! It's not true what he says, is it?

GRAINGER: No!

10 ETHEL *(weeping)*: I couldn't bear it. *(Embracing him.)* I couldn't bear it.

BRENTNALL: That's the ticket. *(Aside.)*

GRAINGER: Never mind, little girl—never mind.

ETHEL: You won't leave me again?

15 BRENTNALL *(aside)*: Good shot!

GRAINGER: What can I do?

ETHEL: I've got seventy pounds, George, I've got seventy pounds.

GRAINGER: I don't want *your* money, Ethel.

ETHEL: You don't mind making a fool of me, and neglecting me, but
20   you won't have my money.

GRAINGER: Now Ethel—

ETHEL *(flashing)*: Isn't it so?

GRAINGER: No Ethel.

ETHEL: Then we'll live together on seventy pounds, till you get a
25   job—?

GRAINGER: But you see.

ETHEL *(turning, flashing, to* BRENTNALL*)*: *Has* he been living straight—*do* they know here he's married?

BRENTNALL: I've told a few of them.

30 ETHEL *(turning slowly to* GRAINGER*)*: Now then—

GRAINGER: You can do what the hell you like.

ETHEL: Then I shall live with you, from this minute onwards.

BRENTNALL: Knocked out.—George!

GRAINGER: Curse you, Brentnall.

35 BRENTNALL: You are a rotter, my dear fellow.

ETHEL *(weeping)*: There's baby crying. *(Exit, weeping.)*

       *(*BRENTNALL *smokes a cigarette—*GRAINGER *fumes.)*

BRENTNALL *(throwing him a dressing gown)*: You'd better clothe yourself—you'll feel stronger.

GRAINGER *(getting into the dressing gown)*: What d'you reckon you're up to.

BRENTNALL: *Don't* be a fool, George, *don't* be a swine. *If* you're going to clear out, stand up and say so honorably: say you'll not abide by your marriage. You *can* do that, with decency. 5

GRAINGER: How the devil can I?

BRENTNALL: *Will* you?

GRAINGER: No, damn it, how can I? I'm not a——

BRENTNALL: Very well then, you won't clear out, you won't renounce your marriage. Very well then, go and live with the 10 girl, and be decent. Have a cigarette! *(GRAINGER takes a cigarette.)*

GRAINGER: It's a cursed rotten hole—

BRENTNALL: Then for the Lord's sake, make it as comfortable as possible, if you're going to stop in it. 15

GRAINGER: Hark!

BRENTNALL: Sally!

GRAINGER: It is, begad!

(ETHEL appears.)

ETHEL: There's a woman enquiring for you. 20

GRAINGER: What for—what does she want?

ETHEL: She wants you.

GRAINGER: Hm! Is it Sally?—She's been running after me ever since I've been here, bless her.

BRENTNALL: Let's have her up. *(Calling)*: Do come upstairs, Miss 25 Magneer. It's quite decent.

GRAINGER: It's a bit thick, Billy. *(Enter SALLY.)*

BRENTNALL *(to SALLY)*: Excuse our appearance, won't you. How do you do. *(Shakes hands.)*

SALLY MAGNEER: How do you do? 30

BRENTNALL: Have you been introduced to Mrs Grainger?—Mrs Doctor Grainger—Miss Magneer.

SALLY MAGNEER: I've been given to understand this is Mrs Doctor Grainger—and that the baby downstairs—

BRENTNALL: Is Master Jimmy Grainger. Quite so. 35

SALLY MAGNEER: I think it *is* quite so. It's happen quite so, but it's not quite the thing.

BRENTNALL: Don't let us quarrel, Sally. Don't be quarrelling with us the last half hour we shall be here.

SALLY MAGNEER: Perhaps not. But what was he masquerading round as not married for, if he had a wife and a child.

ETHEL: You see, Miss Magneer, the fact that Dr Grainger chose to keep his marriage a secret, wouldn't have hurt *you*, unless you'd rushed into hurt.

SALLY MAGNEER: Yes—meaning to say as I ran after him. *(To GRAINGER)*: Eh?

GRAINGER: Well—what else can you call it, Sally?

SALLY MAGNEER: And who wanted me to walk down the fields with him, the first time he saw me—?

GRAINGER: I must say—I think you wanted me quite as much, if not more, than I wanted you, Sally.

SALLY MAGNEER: Oh did I?

ETHEL: I have no doubt about it.

SALLY MAGNEER: And did every single girl you met want you then, Dr Grainger?

GRAINGER: I never said so nor meant so.

SALLY MAGNEER: The one downstairs, for instance.

GRAINGER: Who d'you mean?

SALLY MAGNEER: Annie Calladine.

GRAINGER: What's she doing here?

ETHEL: She met me at the station. I left her holding baby.

SALLY MAGNEER: Let *her* come up, and say *her* share.——No, you daresn't, and you know it.

GRAINGER: Daren't I?—I say, Annie—Annie!

ANNIE'S VOICE: Yes!

GRAINGER: Would you mind coming upstairs a minute.

SALLY MAGNEER: Now you s'll hear *her* side, as well.

(Enter ANNIE.)

BRENTNALL: You will excuse us—we were not expecting callers.

ANNIE CALLADINE: How do you do?

GRAINGER: Annie, Sally wants you to say everything you can against me, in Ethel's hearing.

ANNIE CALLADINE: I don't wish to say everything I can against you, Dr Grainger. But I do wish to say this, that you are a *danger* to every unmarried girl, when you go about as you *have* gone, here. And Mrs Grainger had better look after you very closely, if she means to keep you.

GRAINGER: Thank you Annie, very nice.

ANNIE CALLADINE: Almost as nice as you have been to me.

GRAINGER: I'm not aware that I've done you much damage.

ANNIE CALLADINE: If you haven't, it's not your fault.

(ETHEL *flings herself suddenly on the bed, weeping wildly.*)

SALLY MAGNEER: I'm thankful I'm not his wife.

ANNIE CALLADINE: And I am more than thankful. 5

BRENTNALL: Don't cry, Mrs Grainger. George is all right really.

ANNIE CALLADINE *(fiercely)*: He is *not*, Mr Brentnall.

SALLY MAGNEER: Neither is he.

BRENTNALL: Nay, don't cry, Mrs Grainger.

(Elsa Smith's voice, calling in a jolly singsong: Knabe, Knabe, wo bist 10
du?*)*

BRENTNALL: Gott sei dank, du bist gekommen. Komm hinauf.

ELSA SMITH'S VOICE: Ja!⃰ *(Runs upstairs—enter, chattering in
German.)* Oh!

BRENTNALL *(shaking hands)*: Frightful muddle! Miss Annie Calla- 15
dine— —Mrs Grainger's awfully cut up because George has
been flirting round—

ELSA SMITH: With you, Miss Magneer?—and Miss Calladine?

SALLY MAGNEER: Not to mention the rest.

ELSA SMITH: Oh—oh! I'm sorry. But don't cry, Mrs Grainger, 20
please. He's not a villain if he makes love to the other girls,
surely. Perhaps it's not *nice*. But it was under trying circumstances.

BRENTNALL: That's what I say.

ELSA SMITH: Yes, yes. You're just as bad yourself. *I* know you. 25

BRENTNALL: Nay Elsa, I'm not the same.

ELSA SMITH: Oh—Oh—now. *Don't* try to duck your head in the
white-wash pail with me, no. I won't have it.—Don't cry, Mrs
Grainger, don't cry. He loves you, I'm sure he does, even if he
makes love to the others *(to GRAINGER)* don't you? *(No reply.)* 30
Now you are sulking just like a great baby.—And then that's
your *little* baby downstairs? Ah, the dear! *(Sobbing from ETHEL.)*
Never mind, never mind, cry out your cry, then let me talk to
you.

BRENTNALL: Come by motor-car? 35

ELSA SMITH: Yes, Will Hobson⃰ drove me.

BRENTNALL: Ha!

ELSA SMITH: I like him, so you needn't say Ha!

BRENTNALL: Ha!!

ELSA SMITH *(laughing—putting her hand on his shoulder)*: Not had 40 breakfast, and smoking, and talking to ladies.—Aren't you ashamed, Sir?

BRENTNALL: I've nothing to be ashamed of.

ELSA SMITH *(laughing)*: No—no—hear him! *(Kisses him.)* You are a dear, but a dreadful liar.

BRENTNALL: Nay, I'll be damned—I beg your pardon.

ELSA SMITH: No, you *never* use bad language, do you?

BRENTNALL: Not in presence of ladies.

ELSA SMITH: Well, now listen, I prefer to have you as you are with *men*. If you swear when you are with men, I prefer you to swear when you are with me. Will you—promise me you will!

BRENTNALL: It wouldn't be a hard promise to keep.

ELSA SMITH: Promise me you won't have one philosophy when you are with men, in your smoke room, and another when you are with me, in the drawing room. Promise me you will be faithful to your philosophy that you have with other men, even before me, always.

BRENTNALL: Ha!—not so easy.

ELSA SMITH: Promise me. I want the real you, not your fiction.

BRENTNALL: I promise to do my best.

ELSA SMITH: Yes, and I trust you, you are so decent.

BRENTNALL: Nay Elsa—

ELSA SMITH: Yes you are. Oh I see your faults, I do. But you are decent. *(To* ETHEL, *who has stopped crying, but who still lies on the bed)*: —Don't be *too* cross with Dr Grainger, will you, Mrs Grainger? It's not *very* dreadful. Perhaps Miss Magneer loved him a little.

SALLY MAGNEER: That I never did—

ELSA SMITH *(laughing)*: Yes you did. And *(to* ANNIE*)* you were inclined to love him?

ANNIE CALLADINE: That is the worst part of it.

ELSA SMITH: Well, I, who am a woman, when I see other women who are sweet or handsome or charming, I look at them and think "Well, how can a man help loving them, to some extent. Even if he loves *me*, if I am not there, how can he help loving them?"

ANNIE CALLADINE: But not a married man.

ELSA SMITH: I think a man ought to be fair. He ought to offer his love for just what it is—the love of a man married to another woman—and so on. And, if there is any strain, he ought to tell his wife 'I love this other woman.'

SALLY MAGNEER: It's worse than Mormons.

BRENTNALL: But better than subterfuge, bestiality, or starvation and sterility.

ELSA SMITH: Yes—yes.—If only men were decent enough.

BRENTNALL: And women.

ELSA SMITH: Yes. Don't fret, Mrs Grainger. By loving these two women, Dr Grainger has not lost any of his love for you. I would stay with him.

SALLY MAGNEER: He certainly—never loved me—except for what he could get.

ELSA SMITH: Ha!—ha!— *(Very quaint and very earnest.)* That is *rather* dreadful.—But yes, he must have loved you—something in you.

SALLY MAGNEER: It *was* something.

ELSA SMITH: Yes, I see what you mean—but I don't think you're quite right. No, it's *not quite* so brutal.

BRENTNALL: Shall I walk across to you after lunch.

ELSA SMITH: Yes, do that.

ANNIE CALLADINE: I think I will go. Goodbye Dr Grainger— *(Shakes hands.)* Goodbye Sally—Goodbye Mr Brentnall—

BRENTNALL: Goodbye, Annie. Remember what I told you, and decide for the best. *Don't* be afraid. *(Kisses her.)*

ELSA SMITH: Yes. I think, with a little love, we can help each other so much.

ANNIE CALLADINE *(to* ELSA*)*: Goodbye. *(Crossing and putting her arms round* ETHEL.*)* He* isn't bad, dear. You must bring out the best in him. The baby is a *dear.* And you'll write to me. *(Exit.)*

SALLY MAGNEER: Well, Goodbye all.—And if I were your wife, Dr Grainger, I'd keep the bit between your teeth.

ELSA SMITH: No—no—no one should be driven like a horse between the shafts. Each should live his own life. You are there to *help* your husband, not to drive him.

SALLY MAGNEER: And to watch he doesn't help himself too often. Well goodbye. Shall we be seeing you again, Mr Brentnall.

BRENTNALL: Next week.

SALLY MAGNEER: Right—*do* come: Goodbye. *(Exit.)*

ELSA SMITH *(crossing to* ETHEL*)*: Goodbye. Don't make sorrow and trouble in the world: try to make happiness. I think Satan is in hard judgment, even more than in sin. Try to exonerate.

ETHEL: It's such a shock.

ELSA SMITH *(kissing her)*: Ah yes, it is cruel. But don't let your own suffering blind you, try not to. Goodbye. *(Kisses her.)* Goodbye Dr Grainger. *(Shakes hands.)*

BRENTNALL: I will see you downstairs.—By the way, Grainger and Mrs Grainger are going to stay in my rooms.

ELSA SMITH: How perfectly delightful! Then I shall see you in London. How lovely! Goodbye.

BRENTNALL: I suppose I'm respectable enough to see you downstairs. *(Exit each of them.)*

(GRAINGER and his wife sit silent awhile. They are afraid of each other.)

GRAINGER: Will you go to London to Billy's rooms?

ETHEL: Does he want us to.

GRAINGER: I suppose so.

(Silence.)

GRAINGER: Will you.

ETHEL: Do you want me to?

GRAINGER: You please yourself. I'm not coming to Wolverhampton.

ETHEL: Well— *(Trying not to cry.)* —we'll go to London.

GRAINGER: It's a damned mess.

ETHEL *(crying)*: You'd better do just as you like, then, and I'll go home.

GRAINGER: I didn't mean that.

ETHEL *(crying)*: I'll go home.

GRAINGER: Don't begin again, Ethel.

ETHEL: You hate the thought of being married to me. So, you can be free of me.

GRAINGER: And what about the baby. Don't talk rot, Ethel.

(Puts his arm round her.)

ETHEL: You don't care for that, either.

GRAINGER: Don't I—you don't know. They all make me look as black as I can—

ETHEL: Well, I don't know.

GRAINGER: Yes they do—and they always have done. I never have had anybody to stick up for me. *(Weeps a few tears.)* I've had a rotten time, a rotten time.

ETHEL: And so have I.

GRAINGER: You don't know what it is to be a man.

ETHEL: I know what it is to be your wife.

GRAINGER: Are you going to sling it in my teeth for ever.

ETHEL: No, I'm not. But what did you marry me for. *(Cries.)*

GRAINGER *(embracing her)*: You're the only girl I could have married, Ethel. I've been a rotter to you, I have. *(Weeps.)*

ETHEL: Never mind, we *shall* get on together, we shall.—Mind, somebody is coming. *(A knock—enter* MRS PLUM *with the baby.)*   5

MRS PLUM: He wants you, the precious little lamb, he does. Oh Dr Grainger, let me see you hold him.

   (Gives GRAINGER *the baby. Enter* BRENTNALL.*)*

BRENTNALL: That's the way, George.   10

GRAINGER: Shut up, fool.

(Curtain)

THE FIGHT FOR BARBARA
A COMEDY

JIMMY WESSON

FRANCESCA

BARBARA TRESSIDER

BUTCHER

LADY CHARLCOTE

SIR WILLIAM CHARLCOTE

DR FREDERICK TRESSIDER

5

THE FIGHT FOR BARBARA*

Act I.

Scene: The kitchen of an Italian villa—a big open fire-place of stone, with a little charcoal grate—fornello—on either side—cupboards, table, rush-bottom chairs with high backs—many bright copper pans of all sizes hanging up. 5
Time: 8.30 in the morning. The door-bell rings in the kitchen—rings hard—after a minute a door is heard to bang.
Enter WESSON, *in dressing gown and pyjamas: A young man of about twenty six,* *with thick hair ruffled from sleep. He crosses and goes* 10
through door R. Sounds of voices. Re-enter, followed by Italian maid-servant FRANCESCA—*young, fair, pretty—wears a black lace scarf over her head. She carries a saucepan full of milk. On the table stand a soup-tureen and an enamel jug.*

FRANCESCA: Questa?* *(Puts her hand on the jug.)* 15
WESSON: No, in the other. *(She pours the milk into the tureen.)*
FRANCESCA *(smiling)*: Abondante misura!
WESSON: What's that?—Come?
FRANCESCA: Abondante misura—latte!
WESSON: Oh—full measure—Si!*—running over! 20
FRANCESCA: Ranning ova. *(Both laugh.)*
WESSON: Right you are—you're learning English.
FRANCESCA: Come?
WESSON: Vous apprenez Anglais—voi—inglese—!*
FRANCESCA *(blushing)*: O—non—niente inglese! 25
WESSON: Nothing English? Oh yes!—Er—fa tempo cattivo!*
FRANCESCA: Tempo cattivo—si—
WESSON: Rotten weather—
FRANCESCA: Come?
WESSON: It's all the same. *(She puts the lid on her saucepan and turns* 30
    away.) Er—what day is it?—er—giorno—che giorno—?—
FRANCESCA: Oggi?—domenica.*
WESSON: What is it?

239

FRANCESCA: Domenica!

WESSON: Domenica!—dimanche—Sonntag⃰—Sunday.

FRANCESCA: Come?

WESSON: Sunday?

5   FRANCESCA: Sendy!

WESSON: That's it. *(Both laugh—she blushes and turns away—bows.)*

FRANCESCA: Buon giorno, Signore.⃰

WESSON: Buon giorno.

(Exit FRANCESCA *R.—he drinks some milk, wipes his mouth and begins*

10   *to whistle: 'Put me among the girls'⃰—takes some branches of olive and*
ilex from a box near the fire—puts them in the fireplace. As he is so
*doing, enter—Left—*BARBARA*—age about 26—fair, rather fine young*
woman,⃰ holding her blue silk dressing gown about her. She stands in
doorway L. holding up her finger.)

15   BARBARA⃰: Yes, you may well whistle that! *I* heard you, Giaco-
       metti.⃰

WESSON *(turning around)*: And did it fetch you out of bed?

BARBARA: Yes, it did. *I* heard your dulcet tones.

WESSON: They were no dulcetter than usual.

20   BARBARA: And pray what right had they to be as *dulcet!* *(draws*
      herself up)—to a little servant maid, indeed!

WESSON: She's awfully nice, and quite a lady.

BARBARA: Yes—yes—I know you! She's pretty, is she?

WESSON: Awfully pretty! *(lighting the heap of branches in the fire)*—

25   these matches are the stinking devil.

BARBARA: Aren't they!—I tried to light a cigarette with them, and I
      thought I should have died!

WESSON: You should have waited till the sulphur had burned away.
      (Laughing.)—And the pretty maid had got a mantilla on this

30   morning.

BARBARA: A mantilla?

WESSON: Well, a piece of black lace—so!—à la favourite actress.

BARBARA: Ah! I suppose the poor thing had been to church.

WESSON: It took my breath away when I opened the door, and I

35   said 'Oh!'

BARBARA: *Giacomo!*

WESSON: *Do* call me Jimmy—I hate to be Italianised!—and she
      blushed like fury.

BARBARA: Poor thing! Really, Giacometti, really, you are impossible.

40   WESSON: What for?

BARBARA: Fancy saying 'Oh!' to the young maid! Remember you're a gentleman in her eyes.

WESSON: And what's wrong with saying 'Oh!', when she's got a fascinating mantilla on? I can't say delicate things in Italian—and 'Oh' is all the esperanto I know—and—'Oh'—who can't say 'Oh!'—after all, what is there in it?

BARBARA: What could have been more expressive! Think of the poor thing, how embarrassed she must feel. *(The fire blazes up in the big chimney.)* Oh how beautiful! Now that makes me *perfectly* happy. How *gorgeous!*—how adorable!——No but, Wesson, it's not right, and I don't like it.

WESSON: What's that, the fire?

BARBARA: No, the little servant maid. And you made her feel *so* uncomfortable.

WESSON: I didn't.

BARBARA: You must have done! Think—to her at any rate you're a gentleman.

WESSON: A thundering lot of a gentleman, when she finds me lighting the fire and grinding the coffee—

BARBARA: Yes, but no doubt she thinks that's an eccentricity.

WESSON: There's a lot of eccentricity about living on a hundred and twenty a year,※ the pair of us.

BARBARA: And you must remember how fearfully poor these Italians are—

WESSON: It's enough for me how fearfully poor we are ourselves—you in your silk dressing gown! It'll be some time before you get such a one out of *our* domestic purse.

BARBARA: Well, it doesn't matter—you *are* a gentleman here. Look, this flat is quite grand.

WESSON: It will be when you have to clean it.※

BARBARA: *I* don't mind cleaning it, don't be horrid!—This adorable fire! *(He shakes onto it charcoal out of a big black tin.)*—But you won't do it, will you?

WESSON: What—?

BARBARA: Say 'Oh!' to the little maid. It's not nice, really.

WESSON: Well you see, it popped out, when I saw the mantilla. I s'll be used to it another time.

BARBARA: And you won't say it.

WESSON: I won't say 'Oh', oh dear oh no, never no more, I won't. *(Sings.)*

BARBARA *(kissing him)*: Dear!

WESSON *(kissing her)*: What d'yer want?

BARBARA: I love you.

WESSON: So you ought—is that charcoal burning?

5 BARBARA: Why ought I?

WESSON *(at the fire)*: This is good charcoal.

BARBARA: What do *you* know about charcoal, you—!

WESSON: As much as you. There you are, you see, that's how to set a fornello going.

10 BARBARA *(teasing)*: Oh—oh is it!—and now you're going to make coffee à l'italienne, aren't you? Oh you wonderful person!

WESSON: I am! *(Gets a coffee mill from cupboard—grinds coffee on the table, singing.)*

> Johnny used to grind the coffee-mill
15 > Mix the sugar with the sand,
> But he got run in and all through mixing
> His master's money with his own.*

BARBARA: What is that beautiful and classic song?

WESSON *(sings)*:

20 > Johnny used to grind the coffee-mill
> Mix the sugar with the sand,
> But he got run in and all through mixing
> His master's money with his own.

BARBARA *(laughing)*: Oh you common, common brat! Anybody
25 could tell your father was a coal-miner.

WESSON: A butty collier*—and I wish yours had been ditto—you'd ha' been more use. Think of *me*, Lord of Creation, getting the breakfast ready.* *(She takes his head between her hands, and ruffles his hair.)* —while you stand messing about.

30 BARBARA: Oh your lovely hair!—it makes waves just like the Apollo Belvedere.*

WESSON: And come again tomorrer.

BARBARA: Don't—laugh at yourself—or at me when I say it's nice hair. It *is*, Giacomo, it's really beautiful.

35 WESSON: I know, it's the Apollo Belvedere, and my beautiful nose is Antinous, and my lovely chin is Endymion*—clear out.

BARBARA: You are horrid to yourself! Why won't you let me say you're nice?

WESSON: Because the water's boiling.

BARBARA: You're not a bit nice.

WESSON: Mind!—my water's boiling! *(Breaks away—making coffee in a brass jug.)* If this was Pimlico or Bloomsbury,* and this was a London kitchen, you wouldn't love me, would you?

BARBARA: If you could do anything so horrid as to stifle me in a   5
poor part of London, I would *not* love you—I would hate you for ever. Think of me!

WESSON: But because we come careering to Italy, and the pans are of copper and brass, you adore me, don't you?

BARBARA: Yes—on the whole.   10

WESSON: That is, for the first month or two. We've been here six weeks.

BARBARA: Think of it—Giacomo mio,* it seems like six minutes —it frightens me.

WESSON *(hesitating)*: It doesn't seem three months* since we left   15
England, does it.

BARBARA: I can't believe we're here yet. Giacomo, Giacomo, why is it so new, every day? Giacomo—why is it always more? It's always more, isn't it?

WESSON *(putting his arms round her)*: You're a Judy! *(Kisses her.)*   20

BARBARA: Do you love me?

WESSON: Not a bit.

BARBARA: Not a teenty bit?

WESSON: Not a scroddy* atom. *(Laughs—tightens her in his arms— kisses her.)*   25

BARBARA: You're a *common* thing!

WESSON: Am I no gentleman, as Frederick said?

BARBARA: No, no one could ever accuse you of being a gentleman.

WESSON: Am I a lout?

BARBARA: Oh—*did* it call him a lout! *(Mocking.)*   30

WESSON: Am I a clodhopper?

BARBARA: Now—that makes me happy! That Frederick should call *you* a clodhopper—no, that is too much joy!

WESSON: Am I a miserable worm?

BARBARA: You are!—you *are*!   35

WESSON: Have they called me any more names?

BARBARA: You forget the clumsy clown—

WESSON: That your papa would have kicked downstairs—think of the poor old winded baronet—

BARBARA: Who's had his Selma all his life—   40

WESSON: I wouldn't have a mistress called Selma—no, I wouldn't.
It's too much like some furniture cream or chocolate.

BARBARA: And then says you're a degraded scoundrel for running
away with me.

5   WESSON: Yes—his rotten old cheek. How did *he* manage to keep a
mistress, when all he'd got, work and all, was five hundred a
year?

BARBARA: Poor Selma! I don't suppose she was very expensive.
And you know his illegitimate son is quite a clever author.

10 WESSON: Your half-brother! Didn't your father want a boy—didn't
he wish you were a boy?

BARBARA: Oh, he did, he did, poor Papa!

WESSON: Well, I'm glad you weren't, at any rate.

BARBARA: He's a failure too, you know—papa's a failure! Why are
15 all people failures?

WESSON: Couldn't say.

BARBARA: It's because their women have been so rotten to them.
Mama treated my father badly, she did, just because of his
Selma.

20 WESSON: You'd let *me* have a Selma, wouldn't you?

BARBARA: What!—I'd show you—I'll show you if you try any of
your little games on me. But poor papa—everything he has
done has gone wrong—his money—he had no son—

WESSON: So there'll be no fifth Baronet—how sad—what an awful
25 loss to society!

BARBARA: And Anna married a leather man—

WESSON: Who busted.

BARBARA: Yes! And Maud married a miserable little man papa
hated and despised.

30 WESSON: And whom she hates and despises herself.

BARBARA: She does, poor thing.—And here am I, his favorite
daughter, have run away with the son of a coal-miner, from my
good and loving husband.

WESSON: The right worthy Frederick Tressider, doctor of medi-
35 cine.

BARBARA: Gentleman of means.

WESSON: Worth a dozen of me.

BARBARA: Only so wooden.

WESSON: No Barbara—it's a shame.

40 BARBARA: Oh how I hated his wooden face!

WESSON: Well, you knocked spots off it pretty roughly.*

BARBARA: How common, how unexpressibly common your language is.

WESSON: There goes the milk. *(Dashes to the fire)*: Are you going to have bregger in the kitchen, or in the bedroom.

BARBARA: We'll have it here for once, should we—because of this lovely fire—put some more sticks on.

WESSON: Put 'em on yourself—or wait a minute—want eggs, or don't you?

BARBARA: Yes, let's have eggs.

WESSON: You're a lazy little devil.

BARBARA: Think—think how I worked yesterday!

WESSON: Yes—it nearly killed you, didn't it! *(Silence for a moment.)* You'll have to have a towel on the table, for we've got no tablecloths.

BARBARA *(abstractedly)*: *I* don't mind.

WESSON: Else a newspaper. We often had a newspaper for a tablecloth when I was a kid.

BARBARA *(getting up and kissing)*: —Aw!—aw!—what a shame!

WESSON: Why—don't be sloppy.

BARBARA: I'm *not* sloppy.

WESSON: Yes you are—as if it hurts folks to have a newspaper for a tablecloth. I s'll have to guess the eggs, for I've got no watch.

BARBARA: Poor Frederick!

WESSON *(sighing)*: I wonder what time the butcher boy will come.

BARBARA: He *does* love me! If I'd seen it before I left him—I don't think I could have done it. Why did he always hide it from me.

WESSON: He didn't. You merely never saw it.

BARBARA: Oh but it never came out.

WESSON: What did you *want* him to do! He loved you right enough, you merely didn't love him—and there it stands.

BARBARA: But—I knew he was in love with me—but—why could I never *feel* his love? Why could I never feel it *warm* me.

WESSON: Because you never wanted to. You were non-conductive to his particular form of love, that's all.

BARBARA: Think, I was married to him for three years, and I was no nearer to him than I am to that fornello. Lucy used to roar with laughing when I said to her—"It does seem strange you can be married to a man for years and yet not be a bit intimate with him."

WESSON: Poor devil—it wasn't his fault.

BARBARA: Yes, I have treated him badly.

WESSON: You might have done worse by staying with him.

BARBARA: But think—how he adored me!—*Why* did it never seem
anything to me, his love?—But think, Giacomo, how he must
suffer—such a highly esteemed man, and so proud and
sensitive—!

WESSON: And we'd only known each other three weeks.

BARBARA: Oh Giacomo, it makes me tremble! Do you think we
shall bring it off.

WESSON: We shall if we make up our minds to. But if you keep
footling with the idea of Frederick, and your people, and
duty—then we shan't.

BARBARA: But Giacomo—they loved me so.

WESSON: So do I.

BARBARA: Yes but they needed me more. And I belonged to them!
And they say love wears off—and if it does!

WESSON: You were saying only a minute since it was always more.

BARBARA: Giacomo, I'm frightened.

WESSON: What of?

BARBARA: Of everything—and sometimes I wonder—don't be
cross if I say it, will you!

WESSON: Say what you like.

BARBARA: Sometimes I wonder—it seems horrid—I wonder if I
can trust you.

WESSON: Why?

BARBARA: You are so queer—and I am so all alone—and if you
weren't good to me.

WESSON: I think you needn't be mean—

BARBARA: But look—you seem to want to take me away from
everything and everybody. I feel as if you wanted to swallow me,
and take my will away. You won't do it, will you, Giacomo?

WESSON: You're fatter than I am—ask a cat not to swallow a
camel.

BARBARA: I'm not very fat, am I Giacomo?—Say I'm not very fat!

WESSON: Didon dina dit-on du dos d'un dodu dindon.

BARBARA: Oh you're horrid to me! If you say I'm fat I shall go back
to England—I shall—I shall go straight away.

WESSON: You're as slim as a white herring, straight.

BARBARA: You're so horrid with me—you want to drag me down—
you want to humble me.

WESSON: A white herring's an awfully pretty thing—if the comparison's not odorous.

BARBARA: But I don't like it.—And you're so strong, like the lean 5
Kine of Egypt.☆ You won't swallow me, will you?

WESSON: For my digestion's sake, no.

BARBARA: But do you think Frederick will divorce me?☆

WESSON: You'll have to insist on it.

BARBARA: No—I can't—it seems so cruel. I can't, dear. He's so cut 10
up. You know, he says he can't stand up and publicly accuse me.

WESSON: If he'd hate you, and have done with it, it would be easier.
Or if he loved you, he would offer you divorce. But no, he
messes about between one thing and another, and sentimental-
ises. 15

BARBARA: But he *does* love me, Giacomo—he *does* love me.

WESSON: And a fat lot of use it is to you. But he sees you don't
clearly *want* a divorce, and so he hangs on. Now he talks about
your going to live with your mother, and repenting, then he'll
have you back.—But you like to leave a loop-hole☆ by which 20
you could creep out and go back, don't you?—Ah, you do.

BARBARA: No—no—don't say it—don't say it. Only I'm frightened.

WESSON: You know your people have given out you've gone in a
Convent in France, for a little while, because you had got 25
religious ideas or something like that. And I know they think
you'll come crawling back at last—and Frederick is waiting for
you—he's waiting—and you like to have it so—you do.

BARBARA (*putting her arms round his neck*): No, it's not true
Giacometti, it's not true. I *do* love you, don't I—I *do* love you. 30

WESSON: You only don't want to belong to me.

BARBARA: But I do belong to you.

WESSON: You don't—you tamper with the idea of Frederick—

BARBARA: He'd never do to me what you want to do—

WESSON: What? 35

BARBARA: Humble me, and make me nothing—and then swallow
me. And it's *wrong*. It's *wrong* for you to want to swallow me. I
am myself—and you ought to leave me free.

WESSON: Well, so I do.

BARBARA: You don't. All the time you're at me.—Oh, and I hate you so sometimes Giacomo—now you're cross with me.

WESSON: I should think the eggs are done. Sit down.

BARBARA *(seating herself)*: I'm hungry, Giacomo—are you?

5 WESSON: No—it makes me sick, the way you're always bleeding my self-respect.

BARBARA: *I!*—*I!* Why it's I who've given you your self-respect. Think of the crumpled up, despairing, hating creature that came into Mrs Kelly's drawing room—and now look at your-

10 self.

WESSON: But you *won't* love me—you want to keep upper hand.

BARBARA *(laughing with scorn)*: There you are quite mistaken. *I* want there to be *no* upper hand. I only want both of us to be free to be ourselves—and you seem as if you *can't* have it—you

15 want to bully me, you want to bully me inside.

WESSON: All right—eat your breakfast then, and leave me alone.

BARBARA: And it makes me feel as if I want to run—I want to run from you.

WESSON: Back to Frederick.

20 BARBARA: Yes—poor Frederick—he never made me feel like this. I was always a free woman with him.

WESSON: And mightily you regretted it.

BARBARA: No—no! Not that! Your idea of marriage is like the old savages: hit a woman on the head and run off with her, and if

25 ever she says anything, hit her on the head again.

WESSON: Very well. *(The bell rings noisily)*: There's the butcher. *(Goes out door R.—voices—re-appear* WESSON*)*: What do you want?

BARBARA: I don't know—what do we?

30 WESSON: I!— *(He turns round. The* BUTCHER, *a young handsome fellow of about twenty has followed him and stands in the doorway. He has a cloak with a hood over his head—he is handsome.)*

BARBARA: Oh!—buon giorno!

BUTCHER: Buon giorno, signora.

35 BARBARA: Piove?

BUTCHER: Si.

BARBARA: Ah!—e il lago—?*

BUTCHER: È burrascoso.

BARBARA: Ah!—tempo cattivo per voi.* *(The* BUTCHER *laughs.)*

40 WESSON: What do you want?

BARBARA: Er—ha vitello?

BUTCHER: Si—si—quanto?

BARBARA: How much do we want?

WESSON: Mezzo Chilo.

BARBARA: Mezzo chilo.

BUTCHER *(touching his hood)*: Grazia—buon giorno. *(The door is heard to close.)*

BARBARA: Oh I like him, I like him—you said he wasn't nice.

WESSON: He's not—look at the way he comes in.

BARBARA: I like it. It's so decided, at any rate. I hate English people for the way they always hang fire.

WESSON: Do you?

BARBARA: Yes! I like him as he stands there—he looks like a wild young bull or something, peering out of his hood.

WESSON: And you flirt with him.

BARBARA: *Wesson!*

WESSON: I know it's a great insult to say so. But he *is* good-looking—and see the way you stretch out your arm, and show your throat.

BARBARA: But Wesson, how *can* you. I simply spoke to him. And when you think of yourself with the servant maid—

WESSON: I only laugh—you sort of show yourself.

BARBARA: Well really, this is too much. It is really too much.

WESSON: True, whether or not. And you're always doing it. You always want men to think I don't *keep* you. You write to your mother like that, you write to Frederick like that—always as if I didn't keep you, as if you were rather undecided, you would make up your mind to walk away from me in a little while, probably.

BARBARA: How *can* you be so false. It would serve you right if I *did* leave you.

WESSON: I know that, you've said it before.

BARBARA: Really—no one but a common man would say I flirted with that butcher—

WESSON: Well, I *am* common—what's the odds. You've lived with me for three months.

BARBARA: That doesn't say I shall live with you for ever.

WESSON: You can go the minute you want to go.

BARBARA: Ha, could I! It's easy for you to talk. You'd see, when it came to, how you would let me go.

WESSON: I wouldn't try to stop you, if you really, really wanted to leave me. But you've got to convince me of that first.

BARBARA: You think there's not another like you, don't you?

WESSON: For you, there isn't.

5   BARBARA: I'm not so sure.

WESSON: I am! But try, only try. Only try, and make your mistake. But it'll be too late, once you've done it.

BARBARA: Pooh, you needn't think you'll threaten me.

WESSON: I only tell you.—Can I give you anything?

10   BARBARA: The honey. *(He rises and gets it from the cupboard.)*

WESSON: I wait on you, yet I want to bully you.

BARBARA: Yes, it's subtler than that.

WESSON: If you let me wait on you, you leave yourself in my hands.

15   BARBARA: Not a bit of it—not a bit of it! Do you think it makes any difference to me? Frederick would have waited on me on his knees.

WESSON: Then it's time somebody taught you you're not as great as you think. You imagine you're the one and only phœnix.⁎

20   BARBARA *(laughing)*: And I am, aren't I Giacometti. Say I am.

WESSON: I say you're a pecky scratchy one, at that rate.

BARBARA: No—no!—say I'm nice—say I'm ever so nice.

WESSON: On rare occasions.

BARBARA: Always—say always.

25   WESSON: It wouldn't be true.

BARBARA: Yes—yes it would, Giacomo. See, I'm ever so nice, aren't I? I'm ever so nice! Look at my nice arms, how they love you.

WESSON: Better than you do.

BARBARA: No—not better than I do. Come and kiss them. Come

30   and give them a little kiss.

WESSON *(going and kissing her arms)*: You're cruel, if you're nothing else.

BARBARA: No, I'm not. Say I'm not. Kiss me! *(*WESSON, *laughing shakily, kisses her—. A voice is heard outside, 'La Posta'.)*

35   WESSON: Oh Lord, there's the postman—he's the serpent in my Eden.⁎

VOICE: La Posta! *(*WESSON *goes to the door—re-enters with letters.)*

WESSON: The serpent's left his venom. *(Tearing open an envelope.)*

BARBARA *(making a frightened face)*: Is it Frederick?

40   WESSON: And your mother.

BARBARA: Oh dear, Gia, I can't stand it.

WESSON: Why not?

BARBARA: I can't stand it—I can't—poor Frederick.—If he was ill, Giacomo?

WESSON: He'd have to get better. 5

BARBARA: He might die.

WESSON: He wouldn't be such a fool.* And besides, then we could be married.

BARBARA: Don't say it, Giacomo, don't say it. *(She puts her hand on his. He sits glum. Then they both read their letters.)* 10

WESSON: What's up in your letter?

BARBARA *(wiping her eyes)*: It seems so cruel!

WESSON: Your father's ill.

BARBARA *(starting and snatching the letter from his hand)*: Papa! *(She reads, crying quietly.* WESSON *sits waiting—he has read Frederick's* 15 *letter.)*

BARBARA *(looking up)*: Is he *very* ill, Giacomo?

WESSON: No.

BARBARA: They'll say it's me.

WESSON: Let 'em. It's the whiskey as a matter of fact. 20

BARBARA: But it *will* have upset him, about me.

WESSON: His morals, I suppose?

BARBARA: You sound so cruel.

WESSON: You mess about so!

BARBARA: But if he dies! 25

WESSON: Then his chance of kicking me down the stairs is gone for ever.

BARBARA: But I couldn't bear it—if he died.

WESSON: You'd have to. Besides, he won't.

BARBARA: Look how cruel Mama is. 'Your father is very ill, but he 30 does not wish to see you while you continue your present mode of life.—The doctor says he is to be spared all strain and anxiety.'

WESSON: And they're thinking of going to Harrogate,* so he's not at death's door. 35

BARBARA: Don't you think so?

WESSON: No, I'm sure he's not.

BARBARA: And look at Frederick's letter—'Ever since you drove a spike into my brain, on February the 24th,* I have been mad.'—do you think he *is* mad, Giacomo? 40

WESSON: A bit, perhaps—but so were you while you lived with him
—going clean cracked.

BARBARA: He won't commit suicide, will he?

WESSON: No—no more than I shall.

5   BARBARA *(reading)*: 'There are some nights when I never sleep at
all—I try to work, but my brain has gone.' *(Shudders.)* —Ugh!
—how horrible!

WESSON: It *is*—but I can't help it. Think of the hell if you went
back to him.

10 BARBARA: But not for him.

WESSON: For both of you—you'd torture each other. It is indecent
to think of.

BARBARA *(reading—laughs)*: 'Do not speak to me of Wesson. I do
not wish to hear of his existence, or to know he exists. Only, if
15 ever he crosses my path, I will crush him like a beetle.'

WESSON: His feet aren't as big as all that.

BARBARA: How strong his feelings are!

WESSON: His words, you mean.

BARBARA: No, he *is* passionate—you don't know. And he *can* hate!

20 WESSON: He can sound like it.

BARBARA: But if he came here and killed you!

WESSON: I should offer myself to the knife, of course.

BARBARA: But he might.

WESSON: All right—you like to think so.—But he's got more sense
25 than he sounds.

BARBARA: And you think he wouldn't?

WESSON: I'm sure.

BARBARA: Oh but you don't know him—it's just what he might
do.

30 WESSON: All right—I must practise being daggeroso in readiness.
(Puts a pointed kitchen knife between his teeth.) —So! *(He looks
fierce.)*

BARBARA: Oh you are lovely! *(Laughing.)* Let me kiss you. *(He
takes the knife from between his teeth—she kisses him.)* Oh—the
35 way he submits! Doesn't he like it then?

WESSON: He likes it all right—but he's sick of this bleeding tragedy.

BARBARA: Are you tired of me, Giacomo?

WESSON: Tired of the mess we're in, that's all.

BARBARA: Do you want to be rid of me?

40 WESSON: I want to be sure of you.

BARBARA: Well and you are.—*Do* you think Frederick will ever let me go?

WESSON: He'll have to.

BARBARA: But what can we do?

WESSON: You must insist on his divorcing you.   5

BARBARA: But I daren't, Giacomo, I daren't.

WESSON: Why not?

BARBARA: I don't know.

WESSON: You'd rather remain as we are?

BARBARA: No—no! Only he seems something so sure—you know   10
—like when he said 'you have dishonoured our marriage vow,
but I never will.'

WESSON: That's as he pleases.

BARBARA: But it's rather fine.

WESSON: He *is* fine, in a thousand ways where I'm not. But you   15
never loved him.

BARBARA: No—I *never* loved him. Poor Frederick, it doesn't seem
fair, does it?

WESSON: It does not. You were rottenly unfair to him.

BARBARA: In what way?   20

WESSON: Holding him cheap. Holding his love for you lightly, when
it was the biggest thing about him.

BARBARA: *Why* did it never seem so much to me, till I'd left him!

WESSON: You hated him—While he could keep you, he felt a
man—but you didn't mean to be kept—you tortured him—you   25
fought against him—you undermined him—you were killing
him.*

BARBARA: Oh no—oh no! I never hated him. I did a lot for him.

WESSON: You perhaps had plenty of good will towards him—but
you tortured him like hell. You, with your kindness, are one of   30
the cruellest things going.

BARBARA: How *can* you say so, Giacomo! Am I cruel to you?

WESSON: You are.

BARBARA *(laughing)*: It seems to me only funny when you say I'm
cruel—I, who wouldn't hurt a fly.   35

WESSON: Then I wish I was a fly, and not a man.

BARBARA: Aw, did it be a man!—did it be a little man in trousers,
then, did it!

WESSON: It did it!—I think they're getting a bit impatient, your
people.   40

BARBARA: Impatient—how?

WESSON: Look!—as soon as Frederick knew you'd come away with me, he rushes to the lawyers, sets detectives abroad, starts all the machinery of a divorce—

5 BARBARA: I wish he'd brought it off then, don't you?

WESSON: You know I do.—But no—everything is ripening—when he chucks it up, he can't go on with it, he can't do it.—Then he jaws about repentance: you're to go and live with your mother, and repent—

10 BARBARA *(laughing)*: If he only knew, a great deal of repenting I should have done with Mama.

WESSON: —You're to repent for a year, then go back. Then he's going to have a separation, and will allow you an income, so long as you'll see no more of me: you can do anything but have

15 a lover.

BARBARA: Fancy if I promised to do without you—!

WESSON: And now they're getting desperate. You'll see they'll combine forces just now to get you back—

BARBARA: Even if they did, I'd be gone again in three weeks.

20 WESSON: Not if you promised.

BARBARA: Promised—what's a forced promise to me!—I'd break a thousand promises.

WESSON: But if they got hold of the right handle, they'd get you back and keep you.

25 BARBARA: What handle?

WESSON: Oh, I dunno. Your pity, your self-sacrifice, your desire to be straight.

BARBARA: Self-sacrifice!—there's a lot of self-sacrifice about me. *(Laughs.)* They'd find I don't work well with *that* handle.

30 WESSON: You don't know yourself—*you* keep them dangling.

BARBARA: And if I decided to leave you, you'd kindly help me to pack?

WESSON: I would—but I'd drop your trunk on your head as you went down the stairs.

35 BARBARA *(laughing)*: Imagine me looking up and seeing my trunk descending on my head. I'd have to laugh. And your last vision of me would be a squashed laugh.

WESSON: I hope it 'ud be well squashed.

BARBARA: Aw!—how nasty—think of my *poor* face, that is so nice.

40 Do you hate me, Giacomo?

WESSON: No.

BARBARA *(laughing)*: Oh what a loving way—'*No!*'—Why do you hate me?

WESSON: I wouldn't give you the satisfaction of hating you.

BARBARA: Oh—p-p-pp!—now he's getting lordly. You'd simply wave me disdainfully away. *(She imitates him.)* —With one of your Continental gestures. Think of you, *you*, you common brat, with continental gestures. It makes me die.

WESSON: No, I'd drop the continental trunk on your head.

BARBARA: Why do you hate me?

WESSON: Go to hell.

BARBARA *(plaintive)*: Are you cross with me?

WESSON: No.

BARBARA: But you *are*! *(Very plaintive)*: *Why* are you cross with me, Giacomo, when I love you?

WESSON: You—you only love yourself.

BARBARA: No, Giacometti—no, I don't. See how loving I am, really—see how unselfish I am—

WESSON: So unselfish, you'd rob Peter to pay Paul, then go back to Peter to console him.

BARBARA: You're horrid to me.

WESSON: And you are worse to me.

BARBARA: But I'm not.

WESSON: Hm.

BARBARA *(mocking him)*: 'Hm!'—what common grunts! Kiss me. *(Pleading.)*

WESSON *(clearing the breakfast table)*: You shouldn't waste salt in this country.

BARBARA *(following him)*: Won't you kiss me?

WESSON: You know it's taxed out of reach of poor folk like us.

BARBARA: Don't you want to kiss me?

WESSON: No.

BARBARA *(laughing)*: But why?

WESSON: That's why.

BARBARA *(sadly)*: Aw!

WESSON *(turning and taking her in his arms)*: You're a baggage.

BARBARA: Do you *want* to kiss me? *(She draws back.)*

WESSON: Resigned, I kiss the rod.

BARBARA: And am I the rod?—oh Giacomo, think of *me* a rod—

WESSON: *You* see if Frederick and your mother aren't up to some little trick just now.

BARBARA: I'm frightened, Giacomo.

WESSON: Then you're frightened of yourself, of your own hesitating, half-and-half, neither-fish-flesh-fowl nor good-red-herring self.☆

(Curtain)

Act II.

*Scene: The dining room of the same villa—a rather large room, with
piano, writing desk and old furniture. In the big bay window, which looks
over a garden onto the Lake, is a large couch, very big and broad,
without side or back.*   5
BARBARA *is lying on the couch.* WESSON *with his collar and tie strewn on
the table, sits beside her.*
Time: Evening, several days after the first act.

WESSON: You've got a nice chin.
BARBARA: Frederick used to adore it.   10
WESSON: Then he'd no business to.
BARBARA: You think it ought to be reserved for your lordship.
WESSON: Yes—why wasn't it?
BARBARA *(putting her arms round his neck)*: Dear!
WESSON: Don't you wish there'd never been any Frederick—or   15
    anybody else—
BARBARA: Well, *you* haven't much room to talk; look what a mess
    your women had got you in.
WESSON: But don't you wish we could have come straight to each
    other, and been married simply, before we'd knocked about?   20
BARBARA: I don't trust marriage.
WESSON: Because you were stupid, and married wrong—that's not
    the fault of marriage.
BARBARA: No—but I don't trust it.
WESSON: Folk are such fools, they should marry the right people.   25
BARBARA: Even when the right people are *married*, they go wrong.
WESSON: No—I don't believe it—and I don't believe you love
    me—and whether you do or not, I *do* love you.
BARBARA: Because you've decided to.
WESSON: Yes, because I know. I may hate you, I may rage against   30
    you, I may sneer at you—very well! It doesn't alter the fact that
    I love you.
BARBARA: It seems to me so queer, to make up your mind that you
    love anybody.
WESSON: You poke holes in me—well, I'll patch 'em up—I won't   35
    give in.
BARBARA: Oh— —Oh—the dear! He's on his nice little high horse,
    is he—Oh!—he should be on the round-abouts, on his wooden
    prancer!

WESSON: Or on a round-about chicken—

BARBARA: And he looks so pathetic on his chicken—the dear. *(Kisses him.)*

WESSON: Will you love me, Barbara?

5 BARBARA: Yes, the dear, he shall be loved. *(Kisses him.)*

WESSON: Will you stick to me, Barbara.

BARBARA: Oh, did it want to be stuck to. It shall then—Oh, it's nice hair!

WESSON: Through thick and thin?

10 BARBARA *(half mocking, half caressing)*: Through thick and thin— such nice thick hair!

WESSON: Till death do us part—*

BARBARA: Aw, is it talking about death, is it—aw! *(There is a silence. He looks at his watch.)*

15 WESSON: It's ten past six. What train did your mother say she was coming by?—the five to six.

BARBARA *(starting)*: No, she said half past seven.

WESSON: The six train has just gone. Don't you wish she weren't coming?

20 BARBARA: Are you frightened?

WESSON: No—no—I'm not frightened. Only we're rather raw, really, about the business. It seems funny that we're a scandal.

BARBARA: Doesn't it!

WESSON: I'll go and look if I can see anybody, shall I?

25 BARBARA: Yes! Kiss me first. *(He kisses her—exit. She sits up straightening her hair. She is in Bavarian peasant dress,* with bare arms and throat. He comes running in.)*

WESSON: I don't think it's she—but there *is* a woman—

BARBARA: Good gracious—and look at us! *(She flies out—her voice*
30 *is heard, excited.)* Yes—yes—it's she. Quick, get ready—come and change your coat and put proper slippers on. *

WESSON *(struggling)*: Well, I must get my collar on first. *(In a great flurry, he ties his tie, then runs out. The stage is empty. Their voices are heard.)*

35 VOICE OF BARBARA: The funny little figure! *(Laughs.)*

VOICE OF WESSON: —Struggling along. *(Laughs.)*

VOICE OF BARBARA: Only Mama, *only* Mama, could have such a hat. *(Laughs.)*

VOICE OF WESSON: I thought to myself 'well, if that's Lady
40 Charlcote, Goodness knows what the natives will think.'

VOICE OF BARBARA: Poor Mama. *(They both laugh—there is silence —the door bell rings loudly.* BARBARA *rushes in and stands near the door.* WESSON *is heard outside.)*

VOICE OF WESSON: Oh, how do you do! This is earlier than we thought. It is such a rough road.

VOICE OF LADY CHARLCOTE: How do you do, Mr Wesson. *(Her voice is rather plaintive, and protesting—enter* LADY CHARLCOTE —*about* 60*—white hair, shortish, stout, rather handsome—looks resentful—uglily dressed.)*

BARBARA: Oh—Mama! *(Runs forward, laughing shakily—does not kiss—takes her mother's hand—then stands embarrassed.)*

LADY CHARLCOTE *(looking round)*: Yes—yes—

BARBARA: Take your things off—

LADY CHARLCOTE: But I mustn't stay—I mustn't stay. *(Takes off her hat and her long cloak—*WESSON *takes them.)* —Oh thank you.

BARBARA: Sit down, Mama. We expected you by the later train!

LADY CHARLCOTE: No—no—why.

BARBARA: Laura said in her letter, the half past seven.

LADY CHARLCOTE: No—no—I must go on to Brescia by the 7.15.

BARBARA: I am so glad you would come to see us, Mama. *(Re-enter* WESSON—*seats himself before the writing desk.)*

LADY CHARLCOTE *(taking off her gloves—nervous)*: I want to say to you, Mr Wesson, why don't you do something for Barbara.

WESSON *(astonished)*: But I do!

LADY CHARLCOTE: But you don't. A married woman, and you keep her here with you as she is. It is wrong, quite wrong.

WESSON: But you don't know—you don't understand.

LADY CHARLCOTE: Yes, yes, I do understand. It is you who don't understand. What right have you to do it! Barbara has a husband in England, a good, honest gentleman, who is going mad because of her. She is here, but she can go back. Why do you want to ruin her for ever. You are ruining her life— —

BARBARA: But Mama, what I do I do of myself. *(She is crocheting nervously.)*

LADY CHARLCOTE: Yes. *(Turning to* WESSON*)*: You have not got even enough money to keep her. She has to have money from her sister, from her friends. How can she live here hidden with you. Can you expect it! She is the daughter of a high-born and highly cultured gentleman. Do you expect her to carry your slops and make your beds!* She is not used to such a thing.

BARBARA: But if I choose to do it, Mama, it is my own affair.

LADY CHARLCOTE: No, it isn't. Think of your father—think of Frederick. *(Turning to* WESSON*)*: —And do you expect to build up happiness on the ruins of this life. You cannot. Think of your future. You can do nothing with my daughter. You can't put her in her own station, you can't even give her an honest name.* Is she to live with you, and be your mistress, and take money from her husband and her sister and her friends to keep her.

WESSON: She needn't take any money from anybody.

LADY CHARLCOTE: And you say you will live here. You try it for six months, Mr Wesson, and you will wish yourself dead, you will find it so dull. And Barbara is to be the servant, and she is to have no friends, no, not a friend in the world, but is to live buried here among these common Italians, going under a false name, and any minute you may be turned out—no, it is impossible.

BARBARA: Nobody can kick us out.*

LADY CHARLCOTE *(continuing)*: Another man's wedding ring and engagement ring on her finger at this minute. The very bills of her last dresses left for husband to pay—and he, who has given his whole life up to her. There he is in the town of Chislehurst,* like a madman. What right have you to another man's wife, when you cannot keep her—

BARBARA: But Mama, I'm not a horse that is to be kept. You don't consider me.

LADY CHARLCOTE: Yes, it is you I consider. How can any man say he loves you, when he brings you into this shame. Where will you live. Your father never wants to see you again. It is impossible for you to come to England. This young man's career is ruined, he will have to earn money like a laborer, and you will be like a barmaid, wandering around with her lovers.* Where is it going to end.—And who calls that love? It is selfishness that wants to have its own pleasure regardless of you.

WESSON: But if there were a divorce—

LADY CHARLCOTE *(to him)*: You think only of yourself. Think of her father. He is getting old now. Where will he go, that he can hold his head up. It is a shame that will kill him. It will kill everybody. *(Beginning to cry—looking in her handbag for a hanky.)* We are old, and hoped to live at last in peace. Haven't we had trouble enough in our lives. And how can I sleep at night, thinking of my daughter, and what is to become of her. Her father does not want to see her again. *(Cries.)* There is no rest, and no peace. Her husband comes, and it nearly kills me to see the state he is in. If *you* love her, *he* loves her, and *he* is her husband. He can give her what she wants—her position. A woman *must* have a clear name and a position. What is to become of her, what is to become of her.—And you keep her here. *(Cries.)*

WESSON: No—I don't keep her.

LADY CHARLCOTE: Yes, you keep her here—the daughter of a highly cultured gentleman, as your mistress. It is impossible. And her husband is so good. He will have her back in spite of all, and everything can be hushed up—

BARBARA: I don't want things to be hushed up. What I do I want to be done openly—

LADY CHARLCOTE: Don't be a fool—you can't live on ideas, and your ideas won't make five o'clock company.*

WESSON: No—I don't want people to talk—

LADY CHARLCOTE: But they *will* talk. Sir William and I have come out here because they've started—and his heart so bad! We expect to be considered by our children, but they turn on us. It's not natural that we should have all this trouble, now, when we're not expecting it. Everything begins to look comfortable, and Barbara so well settled, when this happens. As her mother, as a woman older than yourself, I've *got* to tell you it's wrong, absolutely wrong, and can only end in sorrow. You don't know what it means. You're young, and inconsiderate. Be thankful you've got no mother, be thankful she's dead, for if she were here she'd wish you'd never been born. I tell you you're doing yourself a wrong, and your career is ruined. You ought to be in London, to go on with your affairs. You ought to live in London. You forfeit everything. You will see in a few years' time, where you will be. It is my duty to warn you. It is my duty to show you these things. And you must let Barbara go back with me. (WESSON *shakes his head*—BARBARA *crochets nervously—there is silence.*) —Think of your own mother, how she would

have felt. She'll never know now. But think how she would have
felt, and make it right before it's too late. *(She waits—he sits
twisting his fingers, his head is ducked.)*

BARBARA: Has Papa come with you then?

5   LADY CHARLCOTE: Yes—we're staying a month with Laura in
Gardone.*

WESSON *(rising)*: Let me give you something to eat.

LADY CHARLCOTE: No—no—I must be going at once. What time
is it Barbara?

10 WESSON: About twenty-five to seven.

LADY CHARLCOTE: I must be going. It's such a long way to the
station.

WESSON: If you will wait ten minutes, there is a 'corriere' goes by,
and that will take you down to Toscolano.*

15 LADY CHARLCOTE: Yes. But I mustn't be late.

WESSON: You won't be.—What will you eat?

LADY CHARLCOTE: Oh nothing—nothing thank you.

WESSON: Excuse me. *(Exit.)*

BARBARA *(quietly)*: How does Frederick look, mama?

20 LADY CHARLCOTE *(she is flustered, rather pathetic)*: Oh poor fellow.
If you saw him, you could never do it.

BARBARA *(bending her head over her work)*: Is he ill.

LADY CHARLCOTE: Ill!—poor fellow!—he is three parts mad! And
he loves you, Barbara, he loves you! How you can throw away

25 the love of a man like that, is more than I can understand. Why,
if I had had him, instead of your papa—

BARBARA: If I'd had papa, instead of him, I'd never have left him.

LADY CHARLCOTE: You don't know what you're talking about—
Poor fellow, he is quite mad. His eyes! I can't bear to see them.

30 *(She cries.)* And he doesn't sleep. You will be punished for this,
Barbara.

BARBARA: Is he changed?

LADY CHARLCOTE: No—no—he is himself—but—poor fellow—
he looks as if he would dash his brains out against the wall. I'm

35 sure I have to tell him sometimes, you're not worth it, the
suffering he goes through for you.

BARBARA: But I am.

LADY CHARLCOTE: You may think so now—but there will come a
time when you will wish you had him back, when you would

40 give everything to have him back. But it will be too late then.

BARBARA: Does he really want *me*, or does he want his reputation —or rather mine—and his social peace.

LADY CHARLCOTE: Poor fellow—such a position to leave him in. And has he ever been anything but good to you. You have had everything you wanted—. 5

BARBARA: I haven't. He *has* been good to me—I wish he hadn't, it would have been easier. He has been good to me, and he's given me everything he could. But I haven't had what I wanted, no, and he couldn't give it me.

LADY CHARLCOTE: And do you mean that this man can? 10
    (BARBARA *crochets in silence—they wait for each other.*)

BARBARA: Will it kill him?

LADY CHARLCOTE: I tell him, at this rate he won't live long.

BARBARA: Why won't he get another woman.

LADY CHARLCOTE: Ah, you are wicked—a good man's love!— 15
Ah—
    (*Enter* WESSON *with a tray, wine, biscuits, bread and butter.*)

WESSON: Will you have a glass of wine—it's 'vin du pays', but it's—at any rate, it's all right for me, though I'm no connoisseur. 20

LADY CHARLCOTE: No thank you, I won't have any.

WESSON: Could I make you a cup of tea.

LADY CHARLCOTE: No, I must be going. My husband will wait for me for dinner.

WESSON: And won't you have anything at all? 25

LADY CHARLCOTE: Oh no, thank you very much. I'll put my things on. (*He goes out, fetches her cloak and hat.*)

BARBARA: Is Papa in Gardone?

LADY CHARLCOTE: In Brescia—but he doesn't want to see you. (*To* WESSON, *who helps her on with her cloak*): Oh thank you!— 30
But he expects you to come back in a proper state of mind.—I think it's all you can do, to make the best of it now. This *is* impossible. (*Neither of them answers.*) And we are staying at the Monte Baldo.☆

BARBARA: Isn't Gardone cheap but grand? 35

LADY CHARLCOTE: It'll do for me—we shall be comfortable, I think.

WESSON: I'm sorry you have such a tedious journey down to Brescia.

BARBARA (*still crocheting*): I loathe cheap grandeur. 40

LADY CHARLCOTE: Well, we shan't want to see you—unless—unless you are coming back. You will think of it, Mr Wesson.

WESSON: I think Dr Tressider ought to divorce her.

LADY CHARLCOTE: You will write to me, Barbara.

5   BARBARA: Yes—Goodbye, Mama. *(They shake hands.)*

LADY CHARLCOTE: Goodbye— *(To* WESSON*)*: —Oh don't you trouble to come out.

WESSON: I think it is no good for Barbara to go back to Frederick. It would only be misery for them both. They can't—— *(Exit*

10   *talking.* BARBARA *remains alone. Her hands fall in her lap, and she broods. There is sound of a carriage—re-enter* WESSON—*he flings his cap on the table. When* BARBARA *hears him coming she picks up her crocheting. When he enters she looks up with a laugh.)*

BARBARA: Well, there's a storm in a tea-cup!

15   WESSON: I think it would take a bucket to hold it.

BARBARA *(laughing)*: It would!—but poor Mama, she really seemed rather pathetic to me—with her brown eyes, and her tears, and her little fat tootsies shuffling.

WESSON: Yes—it seems rough on her—you couldn't help being

20   sorry for her.

BARBARA: You couldn't, could you!

WESSON: After all, she's old—and it must seem like that to her.

BARBARA: Poor Mama—always full of common sense. She was always a good one at showing you the sensible side of the

25   affair.—But didn't it seem common to you—like any of the women of the common people you've told me about?

WESSON: Just. Only it's natural. At any rate she wasn't lofty.

BARBARA: Oh no—Mama would never have been that. She would have said just the same to a Grand Duke.

30   WESSON: She wouldn't—look at the money business. You *don't* need any of their money—we *can* live on what I earn. And as for you carrying the water to the bedroom—*I* do it as often as not—and *I* clean your boots, and bring the coal in—

BARBARA: And *I* don't mind carrying your slops. I wouldn't do it

35   for any man—no, I wouldn't. But I don't mind doing it.

WESSON: If I can't give you much money—well, I give you everything I've got.

BARBARA: Yes, it was mean of her, bringing that up—it's like kicking a man when he's down.

WESSON: But I suppose anybody would do it. She doesn't seem superior, that's one thing.

BARBARA: No—no. You should have seen the way she treated Barrom when he went bankrupt—and he *was*, oh he *was* elegant—

WESSON: But I hate them! Why can't they leave us alone! What do I care what the old Mrs Baronet says.

BARBARA *(laughing)*: You looked as if you didn't care—the way you sat in that chair. *(Imitates him, half crouching.)*

WESSON: Well—that coming all at once—

BARBARA: When we'd been so happy—yes, it *was* a bit overwhelming!

WESSON: I thought the heavens had opened and the last day had come.

BARBARA: You looked it—the way you sat crumpled up in that chair. *(Laughing.)* I thought you were going to creep underneath it. *(Imitates him, crouching.)*

WESSON: What could I do?

BARBARA *(laughing)*: You looked so frightened, so crumpled up! I expected you every minute to wither away into nothing. *(Laughing uncontrollably.)* I thought there'd be nothing left of you. *(Interrupted by her laughter.)* —You—you seemed to get less and less—till— *(helpless with laughter)* I thought you'd be gone. *(Laughing.)* I was frightened—I wanted to get hold of your coat-tails *(laugh)* to keep you. *(She sits laughing helpless, wiping her eyes.)*

WESSON: Well what could I *do*!

BARBARA: I thought you were going to creep under that desk. *(Shaking and helpless with laughter, she points to the hole under the writing desk, by which he sits.)* I thought you were going to crawl inside like a dog into a kennel *(helpless laughter)* and pop your head out, and look sideways at her, and say 'Yap—yap!' in a little, frightened voice—then rush inside. *(Laughs beyond speech.)*

WESSON: Well—if she'd been a man, I might have shouted—but what else could I do?

BARBARA: You looked so crumpled up with your little tail between your legs. *(Laughs.)* You *did* want to get into that corner. *(Laughs helplessly—then rises.)* —Mind, let me show you.

(Laughing, she almost falls to the floor, then creeps inside the space under the desk—pokes out her head—falls face forward on the floor with laughter—lifts up her face, peering sideways.) —Yap—Yap yap!—yap!—the little dog! *(She shrieks with laughter—he giggles from time to time—she rouses again.)* Poor mama chasing you into the kennel, and you so frightened, looking at her sideways *(growling)* brrr!—Yap!—then darting in again. *(She puts her head on her knees with laughter.)* Yap—yap—yap! *(He giggles.)*

WESSON: No—I wasn't as bad as that.

BARBARA *(shrieking)*: You were, you were! I thought I should have died. And every minute I had visions of you collapsing under the desk and barking at Mama. *(Laughing.)* Poor Mama, what would she have done if you had. *(Laughing with little shrieks.)* Imagine her horror at your head peeping out of there with yap!—yap—yap!

WESSON: I wish I had.

BARBARA: I wish you had, I wish you had! *(Drying her eyes.)* But no, you sat there getting less and less.—You can go so little, like a dying pig. *(She screws herself up in imitation.)*

WESSON: Well *you* were impressed, you know you were.

BARBARA: I wasn't—I wanted to scream.—Why didn't you suddenly get up and flap your arms like a cockerel and crow.—It would have given Mama such a shock.

WESSON: But what good would it have done?

BARBARA: It would have been so beautiful.—Or you might have got astride on a chair and gone riding round the room, shouting. *(She shows him—collapses onto the chair with laughter.)*

WESSON: I might have done a lot of things.

BARBARA: Oh, you might, and you did nothing but crumple up! —What a pity! *(Beginning to laugh again.)* You looked anything but a hero that time.

WESSON: I didn't feel a hero.—And if I'd crowed like a cock I shouldn't have looked a hero.

BARBARA: And you were so cocky before. *(Laughing.)* You didn't think you were going to have your comb cut so soon.

WESSON *(putting his hand on the top of his head)*: It feels as if it had been bitten off.

BARBARA: Mama little thought what havoc she'd work in our little ménage. *(Laughing.)* But why do you take it so seriously?

WESSON: I don't take it seriously.

BARBARA: Then why do you let it shrivel you up so?—When I see you going smaller and smaller, I could die.

WESSON: No, but I reckon it's rather rotten of her. We thought she was coming friendlily, to help, and then this is how it turns out.

BARBARA: What a surprise packet for you! *(Laughing.)* Are you coming back to natural size. Is your poor diminished head swelling again.

WESSON: What will you eat?

BARBARA: I don't mind a bit.

WESSON *(drinking wine)*: Drink?

BARBARA: Thank you. *(She drinks a little.)*

WESSON: I told her the only thing possible was a divorce.

BARBARA: You know what a muddler she is. She blows with every wind.

WESSON: I don't care how she blows, so long as we can get that divorce.

BARBARA: If she goes and sets Frederick's back up now, God knows when you'll get it, I tell you.

WESSON: I don't care—they can all go to hell!—but until you stand up in front of me and say 'I want definitely to go back to Frederick—you're no good to me', I shall tell them to go to blazes with their jaw.

BARBARA: It looks as if you'll tell them a lot. Poor little dog, is his tail coming up again.—Come here and be kissed.

WESSON: I don't want to be kissed.—Will you eat now?

BARBARA: Just as you like.

WESSON: A tray is ready. *(Goes out—returns immediately with the supper tray—drinks wine.)*

BARBARA: Poor Frederick—it does twist my inside to think about him.

WESSON: Then don't think about him.

BARBARA: But I must.

WESSON: And a lot of good may it do you. *(A silence.)*

BARBARA: Do you think he really might go mad.

WESSON: Not unless he's weak-minded to start with.

BARBARA: Well he isn't—his mind is stronger than yours, if it came to.

WESSON *(rather ashamed)*: I know he's not—and he won't go mad.

BARBARA: But he loves me so. *(Plaintively.)*

WESSON: He should have more sense then, for you don't love *him*.

BARBARA: But I do, Giacomo.

WESSON: Very well, you *do* then.

BARBARA: And I can't bear him to suffer.

WESSON: You made him suffer worse underneath, twisting your
5　　　　spear in his secret wound, before you left him, than you do now
　　　　that it's open. He can doctor an open wound. A secret one
　　　　drives him mad.

BARBARA: But I didn't torture him. I was a joy to him. And think
　　　　of it, Giacomo, I was the only joy he'd ever had in his life.

10　WESSON: And the only sorrow, for that matter.

BARBARA: Why do you want to say horrid things about me?

WESSON: I don't.

BARBARA: But you do! Look, you say I tortured Frederick.

WESSON: So you did. So you torture me.

15　BARBARA: But how?—tell me *how*, Giacomo.

WESSON: You know how.

BARBARA: I don't. I don't really, Giacomo mio. I really don't. Tell
　　　　me.

WESSON: You needn't laugh at me, when I'm feeling a fool.

20　BARBARA *(making an explosive sound of derision)*: What, has that
　　　　upset his little equilibrium; can't he bear to be laughed at?

WESSON: You don't laugh as if you loved me, you laugh nastily.

BARBARA: But Wesson—I assure you—it is pure good-humour and
　　　　love. And are you *so* touchy! *(Again exploding with laughter.)*
25　　　　Has *that* upset you!

WESSON: It's neither good-humour nor love.

BARBARA: What is it then?

WESSON: It's trying to make me a fool altogether, when I feel fool
　　　　enough.

30　BARBARA: But it *isn't*—it's just sanity.

WESSON: It's the sanity of a cold douche on a man who's got a
　　　　fever.

BARBARA: Aw!—did it have a fever! And has Mama's little scolding
　　　　put you into a fever. *(Explodes with laughter.)* —You don't know
35　　　　Mama.

WESSON: I'm not keen on knowing her much better.

BARBARA: You hate me, Giacomo.

WESSON: Does it please you?

BARBARA: Why should it please me?—Why *should* it please me,
40　　　　Giacomo?

WESSON: It appears to. You seem to exult.

BARBARA: I exult because you wither away when Mama scolds you! I assure you I don't exult in your heroic appearance *then*!

WESSON: I don't ask you to.

BARBARA: What does he then—does he want me to fall at his feet and worship him, does he then! *(She does so—goes on her knees at his feet, puts her forehead to the ground—raises it up and down—in a consoling, mocking voice)*: La—di-da—di-da!—did it want to be worshipped.

WESSON *(seizing her by the arm)*: Get up, you lunatic.

BARBARA: But don't you like to be worshipped.

WESSON *(gripping her arm)*: Get up. *(She rises slowly—he grips both her arms.)* You love!—you love only *yourself*.

BARBARA *(putting her tongue out at him)*: Tra—la-la—la!

WESSON: Yes.

BARBARA: Tra—la-la—la! *(He remains holding her—she says, almost pleading)*: —Let me go.

WESSON: I won't.

BARBARA: —Why not?

WESSON: Because I don't choose to.

BARBARA: I'll make you.

WESSON: Try!

BARBARA: I *will*!

WESSON: Try! *(A moment of silence.)*

BARBARA *(subduedly)*: You hurt my arms.

WESSON *(through his teeth)*: And why shouldn't I?

BARBARA: Don't be horrid. *(WESSON puts his arms round her, fastens her close.)*

WESSON: Oh, you're not faithful to me! *(His voice is like a cry. He reaches forward his mouth to her throat.)*

BARBARA *(thickly)*: I am.

(Curtain)

Act III.

Scene 1.

Scene: The same.
Time: Morning, the next day.

BARBARA *in walking-out dress,* WESSON *in an old jacket.*

BARBARA: What time did the man say Mama would be here.

WESSON: I understood she would come for you in a carriage at ten
o'clock.

BARBARA: And did she really say you mustn't come?

WESSON: She said she wished to drive alone with you.

BARBARA: Put your coat on and come too—it would serve her
right.

WESSON: No—perhaps she wants to talk to you, and to have you to
herself a bit. It's natural. You needn't do anything that you
don't want to do.

BARBARA: Oh don't you trouble, I shan't do that.

WESSON: Well then it's all right.

BARBARA: Is it, I'm not so sure.

WESSON: Then it can be what the blazes it likes.

BARBARA: Oh can it! Oh can it? Tra—la-la—la!

WESSON: Of course she's late.

BARBARA: Why *should* she ask me for a drive without *you*. It's like
her impudence.—I *won't* go.

WESSON: Yes, you'd better.

BARBARA: You'd say I'd better to any miserable thing they liked to
ask me.

WESSON: All right.

BARBARA: Why don't you say I *oughtn't* to go a drive with Mama
without you.

WESSON: Because I don't care—your mother can use all her persua-
sions and reasons till she's sick of it.

BARBARA: But why should she?—why should we put up with it?

WESSON: It's probably the shortest way, if we stick to ourselves all
through.

BARBARA: A fine lot of sticking to yourself *you* do, don't you. Think
of the shrivelling creature whom Mama scolded yesterday.

WESSON: I *was* true to myself then—and to you.

BARBARA: Were you—were you! Then I'll have another kind of
fidelity, thank you.

WESSON: You won't.—And now you'd better go.

BARBARA: Go!

WESSON: For your drive. You'll find Lady Charlcote before you get to the Piazza.

BARBARA: And if I don't choose to? 5

WESSON *(shrugging)*: You'll please yourself.

BARBARA: Tra—la-la—la!

WESSON: I wish you'd go.

BARBARA: Why do you wish I'd go?—I will then. *(Exit—the door is heard to bang.* WESSON *watches her from the window.)* 10

WESSON: There goes the carriage, and the old lady. I should like to murder the two-pence ha'penny lot of 'em, with their grizzling and whining and chuffing. If they'd leave us alone we should be all right—damn them. Miserable bits of shouters!* My mother was worth a million of 'em, for they've none of 'em the 15 backbone of a flea.—She doesn't *want* to stick to me—she doesn't *want* to love me—she won't *let* herself love me. She wants to save some rotten rag of independence—she's afraid to let herself go and to belong to me—she is—she is—she's afraid to let herself go, and to belong to me— 20

(He goes to the side-board, drinks wine, looks at a book, throws it down, plays a dozen chords on the piano, gets up, drinks more wine, sits down to write, and remains perfectly still, as if transfixed—all the time he has moved quietly—the door-bell rings—he does not hear—it rings louder— he starts up and goes to the door—is heard saying 'how do you do—will 25 *you come in?' Enter* SIR WILLIAM CHARLCOTE—*short, stout, a gentle- man—grey, bristling moustache, has been handsome.)*

WESSON: Will you sit down?

SIR WILLIAM *(taking a seat near the door)*: Thank you.

WESSON *(offering cigarettes in a threepenny packet)*: Excuse the 30 packet.

SIR WILLIAM: Thank you, I have some of my own. *(*WESSON *throws the packet on the table and sits on the couch.)*

WESSON: It's a nice day.

SIR WILLIAM: Yes. *(Clearing his throat.)* I called to hear from 35 yourself an account of what you intend to do.

WESSON *(knitting his fingers)*: I intend to do nothing but what I am doing.

SIR WILLIAM: And what is that?

WESSON: Living here—working— 40

SIR WILLIAM: And keeping my daughter under present conditions?

WESSON: Barbara stays as long as she will. I am here for her while she wants me.

SIR WILLIAM: But you have no right to be here for her to want. Your right is to clear out and to leave her to the people she belongs to.

WESSON: But I say, while ever she wants me, I am here for her.

SIR WILLIAM: Don't you see that is cowardly and base—nothing more than robbery.

WESSON: Is it the morality of it you want to discuss?

SIR WILLIAM: Yes—yes—it is the *right* of it. You may perhaps think I have no room to talk.* That is like your damned impudence.

WESSON: But that's not the point.

SIR WILLIAM: A man has a right to any woman whom he can get, so long as she's not a married woman. Go with all the unmarried women you like. But touch a married woman, and you are a scoundrel.

WESSON: So?

SIR WILLIAM: It destroys the whole family system, and strikes at the whole of society. A man who does it is as much a criminal as a thief, a burglar, or even a murderer.

WESSON: Yes.

SIR WILLIAM: You see my point?

WESSON: Your point of view.

SIR WILLIAM: You see so much. Then you see what you are doing: a criminal act against the state, against the rights of man altogether, against Dr Tressider, and against my daughter— putting aside her mother and all her friends and relatives.

WESSON: So!

SIR WILLIAM: And seeing *that*, only an—only a criminal by conviction can continue in what he is doing—a fellow who deserves to be kicked out of every house, and locked up.

WESSON: If life went according to deserts.

SIR WILLIAM: Yes—yes. And my daughter is a lady—she is not a barmaid.*

WESSON: I never mistook her for one.

SIR WILLIAM: You couldn't have behaved in a commoner fashion if you had.

WESSON: We have both known barmaids we respected, I guess.

SIR WILLIAM: And it is all the same to you.—If I were a younger man I would thrash you, Sir—

WESSON: So!

SIR WILLIAM: If you intend to behave in the least like a man, you will clear out of this place, leave no trace of yourself— 5

WESSON: I've got the house on a six months' lease.*

SIR WILLIAM: I will pay the lease.

WESSON: It is paid.—But I like the place, and prefer to stay.

SIR WILLIAM: That is, you will continue to keep my daughter in—in—in this shame and scandal— 10

WESSON: She chooses to stay.

SIR WILLIAM: If plain reasoning will not convince you, we must try other methods.

WESSON: Very well.

SIR WILLIAM: I shall leave no stone unturned until you are 15 removed.

WESSON: So!

SIR WILLIAM: You—whom I thought to be doing a service by asking you to my house. *(The bell rings.)*

WESSON *(rising)*: Excuse me a moment. *(Exit—voices—enter* 20 BARBARA, *followed by* LADY CHARLCOTE *and* WESSON.*)*

BARBARA: Papa!

SIR WILLIAM: I came to speak with this man.

BARBARA: But why behind my back?

SIR WILLIAM: I will come when I like. I will not have women, and 25 especially women like you, about me when I have anything to say.

BARBARA: Nor more will I have men like you interfering with my affairs behind my back, Papa!

LADY CHARLCOTE: For shame, Barbara. 30

BARBARA *(turning, flashing)*: What right has he to come bullying Wesson behind my back. *I* came away with him—it was *I* who suggested he should come to Italy with me when I was coming to see Laura. So when you have anything to say, Papa, say it to me,—if you dare. 35

SIR WILLIAM: Dare!—dare!—A strumpet like you—!

BARBARA: Whom are you talking to Papa—and you of all people. I did not love Frederick, and I won't live with him—so there —and that is all—and you may go.

SIR WILLIAM: I may what! 40

BARBARA: You may go, if you have no more decency.

SIR WILLIAM *(picking up his hat)*: I never want to see you again.

BARBARA: That is not *my* loss.

LADY CHARLCOTE: Barbara, you should respect your father.

5 BARBARA: Mama—you—you—then let him respect *me*, and the man I live with. *(Exit SIR WILLIAM.)*

LADY CHARLCOTE: What has he said?

WESSON: It does not matter.

LADY CHARLCOTE: Well—now you must make the best of your
10 own affairs—for you've cut off all your own people from you, Barbara, and you deserve what you get.

BARBARA: I have *not* cut myself off—it's you who have left me in the lurch. I was miserable with Frederick. I felt I couldn't stand it. *You* would have helped me to have had lovers, Mama. But
15 because I come away decently and openly, you all turn on me.

LADY CHARLCOTE: You know it is impossible—

BARBARA: Very well, then I will *be* impossible!

LADY CHARLCOTE: I shall never leave you in the lurch. *(Crying.)* You are my daughter whatever happens. *(Exit—WESSON hurries
20 to the door after her—it is heard to close—he returns.)*

BARBARA *(flashing)*: Why do you let them trample on you. *Why* do you play the poor worm! It drives me *mad*.

WESSON: But you don't want me to insult your father.

BARBARA: But why do you let yourself be bullied and treated like
25 dirt?

WESSON: I don't.

BARBARA: You do—you do—and I *hate* you for it.

WESSON: Very well. *(She sits down on the couch, twisting her handkerchief. He seats himself beside her, and takes her hand.)*
30 Never mind, they'll get over it.

BARBARA: Papa won't—and I have loved him so.

WESSON: He will.

BARBARA: He won't! Oh but I hate him—a mean funker. But he always was a funker. He had his Selma on the sly, and when
35 Mama found out—it positively broke him.—What did he say to you.

WESSON: He explained his point of view, which seems to me perfectly logical.

BARBARA: And I suppose you agreed with him?

40 WESSON: No, I didn't agree with him—only I understood.

BARBARA: And you cringed to him, I know you did.

WESSON: I don't think so.

BARBARA: And now they've left me. *(Plaintively.)*

WESSON: But were they very much good to you?

BARBARA: No—no—not lately.—But—*why* is it so hard, Giacomo? 5

WESSON: Never mind—they can slam at us, but we can stand it. If they hit us, we needn't fall down, need we!

BARBARA: But it's so horrible—and I have to fight for you, as if you weren't a man.

WESSON: I don't think you have any need. 10

BARBARA: Yes but I have—and all the burden falls on me—you don't take your share.

WESSON: Surely I do! Never mind, I know it's horrid for you. But you will stick to me, won't you? They'll come round to us in time. 15

BARBARA: I didn't think it would be so hard—I have to fight you, and them, and everybody. Not a soul in the world gives me the tiniest bit of help. I feel as if there wasn't a soul in the world lifted a finger for me.

WESSON: That's only because you feel rotten.—I love you, Barbara. 20

BARBARA: Doesn't it make you hate me, all this horridness?

WESSON: Why should it?—I don't care what comes, so that we get a little closer.

BARBARA: But it's worth it, isn't it Giacomo—say I'm worth it.

WESSON *(putting his arms round her and kissing her)*: You're the only 25
thing in life and in the world that I've got—you are.

BARBARA: Are you sure?

WESSON: I've got my work, which isn't life. Then, there's nothing else but you—not a thing—and if you leave me—well—I've done. 30

BARBARA: How do you mean, done?

WESSON: Only my effort at life. I shall feel as if I had made my big effort—put all my money down—and lost. The only thing remaining would be to go on and make the best of it.

BARBARA: I suppose that's how Frederick feels. 35

WESSON: I suppose it is—if only he would get a grip on and try to make the best of it.

BARBARA: But it's not so easy.

WESSON: No, it isn't, poor devil. But if he's got to do it, he may as well. 40

BARBARA: Oh, do you love me enough, Giacomo?

WESSON: I love you enough for whatever you want me for.

BARBARA: Sure?

WESSON: Sure! The question is, do you love *me* enough?

5 BARBARA: I love you better than you love me.

WESSON: Take your hat off, I can't kiss you.

BARBARA *(obediently removing her hat)*: Mama told me Papa was coming—I was furious, it seemed such a mean dodge. They *are* mean though, and sordid.—Did he say horrid things to you?

10 WESSON: He said he'd thrash me.

BARBARA *(laughing)*: Poor papa.

WESSON: I wanted to tell him his words were bigger than his wisdom. *(He is kissing her ear.)*

BARBARA *(laughing)*: Fancy little Papa—he'd have to get on a stool.

15 WESSON: Are you miserable?

BARBARA: No—no!—why should I be? Are you?

WESSON: Aren't you sick of the eternal battle with them? Don't you wish the fools would let us be.

BARBARA: Oh I do!—you dear. *(Kisses him.)* You *do* love me, don't
20 you?

WESSON *(laughing shakily)*: You know I do.

BARBARA: And you want me?

WESSON: I tell you, I've got nothing else.

BARBARA *(kissing him)*: You dear, Giacomo. But Giacomo, you
25 won't get tired of me?

WESSON: Give me a chance.

BARBARA: It frightens me.

WESSON: What?

BARBARA: I don't know.

30 WESSON: Only love me.

BARBARA: Yes—yes—I will.

WESSON: Are you sorry you're done out of your drive?

BARBARA: No, I'm thankful to be back with you.—If *only* they left us in peace, we could be so happy. Why aren't people allowed to
35 be happy in this life.

WESSON: They seem to grudge it us, don't they.

BARBARA: Yes! And Mama says perhaps Frederick's coming.

WESSON: At any rate we s'll have had 'em all then.

BARBARA: But I couldn't bear to see him, Giacomo!

40 WESSON: Then don't see him.

BARBARA: But if he asked me to?

WESSON: Refuse.

BARBARA: But he might do something mad.

WESSON: Let him.

BARBARA: No—I couldn't bear it. I couldn't bear it if anything   5
happened to him.

WESSON: Why?

BARBARA: Oh don't be cruel—I couldn't.

WESSON: Why *should* anything happen to him?

BARBARA: And what would he do if he saw me?—would he go quite   10
mad?

WESSON: You're not such a magical person as all that.

BARBARA: But you don't know him.

WESSON: Quite sufficiently.

BARBARA: Isn't it funny—when I was first engaged to him, and was   15
reading *Othello*, I thought what a good Othello he'd make,
better than the real one.

WESSON: You feel sure he'll slay you, poor Desdemona.

BARBARA *(laughing)*: Yes!—he's so Othelloish.

WESSON: And you're so Desdemoniacal, aren't you?   20

BARBARA *(laughing)*: What does that mean?

WESSON: It means you sit sighing by a sycamore tree,☆ you poor
soul.

BARBARA *(kissing him)*: Oh I love you!

WESSON: Do you?   25

(Curtain)

Act III.

Scene 2.

Scene: The same—on the table are the dishes, and copper saucepan, from the evening meal.

5 *Time: Evening of the same day:* WESSON *sits alone writing. Enter* BARBARA, *resplendent in an evening dress, with ornament in her hair. She stands in the doorway, looking across at herself in a mirror. He does not look up.*

BARBARA: You've never seen me in this before. *(He looks up—puts*
10 *his pen between his teeth—she preens herself.)* You've never seen me look so grand, have you?
WESSON: No.
BARBARA: Don't I look fine! Do you like it?
WESSON *(after a moment)*: I hate it.
15 BARBARA *(hurt)*: But why?—I look nice.—Don't I look nice?
WESSON: I hate it, take it off.
BARBARA: But why, Giacomo? Doesn't it suit me?
WESSON: I hate it—I hate it—you belong to those others in it.
BARBARA: But how nasty of you, Giacometti! It's only the
20 dress—the woman is just the same.
WESSON: She's not. She's according to her frock, which is Frederick's.
BARBARA *(laughing)*: No she's not, Giacomo, she's the same.
WESSON: I hate it whether or not.—You put it on for Frederick, not
25 for me.
BARBARA: I didn't. I want you to see how grand I can look. Don't you really think I look nice?
WESSON: No—I'd rather see you in your kitchen pinafore.
BARBARA: See how you want to drag me down.—But *you*'ve got an
30 evening suit.
WESSON: I don't care.—It makes me conscious of your class difference.—I wouldn't mind if I'd bought it—but it's Frederick's—you ought to be in his drawing room, not in this bit of a place with me.—Take it off, Barbara.
35 BARBARA *(laughing)*: Does it really hurt you? *(She sits down*⃰ *and begins to play a dance on the piano—it is the Blue Danube*⃰—*she breaks off.)*—It's the dearest dress I ever had, and it wasn't paid for when I came away.
WESSON: How much did it cost?

BARBARA: Eighteen guineas.

WESSON *(pondering)*: And did you leave any more bills for Frederick to pay?

BARBARA *(playing)*: No—I think not—only this. *(The Blue Danube Waltz continues—he sits pondering.)* 5

WESSON: Take it off Barbara.

BARBARA *(slowing down—she is very quiet)*: Yes. *(Rises—exit slowly. He sits chewing his pen—in a moment she rushes back, lays her hands on his shoulder.)*

BARBARA: There's Frederick! 10

WESSON: Rubbish—where?

BARBARA: At the gate—with Mama—I saw them from the bedroom window.

WESSON: No.

BARBARA: Yes—hark! *(Sound of voices.)* Listen, the gate's locked. 15

WESSON: Then let them stay out.

BARBARA: But they'll come to the back door!—What does he want, Wesson, what does he want?

WESSON: To try his hand where your mother and father have failed. *(LADY CHARLCOTE's voice is heard calling 'Barbara!')* 20

BARBARA: Go and open, quick—quick!

WESSON: What for—what's the good?

BARBARA: Quick!

WESSON *(standing stubborn)*: What's the good!

BARBARA: Quick!—I'll call to them from the window *I'm* 25
coming—I will—*(Moves to the window.)*

WESSON: What's the good—let them go away again!

BARBARA: I'll call now—

WESSON: Damn!! *(He moves grudgingly to the door.* BARBARA *stands with her hands clasped over her bare breast, terrified—listening. The* 30
gate is heard to bang open—voices—enter FREDERICK, *alone—a haggard, handsome man of forty, brown moustache, dark brown eyes, greying at the temples. He is dressed in homespun*—*hesitates at the door.)*

FREDERICK *(ironically)*: May I come in? 35

BARBARA *(frightened)*: What do you want?

FREDERICK: Merely permission to speak to you.

BARBARA: You know you may speak to me. *(They hesitate—enter* WESSON——*followed by* LADY CHARLCOTE.*)*

WESSON: Barbara, do you want me to go with Lady Charlcote to 40 the Hôtel Cervo* for half an hour?—she says it would be fair.

BARBARA: I don't know. *(Sinks onto the couch.)*

WESSON: You must *tell* me to go. *(DR TRESSIDER looks at him sideways, and shows his teeth, but does not speak—BARBARA watches the two men in terror.)*

BARBARA: Perhaps you'd better go—Mama can stay with me.

WESSON *(lingering)*: You—

LADY CHARLCOTE: I think Frederick has the right to speak to you alone, Barbara.

BARBARA *(almost whispering)*: But why—?

FREDERICK: Are you afraid that I may abduct you—?*

LADY CHARLCOTE: No, Frederick, I don't think it *is* fair to leave her alone with you.

FREDERICK *(nastily)*: Don't you?—Perhaps it isn't safe—

LADY CHARLCOTE: You might not be responsible for what you did.

FREDERICK: So the only place for me is the lunatic asylum.

BARBARA: If you are like that, Frederick, I don't know what you can want to speak to me at all for.

FREDERICK: It *is* a question for surprise.

BARBARA: I'd much rather you *did* treat me as dirt, and left me alone.

FREDERICK: What is a little dirt to you, hey? *(Showing his teeth.)*
          (There is a pause.)

WESSON: Will you sit down, Lady Charlcote?

FREDERICK *(to WESSON)*: Will you please take yourself away, while I speak to my wife.

BARBARA: Yes, go Wesson. Mama will stay.

WESSON: But—

BARBARA: Yes—go for a little while—I shall be all right.

FREDERICK: You can scarcely refuse to go, since you did not refuse to come.

LADY CHARLCOTE: I would go for a few minutes, Mr Wesson. It can't do you any harm. Things will settle themselves then.

WESSON *(to BARBARA)*: Must I?

BARBARA: Only to the—to one of the other rooms.

WESSON: I'll go to the bedroom, then. *(Exit sullenly.)*

FREDERICK *(taking a seat)*: I'm glad you look so well, Barbara.
          (There is a pause.)

LADY CHARLCOTE: You won't do any good that way, Frederick.

FREDERICK *(turning slowly to her)*: Perhaps you'll tell me what to say!

LADY CHARLCOTE: You needn't behave like a fool, at any rate.
(There is a long silence.)

BARBARA: I'm afraid you've been ill, Frederick.

FREDERICK: Yes—I am ill! I am glad to see you are so well.

BARBARA: Don't Frederick—what *is* the good of this—what *is* the good of it? Let us make the best we can now—

FREDERICK: Exactly!

BARBARA *(turning impatiently to* LADY CHARLCOTE*)*: How is Papa, Mama?

LADY CHARLCOTE: Well, I think the place will suit him.—Of course *you* are impossible, even to mention to him, just now.

BARBARA *(faltering)*: Yes—I'm sorry—

LADY CHARLCOTE: But I tell him—you're *his* daughter, not mine—all haste—and no judgment.

BARBARA: But he *is* well?

LADY CHARLCOTE: Yes, he seems better than I expected.

BARBARA: Thank the Lord! *(Another silence.)*

LADY CHARLCOTE: Have you a drink, Barbara?

BARBARA *(rising and going to the cupboard)*: There's lemon water, and there's red wine. *(Brings two decanters, and three glasses.)*

LADY CHARLCOTE: Give me only lemonade—I'm so thirsty—they gave us a beastly salt *goulash.* (BARBARA *pours her mother's drink, and drinks herself.)*

BARBARA: Will you have some, Frederick?

FREDERICK: Thank you, I won't. ☆

BARBARA: I think you may—

FREDERICK: Thank you.

BARBARA: Then the only sane thing would be to say what you came to say, and let us get it over.

FREDERICK: I came for your instructions, of course.

BARBARA: It seems rather stupid, don't you think?

FREDERICK: I've no doubt I always was stupid—a trusting fool—

BARBARA: You know it wasn't like that. Do you really wish to speak to me?

FREDERICK: Of course I came to pay a friendly call. ☆

BARBARA: But have you *really* anything to say to me?

FREDERICK: Yes, I think I can honestly say I have.—It no doubt surprises you.

BARBARA: Then for God's sake don't torture me any longer.

FREDERICK: It *would* be a pity!—But what I have to say I have to say to my wife, not to the world at large, or even to my mother-in-law, or your paramour.

5 BARBARA: Then *don't* say these unnecessary things to me.

FREDERICK: I know the truth is unnecessary to you.

BARBARA: What does that mean?

LADY CHARLCOTE: Tom-foolery, that's what I call it.

FREDERICK *(turning to her)*: I'm sorry if you are *bored*, Lady
10 Charlcote.

LADY CHARLCOTE: Yes—yes—it *is* boring.

BARBARA: Perhaps you *had* better leave us alone, Mama.

FREDERICK: Hadn't you better consider again, Barbara. Wouldn't that be giving me too much encouragement? I might take a
15 liberty. I might even ask you to livant with me, like a seductive footman, or dustman. *(There is silence—*LADY CHARLCOTE *drinks again.)*

LADY CHARLCOTE: I like these lemons gathered fresh. There is such an aroma about them.

20 BARBARA: Yes! Isn't there! I adore them! *And* the flowers—!

FREDERICK: I am afraid I am keeping you from an interesting chat.

LADY CHARLCOTE: I can go into another room. *(Making signs to* BARBARA.*)*

25 FREDERICK: Oh—thank you—but I don't wish to disturb you. *(Bowing.)*

LADY CHARLCOTE: We have to be back by eight. *(Rising.)*

FREDERICK: Thank you—I will remember.

LADY CHARLCOTE: Where can I go, Barbara? *(*BARBARA *rises—they*
30 *go out together—*FREDERICK *looks round—gnaws the ends of his moustache—re-enter* BARBARA—*she leaves the door open—he glances, sees it, but makes no remark.)*

BARBARA *(taking her former seat)*: Mama is in my bedroom.

FREDERICK: Within call, I hope.

35 BARBARA: Yes. *(There is silence.)*

FREDERICK: Anything to say to me?

BARBARA: What *can* I say!

FREDERICK: I wonder.

BARBARA: Don't be horrid with me Frederick—I *know* I deserve
40 it—

FREDERICK: You might tell me how to behave. The situation is so novel—

BARBARA: Don't be horrid and sarcastic.

FREDERICK (*showing his teeth*): I try not. (*He sits devouring her with his eyes.*) You're in full dress tonight, madam! Was it a great occasion?

BARBARA: No—I put it on—it's the first time.

FREDERICK: You look the thing in it—I turned up to see you on your mettle, by good luck.

BARBARA: Don't.

FREDERICK: Beautiful good luck.—War-paint, I suppose?

BARBARA: No—! You told me once you'd never be hard on a woman.

FREDERICK: I'm sorry if I'm hard on you—that *would* be unjust.

BARBARA: Don't talk like that—Frederick!

FREDERICK: I won't. (*A silence.*)

BARBARA: Let us say what there is to be said.

FREDERICK: What shall we talk about—you or me?

BARBARA: About you.

FREDERICK: Yes—go ahead.

BARBARA: Tell me about yourself—

FREDERICK: Ha!—how I suffered, you mean?

BARBARA: I know it's been awful for you.

FREDERICK: Do you really—I shouldn't have thought it.

BARBARA: Oh but I do! It's nearly driven me cracked sometimes.

FREDERICK: Ha!—It was kind of you.

BARBARA: And I can see— (*Begins to cry.*)

FREDERICK (*with a sob*): Your own work.

BARBARA (*going forward impulsively and putting her hand on his knee*): Don't—don't!

FREDERICK: I won't—but tell me what—I must.

BARBARA: Don't be like this—I can't bear it.

FREDERICK: You might tell me what you can bear.

BARBARA (*rising and going back to her seat*): It is so cruel Frederick.

FREDERICK: Exactly.

BARBARA: Why can't you cast me off—why can't you find some other woman—There's Annabel, who adores you—or Lizzie Burroughs—

FREDERICK: You think they'd make good successors of yours?

BARBARA: They might, Frederick—you don't know.

FREDERICK: You don't know anything in this life, Barbara, and
that's a fact. I thought I had a wife.

BARBARA: You might love them better than me—you might! See, I
was not faithful to you—*

5   FREDERICK *(laughing)*: I wouldn't rub it in, if I were you.

BARBARA *(frightened)*: But I'm not! *(There is a silence.)*

FREDERICK: So you think I might do well to marry again?

BARBARA: I thought—I can't bear—to think of you being lonely.

FREDERICK: Ha—you'd rather I had another woman—I see—

10   BARBARA: You don't know—they adore you—hundreds of women
adore you—

FREDERICK: And you'd give me a wedding present, I dare say, and
give the woman advice how to fool me.*

BARBARA: No—no—I won't let you say these things—

15   FREDERICK *(showing his teeth)*: I daresay.—You were wasted on me,
weren't you?—I didn't appreciate you—

BARBARA: You were *good* to me—but you never understood me—

FREDERICK: I'm sorry! I understood you wanted a decent life, and I
worked hard for you. I understood you wanted some amuse-
20   ment—you did exactly as you liked—you had everything I
had—you had your own way. I was faithful to you from the day
I saw you—and before that. You might have called me a model
husband. I suppose that was my fault. You had better put on my
tombstone 'He was a poor fool and a good husband.'

25   BARBARA *(crying)*: No—it wasn't your fault to be a good husband
—that's why I love you still—in a way—you were so good to
me—but—you weren't near to me—you—you didn't warm
me—

FREDERICK: I think I was as near as ever you'd let me come.

30   BARBARA: No—no—can't you remember—when we were first
married. I thought marriage would be a jolly thing—I thought I
could have lovely games with the man. Can you remember,
when I climbed to the top of the cupboard, in Lucerne.* I
thought you'd look for me, and laugh, and fetch me
35   down.—No, you were terrified. You daren't even come in the
room. You stood in the door looking frightened to death. And I
climbed down.—And that's how it always was. I had to climb
down.—I sat up there in my camisole with my legs dangling,
and you were terrified. I had to climb down. I tell you it *was* a
40   climb down for me.

FREDERICK: But you can scarcely say you left me because I didn't fetch you from the top of a cupboard, where you had climbed like a child—

BARBARA: Yes—yes—because it was always so. You never found *me*—the real me—

FREDERICK: I suppose it sat at the top of a cupboard.

BARBARA: Dangling its legs and feeling down—yes, it did.

FREDERICK: And so you left me?

BARBARA: Yes! I couldn't live with you. It was hopeless.

FREDERICK: Because I didn't drag you by the ankle from the cupboard tops?

BARBARA: Yes—that's it.

FREDERICK: And how long did it take you to find this out? How long have you been deceiving me?

BARBARA: You know very well that I was only introduced to Wesson about a month before—you knew all about it.

FREDERICK: And you began on the first meeting, and betrayed me in my own house.

BARBARA: Never.

FREDERICK: And may I enquire after the predecessors of this clown?

BARBARA: Yourself.

FREDERICK: I enjoy that honor alone, do I?—with the miserable clown—

BARBARA: You were not going to speak of him.

FREDERICK: I was not.

(There is silence.)

FREDERICK: And pray, when did you find out then that I had not —not found the real *you*.

BARBARA: The first night of our marriage—when I stood on that balcony and wanted to drown myself—and you were asleep.

FREDERICK: And afterwards—I suppose you forgot it—

BARBARA: Sometimes. You were good to me—and I didn't think then there *could* be anything else.

FREDERICK: Than what?

BARBARA: Than going on as I was—as your wife.

FREDERICK: Though you didn't exactly like the idea?

BARBARA: No—I never really liked it.

FREDERICK: Ha! *(Another long silence.)*

BARBARA: But I never thought I could be unfaithful to you, or leave you.

FREDERICK: And you *never* loved me?

BARBARA: Sometimes—when you were so nice to me—

5   FREDERICK: Out of gratitude, as it were, and feeling you *ought* to love me.

BARBARA: I always felt I ought to love you.

FREDERICK: But could never bring it off.—Ha!—thank you for the try, at any rate. It may not have been a very desperate one—

10   BARBARA: And of course sometimes I hated you.

FREDERICK: Naturally.

BARBARA: And now it's over.

FREDERICK: As you say—it's over. *(There is a long silence.)*

FREDERICK *(in a sudden outburst)*: Woman, do you know I've given

15   my life to you. Do you know, everything I did, everything I thought, everywhere I went, was for you. I have worked till I reeled, I was so tired. I have tried to fulfil your lightest wish. I have been your slave—

BARBARA: That's it—I didn't want you to be my slave—

20   FREDERICK: I—I—I have done everything. How often have I asked you 'What do you want of me?—' Why didn't you tell me then?—why didn't you say? Why have you deceived me all this while, letting me think you loved me—?

BARBARA: I didn't deceive you. *(Crying.)* I didn't know myself.

25   FREDERICK: How many times have you had your arms round my neck, and said 'Do you love me?'—I might well answer 'Malheureusement.'—What was that but deceit—what was it but lying to me, and falsity—

BARBARA: It wasn't lying to you Frederick—you *did* love me—and

30   I wanted you to love me—

FREDERICK: What right had you to want me to love you, when you cared not a couple of straws about me? Did you want to glory in it, and gloat over it, and make mock over it—

BARBARA: I *did* want you to love me—you were all I had—

35   FREDERICK: Until another came along, and then you threw my love away like a bit of dirty paper wrapping.

BARBARA: No—no—I didn't—

FREDERICK: What else have you done?—You have thrown me away like a bit of paper off a parcel. You got all the goods out of the

40   packet, and threw me away.—I gave you everything, my life,

everything, and it is not worth the stump of a cigarette when it comes to.—I tell you, this is the end of me. I could work then, but now my brain has gone. I may do hack work. Anything original is gone for me. That book, I wanted to dedicate it to you, but I thought it wasn't good enough. I thought I would write a better. I read it through the other day, revising for the third edition,* and I was surprised, it was so good. And I shall do no more. It has gone—I am done—

BARBARA: No, Frederick, no, you will work again.

FREDERICK: I tell you I can no more work now than you can row a boat when you've lost the oars. I am done for—as a man you see me here a ruin.—Some nights I sleep, some nights I never close my eyes. Something goes in my head like a hammer, and nothing I can do will stop it. I keep sane—I force myself to keep sane—But in the end my brain will go—and then I shall make an end—

BARBARA *(going over to him, kneeling with her hand on his knee, crying)*: No—no Frederick—no—no—

FREDERICK: Then I shall go to Wood Norton—do you remember, where I saw you first—a girl of eighteen* with a sash? I shall go to that pine wood where the little grove of larches is, and I shall make an end.—I haven't been since you went. I have wanted to, but I knew I should never come away again. But when it gets unbearable, when things are too bad, then I shall go to my dear Wood Norton.—Do you remember when we caught a squirrel—

BARBARA *(her head on his knee—weeping)*: Oh, what can I do—what can I do?

FREDERICK: I've no doubt it all sounds very melodramatic—but it's the truth for me. Then your work will be finished. I have loved you. When we were engaged, you might have lived on a desert island with me, and you would have been safe.—While we were married, the world didn't hold for me another woman than you.—I would have spilt my blood on every paving-stone in Bromley for you, if you had wanted me to—

BARBARA: But I didn't want you to. I wanted you to come near to me and make me yours and you be mine. But you went on worshipping me instead of loving me—kissing my feet instead of helping me. You put me on a pedestal, and I was miserable.* I didn't want to be on a pedestal, I wanted to be side by side

with a man. And you never thought you were good enough for
me—and so you *weren't* good enough, just because you thought
so—

FREDERICK: And you never loved me all the time. *(He shows his
teeth—his dark eyes glitter.)*

BARBARA: I did love you—I did love you.

FREDERICK *(his fists clenched—shuddering)*: I could strangle you—I
could strangle you.

BARBARA *(terrified)*: Don't—don't—I shall scream—

*(She gets up afraid and draws back. He suddenly gets hold of one of her
arms.)*

FREDERICK: You devil—you devil—you devil. But you belong to
me, do you hear—you belong to me—

BARBARA *(pushing him away)*: Don't—don't—let me go—I shall
call Mama—Oh—

*(He releases her—she flings herself face down on the sofa—he sits
crouching, glaring. Silence for some time.)*

FREDERICK: Well, have you been there long enough?

BARBARA *(sitting up)*: Yes—long enough to know that it never was
any good, and it never would be any good. *(Another long
silence.)*

FREDERICK: 'It never was any good, and never would be any
good'—what?

BARBARA: You and me.

FREDERICK: You and me!—Do you mean to tell me that my life has
been a lie and a falsity—?

BARBARA: Why?

FREDERICK: *You* were my life—you—and you say it was never any
good between us.

BARBARA: But you had your work. Think, if you had to choose
between me and your work.

FREDERICK: You might as well ask an apple-tree to choose between
enjoying the sunshine and growing its own apples: the one
depends on the other and is the result of the other.

BARBARA: No Frederick—why, look how happy you could be with
your work when I was miserable.

FREDERICK: Why were you miserable?

BARBARA: I don't know—but I was.

FREDERICK: But you had no reason to be. I gave you everything
you asked for. What did you want?

BARBARA: I suppose I wanted something you could not give.

FREDERICK *(glaring at her—after a silence, suddenly)*: I had a good mind to murder you.

BARBARA *(frightened)*: Why?

FREDERICK: I had a good mind to murder you as you sit there—it would do me good.* 5

BARBARA *(frightened)*: See—see how you loved me!

FREDERICK: How I loved you!—yes—*you* see!—you see how I loved you, you callous devil! Haven't I loved you with every breath I've fetched—haven't I—haven't I?—and you've not cared a brass button about it, and sit telling me to see how I've loved you—you—*you*! 10

BARBARA: But what was the good of loving me, if you had all the fun out of it. It didn't seem anything to me because I didn't realise—I didn't know— 15

FREDERICK: You didn't *love* me—!

BARBARA: No—well—you should have seen that I did. It doesn't do me any good, if a man *dies* for love of me, unless there is some answer in me, so that it lives in me.

FREDERICK: And it never had any answer from you? 20

BARBARA: Did it?—judge for yourself if it did.

FREDERICK: I ought to have killed myself rather than marry you.

BARBARA: But I couldn't help that, could I?

FREDERICK: No, you could help nothing. You could only throw me away like waste paper that had wrapped up a few years of your 25 life.

BARBARA: I'm sorry Frederick. I'll do what I can, I will really.

FREDERICK: *What* will you do?

BARBARA: Don't you trust me?

FREDERICK: Trust you, yes, you can go on doing as you like with 30 me.

BARBARA: There you are, you see, resigned. Resigned from the very start—resigned to lose. You are, and you always were.

FREDERICK: Very well, you little devil—it seems you were determined— 35

BARBARA: What?

FREDERICK: To destroy me.

BARBARA: How *can* you say so.

FREDERICK: To destroy me.

BARBARA: No—no. 40

FREDERICK: To destroy me.

BARBARA *(going and putting her arms round his neck)*: No—no Frederick. I'd do an awful lot for you—I really would—I have loved you.

5 FREDERICK: What, for example.

BARBARA: I'd help you with the people in Chislehurst—come and live for a time in the same house.

FREDERICK: And then—?

BARBARA: Oh, I don't know—

10 FREDERICK *(holding her by the arms and looking in her eyes)*: Will you give up this man and come back to me?

BARBARA: Oh—what's the good of promising, Frederick—I might only break it again. Don't force me.

FREDERICK: Will you try? Will you try *me* again for three months.

15 BARBARA: Come and live with you again?

FREDERICK: Yes.

BARBARA: As your wife?

FREDERICK: Yes.

BARBARA: Altogether as your wife?

20 FREDERICK: Yes—or even—at first— *(There is a silence.)*

BARBARA *(piteously)*: I don't know, Frederick.

FREDERICK *(slowly)*: You don't know!

BARBARA: No—I don't know—I don't know.

FREDERICK: Will you think about it?

25 BARBARA: But I don't know! What is the good of thinking about it?—But I don't know Frederick.

FREDERICK: You can make up your mind.

BARBARA: But I can't—I can't—it pulls both ways. I don't know, Frederick—I don't know *anything*.

30 FREDERICK: Will you know better tomorrow—will you come then and tell me—will you?

BARBARA: But I shan't know any better tomorrow. It's now! And I can't tell.—Don't make me decide, Frederick.

FREDERICK: What?

35 BARBARA: Which way. Don't make me decide!

(She goes and sits on the couch, hiding her face in a cushion. FREDERICK *suddenly flings his arms on the table and sobs—'Oh Good God*☆*—I can't bear it.'* BARBARA *looks at him, goes and puts her hand on his shoulder.)*

40 Don't Frederick—don't! I *will* make up my mind, I will.

FREDERICK *(his face muffled)*: I can't stand it, Barbara.

BARBARA: No dear. *(He sobs—she touches his hair.)* Don't! Don't! You shall—I will do—what I can—I will—I will do—what I can. *(He stops crying.)*

FREDERICK *(his face still hidden)*: It will kill me Barbara. 5

BARBARA: No dear—no it won't. I must think of something. I will tell you tomorrow. I will come and tell you—

FREDERICK *(his face still hidden)*: What?

BARBARA: I don't know dear—but I will see—I will come. Look at me—look at me. *(He lifts his face.)* Dear! *(He folds her in his* 10 *arms—she puts her head back as he kisses her.)*—There's Mama! *(He listens—hears a sound, snatches his hat and dashes out—* BARBARA *turns to the piano—straightens her hair—stands waiting —enter* LADY CHARLCOTE.*)*

LADY CHARLCOTE: Has Frederick gone? 15

BARBARA: Yes. *(Enter* WESSON.*)*

LADY CHARLCOTE: What have you decided?

BARBARA: I don't know.

LADY CHARLCOTE: That's no answer. Have you decided nothing?

BARBARA: No. 20

LADY CHARLCOTE: I hope he won't go and jump in the lake.

BARBARA: He won't, will he?

LADY CHARLCOTE: It all depends what state you left him in.

BARBARA: I said I'd see him tomorrow.

LADY CHARLCOTE: Then he won't be such a fool. He'll probably 25 be hanging round for me, so I shall have to go. How did he behave?

BARBARA: Oh don't talk about it Mama.

LADY CHARLCOTE: And are you coming to the Monte Baldo tomorrow then? 30

BARBARA: Yes.

LADY CHARLCOTE: What time?

BARBARA: In the morning—about eleven—

LADY CHARLCOTE: And you'll bring him your answer then?

BARBARA: Yes. 35

LADY CHARLCOTE: Well—you must decide for the best for yourself. Only don't go and make a double mess of it, that's all.

BARBARA: How do you mean, a double mess?

LADY CHARLCOTE: You'll have to stick to one or the other now, at any rate—so you'd better stick to the one you can live with, 40 and not to the one you can do without—for if you get the wrong one, you might as well drown two people then instead of one—

BARBARA: I don't know—I shall know tomorrow, Mama. Goodnight.

LADY CHARLCOTE (*kissing her—crying*): Well—all you can do now is to make the best for yourself.—Goodnight!—Oh don't trouble to come out, Mr Wesson—don't.

(WESSON *follows her—exit both—*BARBARA *sits down and begins to play a waltz on the piano—re-enter* WESSON.)

WESSON: Frederick wasn't far off—he hadn't drowned himself.

(BARBARA *goes on playing without taking any notice of him.*)

I don't particularly want to hear that piano, Barbara.

BARBARA: Don't you?— (*Plays a few more bars, then stops.*) What do you want then?

WESSON: So you are going to see him tomorrow.

BARBARA: I am.

WESSON: What for?

BARBARA (*hesitating*): To tell him I'll go back to him.

(*She remains with her back to* WESSON—*he sits at the table. There is dead silence.*)

WESSON: Did you tell him that tonight?

BARBARA: No.

WESSON: Why not?

BARBARA: Because I didn't want to.

WESSON: Did you give him hopes of that answer?

BARBARA: I don't know.

WESSON: You do!—tell me.

BARBARA: I say I don't know—I mean I don't know.

WESSON: Then you're lying.—I don't believe you intended to tell him that. I believe you merely say it to make me wild.

BARBARA: I don't.

WESSON: Then go now.

BARBARA: I said I'd go tomorrow.

WESSON: If you're going back to Frederick in the morning, you're not going to spend a night under this roof—hear that.

BARBARA: Why not?—I've spent a good many nights under this roof—what does one more or less matter?

WESSON: While you've been with me here, I considered you as a woman who wanted to stick to me as a wife—and as anything else I *don't want you*.

BARBARA: Very much as a wife you considered me at first—you were as unsure of us as ever I was.

WESSON: That was at the very first. 5

BARBARA: Was it—was it—

WESSON: Whether or not—that's what I say now.

BARBARA: 'Whether or not!'—you *would* say that—at any rate Frederick wouldn't say 'Whether or not'.

WESSON: And so you want to go back to him? 10

BARBARA: All men are alike. They don't care what a woman wants. They try to get hold of what they want themselves, as if it were a pipe. As for the woman, she's not considered—and so—that's where you make your mistake, gentlemen.

WESSON: Want?—what *do* you want? 15

BARBARA: That's for you to find out.

WESSON: It's for yourself to know first. If an archangel came down and brought you a man, you'd say 'No thank you'.

BARBARA: I probably should—for he'd be a slow piece of goods.

WESSON: What you want is some of the conceit knocking out of 20
you.

BARBARA: You do it, Mr Tuppeny-ha'penny.

WESSON: If Frederick hadn't been such a damn fool, he'd have taken you down a peg or two. Now, you think yourself so blighted high and mighty that nobody's good enough to dangle 25
after you.

BARBARA: Only a little puppy-dog that barks at my skirts.

WESSON: Very well, then the little puppy dog *will* bark. Are you going to see Frederick in the morning?

BARBARA: Yes. 30

WESSON: And are you going to tell him then that you're going back to him.

BARBARA: I don't know.

WESSON: You must know then, because if you are, you're not going to stop the night in this *house*. 35

BARBARA: Pooh—what do I care about your house—poor little house—did it have its little house contaminated!

WESSON: You know it was really *you* who wanted it, and whose it is.

BARBARA: As if *I* care for his house—I'd leave it any minute. I'll leave it now.

WESSON: If you're going to go back to Frederick, *leave* it now. I ask you to—

5   BARBARA: Oh very well—that is soon done. *(She goes out quickly.)*

(Curtain)

Act IV.

Scene: The same.
Time: Ten minutes later.
WESSON *is smoking—enter* BARBARA *dressed, with her hat on.*

BARBARA: Here I am then!   5

WESSON: Are you going straight to Gardone, to the Monte Baldo?

BARBARA: No—I'm going to the Hôtel Cervo.

WESSON: But you can't—she knows us, the landlady—and thinks
we're man and wife. You can't make that mess. If you're going,
go straight to Frederick tonight—I'll see you there.   10

BARBARA: I'm *not* going to Frederick tonight—I'm *not* going to
Gardone—I'm going to the Hôtel Cervo.

WESSON: You are an obstinate fool, and can go to Hell. I won't see
you to the garden gate, not I.

BARBARA *(bowing with deep impudence)*: Then Goodbye, monsieur.   15

WESSON: How much money have you got?

BARBARA: None.

WESSON: Then I won't give you any.

BARBARA: Don't you trouble—I wouldn't take any of your money. I
remember how you begrudged me that sail-cloth I wanted, to   20
cover the couch.

WESSON: I didn't—I thought sail-cloth would be rotten and cold
for a couch—and we *couldn't* afford it, because it was unnecessary.

BARBARA: Couldn't afford it!—it was the *only* thing I ever asked   25
you for, and you were mean, *mean* over it—you were mean over
it, and Frederick wouldn't have dreamed of being so mean—
no—

WESSON: All right—tomorrow you can buy sail-cloth to cover
Frederick's couches.   30

BARBARA: Yes—yes—all right.

WESSON: Have you got your night-things in the hand-bag?

BARBARA: Yes.

WESSON: It's my bag, by the way.

BARBARA: I can leave it at the Hôtel.   35

WESSON: Some soap—some hankys?

BARBARA: No—forgotten 'em.

WESSON: You would *(Exit—comes running back in a moment, puts the
things in her bag.)*

BARBARA: Thank you.

WESSON: And your box I'll pack tomorrow. The things you said
were mine I shall put in.

BARBARA: You needn't.

5   WESSON: I shall. I've never given you anything, so you've nothing
to return to me.

BARBARA: No—you were always stingy.

WESSON: Very well—Frederick isn't.

BARBARA: I suppose it's having been brought up so poor, you can't
10   help it.

WESSON: We won't discuss me, now, nor my upbringing.

BARBARA: Oh all right.

WESSON: I consider that I owe you, of money you had, about eleven
pounds. I'll be stingy and keep one of them. Here's ten out of
15   the forty we'd got.

BARBARA: I shan't have them.

WESSON: You can't go without any money at all.

BARBARA: Yes I can.

WESSON: No you can't. If you don't have these ten pounds, I'll post
20   them to Frederick to you.

BARBARA: All right.

WESSON *(feeling in his pocket)*: Well have ten Lire, at any rate.

BARBARA: No, I won't have anything.

WESSON: You ought to be murdered for your obstinacy.

25   BARBARA: Not twice in one *night.*
                    (A silence ensues.)

WESSON: Very well—then—I will come with you down the village,
since you're frightened of the men.

BARBARA: You needn't—I'm not frightened.

30   WESSON: No—you're too damned high and mighty to possess a
single one of the human virtues or vices, you are. *(A silence.)*
Do you want to go, really?

BARBARA: Yes.

WESSON: Now?

35   BARBARA: Yes.

WESSON: Liar!—liar!—you are showing off! *(Snatches the hand-bag
and flings it into the kitchen.)* Fool's idiotic theatrical game. Take
that hat off.

BARBARA: You're giving your orders.

WESSON: All right. *(Seizes the one pin, pulls off the hat, flings that through the door.)*

BARBARA *(flashing)*: What are you doing?

WESSON: Stopping you being a fool.—Take your coat off.

BARBARA: I shall take my coat off when I please. Indeed, *you* 5
needn't show off, for the minute I want to walk out of this house
I shall walk out, and you nor anybody else will prevent me.

WESSON *(taking up his position with his back to the door)*: All
right—you want to walk out now, and see—

BARBARA: If I want to— 10

WESSON: Want to then—

BARBARA *(with a laugh of scorn)*: Ha—you stop me! *(Marches up to
him with her breast high. He stands immovable.)* Come out! *(He
shakes his head.)* Come out!

WESSON: I told you I wouldn't. 15

BARBARA: Won't you. *(Seizes him. He grapples with her. They
struggle. He forces her backwards, flings her with a smash onto the
couch.)*

WESSON: You shan't! *(Goes and locks the door—stands at a loss.)*

BARBARA *(recovering)*: It's very heroic—but I go tomorrow, 20
whether or not.

WESSON: You'll pass the night in this room then.

*(He sits down—there is silence for some minutes—at last he looks up,
speaks, faltering)*:

You *don't* want to leave me, do you Barbara. *(No answer.)* You 25
don't want to? *(Silence.)* Well, whether you think you do, or not,
I shall never *believe* you want to leave me, not really—so there.
(A silence.) And you shan't—!

BARBARA: A woman couldn't want to leave such a wonder as you,
you think. 30

WESSON: *You* can't want to leave *me*.

BARBARA: Why not?

WESSON *(sulkily)*: Because I don't believe you can.
(There is a silence.)

BARBARA *(with difficulty)*: A sort of faith performance! *(He looks at* 35
her steadily, rises, goes and sits beside her.)

WESSON: Barbican!

BARBARA *(dropping her head on his shoulder with a cry)*: It's so hard
on him, Giacomo, I make him suffer so.

WESSON *(putting his arms round her)*: Never mind, he'll suffer at first, then he'll get better.

BARBARA *(crying)*: He won't.

WESSON: He will—he shall—he shall. And you'll see he will. He'll
5   be all right in the end.—You were too big a mouthful for him to swallow, and he was choking himself.—He'll be all the better in the end.

BARBARA: But I make him suffer so. *(Her head is on his shoulder.)*

WESSON *(kissing and kissing her)*: No—it's my fault.—You don't
10   want to leave me, do you?

BARBARA: I don't know what to do.

WESSON: Stay with me, Barbican, my darling, and we'll manage that he's all right.

BARBARA: But do you think he will be?

15   WESSON: Yes.

BARBARA: It's not fair when a man goes on loving you so much when you don't love him—it makes you feel as if you'd have to go back to him.

WESSON: You can't go back to him—it would be wrong. His love
20   isn't living for you.

BARBARA: It isn't, is it, Giacomo?

WESSON: No—kiss me, Barbara, will you? *(She kisses him.)* I love you Barbara.

BARBARA: Do you really love me?

25   WESSON: *Malheuresement.*

BARBARA: He says that.

WESSON: And I don't mean it. I'm glad I love you, even if you torture me into hell.

BARBARA: But do you love me an awful lot?

30   WESSON: More than enough.

BARBARA: Really?

WESSON: Truly.

BARBARA: But if he dies, I shall torment the life out of you.

WESSON: You'll do that anyhow.

35   BARBARA *(looking up—taking his face between her hands)*: Shall I?—No!—Say no—say I am a joy to you.

WESSON: You are a living joy to me, you are—especially this evening.

BARBARA *(laughs)*: —No—but am I really?

40   WESSON: Yes.

BARBARA: Sure?

WESSON: Yes.

BARBARA: Kiss me—kiss me—and love me—love me a fearful lot —love me a fearful lot.

WESSON: I do.—And tomorrow you'll just say to Frederick 'I can't   5
come back—divorce me if you love me'. You'll say it, won't you. *(Kissing her.)*

BARBARA: Yes.

WESSON: If it kills him—it won't kill him—but you'll say it?

BARBARA *(hiding her face)*: Must I, Giacomo?   10

WESSON: Yes.

BARBARA: Then I s'll have to—oh dear!—But you'll love me—love me a lot. *(She clings to him wildly.)*

WESSON: I do—and I will.

BARBARA: Love me a fearful lot!*   15

(Curtain)

THE DAUGHTER-IN-LAW

MRS GASCOYNE ☆
JOE GASCOYNE
MRS PURDY ☆
MINNIE GASCOYNE
LUTHER GASCOYNE ☆
CABMAN

5

Act I.

Scene 1.

*Scene: A collier's kitchen—not poor—windsor chairs, deal table, dresser
of painted wood, sofa covered with red cotton stuff.*
Time: About half past two of a winter's afternoon.
*Personae: A large, stoutish woman of 65, with smooth black hair parted
down the middle of her head.*—MRS GASCOYNE.

*Enter a young man—about 26—dark, good-looking—has his right arm
in a sling—does not take off his cap—*JOE GASCOYNE.

MRS GASCOYNE: Well, I s'd ha thought thy belly 'ud a browt thee
whoam afore this. *(He sits on the sofa without answering.)*
Doesn't ter want no dinner?

JOE *(looking up)*: I want it if the' is ony.

MRS GASCOYNE: An' if the' isna, tha can go be-out? Tha talks
large, my fine jockey! *(She puts a newspaper on the table, on it, a
plate and his dinner.)* Wheer dost reckon ter's bin?

JOE: I've bin ter th' office for my munny.

MRS GASCOYNE: Tha's niver bin a' this while at th' office.

JOE: They kep' me ower an' hour, an' then gen me nowt.

MRS GASCOYNE: Gen thee nowt!—why how do they ma'e that out?
It's a wik sin' tha got hurt, an' if a man wi' a brokken arm canna
ha'e his fourteen shillin' a week accident pay, who can, I s'd
like to know?

JOE: They'll gi'e me nowt, whether or not.

MRS GASCOYNE: An' for why, prithee?
(He does not answer for some time—then, sulkily):

JOE: They reckon I niver got it while I wor at work.

MRS GASCOYNE: Then when did ter get it, might I ax? I s'd think
they'd like to lay it onto me.

JOE: Tha talks like a fool, mother.

MRS GASCOYNE: Tha looks like one, ma lad.
(She has given him his dinner—he begins to eat with a fork.)

MRS GASCOYNE: Here, hutch up, gammy-leg—gammy arm. *(He
makes room, she sits by him on the sofa, and cuts up his meat for him.)*
It's a rum-un as I should start ha'ein' babies again, an' feedin'
'em wi' spoon-meat. *(She gives him a spoon.)* —An' now let's hear
why they wunna gi'e thee thy pay—another o' Macintyre's
dirty knivey dodges, I s'd think.

JOE *(blurts)*: They reckon I did it wi' foolery, an' not wi' work.

303

MRS GASCOYNE: Oh indeed! An' what by that?

JOE *(eating)*: They wunna gi'e me nowt, that's a'.

MRS GASCOYNE: It's a nice thing! An' what did ter say?

JOE: I said nowt.

5 MRS GASCOYNE: Tha wouldna! Tha stood like a stuffed duck, an'
     said thank yer.

JOE: Well it wor raïght.

MRS GASCOYNE: How right?

JOE: I *did* do it wi' foolery.

10 MRS GASCOYNE: Then what did ter go axin' for pay for?

JOE: I did it at work, didna I? An' a man as gets 'accident at work's
     'titled ter disability pay, isna 'e?

MRS GASCOYNE: Tha said a minnit sin' as tha got it wi' foolery.

JOE: An' so I did.

15 MRS GASCOYNE: I niver 'eered such talk i' my life.

JOE: I dunna care what ter's 'eered an' what t'asna. I wor foolin' wi'
     a wringer an' a pick-heft, ta'e it as ter's a mind.

MRS GASCOYNE: What, down pit?

JOE: I' th' stall, at snap time.

20 MRS GASCOYNE: Showin' off a bit, like?

JOE: Yi.

MRS GASCOYNE: An' what then?

JOE: Th' wringer gev me a rap ower th'arm, an' that's a'.

MRS GASCOYNE: An' tha reported it as a accidint?

25 JOE: It wor accident, worn't it? I niver did it a-purpose.

MRS GASCOYNE: But a pit accident.

JOE: Well, an' what else wor't? It wor a haccident I got i' th' pit, i'
     th' sta' wheer I wor workin.

MRS GASCOYNE: But not *while* tha wor workin'.

30 JOE: What by that—it wor a pit accident as I got i' th' stall.

MRS GASCOYNE: But tha didna tell 'em how it happened.

JOE: I said some stuff fell on my arm, an' brok' it. An' worna that
     trew?

MRS GASCOYNE: It wor very likely trew enough lad, if on'y they'd
35 ha' believed it.

JOE: An' they would ha' believed it, but for Hewett bully raggin
     Bettesworth, 'cos he knowed he was a chappil man. *(He imitates
     the under-ground manager, Hewett, and Bettesworth, a bully.)*
     'About this accident, Bettesworth. How exactly did it occur?' 'I
40   couldn't say for certing, Sir, because I wasn't luikin'.' 'Then tell

me as near as you can.' 'Well, Mester, I'm sure I don't know.'
'That's curious, Bettesworth—I must have a report. Do you
know anything about it, or don't you?* It happened in your stall,
you're responsible for it, and I'm responsible for you.' 'Well
Gaffer, what's right's right, I suppose, ter th' mesters or th' men.   5
An' 'e wor cunjurin' a' snap-time wi' a pick heft an' a wringer,
an' th' wringer catched 'im ower th' arm.' 'I thought you
didn't know'.—'I said *for certain*—I didn't see exactly how twas
done.'

MRS GASCOYNE: Hm!   10

JOE: Bettesworth 'ud non ha' clat-farted but for nosy Hewett. He
says 'Yo know, Joseph, when he says to me—Do you know
anything about that haccident?—then I says to myself,—Take
not the word of truth hutterly outer thy mouth—'*

MRS GASCOYNE: If he took a bit o' slaver out en's mouth, it ud   15
do—

JOE: So this mornin' when I went ter th' office, Mester Salmon he
comm out an' said 'Ow did this haccident occur, Joseph?' and I
said 'Some stuff fell on't' so he says 'Stuff fell on't, stuff fell
on't—you mean coal or rock or what?'—so I says 'Well, it   20
worn't a thripenny bit.' 'No,' he says, '—but what was it?' 'It
wor a piece o' clunch' I says. 'You don't use clunch for wringin''
he says 'do you.' 'The wringin' of the nose bringeth forth
blood,'* I says—

MRS GASCOYNE: Why you know you never did. *(She begins making*   25
a pudding.)

JOE: No—b'r I'd ha meant t'r'a done.

MRS GASCOYNE: We know thee! Tha's done thysen one i' th' eye
this time. When dost think tha'll iver get ter be a butty at this
rate. There's Luther nowt b'r a day man* yet—   30

JOE: I'd as lief be a day man as a butty, i' pits that rat-gnawed
there's hardly a stall worth havin', an' a company as 'ud like yer
ter scrape yer tabs afore yer went home, for fear you took a
grain o' coal.

MRS GASCOYNE: Maybe—but tha's got ter get thy livin' by 'em.   35

JOE: I hanna—I s'll go to Australia.

MRS GASCOYNE: Tha'lt do no such thing, while I'm o' this earth.

JOE: Ah but though, I sholl—else get married, like our Luther.

MRS GASCOYNE: A fat sight better off tha'lt be for that.

JOE: You niver know, mother, dun yer.   40

MRS GASCOYNE: You dunna, ma lad—not till yer find yerself let in. Marriage is like a mouse trap, for either man or woman—you've* soon come ter th' end o' th' cheese.

JOE: Well, ha'ef a loaf's better'nor no bread.

5 MRS GASCOYNE: Why, wheer's th' loaf as tha'd like ter gnawg a' thy life—

JOE: Nay, nowheer yet.

MRS GASCOYNE: Well, dunna thee talk then. Tha's done thysen harm enow for one day, wi' thy tongue—

10 JOE: An' good as well, mother—I've aten my dinner, a'most.

MRS GASCOYNE: An' swilled thy belly afore that, methinks.

JOE: Niver i' this world.

MRS GASCOYNE: An' I'n got thee to keep on ten shillin's a wik club money, han I?

15 JOE: Tha nedna, if ter doesna want. Besides, we s'll be out a strike afore we know wheer we are.

MRS GASCOYNE: I'm sure. You've on'y bin in—

JOE: Now mother, spit on thy hands an' ta'e fresh hold. We s'll be out on strike in a wik or a fortni't—

20 MRS GASCOYNE: Strike's a' they're fit for, a pack o' slutherers as—
(Her words tail off as she goes into the pantry.)

JOE *(to himself)*: Tha goes chunterin' i' th' pantry when somebody's at th' door. *(He rises—goes to the door.)*

MRS PURDY'S VOICE: Is your mother in?

25 JOE: Yi, 'er's in right enough.

MRS PURDY'S VOICE: Well then, can I speak to her?

JOE *(calling)*: Mrs Purdy wants ter speak to thee, mother.

(MRS GASCOYNE crosses the kitchen, heavily, with a dripping pan—stands in the doorway.)

30 MRS GASCOYNE: Good afternoon.

MRS PURDY'S VOICE: Good afternoon.

MRS GASCOYNE: Er—what is it?

MRS PURDY *(appearing—a little fat red-faced body in bonnet and black cape)*: —I wanted to speak to yer rather particler.

35 MRS GASCOYNE *(giving way)*: Oh yes?
(All three enter the kitchen—MRS PURDY stands near the door.)

MRS PURDY *(nodding at JOE)*: Has he had a haccident?

MRS GASCOYNE: Broke his arm.

MRS PURDY: Oh my, that's nasty. When did 'e do that?

MRS GASCOYNE: A wik sin' today.

MRS PURDY: In th' pit?

MRS GASCOYNE: Yes—an 's not goin' to get any accident pay—says as 'e worn't workin', he wor foolin' about.

MRS PURDY: T-t-t-t! Did iver you know—!—I tell you what, Missis, it's a wonder they let us live on the face o' th' earth at all—it's a wonder we don't have to fly up i' th' air like birds.

JOE: There'd be a squark i' th' sky then!

MRS PURDY: But it is indeed. It's somethink awful. They've gave my mester a dirty job o' nights, at a guinea a week, an' he's worked fifty years for th' cumpany, an' isn't but sixty-two now —said he wasn't equal to stall workin', whereas he has to slave on th' roads☆ an' comes whoam that tired he can't put's food i's mouth.

JOE: He's about like me.

MRS PURDY: Yis! But it's no nice thing, a guinea a week.

MRS GASCOYNE: Well, that's how they're servin' 'em a' round— widders' coals stopped—leadin' raised to four an' eight☆—an' ivry man niggled down to nothink—

MRS PURDY: I wish I'd got that Frazer☆ strung up by th' heels—I'd ma'e *his* sides o' bacon rowdy.

MRS GASCOYNE: He's put a new manager to ivry pit,☆ an' ivry one a nigger driver.

MRS PURDY: Says he's got to economise—says the company's not a philanthropic concern—

MRS GASCOYNE: But ta'es twelve hundred a year for his sen.

MRS PURDY: A mangy batchelor wi' 'is iron-men.

JOE: But they wunna work.

MRS PURDY: They say how he did but coss an' swear about them American Cutters. I should like to see one set outer 'im—they'd work hard enough rippin's guts out—even iron's got enough sense for that.

(*She suddenly subsides—there is a pause—*)

MRS GASCOYNE: How do you like living down Nethergreen.☆

MRS PURDY: Well—we're very comfortable—it's small, but it's handy, an' sin' th' mester's gone down t'a guinea—

MRS GASCOYNE: It'll do for you three.

MRS PURDY: Yes!

(*Another pause.*)

MRS GASCOYNE: The men are comin' out again, they say.

MRS PURDY: Isn't it summat sickenin—well, I've werritted an' werritted till I'm soul-sick—

JOE: It sends yer that thin an' threadbare, y'have ter stop sometime.

5 MRS PURDY: There can be as much ache in a motherly body as in bones an' gristle,✫ I'm sure o' that.

JOE: Nay, I'm more than bones an' gristle.

MRS PURDY: That's true as the day.

(Another long pause.)

10 MRS GASCOYNE: An' how have yer all bin keepin'?

MRS PURDY: Oh, very nicely—except our Bertha.

MRS GASCOYNE: Is she poorly then?

MRS PURDY: That's what I comm ter tell yer. I niver knowed a word on't till a Sat'day, nor niver noticed a thing. Then she says

15 to me, as white as a sheet, 'I've been sick every mornin' mother,' an' it com' across me like a shot from a gun. I sunk down i' that chair an' couldna fetch a breath.—An' me as as prided myself. I've often laughed about it, an' said I was thankful my children had all turned out so well, lads an' wenches as well, an' said it

20 was a-cause they was all got of a Sunday—their father was too drunk a-Sat'day an' too tired o' wik days—an' it's a fact, they've all turned out well, for I'd allers bin to chappil. Well, I've said it for a joke, but now it's turned on me. I'd better ha' kep' my tongue still—

25 JOE: It's not me, though, Missis. I wish it wor.

MRS PURDY: There's no occasions to ma'e gam' of it neither, as far as I can see. The youngest an' the last of 'em as I've got, an' a lass as I liked, for she's simple, but she's good natured, an' him a married man. Thinks I to myself 'I'd better go to's mother,

30 she'll ha'e more about 'er than's new wife—for she's a stuck-up piece o' goods as ever trod.'

MRS GASCOYNE: Why, what d'yer mean?

MRS PURDY: I mean what I say—an' there's no denyin' it. That girl—well, it's nigh on breakin' my heart, for I'm that short o'

35 breath—*(Sighs)*—I'm sure!

MRS GASCOYNE: Why don't yer say what you mean?

MRS PURDY: I've said it, haven't I. There's my gal gone four month wi' childt to your Luther.

MRS GASCOYNE: Nay—nay—nay, Missis! You'll niver ma'e me

40 believe it.

MRS PURDY: Glad would I be if I nedna. But I've gone through it all since Sat'day on. I've wanted to break every bone in 'er body —an' I've said I should on'y be happy if I was scraightin' at 'er funeral—an' I've said I'd wring his neck for 'im. But it doesn't alter it—there it is—an' there it will be. An' I s'll be a grand- mother where my heart heaves, an' maun drag a wastrel baby through my old age. An' it's neither a cryin' nor a laughin' matter, but it's a matter of a girl wi' chilt, an' a man six week married.

MRS GASCOYNE: But our Luther never went wi' your Bertha. How d'you make it out?

MRS PURDY: Yea—yea Missis—yea indeed.

JOE: Yi, mother, he's bin out wi' 'er. She wor pals wi' Liza Ann Varley, as went out wi' Jim Horrocks. So Jim, he palled Bertha onter our Luther.—Why, I've had many a glass wi' the four of 'em, i' th' 'Ram'.

MRS GASCOYNE: I niver knowed nowt o' *this* afore.

JOE: Tha doesna know ivrythink, mother.

MRS GASCOYNE: An' it's well I don't, methinks.

JOE: Tha doesna want, neither.

MRS GASCOYNE: Well, I dunno what we're goin' to do, Missis. He's a young married man—

MRS PURDY: An' she's a girl o' mine.

MRS GASCOYNE: How old is she?

MRS PURDY: She wor twenty three last September.

MRS GASCOYNE: Well then, I sh'd a thought she'd ha' known better.

MRS PURDY: An' what about him, Missis, an goes an' gets married t'r another fine madam d'rectly after he's been wi' my long lass.

JOE: But he niver knowed owt about—

MRS PURDY: He'd seen th' blossom i' flower, if he hadna spotted th' fruit a-comin'.

JOE: Yi—but—

MRS GASCOYNE: Yi but what—?

JOE: Well,—you dunna expect—ivry time yer cast yer bread on th' watters, as it'll come whoam to you like—

MRS GASCOYNE: Well, I dunno what we're goin' ter do.

MRS PURDY: I thowt I'd better come to you, rether than—

JOE: Ah, you non want it gettin' about—an' *she*'d best not know, if it can be helped.

MRS GASCOYNE: I can't see for why.

MRS PURDY: No indeed—a man as plays fast an' loose first wi' one an' then goes an' marries another stuck-up piece—

MRS GASCOYNE: An' a wench as goes sittin' i' th' 'Ram' wi' th'
5   fellers mun expect what she gets, Missis.

MRS PURDY: 'Appen so, 'appen so. An' th' man maun abide by what he's gi'en.

MRS GASCOYNE: I dunno *what* we're goin' to do!

JOE: We'd best keep it as quiet as we can.

10 MRS PURDY: I thinks to mysen 'It'll non become *me* to go an' jack up a married couple, for if *he's* at fault, it's her as 'ud ha'e ter suffer.'☆ An' though she's haughty, I knowed her mother, as nice a body as ever stept, an' treated scandylos by Jim Hetherington.☆ An' thinks I, she's a horphan, if she's got money, an'
15 nobbut her husband i' th' world. Thinks I to mysen, it's no good visitin' it on 'er head, if he's a villain. For whatever th' men does, th' women maun ma'e up for. An' though I do consider as it's nowt b'r a dirty trick o' his'n to ta'e a poor lass like my long thing, an' go an' marry a woman wi' money—

20 MRS GASCOYNE: Woman wi' money, ay, an' peace go wi' 'er,☆ 'er an' 'er money. What she's got, she'll keep, you take my word for it, Missis.

MRS PURDY: Yes, an' she's right of it.

JOE: Nay mother, 'er's non close.

25 MRS GASCOYNE: Isn't she—oh isn't she? An' what is she then. All she wanted was as much for her money as she could get. An' when she fun' as nob'dy was for sale, but our Luther, she says 'well, I'll take it.'

JOE: Nay, it worna like that—it wor him as wor that come-day go-
30 day—

MRS PURDY: God send Sunday.☆

MRS GASCOYNE: An' what more can a man do, think yer, but ax a woman? When has *thee* ever done as much.

JOE: No, I hanna, 'cos I've niver seen th' woman as I wanted to say
35 'snap'—but—he slormed an' he—

MRS GASCOYNE: Slormed! Thee slorm but one fiftieth part to any lass tha' likes, an' see if 'er's not all ower thee afore tha's said six words—Slormed! Er wor that high an' mighty, 'er wanted summat bett'nor 'im.

JOE: Nay—I reckon he niver showed the spunk of a sprat-herring to 'er—

MRS GASCOYNE: Did *thee* show any more? Hast iver done? Yet onybody 'ud think tha wor for marryin' 'er thysen.

JOE: If I'd ha' *bin* for marryin' 'er, I'd ha' gone wholesale, not ha' fudged and haffled.

MRS GASCOYNE: But tha *worna* for marryin' neither 'er nor nobody—

JOE: No, I worna.

MRS GASCOYNE: No, tha worna.

(There is a long pause—the mother turns half apologetically, half explanatorily, to MRS PURDY.*)*

MRS GASCOYNE: It's like this 'ere, Missis, if you'll not say nothink about it—sin' it's got to come out atween us. He courted Minnie Hetherington when she wor at her uncle's at th' 'Bell o' Brass',* an' he wor nowt b'r a lad o' twenty two, an' she twenty one. An' he wor gone on 'er right enow. Then she had that row wi' 'er uncle, for she wor iver overbearin' an' chancy. Then our Luther says to me, 'I s'll ax 'er to marry me mother'—an' I says 'Tha pleases thysen, but ter my thinkin', tha'rt a sight too young an' doesna know thy own mind.' Howsoiver, much notice 'e takes o' me.

JOE: He took a lot o' notice on thee, tha knows well enough.

MRS GASCOYNE: An' for what shouldn't he—hadn't I bin a good mother to 'im i' ivry shape an' form. Let *her* make him as good a wife as I made him a mother! Well—we'll see! You'll see *him* repent the day. But they're not to be bidden.—An' so, Missis, he did ax 'er, as 'e'd said 'e should. But Hoity-toity an' no thank yer, she wasn't for havin' him, but mun go an be a nursery governess up i' Manchester. Thinks I to myself 'she's after a town johnny in a Berty-Willie an' a yard o' cuffs.' But he kep' on writin' to 'er, now an' again—an' she answered—as if she wor standin' at top of a flight of steps—

JOE: An' appen on'y wanted fetchin' down.

MRS GASCOYNE: Wi' a kick from behint, if *I'd* ha' had th' doin' on't. So they go mornin' on. He sees 'er once i' a blew moon. If he goes ter Manchester, she condescends to see him for a couple of hours. If she comes here, she ca's i' this house wi' a 'how do you do Mrs Gascoyne' an' off again. If they go f'r a walk,—

JOE: He's whoam again at nine o'clock—

MRS GASCOYNE: If they go for a walk it's 'thank you, I mustn't be
very late. Goodnight Luther.' I thought it ud niver come ter
nothink. Then 'er uncle dies, an' leaves her a hundred pounds,
which considerin' th' way she'd been wi' 'im, was more than *I'd*
ha' gen her—an' she was a bit nicer. She writes ter Luther ter
come an' see her an' stop a couple o' days. He ta'es her ter th'
the-etter, an's for goin' i' th' pit at a shillin', when she says 'It's
my treat, Luther', and five shillin seats apiece, if you please—

JOE: An' 'e couldna luik at th' performance, for fear as the folks was
luikin' at 'im—

MRS GASCOYNE: An' after th' the-etter, it must be supper wi' a
man i' a tail coat an' silver forks, an' she pays.—Yes, says I when
he told me, that's the tricks of servants, showin' off afore decent
folk—

JOE: She could do what she liked, couldn't she.

MRS GASCOYNE: Well, an' after that, he didna write, except to say
thank yer. For it put 'im in a horkard position. That wor four
years ago, an' she's nobbut seen him three times sin' that. If she
could but ha' snapped up somebody else, it 'ud 'a been goodbye
to Luther—

JOE: As tha told him many a time.

MRS GASCOYNE: As I told him many a time, for am I to sit an' see
my own lad bitted an' bobbed, tasted an' spit out by a madam i'
service.—Then all of a suddin, three months back, come a letter
'Dear Luther, I have been thinkin' it over, an' have come to the
opinion that we'd better get married now, if we are ever goin' to.
We've been dallying on all these years, and we seem to get no
further. So we'd better make the plunge, if ever we're going to.
Of course you will say exactly what you think. Don't agree to
anything unless you want to. I only want to say that I think, if
we're ever going to be married, we'd better do it without
waiting any longer.'—Well Missis, he got that letter when he
com' whoam fra work. I seed him porin' an' porin', but I says
nowt. Then he ate some o's dinner, an' went out. When he com'
in, it wor about ha'ef past ten, an' 'e wor white as a sheet. He
gen me that letter, an' says 'What's think o' that, mother?' Well,
you could ha knocked me down wi' a feather when I'd read it. I
says 'I think its tidy cheek, my lad.' He took it back an' put's i's
pocket, an' after a bit, 'e says 'What should ter say, mother?'

'Tha says what's a mind, my lad,' I says. So he begins unlacin's boots. Sudden he stops, an' wi's boot-tags rattlin', goes rummagin' for th' pen an' ink. 'What art goin' ter do?' I says. 'I'm goin' ter write to er', he says. 'An' what art goin' ter say?' I says. 'I'm goin' ter say, 'er can do as 'er's a mind. If 'er wants ter be married, 'er can, an' if 'er doesna, 'er nedna.' So I thinks we could leave it at that. He sits him down, an' doesna write more nor a side an' a ha'ef. I thinks 'that's done it, it'll be an end between them two now.' He niver gev' th' letter to me to read—

JOE: He did ter me. He says 'I'm ready an' willin' to do what you want, whenever yer want. I'm earnin' about thirty five bob a week, an' haven't got any money, because my mother gi'es me what I ax for ter spend. But I can ha'e what I ask for to set up house with. Your loving—Luther.' He says ter me 'Dost think it's a'right'—I says 'I s'd think so, 'er maun ma'e what 'er likes out on't.'

MRS GASCOYNE: On th' Monday after, she wor here livin' at 'er A'nt's, an' th' notice was in at th' registrar.✴ I says What money dost want? He says 'thee buy what tha' thinks we s'll want.' So he tells Minnie, an' she says 'Not biout I'm theer.' Well, we goes ter Nottingham, an' she will ha'e nowt b'r owd fashioned stuff. I says 'that's niver *my* mind, Minnie'—she says 'Well, I like it, an' yo'll see it'll look nice. I'll pay for it.' Which to be sure I never let her.—For she'd had a mester as made a fool of he, tellin' her this an' that, what wor good taste, what wor bad.

JOE: An' it *does* look nice, mother, their house—

MRS GASCOYNE: We'll see how it looks i' ten years' time, my lad, wi' th' racket an' tacket o' children. For it's not serviceable, Missis—

MRS PURDY *(she has been a sympathetic and exclamative listener)*: Then it's no good.

MRS GASCOYNE: An' that's how they got married.

JOE: An' he went about wi's tail atween his legs, scared outer's life.

MRS GASCOYNE: For I said no more. If he axed me owt, I did it, if he wanted owt, I got it. But it wasn't for me to go interferin' where I wasn't wanted.

JOE: If iver I get married, mother, I s'll go i' lodgin's six month afore hand.

MRS GASCOYNE: Tha'd better—ter get thysen a bit case-hardened.

JOE: Yi. But I'm goin' t'r Australia.

MRS GASCOYNE: I come wi'thee then.

JOE: Tha doesna.

MRS GASCOYNE: I dunna fret—tha'lt non go.

5 MRS PURDY: Well, it was what I should call a bit off-hand, I must say—!

MRS GASCOYNE: You can see now how he got married, an' who's to blame.

JOE: Nay, yo' canna ma'e 'er to blame for Bertha. Liza Ann Varley's

10 ter blame for th' lass goin' out o' nights—

MRS PURDY: An' there I thought they wor both i' Varley's, not gallivantin'—

JOE: They often was.—An' Jim Horrocks is ter blame for couplin' 'er onter our Luther, an' him an' her's ter blame for th' rest. I

15 dunno how you can lay it on Minnie. You might as well lay it on 'er if th' childt wor mine.

MRS GASCOYNE *(sharply)*: Tha'd ha'e more sense!

JOE: I'd try.

MRS GASCOYNE: But now she's played fast an' loose wi' him—

20 twice I *know* he axed 'er to ha'e him—now she's asked for what she's got. She's put her puddin' in her mouth, an' if she's burnt herself, serve her right.

MRS PURDY: Well—I didn't want to go to court☆—I thought 'His mother'll be th' best one to go to—'

25 MRS GASCOYNE: No—you mun go to him hisself—go an' tell him i' front of her—an' if she wants anythink, she mun ma'e arrangements herself.

JOE: What was you thinkin' of, Missis Purdy?

MRS PURDY: Well, I was thinkin', she's a poor lass—an' I didn't

30 want 'er to go to court, for they ax such questions—an' I thought it was such a *thing*, him six wik married—though to be sure I'd no notions of how it was—I thought, we might happen say, it was one o' them electricians as was along when they laid th' wires under th' road down to Batford☆—and—

35 JOE: An' arrange for a lump sum, like?

MRS PURDY: Yes—we're poor, an' she's poor—an' if she had a bit o' money of 'er own—for we should niver touch it—it might be a 'inducement to some other young feller—for poor long thing, she's that simple—

40 MRS GASCOYNE: Well, ter my knowledge, them as has had a childt

seems to get off i' marriage better nor many as hasn't. I'm sure, there's a lot o' men likes it, if they think a woman's had a baby by another man—

MRS PURDY: That's nothing to trust by, Missis, you'll say so yourself.

JOE: An' about how much do you want—thirty pound?

MRS PURDY: We want what's fair. I got it fra Emma Stapleton, they had forty wi' their Lucy.*

JOE: Forty pound?

MRS PURDY: Yes.

MRS GASCOYNE: Well then, let *her* find it. She's paid for nothing but the wedding. She's got money enough, if he's none. Let *her* find it. She made th' bargain, she maun stick by it. It was her dip i' th' bran-tub—if there's a mouse nips hold of her finger, she maun suck it better, for nobody axed her to dip.

MRS PURDY: You think I'd better go to him.—Eh Missis, it's a nasty business. But right's right.

MRS GASCOYNE: Right *is* right, Mrs Purdy. And you go and tell him afront of her—that's the best thing you can do. Then ivrything's straight.

MRS PURDY: But for her he might ha' married our Bertha.

MRS GASCOYNE: To be sure, to be sure.

MRS PURDY: What right had she to snatch when it pleased her.

MRS GASCOYNE: That's what I say. If th' woman ca's for th' piper, th' woman maun pay th' tune.

MRS PURDY: Not but what—

JOE: It's a nasty business.

MRS GASCOYNE: Nasty or not, it's hers now, not mine. He's *her* husband. 'My son's my son till he takes him a wife,'* an' no longer. Now let her answer for it.

MRS PURDY: An' you think I'd better go when they're both in.

MRS GASCOYNE: I should go tonight, atween six an' seven, that's what I should do.

JOE: I never should. If I was you, I'd settle it wi'out Minnie's knowin'—it's bad enough—

MRS GASCOYNE: What's bad enough?

JOE: Why that.

MRS GASCOYNE: What?

JOE: Him an' her—it's bad enough as it is.

MRS GASCOYNE *(with great bitterness)*: Then let it be a bit worse, let it be a bit worse. Let her have it then, it'll do her good. Who is she, to trample eggs that another hen would sit warm. No—Mrs Purdy, *give* it her. It'll take her down a peg or two, and My Sirs, she wants it, my sirs she needs it.

5   JOE *(muttering)*: A fat lot o' good it'll do.

MRS GASCOYNE: What has thee ter say, I should like to know. Fed an' clothed an' coddled, tha art, an' not a thing tha lacks. But wait till I'm gone, my lad, tha'lt know what I've done for thee then, tha will.

10   JOE: For a' that, it's no good 'er knowin'.

MRS GASCOYNE: Isna it—isna it. If it's not good for 'er, it's good for '*im*—

JOE: I dunna believe it.

MRS GASCOYNE: Who asked *thee* to believe it! Tha's showed thysèn a wise man *this* day, hasn't ter? Wheer should ter be today, but for me? Wheer should ter iver ha' been? An' then *tha* sets up for to talk. It ud look better o' thee not to spit i' th' hand as holds thy bread an' butter.*

JOE: Neither do I.

20   MRS GASCOYNE: Doesn't ter. Tha has a bit too much chelp an' chunter. It doesna go well, my lad. Tha wor blortin' an' bletherin down at th' office a bit sin', an' a mighty fool tha made o' thysèn. How should thee like to go home wi' *thy* tale o' today, to Minnie, might I ax thee.

25   JOE: If she didna like it, she could lump it.

MRS GASCOYNE: It ud be thee as ud lump, my lad.—But what does thee know about it.—Er'd rip th' guts out on thee like a tiger, an' stan' grinnin' at thee when tha shrivelled up cause tha'd no inside left.

30   MRS PURDY: She looks it, I must admit—every bit of it.

JOE: For a' that, it's no good her knowin'.

MRS GASCOYNE: Well I say it *is*—an' thee, tha shifty little know-all, as blorts at one minute like a suckin' calf an' th' next blethers like a hass, dunna thee come layin' th' law down to me, for I know

35   better.—No, Mrs Purdy, it's no good comin' to me. You've a right to some compensation, an' that lass o' yourn has, but let them as cooked the goose eat it, that's all.—Let him arrange it hisself—an' if he does nothink, put him i' court, that's all.

MRS PURDY: He's not goin' scot free, you may back your life o'

40   that.

MRS GASCOYNE: You go down tonight atween six an' seven, an' let 'em have it straight. You know where they live?

MRS PURDY: I' Simson Street.

MRS GASCOYNE: About four houses up—next Holbrooks.☆

MRS PURDY *(rising)*: Yes. 5

JOE: An' it'll do no good. Gi'e me th' money, mother, I'll pay it.

MRS GASCOYNE: Tha wunna.

JOE: I've a right ter th' money—I've addled it.

MRS GASCOYNE: A' right—an' I've saved it for thee. But tha has none on't till tha knocks me down an' ta'es it out o' my pocket. 10

MRS PURDY: No—let 'em pay themselves—it's not thy childt, is it?

JOE: It isna—but th' money is.

MRS GASCOYNE: We'll see.

MRS PURDY: Well, I mun get back. Thank yer, Missis.

MRS GASCOYNE: An' thank *you*! I'll come down tomorrow—at dark 15 hour.

MRS PURDY: Thank yer.—I hope yer arm'll soon be better.

JOE: Thank yer.

MRS GASCOYNE: I'll come down tomorrow. You'll go tonight—atween six an' seven? 20

MRS PURDY: Yes—if it mun be done, it mun. He took his own way, she took hers, now I mun take mine.—Well—good afternoon. I mun see about th' mester's dinner.

JOE: An' you haven't said nothink to nobody?

MRS PURDY: I haven't—I shouldn't be flig, should I? 25

JOE: No—I should keep it quiet as long's you can.

MRS GASCOYNE: There's no need for a' th' world to know—but them as is concerned maun abide by it.

MRS PURDY: Well—good afternoon—

MRS GASCOYNE *and* JOE: Good afternoon—good afternoon. *(Exit* 30 MRS PURDY.*)*

JOE: Well that's a winder!

MRS GASCOYNE: Serve her right, for tip-callin' wi' im a' those years.

JOE: She niver ought to know. 35

MRS GASCOYNE: I—I could fetch thee a wipe ower th' face, I could.

(He sulks—she is in a rage—Curtain)

Scene 2.

The kitchen of LUTHER GASCOYNE'S *new home. It is pretty—in
'cottage' style*—rush-bottomed chairs, black oak bureau, brass-candle-
sticks, delfi* etc.—green cushions in chairs.*

5   *Time—towards five o'clock—firelight—it is growing dark.* MINNIE
      GASCOYNE *is busy about the fire: a tall, good-looking young woman, in a
      shirt blouse and dark skirt, and apron. She lifts lids of saucepans, etc.—
      hovers impatiently—looks at the clock—begins to trim the lamp.*

MINNIE: I wish he'd come. If I didn't want him he'd be here half
10   an' hour since. But just because I've got a pudding that wants
           eating on the tick—! He—he's *never* up to the scratch, he never
           is.—As if the day wasn't long enough!—
           *(Sound of footsteps—she seizes a saucepan, and is rushing towards the
           door. The latch has clacked.* LUTHER *appears in the doorway in his pit-
15   dirt—a collier of medium height with fair moustache. He has a red scarf
           knotted round his throat, and a cap with a Union Medal.* The two
           almost collide.)*

LUTHER: My word, you're on the hop!
MINNIE *(disappearing into the scullery)*: You *nearly* made me drop
20   the saucepan. Why are you so late?
LUTHER: I'm non late, am I?
MINNIE: You're twenty minutes later than yesterday.
LUTHER: Oh ah, I stopped finishin' a stint, an' com' up wi' a'most
           th' last bantle. *(He takes a tin bottle and a dirty calico snap-bag
25   out of his pocket, puts them on the bureau, goes into the scullery.)*
MINNIE'S VOICE: No! *(She comes hurrying out with the saucepan. In a
           moment,* LUTHER *follows. He has taken off his coat and cap; his
           heavy trousers are belted round his hips, his arms are bare to above
           the elbow, because his pit-singlet of thick flannel is almost sleeve-
30   less.)*
LUTHER: Tha *art* throng!
MINNIE *(at the fire, flushed)*: Yes, and everything's ready, and will be
           spoiled.
LUTHER: Then we'd better eat it afore I wesh me.
35   MINNIE: No—no—it's not nice—
LUTHER: Just as ter's a mind—but there's scarce a collier in a
           thousand weshes his-sèn afore he has his dinner. We niver did
           a-whoam.
MINNIE: But it doesn't look nice.

LUTHER: Eh wench, tha'lt soon get used ter th' looks on me. A bit o' dirt's like a veil on my face—I shine through th' 'andsomer. What hast got? *(He peers over her range.)*

MINNIE *(waving a fork)*: You're not to look.

LUTHER: It smells good. 5

MINNIE: Are you *going* to have your dinner like that?

LUTHER: Ay lass—just for once. *(He spreads a newspaper in one of the green-cushioned arm-chairs, and sits down. She disappears into the scullery with a saucepan. He takes off his great pit-boots. She sets a soup tureen on the table, and lights the lamp. He watches her 10 face in the glow.)* Tha'rt non bad-luikin' when ter's a mind.

MINNIE: *When* have I a mind?

LUTHER: Tha's allers a mind—but when ter lights th' lamp th'art i' luck's way.

MINNIE: Come on then. *(He drags his chair to the table.)* 15

LUTHER: I s'll ha'e ter ha'e a newspaper afront on me, or thy cloth'll be a blackymoor. *(Begins disarranging the pots.)*

MINNIE: Oh you *are* a nuisance! *(Jumps up.)*

LUTHER: I can put 'em a' back again.

MINNIE: I know your puttings back. 20

LUTHER: Tha couldna get married by thysen, could ter—so tha'lt ha'e ter ma'e th' best on me.

MINNIE: But you're such a bother, never here at the right time, never doing the right thing—

LUTHER: An' my mouth's ter wide an' my head's too narrow. Shalt 25 iver ha' come ter th' end o' my faults an' failins?

MINNIE *(giving him soup)*: I wish I could.

LUTHER: An' now tha'lt snap my head off cos I slobber, shanna ter?

MINNIE: Then don't slobber.

LUTHER: I'll try my luck.—What hast bin doin' a' day? 30

MINNIE: Working.

LUTHER: Has our Joe been in?

MINNIE: No. I rather thought he might, but he hasn't.

LUTHER: You've not been up home?

MINNIE: To your mother's?—no, what should I go there for? 35

LUTHER: Eh, I dunno what ter should go for—I thought tha 'appen might.

MINNIE: But what for?

LUTHER: Nay—I niver thowt nowt about what for.

MINNIE: Then why did you ask me? 40

LUTHER: I dunno. *(A pause.)*

MINNIE: Your mother can come here, can't she?

LUTHER: Ay, she can come.—Tha'll be goin' up wi' me tonight—I want ter go an' see about our Joe.

5 MINNIE: What about him?

LUTHER: How he went on about's club money. Shall ter come wi' me?

MINNIE: I wanted to do my curtains.

LUTHER: But tha's got a' day to do them in.

10 MINNIE: But I want to do them tonight—I feel like it.

LUTHER: A' right—I shanna be long, at any rate. *(A pause.)* What dost keep lookin' at?

MINNIE: How?

LUTHER: Tha keeps thy eye on me rarely.

15 MINNIE *(laughing)*: It's your mouth—it looks *so* red and bright, in your black face.

LUTHER: Does it look nasty to thee?

MINNIE: No—no-o!

LUTHER *(pushing his mustache—laughing)*: It ma'es you look like a
20 nigger, i' thy pit-dirt—th' whites o' your eyes!

MINNIE: Just. *(She gets up to take his plate—goes and stands beside him—he lifts his face to her.)* I want to see if I can see you, you look so different.

LUTHER: Tha can see me well enough. Why, dost want to?

25 MINNIE: It's almost like having a stranger.

LUTHER: Would ter rether?

MINNIE: What?

LUTHER: Ha'e a stranger?

MINNIE: What for?

30 LUTHER: Hae!—I dunno.

MINNIE *(touching his hair)*: You look rather nice—an' your hair's so dirty.

LUTHER: Gi'e me a kiss.

MINNIE: But where?—you're all grime.

35 LUTHER: I'm sure I've licked my mouth clean.

MINNIE *(stooping suddenly and kissing him)*: You don't look nearly such a tame rabbit, in your pit-dirt.

LUTHER *(catching her in his arms)*: Dunna I? *(Kisses her.)* What colour is my eyes?

40 MINNIE: Bluey-grey.

LUTHER: An' thine's grey an' black.

MINNIE: Mind! *(She looks at her blouse when he releases her.)*

LUTHER *(timid)*: Have I blacked it?

MINNIE: A bit. *(She goes to the scullery—returns with another dish.)*

LUTHER: They talkin' about comin' out again.   5

MINNIE *(returning)*: Good laws—they've no need.

LUTHER: They are though.

MINNIE: It's a holiday they want.

LUTHER: Nay it isna. They want th' proper scale here,* just as they
  ha'e it ivrywheer else.   10

MINNIE: But if the seams are thin,* and the company can't afford—

LUTHER: They can afford a' this gre't new electric plant; they can
  afford to build new houses for managers,* an' ter give blo—*
  ter give Frazer twelve hundred a year—

MINNIE: If they want a good manager to make the pits pay, they   15
  have to give him a good salary.

LUTHER: So's he can clip down our wages.

MINNIE: Why, what are yours clipped down?

LUTHER: Mine isn't, but there's plenty as is.

MINNIE: And will this strike make a butty of you?   20

LUTHER: You dunna strike to get made a butty on.

MINNIE: Then how *do* you get it. You're thirty one—

LUTHER: An' there's many as owd as me as is day-men yet.

MINNIE: But there's more that aren't, that are butties.

LUTHER: Ay, they've had luck.   25

MINNIE: Luck! You mean they've had some *go* in them.

LUTHER: Why what can I do more than I am doin'.

MINNIE: It isn't what you do, it's how you do it. Sluther through
  any job: get to th' end of it, no matter how. That's you.

LUTHER: I hole a stint as well as any man.   30

MINNIE: Then I back it takes you twice as long.

LUTHER: Nay, nor that neither.

MINNIE: I *know* you're not much of a workman—I've heard it from
  other butties, that you never put your heart into anything—

LUTHER: Who hast heard it fra?   35

MINNIE: From those that know. And I could ha' told it *them*, for I
  know you. You'll be a dayman at seven shillings a day till the
  end of your life—and you'll be satisfied, so long as you can
  shilly-shally through. That's what your mother did for you—
  mardin' you up till you were all mard-soft.   40

LUTHER: Tha's got a lot ter say a' of a suddin. Thee shut thy mouth.

MINNIE: You've been dragged round at your mother's apron-strings, all the lot of you, till there isn't half a man among you.

5   LUTHER: Tha seems fond enough of our Joe.

MINNIE: He is th' best in the bunch.

LUTHER: Tha should ha' married him then.

MINNIE: I shouldn't have had to ask *him*, if he was ready.

LUTHER: I'd axed thee twice afore—tha knowed tha could ha'e it

10   when ter wanted.

MINNIE: *Axed* me! It was like asking me to pull a tooth out for you.

LUTHER: Yi, an' it felt like it.

MINNIE: What?

15   LUTHER: Axin' thee to marry me. I'm blessed if it didna feel like axin' the doctor to pull ten teeth out of a stroke.

MINNIE: And then you expect me to have you!

LUTHER: Well, tha *has* done, whether or not.

MINNIE: I—yes, I had to fetch you, like a mother fetches a kid from

20   school. A pretty sight you looked. Didn't your mother give you a ha'epenny to spend, to get you to go.

LUTHER: No, she spent it for me.

MINNIE: She would! She wouldn't even let you spend your own ha'epenny. You'd have lost it, or let somebody take it from you.

25   LUTHER: Yis, thee.

MINNIE: Me!—me take anything from you! Why you've got nothing worth having.

LUTHER: I dunno—tha seems ter think so sometimes.

MINNIE: Oh!—Shilly-shally and crawl, that's all you can do. You

30   ought to have stopped with your mother.

LUTHER: I should ha' done, if tha hadna hawksed me out.

MINNIE: You aren't *fit* for a woman to have married, you're not.

LUTHER: Then why did thee marry me—it wor thy doin's?

MINNIE: Because I could get nobody better.

35   LUTHER: I'm more class than I thought for then.

MINNIE: Are you—are you—

                 (JOE'S *voice is heard.*)

JOE: I'm commin' in you two, so stop snaggin' an' snarlin'.

LUTHER: Come in, 'er'll 'appen turn 'er tap on thee.

40   JOE (*entering*): Are you eatin' *yet*?

MINNIE: Ay—it ta'es 'er that long ter tell my sins—Tha's just come right for puddin'. Get thee a plate outer t'cupboard—an' a spoon outer t'basket.

JOE *(at the cupboard)*: You've got ivrythink tip-top. What should ter do if I broke thee a plate, Minnie? 5

MINNIE: I should break another over your head.

(He deliberately drops and smashes a plate. She flushes crimson.)

LUTHER: Well, I'm glad it worna me.

JOE: I'm that clumsy wi' my left 'and, Minnie! Why doesna ter break another ower my head. 10

LUTHER *(rising and putting pudding on a plate)*: Here, ta'e this an' sit thee down. *(His brother seats himself.)* Hold thy knees straight, an' for God's sake dunna thee break this. Can ter manage?

JOE: I reckon so. If I canna, Minnie'll feed me wi' a spoon—shonna ter? 15

MINNIE: Why did you break my plate?

JOE: Nay, I didna break it—it wor th' floor.

MINNIE: You did it on purpose.

JOE: How could I. I didn't say ter th' floor 'break thou this plate, oh floor.' 20

MINNIE: You have no right—

JOE *(addressing the floor)*: Tha'd no right to break that plate—dost hear? I'd a good mind ter drop a bit o' puddin' on thy face. *(He balances the spoon—the plate slides down from his knee, smash into the fender.)* 25

MINNIE *(screams)*: It's my best service. *(Begins to sob.)*

LUTHER: Nay, our Joe!

JOE: Er's no occasions ter scraight. I bought th' service, an' I can get th' plates matched. What's her grizzlin' about?

MINNIE: I shan't ask you to get them matched. 30

JOE: Dunna thee, an' then tha runs no risk o' bein' denied.

MINNIE: What have you come here like this for?

JOE: I ha'ena come here like this. I come ter tell yer our Harriet* says, would yer mind goin' an' tellin' 'er what she can do with that childt's coat, as she's made a' wrong. If you'd looked slippy, 35 I'd ha' ta'en yer ter th' Cinematograph* after. But—dearly beloved brethren—let us weep: these our dear departed* dinner-plates. Come Minnie, drop a tear as you pass by.

LUTHER *(to MINNIE)*: Tha needna fret, Minnie—they can easy be matched again. 40

MINNIE: You're just pleased to see him make a fool of me, aren't you?

LUTHER: He's non made a fool o' thee—tha's made a fool o' thysen, scraightin' an' carryin' on.

5 JOE: It's a fact, Minnie. Nay, let me kiss thee better. *(She has risen, with shut face. He approaches with outstretched left arm. She swings round, fetches him a blow over his upper right arm—he bites his lip with pain.)*

LUTHER *(rising)*: Has it hurt thee, lad? Tha shouldna fool wi' 'er.

10 *(MINNIE watches the two brothers, with tears of mortification in her eyes. Then she throws off her apron, pins on her hat, puts on her coat, and is marching out of the house.)*

LUTHER: Are you going to Harriet's?

JOE: I'll come an' fetch you in time for th' Cinematograph.

15   *(The door is heard to bang.)*

JOE *(picking up the broken fragments of plates)*: That's done it.

LUTHER: It's bad luck—ne'er mind. How art goin' on?

JOE: Oh, all right.

LUTHER: What about thy club money?

20 JOE: They wunna gi'e 't me.—But I say, Sorry—tha'rt in for it—

LUTHER: Ay—I dunno what 'er married me for, f'r it's nowt bu' fault she finds wi' me, from th' minnit I come i' th' house to th' minnit I leave it.

JOE: Dost wish tha'd niver done it?—niver got married?

25 LUTHER *(sulky)*: I dunno—sometimes.

JOE: Then it's the blasted devil! *(With tragic emphasis.)*

LUTHER: I dunno—no—I'm married to 'er, an' she's married to me, so she can pick holes i' me as much as she likes—

JOE: As a rule she's nice enough wi' me.

30 LUTHER: She's nice wi' ivrybody but me.

JOE: An' does ter care?

LUTHER: Ay—I do.

JOE: Why doesn't ter go out an' leave 'er?

LUTHER: I dunno.

35 JOE: By the Lord, she'd cop it if I had 'er. *(A pause.)*

LUTHER: I wor' comin' up tonight.

JOE: I thought tha would be. But there's Mrs Purdy commin' ter see thee.

LUTHER: There's who?

JOE: Mrs Purdy. Didna ter ha'e a bit of a go wi' their Bertha, just afore Minnie wrote thee?

LUTHER: Ay—why?

JOE: 'Er mother says 'er's wi' childt by thee. She come up ter my mother this afternoon, an' said she wor commin' here tonight.   5

LUTHER: Says what?

JOE: Says as their Bertha's goin' ter ha'e a childt, an' 'er lays it on ter thee.

LUTHER: Oh my good God!

JOE: Isna it right?   10

LUTHER: It's right if 'er says so.

JOE: Then it's the blasted devil! *(A pause.)* So I come on here ter see if I could get Minnie to go up to our Harriet's.

LUTHER: Oh my good God!

JOE: I thought if we could keep it from 'er, we might settle summat,   15 an' 'er niver know.

LUTHER *(slowly)*: My God alive!

JOE: She said she'd hush it up, an' lay it ont'r a electrician as laid th' cable, an' is gone Goodness knows where—make an arrangement, for forty pound—   20

LUTHER *(thoughtfully)*: I wish I wor struck dead.

JOE: Well tha arena—an' so tha'd better think about it. My mother said as Minnie ought to know, but I say diff'rent, an' if Mrs Purdy doesna tell her, nobody need.

LUTHER: I wish I wor struck dead. I wish a ton o' rock 'ud fa' on   25 me tomorrer.

JOE: It wunna for wishin.

LUTHER: My good God.

JOE: An' so—I'll get thee forty quid, an' lend it thee. When Mrs Purdy comes, tell her she shall ha'e twenty quid this day week,   30 an' twenty quid a year from now, if thy name's niver been mentioned. I believe 'er's a clat-fart.

LUTHER: Me a childt by Bertha Purdy! But—but what's that for—now there's Minnie?

JOE: I dunno what it's for, but theer it is, as I'm tellin' thee. I'll stop   35 for another ha'ef an'hour, an' if 'er doesna come, tha mun see to 'er by hersen.

LUTHER: Er'll be back afore ha'ef an' hour's up. Tha mun go an' stop her.—I—I niver meant—look here, our Joe—I—if I—if she—if she—My God, what have I done now—!   40

JOE: We can stop her from knowin'.

LUTHER *(looking round)*: She'll be comin' back any minnit—nay, I
    niver meant t'r ha'—Joe—

JOE: What?

5   LUTHER: She—she—

JOE: Er never ne'd know.

LUTHER: Ah but though—

JOE: What?

LUTHER: I—I—I'n *done* it.

10   JOE: Well—it might ha happened t'r anybody.

LUTHER: But when 'er knows—an' it's *me* as has done it—

JOE: It wouldn't ha' mattered o' anyhow if it had bin sumb'dy
    else.—But tha knows what ter's got ter say. Arena ter goin' ter
    wesh thee? Go an' get th' panchion.

15   LUTHER *(rising)*: Er'll be comin' in any minnit—

JOE: Get thee weshed, man.

LUTHER *(fetching a bucket and lading-can from the scullery, and
    emptying water from the boiler)*: Go an' ta'e 'er somewheer,
    while Mrs Purdy goes, sholl ter?

20   JOE: D'rectly. Tha heered what I telled thee.

(There is a noise of splashing in the scullery—then a knock. JOE *goes to
    the door—he is heard saying 'Come in'—enter* MRS PURDY.*)*

MRS PURDY: I hope I've not come a-mealtimes.

JOE: No, they've finished. Minnie's gone up t'r our Harriet's.

25   MRS PURDY: Thank the Lord for small mercies—for I didn't fancy
    sittin' an' tellin' her about our Bertha.

JOE: We dunna want 'er ter know—sit thee down.

MRS PURDY: I'm of that mind, Mester, I am. As I says, What's th'
    good o' jackin' up a young married couple? For it won't

30   unmarry 'em nor ma'e things righter. An' yet, my long lass
    oughtner ter bear a' th' brunt.

JOE: Well, an' 'er isn't goin' to.

MRS PURDY: Is that mester weshin'?

JOE: Ah.

35   MRS PURDY: 'As ter towd him?

JOE: Ah.

MRS PURDY: Well, it's none o' my wishin's, I'm sure o' that.—Eh
    dear, you'n bin breakin' th' crockery a'ready!

JOE: Yes—that's me, bein' wallit.

MRS PURDY: T-t-t!—So this is 'ow she fancied it!

JOE: Ah—an' it non luiks bad, does it.

MRS PURDY: Very natty—very nice an' natty.

JOE *(taking up the lamp)*: Come an' look at th' parlour.

(Exit the two, door R.) 5

MRS PURDY'S VOICE: Yis—yis—it's nice an' plain. But a bit o' red plush is 'andsomer, to my mind.—It's th'oldfashioned style, like!—My word, but them three ornyments is gaudy-lookin'.

JOE'S VOICE: An' they reckon they're worth five pound. 'Er mester gen 'em 'er. 10

MRS PURDY'S VOICE: I'd rether had th' money.

JOE'S VOICE: Ah, me an' a'. *(During this time, LUTHER has come hurrying out of the scullery into the kitchen, rubbing his face with a big roller towel. He is naked to the waist. He kneels with his knees on the fender, sitting on his heels, rubbing himself dry. His back is* 15 *not washed—he rubs his hair dry. Enter JOE with the lamp, followed by MRS PURDY.)*

MRS PURDY: It's uncommon, very uncommon, Mester Gaskin— and looks well too, for them as likes it.—But it hardly goes wi' my fancy, somehow, startin' wi' second-hand, owd-fashioned 20 stuff. You dunno *who*'s sotten theirselves on these 'ere chairs now, do you?

LUTHER: It ma'es no diff'rence to me who's sot on 'em an' who 'asna.

MRS PURDY: No—you get used to 'm. 25

LUTHER *(to JOE)*: Shall thee go up t'r our Harriet's?

JOE: If ter's a mind. *(Takes up his cap—to MRS PURDY)*: An' you two can settle as best you can.

MRS PURDY: Yes—yes! I'm not one for baulkin' mysen, an' cuttin' my nose off ter spite my face. 30

(LUTHER has finished wiping himself. He takes a shifting shirt from the bureau, and struggles into it, then goes into the scullery.)

JOE: An' you sure you'll keep it quiet, Missis?

MRS PURDY: Am I goin' bletherin' up street an down street, think yer. 35

JOE: An' dunna tell your Bob.

MRS PURDY: I'n more sense. There's not a word 'e 'ears a-whoam as is of any count, for out it 'ud leak when he wor canned. Yes my guyney—we know what our mester is.

(Re-enter LUTHER—*in shirt and black trousers. He drops his pit-trousers and singlet* beside the hearth.* MRS PURDY *bends down and opens his pit-trousers.)*

MRS PURDY: Nay, if ter drops 'em of a heap, they niver goin' ter get dry an' cosy. Tha sweats o' th' hips, as my lads did!

LUTHER: Well, go thy ways, Joe.

JOE: Ay—well—good luck—an' goodnight Mrs Purdy.

MRS PURDY: Goodnight. *(Exit* JOE.*)*

*(There are several moments of silence—*LUTHER *puts the broken pots on the table.)*

MRS PURDY: It's sad work, Mester Gaskin, f'r a' on us.

LUTHER: Ah.

MRS PURDY:* I left that long lass o' mine fair gaunt, fair chalked of a line, I did, poor thing. Not bu' what 'er should 'a 'ad more sense.

LUTHER: Ah.

MRS PURDY: But it's no use throwin' good words after bad deeds. Not bu' what it's a nasty thing for yer t'r 'a done, it is,—an' yer can scarce look your Missis i' th' face again, I should think. *(A pause.)* But I says t'r our Bertha 'It's his'n, an' he mun pay.' Eh but how 'er did but scraight an' cry. It fair turned me ower. 'Dunna go to 'm, mother,' 'er says, 'Dunna go to 'm for to tell him.' 'Yi,' I says, 'Right's right—tha doesna get off wi' nowt, nor shall 'e neither. 'E wor but a scamp to do such a thing' I says, yes, I did! For you was older nor 'er. Not but what she was old enough ter ha'e more sense. But 'er wor allers one o' th' come-day go-day sort, as 'ud gi'e th' clothes off 'er back an' niver know 'er wor nak'd—a gre't soft looney as she is, an' serves 'er right for bein' such a gabey. Yi, an' I believe 'er wor fond on thee—if a wench *can* be fond of a married man. For one blessin', 'er doesna know what 'er wor an' what 'er worn't. For they ma' talk o' bein' i' love—but you non i' love wi' onybody, wi'out they's a chance o' their marryin' you—howiver much you may like 'em. An' I'm thinkin', th' childt 'll set 'er up again when it comes, for 'er's gone that wezzel-brained an' doited, I'm sure! An' it's a mort o' trouble for me, mester, a sight o' trouble it is. Not as I s'll be hard on 'er. She knowed I wor commin' 'ere tonight, an's not spoke a word for hours, I left her sittin' on th' sofey hangin' 'er 'ead. But it's a weary business mester, an' nowt ter be proud on. I s'd think tha wishes tha'd niver clapt eyes on our Bertha.

LUTHER *(thinking back)*: I dunna—I dunna. An' I dunna wish as I'd niver seen 'er, no I dunna. Er liked me, an' I liked her.

MRS PURDY: An' appen, but for this 'ere marriage o' thine, tha'd 'a married 'er.

LUTHER: Ah, I should. F'r 'er liked me, an' 'er worna neither nice nor near, nor owt else, an' 'er'd 'a bin fond o' me.

MRS PURDY: 'Er would, an' it's a thousand pities. But what's done's done.

LUTHER: Ah, I know that.

MRS PURDY: An' as for your Missis—

LUTHER: 'Er mun do as 'er likes.

MRS PURDY: But tha'rt not for tellin' 'er?

LUTHER: 'Er—'er'll know sometime or other.

MRS PURDY: Nay, nay, 'er ne'dna. You married now, lad, an' you canna please yoursen.

LUTHER: It's a fact.

MRS PURDY: An' Lucy Stapleton, she had forty pound wi' 'er lad, an' it's not as if you hadn't got money. An' to be sure, we've none.

LUTHER: No, an' I'n none.

MRS PURDY: Yea, you've some atween you—an'—well—

LUTHER: I can get some.

MRS PURDY: Then what do yer say?

LUTHER: I say as Bertha's welcome t'r any forty pounds, if I'd got it. For—for—Missis, she wor better to me than iver my wife's bin.

MRS PURDY *(frightened by his rage)*: Niver, lad.

LUTHER: She wor—ah but though she wor. She thought a lot on me.

MRS PURDY: An' so I'm sure your missis does. She naggles thy heart out, maybe. But that's just th' wrigglin' a place out for hersen. She'll settle down comfortable, lad.

LUTHER *(bitterly)*: Will she!

MRS PURDY: Yi—yi.—An' tha's done 'er a crewel wrong, my lad. An' tha's done my gel one as well. For, though she was old enough to know better, yet she's good-hearted and trustin', an' 'ud gi'e 'er shoes off 'er feet. An' tha's landed 'er, tha knows. For it's not th' bad women as 'as bastards nowadays—they've a sight too much gumption. It's fools like our'n—poor thing.

LUTHER: I've done ivrythink that was bad, I know that.

MRS PURDY: Nay—nay—young fellers, they are like that. But it's
wrong, for look at my long lass sittin' theer on that sofey, as if
'er back wor broke.

LUTHER *(loudly)*: But I dunna wish I'd niver seen 'er, I dunna. It
5   wor—it wor—she wor good to me, she wor, an' I dunna wish I'd
niver done it.

MRS PURDY: Then tha ought, that's a'. For I do—an' 'er does.

LUTHER: Does 'er say 'er wishes 'er'd niver seen me?

MRS PURDY: Er says nowt o' nowhow.

10   LUTHER: Then 'er doesna wish it—An' I wish I'd ha' married 'er.

MRS PURDY: Come, my lad, come. Married tha art—

LUTHER *(bitterly)*: Married I am, an' I wish I worna. Your Bertha,
'er'd 'a thought a thousand times more on me than *she* does. But
I'm wrong, wrong, wrong i' ivry breath I take. An' I will be
15   wrong, yi, an' I *will* be wrong—

MRS PURDY: Hush thee—there's somebody comin'.
       (They wait—enter JOE *and* MINNIE, JOE *talking loudly.)*

MINNIE *(entering)*: No you've not, you've no right at all. *(To*
LUTHER*)*: Haven't you even cleared away? *(To* MRS PURDY*)*:
20   Good-evening.

MRS PURDY: Good-evening Missis. I was just goin'.—I've bin
sayin', it looks very nice, th'ouse.

MINNIE: Do you think so.

MRS PURDY: I do indeed.

25   MINNIE: Don't notice of th' mess we're in, shall you. *He (pointing
to* JOE*)* broke the plates—and then I had to rush off up to Mrs
Preston's afore I could clear away. And he hasn't even mended
the fire.

LUTHER: I *can* do—I niver noticed.

30   MINNIE *(to* MRS PURDY*)*: Have a piece of cake? *(Goes to cupboard.)*

MRS PURDY: No thanks, no thanks—I mun get off afore th' Co-op
shuts up. Thank yer very much. Well—Goodnight all.
       (JOE opens her the door—exit.)

MINNIE *(bustling, clearing away—*LUTHER *comes in with coals—to her
35   husband)*: Did you settle it?

LUTHER: What?

MINNIE: What she'd come about?

LUTHER: Ah.

MINNIE: An' I bet you'll go and forget.

40   LUTHER: Oh ah.

MINNIE: And poor old Bob Purdy will go on just the same.

LUTHER: Very likely.

MINNIE: Don't let the dust all go on the hearth. Why didn't you clear away. The house was like a pigsty for her to come into.

LUTHER: Then I wor th' pig.   5

MINNIE *(halting)*: Why—who's trod on your tail now?

LUTHER: There'd be no'b'dy to tread on it if tha wor out.

MINNIE: Oh—oh dear o' me. *(To* JOE*)*: I think we'd better go to the cinematograph, and leave him to nurse his sore tail.

JOE: We better had.   10

LUTHER: An' joy go wi' yer.*

MINNIE: We certainly shan't leave it at home. *(To* JOE*)*: What time does it begin?

JOE: Seven o'clock.

MINNIE: And I want to call in Sisson's shop.* Shall you go with me,   15 or wouldn't you condescend to go shopping with me? *(She has cleared the table, brought a tray and a bowl, and is washing up the pots.)*

JOE: Dost think I'm daunted by Polly Sisson.

MINNIE: You're braver than most men if you dare go in a shop.   20 Here, take a towel and wipe these pots.

JOE: How can I?

MINNIE: If you were a gentleman, you'd hold the plates in your teeth to wipe them.

JOE: Tha wouldna look very ladylike at th' end on't.   25

MINNIE: Why?

JOE: Why, hast forgot a'ready what a shine tha kicked up when I broke them two other plates. *(He has got the towel, and wedging a plate* against his thighs, is laboriously wiping it.)*

MINNIE: I never kicked up a shine.—It *is* nice of you!   30

JOE: What?

MINNIE: To do this for me. *(*LUTHER *has begun sweeping the hearth.)*

JOE: Tha's got two servants.

MINNIE: But I'm sure you want to smoke while you're doing it—don't you now?   35

JOE: Sin' tha says so. *(Fumbles in his pocket.)*

MINNIE *(hastily wiping her hands—puts a cigarette between his lips—gets matches from the mantel-piece, ignoring her husband, who is kneeling sweeping the hearth—lights his cigarette)*: It's so nice to have a lamed man. You feel you've got an excuse for making a   40 fuss of him.—You've got awfully nice eyes and eyebrows. I like dark eyes.

JOE: Oh ah. *(LUTHER rises hastily—goes in the passage—crosses the room quietly. He wears his coat, a red scarf, and a cap.)*

5   MINNIE: There's more go in them than in blue. *(Watches her husband go out. There is silence between the two.)*

JOE: He'll come round again.

MINNIE: He'll have to.—He'll go on sulking now. *(Her face breaks.)* You—you don't know how hard it is.

10   JOE: What?

MINNIE *(crying a few fierce tears)*: This—

JOE *(aghast)*: What?

MINNIE: Why—you don't know. You don't know how hard it is, with a man as—as leaves you alone all the time.

15   JOE: But—he niver hardly goes out.

MINNIE: No but—you don't know—he leaves me alone, he always has done—and there's nobody—

JOE: But he—

MINNIE: He never trusts me—he leaves me so alone—and— *(a*
20   *little burst of tears)* it *is* hard! *(She changes suddenly.)* You've wiped four plates; my word, you are a champion.

JOE: I think so an a'.

MINNIE: I hope the pictures will be jolly—but the sad ones make me laugh more, don't they you?

25   JOE: I canna do wi 'em.

(Curtain)

Act II.

Scene: LUTHER'S *house.*

Time: The same evening—eleven o'clock.

Personae: MINNIE—*alone—weeping—She gets up, fills the kettle, puts it*
on the hob—sits down, weeps again—then hears somebody coming—dries   5
her eyes swiftly—turns the lamp low—enter LUTHER. *He stands in the*
doorway—is rather tipsy—flings his cap down—sits in his chair, lurching
it slightly—neither speaks for some moments.

LUTHER: Well, did yer like yer pictures?

MINNIE: Where have you been?   10

LUTHER: What does it matter wheer I've been!

MINNIE: Have you been drinking?

LUTHER: What's it matter if I have!

MINNIE: It matters a lot to me.

LUTHER: Oh ah!   15

MINNIE: Do you think I'm going to sleep with a man who is half
    drunk?

LUTHER: Nay, I non know who tha'rt goin' ter sleep wi'.

MINNIE *(rising)*: I shall make the bed in the other room.

LUTHER: Tha's no 'casions. I s'll do very nicely on t' sofey. It's   20
    warmer.

MINNIE: Oh, you can have your own bed.

LUTHER: If tha doesna sleep in 't, I dunna.

MINNIE: And if *you do*, I don't.

LUTHER: Tha pleases thysen. Tha can sleep by thysen for iver, if   25
    ter's a mind to't.

MINNIE *(who has stood hesitating)*: Oh very well! *(She goes upstairs,*
    returns immediately with a pillow and two blankets, which she
    throws on the sofa.)

LUTHER: Thank yer kindly.   30

MINNIE: Shall you rake?

LUTHER: I'll rake. *(She moves about—lays the table for the morning's*
    breakfast—a newspaper, cup, plate, etc.—no food because it would
    go dry—rinses his tin pit-bottle, puts it and his snap-bag on the
    table.) I could do it a' for mysen. Tha ned do nowt for me.   35

MINNIE: Why this sudden fit of unselfishness?

LUTHER: I niver want thee to do nowt for me, niver no more. No,
    not so much as lift a finger for me—not if I wor dyin'.

MINNIE: You're not dying, you're only tipsy.

LUTHER: Well, it's no matter to thee what I am.

MINNIE: It's very comfortable for you to think so.

LUTHER: I non know nowt about that.

MINNIE *(after a pause)*: Where have you been tonight?

5   LUTHER: There an' back to see how far it is.

MINNIE *(making an effort)*: Have you been up to your mother's?

LUTHER: Where I've bin I've bin, an' where I haven't I haven't.

MINNIE: Pah!—you needn't try to magnify it and make a mountain. You've been to your mother's, and then to the 'Ram'.

10 LUTHER: All right—if tha knows, tha knows, an' theer's an end on't.

MINNIE: You talk like a fool.

LUTHER: That comes o' bein' a fool.

MINNIE: When were you a fool?

15 LUTHER: Ivry day o' my life, an' ivry breath I've ta'en.

MINNIE *(having finished work, sits down again)*: I suppose you haven't got it in you to say anything fresh.

LUTHER: Why, what dost want me ter say? *(He looks at her for the first time.)*

20 MINNIE *(with a queer catch)*: You might be more of a man if you said you were sorry.

LUTHER: Sorry! Sorry for what?

MINNIE: You've nothing to be sorry *for*, have you?

LUTHER *(looking at her, quickly)*: What art goin' ter say?

25 MINNIE: It's what are *you* going to say. *(A silence.)*

LUTHER *(doggedly)*: I'm goin' ter say nowt.

MINNIE *(bitterly)*: No, you're not *man* enough to say anything—you can only slobber. You do a woman a wrong, but you're never man enough to say you're sorry for it. You're *not* a man, you're

30 not—you're something crawling—!

LUTHER: I'm glad!—I'm glad!—I'm glad! No, an' I wouldna ta'e 't back, no. 'Er wor nice wi' me, which is a thing tha's niver bin. An' so tha's got it, an' mun keep it.

MINNIE: Who was nice with you?

35 LUTHER: *She* was—an' would ha' bin at this minnit, but for thee.

MINNIE: Pah—you're not fit to have a wife. You only want your mother to rock you to sleep.

LUTHER: Neither mother, nor wife, neither thee nor onybody do I want—no—no—

40 MINNIE: No—you've had three cans of beer.

LUTHER: An' if ter niver sleeps i' th' bed wi' me again, an' if ter niver does a hand's turn for me niver no more, I'm glad, I'm glad. I non want thee. I non want ter see thee.

MINNIE: You mean coward. Good God!—I never thought you were such a mean coward as this. 5

LUTHER: An' as for thy money—yi, I wouldna smell on't. An' neither thine, nor our Joe's, nor my mother's will I ha'e. What I addle's my own. What I gi'e thee, I gi'e thee. An' she maun ha'e ten shillin's a month, an' tha maun abide by't.

MINNIE: What are you talking about? 10

LUTHER: My mother wouldna gi'e me th' money. She says she's done her share. An' tha's done thine. An' I'n done mine, begod. An' what yer canna chew yer maun swaller.

MINNIE: You must be quite drunk.

LUTHER: Must I? All right, it's Dutch courage then. A'right, then 15 Dutch courage it is.—But I tell thee, tha does as ter's a mind. Tha can leave me, an' go back inter service, if ter wants. What's it ter me, if I'm but a lump o' muck i' th' ouse wheer tha art. Tha should ha' had our Joe—he's got more *go* than me. An' I should ha' had 'er. I'd got go enough for *her*: 'appen a bit too 20 much.

MINNIE: Her—who?

LUTHER: Her! An' I'm glad 'er's wi' my childt. I'm glad I did it. I'm glad!—For tha's wiped the feet* on me enough. Yi, tha's wiped thy feet on me till what's it to me if tha does it or not. It 25 isna! An' now—tha maun abide by what ter's got, tha maun. *I* s'll ha'e to—an' by plenty I hadna got I've abided. An' so—an' so—yi—

MINNIE: But who is it you—who is she?

LUTHER: Tha knowed a' along. 30

MINNIE: Who is it? *(They are both silent.)* Aren't you going to speak?

LUTHER: What's the good?

MINNIE *(coldly)*: But I must know.

LUTHER: Tha does know. 35

MINNIE: I can assure you I don't.

LUTHER: Then assure thysen an' find out. *(Another silence.)*

MINNIE: Do you mean somebody is going to have a baby by you?

LUTHER: I mean what I've said, an' I mean nowt else.

MINNIE: But you must tell me.* 40

LUTHER: I've boiled my cabbage twice a'ready, hanna I?

MINNIE: Do you mean somebody is going to have a child by you?

LUTHER: Tha can chew it ower, if ter's a mind.

MINNIE *(helpless)*: But— *(She struggles with herself, then goes calm.)*

5 LUTHER: That's what *I* say—*but*! *(A silence.)*

MINNIE: And who is she?

LUTHER: Thee, for a' I know.

MINNIE *(calmly, patiently)*: I asked you a question.

LUTHER: Ah—an' I 'eered thee.

10 MINNIE: Then answer me—who is she?

LUTHER: Tha knows well enow—tha knowed afore they'd towd thee—

MINNIE: Nobody has told me—who is she?

LUTHER: Well, tha's seed 'er mother.

15 MINNIE *(numb)*: Mrs Purdy?

LUTHER: Yi.

MINNIE: Their Bertha?

LUTHER: Yi. *(A silence.)*

MINNIE: Why didn't you tell me?

20 LUTHER: Tell thee what?

MINNIE: This.

LUTHER: Tha knowed afore I did.

MINNIE: I know *now*.

LUTHER: Me an' a'. *(A pause.)*

25 MINNIE: Didn't you know till tonight?

LUTHER: Our Joe told me when tha'd just gone—I niver dreamp afore—an' then 'er mother—

MINNIE: What did her mother come for?

LUTHER: Ter see if we could hush it up a'cause o' thee, an' gi'e her a lump sum.

30

MINNIE: Hush it up because of me?

LUTHER: Ah—lay it ont'r an electrician as wor wi' th' gang as laid th' cable down to Batford—he's gone God knows where—

MINNIE: But it's yours.

35 LUTHER: I know that.

MINNIE: Then why lay it onto somebody else?

LUTHER: Because o' thee.

MINNIE: But why because of me?

LUTHER: To stop thee knowin', I s'd think.

40 MINNIE: And why shouldn't I know?

LUTHER: Eh I dunno. *(A pause.)*

MINNIE: And what were you going to do to stop me knowing?

LUTHER: 'Er axed for forty pound down.

MINNIE: And if you paid forty pounds, you got off scot free?

LUTHER: Summat so.   5

MINNIE: And where were the forty pounds coming from?

LUTHER: Our Joe said 'e'd lend 'em me. I thought my mother
would—but 'er said 'er wouldna—neither would she gie't our
Joe ter lend me, she said. For I wor a married man now, an' it
behoved my wife to look after me. An' I thought tha knowed. I   10
thought tha'd twigged, else bin telled. An' I didna care, an'
dunna care—

MINNIE: And this is what you married me to?

LUTHER: This is what tha married me to. But I s'll niver ax thee
for, no, not so much as the liftin' of a finger—no—   15

MINNIE: But when you wrote and told me you were willing to
marry me—why didn't you tell me this?

LUTHER: Because—as I've telled thee—I didna know till this very
mortal night.

MINNIE: But you knew you'd been with her.   20

LUTHER: Ay, I knowed that. *(A pause.)*

MINNIE: And why didn't you tell me?

LUTHER: What for should I tell thee? What good would it ha' done
thee? Tha niver towd *me* nowt.☆

MINNIE: So that is how you look at it?   25

LUTHER: I non care how I look at it. *(A pause.)*

MINNIE: And was there anybody else?

LUTHER: How dost mean?

MINNIE: Have you been with any other women?

LUTHER: I dunno.—I might.—I dunno.—   30

MINNIE: That means you have.

LUTHER: I'm thirty.

MINNIE: And who *were* they?

LUTHER: I dunno. I've niver bin much wi' anybody—little, very
little—an' then it wor an off-chance. Our Joe wor more that way   35
than me—I worn't that way. *(A pause.)*

MINNIE: —So—this was what I waited for you for!

LUTHER: Tha niver waited for me. Tha had me a-cause tha couldna
get nobody better.

MINNIE: And so—   40

LUTHER *(after a moment)*: Yi, an' so. An' so, I non care what ter does. If ter leaves me—

MINNIE *(in a flash)*: What's the good of me leaving you! Aren't I married to you—tied to you?

5   LUTHER: Tha could leave me whether or not. I should go t'r Australia wi' our Joe.

MINNIE: And what about that girl?

LUTHER: I should send 'er th' money.

MINNIE: And what about me?

10   LUTHER: Tha'd please thysen.

MINNIE: Should you *like* me to leave you, and let you go to Australia?

LUTHER: 'Appen I should.

MINNIE: What did you marry me for?

15   LUTHER: Cos tha axed me.

MINNIE: Did you never care for me? *(He does not answer.)* Didn't you? *(He does not answer.)* Didn't you?

LUTHER *(slowly)*: You niver wanted me—you thought me dirt—

MINNIE: Ha! *(A pause.)* You can have the forty pounds.

20   LUTHER *(very doggedly)*: I shanna.

MINNIE: She's got to be paid.

LUTHER: Tha keeps thy money.

MINNIE: Then where shall you get it from?

LUTHER: I s'll pay 'er month by month.

25   MINNIE: But you can't—think—

LUTHER: Then I'll borrow forty quid somewhere else, an' pay it back i' instalments. Tha keeps thy money.

MINNIE: You can borrow it from me.

LUTHER: I shall not.

30   MINNIE: Very well. I only wanted not to have the bother of paying month by month.—I think I shall go back to my old place.

LUTHER: Tha pleases thysen.

MINNIE: And you can go and live with your mother again.

35   LUTHER: That I should niver do—but tha pleases thysen.—We'n bin married seven wik come Tuesday.

MINNIE: I never ought to ha' done it. ☆

LUTHER: What?

MINNIE: Married you.

40   LUTHER: No.

MINNIE: For you never cared enough.

LUTHER: Yi—it's my fault.

MINNIE: Yes.

LUTHER: It would be. Tha's niver made a fault i' thy life.

MINNIE: Who are you, to talk about my faults. 5

LUTHER: Well— *(A pause.)*

MINNIE: I shall write to Mr Westlake tomorrow.

LUTHER: Tha does as pleases thee.

MINNIE: And if they can't take me back straight away, I shall ask
him if he knows another place. 10

LUTHER: A' right.—An' we'll sell th' furniture.

MINNIE *(looking round at her home)*: Yes.

LUTHER: It'll non bring ha'ef tha gev for't—but it'll bring enough
ter ta'e me out theer.

MINNIE: I'll make up what you lose by it, since I chose it. 15

LUTHER: Tha can gi'e ter them as'll ta'e.

MINNIE: But I shall feel I owe it you.

LUTHER: I'n had six wiks o' married life wi' thee. I mun pay for
that.

MINNIE: You are mean, mean. 20

LUTHER: I know—though tha'rt first as has telled me so.—When
dost reckon tha'lt go?

MINNIE: I'll go tomorrow if you want to get rid of me.

LUTHER: Nay—tha does just as pleases thysen. *I* non want ter get
rid on thee. Nay—nay, it's not that.—It's thee as wants ter go. 25

MINNIE: At any rate, I s'll have a place inside a fortnight.

LUTHER *(dully)*: All right.

MINNIE: So I shall have to trouble you till then.

LUTHER: But I dunna want thee ter do owt for me—no, I dunna.

MINNIE: I shall keep the house, in payment for my board and 30
lodgings. And I'll make the bed up in the back room, and I'll
sleep there, because it's not furnished, and the house is yours.

LUTHER: Th'art—th'art—I wish I might strike thee down.

MINNIE: And I shall keep the account of every penny I spend, and
you must just pay the bills. 35

LUTHER *(rising suddenly)*: I'll murder thee afore tha does. *(He goes
out—She sits twisting her apron. He returns with a large lump of
coal in his hands, and rakes the fire.)*

MINNIE: You cared more for her than for me.

LUTHER: For who? 40

MINNIE: For her. She was the sort of sawney you ought to have had. Did she think you perfect?

LUTHER *(with grim satisfaction)*: She liked me.

MINNIE: And you could do just as you wanted with her?

LUTHER: She'd ha' done owt for me.

MINNIE: And it flattered you, did it? Because a long stalk wi' no flower was at your service, it flattered you, did it? My word, it ought.—As for your Joe, he's not a fool like you, and that's why women think more of him. He wouldn't want a Bertha Purdy. He'd get a woman who was something—and because he knew how to appreciate her. You—what good are you?

LUTHER: I'm no good, but to fetch an' carry.

MINNIE: And a tuppenny scullery girl could do that as well.

LUTHER: All right.

MINNIE: I'll bet even Bertha Purdy thinks what a clown you are. She never wanted you to marry her, did she?

LUTHER: She knowed I wouldn't.

MINNIE: You flatter yourself. I'll bet she never wanted you.—I shouldn't be surprised if the child isn't somebody else's, that she just foists on you because you're so soft.

LUTHER: Oh ah.

MINNIE: It even flatters you to think it's yours.

LUTHER: Oh ah!

MINNIE: And quite right too—for it's the only thing you could have to be proud of. And then really it's not you—

LUTHER: Oh ah!

MINNIE: If a woman has a child, and you think you're the cause, do you think it's *your* doings?

LUTHER: If tha has one, it will be.

MINNIE: And is *that* anything for you to be proud of? Me whom you've insulted and deceived and treated as no snail would treat a woman. And then you expect me to bear your children.

LUTHER: I dunna expect thee. If tha does tha does.

MINNIE: And you gloat over it and feel proud of it.

LUTHER: Yi, I do.

MINNIE: No—no! I'd rather have married a tramp off the streets than you.—And—and I don't believe you *can* have children.

LUTHER: Theer tha knows tha'rt a liar.

MINNIE: I hate you.

LUTHER: All right.

MINNIE: And I *will* leave you, I *will*.

LUTHER: Tha's said so afore.

MINNIE: And I mean it.

LUTHER: All right.

MINNIE: But it's your mother's doing. *She* mollycoddled and   5
marded you till you weren't a man—and now—I have to pay for
it.

LUTHER: Oh ah!

MINNIE: No, you're not a man.

LUTHER: All right. They's plenty of women as would say I am.   10

MINNIE: They'd be lying, to get something out of you.

LUTHER: Why, what could they get outer me.

MINNIE: Yes—yes—what could they— *(She stutters to a close. He
begins to take off his boots.)*

LUTHER: If tha'rt goin', tha'd better go afore th' strike begins. We   15
should be on short commons then—ten bob a wik. *

MINNIE: There's one thing, *you'd* be on short commons without
me. For nobody would keep you for ten shillings a week, unless
you went to your mother's.

LUTHER: I could live at our Harriet's, an' pay 'er off after. An'   20
there'd be th' furniture sold.

MINNIE: And you'd be delighted if there *was* a strike, so you could
loaf about. You don't even get drunk. You only loaf. You're lazy,
lazy, and without the stomach of a louse. You *want* a strike.

LUTHER: All right.   25

MINNIE: And I hope you'll get what you deserve, I do.

LUTHER: Tha'rt gi'en it me.

MINNIE *(lifting her hand suddenly)*: How *dare* you say so—how *dare*
you. I'm too good for you.

LUTHER *(sullenly)*: I know.   30

MINNIE: Yes. *(She gets a candle, lights it, and goes to bed. He flings off
his scarf and coat and waistcoat, throws the pillow on the hearthrug,
wraps himself in the blankets, blows the lamp out, and lies down.)*

(Curtain)

Act III.

Scene: The kitchen of LUTHER GASCOYNE'S *house.*
Time: A fortnight later—afternoon.
Personae: MRS GASCOYNE sen^r, *alone.—Enter* MINNIE GASCOYNE,
5 *dressed from travelling. She is followed by a* CABMAN *carrying a bag.*

MRS GASCOYNE: What—is it you!

MINNIE: Yes, didn't you get my wire?

MRS GASCOYNE: Thy wire! Dost mean a tallygram? No, we'n had
nowt. Though th' house 'as bin shut up.

10 MINNIE *(to the* CABMAN*)*: Thank you—how much?

CABMAN: Ha'ef a crown.

MRS GASCOYNE: Ha'ef a crown for commin' from th' Midland
station! Why tha non know what's talkin' about.

MINNIE *(paying him)*: Thank you.

15 CABMAN: Thank yer. Good afternoon. *(Exit.)*

MRS GASCOYNE: My word, tha knows how ter ma'e th' money fly.

MINNIE: I couldn't carry a bag.

MRS GASCOYNE: Tha could ha' come i' th' 'bus ter Eastwood an'
then a man 'ud 'a browt it on.

20 MINNIE: It is raining.

MRS GASCOYNE: Tha'rt neither sugar nor salt.

MINNIE: I wonder you didn't get my telegram.

MRS GASCOYNE: I tell thee, th' ouse wor shut up last night.

MINNIE: Oh!

25 MRS GASCOYNE: I dunno wheer 'e slep'—wi' some o's pals I
should think.

MINNIE: Oh!

MRS GASCOYNE: Thinks I to mysen, I'd better go an' get some
dinner ready down theer. So I telled our Joe ter come 'ere for's
30 dinner as well, but they'n neither on 'em bin in yet. That's
allers t'road when it's strike. They stop mormin' about,
bletherin' and boozin', an' meals, bless yer, they don't count.—
Tha's bin i' Manchester four days then?

MINNIE: Yes.

35 MRS GASCOYNE: Ay!—Our Luther's niver bin up ter tell me. If I
hadna ha' met Mrs Pervin fra next door here, I should niver ha
knowed a word. That wor yisterday. So I sent our Joe down. But
it seems 'e's neither bin awhoam yesterday nor th' day afore. He

slep' i' th' 'ouse by hissen for two nights. So Mrs Charley☆ said.
He said tha'd gone ter Manchester on business.

MINNIE: Yes.

MRS GASCOYNE: But he niver come ter tell *me* nowt on't.

MINNIE: Didn't he?   5

MRS GASCOYNE: It's trew what they say:

> 'My son's my son till he ta'es him a wife
> But my daughter's my daughter the whole of her life.'

MINNIE: Do you think so?

MRS GASCOYNE: I'm sure.—An' th' men's been out ten days now,   10
an' such carryin's on.

MINNIE: Oh! Why, what?

MRS GASCOYNE: Meetin's ivry mornin'—crier for ever down th'
street wi's bell—an' agitators. They say as Frazer dursn't
venture out o' th' door. Watna' pit-top's bin afire, and there's a   15
rigiment o' soldiers drillin' i' th' statutes ground—bits o' things
they are, an' a', like a lot o' little monkeys i' their red coats
—Staffordshire men. But wiry, so they say. Same as marched
wi' Lord Roberts to Candyhar. But not a man among 'em. If
you watch out fra th' gardin end, you'll see 'em i' th' colliers   20
train goin' up th' line ter Watna'☆—wi' their red-coats jammed
i' th' winders. They say as Frazer's got ten on 'em i 's house ter
guard him—an' they's sentinels at pit top, standin' wi' their
guns, an' th' men crackin' their sides wi' laughin' at em'.

MINNIE: What for?   25

MRS GASCOYNE: Nay. That I canna tell thee. They'n got th' Black
Watch up at Heanor☆—so they sayn—great big Scotchmen i'
kilts. They look well,☆ ha'ein them i' Heanor, wi' a' them lasses.

MINNIE: And what is all the fuss about?

MRS GASCOYNE: Riotin'.—I thought tha'd bobbied off ter Man-   30
chester ter be i' safety.

MINNIE: Oh no—I never knew there was any danger.

MRS GASCOYNE: No more there is, as far as that goes.—What's up
a'tween you an' our Luther?

MINNIE: Oh nothing particular.   35

MRS GASCOYNE: I knowed summat wor amiss, when 'e niver come
up. It's a fortnight last Tuesday sin' 'e set foot i' my house—an'
I've niver clapt eyes on him. I axed our Joe, but he's as stubborn

as a jackass, an' you canna get a word out on 'im, not for love nor money.

MINNIE: Oh!

MRS GASCOYNE: Talks o' goin' t'r Australey. But not if I can help it. An' hints as if our Luther—You not thinkin of it, are you?

MINNIE: No, I'm not—not that I know of.

MRS GASCOYNE: Hm! It's a rum go, when nobody seems ter know where they are, nor what they're goin' ter do. But there's more blort than bustle, i' this world.—What took thee to Manchester?

MINNIE: Oh, I just wanted to go, on business.

MRS GASCOYNE: Summat about thy money, like?

MINNIE: Yes.

MRS GASCOYNE: Our Luther wor axin' me for forty pound, th' last time 'e wor up—but I didna see it! No—I fun him a' as 'e wanted for's marriage, and gen' him ten pound i' hand, an' I thought it 'ud suffice.—An' as for forty pound—it's ter much, that's what I think.

MINNIE: I don't.

MRS GASCOYNE: Oh well, if tha doesna, a' well an' good.—'Appen he's paid it then?

MINNIE: Paid it! Why where was he to get it from?

MRS GASCOYNE: I thought you had it atween you.

MINNIE: We haven't.

MRS GASCOYNE: Why, how dost mean?

MINNIE: I mean we've neither of us got as much as forty pounds.

MRS GASCOYNE: Dost mean *tha* hasna?

MINNIE: No, I haven't.

MRS GASCOYNE: What's a-gait now?

MINNIE: Nothing.

MRS GASCOYNE: What hast bin up to?

MINNIE: I? Nothing. I went to Manchester to settle a little business, that's all.

MRS GASCOYNE: An' wheer did ter stop?

MINNIE: I stayed with my old master.

MRS GASCOYNE: Wor there no Missis then?

MINNIE: No—His wife is dead. You know I was governess for his grandchildren, who were born in India.

MRS GASCOYNE: Hm!—So tha went to see *him*?

MINNIE: Yes—I've always told him everything.

MRS GASCOYNE: So tha went clat-fartin' ter 'im about our Luther, did ter?

MINNIE: Well—he's the only soul in the world that I *can* go to.

MRS GASCOYNE: Hm!—It doesna become thee, methinks.

MINNIE: Well! *(Footsteps are heard.)*   5

MRS GASCOYNE: Here's them lads, I s'd think.

(Enter LUTHER *and* JOE.*)*

JOE *(to* MINNIE*)*: Hello, has thee come?

MINNIE: Yes, I sent a wire, and thought someone might come to meet me.   10

JOE: Nay—there wor no wire. We thought tha'd gone for good.

MINNIE: Who thought so?

JOE: Well—didna tha say so?

MINNIE: Say what?

JOE: As tha'd go, an' he could do what he liked?   15

MINNIE: I've said many things.

MRS GASCOYNE: So that was how it stood!—Tha'rt a fool, our Luther. If ter ta'es a woman at 'er word, well, tha deserves what ter gets.

LUTHER: What am I to do, might I ax?   20

MRS GASCOYNE: Nay, that thy wits should tell thee.—Wheer hast bin these two days.

LUTHER: I walked ower wi' Jim Horrocks ter their Annie's i' Mansfield.

MRS GASCOYNE: I'm sure *she*'d got enough to do, without two men   25
planting themselves on her.—An' how did ter get back?

LUTHER: Walked!

MRS GASCOYNE: Trapsein' thy shoe-leather off thee feet, walkin' twenty miles. Hast had thy dinner?

JOE: We've both 'ad free dinners at th' Methodist chapel.   30

LUTHER: I met Tom Haseldine i' th' 'Badger Box', mother.

MRS GASCOYNE: Oh ay! Wide-mouthed as iver, I reckon.

JOE: Just same. But what dost think, mother? It's leaked out as Frazer's got a lot o' chaps to go tomorrer mornin', ter see after th' roads, an' a' that.   35

MRS GASCOYNE: Th' roads wants keepin' safe, dunna they?

JOE: Yi—but if th' mesters wunna ha'e th' union men, let 'em do it theirselves.

MRS GASCOYNE: Tha talks like a fool.

LUTHER: What right ha' they ter get a lot of scrawdrags an'   40

blacklegs in ter do our work? A' th' pit maun fa' in, if they
wunna settle it fair wi' us.

JOE: Them workins is ours, an' th' mesters'. If th' mesters wunna
treat us fair, then they mun keep 'em right theirselves. They
non goin' ter ha'e no third body in.

MINNIE: But even when it's settled, how are you going back, if the
roof has come in, and the roads are gone?

JOE: Tha mun ax th' mesters that. If we canna go back ter th' rotten
owd pits no more, we mun look elsewhere. An th' mesters can
sit atop o' their pits an' stroke 'em.

LUTHER *(to* MINNIE*)*: If I got a woman in to do th' housework as
tha wunna do for me, tha'd sit smilin, shouldn't ter?

MINNIE: She could do as she liked.

LUTHER: All right. Then mother, 'appen tha'lt boss this house. She
run off ter Manchester, an' left me ter starve. So 'appen tha'lt
come an' do for me.

MRS GASCOYNE: Nay—if ter wants owt tha mun come ter *me*.

JOE: That's right. Dunna thee play blackleg i' this establishment.

MRS GASCOYNE: I s'll mind my own business.

JOE *(to* MINNIE*)*: Now does *thee* think it right, Minnie, as th'
mesters should get a lot o' crawlin' buggers in ter keep their pits
i' order, when th' keepin' o' them pits i' order belongs by right
to us.

MINNIE: It belongs to whosoever the masters pay to do it.

LUTHER: A' right. Then it belongs to me to ha'e any woman in ter
do for me, as I'n a mind. Tha's gone on strike, so I ha'e th' right
ter get anybody else.

MINNIE: When have I gone on strike? I have always done your
housework.

LUTHER: Housework—yi. But we dunna on'y keep th' roof from
comin' in. We *get* as well.—An' even th' housework tha went on
strike wi'. Tha skidaddled off ter Manchester, an' left me to't.

MINNIE: I went on business.

LUTHER: An' we've com'n out on strike 'on business'.

MINNIE: You've not, it's a game.

LUTHER: An' th' mesters 'll ta'e us back when they're ready, or
when they're forced to. An' same wi' thee by me.

MINNIE: Oh!

JOE: We got it fr' Tom Rooks—'e wor goin' ter turn 'em down.* At
four tomorrer mornin, there's ower twenty men goin' down.

MRS GASCOYNE: What a lot of fools men are! As if th' pits didn't
   need ter be kep' tidy, ready for you to go back to 'm.
JOE: They'll be kep' tidy by us then, an' when we'n a mind—an' by
   nobody else.
MRS GASCOYNE: Tha talks very high an' mighty. That's because I   5
   ha'e th' feedin' on thee.
JOE: You put it like our Luther says then. He stands for t'mesters,
   an' Minnie stands for t'men—cos 'er's gone on strike.—Now
   becos she's went ter Manchester, had he got ony right ter ha'e
   Lizzie Charley in for a couple o' nights an' days.   10
MRS GASCOYNE: Tha talks like a fool.
JOE: I dunna.
MINNIE: He's welcome to Lizzie Charley.
JOE: All right—she's a nice gel. We'll ax 'er to come in an' manage
   th' ouse—he can pay 'er.   15
MINNIE: What with?
JOE: Niver you mind. Should ter like it?
MINNIE: He can do just as he likes.
JOE: Then should I fetch her?—should I Luther?
LUTHER: If ter's a mind.   20
JOE: Should I then, Minnie?
MINNIE: If he wants her.
LUTHER: I want somebody ter look after me.
JOE: Right tha art. *(Puts his cap on.)* I'll say as Minnie canna look
   after th' house, will 'er come. That it?   25
LUTHER: Ah.
MRS GASCOYNE: Dunna be a fool. Tha's had a can or two.
JOE: Well—'er'll be glad o' the job.
MRS GASCOYNE: You'd better stop him one of you.
LUTHER: I want somebody ter look after me—an' tha wunna—   30
MRS GASCOYNE: Eh dear o' me!—Dunna thee be a fool our Joe.
   (Exit JOE.) What wor this job about goin' ter Manchester?
LUTHER: She said she wouldna live wi' me, an' so 'er went.—I
   thought 'er'd gone for good.
MINNIE: You didn't—you *knew*—   35
LUTHER: I knowed what tha'd towd me—as tha'd live wi' me no
   longer. Tha's come back o' thy own accord.
MINNIE: I never said I shouldn't come back.
LUTHER: Tha said as tha wouldna live wi' me. An' tha *didna*,
   neither—not for—   40

MRS GASCOYNE: Well Minnie—you've brought it on your own head. You put him off, an' you put him off, as if 'e was of no account, an' then all of a sudden you invited him to marry you—

5　MINNIE: Put him off! He didn't need much putting off. He never came any faster than a snail.

MRS GASCOYNE: Twice to my knowledge he axed thee—an' what can a man do more?

MINNIE: Yes, what! A gramophone in breeches could do as much.

10　MRS GASCOYNE: Oh indeed! What ailed him was, he wor in collier's britches, i'stead o' a stool-arsed Jack's.

MINNIE: No—what ailed him was that *you* kept him like a kid hanging on to you.

MRS GASCOYNE: An' tha bit thy own nose off, when ter said him
15　nay. For had ter married him at twenty three, there'd ha' been none of this trouble.

MINNIE: And why didn't I? Why didn't I? Because he came in his half-hearted 'I will if you like' fashion, and I despised him, yes I did.

20　MRS GASCOYNE: And who are *you* to be despising him, I should like to know.

MINNIE: I'm a woman, and that's enough. But I know now, it was your fault. *You* held him, and persuaded him that what he wanted was *you*. You kept him, like a child. You even gave him
25　what money he wanted, like a child. He never roughed it—he never faced out anything. You did all that for him.

MRS GASCOYNE: And what if I did! If you made as good a wife to him as I made a mother, you'd do.

MINNIE: Should I?—You didn't care what women your sons went
30　with, so long as they didn't *love* them. What do you care really about this affair of Bertha Purdy. You don't. All you cared about was to keep your sons for yourself. You kept the solid meal, and the orts and slarts any other woman could have. But I tell you, I'm *not* for having the orts and slarts, and your leavings from
35　your sons. I'll have a man, or nothing, I will.

MRS GASCOYNE: It's rare to be some folks, ter pick and choose.

MINNIE: I can't pick and choose, no. But what I won't have I won't have, and that is all.

MRS GASCOYNE *(to* LUTHER*)*: Have I ever kept thee from doin' as
40　tha wanted? Have I iver marded and coddled thee?

LUTHER: Tha hasna, beguy!

MINNIE: No, you haven't, perhaps, not by the looks of things. But you've bossed him. You've decided everything for him, really. He's depended on you as much when he was thirty as when he was three. You told him what to do, and he did it. 5

MRS GASCOYNE: My word I've never known all he did.

MINNIE: You have—everything that mattered. You maybe didn't know it was Bertha Purdy, but you knew it was some woman like her, and what did you care? *She* had the orts and slarts, you kept your son. And you want to keep him, even now. Yes—and 10 you do keep him.

MRS GASCOYNE: We're learnin' a thing or two, Luther.

LUTHER: Ah. *(Enter* JOE.*)*

MINNIE: Yes! What did *you* care about the woman who would have to take your sons after you? Nothing! You left her with just the 15 slarts of a man. Yes.

MRS GASCOYNE: Indeed! I canna see as you're so badly off. You've got a husband as doesn't drink, as waits on you hand and foot, as gives you a free hand in everything. It's you as doesn't know when you're well off, madam. 20

MINNIE: I'd rather have had a husband who knocked me about, than a husband who was good to me because he belonged to his mother. He doesn't and can't *really* care for me. You stand before him. His *real* caring goes to *you*. Me he only wants sometimes. 25

JOE: She'll be in in a minute.

MRS GASCOYNE: Tha'rt the biggest fool an' jackanapes, our Joe, as iver God made.

MINNIE: If she crosses that doorstep, then I go for good.

MRS GASCOYNE *(bursting into fury—to* JOE*)*: Tha see what thy 30 bobby interferin' has done.

JOE: Nay—that's how it stood.

MRS GASCOYNE: Tha mun go an' stop her our Luther. Tell 'er it wor our Joe's foolery. An' look sharp.

LUTHER: What should *I* go for. *(Exit—furious.)* 35

MINNIE: You see—you see! His mother's word is law to him. He'd *do* what I told him, but his *feel* would be for you. He's got no *feeling* for me. You keep all that.

MRS GASCOYNE: You talk like a jealous woman.

MINNIE: I do!—And for that matter, why doesn't Joe marry either? 40

Because you keep him too. You know, in spite of his bluster, he cares more for your little finger than he does for all the women in the world—or ever will. And it's wrong—it's wrong. How is a woman ever to have a husband, when the men all belong to their mothers. It's wrong.

MRS GASCOYNE: Oh indeed!—is it? You know, don't you. You know everything.

MINNIE: I know this because I've suffered from it. Your elder sons you let go, and they *are* husbands. But your young sons you've kept. And Luther is your son, and the man that lives with me. But first, he's your son. And Joe never ought to marry, for he'd break a woman's heart.

MRS GASCOYNE: Tha hears, lad! We're bein' told off.

JOE: Ah, I hear. An' what's more, it's true mother.

MINNIE: It is—it is. He only likes playing round me and getting some pleasure out of teasing me, because he knows I'm safely married to Luther, and can never look to *him* to marry me and belong to me. He's safe, so he likes me. If I were single, he'd be frightened to death of me.

JOE: Happen I should.

MRS GASCOYNE: Tha'rt a fool.

MINNIE: And that's what you've done to me—that's my life spoiled—spoiled—ay, worse than if I'd had a drunken husband that knocked me about. For it's dead.

MRS GASCOYNE: Tha'rt shoutin' because nowt ails thee—that's what tha art.

JOE: Nay mother—tha knows it's right. Tha knows tha's got me—an' 'll ha'e me till ter dies—an' after that—yi!

MRS GASCOYNE: Tha talks like a fool.

JOE: An' sometimes, mother, I wish I wor dead, I do.

MINNIE: You see, you see! You see what you've done to them. It's strong women like you, who were too much for their husbands —ah!—

JOE: Tha knows I couldna leave thee, mother—tha knows I couldna. An' me, a young man, belongs to thy owd age. An' there's nowheer for me to go, mother. For tha'rt gettin' nearer to death, an' yet I canna leave thee to go my own road.—An' I wish, yi often, as I wor dead.

MRS GASCOYNE: Dunna, lad—dunna let 'er put these ideas i' thy head.

JOE: An' I can but fritter my days away. There's no goin' forrard for me—.

MRS GASCOYNE: Nay lad, nay—what lad's better off than thee, dost reckon?

JOE: If I went t'r Australia, th' best part on me wouldna go wi' me. 5

MRS GASCOYNE: Tha wunna go t'r Australia.

JOE: If I went, I should be a husk of a man. I'm allers a husk of a man, mother. There's nowt solid about me. The' isna.

MRS GASCOYNE: Whativer dost mean? You've a' set on me at once. 10

JOE: I'm nowt, mother, an' I count for nowt. Yi, an' I know it.

MRS GASCOYNE: Tha does. Tha sounds as if tha counts for nowt, as a rule, doesn't ter?

JOE: There's not much of a man about me. Tother chaps is more of fools, but they more of men an' a'—an' they know it. 15

MRS GASCOYNE: That's thy fault.

JOE: Yi—an' will be—ter th' end o' th' chapter.

(Enter LUTHER.)

MINNIE: Did you tell her?

LUTHER: Yes. 20

MINNIE: We'll have some tea, should we?

JOE: Ay—let's. For it's bin dry work. *(She sets the kettle on.)*

MRS GASCOYNE: I mun be goin'.

MINNIE: Wait and have a cup of tea. I brought a cake.

JOE: But we non goin' ter ha'e it, are we, Luther, these 'ere blacklegs 25
goin' down interferin'.

LUTHER: We arena.

MRS GASCOYNE: But how are you going to stop them?

JOE: We s'll manage it, one road or t'other.

MRS GASCOYNE: You'll non go gettin' yourselves into trouble. 30

LUTHER: We in trouble enow.

MINNIE: If you'd have had Lizzie Charley in, what should you have paid her with?

LUTHER: We should ha' found the money somewhere.

MINNIE: Do you know what I had to keep house on this week, 35
mother?

MRS GASCOYNE: Not much, sin' there wor nowt but ten shillin' strike pay.

MINNIE: He gave me five shillings.

LUTHER: Tha could ha' had what things ter wanted on strap. 40

MINNIE: No—but why should you keep to drink on, as much as you give me to keep house on. Five shillings!

JOE: Five bob's non a whackin' sight o' pocket money for a man's week.

5 MINNIE: It is if he earns nothing.—It was that as finished me off.

JOE: Well, *tha* niver ne'd go short—tha can let *him*.

MINNIE: I knew that was what *he* thought. But if he wouldn't have my money for one thing, he wasn't going to for another.

MRS GASCOYNE: Why, what wouldn't he have it for?

10 MINNIE: He wouldn't have that forty pounds, when I almost went on my knees to beg and beseech of him to have it.

LUTHER: Tha did. Tha throwed it at me as if I wor a beggar as stank.

MINNIE: And you wouldn't have it when I asked you.

15 LUTHER: No—an' I wouldna ha'e it now.

MINNIE: You can't.

LUTHER: I dunna want it.

MINNIE: And if you don't find money to keep the house on, we shall both of us starve. For you've got to keep me. And I've got

20 no money of my own now.

LUTHER: Why, what dost mean?

MINNIE: I mean what I say.

MRS GASCOYNE: Why what?

MINNIE: I was sick of having it between us. It was but a hundred

25 and twenty. So I went to Manchester and spent it.

MRS GASCOYNE: Tha's bin an' spent a hundred and twenty pound i' four days?

MINNIE: Yes, I have.

MRS GASCOYNE: Whativer are we comin' to!

30 JOE: That wor a stroke worth two. Tell us what tha bought.

MINNIE: I bought myself a ring for one thing. I thought if I ever had any children, and they asked me where was my engagement ring, I should have to show them something, for their father's sake. Do you like it? *(Holds her hand out to* JOE.*)*

35 JOE: My word, but that's a bobby-dazzler. Look mother.

MRS GASCOYNE: Hm! *(*JOE *takes the ring off.)*

JOE: My word but that's a diamond if you like. How much did it cost?

MINNIE: Thirty pounds. I've got the bill in my pocket.

40 MRS GASCOYNE: I only hope you'll niver come to want some day.

MINNIE: Luther must see to that.

JOE: And what else did ter buy.

MINNIE: I'll show you. *(Gets her bag—unlocks it—takes out three prints.)*

JOE: I dunna reckon much ter these.   5

MRS GASCOYNE: Nor me neither. An' how much has ter gen for them apiece?

MINNIE: That was twenty-five pounds. They're beautiful prints.

MRS GASCOYNE: I dunna believe a word tha says.

MINNIE: I'll show you the bill. My master's a collector, and he   10
picked them for me. He says they're well worth the money. And I like them.

MRS GASCOYNE: Well I niver seed such a job in my life. T-t-t-t. Well, a' I can say is, I hope tha'll never come ter want. Throwin' good money i' th' gutter like this. Nay—I feel fair bad. Nay!   15
T-t-t-t-t! Such tricks! And such bits o' dirty paper!

JOE: I'd rether ha'e th' Co-op almanack.*

MRS GASCOYNE: So would I any day! What dost say to't, our Luther?

LUTHER: Er does as 'er likes.   20

MINNIE: I had a lovely time with Mr Westlake, choosing them at the dealers'. He *is* clever.

MRS GASCOYNE: Tha towd him tha wanted to get rid o' thy money, did ter.

MINNIE: No—I said I wanted some pictures for the parlour, and   25
asked him if he'd help me choose.

MRS GASCOYNE: Good money thrown away. Maybe the very bread of your children—

MINNIE: Nay, that's Luther's duty to provide.

MRS GASCOYNE: Well, a' I can say is, I hope you may never come   30
to want.—If our Luther died—

MINNIE: I should go back to work.

MRS GASCOYNE: But what if tha'd three or four children?

MINNIE: A hundred and twenty pounds wouldn't make much odds then.   35

MRS GASCOYNE: Well, a' I can say, I hope tha'lt niver live ter rue the day.

JOE: What dost think on 'er Luther?

LUTHER: Nay, she's done as she liked with her own.*

MINNIE *(emptying her purse in her lap)*: I've got just seventeen   40

shillings. You drew your strike pay yesterday. How much have
you got of that Luther?

LUTHER: Three bob.

MINNIE: And do you want to keep it?

5   LUTHER: Ah.

MINNIE: Very well. I shall spend this seventeen shillings till it's
gone, and then we shall have to live on soup tickets.

MRS GASCOYNE: I'll back my life.

JOE: And who'll fetch the soup?

10   MINNIE: Oh, I shall. I've been thinking, that big jug will do nicely.
I'm in the same boat as other men's* wives now, and so I must
do the same.

JOE: They'll gi'e you strap at West's.*

MINNIE: I'm not going to run up bills, no, I'm not.—I'll go to the
15   free teas, and fetch soup, an' with ten shillings a week, we shall
manage.

MRS GASCOYNE: Well, that's one road, lass.

MINNIE: It's the only one.—And now, if he can provide, he
must—and if he can't, he must tell me so, and I'll go back into
20   service, and not be a burden to him.

MRS GASCOYNE: High and mighty, high and mighty! We'll see, my
lass, we'll see.

MINNIE: That's all we can do.

MRS GASCOYNE: Tha doesna care how he takes it.

25   MINNIE: The prints belong to both of us. *(Hands them to* LUTHER.*)*
You haven't said if you like them yet.

LUTHER *(taking them, suddenly rams them in the fire)*: Tha can go to
Hell.

MINNIE *(with a cry)*: Ah—that's my ninety pounds gone. *(Tries to
30   snatch them out.)*

MRS GASCOYNE *(beginning to cry)*: Come Joe, let's go, let's go my
lad. I've seen as much this day as ever my eyes want to see.
Let's go, my lad. *(Gets up, beginning to tie on her bonnet.)*

MINNIE *(white and intense—to* LUTHER*)*: Should you like to throw
35   my ring after them? It's all I've got left. *(She holds out her
hand—he flings it from him.)*

LUTHER: Yi, what do I care what I do— *(clenching his fists as if he
would strike her)* —what do I—what do I—

MRS GASCOYNE *(putting on her shawl)*: A day's work—a day's work!

Ninety pound! Nay-nay, oh nay-nay, oh nay-nay! Let's go, Joe,
my lad. Eh, our Luther, our Luther! Let's go, Joe—come.

JOE: Ah, I'll come mother.

MRS GASCOYNE: Luther!

LUTHER: What? 5

MRS GASCOYNE: It's a day's work, it is, wi' thee. Eh dear—Come,
let's go, Joe. Let's go whoam.

LUTHER: An' I'll go.

MRS GASCOYNE: Dunna thee do nowt as ter'll repent of, Luther—
dunna thee. It's thy mother axes thee.—Come Joe. 10

(Exit, followed by JOE—LUTHER *stands with face averted from his
wife—mutters something—reaches for his cap—goes out.* MINNIE *stands
with her hand on the mantel-piece.)*

(Curtain)

Act IV.

Scene: The same.
Time: The following morning—about 5 a.m.—A candle is burning.
Personae: MINNIE *sits by the fire in a dressing-gown—she is weeping—a*
knock, and MRS GASCOYNE'S *voice—*MINNIE *goes to open the door—re-*
enter with her mother-in-law, the latter with a big brown shawl over her
head.

MRS GASCOYNE: Is Luther a-whoam?

MINNIE: No—he's not been in all night.

MRS GASCOYNE: T-t-t-t! Now whereiver can they be. Joe's not in
neither.

MINNIE: Isn't he.

MRS GASCOYNE: No. He said he might be late, so I went to bed,
and slept a bit uneasy-like till about four aclock. Then I wakes
up a' of a sudden, an' says 'I'm by mysen i' th' house!' It gave
me such a turn I daresn't shout. So I gets me up an' goes ter his
room, an' he'd niver bin i' bed a' night. Well, I went down, but
no signs nowhere. An' 'im wi' a brokken arm. An' I listened an'
I listened—an' then methinks I heered a gun go off. I felt as if I
should die if I stopped by mysen another minute. So I on's wi'
my shawl an' nips down here. There's not a soul astir nowheer.
I a'most dropped when I seed your light. Hasn't Luther bin in
a' night, dost say?

MINNIE: He went out with you, and he never came in again. I went
to bed, thinking perhaps he'd be sleeping on the sofa. And then
I came down and he wasn't here.

MRS GASCOYNE: Well, I've seen nowt of him, for he never come up
to our house.—Now I wonder what's afoot wi' th' silly fools.

MINNIE: I thought he'd gone and left me.

MRS GASCOYNE: It's more like some o' this strike work. When I
heered that gun, I said 'Theer goes one o' my lads.'

MINNIE: You don't think they're killed.

MRS GASCOYNE: Heaven only knows what they are.—But I niver
thought he'd ha' served me this trick—left me by myself
without telling me, and gone cutting off a' th' night through
—an' him wi' a brokken arm.

MINNIE: Where do you think they've gone?

MRS GASCOYNE: The Lord above alone knows—but I's warrant it's

one o' these riotin' tricks—stopping them blacklegs as wor goin'
down to see to th' roads.

MINNIE: Do you think?

MRS GASCOYNE: I'll back anything. For I heered th' winding
engines plain as anything. Hark—! *(They listen.)*

MINNIE: I believe I can hear them.

MRS GASCOYNE: Th' ingines!

MINNIE: Yes.

MRS GASCOYNE: They're winding something down.—Eh dear,
what a dead world it seems, wi' none o' th' pits chuffin', an' no
steam wavin' by day, an' no lights shinin' by night.—You may
back your life there was a gang of 'em going to stop that lot of
blacklegs. And there'd be soldiers for a certainty. If I didn't hear
a shot, I heered summat much like one.

MINNIE: But they'd never shoot them, would they?

MRS GASCOYNE: Haven't they shot men up an' down th' country?
Didn't I know them lads was pining to go an' be shot at. I did.
Methinks when I heard that gun 'They'd never rest till this had
happened.'

MINNIE: But they're not shot, mother. You exaggerate.

MRS GASCOYNE: I niver said they wor.—But if anything happens
to a man, my lass, you may back your life, nine cases out o' ten,
it's a spite on th' women.

MINNIE: Oh what a thing to say—why there are accidents.

MRS GASCOYNE: Yes, an' men verily gets *accidents* to pay us out, I
do believe. They get huffed up, they bend down their faces, and
they say to theirselves 'Now I'll get myself hurt, an' she'll be
sorry'—else 'Now I'll get myself killed, an' she'll ha'e nobody to
sleep wi' 'er, an' nobody to nag at.' Oh my lass, I've had a
husband an' six sons. Children they are, these men, but my
word, they're revengeful children. Children men is a' the days
o' their lives. But they're master of us women when their
dander's up, an' they pay us back double an' treble—they do
—an' you mun allers expect it.

MINNIE: But if they went to stop the blacklegs, they wouldn't be
doing it to spite us.

MRS GASCOYNE: Wouldn't they? Yi but they would. My lads 'ud
do it to spite me, an' our Luther 'ud do it to spite thee.
Yes—and it's trew. For they'd run theirselves into danger and

lick their lips for joy, thinking, if I'm killed, then *she* maun lay me out. Yi—I seed it in our mester. He got killed a' pit. An' when I laid him out, his face wor that grim, an' his body that stiff, an' it said as plain as plain 'Now then, you've done for me.' For it's risky work, handlin' men, my lass, an' niver thee pray for sons.—Not but what daughters is any good. Th' world is made o' men for me, lass—there's only the men for me. An' tha'rt similar. An' so, tha'lt reap trouble by the peck, an' sorrow by the bushel. For when a woman builds her life on men, either husband or sons, she builds on summat as sooner or later brings the house down crash on her head—yi, she does.

MINNIE: But it depends how and what she builds.

MRS GASCOYNE: It depends, it depends. An' tha thinks tha can steer clear o' what I've done. An' perhaps tha can. But steer clear the whole length o' th' road, tha canna, an' tha'lt see.—Nay, a childt is a troublesome pleasure to a woman, but a man's a trouble pure an' simple.

MINNIE: I'm sure it depends what you make of him.

MRS GASCOYNE: Maybe—maybe. But I've allers tried to do my best, i' spite o' what tha said against me this afternoon—

MINNIE: I didn't mean it—I was in a rage.

MRS GASCOYNE: Yi, tha meant it plain enow. But I've tried an' tried my best for my lads, I have.—An' this is what owd age brings me—wi' 'em—

MINNIE: Nay mother—nay. See how fond they are of you.

MRS GASCOYNE: Yi—an' they go now i' their mischief, yea, tryin' to get killed, to spite me. Yi!

MINNIE: Nay—nay—

MRS GASCOYNE: It's true. An' tha can ha'e Luther. Tha'lt get him, an' tha can ha'e him—

MINNIE: Do you think I shall?

MRS GASCOYNE: I can see. Tha'lt get him—but tha'lt get sorrow wi' 'im, an' wi' th' sons tha has. See if tha doesna.

MINNIE: But I don't care. Only don't keep him from me. It leaves me so—with nothing—not even trouble.

MRS GASCOYNE: He'll come to thee—an' he'll think no more o' me as is his mother than he will o' that proker—

MINNIE: Oh no—oh no—

MRS GASCOYNE: Yi—I know well—an' then that other—

(There is a silence—the two women listening.)

MINNIE: If they'd been hurt we should ha' known by now.

MRS GASCOYNE: Happen we should. If they come, they'll come together—an' they'll come to this house first—*(A silence, MINNIE starts.)* Did ter hear owt?

MINNIE: Somebody got over the stile.   5

MRS GASCOYNE *(listening)*: Yi.

MINNIE *(listening)*: It *is* somebody.

MRS GASCOYNE: I' t'street.

MINNIE *(starting up)*: Yes.

MRS GASCOYNE: Comin'?—It's Luther. *(She goes to the door.)* An'   10
it's on'y Luther. *(Both women stand, the mother nearer the door. The door opens—a slight sluther—enter LUTHER, with blood on his face—rather shaky and dishevelled.)* My boy—my boy!

LUTHER: Mother! *(He goes blindly.)* Where's Minnie?

MINNIE *(with a cry)*: Oh!   15

MRS GASCOYNE: Wheer's Joe—wheer's our Joe?

LUTHER *(to MINNIE—queer, stunned, almost polite)*: It worn't 'cause I wor mad wi' thee I didna come whoam—

MRS GASCOYNE *(clenching him sternly)*: Where's Joe?

LUTHER: He's gone up street—he thought tha might ha' wakken-   20
ed—

MRS GASCOYNE: Wakkened enow!* *(Exit.)*

MINNIE: Oh, what have you done?

LUTHER: We'd promised not to tell nobody—else I should. We stopped them blacklegs—leastways—but it worn't because I—I   25
(He stops to think.) I wor mad wi' thee, as I didna come whoam—

MINNIE: What have you done to your head?

LUTHER: It wor a stone or summat catched it. It's gen me a head ache. Tha mun—tha mun tie a rag round it—if ter will. *(He   30
sways as he takes his cap off. She catches him in her arms. He leans on her as if he were tipsy.)* —Minnie!

MINNIE: My love—my love!

LUTHER: Minnie—I want thee ter ma'e what tha can o' me. *(He sounds almost sleepy.)*   35

MINNIE *(crying)*: My love—my love—

LUTHER: I know what tha says is true—

MINNIE: No my love—it isn't—it isn't—

LUTHER: But if ter'lt ma'e what ter can o' me—an' then if ter has a childt—tha'lt happen ha'e enow.   40

MINNIE: No—no—it's you. It's you I want. It's you.

LUTHER: But tha's allers had me.

MINNIE: No—never—and it hurt so.

LUTHER: I thowt tha despised me.

5 MINNIE: Ah—my love!

LUTHER: Dunna say I'm mean, to me—an' got no go—

MINNIE: I only said it because you wouldn't let me love you.

LUTHER: Tha didna love me.

MINNIE: Ha!—it was *you*.

10 LUTHER: Yi. *(He looses himself and sits down heavily.)* I'll ta'e my boots off. *(He bends forward.)*

MINNIE: Let me do them. *(He sits up again.)*

LUTHER: It's started bleedin'. I'll do 'em i' ha'ef a minute.

MINNIE: No—trust me—trust yourself to me. Let me have you

15 now for my own. *(She begins to undo his boots.)*

LUTHER: Dost want me? *(She kisses his hands.)*

MINNIE: Oh my love! *(She takes him in her arms.)*
(He suddenly begins to cry.)

(Curtain)

PREFACE TO
TOUCH AND GO

Preface

A nice phrase: "A People's Theatre."* But what about it? There's no such thing in existence as a People's Theatre: or even on the way to existence, as far as we can tell. The name is chosen, the baby isn't even begotten: nay, the would-be parents aren't married, nor yet courting.

A People's Theatre. Note the indefinite article. It isn't The People's Theatre, but A People's Theatre. Not The people: il popolo, le peuple, das Volk,* this monster is the same the world over: Plebs, the proletariat. Not the theatre of Plebs, the proletariat, but the theatre of A People. What people? Quel peuple donc?*—A People's Theatre. Translate it into French for yourself.

A People's Theatre. Since we can't produce it, let us deduce it. Major premiss: the seats are cheap. Minor premiss: the plays are good. Conclusion: A People's Theatre. How much will you give me for my syllogism? Not a slap in the eye, I hope.

We stick to our guns. The seats are cheap. That has a nasty proletarian look about it. But appearances are deceptive. The proletariat isn't poor. Everybody is poor except Capital and Labour. Between these upper and nether millstones great numbers of decent people are squeezed.

The seats are cheap: in decency's name. Nobody wants to swank, to sit in the front of a box like a geranium on a window-sill—"the cynosure of many eyes."* Nobody wants to profiteer. We all feel that it is as humiliating to pay high prices as to charge them. No man consents in his heart to pay high prices unless he feels that what he pays with his right hand he will get back with his left, either out of the pocket of a man who isn't looking, or out of the envy of the poor neighbour who *is* looking, but can't afford the figure. The seats are cheap. Why should A People, fabulous and lofty giraffe, want to charge or to pay high prices? If it were *the people* now—. But it isn't. It isn't Plebs, the proletariat. The seats are cheap.

The plays are good. Pah!—this has a canting smell. Any play is good to the man who likes to look at it. And at that rate Chu Chin

Chow* is extra-super-good. What about your *good* plays? Whose good? Pfui—to your goodness!

That minor premiss is a bad egg: it will hatch no bird. Good plays? You might as well say mimsy bomtittle* plays, you'd be saying
5   as much. The plays are—don't say good or you'll be beaten. The plays—the plays of A People's Theatre are—oh heaven, what are they?—not popular nor populous nor plebeian nor proletarian nor folk nor parish plays. None of that adjectival spawn.

The only clue-word is People's, for all that. A People's ——.
10   Chaste word, it will bring forth no adjective. The plays of A People's Theatre are People's plays. The plays of A People's Theatre are plays about people.

It doesn't look much, at first sight. After all—people! Yes, people! Not *the people* i.e. Plebs, nor yet the Upper Ten. People. Neither
15   Piccoli nor Grandi* in our republic. People.

People, ah God! Not mannequins. Not lords nor proletariats nor bishops nor husbands nor co-respondents nor virgins nor adulteresses nor uncles nor noses. Not even white rabbits nor presidents. People.
20   Men who are somebody, not men who are something. Men who *happen* to be bishops or co-respondents, women who happen to be chaste, just as they happen to freckle, because it's one of their innumerable odd qualities. Even men who happen, by the way, to have long noses. But not noses on two legs, not burly pairs of gaiters,
25   stuffed and voluble, not white meringues of chastity, not incarnations of co-respondence. Not proletariats, petitioners, presidents, noses, bits of fluff. Heavens, what an assortment of bits! And aren't we sick of them!

People, I say. And after all, it's saying something. It's harder to
30   be a human being, than to be a president or a bit of fluff. You can be a president, or a bit of fluff, or even a nose, by clock-work. Given a rôle, a *part*, you can play it by clockwork. But you can't have a clockwork human being.

We're dead sick of parts. It's no use your protesting that there is a
35   man behind the nose. We can't see him, and he can't see himself. Nothing but nose. Neither can you make us believe there is a man inside the gaiters. He's never showed his head yet.

It may be, in real life, the gaiters wear the man, as the nose wears Cyrano. It may be Sir Auckland Geddes and Mr. J. H. Thomas* are only clippings from the illustrated press. It may be that a miner is a complicated machine for cutting coal and voting on a ballot-paper.

It* may be that coal-owners are like the *petit bleu* arrangement, a system of vacuum tubes for whooshing Bradburys* about from one to the other.

It may be that everybody delights in bits, in parts, that the public insists on noses, gaiters, white rabbits, bits of fluff, automata and jew-jaws.* If they do, then let 'em. Chu Chin Chow for ever.

In spite of them all: A People's Theatre. A People's Theatre shows men, and not parts. Not bits, nor bundles of bits. A whole bunch of rôles tied into one won't make an individual. Though gaiters perish, we will have men.

Although most miners may be pick-cum shovel cum ballot implements, and no more, still, among miners there must be two or three living individuals. The same among the masters. The majority are suction-tubes for Bradburys. But in this Sodom of Industrialism there are surely ten men, all told.—My poor little withered grain of mustard seed,* I am half afraid to take you across to the seed-testing department!—

And if there are ten men, there is a People's Theatre.

How many tragic situations did Goethe say were possible? Something like thirty-two.* Which seems a lot. Anyhow, granted that men are men still, that not all of them are bits, parts, machine-sections, then we have added another tragic possibility to the list: the Strike situation. As yet no one tackles this situation. It is a sort of Medusa head, which turns us,* not to stone, but to sloppy treacle. Mr Galsworthy had a peep, and sank down towards bathos.*

Granted that men are men still, Labour v. Capitalism is a tragic struggle. If men are no more than implements, it is non-tragic and merely disastrous. In tragedy the man is more than his part. Hamlet is more than Prince of Denmark, Macbeth is more than murderer of Duncan. The man is caught in the wheels of his part, his fate, he may be torn asunder. He may be killed, but the resistant, integral soul in him is not destroyed. He goes through, though he dies. He goes through with his fate, though death swallows him. And it is in this facing of fate, this going right through with it, that tragedy lies. Tragedy is not disaster. It is a disaster when a cart-wheel goes over a frog, but it is not a tragedy. Tragedy is the working out of some immediate* passional problem, within the soul of man. If this passional problem, and this working out be absent, then no disaster is a tragedy, not the hugest: not the death of ten million men. It is only a cart-wheel going over a frog. There must be a supreme *struggle*.

In Shakespeare's time it was the people versus king storm that was brewing. Majesty was about to have its head off. Come what might, Hamlet and Macbeth and Goneril and Regan had to see the business through.

Now a new wind is getting up. We call it Labour versus Capitalism. We say it is a mere material struggle, a money-grabbing affair. But this is only one aspect of it. In so far as men are merely mechanical, the struggle is one which, though it may bring disaster and death to millions, is no more than accident, an accidental collision of forces. But in so far as men are men, the situation is tragic. It is not really the bone we are fighting for. We are fighting to have somebody's head off. The conflict is in pure, passional antagonism, turning upon the poles of belief. Majesty was only *hors d'œuvres* to this tragic repast.

So, the strike situation has this dual aspect. First it is a mechanico-material struggle, two mechanical forces pulling asunder from the central object, the bone. All it can result in is the pulling asunder of the fabric of civilisation, and even of life, without any creative issue. It is no more than a frog under a cart-wheel. The mechanical forces, rolling on, roll over the body of life and squash it.

The second is the tragic aspect. According to this view, we see more than two dogs fighting for a bone, and life hopping under the Juggernaut wheel. The two dogs are making the bone a pretext for a fight with each other. That old bull-dog, the British capitalist, has got the bone in his teeth. That unsatisfied mongrel, Plebs, the proletariat, shivers with rage not so much at sight of the bone, as at sight of the great wrinkled jowl that holds it. There is the old dog, with his knowing look and his massive grip on the bone: and there is the insatiable mongrel, with his great splay paws. The one is all head and arrogance, the other all paws and grudge. The bone is only the pretext. A first condition of the being of bully is that he shall hate the prowling great paws of Plebs, whilst Plebs by inherent nature goes mad at the sight of bully's jowl. "Drop it!" cries Plebs. "Hands off!" growls bully. It is hands against head, the shambling, servile body in a rage of insurrection at last against the wrinkled, heavy head.

Labour not only wants his debt. He wants his pound of flesh. It is a quandary. In our heart of hearts we must admit the debt. We must admit that it is long overdue. But this last condition—! In vain we study our anatomy to see which part we can best spare.

Where is our Portia, to save us with a timely quibble? We've plenty of Portias. They've recited their heads off—"The quality of mercy is not strained." But the old Shylock⁎ of the proletariat persists. He pops up again, and says "All right, I can't have my pound of flesh with the blood. But then you can't keep my pound of flesh with your blood—you owe it me. It is your business to deliver the goods. Deliver it then—with or without blood—deliver it." Then Portia scratches her head, and thinks again.

What's the solution? There is no solution. But still, there is a choice. There's a choice between a mess and a tragedy. If Plebs and Bully hang on one to each end of the bone, and pull for grim life, they will at last tear the bone to atoms: in short, destroy the whole material substance of life, and so perish by accident, no better than a frog under the wheel of destiny. That may be a disaster, but it is only a mess for all that.

On the other hand, if they have a fight to fight they might really drop the bone. Instead of wrangling the bone to bits they might really go straight for one another. They are like hostile parties on board a ship, who both proceed to scuttle the ship so as to sink the other party. Down goes the ship, with all the bally lot on board. A few survivors swim and squeal among the bubbles—and then silence—

It is too much⁎ to suppose that the combatants will ever drop the obvious old bone. But it is not too much to imagine that some men might acknowledge the bone to be merely a pretext, another hollow *casus belli.*⁎ If we really could know what we were fighting for, if we could deeply believe in what we were fighting for, then the struggle might have dignity, beauty, satisfaction for us. If it were a profound struggle for something that was coming to life in us, a struggle that we were convinced would bring us to a new freedom, a new life, then it would be a creative activity, a creative activity in which death is a climax in the progression towards new being. And this is tragedy.

Therefore, if we could but comprehend, or feel the tragedy in the great Labour struggle, the intrinsic tragedy of having to pass through⁎ death to birth, our souls would still know some happiness, the very happiness of creative suffering. Instead of which we pile accident on accident, we tear the fabric of our existence fibre by

fibre, we confidently look forward to the time when the whole great
structure will come down on our heads. Yet after all that, when we
are squirming under the débris, we shall have no more faith or hope
or satisfaction than we have now. We shall crawl from under one cart-
wheel straight under another.

The essence of tragedy, which is creative crisis, is that a man
should go through with his fate, and not dodge it and go bumping
into an accident. And the whole business of life, at the great critical
periods of mankind, is that men should accept and be one with their
tragedy. Therefore we should open our hearts. For one thing, we
should have a People's Theatre. Perhaps it would help us in this hour
of confusion better than anything.

Hermitage. June 1919

TOUCH AND GO

GERALD BARLOW

MR BARLOW (*his father*)

OLIVER TURTON

JOB ARTHUR FREER *

WILLIE HOUGHTON *

ALFRED BREFFITT *

WILLIAM (*a butler*)

CLERKS, MINERS, ETC.

ANABEL WRATH

MRS HENRIETTA BARLOW

WINIFRED BARLOW *

EVA (*a maid*)

5

TOUCH AND GO[*]

Act I.

Scene 1.

Sunday morning—market-place of a large mining village in the Mid-lands—a man [WILLIE HOUGHTON] *addressing a small gang of colliers* 5
[including JOB ARTHUR FREER] *from the foot of a stumpy memorial obelisk—church bells heard*[*]—*church-goers passing along the outer pavements.*

WILLIE: What's the matter with you folks, as I've told you before,
and as I shall keep on telling you every now and again, though it 10
doesn't make a bit of difference, is that you've got no idea of
freedom whatsoever. I've lived in this blessed place for fifty
years, and I've never seen the spark of an idea, nor of any
response to an idea, come out of a single one of you, all the
time. I don't know what it is with colliers—whether it's spend- 15
ing so much time in the bowels of the earth—but they never
seem to be able to get their thoughts above their bellies. If
you've got plenty to eat and drink, and a bit over to keep the
Missis quiet, you're satisfied. I never saw such a satisfied
bloomin' lot in my life, as you Barlow and Walsalls men are, 20
really. Of course you can growse as well as anybody, and you do
growse. But you don't do anything else. You're stuck in a sort of
mud of contentment, and you feel yourselves sinking, but you
make no efforts to get out. You bleat a bit, like sheep in a bog—
but you like it, you know. You like sinking in—you don't have 25
to stand on your own feet then.

    I'll tell you what'll happen to you chaps. I'll give you a little
picture of what you'll be like, in the future.—Barlow and
Walsalls'll make a number of compounds, such as they keep
niggers in in South Africa,[*] and there you'll be kept. And every 30
one of you'll have a little brass collar round his neck, with a
number on it. You won't have names any more. And you'll go
from the compound to the pit, and from the pit back again to

the compound. You won't be allowed to go outside the gates, except at week-ends. They'll let you go home to your wives on Saturday nights, to stop over Sunday. But you'll have to be in again by half-past nine on Sunday night; and if you're late, you'll have your next week-end knocked off.—And there you'll be—and you'll be quite happy. They'll give you plenty to eat, and a can of beer a day,* and a bit of bacca—and they'll provide dominoes and skittles for you to play with. And you'll be the most contented set of men alive.—But you won't be men. You won't even be animals. You'll go from number one to number three thousand, a lot of numbered slaves—a new sort of slaves—

VOICE: An' wheer shall tha* be, Willie?

WILLIE: Oh, I shall be outside the palings, laughing at you.—I shall have to laugh, because it'll be your own faults. You'll have nobody but yourself to thank for it. You don't *want* to be men. You'd rather *not* be free—much rather. You're like those people spoken of in Shakespeare—"Oh how eager these men are to be slaves—"* I believe it's Shakespeare—or the Bible—one or the other—it mostly is—*

ANABEL *(she was passing to Church):** It was Tiberius.

WILLIE: Eh?

ANABEL: Tiberius said it.

WILLIE: Tiberius!—Oh did he! *(Laughs.)* Thanks! Well if Tiberius said it, there must be something in it.—And he only just missed being in the Bible, anyway. He was a day late, or they'd have had him in. "Oh, how eager these men are to be slaves."—It's evident the Romans deserved all they got from Tiberius—and you'll deserve all you get, every bit of it. But don't you bother, you'll get it. You won't be at the mercy of Tiberius, you'll be at the mercy of something a jolly sight worse. Tiberius took the skin off a few Romans, apparently. But you'll have the soul taken out of you—every one of you. And I'd rather lose my skin than my soul, any day.—But perhaps you wouldn't.

VOICE: What art ma'ein' for, Willie? Tha seems to say a lot, but tha goes round it. Tha'rt like a donkey on a gin. Tha gets ravelled.

WILLIE: Yes, that's just it. I am precisely like a donkey on a gin—a donkey that's trying to wind a lot of colliers up to the surface. There's many a donkey that's brought more colliers than you up to see daylight, by trotting round.—But do you want to know

what I'm making for! I can soon tell you that. You Barlow and
Walsalls men you haven't a soul to call your own. Barlow and
Walsalls have only to say to one of you, Come, and he cometh,
Go, and he goeth,☆ lie down and be kicked, and he lieth down,
and he *is* kicked—and serve him jolly well right.   5

VOICE: Ay—an' what about it? Tha's got a behind o' thy own,
hasn't ter?

WILLIE: Do you stand there and ask me what about it, and haven't
the sense to alter it. Couldn't you set up a proper government
tomorrow, if you liked? Couldn't you contrive that the pits   10
belonged to you,☆ instead of you belonging to the pits, like so
many old pit-ponies that stop down till they are blind, and take
to eating coal-slack for meadow-grass, not knowing the difference.—If only you'd learn to think, I'd respect you. As you are,
I can't, not if I try my hardest.—All you can think of is to ask   15
for another shilling a day. That's as far as your imagination
carries you. And perhaps you get seven-pence ha'penny:☆ but
pay for it with half-a-crown's worth of sweat. The masters
aren't fools—as you are. They'll give you two-thirds of what
you ask for, but they'll get five-thirds of it back again—and   20
they'll get it out of your flesh and blood, too, in jolly hard work.
Shylock wasn't in it, with them. He only wanted a pound of
flesh.☆ But you cheerfully give up a pound a week, each one of
you, and keep on giving it up.—But you don't seem to see these
things. You can't think beyond your dinners and your 'lowance.   25
You think if you can get another shilling a day you're set up.—
You make me tired, I tell you.

JOB ARTHUR: We think of others besides ourselves.

WILLIE: Hello, Job Arthur—are you there? I didn't recognise you
without your frock coat and silk hat—on the Sabbath.—What   30
was that you said? You think of something else, besides yourselves?—Oh ay—I'm glad to hear it.—Did you mean your own
importance?—*(A motor-car,* GERALD BARLOW *driving,* OLIVER
TURTON *with him, has pulled up.)*

JOB ARTHUR *(glancing at the car)*: No, I didn't.   35

WILLIE: Didn't you though?—Come, speak up, let us have it. The
more the merrier.—You were going to say something.

JOB ARTHUR: Nay, you were doing the talking.

WILLIE: Yes, so I was, till you interrupted, with a great idea on the
tip of your tongue. Come, spit it out. No matter if Mr Barlow   40

hears you. You know how sorry for you we feel, that you've always got to make your speeches twice—once to those above, and once to us here below.—I didn't mean the angels and the devils, but never mind—Speak up, Job Arthur—.

5 JOB ARTHUR: It's not everybody as has as much to say as you, Mr Houghton.

WILLIE: No, not in the open—that's a fact. Some folks says a great deal more, in semi-private. You were just going to explain to me, on behalf of the men, whom you so ably represent and so

10 wisely lead, Job Arthur—we won't say by the nose—you were just going to tell me—on behalf of the men, of course, not of the masters—that you think of others, besides yourself. Do you mind explaining *what* others?

JOB ARTHUR: Everybody's used to your talk, Mr Houghton, and

15 for that reason it doesn't make much impression. What I meant to say, in plain words, was that we have to think of what's best for everybody, not only for ourselves.

WILLIE: Oh, I see. What's best for everybody! I see! Well, for myself, I'm much obliged—there's nothing for us to do, gentle-

20 men, but for all of us to bow acknowledgements to Mr Job Arthur Freer, who so kindly has *all* our interests at heart.

JOB ARTHUR: I don't profess to be a red rag Socialist. I don't pretend to think that if the government had the pits, it would be any better for us. No. What I mean is, that the pits are there,

25 and every man on this place depends on them, one way or another. They're the cow that gives the milk. And what I mean is, how every man shall have a proper share of the milk, which is food and living.—I don't want to kill the cow, and share up the meat. It's like killing the goose that laid the golden egg. I want

30 to keep the cow healthy and strong. And the cow is the pits, and we're the men that depend on the pits.

WILLIE: Who's the cat that's going to lick the cream?

JOB ARTHUR: My position is this—and I state it before masters and men—that it's our business to strike such a balance between the

35 interests of the men and the interests of the masters, that the pits remain healthy, and everybody profits.

WILLIE: You're out for the millennium, I can see—with Mr Job Arthur Freer striking the balance. We all see you, Job Arthur, one foot on either side of the fence, balancing the see-saw, with

40 masters at one end and men at the other. You'll have to give one

side a lot of pudding— But go back a bit, to where we were
before the motor-car took your breath away. When you said, Job
Arthur, that you think of others besides yourself, didn't you
mean, as a matter of fact, the *office men*? Didn't you mean that
the colliers, led—we won't mention noses—by you, were going   5
to come out in sympathy with the office clerks, supposing they
didn't get the rise in wages which they've asked for—the office
clerks? Wasn't that it?

JOB ARTHUR: There's been some talk among the men, of standing
by the office. I don't know what they'll do. But they'll do it of   10
their own decision, whatever it is.

WILLIE: There's not a shadow of doubt about it, Job Arthur.—But
it's a funny thing the decisions all have the same foxy smell
about them, Job Arthur.

OLIVER *(calling from the car)*: What was the speech about, in the   15
first place?

WILLIE: I beg pardon?

OLIVER: What was the address about, to begin with?

WILLIE: Oh, the same old hat—Freedom. But partly it's given to
annoy the Unco Guid,* as they pass to their Sabbath banquet of   20
self-complacency.

OLIVER: What *about* Freedom?

WILLIE: Very much as usual, I believe.—But you should have been
here ten minutes sooner, before we began to read the lessons.
(Laughs.)   25

ANABEL *(moving forward, and holding out her hand)*: You'd merely
have been told what Freedom *isn't*: and you know that
already.—How are you, Oliver?

OLIVER: Good God, Anabel!—are you part of the meeting?—how
long have you been back in England?   30

ANABEL: Some months, now. My family have moved here, you know.

OLIVER: Your family! Where have they moved from?—from the
moon?

ANABEL: No, only from Derby.—How are you, Gerald? *(GERALD
twists in his seat to give her his hand.)*   35

GERALD: I saw you before.

ANABEL: Yes, I know you did. *(JOB ARTHUR has disappeared—the
men disperse sheepishly into groups, to stand and sit on their heels by
the walls and the causeway edge. WILLIE begins to talk to
individuals.)*   40

OLIVER: Won't you get in and drive on with us a little way?

ANABEL: No, I was going to Church.

OLIVER: Going to Church! Is that a new habit?

ANABEL: Not a habit. But I've been twice since I saw you last.

5   OLIVER: I see.—And that's nearly two years ago.—It's an annual thing, like a birthday?

ANABEL: No.—I'll go on then.

OLIVER: You'll be late now.

ANABEL: Shall I?—It doesn't matter.

10   OLIVER: We are going to see you again, aren't we?

ANABEL *(after a pause)*: —Yes, I hope so, Oliver.

OLIVER: How have you been these two years—well?—happy?

ANABEL: No, neither.—How have you?

OLIVER: Yes, fairly happy.—Have you been ill?

15   ANABEL: Yes—in France, I was very ill.

OLIVER: Your old neuritis?

ANABEL: No. My chest. Pneumonia—oh, a complication.

OLIVER: How sickening. Who looked after you? Is it better?

ANABEL: Yes, it's a great deal better.

20   OLIVER: And what are you doing in England—working?

ANABEL: No, not much.—I won't keep the car here, Goodbye.

GERALD: Oh, it's all right.

OLIVER: But Anabel—we must fix a meeting.—I say.—Wait just a moment.—Could I call on your people?—Go in to town with

25   me one day.—I don't know whether Gerald intends to see you—whether he intends to ask you to Lilley Close—

GERALD: I—

ANABEL: He's no need. I'm fixed up there already.

GERALD: What do you mean?

30   ANABEL: I am at Lilley Close every day—or most days—to work with your sister Winifred in the studio.

GERALD: What?—Why how's that?

ANABEL: Your father asked me. My father was already giving her some lessons.

35   GERALD: And you're at our house every day?

ANABEL: Most days.

GERALD: Well I'm—well I'll be—. You managed it very sharp, didn't you? I've only been away a fortnight.

ANABEL: Your father asked me—he offered me twelve pounds a

40   month—I wanted to do something.

GERALD: Oh yes, but you didn't hire yourself out at Lilley Close as a sort of upper servant, just for twelve pounds a month.

ANABEL: You're wrong—you're wrong. I'm not a sort of upper servant at all—not at all—

GERALD: Oh yes you are, if you're paid twelve pounds a month— three pounds a week. That's about what father's sick nurse gets, I believe.—You're a kind of upper servant, like a nurse.—You don't do it for twelve pounds a month. You can make twelve pounds in a day, if you like to work at your little models—I know you can sell your little statuette things as soon as you make them—

ANABEL: But I *can't* make them. I *can't* make them. I've lost the spirit—the *joie de vivre*—I don't know what, since I've been ill.—I tell you I've *got* to earn something.

GERALD: Nevertheless, you won't make me believe, Anabel, that you've come and buried yourself in the provinces—*such* provinces—just to earn father's three pounds a week.—Why don't you admit it, that you came back to try and take up the old threads—?

OLIVER: Why not, Gerald? Don't you think we ought to take up the old threads?

GERALD: I don't think we ought to be left without choice. I don't think Anabel ought to come back and thrust herself on me—for that's what it amounts to, after all—when one remembers what's gone before.

ANABEL: I *don't* thrust myself on you, at all. I know I'm a fool, a fool, to come back. But I wanted to. I wanted to see you again. Now I know I've presumed. I've made myself *cheap* to you. I wanted to. I wanted to. And now I've done it, I won't come to Lilley Close again—nor anywhere where you are. Tell your father I have gone to France again—it will be true.

GERALD: You play tricks on me—and on yourself. You know you do. You do it for the pure enjoyment of it. You're making a scene here in this filthy market-place, just for the fun of it.— You like to see these accursed colliers standing eyeing you—and squatting on their heels. You like to catch me out, here where I'm known, where I've been the object of their eyes since I was born. This is a great *coup de main*⃰ for you. I knew it the moment I saw you here.

OLIVER: After all, we *are* making a scene in the market-place. Get

in, Anabel, and we'll settle the dispute more privately. I'm glad
you came back, anyhow. I'm glad you came right down on us.—
Get in, and let us run down to Whatmore—*

ANABEL: No, Oliver. I don't want to run down to Whatmore. I
5   wanted to see you—I wanted to see Gerald—and I've seen
him—and I've heard him. That will suffice me. We'll make an
end of the scene in the market-place. *(She turns away.)*

OLIVER: I knew it wasn't ended. I knew she would come back and
tell us she'd come. But she's done her bit—now she'll go again.
10   My God, what a fool of a world!—You go on, Gerald—I'll just
go after her and see it out. *(Calls.)* One moment, Anabel.

ANABEL *(calling)*: Don't come, Oliver. *(Turns.)*

GERALD: —Anabel! *(Blows the horn of the motor car violently and
agitatedly—she looks round—turns again as if frightened.)* God
15   damn the woman.— *(Gets down from the car.)* Drive home for
me, Oliver.

(Curtain)

Scene 2.

WINIFRED's *studio at Lilley Close.* ANABEL *and* WINIFRED *working at a model in clay.*

WINIFRED: But isn't it lovely to be in Paris, and to have exhibitions, and to be famous? 5

ANABEL: Paris *was* a good place. But I was never famous.

WINIFRED: But your little animals and birds were famous. Gerald* said so. You know he brought us that bronze thrush, that is singing, that is in his room. He has only let me see it twice. It's the loveliest thing I've ever seen. Oh if I can do anything like 10 that—. I've worshipped it, I have.—Is it your best thing?

ANABEL: One of the best.

WINIFRED: It must be. When I see it, with its beak lifted, singing, something comes loose in my heart, and I feel as if I should cry, and fly up to heaven.—Do you know what I mean?—Oh, I'm 15 sure you do, or you could never have made that thrush.—Father is so glad you've come to show me how to work. He says now I shall have a life-work, and I shall be happy. It's true too.

ANABEL: Yes, till the life-work collapses.

WINIFRED: Oh, it can't collapse. I can't believe it could collapse. 20 Do tell me about something else you made, which you loved: something you sculpted. Oh, it makes my heart burn to hear you.—Do you think I might call you Anabel? I should love to.—You do call me Winifred already.

ANABEL: Yes, do. 25

WINIFRED: Won't you tell me about something else you made— something lovely.

ANABEL: Well—I did a small kitten—asleep—with its paws crossed. You know, Winifred, that wonderful look that kittens have, as if they were blown along like a bit of fluff,—as if they weighed 30 nothing at all—just wafted about*—and yet so *alive*—do you know—

WINIFRED: Darlings—darlings—I love them.

ANABEL: Well my kitten really came off—it had that quality. It looked as if it had just wafted there. 35

WINIFRED: Oh yes!—Oh, I know!—And was it in clay?

ANABEL: I cut it in soft grey stone as well.—I loved my kitten. An Armenian bought her.

WINIFRED: And where is she now?

ANABEL: I don't know—in Armenia, I suppose, if there is such a place.*—It would have to be kept under glass, because the stone wouldn't polish—and I didn't want it polished. But I dislike things under glass, don't you?

5 WINIFRED: Yes, I do.—We had a golden clock, but Gerald wouldn't have the glass cover, and Daddy wouldn't have it without. So now the Clock is in Father's room.—Gerald often went to Paris. Oliver used to have a studio there.—I don't care much for painting, do you?

10 ANABEL: No. I want something I can touch, if it's something outside me.

WINIFRED: Yes, isn't it wonderful, when things are substantial.— Gerald and Oliver came back yesterday from Yorkshire. You know we have a colliery there.

15 ANABEL: Yes, I believe I've heard.

WINIFRED: I want to introduce you to Gerald, to see if you like him. He's good at the bottom, but he's very overbearing and definite.

ANABEL: Is he?

20 WINIFRED: Terribly clever in business—he'll get awfully rich.

ANABEL: Isn't he rich enough already?

WINIFRED: Oh yes, because Daddy is rich enough, really.—I think if Gerald was a bit different, he'd be really nice. Now he's so *managing*. It's sickening.—Do you dislike managing people,

25 Anabel?

ANABEL: I dislike them extremely, Winifred.

WINIFRED: They're such a bore.

ANABEL: What does Gerald manage?

WINIFRED: Everything. You know he's revolutionised the collieries

30 —and the whole company. He's made a whole new thing of it, so *modern*.* Father says he almost wishes he'd let it die out—let the pits be closed.—But I suppose things *must* be modernised, don't you think?—Though it's very unpeaceful, you know, really.

35 ANABEL: Decidedly unpeaceful, I should say.

WINIFRED: The colliers* work awfully hard. The pits are quite wonderful now. Father says it's against nature: all this electricity and so on. Gerald adores electricity. Isn't it curious?

ANABEL: Very.—How are you getting on?

WINIFRED: I don't know. It's so hard to make things *balance* as if they were alive.—Where *is* the balance in a thing that's alive?

ANABEL: The poise? Yes, Winifred—to me, all the secret of life is in that—just the—the inexpressible poise of a living thing, that makes it so different from a dead thing. To me, it's the soul, you know—all living things have it, flowers, trees as well. It makes life always marvellous.

WINIFRED: Ah yes—ah yes. If only I could put it in my model.

ANABEL: I think you will. You are a sculptor, Winifred.—Isn't there someone there?

WINIFRED *(running to the door)*: Oh Oliver—

OLIVER [*at the door*]: Hello Winnie. Can I come in? This is your sanctum, you can keep us out if you like.

WINIFRED: Oh no.—Do you know Miss Wrath, Oliver? She's a famous sculptress.

OLIVER: Is she? We have met.—Is Winifred going to make a 'sculptress', do you think?

ANABEL: I do.

OLIVER: Good.—I like your studio, Winnie. Awfully nice up here over the out-buildings. Are you happy in it?

WINIFRED: Yes, I'm *perfectly* happy—only I shall *never* be able to make real models, Oliver—it's so difficult.

OLIVER: Fine room for a party—give us a studio party one day, Win.—and we'll dance.

WINIFRED *(flying to him)*: Yes Oliver—do let us dance. What shall we dance to?

OLIVER: Dance?—Dance *vigni-vignons*, we all know that. Ready?

WINIFRED: Yes. *(They begin to sing, dancing meanwhile, in a free little ballet-manner, a wine-dance, dancing, separate, and then together—.)*

> De terre en vigne
> La voilà la jolie vigne
> Vigni-vignons—vignons le vin
> La voilà la jolie vigne au vin
> La voilà la jolie vigne.

OLIVER: Join in—join in, all. (ANABEL *joins in—the three dance and move in rhythm.)*

WINIFRED: I love it——I love it.—Do—*ma capote a trois boutons*

—you know it, don't you, Anabel?—ready—now— *(They begin to dance to a quick little march-rhythm, all singing and dancing till they are out of breath.)*

OLIVER: Oh—tired—let us sit down.

5 WINIFRED: Oliver—oh Oliver—I *love* you and Anabel.

OLIVER: Ah Winifred, I brought you a present—you'll love me more now.

WINIFRED: Yes, I shall. Do give it me.

OLIVER: I left it in the morning room—I put it on the mantel-piece
10 for you.

WINIFRED: Shall I go for it?

OLIVER: There it is, if you want it.

WINIFRED: Yes—do you mind?—I won't be long. *(Exit.)*

OLIVER: She's a nice child.

15 ANABEL: A *very* nice child.

OLIVER: Why did you come back, Anabel?

ANABEL: Why does the moon rise, Oliver?

OLIVER: For some mischief or other, so they say.

ANABEL: You think I came back for mischief's sake?

20 OLIVER: Did you?

ANABEL: No.

OLIVER: Ah.

ANABEL: Tell me, Oliver, how is everything now—how is it with
you?—how is it between us all?

25 OLIVER: How is it between us all?—How *isn't* it is more the mark.

ANABEL: Why?

OLIVER: You made a fool of us.

ANABEL: Of whom?

OLIVER: Well—of Gerald particularly—and of me.

30 ANABEL: How did I make a fool of you, Oliver?

OLIVER: That you know best, Anabel.

ANABEL: No, I don't know.—Was it ever right between Gerald and
me, all the three years we knew each other—we were together—?

OLIVER: Was it all wrong?

35 ANABEL: No—not all. But it was terrible. It was terrible, Oliver.
You don't realise. You don't realise how *awful* passion can be,
when it never resolves, when it never becomes anything else. It
is hate, really.

OLIVER: What did you want the passion to resolve into?

40 ANABEL: I was blinded—maddened. Gerald stung me and stung me

till I was mad. I left him for reason's sake, for sanity's sake. We should have killed one another.

OLIVER: You stung him too, you know: and pretty badly, at the last: you dehumanised him.

ANABEL: When? When I left him, you mean?

OLIVER: Yes—when you went away with that Norwegian,*— playing your game a little too far.

ANABEL: Yes, I knew you'd blame me. I knew you'd be against me. But don't you see, Oliver, you helped to make it impossible for us.

OLIVER: Did I? I didn't intend to.

ANABEL: Ha—ha—Oliver! Your good intentions! They are too good to bear investigation, my friend. Ah, but for your good and friendly intentions—

OLIVER: You might have been all right—?

ANABEL: No—no—I don't mean that.—But we were a vicious triangle, Oliver, you must admit it.

OLIVER: You mean my friendship with Gerald went against you?

ANABEL: Yes. And your friendship with me went against Gerald.

OLIVER: So I am the devil in the piece.

ANABEL: You see, Oliver, Gerald loved you far too well ever to love me altogether. He loved us both. But the Gerald that loved you so dearly, old, old friends as you were, and *trusted* you, he turned a terrible face of contempt on me. You don't know, Oliver, the cold edge of Gerald's contempt for me—because he was so secure and strong in his old friendship with you. You don't know his sneering attitude to me, in the deepest things— because he shared the deepest things with you. He had a passion for me. But he loved you.

OLIVER: Well, he doesn't any more. We went apart after you had gone. The friendship has become almost casual.

ANABEL: You see how bitterly you speak.

OLIVER: Yet you didn't hate me, Anabel.

ANABEL: No Oliver—I was *awfully* fond of you. I trusted you—and I trust you still.—You see I knew how fond Gerald was of you. And I had to respect this feeling. So I *had* to be aware of you: I *had* to be conscious of you: in a way, I had to love you. You understand how I mean. Not with the same fearful love with which I loved Gerald. You seemed to me warm and pro- tecting—like a brother, you know—but a brother one *loves*—

Plays

OLIVER: And then you hated me—

ANABEL: Yes, I had to hate you.

OLIVER: And you hated Gerald—

ANABEL: Almost to madness—almost to madness.

5   OLIVER: Then you went away with that Norwegian. What of him?

ANABEL: What of him?—Well, he's dead.

OLIVER: Ah.—That's why you came back?

ANABEL: No—no.—I came back because my only hope in life was in coming back.—Baard was beautiful—and awful. You know

10   how glisteningly blond he was. Oliver, have you ever watched the polar bears? He was cold as iron when it is so cold that it burns you. Coldness wasn't negative with him. It was positive—and awful beyond expression—like the aurora borealis.

OLIVER: I wonder you ever got back.

15   ANABEL: Yes, so do I. I feel as if I'd fallen down a fissure in the ice. Yet I have come back, haven't I?

OLIVER: God knows.—At least, Anabel, we've gone through too much ever to start the old game again. There'll be no more sticky love between us.

20   ANABEL: No, I think there won't, either.

OLIVER: And what of Gerald?

ANABEL: I don't know. What do you think of him?

OLIVER: I can't think any more. I can only blindly go from day to day, now.

25   ANABEL: So can I. Do you think I was wrong to come back? Do you think I wrong Gerald?

OLIVER: No. I'm glad you came. But I feel I can't *know* anything. We must just go on.

ANABEL: Sometimes I feel I ought never to have come to Gerald

30   again—never—never—never—

OLIVER: Just left the gap?—Perhaps, if everything has to come asunder.—But I think, if ever there is to be life—hope—then you had to come back. I always knew it. There is something eternal between you and him—and if there is to be any

35   happiness, it depends on that.—But perhaps there is to *be* no more happiness, for our part of the world.

ANABEL *(after a pause)*: Yet I feel hope, don't you?

OLIVER: Yes—sometimes.

ANABEL: It seemed to me, especially that winter in Norway, I can

40   hardly express it—as if any moment life might give way under

one, like thin ice—and one would be more than dead.—And
then I knew, my only hope was here—the only hope.

OLIVER: Yes. I believe it. And I believe— *(Enter* MRS HENRIETTA
BARLOW.*)*

MRS BARLOW: Oh, I wanted to speak to you, Oliver.

OLIVER: Shall I come across?

MRS BARLOW: No—not now. I believe Father is coming here with
Gerald.

OLIVER: Is he going to walk so far?

MRS BARLOW: He will do it.—I suppose you know Oliver?

ANABEL: Yes, we have met before.

MRS BARLOW *(to* OLIVER*)*: You didn't mention it.—Where have
you met Miss Wrath?—She's been about the world, I believe.

ANABEL: About the world—no, Mrs Barlow. If one happens to
know Paris and London—

MRS BARLOW: Paris and London! Well, I don't say you are
altogether an adventuress. My husband seems very pleased with
you—for Winifred's sake, I suppose—and he's wrapped up in
Winifred.

ANABEL: Winifred is an artist.

MRS BARLOW: All my children have the artist in them. They get it
from my family. My father went mad in Rome.—My family is
born with a black fate—they all inherit it—

OLIVER: I believe one is master of one's fate* sometimes, Mrs
Barlow. There are moments of pure choice.

MRS BARLOW: Between two ways to the same end, no doubt.
There's no changing the end.

OLIVER: I think there is.

MRS BARLOW: Yes, you have a *parvenu's** presumptuousness somewhere about you.

OLIVER: Well, better than a blue-blooded fatalism.

MRS BARLOW: The fate is in the blood: you can't change the
blood.

(Enter WINIFRED.*)*

WINIFRED: Oh, thank you, Oliver, for the wolf and the goat, thank
you so much. The wolf has sprung on the goat, Miss Wrath,
and has her by the throat.

ANABEL: The wolf!

OLIVER: It's a little marble group—Italian—in hard marble.

WINIFRED: The wolf—I love the wolf—he pounces so beautifully.

His back-bone is so terribly fierce.—I don't feel a bit sorry for the goat, somehow.

OLIVER: I didn't. She is too much like the wrong sort of clergyman.

WINIFRED: Yes—such a stiff long face. I wish he'd kill her.

MRS BARLOW: There's a wish.

WINIFRED: Father and Gerald are coming.—That's them, I suppose.

(Enter MR BARLOW *and* GERALD.*)*

MR BARLOW: Ah, Good Morning—Good-morning—quite a little gathering. Ah—

OLIVER: The steps tire you, Mr Barlow.

MR BARLOW: A little—a little.—Thank you.—Well, Miss Wrath, are you quite comfortable here?

ANABEL: Very comfortable, thanks.

GERALD: It was clever of you, father, to turn this place into a studio.

MR BARLOW: Yes, Gerald. You make the worldly schemes and I the homely.—Yes, it's a delightful place. I shall come here often if the two young ladies will allow me.—By the way, Miss Wrath, I don't know if you have been introduced to my son Gerald. I beg your pardon. Miss Wrath, Gerald—my son, Miss Wrath. *(They bow.)* Well, we are quite a gathering, quite a pleasant little gathering. We never expected anything so delightful a month ago, did we Winifred darling?

WINIFRED: No Daddy. It's much nicer than expectations.

MR BARLOW: So it is, dear—to have such exceptional companionship and such a pleasant retreat. We are very happy to have Miss Wrath with us: very happy.

GERALD: A studio's awfully nice, you know, it is such a retreat. A newspaper has no effect in it, falls quite flat, no matter what the headlines are.

MR BARLOW: Quite true, Gerald dear. It is a sanctum the world cannot invade—unlike all other sanctuaries, I am afraid.

GERALD: By the way, Oliver—to go back to profanities—the colliers really are coming out in support of the poor ill-used clerks.

MR BARLOW: No-no, Gerald, no-no. Don't be such an alarmist. Let us leave these subjects before the ladies.—No-no—the clerks will have their increase quite peacefully.

GERALD: Yes, dear father—but they can't have it peacefully now. We've been threatened already by the colliers—we've already received an ultimatum.

MR BARLOW: Nonsense, my boy—nonsense. Don't let us split words. You won't go against the clerks, in such a small matter. Always avoid trouble over small matters. Don't make bad feeling, don't make bad blood.

MRS BARLOW: The blood is already rotten in this neighbourhood. What it needs is letting out. We need a few veins opening, or we shall have mortification setting in. The blood is black.

MR BARLOW: We won't accept your figure of speech literally, dear. No, Gerald, don't go to war over trifles.

GERALD: It's just over trifles that one must make war, father. One can yield gracefully over big matters. But to be bullied over trifles is a sign of criminal weakness.

MR BARLOW: Ah, not so, not so, my boy. When you are as old as I am you will know the comparative insignificance of these trifles.

GERALD: The older *I* get, father, the more such trifles stick in my throat.

MR BARLOW: Ah, it is an increasingly irritable disposition in you, my child. Nothing costs so bitterly, in the end, as a stubborn pride.

MRS BARLOW: Except a stubborn humility—and that will cost you more. Avoid humility, beware of stubborn humility: it degrades. Hark, Gerald, fight! When the occasion comes, fight! If it's one against five thousand, fight! Don't give them your heart on a dish! Never! If they want to eat your heart out, make them fight for it, and then give it them poisoned at last, poisoned with their own blood.—What do you say, young woman!

ANABEL: Is it for me to speak, Mrs Barlow?

MRS BARLOW: Weren't you asked?

ANABEL: Certainly I would *never* give the world my heart on a dish.—But can't there ever be peace—real peace—?

MRS BARLOW: No—not while there is devilish enmity.

MR BARLOW: You are wrong, dear, you are wrong. The peace can come, the peace that passeth all understanding.

MRS BARLOW: That there is already between me and Almighty God. I am at peace with the God that made me, and made me proud. With men who humiliate me I am at war. Between me and the shameful humble there is war to the end, though they are millions and I am one. I hate the people. Between my race and them there is war, between them and me, between them and my children, for ever war, for ever and ever.

MR BARLOW: Ah, Henrietta—you have said all this before.

MRS BARLOW: And say it again. Fight, Gerald. You have my blood
in you, thank God. Fight for it, Gerald. Spend it as if it were
costly,* Gerald, drop by drop. Let no dogs lap it.—Look at your
father. He set his heart on a plate at the door, for the poorest
mongrel to eat up. See him now, wasted and crossed out like a
mistake—and swear, Gerald, swear to be true to my blood in
you. Never lie down before the mob, Gerald. Fight it and stab it
and die fighting. It's a lost hope—but fight.

GERALD: Don't say these things here, mother.

MRS BARLOW: Yes I will—I will. I'll say them before you, and the
child Winifred. She knows. And before Oliver and the young
woman—they know too.

MR BARLOW: You see, dear, you can never understand that,
although I am weak, and wasted, although I may be crossed out
from the world like a mistake, I still have peace in my soul, dear,
the peace that passeth all understanding.

MRS BARLOW: And what right have you to it? All very well for you
to take peace with you into the other world. What do you leave
for your sons to inherit?

MR BARLOW: The peace of God, Henrietta, if there is no peace
among men.

MRS BARLOW: Then why did you have children? Why weren't you
celibate! They have to live among men. If they have no place
among men, why have you put them there? If the peace of God
is no more than the peace of death, why are your sons born of
you? How can you have peace with God, if you leave no peace
for your sons—no peace, no pride, no place on earth.

GERALD: Nay, mother, nay. You shall never blame father on my
behalf.

MRS BARLOW: Don't trouble—he is blameless.—I, a hulking, half-
demented woman, I am *glad* when you blame me.—But don't
blame me when I tell you to fight. Don't blame me when I call
on your pride. Don't do that, or you will regret it when you
must die. Ah, your father was stiff and proud enough before
men of better rank than himself. He was overbearing enough
with his equals and his betters. But he humbled himself before
the poor, he made me ashamed. He must hear it—he must hear
it. Better he should hear it than die coddling himself with peace.
His humility, and my pride, they have made a nice ruin of each

other. Yet he is the man I wanted to marry—he is the man I would marry again. But never, never again would I give way before his goodness.—Gerald, if you must be true to your father, be true to me as well. Don't set me down at nothing because I haven't a humble case.   5

GERALD: No, mother, no, dear mother.—You see, dear mother, I have rather a job between the two halves of myself. When you come to have the wild horses in your own soul, mother—it makes it difficult.

MRS BARLOW: Never mind, you'll have help.   10

GERALD: Thank you for the assurance, darling.—Father, you don't mind what mother says, I hope—I believe there's some truth in it, don't you?

MR BARLOW: I have nothing to say.

WINIFRED: *I* think there's some truth in it, Daddy. You were always   15
worrying about those horrid colliers, and they didn't care a bit about you. And they *ought* to have cared a million pounds.

MR BARLOW: You don't understand, my child.

(Curtain)

Act II.

SCENE: Evening of the same day—drawing-room at Lilley Close—MR
BARLOW, GERALD, WINIFRED, ANABEL, OLIVER *present*—WILLIAM
pours coffee.

5   MR BARLOW: And you are quite a stranger in these parts, Miss
       Wrath?
       ANABEL: Practically. But I was born at Derby.
       MR BARLOW: I was born in this house—but it was a different affair
       then. My father was a farmer, you know. The coal has brought
10   us what moderate wealth we have.—Of course, we were never
       poor or needy—farmers, substantial farmers. [*Exit* WILLIAM.]
       And I think we were happier so—yes.—Winnie, dear, hand
       Miss Wrath the sweets. I hope they're good. I ordered them
       from London for you.—Oliver, my boy, have you everything
15   you like?—That's right.—It gives me such pleasure to see a
       little festive gathering in this room again. I wish Bertie and
       Elinor might be here.—What time is it, Gerald?
       GERALD: A quarter to nine, father.
       MR BARLOW: Not late yet. I can sit with you another half-hour. I
20   am feeling better today. Winifred, sing something to us.
       WINIFRED: Something jolly, father?
       MR BARLOW: Very jolly, darling.
       WINIFRED: I'll sing the "Lincolnshire Poacher", shall I?
       MR BARLOW: Do, darling—and we'll all join in the chorus. Will
25   you join in the chorus, Miss Wrath?
       ANABEL: I will. It is a good song.
       MR BARLOW: Yes, isn't it!
       WINIFRED: All dance for the chorus, as well as singing.
          (They sing—some pirouette a little for the chorus.)
30   MR BARLOW: Ah splendid, splendid! There is nothing like gaiety.
       WINIFRED: I do love to dance about. I know, let us do a little
       ballet—four of us—oh do—
       GERALD: What ballet, Winifred?
       WINIFRED: Any: Eva can play for us. She plays well.
35   MR BARLOW: You won't disturb your mother. Don't disturb Eva if
       she is busy with your mother. *(Exit* WINIFRED.*)*—If only I can
       see Winifred happy, my heart is at rest: if only I can hope for
       her to be happy in her life.

GERALD: Oh, Winnie's all right, father—especially now she has Miss Wrath to initiate her into the mysteries of life and labour.

ANABEL: Why are you ironical?

MR BARLOW: Oh, Miss Wrath, believe me, we all feel that—it is the greatest possible pleasure to me that you have come. 5

GERALD: I wasn't ironical, I assure you.

MR BARLOW: No indeed, no indeed! We have every belief in you!*

ANABEL: But why should you have.

MR BARLOW: Ah, my dear child, allow us the credit of our own discernment.—And don't take offence at my familiarity. I am 10
afraid I am spoilt since I am an invalid.

(Re-enter WINIFRED, with EVA.)

MR BARLOW: Come, Eva, you will excuse us for upsetting your evening. Will you be so good as to play something for us to dance to? 15

EVA: Yes Sir. What shall I play?

WINIFRED: Mozart—I'll find you the piece. Mozart's the saddest musician in the world—but he's the best to dance to.—

MR BARLOW: Why, how is it you are such a connoisseur in sadness, darling? 20

GERALD: She isn't. She's a flagrant amateur.

(EVA plays—they dance a little ballet.)

MR BARLOW: Charming—charming. Miss Wrath—will you allow me to say Anabel, we shall all feel so much more at home?— Yes—thank you—er—you enter into the spirit of it wonderfully, 25
Anabel dear. The others are accustomed to play together. But it is not so easy to come in on occasion as you do.

GERALD: Oh, Anabel's a genius—I beg your pardon, Miss Wrath—familiarity is catching.

MR BARLOW: Gerald, my boy, don't forget that you are virtually 30
host here—

EVA: Did you want any more music, Sir?

GERALD: No, don't stay, Eva. We mustn't tire father. *(Exit EVA.)*

MR BARLOW: I am afraid, Anabel, you will have a great deal to excuse in us, in the way of manners. We have never been a 35
formal household. But you have lived in the world of artists, you will understand, I hope.

ANABEL: Oh, surely—.

MR BARLOW: Yes, I know.—We have been a turbulent family, and we have had our share of sorrow, even more, perhaps, than of 40 joys. And sorrow makes one indifferent to the conventionalities of life.

GERALD: Excuse me, father, do you mind if I go and write a letter I have on my conscience?

5 MR BARLOW: No my boy. *(Exit* GERALD.*)* We have had our share of sorrow and of conflict, Miss Wrath, as you may have gathered.

ANABEL: Yes—a little.

MR BARLOW: —The mines were opened when my father was a boy—the first—and I was born late, when he was nearly fifty.

10 So that all my life has been involved with coal and colliers. As a young man, I was gay and thoughtless. But I married young, and we lost our first child, through a terrible accident. Two children we have lost through sudden and violent death.[☆] *(*WINIFRED *goes out unnoticed.)* —It made me reflect. And when

15 I came to reflect, Anabel, I could not justify my position in life. If I believed in the teachings of the New Testament—which I did, and do—how could I keep two or three thousand men employed underground in the mines, at a wage, let us say, of two pounds a week,[☆] whilst I lived in this comfortable house,

20 and took something like two thousand pounds a year—let us name any figure—

ANABEL: Yes, of course.—But is it money that really matters, Mr Barlow?

MR BARLOW: My dear, if you are a working man, it matters. When

25 I went into the homes of my poor fellows, when they were ill or had had accidents—then I knew it mattered. I knew that the great disparity was wrong—even as we are taught that it is wrong.[☆]

ANABEL: Yes, I believe that the great disparity is a mistake.—But

30 take their lives, Mr Barlow. Do you think they would *live* more, if they had more money? Do you think the poor live less than the rich—is their life emptier?

MR BARLOW: Surely their lives would be better, Anabel.

OLIVER: All our lives would be better, if we hadn't to hang on in the

35 perpetual tug of war, like two donkeys pulling at one carrot. The ghastly tension of possession,[☆] and struggling for possession, spoils life for everybody.

MR BARLOW: Yes, I know now, as I knew then, that it was wrong. But how to avoid the wrong? If I gave away the whole of my

40 income, it would merely be an arbitrary dispensation of charity.

The money would still be mine to give, and those that received it would probably only be weakened instead of strengthened. —And then my wife was accustomed to a certain way of living, a certain establishment. Had I any right to sacrifice her, without her consent?

ANABEL: Why no!

MR BARLOW: Again, if I withdrew from the Company, if I retired on a small income, I knew that another man would automatically take my place, and make it probably harder for the men.

ANABEL: Of course—while the system stands, if one makes self-sacrifice one only panders to the system, makes it fatter.

MR BARLOW: One panders to the system, one panders to the system. And so, you see, the problem is too much. One man cannot alter or affect the system, he can only sacrifice himself to it. Which is the worst thing probably that he can do.

OLIVER: Quite. But why feel guilty for the system—everybody supports it, the poor as much as the rich. If every rich man withdrew from the system, the working classes and socialists would keep it going, every man in the hope of getting rich himself, at last.—It's the people that are wrong. They want the system much more than the rich do—because they are much more anxious to be rich—never having been rich, poor devils.

MR BARLOW: Just the system.—So I decided at last that the best way was to give every private help that lay in my power. I would help my men individually and personally, wherever I could.—Not one of them came to me and went away un-heard—and there was no distress which could be alleviated, that I did not try to alleviate.—Yet I am afraid that the greatest distress I never heard of, the most distressed never came to me. They hid their trouble.

ANABEL: Yes, the decent ones.

MR BARLOW: But I wished to help—it was my duty.—Still, I think that, on the whole, we were a comfortable and happy com-munity. Barlow and Walsalls' men were not unhappy in those days, I believe. We were liberal, the men lived.

OLIVER: Yes, that is true. Even twenty years ago the place was still jolly.

MR BARLOW: And then, when Gerald was a lad of thirteen, came the great lock-out. We belonged to the Masters Federation—I was but one man on the Board. We had to abide by the decision.

The mines were closed till the men would accept the reduction.
—Well, that cut my life across. We were shutting the men out
from work, starving their families, in order to force them to
accept a reduction. It may be, the condition of trade made it
imperative. But for myself, I would rather have lost everything.—Of course, we did what we could. Food was very
cheap—practically given away. We had open kitchen here. And
it was mercifully warm summer time.—Nevertheless, there was
privation and suffering—and trouble and bitterness. We had the
red-coats down—even to guard this house. And from this
window I saw Whatmore head-stocks ablaze, and before I could
get to the spot the soldiers had shot two poor fellows—they
were not killed, thank God—

OLIVER: Ah, but they enjoyed it—they enjoyed it immensely; I
remember what grand old sporting weeks they were. It was like
a fox-hunt, so lively and gay—bands and tea-parties and excitement everywhere, pit-ponies loose, men all over the country-
side—✻

MR BARLOW: There was a great deal of suffering which you were
too young to appreciate.—However, since that year, I have had
to acknowledge a new situation—a radical, if unspoken opposition between masters and men. Since that year we have been
split into opposite camps. Whatever I might privately feel, I was
one of the owners, one of the masters, and therefore in the
opposite camp. To my men I was an oppressor, a representative
of injustice and greed. Privately, I like to think that even to this
day they bear me no malice, that they have some lingering
regard for me. But the master stands before the human being,
and the condition of war overrides individuals.—They hate the
master, even whilst, as a human being, he would be their friend.
I recognise the inevitable justice. It is the price one has to pay.

ANABEL: Yes, it is difficult—very.

MR BARLOW: Perhaps I weary you?

ANABEL: Oh no—no.

MR BARLOW: Well—then the mines began to pay badly—the seams
ran thin and unprofitable, work was short. Either we must close
down, or introduce a new system, American methods, which I
dislike so extremely. Now it really became a case of men
working against machines, flesh and blood working against iron,
for a livelihood. Still, it had to be done—the whole system

revolutionised. Gerald took it in hand—and now I hardly know my own pits, with the great electric plants, and strange machinery, and the new coal-cutters, iron-men as the colliers call them, everything running at top speed, utterly dehuman- ised, inhuman. Well, it had to be done—it was the only   5 alternative to closing down, and throwing three thousand men out of work. And Gerald has done it.—But I can't bear to see it. The men of this generation are not like my men. They are worn, and gloomy, they have a hollow look that I can't bear to see. They are a great grief to me. I remember my men even   10 twenty years ago—a noisy, lively, careless set, who kept the place ringing. Now it is too quiet—too quiet. There is some- thing wrong in the quietness, something unnatural. I feel it is unnatural, I feel afraid of it. And I cannot help feeling guilty.

ANABEL: Yes—I understand. It terrifies me.   15

MR BARLOW: Does it—does it?—Yes.—And as my wife says, I leave it all to Gerald—this terrible situation. But I appeal to God, if anything in my power could have averted it, I would have averted it. I would have made any sacrifice. For it is a great and bitter trouble to me.   20

ANABEL: Ah well, in death there is no industrial situation. Some- thing must be different, there.

MR BARLOW: Yes—yes.

OLIVER: And you see sacrifice isn't the slightest use. If only people would be sane and decent—   25

MR BARLOW: Yes—indeed. Would you be so good as to ring, Oliver.—I think I must go to bed.

ANABEL: Ah, you have over-tired yourself.

MR BARLOW: No my dear—not over-tired. Excuse me if I have burdened you with all this. It relieves me to speak of it.   30

ANABEL: I realise *how* terrible it is, Mr Barlow—and how helpless one is.

MR BARLOW: Thank you, my dear, for your sympathy.

OLIVER: If the people for one minute pulled themselves up and conquered their mania for money* and machine-excitement,   35 the whole thing would be solved.—Would you like me to find Winnie and tell her to say Goodnight to you?

MR BARLOW: If you would be so kind. *(Exit* OLIVER.*)* Can't you find a sweet that you would like, my dear. Won't you take a little cherry brandy? *(Enter* WILLIAM.*)*   40

ANABEL: Thank you—

WILLIAM: You will go up, Sir.

MR BARLOW: Yes, William—

WILLIAM: You are tired, tonight, sir.

5   MR BARLOW: It has come over me just now.

WILLIAM: I wish you went up before you came over so tired, Sir. Would you like nurse?

MR BARLOW: No, I'll go with you, William.—Good night, my dear.

10   ANABEL: Good night, Mr Barlow. I am so sorry if you are over tired.

    (Exit WILLIAM *and* MR BARLOW—ANABEL *takes a drink and goes to the fire.—Enter* GERALD.*)*

GERALD: Father gone up?

15   ANABEL: Yes.

GERALD: I thought I heard him. Has he been talking too much?— Poor father, he will take things to heart.

ANABEL: Tragic, really.

GERALD: Yes, I suppose it is.—But one can get beyond tragedy,

20   beyond the state of feeling tragical, I mean. Father himself is tragical. One feels he is mistaken—and yet he couldn't be any different, and be himself, I suppose. He's sort of crucified on an idea of the working people. It's rather horrible when he's one's father.—However—apart from tragedy, how do you like being

25   here—in this house?

ANABEL: I like the house. It's rather too comfortable—

GERALD: Yes. But how do you like being here?

ANABEL: How do you like my being in your home?

GERALD: Oh, I think you're very decorative.

30   ANABEL: More decorative than comfortable?

GERALD: Perhaps. But perhaps you give the necessary finish to the establishment.

ANABEL: Like the correct window-curtains.

GERALD: Yes—something like that.—I say, why did you come,

35   Anabel? Why did you come slap bang into the middle of us?—It's not expostulation—I want to know.

ANABEL: You mean you want to be told.

GERALD: Yes, I want to be told.

ANABEL: That's rather mean of you.—You should savvy, and let it

40   go without saying.

GERALD: Yes, but I don't savvy.

ANABEL: Then wait till you do.

GERALD: No, I want to be told.—There's a difference in you, Anabel, that puts me out, rather. You're sort of softer and sweeter—I'm not sure whether it isn't a touch of Father in you. There's a little sanctified smudge on your tongue. Are you really a bit sanctified?

ANABEL: No, not sanctified. It's true I feel different. I feel I want a new way of life—something more dignified, more religious, if you like—anyhow, something *positive*.

GERALD: Is it the change of heart, Anabel?

ANABEL: Perhaps it is, Gerald.

GERALD: I'm not sure that I like it. Isn't it like a berry that decides to get very sweet, and goes soft?

ANABEL: I don't think so.

GERALD: Slightly sanctimonious.—I think I liked you better before. I don't think I like you with this touch of aureole. People seem to me so horribly self-satisfied when they get a change of heart—they take such a fearful lot of credit to themselves on the strength of it.

ANABEL: I don't think I do.—Do you feel no different, Gerald?

GERALD: Radically, I can't say I do. I feel very much more *in*different.

ANABEL: What to?

GERALD: Everything.

ANABEL: You're still angry, that's what it is.

GERALD: Oh yes, I'm angry. But that is part of my normal state.

ANABEL: Why are you angry?

GERALD: Is there any reason why I shouldn't be angry? I'm angry because you treated me—well, so impudently, really—clearing out and leaving me* to whistle to the empty walls—

ANABEL: Don't you think it was time I cleared out, when you became so violent, and really dangerous, really like a madman?

GERALD: Time or not time, you went—you disappeared and left us high and dry—and I am still angry.—But I'm not only angry about that. I'm angry with the colliers, with Labour, for its low-down impudence—and I'm angry with father for being so ill —and I'm angry with mother for looking such a hopeless thing —and I'm angry with Oliver because he thinks so much—

ANABEL: And what are you angry with yourself for?

GERALD: I'm angry with myself for being myself.—I always was that. I was always a curse to myself.

ANABEL: And that's why you curse others so much.

GERALD: You talk as if butter wouldn't melt in your mouth.

5   ANABEL: You see, Gerald, there has to be a change. You'll have to change.

GERALD: Change of heart?—Well, it won't be to get softer, Anabel.

ANABEL: You needn't be softer. But you can be quieter,—more sane even. There ought to be some part of you that can be quiet and 10   apart from the world, some part that can be happy and gentle—

GERALD: Well, there isn't. I don't pretend to be able to extricate a soft sort of John Halifax Gentleman* out of the machine I'm mixed up in, and keep him to gladden the connubial hearth. I'm angry, and I'm angry right through, and I'm not going to play 15   bo-peep with myself,* pretending I'm not.

ANABEL: Nobody asks you to. But is there no part of you that can be a bit gentle and peaceful and happy with a woman?

GERALD: No there isn't.—I'm not going to smug with you, no, not I. You're smug in your coming back. You feel virtuous, and 20   expect me to rise to it. I won't.

ANABEL: Then I'd better have stayed away.

GERALD: If you want me to virtuise* and smug with you, you had.

ANABEL: What *do* you want, then?

GERALD: I don't know. I know I don't want *that*.

25   ANABEL: Oh very well.— *(Goes to the piano, begins to play. Enter* MRS BARLOW.*)*

GERALD: Hello mother! Father *has* gone to bed.

MRS BARLOW: Oh. I thought he was down here talking.—You two alone?

30   GERALD: With the piano for chaperone, mother.

MRS BARLOW: That's more than I gave you credit for.—I haven't come to chaperone you, either, Gerald.

GERALD: Chaperone *me*, mother? Do you think I need it?

MRS BARLOW: If you do you won't get it. I've come too late to be of 35   any use in that way, as far as I hear.

GERALD: What have you heard, mother?

MRS BARLOW: I heard Oliver and this young woman talking.

GERALD: Oh did you? When? What did they say?

MRS BARLOW: Something about married in the sight of heaven, but 40   couldn't keep it up on earth.

GERALD: I don't understand.

MRS BARLOW: That you and this young woman were married in the sight of heaven, or through eternity, or something similar, but that you couldn't make up your minds to it on earth.

GERALD: Really! That's very curious, mother.   5

MRS BARLOW: Very common occurrence, I believe.

GERALD: Yes, so it is. But I don't think you heard quite right, dear. There seems to be some lingering uneasiness in heaven, as a matter of fact. We'd quite made up our minds to live apart, on earth.—But where did you hear this, mother?   10

MRS BARLOW: I heard it outside the studio door, this morning.

GERALD: You mean you happened to be on one side of the door while Oliver and Anabel were talking on the other?

MRS BARLOW: You'd make a detective, Gerald, you're so good at putting two and two together.—I listened till I'd heard as much   15
as I wanted.—I'm not sure I didn't come down here hoping to hear another conversation going on.

GERALD: Listen outside the door, darling?

MRS BARLOW: There'd be nothing to listen to if I were inside.

GERALD: It isn't usually done, you know.   20

MRS BARLOW: I listen outside doors when I have occasion to be interested—which isn't often, unfortunately for me.

GERALD: But I've a queer feeling that you have a permanent occasion to be interested in me. I only half like it.

MRS BARLOW: It's surprising how uninteresting you are, Gerald,   25
for a man of your years. I have not had occasion to listen outside a door, for you, no, not for a great while, believe me.

GERALD: I believe you implicitly, darling. But do you happen to know me through and through, and in and out, all my past and present doings, mother? Have you a secret access to my room,   30
and a spy hole, and all those things?—This is uncomfortably thrilling. You take on a new lustre.

MRS BARLOW: Your memoirs wouldn't make you famous, my son.

GERALD: Infamous, dear?

MRS BARLOW: Good heavens, no. What a lot you expect from your   35
very mild sins.—You and this young woman have lived together, then?

GERALD: Don't say 'this young woman', mother dear—it's slightly vulgar.—It isn't for me to compromise Anabel by admitting such a thing, you know.   40

MRS BARLOW: Do you ask me to call her Anabel? I won't.

GERALD: Then say 'this person', mother. It's more becoming.

MRS BARLOW: I didn't come to speak to you, Gerald. I know you. I came to speak to this young woman.

5 GERALD: 'Person', mother.—Will you curtsey, Anabel?—and I'll twist my handkerchief. We shall make a Cruikshank drawing,* if mother makes her hair a little more slovenly.

MRS BARLOW: You and Gerald were together for some time?

GERALD: Three years, off and on, mother.

10 MRS BARLOW: And then you suddenly dropped my son, and went away?

GERALD: To Norway, mother, so I have gathered.

MRS BARLOW: And now you have come back because that last one died?

15 GERALD: Is he dead, Anabel? How did he die?

ANABEL: He was killed on the ice.

GERALD: Oh God.

MRS BARLOW: Now, having had your fill of tragedy, you have come back to be demure, and to marry Gerald.—Does he thank you?

20 GERALD: You must listen outside the door, mother, to find that out.

MRS BARLOW: Well, it's your own affair.

GERALD: What a lame summing up, mother—quite unworthy of you.

ANABEL: What did you wish to say to me, Mrs Barlow? Please say
25 it.

MRS BARLOW: What did I wish to say! Ay, what did I wish to say! What is the use of my saying anything! What am I but a buffoon and a slovenly caricature in the family.

GERALD: No, mother dear, don't climb down—please don't. Tell
30 Anabel what you wanted to say.

MRS BARLOW: Yes—yes—yes.—I came to say—don't be good to my son—don't be good to him—

GERALD: Sounds weak, dear—mere contrariness.*

MRS BARLOW: Don't presume to be good to my son, young woman.
35 I won't have it, even if he will. You hear me.

ANABEL: Yes. I won't presume, then.

GERALD: May she presume to be bad to me, mother?

MRS BARLOW: For that you may look after yourself.—But a woman who was good to him would ruin him in six months, take the
40 manhood out of him. He has a tendency, a secret hankering, to

make a gift of himself to somebody.—He shan't do it. I warn
you. I am not a woman to be despised.

ANABEL: No, I understand.

MRS BARLOW: Only one other thing I ask. If he must fight, and
fight he must, let him alone, don't you⃰ try to shield him or   5
save him. *Don't interfere*—do you hear?

ANABEL: Not till I must.

MRS BARLOW: *Never.* Learn your place—and keep it. Keep away
from him, if you are going to be a wife to him. Don't go too
near. And don't let him come too near. Beat him off if he tries.   10
Keep a solitude in your heart even when you love him best.
Keep it. If you lose it you lose everything.

GERALD: But that isn't love, mother.

MRS BARLOW: What?

GERALD: That isn't love.   15

MRS BARLOW: *What?* What do you know of love, you ninny? You
only know the feeding-bottle. It's what you want, all of you, to
be brought up by hand, and mew about love.—Ah God, Ah
God—that you should none of you know the only thing⃰ which
would make you worth having.   20

GERALD: I don't believe in your only thing, mother. But what is it?

MRS BARLOW: What you haven't got—the power to be alone.

GERALD: Sort of megalomania, you mean?⃰

MRS BARLOW: What? Megalomania! What is your *love* but a
megalomania, flowing over everybody and everything like spilt   25
water. Megalomania! I hate you, you softy. I would *beat* you
(suddenly advancing on him and beating him fiercely) —beat you
into some manhood—beat you—

GERALD: Stop mother—keep off—

MRS BARLOW: It's the men who need beating nowadays, not the   30
children. Beat the softness out of him, young woman. It's the
only way if you love him enough—if you love him enough.

GERALD: You hear, Anabel.

> Speak gently to your little boy
> And beat him when he sneezes.⃰   35

MRS BARLOW *(catching up a large old fan, and smashing it about his
head)*: You softy—you piffler—you will never have had
enough. Ah, you should be thrust in the fire, you should, to
have the softness and the brittleness burnt out of you. *(The door*

opens—OLIVER *enters, followed by* JOB ARTHUR. MRS BARLOW *is still attacking* GERALD. *She turns infuriated.*) Go out. Go out! What do you mean by coming in unannounced. Take him upstairs—take that fellow into the library, Oliver Turton. [*Exit*

5   OLIVER *and* JOB ARTHUR.]

GERALD: Mother, you improve our already pretty reputation. Already they say you are mad.

MRS BARLOW (*ringing violently*): Let me be mad then. I am mad—driven mad. One day I shall kill you, Gerald.

10   GERALD: You won't, mother, because I shan't let you.

MRS BARLOW: Let me—let me! As if I should wait for you to let me.

GERALD: I am a match for you even in violence, come to that.

MRS BARLOW: A match! A damp match. A wet match. (*Enter*

15   WILLIAM.)

WILLIAM: You rang, Madam?

MRS BARLOW: Clear up those bits.—Where are you going to see that white-faced fellow? Here?

GERALD: I think so.

20   MRS BARLOW: You will *still* have them coming to the house, will you? You will still let them trample in our private rooms, will you? Bah, I ought to leave you to your own devices. (*Exit.*)

GERALD: When you've done that, William, ask Mr Freer to come down here.

25   WILLIAM: Yes sir. (*A pause—exit* WILLIAM.)

GERALD: So—o—o:—You've had another glimpse of the family life.

ANABEL: Yes.—Rather—disturbing—frightening.

GERALD: Not at all, when you're used to it.—Mother isn't as mad

30   as she pretends to be.

ANABEL: I don't think she's mad at all.—I think she has most desperate courage.

GERALD: 'Courage' is good. That's a new term for it.

ANABEL: Yes, courage. When a man says courage he means the

35   courage to die. A woman means the courage to live. That's what women hate men most for: that they haven't the courage to live.

GERALD: Mother takes her courage into both hands rather late.

ANABEL: We're a little late ourselves.

40   GERALD: We are, rather. By the way, you seem to have had plenty of

the courage of death—you've played a pretty deathly game, it
seems to me—both when I knew you and afterwards, you've
had your finger pretty deep in the death-pie.

ANABEL: That's what I want a change of—of—

GERALD: Of heart?—Better take mother's tip, and try the poker. 5

ANABEL: I will.

GERALD: Ha—corraggio!

ANABEL: Yes—corraggio!

GERALD: Corraggiaccio!

ANABEL: Corraggione!☆ 10

GERALD: Cock-a-doodle-doo—! *(Enter OLIVER and JOB ARTHUR.)*
Oh, come in. Don't be afraid, it's a charade. *(ANABEL rises.)* No,
don't go, Anabel. Corraggio! Take a seat, Mr Freer.

JOB ARTHUR: Sounds like a sneezing game, doesn't it?

GERALD: It is. Do you know the famous rhyme 15

> Speak gently to your little boy
> And beat him when he sneezes—?

JOB ARTHUR: No, I can't say I do.

GERALD: My mother does.—Will you have anything to drink? Will
you help yourself? 20

JOB ARTHUR: Well—no—I don't think I'll have anything, thanks.

GERALD: A cherry brandy?—Yes?—Anabel, what's yours?

ANABEL: Did I see Kümmel?☆

GERALD: You did. *(They all take drinks.)*—What's the latest, Mr
Freer? 25

JOB ARTHUR: The latest? Well, I don't know, I'm sure—

GERALD: Oh yes. Trot it out. We're quite private.

JOB ARTHUR: Well—I don't know. There's several things.

GERALD: The more the merrier.

JOB ARTHUR: I'm not so sure.—The men are in a very funny 30
temper, Mr Barlow—very funny.

GERALD: Coincidence—so am I. Not surprising, is it?

JOB ARTHUR: The men, perhaps not.

GERALD: What else, Job Arthur.

JOB ARTHUR: You know the men have decided to stand by the 35
office men?

GERALD: Yes.

JOB ARTHUR: They've agreed to come out next Monday.

GERALD: Have they!

JOB ARTHUR: Yes, there was no stopping them. They decided for it like one man.

GERALD: How was that?

JOB ARTHUR: That's what surprises me. They're a jolly sight more certain over this than they've ever been over their own interests.

GERALD: All their love for the office-clerks coming out in a rush.

JOB ARTHUR: Well, I don't know about love—but that's how it is.

GERALD: What is it, if it isn't love?

JOB ARTHUR: I can't say. They're in a funny temper. It's hard to make out.

GERALD: A funny temper, are they? Then I suppose we ought to laugh.

JOB ARTHUR: No, I don't think it's a laughing matter. They're coming out on Monday, for certain.

GERALD: Yes. So are daffodils.

JOB ARTHUR: Beg pardon?

GERALD: Daffodils.

JOB ARTHUR: No, I don't follow what you mean.

GERALD: Don't you?—But I thought Alfred Breffitt and William Straw* were not very popular.

JOB ARTHUR: No, they aren't—not in themselves. But it's the principle of the thing—so it seems.

GERALD: What principle?

JOB ARTHUR: Why, all sticking together, for one thing—all Barlow and Walsalls men holding by one another—

GERALD: United we stand—

JOB ARTHUR: That's it.—And then it's the strong defending the weak, as well. There's three thousand colliers standing up for thirty-odd office-men.—I must say I think it's sporting, myself.

GERALD: You do, do you. United we stand, divided we fall. What do they stand for, really? What is it?

JOB ARTHUR: Well—for their right to a living wage. That's how I see it.

GERALD: For their right to a living wage! Just that?

JOB ARTHUR: Yes sir, that's how I see it.

GERALD: Well, that doesn't seem so preposterously difficult, does it.*

JOB ARTHUR: Why, that's what I think myself, Mr Gerald. It's such a little thing—

GERALD: Quite.—I suppose the men themselves are to judge what is a living wage?

JOB ARTHUR: Oh, I think they're quite reasonable, you know.

GERALD: Oh yes, eminently reasonable. Reason's their strong point. —And if they get their increase they'll be quite contented?

JOB ARTHUR: Yes, as far as I know, they will.

GERALD: As far as you know? Why, is there something you don't know?—something you're not sure about?

JOB ARTHUR: No—I don't think so. I think they'll be quite satisfied, this time.

GERALD: Why this time? Is there going to be a next time—every-day-has-its-tomorrow kind of thing?

JOB ARTHUR: I don't know about that. It's a funny world, Mr Barlow.

GERALD: Yes, I quite believe it. How do you see it funny?

JOB ARTHUR: Oh, I don't know. Everything's in a funny state.

GERALD: What do you mean by everything?

JOB ARTHUR: Well—I mean things in general—Labour, for example.

GERALD: You think Labour's in a funny state, do you? What do you think it wants? What do you think, personally?

JOB ARTHUR: Well, in my own mind, I think it wants a bit of its own back.

GERALD: And how does it mean to get it?

JOB ARTHUR: Ha, that's not so easy to say. But it means to have it, in the long run.

GERALD: You mean by increasing demands for higher wages?

JOB ARTHUR: Yes, perhaps that's one road.

GERALD: Do you see any other?

JOB ARTHUR: Not just for the present.

GERALD: But later on?

JOB ARTHUR: I can't say about that.—The men will be quiet enough for a bit, if it's all right about the office-men, you know.

GERALD: Probably.—But have Barlow and Walsalls men any special grievance, apart from the rest of the miners?

JOB ARTHUR: I don't know. They've no liking for you, you know, sir.

GERALD: Why?

JOB ARTHUR: They think you've got a down on them.

GERALD: Why should they?

JOB ARTHUR: I don't know, sir, but they do.

GERALD: So they have a personal feeling against me?—You don't think all the colliers are the same, all over the country?

JOB ARTHUR: I think there's a good deal of feeling—

5   GERALD: Of wanting their own back?

JOB ARTHUR: That's it.

GERALD: But what can they do? I don't see what they can do. They can go out on strike—but they've done that before, and the owners, at a pinch, can stand it better than they can. As for the

10   ruin of the industry, if they do ruin it, it falls heaviest on them. In fact it leaves them destitute. There's nothing they can do, you know, that doesn't hit them worse than it hits us.

JOB ARTHUR: I know there's something in that.—But if they had a strong man to head them, you see—

15   GERALD: Yes, I've heard a lot about that strong man—but I've never come across any signs of him, you know. I don't believe in one strong man appearing out of so many little men. All men are pretty big in an age, or in a movement which produces a really big man. And Labour is a great swarm of hopelessly little

20   men. That's how I see it.

JOB ARTHUR: I'm not so sure about that.

GERALD: I am.—Labour is a thing that can't have a head. It's a sort of unwieldy monster that's bound to run its skull against the wall sooner or later, and knock out what bit of brain it's got. You

25   see you need wit and courage and real understanding, if you're going to do anything positive. And Labour has none of these things—certainly it shows no sign of them.

JOB ARTHUR: Yes, when it has a chance, I think you'll see plenty of courage, and plenty of understanding.

30   GERALD: It always has a chance. And where one sees a bit of courage, there's no understanding, and where there's some understanding, there's absolutely no courage. It's hopeless, you know.—It would be far best if they'd all give it up, and try a new line.

35   JOB ARTHUR: I don't think they will.

GERALD: No, I don't, either.—They'll make a mess, and when they've made it, they'll never get out of it.—They can't, they're too stupid.

JOB ARTHUR: They've never had a try yet.

40   GERALD: They're trying every day. They just simply couldn't

control modern industry—they haven't the intelligence. They've no *life* intelligence. The owners may have little enough, but Labour has none. They're just mechanical little things that can make one or two motions, and they're done. They've no more idea of life than a lawn-mower has. 5

JOB ARTHUR: It remains to be seen.

GERALD: No, it doesn't. It's perfectly obvious—there's nothing remains to be seen. All that Labour is capable of, is smashing things up. And for that I don't believe it has either the energy or the courage or the bit of necessary passion, or slap dash, call it 10 whatever you will.—However, we'll see.

JOB ARTHUR: Yes sir.—Perhaps you see now why you're not so very popular, Mr Gerald.

GERALD: We can't all be popular, Job Arthur. You're very high up in popularity, I believe. 15

JOB ARTHUR: Not so very. They listen to me a bit. But you never know when they'll let you down. I know they'll let me down one day—so it won't be a surprise—

GERALD: I should think not.

JOB ARTHUR: —But about the office men, Mr Gerald. You think 20 it'll be all right.

GERALD: Oh yes, that'll be all right.

JOB ARTHUR: Easiest for this time, anyhow, sir.—We don't want bloodshed, do we.

GERALD: I shouldn't mind at all. It might clear the way to some- 25 thing.—But I have absolutely no belief in the power of Labour even to bring about anything so positive as bloodshed.

JOB ARTHUR: I don't know about that. I don't know.—Well.

GERALD: Have another drink before you go.—Yes, do.—Help your-self. 30

JOB ARTHUR: Well—if you're so pressing.— *(Helps himself.)* Here's luck, all.

ALL: Thanks.

GERALD: Take a cigar—there's the box. Go on—take a handful—fill your case. 35

JOB ARTHUR: They're a great luxury nowadays, aren't they. Almost beyond a man like me.

GERALD: Yes, that's the worst of not being a bloated capitalist. Never mind, you'll be a Cabinet Minister some day.—Oh, all right—I'll open the door for you— 40

JOB ARTHUR: Oh, don't trouble.—Good night—good-night. [*Exit*
GERALD *and* JOB ARTHUR.]

OLIVER: Oh God, what a world to live in!

ANABEL: I rather liked him. What is he?

5 OLIVER: Checkweighman—local secretary for the Miners Federation*—plays the violin well, although he was a collier, and it
spoilt his hands. They're a musical family.

ANABEL: But isn't he rather nice?

OLIVER: I don't like him. But I confess he's a study. He's the
10 modern Judas.

ANABEL: Don't you think he likes Gerald?

OLIVER: I'm sure he does.—The way he suns himself here—like a
cat purring in his luxuriation.*

ANABEL: Yes, I don't mind it. It shows a certain sensitiveness—and
15 a certain taste—

OLIVER: Yes, he has both—touch of the artist, as Mrs Barlow says.
He loves refinement, culture, breeding, all those things—loves
them—and a presence, a fine free manner—

ANABEL: But that is nice in him.

20 OLIVER: Quite. But what he loves, and what he admires, and what
he aspires to, he *must* betray. It's his fatality. He lives for the
moment when he can kiss Gerald in the Garden of Olives,* or
wherever it was.

ANABEL: But Gerald shouldn't be kissed.

25 OLIVER: That's what I say.

ANABEL: And that's what his mother means as well, I suppose.

(Enter GERALD.*)*

GERALD: Well—you've heard the voice of the people.

ANABEL: He isn't the people.

30 GERALD: I think he is, myself—the epitome.

OLIVER: No, he's a special type.

GERALD: Ineffectual, don't you think?

ANABEL: How pleased you are, Gerald! How pleased you are with
yourself! You love the turn with him.

35 GERALD: It's rather stimulating, you know.

ANABEL: It oughtn't to be, then.

OLIVER: He's your Judas, and you love him.

GERALD: Nothing so deep. He's just a sort of Aeolian harp* that
sings to the temper of the wind.—I find him amusing.

40 ANABEL: I think it's boring.

OLIVER: And I think it's nasty.

GERALD: I believe you're both jealous of him.—What do you think of the British working man, Oliver?

OLIVER: It seems to me he's in nearly as bad a way as the British employer: he's nearly as much beside the point.   5

GERALD: What point?

OLIVER: Oh, just life.

GERALD: That's too vague, my boy.—Do you think they'll ever make a bust-up?

OLIVER: I can't tell. I don't see any good in it, if they do.   10

GERALD: It might clear the way—and it might block the way for ever: depends what comes through. But sincerely, I don't think they've got it in them.

ANABEL: They may have something better.

GERALD: That suggestion doesn't interest me, Anabel.—Ah well,   15 we shall see what we shall see.—Have a whiskey and soda with me, Oliver, and let the troubled course of this evening run to a smooth close.—It's quite like old times. Aren't you smoking, Anabel?

ANABEL: No thanks.   20

GERALD: I believe you're a reformed character.—So it won't be like old times after all.

ANABEL: I don't want old times. I want new ones.

GERALD: Wait till Job Arthur has risen like Antichrist, and pro-claimed the resurrection of the gods—do you see Job Arthur   25 proclaiming Dionysos and Aphrodite?*

ANABEL: It bores me. I don't like your mood. Good-night.

GERALD: Oh, don't go.

ANABEL: Yes, Good-night. *(Exit.)*

OLIVER: She's *not* reformed, Gerald. She's the same old moral   30 character—moral to the last bit of her, really—as she always was.

GERALD: Is that what it is?—But one must be moral.

OLIVER: Oh yes.—Oliver Cromwell wasn't as moral as Anabel is—nor such an iconoclast.*   35

GERALD: Poor old Anabel.

OLIVER: How she hates the dark gods!

GERALD: And yet they cast a spell over her.—Poor old Anabel.— Well, Oliver, is Bacchus the father of whiskey?*

OLIVER: I don't know.—I don't like you either. You seem to smile all over yourself. It's objectionable.—Good night.

GERALD: Oh, look here, this is censorious.

OLIVER: You smile to yourself. *(Exit.)*

5 *(Curtain)*

Act III.

Scene 1.

An old park—early evening. In the back-ground a low Georgian hall which has been turned into offices for the Company, shows windows *already lighted.* GERALD *and* ANABEL *walk along the path.*

ANABEL: How beautiful this old park is!

GERALD: Yes, it is beautiful—seems so far away from everywhere, if one doesn't remember that the hall is turned into offices.—No one has lived here since I was a little boy. I remember going to a Christmas party at the Walsalls.

ANABEL: Has it been shut up so long?

GERALD: The Walsalls didn't like it—too near the ugliness—they were county, you know*—we never were: father never gave mother a chance, there.—And besides, the place is damp, cellars full of water.

ANABEL: Even now?

GERALD: No, not now—they've been drained. But the place would be too damp for a dwelling-house. It's all right as offices—they burn enormous fires. The rooms are quite charming.—This is what happens to the stately homes of England*—they buzz with inky clerks, or their equivalent. Stateliness is on its last legs.

ANABEL: Yes—it grieves me—though I should be bored if I had to be stately, I think.—Isn't it beautiful in this light, like an eighteenth-century aquatint?—I'm sure no age was as ugly as this, since the world began.

GERALD: For pure ugliness, certainly not. And I believe none has been so filthy to live in.—Let us sit down a minute, shall we, and watch the rooks fly home. It always stirs sad sentimental feelings in me.

ANABEL: So it does in me.—Listen, one can hear the coal-carts on the road,—and the brook—and the dull noise of the town—and the beating of New London pit*—and voices—and the rooks—and yet it is so still. We seem so still here, don't we.

GERALD: Yes.

ANABEL: Don't you think we've been wrong?

GERALD: How?

ANABEL: In the way we've lived—and the way we've loved.

GERALD: It hasn't been heaven, has it? Yet I don't know that we've been wrong, Anabel. We had it to go through.

ANABEL: Perhaps.—And yes, we've been wrong too.

GERALD: Probably. Only I don't feel it like that.

ANABEL: Then I think you ought. You ought to feel you've been wrong.

5 GERALD: Yes, probably. Only, I don't. I can't help it.—I think we've gone the way we had to go, following our own natures.

ANABEL: And where has it landed us?

GERALD: Here.

ANABEL: And where is that?

10 GERALD: Just on this bench in the park, looking at the evening.

ANABEL: But what next?

GERALD: God knows. Why trouble?

ANABEL: One must trouble. I want to feel sure.

GERALD: What of?

15 ANABEL: Of you—and of myself.

GERALD: Then *be* sure.

ANABEL: But I can't. Think of the past—what it's been.

GERALD: This isn't the past.

ANABEL: But what is it? Is there anything sure in it? Is there any
20 real happiness?

GERALD: Why not?

ANABEL: But how can you ask!—Think of what our life has been.

GERALD: I don't want to.

ANABEL: No, you don't.—But what *do* you want?

25 GERALD: I'm all right, you know, sitting here like this.

ANABEL: But one can't sit here for ever, can one?

GERALD: I don't want to.

ANABEL: And what will you do when we leave here?

GERALD: God knows.—Don't worry me. Be still a bit.

30 ANABEL: But *I'm* worried.—You don't love me.

GERALD: I won't argue it.

ANABEL: And I'm not happy.

GERALD: Why not, Anabel?

ANABEL: Because you don't love me—and I can't forget.

35 GERALD: I do love you.—And tonight I've forgotten.

ANABEL: Then make me forget too. Make me happy.

GERALD: I *can't* make you—and you know it.

ANABEL: Yes you can. It's your business to make me happy. I've made you happy.

40 GERALD: You want to make me unhappy.

ANABEL: I *do* think you're the last word in selfishness.—If I say I can't forget, you merely say "*I've* forgotten," and if I say I'm unhappy, all you can answer is that I want to make *you* unhappy. I don't in the least. I want to be happy myself. But you don't help me. 5

GERALD: There is no help for it, you see.—If you *were* happy with me here you'd *be* happy—as you aren't, nothing will make you —not genuinely.

ANABEL: And that's all you care.

GERALD: No—I wish we could be both happy at the same moment. 10 But apparently we can't.

ANABEL: And why not?—because you're selfish, and think of nothing but yourself and your own feelings.

GERALD: If it is so it is so.

ANABEL: Then we shall never be happy. 15

GERALD: Then we shan't. *(A pause.)*

ANABEL: But what are we going to do?

GERALD: Do?

ANABEL: Do you want me to be with you?

GERALD: Yes. 20

ANABEL: Are you sure?

GERALD: Yes.

ANABEL: Then why don't you want me to be happy?

GERALD: If you'd only *be* happy, here and now,—

ANABEL: How can I? 25

GERALD: How can't you?—You've got a devil inside you.

ANABEL: Then make me not have a devil.

GERALD: I've known you long enough—and known myself long enough—to know I can make you nothing at all, Anabel: neither can you make me. If the happiness isn't there—well, we shall 30 have to wait for it, like a dispensation. It probably means we shall have to hate each other a little more.—I suppose hate is a real process.

ANABEL: Yes, I know you believe more in hate than in love.

GERALD: Nobody is more weary of hate than I am.—And yet we 35 can't fix our own hour, when we shall leave off hating and fighting. It has to work itself out in us.

ANABEL: But I don't *want* to hate and fight with you any more. I don't *believe* in it—not any more.

GERALD: It's a cleansing process—like Aristotle's Katharsis.※ We shall hate ourselves clean at last, I suppose.

ANABEL: Why aren't you clean now?—Why can't you love? *(He laughs.) Do* you love me?

5   GERALD: Yes.

ANABEL: Do you want to be with me for ever?

GERALD: Yes.

ANABEL: Sure?

GERALD: Quite sure.

10 ANABEL: Why are you so cool about it?

GERALD: I'm not. I'm only sure—which you aren't.

ANABEL: Yes I am.—I *want* to be married to you.

GERALD: I know you want me to want you to be married to me. But whether off your own bat you have a positive desire that way, I'm not sure.—You keep something back—some sort of female

15 reservation—like a dagger up your sleeve—You want to see me in transports of love for you—

ANABEL: How can you say so? There—you see—there—this is the man that pretends he loves me, and then says I keep a dagger up

20 my sleeve. You liar—

GERALD: I do love you—and you do keep a dagger up your sleeve—some devilish little female reservation which spies at me from a distance, in your soul, all the time, as if I were an enemy—

25 ANABEL: How *can* you say so?—Doesn't it show what you must be yourself. Doesn't it show?—What is there in *your* soul?

GERALD: I don't know.

ANABEL: Love, pure love?—Do you pretend it's love—

GERALD: I'm so tired of this.

30 ANABEL: So am I, dead tired: you self-deceiving, self-complacent thing. Ha—aren't you just the same. You haven't altered one scrap, not a scrap.

GERALD: All right, you are always free to change yourself.

ANABEL: I *have* changed, I *am* better, I *do* love you—I love you

35 wholly and unselfishly, I do, and I want a good new life with you—

GERALD: You're terribly wrapped up in your new goodness. I wish you'd make up your mind to be downright bad.

ANABEL: Ha!—do you!—you'd soon see. You'd soon see where

40 you'd be if— — There's somebody coming. *(Rises.)*

GERALD: Never mind, it's the clerks leaving work, I suppose. Sit still.

ANABEL: Won't you go?

GERALD: No.— *(A* CLERK *draws near, followed by another.)*

GERALD: Good-evening.

CLERK: Good-evening, Sir. *(Passes on.)* Good-evening Mr Barlow.

ANABEL: They are afraid.

GERALD: I suppose their consciences are uneasy about this strike.

ANABEL: Did you come to sit here just to catch them, like a spider waiting for them?

GERALD: No. I wanted to speak to Breffitt.

ANABEL: I believe you're capable of any horridness.

GERALD: All right, you believe it. *(Two more figures approach.)*

GERALD: Good-evening.

CLERKS: Good-night Sir. *(One passes, one stops.)* —Good-evening, Mr Barlow—er—did you want to see Mr Breffitt, Sir—?

GERALD: Not particularly.

CLERK: Oh. He'll be out directly, Sir—if you'd like me to go back and tell him you wanted him.

GERALD: No thank you.

CLERK: Goodnight Sir. Excuse me asking.

GERALD: Goodnight.

ANABEL: Who is Mr Breffitt.

GERALD: He is the chief clerk—and cashier—one of father's old pillars of society.*

ANABEL: Don't you like him?

GERALD: Not much.

ANABEL: Why?—You seem to dislike very easily.

GERALD: Oh, they all used to try to snub me, these old buffers. They detest me like poison, because I am different from father.

ANABEL: I believe you enjoy being detested.

GERALD: I do. *(Another* CLERK *approaches—hesitates—stops—.)*

CLERK: —Good-evening Sir—Good-evening Mr Barlow—er—did you want anybody at the office, Sir?—We're just closing.

GERALD: No, I didn't want anybody.

CLERK: Oh no Sir. I see.—Er—by the way, Sir—er—I hope you don't think this—er—bother about an increase—this strike threat—started in the office—

GERALD: Where did it start?

CLERK: I should think it started—where it usually starts, Mr

Barlow, among a few loud-mouthed people as thinks they can do as they like with the men. They're only using the office-men as a cry—that's all. They've no interest in us. They want to show their power.—That's how it is, Sir.

5   GERALD: Oh yes.

CLERK: We're powerless, if they like to make a cry out of us—

GERALD: Quite.

CLERK: We're as much put out about it as anybody.

GERALD: Of course.

10   CLERK: Yes.—Well—Good-night, Sir. *(CLERKS draw near—there is a sound of loud young voices, and bicycle bells. Bicycles sweep past.)*

CLERKS: Goodnight Sir. Goodnight, Sir.

GERALD: Goodnight.—They're very bucked to see me sitting here with a woman—a young lady, as they'll say. I guess your name

15   will be flying round tomorrow.—They stop partly to have a good look at you. Do they know you, do you think.

ANABEL: Sure.

CLERKS: Mr Breffitt's just coming, Sir.—Good-night Sir—Goodnight Sir. *(Another bicycle passes.)*

20   ANABEL: The bicycles don't see us.—Isn't it rather hateful to be a master? The attitude of them all is so ugly. I can quite see that it makes you rather a bully.

GERALD: I suppose it does. *(Figure of a large man approaches.)*

BREFFITT: Oh—Ah—it's Mr Gerald!—I couldn't make out who it

25   was.—Were you coming up to the Office, Sir?—Do you want me to go back with you.

GERALD: No thank you.—I just wanted a word with you about this agitation. It'll do just as well here. It's a pity it started—that the office should have set it going, Breffitt.

30   BREFFITT: It's none of the office's doing, I think you'll find, Mr Gerald. The office-men did nothing but ask for a just advance —at any rate, times and prices being what they are, I consider it a fair advance. If the men took it up it's because they've got a set of loud-mouthed blatherers and agitators among them like Job

35   Arthur Freer, who deserve to be hung, and hanging they'd get, if I could have the judging of them.

GERALD: Well—it's very unfortunate—because we can't give the clerks their increase now, you know.

BREFFITT: Can't you—can't you? I can't see that it would be

40   anything out of the way, if I say what I think.

GERALD: No. They won't get any increase now. It shouldn't have been allowed to become a public cry with the colliers. We can't give in now.

BREFFITT: Have the board decided that?

GERALD: They have—at my advice. 5

BREFFITT: Hm!—Then the men will come out.

GERALD: We will see.

BREFFITT: It's trouble for nothing—it's trouble that could be avoided. The clerks could have their advance, and it would hurt nobody. 10

GERALD: Too late now.—I suppose if the men come out the clerks will come out with them?

BREFFITT: They'll have to—they'll have to.

GERALD: If they do, we may then make certain alterations in the office staff, which have needed making for some time. 15

BREFFITT: Very good—very good. I know what you mean.—I don't know how your father bears all this, Mr Gerald.

GERALD: We keep it from him as much as possible.—You'll let the clerks know the decision. And if they stay out, with the men, I'll go over the list of the staff with you. It has needed revising for a 20 long time.

BREFFITT: I know what you mean—I know what you mean. I believe I understand the firm's interest in my department. I ought, after forty years studying it. I've studied the firm's interests for forty years, Mr Gerald. I'm not likely to forget 25 them now.

GERALD: Of course.

BREFFITT: But I think it's a mistake, I think it's a mistake, and I'm bound to say it, to let a great deal of trouble rise for a very small cause.—The clerks might have had what they reasonably asked 30 for—

GERALD: Well, it's too late now.

BREFFITT: I suppose it is, I suppose it is. I hope you'll remember, Sir, that I've put the interest of the firm before everything, before every consideration. 35

GERALD: Of course, Breffitt.

BREFFITT: But you've not had any liking for the office staff, I'm afraid, Sir, not since your father put you amongst us for a few months.—Well, sir, we shall weather this gale, I hope, as we've weathered those in the past. Times don't become better, do 40

they? Men are an ungrateful lot, and these agitators should be
lynched. They would if I had my way.

GERALD: Yes, of course. Don't wait.

BREFFITT: Goodnight to you. *(Exit.)*

GERALD: Goodnight.

ANABEL: He's the last, apparently.

GERALD: We'll hope so.

ANABEL: He puts you in a fury.

GERALD: It's his manner. My father spoilt them—abominable old
limpets. And they're so self-righteous. They think I'm a sort of
criminal who has instigated this new devilish system which runs
everything so close and cuts it so fine:—as if they hadn't made
this inevitable by their shameless carelessness and wastefulness
in the past. He may well boast of his forty years—forty years'
crass stupid wastefulness. *(Two or three more* CLERKS *pass,
talking till they approach the seat, then becoming silent after bidding
goodnight.)*

ANABEL: But aren't you a bit sorry for them?

GERALD: Why? If they're poor, what does it matter, in a world of
chaos.

ANABEL: And aren't you an obstinate ass not to give them the bit
they want. It's mere stupid obstinacy.

GERALD: It may be. I call it policy.

ANABEL: Men always do call their obstinacy policy.

GERALD: Well, I don't care what happens. I wish things would come
to a head. I only fear they won't.

ANABEL: Aren't you rather wicked? *Lusting* for strife.

GERALD: I hope I am. It's quite a relief to me to feel that I may be
wicked. I fear I'm not. I can see them all anticipating victory, in
their low-down fashion—wanting to crow their low-down crow-
ings. I'm afraid I feel it's a righteous cause, to cut a lot of little
combs before I die.

ANABEL: But if they're in the right in what they want.

GERALD: In the right—in the right—they're just greedy, incompe-
tent, stupid, gloating in a sense of the worst sort of power.
They're like vicious children, who would like to kill their
parents so that they could have the run of the larder.—The rest
is just cant.

ANABEL: If you're the parent in the case, I must say you flow over
with lovingkindness for them.

GERALD: I don't, I detest them. I only hope they will fight. If they would I'd have some respect for them. But you'll see what it will be.

ANABEL: I wish I needn't, for it's very sickening.

GERALD: Sickening beyond expression. 5

ANABEL: I wish we could go right away.

GERALD: So do I—if one could get oneself out of this.—But one can't. It's the same wherever you have industrialism—and you have industrialism everywhere, whether it's Timbuctoo or Paraguay or Antananarivo.* 10

ANABEL: No it isn't, you exaggerate.

JOB ARTHUR *(suddenly approaching from the other side)*: Good-evening, Mr Barlow. I heard you were in here. Could I have a word with you.

GERALD: Get on with it, then. 15

JOB ARTHUR: Is it right that you won't meet the clerks.

GERALD: Yes.

JOB ARTHUR: Not in any way.

GERALD: Not in any way whatsoever.

JOB ARTHUR: But—I thought I understood from you the other 20
night ...*

GERALD: It's all the same what you understood.

JOB ARTHUR: Then you take it back, Sir.

GERALD: I take nothing back, because I gave nothing.

JOB ARTHUR: Oh, excuse me, excuse me, Sir.—You said it would 25
be all right about the clerks. This lady heard you say it.

GERALD: Don't you call witnesses against me.—Besides, what does
it matter to you? What in the name of—

JOB ARTHUR: Well, Sir, you said it would be all right, and I went
on that— 30

GERALD: You went on that! Where did you go to?

JOB ARTHUR: The men'll be out on Monday.

GERALD: So shall I.

JOB ARTHUR: Oh yes but—where's it going to end?

GERALD: Do you want me to prophesy? When did I set up for a 35
public prophet?

JOB ARTHUR: I don't know, Sir.—But perhaps you're doing more
than you know. There's a funny feeling just now among the
men.

GERALD: So I've heard before. Why should I concern myself with 40 their feelings? Am I to cry when every collier bumps his funny bone—or to laugh?

JOB ARTHUR: It's no laughing matter, you see.

GERALD: And I'm sure it's no crying matter—unless you want to cry, do you see.

JOB ARTHUR: Ah but, very likely, it wouldn't be me who would cry.—You don't know what might happen, now.

GERALD: I'm waiting for something to happen. I should like something to happen—very much—very much indeed.

JOB ARTHUR: Yes, but perhaps you'd be sorry if it did happen.

GERALD: Is that a warning or a threat—

JOB ARTHUR: I don't know—it might be a bit of both.—What I mean to say—

GERALD *(suddenly seizing him by the scruff of the neck, and shaking him)*: What you mean to say—I mean you to say less, do you see —a great deal less—do you see—you've run on with your saying long enough, that clock had better run down. So stop your sayings—stop your sayings, I tell you—or you have them shaken out of you—shaken out of you—shaken out of you, do you see— *(Suddenly flings him aside—*JOB ARTHUR, *staggering, falls.)*

ANABEL: Oh no—oh no—

GERALD: Now get up, Job Arthur; and get up wiser than you went down. You've played your little game and your little tricks and made your little sayings long enough. You're going to stop now.—We've had quite enough of strong men of your stamp, Job Arthur—quite enough—such Labour leaders as you.

JOB ARTHUR [*getting up*]*: You'll be sorry, Mr Barlow—you'll be sorry. You'll wish you'd not attacked me.

GERALD: Don't you trouble about me and my sorrow. Mind your own.

JOB ARTHUR: You will, you'll be sorry. You'll be sorry for what you've done. You'll wish you'd never begun this—

GERALD: Begun—begun—I'd like to finish too, that I would. I'd like to finish with you too—I warn *you*—

JOB ARTHUR: I warn you—I warn you. You won't go on much longer. Every parish has its own vermin.

GERALD: Vermin?

JOB ARTHUR: Every parish has its own vermin, it lies with every parish to destroy its own. We shan't have a clean parish till we've destroyed the vermin we've got.

GERALD: Vermin? The fool's raving. Vermin!—Another phrase-maker, by God. Another phrase-maker to lead the people.—Vermin? What vermin. I know quite well what *I* mean by vermin, Job Arthur. But what do you mean? Vermin? Explain yourself. 5

JOB ARTHUR: Yes. Vermin. Vermin is what lives on other people's lives, living on their lives and profiting by it. We've got 'em in every parish—vermin, I say—that live on the sweat and blood of the people—live on it, and get rich on it—get rich through living on other people's lives, the lives of the working men— 10 living on the bodies of the working men—that's vermin—if it isn't, what is it—And every parish must destroy its own, every parish must destroy its own vermin.

GERALD: The phrase, my God, the phrase.

JOB ARTHUR: Phrase or not phrase, there it is, and face it out if you 15 can. There it is—there's not one in every parish—there's more than one—there's a number—

GERALD *(suddenly kicking him)*: Go—! *(Kicks him.)* Go! *(Kicks him.)* Go—! *(*JOB ARTHUR *falls.)* Get out! *(Kicks him.)* Get out, I say!—Get out, I tell you!—Get out!—Get out!—Vermin!— 20 Vermin!—I'll vermin you!—I'll put my foot through your phrases.—Get up, I say, get up and go—*go*—

JOB ARTHUR: It'll be you as'll go, this time.

GERALD: What? What!—By God, I'll kick you out of this park like a rotten bundle if you don't get up and go. 25

ANABEL: No, Gerald, no. Don't forget yourself. It's enough now.—It's enough now.—Come away. Do come away. Come away, leave him.

JOB ARTHUR *(still on the floor)*: It's your turn to go. It's you as'll go, this time. 30

GERALD *(looking at him)*: One can't even tread on you.

ANABEL: Don't, Gerald, don't—don't look at him.—Don't say any more, you Job Arthur.—Come away, Gerald—come away—come—do come.

GERALD *(turning)*: *That* a human being!—My God!—But he's right 35 —it's I who go. It's we who go, Anabel. He's still there.—My God, a human being—!

(Curtain)

Scene 2.

Market-Place as in Act I. WILLIE *addressing a large crowd of men* [*including* JOB ARTHUR] *from the foot of the obelisk.*

WILLIE: And now you're out on strike—now you've been out for a
5   week, pretty nearly, what further are you? I heard a great deal of
talk about what you were going to do. Well, what *are* you going
to do? You don't know. You've not the smallest idea. You
haven't any ideas whatsoever. You've got your leaders. Now
then, Job Arthur, throw a little light on the way in front, will
10   you: for it seems to me we're lost in a bog. Which way are we to
steer? Come—give the word, and let's gee-up.

JOB ARTHUR: You ask me which way we are to go. I say we can't go
our own way, because of the obstacles that lie in front. You've
got to remove the obstacles from the way.

15 WILLIE: So said Balaam's ass.—But you're not an ass—beg pardon;
and you're not Balaam—you're Job.* And we've all got to be little
Jobs, learning how to spell patience backwards. We've lost our
jobs and we've found a Job. It's picking up a scorpion when you're
looking for an egg.*—Tell us what you propose doing.— Remove
20   an obstacle from the way! What obstacle?—and whose way?

JOB ARTHUR: I think it's pretty plain what the obstacle is.

WILLIE: Oh ay. Tell us then.

JOB ARTHUR: The obstacle to Labour is Capital.

WILLIE: And how are we going to put salt on Capital's tail?

25 JOB ARTHUR: By Labour we mean us working men; and by Capital
we mean those that derive benefit from us, take the cream off us
and leave us the skim.

WILLIE: Oh yes.

JOB ARTHUR: So that if you're going to remove the obstacle, you've
30   got to remove the masters, and all that belongs to them. Does
everybody agree with me.

VOICES (*loud*): Ah, we do—yes—we do that—we do an' a'—yi—yi,
that's it.

WILLIE: Agreed unanimously. But how are we going to do it? Do
35   you propose to send for Williamson's furniture van, to pack
them in? I should think one pantechnicon would do, just for
this parish. I'll drive. Who'll be the van men, to lift and
carry?

JOB ARTHUR: It's no use fooling. You've fooled for thirty years, and

we're no further. What's got to be done will have to be begun.
It's for every man to sweep in front of his own doorstep. You
can't call your neighbour dirty till you've washed your own face.
Every parish has got its own vermin, and it's the business of
every parish to get rid of its own.

VOICES: That's it—that's it—that's the ticket—that's the style—

WILLIE: And are you going to comb 'em out, or do you propose to
use Keatings?

VOICES: Shut it. Shut it up. Stop thy face. Hold thy gab.—Go on,
Job Arthur.

JOB ARTHUR: How it's got to be done is for us all to decide. I'm not
one for violence, except it's a force-put. But it's like this. We've
been travelling for years to where we stand now—and here the
road stops. There's only room for one at a time on this path.
There's a precipice below and a rock-face above. And in front
of us stands the masters. Now there's three things we can do.
We can either throw ourselves over the precipice: or we can lie
down and let the masters walk over us: or we can *get on*.

WILLIE: Yes. That's all right. But how are you going to get on?

JOB ARTHUR: Well—we've either got to throw the obstacle down
the cliff—or walk over it.

VOICES: Ay—ay—ay—yes—that's a fact—

WILLIE: I quite follow you, Job Arthur. You've either got to do for
the masters—or else just remove them, and put them somewhere else.

VOICES: Get rid on 'em—drop 'em down th' shaft—sink 'em—ha'
done wi' 'em—bust the beggars—what do you do wi' vermin—

WILLIE: Supposing you begin. Supposing you take Gerald Barlow,
and hang him up from this lamp-post, with a piece of coal in his
mouth for a sacrament—

VOICES: Ay—serve him right—serve the beggar right—shove it
down's throttle—ay—

WILLIE: Supposing you do it—supposing you've done it—and
supposing you aren't caught and punished—even supposing
that—what are you going to do next?—*that's* the point.

JOB ARTHUR: We know what we're going to do. Once we can get
our hands free, we know what we're going to do.

WILLIE: Yes, so do I. You're either going to make *such* a mess that
we shall never get out of it—which I don't think you will do, for
the English working-man is the soul of obedience and order,

and he'll behave himself tomorrow as if he was at Sunday school, no matter what he does today—No, what you'll do, Job Arthur, you'll set up another lot of masters, such a jolly sight worse than what we've got now. I'd rather be mastered by Gerald Barlow, if it comes to mastering, than by Job Arthur Freer—oh, *such* a lot! You'll be far less free with Job Arthur for your boss than ever you were with Gerald Barlow. You'll be far more degraded.—In fact, although I've preached socialism in this market-place for thirty years—if you're going to start killing the masters to set yourselves up for bosses—why, kill me along with the masters. For I'd rather die with somebody who has one tiny little spark of decency left—though it *is* a little spark—than live to triumph with those that have none.

VOICES: Shut thy face, Houghton—shut it up—shut him up— hustle the beggar—Hoi—hoi-ee—whoo—whoam-it, whoam-it,—whoo!—bow-bow—wet-whiskers—

WILLIE: And it's no use you making fools of yourselves— *(His words are heard through an ugly, cold, jeering commotion.)*

VOICE *(loudly)*: He's comin'—

VOICES: Who?

VOICE: Barlow—See's motor?—comin' up—sithee?—

WILLIE: If you've any sense left— *(Suddenly and violently disappears.)*

VOICES: Sorry!—he's comin'—s'comin'—sorry ah!—who's in?— that's Turton drivin'—yi, he's behind, wi' a woman—ah, he's comin'—he'll none go back—hold on, Sorry—wheer's 'e comin'?—up from Lodnor?—ay— *(The cries die down—the motor-car slowly comes into sight, OLIVER driving, GERALD and ANABEL behind. The men stand in a mass in the way.)*

OLIVER: Mind yourself, there. *(Laughter.)*

GERALD: Go ahead, Oliver.

VOICE: What's yer urry! *(Crowd sways and surges on the car. OLIVER is suddenly dragged out—GERALD stands up—he too is seized from behind—he wrestles—is torn out of his great-coat—then falls, disappears—loud cries—Hi—hoi—hoiee—all the while—the car shakes and presses uneasily.)*

VOICE: Stop the blazin' motor, somebody.

VOICE: Here y'are!—hold a minute— *(A man jumps in and stops the engine—he drops in the driver's seat.)*

COLLIER *(outside the car)*: Step down Miss.

ANABEL: I am Mrs Barlow.

COLLIER: Missis, then. *(Laugh.)* Step down.—Lead 'er forrard.

VOICES: Take 'em forrard—take 'em forrard—

JOB ARTHUR: Ay, make a road—

GERALD: You're makin' a proper fool of yourself now, Freer. 5

JOB ARTHUR: You've brought it on yourself. *You've* made fools of plenty of men—

COLLIERS: Come on, now—come on—whoa!—whoa!!—he's a jibber—go pretty now, go pretty—

VOICES *(suddenly)*: Lay hold o' Houghton—nab 'im—seize 'im— 10 rats!—rats!—bring 'im forrard.

ANABEL *(in a loud, clear voice)*: I never knew anything so *ridiculous.*

VOICES *(falsetto)*: Ridiculous! Oh, ridiculous! Mind the step dear!—I'm Mrs Barlow!—Oh are you!—Tweet-tweet!*—

JOB ARTHUR: Make a space, boys—make a space— *(He stands with* 15 *prisoners in a cleared space before the obelisk.)* —Now—Now— Quiet a minute—we want to ask a few questions of these gentlemen—

VOICES: Quiet!—quiet!—Sh-h-h! Shh-h-h!—Answer pretty—answer pretty now!—Quiet!—shh-h-h— 20

JOB ARTHUR: We want to ask you, Mr Gerald Barlow, why you have given occasion for this present trouble—

GERALD: You are a fool.

VOICES: Oh—Oh!—naughty Barlow!—naughty Baa-lamb—answer pretty—answer pretty—be good Baa-lamb—baa—baa!—answer 25 pretty when gentleman asks you.—

JOB ARTHUR: Quiet a bit.—Sh-h-h!—We put this plain question to you, Mr Barlow.—Why did you refuse to give the clerks their just and fair advance, when you knew that by refusing you would throw three thousand men out of employment—? 30

GERALD: You are a fool, I say.

VOICES: Oh—Oh—won't do—won't do Barlow—wrong answer— wrong answer—be good baa-lamb—naughty boy—naughty boy—

JOB ARTHUR: Quiet a bit—now!—If three thousand men ask you a 35 just, straightforward question, do you consider they've no right to an answer—?

GERALD: I would answer you* with my foot—

VOICES *(amid a threatening scuffle)*: La-di-da! Hark ye—hark ye!—Oh—whoa—whoa a bit!—won't do!—won't do!—naughty 40

—naughty—say you're sorry—say you're sorry—kneel and say you're sorry—kneel and beg pardon—

JOB ARTHUR: Hold on a bit—keep clear—

VOICES: Make him kneel—make him kneel—on his knees with him—

JOB ARTHUR: I think you'd better kneel down. *(The crowd press on* GERALD—*he struggles—they hit him behind the knees, force him down.)*

OLIVER: This is shameful and unnecessary—

VOICES: All of 'em—on your knees—all of 'em—on their knees.— *(They seize* OLIVER *and* WILLIE *and* ANABEL, *hustling—*ANABEL *kneels quietly—the others struggle.)*

WILLIE: Well of all the damned, dirty, cowardly—

VOICES: Shut up, Houghton—shut him up—squeeze him—

OLIVER: Get off me—let me alone—I'll kneel—

VOICES: Good little doggies—nice doggies—kneel and beg pardon —yap-yap—answer—make him answer—

JOB ARTHUR *(holding up his hand for silence)*: It would be better if you answered straight off, Barlow. We want to know why you prevented that advance.

VOICES *(after a pause)*: Nip his neck. Make him yelp.

OLIVER: Let me answer, then.—Because it's worse, perhaps, to be bullied by three thousand men, than by one man.

VOICES: Oh!—Oh!—dog keeps barking—stuff his mouth—stop him up—here's a bit of paper—answer Barlow—nip his neck— stuff his mug—make him yelp—cork the bottle. *(They force a lump of newspaper into* OLIVER'S *mouth, and bear down on* GERALD.)

JOB ARTHUR: Quiet—quiet—quiet a minute, everybody. We give him a minute—we give him a minute to answer—

VOICES: Give him a minute—a holy minute—say your prayers, Barlow—you've got a minute—tick-tick says the clock—time him—

JOB ARTHUR: Keep quiet—

WILLIE: Of all the damned, cowardly—

VOICES: Sh-h-h! Squeeze him, throttle him. Silence is golden, Houghton. Close the shutters, Willie's dead.—Dry up, wet whiskers—

JOB ARTHUR: You've fifteen seconds.

VOICES: There's a long, long trail a-winding—

JOB ARTHUR: The minute's up.—We ask you again, Gerald Barlow, why you refused a just and fair demand, when you knew it was against the wishes of three thousand men all as good as yourself—

VOICES: And a sight better—I don't think—we're not all vermin— 5
we're not all crawlers, living off the sweat of other folks—we're not all parish vermin—parish vermin—

JOB ARTHUR: —And on what grounds you think you have no occasion to answer the straightforward question we put you here. 10

ANABEL *(after a pause)*: Answer them, Gerald. What's the use of prolonging this.

GERALD: I've nothing to answer.

VOICES: Nothing to answer—Gerald darling—Gerald duckie—oh lovey-dovey—I've nothing to answer—No by God—No by 15
God, he hasna—nowt to answer—ma'e him find summat, then—answer for him—gi'e him 's answer—let him ha'e it—go on—mum—mum—lovey-dovey—rub his nose in it—ay, rub his nose in it—kiss the dirt, ducky—bend him down—rub his nose is—he's saying something—oh no he isn't—sorry I spoke 20
—bend him down—

JOB ARTHUR: Quiet a bit—quiet everybody—he's got to answer— keep quiet—Now— *(A silence.)* Now then, Barlow—will you answer, or won't you?— *(Silence.)*

ANABEL: Answer them, Gerald—never mind— 25

VOICES: Sh-h-h! Sh-h-h! *(Silence.)*

JOB ARTHUR: You won't answer, Barlow?

VOICE: Down the beggar.

VOICES: Down him—put his nose down—flatten him— *(The crowd surges and begins to howl—they sway dangerously—*GERALD *is* 30
spread-eagled on the floor, face down.)

JOB ARTHUR: Back—back—back a minute—back—back— *(They recoil.)*

WILLIE: I *hope* there's a God in heaven—

VOICES: Put him down—flatten him. (WILLIE *is flattened on the* 35
ground.)

JOB ARTHUR: Now then—now then—if you won't answer, Barlow, I can't stand here for you any more.—Take your feet off him, boys, and turn him over. Turn him over—let us look at him. Let us see if he *can* speak. *(They turn him over, with another* 40

scuffle.) —Now then, Barlow—you can see the sky above you.
Now do you think you're going to play with three thousand
men, with their lives and with their souls—now do you think
you're going to answer them with your foot—do you—do you.
5   *(The crowd has begun to sway and heave dangerously, with a low,
muffled roar, above which is heard* JOB ARTHUR'S *voice. As he
ceases the roar breaks into a yell, the crowd heaves.)*

VOICES: Down him—crack the vermin—on top of him—put your
foot on the vermin—

10 ANABEL *(with a loud, piercing cry, suddenly starting up)*: Ah no! Ah no!
Ah-h-h-h no-o-o-o! Ah-h-h-h no-o-o-o! Ah-h-h-h no-o-o-o!
No-o-o-o! No-o-o! No-o! No-o! No-o-o!—Ah-h-h-h!—it's
enough, it's enough, it's enough! It's enough, he's a man as you
are. He's a man as you are. He's a man as you are. He's a man as
15   you are. *(Weeps—a breath of silence.)*

OLIVER'S VOICE: Let us stop now—let us stop now. Let me stand
up. *(Silence.)* I want to stand up. *(A muffled noise.)*

VOICE: Let him get up. *(*OLIVER *rises.)*

OLIVER: Be quiet. Be quiet.—Now—choose! Choose! Choose!
20   Choose what you will do! Only choose! Choose!—it will be
irrevocable. *(A moment's pause.)* Thank God we haven't gone
too far.—Gerald, get up. *(Men still hold him down.)*

JOB ARTHUR: Isn't he to answer us? Isn't he going to answer us?

OLIVER: Yes, he shall answer you. He shall answer you. But let him
25   stand up. No more of this. Let him stand up.—He must stand
up. *(Men still hold* GERALD *down.* OLIVER *takes hold of their
hands, and removes them.)* Let go—let go now. Yes, let
go,—yes—I ask you to let go. *(Slowly, sullenly the men let go.*
GERALD *is free—but he does not move.)* There—get up Gerald!
30   Get up! You aren't hurt, are you? You must get up, it's no use.
We're doing our best—you must do yours. When things are like
this,* we have to put up with what we get. *(*GERALD *rises slowly,
and faces the mob. They roar dully.)* —You ask why the clerks
didn't get their increase? Wait! Wait! Do you still wish for any
35   answer, Mr Freer?

JOB ARTHUR: Yes, that's what we've been waiting for.

OLIVER: Then answer, Gerald.

GERALD: They've trodden on my face.

OLIVER: No matter. Job Arthur will easily answer that you've trodden on their souls. Don't start an altercation. *(The crowd is beginning to roar.)*

GERALD: You want to know why the clerks didn't get their rise?—because you interfered and attempted to bully about it, do you see. That's why.

VOICES: You want bullying.—You'll get bullying, you will—

OLIVER: Can't you see it's no good, either side. It's no mortal use. We might as well all die tomorrow, or today, or here this minute, as go on bullying one another, one side bullying the other side, and the other side bullying back. We'd *better* all die.

WILLIE: And a great deal better. I'm damned if I'll take sides with anybody against anything, after this. If I'm to die, I'll die by myself. As for living, it seems impossible.

JOB ARTHUR: Have the men nothing to be said for their side?

OLIVER: They have—a great deal—but not *everything*, you see.

JOB ARTHUR: Haven't they been wronged?—and *aren't* they wronged.

OLIVER: They have—and they are.—But haven't they been wrong themselves, too?—and *aren't* they wrong, now?

JOB ARTHUR: How?

OLIVER: What about this affair? Do you call it right?

JOB ARTHUR: Haven't we been driven to it?

OLIVER: Partly. And haven't you driven the masters to it, as well?

JOB ARTHUR: I don't see that.

OLIVER: Can't you see that it takes two to make a quarrel?—And as long as each party hangs on to its own end of the stick, and struggles to get full hold of the stick, the quarrel will continue? It will continue till you've killed one another. And even then, what better shall you be? What better would you be, really, if you'd killed Gerald Barlow just now? You wouldn't, you know. We're all human beings, after all. And why can't we try really to leave off haggling against one another, and set up a new state of things?

JOB ARTHUR: That's all very well, you see, while you've got the goods.

OLIVER: I've got very little, I assure you.

JOB ARTHUR: Well, if you haven't, those you mix with have. They've got the money, and the power, and they intend to keep it.

OLIVER: As for power, somebody must have it, you know. It only
   rests with you to put it into the hands of the best men, the men
   you *really* believe in.—And as for money, it's life, it's living that
   matters, not simply having money.

5 JOB ARTHUR: You can't live without money.

OLIVER: I know that. And therefore why can't we have the decency
   to agree simply about money, just agree to dispose of it so that
   all men could live their own lives.

JOB ARTHUR: That's what we want to do. But the others, such as
10   Gerald Barlow, they keep the money—*and* the power—

OLIVER: You see, if you wanted to arrange things so that money
   flowed more naturally, so that it flowed naturally to every man,
   according to his needs, I think we could all soon agree. But
   you don't. What you want is to take it away from one set and
15   give it to another—or keep it yourselves.

JOB ARTHUR: We want every man to have his proper share.

OLIVER: I'm sure *I* do. I want every man to be able to live and be
   free. But we shall never manage it by fighting over the
   money.—If you want what is natural and good, I'm sure the
20   owners would soon agree with you.

JOB ARTHUR: What? Gerald Barlow agree with us?

OLIVER: Why not? I believe so.

JOB ARTHUR: You ask him.

OLIVER: Do you think, Gerald, that if the men really wanted a
25   whole, better way, you would agree with them.

GERALD: I want a better way myself—but not their way.

JOB ARTHUR: There, you see!

VOICES: Ah-h! Look you!—That's him—that's him all over.

OLIVER: You want a better way—but not his way: he wants a better
30   way—but not your way. Why can't you both drop your buts,
   and simply say you want a better way, and believe yourselves
   and one another when you say it? Why can't you?

GERALD: Look here! I'm quite as tired of my way of life as you are
   of yours. If you make me believe you want something better,
35   then I assure you I do, I want what you want.—But Job Arthur
   Freer's not the man to lead you to anything better. You can tell
   what people want, by the leaders they choose, do you see. You
   choose leaders whom I respect, and I'll respect you, do you see.
   As it is, I don't.—And now I'm going—

40 VOICES: Who says?—Oh ay!—Who says goin'?

GERALD: Yes, I'm going.—About this affair here we'll cry quits; no more said about it.—About a new way of life, a better way all round, I tell you I want it and need it as much as ever you do. I don't care about money really. But I'm never going to be bullied. 5

VOICE: Who doesn't care about money—?

GERALD: I don't. I think we ought to be able to alter the whole system—but not by bullying, not because one lot wants what the other has got.

VOICE: No, because you've got everything. 10

GERALD: Where's my coat? Now then, step out of the way—

(They move towards the car.)

(Curtain)

DAVID

AGAG

MEN WITH SPEARS

MERAB

MICHAL   5

1ST MAIDEN

2ND MAIDEN

3RD MAIDEN

4TH MAIDEN

SAUL   10

MAN

JONATHAN

ABNER

SAMUEL

PROPHETS   15

1ST HERDSMAN

JESSE

ELIAB

1ST ELDER

2ND ELDER   20

3RD ELDER

4TH ELDER

ABINADAB

SHAMMAH

FOURTH SON   25

FIFTH SON

SIXTH SON

SEVENTH SON

DAVID

NEIGHBOURS   30

WATCHMAN

1ST SOLDIER

LITTER-BEARERS

2ND SOLDIER

1ST CAPTAIN
SOLDIERS
3RD SOLDIER
GOLIATH
5   ARMOUR-BEARER
HERALD
CAPTAINS
ADRIEL
SINGER
10   MEN
2ND HERDSMAN
2ND CAPTAIN
WOMAN-SERVANT
BOY
15   4TH SOLDIER
5TH SOLDIER
1ST PROPHET
2ND PROPHET
LEADER OF ARMED MEN
20   6TH SOLDIER
7TH SOLDIER
LAD

D. H. Lawrence's list of characters

DAVID, Son of Jesse
25   SAUL, King of Israel
SAMUEL, Prophet of God.
JONATHAN, Son of Saul.
ABNER, leader of Saul's host
AGAG, King of Amalek

30   Merab, daughter of Saul
Michal, daughter of Saul
Woman-servant
Maidens

Jesse, father of David
35   Eliab, Abinadab, Shammah, brothers of David
Fourth, fifth, Sixth & seventh brothers of David
Adriel the Meholathite
Captains, Fighting-men, Herald, Armour-Bearer, Elders, Neighbours,
Prophets, Herdsmen & Lad.

DAVID*

Scene 1.

Courtyard of SAUL'S *house in Gilgal—sort of compound with an adobe house* * *beyond—*AGAG, *bound, seated on the ground, and fastened by a rope to a post of the shed—*MEN WITH SPEARS*—enter* MERAB *and* MICHAL, *daughters of* SAUL, *with tambourines:* *—MAIDENS—   5

MICHAL *(running and dancing)*: Saul came home with the spoil of the Amalekite!*

MAIDENS: Hie! Amalekite! Hie! Amalekite.

MICHAL: Saul threw his spear into the desert of Shur,* through the   10
heart of the Amalekite.

MAIDENS: Stuck the Amalekite, pierced him to the ground.*

MICHAL: Wind of the desert blows between the ribs of Amalek, only the jackal is fat in that land. Who smote the Amalekite, as a sand-storm smites the desert?   15

MAIDENS: Saul! Saul! Saul is the slayer and the death of Amalek.

MERAB *(before* AGAG*)*: What is this dog with a string round his neck?

MAIDENS: What dog is this?

MICHAL: I know this dog, men used to call it king.   20

MAIDENS: Look at this King!

MERAB: Agag, Agag, King of the Amalekites! Dog on a string at the heels of mighty Saul!

MICHAL *(speaking to* AGAG*)*: Are you the King of the Amalekites?

AGAG: I am he, maiden!   25

MICHAL: I thought it was a dog my father had brought home, and tied to a post.

MERAB: Why are you alone, Agag? Where are all your armed men, that ran like lions* round the road to Egypt? Where are your women, with gold on their foreheads? Let us hear the tinkle of   30
the bracelets of your women, O King, King Agag, King of mighty Amalek!

435

MAIDENS *(laughing—shaking tambourines in* AGAG's *face—spitting on him)*: Dog! Dog! Dog of an Amalekite!

MICHAL: Who hung on the heels of Israel when they journeyed out of the wilderness of Shur, coming from Egypt,* in the days of our fathers, in the day of Moses our great deliverer?

MAIDENS: Ay! Ay! Who threw spears in the backs of the wandering Israelites?

MICHAL: Who killed our women, and the weary ones, and the heavy-footed?* In the bitter days of wandering, when we came up out of Egypt?

MERAB: Who among our enemies was accursed like the Amalekite? When Moses held the rod of God uplifted in his hand, Joshua smote the Amalekite till the sun went down. But even when the sun was gone, came the voice of the Almighty: *War, and war with Amalek, till Amalek is put out from under heaven.*

MICHAL: Dog! Son of dogs that lay in wait for us as we passed by! Dog! Why has Saul left you eyes to see, and ears to hear!

SAUL *(coming from house)*: Agag is among the maidens!

MICHAL: See, Father, is *this* a king?

SAUL: Even so.

MICHAL: It is a dog that cannot scratch his own fleas.

SAUL: Even so, it is a king: king of rich Amalek. Have you seen the presents he has brought for the household of Saul?

MICHAL: For the daughters of Saul, Father?

SAUL: Surely for Merab and Michal, daughters of Saul. *(To* MAN.) Ho! Bring the basket of spoils for the daughters of the King.

MICHAL: Listen! Listen! King Agag seeks a wife in Gilgal! Oh Father, I do not like him! He looks like a crow the dogs have played with. Merab, here is a King for your hand!

MERAB: Death is his portion, the Amalekite.

MICHAL: Will you put him to death,* Father? Let us laugh a little longer at his Amalek nose.

(Enter MAN *with basket—also* JONATHAN *and* ABNER.*)*

SAUL: See the gifts of Agag, King of Amalek, to the daughters of Saul! Tissue from Egypt, head-veils from Pharaoh's house! And see, red robes from Tyre, yellow from Sidon.*

MICHAL *(screams)*: That for *me*, Father, that for me! Give the other to Merab.—Ah! Ah! Ah! Ah!—Thank you, King Agag, thank you, King of Amalek.

SAUL: Goldsmith's work for arms and ankles, gold and dropping silver, for the ears.[☆]

MICHAL: Give me those! Give me those! Give the others to Merab! Ay! Ay! Maidens! How am I?—See, Agag, noble Agag, how am I now? Listen! *(She dances, the ornaments clink.)* They say: 5
Noble Agag!—King of Givers!—Poor draggled crow that had gold in its nest! Caw! King Agag! Caw! It's a daughter of Saul, of long-limbed Saul, smiter of Amalek, who tinkles with joys of the Amalekite.

JONATHAN: Peace, maiden! Go in and spin wool with the women.[☆] 10
You are too much among the men.

MICHAL: Art thou speaking, Oh Jonathan, full of thine own manhood?

JONATHAN: Take in these spoils from the eye of men, and the light of day.—Father, there came one saying that Samuel sought you 15
in Carmel.[☆]

SAUL: Let him find me in Gilgal.

ABNER: They are calling even now at the gate.
(Moves to gate.)

SAUL *(to girls)*: Go to the house and hide your spoil, for if this 20
prophet of prophets[☆] find the Treasure of the Amalekite upon you, he will tear it away, and curse your youth.

MICHAL: That he shall not! Oh Merab, you got the blue shawl from me!—Run! Maidens! Run!—Farewell, King Agag, your servant thanks your lordship!—Caw!—Nay, he cannot even say caw! 25
(Exit, running, MICHAL—*and other* MAIDENS *follow.)*

ABNER: It is so, my lord. Samuel even now has passed the stone of directions, seeking Saul in Gilgal.[☆]

SAUL: It is well. He has come to bless our triumph.

JONATHAN: Father, will you leave that man in the sight of Samuel? 30

SAUL: No! Go you quietly into the house, Oh Agag! Take him quickly, men, and let no mouth speak his name.
(Exeunt AGAG *and* MEN WITH SPEARS.*)*

JONATHAN: I have a misgiving, Father, that Samuel comes not in peace, after Saul in Gilgal. 35

SAUL: Has Saul laid low the Amalekite, to fear the coming of an old prophet?

ABNER: Samuel is a jealous man, full of the tyranny of prophecy. Shall we wait him here, or go into the house and be seated on the mats? Or shall we go forth from the gate towards him? 40

SAUL: I will stay here, and brighten my sword-edge in the waiting.

ABNER *(at the gate—calling)*: He is coming across the field: an old man in a mantle,* alone, followed by two of the prophets.

JONATHAN *(joining ABNER)*: It is he. And coming in anger.

5   ABNER: In anger against whom?

JONATHAN: Against my father. Because we have not destroyed the Amalekite utterly, but have saved the best spoil.

ABNER: Nay, but it is a foolish thing, to throw fine linen into the fire, and fat young oxen down a dry well.

10   JONATHAN: It was the commandment.

ABNER: Why should the maidens not rejoice in their ornaments, and the God of the Unknown Name* enjoy the scent of blood-sacrifice?

(They retreat from the gate; SAUL sharpens his sword. After a pause,
15   *enter SAMUEL, followed by the PROPHETS.)*

SAUL *(laying down his sword)*: Blessed be thou of the Lord! I have performed the commandment of the Lord.

SAMUEL: What meaneth this bleating of the sheep in my ears, and the lowing of the oxen which I hear?

20   SAUL: They have brought them from the Amalekites. The people spared the best of the sheep, and of the oxen, to sacrifice unto thy God.—But the rest we have utterly destroyed.

SAMUEL: Stay, and I will tell thee what I have heard out of the inner darkness, this night.

25   SAUL: Say on.

SAMUEL: When thou wast little in thine own sight, wast thou not made the chieftain of the tribes of Israel, and the Deep poured his power over thee, to anoint thee king? And the voice out of the deeps sent thee on a journey, saying: Go and utterly destroy
30   the sinners the Amalekites, and fight against them until they be consumed.—Why then did you not obey the voice, instead of flying upon the spoil, and doing evil in the sight of the unclosing eyes?

SAUL: Yea, I have obeyed the voice from the beyond. I have gone
35   the way which the Great One sent me, and have brought Agag the king of Amalek prisoner, and have utterly destroyed the Amalekites. But the people took of the spoil, sheep and oxen, the chief of the things which should have been utterly destroyed, to sacrifice in Gilgal unto the Lord thy God.

40   SAMUEL: Does the Breather of the skies take as great delight in

sacrifice and burnt offerings, as in obedience to the voice that
spoke on the breath of the night? Behold, to obey is better than
sacrifice, and to hearken than the fat of rams.

SAUL: Is not thy God the sender of life, and the bread of life? And
shall we deny the meat and destroy the bread that is sent? 5

SAMUEL: Behold, is the Lord my God a sutler,* to stock the larders
of Saul?—Lo, he heeds not the fat beef nor the fine raiment,
but threshes out his anger in the firmament. Amalek has defied
the Living Breath, and cried mockery on the Voice of the
Beyond. Therefore the living Wrath will wipe out the Amale- 10
kite, by the hand of his servant Israel. And if the Nameless is
without compunction, whence this compunction of Saul?

SAUL: I feared the people, and obeyed their voice.

SAMUEL: Yea, that was bravely done! Thou didst not fear the Great
Lord, thou fearedst* the people, smaller than thyself. Thou 15
didst not obey the cry from the midst of the dark, but the voice
of the people!—I tell you,* rebellion is as the sin of witchcraft,
and stubbornness is as iniquity and idolatry. Because thou hast
rejected the word of the Lord, the Lord hath also rejected thee
from being king. 20

SAUL: Shall a king not hearken to the voice of his people?

SAMUEL: The people cried for a king, in the frowardness of their
hearts.* But can they make a king out of one of themselves?
Can they whistle a lion forth from a litter of dogs? The people
cried for a king, and the Lord gave to them. Even thee, 25
Saul.—But why art thou king? Because of the voice of the
people?

SAUL: Thou didst choose me out.

SAMUEL: The finger of the Thunder pointed me to thee, and the
Wind of Strength* blew me in thy way. And thou art king 30
because from out of the middle world, the great Wish* settled
upon thee. And thou art king because the Lord poured the oil
of his might over thee.—But thou art disobedient, and shuttest
thine ears to the Voice. Thou hearest the barking of dogs and
the crying of the people, and the Voice of the midmost is 35
nothing to thee. Therefore thou hast become as nothing unto
the Lord, and he that chose thee rejecteth thee again. The
power of the Lord shall fall away from thee, and thou shalt
become again a common man, and a little thing, as when the
Lord first found thee. 40

SAUL: I have sinned. For I have transgressed the commandment of the Lord, which thou didst hear out of the deeps of the night. Because I feared the people, and obeyed their voice.—But now, I pray thee, pardon my sin, and turn again with me, that I may find the Lord, to worship him.

SAMUEL: I will not return with thee: for thou hast rejected the word of the Lord; and the Lord hath rejected thee from being king over Israel.

(SAMUEL turns away. SAUL catches hold of the hem of SAMUEL'S garment, and it tears, in his hand.)

SAMUEL: The Lord hath rent the kingdom of Israel away from thee this day, and hath given it to a neighbour of thine, that is better than thou.— *(Pause.)* For the Mighty One that moveth Israel will not lie, nor repent towards thee again: for he is not a man, that he should repent.

SAUL: I have sinned, I have sinned. I have turned my face the wrong way.—Yet honour me now, I pray thee!—Honour me before the elders of my people, and before Israel, and turn again with me, that I may find the Lord thy God, and worship him.

SAMUEL *(turning)*: Thou hast turned away from the Hidden Sun, and the gleam is dying from out of thy face. Thou hast disowned the Power that made thee, and the glow is leaving thy limbs, the glisten of oil is waning on thy brow, and the vision is dying in thy breast.—Yet because thou art the Lord's anointed, I will bless thee again in the sight of the elders. Yet if the Lord hath decided against thee, what avails an old man's blessing?

SAUL: Yet bless me, my father.

SAMUEL *(lifting his hand)*: The Lord be with thee! The Lord's strength strengthen thee! The power and the might of the Lord, brighten thine eyes and light thy face! the Lord's life lift thy limbs and gladden the walls of thy breast, and put power in thy belly and thy hips! The Lord's haste strengthen thy knees and quicken thy feet!*

SAUL *(lifting both hands to heaven)*: Lo, I have sinned, and lost myself. I have been mine own undoing. But I turn again to Innermost, where the flame is, and the wings are throbbing. Hear me, and take me back! Brush me again with the wings of life, breathe on me with the breath of thy desire, come in unto me, and be with me, and dwell in me. For without the presence

of the awful* Lord, I am an empty shell.—Turn to me, and fill
my heart, and forgive my transgression. For I will wash myself
clean of Amalek, to the last speck, and remove the source of my
sinning. *(Drops his hands—turns to* SAMUEL.*)* Is it well, O
Samuel!   5

SAMUEL: May it be well.—Bring me hither Agag, King of the
Amalekites.

SAUL: Ho, Jonathan, send here Agag the Amalekite. And send thou
the chief of the herdsmen, oh Abner. We* must wipe away the
stain of Amalek swiftly, out of Gilgal. *(Exeunt* JONATHAN *and*   10
ABNER.*)*

SAUL *(to* SAMUEL*)*: The Lord shall be with me again this day, that
the kingdom be not rent from me.

SAMUEL: Who knoweth the ways of the Deep?* I will entreat, ah!
for thee in the night-time, and in the day. But if he hath turned   15
his face away, what am I but an old man crying like an infant in
the night!*

(Enter AGAG—*coming forward delicately.)*

AGAG: Surely the bitterness of death is past.

SAMUEL *(seizing* SAUL'S *sword)*: As thy sword hath made women   20
childless, so shall thy mother be childless among women.

(Rushes on AGAG *with sword—*AGAG *steps behind a wall,* SAMUEL *upon*
him. Enter [JONATHAN, ABNER *and*] 1ST HERDSMAN.*)*

JONATHAN: Better it had been in battle, on the field of the fight.

ABNER: It is as a sacrifice.   25

SAUL *(to* 1ST HERDSMAN*)*: Gather together the cattle of the Amalekite, which came as spoil, and fasten them in a pen. Leave out
no sheep and no calf, nor any goat, but put them all in.

1ST HERDSMAN: It shall be as Saul says. *(Exit.)*

SAMUEL *(entering with red sword)*: I have hewed him in pieces   30
before the Lord, and his blood has gone up to the Most High,*
it is in the nostrils of the God of Wrath.*

SAUL: Come now, I pray thee, within the house, and let them bring
water for thy feet and food to glad thine heart.

SAMUEL: It may not be. But I must go to Ramah* to entreat for   35
thee before the Lord, and even now must I go. And may the
Might be with thee—*

(Curtain)

Scene 2.

A room in Ramah. Night. SAMUEL *in prayer.*

SAMUEL: Speak to me out of the whirlwind, come to me from
behind the sun, listen to me where the winds are hastening.—
When the power of the whirlwind moves away from me, I am a
worthless old man. Out of the deep of deeps comes a breath
upon me, and my old flesh freshens like a flower, I know no age.
Oh, upon the wings of distance, turn to me, send the fanning of
strength into my hips.—I am sore for Saul, and my old bones
are weary for the king. My heart is like a fledgling in a nest,
abandoned by its mother. My heart opens its mouth with vain
cries, weak and meaningless, and the Mover of the deeps will
not stoop to me.—My bowels are twisted in a knot of grief, in a
knot of anguish for my son, for him whom I anointed beneath
the firmament of Might.—On earth move men and beasts, they
nourish themselves and know not how they are alive. But in all
the places moves unseen almighty, like a breath among the
stars, or the moon, like the sea turning herself over. I eat bread,
but my soul faints, and wine will not heal my bones. Nothing is
good for me but God. Like waters he moves through the world,
like a fish I swim in the flood of God Himself.—Answer me,
mover of the waters, speak to me as waves speak, without
mouths. Saul has fallen off, as a ripe fig falls and bursts. He,
anointed, he moved in the flood of power, he was God's, he was
not his own. Now he is cast up like a fish among the dry stones,
he beats himself against the sun-licked pebbles. He has jumped
out from the deeps of the Lord, the sea of God has seen him
depart. He will die within the smell of his own violence.—Lord,
Lord, Ocean and Mover of Oceans, lick him up again into the
flood of thy self. Wilt thou not reach for him with the arm of a
long wave, and catch him back into the deeps of living God? Is
he lost from the sway of the tide for ever?—When the rain wets
him, will it wet him godless, and will the wind blow on him
without god in it? Lord, wilt thou not reach for him, he is thine
anointed?—Bitter are the waters of old age, and tears fall
inward on the heart.—Saul is the son whom I anointed, and
Saul has crawled away from god, he creeps up the rocks in
vanity, the stink of him will rise up like a dead crab.—Lord, is
it verily so with Saul, is he gone out from thee for ever, like a

creeping thing crawled in vanity from its element of elements?—I am old, and my tears run inward, they deaden my heart because of Saul. For Saul has crawled away from the Fountain of Days, and the Ancient of Days* will know him no more.—I hear the voice of the Lord like waters washing through the night, saying: *Saul has fallen away, and is no more in the way of the power of God.*—Yea, what is love, that I should love him! He is fallen away, and stinketh like a dead crab, and my love stinks with him. I must wash myself because of Saul, and strip myself of him again, and go down into the deeps of God.—Speak, Lord, and I will obey. Tell me, and I will do it. I sink like a stone in the sea, and nothing of my own is left me. I am gone away from myself, I disappear in the deeps of God. And the oracle of the Lord stirs me, as the fountains of the deep.—Lo! I am not mine own. The flood has covered me, and the waters of the beginning sound in the shell of my heart. And I will find another king for Israel, I shall know him by the whisper of my heart. Lo, I will fill the horn with oil again,with the oil from the body of him, and I will go into the hills of Judah.* I will find out one, in whom the power sleeps. And I will pour potency over his head, and anoint him with God's fecundity, and place him beyond forgetting. I will go into the hills of Judah, where the sheep feed among the rocks, and find a man fresh in the morning of God. And he shall be king. On the morrow I will gather myself and go, silently, carrying the kingship away from Saul, because the virtue is gone out of him.* And Saul will kill me with a spear, in one stroke, for rage he will kill me,* if I tell him. But I shall not tell him. I shall say: I must away to the land of Judah, it is the time to sacrifice in the place Bethlehem,* the appointed time is at hand.—So I shall go away from Saul for ever, and never shall I see his face again. I shall hide myself away from his face, lest he hurt himself, slaying me.—I shall go in the morning with sure feet, but the shell of my heart will be weary. For I am the Lord's and servant of the Lord, and I go in obedience, even with the alacrity of willingness. But alas, that I should have loved Saul, and had pride in him! I am old—

(Curtain)

Scene 3.

*Bethlehem—an open place in the village—an old man on a roof calling
aloud, and kindling a signal fire.* [*Enter* JESSE *and* ELIAB.][☆]

1ST ELDER *(calling on the roof)*: Come in! Come in! Come in!
5   Come all men in! Come all men in to the place of counsel!
Gather in to the place of counsel, all men gather now. Come in!
Come in![☆]

2ND ELDER *(on the Plaza)*[☆]: What now?

3RD ELDER: The watchman on the fourth hill saw a host of
10   prophets coming, even Samuel among them.

2ND ELDER: Yea! What does this bode?

JESSE: What have we done wrong, that Samuel comes down upon
us? If he curse us, we are dead men.

4TH ELDER: Dread is on me. The sun looks darkened.

15 3RD ELDER: Nay, let us wait. It may be he comes in peace.

ELIAB *(brother of* DAVID*)*: Why do we, who are men that fear not
the lion nor the bear, nor even the Philistine,[☆] tremble before
the raging of these prophets?

2ND ELDER: Hush then! For the Bolt is above us, and can strike
20   out of a clear sky. Canst thou hear his meaning, or know his
vision, who is secret save to the prophets? Peace then, hush thy
mouth—

JESSE: Verily, there is no open vision, and the word of One is
precious. Without Samuel, we should stare with the stare of
25   deaf men, and the fixed eyes of the blind. We should run our
faces against the wall, and fall with our feet into a hole. We
should not hear the lion roaring upon us—

ELIAB: Not so, my father. Without a prophet I seek the lion when
he roars about the herd, I slay him without advice from the
30   Lord. We live our lives as men, by the strength of our right
hand. Why heed the howlings of priests in linen ephods,[☆] one
or many!

JESSE: My son, shut thy teeth upon such words. Seal thy heart to
silence.—The strength of a man lasts for a little time, and
35   wastes like the oil in a lamp. You are young, and your lamp is
unbroken. But those that live long needs must renew their
strength again, and have their vessel replenished. And only
from the middle-middle of all the worlds, where God stirs amid
his waters, can strength come in to us.

ELIAB: Will it not come without Samuel?

JESSE: There is a path that the gazelle cannot follow, and the lion knows not, nor can the eagle fly it. Rare is the soul of the prophet, that can find out the hidden path of the Lord. There is no open vision, and we, who can see the lion in the thicket, cannot see the Lord in the darkness, nor hear him out of the cloud. But the word of One is precious, and we perish without it.

ELIAB: *I* cannot bow my heart to Samuel. Is he a King to lead us to battle, and share the spoil with us? Why should we fare worse without him?

JESSE: My son, day follows day, and night travels between the days. But the heart of man cannot wander among the years like a wild ass in the wilderness, running hither and thither. The heart at last stands still, crying: *Whither? Whither?* And though the feet walk the ways of the earth, the heart keeps on crying: *Whither? Whither?* Like a lost foal whinneying for his dam, the heart cries and nickers for God, and will not be comforted. Then comes the prophet with the other vision in his eyes, and the inner hearing in his ears, and he uncovers the secret path of the Lord, who is at the middlemost place of all. And when the heart is in the way of God, it runs softly and joyously, without weariness.

ELIAB: I would sooner follow the king, with spear and shield.

JESSE: Samuel is more precious than the king, and more to be obeyed. As God is to Samuel, Samuel to the king is God. The king is as a boy awaiting his father's bidding, uneasy till he is told what he shall do. Even so Samuel speaks to Saul, with the mouth of authority, to be obeyed. For he is the lips of God.

ELIAB: For me, give me⸎ the right arm of Saul.

(SAMUEL enters—followed by wild PROPHETS. The ELDERS go to meet him.)

1ST ELDER: The Lord be with thee!⸎

SAMUEL: The Lord keep this people!

1ST ELDER: Comest thou in peace?

SAMUEL: In peace. I come to sacrifice unto the Lord. Sanctify yourselves, and come to sacrifice, according to your families. Renew your clothes and purify yourselves.

1ST ELDER: Into which house will you go?

SAMUEL: Into the house of Jesse.

JESSE: I am here, my Lord.

SAMUEL: Call your household together, and sanctify yourselves, for we will sacrifice a heifer to the Lord this day, in your house. And it shall be a feast unto you.

5   *(Curtain)*

Scene 4.

JESSE'S *house—a small inner courtyard: a rude altar smoking, and blood sprinkled round:* SAMUEL *before the altar, hands bloody. In another part a large red fire with great pot seething, and pieces of meat roasting on spits.* JESSE *turning the spits. It is evening, sun going down.*   5

SAMUEL: Call your sons. Call them one by one to pass before me. For I will look on them, before we sit around to the feast of the sacrifice.

JESSE: They are in the house, waiting. I will call the first-born first. *(Calling.)* Eliab, come forth! Samuel asks for thee!   10

ELIAB *(entering)*: The Lord be with you.

SAMUEL *(aside)*: Surely the Lord's anointed is before him! *(Gazes at* ELIAB, *who is big and handsome.)*

SAMUEL *(aside)*: I shall not look on his countenance, nor on the height of his stature. For the voice of my soul tells me he is   15
rejected.—The Lord sees not as men see. For man looketh on the outward appearance, but the Lord looketh on the heart.

SAMUEL *(to* JESSE): Him hath the Lord not chosen. Call thy other son.

JESSE: Ha! Abinadab!—And Eliab, gather all thy brothers together,   20
for the feast shall be set forth. *(Exit* ELIAB.)

ABINADAB *(entering)*: The Lord be with you.

SAMUEL *(gazing on* ABINADAB): Neither hath the Lord chosen this.

JESSE: Go thou, Abinadab!—Be all thy brethren ready in the house?   25

ABINADAB: They be all there, waiting for the sacrifice meat.

JESSE *(calling)*: Come, Shammah! And when I call, come you others in your order, one by one.

SHAMMAH *(entering)*: The Lord be with you.

SAMUEL *(slowly)*: Neither hath the Lord chosen this.   30

JESSE: Go thou! Nay! Rather go to the fire, and turn the spitted meat.

SHAMMAH: Yea! For it should not singe.

JESSE *(calling)*: Ho! Son! Come forward!

FOURTH SON: The Lord be with you!   35

SAMUEL: Neither hath the Lord chosen this.

JESSE: Go thou hence, and wait yet a while.

FOURTH SON: What wouldst thou then with me?

JESSE *(calling)*: Ho! Son! *(To him who waits.)* Nay, go or stay, as
    thou wilt. But stand aside. *(He stands aside.)*

FIFTH SON: The Lord be with you.

JESSE: Turn thy face to the sun, that it may be seen.

5   SAMUEL: Neither hath the Lord chosen this.

JESSE: Thou art not he, whom Samuel seeks. Stand thou aside!
    (Calling.) Ho! Son! *(To him who waits.)* Bring in thy brother.
    (Enter SIXTH SON—all the other brothers edge in after him.)

SIXTH SON: The Lord be with you!

10   SAMUEL: Neither hath the Lord chosen this.

SIXTH SON: Wherefore hast thou called me, my father?

JESSE: Samuel would look on the faces of all my sons. Go now!
    Who then was not called? Who among you has not come
    forward?

15   SEVENTH SON: I! Wilt thou me?

JESSE: Nay, but come into the light, before the prophet of God.

SAMUEL: Neither hath the Lord chosen this.

JESSE: Nay, then it is finished, for there be no more.

SAMUEL: Are here all thy children?

20   JESSE: Yea verily, there remaineth yet the youngest. And behold, he
    keepeth the sheep.※

SAMUEL: Send and fetch him. For we will not sit down till he come
    hither.

JESSE: Go thou Shammah, for he will be coming in now.—I will

25   see!

                     (Exit JESSE, also SHAMMAH.)

ELIAB: My Lord, will the Lord of Hosts※ anoint a king, while Saul
    yet liveth?

SAMUEL: My son, out of the deep cloud the lightning cometh, and

30   toucheth its own. Even so from the whirlwind at the whole
    world's middle, leaneth out the Wonderful and toucheth his
    own. But※ whether the anointing be for prophecy or priesthood,
    or for a leader or a king over Israel, the Mover of all hath it in
    his own deeps.

35   ELIAB: Yea! But if the Lord anoint a man to be king, can the Lord
    again take back the anointing, and wipe out the oil, and remove
    the gift, and undo the man he has made?

SAMUEL: The power is beyond us, both before and after. Am I not
    anointed before this people? But if I should say: *The power is*

40   *mine own. I will even do my own bidding*, then this is the sin of

witchcraft, which stealeth the power of the whirlwind for its own. And the power will be taken from me, and I shall fall into a pit.

ELIAB: It is a hard thing, to be the Lord's anointed.

SAMUEL: For the froward and irreverent spirit, it is a thing well-nigh impossible.

(Enter JESSE *and* DAVID.*)*

JESSE: This is David, the last of the sons of Jesse. *(Enter* SHAMMAH.*)*

SAMUEL *(aside)*: I shall arise and anoint him. For this is he.

SAMUEL *(aloud)*: The Lord hath chosen this one. *(Takes the horn of oil and holds it over* DAVID'*s head.)* The skies will anoint thee with their glory, the oil of the sun is poured over thee, and the strength of his power. Thou shalt be a master of the happenings among men.—Answer then. Does thy soul go forth to the Deep, does the Wonderer move in thy soul?

DAVID: Yea, my Lord. Surely my soul leaps with God!*

SAMUEL *(anointing* DAVID*)*: The Glory pours himself out on thee. The Chooser chooseth thee. Thou shalt be no more thine own, for the chosen belongs to the Chooser.* When thou goeth in, it shall be at the whisper of the Mover, and when thou comest out,* it shall be the Lord. Thy strength is at the heart of the world, and thy desires are from thence. The walls of thy breast are the front of the Lord, thy loins are the Deep's, and the fire within them is His. The Lord looketh out of thine eyes and sits on thy lips. Thou closest thy fist on the Deep, and thy knees smile with his strength. He holdeth the bow of thy body erect, and thy thighs are the pillars of his presence.—Henceforward thou art not thine own. The Lord is upon thee, and thou art his.

DAVID *(making an obeisance)*: I am thy servant, my Lord.

SAMUEL: Ye shall sit around, and divide the meat, and eat of the feast, and bid the neighbours to your feast of sacrifice, this night.

(They move around, fetching trenchers of wood, and a huge dish, and a heap of flat bread. They begin to take the meat from the fire, and with a cry, lift down the pot.)*

JESSE: David is a child, and the Lord hath chosen him. What shall become of him? Make it plain to us, Oh Samuel, this night!

SAMUEL: Ask not, for none knoweth. Let him live till such time as the Unseen stretcheth out his hands upon him. When the time is fulfilled, then we shall know. Beforehand no man knoweth.— And now the meat is ready from the fire, and the feast of sacrifice is prepared, and I have done. Eat you, of the feast, and

5 live before the Lord, and be blessed. Speak nothing of this hour, lest mischance befall you. I go my way. Do not seek to stay me. Call whom ye will to meat, eat then what is before you, for this is your hour.

JESSE: The sun has gone down, and it is night. Wilt thou verily go

10 forth?

(Exit SAMUEL.)

ELIAB: He has anointed the youngest, and the eldest he has passed over.

JESSE: It is the Lord.—Go, Abinadab, and bid in the neighbours to

15 the feast. [*Exit* ABINADAB.]

ELIAB: Nay, it is Samuel, who envies a strong man his strength, and settles on the weak.

JESSE: These things, at this hour, thou shalt not say. Is my son David chosen beneath the heavens, and shall Eliab his brother

20 cast it up a reproach at him?—Yea! pile up the dish from the pot, that it may cool, and not burn the hand of him that tasteth.

ELIAB *(to* DAVID*)*: Wilt thou be a priest in a blue ephod?

DAVID: I know not. Today, and tomorrow I shall keep my father's sheep. More I know not.

25 ELIAB: Canst thou see the Bolt within the cloud? Canst thou hear his Voice out of the ground?

DAVID: I know not. I wish the Lord be with me.

ELIAB: Is he nearer thee than thine own father?

DAVID: My father sits before me and I see his face. But the Lord is

30 in my limbs as a wind in a tree, and the tree is shaken.

ELIAB: Is not the Lord also in me, thou stripling? Is thine the only body that is visited?

DAVID: I know not. My own heart I know. Thou knowest thine own.—I wish the Lord be with me.

35 ELIAB: Yea, I know my own heart indeed. Neither is it the heart of a whelp that minds the sheep, but the heart of a man that holds a spear.—Canst thou draw my bow, or wield my sword?

DAVID: My day is not yet come. [*Enter* NEIGHBOURS.]

JESSE: It is enough! The guests we have bidden are here! Oh David,

40 my son, even carry now their portion to the women-folk, for

they may not come here. And think thou no more of this day. The Lord will move in his own time, thou canst not hasten him. *(To the* NEIGHBOURS.*)* Yea* come! and sit ye to meat! For we will eat this night of the sacrifice that Samuel hath slain before the Lord.   5

NEIGHBOURS: Peace be to this house! And is Samuel at once gone forth! Yea! Good seemeth thy feast, oh Jesse!

JESSE: An heifer, of the first year, fat and goodly! Reach forth thy hand.*

(They all sit around the huge, smoking platter. JESSE *dips in his hand,*   10
and carries the mess *to his mouth.)*

NEIGHBOUR: Yea! Good is the feast! And blessed be Samuel, who came to Bethlehem this day!

(Re-enter DAVID: *sits down and eats. They all dip their hands in the*
great platter, and eat in silence.)   15

NEIGHBOUR: Verily, this is a great feast! Surely the Lord hath visited* thy house this day, O Jesse!

(Curtain)

Scene 5.

SAUL'S *house in Gilgal*—MERAB *and* MICHAL *in the courtyard, spinning wool, with their* MAIDENS. *They are laughing and giggling.*

3RD MAIDEN: Now I'll ask one! I'll ask one.

5   MERAB: Ask then!

3RD MAIDEN: Why does a cow look over a wall?

MICHAL: Yah! Yah! We know that old one. We all know it.—

MERAB: Who knows the answer? Hold your hand up.
(Only MICHAL *holds up her hand.)*

10   3RD MAIDEN: There! There! They don't know it! Why does a cow look over a wall?

1ST MAIDEN: To see what's on the other side.

MICHAL: Wrong! Wrong! How silly! *(Laughter.)*

2ND MAIDEN: Because it wants to get out.

15   MICHAL: Wrong! And it's such an easy one.

3RD MAIDEN: Why does a cow look over a wall?

4TH MAIDEN: To scratch its neck— *(Much laughter.)*

3RD MAIDEN: Wrong! Wrong! All wrong! Give it up!

MICHAL: No! No! Let them guess again.—Why does a cow look

20   over a wall?

1ST MAIDEN: To see if David's coming to drive her to pasture. *(Wild laughter.)*

MICHAL: That's wrong! That's not the answer!

MERAB: Give it up?

25   2ND MAIDEN *(laughing wildly)*: *To see if David's coming to drive her to pasture!*

MICHAL: That's not the answer. *Stupid!*

1ST MAIDEN: Why not? Say I, it's as good as the real answer.—The cows of Jesse will have to look a long time over a wall. *(Much laughter.)*

30   No doubt they're looking at this moment. *(Shrieks of laughter.)* Moo-oo! Moo-oo! David, come home? *(Hysterical laughter.)*

MICHAL: Fool! Fool! That's not the answer.

1ST MAIDEN: Yes. That's the answer in Bethlehem.—Why does a Bethlehem cow look over a wall?—Because David's come to

35   Gilgal. *(Much laughter.)*

MICHAL: That's wrong! That's wrong!

2ND MAIDEN: It's not wrong for a Bethlehem cow.

MICHAL: But it's not a Bethlehem cow. *(Loud laughter.)*

1ST MAIDEN: Is it the heifers of Gilgal? *(Wild laughter.)*

4TH MAIDEN: Why do the heifers of King Saul look over the wall in Gilgal?

1ST MAIDEN: Listening to the music. *(Wild laughter.)*

MERAB *(amid her laughter)*: If my father hears us!

MICHAL: You are all fools! You don't know the right answer. You can't guess it! You can't guess it. 5

2ND MAIDEN: Well, what is it then? Only Michal knows what the cow is looking for! *(Laughter.)*

MAIDENS: Go on! Go on! Tell us Michal!

MICHAL: Because she can't see through it. *(Laughter.)* 10

1ST MAIDEN: See through what? *(Wild laughter.)*

MAIDENS: See through what? *(All laughing.)*

2ND MAIDEN: Because who can't see through what? *(Shrieks of laughter.)*

4TH MAIDEN: What a senseless answer! 15

1ST MAIDEN: *Because she can't see through it*! *(Shrieks of laughter.)*

MICHAL: You are all fools! fools! fools! You know *nothing*. You don't know *anything*!

(Enter SAUL—*angry.)*

SAUL: Enough! Enough! What is all this! Is there a madness among the women? Silence, I say! 20

MICHAL: We are but telling riddles.

SAUL: It shall not be! What, am I to hear the shrieks of my daughters' folly spoiling the morning. I will riddle you a riddle* you shall not care for. *(*MAIDENS *steal away.)* 25

MERAB: We had thought my father was abroad among the men.

SAUL: You had thought, had you! And your father's being abroad was timely to let loose your ribaldry!

MICHAL: Nay, Father, there was no ribaldry. The maid did only ask, Why does a cow look over a wall? 30

SAUL *(shouting)*: Be still! Or I will run this spear through your body.—Am I to wrestle with the Lord, and fail because of the wantoning of my daughters among their maidens! Oh, cursed in my offspring as in all things! *(*MERAB *steals away.)* Cursed above all in my women-folk! 35

MICHAL: Could we not help you, Father, to strive with the Lord? They say the wise women can command the spirits of the deep.*

SAUL: Art thou then a seeress? art thou amongst the witches?

MICHAL: Not so. But Saul my father is among the wondrous. 40

Should not his daughter be as wise as the wise women who can see into the mysteries?

SAUL *(groaning)*: This is the sin of witchcraft! The hand of my children is against me!

⁵ MICHAL: Nay, Father, we would indeed be for you, and not against you.

SAUL: I have sworn to wipe out the sin of witchcraft from the land. I have sworn the death of all who lure the people with spirits and with wizardry. I have killed the soothsayers in the towns

¹⁰ and the villages—

MICHAL: But Father, might I not see the Bolt in a cloud, or call the spirits out of the earth? I am your daughter.—Is that to be a witch?

SAUL: Thou art a spawn of evil, and I will run thee through.

¹⁵ MICHAL: But why! oh why!

SAUL: Thy soul is a soul of a witch that workest against thy father. I call on the Lord, and my heart foams, because he will not hear me. I know it now. It is thee, thou witch! *(Wanting to strike her with the spear.)*

²⁰ MICHAL *(weeping)*: It is not so! It is not so!—The people say of thee, the Lord has departed from thee, and I would only help thee with the Lord, as Jonathan helps thee against the Philistine.

SAUL *(horrified)*: Is the Deep a Philistine! Nay, now I know thou art

²⁵ the brood of witches, who catch the powers of earth by cunning. Now I will surely pierce thee through, that my house may be pure, and the Fire may look on me again.

MICHAL *(screams)*: My Lord! My Lord!

SAUL: I will pierce thee through. For I have sworn the death of all

³⁰ witches, and such as steal the powers of earth and sky, by their cunning. It will be as good a deed in the sight of the Lord, as when the prophet of God slew Agag, and Samuel will turn to me again. For I am empty when the Lord abandons me. And evil spirits break into my empty place, and torture me.—I will

³⁵ surely slay this witch, though she were seven times my youngest. For she lifts the latch to the evil spirit that gets into my soul unawares.

MICHAL: My Lord! My Lord! I am no witch! I am not!

SAUL: Thou art a witch, and thy hand worketh against me, even

⁴⁰ when thou knowest not. Nay, thou art a witch, and thy soul

worketh witchcraft even when thou sleepest.—Therefore I will
pierce thee through. And I will say unto the people: Saul hath
slain the witch that gnawed nearest into his heart.

MICHAL: I will not be slain! *(Shrieks.)*

(Enter JONATHAN *and* DAVID, *running.)*

JONATHAN: My Father!

DAVID: Oh King!

SAUL: This is the witch that hinders me with the Lord!

JONATHAN: This, Father! Why Michal is a child, what can she
know of witchcraft?

SAUL: It is in her will. My soul tells me that women with their evil
intentions are playing against me, with the Lord. And this is
she. She shall die as the other seeresses died, to cleanse the land
before the Lord God.

DAVID: But yet, Oh King! thy servant has heard it is a hard thing to
be a witch, a work of silent labour and of years. And this
maiden your daughter is not silent, I think, nor does she seem
to waste her young brows in secret labours.

JONATHAN: That is true enough. She is a feather-brain. *

SAUL: Yet is her spirit against her father's.

MICHAL *(still weeping)*: No! No! I would help him.

DAVID: If some spirit of evil hinder King Saul with the Lord of
Hosts, it will be more than the whims of a girl. The spirits that
hamper the soul of the king cannot be children and girls.

SAUL: It may be so. Yet though I wrestle, the spirit of the Deep will
not come to me. And the wound is greater than a wound in
battle, bleeding inwardly. I am a strange man unto myself.

DAVID: Yet Saul is king, comely in his pride, and a great leader in
battle. His *deeds* cry into the whirlwind and are heard. Why
should Saul wrestle with the Lord? Saul speaks in actions, and
in the time of action the Spirit of God comes upon him, and he
is king in the sight of all men.

SAUL: It is even so. Yet my soul does not cease to ache, like the soul
of a scorned woman, because the Lord will not descend upon
me and give me peace in strength.

DAVID: Who is strong like Saul, in Israel?

SAUL: Yet his strength is as a drunken man's, great with despair.

DAVID: Nay, Oh King! These are fancies. How can my Lord speak
of despair, when victory is with him, and the light is on his
brow in the sight of all Israel.

SAUL: Can I so deceive myself?

DAVID: Surely the king deceives himself.

JONATHAN: Surely, Father, it is a strange self-deception you put on yourself.

5 SAUL: Can it be so? Yet if so, why does Samuel visit me no more, and withhold his blessing? And why do I feel the ache in me, and the void, where the Full should be? I cannot get at the Lord.

MICHAL: May I speak, my Father?

10 SAUL: Yea!

MICHAL: Why not laugh as you used to laugh, Father, and throw the spear in sport, at a mark, not grip it in anger. Saul is beautiful among men, to make women weep for joy if he smile at them. Yet his face is heavy with a frown.

15 SAUL: Why should I smile at thee, witch?

MICHAL: To gladden me, Father. For I am no witch.

SAUL: And when dost thou need gladdening, say?

MICHAL: Now, Father, even here!

SAUL: Thy sorrows are deep, I warrant me. *(Touches her cheek with*
20 *his fingers.)*

MICHAL: Yea! Did not this strange young man: indeed he is but a boy: find me chidden and disgraced and in tears before the king?

SAUL: And what then?

25 MICHAL: Who is this boy from the sheep-folds of Bethlehem, that he should think lightly of the king's daughter in Gilgal!

DAVID: Nay! What man could think lightly of Michal, the daughter of Saul? Her eyes are like stars shining through a tree at midnight.

30 MICHAL: Why through a tree?

SAUL *(laughing suddenly)*: Thou bird of the pert whistle! Run! Run, quail! Get thee among the maidens! Thou hast piped long enough before the men.

MICHAL: Even if I run, my thoughts run with me?

35 SAUL: What thoughts, bird of mischief?

MICHAL: That this boy ruddy* with the shepherd's sun has seen my tears and my disgrace.

DAVID: Surely, the tears of Michal are like falling stars in the lonely night—

40 MICHAL: Why, again, in the night?

SAUL *(laughing aloud)*: Be gone! Be gone! No more!

(Exit MICHAL.*)*

SAUL: She is a chick of the king's nest! Think not of her, David!

DAVID: But she is pleasant to think of.

SAUL: Even when she mocks thee? 5

DAVID: Very pleasant.

SAUL: The young men flee from a mocking woman.

DAVID: Not when the voice is sweet.

SAUL: Is Michal's voice sweet? To me, at times, it is snarling and
bad in my ears. 10

DAVID: That is only when the harp-strings of the king's ears are
unstrung.

SAUL: It may be. Yet I think I am cursed in my women-folk. Was
not the mother of Jonathan* a thorn in my heart?—What dost
thou prescribe for a thorn in the heart, young wiseling? 15

DAVID: Pluck it out,* Oh King, and throw it aside, and it is
forgotten.

SAUL: But is it easy to pluck out a rancorous woman from the
heart?

DAVID: I have no certain knowledge. Yet it should not be hard, I 20
think.

SAUL: How?

DAVID: A man asks in his heart: Lord, who fannest the fire of my
soul into strength, does this woman cast fuel on the Lord's fire
within me, or does she cast wet sand?—Then if the Lord say: 25
She casts wet sand: she departs forever from a man's presence,
and a man will go in unto* her no more, because she seeks to
quench the proper fire which is within him.

SAUL: Thou art wiser than if thou hadst been many times wived.
Thou art a cocksure stripling. 30

DAVID: My brothers say of me, I am a cocksure malapert.* Yet I do
not wish to be! Why am I so, my Lord?

SAUL *(laughing)*: It must be the Lord made thee so.

DAVID: My brother has struck me in the face, before now, for words
in which I saw no harm. 35

SAUL *(laughing)*: Didst see the harm afterwards?

DAVID: Not I. I had a bruised mouth, and that was harm enough.
But I thought still the words were wise.

SAUL *(laughing)*: Dost think so even yet?

DAVID: Yea, they were wise words. But unwisely spoken. 40

SAUL *(laughing heartily)*: The Lord sends the wisdom, and leaves thee to spend it! You offer a tit-bit to a wolf, and he takes your fingers as well.

DAVID: I shall learn in the king's household.

5 SAUL: Among the wolves?

DAVID: Nay, the lion is nobler than the wolf.

SAUL: He will not grudge thee thy callow wisdom.—I go to speak with Abner.✳

DAVID: Can I serve the King in anything?

10 SAUL: Not now. *(Exit.)*

DAVID: He has gone in good humour.

JONATHAN: We found him in an evil one.

DAVID: Evil spirits out of the earth possess him, and laughter of a maiden sounds to him as the voice of a hyena sounds to a

15 wounded man, stricken in the feet.

JONATHAN: It is so. He rails at his daughters, and at the mother who bore me, till my heart swells with anger—Yet he was not always so. Why is it?

DAVID: He has lost the Lord, he says.

20 JONATHAN: But how? Have I lost the Lord, too?

DAVID: Nay! You are good.

JONATHAN: I wish I knew how my father had lost the Lord.—You, David, the Dawn is with you. It is in your face.—Do you wrestle before the Lord?

25 DAVID: Who am I, that I should wrestle before the Lord?—But when I feel the Glory is with me, my heart leaps like a young kid, and bounds in my bosom, and my limbs swell like boughs that put forth buds.—Yet I would not be vainglorious.

JONATHAN: Do you dwell willingly here in Gilgal?

30 DAVID: I am strange here, and I miss my father, and the hills where the sheep are, in Bethlehem.—Yet I comfort myself, turning my soul to the Nameless, and the flame flares up in my heart, and dries my tears, and I am glad.

JONATHAN: And when my father has been bitter and violent, and

35 you go alone in tears in a strange place—I have seen the tears, and my heart has been sad—then do you yearn for Bethlehem, and your own?

DAVID: I am weak still.—But when I see the stars, and the Lord in darkness alive between them, I am at home, and Bethlehem or

40 Gilgal is the same to me.

JONATHAN: When I lie alone in camp, and see the stars, I think of my mother, and my father, and Michal, and the home place.— You, the Lord becomes a home to you, wherever you are.

DAVID: It is so. I had not thought of it.

JONATHAN: I fear you would never love man nor woman, nor wife nor child, dearly.

DAVID: Nay! I love my father dearly, and my brother, and my mother.

JONATHAN: But when the Lord enters your soul, father or mother or friend is nothing to you.

DAVID: Why do you say so?—They are the same. But when the Lord is there, all the branches are hidden in blossom.

JONATHAN: Yea!—I, alas, love man or woman with the heart's tenderness, and even the Lord cannot make me forget.

DAVID: But nor do I forget.—It is as if all caught fire at once, in the flame of the Hope.

JONATHAN: Sometimes I think the Lord takes from me the flame I have. I love my father. And my father lifts the short spear at me,* in wild anger, because, he says, the Fire has left him, and I am undutiful.

DAVID: The king is the Lord's anointed. The king has known, as none know, the strong gladness* of the Lord's presence in his limbs. And then the pain of wanting the Lord, when he cometh not, passes the pain of a woman moaning for the man she loves, who has abandoned her.

JONATHAN: Yet we love the king. The people look up to him. Abner, the chief captain, is faithful to him unto death. Is this then nothing, to a man?

DAVID: To a man, it is much. To the Lord's anointed, it is much riches. But to the king whom the Lord hath rejected, even love is a hurt.

JONATHAN: Is my father truly rejected from being king, as Samuel said? And merely that he spared Agag and a few Amalekite cattle? Myself, I would not willingly have drawn the sword on naked Agag.

DAVID: Who knows? I know not.—When a people choose a king, then the will of the people is as God to the king. But when the Lord of All chooses a king, then the king must answer to the Lord of All.

JONATHAN: And the Lord of All required the death of defenceless Agag?

DAVID: Amalek has set his will against the Whirlwind. There are two motions in the world. The will of man for himself, and the
5 desire that moves the Whirlwind. When the two are one, all is well. But when the will of man is against the Whirlwind, all is ill, at last. So all is decreed ill, that is Amalek. And Amalek must die, for he obstructs the desire of the breathing God.

JONATHAN: And my father?

10 DAVID: He is king, and the Lord's anointed.

JONATHAN: But his will is the will of a man, and he cannot bend it with the Lord's desire?

DAVID: It seems he cannot. Yet I know nothing.

JONATHAN: It grieves me for my father. Why is it, you can soothe
15 him? Why cannot I?

DAVID: I know not. It is the Lord.

JONATHAN: And why do I love thee?

DAVID: It is the Lord.

JONATHAN: But do you love me again, David?

20 DAVID: If a man from the sheep dare love the king's son, then I love Jonathan. But hold it not against me, for presumption.

JONATHAN: Of a surety, lovest thou me, David?

DAVID: As the Lord liveth.

JONATHAN: And it shall be well between us, for ever?

25 DAVID: Thou art the king's son. But as the Lord liveth and keepeth us, it shall be well between me and thee. And I will serve thee.

JONATHAN: Nay, but love my soul.

DAVID: Thy soul is dear to my soul, dear as life.

(They embrace in silence.)

30 JONATHAN: And if my father sends thee away, never forget me.

DAVID: Not while my heart lives, can I forget thee.—But David will easily pass from the mind of the son of the king.

JONATHAN: Ah never! For my heart is sorrowful, with my father, and thou art my comfort. I would thou wert king's son, and I
35 shepherd in Bethlehem.

DAVID: Say not so, lest thine anger rise on me at last, to destroy me.

JONATHAN: Nay, it will not.

(Curtain)

Scene 6.

Yard of SAUL'S *house in Gilgal.* MICHAL, *with tambourine, singing, or talking to herself.*

MICHAL: As for me, I am sad. I am sad, I am sad, and why should I not be sad?—All things together want to make me sad.—I hate the house when the men are gone to war. All the men gone out against the Philistine.* Gone these many days. And never a victory. No-one coming home with spoil, and no occasion to dance. I am sad, I am sad, my life is useless to me.—Even when they come, they will not bring David. My father looked pleasantly on him for a while, then sent him away.* So are men! Such is a king! Sent him away again! And I know, some day when the Lord has left Saul, he will marry me to some old Sheik.—Unless he dies in the war.—Anyhow everybody is gone, and I am dull, dull.—They say it is the Lord. But why should the Lord make the house of Saul dreary? As for me, I don't know whether the Lord is with me, or whether he is not with me. How should I know?—Why should I care! A woman looks with different eyes into her heart, and Lord or no Lord, I want what I want.—I wish I had a sure charm to call back David, son of Jesse. The spells I have tried were no good. I shall try again with the sand and the bones. *(She puts a little sand, and three small white bones, in her tambourine—mutters and bends—tosses her tambourine softly and drops it on the ground. Kneels and gazes intently.)* Bones, bones, show me the ways in the sand.* Sand, lie still, sand, lie still and speak.—Now then, I see the hills of Judah, where Bethlehem is. But David is not there, he is gone. At least I don't see him. In the sand is a road to Gilgal, by the white crown-bone.* But he is not coming this way, that *I* can see.—Where else? Where else?—This must be Elah in the sand, where my father is. And there is Shochoh, opposite, where the Philistines are. Ah yes, two hills, and a valley between, with a brook in the bottom.* And my father with our men on one slope, the Philistines on the other.—Ah yes, that will be my father among our men; at least, that is his black tent. But Jonathan is not there. Oh* woe, if Jonathan were killed! My heart is afraid for Jonathan. Though how should I know Jonathan as a speck of sand, anyhow?—There is nothing in the sand. I am no wise woman, nor a seeress, even though I

would like to be!—How dull it is! How dull it is here! How dull
it is to be a woman! *(Throws away her tambourine.)* Why do they
sit in front of the Philistines, without defeating them!

WATCHMAN *(entering from the gate)*: Men are coming, from the
host of Saul. They come with a litter.

1ST SOLDIER *(entering)*: The Lord strengthen you.

MICHAL: Who comes? Is it news of victory?

1ST SOLDIER: No, Lady! Jonathan is wounded in the knee, and
comes home to rest.⸱

MICHAL: Wounded in the knee? And what else?

1ST SOLDIER: How, else?

MICHAL: Oh slow-witted! What other news? Are the Philistines
defeated and slaughtered?

1ST SOLDIER: Nay!—they are not.

MICHAL: Then what has happened?

1ST SOLDIER: Nought⸱ has happened.

MICHAL: Where is the king? Is all well with him?

1ST SOLDIER: The king is with the host at Elah, and all is well with
him.

MICHAL: Then where are the Philistines?

1ST SOLDIER: The Philistines are arrayed over against us, on the
opposite hill, at Shochoh.

MICHAL: And what happens? Do Israel and the Philistine sing
songs to one another?

1ST SOLDIER: Nay! A portion of the men go forth to fight, wellnigh
each day. And the champion of the Philistine comes each day to
challenge us.

MICHAL: And who answers out of Israel?

1ST SOLDIER: None answers.

MICHAL: None answers! Yea, that is news to hear! Has Israel never
a champion? Is my father the king sick?

1ST SOLDIER: Many champions have we, forsooth.—But we are
men. And this Philistine is huge, he is one of those of the old
days, before the Flood. He is a huge giant, whose great voice
alone shakes the tents.

MICHAL: And not one man answers his challenge?

1ST SOLDIER: Nay, where shall we find a huge giant among us, to
answer him?

MICHAL: If he were a mountain, I would prick him with my needle.

1ST SOLDIER: Yea, and would you might prick the eyeballs of him.
(*Enter* LITTER-BEARERS *with* JONATHAN.)

MICHAL: This is most strange!—Ah, Jonathan, and art thou
wounded in the knee?

JONATHAN: Yea! 5

MICHAL: The Lord be praised, it is not in the calf.*

JONATHAN: Hush, shrew!

MICHAL: Did the Philistine giant wound thee in the knee, Oh
Jonathan?

JONATHAN: A Philistine wounded me. 10

MICHAL: But I hear they boast a giant, a champion.

JONATHAN: Yea, verily.

MICHAL: A huge, unheard-of giant.

JONATHAN: Huge enough: and heard daily.

MICHAL: What does he say daily? 15

JONATHAN: Oh—he asks that we send down a man to fight with
him. And if he, the Philistine of Gath, slay our man, then shall
all Israel be servant to the Philistines. But if our man slay this
Goliath, then the Philistines shall be our servants.—And seeing
that this giant be so large, no ordinary man can get past his 20
sword to attack him, therefore the king is not willing that the
fight be settled between champions, lest we lose our freedom in
a moment.

MICHAL: And dare no man go up against this huge one?

JONATHAN: Nay, many dare. And many a man seeks to go. I myself 25
would willingly go. Though I know I should die. But what
would I care about dying, if the Philistine died first? Yet I
doubt* *I* should die first, and Israel be delivered into bond-
age.—Hence the king will accept no champion from our midst.
But we shall sally forth in daily companies, and defeat the 30
Philistine at length.

MICHAL: At a great length.

JONATHAN: Hast thou wounds or pain, to find it so?

MICHAL: Yea, the wound of shame, that Israel, challenged, is dumb.
Israel has no champion! What wound of shame for the woman! 35

JONATHAN: Why risk the nation in a fight between champions? We
are all champions, and we all fight the Philistine.

MICHAL: Only not this big one.

JONATHAN: In single combat, with the fate of the nation hanging on the issue, no! But if Goliath mingle in the battle ranks, then every man of Benjamin⁎ will have at him.

MICHAL: And mingles he not in the battle ranks?

JONATHAN: Ah no! He saves himself for the single combat, for this bawling of the challenge and the rattling of his oversized shield.⁎

MICHAL: Some man should think of a way.

JONATHAN: Think thou! I must rest, and recover, and return to the field of battle.

(Curtain)

Scene 7.

*The camp of the Israelites at Elah—in the background black tents of
worsted—morning.—Men assembling in arms, to battle—much shouting
of war-cries—much noise of war-like anticipation.* DAVID *entering,
carrying a staff.*   5

DAVID: Is yon the tent of Eliab of Bethlehem?

2ND SOLDIER: The tent of the sons of Jesse.

SHAMMAH *(coming armed from the tent)*: Is not this our brother
   David! *(Calling.)* Ho, David is here! *(Embracing* DAVID.*)* And
   art thou also come to the fight?   10

ELIAB *(also armed)*: What, David! Hast thou left the sheep to come
   among the men-at-arms? *(They embrace.)*

DAVID: My father sent me here to enquire of you, and to bring you
   bread, and ten cheeses for the captain of your thousand. The
   loaves and the parched corn and the cheeses have I left with the   15
   keeper of the victuals.*—But where is Abinadab?

ELIAB: With the host, where we must form to battle. *(The men are
   forming in loose array.* ABINADAB *comes and embraces* DAVID.*)*

ABINADAB: Hast thou come from Bethlehem? And how is our
   father, and all the homestead?   20

DAVID: Yea, all are well. My father sent me with victual, and to see
   how you fare, and to take your pledge.*

ELIAB: The pledge we will give you after the fight? And how fares
   my young son at home?

1ST CAPTAIN *(calling)*: The thousand of Judah, get you to your   25
   hundreds: get you to your place.
                    (Bustle of men falling into rank.)

DAVID *(following his brothers)*: Your son was bitten by a hound, but
   all is well.*

ELIAB: What hound, forsooth? And lives the dog yet?   30

SAUL *(passing)*: Five hundred of Benjamin, lead into the valley!

SOLDIERS: Ah! Ah! The five hundred are moving forth!
                    (Loud shouting of SOLDIERS.*)*

DAVID: And how goes the fight?

SHAMMAH: Wellah,* this way and that, as wind bloweth!   35

DAVID: The days are many, that you are afield. My father grew
   uneasy, and could stay no longer. Long days and no news are ill
   to live, said he.

ELIAB: Tell my father, this is no folding of sheep, out here.

DAVID: And has no weighty blow been struck, on either side?

SOLDIERS *(calling)*: Ha! Ha! The five hundred are near the brook! And behold, the Philistine champion cometh forth from the ranks, to meet them. *(Hush in the camp.)*

5 MIGHTY VOICE OF GOLIATH: Ho! Ho there! Israel! Why are ye come out to set your battle in array?—am I not a Philistine, and ye servants to Saul? Choose you a man for you, and let him come down to me.

DAVID *(in the hush)*: But who is this?

10 SOLDIERS: Ha! Ha! The five hundred are fleeing back from him! They are sore afraid. *(A hush.)*

SHAMMAH: This is Goliath, their champion.

VOICE OF GOLIATH: Ha-ha! Why run ye? Choose you a man for you, and let him come down to me. If he can fight with me, and 15 kill me, then will we be your servants. But if I prevail against him, and kill him, then shall ye be our servants, and serve us. It is fairly said. Choose you a man for you!

DAVID *(in the hush)*: Surely he is a huge man! Goeth no man forth to meet him?

20 2ND SOLDIER: Have you seen this man! Surely, forty days has he come up to defy Israel. And it shall be, that the man who killeth him, the king will enrich him with great riches, and will give him his daughter, and make his father's house free in Israel.

DAVID: What will the king do, to the man that killeth this Philistine, 25 and taketh away the reproach from Israel?—Will he surely give him his daughter, the daughter of his house in Gilgal?

2ND SOLDIER: Ay, surely he will. And much riches. And make his father's house free in Israel.

DAVID: Who is this uncircumcised Philistine, that he should defy 30 the armies of the living God?

SOLDIERS: Ah! He is what thou seest.

DAVID: As the Lord liveth, there shall be an end to him.

SOLDIERS: Would it were so. But who shall do it?

DAVID: Is the Lord nought in the reckoning?—The Lord is with 35 me, and I will do it.

SOLDIERS: Thou? How canst thou kill this great giant?

DAVID: I can do it. I will kill him, as the Lord liveth in me, were his name six times Goliath.

SOLDIERS: Nay, but how?

40 DAVID: The Lord will show you how. I, I will kill him.

ELIAB *(coming forward)*: What art thou doing here? Why camest thou hither, and with whom hast thou left those few sheep in the wilderness? I know thy pride, and the naughtiness of thy heart. For thou art come down that thou mightest see the battle. 5

DAVID: What have I now done? Was I not sent by my father, for a cause?

ELIAB *(turning away in anger)*: Thou didst persuade him, in the vanity of thy mind.

2ND SOLDIER: Shall we say to Saul of thee, that thou art minded to kill the giant? 10

DAVID: Say so to him. For the Lord is with me.

3RD SOLDIER: Verily!—feelest thou in thee the power to kill this mighty man?

DAVID: Verily! And is it sooth,* the king will give his daughter to him that slayeth the roaring Philistine? 15

SOLDIERS: Yea, it is sooth, for it is so proclaimed. But tell us how thou wilt come nigh him, to slay him?

DAVID: The Lord will show you.

SOLDIERS: Saul is coming. 20

SAUL *(approaching)*: Which is this man, will go forth against the Philistine?

DAVID: Let no man's heart fail because of this giant, for thy servant will go and fight with him.

SAUL: Thou? Thou art not able to go against this Philistine to fight with him, for thou art but a youth, and he a man of war from his youth. 25

DAVID: Thy servant slew both the lion and the bear; and this uncircumcised Philistine shall be as one of them, seeing he hath defied the armies of the living God. 30

SAUL: But neither lion nor bear came against thee in greaves of brass, nor armed with sword a man's length. How shallst thou fight with this giant in panoply?*

DAVID: The Lord that delivered me out of the paw of the lion, and out of the paw of the bear, he will deliver me out of the hand of this Philistine. 35

SAUL: Thou shalt go. And the Lord be with thee. *(To* ARMOUR-BEARER.*)* Fetch hither my armour, and bring another sword. For we will put them on him. *(Exit* ARMOUR-BEARER.*)*

DAVID: Shall thy servant go in armour clad? 40

SAUL: How else canst thou keep thy life?

VOICE OF GOLIATH: Ho! men of Saul! Is there no man among you, to answer when a fighter calls? Are you all maidens, combing your hair? Where is Saul, the slayer of foemen? Is he crying like a quail to his God? Call to Baal, and call to Ashtaroth, for the God of Israel is a pigeon in a box.*

DAVID: Ha! Lord God! Deliver him into my hand this day!

SAUL: Yea! *(Enter* ARMOUR-BEARER.*)* Put the coat of proof upon him, and the helmet of brass.

(They put the armour of SAUL *on* DAVID.*)**

DAVID: I am not used to it.

SAUL *(unbuckling his sword)*: Take thou my sword.

DAVID *(girding it on)*: Thy servant hath honour beyond his lot. Lo! I am strange in this array! The Lord hath not intended it for me. *(Takes shield.)*

SAUL: Now thou art ready. A man shall bear thy shield.

DAVID: Then let me go. But let me assay this sword* and battle harness that is on me. *(Sets forth. Tries his sword. Goes a little way. Turns suddenly back.)* —I cannot go with these, for I have not proved them. *(Drops his shield. Hastily unbuckles sword, and gives it to* SAUL. *Unfastens the helmet. The* ARMOUR-BEARER *disarms* DAVID.*)*

SAUL: Then thou goest not! Uncovered thou canst not go.

DAVID: The Lord shall be my shield. I will surely go. Give me my staff. My brother hath my staff.

SAUL: As thy soul livest, naked thou canst not go.

DAVID: As the Lord liveth, I will go with nought but God upon me.

VOICE OF GOLIATH: The God of Israel is a blue pigeon in a box, and the men of Israel are quails in the net of the Philistine. Baal is laughing aloud, and Astarte* smiles behind her sleeve, for Israel is no more than worms in a dung-hill.

DAVID: I shall go. Sound the trumpet!

(He [takes] his staff—crosses hastily to the back of the stage, downwards as to a valley. Stoops in the distance—meanwhile trumpet sounds, and the voice of the* HERALD *is heard, crying.)*

HERALD: Come down, Goliath! Come forward, Philistine! For Israel sendeth a champion against thee. *(Noise of shouting in both camps.)*

SHAMMAH: See, David is picking smooth stones from the brook bed.

ABINADAB: He has put them in his leather pouch, and taken his sling in his hand. Surely he will go after the Philistine as after a wolf.

SAUL: The Philistine cometh down,* with his shield-bearer before him.—Yea, but the youth is naked and unafraid.

VOICE OF GOLIATH: Where art thou, champion of Israel? I see thee not. Hast thou already perished of thy dread?

VOICE OF DAVID *(small)*: Yea, I am coming.

VOICE OF GOLIATH: Thou!

SAUL: How he disdains the youth! If we have lost all on this throw!

VOICE OF GOLIATH: Am I a dog, that thou comest to me with staves? Now shall Astaroth slay thee with spittle, and Baal shall break thy bones with a loud laugh.

VOICE OF DAVID: Thou comest to me with a sword, and with a spear, and with a shield: but I come to thee in the name of the Lord of hosts, the God of the armies of Israel, whom thou hast defied.

VOICE OF GOLIATH: Come! Ha-ha! Come to me, and I will give thy flesh to the fowls of the air, and to the wild beasts of the hills.

(Meanwhile the by-standers, SHAMMAH, ABINADAB, SOLDIERS, all save the ARMOUR-BEARER and SAUL, have been running to the far background, to look closer.)

VOICE OF DAVID: This day will the Lord deliver thee into my hand; and I will smite thee, and take thy head from thee.

(Loud shouting of Israel.)

VOICE OF GOLIATH: Ha! Ha! Canst thou chirp? Come over, thou egg,* that they see me swallow thee.

(Loud yelling from Philistines.)

VOICE OF DAVID: I will give the carcases of the host of the Philistines this day to the fowls of the air, and to the beasts of the earth. That all the earth may know there is a God in Israel.

(Loud yelling of Israel.)

VOICE OF GOLIATH: Come, thou whistling bird! Come! Seest thou this sword?

(Loud yelling of Philistines.)

VOICE OF DAVID: Yea! and all this people shall know that the Lord saveth not with sword and spear: for the battle is the Lord's, and he will give you into our hands.

(Great defiance heard in Israel.)

5 VOICE OF GOLIATH: Must we die of thy talking? And wilt thou not come forth? Then must I fetch thee—

(Tumult in Philistia.)

ARMOUR-BEARER: The Philistine is hastening down!—Oh, and behold, the youth is running at him fast! Ha-a-a!

(ARMOUR-BEARER rushes away, leaving SAUL alone.)

10 SAUL *(in a pause)*: Ah!—Ah!—Lord, my Lord!—Is he down? *(Great shouting heard—men running.)* What?—Yea, the Philistine has fallen! The boy but slang a stone at him! It is the Lord!—Nay, he riseth not!—Ah God! was it so easy a thing? Why had I not done it!—See, see, Saul, see, thou king of Israel, 15 see this nameless boy who hath run upon the fallen Philistine, and seized his sword from his hand, and stands upon his body hewing at the neck of the giant!—Ah, sight for the king of Israel, who stands alone, in safety, far off, and watches this thing done for him!—Yea, they may shout! It is not for me. It is 20 for that boy, whom I know not. How should I know him, with his young beard on his lip!—It is a hard thing to hack off the head of such a giant, and he cannot find the neck joint. I see him stooping! *(A great wild shout is heard.)* Ah! Even so! Even so!

25 ABNER *(entering running)*: The youth hath slain the Philistine with a stone from a sling, and even now has hewn his head loose, and is holding it up before the armies.

SAUL: Even so!

ABNER: Yea! He stands upon the body of that which was Goliath, 30 and holds up the head to Israel!—The Lord has prevailed. *(Wild shouting.)*

SOLDIERS *(running past)*: The host of the Philistine is in flight! After them! After them!

ABNER: Shall we not pursue? Will not the king lead the pursuit? 35 —Lo! they flee in abandon, flinging away their spears in their haste.

SAUL: This needs no leader. Any man can strike in the back of a running enemy.—What of the youth?

ABNER: He hath stripped the Philistine of his gear. Yea, I see the 40 body of the giant naked in blood upon the ground.

SAUL: Who is this youth? Whose son is he?

ABNER: As thy soul liveth, O King, I cannot tell.

SAUL: Enquire thou whose son the stripling is.

ABNER: He is coming towards the brook. I will bring him hither. *(Exit.)*

SAUL: Yea, is he coming! And alone up the slope, for the men have gone like hounds after the Philistine, and to the stripping of the tents. Yea, as bees swarm in upon the sweet-meats, when the window is opened.—This is a day to make songs for.—But not in the name of Saul. Whom will the maidens sing to? To him yonder, coming up the hill slowly, with the swinging head, and the bright brass armour of the Philistine. To that ruddy-faced fair youth, with a young beard on his mouth.—It seems I should know him, if I would. Yea, I shall know him in my hour!—Ah the blithe thing! Ah the blithe boy! Ah God! God! was I not blithe? Where is it gone? Yea, where!—Blitheness in a man is the Lord in his body. Nay, boy, boy! I would not envy thee the head of the Philistine. Nay, I would not envy thee the kingdom itself. But the blitheness of thy body, that is thy Lord in thee, I envy it thee with a sore envy. For once my body too was blithe. But it hath left me. It hath left me. Not because I am old. I am not old. And were I ancient as Samuel is, I could still have the alertness of God in me, and the blithe bearing of the living God upon me.—I have lost the best. I had it, and have let it go.—Ha! whither is he going? He turns aside, among the tents. Aha! Aha! So it is. Among the tents of Judah, and to the booth* of the Bethlehemite! So, he has gone in to lay down his spoil, the helmet of brass, and the greaves of brass, the coat, the great sword, and the shirt fringed with scarlet.—Lay them by, they are thine. Yea, they are thine, lay them in thy tent. No need to bring them unto the king. They are no king's spoil.— Yea, lead him hither, Abner! Lead him hither! He is bringing the head in his hand, oh yes, the champion, the victor! He is bringing the head in his hand, to swing it under the nose of the king.—But the sword, the great sword, and the greaves of brass and the body-spoil he has e'en laid by in his own tent, where no man may lay hand on it.—Oh, it is a shrewd youth, and a canny youth, cunning* as the Lord makes them.

(Enter DAVID, *with head of* GOLIATH—*and* ABNER.*)*

SAUL: So! Comest thou again?

DAVID: Even so! To lay the head of thine enemy before thee, Oh King!

SAUL: Whose son art thou, thou young man?

DAVID: I am the son of thy servant Jesse the Bethlehemite.

5 SAUL: Art thou so! Ay, thou art David! And brother to Eliab, and Abinadab, and Shammah, three men of war!—Thou hast put cunning in thy skill, and slain thine enemy as he were a hare among the bushes.

ABNER: See! the place where the stone sunk in, in the side of the
10 forehead bone! It lies still there, the stone of David.

SAUL: Yea, that was death without weapons meeting, indeed.

ABNER: Surely the Lord was in that round stone, that digged the pit of death in Goliath's head-bone!

DAVID: Except the Lord had been with me, I had not done it.

15 SOLDIERS *(standing round)*: Yea, the Lord sped the hand of David. The Lord is with this young man.

SAUL: Praise we must give to the Lord, and to David the promised reward.—Seekest thou thy reward at the king's hand, thou young man?

20 DAVID: It is as the king willeth.—Yet what should the reward be?

SAUL: Hast thou not heard it proclaimed?

DAVID: Nay, I arrived but in the dawn, with provender from my father to my brethren.

SAUL: Didst thou not set forth even now against the Philistine,
25 hoping big for the reward?

DAVID: Not so, Oh King. But the Lord moved me to go, to take off the shame and the reproach from the army of the living God.

SAUL: Thou hast done well!—Yet claimest thou thy reward?

DAVID: Shall I not hear from the king's mouth, what the reward
30 should be?

SAUL: How was it said, Abner? Recallest thou?

ABNER: Yea, Oh king! Riches, and the king's daughter, and freedom for his father's house, to the man that should slay Goliath in the single combat.

35 SAUL: Single-handed hath David slain Goliath, indeed! Even without any combat at all.—But how likest thou thy reward, thou young man?

DAVID: Were it mine, oh king, I should rejoice for my father's sake, and fall to the ground beneath the honour put upon me, being
40 son-in-law to the king.

SAUL: Even so! Now thou shalt stay with me, and live in my house, and return no more to thy father's house. And all shall be done to thee, as was said.—For surely thou hast brought much honour upon Israel. And we will make much of thee. For thou art champion of Israel in the sight of all the people. And thou shalt sit at the king's right hand, that all men may delight in thee. Yet, since thou art young, and fresh from the sheep-folds, we will not hasten thee to thy confusion. But thou shalt dwell as a son among us, and rise in degree as a son rises, sitting at the king's meat.—And behold, my elder daughter Merab, her will I give thee to wife. Only be thou valiant for me, and fight the Lord's battles.

DAVID: Let but thy servant serve thee, oh King, in the sight of the Lord.

SAUL: Come with us now to the tent.

DAVID: And my Lord will take the head of this Philistine, to put it on a pole?

SAUL: Nay! Thou thyself shalt bring it before the people, in Jerusalem of Judah.

(Curtain)

Scene 8.

*The King's tent at Elah—a square tent of dark worsted, with the wide
front open—heaps of panoply and spoil without—within, in the public
part of the tent,* SAUL, *with* DAVID *on his right hand,* JONATHAN *on his
left—and sitting around, the* CAPTAINS *of the armies of Israel.*

SAUL: We have numbered the army in tens, in hundreds, and in
thousands. And now are all the men returned from pursuing
after the Philistine, and the spoil is all brought in. And the
wounded of the Philistine have fallen by the way, even to the
valley of Ekron and the gates of Gath, their dead are more than
their living. Yet are their princes within the land, holding on to
strong places. Therefore we will rejoice not yet, nor go home to
the feasting. But while his heart is sunk low, we will follow up
the Philistine in every place where he holds out. Is it sooth?

CAPTAINS: It is good, Oh King.

ABNER: The blow that was struck with a pebble, we will follow up
with swords and spears, till in the Lord's name not one
uncircumcised remains in the land.

CAPTAINS: It is good! It is good! *(They strike their shields.)*

SAUL: And shall not the hand that begun the good work, bring it to
a finish?

CAPTAINS: Yea! Yea! Even so!

SAUL *(presenting* DAVID*)*: This is David, son of Jesse the Bethlehemite. This is David, that slew Goliath the Philistine, and delivered Israel from reproach. Sits not David high in the heart of
every man in Israel, this day?

CAPTAINS: Yea! David! David! *(Striking shields.)*

SAUL: Who is first among the men of war this day? Is it not David,
my son David?

CAPTAINS: David! David! It is David!

SAUL: Yea Captains! Your king is but captain of the captains! Whom
shall we set over the men of war this day? Shall it not be
David? This time, shall not David lead the hosts? Is he not first
against the Philistine? Yea, in this foray of triumph and this
campaign of victory, should any man lead but David?

CAPTAINS: It is good! David shall command, till we return home
this time from smiting the Philistine. *(They clash shields with
martial noise.)*

SAUL *(to* DAVID*)*: Hearest thou, David, son of my delight?

DAVID: Oh King, I am no leader of men of war. I have no skill in arts of battle. Honour me not to my confusion.

SAUL: Nay, this time shalt thou take the charge. For in *this* fight art thou the first man among the men of war in Israel.—Answer, Captains! Is it not so? 5

CAPTAINS: Verily! This time we will have David.

ABNER: Verily, save David lead us, we will not go. *(The* CAPTAINS *rise, and lift locked shields* before DAVID *as if to raise him up.)*

SAUL: If we go not now, we lose the golden hour. The choice is upon thee, David. 10

DAVID: Thy servant will do according to thy will, oh King, and according to the will of Abner, and of the captains. *(He rises before the* CAPTAINS.*)* But I am young, and not brought up to war. And the captains and the strong men will laugh at me, seeing my inexperience, and my presumption. 15

ABNER: Nay! No man shall find occasion to laugh at thee, for the fight is in thee as in a young eagle. Leading to war shalt thou learn war.

DAVID: It is as the king and the Captains shall bid me.

SAUL *(rising)*: We will make ready, and send out the news through 20 the camp: *In this is David our leader*! Then David shall choose his men, and go forth. He shall give his orders, and the captains shall march at his bidding. David, the day is thine! *(Salutes.)*

(The CAPTAINS *again salute* DAVID *with spear on shield, then they go* 25 *out.)*

CAPTAINS: To thee, David! *(Exeunt.)*

DAVID *(to* JONATHAN*)*: How shall I bring this to a pass?

JONATHAN: Thy soul will not fail thee. Thou art the young lion of Judah, thou art the young eagle of the Lord.—Oh David, is it 30 well between me and thee, and hast thou verily not forgotten me?

DAVID: Verily, thou hast not left my soul.—But how shall I go before these men?

JONATHAN: We have sworn a covenant, is it not between us?—Wilt 35 thou not swear with me, that our souls shall be as brothers, closer even than the blood?—Oh David, my heart hath no peace save all be well between thy soul and mine, and thy blood and mine.

DAVID: As the Lord liveth, the soul of Jonathan is dearer to me 40 than a brother's.—Oh brother, if I were but come out of this pass, and we might live before the Lord, together!

JONATHAN: What fearest thou then?

DAVID: In the Lord, I fear nothing. But before the faces of men, my heart misgives me.

JONATHAN: Sittest thou not high in the hearts of all Israel?

DAVID: Yea, but who am I, to be suddenly lifted up! Will they not throw me as suddenly down?

JONATHAN: Who would throw thee down, that art strong as a young eagle, and subtle as the leopard?

DAVID: I will rest in the Lord.

JONATHAN: And in me wilt thou not trust?

DAVID: I will trust thee, Jonathan, and cleave to thee till the sun sets on me. Thou art good to me as man never before was good to me, and I have not deserved it. Say thou wilt not repent of thy kindness towards me!

JONATHAN: Oh brother, give me the oath, that nought shall sunder our souls, for ever.

DAVID: As the Lord liveth, my soul shall not part for ever from the soul of my brother Jonathan; but shall go with him up the steeps of heaven, or down the sides of the pit. And between his house and my house, the covenant shall be everlasting.—For as the hearts of men are made on earth, the heart of Jonathan is gentlest and most great.

JONATHAN: The covenant is between us. *(Covers his face.)*

DAVID *(after a pause)*: But how shall I go before these captains, oh my brother? Comest thou not with me? Wilt thou not stand by me? Oh, come!

JONATHAN: I am limping still in the knee, and how shall I lead a foray? But thou art mine and I am thine. And I will clothe thee in my clothes, and give thee my sword and my bow, and so shall my spirit be added to thy spirit, and thou shalt be as the king's son and the eagle of the Lord, in the eyes of the people.

(Takes off his striped coat, or wide-sleeved long tunic.)

DAVID: But can I do this thing?

JONATHAN: Yea! That all men know thou art as the king's son in the world. For the eagle hath gold in his feathers, and the young lion is bright. So shall David be seen in Israel.

*(*DAVID *slowly pulls off his loose robe, a herdsman's tunic, cut off at the*

knee. JONATHAN *takes off his sleeveless shirt, and is seen in his leathern loin-strap. From his upper arm he takes a metal bracelet.)*

JONATHAN: Even all my garments thou shalt take, even the armlet that should not leave me till I die. And thou shalt wear it for ever. And thy garments will I take upon me, so the honour shall be mine.   5

*(*DAVID *pulls off his shirt, and is seen in the leathern loin-strap,* JONATHAN *puts his bracelet on* DAVID'S *arm, then his own shirt over* DAVID'S *head; and holds up his coloured robe.* DAVID *robed,* JONATHAN *brings him a coloured head-kerchief, and girdle: then his sword, and his*   10 *bow and quiver, and shoes.* JONATHAN *puts on* DAVID'S *clothes.)*

DAVID: How do I now appear?

JONATHAN: Even as the eagle in his own plumage.—It is said, David, that thou art anointed of Samuel, before the Lord. Is it so?   15

DAVID: Yea.

JONATHAN: Thou hast the sun within thee, who shall deny thee?

DAVID: Why speakest thou sadly, Jonathan, brother?

JONATHAN: Lest thou go beyond me, and be lost to me.

DAVID: Lord! Lord! Let not my soul part from the soul of Jonathan   20 for ever, for all that man can be to man on earth, is he to me.

JONATHAN: Would I could give thee more!

SAUL *(entering)*: Yea! And which now is the king's son, and which the shepherd?

DAVID: Thy son would have it so, Oh King.   25

JONATHAN: It is well, father! Shall not the leader shine forth?

SAUL: Even so. And the young king-bird shall moult his feathers in the same hour.

JONATHAN: The robe of David honours the shoulders of Jonathan.

SAUL: Art thou ready, thou brave young man?   30

DAVID: I am ready, Oh King.

SAUL: The host is in array, awaiting thy coming.

DAVID: I will come where the king leads me.

SAUL *(to* JONATHAN*)*: Put another robe upon thee, ere thou come forth.   35

JONATHAN: I will not come forth. *(Turns abruptly—*DAVID *follows* SAUL *from the tent—loud shouting of the army.)*

JONATHAN *(alone)*: If the Lord hath anointed him for the kingdom, Jonathan will not quarrel with the Lord. My father knoweth. Yet Saul will strain against God.—The Lord hath not revealed himself unto me: save that once I saw the glisten in my father, that now I see in David. My life belongs to my father, but my soul is David's. I cannot help it. The Lord sees fit to split me between king and king-to-be, and already I am torn asunder as between two wild horses⃰ straining opposite ways.—Yet my blood is my father's. And my soul is David's.—And the right hand and the left hand are strangers on me.

(Curtain)

Scene 9.

Outside the courtyard of SAUL'S *house in Gilgal: doorway of courtyard
seen open—*MAIDENS *running forth with instruments of music—menservants gazing into the distance—people waiting.*

MAIDENS: Lu-lu-a-li-lu-lu-lu! Lu-lu-lu-li-a-li-lu-lu! A-li-lu-lu-lu!   5
    Lu-a-li-lu! Lu-al-li-lu! Lu-al-li-lu-a!
MERAB: Out of Judah Saul comes in!
MICHAL: David slew the Philistine.⁂
MERAB AND HER MAIDENS: Out of Judah Saul comes in.
MICHAL AND HER MAIDENS: David slew the Philistine.   10
              (Repeat several times.)
ALL: A-li-lu-lu! A-li-lu-lu-lu! Lu! lu! lu! lu! li! lu! lu! a! li! lu! lu! lu!
MERAB: All the Philistine has fled.
MICHAL: By the roadside fell their dead.
MERAB: Wounded fell down in the path.   15
MICHAL: Beyond Ekron unto Gath.
MERAB AND HER MAIDENS: All the Philistine has fled.
MICHAL AND HER MAIDENS: By the roadside fell their dead.
MERAB AND HER MAIDENS: Wounded fell down in the path.
MICHAL AND HER MAIDENS: Beyond Ekron unto Gath.   20
            (They repeat this continuously.)
ALL: Lu-li-lu-lu-lu! Lu-lu-li-a-lu-lu! Li-a-li-lu-lu-lu! Lu! Lu!
    Lu! A! li! Lu! Lu! Lu! Lu! Li! A! Lu! Lu! Li! Lu! A! Li! Lu!
    Lu! Lu! Lu! u!
MERAB: Saul in thousands slew their men!   25
MICHAL: David slew his thousands ten!
MERAB AND MAIDENS: Saul in thousands slew their men!
MICHAL AND MAIDENS: David slew his thousands ten!—Oh! Lu!
    Lu! Lu! Lu! Lu! Lu! A! Li! Lu! Lu! Lu!
ALL: Lu! Lu! Lu! Li! Lu! Lu! Lu!—A-li-lu-lu-a-li-lu-lu! Lu-a-li-   30
    lu-lu-lu! Lu-lu-lu!
MERAB: Out of Judah Saul comes in.
MICHAL: David slew the Philistine.
MERAB AND MAIDENS: Out of Judah Saul comes in.
MICHAL AND MAIDENS: David slew the Philistine.   35
ALL: Lu-li-lu-lu-lu-li-lu! Lu-lu-a-li-lu-lu-lu!
(They continue the repetition of the simple rhymes, and the refrain, as
SAUL *draws near, followed by* DAVID, JONATHAN, ABNER, *and the
armed men. The* MAIDENS *keep up the singing all the time, dancing,*

MERAB *with her* MAIDENS *on one side of the men,* MICHAL *and her*
MAIDENS *on the other, singing loudly back and forth all the time. The*
men pass slowly into the gate, without response. The MAIDENS *run*
peering at the spoil the servant-men are carrying in. All pass in at the
5   *gate.)*

                              (Curtain)

                    (Must be kept simple—plain—naïve—villagers.) *

Scene 10.

Courtyard of SAUL'S *house in Gilgal—confusion of people and men just come in—*MAIDENS *still singing outside.*

ABNER: The king is returned to his own house once more full of victory. When shall ye slay the sacrifice? 5

SAUL: Tonight I will slay a bull calf for my house, and an ox will I sacrifice for my household. And for the men will we slay oxen and sheep and goats.

ABNER: Yea! For this is a great day before the Lord in Israel! And we will sprinkle the spoil with the sacrifice. 10

SAUL: Hast thou heard the song of the women?—Nay, hearest thou? Hark!

(In the distance is heard the singing.)

VOICE OF MERAB: *Saul in thousands slew his men.*

VOICE OF MICHAL: *David slew his thousands ten.* 15

VOICES OF MAIDENS: *Lu-lu-lu-li-lu-lu-a! A-li-lu-lu-a-li-lu!*

ABNER: Ay!

SAUL: May such mouths be bruised!

ABNER: Nay! Nay! King Saul! In this hour!

SAUL: In this instant!—They have ascribed to David ten thousands, 20 and to me they have ascribed but thousands. And what can he have more, but the kingdom?

ABNER: Nay, nay, Oh Saul! It is but the light words of women. Ay, let them sing! For as vain women they fancy nought but that head of Goliath, with the round stone sunken in.—But the king 25 is king.

SAUL: Shall that shepherd oust me, even from the mouths of the maidens?

ABNER: Nay, this is folly, and less than kingly.

MICHAL *(followed by* MERAB—*running round* SAUL *with their tam-* 30 *bourines)*: Lu-lu-lu-lu-a-li-lu! A-li-lu-lu-a-li-lu-lu-lu!

SAUL: Away!

MERAB AND MICHAL: Lu-lu-lu-lu! Saul the King! Lu-lu-lu-lu-al-li-lu-lu! Saul! Saul! Lu-lu-lu! Saul! Saul! Lu-lu-lu!

SAUL: Peace, I say! *(Exit, passing into house.)* 35

MERAB AND MICHAL: Jonathan and David. Lu-lu-lu! Here they come, the friendly two!—Lu-lu-lu-lu-a-li-lu! Lu-lu-a-li-lu-lu-lu!

MERAB: Jonathan is kingly bred.

MICHAL: David took Goliath's head.

BOTH: Jonathan and David! Lu-lu-lu-a!
          Here they come, the loving two-a!

5   MICHAL *(to* DAVID*)*: Where is the giant's head?

DAVID: It is in Jerusalem of Judah, oh Maiden.

MICHAL: Why did you not bring it here, that we might see it?

DAVID: I am of Judah; and they would have it there.

MICHAL: But Saul is king, and could have it where he would.

10 DAVID: Saul would leave it in Jerusalem.

MICHAL: And the armour, and the greaves of grass, and the shield, and the sword? The coat of brass that weighs five thousand shekels? Where are these? I want to see them, Oh David!

DAVID: The armour is in my father's house, and in Jerusalem. The
15 sword lies before the Lord, in Ramah;* with Samuel, Oh Maiden!

MICHAL: Why take it to Samuel?—Do you not know my name, Oh David?

DAVID: You are Michal.

20 MICHAL: I am she.—And this is Merab! Look at him, Merab, and see if you like him.—Is it true, oh my brother Jonathan, that the king will give Merab his daughter to the slayer of the Philistine?

JONATHAN: He hath said so.—

25 MICHAL: To us he has said not one word.—Oh Merab, look at thy man! How likest thou him?

MERAB: I will not look at him yet.

MICHAL: Oh thou! Thou hast spied out every hair in his beard. Is he not fox-red? I think the beard of a man should be black as a
30 raven. Oh Merab, thy David is very ruddy.

MERAB: Nay! As yet he is not mine, nor I his.

MICHAL: Thou wouldest it were so! Aiee! Thou art hasty and beforehand with the red youth! Shame on thee, that art a king's daughter!

35 MERAB: Nay, now, I have said nought.

MICHAL: Thou shouldst have said somewhat, to cover thy un-maidenly longing.—Oh David, this Merab sighs in her soul for you. How like you her?

DAVID: She is fair, and a modest maiden.

40 MICHAL: As am not I!—Oh, but I am Saul's very daughter, and a

hawk that soars king high.—And what has David brought, to lay before Merab?

DAVID: All I have is laid before the king.

MICHAL: But naught of the Philistine Goliath! All that spoil you took home to your father's house, as the fox brings his prey to his own hole.—Ah David, the wary one!

MERAB: It was his own! Where should he take it, but to his father's house!

MICHAL: Is not the king his father!—Why could he not bring it here?—Is Merab not worth the bride-money?

JONATHAN: Oh, peace! Thou art all mischief, Michal. Thou shouldst be married to a Philistine, for his undoing.

MICHAL: Ayee! This David has come back to trouble us!—Why didst not *thou* slay the Philistine, Jonathan?

JONATHAN: Peace!—Let us go in, David! These maidens are too forward. My father did never succeed in ruling his household of women.

MICHAL: Ayee!—his household of women! Thou Jonathan!—Go in, oh David! They shall not put poison in your meat. *(As* DAVID *and* JONATHAN *depart, she sings.)*

> Empty-handed David came!
> Merab saw him full of shame!
> Lu-lu-lu-lu-lu-li-lu! A-li-lu-ia! A-li-lu!
> Empty handed David came!
> Merab saw him full of shame!
> A-li-lu-lu!—A-li-lu-lu!—Lu-lu-li-lu-a!

(To MERAB.*)* So, he has come!

MERAB: Even so!—Yet his brow says: *Have a care!*

MICHAL: Have a care, Merab! Have a care, David! Have a care, Michal! Have a care, Jonathan! Have a care, King Saul!—I do not like his brow, it is too studied.

MERAB: Nay, it is manly, and grave.

MICHAL: Ayee! Ayee! He did not laugh. He did not once laugh. It will not be well, Merab.

MERAB: What will not be well?

MICHAL: The king will not give thee to him.

MERAB: But the king hath spoken.

MICHAL: I have read the brow of Saul, and it was black.—I have looked at David's brow, and it was heavy and secret.—The king will not give thee to David, Merab, I know it, I know it.

MERAB: A king should keep his word!

MICHAL: What! Art thou hot with anger against thy father, lest he give thee not to this shepherd boy!—David hath cast a spell on Merab! The ruddy herdsman out of Judah has thrown a net over the king's daughter!—Oh poor quail!—poor partridge!

MERAB: I am not caught! I am not!

MICHAL: Thou art caught!—And not by some chieftain, nor by some owner of great herds. But by a sheep-tending boy! Oh fie!

MERAB: Nay, I do not want him.

MICHAL: Yea, thou dost. And if some man of great substance came, and my father would give thee to him, thou wouldst cry: *Nay! Nay! Nay! I am David's!*

MERAB: Never would I cry this that thou sayst. For I am not his.—And am I not first daughter of the king!

MICHAL: Thou waitest and pantest after that red David. And he will climb high in the sight of Israel, upon the mound of Merab. I tell thee, he is a climber who would climb above our heads.

MERAB: Above my head he shall not climb.

MICHAL: Empty-handed David came!
             Merab saw him full of shame!
             Lu-li-lu-lu! Lu-li-lu-lu-lu! A-li-lu-lu!

(Curtain)

Scene 11.

Room in King's house at Gilgal—bare adobe room, mats on the floor—
SAUL, ABNER *and* ADRIEL *reclining around a little open hearth.*

SAUL: And how is the slayer of Goliath looked upon, in Gilgal?

ABNER: Yea! he is a wise young man, he brings no disfavour upon 5
himself.

SAUL: May Baal finish him!—And how looks he on the king's
daughter? Does he eye Merab as a fox eyes a young lamb?

ABNER: Nay, he is wise, a young man full of discretion, watching
well his steps. 10

SAUL: Ay is he! Smooth faced and soft-footed, as Joseph in the
house of Pharaoh!* I tell you, I like not this weasel.*

ABNER: Nay, he is no enemy of the king. His eyes are clear, with the
light of the Lord God. But he is alone and shy, as a rude young
shepherd. 15

SAUL: Thou art his uncle, surely.—I tell you, I will send him back
to Bethlehem, to the sheep-cotes.

ABNER: He is grown beyond the sheep-cotes, Oh King!—And wilt
thou send him back into Judah, while the giant's head still
blackens above the gates of Jerusalem, and David is darling of 20
all Judaea, in the hearts of the men of Judah?—Better keep him
here, where the king alone can honour him.—

SAUL: I know him! Should I send him away, he will have them
name him king in Judah, and Samuel will give testimony.—Yea,
when he carried the sword of the giant before Samuel in 25
Ramah, did not Samuel bless him in the sight of all men,
saying: Thou art chosen of the Lord out of Israel!

ABNER: If it be so, Oh King, we cannot put back the sun in
heaven.—Yet is David faithful servant to the king, and full of
love for Jonathan. I find in him no presumption.* 30

SAUL: My household is against me. Ah, this is the curse upon me!
My children love my chief enemy, him who hath supplanted me
before the Lord. Yea, my children pay court to David and my
daughters languish for him.—But he shall not rise up upon me.
I say he shall not! Nor shall he marry my elder daughter Merab. 35
Wellah, and he shall not.

ABNER: Yet Saul has given his word.

SAUL: And Saul shall take it back.—What man should keep his
word with a supplanter?—Abner, have we not appointed him

captain over a thousand? Captain over a thousand, in the army of Saul, shall he be. Oh yes!—And tomorrow I will say to him, I will even say it again: *Behold Merab, my elder daughter, her will I give thee to wife: only be thou valiant for me, and fight the Lord's battles.* And then he shall go forth with his thousand again, quickly, against the Philistine. Let not my hand be upon him, but let the hand of the Philistines be upon him.

ABNER: But if the Lord be with him, and he fall not, but come back once more with spoil, wilt thou then withhold the hand of thy daughter Merab from him?

SAUL: He shall not have her!—Nay, I know not. When the day comes that he returns back to this house, then Saul will answer him.—We will not tempt the Thunderer.

ABNER: I have it sure, from Eliab his brother, that David was anointed by Samuel to be king over Israel, secretly, in the house of his father Jesse. And Eliab liketh not the youngster, saying he was ever heady, naughty-hearted, full of a youngling's naughty pride, and the conceit of the father's favourite.—Now the tale is out in Judah, and many would have him king, saying: Why should Judah look to a king out of Benjamin? Is there no horn-anointed among the men of Judah!

SAUL: So is it! So is it!—Tomorrow he shall go forth with his men, and the hand of the Philistine shall be upon him. I will not lift my hand upon him, for fear of the Dark!—Yet where is he now? What is he conniving at this moment, in the house of Saul?—Go, see what he is about, O Adriel! *(Exit* ADRIEL.*)*

ABNER: It is a bad thing, Oh Saul, to let this jealous worm eat into a king's heart, that always was noble!

SAUL: I cannot help it. The worm is there. And since the women sang—nay, in all the cities they sang the same: *Saul hath slain his thousands, but David hath slain his tens of thousands*, it gnaws me, Abner, and I feel I am no longer king in the sight of the Lord.

ABNER: Canst thou not speak with the Morning Wind? And if the Lord of Days have chosen David to be king over Israel after thee, canst thou not answer the great Wish of the heavens, saying: '*It is well!*'

SAUL: I cannot! I cannot deny my house, and my blood! I cannot cast down my own seed, for the seed of Jesse to sprout. I cannot! Wellah, and I will not! Speak not to me of this!

ABNER: Yet wert *thou* chosen of God! And always hast thou been a man of the bright horn.✡

SAUL: Yea, and am I brought to this pass!—Yea, and must I cut myself off?—Almost will I rather be a man of Belial,✡ and call on Baal. Surely Ashtaroth were better to me. For I have kept the faith, yet must I cut myself off! Wellah, is there no other strength?

ABNER: I know not. Thou knowest, who hast heard the thunder and hast felt the Thunderer.

SAUL: I hear it no more, for it hath closed its lips to me.—But other voices hear I in the night—other voices—!

(Enter ADRIEL.)

SAUL: Well, and where is he?

ADRIEL: He is sitting in the house of Jonathan, and they make music together, so the women listen.

SAUL: Ah! And sings the bird of Bethlehem? What songs now?

ADRIEL: Even to the Lord: *how excellent is thy name in all the earth*! And men and women listen diligently, to learn as it droppeth from his mouth. And Jonathan for very love writes it down.

SAUL: Nay, canst thou not remember?

ADRIEL: I cannot, Oh King.—Hark!

(A man is heard in the courtyard, singing loud and manly, from Psalm 8.)

VOICE OF SINGER: "What is man, that thou art mindful of him? and the son of man, that thou visitest him?
For thou hast made him a little lower than the angels, and hast crowned him with glory and honour.
Thou madest him to have dominion over the works of thy hands, thou hast put all things under his feet;
All sheep and oxen, yea, and the beasts of the field;
The fowl of the air, and the fish of the sea, and whatsoever passeth through the paths of the seas.
O Lord our Lord, how excellent is thy name in all the earth!"✡

(SAUL listens moodily.)

SAUL: I hear him! Yea, they sing after him! He will set all Israel singing after him, and all men in all lands. All the world will sing what he sings.—And I shall be dumb. Yea, I shall be dumb, and the lips of my house will be dust!—What, am I naught! And set at naught! What, do I not know? Shall I go down into the grave silenced, and like one mute with ignorance.—Ha!

Ha!—there are wells in the desert, that go deep. And even there
we water the sheep, when our faces are blackened with drought.
Hath Saul no sight into the unseen? Ha look! look down the
deep well, how the black water is troubled.—Yea, and I see
death, death, death! I see a sword through my body, and the
body of Jonathan gaping wounds, and my son Abinadab, and
my son Melchishua, and my son Ishbosheth* lying in blood.
Nay, I see the small pale issue of my house creeping on broken
feet,* as a lamed worm. Yea, yea, what an end!—And the seed
of David rising up and covering the earth, many, with a glory
about them, and the wind of the Lord in their hair. Nay, then
they wheel against the sun, and are dark, like the locusts
sweeping in heaven, like the pillar of locusts moving, yea, as
tall, dark cloud* upon the land. Till they drop in drops of
blood, like thunder-rain, and the land is red.—Then they turn
again into the glory of the Lord.—Yea, as a flight of birds down
all the ages, now shedding sun and the gleam of god, now
shedding shadow and the fall of blood.—Now as quails chirping
in the spring: now as the locust-pillars of cloud, as death upon
the land.—And they thicken and thicken, till the world's air
grates and clicks as with the wings of locusts. And man is his
own devourer, and the Deep turns away, without wish to look
on him further. So the earth is a desert, and manless, yet
covered with houses and iron.—Yea David, the pits are digged
even under the feet of thy God, and thy God shall fall in. Oh,
their God shall fall into the pit, that the sons of David have
digged. Oh, men can dig a pit for the most high God, and he
falls in, as they say of the huge elephant in the lands beyond the
desert.—And the world shall be godless, there shall no god walk
on the mountains, no whirlwind shall stir like a heart in the
deeps of the blue firmament. And God shall be gone from the
world. Only men there shall be, in myriads, like locusts, clicking
and grating upon one another, and crawling over one another.
The smell of them shall be as smoke, but it shall rise up into
the air, without finding the nostrils of God. For God shall be
gone! gone! gone! And men shall inherit the earth!* Yea, like
locusts, and whirring on wings like locusts. To this the seed of
David shall come, and this is their triumph, when the house of
Saul has been swept up, long, long ago, into the body of God.—
Godless the world! Godless the men in myriads even like

locusts.—No God in the air! No God on the mountains! Even
out of the deeps of the sky they lured him, into their pit! So the
world is empty of God, empty, empty, like a blown egg-shell
bunged with wax and floating meaningless. God shall fall
himself into the pit these men shall dig for him! Ha! Ha! O   5
David's Almighty, even he knows not the depth of the dark
wells in the desert, where men may still water their flocks! Ha-
ha! Lord God of Judah, thou peepest not down the pit where
the black water twinkles. Ha-ha! Saul peeps, and sees the fate
that wells up from below! Ha! Lo! Death and blood, what is this   10
Almighty that sees not the pits digged for him by the children
of men?—Ha-ha! saith Saul. Look in the black mirror! Ha!

ABNER: It is not well, Oh King.

SAUL: Ha! It is very well! It is very well. Let them lay their trap for
his Lord, for his Lord will fall into it. Aha! Aha! Give them   15
length of days. I do not ask it.

ABNER: My lord, the darkness is over your heart—

SAUL: And over my eyes! Ha! And on the swim of the dark are
visions! What? Are the demons not under all the works of God,
as worms are under the roots of the vine? Look! *(Stares*   20
transfixed.)

ABNER *(to* ADRIEL*)*: Go quickly and bring Jonathan, and David, for
the king is prophesying with the spirits of the under-earth.
(Exit ADRIEL.*)*

SAUL: The room is full of demons! I have known it filled with the   25
breath of Might. The glisten of the dark, old movers that first
moved the world into shape. They say the God was once as a
beetle, but vast and dark. And he rolled the earth into a ball,
and laid his seed in it. Then he crept clicking away to hide for
ever, while the earth brought forth after him.—He went down a   30
deep pit.—The gods do not die. They go down a deep pit, and
live on at the bottom of oblivion. And when a man staggers, he
stumbles and falls backwards down the pit, down through
oblivion after oblivion, where the gods of the past live on. And
they laugh, and eat his soul.—And the time will come when   35
even the God of David will fall down the endless pit, till he
passes the place where the serpent lies living under oblivion, on
to where the beetle of the beginning lives yet under many layers
of dark.—I see it! Aha! I see the beetle clamber upon him, who
was Lord of Hosts—   40

ABNER: I cannot hear thee, Oh King. I would e'en be deaf in this hour! Peace! I bid thee! Peace!

SAUL: What? Did someone speak within the shadow? Come thou forth then from the shadow, if thou hast aught to say.

5 ABNER: I say Peace! Peace, thou! Say thou no more!

SAUL: What? Peace! saith the voice? And what is peace? Hath the Beetle of the Beginning peace, under many layers of oblivion? Or the great Serpent coiled forever, is he coiled upon his own peace?*

10 *(Enter* JONATHAN, DAVID, *and* MEN.*)*

SAUL *(continuing)*: I tell you, till the end of time, unrest will come upon the serpent of serpents, and he will lift his head and hiss against the children of men—Thus will he hiss! (SAUL *hisses.)* *Hiss! Hiss!*—and he will strike the children of men—thus—

15 *(*SAUL *strikes as a serpent, and with his javelin.)*

JONATHAN: Father, shall we sound music?

SAUL: Father! Who is father? Know ye not, the vast, dark, shining beetle was the first father, who laid his eggs in a dead ball of the dust of forgotten gods. And out of the egg the serpent of gold,

20 who was Great Lord of Life,* came forth—

JONATHAN *(to* DAVID*)*: Now sing, that peace may come back upon us.

DAVID: —If he heed me. *(Sings Psalm 8.* SAUL *meanwhile raves— then sinks into gloom, staring fixedly.)*

25 SAUL: And the serpent was golden with life. But he said to himself: I will lay an egg. So he laid the egg of his own undoing. And the Great White Bird* came forth. Some say a dove, some say an eagle, some say a swan, some say a goose, all say a bird. And the serpent of the sun's life turned dark, as all gods turn dark.

30 Yea, and the great White Bird beat wings in the firmament, so the dragon slid into a hole, the serpent crawled out of sight, down to the oblivion of oblivion, yet above the oblivion of the Beetle—

*(*DAVID *meanwhile sings.)*

35 SAUL *(striking with his hands as if at a wasp)*: Na-a! But what is this sound that comes like a hornet at my ears, and will not let me prophesy! Away! Away!

JONATHAN: My father, it is a new song to sing.

SAUL: What, art thou Jonathan, thy father's enemy?

40 JONATHAN: Listen to the new song, Father.

SAUL: What? *(Hearkens a moment.)* I will not hear it! What! I say! —I will not hear it! Trouble me not, nor stop the dark fountain of my prophecy!—I will not hearken! *(Listens.)*

DAVID *(singing)*: "When I consider the heavens, the work of thy fingers, the moon and the stars, which thou hast ordained—"

SAUL: What! Art thou there, thou brown hornet, thou stealer of life's honey! What, shalt thou stay in my sight! *(Suddenly hurls his javelin at DAVID.—DAVID leaps aside.—)*

JONATHAN: My Father, this shall not be!

SAUL: What! art thou there? Bring me here my dart.☆

JONATHAN *(picking up the javelin)*: Look then at the hole in the wall! Is not that a reproach against the house of the king for ever? *(Gives the javelin to SAUL. SAUL sinks into moody, silent staring. DAVID begins to sing very softly.)*

DAVID *(singing)*: Oh Lord our Lord, how excellent is thy name in all the earth! Who hast set thy glory above the heavens—

(SAUL very softly, with the soft, swift suddenness of a great cat leaps round and hurls the javelin again. DAVID as swiftly leaps aside.)

SAUL: I will smite David even to the wall.

ABNER: Go hence, David! Swiftly hence!

JONATHAN: Twice, Father! *(Exit DAVID.)*

ABNER *(seizing javelin)*: The evil spirits upon thee have done this, Oh Saul! They have not prevailed.

SAUL: Have I pierced him? Is he down with the dead? Can we lay him in the sides of the pit?

ABNER: He is not dead! He is gone forth.

SAUL *(wearily)*: Gone forth! Ay! He is gone forth!—What, did I seek to slay him?

JONATHAN: Yea, twice.

SAUL: It was not of myself.☆ I was then beside myself.

ABNER: Yea, the evil spirits were upon thee.

SAUL: Tell him, Oh Jonathan, Saul seeks not his life. Nay! Nay! Do I not love him, even as thou dost, but more, even as a father!—Oh David! David! I have loved thee. Oh I have loved thee and the Lord in thee.—And now the evil days have come upon me, and I have thrown the dart against thee, and against the Lord!—I am a man given over to trouble, and tossed between two winds!—Lo, how can I walk before the faces of men? *(Covers his face with his mantle.)*

ABNER: The evil spirits have left him. Peace comes with sorrow.

JONATHAN: Ay! And only then.

SAUL: Bring David hither to me, for I will make my peace with him, for my heart is very sore.

JONATHAN: Verily, shall it be peace?

5   SAUL: Yea! For I fear the Night. *(Exit* JONATHAN.*)* Surely now will David publish it in Judah: *Saul hath lifted his hand to slay me*!

ABNER: He will not publish it in Judah.

SAUL: And wherefore not? Is he not as the apple of their eyes, to the men of Judah, who love not overmuch the tribe of
10   Benjamin?

ABNER: But David is the king's man.

SAUL: Ah, would it were verily so.

(Enter JONATHAN *and* DAVID.*)*

DAVID: The Lord strengthen the king!

15   SAUL: Ah David, my son, come, and come in peace. For my hands are bare and my heart is washed and my eyes are no longer deluded. May the Lord be with thee, David! and hold it not against me, what I have done. Spirits of the earth possess me, and I am not my own. Thou shalt not cherish it in thy heart,
20   what Saul did against thee, in the season of his bewilderment?

DAVID: Nought has the king done against me. And the heart of thy servant knoweth no ill.

SAUL: Hatest thou me not, David?

DAVID: Let the word be unspoken, my Father!

25   SAUL: Ah David! David! Why can I not love thee untroubled?—But I will right the wrong.—Thou shalt henceforth be captain of the thousand of Hebron, and dwell in thine own house, by thy men. And behold, Merab, my elder daughter, I will give thee to wife.

30   DAVID: Who am I? and what is my life, or my father's family in Israel, that I should be son-in-law to the king?

SAUL: Nay, thou art of mine own heart. And the Lord is thy great strength. Only be valiant for me, and fight the Lord's battles!

DAVID: All my life is the King's, and my strength is to serve.

35   SAUL: It shall be well. And with thy thousand shalt thou succour Israel.

(Curtain)

Scene 12.

The well in Gilgal—MAIDENS *coming with water-jars*—*Two*
HERDSMEN[*] *filling the trough*—*one below, at the water, one on the*
steps—*They swing the leathern bucket back and forth with a rough*
chant; the lower HERDSMAN *swinging the load to the upper, who swings*   5
it to the trough, and hands it back. DAVID *approaching.*

1ST HERDSMAN: Ya! David missed her.

2ND HERDSMAN: Let him get her sister—Oh-Oh-Oh-h-!

1ST HERDSMAN: Ya! David missed her.

2ND HERDSMAN: Let him get her sister—Oh-h-h-h!   10

        (Continue several times.)

1ST MAIDEN: How long, oh Herdsmen!

2ND HERDSMAN: Ho-o-o! Enough!

1ST HERDSMAN *(coming up)*: —Ya! David missed her!

        (MAIDENS run away from him.)   15

1ST MAIDEN: Ho thou! Seest thou not David?

1ST HERDSMAN: Yea, he is there! Ho! David! And hast thou missed
    her? *(MAIDENS laugh.)*

DAVID: What sayest thou, Oh Man?

1ST HERDSMAN: Thou hast missed her—say!—am I not right!   20

DAVID: And whom have I missed?

1ST HERDSMAN: Wellah! And knowest thou not?

DAVID: Nay!

1ST HERDSMAN: Wellah! But Merab, the king's elder daughter!
    Wellah! We feasted her week[*] half a moon ago, whilst you and   25
    your men were gone forth against the Philistine.—Wellah, man,
    and didst thou not know?

DAVID: Sayest thou so?

1ST HERDSMAN: Wellah! And is it not so?—Say, Maidens, hath not
    Adriel the Mehólathite got Merab, Saul's daughter, to wife?[*]   30
    And hath he not spent his week with her?—Wellah, thou art
    ousted from that bed, Oh David.

DAVID: And hath the king given his daughter Merab unto Adriel
    the Meholathite! Wellah, shall he not do as he choose, with his
    own?   35

1ST HERDSMAN: Ay, wellah, shall he! But thou wert promised. And
    in thy stead, another hath gone in unto her.—Is it not so, Oh
    Maidens? Sleeps not Merab in the tent of Adriel the Mehola-
    thite?

1ST MAIDEN: Yea, the king hath married her to the man.

DAVID: And sings she as she shakes his butter-skin?*

1ST MAIDEN: Nay, as yet she sings not.—But if David sits here beneath the tree, she will come with her jar.—Nay, is that not Adriel the Meholathite himself, coming forth?—Oh herdsman, drive not the cattle as yet to the drinking troughs! *(Goes down and fills her pitcher.)*

2ND MAIDEN: Will David sit awhile beneath the tree?

DAVID: Yea!

2ND MAIDEN: Then shall Michal, daughter of Saul, come hither with her water-jar. Is it well, Oh David!

DAVID: Yea, it is very well.

[*Enter* ADRIEL.] *(*2ND MAIDEN *goes down with her pitcher.)*

ADRIEL: Ha David! And art thou returned? I have not seen thee before the king.

DAVID: I returned but yesterday. And I saw the king at the dawn.—Now art thou become a great man in Israel, Oh Adriel, and son-in-law to the king.—How fareth Merab in the tents of the Meholathite?

ADRIEL: Yea, and blithely. And tomorrow even in the early day will I set her on an ass, and we will get us to my father's house. For he is old, and the charge of his possessions is heavy upon him, and he fain would see* his daughter Merab, who shall bring him sons—sons to gladden him. And she shall have her hand-maidens about her, and her store-barns of wool, and corn, and clotted figs,* and bunches of raisins, all her wealth she shall see in store!

DAVID: May she live content, and bring thee sons, even males of worth.

ADRIEL: The Lord grant it!—And thou hast come home once more with spoil! How thou chastenest the Philistine!—Yea, and behold, the king hath delight in thee, and all his servants love thee!—Lo! I am the king's son-in-law, of Merab. Now therefore be thou also the king's son-in-law, for there is yet a daughter.

DAVID: Seemeth it to you a light thing, to be the king's son-in-law, seeing that I am a poor man, and lightly esteemed?

ADRIEL: By my beard, the king delighteth in thee, and all his servants love thee.* There is no man in Israel more fit to take a daughter of the king.

DAVID: Yea, there be men of mighty substance such as thou, whose flocks have not been counted, and who send men-at-arms pricking* with iron lance-points, to the king's service. But what have I, save the bare hands and heart of a faithful servant?

ADRIEL: Nay, thy name is high among men.—But Lo! Here cometh Saul, as he hath promised. He is coming out to my tents.—I will go forward to bring him in. Come thou? 5

DAVID: Nay! Leave me here. *(Exit* ADRIEL.*)*

1ST HERDSMAN: I have heard the mouth of Adriel, oh David! Surely he is the king's listener.

DAVID: And thou! Who made *thee* a listener? 10

1ST HERDSMAN: Nay, I must guard the water-troughs till the cattle have drunk.—Adriel hath flocks and menservants! But David hath the Lord, and the hearts of all Israel!—Better a brave and bright man, with a face that shines to the heart, than a great owner of troops and herds, who struts with arms akimbo.—As I 15 plant this driving-stick in the soft earth, so hath the Lord planted David in the heart of Israel,—I say, Stick, may thou flourish! May thou bud and blossom and be a great tree.*—For thou art not as the javelin of Saul, levelled at David's bosom.

DAVID: Peace! Saul cometh. 20

1ST HERDSMAN: Wellah! And I will go down to the water. *(Goes to the well.)*

[*Enter* SAUL *and* ADRIEL.]*

DAVID: The Lord strengthen the king.

SAUL: Art thou my son, David?—Yea David, have they told thee, I 25 have married my daughter Merab unto Adriel the Meholathite, even to him who stands here?

DAVID: Yea, Oh Saul! They told me the king's pleasure. May the Lord bless thy house for ever!

SAUL: Have I not promised my daughter unto thee! But my servants 30 tell me, the heart of Michal goes forth wishful unto David. Say now, is she fair in thine eyes?

DAVID: Yea! Yea, oh king, yea!

SAUL: When the new moon* shows her tender horns above the west, thou shalt this day be my son-in-law in one of the twain. 35

DAVID: Let thy servant but serve the king!

SAUL: Yea, and thou serve me, it shall be on the day of the new moon.

DAVID: Yea, will I serve, without fail.

SAUL: So be it! *(Exit, with* ADRIEL.*)* 40

1ST HERDSMAN *(coming up)*: Now is David the richest man in Israel—in promises! Wilt thou not sell me a king's promise, for this my camel-stick?

DAVID: It is well.

5   1ST HERDSMAN: Sayest thou? Then it is a bargain?—Wellah! take my stick! It is worth the word of a king.

DAVID: Peace!

1ST HERDSMAN: Thou meanest *war*!

DAVID: How?

10   1ST HERDSMAN: If thou get her, it is war. If thou get her not, it is more war. Sayest thou peace?

MAIDENS *(running)*: Oh master David, hath Saul passed with Adriel?

1ST HERDSMAN: They have passed, letting fall promises as the goat
15   droppeth pills.

DAVID: Peace, oh man!

3RD MAIDEN: Oh master David, shall Michal come forth to fill her water-jar? For Merab is setting meats before the king, in the booth of Adriel. Oh David, shall Michal bring her jar to the well?

20   1ST HERDSMAN: Ay wellah! shall she! And I will hold back the cattle this little while, for I hear their voices.

(Exit.)

DAVID: Run back quickly, and let her come.

(Exit 3RD MAIDEN.)

25   DAVID *(alone)*: Lord! dost thou send this maiden to me?—My entrails strain in me, for Michal, daughter of Saul.—Lord God of my salvation, my wanting of this maiden is next to my wanting thee. My body is a strong-strung bow. Lord, let me shoot mine arrow unto this mark!—Thou fillest me with desire
30   as with thunder, thy lightning is in my loins, and my breast like a cloud leans forward for her.—Lord! Lord! thy left hand is about her middle, and thy right hand grasps my life. So thou bringest us together in thy secret self, that it may be fulfilled for thee in us.—Lord of the Great Wish, I will not let her go.

35   MICHAL *(entering—covering her chin and throat with her kerchief)*: Wilt thou let me pass to fill my jar, Oh thou stranger?

DAVID: Come, Michal, and I will fill thy jar.

(She comes forward—he takes her jar and goes down the steps. Returning, he sets it on the ground at his feet.)

40   MICHAL: Oh David! And art thou still unslain?

DAVID: As the Lord wills, no man shall slay me.—And livest thou in thine house lonely, without thy sister Merab?

MICHAL: Is thy heart sore in thee, David, that thou hast lost Merab?—Her heart is gentle, and she sighed for thee. But e'en she obeyed. 5

DAVID: She hath a man of more substance than David. And my heart is very glad on her account.

MICHAL: It is well.

DAVID: Oh Michal, didst thou come willingly to the well, when the maiden told thee I waited here? 10

MICHAL: Yea, willingly.

DAVID: Oh Michal, my heart runs before me, when it sees thee far off, like one eager to come to his own place. Oh thou with the great eyes of the wilderness, shall my heart leap to thee, and shalt thou not say Nay! to it? 15

MICHAL: What said my father, Oh David, when he passed?

DAVID: He said: When the new moon showeth her horns in the west, on this day shalt thou surely be my son-in-law of one of the twain!

MICHAL: Yea, and is thy heart uplifted, to be a king's son-in-law? 20

DAVID: So she be Michal, my body is uplifted like the sail of a ship when the wind arouses.

MICHAL: Nay, thou art a seeker of honours! Merab had been just as well to thy liking.

DAVID: Ah no! Ah no! Ah no! Merab is gentle and good, and my 25 heart softened with kindness for her, as a man unto a woman. —But thou art like the rising moon, that maketh the limbs of the mountain glisten.—Oh Michal, we twain are upon the hillsides of the Lord, and surely he will bring our strength together! 30

MICHAL: And if the Lord thy God say thee nay!

DAVID: He will not. He hath thy life in his left hand, and my life he holdeth in his right hand. And surely he will lay us together in the secret of his desire, and I shall come in unto thee* by the Lord's doing. 35

MICHAL: But if he say thee nay, thou wilt let me go?

DAVID: Thou knowest not the Lord my God. The flame he kindles he will not blow out. He is not yea-and-nay! But my Lord my God loveth a bright desire and yearneth over a great Wish, for its fulfilment. Oh the Lord my God is a glowing flame and he 40

loveth all things that do glow. So loves he thee, Michal, oh
woman before me, for thou glowest like a young tree in full
flower, with flowers of gold and scarlet, and dark leaves. Oh
thou young pomegranate tree, flowers and fruit together show
on thy body.—Nay, it is the glow of the Lord God's presence,
and flame calleth to flame, for flame is the body of God,* like
flowers of flame. Oh, and God is a great Wish, and a great
Desire, and a pure flame for ever.—Thou art kindled of the
Lord,* Oh Michal, and he will not let thee go.

MICHAL: Yet the Lord himself will not marry me.

DAVID: I will marry thee, for the Lord hath kindled me unto thee,
and hath said: Go to her, for the fruits of the pomegranate* are
ripe.

MICHAL: Wilt thou not seek me for thyself?

DAVID: Yea, for my very self; and for my very self; and for the
Lord's own self in me.

MICHAL: Ever thou puttest the Lord between me and thee.

DAVID: The Lord is as a sweet wind that fills thy bosom and thy
belly as the sail of a ship, so I see thee sailing delicately towards
me, born onward by my Lord.

MICHAL: Oh David, would the new moon were come! For I fear my
father, and I misdoubt his hindrances.

DAVID: Thinkest thou, he would marry thee away, as Merab?

MICHAL: Nay, but thou must make a song, and sing it before all
Israel, that Michal is thine by the king's promise, no man shall
look on her but David.

DAVID: Yea! I will make a song. And yea, I will not let thee go.
Thou shalt come to me as a wife, and I will know thee, and
thou shalt lie in my bosom.* Yea! As the Lord liveth!

MICHAL: And as the Lord liveth, not even my father shall constrain
me, to give me to another man, before the new moon showeth
her horns.

DAVID: It is well, Oh Michal! Oh Michal, wife of David, thou shalt
sleep in my tent! In the tent of the men of war, beside the sword
of David, Michal sleeps, and the hand of David is upon her hip.
He has sealed her with his seal,* and Michal of David is her
name, and kingdoms shall he bring down to her. Michal of
David shall blossom in the land, her name shall blossom in the
mouths of soldiers as the rose of Sharon after rain. And men-
at-arms shall shout her name, like a victory cry it shall be heard.

And she shall be known in the land but as Michal of David;
blossom of God, keeper of David's nakedness. ☆

MICHAL: They shall not reive☆ me from thee.—I see men coming.

DAVID: Wilt thou go?

MICHAL: I shall call my maidens. So ho! So ho! *(Waves the end of*   5
her kerchief.)

1ST HERDSMAN *(entering):* There are two captains, servants of
Saul, coming even now from the booths of the Meholathite,
where the king is.

MICHAL: Yea, let them come, and we will hear the words they put   10
forth.

1ST HERDSMAN: And the cattle are being driven round by the
apricot garden. They will soon be here—

DAVID: In two words we shall have the mind of Saul, from these
captains.   15

MAIDENS *(entering running):* Oh Michal, men are approaching!

MICHAL: Fill you your jar, and with one ear let us listen. David
stays under the tree.

1ST MAIDEN: Stars are in thine eyes, Oh Michal, like a love night!

2ND MAIDEN: Oh! and the perfume of a new opened flower! What   20
sweetness has she heard?

3RD MAIDEN: Oh say, what words like honey, and like new sweet
dates of the oasis, hath David the singer said to Michal? Oh,
that we might have heard!

1ST CAPTAIN *(entering):* David is still at the well?   25

DAVID: Yea, after war and foray, happy is the homely passage at the
well.

2ND CAPTAIN: Wilt thou return to the king's house with us, and
we will tell thee what is toward: even the words of Saul
concerning thee.   30

DAVID: Say on! For I must in the other way.

1ST CAPTAIN: The king delighteth in thee more than in any man
of Israel. For no man layeth low the king's enemies, like David
in the land.

DAVID: Sayest thou so?   35

1ST CAPTAIN: Yea! And when the new moon shows her horns,
shalt thou be son-in-law to Saul, in his daughter Michal.

DAVID: As the Lord, and the king, willeth.—Saul hath said as much
to me, even now.—Yet am I a poor man, and how shall the king
at last accept me?   40

2ND CAPTAIN: This too hath Saul considered. And he hath said: Tell my son David, the king desireth not any bride money, nay, neither sheep nor oxen nor asses, nor any substance of his. But an hundred foreskins of the Philistines shall he bring to the king, to be avenged of his enemies.

1ST CAPTAIN: So said the king: Before the new moon as she cometh sets on her first night, shall David bring the foreskins of an hundred Philistines unto Saul. And that night shall Saul deliver Michal his daughter unto David, and she shall sleep in David's house.

2ND CAPTAIN: And Israel shall be avenged of her enemies.

DAVID: Hath the King verily sent this message to me?

1ST CAPTAIN: Yea, he hath sent it, and a ring* from his own hand.—Lo! here it is! For said Saul: Let David keep this for a pledge between me and him, in this matter. And when he returneth, he shall give me my ring again, and the foreskins of the Philistine, and I will give him Michal my daughter to wife.

DAVID: Yea! Then must I hence, and call my men, and go forth against the Philistine. For while the nights yet are moonless and without point of moon, will I return with the tally. *(Exit.)*

2ND CAPTAIN: Yea, he is gone on the king's errand.

1ST CAPTAIN: Let him meet what the king wishes.

(Exeunt.)

1ST HERDSMAN: Yea, I know that ye would have.—Ye would slay David with the sword of the Philistine. For who keeps promise with a dead man! *(*MICHAL *and* MAIDENS *edge in.)* Hast thou heard, Oh Michal! David is gone forth again against the Philistine. For Saul asketh an hundred foreskins of the enemy, as thy bride-money. Is it not a tall dowry?

MICHAL: Yea, hath my father done this!

1ST HERDSMAN: Wellah, hath he! For dead men marry no King's daughters. And the spear of some Philistine shall beget death in the body of David.—Thy father hath made thee dear!

MICHAL: Nay, he hath made my name cheap in all Israel.

2ND HERDSMAN *(entering)*: Run, maidens! The cattle are coming round the wall, athirst!

MAIDENS *(shouldering their jars)*: Away! Away!

(Exeunt.)

(Curtain)

Scene 13.

A room in DAVID'S *house in Gilgal—almost dark—*DAVID *alone, speaking softly:—an image* in a corner.*

DAVID: Give ear to my words, O Lord; consider my meditation.

Hearken unto the voice of my cry, my King, my God: for unto 5
thee will I pray.

My voice shalt thou hear in the morning, O Lord: in the
morning will I direct my prayer unto thee, and will look up.

For thou art not a God that hath pleasure in wickedness: neither
shall evil dwell with thee. 10

The foolish shall not stand in thy sight: thou hatest all workers
of iniquity.

Thou shalt destroy them that speak leasing: the Lord will abhor
the bloody and deceitful man.

But as for me, I will come into thy house in the multitude of 15
thy mercy: and in thy fear will I worship toward thy holy
presence.*

Lead me, O Lord, in thy righteousness, because of mine
enemies: make the way straight before my face.

For there is no faithfulness in their mouth: their inward part is 20
very wickedness; their throat is as an open sepulchre: they
flatter with their tongue.

Destroy thou them, O God; let them fall by their own counsels;
cast them out in the multitude of their transgressions, for they
have rebelled against thee. 25

But let all those that put their trust in thee rejoice: let them ever
shout for joy, because thou defendest them; let them also that
love thy name be joyful in thee.

For thou, Lord, wilt bless the righteous; with favor wilt thou
compass him, as with a shield.* 30

(Pause.)

Nay Lord, I am thine anointed, and thy son. With the oil of
anointment hast thou begotten me. Oh, I am twice begotten: of
Jesse, and of God! I go forth as a son of God, and the Lord is
with me.*—Yet for this they hate me, and Saul hath me in 35
abhorrence, and the men that are with Saul seek to destroy
me.—What can I do, Oh Lord, in this pass?

(Enter MICHAL, *through curtain at side, with tray and lamp.)*

MICHAL: The dawn is at hand. Art thou not faint with this long watching before the Lord? Oh! why wilt thou leave thy bed and thy pleasure of the night, to speak thyself out into the empty chill hours towards morning?—Come then, eat of the food which I have brought.

DAVID: I will not eat now, for my soul still yearns away from me.

MICHAL: Art thou sick?

DAVID: Yea! My soul is sick.

MICHAL: Why?

DAVID: Nay, thou knowest. Thy father hates me beyond measure.

MICHAL: But I, I love you.

DAVID *(takes her hand)*: Yea!

MICHAL: Is it nothing to you, that Michal is your wife, and loves you?

DAVID: Verily, it is not nothing.—But Michal, what will come to me at last? From moon to moon Saul's anger waxes. I shall lose my life at last. And what good shall I be to thee then?

MICHAL: Ah no! Ah no! Never shall I see thee dead. First thou shalt see me dead. Never, never shall I tear my hair for thee, as a widow. It shall not be. If thou go hence, it shall not be into death.

DAVID: Yet death is near.—From month to month, since I came back with the foreskins of the Philistine, and got thee to wife, Saul has hated me more. Michal loves David, and Saul's hate waxes greater. Jonathan loves David, and the king commands Jonathan, saying: There, where thou seest him, there shalt thou slay David.

MICHAL: My father is no more a man. He is given over entirely to evil spirits.—But Jonathan will save thee through it all.

DAVID: The Lord will save me. And Jonathan is dearer to me than a heart's brother.

MICHAL: Think, Oh husband! if Saul hateth thee, how Michal and Jonathan, who are children of Saul, do love thee.

DAVID: Yea verily! It is like the rainbow in the sky unto me. But oh, Michal, how shall we win through? I have loved Saul. And I have not it in me, to hate him. Only his perpetual anger puts on me a surpassing heaviness, and a weariness, so my flesh wearies upon my bones.

MICHAL: But why? Why? Why does it matter to thee?—I love thee, all the time.—Jonathan loves thee.—Thy men love thee.—Why

does the frenzy of one distracted man so trouble thee?—Why?
It is out of all measure.

DAVID: Nay, he is Saul, and the Lord's anointed. And he is king
over all Israel.

MICHAL: And what then? He is no man among men any more. Evil
possesses him. Why heed him, and wake in the night for him?

DAVID: Because he is the Lord's anointed, and one day he will kill
me.

MICHAL: He will never kill thee. Thou sayst thyself, the Lord will
prevent him. And if not the Lord, then I will prevent him—for
I am not yet nothing in Gilgal. And Jonathan will prevent
him.—And the captains will prevent him.—And art thou not
also the Lord's anointed? And will not the Lord set thee king
on the hill of Zion, in thine own Judah?

DAVID: Oh Michal! Oh Michal! That the hand of the Lord's
anointed should be lifted against the Lord's anointed!—What
can I do? For Saul is the Lord's, and I may not even see an
enemy in him! I cannot, verily!—Yet he seeks to slay me.—All
these months since he gave thee to me, after I brought the
foreskins of the Philistine for thy dowry, he has hated me more,
and sought my life.—Before the moon of our marriage was
waned away, thy father commanded his servants, and even
Jonathan, to slay David on that spot where they should find
him. So Jonathan came to me in haste and secret, and sent me
away into the fields by night and hid me. Yea, before the month
of our marriage was finished, I had to flee from thee in the
night, and leave my place cold.

MICHAL: But not for long. Not for long. Jonathan persuaded my
father, so he took thee back. Even he loved thee again.

DAVID: Yea, he also loves me! But Saul is as a man falling backward
down a deep pit, that must e'en clutch what is nearest him, and
drag it down along with him.

MICHAL: But Saul swore: As the Lord liveth, David shall not be
slain.

DAVID: Ay, he swore. But before two moons were passed, his brow
was black again. And when the season of the year came, that the
kings of the Philistine go forth, I went up against them, and
fought. The months of the fighting I fought with them, and
prevailed.—And thou didst wait for me!—But when at length I
came home with my men to Gilgal, and all the people rejoiced,

I saw* with a sinking heart the face of Saul blacken, blacken darker with greater hate!—Yea, he hath loved me, as the Lord's anointed must love the Lord's anointed. But Saul is slipping backward down the pit of despair, away from God. And each time he strives to come forth, the loose earth yields beneath his feet, and he slides deeper.—So the upreach of his love fails him, and the downslide of his hate is great and greater in weight.—I cannot hate him—nor love him.—But Oh, Michal, I am oppressed with a horror of him.

MICHAL: Nay, do not dwell on him.

DAVID: And the year went round its course, and once more there was war with the Philistine. And once more we prevailed, in the Lord. And once more the armies shouted my name. And once more I came home to thee—and thou didst sing. And my heart did sing above thee.—But as a bird hushes when the shadow of the hawk dances upon him from heaven, my heart went hushed under the shadow of Saul. And my heart could not sing between thy breasts, as it wanted to, even the heart of a bridegroom. For the shadow of Saul was upon it—

MICHAL: Oh, why do you care? Why do you care? Why do you not love me, and never care?

DAVID: It is not in me. I have been blithe of thy love and thy body. But now three days ago, even in the midst of my blitheness, Saul again threw his javelin at me—yea, even in the feast. And I am marked among all the men.*—And the end draws nigh. —For scarce may I leave this house, lest at some corner they slay me.

MICHAL: What end, then? What end draws nigh?

DAVID: I must get me gone. I must go into the wilderness.

MICHAL *(weeping)*: Oh bitter! bitter! My joy has been torn from me, as an eagle tears a lamb from the ewe. I have no joy in my life, nor in the body of my lord and my husband. A serpent is hid in my marriage bed, my joy is venomed. Oh that they had wed me to a man that moved me not, rather than be moved to so much hurt.

DAVID: Nay, nay! Oh nay nay! Between me and thee is no bitterness, and between my body and thy body there is constant joy.—Nay nay! Thou art a flame to me of man's forgetting, and God's presence. Nay nay! Thou shalt not weep for me, for thou art a delight to me, even a delight and a forgetting.

MICHAL: No! No! Thou leavest me in the night, to make prayers and moaning before the Lord. Oh, that thou hadst never married in thy body the daughter of thine enemy!

DAVID: Say not so, it is a wrong thing. Thou art sweet to me, and all my desire. 5

MICHAL: It is not true! Thou moanest, and leavest me in the night,* to fall before the Lord.

DAVID: Yea, trouble is come upon me. And I must take my trouble to the Lord. But thy breasts are my bliss and my forgetting. —Oh, do not remember my complaining! But let thyself be 10 sweet to me, and let me sleep among the lilies.

MICHAL: Thou wilt reproach me again with my father.

DAVID: Ah no! Ah never I reproached thee! But now I can forget, I can forget all but thee, and the blossom of thy sweetness. Oh come with me, and let me know thee. For thou art ever again as 15 new to me.

MICHAL *(rising as he takes her hand)*: Nay, thou wilt turn the bitterness of thy spirit upon me again.

DAVID: Ah no! I will not! But the gates of my life can I now open to thee again, and the world of bitterness shall be gone under, as 20 in a flood.

MICHAL: And wilt thou not leave me?

DAVID: Nay, lift up thy voice no more, for the hour of speech has passed.

(Exeunt through curtain at back.) 25

(Curtain)

Scene 14.

The same room, unchanged, an hour or so later—but the grey light of
day. A WOMAN-SERVANT *comes in.—There is a wooden image in a*
corner.

5   WOMAN-SERVANT: Yea, the lighted lamp, and the food!—My lord
      David hath kept watch again before the Lord, and tears will fall
      on Michal's bosom, and darken her heart!—Aiee! Aiee! That
      Saul should so hate the life of David! Surely the evil spirits are
      strong upon the king.

10 BOY *(entering)*: Jonathan, the king's son, is below, knocking softly at
      the door.☆

      WOMAN-SERVANT: Go! Open swiftly, and make fast again!—Aiee!
      Aiee! My lord Jonathan comes too early for a pleasure visit.—I
      will see if they sleep.

15 *(Goes through the curtain—enter* JONATHAN. JONATHAN *stands silent,*
    pensive. Goes to a window.—Re-enter WOMAN-SERVANT. *She starts,*
              seeing JONATHAN—*then puts her hand on her mouth.)*

      WOMAN-SERVANT: Oh my lord Jonathan! Hush!

      JONATHAN: They are sleeping still?

20 WOMAN-SERVANT: They are sleeping the marriage sleep.—David
      hath even watched before the Lord, in the night. But now with
      Michal he sleeps the marriage sleep, in the lands of peace. Now
      grant a son shall come of it, to ease the gnawing of Michal's
      heart.

25 JONATHAN: What gnaws in Michal's heart?

      WOMAN-SERVANT: Ah my Lord, her love even for David, that will
      not be appeased. If the Giver☆ gave her a son, so should her
      love for David abate, and cease to gnaw in her.

      JONATHAN: But why should it gnaw in her? Hath she not got him,
30   and the joy of him?

      WOMAN-SERVANT: Oh Jonathan, she is even as the house of Saul.
      What she hath, cannot appease her.

      JONATHAN: What then would she more?

      WOMAN-SERVANT: She is of the house of Saul, and her very love
35   is pain to her. Each cloud that crosses her is another death of
      her love.—Ah, it is better to let love come and to let it go, even
      as the winds of the hills blow along the heavens. The sun
      shines, and is dulled, and shines again. It is the day, and its
      alterings; and after, it is night.

JONATHAN: David and Michal are asleep?

WOMAN-SERVANT: In the marriage sleep. Oh, break it not!

JONATHAN: The sun will soon rise. Lo! this house is upon the wall
of the city, and the fields and the hills lie open.

WOMAN-SERVANT: Shall I bring food to Jonathan? 5

JONATHAN: Nay!—Hark! Men are crying at the city's western gate,
to open. The day is beginning.

WOMAN-SERVANT: May it bring good to this house!

JONATHAN: It is like to bring evil.

WOMAN-SERVANT: Ah, my Lord! 10

DAVID *(appearing through the curtain at the back)*: Jonathan!

JONATHAN: David! Thou art awake!

DAVID *(laughing)*: Yea! Am I not? Thou art my brother Jonathan,
art thou not? *(They embrace.)*

JONATHAN: Oh David, the darkness was upon my father in the night, 15
and he hath again bid slay thee.—Leave not the house.—Unbar
not the door!—Watch! And be ready to flee!—If armed men stand
round the door, (MICHAL *appears*) —then let down the boy from
the window, and send instantly to me. I will come with thy men,
and with mine, and we will withstand the hosts of Saul, if need be. 20

MICHAL: Is something new toward?

JONATHAN: My father bade his men take David, and slay him in
the dawn. I must away, lest they see that I have warned
thee.—Farewell, Oh David!

DAVID: Farewell, my brother Jonathan!—But I will come down the 25
stair with thee. *(Exeunt.)*

MICHAL: Yea! Yea! So sure as it is well between me and him, so
sure as we have peace in one another, so sure as we are together,
yea together, as man and woman are together!—comes this evil
wind and blows upon us! And oh, I am weary of my life, 30
because of it!

WOMAN-SERVANT: Aiee! Aiee! Say not so, Oh Michal! For thy
days are many before thee.

MICHAL: This time, an' they take him, they will surely kill him.

WOMAN-SERVANT: Sayst thou so! Oh why, in the Lord's name! 35

MICHAL: I know it. If they take him this time, he is lost.

WOMAN-SERVANT: Oh, then shall they surely not take him! Oh,
but what shall we do?

MICHAL: Creep thou on the roof! Let no man see thee. And there
lie, watch if armed men approach the house. 40

DAVID *(entering)*: There is no one there.

MICHAL: They will come as the sun comes. *(To* WOMAN-SERVANT.*)* Go thou and watch.

WOMAN-SERVANT: Verily, I will! *(Exit.)*

5   MICHAL: Oh David! So sure as it is spring-time in me, and my body blossoms like an almond tree, comes this evil wind upon me, and withers my bud!—Oh how can I bring forth children to thee, when the spear of this vexation each time pierces my womb.

DAVID: Trouble not thyself, my flower. No wind shall wither thee.

10   MICHAL: Oh, but I know. This time, an' they take thee, thou shalt lose thy life.—And Jonathan will not save thee.

DAVID: Nay! Be not afraid for me.

MICHAL: Yes! I am afraid! I am afraid! Ho! Ho! there! *(Claps her hands—enter* BOY. *To* BOY.*)* Bring the water skin for thy
15   master, filled with water. And his pouch with bread. For he goeth on a journey.—Oh David! David! Now take thy cloak, and thy bow, and thy spear, and put on thy shoes. For thou must go! Jonathan cannot avail thee this time.

DAVID: Nay! Why shall I flee, when the sun is rising?

20   MICHAL: Yea! If thou go not before the sun is here, in the morning thou shalt be slain. Oh make ready! Thy shoes! Put them on! *(*DAVID *reluctantly obeys.)* Thy cloak, so they shall not know thee! *(He puts it on.)* Thy spear and bow!

BOY *(entering)*: Here is the pouch and the water-flask.

25   MICHAL: Run, bring figs and dry curds. Dost thou hear ought at the door?

BOY: Nought! *(Exit.)*

MICHAL: Oh David, art thou ready! Oh, that thou leavest me!

DAVID: I need not go! Yea, to comfort thee, I will go to the place
30   that Jonathan knoweth of, and thou shalt send thither for me. Or wilt thou—

WOMAN-SERVANT *(re-entering)*: Oh Michal! Oh David, master! There be men at arms approaching, under the wall, and walking by stealth. Oh flee! flee! for they mean thy life.

35   MICHAL: Now must thou go by the window, into the fields. I see the sun's first glitter.—Even for this hour have I kept the new rope ready.—

(She fastens the rope to a stout stake, and flings the end from the window.
                                            —*To* DAVID.*)*

40   —Go! Go! Swiftly be gone!

DAVID: I will come again to thee. Sooner or later, as the Lord liveth, I will take thee again to me, unto my bed and my body.

MICHAL: Hark! They knock! Ha-a!

BOY *(entering)*: There are men at the door!

MICHAL: Go! Call to them! Ask what they want! But touch thou not the door! 5

(DAVID meanwhile climbs through the window—the stake across the window-space holds the rope.)

WOMAN-SERVANT *(climbing with her hands)*: So! So! So! My lord David! So! So! Swing him not against the wall, oh spiteful rope! 10 So! So! He kicks free! Yea! And god be praised, he is on the ground, looking an instant at his hands. So he looks up and departs! Lifts his hand and departs!

MICHAL: Is he gone? Draw in the rope, and hide it safe.

WOMAN-SERVANT: That will I! 15

(Meanwhile MICHAL has flung back the curtain of the recess where the low earthen bank of the bed is seen, with skins and covers. She takes the wooden image of a god and lays it in the bed, puts a pillow at its head, and draws the bed-cover high over it.)

MICHAL *(to herself)*: Yea, and my house's god which is in my house, 20 shall lie in my husband's place, and the image of my family god, which came of old from my mother's house, shall deceive them. For my house has its own gods, yea, from of old, *(enter BOY)* and shall they forsake me?

BOY: They demand to enter. The king asketh for David, that he go 25 before the king's presence.

MICHAL: Go thou, say to them: My lord and my master, David, is sick and in his bed.

BOY: I will say that. *(Exit.)*

WOMAN-SERVANT: Sit thou nigh the bed. And if they still will 30 come up, thou shalt say he sleepeth.

MICHAL: Yea, will I.— *(Sits by bed.)* Oh god of my household, oh god of my mother's house, Oh god in the bed of David, save me now! *(Enter BOY.)*

BOY: They will e'en set eyes on my master. 35

MICHAL: Stay! Say to them, that their captains shall come up, two only: but softly, for my lord David hath been sick these three days, and at last he sleepeth.

BOY: I will tell them. *(Exit.)*

WOMAN-SERVANT: And I too will go bid them hush! 40

(Exit—MICHAL *sits in silence. Enter* 1ST *and* 2ND CAPTAINS—*with the*
WOMAN-SERVANT.*)*

WOMAN-SERVANT: There he sleepeth in the bed.

MICHAL: Sh-h-h!

5   1ST CAPTAIN: I will go even now and tell the king.

(Exeunt the CAPTAINS—*after a pause—Curtain.)*

(Curtain rises, after short time, on same scene.)

WOMAN-SERVANT *(rushing in)*: They are coming again down the
street, but boldly now.

10   MICHAL: Yea! Let them come! By this time is David beyond their
reach, in the secret place.

WOMAN-SERVANT: Oh, and what shall befall thee! Oh!

MICHAL: I am the king's daughter. Even Saul shall not lift his hand
against me.—Go down thou to the door, and hold the men

15   whilst thou mayst. Why should we admit them forthwith? Say
that Michal is performing her ablutions.

WOMAN-SERVANT: Will I not! *(Exit.)*

MICHAL: And shall I strip the bed? Then will they search the house
and the fields.—Nay, I will leave it, and they shall see how they

20   were fools.—Oh teraphim, oh my God of my own house,
hinder them and help me. Oh thou my teraphim, watch for me!

(Sound of knocking below.)

VOICE OF WOMAN-SERVANT: Ho ye! Who knocks, in the Lord's
name?

25   VOICE OF 1ST CAPTAIN: Open! Open ye! In the name of the king.

VOICE OF WOMAN-SERVANT: What would ye, in this house of
sickness?

VOICE OF 1ST CAPTAIN: Open, and thou shalt know.

VOICE OF WOMAN-SERVANT: I may not open, save Michal bid me.

30   VOICE OF 1ST CAPTAIN: Then bid Michal bid thee open forthwith.

VOICE OF WOMAN-SERVANT: Oh thou captain of the loud shout,
surely thou wert here before! Know then, my master is sick,
and my mistress performeth her ablutions in the sight of the
Lord. At this moment may I not open.

35   VOICE OF 1ST CAPTAIN: An' thou open not, it shall cost thee.

VOICE OF WOMAN-SERVANT: Nay now, is not my mistress king's
daughter, and is not her command laid on me! Oh Captain, wilt
thou hold it against me, who tremble between two terrors?

VOICE OF 1ST CAPTAIN: Tremble shalt thou, when the terrors nip thee.—E'en open the door, lest we break it in.

VOICE OF WOMAN-SERVANT: Oh what uncouth man is this, that will break down the door of the king's daughter, and she naked at her bath,* before the Lord! 5

VOICE OF 1ST CAPTAIN: We do but the king's bidding.

VOICE OF WOMAN-SERVANT: How can that be? What, did the king indeed bid ye break down the door of his daughter's house, and she uncovered in the Lord's sight, at her ablutions?

VOICE OF 1ST CAPTAIN: Yea! The king bade us bring before him 10 instantly the bed of David, and David upon the bed!

VOICE OF WOMAN-SERVANT: Oh now, what unseemly thing is this! Hath not the king legs long enough! And can he not walk hither on his feet? Oh send, fetch the king, I pray thee, thou Captain.—Say, I pray thee, that Michal prays the king come 15 hither.

VOICE OF 1ST CAPTAIN: Word shall be sent.—Yet open now this door, that the bird escape us not.

VOICE OF WOMAN-SERVANT: Oh Captain! And is my master then a bird? Oh, would he were, even the young eagle, that he might 20 spread wing! Oh man, hast thou no fear what may befall thee, that thou namest David a bird? Oh Israel, uncover now thine ear!

VOICE OF 1ST CAPTAIN: I name him not.

VOICE OF WOMAN-SERVANT: And what would ye, with this bird 25 my master! Oh, the Lord forbid that any man should call him a bird!

VOICE OF 1ST CAPTAIN: We e'en must bring him upon his bed, before the king.

VOICE OF WOMAN-SERVANT: Now, what is this! Will the king heal 30 him with mighty spells? Or is David on his sick-bed to be carried before the people, that they may know his plight? What new wonder is this?

VOICE OF 1ST CAPTAIN: I cannot say: yet will I wait no longer.

MICHAL: Open, Maiden! Let them come up. 35

VOICE OF WOMAN-SERVANT: Oh, my mistress crieth unto me, that I open.—Yea, Oh Michal, I will e'en open to these men. For who dare look aslant at the king's daughter.

1ST CAPTAIN *(entering, followed by* [WOMAN-SERVANT *and]* *sol-*

diers): Is David still in the bed? An' he cannot rise, will we carry him upon the bed, before the king.

MICHAL: Now, what is this?

1ST CAPTAIN*: Sleeps he yet? Ho David, sleepest thou?

4TH SOLDIER: We will take up the bed, and wake him.

5TH SOLDIER: He stirs not at all.

1ST CAPTAIN *(to* MICHAL*)*: Yea, rouse him and tell him the king's will.

MICHAL: I will not rouse him.

1ST CAPTAIN *(going to the bed)*: Ho thou! Ho! David!— *(He suddenly pulls back the bed-cover.)* What is this? *(Sudden loud shrilling laughter from the* WOMAN-SERVANT, *who flees when the men look round.)*

SOLDIERS *(crowding)*: We are deceived.—Ha-ha! It is a man of wood and a goat's hair bolster!—Ha-ha-ha! What husband is this, of Michal's?

MICHAL: My teraphim, and the god of my house.

1ST CAPTAIN: Where hast thou hidden David?

MICHAL: I have not hidden him.

(Pause—Voice of SAUL* *on the stair.)*

VOICE OF SAUL: Why tarry ye here? What! Must the king come on his own errands? *(Enter* SAUL.*)* And are ye here?

MICHAL: The Lord strengthen thee, my father.

SAUL: Ha! Michal! And can then David not rise from his bed, when the king sendeth for him?

1ST CAPTAIN: Lo! O King! Behold the sick man on the bed! We are deceived of Michal.

SAUL: What is this? *(Flings the image across the room.)*

MICHAL: Oh, my teraphim! Oh God of my house! Oh alas, alas, now will misfortune fall on my house! Oh woe is! Woe is me! *(Kneels before teraphim.)*

SAUL: Where is David? Why hast thou deceived me?

MICHAL: Oh, God of my house, god of my mother's house, visit it not upon me!

SAUL: Answer me, or I will slay thee!

MICHAL: God of my house, I am slain, I am slain!

SAUL: Where is David?

MICHAL: Oh my Lord, he is gone; he is gone ere the sun made day.

SAUL: Yea, thou hast holpen him against me.

MICHAL *(weeping)*: Oh! Oh! He said unto me: *Let me go; why shouldst thou make me slay thee, to trouble my face in the sight of men.*—I could not hinder him, he would have slain me there!

SAUL: Why hast thou deceived me so, and sent away mine enemy, that he is escaped? 5

MICHAL *(weeping)*: I could not prevent him.

SAUL: Even when did he go?

MICHAL: He rose up before the Lord, in the deep night. And then he would away, while no man saw.

SAUL: Whither is he gone? 10

MICHAL: Verily, and verily, I know not.

(Pause.)

SAUL: So! He hath escaped me! And my flesh and my blood hath helped mine enemy. Woe to you, Michal! Woe to you! Who have helped your father's enemy, who would pull down thy father to 15 the ground. Lo! my flesh and my blood rebel against me, and my seed lies in wait for me, to make me fall!

MICHAL: Oh, why must David be slain?

SAUL: Woe to you, Michal! And David shall bring woe to you, and woe upon you. David shall pull down Saul, and David shall pull 20 down Jonathan, thee, Michal, he will pull down, yea, and all thy house. Oh, thou mayst call on the teraphim of thy house. But if thy teraphim love thy house, then would he smite David speedily to the death. For if David liveth, I shall not live, and thou shalt not live, and thy brothers shall not live. For David 25 will bring us all down in blood.

MICHAL *(weeping)*: Oh my father, prophesy not against him.

SAUL: It shall be so.—What, have I no insight into the dark!—And thou art now a woman abandoned of her man, and thy father castest thee off, because thou hast deceived him, and brought 30 about his hurt.

MICHAL: Oh my father, forgive me! Hold it not against me!

SAUL: Nay, thou hast bent thy will against thy father, and called destruction upon thy father's house.

MICHAL: Ah no! Ah no! 35

(Curtain)

Scene 15.

Naioth in Ramah—*a round, pyramid-like hill, with a stair-like way to
the top, where is a rude rock altar. Many* PROPHETS, *young and old,
wild and lusty, dressed in blue ephods without mantle, on the summit of*
5   *hill and down the slope. Some have harps, psalteries, pipes and tabrets.*
*There is wild music and rough, ragged chanting. They are expecting
something. Below,* SAMUEL *and* DAVID, *talking. Not far off* 1ST
PROPHET *in attendance.*

PROPHETS (*on hill—irregularly crying and chanting*): This is the
10   place of the Lord! Upon us shines the Unseen! Yea, here is Very
God! Who dares come into the glory! Oh thou, filled with the
Lord, sing with me on this high place. For the egg of the world
is filled with God.

SAMUEL (*speaking to* DAVID): It is time thou shouldst go. As a fox
15   with the dogs upon him, hast thou much fleeing to do.

DAVID: Must I always flee, my Father. I am already weary of flight.

SAMUEL: Yea, to flee away is thy portion. Saul cometh hither to
seek thee. But surely shall he fall before the Lord. When he
gets him back to his own city, enquire thou what is his will
20   towards thee. And if it still be evil, then flee from him diligently,
while he lives.

DAVID: And shall there never be peace between Saul's house and
mine?

SAMUEL: Who knows the Lord utterly! If there be not peace this
25   time, then shall there never in life be peace between thee and
him, nor thy house and his.

DAVID: Yet am I his son-in-law, in Michal my wife. And my flesh
yearneth unto mine own.

SAMUEL: Is the house of Saul thine own?

30   DAVID: Yea, verily—

SAMUEL: Dost thou say, *yea, verily!*—Hark now! If this time there
be peace between thee and him, it shall be peace. But if not,
then think of nought but to flee, and save thyself, and keep on
fleeing while Saul yet liveth.—The Lord's choice is on thee, and
35   thou shalt be king in thy day.—As for me, I shall never see thy
day.

DAVID: Would I could make my peace with Saul! Would I could
return to mine own house, and to mine own wife, and to the
men of my charge!

SAMUEL: My son, once the Lord chose Saul. Now hath he passed Saul over, and chosen thee. Canst thou look guiltless into the face of Saul? Can he look guiltless into thy face? Can ye look into each other's faces, as men who are open and at peace with one another? 5

DAVID: Yet would I serve him faithfully.

SAMUEL: Yea, verily! And in thine heart, art thou king, and pullest the crown from his brow with thine eyes.

DAVID: Oh my Father, I would not!

SAMUEL: Wouldst thou not?—Willst thou say to me here and now: 10 *As the Lord liveth, I will not be king! But Saul and his house shall rule Israel for ever: and Jonathan my friend shall be king over me!*—Wilt thou say that to me?

DAVID: Doth Samuel bid me say this thing?

SAMUEL: He bids thee not.—But for Saul's sake, and for Jonathan's, 15 and for Michal's, and for peace, wilt thou say it?—Answer me from thine heart, for I know the smell of false words.—Yea, I bid thee, speak!

DAVID: The Lord shall do unto me as he will.

SAMUEL: Yea, for the Lord hath anointed thee, and thou shalt rule 20 Israel when Saul is dead, and I am dead, and the Judges of Israel are passed away.—For my day is nearly over, and thine is another day. Yea, Saul has lived in my day, but thou livest in thine own day, that I know not of.

DAVID: Oh my Lord, and is there nought but wrath and sorrow, 25 between me and Saul henceforth?

SAMUEL: The Lord will show! Knowest thou not?

DAVID: I would it were peace!

SAMUEL: Wouldest thou verily?—When the wind changes, will it not push the clouds its own way? Will fire leap lively in wet 30 rain?—The Lord is all things. And Saul hath seen a tall and rushing flame, and hath gone mad, for the flame rushed over him. Thou seest thy God in thine own likeness, afar off, or as a brother beyond thee, who fulfils thy desire.—Saul yearneth for the flame: thou for thy tomorrow's glory. The God of Saul hath 35 no face. But thou wilt bargain with thy God. So be it! I am old, and would have done.—Flee then, thou, and flee again, and once more, flee. So shalt thou at last have the kingdom and the glory in the sight of men.—I anointed thee, but I would see thee no more, for my heart is weary of its end. 40

DAVID: Wilt thou not bless me?

SAMUEL: Yea, I will bless thee! Yea, I will bless thee, my son. Yea, for now thy way is the way of might, yea, and even for a long space of time it shall be so.—But after many days, men shall come again to the faceless flame of my Strength, and of Saul's.—Yea, I will bless thee! Thou art brave, and alone, and by cunning must thou live, and by cunning shall thy house live for ever.—But hath not the Lord created the fox, and the weasel that boundeth and skippeth like a snake!

DAVID: Oh Samuel, I have but tried to be wise! What should I do, and how should I walk in the sight of men! Tell me, my father, and I will do it.

SAMUEL: Thou wilt not. Thou walkest wisely, and thy Lord is with thee. Yea, each man's Lord is his own, though God be but one. I know not thy Lord. Yet walk thou with him. Yea, thou shalt bring a new day for Israel. Yea, thou shalt be great, thou shalt fight as a flower fighteth upwards, through the stones, and alone with God, to flower in the sun at last. For the yearning of the Lord streameth as a sun, even upon the stones. *(A tumult above, among the* PROPHETS. SAMUEL *looks up—continues abstractedly.)* Yea, and as a flower thou shalt fade. But Saul was once as a burning bush, afire with God. Alas, that he saw his own image mirrored in the faces of men! *(A blare of music above.)*

SAMUEL *(to* 1ST PROPHET*)*: What see ye?

PROPHETS *(shouting)*: The sun on the arms of the king.

SAMUEL *(to* DAVID*)*: Now shalt thou go! For I too will not set mine eyes upon Saul the king.

DAVID: Bless me then, Oh my Father!

SAMUEL: The Lord fill thy heart and thy soul! The Lord quicken thee!* The Lord kindle thy spirit, so thou fall into no snare!—And now get thee gone!—And when Saul is returned to his own place, enquire thou secretly his will towards thee. And then act wisely, as thou knoweth.

DAVID: I go forth into the fields, as a hare when the hound gives mouth! But if the Lord go with me— *(Exit.)*

SAMUEL *(to* 1ST PROPHET*)*: Is Saul surely in sight?

1ST PROPHET: Verily, he is not far off. He has passed the well of Shecu.*

SAMUEL: Has he company of men?

1ST PROPHET: Ten armed men has he.

SAMUEL: Will he still bring armed men to the high place?—Lo! say
thou to him, Samuel hath gone before the Lord, in the hidden
places of the Hill.

1ST PROPHET: I will e'en say it.

SAMUEL: Say also to him, David, the anointed, is gone, we know 5
not whither.—And let the company of the prophets come down
towards the king.

1ST PROPHET: It shall be so. *(Exit* SAMUEL*).*

1ST PROPHET *(climbing hill and calling)*: O ye Prophets of the
Lord, put yourselves in array, to meet Saul the king. 10

2ND PROPHET *(with flute—on the hill—sounds flute loudly, with a
strong tune—shouts)*: Oh come, all ye that know our God! Oh
put yourselves in array, ye that know the Name. For that which
is without name is lovelier than anything named! *(Sounds the
tune strongly—*PROPHETS *gather in array, musicians in front—* 15
they chant slowly. As SAUL *approaches, they slowly descend.)*

CHORUS OF PROPHETS:

Armies there are, for the Lord our God!
Armies there are against the Lord!
Wilt thou shake spears in the face of Almighty God? 20
Lo! in thy face shakes the lightning. *(Bis.)*
Countest thou thyself a strong man, sayst thou Ha-ha!
Lo! We are strong in the Lord! Our arrow seest thou not!
Yet with the unseen arrows of high heaven⸙
Pierce we the wicked man's feet, pierce we his feet in the fight. 25
Lo! the bow of our body is strung by God.
Lo! how he taketh aim with arrow-heads of our wrath!
Prophet of God is an arrow in full flight
And he shall pierce thy shield, thou, thou Lord's enemy.
Long is the fight, yet the unseen arrows fly 30
Keen to a wound in the soul of the great Lord's enemy.
Slowly he bleeds, yet the red drops run away
Unseen and inwardly, as bleeds the wicked man,
Bleeding of God! Secretly, of God.

SAUL *(entering with* ARMED MEN*—*PROPHETS *continue to chant)*: 35
Peace be with you!⸙

1ST PROPHET: Peace be with the king.

SAUL: Lo! ye prophets of God! Is not Samuel set over you?

1ST PROPHET: Yea! Oh King!

SAUL *(beginning to come under the influence of the chant,⸙ and to take* 40
the rhythm in his voice): Is Samuel not here?

1ST PROPHET: He hath gone up before the Lord!

SAUL: Surely the Lord is in this place! Surely the great brightness! *(looks around)* —And the son of Jesse, is he among the prophets?

5   1ST PROPHET: Nay, he has gone hence.

SAUL: Gone! Gone! What, has he fled from the high place! Surely he feared the Glory! Yea, the brightness! So! He has fled before the flame! Thus shall he flee before the flame!—But gone? Whither gone?

10   1ST PROPHET: We know not whither.

SAUL: Even let him go! Even let him go whither he will! Yea, even let him go! Yea! Come we forth after such as he? Let him go!—Is not the Lord here? Surely the brightness is upon the hill! Surely it gleams upon this high place!

15   LEADER OF ARMED MEN: Tarry⁎ we here, Oh King? Where shall we seek the son of Jesse?

SAUL: Even where ye will.

LEADER OF ARMED MEN: Tarrieth the king here?

SAUL: Yea! I will know if the Lord is verily in this place.

20   1ST PROPHET: Verily he is here. *(Company of* PROPHETS *still chant.)*

SAUL *(going slowly forward)*: Art thou here, Lord! What? Is this thy brightness upon the hill? What? Art thou here in thy glory?

COMPANY OF PROPHETS:

25   Fire within fire is the presence of the Lord!
                Sun within the sun is our god! *(Bis.)*
                Rises the sun among the hills of thy heart
                Rising to shine in thy breast? *(Bis.)*

SAUL: Yea! Oh Prophets! Am I not king? Shall not the sun of suns

30   rise among the hills of my heart, and make dawn in my body? What! Shall these prophets know the glory of the Lord, and shall the son of Kish stay under a cloud! *(Sticks his spear into the ground, and unbuckles his sword-belt.)*

LEADER OF ARMED MEN: Wilt thou go up before the Lord, Oh

35   King! Then camp we here, to await thy pleasure.

SAUL: I will go up. Camp an' ye will.

LEADER OF ARMED MEN: Even camp we here. *(They untackle.)*⁎

SAUL: Ha!—Ha!—Is there a glory upon the prophets? Do their voices resound like rocks in the valley! Ha! Ha!—Thou of the

40   sudden fire! I am coming! Yea! I will come into the glory!

(Advancing, throws down his woolen mantle. The 1ST PROPHET *takes it up.)*

CHORUS OF PROPHETS:

> Whiteness of wool helps thee not in the high place,
> Colours on thy coat* avail thee nought. *(Bis.)*
> Fire unto fire only speaks, and only flame
> Beckons to flame of the Lord! *(Bis.)*

(The PROPHETS *divide and make way, as* SAUL *comes up.)*

SAUL: Is my heart a cold hearth? is my heart fireless unto thee? Kindler! It shall not be so! My heart shall shine to thee, yea, unshadow itself. Yea, the fire in me shall mount to the fire of thee, thou Wave of Brightness!

6TH SOLDIER *(below—with loud and sudden shout)*: The sun is in my heart. Lo! I shine forth!

SAUL *(with suddenness)*: I will come up! Oh! I will come up! Dip me in the flame of brightness, thou Bright One, call up the sun in my heart, out of the clouds of me. Lo! I have been darkened, and deadened with ashes! Blow a fierce flame on me, from the middle of thy glory, oh thou of the faceless flame! *(Goes slowly forward.)* Oh dip me in the ceaseless flame! *(Throws down his coat, or wide-sleeved tunic, that came below the knee and was heavily embroidered at neck and sleeves in many colours. Is seen in the sleeveless shirt that comes half way down the thigh.)*

6TH SOLDIER *(below)*: Kings come and pass away, but the flame is flame forever. The Lord is here, like a tree of white fire! Yea, and the white glory goes in my nostrils like a scent.

SAUL: Shall a soldier be more blessed than I? Lo! I am not dead, thou Almighty! My flesh is still flame, still steady flame. Flame to flame calleth, and that which is dead is cast away! *(Flings off his shirt: is seen, a dark-skinned man in leathern loin-girdle.)* Nay, I carry nought upon me, the long flame of my body leans to the flame of all glory!—I am no king, save in the Glory of God. I have no kingdom, save my body and soul. I have no name. But as a slow and dark flame leaneth to a great glory of flame, and is sipped up, naked and nameless lean I to the glory of the Lord.

CHORUS OF PROPHETS:

> Standeth a man upon the stem of upright knees
> Openeth the navel's closed bud, unfoldeth the flower of the breast!
> Lo! Like the cup of a flower, with morning sun
> Filled is thy breast with the Lord, filled is thy navel's wide flower!

6TH SOLDIER: Oh come! For a little while the glory of the Lord stands up on the high place! Oh come! before they build him houses, and close him within a roof! Oh, it is good to live now, with the light of the first day's sun upon the breast. For when the seed of David have put the Lord inside a house, the glory will be gone, and men will walk with no transfiguration!* Oh come to this high place! Oh come!

SAUL: Surely I feel my death upon me! Surely the sleep of sleeps descends. *(Casts himself down.)* I cast myself down, night and day, as in death, lie I naked before God.—Ah, what is life to me! Alas, that a man must live till death visit him!—that he cannot walk away into the cloud of Sun! Alas! for my life! For my children and my children's children, alas! For the son of Jesse will wipe them out! Alas! for Israel! For the fox will trap the lion of strength, and the weasel that is a virgin, and bringeth forth her young from her mouth,* shall be at the throats of brave men! Yea! by cunning shall Israel prosper, in the days of the seed of David: and by cunning, and lurking in holes of the earth,* shall the seed of Jesse fill the earth. Then the Lord of Glory will have drawn far off, and gods shall be pitiful, and men shall be as locusts.—But I, I feel my death upon me, even in the glory of the Lord. Yea! leave me in peace before my death, let me retreat into the flame!*

(A pause.)

7TH SOLDIER: Saul hath abandoned his kingdom and his men! Yea! he puts the Lord between him and his work!

PROPHET: E'en let him be! For his loss is greater than another's triumph.

7TH SOLDIER: Yea! But wherefore shall a man leave his men leaderless! Even for the Lord!

6TH SOLDIER *(prophesying)*: When thou withdrawest thy glory, let me go with thee, Oh Brightest, even into the fire of thee!

CHORUS OF PROPHETS:

> Cast thyself down, that the Lord may snatch thee up.
> Fall before the Lord, and fall high.
> All things come forth from the flame of Almighty God.
> Some things shall never return! *(Bis.)*
> Some have their way and their will, and pass at last
> To the worm's waiting mouth *(Bis.)*

But the high Lord he leans down upon the hill
And wraps his own in his flame,
Wraps them as whirlwind from the world.
Leaves not one sigh for the grave . . .

(Curtain) 5

Scene 16.

*Late afternoon—a rocky place outside Gilgal—*DAVID *in hiding near the stone Ezel.*

DAVID *(alone)*: Now if Jonathan comes not, I am lost.—This is the
5   fourth day, and evening is nigh. Lo! Saul seeketh my life.—Oh
         Lord! look upon me; and hinder mine enemies. Frustrate them,
         make them stumble, Oh my God!—So near am I to Gilgal, yet
         between me and mine own house lies the whole gap of death.
         Yea Michal, thou art not far from me. Yet art thou far away even
10   as death.—I hide and have hidden. Three days have I hidden,
         and eaten scant bread. Lo! is this to be the Lord's anointed!
         Saul will kill me, and I shall die!—There! Someone moves
         across the fields!—Ah watch! watch!—Is it Jonathan?—It is two
         men, yea, it is two men. And one walks before the other.—
15   Surely it is Jonathan and his lad! Surely he has kept his
         word!—Oh Lord, save me now from mine enemies, for they
         compass me round. Oh Lord my God, put a rope round the
         neck of my enemy, lest he rush forward and seize me in the
         secret place.—Yea, it is Jonathan, in a striped coat. And a man
20   behind him carryeth the bow. Yea, now must I listen, and
         uncover my ears, for this is life or death.—Oh that he may say:
         Behold! the arrows are on this side of thee, take them!—For then
         can I come forth and go to my house, and the king will look
         kindly on me.—But he comes slowly, and sadly. And he will say:
25   *The arrows are beyond thee*—and I shall have to flee away like a
         hunted dog, into the desert.—It will be so!—Yea!—And I must
         hide lest that lad who follows Jonathan should see me, and set
         Saul's soldiery upon me. *(Exit—after a pause, enter* JONATHAN,
         with bow, and LAD *with quiver.)*
30 JONATHAN *(stringing his bow)*: Lo! this is the stone Ezel. Seest thou
         the dead bush, like a camel's head? That is a mark I have shot
         at, and now before the light falls, will I put an arrow through
         his nose. *(Takes an arrow.)* Will this fly well? *(Balances it.)*
    LAD: It is well shafted, Oh Jonathan.
35 JONATHAN: Ay! let us shoot. *(Takes aim—shoots.)* Yea! it touched
         the camel's ear, but not his nose! Give me another! *(Shoots.)*
         Ah! Hadst thou a throat, thou camel, thou wert dead.—Yet is
         thy nose too cheerful! Let us try again! *(Takes another arrow—
         shoots.)* Surely there is a scratch upon thy nose-tip.—Now this

time! *(Takes another arrow, shoots again.)* Nay, I am not myself! Give me the quiver. And run thou, take up the arrows e'er the shadows come.

LAD: I will find them. *(He runs—as he goes,* JONATHAN *shoots an arrow over his head. The* LAD *runs after it—stops.)*

JONATHAN: Is not the arrow beyond thee?

LAD: One is here!—Here another!

JONATHAN: The arrow is beyond thee! Make speed! Haste! Stay not!

LAD: Three have I! But the fourth—

JONATHAN: The arrow is beyond thee! Run, make haste!

LAD: I see it not! I see it not!—Yea, it is there within a bush!—I have it, and it is whole. Oh master, is this all?

JONATHAN: There is one more. Behold, it is still beyond thee.

LAD *(running)*: I see it not! I see it not! Yea, it is here!

JONATHAN: It is all! Come then! Come! Nay, the light is fading and I cannot see. Take thou the bow and the arrows, and go home. For I will rest here a while by the stone Ezel.

LAD: Will my master come home alone?

JONATHAN: Yea will I, with the peace of day's-end upon me.—Go now, and wait me in the house. I shall soon come. *(Exit* LAD. JONATHAN *sits down on a stone till he is gone.)*

JONATHAN *(calling softly)*: David! David!

*(*DAVID *comes forth, weeping. Falls on his face to the ground, and bows himself three times before* JONATHAN. JONATHAN *raises him. They kiss one another, and weep.)*

DAVID: Ah, then it is death, it is death to me from Saul.

JONATHAN: Yea, he seeks thy life, and thou must flee far hence.

DAVID *(weeping)*: Ah Jonathan! Thy servant thanks thee from his heart. But ah, Jonathan, it is bitter to go, to flee like a dog, to be houseless and homeless and wifeless, without friend or helpmate! Oh, what have I done, what have I done! Tell me, what have I done! And slay me if I be in fault.

JONATHAN *(in tears)*: Thou art not in fault. Nay, thou art not! But thou art anointed, and thou shalt be king. Hath not Samuel said it even now, in Naioth, when he would not look upon the face of Saul!—Yea, thou must flee until thy day come. Till there comes the day of the death of Saul, and the day of the death of Jonathan.

DAVID *(weeping)*: Oh, I have not chosen this. This have I not taken upon myself. This is put upon me, I have not chosen it! I do not want to go! Yea, let me come to Gilgal and die, so I see thy face, and the face of Michal my wife, and the face of the king. Let me die! Let me come to Gilgal and die! *(Flings himself on the ground in a paroxysm of grief.)*

5

JONATHAN: Nay! Thou shalt not die. Thou shalt flee! And till Saul be dead, thou shalt flee. But when Saul has fallen, and I have fallen with my father—for even now my life follows my father's—then thou shalt be king.

10 DAVID: I cannot go!

JONATHAN: Yea! Thou shalt go now. For they will send forth men to meet me, ere the dark. Rise now, and be comforted. *(DAVID rises.)*

DAVID: Why shouldst thou save me! Why dost thou withhold thy hand! Slay me now!

15

JONATHAN: I would not slay thee, nor now nor ever.—But leave me now, and go. And go in peace, forasmuch as we have sworn both of us in the name of the Lord, saying, *The Lord be between me and thee, and between my seed and thy seed for ever.*

20 DAVID: Yea! the covenant is between us. And I will go, and keep it.

(They embrace in silence, and in silence DAVID goes out.)

JONATHAN *(alone in the twilight)*: Thou goest, David! And the hope of Israel with thee!—I remain, with my father, and the star-stone* falling to despair. Yet what is it to me! I would not

25 see thy new day, David. For thy wisdom is the wisdom of the subtle, and behind thy passion lies prudence.* And naked thou wilt not go into the fire.—Yea, go thou forth, and let me die. For thy virtue is in thy wit and thy shrewdness. But in Saul have I known the splendour and the magnanimity of a

30 man.—Yea, thou art a smiter down of giants, with a smart stone! Great men and magnanimous, men of the faceless flame, shall fall from Strength, fall before thee,* thou David, shrewd whelp of the lion of Judah!—Yet my heart yearns hot over thee, as over a tender, quick child.* And the heart of my father

35 yearns, even amid its dark wrath. But thou goest forth, and knowest no depth of yearning, thou son of Jesse.—Yet go!* For my twilight is more to me than thy day, and my death is dearer to me than thy life! Take it! Take thou the kingdom, and the days to come. In the flames of death where Strength is, I will

40 wait and watch till the day of David at last shall finish, and

wisdom no more be fox-faced, and the blood gets back its flame.
—Yea, the flame dies not, though the sun's red dies!—And I
must get me to the city—
> *(Rises and departs hastily.)*

(Curtain)

APPENDIX I

EDWARD GARNETT'S INTRODUCTION TO *A COLLIER'S FRIDAY NIGHT*

EDWARD GARNETT'S INTRODUCTION
TO *A COLLIER'S FRIDAY NIGHT*[1]

His first play, *A Collier's Friday Night*, Lawrence tells us, in a note
pencilled on the MS., 'was written when I was twenty-one, almost
before I'd done anything. It is most horribly green.'[2] From the
biographical details contributed by D.H.L. to the American edition
of *The Widowing of Mrs. Holroyd* (New York, 1914) we learn that 'at
twenty-three he left the (Nottingham Day Training) College and
went to London to teach school, to study French and German and to
write.'[3] So, *A Collier's Friday Night* was written at Eastwood,
1906–7.[4] When, five years or so later, April 1912, he sent me the
MS.,[5] looking back at his provincial inexperience it was natural that
both the piece and the youth who wrote it should seem to him
'horribly green.' But what strikes one critically is the sureness of
touch and penetrating directness of this dramatic chronicle of family
life. As a theatre piece it is a bit too artless and diffuse, too lacking in
concentration and surprise, and its interest lies in the strongly drawn
characters, their relations and the clash of their personalities. The
life of this household warring within itself is, of course, a transcript
of the life of the Lawrence family. The situation is the same that
D.H.L. handled later in *Sons and Lovers*, viz. the enmity between the
father and the mother, and the latter's jealousy of her son's sweetheart. If 'greenness' there be, it lies in the cocksureness of the
author's tone and not in the delineation of the situation and
characters. The opening scene between Nellie, the mother, and the
father, exposes admirably the latter's stormy bitterness against his
family, who despise him. And the closing scene between the parents
and Ernest (pp. 70–76)[6] is as dramatically powerful as the passage

5

10

15

20

25

---

[1] Pp. v–vii of the first English edition of the play, published by Martin Secker, June
1934.
[2] See p. xxviii for the correct wording.
[3] See Edwin Björkman's Introduction to *The Widowing of Mrs. Holroyd*, reprinted as
Appendix II to this edition.
[4] See Introduction, p. xxviii.
[5] Cf. *Letters*, i. 381 and n. 3.
[6] Pp. 49–52 in this edition.

following between mother and son (pp. 77–82)[7] is delicate and poignant. Whether the psychological veracity of these characters and their behaviour can offset the discursiveness of the play will be interesting to watch. The warp and woof of the drama out of which the situations are spun are the bitterness between the parents and Ernest's relations with the women round him. At twenty-one Lawrence had not yet evolved his philosophical doctrines about sex, nor had he developed the 'inner conflict' between his selves. But his uncanny clairvoyance about women and the sex duel generally is declared in every scene of *A Collier's Friday Night*, as when Ernest says sadly to Maggie (p. 45):[8]

'You know you think too much of me—you do, you know.' (She looks at him with a proud, sceptical smile.)

(He waxes suddenly wroth)— 'It's just like a woman, always aching to believe in somebody or other, or something or other.' (She smiles.)

Then you have the difference between the attitude of the sexes. And later (p. 72)[9] woman's secret is declared in the mother's cry:

'No, my boy, because she doesn't mean the same to me. She has never understood—she has not been like you. And now—you seem to care nothing—you care for *any*thing more than home: you tell me nothing but the little things: you used to tell me everything; you used to come to me with everything; but now—I don't *do* for you now. You have to find somebody else.'

With what a light dexterous hand D.H.L. has touched off the flirtatious relations between himself and the feminine bevy round him, in the scene between Beatrice, Ernest and Maggie, with the cattish innuendoes about the College girls (pp. 49–51).[10] There is no 'greenness' in this scene done straight from the life by a man with a genius for attracting the sex. And if anybody wishes to see the difference in expression between this young author of twenty-one and the D.H.L. of twenty-seven, let him compare the two portraits given in *The Early Life of D. H. Lawrence*.[11] The alertness, directness and stubborn pride in the gaze of the youth who wrote *A Collier's*

---

[7] Pp. 53–7 in this edition.
[8] P. 32 in this edition.
[9] P. 56 in this edition.
[10] Pp. 35–7 in this edition.
[11] Garnett refers to the photographs in Lawrence and Gelder, *The Early Life of D. H. Lawrence*, frontispiece and opposite p. 96.

Friday Night has been enriched by something more speculative and roguishly aware of himself and others in the later photograph of 1911. The latter is a marvellously faithful portrait of D. H. Lawrence as I first knew him when he came to the Cearne[12] and his love-ableness, cheekiness, intensity and pride are all there for the dis-   5
cerning eye.

April, 1934.

[12] The Garnetts' cottage s. of London near Edenbridge, Kent; see *Letters,* i. 314. The photograph actually dates from 1913.

APPENDIX II

EDWIN BJÖRKMAN'S INTRODUCTION
TO *THE WIDOWING OF MRS. HOLROYD*

EDWIN BJÖRKMAN'S INTRODUCTION TO *THE WIDOWING OF MRS. HOLROYD*[1]

D. H. Lawrence is one of the most significant of the new generation of writers just beginning to appear in England. One of their chief marks is that they seem to step forward full-grown, without a history to account for their maturity. Another characteristic is that they frequently spring from social layers which in the past had to remain largely voiceless. And finally, they have all in their blood what their elders had to acquire painfully: that is, an evolutionary conception of life.

Three years ago the author of 'The Widowing of Mrs. Holroyd' was wholly unknown, having not yet published a single work. To-day he has to his credit three novels—'The White Peacock,' 'The Trespasser' and 'Sons and Lovers'—a collection of verse entitled 'Love Poems,' and the play contained in this volume. All of these works, but in particular the play and the latest novel, prove their author a man gifted with a strikingly original vision, a keen sense of beauty, an equally keen sense of verbal values, and a sincerity which makes him see and tell the truth where even the most audacious used to falter in the past. Flaubert himself was hardly less free from the old curse of sentimentalizing compromise—and yet this young writer knows how to tell the utmost truth with a daintiness that puts offence out of the question.

He was born twenty-seven years ago in a coal-miner's cottage at the little colliery town of Eastwood, on the border line between Nottingham and Derbyshire. The home was poor, yet not without certain aspirations and refinements. It was the mother who held it together, who saved it from a still more abject poverty, and who filled it with a spirit that made it possible for the boy—her youngest

---

[1] Pp. vii–x of the first American and English edition of the play, published by Mitchell Kennerley, New York, and Duckworth, London (April 1914). Edwin August Björkman (1866–1951), Swedish-born novelist, translator and critic, editor of Kennerley's Modern Drama Series (1912–15). The series was meant to bring the dramatic production of the last fifty years to the American public's notice; it included American and English plays as well as translations, among them plays by Ibsen, Strindberg, Björnson, Andreyev, Schnitzler, etc.

son—to keep alive the gifts still slumbering undiscovered within him. In 'Sons and Lovers' we get the picture of just such a home and such a mother, and it seems safe to conclude that the novel in question is in many ways autobiographical.

At the age of twelve the boy won a County Council Scholarship[2] —and came near having to give it up because he found that the fifteen pounds a year conferred by it would barely pay the fees at the Nottingham High School and the railway fares to that city. But his mother's determination and self-sacrifice carried him safely past the seemingly impossible. At sixteen he left school to earn his living as a clerk. Illness saved him from that uncongenial fate. Instead he became a teacher, having charge of a class of colliers' boys in one of those rough, old-fashioned British schools where all the classes used to fight against one another within a single large room. Before the classes convened in the morning, at eight o'clock, he himself received instruction from the head-master; at night he continued his studies in the little kitchen at home, where all the rest of the family were wont to foregather. At nineteen he found himself, to his own and everybody else's astonishment, the first on the list of the King's Scholarship examination, and from that on he was, to use his own words, 'considered clever.' But the lack of twenty pounds needed in a lump sum to pay the entrance fee at the training college for teachers made it impossible for him to make use of the gained advantage.

Two years later, however, he succeeded in matriculating at the Nottingham Day Training College.[3] But by that time the creative impulse had already begun to stir within him, aided by an early love affair, and so he wrote poems and worked at his first novel when he should have been studying. At twenty-three he left the college and went to London to teach school, to study French and German, and to write. At twenty-five he had his first novel—'The White Peacock' —accepted and printed. But the death of his mother only a month before that event made his victory seem useless and joyless. After the publication of his second novel, in 1912, he became able to give up

---

[2] For the exact dates and details of the following summary of DHL's early life see the 'Chronology' in this volume; see also *Letters*, i. xxviff., and *Early Years*. The scholarship only paid £12 a year.

[3] It was actually in July 1905 that he passed the London Matriculation examination for admission to University College, Nottingham. He went on teaching at Eastwood in order to save money.

teaching in order to devote himself entirely to his art.[4] Out of that leisure—and perhaps also out of the sorrow caused by the loss of her who until then had been the mainspring of his life—came 'Sons and Lovers' and 'The Widowing of Mrs. Holroyd.'[5]

What has struck me most deeply in these two works—apart from their splendid craftsmanship—is their psychological penetration, so closely paralleling the most recent conclusions of the world's leading thinkers. In the hands of this writer, barely emerged out of obscurity, sex becomes almost a new thing. Not only the relationship between man and woman, but also that of mother and child is laid bare in a new light which startles—or even shocks—but which nevertheless compels acceptance. One might think that Mr. Lawrence had carefully studied and employed the very latest theories of such men as Freud, for instance, and yet it is a pretty safe bet that most of his studies have been carried on in his own soul, within his own memories.[6] Thus it is proved once more that what the student gropingly reasons out for abstract formulation is flashed upon the poetic dreamer in terms of living reality.

Another thing that has impressed me is the aspect in which Mr. Lawrence presents the home life of those hitherto submerged classes which are now at last reaching out for a full share in the general social and cultural inheritance. He writes of that life, not only with a knowledge obtained at first hand, but with a sympathy that scorns any apologetic phrase-mongering. Having read him, one feels inclined to conclude, in spite of all conflicting testimony, that the slum is not a location, but a state of mind, and that everywhere, on all levels, the individual soul may create around itself an atmosphere expressive of its ideals. A book like 'Sons and Lovers' ought to go far to prove that most of the qualities held peculiar to the best portion of

---

[4] Björkman does not mention DHL's serious illness of 1911–12 which in fact was the cause of his quitting.

[5] Björkman links the writing of *Sons and Lovers* and *The Widowing of Mrs. Holroyd* and relates both works to the death of DHL's mother in December 1910; however, DHL worked on the short story 'Odour of Chrysanthemums' and on the play before that date and he started writing the first version of the novel in the autumn of 1910.

[6] DHL comments on this evaluation in a letter of 5 October 1913: 'Of course I take unto myself all the beautiful and laudatory things he [Björkman] says about me in the preface: they seem to me very just. I never did read Freud, but I have heard about him since I was in Germany' (*Letters*, ii. 80); in a different mood, only seven months later, he called the 'Introduction' rather unfairly a 'filthy little notice on me' (*Letters*, ii. 174).

the 'ruling classes' are nothing but the typical marks of normal humanity.

EDWIN BJÖRKMAN.

APPENDIX III

ALTITUDE

Altitude

Scene 1.

MARY A. *in kitchen doorway at Taos.*

MARY *(chants to herself—says Om! resoundingly)*: —This country
is waiting. It lies spell-bound, waiting. The great South-West,   5
America of America. It is waiting. What for? What for?
SPUD *(entering)*: Hello! Hasn't the cook come?
MARY: Goodmorning! No sign of her as yet.—Isn't morning won-
derful, here at this altitude, in the great South-West? Does it
kindle no heroic response in you, young Intellectual?   10
SPUD: I don't know. Maybe I'd better kindle a fire in the stove.
MARY: Quite right! Homage to the god of fire. Wait! An apron! Let
me do it. The fire in this house is the woman's fire, the fire in
the camp is the man's fire. You know the Indians say that?
SPUD: No, I didn't know it till you told me.   15
MARY: Ah, young Intellectual! It is a Woman Mediator you are
pining for. The Woman Redeemer!
SPUD: Maybe! Does this look like an apron? *(MARY girds it on.)*
MARY: To do, to know, and to be! Hamlet had hold of only one-
third of the twisted string. *(Busy at the stove.)*   20
(Enter CLARENCE in rose-coloured trousers and much jewellery.)
CLARENCE: Oh Good-morning, Mary! Good morning Spud.—
Why, Mary, won't you let Emilia do that?
MARY: Do you see any Emilia in the neighbourhood.
CLARENCE: Why no, I don't. Is it possible she's not coming! Oh,   25
what a calamity!
MARY: A contretemps, not a calamity, young Idealist. The heroic
nature is ready for every emergency. Woman is the great go-
between. When the cook does not turn up, *I* am cook. Mary and
Martha should be one person.   30
SPUD: What about Magdalene?
MARY: The men will play *her* rôle.
CLARENCE: Oh, but do let me do this.

541

MARY: Do what?

CLARENCE: Make a fire and all that.

MARY: The wood-box is empty: bring in some wood.

SPUD: Oh, I wish Mabel weren't so temperamental.

5   MARY: Thank God for Mabel's temperament, young Intellectual. Where would you be without it?

SPUD: Why I might get my coffee.

MARY: You get more than coffee from Mabel.

SPUD: Maybe I do. But it's rough on an empty stomach.

10   *(Enter* CLARENCE, *lays wood on kitchen table.)*

MARY: In the wood-box, young dreamer!

CLARENCE: Oh, so sorry!

MARY: Brains and dreams won't start a stove. Hands, muscle, and commonsense must be ready for any emergency, in the new

15   mystic we are bringing into the world.

CLARENCE: I'll take Mabel her breakfast in bed. That will be much the best.

                *(*MILKMAN *suddenly at the door.)*

MILKMAN: How much? Got the empty bottles? Any cream?

20 SPUD: Oh yes, let's have cream.

CLARENCE: Mabel only lets us have it on Sundays.

MARY: A pint of cream, two quarts of milk. The cook will give you the bottles tomorrow. *(*MILKMAN *slams wire door.)*

                *(*CLARENCE *goes out: loudly rings the gong.)*

25 SPUD: Why, what is he ringing for?

MARY: No doubt he thinks the bell will bring the breakfast, as the rooster thinks he brings the sun with his noise. It is all part of the male vanity. Woman brings the breakfast, meanwhile—

SPUD: And I suppose she has some hand in making the sun rise too?

30 MARY: Certainly. It is the great creative spirit of Woman, the perfected Woman, that keeps the sun in stable equilibrium.

SPUD *(sniggering)*: Do you say she keeps the sun in her stable.

IDA *(entering)*: Oh-h! I thought it was breakfast.

MARY: Lay the table, Ida.

35 IDA: For *everybody*?

(Enter MRS SPRAGUE *in white muslin—hovers—sits at table and looks benignly at the stray bits of wood left there by* CLARENCE.*)*

CLARENCE *(entering)*: Oh—er! Goodmorning! Goodmorning Mrs Sprague, how did you sleep?—Goodmorning Ida!

40 IDA: We're supposed to be laying the table.

MRS SPRAGUE: Oh yes! Oh yes! *(Hunts round, finds a tumbler, and wanders round with it.)*

MABEL *(in doorway)*: Where's breakfast? Where's Emilia? Who rang that bell?

CLARENCE: I rang the bell, Mabel. I thought we might as well all know that cook isn't coming.—*Won't* you go back to bed. *Please* do! You'll be *so* much more comfortable. 5

MABEL *(rushing at stove)*: Where's the coffee? Where's the coffee-pot? Is that water boiling?

MARY: Mabel, *I* am making the coffee. 10

MABEL: It's got to boil. It's got to boil several minutes. I want it *strong*, so it's got to boil.

MARY: Mabel, you may trust many things to me, the least of them being the coffee.—Won't you all sit down and discuss the situation, while I solve it. 15

MABEL: The bacon! *(Rushes into pantry and emerges with a side of bacon.)* Who can cut bacon *thin*? It's got to be cut *thin*. I want it dry. Cut it, somebody, and *I'll* cook it.

CLARENCE *(with dignity)*: I'll cut it, Mabel. Where is a knife.

(MABEL rushes across and produces a huge knife. CLARENCE proceeds to saw bacon, on the table-cloth.) 20

IDA: Not on the table-cloth, Clarence.

MABEL *(snatching knife)*: Not so *thick*! Somebody cut the bacon who can cut it *thin*. *(Silence.)* Spud, come and cut the bacon.

SPUD *(reluctantly)*: I'll try.—My God, be careful with that knife, you look like a Chicago aesthetic.☆ *(Crouches on floor to cut bacon.)* 25

INDIAN *(in doorway)*: Hello!

MABEL: Hello Joe! No cook this morning. You know how to cook?

INDIAN: No.

MARY: Will one of our young Intellectuals go to the well for water? 30

MABEL *(to Indian)*: Fetch a pail of water, Joe.

MARY: Don't you notice, the moment an Indian comes into the landscape, how all you white people seem so *meaningless*, so ephemeral?☆

IDA: Why yes! I was just thinking how ephemeral you all looked when Joe picked up the pail. 35

MABEL *(snorts)*: It *is* extraordinary! It's because the Indians have *life*. They have *life*, where we have *nerves*. Haven't you noticed, Mary, at an Indian dance, when the Indians all sit banked up on one side, and the white people on the other, how *all* the life is on 40 the Indian side, and the white people seem so dead. The Indians are like glowing coals, and the white people are like ashes.

IDA: Well Mabel, and which side are you on?

MABEL *(snorts)*: The Indian.

5 MARY: There is something which *combines* the red and the white, the Indian and the American, and is greater than either.

MABEL *(rushing at* SPUD*)*: That's enough bacon, Spud.

SPUD *(rising)*: I don't know that I feel so *ashy* at an Indian dance. *(Looks at his finger.)*

10 IDA: No, neither do I, Spud.

CLARENCE: And *I certainly* don't get any glow from the Indians.

MABEL: Well, you all know what I mean. And you do *all feel* it. Anyway you *look* it.

IDA: Perhaps we're the ashes of your stormy past, Mabel, and you
15 see in the Indians the red glow of your future.—But my dear, it's all red paint.

CLARENCE: Exactly. The paint they've daubed on their faces.

SPUD: The danger signal!

MRS SPRAGUE: Have you cut your finger?

20 SPUD: A little.

IDA: Suck it Spud.

SPUD: I *am* sucking it.

JOE *(entering)*: Here's the water.

MABEL: All right, Joe. You can go and chop some wood if you like.

25   (JOE *grunts, and doesn't like.)*

MABEL *(rushing at the stove)*: I'll fry the bacon, Mary!

MARY: Mabel, *I am* officiating at this altar.

MABEL: But I want my bacon dry, *dry*! You others can have it as you want it, but I want mine dry.

30 MARY: You shall have it as dry as the Arizona desert, Mabel.

IDA: Oh, what about Professor Mack?⃰ Is he still desiccating in the Arizona desert, studying the habits and misbehaviours of the Cactus?

MABEL: He's coming here.

35 IDA: Why how thrilling! Don't you feel awfully bucked, Mary?

MARY: Professor Mack and I have had a perfect correspondence all our lives. This is the first time we shall have slept under the same roof.

IDA: Why how extraordinary! I wonder what the *roof* will feel about
40   it.

MABEL: Let's sit down now. *(They all sit at table—)*

MABEL *(ominously)*: Well, here we all are.

SPUD: Minus a few of us.

MABEL: How are you, Alice? You've not said anything yet.

MRS SPRAGUE: Why I'm fine, Mabel. How are you? 5

MABEL: Fine! *(snorts)* How is everybody? How are you, Spud? Ida?

SPUD: Fine!

IDA: Fine!

MABEL: Mary, how d'you feel this morning? 10

MARY: Why fine!

CLARENCE: If you were going to ask me how I feel, Mabel, I feel fine, perfectly fine. It's *wonderful* to be here.

MABEL: Ye-es! You're *looking* marvellous. But you're not going down to the Plaza* in those trousers! 15

CLARENCE: Why yes. I wasn't going to take them off to go down town.

MABEL: What's the idea?

CLARENCE: As you said, we all *feel* so fine, I thought I'd try to look as fine as I felt. 20

MABEL: But why in trousers. Why look it in trousers?

CLARENCE: But why not? You wouldn't have me try to look it *without* trousers. No Mabel! If we *feel* wonderful, and we *are* perhaps rather wonderful, I think it's up to us to come out in our own feathers. 25

MABEL: Yes, but why feather your legs?

CLARENCE: But why not.

MABEL: It's an exhibitionist complex.

IDA: Mabel, I don't think you can quite say that. I *admire* rose-coloured trousers. 30

MABEL: Yes, all right, indoors. But not to go down to the Plaza. They're all wrong in the Plaza. Think how the people will *jeer* —and then talk. Another sign of vice from over here.

CLARENCE: But what does it matter whether they jeer or talk. I shall go perfectly unconscious of them, in my rose-coloured 35 trousers.

MABEL: You won't! You can't! You'll be conscious all the time. You'll be conscious all the time that they're jeering at you, and then you'll get all tied up over it afterwards.

CLARENCE: I assure you, Mabel, I *should* have gone to the Plaza in 40 my rose-coloured trousers *perfectly* unconscious of everybody, if you hadn't started this difficulty.

MABEL: I bet you you wouldn't. You *couldn't*. Anyhow, what do you want to go to the Plaza for in rose-coloured trousers? *What* are

5   you conscious of, when you wear them?

CLARENCE *(with hauteur)*: Of *feeling* wonderful, and, I hope, of looking it.

MABEL: Clarence! You know everybody will just say you look a fool. Not wonderful at all.

10 CLARENCE: I thought it didn't matter what the crowd in the Plaza says.—Anyhow, you've squashed my effort. I shall go and take off my trousers and never put them on again.

IDA: But you'll put on others, won't you?

CLARENCE: Yes, *grey* ones.

15 IDA: But Clarence! Wait! Why don't you walk up and down this room a few times before *us*, and see how you feel: and we'll say whether you're wonderful, or exhibitionist or whatever it is.

CLARENCE: No. I shall go and take them right off.

MARY: Stick to your guns, young aesthete.

20 IDA: Stick to your trousers, anyhow. No, I mean it quite fairly. Walk up and down a few times past the sink—yes!—there! *(CLAR-ENCE walks. Enter JOE, who goes in and out vaguely.)*

MABEL *(irritably)*: Hullo Joe! How're you feeling, hm!

JOE: Fine!

25 MABEL: Can you stay help wash dishes? Put some water in the kettle.

(JOE crosses in front of CLARENCE, who is walking up and down.)

CLARENCE: Excuse me, Joe, will you keep still a minute.

MABEL: I *told* him to fill the kettle.

30 CLARENCE: Mabel, I am acting at the request of the majority.

MABEL: You're a pure exhibitionist. I don't care about majorities, anyhow. Leave off exhibiting yourself.

IDA: Oh but you're *fine*, Clarence! I'm *all* for rose-coloured trousers.

CLARENCE: I shall go and take them right off.

35 CHORUS: No! No! They're wonderful.

MARY: Let us appeal to true, unspoiled taste, and hear what the vital American has got to say.—Joe, what do you think of Clarence's trousers.

JOE: Fine!

40   *(Enter TONY.)*

MABEL: Here's Tony! Let's ask Tony. He sees both sides. Tony!
Tony! Clarence is going down to the Plaza in those trousers.
What you think of it.

TONY *(seating himself at table)*: Make a guy[*] of himself, sure.

MARY: You wouldn't go down to the Plaza in them, Tony?   5

TONY: Me? No, I wouldn't.

MARY: And you, Joe, would you go to the Plaza in those trousers?

JOE: No Mam! They're fine for a dance, for an Indian.

MABEL: That's it! You give them to Joe, Clarence.

CLARENCE: I shall not, Mabel. But I shall go and take them *right*   10
off, and never put them on again.

IDA: Don't Clarence! Oh don't!

MARY: The Indian has spoken.

IDA: Then let the Jew speak. I'm a Jew, and my people are good at
speaking. Clarence, I implore you, don't haul down your flag.   15
Keep your trousers. *I'll* walk down the Plaza with you.

MABEL: *Ida!* Prepare for the consequences.

IDA: What consequences, Mabel!

MABEL: All the *talk!* What'll Andrew[*] say?

IDA: Why I'll make him paint a portrait of Clarence *in* the trousers.   20

SPUD: Keep them, Clarence.

MRS SPRAGUE: They're a lovely colour. They make a bright note.

MARY: I wash my hands of them.

MABEL: But it's so *babyish!*

CLARENCE: I shall take them *right* off! *(Flounces out. A silence.)*   25

MRS SPRAGUE: Do you know, voices have told me that Clarence is a
great Initiator.

MABEL: Initiator of *what*, Alice?

IDA: The fashion in rose-coloured trousers. I agree with him entirely.

MRS SPRAGUE: No. If we take care of him, and protect him, and   30
love him, he may be a Great Teacher.

MABEL: Well I protect him preventing him making a guy of himself.

MARY: I think the Indians are almost *always* right. I doubt if any
young man is capable of having a revelation. I doubt *really* if
any *man* is capable of having a revelation. The next time, I *really*   35
believe it will be a *Woman*. The next Redeemer will probably,
almost certainly, be a Woman.

MABEL: Meaning yourself, Mary? Why shouldn't *I* have the revelation.

MARY: You're not perfect, Mabel. And I'm glad you're not. I have   40 hardly any place in my life for a woman who is both rich and perfect.

MARY: Tony!

TONY: What?

5 MABEL: Like a fried egg?

TONY: Yes, I think so.

MABEL: Well get up and fry it then. There's no cook today.

(TONY *gets up.*)

MARY: How are you this morning, Tony? It is so good to sit next to

10 you.

TONY: I'm fine.

MABEL: The Indians *do* feel fine. They always feel fine. That's because they live right. They've got something that white people haven't got. We've got to get it. That's what we're here

15 for. That's what I married Tony for. To try and get that wonderful something that they've got and that white people haven't.

TONY: Where the eggs?

MABEL: Can't you find any? Well, maybe there aren't any. Have

20 some marmalade.

TONY: Well, I guess I eat a can of sardines.

MABEL: Tony, you don' want a can of sardines for breakfast.

TONY: Guess I do!

MABEL: Oh dee—ar! (TONY *unwinds sardines.*)

25 MARY: Mabel, when you say the Indians have that wonderful thing that white people haven't got, I think *I* have it.—Joe, more wood on the fire.—The Indians have the rhythm of the earth. The earth in America has a *special* rhythm, the marvellous American rhythm. And here in Taos that rhythm is at its height.

30 IDA: You mean altitude?

MARY: I mean the *perfect* rhythm. The white people still haven't got the rhythm of America, the perfect rhythm of American earth. The Indians have had it so long, maybe they are in danger of losing it. The new revelation will come when the white people,

35 when some white *Woman*, gets the perfect rhythm of the American earth. And I think, if I stay here all summer (*looks meaningly at* MABEL) I shall get it.

MABEL: Well, *stay* all the summer, and let's see you get it. We want something to happen. Here we all are, a group of more or less

40 remarkable people, in a remarkable place, at a remarkable

altitude. If something doesn't happen of itself, let's *make* it happen. Let's make a Thing!

(Enter ELIZABETH *eating an apple, and shedding large tears.)*

MABEL: What's the matter?

ELIZABETH: Why I'm so mad at Contentos.* 5

MABEL: What's he done, then?

ELIZABETH: Why he's broken his bridle *again*, and got away.

MABEL: Where is he?

TONY: I tell you to take a rope—

MABEL: Go get a rope and catch him. 10

(Enter CLARENCE *in grey flannel trousers.)*

IDA: Oh dear;—The glory has departed.*

CLARENCE: Yes, it intended to depart.

IDA: Too bad.

MABEL: Spud, you finished? Go get the poppies before the sun 15
spoils them.*

SPUD: Let me drink my coffee. *(Drinks and departs.)*

IDA: Spud's queer this morning.

CLARENCE: Spud always seems queer, to *me*.

MABEL: Spud *is* queer*—I wonder what it is. Whether we can't fix 20
it.

MRS SPRAGUE: He has such a sweet disposition. I wonder what it can be?

CLARENCE: I don't know. Of course, it mayn't *mean* anything, but I heard his door banging *all* night last night. It really seemed 25
mysterious.

MRS SPRAGUE: It was my door. There's no catch on it. It makes me nervous in the night.

IDA: Oh! Why doesn't Mabel have a catch *put* on the door? Of course it makes you nervous, banging in the wind. 30

MABEL: I forget about it, every day.

CLARENCE: *I'll* put a catch on the door. *(Exit.)*

IDA: Will he do it, do you think?

MABEL: Who? Clarence? Maybe he will. But he's more likely to try a safety-pin. 35

IDA: Mabel, you say the Indians feel fine *all the time*, and that we ought to feel the same. What I want to know is, what do you mean by feeling fine? Feeling up to the mark, and so on?

MABEL: Oh, no, none of those dreary things. I mean feeling good. You have that good feeling, don't you know, when you expand 40

—and you make everybody around you feel wonderful. I know I do it myself. You can't help it—they've *got* to feel good, just because of the thing that's in you. You radiate life, and the people around you feel good. Haven't you seen me do it. Don't you feel it come from me?

IDA: Ye—es—! Maybe I do. But what does this feeling good mean? Is it just good spirits?

MABEL: No! Not any of that. Tony, you explain how the Indians feel when they feel good.

TONY *(chewing a sardine)*: Well—the Indians—they feel the sun. They feel the sun inside them, and they feel good. Like what the sun shine inside them, and they love everybody.

IDA: Sunshine, Tony, or moonshine inside them?

MARY *(heavily)*: Let *me* explain what it is. The sun is overhead, and the earth is underfoot. We live between the two— *(At that moment, telephone rings, and enter* SPUD *with poppies and* ELIZABETH. MABEL *jumps to telephone.* SPUD *poses with poppies* —ELIZABETH *gets a cup and pours herself coffee.* MABEL: Hallo! ELIZABETH: Guess I'll have a cup of coffee. SPUD: Aren't the poppies beautiful!—*all at once.)*

MABEL *(at telephone)*: You Ida!— *(*IDA *goes.)* —Elizabeth, you drinking coffee? Leave off! It's not good for you. Go get some vases for the poppies.

ELIZABETH: Why I can drink just a cup! *(Exit* ELIZABETH *and* SPUD.*)*

IDA *(from phone)*: Telegram from Andrew.

MABEL: What saying?

*(*IDA *hangs up receiver and holds her head in both hands.)*

(Curtain)

Scene 2.

SPUD *and* ELIZABETH *getting vases in next room.*

ELIZABETH: Spud, why don't you come and ride with me now?

SPUD: Why, I don't know, Elizabeth. I guess I'm busy.

ELIZABETH: Oh, busy! Busy what at? 5

SPUD: I don't know.—Write a *pome.*

ELIZABETH: A pome! Why don't you do that after dinner?

SPUD: I might not feel like it.

ELIZABETH: Well, why do it at all?

SPUD: Oh I don' know. Why do anything? 10

ELIZABETH: Because it's fun! Let's go riding up the canyon. Yes do! It'll be lots of fun. Won't you?

SPUD: No, I don't think so—really!

ELIZABETH: Oh, why do you always act *mean?*

SPUD: I don't, do I? I don't want to. 15

ELIZABETH: But you do. Why do you if you don't want to? What do you say you want to write a *pome* for, instead of going a ride up the canyon with me. I call that acting mean—

SPUD: But how—?

ELIZABETH: Why, because it is. 20

SPUD: Because you want me to go riding up the canyon when I don't want to. Isn't that acting mean, when you want me to do a thing I don't want to.

ELIZABETH: Well you ought to want to. You don't want to want to. That's where it's so mean of you. If you wanted to want to 25 you'd want to.

SPUD: Why?

ELIZABETH: Because it would be *fun.* Lots of fun.

SPUD: Not necessarily for me. I might be bored.

ELIZABETH: No you wouldn't be bored, Spud. Go on—let's do it. 30 Think of the *fun.*

SPUD: But I tell you I don't like fun. I don't care for it.

ELIZABETH: Oh go on! Oh my, don't you just act *mean!*

SPUD: And I *hate* lots-of-fun.

ELIZABETH: Why it's *impossible,* and so you don't hate it. You just 35 want to act mean to me.

SPUD: I don't see that *at all.*

ELIZABETH: Of course you do—

(Enter IDA *with a tragic face.)*

IDA: The poppies are all coming to pieces while you two children stay flirting here. Sic transit gloria mundi.

ELIZABETH: Who's sick then?

5 SPUD: And we're not flirting—

ELIZABETH: If people are so *mean*—

SPUD: Do you mean me? Am I mean?

ELIZABETH: Yes I do mean you. You are mean.

SPUD: Why am I?

10 ELIZABETH: Oh goodness, starting that all over again.

IDA: Why *are* you mean, anyway Spud.

SPUD: Because I won't go riding up the canyon with Elizabeth when I don' want to.

ELIZABETH: But he *ought* to want to.

15 SPUD: Well I *don't* want to.

IDA: Why not sacrifice yourself, Spud?

SPUD: I won't.

IDA: Why won't you?

SPUD: Because I *don' want to.*

20 IDA: But there must be a reason why you don't want to.

SPUD: Why? Does everything have a reason.

IDA: Yes. How not?

SPUD: Well *I* don't know the reason why I don't want to, if there is any reason beyond just not wanting to.

25 ELIZABETH: The reason is *meanness!*

IDA *(sighing)*: I should have thought it would be awfully nice to ride up the canyon on a lovely summer morning with a fair and bonny maid—love's young dream and all that sort of thing.

ELIZABETH: Ugh! Ida! For goodness sake!

30 SPUD: That's exactly it. I don't *want* to fall in love with Elizabeth, and possibly have her falling in love with me.

ELIZABETH: *Im*possibly, not possibly, Spud don't-wanter! All *I* want is to have *fun.*

SPUD: And every time you say it, I loathe *fun* more. I hate *fun!* I

35 loathe it.

ELIZABETH: Well then, you must be just crazy. Everyone wants fun when they're young. It's only natural.

SPUD: Well then I don't. Maybe I'm not young and natural.

ELIZABETH: You don't *act* young, so you can't be natural. A don't-

40 wanter isn't natural.

IDA: But Spud, why shouldn't you fall in love with Elizabeth? She's a very nice girl.

ELIZABETH *(shouts)*: Why sure!

IDA: Wouldn't it be awfully *good* for you to fall in love with her? Wouldn't it mean much more life for you?   5

SPUD: No!!! It wouldn't! I tell you I'm *not going* to fall in love with a *girl*, and go dangling around. I object to it all.

IDA: But suppose you couldn't help yourself?

ELIZABETH: Yea-a! What then?

SPUD: But I *can* help myself—and I *intend* to help myself. I'm not   10
going to fall in love with some fool girl, and get *married*! Married! Ugh! The very thought of it makes me sick with myself.

ELIZABETH: Ida's been married twice: and she's married now, and her husband's coming here to stay. Nice sort of manners *you've*   15
got, Spud Johnson.

SPUD: I'm awfully sorry about Ida. I mean I don't want to hurt her feelings. But the very word *marriage* does something to me. Marriage! Marriage! Marriage!

ELIZABETH: Marriage!   20

IDA: Marriage! Perhaps you're right, Spud. But *we* were always brought up to think it the most desirable thing on earth.

ELIZABETH: Oh I don't think that. Only I *do* want some fun while I'm young. Spud!

SPUD: Well I don't. I always avoid fun, if I can.   25

IDA: And you don't want *love*, Spud?

SPUD: Lo-o-ve! God, no! I'd rather take castor oil.☆

ELIZABETH: Love! Lo-o-ve! Much you know about it.

IDA: Well I hope you don't know much more, child.

ELIZABETH: I don't know anything at all, but it might be fun! Lots   30
of fun.

IDA: Yes, it might. What a pity it so rarely is.

SPUD: There you are, Ida. You only want me to touch pitch☆
because you've touched it.

IDA: Maybe it's because I'm a woman.—But what *do* you want,   35
Spud.

SPUD: I tell you, I don't know myself.

ELIZABETH: He's only a don't-wanter, he is. All he wants is to act mean, that's all he wants. He's worse than Contentos.

IDA: Well, we all have our own difficulties.   40

ELIZABETH: I should say we do!

MABEL *(suddenly, through door)*: Oh de—ar! What are you all *doing*! Where are those *vases*?

(ELIZABETH *drops vase.*)

5　ELIZABETH: There goes one of them.

(Curtain)

Suggested emendations of stage directions for performances of *Altitude*

542:3 following wood. insert *(*CLARENCE *goes out.)*
543:26 following *bacon.* insert *Enter* JOE.
543:27 delete INDIAN insert JOE
543:29 delete INDIAN insert JOE
543:31 delete *Indian* insert JOE
543:31 following Joe. insert *(Exit* JOE.*)*
544:25 following *like.* insert *Exit* JOE.

APPENDIX IV

NOAH'S FLOOD

[1ST MAN
2ND MAN
3RD MAN   5
NOAH
MEN AND WOMEN
SHEM
HAM
JAPHET   10
COSBY*]

Noah.   Shem   the Utterer   +   Kanah   the echoer
               I am. it is   it was. it shall be

        Ham   (Heat)   +   Shelah   (Flux)

Japhet (encompassing, spreading, Father of All: also Destroyer)   15
                        +   Cosby
                        (female-male. Kultur-träger)

Noah's Flood

1ST MAN: What ails the sun, that his mornings are so sickly?

2ND MAN: You heard what the Old One* said: the sun is dark with the anger of the skies.

1ST MAN: The Old One is sly. Himself is angry, so he says the anger breathes from the hollows of the sky. We are not fools altogether. What think you? Are the sons of men more stupid than the sons of God.*

3RD MAN: I don't think!—The Old One and his demi-god sons, what are they? They are taller than the sons of men, but they are slower. They are stronger, but it seems to me they are duller. Ask women what they think of the sons of Noah, the demi-gods! Ah, the Sons of God! They follow at the heels of the daughters of men, and the daughters of men laugh beneath the black beards, as they laugh when the bull snorts, and they are on the safe side of the wall. Big is the bull by the river, but a boy leads him by the nose. So, if you ask me, do we lead these big ones, these demi-gods, old Noah and his sons, Shem and Ham and Japhet.

1ST MAN: If we had the secret of the red flutterer.

3RD MAN: Ha! I have the name of that Bird. Ham told a woman that the name is Fire.

1ST MAN: Fire! It is a poor name! What is its father, and who its mother?

3RD MAN: Nay, that Ham did not tell. It is a secret of these demi-gods. But I tell you. It comes out of an egg. And the Old One knows where the eggs of that bird called Fire are laid. So he gathers them up, for his house.

2ND MAN: He shall tell us.

3RD MAN: No, he will never tell us. But his sons may. Because if we knew the secret of the red bird they call Fire, and could find her eggs and have the young ones flutter in our houses, then we should be greater than Noah and his sons. The sons of men already are wittier* than the sons of god. If we had the scarlet

chicken they call Fire, between our hands, we could do away
with the sons of god, and have the world for our own.

1ST MAN: So it should be. The sons of men are numberless, but
these sons of god are few and slow. The sons of men know the
secret of all things, save that of the red flutterer. The sons of
men are the makers of everything. The sons of god command
and chide, but what can they make, with their slow hands? Why
are they lords, save that they guard the red bird which should
now be ours. What name do they give it, again?

3RD MAN: Fire.

1ST MAN: Fire! Fire! And that is all their secret and their power:
merely Fire! Already we know their secret.

3RD MAN: Ham told it to a woman, and even as she lay with him
she laughed beneath his beard, and mocked him.

1ST MAN: Yet this red bird hatches the pale dough into bread, into
good dark bread. Let us swear to catch the red bird, and take it
to our houses. And when it has laid its eggs, we will kill the
demi-gods, and have the earth to ourselves. For the sons of men
must be free.

2ND MAN: Yes indeed! Free! Free! Is it not a greater word than
Fire! We will kill the demi-gods, and be free. But first we must
catch the red bird, take him alive, in a snare.

1ST MAN: Ah, if we could! For Ham has told us, that the feathers
shine like feathers of the sun, with warmth, even hotter than the
sun at noon.

2ND MAN: Then it were very good if we had him, seeing the sun in
heaven has lost his best feathers, and limps dustily across the
heavens like a moulting hen. Ah men, have you learnt what it is
to shiver?

3RD MAN: Have we not! Even in the day-time shivers seize us, since
the sun has moulted his rays. And shivering in the daytime is
like dying before one's hour. The death-shiver is on us. We
must capture the red bird, so that he flutters his wings in our
houses and brightens our flesh, as the moulting sun used to do,
till he fell poor and mean.

2ND MAN: You know what Shem says? He says there are three
birds: the little red bird in the houses of the demi-gods—

3RD MAN: The one Ham calls Fire. We must lay hold of that one.

2ND MAN: Then the bigger bird of the sun, that beats his yellow wings and makes us warm, and makes the ferns unroll, and the fern-seed fall brown; for bread.＊

3RD MAN: Ay, the bird of the sun! But he is moulting, and has lost his ray-feathers, and limps through grey dust across the sky. He is not to be depended on. Let us once get hold of the red chick Ham calls Fire, and we will forget the sick sun of heaven. We need our sun in our grasp. A bird in the hand is worth two in the bush.＊

2ND MAN: Yet you know what Shem says. Far, far away beyond the yellow sun that flies across the sky every day, taking the red berries to his nest, there lives the Great White Bird,＊ that no man has ever seen.

3RD MAN: Nor no demi-god either.

2ND MAN: In the middle of the tree of darkness is a nest, and on the nest sits the Great White Bird. And when he rises on his nest and beats his wings, a glow of strength goes through the world. And the stars are the small white birds that have their nests among the outer leaves. And our yellow sun is a young one that does but fly across from the eastern bough to the western, near us, each day, and in his flight stirs with his feathers the blue dust of space, so we see him in the blue of heaven, flashing his sun-pinions.—But beyond the blue fume of the sky, all the time, beyond our seeing, the Great White Bird roosts at the centre of the tree.

3RD MAN: Hast thou seen thy Great White Bird, fool?

2ND MAN: I? No!

3RD MAN: When dost thou expect to see him?

2ND MAN: I? Never!

3RD MAN: Then why dost thou talk of him?

2ND MAN: Because Shem told me.

3RD MAN: Shem! He is fooling thee. Did he tell thee the secret of the little red bird?

2ND MAN: That, no!

3RD MAN: That, no! Rather will he tell thee of a great White Duck that no man ever did see or ever will see. Art thou not a fool?

2ND MAN: Nay! for listen! Shem says that even the yellow sun cannot fly across from the eastern bough to the western, save on the wind of the wings of the Great White Bird. On the dead air he cannot make heading. Likewise, Shem says, the air men

breathe is dead air, dead in the breast, save it is stirred fresh
from the wings of the Great White Bird.

3RD MAN: The air in my breast is not dead.

2ND MAN: And so it is, the sun struggles in grey dust across the
heavy sky,* because the wings of the Great White Bird send us
no stir, there is no freshness for us. And so we shiver, and feel
our death upon us beforehand, because the Great White Bird has
sunk down, and will no more wave his wings gladly towards us.

1ST MAN: And pray, why should *he* be moping?

2ND MAN: Because the sons of men never breathe his name in
answer. Even as the ferns breathe fern-seed, which is the fume
of their answer to the sun, and the little green flowers that are
invisible make a perfume like the sky speaking with a voice,
answering deep into heaven, so the hearts of men beat the
warmth and wildness of an answer to the Great White Bird,
who sips it in and is rejoiced, lifting his wings.—But now the
hearts of men are answerless, like slack drums gone toneless.
They say: We ourselves are the Great White Birds of the
universe. It is we who keep the wheel going!—So they cry in
impertinence, and the Great White Bird lifts his wings no more,
to send the wind of newness and morning into us. So we are
stale, and inclining towards deadness. We capture the yellow
metal, and the white, and we think we have captured the
answerer. For the yellow gold and the white silver are pure
voices of answer calling still from under the oldest dawn, to the
Great White Bird, as the cock crows at sunrise. So we capture
the first bright answerers, and say: Lo! we are lords of the
answer.—But the answer is not to us, though we hold the gold
in our fist. And the wings of the Bird are slack.

1ST MAN: What is all this talk? Is the humming-bird less blue-
brilliant?

2ND MAN: It is Shem's word, not mine. But he says, the Great
White Bird will waft his wings even to the beast, for the beast is
an answerer. But he will withhold his draught of freshness from
the new beast called man, for man is impertinent and answerless.—And the small white birds, the stars, are happy still in the
outer boughs, hopping among the furthest leaves of the tree,
and twittering their bright answer. But men are answerless, and
dust settles on them, they shiver, and are woe-begone in spite of
their laughter.

1 ST MAN: Nay, thou art a mighty talker! But thy Great White Bird is only a decoy-duck, to decoy thee into obedience to these demi-gods, who cannot stoop to sweep the fern seed for themselves, but must bid the children of men.—And thou art a fool duck decoyed into their net.—Did Japhet ever talk of a Great White Bird? And Japhet is shrewd. Japhet says: Ah, you sons of men, your life is a predicament. You live between warm and cold, take care. If you fall into great heat, you are lost, if you slip down the crevices of cold, you are gone for ever. If the waters forsake you, you are vanished, and if the waters come down on you, you are swept away. You cannot ride on the heat nor live beneath the waters. The place you walk on is narrow as a plank across a torrent. You must live on the banks of the stream, for if the stream dries up, you die, but if the stream flows over its banks, likewise you die. Yet of the stream you ask not whence it cometh nor whither it goeth. It travels forever past you, it is always going, so you say: The stream is there! I tell you, watch lest it be not there. Watch lest the banks be gone beneath the flood.* For the waters run past you like wolves which are on the scent. And waters come down on you like flocks of grasshoppers from the sky, alighting from the invisible. But what are the wolves running for, and what hatched the flying waters in mid-heaven? You know not. You ask not. Yet your life is a travelling thread of water forever passing.* Ask then, and it shall be answered you. Know the whither and the whence, and not a wolf shall slip silently by in the night, without your consent. Ask, and it shall be answered unto you. Ask! Ask! and all things shall be answered unto you, as the cock answers the sun. Oh wonderful race of Askers, there shall be no answer ye shall not wing out of the depths. And who answers, serves.—So says Japhet, and says well. And if we had the red flutterer, it should answer to us, and all things after should answer to us for their existence. And we should be the invincible, the Askers, those that set the question.

3 RD MAN: It is so. If we had the red bird in our hand, we could force the sun to give himself up in answer; yea, even the Great White Bird would answer in obedience. So we could unleash the waters from the ice, and shake the drops from the sky, in answer to our demand. The demi-gods are dumb askers, they get half-answers from us all. What we want is the red bird.

1ST MAN: It is true. That is all we need.

2ND MAN: Then let us take it. Let us steal it from their house, and be free.

3RD MAN: It is the great word: let us be free. Let us yield our answer no more, neither to gods nor demi-gods, sun nor inner sun.

1ST MAN: Men masters of fire, and free on the face of the earth. Free from the need to answer, masters of the question. Lo, when we are lords of the question, how humbly the rest shall answer. Even the stars shall bow humbly, and yield us their reply, and the Sun shall no more have a will of his own.

2ND MAN: Can we do it?

1ST MAN: Can we not? We are the sons of men, heirs and successors of the sons of god. Japhet said to me: The sons of men cannot capture the gift of fire: for it is a gift. Till it is given to them, by the sons of god, they cannot have it.—I said to him: Give us the gift!—He said: Nay! for ye know not how to ask. When ye know how to ask, it shall be given you.

3RD MAN: So! What they will not give, we will take.

2ND MAN: Yes, we will take it, in spite of them. We are heirs of the gods and the sons of god. We are heirs of all. Let us take the flutterer, and be free. We have the right to everything; so let us take.

1ST MAN: Japhet said, it is a gift!

(Enter NOAH.)

NOAH: The women are sweeping the fern-seed for bread, what are the men about?

3RD MAN: The men are cold, my Lord.

NOAH: Will their own words warm them?

3RD MAN: Yea, my Lord: for they were talking of the bird called Fire.

NOAH: It is but a word in the mouths of men.

3RD MAN: Yea, but we have learned the word. Cannot we call the bird by name, and will it not come?

NOAH: This is a bird that comes not for calling, nor for being named, nor will a word cover it. Summon all the men to this place beneath the tree, and all the women. *(A conch-shell sounds—MEN AND WOMEN begin to drift in to the open space under the tree—the sons of NOAH come from the house—wearing robes. NOAH's robe black and white: SHEM's robe is yellow, HAM's red, JAPHET's blue and white. HAM is dark, like a negro.)*

NOAH: Bring your mother, and bring your wife Kanah, Shem. Ham, bring your wife Shelah. We will all be here, to the counsel. *(The people sit upon the ground, under the fringes of the great tree. The demi-gods stand by the trunk. Enter* 1ST MAN, *followed by a strange woman.)*

1ST MAN: My Lord, here is a stranger-woman wishes to be present.

NOAH: Yea, son of man, one more stranger-woman?

1ST MAN: We have not known her, my Lord. She will have none of us. She seeks the sons of God, this one.

NOAH: Son of man, upon every high hill and under every green tree ye have committed adultery. Are you then prouder each day, to prostitute yourselves? Is there no shame between your eyes?

1ST MAN: Son of God, it is the way of men with women: the way of the sons of God with women too. Wherein is the shame?

NOAH: The shame that cannot darken your brow will darken the sky. Is your manhood a toy, that you play with it? And the secret places of the woman, are they for you to wallow in? I tell you again, whosoever goes in unto a woman, unless the Lord of Hosts goes with him, goes towards his own death.

1ST MAN: Ay, my Lord, and when he rises up, he triumphs in another little resurrection.—But this woman will have none of us. She seeks the Sons of God.

NOAH: Who are you, daughter of men? Where do you come from?

COSBY: My name is Cosby, my Lord. I come from my wanderings, for I am weary of the world of men.

NOAH: What would you, then?

COSBY: Oh my Lord, the children of men have turned my heart to dust, and yet I cannot die and let be. They told me the last of the Sons of God lived here in this valley below the sun.

NOAH: Even so—and what then?

COSBY: The world of men is like a fenced field, and even the sky is fenced off. And the love of men is like a fowler's net, where one breaks one's feathers and one's heart. And freedom is like a revolving cage, where the squirrel climbs without escaping, and runs without moving away. Oh my Lord, I thought the Sons of God would be a gate leading out from the world of men, whereby one could pass out.

NOAH: From a little cage to a larger cage, daughter of men? For what is the revolving world but a squirrel's cage that spins, and the farthest stars wheel round upon the bars of the cage. And the clambering of the children of men keeps the cage still turning, for men must clamber as the squirrel must. And clambering, he wheels the universe into motion.

COSBY: Is it so?

NOAH: To the children of men, it is so.—But sit down here, for I must speak once more to the children of men.

3RD MAN: My Lord, all the people that will come, are here. The rest say they have no time.—My Lord, may we speak before you and the Lords Shem, Ham, and Japhet?

NOAH: So you speak briefly.

3RD MAN: It shall be brief. Sons of God, the sons of men and the daughters of men sit in the curve of the world before you. Sons of God, you are taller than we, and slower. You are greater than we, and less nimble—You utter words, and we do deeds. —Sons of God, you look into the heavens. Sons of men, daughters of men, we sweep the bread beneath the fern-leaves, we put seed in the heavy earth. We watch the flocks, we take milk in gourds, we make cheese in the butter-skins. We weave white wool and dip it in colour. We build houses of wood, we press the glass of earth into knives.✶ All these things we do, with wit and with nimble fingers. We labour, and then we sing, we dance, we have pleasure among the limbs of women. All this is ours.—Sons of God, you toil not, neither will you dance.✶ You dwell apart, and your silence is like a cloud. You speak to command and to chide. Your hearts are dark to the children of men. One treasure alone you have on earth, the secret red bird whose name is Fire, the bird whose dead white feathers alone are left to us.

Sons of god, you have now no pleasure in the earth. Our daughters are no longer fair in your eyes, our singing is not sweet to you, our works are not goodly in your esteem. Therefore, sons of god, why will you dwell any longer in the world of the children of men, when you like it not? This is the world of men. Is there no world for the Sons of God? Must they dwell forever like a cloud among the children of men?

NOAH: Would you have us go? Would you have us leave you?

PEOPLE: Yea!

3RD MAN: Yea, it is our will. But leave us the red bird, that it hatch in our homes. Japhet hath said to us, the bird can not be caught, it will die in our hands, if we seize it. It is the last gift from the

sons of God to the sons of men. Give us the gift, that the sons
of men may be perfect, and heirs of the sons of god.

NOAH: There is a time to give, and a time to withhold.* The time
to give is not yet; I have looked into the heavens, sons of men,
and into the deeps, and I have heard a word from the Great   5
One, greater than we. Surely the secret of fire shall be given
you, the sons of god shall despoil themselves. The Great One
breathed upon me, and I felt the end. Yet the end will not be
utterly an end.

3RD MAN: Make us the gift, my Lord, and the sons of men shall be   10
grateful to the Sons of God.

NOAH: I cannot open my hand, Son of man, till the Great One
breathes on it. And even if I give you the gift of fire, think you
you can live by it for ever?

3RD MAN: For ever is a long day, my Lord. Give us the red flutterer,   15
that it flutters in our houses, and we will live by it long enough.

NOAH: Long enough! But at last you will drown it in blood, and
quench it in tears.

[end of manuscript]

Suggested emendations of stage directions for performances of *Noah's Flood*

559:1 **following** *Noah's Flood* **insert** / *Enter* 1ST MAN, 2ND MAN *and* 3RD MAN.

564:36 **preceding** *A conch-shell sounds* **insert** *Exit* 1ST MAN.

565:3 **for** *The people* **read** MEN AND WOMEN

565:5 **for** *a strange woman* **read** COSBY

566:36 **for** PEOPLE **read** MEN AND WOMEN

APPENDIX V

i THE ORIGINAL ENDING TO *DAVID*

The original manuscript of *David* (MS) today exists in the form of notebook pages held loosely within the covers of the notebook from which at some stage most of the pages were torn out, or fell out as the notebook's stitched binding disintegrated. As well as – at different times – being given page numbers by Lawrence, not always accurately, the individual leaves of the notebook also have stamped numbers on the top right-hand corner of the recto, which show their original location. The notebook was originally also the home for a number of essays and drafts of essays written in the summer of 1925; a reconstruction of the complex sequence of writing and revision at the end of the play can confirm a probable compositional *terminus ad quem* for three essays – 'Art and Morality', 'Morality and the Novel' and 'The Novel' – originally inscribed in the notebook.[1]

The notebook also still holds two scenes of the play which – although not deleted, and bearing stamped numbers interrupting sequences of numbers belonging to the main body of the text – are certainly discards. Any doubt about their status is resolved by the circumstances of *David*'s composition. Lawrence tore out batches of leaves from the notebook when he had finished working on them, and gave them to Dorothy Brett for typing: she was then living in a cabin a mile and a half from the Lawrence cabin on Kiowa Ranch. The only used leaves not torn out but still integral with the notebook binding are those stamped 86–91, from scenes which Lawrence discarded; thus demonstrating that these were leaves he had decided not to have typed. (Leaves 92–4, the end of the second scene to be discarded, probably came loose on their own.)

The whole notebook can be reconstructed as follows:

Leaves	Contents	Composition date
1–6	*David* (start, loose within covers)	?March 1925
7–10	*missing*	?March 1925

[1] These essays have previously been dated 'between 7 May and the end of June' purely on the grounds that DHL would probably not have had time to write them before 7 May (*Hardy* xlvii).

571

11–79	*David* (loose within covers)	April 1925
80–82	*missing* (discarded part of *David* MS)	April–May 1925
83	*David* (re-used leaf, loose within covers)	April–May 1925
84–85	*missing* (discarded part of *David* MS)	April–May 1925
86–91	*David* (discarded scene, still held in binding)	April–May 1925
92–94	*David* (discarded scene, loose within covers)	April–May 1925
95–98	*David* (new ending, loose within covers)	May 1925
99	*missing* (used for pp. 1–2 of the fragmentary draft essay on art whose p. 3 survives on the next leaf)	?May 1925
100	p. 3 of draft essay on art (E177.4, loose within covers: Tedlock 163–4)	?May 1925
101	untitled paragraph draft for essay on art and morality (E24a, loose within covers: Tedlock 164)	?May 1925
102–106	'Art and Morality' I (E24b, now detached from the notebook: *Hardy* 233–7)	?June 1925
107–111	'Morality and the Novel' I (E244a, now detached from the notebook: *Hardy* 241–5)	?June 1925
112–116	'Art and Morality' II (E24e, now detached from the notebook: *Hardy* 163–8)	June–July 1925
117–121	'Morality and the Novel' II (E244d, now detached from the notebook: *Hardy* 171–6)	June–July 1925
122–123	*blank leaves* (still held in binding)	
124	*missing*	
131–125 [reversed]	'The Modern Novel' (E280a, now detached from the notebook: *Hardy* 179–90 as 'The Novel'; page stubs show where torn out)	June 1925
132–138	*David* (revisions, removed out of sequence, loose within covers)	April–May 1925
139–?160	*missing* (probably removed at an early stage, before leaves 132–8 were used for revisions to *David*: original notebook length either 1–144 or 1–160)	before April 1925

Lawrence began to write *David* from the front of what was probably a completely empty notebook, on the first numbered recto leaf (numbering hereafter given in the form 'leaf 1r'), and apparently wrote with relatively few breaks up to leaf 94v. Three hiatuses however occur in the sequence. (1) Leaves 7–10 are missing from the notebook, having been torn out (and probably used for another purpose) before the text of *David* had reached them: no text is missing. (2) Leaves 13–14 are reversed in the printed numbering. (3) Leaves 80–2 and 84–5 are missing, Lawrence having discarded them when he undertook a major revision of the fifteenth scene.

Having reached leaf 94v, however – the first page of what he had originally meant to be the eighteenth and last scene – he appears to have stopped writing. The play was getting extremely long, and he was probably unsure whether the role which Saul was starting to play – as tragic representative of an earlier kind of being than David – was altogether clear, given that Saul had held the stage untragically during the preceding scene. Lawrence probably realised that the problem lay not with what he was about to write in the last scene but further back – in what had happened to Saul in the potentially tragic fifteenth scene. Accordingly he went back and embarked on an extensive revision of that scene.

The new fifteenth scene is written on a sequence of leaves running 136v–138v, 133r–133v, 83r–83v, 134r–135v, 132r–132v. Leaf 136r also bears a deleted version of a page of text[2] which also appears – almost unchanged, and undeleted – on leaf 132r. It is, however, possible to explain the sequence and to account for the deleted and repeated page.

Lawrence needed fresh notebook leaves for his revision of the fifteenth scene; he began to take them from later in the notebook. The latter would originally have had 144 or 160 numbered leaves;[3] the original final pages of the notebook had, therefore, almost certainly been removed. He first tore out the blank leaves 136–8 (pp. 157–61), presumably thinking that they would be enough for the revision. He needed more, however: accordingly, he returned to the back of the book and tore out another batch, leaves 133–5 (pp. 162–3, 166–9). He must then have realised that – if he compressed his writing to fit the slightly expanded text into the lower half of leaf 133v – he could then re-employ leaf 83 from the original writing, with a substantial saving of time (leaf 83r contained several lines of musical notation he would have had to re-copy). Old leaf 83, revised, therefore kept its position in the sequence (pp. 164–5), being followed by new leaves 134–5.

The revised scene was still growing, however, and Lawrence needed yet more paper to complete it. He must have started to use leaf 136r, not

---

[2] See Explanatory note on 520:23 for transcription.
[3] There being 16 leaves in a stitched gathering, and at least 138 leaves in the book, the total number would have been either 144 or 160. The previous notebook which DHL had used (the so-called 'Hopi Snake Dance' notebook: Tedlock 184–5) had had 160 stamped and numbered leaves.

noticing that he had already used the other side for the start of the scene. An almost clean draft of his new text of the penultimate page of the scene (p. 170) thus survives on leaf 136r, cancelled: Lawrence must have turned the leaf over and found the verso already used. He lightly cancelled the abortive side of text on leaf 136r and noted '(*turn over, for page 157.*' (The number '157' also appears on the inside of the front notebook cover, presumably as a further reminder.) To finish his work he still needed more paper, so he had to tear out yet another leaf from the back – leaf 132. The fifteenth scene's final two pages (pp. 170–1) appear upon it.

Leaves 80r–82v and 84r–85v were discarded, so that we cannot say much about the original version of the scene. It did, however, grow two whole MS pages longer in the course of revision. We can tell this because the scene had originally started (Lawrence's numbering) on p. 157, ending on p. 169, but in its revised form ran from p. 157 to p. 171.

Having completed his rewriting of the fifteenth scene – still, of course, headed 'Scene XIV' (see Introduction, footnote 128) – Lawrence then decided to omit the next two scenes (his old sixteenth and seventeenth). This was because of Saul's now tragic realisation of his own fate in the revised fifteenth scene: Lawrence would no longer have wanted him to reappear. (The old sixteenth scene had been little more than a reworking of 1 Samuel xx. 1–23.)

Lawrence needed to ensure, however, that the discarded scenes did not get mixed up with the sequence he had now established. First, he clearly headed his next (and final) scene 'Scene XV' (p. 172); secondly, he ensured that the pagination he had given his new fifteenth scene was continued into his new sixteenth. Thirdly, he left the pages of the old sixteenth and seventeenth scenes in the notebook: the rest was torn out to give to Dorothy Brett, including the leaves already torn out to complete the revision. Of course, Lawrence was in the rather unusual position for an author of being able to ensure that his typist got the correct pages in sequence: he passed them on to her himself. Leaving the rejected scenes in the notebook, however, ensured their survival.

He must then – if he had not already done so – have assembled all his new leaves in their proper sequence following leaf 79r (the last page of the fourteenth scene, p. 156). (The original – deleted – text of the start of the first draft of the fifteenth scene on leaf 79v therefore survives facing the abortive draft text of p. 170 on leaf 136r, also deleted.) He would then have written the new sixteenth and final scene into the notebook (heading it 'XV') on leaves 95–8, numbering its first page '157' and deleting the original half-page fragment of its opening on leaf 94v. When, on 7 May 1925,

Lawrence told Ida Rauh that he had finished writing *David*, he probably meant that he had completed his revision of the fifteenth scene, had omitted the old sixteenth and seventeenth scenes, and had completed his new final scene.

Printed below are diplomatic transcripts of the original sixteenth and seventeenth scenes, and the first-page fragment of the eighteenth (and final) scene (misnumbered 'xv', 'xvi' and xvii'). Preceding them is the surviving deleted fragment of the first page of the original fifteenth scene (mis-numbered 'xiv'). None of them has previously been published. Characters' names as speech headings for the dialogue are printed in small capitals. Unspaced em dashes have been employed throughout. The symbols < > denote deletions in the manuscript, ⌈ ⌉ are insertions, [ ] denote editorial interventions and [. . .] are illegible passages.

Scene XIV

(Naioth in Ramah – numerous ⌈vigorous, young & old⌉ prophets, in
blue ephods, drawn up on a <little hill, crying at times> ⌈round hill
crowned with a ⌈⌈rough⌉⌉ stone altar, <rude>) They have pipes and
5   psalteries, tabrets & harps, and chant rude chants, in unison and out
of unison⌉ *The Lord is God! Behold! The Lord in the heavens. Out of
the blue he leaneth. Yea Lord. I am here—The Lord is God, and only
he! God is One God!*—In the foreground Samuel and David)

PROPHETS: This is the place of the Lord. ⌈Near is the Unseen
10   One.⌉ Out of the cloud he leans, and <pours> ⌈claims⌉ himself
upon his own. Oh thou, filled with God, sing with me on this
high place. Sing, for <in all the world there is but God.> ⌈the
egg of the world is full of God.⌉

SAMUEL: <Thou leavest me now, and it may be I shall never see
15   thee more. For I am old. And thou hast much fleeing before
thee.> ⌈It is time thou shouldst go. And thou too wilt go from
me forever, for I am old, and shall shortly die. And as a fox
when hunters pursue him, hast thou much fleeing before thee.⌉

DAVID: Must I ever flee, my Father? I am already weary of flight—

20   SAMUEL: <Yea, t> ⌈T⌉hou shalt enquire of Saul once more. Now
he comes hither to seek thee. But he will fall before the Lord.
When he <gets> ⌈gets him⌉ back to his own city, then enquire
of him again what is his will concerning thee. And if it still be
<the> ⌈against thee,⌉ then flee from him diligently, while he
25   lives.

DAVID: And shall there never be peace between Saul's house

[end of manuscript]

Scene XV

(A black tent under a tree—Jonathan, stringing a bow. Enter man
with a spear)

MAN: The Lord strengthen thee!

JONATHAN: What wouldest thou?   5

MAN: <One whom thou knowest.> ⌈There is one would speak with
thee!⌉

JONATHAN <(coming forth)>: Wh<ere>o is he?

MAN: One whom thou knowest.

JONATHAN: Where then?   10

MAN: He waiteth among the trees.

JONATHAN: Let him come.

MAN: Of a surety?

JONATHAN: Yea! How now?

MAN: Lest he be delivered over to the king, who would slay him.   15

JONATHAN: It is David! Bring him hither! These be my own very
men, and none other.

MAN: As the Lord liveth?

JONATHAN: Hasten thou! (Waves <arrow> <Qu> ⌈hand⌉ towards
trees in signal of friendship—the man signals with his spear—   20
David emerges)

JONATHAN: Ha David! And where wast thou?

DAVID: Jonathan! Thou art glad in my sight.

(they embrace)

JONATHAN: Where wast thou, David, my brother?   25

DAVID: I fled from Naioth, before the king, and hid till I might
come to thee.—Is the King returned to his house?

JONATHAN: He is returned.

DAVID: And how?

JONATHAN: Who can know!—In Naioth he stripped himself, and   30
prophesied, and lay night and day naked before the Lord, on
the high place.—So he came back silent, but sombre, and sunk
in shadow. Sometimes methinks I see the wings of <death>
⌈doom⌉ spread between his brows.

DAVID: And towards me, how is he?   35

JONATHAN: Nay, I know not. For when I see the black eyebrows of
Saul like the wings of <death> ⌈doom⌉ alighting, my heart
fails, and I must go away from before him.—But how is it with
thee?

DAVID: Lo! I am a hare pursued by the hounds, and shadowed by the hawk. I know not where to lay my head, lest suddenly the sword be in me, and the death-scream issue from my mouth.

JONATHAN: \<This shall not be!\> ⌈Far be it from thee!⌉

5 DAVID: Oh Jonathan, what have I done? What is mine iniquity? And what is my sin before thy father, that he seeketh my life?

JONATHAN: \<God forbid!\> Thou shalt not die. Behold, my father will do nothing either great or small, but he will show it me. And why should my father hide this thing from me?—It is not

10 so! He seeketh not thy life.

DAVID: Yea, he seeketh it. So he sent the messengers, thrice, to Naioth. And the messengers fell before the Lord, and prophesied. But they came, as Saul came, to take David and to slay him.

15 JONATHAN: Nay! For my father said: *I go to the high place in Naioth in Ramah, even unto the Lord*!

DAVID: Thy father certainly knoweth that I have found grace in thine eyes: and he saith: *Let not Jonathan know this, lest he be grieved*.—But truly, as thy soul liveth, and as the Lord liveth,

20 there is but one step between me and death.

JONATHAN: Nay, brother!—Tell me then, what shall I do?—Whatsoever thy soul desireth, I will even do it for thee.

DAVID: Behold! tomorrow is the new moon, and I should not fail to sit with the king at meat, among the captains. For the king

25 seeth us all with his eye, at the new moon.—But let me go, that I may hide myself in the field unto the third day at even.—If thy father at all miss me, then say: *David earnestly asked leave of me that he might run to Bethlehem his city: for this moon there is a yearly sacrifice there, for all the family*. If he say thus: *It is well*

30 \<,\>! thy servant shall have peace. But if he be very wrath, then be sure that evil is determined by him.—But thou, deal thou kindly with thy servant. For thou hast brought thy servant into a covenant of the Lord with thee.—Nevertheless, if there be evil in me, slay me thyself. For why shouldest thou bring me

35 \<before\> ⌈to⌉ thy father?

JONATHAN: Far be it from thee!—For if I knew certainly that evil were determined by my father to come upon thee, then would I not tell thee?—Why should I bring thee to my father, against thy will?—And yea, why shouldst thou bid me slay thee?

40 DAVID: I feel my death is very near me.—And who should tell me

what thy father hath determined? And what if he answer thee
roughly, how shalt thou come openly to me?

JONATHAN: Come, let us go aside! (they go aside under a tree)

JONATHAN<:> (lifting his hand) Oh Lord God of Israel, when I
have sounded my father, tomorrow at any time, or else the third   5
day hence, and, behold, if there be good toward David, and I
[then] send not unto David, and show it him:—the Lord do so
and much more to Jonathan.—But if it please my father to do
thee evil, then I will show it thee, and send thee away, that thou
mayest go in peace. And the Lord be with thee, who art   10
anointed to be king, as he hath been with my father in times
past.—For Samuel hath again assured thee in Naioth, thou
shalt be king in the sight of the Lord.⁺ Is it not so?

DAVID: It pleased Samuel so to speak. But oh, what am I, but a dog
fleeing before the stones of angry men.   15

JONATHAN: The word of Samuel will come to pass. Therefore shalt
thou show me the kindness of the Lord, not only while yet I
live, that I die not; but also shalt thou not cut off thy kindness
from my house for ever; no, not when the Lord hath cut off the
enemies of David every one from the face of the earth.—And   20
thou shalt swear to me, as the Lord liveth, and as thy soul
liveth, and upon the stem of the herb. (takes a stem)

DAVID: Ah Jonathan, needs it to swear! Lo! what am I!

<(receives>

JONATHAN: Yet shalt thou swear it unto me. [(gives stem to   25
David)]

DAVID: As the Lord liveth, and as my soul liveth, and here upon
the stem of the herb, swear I unto thee, that <th> I will love
Jonathan, and give him the kindness of my heart, while I live,
and his house will I love and dea<lt>l [gently] with <in   30
kindness> for ever, and never will I look on the house of
Jonathan save to do good [,]<towards it,> in the sight of the
Lord, all my days.

JONATHAN: And my soul shall love David, and David's issue, and
all David's house, for ever and ever!   35

(They embrace, kissing in silence. David covers his face)

JONATHAN (slowly) Tomorrow is the new moon. And thou shalt be
missed, because thy seat will be empty.—For the days of the
new moon are solemn days, when the sacrifice is slain, and all
the king's men feast solemnly with the king.—So will I watch   40

what my father will say!—And ⌈when⌉ thou hast stayed three
days in the wilderness, then go down swiftly, secretly, to the
secret place which we have between us, nigh unto Gilgal. There
thou shalt remain, by the stone Ezel.—And on the fourth day I
5   will come forth to shoot with the bow. And I will shoot three
arrows on the side of the stone Ezel, as if I shot at a mark. And
behold, I will send a lad, saying: *Go, find out the arrows.* If I
expressly say unto the lad: *Behold, the arrows are on this side of
thee, take them!*—then come thou forth from hiding, for there is
10 peace to thee, and no hurt, as the Lord liveth. But if I say thus
unto the young man: *Behold, the arrows are beyond thee!*—then
go thou thy way; for the Lord hath sent thee away. Is it well?

DAVID: Ay! If thou sayst, *Behold, the arrows are on this side of thee,
take them!* then shalt I come forth to thee. But if thou sayst: *The*
15 *arrows are beyond thee,* then I will flee away, in secret.—But oh,
my heart shall stay with thee for ever, for thou savest me, and
savest me again!

JONATHAN: It is well! And touching the matter which thou and I
have sworn to, the Lord be between me and thee for ever.—
20 No[w] go swiftly into the bushes. I return to the tent. Till the
fourth day of the new moon—

(Curtain)

Scene XVI

< <<Room>> ⌈A long clay room⌉ in Saul's house in Gilgal, <<great
platters of food steaming—men reclining, eating—Saul at the head of
the circle upon the mats, <<<night—dusky lamps burning—>>>
upon a clay bench raised a little above the rest, against the wall: a   5
broad clay seat against the wall—>> ⌈dimly lighted. Men reclining
⌈⌈or sitting⌉⌉ on mats along the two walls. At the head of the room,
Saul, upon a ⌈⌈slightly⌉⌉ raised clay bench or platform, against the
wall. Servants carrying huge platters of food, which they set down at
intervals, before the guests⌉>   10

(A rather long clay room in Saul's house in Gilgal—At the end of
the room, a low clay bench or platform, on which Saul <lies>
reclines or sits—Jonathan ⌈below,⌉ on his right—Jonathan moves,
and Abner takes his place: but not on the raised place. A fire of
bushes and twigs burns in a fire-pit⃰ ⌈a long pit like a grave, across⌉   15
near Saul's seat. Dull lamps set on the floor illuminate the room
feebly. Eight or ten men, captains, guests of importance, recline on
mats on the floor, more or less in two rows. <Servants carry huge
platters, and set them down steaming, at intervals, before the men.>
⌈Slave servants bring ewer and basin, and pour water over the hands   20
of the men, one by one.⌉ The place on Saul's left, facing Abner, is
empty. Jonathan moves nearer the door. Slaves enter with ⌈a⌉ huge
platter of steaming food. All rise and sit round on the mats, Saul
comes down from his place. The place on his left is still empty. The
men sit cross-legged round the platter)   25

SAUL: Reach forth thine hand!
MEN: In the Lord's name! (they begin to eat with their fingers,<)>
    from the huge central mess<)>: for a while they eat in silence)
ABNER: Is not Phaltiel the son of Laish⃰ bidden to the feast, Oh
    King?   30
SAUL: I have not seen him this day.
ABNER: He hath arrived towards evening, with asses laden for the
    king, and hath pitched by the well of the gate.
SAUL: Tomorrow we will bid him to the feast of the sacrifice, for it
    is the last day.   35
ABNER: Wilt thou not see him this night? He comes from the
    borders of Gath, and is a mighty man, strong in possessions,

and with many armed servants. He hath been up among the
Philistine, and knoweth their strength

SAUL: We will call him. (Abner sends a servant) And he shall sit
here, in this empty place, which is <David's> ⌈empty again

5   today.⌉—Yea, oh Jonathan, wherefore cometh not the son of
Jesse to meat, neither yesterday nor today? Hath something
befallen him? Is he not clean?✻

JONATHAN: David earnestly asked leave of me, to go to Bethlehem.
He said: *Let me go, I pray thee; for our family hath a sacrifice in*

10   *the city; and my brother, he hath commanded me to be there. And*
now, if I have found favour in thine eyes, let me get away, I pray
thee, and see my brethren. Therefore he cometh not to the king's
table.

SAUL: Yea,verily is he gone forth to work more mischief in Israel,

15   this fox who w<ho>ould be a lion.

JONATHAN: Surely he is a faithful servant to the king!

SAUL: Sayst thou so! Wouldst thou even say it again to me?—This
fox, that peepeth round the corners! This sly one, that slingeth
stones unexpectedly at his enemy, and the like, unexpectedly, at

20   his friends. This champion, who is champion because he can
knock a bird off a bough, with a smart stone. This meek
shepherd who hides his purpose up his wide sleeve, and creeps
on by cunning.—Say thou, hath Samuel anointed him to be
king? And hath he not laid it up in store, in his sly mind? Can

25   he not play on the hearts of Israel cunningly, as on the harp-
strings, this bird that chirpeth his own vanity?—Oh yes! Oh
ye<s>a! Brave and flush as a man he goeth not forth: but sly,
and with belly to the ground, and peeping erst round the
corner, before he ventureth.—Hast thou taken this to thy

30   bosom?

JONATHAN: Verily, hast thou no cause against him. For ever is he
true servant <against> ⌈for⌉ the king, and valiant against the
king's enemies.

SAUL: Yea, valiant! Yea, true! Eateth he not my bread? and hath he

35   not in his mind, to eat up the kingdom also <—>?

JONATHAN: If the Lord will have him king, in the days to come—

SAUL: Thou son of a perverse, rebellious woman! Do I not know
⌈that⌉ thou hast chosen the son of Jesse to thine own confusion,
and to the confusion of thy mother's nakedness?—For as long

40   as the son of Jesse liveth upon the ground, thou shalt not be

established, nor thy kingdom.—Wherefore now send and fetch
him unto me, for he shall surely die.

JONATHAN: Wherefore shall he be slain? What hath he done?

SAUL (rising): Cursed be thy mother's nakedness, thou <mis-
begotten> ⌈mis-born⌉—(hurls javelin at Jonathan)   5

JONATHAN: Hast thou cursed my mother's nakedness!—Thy meat
of sacrifice will I not eat! (goes forth in fierce anger) (Phaltiel
has entered during the scene. Jonathan gone, <after> ⌈ensues⌉ a
pause of dead silence, in which a servant brings back the javelin
to Saul, who sticks it in the ground.)   10

ABNER: Art thou here, Phaltiel? The king bids thee sit by him.

PHALTIEL (a big handsome man): The Lord reward it unto you.
(sits in David's place)

SAUL: Reach forth thine hand.

PHALTIEL: In the Lord's name.   15

ABNER: Thou sittest in the place of the son of Jesse, the killer of
Goliath—He hath turned his <hand> ⌈heart⌉ against the king,
and is not come to meat.

PHALTIEL: Yea, I have heard, he will be king. Will he sling stones
at all of us? Or will he even dig a pit, as for the bear? For it   20
seems, by David men should be trapped and slain as beasts of
the field.—He is indeed no man of war, to become king.

ABNER: Yet even now, Samuel hath said to him in Naioth, <ere>
e'er Saul came: *Thou, David, shalt surely be king, for the Lord
hath said it.*   25

PHALTIEL: The king was in Naioth. And the Lord spoke likewise
to the king.

ABNER: Wilt thou not tell us, Oh King, the word of the Lord to
thee in Naioth?

SAUL: Is the Lord a man, to babble words on his lips? Or is he a   30
prophet, or a priest, or a leader of fighting men, to shout
commands? Lo, to me is the Lord God a flame that f<lo>illeth
me. And if out of the flame I speak, it is *I* who frame the words
and shape the speech. God doth not speak.

ABNER: Yet he spoke to Moses.   35

SAUL: Nay! Moses was in the flame. And out of the flame Moses
spoke. But the words and the speech are man's, and the man
was Moses. God speaketh not, and commandeth not, any more
than the flame of the fire <speaketh,> ⌈<sounds,> openeth its
mouth in words,⌉ when it warms my body. So the Lord warms   40

my soul. But never doth he prate at me. I will put no words into the mouth of travelling flame, for they belong not there. Doth the fire of my hearth warm me <with words?> ⌈speechfully?⌉

ABNER: Then how shall a man know what he doeth?

SAUL: What he doeth he doeth from the heart that is in him, warm with God.—There is no commandment from God, save one, which is the commandment of the fire: *Oh, <nourish> ⌈take⌉ my flame <with> ⌈into⌉ the fuel of your life.*—There is but one sin, to deny the <bright> flame of God its rushing leap in my body, as Jonathan denies it. Nay, he throws damp sand on the fire of God in him, and I must see it. He quenches his own loins, and I must bear it. He lets the foxy son of Jesse steal his life, and I must allow it.

ABNER: Is not the Lord with David?

SAUL: Yea, but a little Lord, with a face like David's own, and a cunning sling in his hand, charged with a round pebble.—Oh David hath put the face of David upon the rushing flame that is God. And for a time, this shall prevail. For men put masks on the flame of God, as Baal and Ashtaroth. And David puts the mask of David. And the house of David will put other masks.—But at last the flame shall sweep them all up. And Saul will be in the flame. For the flame of God will not stay shut behind a mask, for ever—

PHALTIEL: Yea, it is good to me to think, that the flame is very god: that I am the bush that burns and burns not down. Yea, the flame, the many flames! The thorns becoming god in the fire, crackling to god! The sun wheeling godly in heaven! The unseen flame in the wine, the unseen flame in the sea! The flame in my heart, when I take the sword and hear the call of the king! The flame in my eyes when I see Israel in victory. The soft flame in my knees, when my little son clings to them. The goodly flame in my thighs when the woman touches me, and I turn to her, and my loins rush up in flame like a fire of thorns! And the steady flame in my bowels, when I see my camels coming to drink, after a long journey, come safely back.—Yea, it is good to know there is no face to our God, that he changes as the manifold fire, and speaks not, only surges and warms and burns, and uttereth nothing, only subtly flames.

SAUL: Ah, if Jonathan but knew! And if the mother of Jonathan had not shut her womb to the flame, leaving the small mouth open only to the man, we had not lost the kingdom, and the house of David had not masked the flame for all the world.—But the masks at last will melt into ash. And Saul will be in the flame. —Yet my doomed heart hates this David. Yet he must have his hour! And I shall be in the flame that consumes his house at last. 5

(Curtain)

Scene XVII

(Morning—Rocky place outside Gilgal—the rock Ezel. <Jonathan
and a boy—Jonathan shooting arrows at the rock Ezel)

JONATHAN (to the lad): Run, find out the arrows which I shoot. (as
5   the boy runs, Jonathan shoots an arrow over his head, beyond
           him)
JONATHAN: Is not the arrow beyond thee? (boy runs looking)>

⌈David alone.—After a while Jonathan enters, with a boy bearing a
quiver.)⌉

10   DAVID (alone): Now if Jonathan come out, I am lost. For this is the
           third day, when he should be here.—Lord, hast thou
           <crowned> anointed me king, to drive me into a hole like a
           jackal, there to live hungry and faint, and outcast!
      JONATHAN: Behold, the arrows are beyond thee! Run, make haste,
15   stay not.
           (boy hunts for arrows, gathers them up, comes running

[end of manuscript]

ii. THE MUSIC FOR *DAVID*

Between the spring of 1925 and the autumn of 1926, Lawrence composed music for *David*, ending up with ten pieces in all. He began in the manuscript (Roberts E87a: hereafter MS), into which he inscribed two pieces (nos. 4 and 6 in the table below): no. 6 he preserved on an old leaf and re-used when he revised the fifteenth scene and discarded most of the old leaves.[1] When he read the play to Ida Rauh on 17–18 May 1925, he apparently sang these two pieces and perhaps others.[2] Brett carefully wrote out nos. 4 and 6 in the surviving typescript (Roberts E87b: hereafter TS) which she made in May–June 1925, while Lawrence at some stage added nos. 1 and 2 to the TS. It is not known whether either of them did the same in the carbon copy.

Fifteen months later, he offered to send music for the play to Robert Atkins, who was planning to direct it in London in the autumn of 1926 (v. 543). However, Lawrence no longer had access either to MS or to TS and therefore had to remember (or to re-invent) the music he had already composed, as well as to add some new pieces. In the notebook which he would shortly use for writing the first version of *Lady Chatterley's Lover*,[3] he re-drafted nos. 2, 4 and 6 and wrote out no. 3, as well as making preliminary sketches for nos. 5 and 7: the number of musical items thus grew to six. He may have used other paper for drafts which no longer survive. On 13 October, he went to his neighbours, the Wilkinsons, in Scandicci 'to borrow the use of the piano and sat for more than an hour very happily composing a chant for his play'. The following day he went back with 'the manuscript score for the Psalm in his David' – i.e. no. 4 – 'and we were able to find a good many mistakes and A[rthur] did a great deal of neat scratching out for him. He went off very happy to have his M.S ready for the post'.[4] On 16 October he posted nos. 2–10 to Atkins (v. 557). For some reason, at this stage he omitted no. 1, which survives

---

[1] See Appendix v i.
[2] See Introduction, p. lxxii.
[3] Roberts E186a.
[4] Unpublished diary of Lilian Wilkinson, quoted by kind permission of Mrs Lisa Smith; Arthur Gair Wilkinson (1882–1957) was her husband.

587

only in TS, and which he had either decided not to use or (more likely) forgotten.[5] It is not known whether Atkins passed on the music to Phyllis Whitworth, as Lawrence suggested.[6] The complete list of all Lawrence's music pieces, in their different versions, is as follows:

No.	Scene	Title	MS E87a	TS E87b	Notebook E186a	Atkins letter	Edition text
1	1	'Saul came home'		108a [DHL]			435:7
2	9	'Lu-lu-a-li-lu-lu-lu!'		44a [DHL]	221c	1	479:5
3	10	'Jonathan and David'			221c	1	482:3
4	11	'What is man'	52v	56 [Brett]	221c–221c	1	487:24
5	12	'Yah! David missed her'			221c	2	493:7
6	15	'Armies there are'	83r	97 [Brett]	221a	2	517:18
7	15	'Fire within fire'			221b	3–4	518:25
8	15	'Whiteness of wool'				3	519:4
9	15	'Standeth a man'				4	519:37
10	15	'Cast thyself down'				3	520:34

The May 1927 performances of the play, however, ignored Lawrence's music. 'The Incidental Music' – which probably included music for the sung items – was composed by Richard Austin, and – for example – in the performance of no. 4, Psalm viii in Scene 11, Edward Marsh heard 'the tune we all know so well from Morning Prayer' rather than 'the church-bell tune of the Indians' Lawrence had adapted and sent to Atkins.[7] The first public performance of Lawrence's own music, with pipe, drum and tambourine parts composed by Bethan Jones, took place at the D. H. Lawrence Centre of the University of Nottingham on 20 April 1996.[8]

The music printed below has slightly regularised Lawrence's notation and extended the musical settings to cover all the text which Lawrence clearly wished to be sung. The base-text for the words printed is the edited text above; when, however, he copied the words on to the music pages he sent to Atkins for items 2–10, Lawrence made a small number of changes to words and punctuation, and these have been incorporated as representing his own final thoughts about the text of the songs. The music text

---

[5] The pages he sent were reproduced in *A D. H. Lawrence Miscellany*, ed. Harry T. Moore (1961), illustrations between pages 150 and 151.

[6] Unpublished letter to Phyllis Whitworth, 15 November 1926.

[7] Programme, p. [v]; see Introduction, p. lxxxi; see Explanatory note on 487:7.

[8] Voices – Philip Weller, Catharine Williams, Jenny Smith; instrumentalists – Bethan Jones, Kieran O'Riordan, Jo Castle; narration – John Worthen. The music was performed again on 15 July 1996 at the 6th International D. H. Lawrence Conference at the University of Nottingham. The D. H. Lawrence Centre holds a tape of the first performance, and a set of the parts for tambourine, drum and pipe.

of piece no. 1 is published here for the first time, from the music setting in TS; the words and punctuation have been emended from those written into that setting. No apparatus of DHL's variants in his musical settings is provided: as Enlister Fowler noted, 'Musical settings are not texts, and should not be treated as such in editing a literary *oeuvre*'.[9]

[9] *Times Literary Supplement*, 27 August 1993, p. 4.

1 'Saul came home' (435:7)

2 'Lu-lu-a-li-lu-lu-lu!' (479:5)

Scene IX – to be sung rather nasal & monoto[no]us

MAIDENS

Lu-lu - a - li - lu - lu - lu! Lu-lu - lu - li - a - li - lu - lu! A - li - lu - lu - lu - lu!

Lu - a - li - lu! Lu - a - li - lu! Lu - al - li - lu - a!

MERAB   MICHAL

Out of Ju - dah Saul comes in! Da - vid slew the Phil - is - tine.

MERAB AND HER MAIDENS   MICHAL AND HER MAIDENS

Out of Ju - dah Saul comes in. Da - vid slew the Phil - is - tine.

ALL

A - li - lu - lu! A - li - lu - lu - lu! Lu! lu!lu! lu! li! lu! lu! a! li! lu! lu! lu! lu!

MERAB   MICHAL

All the Phil - is - tine has fled. By the road-side fell their dead.

MERAB   MICHAL

Woun - ded felldown in the path. Be - yond Ek - ron un - to Gath.

MERAB AND MAIDENS   MICHAL AND MAIDENS

All the Phil - is - tine has fled. By the road-side fell their dead.

MERAB AND MAIDENS   MICHAL AND MAIDENS

Woun - ded felldown in the path. Be - yond Ek - ron un - to Gath.

3 'Jonathan and David' (482:3)

Scene X

MERAB AND MICHAL

Jo-na-thanand Da - vid!   Lu - lu - lu - a!   Here they come, the   lo - ving two-a!

4 'What is man' (487:24)

Scene XI – rather gay and lilting

5 'Yah! David missed her' (493:7)

Scene XII – very nasal

6 'Armies there are' (517:18)

Scene XV

strungby God Lo! how he ta - k - eth aim With ar - row - heads of our

wrath Pro - phet of God isan ar - row in full flight And he shall

pi - ercethy shield, thou, thou Lord's en - e - my. Long is the fight yet the

un - seen a - rrows fly keen toa wound inthe soul of the great

Lord's en - em - y Slow-lyhe bleedsyet the red drops runa - way

un - seen and i - n - ward-ly As bleeds the w - i - cked man

bleeding ofGodsecret - -ly ofGod.

7 'Fire within fire' (518:25)

Scene XV

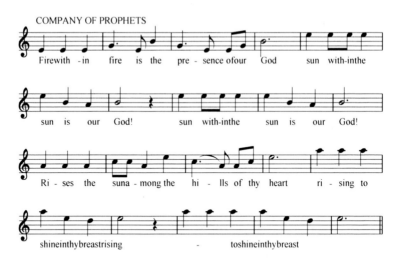

COMPANY OF PROPHETS

Firewith - in fire is the pre - sence ofour God sun with-inthe

sun is our God! sun with-inthe sun is our God!

Ri - ses the suna - mong the hi - lls of thy heart ri - sing to

shineinthybreastrising - toshineinthybreast

8 'Whiteness of wool' (519:4)

Scene XV (contd)

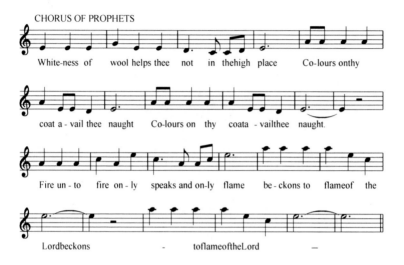

CHORUS OF PROPHETS

White-ness of wool helps thee not in thehigh place Co-lours onthy

coat a - vail thee naught Co-lours on thy coata - vailthee naught.

Fire un - to fire on - ly speaks and on-ly flame be - ckons to flameof the

Lordbeckons - toflameoftheLord —

9 'Standeth a man' (519:37)

Scene XV –

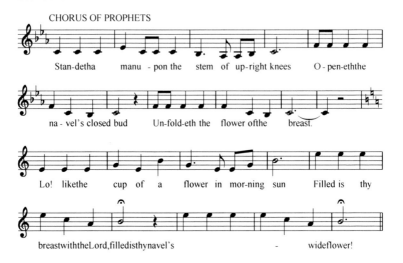

CHORUS OF PROPHETS

Stan-deth a   man u - pon the   stem of up-right knees   O - pen-eth the

na - vel's closed bud   Un-fold-eth the   flower of the   breast.

Lo! like the   cup of a   flower in mor-ning sun   Filled is   thy

breast with the Lord, filled is thy navel's   -   wide flower!

10 'Cast thyself down' (520:34)

Scene XV cont.

CHORUS OF PROPHETS

Cast thy - self down that the Lord may take thee up Fall be-fore the

Lord and fall high All things come forth from the flame of al-migh-ty

God somethings will ne - ver re - turn some things will ne - ver re -

turn Somehave their will and their way and come at last

tothe worm's wa - i - ting mouth— To theworm's wa - i - ting mouth

Butthe high Lord heleans down u - pon the hill and wrapshis

ownin his flame wraps themas whirl-wind from the world

leavesnotonesighforthegrave

iii. THE GERMAN TEXTS OF *DAVID*

The texts of *David* include an extensively authorially revised text which cannot, however, be employed to correct earlier texts: it is Lawrence's revision of his wife Frieda's German translation.

The first indication we have that Frieda wanted to translate *David* came on 2 July 1925, less than two months after Lawrence had finished writing it, and less than six weeks after he had read it aloud to Ida Rauh (see Introduction, pp. lxxii–lxxiii). The latter had taken the bulk of the play's manuscript (MS) away with her after the reading, and Lawrence had sent her the final part of MS when Dorothy Brett had finished typing it; but at the start of July he asked her to send MS back, because 'Frieda is set on translating it' (v. 275). Both the typescripts made by Brett were by then in the hands of his agent (v. 268). MS arrived back on 13 July, and the same day Lawrence reported that Frieda was 'already immersed' in the work of translation (v. 276): she was writing her translation into the first of two feint-lined exercise books (hereafter GMS).[1]

However, having recovered MS, Lawrence decided that, as a priority, he ought to use it as a copy of the play to be sent around potential theatre producers. Just over a fortnight later (31 July), he sent MS to his literary agent in London (v. 283). Frieda's creation of GMS must have stopped at that point; no other copy of the play was available to her.

In spite of her initial enthusiasm, she probably did rather little. In the summer of 1925 she was using a peculiarly thick pen nib and – with one exception – employed only the rectos of pages, whereas in scenes 2–16 she would use a much thinner nib, and inscribe both rectos and versos. It seems likely that she finished Scene 1, wrote out the heading 'II Scene' and the character heading 'Samuel', and then stopped. The second half of July had turned out particularly hot (v. 277, 278), which may have affected her progress.[2]

---

[1] Roberts E87.1a, 254pp. (UCB).

[2] A word in scene 3 she would translate as 'Blitz' ('lightning') had appeared as 'Lord' in MS and the surviving typescript, and would only be changed to 'Bolt' in DHL's proof correction of December 1925 – January 1926 (see below), thus proving she was using the proofs to translate scene 3.

She now had to wait until another text of the play was available; and that cannot have been until December 1925, by which time she and Lawrence had left America and were living in the Villa Bernarda, Spotorno, in northern Italy. Lawrence received two sets of first proofs of the play (hereafter PPI) sometime between 8 and 20 December (see Introduction, p. lxxvii), and it would then have been possible for Frieda to recommence work. She did not yet start, however. Lawrence may have warned her that he would be revising the play while correcting its proofs, and that she should wait for the revised text.

Lawrence returned his corrected set of first proofs to the printers well before the end of December, and – incidentally – gave away his almost uncorrected duplicate set (PPI) on 11 January 1926 (v. 376). Being uncorrected, PPI would have been of no use to Frieda. But, early in January, Lawrence acquired two sets of second proofs; and the duplicate set (PPII) which, again, remained mostly uncorrected (but which of course incorporated the changes he had made in PPI) remained in his possession until December 1926 (see Introduction, p. lxxvii).[3]

No other texts of the play were available in Spotorno until a copy of the first English edition arrived towards the end of March – Lawrence thanked Secker for it on 4 April (v. 413) though it may have come a little earlier. When Frieda restarted her translation, therefore, sometime in January, she must have been working either from the duplicate set of PPII, or from Lawrence's corrected set of first proofs. She left tell-tale traces, however, in the surviving duplicate set of PPII. At the bottom of p. 115 she wrote her name, 'Frieda', and on p. 41 the date '1912' in the print-like script she sometimes employed,[4] while blue ink smudges and mostly unreadable words in 'mirror-writing' on pp. 26, 36, 49, 50, 60, 63, 68, 76, 96 and 100 of PPII record occasions when she turned over still wet blue ink pages of GMS on to the proofs she was using.[5]

Lawrence wrote to Martin Secker on 1 February that she was 'crazy,

---

[3] His corrected set of PPI (Roberts E87.1d) was also returned to him at some stage: it was in his possession in April 1928, when he had it bound (as he did Frieda's translation) (*Letters*, vi. 348 n. 4). These proofs are now unlocated.

[4] Seen, for example, in the 1913 manuscript of Lawrence's short story 'The Primrose Path' (Roberts E322.7a, UN), p. 9. DHL described exactly such handwriting – as well as recreating Frieda's habit of writing out her name – in his story 'The Mortal Coil', where the character Marta 'began writing her name in stiff Gothic characters, time after time' (*England, My England and Other Stories*, ed. Bruce Steele, Cambridge, 1990, 172:14–15).

[5] The word 'auch' is probable on PPII, p. 49, and a peculiar, smudged central 't' in the first of two examples of the word 'finstrer' in GMS (p. [193]) clearly appears (reversed) below the equivalent passage on PPII, p. 100.

translating it. She loves it, and has become the authoress, I the cook and the captain bold, and housemaid of the Villa B.' (v. 388). Around this point she must have started work in the second exercise book. By 2 February, 'wildly translating' – hence the smudges, perhaps – she had completed half the play, probably Scenes 2–8, to add to her existing translation of Scene 1. This suggests that she must have started work two or three weeks earlier, probably soon after PPII had arrived in Spotorno. At the start of February, Lawrence arranged for his typewriter to be sent to him so that Frieda's daughter, Elsa Weekley (shortly to be arriving in Spotorno), would be able to start typing the translation from what Lawrence disparagingly called 'F's rather muddled books' (v. 389). The two-notebook manuscript remained without page numbers, and contained numerous deletions and substitutions – not always clearly marked, at least to the eye of a professional author. It contained gaps which she presumably expected him to fill with translations of the play's rhyming chants; and between p. [96] and p. [97] it omitted, apparently by accident, one passage of three-quarters of a page (PPII, p. 52) (see below).

She was still at work on 15 March, when she remarked that 'I am translating it quite well into German!'[6] It is not known exactly when she finished; her translation occupied 256 pages of the 2 notebooks, in all. She ignored the archaisms of Lawrence's biblical English, and made no attempt to reproduce the passages taken directly from *KJB* with their equivalents from a German Bible. She produced a rather literal translation which added very little to Lawrence's original. Sentences obscure in Lawrence's archaic English remain obscure in Frieda's German, which suggests that she did not ask him what they meant. However, Lawrence's handwriting appears frequently in her manuscript. He regularly made small changes, altering her translation of 'wilderness' from 'Wildnis' to 'Wüste', for example (p. [32]); he added extra words and phrases, and inserted translations of a number of the play's short rhyming chants.[7] His contributions appear more often in the first half of GMS than in the second; in Scene 12, for example, the gaps Frieda left for him to fill remain blank. On the other hand, in Scene 15 he inserted a number of lengthy choral chants.

Before Elsa Weekley left Italy for London on 27 April, she had completed the first 26 pages of a typescript (v. 464) – about a quarter of the whole. But the typing then remained at a standstill until the end of May,

[6] Frieda Lawrence, *Memoirs*, 232.

[7] 'Tausend Männer Saul erschlug / Doch zehn Tausend David schlug' (p. [126]), for example, in his version of 'Saul in thousands slew their men! / David slew his thousands ten!' (479:25–6).

when Lawrence took it up. This was 'a slow business, I'm no typist', as he told Frieda's sister, Else Jaffe (v. 464). He was, however, well aware that no one would have been able to work from GMS. The Lawrences were feeling hard-up in the spring of 1927, too, and he may have been trying to economise by doing the typing. To Frieda's sister he rather unconvincingly explained that 'it is good for me to learn some German, I suppose'. Significantly, however, he also remarked 'it is just as well for me to go through the MS myself' (v. 464). Not only did he go on with the revision he had started in GMS: he probably typed GMS because he wanted to recreate it – as he put it a fortnight later, 'alter F's translation all the way' (v. 473). He probably used the same copy of PPII as Frieda; a passage on p. 52 which she had left out is marked in pencil, almost certainly by Lawrence, who added that passage to his typescript.

On 8 June he told Frieda's mother that the typing would take another week: 'Ein schwieriges Arbeit, ich "tippe" sehr ungern, und mache viele Fehler' ['a difficult job, I really don't enjoy typing, and make lots of mistakes'] (v. 469). 'I loathe the typewriter' (v. 472), he remarked to Secker: typing English was bad enough, but German was much worse, as he told Brett: 'be glad you don't have to do it – every noun in German a capital letter!' But the real problem was 'having to re-translate F's translation' (v. 470). He frequently adjusted it (not always for the better); but he was mainly concerned to add new passages and phrases in his often incorrect but always individual German. It is possible that Frieda helped him: his vocabulary at times shows signs of unusual quality. The typing, however, was 'a labour, I assure you. I wonder the typewriter hasn't gone off with a bang and a smell of sulphur' (v. 473). He finished work by 14 June (v. 474).[8] A year later, describing it to his German friend Max Mohr (who was trying to set up a performance of the play in Berlin), he made it sound entirely his own work: 'I know the translation is very unsatisfactory: my sort of German, which, like your English, must go into a class by itself' (vi. 204). When, not much to his surprise, Mohr's hopes for a production came to nothing – 'I knew too well that you would never get past the commercial *Wurm* with it' – Lawrence, however, gave credit where credit was due: 'Only my wife is sad' (vi. 248).

The fact that the German which Frieda and Lawrence used – unlike the

---

[8] Roberts E87.1b, the typescript made by Elsa Weekley and DHL, was of 94 pages and contained a number of handwritten additions by DHL: it was described by Powell, *the manuscripts*, p. 44, and Tedlock 124–5. Roberts's *Bibliography*, however, confuses E87.1b with the later re-typing, located at UCB, of 104 pages and without any handwritten corrections (see note 11 below).

language of *KJB* – was not an archaic language means that the play is slightly more accessible in its German form, for all its oddities. As Lawrence told Else,

I am interested, really, to see the play go into German, so much simpler and more direct than in English. English is really very complicated in its *meanings*. Perhaps the simpler a language becomes in its grammar and syntax, the more subtle and complex it becomes in its suggestions. Anyhow this play seems to me much more direct and dramatic in German, much less poetic and suggestive than in English.

(v. 464)

Frieda's original manuscript notebooks[9] still survive; but the 94-page typescript Lawrence and Elsa Weekley made is unfortunately missing, so that it is impossible to see whether Lawrence made any alterations to the 26 pages typed by Elsa. All we can guess is that some at least of the 'few corrections hand-printed in ink' recorded by Tedlock in 1948 when he described the missing typescript appeared in her part of the typing. The original title-page – presumably Elsa's – read 'David / ein Schauspiel / von / D. H. Lawrence / übersetzt von Frieda Lawrence / (geb. Freiin von Richthofen)' ['David / a play / by / D. H. Lawrence / translated by Frieda Lawrence / (born Baroness von Richthofen)']. It was almost certainly Lawrence who added 'und D. H. L.' in ink after 'Frieda Lawrence'.[10] The typescript made by Lawrence and Elsa Weekley was, however, re-typed before it vanished, and that typescript (hereafter GTSII) survives.[11]

It is not, of course, possible to emend the 1925–6 English text of *David* from the 1926 German translation by Lawrence and Frieda; but some of the most interesting alterations in GTSII, especially cuts and additions, are translated into English in the Explanatory notes.[12] As an example of what Frieda did, and what Lawrence did to her work, what follows is the last speech of the play: Frieda's GMS is in the left-hand column, and Lawrence's GTSII on the right. The major differences are printed in bold. Deletions in the manuscript are marked < > and insertions are marked [ ].

---

[9] Subsequently bound together within grey, black and white decorated boards by Orioli (see note 3 above).

[10] Tedlock 124.

[11] GTSII (UCB), 104 pp., no number in Roberts. The title-page addition reads 'and D. H. L.', not 'und D. H. L.' and is typed in GTSII (it was handwritten in E87.1b) while there are no ink additions in the text.

[12] See entries at 437:2, 443:28, 444:3, 444:4, 448:21, 451:3, 524:26, 524:34 and 524:36.

GMS

Du gehst, David! Und die Hoffnung Israels mit Dir! Ich bleibe, mit meinem Vater und der Stern<schein>⌈stein⌉ fällt in Verzweiflung. Und doch was liegt daran? Ich möchte Deinen neuen Tag nicht sehen, David. Denn Deine Weisheit ist die Weisheit der Schlauen und hinter Deiner Leidenschaft steht Vorsicht. Und nackt gehst Du nicht ins Feuer. Ja, geh denn hin<aus> und lass mich sterben. Denn Deine Jugend liegt in Deiner Klugheit und Deiner Schläue. Aber in Saul hab ich die Hochherzigkeit eines Mannes gekannt. Ja, Du schlägst die Riesen mit einem schlauen Stein! Grosse und hochherzige Männer, Männer der antlitzlosen Flamme werden fallen in ihrer Stärke, vor Dir werden sie fallen, Dir David dem klugen Jungen des Löwen von Judah! Ja; mein Herz brennt für Dich in mir wie über einem zarten, klugen Kind. Und mein Herz brennt in meinem Vater selbst sogar in seinem dunklen Zorn. Aber ⌈Du⌉ geh⌈st⌉ <Du> hin<aus> und kenn⌈st⌉ kein dunkles Sehnen, Du Sohn Isais. Doch geh! Denn mein<e> Zwielicht gilt mir mehr denn Dein Tag und mein Tod ist mir lieber wie Dein Leben. Nimm es! Nimm Du das Königreich, und die Tage, die kommen. In den Flammen des Todes, wo die Kraft ist, will ich warten bis der Tag Davids endlich vorüber ist und die

GTSII

Du gehst, David! und die Hoffnung Israels mit dir! Ich bleibe mit meinem Vater, und der Sternstein fällt in Verzweiflung. Und doch was liegt daran? Ich möchte deinen neuen Tag nicht sehen, David. Denn deine Weisheit ist die Weisheit der Schlauen, und hinter deiner Leidenschaft steht Vorsicht. **Ehrsucht liegt dir im Innersten des Herzens, Ehrsucht und Eigenwille. Doch bist du mir vielleicht nicht ganz kalt, und das, was wir geschworen haben, wirst du nicht ganz vergessen.** Aber in Saul hab' ich **die Grossmut** eines Mannes gekannt. – Ja, du schlägst den Riesen mit einem **gewandten** Stein, du! **Aber** grosse Männer und hochherzige Männer der antlitzlosen Flamme, werden fallen von ihrer Stärke, vor dir werden sie fallen, David, dem klugen Jungen des Löwen von Juda. **Doch** brennt mein Herz für dich, wie für ein zartes, kluges Kind. **Denn du bist so mutig, und allein Ja,** und das Herz brennt für dich in meinem Vater selbst, sogar in seinem dunklen Zorn. Aber du, du gehst fort und kennst keine **tiefe Antwort, kein stilles** Sehnen, du Sohn Isais! Doch geh! **Auch du wirst nicht ganz und gar vergessen, du kannst es nicht, auch wenn du willst. Etwas aus mir soll in dir leben, und in deinem Samen bis an das Ende, und an den neuen**

Weisheit nicht mehr fuchsschlau ist und das Blut seine Flamme wieder erhält. Ja, die Flamme stirbt nicht wenn auch der Sonne Rot stirbt! – Und nun muss ich zur Stadt gehn!

(Steht auf und geht schnell fort -.)[13]

[13] E87.1a, pp. [255–6].

Anfang. Ja geh! Denn mein Zwielicht gilt mir mehr **wie** dein Tag, und mein Tod ist mir lieber wie dein Leben. Nimm es! Nimm du das Königreich, und die Tage, die kommen. In den Flammen des Todes, wo die Kraft **lebt**, will ich warten bis der Tag Davids endlich vorüber ist, und die Weisheit nicht mehr fuchsschlau ist, **und kalt,** und das Blut wieder seine Flamme erhält. Ja, die Flamme stirbt nicht, wenn auch der Sonne Rot stirbt Und nun muss ich zur Stadt gehen. (**er** steht auf und geht schnell fort)[14]

[14] GTSII (p. 104); see Explanatory notes on 524:26, 34 and 36.

EXPLANATORY NOTES

EXPLANATORY NOTES

Note: Explanatory notes are signalled by asterisks in the text except in the case of *David*, where notes wholly devoted to biblical parallels are not signalled.

A Collier's Friday Night

3:10 MOTHER ... WYLD   The characters and the events of the play are closely based on DHL's family and experience. See *Letters*, i. 174, 190–1; the autobiographical sketches, especially 'Nottingham and the Mining Countryside', in *Phoenix*, ed. Edward D. McDonald (New York, 1936), and *Phoenix II*, ed. Warren Roberts and Harry T. Moore (1968), and Ada Lawrence and Stuart Gelder, *The Early Life of D. H. Lawrence* (1932). Chaps. IV and VIII of *Sons and Lovers* (1913) are also prefigured.

The setting is a mining community and various clues point to a recreated Eastwood, DHL's birthplace, a small mining town 9 miles n.w. of Nottingham. The setting is closely modelled on the Lawrence family homes in Walker Street and Lynn Croft, Eastwood (cf. *Letters*, i. 174; Lawrence and Gelder, *The Early Life*, pp. 19–20; E.T. 166). The action takes place in the autumn, most probably during November (see note on 25:23).

Mrs and Mr Lambert are recreations of DHL's parents, Lydia Lawrence, née Beardsall (1851–1910), and Arthur John Lawrence (1846–1924). In the MS the character Mr Lambert is addressed as 'Walter' (once, p. [35], which is emended) and 'George' (twice, pp. [39], [43]). DHL does not seem to have noticed the inconsistency; cf. Arthur Lawrence's brothers, George (1853–1929) and Walter (1856–1904), and Walter Morel, the father in *Sons and Lovers*.

Ernest Lambert is a recreation of DHL, with the name of DHL's elder brother, William Ernest (1878–1901). On three occasions, however, DHL wrote or started to write 'Cyril' instead of 'Ernest' (MS, pp. [43], [110], [133]); the character is thus linked to the DHL figures, Cyril Beardsall in *The White Peacock* (1911) and Cyril Mersham in 'A Modern Lover' (1909: see *Love Among the Haystacks and Other Stories*, ed. John Worthen, Cambridge, 1987, pp. 28–48). The name Ernest Lambert also appears in the MS of DHL's novel, *The Trespasser* (1912), where on one occasion it replaced that of the narrator, Cecil Byrne (see *The Trespasser*, ed. Elizabeth Mansfield, Cambridge, 1981, note on 42:28, and Bruce Steele, 'The Manuscript of D. H. Lawrence's *Saga of Siegmund*', *Studies in Bibliography*, xxxiii 1980, 193–205).

Nellie Lambert is modelled on DHL's younger sister, Lettice Ada (1887–1948), who was a full-time teacher from June 1907. In MS, DHL twice wrote 'Ada' instead of 'Nellie' (pp. [83], [117]), but recognized the slip of the pen and corrected it. Ada's fiancé, William Edwin Clarke (1889–1964), appears as 'Eddie' in the play; they married in 1913.

Maggie Pearson is based on DHL's friend, Jessie Chambers (1887–1944). Gertie Coomber represents Gertrude ('Gertie') Cooper (1885–1942) who lived next door to the Lawrences in Lynn Croft, Eastwood; her sister Frances (1884–1918) is also mentioned in the play. Beatrice Wyld is based on Alice Beatrice Hall (b. ?1880), a friend of the Coopers and the Lawrences whom DHL hardly disguises: he uses her second name and her mother's maiden name (cf. George Hardy and Nathaniel Harris, *A D. H. Lawrence Album*, Ashbourne, 1985, p. 124; *Letters*, i. 68–9, 71; *The White Peacock*, ed. Andrew Robertson, Cambridge, 1983, notes on 21:30, 23:38, 118:29, and Introduction, pp. xliii–xliv; cf. Alice Gall in *The White Peacock* and Beatrice Wyld in *Sons and Lovers*, ed. Helen Baron and Carl Baron, Cambridge, 1992, note on 242:8). In MS (p. [77]), DHL wrote 'Alice Ga' instead of 'Beatrice' and then deleted it.

5:1 **A COLLIER'S FRIDAY NIGHT**   Cf. the poem 'The Cotter's Saturday Night' (1786) by Robert Burns (1759–96), showing a family joyfully and piously preparing for and having supper (*The Poems and Songs of Robert Burns*, ed. James Kinsley, 3 vols., Oxford, 1968, i. 145–52). In Eastwood, however, Friday nights had an importance of their own, as Friday was pay-day for the miners: Friday night was baking night, market night and also courting night.

5:3 *The kitchen or living room*   The kitchen was the centre of a miner's home; family life centred there.

5:9 *edition of Lessing,*   Gotthold Ephraim Lessing (1729–81), German dramatist, critic and essayist, particularly noted for his treatise on aesthetics, *Laokoon* (1766), which DHL knew. Bohn's Standard Library published an edition of Lessing's works 'florid in green and gilt' in three volumes (1878–99).

5:14 *clothes*   Second part of the word is illegible and corrected to 'clothes' by a different hand in pencil (MS, p. [1]). Further down at 5:16–17, 'that' and 'and below' (MS, p. [1]) are slightly mutilated; TCCI is the source of the readings.

5:19 *Reeve's silver trade mark.*   Reeves & Sons Ltd were manufacturers of colours and paint boxes; the round silver trade mark showed the company's name and a greyhound as the crest of the Reeves family.

5:21 *ragged pink chrysanthemums.*   Interlinear revision; deleted MS reading (p. [2]) was 'dahlias', replaced by 'michaelmas daisies' which was also crossed out.

5:24 *the "World's Famous Literature"*   The International Library of Famous Literature, ed. Richard Garnett (1899), 20 vols. DHL's brother, William Ernest, owned a set which deeply influenced DHL's early reading (see *Letters*, i. 4–6).

5:28 *prints from water colours,*   On his twenty-first birthday, DHL received from the Chambers family six parts of *English Water-Colour*, ed. Charles Holme (1902). DHL used the reproductions when making copies of paintings (see 'Making Pictures', *Phoenix II*, pp. 604–5).

6:1 *'Coronation' tumblers*   Commemorating the coronation of King Edward VII (1841–1910) in 1902. DHL first wrote ' "Coronation" drinking "glasses" ' (MS, p. [3]).

6:2 *Venice ... Stead's Christmas Numbers,*   Probably a keepsake from one of William Thomas Stead's newspapers, magazines or Christmas annuals.

6:4 *'New Age'.*   The radical socialist 'Weekly Review of Politics, Literature and

Art', started in 1907, ed. A. R. Orage; it supported Labour politics, the Fabian Society, women's interests and the Suffragists. DHL took it regularly for a time 1908–9 (E.T. 120); see also *Hardy*, note on 135:2, and *Mr Noon*, ed. Lindeth Vasey (Cambridge, 1984), note on 3:6.

6:22 **"Oh ... weary!"/MOTHER** Here (MS, p. [4]) and in a few other instances, DHL used quotation marks to indicate direct speech before remembering the normal convention for play-writing.

6:25 **old Tommy** Probably refers to Thomas Alfred Beacroft, Head of Ilkeston Pupil-Teacher Centre, 1899–1913; DHL, his sister Ada and Jessie Chambers all attended the Centre before qualifying as teachers.

7:23 *'The Scarlet Pimpernel',* The best-selling novel (1905) by Baroness Emmuska Orczy (1865–1947), Hungarian writer of spy novels and historical romances who wrote in English (cf. *Letters*, i. 223).

7:38 **Selson,** I.e. Selston colliery, 2 miles n. of Eastwood; DHL's spelling represents local pronunciation.

8:4 **Miner's Arms,** Cf. the Miners' Arms, a public house, in Mansfield Road, Eastwood.

8:28 *'prunes and prisms' manner,* A prim and affectedly elegant mode of speech; an allusion to the novel *Little Dorrit*, Book II, chap. v (1857) by Charles Dickens (1812–70).

8:38 NELLIE LAMBERT ... **Johnny Grocock.** Omitted by the typist of TCCI (Act I, p. 6) so that in all subsequent texts the following reference to 'name' became incomprehensible.

8:40 **Carooso.** Enrico Caruso (1873–1921), celebrated Italian tenor: the spelling indicates Nellie's pronunciation.

9:2 *the Gibson bend.)* The 'Gibson Girl' of Charles Dana Gibson (1867–1944), American artist and illustrator, delineated the American ideal of femininity of the period (slender, beautiful, with glamour and grace); his drawings had an enormous vogue between the late 1890s and the First World War and appeared in leading magazines and as illustrations in novels.

9:26 *drags his heavily shod feet ... limps slightly,* DHL originally wrote 'tramps with his heavy shoes' (MS, p. [11]) ... after an accident at work in 1903, DHL's father limped; see *Early Years* 43.

10:3 *disagreeably.)* Revised in MS (p. [12]) from 'with a snarling bitterness'.

10:17 **dotty** *(dirty)* DHL provides the meaning of a word as spoken locally; only 'dotty' should be spoken by the actor.

12:16 *sniffing,* Her disdainful sniff was a distinctive trait of DHL's mother; cf. George Henry Neville, *A Memoir of D. H. Lawrence*, ed. Carl Baron (Cambridge, 1981), p. 56.

13:34 **Derby,** In September 1906, DHL began a two-year teacher-training course at University College, Nottingham. Derby, a city 10½ miles s.w. of Eastwood, also had a training college, the Lichfield and Southwell Diocesan Training College.

14:15 **hippotamus.**   If not a slip of the pen, this may represent the pronunciation.

15:1 **Mater,**   A word commonly used by DHL for his mother; cf. below Mater, Mutter, Mutterchen, Matoushka and Matkha (Latin, German, Russian), Little Woman, little Ma, Little. These forms were used by DHL and his friends following educated middle-class use (cf. *Letters*, i. 173, 202; E.T. 149; Neville, *A Memoir*, p. 337; *The White Peacock*, ed. Robertson, 7:15, 8:6, 173:32, 37; *Sons and Lovers*, ed. Baron and Baron, 74:22, 197:33, 244:31). See too note on 50:13.

15:3 **middle of the term**   One of the few specific clues to the play's time-scheme; see note on 25:23 and Introduction, p. xxviii.

15:6 **Piers the Ploughman ... Horace: Quintus Horatius Flaccius,** *Piers Plowman*, the Middle English alliterative allegorical poem (*c.* 1360–87) by William Langland (*c.* 1303–90) ... Quintus Horatius Flaccus (Horace), Roman poet (65–8 BC).

15:22 **Mutterchen?**   Little mother? (German); diminutive and term of endearment; the correct form is 'Mütterchen'. DHL first wrote 'Mutterschen' and then corrected it (MS, p. [25]).

15:25 **nap:**   A card game in which each player receives five cards, and declares the number of hands (or 'tricks') s/he is going to win; to call five is to 'go nap'.

15:29 **Burke.**   Edmund Burke (1729–97), Whig statesman, orator and political theorist.

15:36 **Professor Staynes**   Family name with which DHL was familiar: Lydia Lawrence's younger sister, Ellen Beardsall (1855–1908), married John Richard Staynes. DHL also used the name for Miriam in the second version of 'Paul Morel' (later *Sons and Lovers*).

16:18 **blessed**   DHL first wrote 'blooming' (MS, p. [28]) and then inserted 'blessed' over it.

16:27 **Your grandfather** [16:5] **... repeat such—** Apparently a fictionalised version of the myth of the superior social background of Lydia Lawrence: see *Early Years* 25–6.

16:38 **the 'Savoy'**   Vegetarian restaurant at 38a, Wheeler Gate, Nottingham.

17:11 **Lois?**   Possibly a reference to Sara Lois Mee, a fellow-student of DHL at University College, Nottingham (cf. *Letters*, i. 142).

18:2 **Swinburne's dead!**   DHL wrote 'George Mere' (MS, p. [31]) which he immediately crossed out and replaced with 'Swinburne's'. George Meredith (1828–18 May 1909), journalist, poet, novelist, playwright and critic. Algernon Charles Swinburne (1837–10 April 1909), playwright, poet and critic. The reference helps to date MS; see Introduction, p. xxviii.

18:18 **Count it.**   Cf. *Sons and Lovers*, ed. Baron and Baron: 'Friday night was reckoning night for the miners. Morel "reckoned"—shared up the money of the stall—either in the New Inn at Bretty, or in his own house, according as his fellow butties wished ... It was decorum for the women to absent themselves while the men reckoned' (234:22–33).

18:31 **Dixon**   Cf. the Eastwood doctor, Francis Dixon of Church Street.

19:27 **Onoto.** The Onoto pen, made by Thomas De La Rue & Co., Ltd, was the first plunger-filled fountain pen; it excited much comment when it was first produced towards the end of the nineteenth century.

19:39 *"butty"*, The 'butty' or 'butty collier' – a 'mining contractor' – was in charge (often with one or two other butties) of a small team working a 'stall' – a section of the coal-face – in the nineteenth-century and early twentieth-century pit. He was paid directly by the company for the weight of coal produced by his stall, and distributed the wages to his team (the day men). Cf. *Sons and Lovers*, ed. Baron and Baron:

> A butty is a contractor. Two or three butties are given a certain length along a seam of coal, which they are to mine forward to a certain distance. They were paid something like 3/4 [i.e. three shillings and four pence] for every ton of coal they turned out. Out of this, they had to pay the men, holers and loaders, whom they hired by the day, and also for tools, powder, and so on. (26:5–10)

See also *The Daughter-in-Law*, note on 305:30; A. R. Griffin, *Mining in the East Midlands 1550–1947* (1971), pp. 32–3, and *The Miners of Nottinghamshire, 1818–1914* (Nottingham, 1956), p. 138; Roy Spencer, *D. H. Lawrence Country: A Portrait of His Early Life and Background with Illustrations, Maps and Guides* (1979), pp. 57–9.

20:8 *Ready Reckoner,* A book of mathematical tables to facilitate simple calculations; especially useful in the days of 12 pence to the shilling and 20 shillings to the pound. See 'A note on pounds, shillings and pence'.

21:20 **Grieg** Edvard Grieg (1843–1907), Norwegian composer.

21:22 **'The Maiden's Prayer'?** Piano piece by the Polish composer Tekla Badarzewska-Baranowska (1838–61), published under the French title 'La Prière d'une Vierge' (1856), sung and played by 'the whole world'. Cf. DHL in 'Nottingham and the Mining Countryside':

> The human soul needs actual beauty even more than bread. The middle classes jeer at the colliers for buying pianos—but what is the piano, often as not, but a blind reaching out for beauty. To the woman it is a possession and a piece of furniture and something to feel superior about. But see the elderly colliers trying to learn to play, see them listening with queer alert faces to their daughter's execution of *The Maiden's Prayer*, and you will see a blind, unsatisfied craving for beauty. (*Phoenix*, p. 138)

21:35 *the miner's banging* DHL first wrote (MS, p. [39]) 'sound of the heavy stumbling of the miner's through'; he then deleted 'heavy stumbling' and inserted 'banging' but did not cross out the first 'of the'; this has been emended.

22:8 *husband* In MS, DHL wrote 'fat husband'; he then deleted 'fat' (p. [39]).

22:21 **club to pay,** I.e. the so-called club (or insurance scheme) to which many miners subscribed a weekly amount ('club-money'), for sick-pay or payment during unemployment, etc., before either the company or the state made such provision.

22:25 **the Tunns** Cf. The Three Tuns (or Tunns) Inn, public house in Eastwood close to the Lawrences' family house in Walker Street; see *The White Peacock*, ed. Robertson, 35:14.

22:36 *Norfolk costume:* A loosely fitting country or sporting suit; the jacket has a waistband and the trousers are knee-breeches. In *Sons and Lovers* Paul Morel wears a 'norfolk suit' (ed. Baron and Baron, 119:12).

22:37 *Grieg's 'Anitra's Tanz' and then 'Åse's Tod'* Two parts of the well-known *Peer Gynt* music (1876, 1888): 'Anitra's Dance' and 'Aase's Death'. Grieg's music was usually published in Germany, hence the German titles.

24:11 **Cornell's** Cf. Frederick Cornell's Provision Dealer's business, Nottingham Road, Eastwood's main shopping street.

25:23 **little Margaret?** A reference to the daughter Margaret Emily (b. 9 February 1909) of DHL's elder sister, Emily Una (1882–1962), and her husband, Samuel Taylor King (1880–1965). 'I suppose Emma & Joe are my parents in the play. As a matter of interest my Mother's name was Emily & my Father had a brother called Joe. "The lads" referred to [see 25:32] would be the sons of George Lawrence [1876–1967]. Their real names were Ernest [1897–1972] & Arthur [1900–74]' (Margaret Needham, letter to eds., 30 April 1984). The mention of Christmas helps place the action in November; see note on 15:3 and Introduction, p. xxviii.

27:31 **Coll's all foolery and flummery.** See Glossary; and cf. DHL's disenchantment with University College, Nottingham: *Letters*, i. 49, 72; *The Rainbow*, ed. Mark Kinkead-Weekes (Cambridge, 1989), 402:39ff.; E.T. 76–88.

28:40 *a little note book ... Verses.* DHL used at least two Nottingham University College notebooks for drafts and fair copies of his poems (Roberts E317 and E320.1). See next note.

29:32 **the almond tree ... 'A Life History' 's – best.** DHL originally wrote 'this about the cherries' (MS, p. [57]), then crossed out 'cherries' and substituted 'almond tree'. He had written poems about cherries by December 1908 and January 1909 ('Song: Up in the high swinging cherry-tree' and 'Cherry Robbers'); poems on almond blossom and 'A Life History' date from April and November 1909 respectively ('Letters from Town. The Almond Tree' and 'A Life History in Harmonies and Discords'). Drafts appear in DHL's University College notebooks (see note on 28:40). Cf. *Early Years* 274–6, 480–1, 495–9.

30:12 **diary in French?** Cf. Jessie Chambers's account, to some extent a summary of the second act of the play:

> he had started giving me French lessons ... It was arranged that I should call at his home for my French lesson on Friday evenings as I returned from the Centre. Friday was the night when the little market was held in the open space in front of the Sun Inn, and we were often left alone while Mrs. Lawrence went to the market. The father I rarely saw. He was always out in the evenings.
>
> We talked of many things besides French once the door was closed and there arose the magical sense of being alone together. We tried to find out the differences in our own characters. Lawrence told me that I was high and very deep, whereas he was very broad but comparatively shallow...
>
> Our Friday evening lessons were not always undisturbed. Occasionally, one or other of the girls who drifted so casually in and out of the house would come in and sit watching us quizzically, and the atmosphere would become charged with curious cross-currents of feeling. There was one girl in particular who delighted to create this electric atmosphere. She had a ready wit and a caustic tongue, and her gibes flew like

arrows ... and Lawrence suggested we should each keep a diary in French. He insisted on my keeping one, but I never saw his. I was to put down my *thoughts* (he was emphatic about that) and he would correct and reply in French. He used to ask for my diary each week with a pedagogical air. (E.T. 56–60, 135)

30:33 you drink me up, A recurring image DHL used to describe his relationship with Jessie Chambers. In December 1910 he wrote: '*Muriel* [Jessie] is the girl I have broken with. She loves me to madness, and demands the soul of me ... Nobody can have the soul of me. My mother has had it, and nobody can have it again ... Louie ... would never demand to drink me up and have me' (*Letters*, i. 190–1). See note on 35:28.

31:15 short sighted. Deleted MS reading was 'excited' (p. [61]). Miriam in *Sons and Lovers* is also short-sighted (ed. Baron and Baron, 187:27).

31:18 French verse ... for fourpence. DHL first read poems by Charles Baudelaire (1821–67) and Paul Verlaine (1844–96) during 1909. In 1910 he noted: 'I've got Baudelaire's *Fleurs du Mal* – got them for 9d in Charing Cross Rd on Friday ... They are better than Verlaine' (*Letters*, i. 179). *Les Fleurs du Mal* (1857) contained the poems referred to below.

31:25 Your hair did tickle me. Cf. *Sons and Lovers*, ed. Baron and Baron: 'She bent forward, trying to see and to understand. Her free, fine curls tickled his face. He started as if they had been red hot, shuddering' (247:14–16).

32:2 'Eurent.' [31:34] ... être ... the imperfect. Maggie's first mistake is to have used 'avoir' rather than 'être' with her verb: she has tried to express something like 'Every day, they went out', originally writing (e.g.) 'Chaque jour, ils avaient sorti'. Her second mistake is now to try to correct herself by using the 'passé simple' – what Ernest calls 'the *preterite*' (31:36) – still using 'avoir': 'Chaque jour, ils eurent sorti'. Ernest explains that with a verb of motion such as she has used, the correct auxiliary would have been 'être' but that she should (anyway) have used the imperfect of the main verb and so simply have written 'Chaque jour, ils sortaient'.

32:10 a Saturday child? Cf. the traditional rhyme about birthdays: 'Saturday's child works hard for a living.'

32:20 Francis Thompson's 'Shelley': The essay 'Shelley' by Francis Thompson (1859–1907), poet and essayist, was first published in the *Dublin Review* (July 1908) and as a book early in 1909; DHL sent a copy to Jessie Chambers (E.T. 119): 'Shelley's life frequently exhibits in him the magnified child. It is seen in his fondness for apparently futile amusements, such as the sailing of paper boats. This was, in the truest sense of the word, child-like; not ... childish' (2nd edn 1909, p. 35).

32:24 coloured DHL first wrote 'glib' (MS, p. [64]).

33:15 'Maîtresse des Maîtresses' ... 'le Balcon', Ernest quotes part of the first line of Baudelaire's 'Le Balcon': 'Mère des souvenirs, maîtresse des maîtresses' (Mother of memories, mistress of mistresses).

33:19 like oranges DHL's initial evaluation of the poem's rich imagery read (MS, p. [67]): 'like oranges when they're ripe falling and rolling a little way along a dark carpet, all full of rich colour held on another darker, dark <blue> colour, like twilight ...' Here and elsewhere in the notes, < > denote deletions, ⌈ ⌉insertions.

33:24 the 'Albatross'! Baudelaire's 'L'Albatros'.

34:7 sickenin'? DHL described the girl's mocking and teasing manners in a letter: 'Alice Gall ... and I always talk in the broadest slang; she sits on my knee and makes mocking love to me; she is a delightful little devil' (*Letters*, i. 71).

35:5 too lovly f'r anyfing! 'Too lovely for anything', i.e. marvellous (imitating Cockney).

35:7 *revenant à son mouton)*: DHL's singular modification of 'Revenons à nos moutons' (let us return to our sheep, i.e. let us get back to the subject; French). Cf. *The White Peacock*, ed. Robertson, 29:6.

35:28 the Gypsy Perhaps an allusion to Louie Burrows (1888–1962): ' "my girl" in Coll' and later DHL's fiancée, 'big, and swarthy, and passionate as a gipsy' (*Letters*, i. 190, 193, 343).

35:31 an Erewhonian. Allusion to the anti-utopian novel *Erewhon* (1872) by Samuel Butler (1835–1902).

35:34 'Sigh no more ladies.' See Shakespeare's *Much Ado About Nothing*, II. iii. 62–5:

> Sigh no more, ladies, sigh no more,
> Men were deceivers ever:
> One foot in sea, and one on shore,
> To one thing constant never.

36:16 like an Amazon, Perhaps also a reference to Louie Burrows; DHL once called her 'you lucky young Amazon' (*Letters*, i. 113).

37:12 ennui. Vous m'agacez ... au diable. Boredom. You make me nervous. Go to the devil (French).

39:15 'What the heart doesn't——.' Popular saying: 'What the eye doesn't see, the heart doesn't grieve over.'

39:23 The Staff of Life——! I.e. bread is the staff of life; a biblical allusion and proverbial saying (cf. Ezekiel iv. 16; v. 16; xiv. 13; Psalm cv. 16).

40:3 'adsum' 'I am present' (Latin), usually in answer to a roll call.

41:19 *lighting up)*: DHL first wrote 'lighting up cruelly' (MS, p. [86]).

42:22 She said DHL first wrote 'told me', then crossed out 'told' and wrote 'said' over it, but forgot to delete the 'me' (MS, p. [88]); the sentence has been editorially emended.

44:2 hour ago. DHL failed to indicate that Nellie Lambert leaves the kitchen before Mrs Lambert and Beatrice Wyld begin their confidential talk. A stage direction has been supplied editorially.

44:19 the Old Lad ... that lad Reference to the devil, misinterpreted by the typist of TCCI who wrote 'Old Dad' (Act III, p. 4) ... i.e. Ernest: DHL first wrote '*he*' and then revised it (MS, p. [92]).

48:21 the Ram. Cf. the Ram Inn, public house at Moorgreen, 1 mile e. of

Eastwood, also mentioned and recreated in *The White Peacock*, ed. Robertson, 139:1–11, and Part III, chap. iv, 'Domestic Life at the Ram', pp. 269–78.

50:1 **begrudging** Interlinear revision in MS (p. [106]), replacing 'prowling'.

50:11 **care of it!** The following stage direction has been added editorially; although the father jumps up from his chair at 51:22, there is no stage direction indicating that he has sat down.

50:13 MOTHER DHL originally wrote (MS, p. [107]) 'Matkha' (Matka, Russian for mother).

51:33 **little— —.** MS originally read 'little sniveller?' (p. [111]).

52:38 *a Waterbury watch* A product of the Waterbury Watch Company; a cheap watch for use in the pit, contrasted with the silver watch used on social occasions (see 53:2–3).

54:22 **Frank Brangwyn ... Impressionism,** Frank Brangwyn (1867–1956), decorative painter, whose work *The Orange Market* (1901) DHL knew very well, called 'impressionist' and copied for his sister Ada in December 1910 (*Letters*, i. 196 and n. 4 and n. 5). The 'Exhibition' may be an allusion to the winter exhibition at the Royal Academy in London early in 1909 (cf. *Letters*, i. 113, 115, 120, 124). 'Impressionism' here refers to paintings designed to convey general impressions without necessarily providing detail; it is not a reference to French Impressionism of the late nineteenth century.

54:26 **Pre-Raphaelitism** The shared faith in painting of clarity, precision and honest realism (a realism totally identified with symbolism) of the 'Pre-Raphaelite Brotherhood', started in 1848 by Dante Gabriel Rossetti (1828–82), William Holman Hunt (1827–1910) and John Everett Millais (1829–96). See *Letters*, i. 80, 86; *The White Peacock*, ed. Robertson, pp. 69, 85, 150.

56:16 **Herod's Farm.** DHL's recreation of Haggs Farm, 3 miles n. of Eastwood, where the Chambers family lived until 1910 (cf. also 'Herod's Farm' in *Sons and Lovers*, ed. Baron and Baron, 194:20, a reference to Coneygrey Farm, 1 mile n. of Eastwood).

57:6 *having ... torment him).* Interlinear revision replacing 'and calm reassurance' (MS, p. [125]).

58:38 **The sad history ... shuttlecock—Amen.'** Apparently invented; drawing on the poems 'O my Luve's like a red, red rose' (1794) by Robert Burns (*The Poems and Songs of Robert Burns*, ed. Kinsley, ii. 734–5), and 'Meeting at Night' (1845; 'the two hearts beating each to each') by Robert Browning (1812–89).

58:41 **Weep over it.** Replacing 'Put it in the fire' (MS, p. [130]).

59:2 **And pickle ... German girls do.** Perhaps a reference to the common practice of pressing and drying flowers; English youth apparently (but wrongly) believed that their German equivalent used more advanced technology.

The Widowing of Mrs. Holroyd

61:12 MRS. HOLROYD ... TWO MINERS DHL introduces similar characters to those in his short story 'Odour of Chrysanthemums' (see Introduction) with which the play, especially in Act III, has much in common. He mostly uses different names, but keeps 'Rigley' (with another first name) and 'Lizzie' (or 'Elizabeth') as the first name of the miner's wife. The play includes four new characters: Holroyd, Blackmore, Clara and Laura. See 'Odour of Chrysanthemums', *The Prussian Officer and Other Stories*, ed. John Worthen (Cambridge, 1983), pp. 181–99 and note on 181:1.

63:1 **THE WIDOWING OF MRS. HOLROYD**   The pit referred to in the play is Brinsley colliery, 1 mile n. of Eastwood, where DHL's father Arthur was a miner for many years. DHL's uncle, James Lawrence (b. 1851), was killed underground at Brinsley colliery in February 1880; his widow Polly (1854–95) was left with two children, Sarah Ann (b. 1876) and John (b. 1877); DHL, his brothers and sisters visited her frequently, as they did their paternal grandparents, John (1815–1901) and Louisa (1818–98), and two other aunts, all of whom lived in Brinsley.

DHL remarked upon the real-life background ('Holroyd … was my uncle') which he used again in 'Odour of Chrysanthemums' – 'a story full of my childhood's atmosphere' (*Letters*, i. 199, 471, v. 593); see note on 109:9 below. Photographs of Brinsley colliery are in Harry T. Moore, *The Priest of Love* (New York, 1974), following p. 170; *Early Years* plate 9; Hardy and Harris, *A D. H. Lawrence Album*, p. 23. A photograph of the now-rebuilt cottage of DHL's Aunt Polly appears in Claude M. Sinzelle, *The Geographical Background of the Early Works of D. H. Lawrence* (Paris, 1964), plate 6.

64:4 **electricians, … gentlemen on a mine:**   Changes in coal-mining technique profoundly affected the working conditions of miners in the Eastwood collieries of Barber Walker and Co. during the first two decades of the century. Coal-cutting machines, 'American Cutters' or – as the miners called them – 'iron-men' (307:27) were brought in, 'not only with the object of superseding hand-holing, by the introduction of coal-cutting machines, but also to replace the obsolete steam driven haulages and to reduce the large number of ponies underground and their drivers' (G. C. H. Whitelock, *200 Years in Coal: The History of Barber Walker and Company Limited* (n.p., n.d. [1957]), pp. 44, 47). By January 1910, five of the forty stalls at Brinsley were being worked with the aid of mechanical and electrically powered coal-cutting machines. See Storer 103. The introduction of electricity into the mine also affected lighting, haulage, underground traffic and ventilation. For this period of change see also notes on 307:22, 321:11 and 13, and *WL*, notes on 230:28 and 35.

65:13 **New Inn,**   Public house in Old Brinsley, near DHL's aunt's cottage and his grandparents' house, and close to the other public house mentioned in the play, the Prince of Wales.

66:22 **a dog's-nose**   A drink of beer mixed with whisky, gin or rum, popular in the north of England: Clara explains the meaning at 75:6.

67:27 **Selvidge to selvidge.**   Standard spellings are 'selvage' and 'selvedge'; folding sheets with the hemmed, non-fraying edges of cloth against each other.

67:38 **Bestwood.**   DHL's regular fictional name for Eastwood; cf. *Sons and Lovers*, ed. Baron and Baron, 9:16.

69:26 **uncle John's**   A fictionalisation; DHL's father, Arthur John, was always called Arthur; but cf. John Lawrence, father of Arthur and James.

71:14 **Rest for the weary.** A common saying, based on Job iii. 16–17.

78:2 **points down th' line.** Tapering, movable rails where one railway track joins another.

83:11 **It's him tha cuts thy cloth by,** It's his advice you follow; variation of the proverbial saying 'cut one's coat according to one's cloth', adapt oneself to circumstances.

86:6 **more mark than mar.** Looking worse than it really is.

86:31 **the drawn sword between us.** Very likely a reference to the *Nibelungen-lied*, the German epic poem (*c.* 1200) which was a source of Richard Wagner's opera cycle, *Der Ring des Nibelungen* (1869–76). King Gunther is assisted in the wooing of Queen Brunhild by Siegfried. On the wedding-night Siegfried again has to come to Gunther's rescue and later puts a sword between himself and Brunhild until the husband Gunther takes his place. DHL was familiar with this story through Wagner's adaptation and through Helen Corke (see *The Tresspasser*, ed. Mansfield, Introduction and Appendix 6). He may also have had in mind the medieval romance of Tristram and Iseult, where the sword is again employed as a symbol of chastity; he knew Wagner's 1865 opera *Tristan und Isolde* (*Letters*, i. 140, and *The Trespasser*, ed. Mansfield, Introduction and Appendix 6).

92:18 **Rainsworth ... Mansfield Grammar School ... Berryman's.** Rainsworth is a village about 3 miles s.e. of Mansfield and 12 miles n. of Nottingham ... the Queen Elizabeth's Grammar School for Girls in Mansfield opened in January 1885 ... Berryman was a common local name; DHL uses it in 'The Christening' for a baker in Eastwood (see *The Prussian Officer and Other Stories*, ed. Worthen, 172:17 and n.).

92:37 **My uncle ... a hundred and twenty pounds.** In *The Daughter-in-Law* Minnie also has £120 of saved money (see 352:24–5): approaching a year's salary even for lower-middle-class people.

94:16 **you have to go and steal the baby.** Tinkers and gypsies who called at houses to sell and do repairs (e.g. sharpening knives) were popularly suspected of stealing (see 94:18) small children.

99:34 **He butties** He works as a butty in the same team as; see note on 19:39.

100:32 **the night deputy,** The Deputy Manager underground during the night shift, responsible for safety.

101:4 **Union-pay, and sick-pay** Money paid out of funds of the trades union and the workmen's clubs (benefit societies and sick-clubs) in cases of illness or accident; see too note on 22:21.

101:17 *fan engine ... driving engine ... skirr of brakes on the rope* The ventilation system of the mine ... the engine which draws the cage or chair with men or wagons up and down (see 101:18) ... sound of the brakes being applied to the winding cable.

101:31 **It's an ill wind brings no good.** Variation of the saying 'It's an ill wind that blows nobody good', i.e. most events benefit someone.

104:4 **after-damp—** A poisonous gas (also known as choke-damp) formed after the explosion of firedamp (a dangerous combination of air and the methane gas endemic in coal-mines). No explosion has, however, occurred; either DHL or Rigley may therefore actually mean firedamp (methane in a concentrated form can be fatal), or Rigley is using a technical term to divert attention from the actual cause of death.

When revising the play for publication in 1913, DHL considered using 'Afterdamp' as the play's title. He asked his American publisher Kennerley: 'I don't know what you think of the title – *The Widowing of Mrs. Holroyd*. Garnett said it wasn't good. I suggested "Afterdamp" on the last MS., but am by no means keen on it. It would do exceedingly well, in idea, but I don't like the word. I wish it were the German: "Schlagender Wetter"' (*Letters*, ii. 72). The correct German for firedamp would be 'schlagende Wetter': very expressive in German.

The Austrian poetess, novelist and playwright Marie Eugenie delle Grazie (1864–1931) wrote a naturalistic colliery play with the title *Schlagende Wetter* (1899) dealing with the capital-labour conflict; it ends with a mine catastrophe. It is not certain whether DHL knew of this play, but it seems likely.

109:9 **to be smiling.** Cf. DHL in 1910 about Louisa and James Lawrence: 'I heard my Grandmother say, 18 years ago, "Like a blessed smiling babe he looked – he did that"' (*Letters*, i. 199).

110:14 **rods o' trouble,** I.e. 'rods for your own back': they will make you suffer.

110:15 **We** An editorial correction. E1 printed 'Me' (p. 93), which makes no sense in Midlands dialect; and as DHL's handwritten 'W' could fairly easily be misread as 'M', it has been assumed that an error was made either by the typist who – working from DHL's manuscript – produced the now missing typescript which Kennerley used to correct the proofs, or that DHL's handwritten correction was misread at some other stage (see Introduction, pp. xxxix–xli).

The Merry-go-Round

111:18 MRS HEMSTOCK ... PATTY, A GOOSE Some particulars of the Lawrence family appear to have been recreated in the Hemstocks, and some real-life people, names and circumstances appear. Mrs Hemstock's illness can be related to Mrs Lawrence's fatal illness in late 1910 when DHL was working on the play. The real-life Nurse Broadbent was Greasley district nurse in 1910; Nurse Broadbanks of the play, 'some thirty years old', probably also draws upon Florence ('Flossie') Cullen (1879–1924), who nursed Mrs Lawrence (*Letters*, i. 234 and n. 1; *The Lost Girl*, ed. John Worthen, Cambridge, 1981, note on 2:20). Dr Foules is perhaps a recreation of the Eastwood doctor, Duncan Macdonald Forbes (1838–1911).

The Rev. Rodolph Baron von Hube (?1834–1910) was Vicar of Greasley (1866–1907), next to the parish of Eastwood; he died on 23 November 1910, immediately before DHL wrote the play. Von Hube was the son of a Polish nobleman, had fought in an insurrection against the Prussians, became a missionary in South Africa, then returned to Britain and was eventually appointed Vicar of Greasley (see *The Rainbow*, ed. Kinkead-Weekes, note on 49:14). His wife was English. In 1901 he published a history of the parish of Greasley, *Griseleia in Snotinghscire* (Nottingham). He learnt his English late in life and his obituary ('Close of a Romantic Career') remarked that he was 'a man of great natural eloquence and ability, who fought most successfully against the difficulties of language, and, although he laboured under the disadvantage ... of being a foreigner, he was essentially a gentleman, and was widely respected and admired as such' (*Eastwood & Kimberley Advertiser*, 25 November 1910, p. 3). See too DHL's 1908 poem 'The Death of the Baron', stanzas vii–ix:

> He was a soldier once, our fierce little Baron—a Pole
> Fleeing in exile to England at the end of the fight.
> He was a soldier always; in church it was a sight
> To see him flash and tremble with the fire of his soul.

> They are tolling his failure, after all these years, to the tired birds.
> He had hoped to die in the pulpit, to conquer in death.—
> For his mission had cruelly failed, while his passionate foreign breath
> Refused to be moulded in arrows of English words.

> Sunday after Sunday they carried him trembling to his place
> In the pulpit, where, shrivelled and ghastly, in unintelligible speech
> He preached to the stolid farmers, till at last he could preach
> No more, and he lay at home, unutterable despair in his face.

> (*Complete Poems*, ii. 858–9)

113:1 **THE MERRY-GO-ROUND** DHL first experimented with 'The Goose' and then 'Nurse' as titles (MS, p. 1), both heavily crossed out; he then wrote 'The Merry-go-Round—by D H Lawrence.' The title had been used by W. Somerset Maugham (1874–1965) for a novel published in 1904. The right-hand top corner of p. 1 bears the inscription in pencil, not in DHL's hand, 'Ford Maddox [*sic*] Hueffer' (see Introduction).

113:33 **as snug as a bug in a rug.** Very comfortable.

114:13 **nine** DHL wrote 'five' and then 'nine' over it in MS (p. 3), but the typist of TSI misread the word as 'five' (p. 3).

114:23 **Jonah back-ards.** I.e. Jonah in reverse; see Jonah i. 17: 'Now the Lord had prepared a great fish to swallow up Jonah. And Jonah was in the belly of the fish three days and three nights.'

115:27 **'ae'-porth,** A more common colloquial form is ha'porth (half-penny-worth); DHL's phonetic rendering of the dialect here and elsewhere caused problems for his copyists and typesetters. See Glossary.

115:29 **talk the leg off an iron pot,** Talk non-stop.

116:25 **on strike.** Eastwood miners were on strike from June to November 1910.

117:32 **fourteen stone** About 89 kilograms; a stone is 14 pounds or 6.35 kilograms.

118:6 **doctor and Mr Leaky.** A recreation of Charles J. Leakey, assistant to the two Eastwood doctors, Duncan Macdonald Forbes (see note on 111:18) and Francis Dixon (see note on 18:31).

118:26 **Northrop** Phonetic variant of Newthorpe, part of Greasley parish; see note on 111:18.

120:21 **like butter ... away in** Deleted MS reading (p. 16): 'till he feels like a pearl-button swimmin' to nowt in'; DHL failed to remove the 'in', now editorially emended.

121:19 **I wish—I wish** DHL may perhaps have duplicated the words unintentionally when starting a new page (MS, pp. 18–19), but they have been retained.

122:18 **Foules.** See note on 111:18. DHL first wrote 'MacCleod', but wrote 'Foules' over it (MS, p. 20). He may have been thinking of his close friend, Arthur McLeod (1885–1956), a fellow teacher at Davidson Road School, Croydon.

123:25 **the Baron von Ruge,** In MS (p. 22) DHL used the Baron's real name 'von Hube' for the first and only time; it has been emended in accordance with his majority usage.

124:36 **your eye ... a look.** Being uncompromising; cf. Exodus xxi. 24 ('Eye for eye, tooth for tooth').

125:2 *Old* **Harry.** The devil.

125:36 *(Enter* SUSY, DHL wrote '(enter Susy,' in MS (p. 27) but deleted '(enter', which has been restored.

126:5 **in th' parsley bed ... find** *babies* Cf. the story told to little children, to explain their origins, that they were 'found in the parsley bed'.

126:10 **There's a ... about thee—!** Deleted in MS: 'Luthee at the helpless widder—!' (p. 28).

128:22 **Vox, et ... nothing more.'** Latin axiom originally applying to the nightingale. DHL's spelling has been corrected. The large number of sayings and quotations in the play may suggest that DHL made use of a dictionary; e.g. the appendix 'Words and Phrases in More or Less Current Use from Latin, Greek, and Modern Foreign Languages', *Chambers's English Dictionary* (1898).

128:31 **Damnosa quid ... time impaired.'** Horace, *Carmina*, III. vi. 45, usually translated as 'what does not destructive time destroy?' (Latin)

128:33 **Suum Cuique.** 'To every man his due, to each his own'. (Latin)

128:39 **Verbum sat sapienti.** 'Verbum sapienti sat est' – a word to the wise is enough. (Latin)

129:7 **Rem acu ... your needle.'** More accurately: 'you have touched the thing with a needle, hit it directly'. (Latin)

129:10 **Semper idem** 'Always the same'. (Latin)

129:25 **Quid rides?** Horace, *Satires*, I. i. 69.

131:5 **he used ter court Nurse!** Replacing 'him being Nurse's old fellow!' in MS (p. 37 [38]).

135:30 **"Dilly-Dilly ... be killed.'** From the nursery rhyme 'Dilly Dilly':

> Oh, what have you got for dinner, Mrs Bond?
> There's beef in the larder, and ducks in the pond;
> Dilly, dilly, dilly, dilly, come to be killed,
> For you must be stuffed and my customers filled!

136:30 **'You've [136:21] ... Oh Ho."'** Popular music-hall comic song by F. W. Carter and A. J. Mills.

139:9 **the taste ... mouth into.** DHL first wrote 'in when tha's done kissin' somebody clse.' in MS (p. 54 [55]).

142:27 **bug** The dialect word (conceited, vain, stuck up) was deleted in pencil and replaced by 'big' in MS (p. 59 [61]) in an unknown hand, probably when it was first being copied in London; TSI adopts the change. See also TA entry at 152:8 for another alteration also made in pencil (MS, p. 76 [78]).

143:39 **faces of brass.** Shamelessness, impudence.

144:35 **the boughs ... arms of God.** Suggests Deuteronomy xxxiii. 27 and v. 15, Exodus vi. 6 and Isaiah lii. 10. The Baron does not in general use exact quotations, but recalls biblical texts in a pseudo-biblical style.

145:18 **I keep ... this stick.** Deleted MS reading was 'Let go my wrists, wretch, are you a man to fight thus?' (p. 65 [67]).

145:22 **If I ... were killed.** Deleted MS reading was 'Let go my wrists, foul, base fighter.' (p. 65 [67]).

151:36 **savation.** I.e. 'saving' in the Baroness's inaccurate English.

152:6 *(Conning)* Perusing, poring over; misread in TSI as 'counting' (p. 56).

152:14 *cries on the Lord in German.)* 'Oh Gott' or 'Mein Gott' (Oh God, my God).

152:31 **The power of evil is strong,** Perhaps alluding to Genesis viii. 21.

152:39 **cloak of mercy** Psalm xxxii. 1.

153:5 **pull us down ... the land—?** Psalm lxxix. 7, Isaiah i. 7.

153:9 **Throttle-ha'penny'.** I.e. the Baroness's thin throat; the local name for the small colliery at Hill Top, Eastwood (see *The Lost Girl*, ed. Worthen, note on 17:33).

153:15 **Under the sword ... find wisdom.** Cf. Psalm cxi. 10 (*Book of Common Prayer*).

153:32 **my father** DHL first wrote 'Tom Beardsall' and then deleted it (MS, p. 79 [81]). Beardsall was DHL's mother's maiden name, used for the main characters in *The White Peacock*.

155:12 **By gum ... begin of.** Deleted in MS: 'You don't flatter the men, Baroness. They must be proud of what they've made.' (p. 82 [84]).

155:36 **parish of Greenway** DHL uses two different names to recreate Greasley: Greenway and Greenstone (see 180:4).

156:16 **Greenhills** I.e. Greenhills Road, Eastwood.

157:40 **say anything.** In MS, originally followed by 'Their throats are full of untruth like a bird's crop, Baron.' (p. 88 [90]); cf. 158:6–7.

162:8 **chapel-going ... church** Common distinction between nonconformists and those attending the Church of England.

163:12 **'Ora pro Nobis'** Pray for us (Latin).

163:13 **'Gentle Annie'?** Mid-nineteenth-century love-song ('Thou wilt come no more, Gentle Annie') by the American songwriter Stephen Foster (1826–64); see ' "Burns Novel" fragments', *Love Among the Haystacks*, ed. Worthen, 208:38.

163:17 *'What are the Wild Waves Saying'.* Popular Victorian duet (1850) by

Stephen Glover and J. E. Carpenter, inspired by Charles Dickens's *Dombey and Son* (1846–8); see *Letters*, ii. 62 and n. 2.

> What are the wild waves saying,
>   Sister, the whole day long,
> That ever amid our playing
>   I hear but their low lone song? . . .
>
> Brother, I hear no singing!
>   'Tis but the rolling wave,
> Ever its lone course winging
>   Over some ocean cave! . . .

163:18 *'lamentoso'.)*   Expressing sorrow, mournfully (Italian).

163:24 'Music when ... the memory.'   'To —' (1821) by Percy Bysshe Shelley (1792–1822), ll. 1–2.

163:30 'By rapture's ... artless lay.'   An invented 'quotation' using elements of other poetry: thirteen poems in English contain the phrase 'artless lay'.

164:7 'For pity ... to love—'   From 'Alexander's Feast' (1697) by John Dryden (1631–1700), l. 6.

164:23 Pears Soap ... gets it'   One of the most famous and successful advertisements of the late nineteenth century showed a baby leaning out of his shallow bath tub in order to reach a cake of Pears' Transparent Soap; see *Letters*, i. 252 and n. 3, 269.

165:25 the light ... a bushel.   Concealed; cf. the proverb 'to hide one's light under a bushel', to conceal one's merits.

165:26 'Blown to ... breath of—'   An invented 'quotation' using elements of other poetry: eight poems in English contain the phrase 'awful breath', and l. 191 of 'Pompilia' (in *The Ring and the Book*, 1868–9) by Robert Browning (1812–89) starts 'Blown to a . . .'.

166:17 I have avoided ... the 'Matrimonial Post.'   I.e. not yet appeared in the marriage announcements in the newspaper.

166:18 It never ... it pours.   The proverbial saying replaced 'Life, in short.' in MS (p. 104 [106]).

166:20 The third time ... they say.   Proverbial: third time lucky. Deleted in MS: 'I am glad to make its acquaintance.' (p. 104 [106]).

166:21 I will tell you tomorrow.   DHL originally wrote 'I think we are fairly representative.' (MS, p. 104 [106]).

168:8 'Er bites ... her face.   Cf. 'to cut off one's nose to spite one's face': taking revenge but simultaneously hurting oneself.

168:33 the quiet vessels are the full ones.   I.e. reliable; cf. the proverb 'empty vessels make the most noise'.

170:25 pair of breeches on a clothesline   I.e. would take any sort of man. Deleted in MS: 'scarecrow in a field' (p. 111 [114]).

173:39 driving engines   The winding engines at the pit-head.

174:20 Tha hasna ... boot-tops.   You've taken practically no interest yourself.

175:8 *front room.)*   The next line (deleted by DHL) originally read '(Curtain for a minute, or two)' (MS, p. 119 [123]).

177:11 **lap at a full saucer.**   Deleted in MS: 'slide into a warm place.' (p. 123 [127]).

177:27 **And now ... you've been.**   DHL first wrote 'I'm here—an' she can wait.' (MS, p. 124 [128]).

178:7 **If I say 'snip' ... Snip?**   To say snip to another's snap: to accept readily an offer of marriage; with perhaps a reference to the card-game, snap.

178:28 **Derby.**   A city 10½ miles s.w. of Eastwood.

181:29 **my ewe lamb**   My most cherished possession, cf. 2 Samuel xii.1–6.

182:38 **the mote ... the church,**   Cf. Matthew vii. 3.

183:4 **You died ... shoes on.**   If the worst comes to the worst; perhaps combining the phrases 'die in a ditch' and 'die with one's boots on'.

183:6 **a pound of flesh ... cut judiciously.**   Cf. Shakespeare's *The Merchant of Venice*, IV. i. 228–9.

185:2 **I've built my house on the sand.**   I've been improvident; see Matthew vii. 26–7.

187:10 **Methodist's**   Deleted in MS: 'Wesleyan' (p. 140 [144]).

188:12 **All's fair in love and war,**   Proverbial: any method is allowed.

189:19 **Hude—?**   Deleted in MS: 'Huge' (p. 145 [149]), both suggesting Mr Wilcox's mockery of the Baron's name.

190:14 **play Duke to our 'As You Like It'.**   The final act of Shakespeare's play ends with marriages overseen by the Duke. DHL taught the play at his Croydon school early in 1911 (cf. *Letters*, i. 242, 245, 247).

The Married Man

191:14 DR GEORGE GRAINGER ... ETHEL, GRAINGER'S WIFE   Dr George Grainger is modelled on DHL's early and close friend, George Henry Neville (1886–1959): their friendship began in 1893, and they attended Nottingham High School together; both became teachers. DHL visited Neville at Bradnop near Leek in Staffordshire between 25 and 31 March 1912 (*Letters*, i. 373 and n. 4, 374, 377, 379, 386). Cf. also Neville, *A Memoir*, pp. 38ff. and E.T. 206–8; Gilbert Noon of Part 1 of DHL's novel, *Mr Noon*, is partly based on Neville, and Leslie Tempest in *The White Peacock* has some of his characteristics. Grainger's wife and son are given the first names of their real-life originals (see note on 206:15).

William ('Billy') Brentnall is based on DHL himself; his family nicknames included 'William' and 'Billy' (*Early Years* 55, 279 and 551).

Elsa Smith is a recreation of Frieda Weekley, née von Richthofen (1879–1956), whom DHL had met shortly before writing the play; she had an elder sister Else (1874–1973) and a daughter named Elsa (1902–85). See notes on 237:9 and 251:39.

Mrs Plum is based on Mrs Plumb, Neville's landlady at Bradnop; the Magneer family is to some extent based on Mrs and Mr Titterton (see *Letters*, i. 377).

193:1 **THE MARRIED MAN**   The first five pages of MS are missing. The first surviving page is numbered '6' in DHL's hand; it has a note in pencil '? MARRIED MAN'.

193:5 Bring me some collars up.　The setting, characters and action in the missing pages of MS can only be guessed at. According to the initial stage direction of Act IV, the setting is a bedroom in Mrs Plum's cottage. Dr Grainger has been staying there for some time. Brentnall is Grainger's friend, visiting and staying overnight in the same room. When Mrs Plum enters she refers to a conversation with Grainger, presumably about his family situation. Brentnall and Grainger are discussing Grainger's future because his stay as a doctor's locum has come to an end. The action takes place on two successive days.

194:16 Wolverhampton.　Town in Staffordshire, about 12 miles n.w. of Birmingham; Neville met and married his wife in Stourbridge, also in Staffs., about 10 miles w. of Birmingham.

195:4 a gay bachelor.　Cf. DHL on Neville: 'His wife is with her parents in Stourbridge . . . He lives "en bachelier". Which is quite a story!' (*Letters*, i. 379).

195:37 *fine*　In MS (p. 10) DHL replaced 'pretty' by 'real fine' (195:36) and '*pretty*' by 'fine'; he did not underline the word but the original stress has been retained editorially.

196:16 Thanks for your caution, Mr Magneer.　DHL originally wrote 'You caution me, Mr Magneer?' (MS, p. 11); in revision he failed to delete the question mark, which has been emended editorially.

196:33 Ashbourne.　Town in Derbyshire, about 25 miles n.w. of Nottingham.

197:5 *Parma violets*,　A variety of especially sweet-smelling violet with pale-blue double flowers; worn as decoration, often suggesting an aspiration towards superiority and ladylike refinement.

197:13 Emily . . . Ada　DHL uses his own sisters' first names.

200:26 a poem about a couch . . . Cowper　The long reflective poem 'The Task' (1785) by William Cowper (1731–1800); Book I is entitled 'The Sofa' ('I sing the sofa . . .').

201:25 Wherein must . . . To run away,　The original MS reading (p. 19) was 'Unto what must . . . A little back-bone,'.

201:26 Annie!　This line originally read 'He must help you along, I think' (MS, p. 19); the following line originally read 'To come to the scratch, I should say'.

201:31 Mine!　Deleted MS reading (p. 19) was 'Got none.'

202:26 *sotto voce*　'In a low or soft voice' (Italian).

202:32 Dog in the manger.　Proverbial from Aesop: people begrudge others what they cannot enjoy themselves.

204:14 mine's pistols.　Jocular version of a reply to a challenge to a duel; the person challenged chooses the weapons.

206:15 January . . . March . . . June.　DHL originally wrote 'November . . . January . . . April' (MS, p. 27), using the actual months of Neville's marriage to Ethel Gertrude Piper on 4 November 1911, the birth of their son James in January 1912 and the writing of the play in April 1912.

207:7 **whistles quickly a private call**   Cf. Neville, *A Memoir*, p. 42: 'If I reached the fields before meeting him, our old High School whistle call ... prevented us from missing each other in the darkness'.

208:30 **Billy's ... convalescent,**   On his visit to Bradnop in March 1912, DHL was still recovering from pneumonia.

208:34 **thing!**   Replaced 'scoundrel' (MS, p. 31).

209:16 **running the rig**   See Glossary, and cf. *Letters*, i. 377, with DHL's report of his and Neville's activities and his remark that Jack Titterton (recreated as Jack Magneer in the play) 'runs the rig in Leek occasionally'.

212:4 **crib,**   Cribbage, a game of cards; discarded cards form the 'crib' of 212:12; the game is scored with wooden pegs on a board (see 213:10).

212:31 **Take your ... love lies.**   Proverbial: If you feel sorrow, don't tell your enemy.

216:1 **Waltz valeta—**   Ballroom round dance of English origin in waltz time.

225:18 **what a ... ingratitude!'**   Proverbial: ingratitude is the worst of all vices.

226:1 **"On the banks of Allan Water".**   Traditional Scottish song, well-known throughout the late-Victorian period, telling a tragic love story; words by M. G. ('Monk') Lewis (1775–1818).

226:2 ETHEL   DHL first wrote 'Ethel, with the baby', then deleted 'with the baby' (MS, p. 57).

227:36 **your friend, Mrs Grainger.**   DHL never met Neville's wife; cf. Neville, *A Memoir*, p. 31.

231:13 **Knabe, Knabe ... Gott sei dank ... Ja!**   Boy, boy, where are you? ... thank goodness you have come. Come upstairs ... Yes! (German).

231:36 **Will Hobson**   Probably a reference to the Nottingham lace manufacturer, Will Dowson (1864–1934), who had an affair with Frieda Weekley and took her out in his motor car (cf. *Early Years* 379, 565 n. 28).

233:28 **He**   DHL first wrote 'Ne', most probably for Neville, deleted it and substituted 'He' (MS, p. 69).

The Fight for Barbara

237:9 JIMMY WESSON ... DR FREDERICK TRESSIDER   Although the characters' names are fictional, characters and action are thoroughly autobiographical; see Introduction, pp. xxxiii–xxxiv and DHL's letters of March to December 1912 (*Letters*, i.); *"Not I, But the Wind ..."* and *Memoirs*; *Mr Noon*, ed. Vasey; and Nehls, i. 180–3, 561 nn. 29–34.

Jimmy Wesson is modelled on DHL, and Barbara Tressider on Frieda Weekley. Her name in the play echoes that of her younger daughter Barbara Joy ('Barby') (1904–98).

Lady Charlcote is modelled on Frieda's mother, the Baronin Anna von Richthofen (1851–1930); the visit in the play to Barbara and Wesson is drawn from real life: see *Letters*, i. 429–30. Sir William Charlcote is a recreation of Baron Friedrich von Richthofen (1845–1915), Frieda's father, an officer in the Prussian army and later garrison administrative officer in Metz. DHL met him in early May 1912; cf. Frieda's recollection: 'He met my father only once, at our house. They looked at each other fiercely – my father, the pure aristocrat, Lawrence, the miner's son. My father, hostile, offered a cigarette to Lawrence' (*"Not I, But the Wind ..."* 26).

Frederick Tressider is based on Ernest Weekley (1865–1954), etymologist and Professor of Modern Languages at University College, Nottingham, and husband of Frieda; DHL attended his lectures as a student. DHL spelled the name both 'Tressidder' (MS, pp. 5, 21) and 'Tressider' (MS, pp. 28 [28B], 35); the latter form (arguably a revision) has been adopted.

239:1 **THE FIGHT FOR BARBARA**   In MS (p. 1) DHL wrote: 'The Fight for Barbara/A Comedy by D. H. Lawrence'. The title was altered for the periodical publication in 1933 to 'Keeping Barbara'; see Introduction, p. xci.

239:6 *Scene: The kitchen ... fornello ... hanging up.*   The setting is similar to the flat in the Villa Igéa at Villa di Gargnano on the Lago di Garda in Italy, where Frieda and DHL moved on 18 September 1912. Cf. *Letters*, i. 457–8: 'We're settled in a lovely flat, looking at the lake ... And in the kitchen there's a great open fireplace, then two little things called fornelli – charcoal braziers – and we've got lots of lovely copper pans, so bright. Then I light the fornello and we cook.' Frieda recalled: 'At Gargnano we found Villa Igea to spend the winter. Lawrence for the first time had a place of his own. The first floor of a large villa, our windows looking over the lake, the road running underneath, opposite us the Monte Baldo in rosy sunsets ... that big bare kitchen with the "fornelli" and the big copper pans' (*"Not I, But the Wind ..."* 73). DHL first wrote 'with two' in MS (p. 1) thinking of the two fornelli, but then changed the description to 'with a little charcoal grate'. See also *Letters*, i. 453, 456–8, 475; *Memoirs* 96.

239:10 *about twenty six,*   DHL's age in the summer of 1912.

239:15 **Questa?**   'This one?' (Italian). See *Letters*, i. 450, 464, 474 and 483 for details of DHL and Frieda learning Italian.

239:20 **Abondante misura** [239:17] ... **Come ... latte ... Si!**   Plentiful, good measure [abbondante] ... What, what did you say ... Milk ... Yes! ['Sì'] (Italian).

239:24 **Vous apprenez ... inglese—!**   You are learning English – you – English – ! (French, Italian).

239:26 **non—niente ... fa tempo cattivo!**   Not – no, not English at all ... (it is) bad, wretched, unpleasant weather! (Italian).

239:32 **giorno—che giorno ... Oggi?—domenica.**   The day – what day is it ['che giorno è oggi'] ... 'Today? – Sunday' (Italian).

240:2 **Domenica! ... Sonntag**   (Italian, French, German).

240:7 **Buon giorno, Signore.**   'Good morning, Sir' (Italian).

240:10 *'Put me among the girls'*   Music-hall song by C. W. Murphy, music by Dan Lipton, first performed by Charles R. Whittle in 1907: 'Put me amongst the girls! / Put me amongst the girls! / Do me a favour, do, / You know I'd do as much for you. / Put me amongst the girls, / Those with the curly curls; / They'll enjoy themselves and *so will I*, / If you put me amongst the girls.' Cf. *Sons and Lovers*, ed.

Baron and Baron, 391:38 and note; Paul Morel whistles the song.

In Frieda's hand in pencil (MS, p. 2), there is an interpolation after 'whistle:': 'Du schönes Fischer-', suggesting 'Du schönes Fischermädchen' ('You beautiful fishergirl'), a poem (1824) by the Romantic poet Heinrich Heine (1797–1856), set to music (D957 no. 10) by Franz Schubert (1797–1828).

240:13 **rather fine young woman,** These words are crossed out in pencil, probably by Frieda (MS, p. 2).

240:15 BARBARA In MS (p. 2) 'smiling' has been inserted between the character's name and the dialogue; another addition by Frieda.

240:16 **Giacometti.** Barbara creates an affectionate form of 'Giacomo', the Italian for James; the correct form would be Giacomino (Jimmy).

241:22 **a hundred and twenty a year,** When DHL started work as a teacher in Croydon he earned £95 a year (see *Letters*, i. 79–80); later he thought that '£120 a year income' (ibid., 223) or rather an 'assured income of £150' (ibid., 293) was necessary for marriage. He and Frieda lived on far less: see, e.g., *Letters*, i. 390, 401, 424, 430, 453, and *"Not I, But the Wind ..."* 53: 'We had very little money, about fifteen shillings a week.'

241:30 **clean it.** See *"Not I, But the Wind ..."* 73, for an account of Frieda's attempts at housekeeping.

242:17 **Johnny used ... his own.** Unidentified.

242:26 **butty collier** See note on 19:39.

242:28 **breakfast ready.** Cf. *Letters*, i. 466: 'I generally get up about 8.0 and make breakfast ...'

242:31 **Apollo Belvedere.** A Roman copy of a celebrated Greek statue, in the Vatican Museum, Rome. Apollo, Graeco-Roman deity of the sun, of music, poetry, healing, light and youth, is usually represented in art as a handsome young man. Cf. 'New Eve and Old Adam': 'He loved that dearly, to feel the ... touch-touch of her finger-tips making his hair, as she said, like an Apollo's': (*Love Among the Haystacks*, ed. Worthen, 182:12–14).

242:36 **Antinous ... Endymion** Beautiful youths: Antinous, one of the Roman Emperor Hadrian's favourites, was deified after his death; in Greek mythology, Endymion was loved by the moon goddess, Selene.

243:3 **Pimlico ... Bloomsbury,** Pimlico, then a poor district in the City of Westminster, situated between Victoria and the river Thames ... Bloomsbury, the residential and academic area around the British Museum, then associated with artists and literati (cf. later Bloomsbury Group).

243:13 **mio,** My (Italian).

243:15 **six weeks ... three months** For the real-life dates, see Chronology. 'Six weeks' is equivalent to the period between DHL and Frieda settling in the Villa Igéa and DHL writing the play at the end of October 1912.

243:24 **teenty ... scroddy** See Glossary, and cf. 'tinty' as used by Frieda (*Letters*, i. 439 and n. 2) when apparently imitating DHL's pronunciation. See too 'The Miner at Home' (1912; *Love Among the Haystacks*, ed. Worthen, 126:25 and note) and from October 1912, *Letters*, i. 463; cf. *OED2*.

244:2 **Selma ... chocolate.** Frieda's father had a mistress called Selma who probably had an illegitimate son (cf. 244:9); see *Early Years* 374, 564 n. 10. In *Mr Noon* the Baron has a mistress named Elena, an illegitimate son and is a gambler (ed. Vasey, pp. 179, 180, 215). Wesson puns on a then well-known brand of Swiss chocolate ('Velma Suchard').

244:29 **Anna ... Maud ... despised.** Perhaps referring to Frieda's two sisters Else and Johanna (1882–1971); each had a troubled marriage.

245:1 **from my good [244:33] ... pretty roughly.** See Introduction, p. xxxiv, n. 31; revised in MS (p. 5) from:

> Barbara: ... have run away with the son of a coal-miner, on the eve of my wedding.
> Wesson: The right worthy Frederick Walker, doctor of medicine
> Barbara: And gentleman of means.
> Wesson: —And old stager of thirty nine—
> Barbara: But handsome, oh handsome
> Wesson: And wooden, oh wooden
> Barbara: And esteemed—oh, esteemed up to heaven
> Wesson: You'd have to steam a long time at that pudding before it riz.

246:6 **such a highly esteemed man,** The insertion 'so well known' in pencil in MS (p. 6), most probably in Frieda's hand, was apparently meant to replace DHL's phrase.

246:8 **Think, I was married [245:36] ... And we'd only** See Introduction, p. xxxiv, n. 31; heavily revised in MS (p. 6) from:

> Barbara: Think, I was engaged to him for eighteen months, and I was no nearer to him than I am to that fornello. He used to have me on his knee, and kiss me, and I thought it was very nice—but as for touching me not a bit, not a bit.
> Wesson: Poor devil—it wasn't his fault.
> Barbara: Yes, I have treated him badly.
> Wesson: You might have done worse by marrying him.
> Barbara: But think—a week before the wedding—everything ordered—and since I am with you I know how he must have been suffering, waiting for me—
> Wesson: Fancy we'd only known each other three weeks.

See *Memoirs* 73–4 for Frieda's account of Weekley's awkwardness when close to her.

246:10 **bring it off.** Cf. *Letters*, i. 498, where Frieda writes: '... we are *really* happy; though we fight like blazes, we shall bring it off – '; i.e. succeed.

246:34 **cat ... swallow a camel.** Probably a pun on 'cat' and 'gnat'; see Matthew xxiii. 24 ('Ye blind guides, which strain at a gnat, and swallow a camel.').

246:36 **Didon dina ... dindon.** A well-known tongue-twister used in classroom drill by students of French, also quoted in 'Study of Thomas Hardy' (1914), *Hardy*, 11:10 and note.

247:6 **the lean Kine of Egypt.** See Genesis xli. 1–4, 17–21 ('And the ill favoured and leanfleshed kine did eat up the seven well favoured and fat kine').

247:8 **divorce me?** See *Letters*, i. 401ff. Weekley divorced Frieda on 27 April 1914, and she and DHL married on 13 July 1914.

247:20 **But do** [247:8] ... **a loop-hole** MS (p. 7) is extensively revised. The deleted text read:

> Barbara: You know I don't believe it's a proper marriage, so I can leave you.
> Wesson: I do wish you'd let me go to the Consul in Brescia.
> Barbara: No dear—no—I'm frightened—we're married enough for Italy, at any rate.
> Wesson: We're married according to the civil law of France, that's all. And we neither of us feel it's very sure, either.
> Barbara: But it'll do, Giacomo—it'll do.
> Wesson: If you really loved me, Barbara, you'd want me to make sure it's right. But you're *afraid* of loving me. You want to leave a loop-hole open by which you could creep out and go back, don't you?—Ah, you do.

248:37 **signora ... Piove ... Si ... e il lago—?** Madam ... Is it raining ... Yes ... and the lake—? (Italian).

248:39 **È burrascoso ... tempo cattivo per voi.** It is stormy ... bad weather for you (Italian).

249:6 **ha vitello ... quanto ... Mezzo Chilo ... Grazia** Does he have any veal ... how much ... Half a kilo ... Thanks ['grazie'] (Italian).

250:19 **the one and only phœnix.** Cf. *"Not I, But the Wind ..."* 73: 'When Lawrence found me all misery he called: "The One and Only (which name stood for the one and only phoenix, when I was uppish) is drowning, oh, dear!"'

250:36 **'La Posta' ... serpent ... Eden.** 'The post'. (Italian) See *Memoirs* 96: '"*La posta*," rang from the gate the deep voice of the Italian postman that they liked so much' ... See Genesis ii. 8 and iii; cf. too *"Not I, But the Wind ..."* 58: 'Then again we would be thrown out of our paradisial state. Letters would come.' The arriving mail ('storms', 'a cyclone' or 'yards and yards and yards' of letters) regularly caused disturbance and passionate scenes. See *"Not I, But the Wind ..."* 25, 78; *Memoirs* 96–7, 178–81; *Letters*, i. 420–2, 424.

251:7 **a fool.** The original stage direction after 'fool' – '(They both read the letters – Barbara begins to cry)' – was crossed out by DHL when revising MS (p. 11).

251:34 **Harrogate,** A spa in North Yorkshire.

251:39 **February the 24th,** In 1912, a Saturday; if an autobiographical reference, it may denote some significant date in the relationship between Frieda, Weekley and DHL. It does not establish the date for the first meeting of DHL and Frieda, which apparently occurred on a Sunday early in March 1912 – see *Early Years* 380, 562–3 n. 5; *"Not I, But the Wind ..."* 22–4; and *Letters*, i. 374 n. 4.

252:30 **daggeroso in readiness.** DHL's coinage, 'dagger' with Italian suffix '-oso' (carrying a dagger, inclined or ready to use a dagger); Paul Morel uses the same word in *Sons and Lovers*, ed. Baron and Baron, 390:23 and note.

253:27 **While he ... killing him.** Replacing the earlier MS reading (p. 12): 'you cheapened him in his own eyes—you never established him but you tortured him—as a real man, you almost broke him.'

255:19 **rob Peter to pay Paul,** Proverbial: to take from one person to give to another.

255:38 **I kiss the rod.** Proverbial: to take punishment meekly or gladly; cf. Alexander Pope (1688–1744), 'An Epistle to Dr. Arbuthnot' (1735), l. 158.

256:6 **neither-fish-flesh-fowl ... good-red-herring self.** Proverbial: something strange or partial is neither fish nor flesh, nor good red herring.

258:12 **Till death do us part—** 'Till death us do part'; final line of the marriage vow in *The Book of Common Prayer*.

258:26 *Bavarian peasant dress*, Dirndl, a fashionable dress for women, neither lower-class nor informal; suggesting the real-life Frieda rather than Barbara, who is English. See the photograph of 'Frieda in Bavarian costume' in *"Not I, But the Wind ..."*, facing 60.

258:31 **slippers on.** The following recreates the Baronin von Richthofen's unexpected visit to DHL and Frieda at Icking, s. of Munich, on 2 August 1912. DHL described the meeting in a letter two days later (*Letters*, i. 429–30) and used it in *Mr Noon*, ed. Vasey, pp. 216–20.

259:8 LADY CHARLCOTE—*about 60* Baronin Anna von Richthofen's actual age in 1912.

259:19 **Laura** Perhaps a fictionalisation of Frieda's elder sister, Else; presumably not 'Laura, the friend' who introduced Frieda to the bohemian lifestyle in Munich (*Memoirs* 82–3).

259:20 **Brescia** Provincial capital in northern Italy at the foot of the Alps, about 20 miles w. of Lago di Garda.

260:2 **daughter ... beds!** Cf. *Letters*, i. 429.

260:9 **an honest name.** DHL seems to have crossed out 'an' by mistake in MS (p. 17).

260:20 **kick us out.** Barbara's reply refers to the earlier MS reading (p. 18) 'may be kicked out', altered to the less harsh 'may be turned out' (260:18).

260:25 **Chislehurst,** Replaces the deleted MS reading (p. 18) 'Norwich' (perhaps a substitution for the real-life Nottingham: it was also deleted on pp. 43 and 46 of MS). Chislehurst (see too 290:6), like Bromley (287:35), was a s.e. London suburb, but notably more genteel; DHL had worked in Croydon (1908–11) and would have known the difference.

260:34 **with her lovers.** In MS (p. 18) 'in this miserable country' is replaced by 'with her lovers', but 'with' was also inadvertently deleted; it has been restored. 'Like a barmaid' (260:34) replaces the earlier 'a tramp'.

261:21 **five o'clock company.** I.e. people coming to formal five o'clock tea; Barbara's status as a woman openly living in adultery makes her unacceptable in polite society.

262:6 **Gardone.** A resort on the w. shore of Lago di Garda, s. of Gargnano; see *Letters*, i. Map 7.

262:14 **a 'corriere' ... Toscolano.** The 'post-omnibus', for people and mail (Italian) ... a village on the Lago di Garda between Gargnano and Gardone.

263:34 **the Monte Baldo.** Baedeker mentions the 'Hôt. Monte Baldo' in Gardone as being 'well spoken of' (Baedeker's *The Eastern Alps*, Leipzig, 1907, p. 374). Monte Baldo is to the e. of Lago di Garda; see note on 239:6.

271:14 **of shouters!** Replacing the deleted MS reading (p. 28) 'of cheap aristo-crats!'

272:12 **room to talk.** To have a (moral) right to judge or speak; 'room' replacing the earlier 'right' in MS (p. 28 [28B]).

272:36 **barmaid.** 'My father had written: "You travel about the world like a barmaid"' (*"Not I, But the Wind ..."* 58); DHL reported an identical reproach by the Baronin in *Letters*, i. 429–30. See note on 260:34.

273:6 **six months' lease.** DHL and Frieda probably rented the Villa Igéa from mid-September 1912 until mid-March 1913; they actually stayed an extra fortnight (*Letters*, i. 456, 535).

276:31 **I will.** In MS (p. 32) originally followed by the stage direction '(curtain)' which DHL deleted.

277:22 *Othello* [277:16] ... **Desdemona** ... **sycamore tree,** Cf. *Othello* iv. iii. 40ff., Desdemona's 'willow' song: 'The poor soul sat sighing by a sycamore tree ...'.

278:35 *(She sits down* Replacing '(she is hurt nevertheless)' in MS (p. 34).

278:36 *the Blue Danube* Waltz (1867) ('An der schönen, blauen Donau') by Johann Strauss II (1825–99).

279:33 *homespun* In her fictional account of her honeymoon with Ernest Weekley, Frieda described how, in a hotel in Lucerne she 'came and sat on his knee. She could feel his legs tremble underneath her, she could smell his homespun' (*Memoirs* 73).

280:1 **Hôtel Cervo** Gargnano hotel where the German-born landlady (Maria Samuelli) was one of DHL's and Frieda's first acquaintances (*Letters*, i. 466, 474, 520). See also Baedeker, *Eastern Alps*, p. 375.

280:12 **Are you ... abduct you—?** MS (pp. 35–9) has a large number of deletions. Frederick's question (280:12) replaced the deleted MS (p. 35) reading '*I shan't rape you*'. The original reading, 'I might do her some damage—?' (MS, p. 36) became 'Perhaps ... safe—' (280:15); 'did not refuse to come.' (280:32) replaced the original 'only came when you were bidden' (MS, p. 36); 280:20 was followed by a stage direction which DHL deleted: '(laughs overwrought)' (MS, p. 36); 'I'm glad ... Barbara.' (280:38) superseded 'I must first compliment you on your appearance, Barbara' (MS, p. 36).

281:27 **Thank you, I won't.** From here to 283:28, DHL heavily revised MS (pp. 37–9); it originally read:

> Frederick: Thanks, I will not.
> Barbara: Oh, you easily may—it's not like the Arabs' Salt.
> Frederick: Thank you <<<, but I did not want <<don't come>> <wish to> to drink>>> ⌈. I will drink later.⌉
> Barbara: Then the only sane thing would be to say what you did come for.
> Frederick: I came for you to put me in my place, of course.
> Barbara: It seems rather stupid, don't you think?
> Frederick: Probably I have always seemed stupid to you—naturally.
> Barbara: I don't see why you should be wilfully stupid *now*. Do you really wish to speak to me?

Frederick: You don't suppose I intended merely to pay a friendly call?

Barbara: But have you *really* anything to say to me?

Frederick: Yes, I think I can honestly say I have. I don't want to fritter your valuable time away, as you may imagine—but—

Barbara: <And> Then will you say what you have to say?

Frederick: What I have to say I have to say to my wife, not to the world at large, or even to my mother-in-law, or your paramour.

Barbara: But if that is the way you want to behave, why should I listen?

Frederick: Your method of reasoning is your own.

Barbara: What does that mean? [282:7]

[282:20] Barbara: Yes! Isn't there! <And the> I adore them! *And* the flowers—!

Frederick: Barbara, if you would show <Lady Charlcote> Mama into the study for a few moments, I should like to speak to you.

Lady Charlcote: <I can trust you not to be brutal, Frederick?> I can go <by myself (making a sign> to Barbara)

Frederick: I hope you may trust me to be a gentleman, Mama.

Lady Charlcote: Then I leave Barbara to you, and for you to speak to her and behave as a gentleman. (rising)

Frederick: <It's very good of you.> Thank you—<good of you.> I will remember [282:28]

[283:11] Frederick: Beautiful good luck.—I suppose you were being particularly charming to—

Barbara: He didn't like it No—! <only accident, I'm afraid> ⌈do try not to be hard on me!⌉

Frederick: So—he's exacting, is he.

Barbara: Don't let's talk about him, Frederick.

Frederick: Oh very well—he's beside the point—

Barbara: Yes

Frederick: Then whom *shall* we talk about, you or me? [283:18]

[283:26] Frederick: Ha!—so you went to—that worm—for comfort?

Barbara: He couldn't always comfort me, Frederick.

Frederick: You surprise me. [283:28]

281:37 **call.** In MS (p. 37) this line was originally a question (see note on 281:27); DHL neglected to delete the question mark.

282:36 **to me?** DHL first wrote 'to me, Babs?', then deleted the affectionate 'Babs', as at 283:1 (MS, p. 38).

283:38 **Lizzie Burroughs—** DHL uses a version of the name of his former fiancée, Louie Burrows, whom he broke with in February 1912.

284:4 **not faithful to you—** For Frieda's love affairs, before and after she met DHL, see *"Not I, But the Wind . . ."* 20ff.; *Memoirs* 79–91; *Early Years* 378ff.

284:13 **to fool me.** Replaces earlier 'to cuckold me' (MS, p. 39).

284:33 **when I climbed ... Lucerne.** Frieda wrote two slightly differing accounts of her honeymoon trip with Ernest Weekley (*Memoirs* 73–4, 'at Lucerne', and 423–4, 'in Como').

286:27 **'Malheureusement.'** 'Regrettably, unfortunately'. (French); see too 298:25–8 for Wesson's inaccurate version.

287:7 **the third edition,** DHL imagines the real-life academic author, Weekley, rather than the medical doctor, Frederick Tressider. Weekley's *The Romance of Words*, 1st edn, March 1912, was reprinted June 1912; a revised and enlarged 2nd edn appeared in November 1913. Neither has a dedication.

287:20 **Wood Norton ... saw you first ... eighteen** Wood Norton is a village in Norfolk, 18 miles n.w. of Norwich (see note on 260:25). Weekley met Frieda in Germany in the Black Forest in the summer of 1898 (Frieda was born on 11 August 1879).

287:39 **worshipping me ... kissing my feet ... on a pedestal ... miserable.** Cf. similar accounts in *Memoirs* 70 and *Mr Noon*, ed. Vasey, 124:29–125:13, and 314 n. on 125:4.

288:11 *(his fists* [288:7] *... her arms.)* The stage directions originally read: '(his hands on her throat)' and '(... He suddenly flings his arms round her, holds her fast, kissing her)' (MS, p. 44).

289:6 **do me good.** DHL first wrote in MS (p. 45): 'be good to get my thumbs in your throat.' He used a similar expression in a letter to Helen Corke in 1910 (*Letters*, i. 160).

290:37 **'Oh Good God'** Replaces the earlier 'I can't bear it' (MS, p. 47).

297:37 **Barbican!** Term of endearment and play on her name.

299:15 **a fearful lot!** It is clear from MS (p. 55) that DHL inserted the play's final line – giving Barbara the last word – after originally finishing the play with Wesson's 'I do – and I will.'

The Daughter-in-Law

301:2 MRS GASCOYNE A common name in DHL's home town of Eastwood (mentioned at 342:18 and from which many of the names, places and situations in the play are drawn); John Gascoigne was a deputy at Brinsley colliery near Eastwood in 1874 (Storer 17), and George Gascoigne was a well-known dairyman and carter at 98, Nottingham Road, Eastwood, in the early 1900s. 'Gascoyne' was sometimes pronounced 'Gaskin' (see 327:18, 328:11 etc.).

301:4 MRS PURDY A common Eastwood name; William Purdy (1843–1928) was locally famous as the designer of a miners' safety lamp, and had a son Luther (see Storer 63–6); in 1903 another William Purdy was on the office staff of the local mining employers, Barber Walker and Co. Jerry Purdy is a character in *Sons and Lovers*, ed. Baron and Baron, 28:12.

301:6 LUTHER GASCOYNE DHL's uncle, George Lawrence, had a son named Luther John, b. 22 October 1877.

303:17 **th' office** I.e. the colliery company office. DHL draws many details from the personnel and arrangements of Barber Walker and Co.; their Eastwood office was, until 1917, at the corner of Mansfield Road and Greenhills Road (cf. note on 411:4).

303:22 **fourteen shillin' a week accident pay,** The rate would naturally depend on the level of the injured man's wages; compensation pay per week recorded at Brinsley pit in 1908 varied between 10s 8d and – for a butty (see note on 19:39) – 18s 1d (Storer 106).

303:37 **Macintyre's**   Perhaps DHL's recreation of the Barber Walker and Co. General Manager, John William Fryar (d. 1915); see note on 369:5.

304:37 **Hewett ... Bettesworth ... a chappil man.**   Leonard Hodges (b. 1880) was appointed Manager of Brinsley and Selston colliery in 1907 ... Bettesworth was a common local name ... i.e. one who is active in one of the local nonconformist chapels.

305:3 **That's curious ... don't you?**   Substituted in MS for 'But look here, Bettesworth—You sound a bit fishy—I have a right to know. Now then, I put it to you plainly: Will you <tell me simply> please tell me what you know about that accident<?>, or won't you?' (pp. 2–3).

305:14 **Take not ... hutterly outer thy mouth—'**   Psalms cxix. 43 ['And take ... utterly out of my mouth'].

305:24 **'The wringin' ... forth blood,'**   Proverbs xxx. 33 ['the wringing ...'].

305:30 **a butty ... a day man**   See note on 19:39. DHL's father Arthur was a butty at the age of 28: see 321:22–4 ... day men were paid at a daily rate (7s a day in Nottinghamshire: see 321:37) for their work in the butties' team. See 'A note on pounds, shillings and pence'.

306:3 **either man or woman—you've**   DHL turned from p. 3 of MS to p. 4 after writing 'woman', putting no punctuation either after 'woman' or before 'you've': a dash is more appropriate than the full stop and new sentence of TCCI (p. 6).

307:13 **a guinea a week ... fifty years for th' cumpany ... sixty-two now ... th' roads**   A miner working at the coal-face in the Midlands collieries before the First World War might earn between 5s and 8s a shift; 21s a 6-day week could therefore mean an income cut by half ... DHL's father Arthur had worked underground for various colliery companies (including Barber Walker and Co.) for 52 years by 1909, when he stopped working as a butty; he continued until at least 1912, when he was 65. It was not uncommon for colliers still to be at work in their middle sixties, though often on the 'roads' – underground connecting tunnels – rather than at the coal-face 'stall' (see e.g. Storer 101).

307:18 **widders' coals stopped—leadin' raised to four an' eight**   Widows of coal-miners were frequently allowed a certain quantity of free (or cheap) coal, while miners themselves could buy coal from the pit-head at special rates. The commercial price per ton of coal in 1912 was around 5s 6d, so 'leading' (pronounced as in the verb 'to lead') at 4s 8d represented a saving of 10d a ton.

307:20 **Frazer**   DHL's recreation of Thomas Philip Barber (1876–1961), joint owner and director of Barber Walker and Co. after his father's death in 1893. DHL spelled the name in MS twice with an 's' (pp. 5, 43), but three times with a 'z' (pp. 20, 43 and 46), which is the form adopted here. On one occasion (p. 43) he began to write the name with another initial letter, possibly a 'B'.

307:22 **a new manager to ivry pit,**   The Eastwood collieries of Barber Walker and Co. were extensively modernised in the period 1905–8, under the new general managership of John William Fryar (see note on 369:5); electric power and mechanical coal-cutters were introduced (see note on 64:4 and 307:27–30, 395:3–4), and many of the older underground managers were replaced, along with many of the older office staff; Brinsley Colliery had a new manager from 1907 (see note on 304:37). See Whitelock, *200 Years in Coal*, pp. 43–5.

307:34 **Nethergreen.** ½ mile n. from Eastwood on the Mansfield Road, going towards Brinsley.

308:6 **motherly ... bones an' gristle,** Substituted in MS (p. 6) for 'cosy' ... substituted in MS (p. 6) for 'a scratchetty, scrattlin' corpse'.

309:36 **cast yer bread ... come whoam to you like—** Cf. Ecclesiastes xi. 1 ('Cast thy bread upon the waters; for thou shalt find it after many days').

310:12 **suffer.'** DHL failed to indicate in MS (p. 8) where Mrs Purdy's thoughts (signalled by the opening inverted comma at line 25) come to an end; the place chosen by the typist of TCCI (l.14) has been accepted.

310:14 **Jim Hetherington.** Minnie Gascoyne's father.

310:20 **peace go wi' 'er,** See note on 331:11.

310:31 **come-day go-day ... God send Sunday.** Proverbial: 'spoken to lazy servants who only mind to serve out their time and get their wages': 'the sluggard's daily prayer'. Cf. Nehls, iii. 609.

311:16 **th' 'Bell o' Brass',** An unidentified public house. Also proverbial: see *The Married Man*, 193:30 ('as clear as a bell o' brass').

312:7 **days.** A deleted phrase in MS reads, 'She pays for th' theatres' (p. 10).

313:19 **th' notice was in at th' registrar.** Notice of intention to marry must be given either to the local registrar of marriages or to the vicar of the parish of residence, who publishes the 'banns' for three successive Sundays. Minnie and Luther were clearly not married in church.

314:23 **to court** I.e. for a paternity order to be served on Luther.

314:34 **Batford** In MS (p. 13) DHL first wrote 'Basford', then altered it to 'Batford'; the typist of TCCI produced 'Batsford' here (l.20) and 'Balford' at 38:8 (ll.8); Basford was first a village and then a suburb to the n. of Nottingham: DHL re-created it as 'Barford' in his story 'Daughters of the Vicar' (*The Prussian Officer*, ed. Worthen, 87:30).

315:8 **Lucy.** Later in MS (p. 29) DHL referred to the daughter as 'Lizzie': that reference has been emended editorially to 'Lucy'.

315:29 **'My son's ... a wife,'** Quoted in full at 343:7–8; proverbial. It provided Walter Greenwood with the title for his 1936 version of the play; see Introduction, p. xciii.

316:18 **to spit ... an' butter.** A version of the proverbial 'to bite the hand that feeds you'.

317:4 **Simson Street ... next Holbrooks.** DHL invents the street name, which does not occur in Eastwood; to judge however by the reference in Act IV to the stile outside the house, his creation can be placed in the region of the Breach in Eastwood: the Lawrences' house there (1887–92) faced the stile at the end of the footpath from the common gardens (cf. the stile in *Sons and Lovers*, ed. Baron and Baron, 14:6). There were numerous Holbrook families in Eastwood.

318:3 *'cottage' style*   See *OED2* 4.a., quoting an 1845 publication: 'The term cottage has for some time past been in vogue as a particular designate for small country residences and detached suburban houses, adapted to a moderate scale of living, yet with all due attention to comfort and refinement ... in this sense of it, the name is divested of all associations with poverty.'

318:4 *delft*   Glazed earthenware first made at Delft in the Netherlands and exported in large quantities; also manufactured in Britain from the eighteenth century. While not china, it was regarded as superior to ordinary earthenware.

318:16 *a Union Medal.*   I.e. the badge of the Nottinghamshire Miners' Association.

321:9 **th' proper scale here,**   In the period up to 1912, the Miners' Federation of Great Britain campaigned for a 5s a day minimum wage for all mine-workers and 7s for face-workers; the Nottinghamshire and Yorkshire Associations were fighting in 1912 for a 7s 6d minimum wage for their day-men face-workers, who were currently paid 7s a day.

321:11 **seams are thin,**   After the Top Hard Seam had been worked out, almost all the coal seams in the Eastwood region were comparatively thin (ranging, e.g., from 2ft 1in to 3ft 10in at Brinsley). The mechanisation of the Eastwood collieries was particularly important for the working of thin seams; at High Park colliery, e.g., the working height on the coal-face after the Top Hard Seam was exhausted was reduced from 4ft 9in to 2ft 9in.

321:13 **gre't new electric plant ... new houses for managers,**   Moorgreen Electrical Plant, designed to supply power for all the Eastwood collieries of Barber Walker and Co., started operation at Easter 1907 ... a new house (Moorlands, Brinsley) was, for example, built for the new Manager of Brinsley pit (see note on 304:37).

321:13 **blo—**   Obviously 'bloody', but Luther interrupts himself. The word would have been a problem on stage. When George Bernard Shaw gave Eliza Doolittle the words 'Not bloody likely' in *Pygmalion* (1914), during rehearsals Beerbohm Tree had been 'in a pitiful state of nerves, begging Shaw to substitute "blooming" or "ruddy" for his dreadful word' (Michael Holroyd, *Bernard Shaw: Volume II. 1898–1918. The Pursuit of Power*, 1989, p. 338). Mrs Gascoyne uses 'bobby' at 349:31 as a euphemism for 'bloody'. The text does, however, contain the words 'clat-farted' (305:11), 'buggers' (346:21) and 'stool-arsed' (348:11), which in 1913 would probably all have been excised before public performance.

323:33 **our Harriet**   Apparently a married sister of Luther and Joe, the 'Mrs Preston' of 330:26–7.

323:36 **th' Cinematograph**   Parker's Picture Pavilion in the Sun Inn Croft, Eastwood, had been showing films from 1910; George Henry Cullen's Picture Palace in Langley Mill had been in operation from 1912 (see *The Lost Girl*, ed. Worthen, pp. 85–112). The purpose-built Empire Picture House at the corner of King Street and Nottingham Road in Eastwood opened in 1913.

323:37 **dearly beloved brethren ... our dear departed**   The opening words – after the introductory sentences – of the services of Morning Prayer and Evening Prayer in the *Book of Common Prayer*: 'Dearly beloved brethren, the Scripture moveth us in sundry places ...' ... popular phrase, originally from the *Book of Common Prayer* Burial service: 'the soul of our dear brother/sister here departed ...'

324:20 **Sorry** See Glossary. ' "Sorry" is a common form of address. It is perhaps a corruption of "Sirrah" ' (*Sons and Lovers*, ed. Baron and Baron, 41:40).

327:31 *a shifting shirt* A clean shirt, to be changed into after work; cf. Mr Morel's 'shifting-trousers' in *Sons and Lovers* (ed. Baron and Baron, 236:30).

327:36 **your Bob.** I.e. Bob Purdy.

328:2 *singlet* DHL's MS spelling 'singlit' (p. 27) has no precedent; it may incorporate a memory of Midlands pronunciation.

328:13 MRS PURDY: In the margin of MS (p. 28), against this speech-heading, is written 'Begin' (with a cross) in an unidentified hand; the typist of TCCI started a new page (1.46) at this point.

330:32 **afore th' Co-op shuts up.** The Co-operative Wholesale Society shop, the centre of local shopping (and economising) in the working-class community, normally closed at 7.00 p.m.: see too 353:17.

330:33 JOE In MS, DHL twice wrote 'Harry' instead of Joe (pp. 30, 35): the mistakes have been emended editorially. It is possible that Harry had been the character's name in a previous draft of the play, or that DHL was thinking of some unidentified real-life original; but more likely that he had in mind Harry Hemstock, the mother-dominated son he created in *The Merry-go-Round*.

331:11 **An' joy go wi' yer.** A common Midlands dialect phrase (cf. 'an' peace go wi' 'er' at 310:20), sometimes extended to 'joy go with you and sixpence, and then you'll want neither love nor money'. At least two nineteenth-century poems also contain the phrase; it is impossible to say if DHL knew them. See A. P. Graves (1846–1932), 'Companions', l. 12, *Irish Songs and Ballads* (Manchester 1880), p. 198 ('Joy go with you ever'); J. Moultrie (1799–1874), 'Sonnet XXII', l. 2, *Poems* (1876), p. 260 ('All joy go with you'). In 1928, DHL suggested '*Joy Go With You – by Norman Kranzler. (The Ponte Press)*' (*Letters*, vi. 525) for the covers and title-pages of copies of *Lady Chatterley's Lover*, to try and evade postal and customs officials.

331:15 **Sisson's shop.** Perhaps the grocer and beer retailer, Albert E. Sisson, of Nottingham Road, Eastwood, or the similar shop owned by Enoch Sisson in Princes Street; it is not known whose wife Polly Sisson was.

331:29 *plate* In MS (p. 31) 'plates'; DHL first wrote 'the plates', then altered 'the' to 'a' but failed to change 'plates'.

334:3 **I non know nowt** The double negative is a dialect characteristic; TCCI however misread 'non' as 'now' (II.3) and TSII, probably suspecting an uncorrected mistyping of 'know', omitted the word (p. 57).

335:24 **tha's wiped the feet** TSII (p. 60) emended 'the' to 'tha' – a grammatically impossible change. DHL's 'the' is clearly an attempt to represent the pronunciation of a reduced form of 'thy', although standard orthography leads to a potentially confusing word.

335:40 **tell me.** MS (p. 36) reads 'tell thee'. A reflexive use of 'tell' would, however, be extremely unlikely, and the emendation of 'thee' to 'me' made by TSII (p. 60) has been accepted.

337:24 What good ... *me* nowt. Revised in MS (p. 37) from 'Tha didna want ter know how many times I'd bin drunk.'

338:37 I never ought to ha' done it. DHL maintained Minnie's dialect speech at a lighter level than that of the other characters; in MS (p. 38), e.g., he first wrote 'I never ought t'', giving her the dialect 't' for 'to', before revising it to the present reading; while at 359:5 he first wrote 'got ower' (MS, p. 61) before revising the second word to 'over'.

339:7 Mr Westlake Minnie's old employer or 'master' (344:35): see 353:10–11, 21–2.

341:16 ten bob a wik. I.e. strike-pay; full members of the Union during the 1912 strike were entitled to 10s per week, with 1s extra for each child aged under 13. See 'Strike-Pay', *Love Among the Haystacks*, ed. Worthen, pp. 134–42.

342:13 th' Midland station! I.e. the Nottingham station of the Midland Railway, in Carrington Street.

342:21 neither sugar nor salt. I.e. you won't melt.

343:1 Mrs Pervin [342:36] ... Mrs Charley Name used again by DHL in both his 1916 story, 'The Horse-Dealer's Daughter', and his 1919 story, 'The Blind Man', *England, My England and Other Stories*, ed. Bruce Steele (Cambridge, 1990), pp. 46–63 and 137–52 ... presumably identical with (or mother of) the 'Lizzie Charley' of 347:10: living about a minute away, to judge by the length of Joe's absence later in the scene.

343:21 Watna' pit-top's [343:15] ... ter Watna' In his novel *Women in Love* and in his play *Touch and Go* (both published in 1920) many of the same details appear in an account of the miners' lock-out of 1893, which DHL knew from local memory: see too 393:38–394:13, and note on 394:18. Here he uses the materials to recreate the unrest in the Eastwood collieries between 1908 and 1912. At New Watnall colliery in 1893 the one serious riot in Nottinghamshire took place; on 6 September, wagons standing in the railway sidings and various buildings were set on fire; seven ringleaders were arrested. Large detachments of police and soldiers were brought into the area; 115 officers and men of the Staffordshire regiment were quartered at the Sun Inn; the regiment (the 17th Lancers) had served at Kandahar (the capital of a province of Afghanistan) 1880–1, during British attempts to retain it. General Sir Frederick Sleigh Roberts (1832–1914), with a picked body of 10,000 men, had marched from Kabul on 9 August 1880 to relieve Kandahar, and became a popular hero when he succeeded in doing so: he was made a baronet. See *The White Peacock*, ed. Robertson, 35:28 and note; the exploit was commemorated in the song 'Marching to Candahar' which DHL would have known from the *National Song Book*. Kandahar was eventually evacuated in April 1881. The statutes ground, next to the Sun Inn in Eastwood, was named after the annual fairs originally held there for the hiring of servants and labourers.

343:27 th' Black Watch up at Heanor There is no other report of the Black Watch (the famous British Highland Regiment dating from 1729, distinctive for its sombre tartan – see 'kilts' at 343:28) being present at Heanor either at the 1893 lock-out or at any subsequent disturbances.

343:28 **They look well**, Common, ironical, local phrase meaning 'They're clearly stupid.'

345:24 **Mansfield.** 12 miles n.e. of Eastwood; when Mrs Gascoyne refers to walking 'twenty miles' (345:29), she presumably means there and back.

345:30 **free dinners at th' Methodist chapel.** During strikes, such dinners were provided in the schoolroom of the Primitive Methodist chapel in the Squares, Eastwood, just off Wellington Street; 'soup tickets' (354:7) were also distributed.

345:31 **th' 'Badger Box',** Lawrence uses the original (and current) name for a public house then normally called 'The Robin Hood', on the main road between Mansfield and Eastwood, 1 mile s. of Kirkby-in-Ashfield; the name derived from the fact that in the late nineteenth century the pub kept a badger in an empty beer barrel and men would bring in dogs to fight it in the inn yard.

345:35 **th' roads, an' a' that.** A mine needs constant maintenance to keep its roads workable and safe: see note on 307:13.

346:39 **Tom Rooks—e' wor goin' ter turn 'em down.** Rooks would be the engine driver, in charge of the shaft's winding machinery, and responsible for raising and lowering coal, men and supplies.

348:9 **gramophone** By 1913, the distinction between 'gramophone' (using discs) and 'phonograph' (using cylinders) was established. The spelling 'gramaphone' of MS (p. 48), however, may reproduce Minnie's uncertain pronunciation of what was still a relatively new word.

348:11 **collier's britches ... stool-arsed Jack's.** I.e. a working man rather than a clerk; cf. *Sons and Lovers*: 'What dost want ter ma'e a stool-harsed Jack on 'im for? ... All he'll do is to wear his britches behind out an' earn nowt' (ed. Baron and Baron, 70:1–2).

353:17 **almanack.** A broadsheet year's calendar, usually decorated and pictorial; cf. *Lady Chatterley's Lover*, when Constance decorates Mellors with flowers and he comments 'Make a calendar of me!' (ed. Michael Squires, Cambridge, 1993, 227:23).

353:39 **her own.** Minnie's revelation is very similar to that in DHL's short story 'Her Turn', written in March 1912 (see *Love Among the Haystacks*, ed. Worthen, 132:35–133:13).

354:11 **men's** In MS (p. 56) DHL first wrote 'men's', then deleted the apostrophe and placed it after the 's', to create 'mens''. In spite of the evidence of his final preference (typed by TCCI, III.23), this edition has returned to the grammatically correct form, typed in TSII (p. 95).

354:13 **West's.** Cf. James West & Son, grocers, Nottingham Road, Eastwood.

359:22 **Wakkened enow!** In MS (p. 62) Mrs Gascoyne's parting remark originally ran 'An' me down here!', which DHL adjusted to 'Wakkened indeed!' before deciding on the final reading.

360:18 *begins to cry.* In MS (p. 63) DHL originally wrote 'begins to cry, saying Minnie, Minnie!'

Preface to *Touch and Go*

363:2 **"A People's Theatre."** Title invented by Douglas Goldring (see Introduction, p. xlix).

363:9 **il popolo, le peuple, das Volk,** The people (Italian, French, German).

363:11 **Quel peuple donc?** What people, then? (French).

363:24 **"the cynosure of many eyes."** Cf. Milton, 'L'Allegro' (1632), 'Where perhaps some beauty lies,/ The cynosure of neighbouring eyes' (ll. 79–80); 'cynosure' is a person or thing attracting notice because of its beauty.

364:1 **Chu Chin Chow** Musical extravaganza (1916) based on the story of Ali Baba and the Forty Thieves, music by Frederic Norton and book by Oscar Asche; for many years holder of the record for the longest run in the London theatre (2,238 performances).

364:4 **mimsy bomtittle** Nonsense words, the first from *Through the Looking Glass and What Alice Found There* (1872), by Lewis Carroll (C. L. Dodgson, 1832–98), chap. VI: 'All mimsy were the borogoves'.

364:15 **the Upper Ten ... Piccoli ... Grandi** I.e. the upper ten per cent ... little ones ... big ones (Italian).

364:39 **Cyrano ... Sir Auckland Geddes ... J. H. Thomas** Cyrano de Bergerac (1619–55), French writer, notorious for his large nose: hero of the eponymous popular verse drama (1897) by Edmond Rostand (1868–1918) ... Sir Auckland Campbell Geddes (1879–1954), Scottish politician and surgeon, brought into the Government by Lloyd George, Minister of National Service in 1917 and President of the Board of Trade (thus in regular contact with the mining industry) in 1919 ... J. ('Jimmy') Thomas (1874–1949), son of an engine driver, General Secretary of the National Union of Railwaymen (1918–24) and a noted political figure, was to become Colonial Secretary in the Labour Government of January 1924. See too 407:39.

365:3 **ballot-paper. It** DHL introduced an odd, slanting stroke into MS (p. 3) following 'ballot-paper', and covering his previously inserted full-stop. The compositor of E1 (Gallagher) ignored the mark, but DHL may well have been indicating a paragraph break, which has been inserted here.

365:4 ***petit bleu* arrangement ... vacuum tubes ... Bradburys** Telegram system (French) ... used in shops and offices for transferring money, etc., from counter to till ... Treasury notes bearing the signature of Sir John Bradbury (1872–1950), Secretary to the Treasury 1913–19, were often called Bradburys.

365:8 **jew-jaws.** DHL's spelling of the word 'gewgaws' ('gaudy trifles, playthings'), also used in proof correction for *The Rainbow* (ed. Kinkead-Weekes, p. 653, Textual apparatus for 404:24). The word apparently lacks anti-Semitic ironisation.

365:18 **in this Sodom ... ten men ... grain of mustard seed,** See Genesis xvii. 32: God promised not to destroy Sodom if ten righteous men could be found there ... Matthew xiii. 31 ('The kingdom of heaven is like to a grain of mustard seed ...') or xvii. 20 ('If ye have faith as a grain of mustard seed').

365:22 **How many ... thirty-two.** In conversation with his friend Eckermann on Sunday 14 February 1830 (Johann Peter Eckermann, *Gespräche mit Goethe*, ed. H. H. Houben, Leipzig, 1905, p. 314), Johann Wolfgang von Goethe (1749–1832) is reported as saying: 'Gozzi habe die Meinung gehabt, es gebe nur sechs und dreissig tragische Situationen; Schiller habe geglaubt, es gebe mehr, allein es sei ihm nicht einmal gelungen, nur so viele zu finden.' ['Gozzi was of the opinion that there were only thirty-six tragic situations; Schiller believed there were more, but not once did he manage to discover even that many.'] Carlo Gozzi (1720–1806), Italian dramatist; Friedrich Schiller (1759–1805), German poet and dramatist.

365:26 **turns us,** The compositor (Gallagher) misread DHL's 'us' as 'no' and introduced a dash before it to make sense of the sentence: see Textual apparatus.

365:27 **Mr Galsworthy ... bathos.** A reference to the play *Strife* (performed 1909, pub. 1910), by John Galsworthy (1867–1933), which dealt with a strike situation: DHL saw it in Nottingham in 1909 (E.T. 172). At 365:27, he replaced 'melted' with 'sank down' in MS (p. 4); 'merely disastrous' (365:30) replaced 'boring' in MS (p. 5).

365:39 **immediate** Replacing 'immense' in MS (p. 5); 'people versus king' (366:4) replaced 'king versus people' in MS (p. 5).

366:6 **Majesty was ... Goneril and Regan** In 1649, thirty-three years after Shakespeare's death, King Charles I (b. 1600, ruled 1625–49) was executed (see *Twilight in Italy and Other Essays*, ed. Paul Eggert, Cambridge, 1994, 120:15) ... Lear's two eldest daughters in Shakespeare's *King Lear*.

367:6 **his pound of flesh** [366:40] **... Portia ... "The quality ... the old Shylock** The central situation, characters and Portia's central speech (IV. i. 180) from Shakespeare's *The Merchant of Venice*; see too 183:6 and note.

367:26 **too much** Replacing 'useless' in MS (p. 8).

367:29 *casus belli.* Act or event used to justify a war.

367:38 **having to pass through** Revised from 'an impending death which' in MS (p. 8).

368:13 **Hermitage. June 1919** DHL was resident in Hermitage, near Newbury, Berkshire, 25 April–23 July 1919; see, however, Introduction, pp. xlix–l.

Touch and Go

369:4 GERALD BARLOW ... WINIFRED BARLOW Gerald Barlow, his father, mother (Henrietta) and sister (Winifred) are versions of members of the Crich family which DHL first created in *WL* (cf. Gerald, Thomas, Christiana and Winifred Crich), and both families are based on the real-life Barber family of Eastwood. Mr Barlow corresponds to Thomas Barber (1843–93), Henrietta Barlow to his wife Frances Ann (née Spragge) – whose father was reputed to have gone 'mad' (385:22) in Italy – and Gerald in some respects resembles Thomas Philip Barber (see note on 307:20). Like the Barbers, the Barlows have lost two children 'through sudden and violent death' (see note on 392:13). Their house Lilley Close (376:26) corresponds to the Barber home, Lambclose House; like Lambclose, it was once a farm (390:9–11), with its name suggested by Willey Wood, just to the n. of Lambclose. Mr Barlow's reference to 'The mines ... opened when my father was a boy' (392:8–9) suggests the opening of new and deeper Barber Walker and Co. pits in the period 1839–60, though Thomas Barber's father and Mr Barlow's father would have been boys in the period 1795–1810, when Barber Walker worked a large number of small pits in the neighbourhood of Eastwood, having started in the mid-eighteenth century (see Whitelock, *200 Years in Coal*, p. 22). The modernisation (380:29–33, 394:38–395:7) and electrification (380:36–8, 395:2–5) of Barlow and Walsalls collieries, however, corresponds to the modernisation of the Barber Walker collieries 1905–8 (ibid., p. 44); and the Barlow colliery in Yorkshire (380:13–14) is a version of Barber Walker and Co.'s Bentley colliery. Other details of Barber family history are also paralleled by events in both play and novel; see note on 394:18 and *WL*, note on 12:38, DHL used the name 'Bennett' in MS six times (pp. 16–17) before finally deciding on 'Barlow' and emending accordingly (he used it again – and deleted it – on pp. 20, 23 and 27).

There are numerous further similarities to the names, events and conversations of *WL*; for example, Gerald's response to his mother's threat to kill him – 'I shan't let you' (402:10) – parallels Birkin's response to Hermione Roddice when she tries to kill him ('I don't let you' – *WL* 106:4–5); the description of the 'Georgian hall' as an 'eighteenth-century aquatint' (411:3, 24) is reminiscent of DHL's description of the Georgian Breadalby in the novel as 'an old English aquatint' (*WL*, note on 82:25).

Oliver Turton and Anabel Wrath plays the same roles in *Touch and Go* as Rupert Birkin and Gudrun Brangwen in *WL* (see *WL*, notes on 16:6 and 7:3). As in the novel, Anabel teaches Winifred sculpture in a studio made 'over the out-buildings' (381:20); Anabel, as Gudrun does, specialises in small sculptures of animals and birds; in both novel and play Winifred is given a present of a small sculpture (385:35–386:4); like Gudrun's father, Will, in *The Rainbow* and *WL*, Anabel's father teaches art (376:33–4). Anabel, like Gudrun, has had an affair with Gerald; her lover Baard (like Gerald in *WL*) is associated with the north and has died frozen (400:15–16). The name Anabel, however, also recalls the gamekeeper Annable of DHL's first novel, *The White Peacock*, while 'Wrath' is a common Eastwood name (Sam King, husband of DHL's sister Emily, had a sister Sarah who married Fred Wrath in December 1903).

369:5 JOB ARTHUR FREER Reminiscent (in name) of the Barber Walker and Co. General Manager, John William Fryar (see note on 307:22), but a recreation of the Eastwood miners' leader Joseph Birkin (see Introduction, p. xlv), like Freer (408:6–7) a noted violinist. Freer appears in the same role in DHL's 1922 novel, *Aaron's Rod*, ed. Mara Kalnins (Cambridge, 1988), 8:5–9.

369:6 WILLIE HOUGHTON DHL's recreation of Eastwood's socialist, journalist and tradesman, William Edward ('Willie') Hopkin (1862–1951), by 1918 resident in Eastwood for fifty-six years (cf. 371:12–13, note on 371:7 and Introduction, pp. xlv–xlvi).

369:7 ALFRED BREFFITT A recreation of the long-serving Estate Agent and Cashier of Barber Walker and Co., Alfred W. Brentnall (1834–1924); see too *Aaron's Rod*, ed. Kalnins, 26:15–19 and note.

371:1 TOUCH AND GO Proverbial: a critical state of things.

371:7 *market-place ... memorial obelisk ... bells heard* Eastwood's old market-place was at the junction of Nottingham Road, Mansfield Road, Church Street and Derby Road ... the 'memorial obelisk' (see photograph in *Around Old Eastwood*, Eastwood, 1991, p. 9) was erected in 1896 in memory of Edward Lindley, first Chairman of Eastwood Council and General Manager of Barber Walker and Co. ... the Parish church of St Mary stands 100 yards away, down Church Street. The Independent Labour Party (ILP) held regular 11.00 a.m. Sunday meetings in Eastwood market-place each year from late spring until autumn; Willie Hopkin (see note on 369:6) was a member of the ILP and spoke regularly. In 1909, for example, he gave addresses on 30 May and 29 August (see *Eastwood & Kimberley Advertiser*, 4 June and 3 September 1909, p. 2). DHL's recreation of Hopkin as Lewie Goddard in *Mr Noon* – ed. Vasey, 36:15 – shows him going to an ILP meeting in 'Knarborough' (Nottingham).

371:30 **compounds ... in South Africa,** I.e. 'concentration camps', invented by the 1st Earl Kitchener of Khartoum (1850–1916); the non-combatants of a district were forced into them during the Boer War (1899–1902).

372:7 **a can of beer a day,** Not, of course, the can of beer invented in the 1960s, but the large metal can used to fill a number of beer glasses at a public house; see Glossary, 'can', 'canned'.

372:13 **tha** DHL first wrote 'thee' in MS (p. 2), then altered it to 'tha' by writing the 'a' over the double 'e': TCC (1.2) misread as 'thee'.

372:19 **"Oh how eager these men are to be slaves—"** 'Memoriae proditur Tiberium ... Graecis verbis in hunc modum eloqui solitum: "O homines ad servitutem paratos!" ' (Tacitus, *Annals*, III.65) ['Tradition says that Tiberius ... had a habit of exclaiming in Greek: "O, how ready these men are to be slaves!" ']; the Roman emperor Tiberius Claudius Nero (42 BC–AD 37) 'took the skin off a few Romans' (372:31–2): *Annals*, VI, refers to his 'unrestrained crime and infamy'. DHL – who had recently read Tacitus – twice added the saying to the manuscript of *Movements in European History* during revision in April 1919, noting that Tiberius 'is supposed to have been very cruel' (ed. Philip Crumpton, Cambridge, 1989, 14:22, 24 and 15:6–7).

372:20 **Shakespeare—or the Bible ... mostly is—** Cf. T. R. Eaton, *Shakespeare and the Bible* (1858), p. 5: 'A passage rises in our thoughts, unaccompanied by a clear recollection of its origin. Our first impression is that it *must* belong *either* to the *Bible* or to *Shakespeare*.'

372:21 *(she was passing to Church):* Complete Plays 326 modified to '*(passing to church)*'.

373:4 **Come, and ... he goeth,** Cf. Matthew viii. 9 ('I say to this man, Go, and he goeth; and to another, Come, and he cometh') and Luke vii. 8.

373:11 **contrive that ... belonged to you,** The nationalisation of the British coal industry (which finally took place in 1947) was frequently discussed 1918–26: 'A near revolutionary situation developed in the early months of 1919, when the demand for mines' nationalisation became insistent' (A. R. Griffin, *Mining in the East Midlands 1550–1947*, 1971, p. 278). DHL originally wrote 'see' and revised to 'contrive' in MS (p. 3).

373:17 **shilling a day ... seven-pence ha'penny:** Wage negotiations in the coal industry had been made more acute by the steeply rising cost of food and of living towards the end of the First World War; the average retail price of food had risen by 133% and the cost of living by 125% by November 1918, compared with 1914 levels.

373:23 Shylock ... pound of flesh.   See note on 367:6.

375:20 the Unco Guid,   'The all-too good': from Robert Burns, 'Address to the Unco Guid, or the Rigidly Righteous' (*The Poems and Songs of Robert Burns*, ed. Kinsley, i. 52–4).

376:9 doesn't matter.   Revised in MS (p. 6) from 'doesn't matter, does it?'

377:38 *coup de main*   'Surprise attack' (French).

378:3 Whatmore—   DHL's recreation of Watnall, 4 miles s.e. of Eastwood, and of the colliery there (see 394:11).

379:7 Gerald   Squeezed up against the right-hand edge of the page in MS (p. 9) and misread as 'Jack' by the typist of TCC (I.12).

379:31 wafted about   Revised in MS (p. 9) from 'wafted about like little quick puffs of air'.

380:2 Armenia ... if there is such a place.   Not actually a country but a land-locked region of Transcaucasia, in the news because of massacres there by Turkish soldiers in 1915; occupied 1918–19 by Turkey and Russia. Recognised as a free independent state in 1920, it never existed as such, being incorporated in the Union of Soviet Socialist Republics.

380:31 so *modern*.   See note on 64:4.

380:36 The colliers   Preceded in MS (p. 11) by the deleted sentence 'But Gerald says you've got to put blue fire into people, to make them <work.> ⌜spring⌝'.

381:17 'sculptress',   Although Oliver may question Winifred's word, it is of seventeenth-century origin; with a history, however, of disparaging usage.

381:37 De terre [381:31] ... *move*   'From earth to vine / That's the lovely vine / Vine, vine, let us vine the wine / That's the wine's lovely vine / That's the lovely vine'; from 'La vigne au vin', popular French song with numerous stanzas and surviving in many versions, tracing the course of the wine from earth to vine, vine to bud, bud to flower, flower to grape, etc., etc. The final stanza of one common version runs:

> De bouche en pisse
> La voilà la jolie pisse
> Pissi, pissons, pissons le vin
> La voilà la jolie pisse au vin
> La voilà la jolie pisse!

['From mouth to piss / That's the lovely piss / Piss, let us piss, let us piss the wine / That's the wine's lovely piss / That's the lovely piss!'] ... revised in MS (p. 12) from 'twine'.

381:39 *ma capote a trois boutons*   Popular French round song: 'Ma capote a [un/deux/trois, etc.] boutons, Marchons, / Marchons légèr', légère, Marchons légèrement' ['My cloak has [one/two/three, etc.] buttons, let us march / let us march ligh', light, let us march lightly'].

383:6 **that Norwegian,** Named as 'Baard' at 384:9: see note on 369:4.

384:30 **never—never—never—** Cf. *King Lear* v. iii. 307.

384:35 **on that.** Revised in MS (p. 16) from 'on that, and that only.'

385:24 **one is master of one's fate** A favourite quotation of DHL's: 'I am the master of my fate', from 'Invictus' by W. E. Henley (1849–1903), l. 15.

385:29 **a** *parvenu's* That of an upstart, obtaining wealth or position well beyond his obscure origins.

387:9 **go to war** Revised in MS (p. 19) from 'make trouble'.

387:33 **the peace that passeth all understanding.** Philippians iv. 7 ['The Peace of God, which passeth . . .'].

387:37 **shameful** Revised in MS (p. 20) from 'arrogant'.

388:4 **Spend it . . . were costly,** Revised in MS (p. 20) from 'Spill it hard,'.

390:11 **[*Exit* WILLIAM.]** DHL provides no stage direction for William's exit, but he enters again at 395:40. He must leave here, or a little earlier: his pouring coffee for five people (390:3–4) cannot last long, and at 390:12–13 Mr Barlow asks Winifred, not William, to hand Anabel the sweets.

390:17 **Bertie and Elinor** Presumably other Barlow children. In *WL* there are seven Crich children: see *WL*, note on 12:38.

390:23 **the "Lincolnshire Poacher",** English traditional song: 'When I was bound apprentice / In famous Lincolnshire, / Full well I served my master / For more than seven year, / Till I took up to poaching, / As you shall quickly hear. / [*Chorus*] Oh—'tis my delight / On a shining night / In the season of the year.'

391:7 **in you!** MS (p. 24) reads 'in you?' but Mr Barlow is not querying his belief in Anabel. It seems more likely that DHL intended to inscribe an exclamation mark, which has been editorially substituted.

392:13 **lost our first child . . . violent death.** The eldest son of the Barber family, Thomas Philip Barber (see note on 307:20), had accidentally killed his brother, Kenneth Forbes Barber (b. 1877), on 23 April 1890, while his sister Cecily Frances Barber (b. 1886) drowned on 12 August 1892; see *WL*, notes on 26:10 and 180:27.

392:19 **a week,** Revised in pencil in MS (p. 25) from 'a year'.

392:28 **we are taught that it is wrong.** Cf. Matthew xxii. 39: 'Thou shalt love thy neighbour as thyself.'

392:36 **tension of possession,** DHL first wrote 'tension of possessions', but then deleted (or just possibly smudged) the final 's' (MS, p. 26): the typist of TCC inserted it (II.6). Given the sentence's parallel construction ('of possession . . . for possession'), deletion is more probable.

394:18 **great lock-out [393:39] . . . the country-side—** In July 1893 the Midland Counties members of the Coal-Owners' Federation (the 'Masters Federation' of 393:39) attempted to enforce a reduction in wages; this led, from 28 July, to a sixteen-week lock-out and stoppage. Buns, soup and other food were distributed. See notes on 343:21 and 27, and *WL*, notes on 224:33, 226:2 and 18.

395:35 **money** Revised in MS (p. 26a) from 'possession'.

397:31 **me**   The typist of TCC (II.13) read the word in MS (p. 28a) as 'one': there is an enclosed loop at the start of the first letter which looks like an 'o' preceding an 'n'. But another example in MS of an undoubted 'me' also starting with an enclosed loop (p. 38, line 29), and the context here, strongly suggest that the word here too is 'me'.

398:12 **John Halifax Gentleman**   The novel (*John Halifax, Gentleman*, 1856) by Dinah Maria Mulock, later Mrs Craik (1826–87); Halifax is a boy of humble origins whose high principles and nobility of character bring him prosperity and happiness.

398:15 **play bo-peep with myself,**   The nursery game in which the child is amused by someone concealing his or her face, peeping out for a second, then again hiding. There may be an allusion to *King Lear* I. iv. 181, with its suggestions of blindness and folly.

398:22 **virtuise**   The only example of this nonce-word in *OED2*: presumably invented to mean 'pretend to be virtuous'. For 'smug', see Glossary.

399:4 **to it**   DHL's pencil revision in MS (p. 30): his original version read 'to live together', which clarifies 'to live apart' at 399:9. Mrs Barlow refers to 384:33–4, shortly before her entrance at 385:3.

400:6 **a Cruikshank drawing,**   George Cruikshank (1792–1878), artist and illustrator with a reputation for depicting low life, illustrating (for example) *Sketches by Boz* (1836) and *Oliver Twist* (1838) by Charles Dickens.

400:33 **Sounds weak ... mere contrariness.**   Pencil revision in MS for 'Too bad, dear—I'll never marry her if she listens.' (p. 32).

401:5 **let him alone, don't you**   Pencil revision in MS for 'wait for him till he wins, do not' (p. 33).

401:19 **only thing**   Pencil revisions in MS (p. 33) here and at 401:21 for 'fierce isolation'.

401:23 **But what ... you mean?**   Pencil revision in MS (p. 33) for 'It's a kind of megalomania.'

401:35 **Speak gently ... he sneezes.**   DHL's version of the lullaby sung by the Duchess in the pepper-filled kitchen of chap. VI of *Alice's Adventures in Wonderland* (1865) by Lewis Carroll. E1 corrected 'gently' to 'roughly' here and below (pp. 56, 59), but the misquotation is probably deliberate. The lullaby continues 'For he can perfectly enjoy / The pepper when he pleases.'

403:10 **corraggio ... Corraggiaccio ... Corraggione!**   Courage ... poor sort of courage ... great courage (Italian).

403:23 **Kümmel?**   Cumin-flavoured liqueur (see *Letters*, ii. 536).

404:21 **William Straw**   W. Straw (b. 1870) worked as a wagoner in Barber Walker and Co.'s Brinsley colliery in 1885, as a member of DHL's father's coal-getting team, but the name was common locally.

404:38 **it.**   DHL wrote the word on the extreme right-hand edge of the paper in MS (p. 37), leaving no space for punctuation. TCC (II.26) supplied the conventional question mark, but as DHL did not add one below the word (his practice when running out of space in MS) he is more likely to have implied a full stop.

407:39 **a Cabinet Minister some day.** See note on 364:39.

408:6 **Miners Federation** The Miners' Federation of Great Britain (founded 1889) was the most active and socialist of the various miners' unions: it led the campaign to secure a minimum wage in 1912 which provoked a widespread strike.

408:13 **luxuriation.** The 'action or process of luxuriating; exuberant efflorescence' (*OED2*); Thomas de Quincey is the source of the only two citations in *OED2* of an uncommon word which DHL may well have learned from an author he was very fond of. He gave his set of De Quincey's complete works to Catherine and Donald Carswell (see Introduction, footnote 64) in October 1919 (iii. 407).

408:22 **Garden of Olives,** The location of Judas's kiss betraying Christ is the 'mount of Olives' in Matthew's, Mark's and Luke's Gospels, an unnamed 'garden' in John's Gospel.

408:38 **Aeolian harp** A stringed instrument that produces musical sounds in response to air currents.

409:26 **risen like Antichrist ... Dionysos ... Aphrodite?** Revelation xiii. 1 ... Greek god of wine, fruitfulness and vegetation ... Greek goddess of love and beauty.

409:35 **Oliver Cromwell ... iconoclast.** General and statesman (1599–1658) who ruled England as Lord Protector of the Commonwealth 1653–8 following the execution of Charles I (see note on 366:6). During the interregnum Puritan iconoclasts defaced or destroyed many images in churches.

409:39 **is Bacchus the father of whiskey?** I.e. is the (Greek and Roman) god of wine also responsible for whiskey?

411:4 **a low Georgian hall ... offices for the Company,** Eastwood Hall, dating from the early nineteenth century and owned by the Walker family (see next note), who resided there 1843–71, was empty for many years; it was turned into offices for Barber Walker and Co. in 1917, replacing the old company office (cf. note on 303:17).

411:13 **Walsalls ... county, you know** The Walker family were a 'county' family, originally lords of the manor in Eastwood, but not as active as the Barber family in Barber Walker and Co.

411:20 **the stately homes of England** 'The Homes of England' (1827) by Mrs Felicia Dorothea Hemans (1793–1835), l. 1.

411:32 **the road ... the brook ... the town ... New London pit** Recreations of Mansfield Road, Beauvale Brook, Eastwood and New England colliery.

414:1 **Aristotle's Katharsis.** Aristotle's *Poetics*, section VI, describes κάθαρσιν as 'through pity and fear effecting the proper purgation of those emotions' (tr. S. H. Butcher, 1895).

415:25 **pillars of society.** The title of William Archer's English translation (1888) of the play *Samfundets støtter* (1877) by Henrik Ibsen (1828–1906).

417:15 **alterations in the office staff,** The modernisation of Eastwood collieries under Thomas Philip Barber involved, in 1906–7, 'the appointment of a young up-to-date management staff' (Whitelock, *200 Years in Coal*, p. 44); see *WL*, note on 229:13.

419:10 **Timbuctoo ... Paraguay ... Antananarivo.**   Town in Mali, n.w. Africa, on the edge of the Sahara ... state in central s. America ... town (now called Tananarivo) in central Madagascar.

419:21 **the other night** ...   DHL inscribed a smudged full stop after 'night' in MS (p. 58) at the right-hand margin and two further dots below the word. The typist of TCC (III.15) ended the line at the right-hand margin and left no space for punctuation: E1 (p. 79) inserted an unspaced double m-dash. As DHL sometimes inserted punctuation below the word in such cases (see note on 404:38), the dots – unique in MS – may have been his way of showing that Job Arthur's words tail away.

420:27 **[*getting up*]**   Although DHL inserted no stage direction, it is clear from 421:19 that Job Arthur has got up after Gerald's initial assault; and he could reasonably do so while speaking 420:27–8.

422:16 **Balaam's ass ... Job.**   Numbers xxii. 28–30: the ass refused to go forward because of an angel standing in its path, and eventually spoke to Balaam. A favourite allusion of DHL's; see e.g. *Letters*, iv. 177, 180–1, 479 ... Job was 'one that feared God, and eschewed evil' (Job i. 1) and an exemplar of patience (James v. 11).

422:19 **picking up a scorpion ... looking for an egg.**   Cf. Luke xi. 12 ('if he shall ask an egg, will he offer him a scorpion?').

423:8 **Keatings?**   Keating's powder was a famous brand of household insecticide, specifically for killing fleas (see *Letters*, i. 240).

423:9 **Stop thy face. Hold thy gab.**   See Glossary. DHL's father is reported as using the expression 'Hoad the faece, woman'; a local woman commented, 'Thee calls it "shut up." That's what he meant, "Shut your faece." Aye, that an old 'un, "Hoad the faece!" ' (Nehls, iii. 579).

423:15 **only room ... rock-face above.**   Revised in MS (p. 63) from 'a precipice in front. And if ever we're going to get any further, we've got to jump it'.

424:12 **little**   Although DHL deleted 'tiny' in MS (p. 64) and wrote 'little' above it, TCC typed both words (III.23).

424:27 **Lodnor?**   DHL's recreation of Codnor, 1½ miles to the n.w. of Eastwood: a car from Codnor would come up the Derby Road into Eastwood market-place.

425:14 **Tweet-tweet!**   From at least the 1890s (*OED2*), the sound of the would-be superior but ineffectual upper-class voice: cf. Leslie Sarony, music-hall artiste *c.* 1940: 'I lift up my finger and I say "Tweet tweet"!'

425:38 **I would answer you**   Pencil revision in MS (p. 66) of 'You want answering'.

426:37 **Close the shutters, Willie's dead.**   Celebrated minstrel ballad, *c.* 1875, words and music by James E. Stewart: 'Close the shutters, Willie's dead, / Whom we lov'd so dear. / Like a dream his spirit fled / From our home, now sad and drear.'

426:40 **There's a long, long trail a-winding**   Famous First World War song, music by Alonzo Elliot, words by S. King (1914), continuing 'Into the land of my dreams— / Where the nightingales are singing / And the white moon beams'. In a reference to the Midlands in 1917 in *Kangaroo*, DHL referred to it as 'This ghastly trailing song, like death itself. The colliers seemed to tear it out of their bowels, in a long, wild chant' (ed. Bruce Steele, Cambridge, 1994, 230:12, 229:31–2). The only certain authorial revision of the text of *Touch and Go* between MS and E1 (see Introduction, p. liii): the reading of MS (p. 67) and TCC (III.27) had been the counting nursery rhyme 'One—two—buckle my shoe', no. 385 in the *Oxford Book of Nursery Rhymes*, ed. I. and P. Opie (Oxford, 1951).

428:32 **are like this,** Pencil revision in MS (p. 69) for 'have come to this pass'.

429:4 **attempted to ... about it,** Replacing the MS reading 'wanted to bully <me> it out of us' (p. 69): the revision of 'about it' in pencil, the rest in ink.

430:13 **to every ... his needs,** An echo of Karl Marx's *Critique of the Gotha Programme* (1875), itself an echo of Mikhail Bakunin's Declaration after the failure of the Lyons uprising of 1870: 'From each according to his abilities, to each according to his needs'.

431:13 **Yes, I'm going** [431:1] **... (Curtain)** The end of the play, as first written in MS (p. 71) read:

Gerald: Yes, I'm going.—I'm not going to make any bother about this business. You've had you're whack at me—now we're quits. My wife'll give you her word that what I say I mean.
Anabel: Yes—you can trust him, if only you will.
Gerald: And that's more than I can say of them—I can't trust   5
them. Has somebody got my coat?—
Job Arthur: What about the clerks wages, Mr Barlow?
Gerald: You hold your tongue, do you see.—I'll put up notices tomorrow, about what we'll do. *I'm* the Justice of the Peace for this district, you know—so we'll keep the peace for as long as   10
we can—I've said we're quits—

                    (curtain)
                    The End.

DHL revised this ending twice in MS. On the first occasion, in pencil, he rewrote lines 1–3 to create the reading of the final text as far as 'about money really.' in the final text (431:4); he then deleted Anabel's speech at line 4 and the speech heading for Gerald on line 5, so that 'about money really.' was followed by line 5's 'And that's more' and the rest of the scene as above. In his second revision, in black ink, he added the sentence 'But I'm never going to be bullied.' to Gerald's first speech, deleted everything from 'And that's more' to the end of the scene, and inserted the speeches for VOICE, GERALD, VOICE and GERALD which constitute the final ending.

David

Note A great deal of *David* consists of language influenced by the 1611 (Authorised or King James) translation of the Bible (hereafter *KJB*): all references to the Old Testament (OT) and the New Testament (NT) Bible are to *KJB*, unless otherwise noted. Explanatory notes to the play (and to the passages from it printed in Appendix v) are asterisked in the text when they contain something other than biblical quotation or reference (e.g. textual notes are asterisked, as are names of people and places in *KJB*). Direct quotations from *KJB* are annotated without asterisks in the text: *KJB* is only quoted in the note (in square brackets) if DHL altered it. Close references to *KJB* have also been annotated, with appropriate quotations following in round brackets. The word 'etc.' in an entry signifies that there may be several sources; e.g. at 450:5 the phrase 'before the Lord' appears: Genesis x. 9 is the first of 254 occurrences in *KJB*. Simple *KJB* linguistic parallels have not normally been annotated; e.g. 'no man knoweth' at 450:2 appears at Deuteronomy xxxiv. 6 ('no man knoweth of his sepulchre unto this day'), but DHL was almost certainly not drawing upon that source.

434:22 AGAG [433:2] ... LAD   No list of characters appears in MS or TS: DHL's own list in PPI (see next note) is incomplete and inconsistent. The list provided here – in the order of the characters' appearance – assumes, for example, that the characters DHL describes in speech-headings more than once as 'MAIDENS' are identical with the characters he names as '1ST MAIDEN', '2ND MAIDEN', '3RD MAIDEN' and '4TH MAIDEN', but that the characters described as 'PROPHETS' at 445:31 are more numerous than the two individually named as '1ST PROPHET' and '2ND PROPHET'. The list also makes sense of the appearance of characters named only as 'SOLDIER' or 'ANOTHER SOLDIER' in the text; there is no reason to assume that the down-to-earth 'SOLDIER' of 462:6–16 is identical with the entranced 'SOLDIER' of 519:13–14.

434:39 DAVID [434:24] ... **Lad.**   This is the list of characters DHL inscribed on p. [v] of PPI below the printer's setting '**CHARACTERS**'; he must have inserted a very slightly different list in the set of proofs he returned to the printer, which appeared in E1.

David was anointed by Samuel (1 Samuel xvi. 13: hereafter 1 Sam.): later husband of Michal (1 Sam. xviii. 27) and friend of Jonathan (1 Sam. xviii. 1), he became king of Judah (2 Samuel ii. 4: hereafter 2 Sam.: see note on 443:20). See 1 Sam. xvi–xxx, 2 Sam. i–xxiv, 1 Kings i–ii, 1 Chronicles iii, xi–xxix; see also Introduction, pp. lx–lxi.

Saul was the son of 'a man of Benjamin whose name was Kish' (1 Sam. ix. 1); anointed by Samuel to be 'captain over ... Israel' (1 Sam. ix. 16: see note on 436:4) and made king by the people of Israel (1 Sam. xi. 15); the father of Jonathan, Merab and Michal (1 Sam. xiv. 49). See 1 Sam. ix–xxxi.

Samuel was a Levite, last of the Judges (those – often military leaders – invested with temporary authority in Israel in the period between Joshua and the Kings), first of the Prophets of the Lord (1 Sam. iii. 20); son of Hannah (1 Sam. i. 20); served God from childhood (1 Sam. iii); anointed Saul and David as kings. See 1 Sam. i–iv, viii–xiii, xv–xvi, xxiv–xxv.

Jonathan was the eldest son of Saul (1 Sam. xiii. 16) and friend of David (1 Sam. xviii. 1). See 1 Sam. xiii–xxxi and note on 488:7.

Abner was Saul's 'captain of his host ... the son of Ner, Saul's uncle' (1 Sam. xiv. 50).

Agag was a common title of the kings of Amalek (as Pharaoh was of the Egyptian kings) but here one particular ruler; see 1 Sam. xv. 8–9, 32–3.

Merab was the elder daughter of Saul (1 Sam. xiv. 49) and originally promised to David in marriage (1 Sam. xviii. 17–19); married to Adriel the Meholathite (see below).

Michal was the younger daughter of Saul (1 Sam. xiv. 49) and the first wife of David (1 Sam. xviii. 20, 27–8). DHL refers to her in *The Rainbow*, when Anna Brangwen – admiring David – wonders 'Why should he uncover himself to Michal, a common woman?' (ed. Kinkead-Weekes, 170:10–11).

Jesse was an Ephrathite of Bethlehem in Judah (1 Sam. xvii. 12) and the father of David (1 Sam. xvi. 1, 13).

Eliab, Abinadab and Shammah were the three eldest sons of Jesse: the fourth, fifth, sixth and seventh sons are not named in *KJB* (1 Sam. xvi. 6–10).

Goliath, from Gath, was the (giant) champion of the Philistines (1 Sam. xvii. 4); see notes on 444:17 and 462:34.

Adriel the Meholathite was given Merab as his wife by Saul (1 Sam. xviii. 19).

The Elders – usually heads of families – helped in the government of the Israelites; every city had a ruling body of elders, whose duties including acting as judges; later they shared with the priests the responsibility of determining religious affairs.

435:1 DAVID At some stage, in pencil, DHL revised the title in the heading for Scene 1 (MS, p. 1) from 'David' to 'Saul'. The title in TS (p. [1]) was however corrected in ink from 'SAUL' to 'DAVID' and there is no other evidence, from any later stage of the play's development, that DHL wished it to be called anything but *David*. The title-page of MS (perhaps not in DHL's hand) reads: '*DAVID / A PLAY /* by / D H LAWRENCE'.

435:4 *Gilgal ... compound ... adobe house* W. of the Jordan, near Jericho; where Saul was made king (1 Sam. xi. 14–15) and often associated with him (see 1 Sam. x. 8, xiii. 7–8, 12, 15, xv. 12) ... early indications that DHL was drawing on the culture, religion and civilisation he had seen in the Indian settlements of Arizona and New Mexico, 1922–5. Frieda Lawrence remarked in 1938 that 'The outer form of the life of these old testament people Lawrence believed to have been much like the near Taos Indians' (*D. H. Lawrence's Manuscripts*, ed. Squires, p. 174). Indian associations include the non-*KJB* words 'compound' (435:3) and 'adobe' (sun-dried brick: here and at 485:2), the flat roofs of the houses (444:2, though also implied in many Bible episodes), the 'flat bread' (449:36), the black tents (461:36) of 'worsted' (465:2–3, 474:2) and Saul's final appearance as '*a dark-skinned man*' (519:30). See also notes on 439:30, 444:8, 449:36, 464:6, 487:33, 490:27 and 581:16.

435:6 MEN WITH SPEARS ... *tambourines:* A liberty with the OT story, for at this time only Saul and Jonathan had spears (cf. 1 Sam. xiii. 19, 22) ... In OT, women often sound 'timbrels' at times of triumph (e.g. Exodus xv. 20 and Psalms lxviii. 25): *KJB*'s 'timbrels' are now generally translated as 'tambourines'. See note on 514:5.

435:8 the Amalekite! The Amalekites – or Amalek, a people and a country in the Negeb and Sinai area, e. of Egypt (see next note) – attacked the Israelites on their way from Egypt (see 436:4 and note) and were not forgiven; they were twice defeated by Saul (see 1 Sam. xiv. 48, xv. 2–8).

435:10 the desert of Shur, The 'wilderness of Shur' (Exodus xv. 22) extended from the e. border of Egypt as far as the Negeb area; see 1 Sam. xv. 7.

435:12 Saul came home [435:7] ... to the ground. DHL's musical setting of these lines (and of the music he wrote for texts at 479:5, 482:3, 487:24, 493:7, 517:18, 518:25, 519:4, 519:37, 520:34) appears in Appendix v ii.

435:17 **this dog** Cf. 1 Sam. xvii. 43 ('*Am* I a dog ...').

435:29 **ran like lions** Revised in MS (p. 2) from 'hung like jackals'.

436:4 **hung on the heels of Israel ... coming from Egypt,** The Israelites – their name derived from the new name given to Jacob and the territory they occupied – fought with the Amalekites (see Exodus xvii. 8–16); cf. 1 Sam. xv. 2 ('I remember *that* which Amalek did to Israel, how he laid *wait* for him in the way, when he came up from Egypt'): see too 436:16 ... Exodus xvii. 1 ['... from the wilderness'].

436:7 MAIDENS: ... **wandering Israelites?** Although 'wandering' is not a *KJB* word, cf. Numbers xiv. 33 ('And your children shall wander in the wilderness forty years'), Numbers xxxii. 13 and Joshua xiv. 10.

436:9 **heavy-footed?** DHL's question mark, added in TS (p. 2), was probably not inserted in the missing carbon-copy typescript, the source of all subsequent texts.

436:13 **When Moses ... the sun went down.** Cf. Exodus xvii. 9, 11–12 ('And Moses said unto Joshua, Choose us out men, and go out, fight with Amalek: to morrow I will stand on the top of the hill with the rod of God in mine hand ... And it came to pass, when Moses held up his hand, that Israel prevailed: and when he let down his hand, Amalek prevailed ... and Aaron and Hur stayed up his hands, the one on the one side, and the other on the other side; and his hands were steady until the going down of the sun').

436:15 *war with Amalek ... from under heaven.* See Exodus xvii. 16 and Genesis vi. 17, etc.

436:17 **eyes to see, and ears to hear!** Deuteronomy xxix. 4.

436:20 **Even so.** Revelation i. 7, etc.

436:32 **put him to death,** Although there are non-*KJB* antecedents, a phrase commonly thought of as biblical, especially in connection with the crucifixion of Jesus (cf. Matthew xxvi. 59, xxvii. 1, etc.).

436:37 **Tyre ... Sidon.** Cities on the Mediterranean coast of present-day Lebanon: Tyre is 3 miles w. of Ramah (see note on 441:35).

437:2 **Goldsmith's work ... the ears.** More detailed in the typescript DHL made following Frieda's translation of the play into German (hereafter GTSII) (p. 3): 'Goldschmuck, Reifen und Spangen, und Armbänder: Ohrringe mit Tropfen von Gold [Gold ornaments, clasps and bangles, and bracelets: earrings with drops of gold]' and in MS (p. 4) before revision ('... dropping stones of ruby, for ...').

437:10 **Go in ... the women.** Revised in MS (p. 5) from 'Go to our mother and spin wool with her.' In her reply (437:12–13), Michal originally mentioned 'thine own little manhood' (p. 20).

437:16 **Carmel.** A mountain which forms a characteristic feature of Canaan; see note on 437:28.

437:21 **this prophet of prophets** The first of the play's examples of DHL imitating the form of the Hebraic superlative: cf. 'deep of deeps' (442:6), 'serpent of serpents' (490:12), etc.

437:27 **It is so,** Job ix. 2 (and *Hardy*, 105:5); but 'it was so' is extremely common in *KJB*: see Genesis i. 7, etc.

437:28 **Samuel ... seeking Saul in Gilgal.** Cf. 1 Sam. xv. 12 ('And when Samuel rose early to meet Saul in the morning, it was told Samuel, saying, Saul came to Carmel, and, behold, he ... is gone about, and passed on, and gone down to Gilgal'). The 'stone of directions' is presumably the equivalent of a sign-post.

437:29 **It is well.** See 1 Sam. xx. 7, etc.

437:30 **in the sight of** Extremely common in *KJB* (152 occasions): see Genesis xxxiii. 8, etc.

437:32 **let no mouth speak his name.** Cf. Psalms xlix. 3 ('My mouth shall speak ...'), etc.

437:36 **laid low** Cf. Isaiah xiii. 11 ('lay low the haughtiness ...').

438:1 **sword-edge** *KJB* frequently refers to the 'edge of the sword' (38 occasions): see Genesis xxxiv. 26, etc.

438:3 **an old man in a mantle,** 1 Sam. xxviii. 14 ['An old man ... covered with a mantle']. Samuel's mantle – a garment particularly associated with the prophets Elijah and Elisha (see 2 Kings ii. 8, 13–14) – becomes significant at 440:9–10, when Saul tears '*the hem of* SAMUEL's *garment*' (see note on 440:20); it is what distinguishes him when the witch at Endor raises his spirit (1 Sam. xxviii. 11–20).

438:8 **destroyed and Amalekite utterly ... fine linen** Cf. 1 Sam. xv. 3 ('Now go and smite Amalek, and utterly destroy all that they have') ... see 1 Chronicles iv. 21, xv. 27, etc.

438:12 **the God of the Unknown Name** The tetragrammaton YHWH – 'Yahweh', the incommunicable name of the God of Israel ('Jehovah' was a twelfth-century AD version) – was considered too sacred to pronounce. When Moses asked God how to answer Israelites who asked 'What *is* his name?', 'God said unto Moses, I AM THAT I AM: and he said, Thus shalt thou say unto the children of Israel, I AM hath sent me unto you' (Exodus iii. 13–14). See too Exodus vi. 2–3 ('And God spake unto Moses, and said unto him, I *am* the LORD: And I appeared unto Abraham, unto Isaac, and unto Jacob, by *the name of* God Almighty, but by my name JEHOVAH was I not known to them').

438:25 **Blessed be [438:16] ... Say on.** 1 Sam. xv. 13–16 ['And Samuel came to Saul: and Saul said unto him, Blessed *be* ... the LORD: I have ... / And Samuel said, What *meaneth* then this bleating ... / And Saul said, They have ... Amalekites: for the people spared ... the sheep and of ... unto the LORD thy God; and the rest ... / Then Samuel said unto Saul, Stay, and ... what the LORD hath said to me this night. And he said unto him, Say on'].

438:33 **When thou [438:26] ... unclosing eyes?** 1 Sam. xv. 17–19 ['And Samuel said, When thou ... *made* the head of ..., and the LORD anointed thee king over Israel? / And the LORD sent thee on a journey, and said, Go and ... be consumed. / Wherefore then didst thou not obey the voice of the LORD, but didst fly upon the spoil, and didst evil in the sight of the LORD?'].

439:3 **Yea, I [438:34] ... fat of rams.** 1 Sam. xv. 20–2 ['And Saul said unto Samuel, Yea, I ... voice of the LORD, and have gone ... which the LORD sent ... of Amalek, and ... / ... to sacrifice unto the LORD thy God in Gilgal. / And Samuel said, Hath the LORD *as great* delight in burnt offerings and sacrifices, as in obeying the voice of the LORD? Behold, to ...]' For 'the Great One', cf. Isaiah xix. 20 ('he shall send them a saviour, and a great one').

439:4 **the bread of life?** John vi. 35, 48.

439:6 **a sutler,** One who follows an army and sells provisions to soldiers. Not a *KJB* word, although dating from the 1590s.

439:9 **the Living Breath,** Cf. Genesis ii. 7 ('And the LORD God ... breathed into his nostrils the breath of life'), etc.

439:11 **his servant Israel.** See 1 Chronicles xvi. 13, Psalms cxxxvi. 22, etc.

439:13 **I feared ... their voice.** 1 Sam. xv. 24.

439:15 **fearedst** Printed as 'feardest' in PPI and PPII (p. 13) and (probably as a result) altered to 'fearest' by DHL in the first of the authorial corrections surviving in PPII. See Introduction, footnote 326.

439:17 **you,** PPI (p. 13) reads 'thee'; it is possible that, in the carbon-copy typescript, DHL was responsible for bringing this word into line with the 'thee' and 'thou' used elsewhere in the paragraph, but it is more likely to be a regularisation by the compositor of PPI.

439:21 **rebellion is ... being king ... voice of his people?** 1 Sam. xv. 23 ['For rebellion ... the LORD, he hath ...'] ... cf. 1 Sam. xv. 24 ('I feared the people, and obeyed their voice') and 1 Sam. viii. 7 ('Hearken unto the voice of the people').

439:23 **in the frowardness of their hearts.** Cf. Proverbs vi. 14 ('Frowardness *is* in his heart'). 'Frowardness' – like 'froward' a common *KJB* word – means 'perversity' or 'ungovernableness'. See 449:5 below.

439:24 **a lion ... dogs.** Cf. Ecclesiastes ix. 4 ('for a living dog is better than a dead lion').

439:25 **The people ... to them.** Cf. 1 Sam. xii. 12–13.

439:28 **Thou didst choose me out.** Cf. 1 Sam. ii. 28 ('And did I choose him out of all the tribes of Israel ...').

439:30 **the Thunder ... the Wind of Strength** Especially in his revision of the play in PPI, DHL combined elements of North American Indian animist religion concerning the life of Fire, Water, Thunder, Light, Dark, etc., with fragments of pre-Socratic thought and *KJB* reference. Here he uses, in particular, David's song of thanksgiving in Psalms xviii. 13 ('The LORD also thundered in the heavens'). See too 1 Sam. vii. 10 ('the LORD thundered with a great thunder'), Psalms xxix. 3 ('the God of glory thundereth'), Psalms lxxvii. 18 ('The voice of thy thunder *was* in the heaven') and Psalms lxxxi. 7 ('I answered thee in the secret place of thunder'). In his work on PPI, he replaced the words 'God' and 'Lord' with 'Deep' (441:14, 449:16, 449:24, 26, 454:24, 455:25, 488:22), 'Might' (441:37, 489:26), 'Bolt' (444:19, 450:25, 454:11), 'One' (444:23, 445:7), 'Fire' (454:27, 459:19), 'Full' (456:7), 'Dawn' (458:23), 'Hope' (459:16), 'Thunderer' (486:13, 487:9), 'Morning Wind' (486:34), 'Lord of Days' (486:35), 'the bright horn' (487:2), 'Night' (492:5),

'Giver' (506:27), 'hills' (506:37), 'day' (506:38), 'Strength' (516:5, 524:32, 39), 'Hill' (517:3), 'Name' (517:13), 'Kindler' (519:10), 'Wave' (519:12) and 'Sun' (520:12); he also altered 'Lord's anointed' to 'horn-anointed' (486:20) and 'the Lord's way' to 'the way of might' (516:3). In such ways he could replace the concept of a personal God with something more primitive. For DHL on animism, see 'The Hopi Snake Dance', *Mornings in Mexico* (1927), pp. 140–5, and 'New Mexico', *Phoenix*, pp. 146–7 ... cf. Hosea xiii. 15 ('the wind of the LORD ...') and Isaiah xi. 15 ('And the LORD ... with his mighty wind').

439:31 **the great Wish** Perhaps a reminiscence of the Norse 'God Wish' described in lecture 1 ('The Hero as Divinity') of *Lectures on Heroes* (1840), by Thomas Carlyle, which DHL knew by Spring 1906 (E.T. 102); the immediately preceding mention of 'middle world' (suggestive of 'middle earth', an archaic and mythological view of earth situated between heaven and hell) strengthens the probability of a link with Carlyle's description of the Norse view of the Gods and of the world.

439:33 **the Lord ... over thee.** Cf. 1 Sam. x. 1 ('Then Samuel took a vial of oil, and poured *it* upon his head ...').

440:20 **I have sinned** [440:1] ... **worship him.** 1 Sam. xv. 24–30 ['And Saul said unto Samuel, I have sinned: for I ... the LORD, and thy words: because I feared their voice. / Now therefore, I pray ... that I may worship the LORD. / And Samuel said unto Saul, I will ... over Israel. / And as Samuel turned about to go away, he laid hold upon the skirt of his mantle, and it rent. / And Samuel said unto him, The LORD hath ... than thou. / And also the Strength of Israel will not lie nor repent: for he is not ... should repent. / Then he said, I have sinned: *yet* honour ... pray thee, before the ... that I may worship the LORD thy God'].

440:23 **the Hidden Sun ... the Power** Cf. Psalms lxxxiv. 11 ('For the LORD god *is* a sun ...') ... cf. Deuteronomy iv. 37 ('with his mighty power'), Psalms cxlvii. 5 ('Great *is* our Lord, and of great power') and Psalms lxii. 11 ('power *belongeth* unto God').

440:25 **the Lord's anointed,** 1 Sam. xvi. 6, xxiv. 6, etc.

440:28 **Yet bless me, my father.** Cf. Genesis xxvii. 34, 38 ('Bless me, *even* me also, O my father').

440:30 **The Lord ... strengthen thee!** 1 Sam. xvii. 37, the source of this traditional blessing ... cf. Psalms xx. 1–2.

440:34 **strengthen thy knees ... quicken thy feet!** Cf. Job iv. 4 and Isaiah xxxv. 3 ... Psalms contains numerous references to 'quicken' (i.e. enliven). For the potential significance of knees, see R. B. Onions, *The Origins of European Thought*, 2nd edn (Cambridge, 1954), pp. 174–86.

440:36 **I have sinned ... own undoing.** 1 Sam. xv. 24, 30 ... cf. Isaiah vi. 5 ('I am undone').

441:1 **awful** In TS (p. 8), DHL deleted 'unknown', inserted and then deleted 'awful'. In the carbon-copy typescript, he must have allowed 'awful' to stand.

441:2 **forgive my transgression.** Cf. Joshua xxiv. 19 ('he will not forgive your transgressions') and Psalms li. 1 ('blot out my transgressions').

441:6 **Is it well ... May it be well.** Cf. 2 Kings iv. 26 ('*Is it* well ... *It is* well').

441:7 **Bring me ... the Amalekites.**   1 Sam. xv. 32 ['Then said Samuel, Bring ye hither to me Agag the king of ...'].

441:9 **Abner. We**   Brett left TS reading 'Abner, we' (p. 8); DHL corrected TSR to 'Abner, for we'. This has however been judged a response to the errors in TS, and the MS reading (p. 13) has been restored.

441:13 **The Lord ... rent from me.**   Cf. 1 Sam. xv. 28 ('And Samuel said unto him [Saul], The LORD hath rent the kingdom of Israel from thee this day').

441:14 **Who knoweth ... the Deep?**   Cf. Jeremiah v. 4–5 ('they know not the way of the LORD ... they have known the way of the LORD'): DHL replaced 'Lord' with 'Deep' in his correction of PPI (p. 15).

441:16 **turned his face away,**   Cf. 2 Chronicles vi. 42 ('turn not away the face of thine anointed') and Ezekiel vii. 22 ('My face will I turn also from them').

441:17 **crying like an infant in the night!**   A favourite DHL allusion: Tennyson, *In Memoriam* (1850), liv, ll. 17–18: '... what am I? / An infant crying in the night ...'

441:21 *coming forward* ... **among women.**   1 Sam. xv. 32 ['And Agag came unto him delicately. And Agag said, Surely the ...'] ... 1 Sam. xv. 33.

441:31 **I have hewed ... before the Lord,**   1 Sam. xv. 33 ['And Samuel hewed Agag in pieces before the LORD in Gilgal'].

441:31 **the Most High,**   Cf. Mark v. 7, Acts xvi. 17 ('the most high God'), but DHL's source may well have been the closing words ('Glory be to thee, O Lord most high') of the prayer 'Therefore with Angels and Archangels' in the Church of England communion service.

441:32 **the nostrils ... God of Wrath.**   Cf. 2 Sam. xxii. 8–9 ('he was wroth. / There went up a smoke out of his nostrils'); see too *Paradise Lost* ix. 196 ... cf. Psalms lxxviii. 31, etc. ('The wrath of God').

441:35 **Ramah**   A city in Ephraim, near Bethel, where Samuel lived (see 1 Sam. xv. 34).

441:37 **And may the Might be with thee—**   'Might' is a common *KJB* word: cf. 1 Chronicles xxix. 12 ('in thine hand *is* power and might') and Revelation vii. 12 ('... honour, and power, and might, *be* unto our God for ever and ever'); see too note on 439:30. The dash at the end of a speech with no other punctuation, here and elsewhere, is very frequently an indication that the speech is being interrupted, either by another speech or by an action or by an exit; see, e.g., 444:22, 27, 452:17, 454:10, etc.

442:3 **out of the whirlwind,**   Job xxxviii. 1 and xl. 6.

442:6 **the deep of deeps**   Cf. Psalms xviii. 15–16 ('Then the channels of waters were seen, and the foundations of the world were discovered ... he drew me out of many waters') and Psalms cvii. 24 ('the works of the LORD, and his wonders in the deep'), 1 Corinthians ii. 10 ('the deep things of God'), Psalms xlii. 7 ('Deep calleth unto deep'), etc. Cf. too Psalms lxxxviii. 6 ('in the deeps'), etc. See also notes on 439:30 and 443:12.

442:9 **I am sore for Saul,**   Cf. 1 Sam. xvi. 1 ('And the LORD said unto Samuel, How long wilt thou mourn for Saul ...?').

442:13 **My bowels ... a knot of grief,** Cf. Lamentations i. 20 ('I *am* in distress: my bowels are troubled; mine heart is turned within me'). 'Knot' is not a *KJB* word. See too note on 496:26.

442:17 **unseen almighty,** Genesis xvii. 1 ('the Almighty God'), etc. In MS (p. 15), DHL first wrote 'moves the Mighty One', then inserted an unclear 'unseen' after 'moves', deleted 'the' and 'One', and altered 'Mighty' to 'almighty'. Brett read 'unseen' as 'Unseen' and capitalised 'almighty' (TS, p. 10).

442:20 **Like waters** Cf. Job xxiv. 18 ('He *is* swift as the waters').

442:31 **living God?** 1 Sam. xvii. 26, 36, etc.

442:38 **the stink ... rise up** Cf. Isaiah xxxiv. 3 ('their stink shall come up'), Joel ii. 20 ('his stink shall come up') and Amos iv. 10 ('I have made the stink of your camps to come up into your nostrils').

443:1 **creeping thing** Genesis i. 26.

443:4 **the Fountain of Days ... the Ancient of Days** Cf. Jeremiah xvii. 13 ('the LORD, the fountain of living waters') ... Daniel vii. 9, 13, 22; cf. too the frontispiece (plate i) 'The Ancient of Days' to 'Europe' (1794) by William Blake (1757–1827) and the hymn 'O Worship the King' by Robert Grant (1779–1838) ('the Ancient of Days / Pavilioned in splendour, / And girded with praise').

443:12 **the deeps of God ... I sink ... stone in the sea,** Cf. Psalms lxix. 2 and 14 ('I sink in deep mire ... let me not sink: let me be delivered ... out of the deep waters') and Exodus xv. 10 ('the sea covered them: they sank as lead in the mighty waters'). See also note on 442:6.

443:15 **the oracle of the Lord ... fountains of the deep.** Cf. Psalms xxviii. 2 ('thy holy oracle'), Romans iii. 2 ('the oracles of God'), etc. ... Genesis viii. 2 ['... fountains also of ...'].

443:18 **I will fill the horn with oil again,** 1 Sam. xvi. 1 ['fill thy horn with oil'].

443:20 **Judah.** The territory of the tribe originating from Judah, fourth son of Jacob.

443:27 **the virtue is gone out of him.** Mark v. 30 ['... had gone ...']. See *Love Among the Haystacks*, ed. Worthen, 149:38; *The Trespasser*, ed. Mansfield, 155:39; *St. Mawr and Other Stories*, ed. Brian Finney (Cambridge, 1983), 64:4–5.

443:28 **with a spear ... kill me,** Omitted in GTSII (p. 11), where the whole sentence runs 'Und Saul wird mich töten wollen, wenn ich es ihm sage' ['And Saul will want to kill me, if I tell him'].

443:30 **Bethlehem,** Town six miles n. of Jerusalem, home town of Jesse and birthplace of David and Jesus, who fulfilled the prophecy (Micah v. 2, Matthew ii. 5) that the Messiah would be born there 'of the house and lineage of David' (Luke ii. 4). Samuel went there on God's direction (1 Sam. xvi. 1, 4).

443:32 **from Saul ... never ... face again.** Cf. 1 Sam. xv. 35 ('And Samuel came no more to see Saul until the day of his death'). See too 456:5–6.

443:36 **But alas ... loved Saul,** Cf. 1 Sam. xv. 35 ('Samuel mourned for Saul').

444:3 **[*Enter* JESSE *and* ELIAB.]** Not in MS or E1; GTSII (p. 12), however, includes the stage direction 'Männer kommen, auch Isai, Davids Vater, und Eliab,

Davids Bruder' ['Men enter, including Jesse, David's father, and Eliab, David's brother'].

444:7 **Come in! ... Come in!**   No such gathering as the Elder calls for actually occurs: GTSII (p. 12) omitted.

444:8 *(on the Plaza)*   DHL is apparently thinking of New Mexico and Mexico, and perhaps specifically of Taos Plaza, which is the main square in the centre of the town. See note to 545:15.

444:14 **The sun looks darkened.**   Cf. Luke xxiii. 45 ('And the sun was darkened ...'); also Matthew xxiv. 29, Mark xiii. 24, Isaiah xiii. 10, etc.

444:17 **not the lion nor the bear ... the Philistine,**   Cf. 1 Sam. xvii. 36 ('both the lion and the bear') ... neighbouring, non-Semitic people, constant enemies of Israel, ruling the Negeb, much of the hill country and the coastal plain with the five royal cities of Gaza, Gath, Ashkelon, Ashdod and Ekron (now Akir: the most northerly). See too note on 474:10.

444:24 **there is ... is precious.**   1 Sam. iii. 1 ['And the word of the LORD was precious in those days; *there was* no open vision'].

444:27 **the lion roaring upon us**   Cf. Isaiah xxxi. 4 ('Like as the lion ... roaring on his prey').

444:31 **the strength of our right hand ... linen ephods,**   Cf. Psalms xx. 6 ('the saving strength of his right hand'): *KJB* contains many references to 'right hand' ... priestly garments, like surplices, worn by prophets (see 514:4); Samuel wore one as a child (1 Sam. ii. 18), as did David when dancing before the Lord (2 Sam. vi. 14). The 'blue ephod' of 450:22 suggests Exodus xxxix. 2 ('he made the ephod *of* gold, blue, and purple').

444:37 **those that ... renew their strength**   Cf. Isaiah xl. 31 and xli. 1 ('they that wait upon the LORD shall renew *their* strength ... let the people renew *their* strength').

444:39 **God stirs amid his waters,**   Cf. Psalms xxix. 3 ('The voice of the LORD is upon the waters ... the LORD *is* upon many waters').

445:5 **lion in the thicket,**   Cf. Jeremiah iv. 7 ('The lion is come up from his thicket') and Genesis xxii. 13 ('a ram caught in a thicket').

445:7 **hear him out of the cloud.**   Cf. Mark ix. 7 ('a voice came out of the cloud'), Matthew xvii. 5, etc.: the NT references relate to the OT archetype at Exodus xxiv. 16.

445:12 **day follows day ... between the days.**   Cf. Psalms xix. 2 ('Day unto day uttereth speech, and night unto night sheweth knowledge').

445:14 **a wild ass in the wilderness,**   Jeremiah ii. 24 ['... ass used to the ...'].

445:18 **will not be comforted.**   Cf. Matthew ii. 18 ('Rachel weeping *for* her children, and would not be comforted').

445:29 **give me**   In MS (p. 22), DHL originally wrote 'I prefer', but deleted 'prefer' and inserted 'give me' without deleting the redundant 'I'. TS (p. 15) omitted it.

445:32 **The Lord be with thee!**   Ruth ii. 4: also a frequently used blessing spoken by a minister to a congregation, e.g. in Morning Prayer, Evening Prayer, etc. ['... with you'] in the *Book of Common Prayer*.

445:36 **Comest thou ... come to sacrifice,** 1 Sam. xvi. 4–5 ['Comest thou peaceably? / And he said, Peaceably: I am come ... the LORD: sanctify yourselves, and come with me to the sacrifice'].

445:37 **Renew your ... purify yourselves.** Cf. 1 Sam. xi. 14 ('let us go to Gilgal, and renew the kingdom') and Numbers xxxi. 19–20 ('purify *both* yourselves and your captives ... And purify all *your* raiment').

446:3 **Call your household ... in your house.** Cf. 1 Sam. xvi. 5 ('And he sanctified Jesse and his sons, and called them to the sacrifice').

447:17 **Surely the Lord's** [447:12] **... on the heart.** 1 Sam. xvi. 6–7 ['he looked on Eliab, and said, Surely the ... / But the LORD said unto Samuel, Look not on his countenance, or on the ... his stature; because I have refused him: for *the LORD seeth* not as man seeth; for man ...'].

447:23 **Ha! Abinadab ... chosen this.** 1 Sam. xvi. 8 ['Then Jesse called Abinadab, and made him pass before Samuel. And he said, Neither hath ...'].

447:26 **the sacrifice meat.** Cf. Numbers xxviii. 20 and 24 ('their meat offering ... the meat of the sacrifice made by fire').

447:30 **Come, Shammah ... Lord chosen this.** 1 Sam. xvi. 9 ['Then Jesse made Shammah to pass by. And he said, Neither hath ...'].

448:17 FOURTH SON: [447:35] **... Lord chosen this.** 1 Sam. xvi. 10 ['Again, Jesse made seven of his sons to pass before Samuel. And Samuel said unto Jesse, the LORD hath not chosen these'].

448:21 **the sheep.** GTSII (p. 16) adds 'Er ist nur ein Knabe' ['He is only a boy'].

448:23 **Are here all ... he come hither.** 1 Sam. xvi. 11 ['... And he said, There remaineth ... youngest, and, behold, he ... And Samuel said unto Jesse, Send and fetch him: for we ...'].

448:27 ELIAB: **... Lord of Hosts** DHL inserted '(coming forward from the fire)' after the speech-heading in TSR (p. 17) but presumably failed to insert it in the carbon-copy typescript, as it does not appear in PPI ... i.e. 'God of the armies of Israel' (1 Sam. xvii. 45): a very common OT phrase (see, e.g., 1 Sam. i. 3, xv. 2).

448:32 **the Wonderful ... own. But** Cf. Isaiah ix. 6 ('and his name shall be called Wonderful') ... it is possible that the variant ('own, but') in PPI (p. 25) was introduced in the carbon-copy typescript: DHL had made several changes in TS (p. 17) in this speech. However, it is more likely that the compositor regularised a sentence starting 'But'. The reading of MS (p. 25) and TS has been retained.

449:1 **the sin of witchcraft,** 1 Sam. xv. 23.

449:3 **I shall fall into a pit.** Cf. Isaiah xxiv. 18 ('he who fleeth from the noise of the fear shall fall into the pit') and Jeremiah xlviii. 44 ('He that fleeth from the fear shall fall into the pit'). See too 476:21.

449:6 **a hard thing ... well-nigh** 2 Kings ii. 10 ... cf. Psalms lxxiii. 2 ('my steps had well nigh slipped').

449:10 **I shall ... is he.** 1 Sam. xvi. 12 ['And the LORD said, Arise, anoint him: for this ...'].

449:11 **The Lord hath chosen this one.** Cf. Deuteronomy vii. 6 ('the LORD thy God hath chosen thee').

449:13 *the horn of oil ... their glory,* 1 Sam. xvi. 13 ... cf. Isaiah xlv. 8 ('let the skies pour down righteousness').

449:17 **Surely my soul leaps with God!** Probably suggested by part of the David story not used by DHL: see 2 Sam. vi. 16 ('king David leaping and dancing before the LORD'). Cf. also Isaiah lxi. 10 ('my soul shall be joyful in my God'). The sentence did not appear in MS but was written into TS (p. 18).

449:20 **The Glory pours ... the Chooser.** In MS (p. 27) these sentences originally ran: 'The Lord pours himself out on thee. The Lord waketh thee. Thou art no more thine own, for the Lord hath claimed thee for the length of thy days.'

449:22 **When thou goeth in ... when thou comest out,** DHL's reversal of the common *KJB* formula 'go out / come in': e.g. 1 Sam. xxix. 6 and 2 Sam. iii. 25 ('thy going out and thy coming in') and Psalms cxxi. 8 ('The LORD shall preserve thy going out and thy coming in from this time forth'). An important text for DHL: see, e.g., *The Rainbow*, ed. Kinkead-Weekes, 20:13.

449:30 **not thine own ... thou art his.** Cf. 1 Corinthians vi. 19 ('ye are not your own') and *The Rainbow*, ed. Kinkead-Weekes, 40:4 and 302:37 ... cf. 1 Sam. xvi. 18, etc. ('the LORD *is* with him').

449:31 **I am thy servant, my Lord.** Cf. Psalms cxvi. 16, etc. ('O LORD, truly I *am* thy servant').

449:36 *flat bread.* DHL is probably thinking of Mexican and Indian tortillas – flat round cakes of corn meal – as well as of Jewish unleavened bread.

449:38 **the Lord hath chosen him,** Cf. 1 Kings viii. 16 ('I chose David'), 1 Kings xi. 13 ('which I have chosen'), etc.

450:2 **the time is fulfilled,** Mark i. 15 ['The ...'], etc.

450:5 **before the Lord,** Genesis x. 9, etc.

450:13 **He has anointed ... passed over.** Cf. Genesis xxv. 23 ('and the elder shall serve the younger') and Luke i. 52–3 ('He hath put down the mighty from *their* seats, and exalted them of low degree. / He hath filled the hungry with good things; and the rich he hath sent empty away').

450:20 **cast it up a reproach** Almost the language of *KJB*: cf. 1 Sam. xi. 2 ('lay it *for* a reproach').

450:24 **I shall ... father's sheep.** Cf. 1 Sam. xvii. 15 ('But David went ... to feed his father's sheep'); there are many NT references too.

450:31 **stripling?** Lad; 1 Sam. xvii. 56 (referring to David: 'Inquire thou whose son the stripling *is*') is the word's only occurrence in *KJB*. See too 457:30.

450:38 **My day is not yet come.** Cf. John ii. 4 ('mine hour is not yet come').

450:40 **now** The reading of TSR (p. 20): the reading of PPI ('out') may derive from an interlinear insertion in the carbon-copy typescript, but is more likely to be a compositor's (normalising) error.

451:3 *(To the* NEIGHBOURS.*)* **Yea** Replaced in GTSII (p. 19) by a speech from the Neighbours: 'Der Herr stärke Euch heut' Abend' ['The Lord strengthen you this night'] ... the reading of TSR (p. 20). PPI prints 'Nay', which may have been the word in the carbon-copy typescript, but is more likely to be the result of a compositor seeing DHL's rather unclear 'Y' as an 'N', and altering the rest of the word to fit.

451:6 **Peace be to this house!** 1 Sam. xxv. 6 ['peace *be* to thine house'].

451:8 **An heifer,** Cf. 1 Sam. xvi. 2 ('Take an heifer with thee ...').

451:9 **Reach forth thy hand.** The sentence appears in PPI. In TSR (p. 20), the words 'Eat then! have been deleted following 'and goodly!', and Jesse's speech 'Reach forth thy hand' appears as an interlinear insertion in pencil immediately before the stage direction noting David's re-entrance. This makes it likely that TS was emended first and that PPI reflects the revised reading of the carbon-copy typescript. The ending of this scene was written into the typescripts. See Textual apparatus, entries for 451:3, 451:8 and 451:13.

451:11 *the mess* A serving or measure of food sufficient to make a dish: see, e.g., 2 Sam. xi. 8 ('a mess *of meat*').

451:17 **visited** Common *KJB* sense of 'looked after, taken care of' (see, e.g., Genesis l. 24–5).

452:35 **David's come to Gilgal.** Cf. 1 Sam. xvi. 19–20 ('... Saul sent messengers unto Jesse, and said, Send me David thy son, which *is* with the sheep. / And Jesse took an ass *laden* with bread, and a bottle of wine, and a kid, and sent *them* by David his son unto Saul').

453:24 **riddle you a riddle** The play's first example of DHL imitating the well-known form of the Hebraic cognate accusative: cf. 'they dreamed a dream' (Genesis xl. 5). Later examples are not annotated.

453:32 **wrestle with the Lord,** Cf. Jacob's wrestling with 'God, face to face' (Genesis xxxii. 24–30).

453:38 **wise women ... the spirits of the deep.** I.e. soothsayers: later, one interceded with David (2 Sam. xiv. 2) ... cf. Glendower in Shakespeare's *Henry IV Pt 1*, III. i. 53: 'I can call spirits from the vasty deep'.

453:40 **among the wondrous.** Cf. 1 Sam. x. 11–12 ('*Is* Saul also among the prophets?'): MS reads 'among the prophets' (p. 33).

454:3 **the sin of witchcraft!** 1 Sam. xv. 23.

454:6 **for you ... not against you.** Cf. Matthew xii. 30 ('He that is not with me is against me').

454:9 **from the land ... and with wizardry.** Cf. 1 Sam. xxviii. 3 ('And Saul had put away those that had familiar spirits, and the wizards, out of the land').

454:18 **I call ... he will not hear me.** Cf. Psalms lxxxviii. 9, 14 ('LORD, I have called daily upon thee ... LORD, why casteth off my soul? *why* hidest thou thy face from me?').

454:21 **departed from thee,** 1 Sam. xvi. 14 ['the Spirit of the LORD departed from Saul'].

454:27 **the Fire** For DHL's combination of elements of North American Indian and other animist religions with *KJB* reference, see note on 439:30. Cf. Psalms xviii. 8 ('There went up a smoke out of his nostrils, and fire out of his mouth devoured'). See also Exodus xix. 18 ('And mount Sinai was altogether on a smoke, because the LORD descended upon it in fire') and Deuteronomy iv. 24 ('For the LORD thy God *is* a consuming fire . . .').

454:30 **I have . . . all witches,** Cf. note on 454:9 and Exodus xxii. 18 ('Thou shalt not suffer a witch to live').

454:31 **as good a deed** Brett's typed rendition (TS, p. 24) of DHL's 'a good deed' (MS, p. 35); DHL's added phrase in TSR – see Textual apparatus for 454:31(ii) – makes it impossible to return to the reading of MS.

454:35 **my empty place . . . seven times** For the meaning of 'empty' see Matthew xii. 43–5 . . . the number seven – symbolic of perfect order, and of the union of the ternary and the quaternary – entered extensively into the religious life and observances of the Jews: e.g. cf. Matthew xviii. 21–2.

454:36 **spirit that gets** DHL's revision of 'steals' to 'gets' (TSR, p. 24) marks, in effect, his adoption of Brett's 'spirit that steals' for his own 'spirits that steal' (MS, p. 35); it would be inadvisable to return to his MS reading or to modify the TSR reading.

455:19 **a feather-brain.** Giddy, light-headed. Not in *KJB*: nineteenth-century archaic. *OED2* cites Carlyle using it in 1839, following the adjective 'feather-brained' used by Scott in 1820 (see notes on 457:31 and 467:15).

455:27 **I am a strange man unto myself.** Cf. Psalms lxix. 8 ('I am become a stranger unto my brethren').

455:31 **the Spirit of God comes upon him,** Common OT phrase, taking many forms: e.g. 1 Sam. x. 10 ['. . . God came . . .'], etc.

455:37 **great with** Cf. Psalms lxxviii. 71 ('great with young') and Luke ii. 5 ('great with child').

455:40 **in the sight of all Israel.** Deuteronomy xxxi. 7, etc.

456:13 **beautiful among men,** Cf. 1 Sam. ix. 2 ('Saul . . . a choice young man, and a goodly; and *there was* not among the children of Israel a goodlier person than he . . .').

456:36 **ruddy** Used three times in *KJB*, twice with reference to David (1 Sam. xvi. 12, xvii. 42). See also note on 471:13. DHL's first reference appears to have been in 'A Prelude', *Love Among the Haystacks*, ed. Worthen, 5:2; the word subsequently appears frequently in his work, indicating health, vigour and vitality.

457:14 **the mother of Jonathan** Ahinoam (1 Sam. xiv. 50), mother of Jonathan and of Saul's two daughters Merab and Michal: according to Saul 'a perverse rebellious *woman*' (1 Sam. xx. 30).

457:16 **wiseling . . . Pluck it out,** I.e. a pretender to wisdom ('*rare*' in *OED2*) . . . Matthew v. 29, etc.

457:27 **in unto** Brett typed 'into' (TS, p. 28) and DHL emended to 'nigh unto'. His emendation has been judged an attempt to return his text to the MS reading (p. 41), a phrase common in OT: see Genesis xvi. 4, etc.

457:31 **malapert.** David's brother Eliab says to him 'I know thy pride, and the naughtiness of thine heart' (1 Sam. xvii. 28). A malapert is a presumptuous, impudent, saucy person (last previous use as a noun in 1765): DHL may have adapted the adjective used by Shakespeare (*Twelfth Night*, IV. i. 47) and revived as a literary archaism by Sir Walter Scott (1771–1832) in *The Betrothed* (1825), chap. VIII.

458:1 **The Lord sends the wisdom,** Cf. 1 Chronicles xxii. 12 ('Only the LORD give thee wisdom and understanding . . .').

458:8 **I go to speak with Abner.** DHL first wrote 'I will go and find Ahab' (MS, p. 42): Ahab was the seventh king of Israel and the husband of Jezebel (1 Kings xvi–xxii), but DHL may have been thinking of Captain Ahab in Melville's *Moby Dick* (1851).

458:17 **the mother who bore me,** Cf. Jeremiah xxii. 26 ('thy mother that bare thee').

458:23 **the Dawn is with you.** Cf. 1 Sam. xvi. 13 ('and the Spirit of the LORD came upon David from that day forward').

459:10 **father or mother . . . nothing to you.** Cf. Matthew x. 37 ('He that loveth father or mother more than me is not worthy of me . . .') and xii. 48 ('Who is my mother? and who are my brethren?').

459:16 **the Hope.** *KJB* regularly associates God with hope: e.g. Psalms lxxi. 5 ('For thou *art* my hope, O Lord GOD') and Jeremiah xvii. 13 ('O LORD, the hope of Israel'). See also note on 439:30.

459:19 **my father . . . spear at me,** Saul's threats and homicidal attempts with the javelin, described at 1 Sam. xviii. 10–11, xix. 9–10 and xx. 33, are mentioned four more times in the play: see 490:15, 491:7–8, 491:17–18 and 504:24. See too 583:5–10.

459:22 **strong gladness** Not *KJB*; but see *The Rainbow*, ed. Kinkead-Weekes, 262:24.

459:27 **faithful . . . unto death.** Revelation ii. 10 ('faithful unto death').

459:30 **the Lord hath rejected,** 1 Sam. xv. 23 ['Because thou hast rejected the word of the LORD, he hath also rejected thee from *being* king'].

459:36 **a people choose a king,** The people of Israel had – in spite of Samuel's arguments – insisted 'Nay; but we will have a king over us' (1 Sam. viii. 19; see too viii. 5–22.)

459:38 **Lord of All** Acts x. 36, Galatians iv. 1.

460:17 **why do I love thee?** For the love of David and Jonathan, see 1 Sam. xviii. 1–3, xx. 17 and 2 Sam. i. 26. Cf. *The White Peacock*, ed. Robertson, 223:1–3.

460:26 **between me and thee.** 1 Sam. xx. 42 ['The LORD be between me and thee, and between my seed and thy seed for ever'].

460:27 **love my soul.** Cf. 1 Sam. xviii. 1 ('Jonathan loved him as his own soul').

461:5 **why should I not be sad?** Nehemiah ii. 3 ['. . . not my countenance be . . .'].

461:7 **gone out against the Philistine.** Cf. 1 Sam. iv. 1 ('Now Israel went out against the Philistines to battle'). The preparations of this battle are recorded at 1 Sam. xvii. 1–2. The Philistines were the descendants of Casluhim (Genesis x. 14): they migrated northward from Egypt to Canaan, keeping by the sea coast.

461:9 **victory ... dance.** 1 Sam. xxx. 16 portrays a reaction to victory: 'eating and drinking, and dancing, because of all the great spoil that they had taken out of the land of the Philistines'.

461:11 **sent him away.** DHL invents this detail where the Bible offers two contradictory versions of Saul's acquaintance with David. In the first part of the David story, David is originally sent to Saul because of his skill as a harp-player, and rises to the position of Saul's armour-bearer (1 Sam. xvi. 21); when, however, the war with the Philistines starts and his three elder brothers follow Saul, David 'returned from Saul to feed his father's sheep at Bethlehem' (1 Sam. xvii. 14–15). When David reappears in both Bible and play, Saul arms him for combat without recognising him; even when David kills Goliath, neither in the Bible nor in the play is Saul aware of who he is. DHL invents a sending-away to deal with the first problem, supplies a reason for Saul not recognising David – 'How should I know him, with his young beard on his lip!' (470:20–1) – then has Saul suddenly recognise him after the death of Goliath: 'Ay, thou art David!' (472:5).

461:26 **show me the ways in the sand.** Divination was forbidden to the Jews (Deuteronomy xviii. 9–14) but was common among their neighbours (see, e.g., Ezekiel xxi. 21).

461:29 **white crown-bone.** Technically part of the skull of a whale, but here probably the part of a tooth projecting beyond the gum.

461:33 **Elah ... Shochoh ... two hills ... a valley ... a brook in the bottom.** Cf. 1 Sam. xvii. 1–3 ('Now the Philistines ... were gathered together at Shochoh, which *belongeth* to Judah ... / And Saul and the men of Israel were gathered together, and pitched by the valley of Elah ... / And the Philistines stood on a mountain on the one side, and Israel stood on a mountain on the other side: and *there was* a valley between them'). The brook (466:2) is where David selects his sling stones (469:1–2).

461:36 **Oh** One of the occasions where it is possible that DHL was responsible for a change in the revised set of second proofs: see, e.g., Textual apparatus entries at 439:15(ii), 439:33, 442:2, 449:19(i), 459:5, 459:6, 462:8, 465:15, 468:8 and 471:28 (cf. note on 468:10), 517:12(i), 517:12(ii). Although the change here obliged the Riverside Press to fill out an already widely spaced line by moving a word down from the previous line, replacing 'Oh' by 'O' was one of the tasks to which the printers devoted themselves at the second-proof stage (see, e.g., entries at 450:39, 455:7, 512:33); it is therefore likely that the printers made this change and the consequent lineation adjustment without consulting DHL.

462:6 **The Lord strengthen you.** Psalms xx. 1–2 ['The LORD ... strengthen thee out of Zion'].

462:9 **Jonathan is wounded ... home to rest.** Neither wounding nor return home is in the Bible.

462:16 **Nought** PPI and PPII regularly altered DHL's 'nought' to 'naught' (see list of silent emendations), as they did 'ought' and 'aught'; but DHL's spelling for the meaning 'nothing' is sanctioned by *OED2* A.*sb.*1. as 'Now only literary' while 'naught' is 'Now *arch.*' Three occasions (483:4, 487:38 and 39) where DHL himself used the spelling 'naught' have not been altered.

462:21 **arrayed** Cf. 1 Sam. xvii. 21 ('For Israel and the Philistines had put the battle in array . . .'), 466:6 and note on 466:8.

462:27 **the champion ... to challenge us.** 1 Sam. xvii. 4 ['And there went out a champion out of the camp of the Philistines . . .'].

462:34 **Philistine is huge ... before the Flood.** Goliath's height according to 1 Sam. xvii. 4 was 'six cubits and a span' ($3\frac{1}{2}$ metres: $11\frac{1}{2}$ feet) . . . cf. Genesis vi. 4 ('There were giants in the earth in those days . . .'). For the Flood, see Genesis vi–ix.

463:6 **in the calf.** I.e. in a stupid, doting, brainless person (*OED2* 1.c.).

463:19 **he asks ... our servants.** 1 Sam. xvii. 8–9 ['choose you a man for you, and let him come down to me. / If he be able to fight with me, and to kill me, then will we be your servants: but if I prevail against him, and kill him, then shall ye be our servants, and serve us'].

463:28 **I doubt** I.e. 'I am afraid', the original reading of MS (p. 53). DHL habitually used the word in this sense: e.g. to his sister Ada, 14 July 1925, 'I doubt there'll be no wild strawberries' (*Letters*, v. 279).

464:2 **Benjamin** Saul's tribe (1 Sam. ix. 1–2); see too 486:20.

464:6 **his oversized shield.** Cf. 1 Sam. xvii. 7 ('and one bearing a shield went before him'). DHL adds the detail of the rattling of the shield: perhaps from his observation of North American Indian ceremonies (see note on 435:4).

465:7 **the sons of Jesse.** Cf. 1 Sam. xvii. 13 ('the three eldest sons of Jesse went *and* followed Saul to the battle').

465:15 **My father ... bread ... ten cheeses for the captain of your thousand ... parched corn** 1 Sam. xvii. 17–18 ['Take now for thy brethren an ē'phàh of this parched *corn*, and these ten loaves . . . / And carry these ten cheeses unto the captain of *their* thousand . . .'].

465:16 **left with the keeper of the victuals.** 1 Sam. xvii. 22 ['And David left his carriage in the hand of the keeper of the carriage . . .']; 'carriage' means 'vessel' or 'instruments', but DHL clearly assumes that it means 'food'.

465:17 **With the host ... to battle.** Cf. 1 Sam. xvii. 20 ('he came to the trench, as the host was going forth to the fight, and shouted for the battle').

465:22 **see how you fare, and to take your pledge.** 1 Sam. xvii. 18 ['look how thy brethren fare, and take their pledge']. The meaning of *KJB* is unclear; 'pledge' has been defined as 'security offered (ten cheeses in this case) for the safety of men in an armed camp' (*Black's Bible Dictionary*, ed. Madeline S. Miller and J. Lane Miller, 1954, p. 564); it may, however, mean 'some token of your welfare'. DHL favours the latter: Eliab's query at 465:23 shows that he will give no assurances about their welfare until after the battle.

465:24 **my young son** In the Bible, Eliab's only child is his daughter Abihail (2 Chronicles xi. 18).

465:29 **but all is well.** In MS (p. 56) and TS (p. 38) the phrase reads 'but is well.' It has been assumed, with some misgivings, that DHL made the alteration in the carbon-copy typescript when completing the line (TS was typed as 'but is we'); it appeared in PPI (p. 48).

465:35 Wellah, Here and elsewhere (see e.g. 485:36, 486:40; 487:6 and 493:22) clearly an emphasiser, perhaps a version of the Old English 'wella' (*OED2* A.a.), 'Well then', last *OED2* citation 1205. Later recorded variants – 'Welladay', 'Wellaway' and 'Wellaneer' – all means 'Alas', which is a possible meaning only at 486:40 and 487:6. Either Nottinghamshire-Derbyshire dialect had preseved an otherwise unrecorded meaning akin to the Old English, or DHL is coining an archaic emphasiser based on 'Well'.

466:4 the Philistine ... from the ranks, Cf. 1 Sam. xvii. 23 ('there came up the champion, the Philistine ... out of the armies of the Philistines').

466:8 Why are ye ... down to me. 1 Sam. xvii. 8 ['... array? *am* not I a ... choose ...'].

466:11 fleeing back ... sore afraid. 1 Sam. xvii. 24 ['fled from him, and were sore afraid'].

466:16 Choose you ... serve us. 1 Sam. xvii. 8–9 ['choose you ... If he be able to fight ... and to kill me ... servants: but ...'].

466:21 Surely, forty ... defy Israel. 1 Sam. xvii. 16 ['presented himself forty days'] and xvii. 25 ['surely to defy Israel is he come up: and it ...'].

466:25 And it ... from Israel? 1 Sam. xvii. 25 ['and it ...'] and xvii. 26 ['What shall be done to the ...'].

466:30 Who is this ... the living God? 1 Sam. xvii. 26 ['who *is* ...'].

466:32 As the Lord liveth, Very common in OT: Judges viii. 9, Ruth iii. 13, etc.

467:7 Why camest [467:1] ... a cause? 1 Sam. xvii. 28 ['... thou down hither? and ... of thine heart; for thou ...'] and 29 ['... done? *Is there* not a cause?'].

467:8 turning Cf. 1 Sam. xvii. 30 ('And he turned from him ...').

467:12 For the Lord is with me. Jeremiah xx. 11 ['But the ...'].

467:15 sooth, 'True': obsolete and not in *KJB*, but revived as a literary archaism, e.g. by Sir Walter Scott (see 'Marmion' I. xv): cf. notes on 457:31 and 455:19.

467:27 Let no ... his youth. 1 Sam. xvii. 32 ['... because of him; thy servant ... with this Philistine'] and 33 ['Thou art ...'].

467:30 Thy servant ... living God. 1 Sam. xvii. 34 ['... bear, and ...']; DHL omits the first part of David's explanation from 1 Sam. xvii. 34–5: 'Thy servant kept his father's sheep, and there came a lion, and a bear, and took a lamb out of the flock: / And I went out after him, and smote him, and delivered *it* out of his mouth; and when he arose against me, I caught *him* by his beard, and smote him, and slew him.'

467:33 greaves of brass ... panoply. 1 Sam. xvii. 6 ... A complete suit of armour, of ancient or medieval times. Not in *KJB*: DHL's source may have been the hymn 'Soldiers of Christ, arise' (1749) by Charles Wesley (1707–88), ll. 11–12 ['And take, to arm you for the fight, / The panoply of God'], with its reference to Ephesians vi. 11. See too 474:3.

467:37 The Lord ... with thee. 1 Sam. xvii. 37 ['Go, and the ...'].

468:6 Baal ... Ashtaroth ... pigeon in a box. The chief masculine deity of the Phoenicians and Canaanites ... the female idol of the Philistines, Phoenicians and

Zidonians: cf. 469:14 'Astaroth' and 487:5, 584:19 'Ashtaroth' (both spellings in *KJB*) ... 'box' refers to the 'ark of the covenant' captured by the Philistines (1 Sam. iv. 11–22) but returned to the Israelites (1 Sam. vi–vii), the 'pigeon' being the God (or Holy Spirit) supposedly within it. The ark was the depository of the two tablets of the decalogue and other sacred objects.

468:7 **Deliver him into my hand**   Common OT phrase, e.g. 1 Sam. xiv. 10, 12, 37, etc.

468:10 **the coat of proof ... *on* DAVID.)**   I.e. proved and tested ... cf. 1 Sam. xvii. 38 ('And Saul armed David with his armour'). E1's alteration of PPII's 'mail' (to 'proof' at 468:8 and 'coat' at 471:28), two of the only three clearly authorial emendations of words at the second proof stage, presumably derive from DHL becoming convinced that chain-mail armour was an anachronism, although 'mail' appears twice in *KJB* in this episode (1 Sam. xvii. 5 and 38).

468:13 *girding*   Cf. 1 Sam. xvii. 39 ('And David girded his sword upon his armour ...').

468:17 **thy shield ... assay this sword**   There is no reference to David's shield in *KJB*: DHL may have been following 1 Sam. xvii. 41 ('the man that bare the shield *went* before him') referring to Goliath's shield-bearer. See also 1 Sam. xvii. 7 ... At 1 Sam. xvii. 39 David 'assayed to go' (*OED2* III.17.a.), meaning 'set himself to do something', but in the light of the following s.d., DHL clearly means here 'put to the proof, try' (*OED2* I.1.a.).

468:22 **I cannot ... proved them ... *disarms* DAVID.)**   Cf. 1 Sam. xvii. 39 ['... with these; for I ...'].

468:25 **The Lord shall be my shield ... staff.**   Psalms xxviii. 7 ['... *is* my strength and my...'] ... 1 Sam. xvii. 40.

468:31 **Astarte**   Greek name for the Sumerian divinity Ishtar: the great goddess, especially of love and fertility, equivalent to Aphrodite, 'the great goddess of destruction in sex' ('The Crown', *Reflections on the Death of a Porcupine and Other Essays*, ed. Michael Herbert, Cambridge, 1988, 292:16).

468:34 *He [takes] his staff—crosses*   In TS (p. 42), Brett omitted the reference to David's staff being held by his brother (468:25). As David should carry a staff (see 1 Sam. xvii. 40: 'And he took his staff in his hand ...'), DHL inserted a sentence ('He picks up his staff') in this stage direction in TSR (see Textual apparatus 468:24, 34). To allow DHL's reference to the staff at 468:25 to remain, this stage direction has been editorially adjusted.

469:4 **smooth stones ... the brook bed ... his leather pouch ... sling in his hand.**   Cf. 1 Sam. xvii. 40 ('chose him five smooth stones out of the brook and put them in a shepherd's bag which he had ... and his sling *was* in his hand').

469:6 **a wolf ... cometh down,**   Cf. 'The Destruction of Sennacherib' (1815) by Lord Byron (1788–1824) ['The Assyrian came down like the wolf on the fold'].

469:14 **Am I ... with staves?**   1 Sam. xvii. 43.

469:19 **Thou comest ... hast defied.**   1 Sam. xvii. 45.

469:22 **Come to ... the hills.**   1 Sam. xvii. 44 ['... flesh unto the ... to the beasts of the field'].

469:27 **This day ... from thee.** 1 Sam. xvii. 46 ['... into mine hand ... take thine head ...'].

469:30 **thou egg,**   Cf. *Macbeth* iv. ii. 81: 'What, you egg!'

469:34 **I will ... in Israel.** 1 Sam. xvii. 46 ['... day unto the ... the wild beasts ... earth; that ... know that there ...'].

470:2 **and all [469:39] ... our hands.** 1 Sam. xvii. 47 ['And all this assembly shall ...'].

470:8 **The Philistine ... him fast!** Cf. 1 Sam. xvii. 48 ('when the Philistine arose, and came and drew nigh to meet David, that David hasted, and ran toward the army to meet the Philistine').

470:12 **The boy but slang a stone at him!** Cf. 1 Sam. xvii. 49 ('And David ... took thence a stone, and slang *it*').

470:17 **who hath run ... of the giant!** Cf. 1 Sam. xvii. 51 ('Therefore David ran, and stood upon the Philistine, and took his sword, and drew it out of the sheath thereof, and slew him, and cut off his head therewith').

470:32 ***Wild shouting* ... in flight!** Cf. 1 Sam. xvii. 51–2 ('And when the Philistines saw their champion was dead, they fled. / And the men of Israel and of Judah arose, and shouted, and pursued the Philistines ...').

471:3 **Who is ... stripling is.** 1 Sam. xvii. 55–6 ['whose son *is* this youth? ... O king ... cannot tell. / And the king said, Inquire ...'].

471:8 **stripping of the tents.** Cf. 1 Sam. xvii. 53 ('and they spoiled their tents').

471:13 **brass armour ... ruddy-faced fair youth,** 1 Sam. xvii. 5–6 ... cf. 1 Sam. xvii. 42 ('he was *but* a youth, and ruddy, and of a fair countenance'): see too note on 456:36.

471:27 **booth**   Temporary structure, originally covered with canvas: a tent; cf. Jonah iv. 5 (and see below, 496:19 and 499:8).

471:30 **lay them in thy tent.** Cf. 1 Sam. xvii. 54 ('but he put his armour in his tent').

471:38 **cunning**   This word – crucial to DHL's interpretation of David – probably owes its origin to 1 Sam. xvi. 16, 18 ('a cunning player on an harp ... cunning in playing'). *KJB*, following the Geneva Bible of 1560, uses 'cunning' in its old sense, to describe skilful, inventive musical performance (cf. 1 Chronicles xxv. 7), craftsmanship and knowledge. The sense 'crafty' dates only from the 1590s. Cf. note on 485:5.

471:39 ***(Enter* DAVID *... and* ABNER.*)*** Cf. 1 Sam. xvii. 57 ('Abner took him, and brought him before Saul with the head of the Philistine in his hand').

472:4 **Whose son ... the Bethlehemite.** 1 Sam. xvii. 58.

472:10 **the stone sunk ... forehead bone!** 1 Sam. xvii. 49 ['... into his forehead'].

472:14 **Except the Lord**   Psalms cxxvii. 1.

472:16 **The Lord is with this young man.** Cf. 1 Sam. xviii. 14 ('and the LORD *was* with him').

472:22 **in the dawn,** Cf. 1 Sam. xvii. 20 ('early in the morning').

472:37 **thou young man?** 1 Sam. xvii. 58.

472:40 **I should ... the king.** Cf. 1 Sam. xviii. 18 ('what *is* my life, *or* my father's family in Israel, that I should be son in law to the king?').

473:2 **Now thou ... father's house.** Cf. 1 Sam. xviii. 2 ('And Saul took him that day, and would let him go no more home to his father's house').

473:8 **to thy confusion.** Cf. 1 Sam. xx. 30 ('to thine own confusion').

473:12 **behold, my ... Lord's battles.** 1 Sam. xviii. 17 ['Behold ... wife: only ...'].

474:8 **pursuing after ... brought in.** Cf. 1 Sam. xvii. 53 ('And the children of Israel returned from chasing after the Philistines, and they spoiled their tents').

474:10 **And the ... of Gath,** Cf. 1 Sam. xvii. 52 ('And the wounded of the Philistines fell down by the way to Shaaraim, even unto Gath, and unto Ekron'). See note on 444:17.

474:11 **their princes** Cf. 1 Sam. xviii. 30 ('the princes of the Philistines').

474:32 **set over the men of war** Cf. 1 Sam. xviii. 5 ('And Saul set him over the men of war'). In the Bible, however, David has had a reputation as 'a mighty valiant man, and a man of war' from the start, has been Saul's 'armour-bearer' (1 Sam. xvi. 18, 21) and is only made leader some time after the death of Goliath (1 Sam. xviii. 1–5). Saul's sudden elevation of him here suggests the duplicity of 486:6–7.

475:2 **my delight** [474:39] **... my confusion.** Cf. 1 Sam. xviii. 22 ('the king hath delight in thee') ... cf. Psalms xliv. 15 ('My confusion *is* continually before me ...'): see too 473:8.

475:8 *locked shields* I.e. linked to form a defensive wall or platform.

475:30 **young lion of Judah,** Cf. Revelation v. 5 ('the Lion of the tribe of Judah') and Hosea v. 14 ('as a young lion to the house of Judah').

475:33 **not left my soul.** Cf. 1 Sam. xviii. 1 ('the soul of Jonathan was knit with the soul of David').

475:36 **sworn a covenant ... as brothers,** Cf. 1 Sam. xviii. 3 ('Then Jonathan and David made a covenant, because he loved him as his own soul').

476:11 **I will ... the Lord.** Psalm xxxvii. 7 ['Rest ...'].

476:21 **the sides of the pit.** I.e. hell: Isaiah xiv. 15; see too 449:3.

476:22 **between his house ... be everlasting.** Cf. 1 Sam. xx. 16 and 42 ('Jonathan made *a covenant* with the house of David', 'The LORD be between me and thee, and between my seed and thy seed for ever'); cf. also 2 Sam. xxiii. 5 ('Although my house *be* not so with God; yet he hath made with me an everlasting covenant ...') and Genesis ix. 16 ('the everlasting covenant').

476:31 **I will clothe thee ... my bow,** Cf. 1 Sam. xviii. 4 ('And Jonathan stripped himself of the robe that *was* upon him, and gave it to David, and his garments, even to his sword, and to his bow, and to his girdle'). See also 476:34–477:11.

478:6 **torn asunder as between two wild horses** A primitive form of execution: the French queen Brunhilde, who ruled over the eastern part of the empire of the Merovingian kings, was overthrown and so executed in 613.

478:9 **right hand ... on me.** Replacing, in MS, 'sweet and the bitter are mingled for me.' (p. 88).

479:3 *instruments of music* 1 Sam. xviii. 6.

479:8 **Lu-lu-a-li-lu-lu-lu! ... slew the Philistine.** The dialogue form (see 480:1–2) is suggested by 1 Sam. xviii. 7: 'And the women answered *one another* as they played'. Cf. also 1 Sam. xviii. 6 ('the women came out of all cities of Israel, singing and dancing, to meet king Saul, with tabrets, with joy ...': see note on 514:5).

479:26 **Saul in thousands ... thousands ten!** Cf. 1 Sam. xviii. 7 ('Saul hath slain his thousands, and David his ten thousands').

480:7 *(Must be ... naïve—villagers.)* Not printed in PPI (p. 67), so possibly deleted in the carbon-copy typescript; but more likely ignored by the compositors of PPI as inappropriate for a printed play.

481:18 **May such mouths be bruised!** Cf. 1 Sam. xviii. 8 ('And Saul was very wroth, and the saying displeased him ...').

481:22 **They have ... the kingdom?** 1 Sam. xviii. 8 ['... unto David ... thousands: and ... more but ...'].

482:6 **Jerusalem** 1 Sam. xvii. 54.

482:15 **The sword ... in Ramah;** In *KJB* the sword is deposited in Nob with the priest Ahimelech, 'wrapped in a cloth behind the ephod' (1 Sam. xxi. 1, 9).

485:5 **wise** See 1 Sam. xviii. 5, 14, 15, 30 ('behaved himself wisely ... behaved himself wisely in all his ways ... behaved himself very wisely ... behaved himself more wisely than all the servants of Saul'). Cf. 485:9–10 and note on 471:38.

485:12 **Smooth faced ... of Pharaoh!** Nothing in *KJB* shows Joseph either 'Smooth faced' or 'soft-footed'. Saul may be thinking of how Joseph 'got him out' after Potiphar's wife's attempt to seduce him when he was overseer of her husband's house (Genesis xxxix. 4, 7–20), or of Joseph's behaviour towards his brothers when he was Pharaoh's chief minister (Genesis xlii–xlv). Joseph's father Jacob is, however, distinguished as a 'smooth man' (Genesis xxvii. 11). Jael, the wife of Heber, is the only OT character to move 'softly', on her way to kill Sisera (Judges iv. 21).

485:12 **this weasel.** An unclean animal (see Leviticus xi. 29), renowned for its ferocity, blood-thirstiness, cleverness and slimness: DHL's description of Baroness Skrebensky in *The Rainbow*, ed. Kinkead-Weekes, as having 'a kind of joyous coldness, laughing, delighted, like some weasel' (184:21–2), altered from the manuscript reading 'the charm of naïvete born of sang-froid and subtlety' (p. 589) suggests the significance here. The specifically twentieth-century sense (originally US) implying sneaking, untrustworthy behaviour is not appropriate. See also note on 520:16.

485:17 **his uncle ... sheep-cotes.** David's uncle was 'Jonathan ... a counseller, a wise man, and a scribe' (1 Chronicles xxvii. 32) ... associated with David at 1 Sam. xxiv. 3.

485:30 **I find in him no presumption.** Cf. John xviii. 38 ('I find in him no fault *at all*'). 'Presumption' is not a *KJB* word, though 'presumptuous' is. The well-known nature of the Gospel passage argues in favour of DHL repeating it, consciously or unconsciously (Jesus descended from the house of David).

485:32 **my chief enemy,**   Cf. 1 Sam. xviii. 29 ('and Saul became David's enemy continually').

486:1 **captain over a thousand?**   1 Sam. xviii. 13.

486:5 *Behold Merab ... Lord's battles.*   See note on 473:12.

486:7 **Let not ... upon him.**   1 Sam. xviii. 17 ['... mine hand ...'].

486:18 **naughty-hearted ... naughty pride,**   Cf. 1 Sam. xvii. 28 ('I know thy pride, and the naughtiness of thine heart').

486:24 **the Dark!**   See note on 439:30. Cf. Psalms xviii. 11 ('He made darkness his secret place') and Psalms cv. 28 ('He sent darkness, and made it dark'). God existed before he created light (Genesis i. 1–5).

486:31 *Saul hath ... of thousands,*   1 Sam. xviii. 7 ['... and David his ten thousands'].

486:35 **the Morning Wind ... the Lord of Days**   See note on 439:30; cf. Psalms xviii. 10 ('he did fly upon the wings of the wind') ... see note on 443:4.

486:39 **I cannot ... to sprout.**   Cf. 1 Sam. xxiv. 21 ('Swear now ... that thou wilt not cut off my seed after me').

487:2 **of the bright horn.**   Cf. 1 Sam. ii. 1 ('mine horn is exalted in the LORD'); DHL originally wrote 'of God' (MS, p. 102).

487:4 **cut myself off ... man of Belial.**   Common OT formula: cf. Exodus xxiii. 23 ('I will cut them off'), Psalms xxxi. 22 ('I am cut off from before thine eyes'), etc. ... in OT, neither place nor proper name, but a common way of saying 'worthless': e.g. 1 Sam. xxv. 17 ('he *is such* a son of Belial, that *a man* cannot speak to him'). From the thirteenth century (and in NT translation) treated as a devil's name: see Milton, *Paradise Lost*, i. 490 ('*Belial* came last, than whom a Spirit more lewd / Fell not from Heaven ...').

487:17 **Even to the Lord: ... the earth!**   Isaiah xix. 22 ['*even* ... Lord,'] and Psalms viii. 9 ['O LORD our Lord, how ...'].

487:33 **"What is [487:24] ... the earth!"**   Psalms viii. 4–9. Musical settings of these lines – see Appendix v ii. – appear in MS (p. 104) and TS (p. 56), as does a note 'tune the church-bell of the Indians' (mistyped and deleted in TS). However, like the note referring to 'the music above' (see Textual apparatus at 490:23(ii)), such notes and music have not been accepted as part of the play's text. Cf. 'Indians and Entertainment', *Mornings in Mexico*: 'The Indian, singing, sings without words or vision ... He will tell you it is ... quite modern, the song of the church bell on Sunday morning' (p. 104).

488:7 **Jonathan ... Abinadab ... Melchishua ... Ishbosheth**   All four of Saul's sons died violently. Jonathan (the eldest), Abinadab (the fourth; also the name of a son of Jesse – see 447:20–4 and 1 Sam. xvii. 13) and Melchischua (the third) were all killed with their father at Mount Gilboa (1 Sam. xiv. 49, xxxi. 2). Ishbosheth (second son) – the 'Ishui' of 1 Sam. xiv. 49 – became king of Israel but was eventually murdered in his bed (2 Sam. ii. 8–10, iv. 6–7).

488:9 on broken feet, I.e. Jonathan's son Mephibosheth, 'lame on both his feet' (2 Sam. iv. 4, ix. 13).

488:10 And the seed ... covering the earth, Cf. Genesis xiii. 16 and xxvi. 4 ('I will make thy seed as the dust of the earth ... I will make thy seed to multiply as the stars of heaven') and Numbers xxii. 11 ('*there is* a people come out of Egypt, which covereth the face of the earth'). *KJB* contains many references to the 'seed of David': e.g. 1 Kings xi. 39, Psalms xviii. 50, Jeremiah xxxiii. 22, etc. See also note on 476:22.

488:14 the pillar ... as tall, dark cloud The plague of locusts in Egypt (Exodus x. 4–19) apparently combined with the pillar of cloud which led the Israelites out of Egypt (Exodus xiii. 21).

488:24 pits are digged Cf. Psalms xciv. 13 and cxix. 85 ('the pit be digged for the wicked ... The proud have digged pits for me').

488:36 And men ... the earth! Cf. Matthew v. 5 ('the meek ... shall inherit the earth'); see too *WL* 361:12–13 and note.

489:3 blown egg-shell First in a sequence of references (and re-imaginings) of the primordial 'mundane egg' of Indian and other cosmogenies, from which the world was hatched. See 'the egg' (490:19), 'the egg of his own undoing' (490:26) and 'the egg of the world' (514:12).

489:16 length of days. Proverbs iii. 2.

489:23 prophesying ... spirits of the under-earth. Cf. 1 Sam. xviii. 10 ('the evil spirit from God came upon Saul, and he prophesied in the midst of the house').

489:28 God was ... into a ball, In Ancient Egypt, the scarab – the sacred dung-beetle – was venerated as a type of the sun-god, probably because the ball of dung rolled by the beetle to provide a place for its eggs was regarded as an image of the sun tracing its course across the heavens: DHL is combining Egyptian mythology with Judaic, Romano-Graeco and American Indian mythology.

489:35 soul. Revised in MS (p. 109) from 'body'.

490:9 Serpent coiled ... his own peace? Hindu rather than Judaic in origin, the image being taken initially from James Pryse's *Apocalypse Unsealed* (New York, 1910), where 'cosmic energy' is said to 'lie coiled-up like a slumbering serpent' (p. 16); Pryse was influenced by Hindu theories of the chakras, the bodily centres of awareness. Cf. *WL* 451:15–16 ('the central serpent that is coiled at the base of life').

490:20 the serpent ... Lord of Life, Cf. DHL's poem 'Snake', ll. 71–2 ('And so, I missed my chance with one of the lords / Of life').

490:23 *Sings Psalm 8.* On two occasions in *KJB*, David plays the harp to calm Saul, but on neither occasion does he sing: cf. 1 Sam. xvi. 23 ('when the *evil* spirit from God was upon Saul ... David took an harp, and played with his hand: so Saul was refreshed, and was well, and the evil spirit departed from him') and 1 Sam. xviii. 10 ('and he prophesied in the midst of the house: and David played with his hand, as at other times'). For Psalm viii. 4–9, see 487:24–33; see too notes on 491:5 and 16.

490:27 **the Great White Bird**   Probably a version of the Eagle or Thunderbird in North American Indian mythology.

490:31 **the dragon**   Frequent image in Revelation xii–xiii.

490:38 **a new song**   Psalms xxxiii. 3, xl. 3, xcvi. 1, etc.

491:5 **"When I consider ... hast ordained—"**   Psalms viii. 3 ['... thy heavens...'].

491:10 *hurls his javelin* **... my dart.**   1 Sam. xviii. 10–11 ['And Saul cast the javelin ...']: see note on 459:19 ... see Job xli. 26 ('the spear, the dart'), the word – meaning a light spear or javelin – used primarily with reference to the archaic period.

491:16 **Oh Lord ... the heavens—**   Psalms viii. 1 ['... who ...'].

491:19 **I will ... to the wall.**   1 Sam. xviii. 11 ['... wall *with it*'] and xix. 10 ['And Saul sought to smite ...'].

491:21 **Go hence ... Twice, Father!**   Cf. 1 Sam. xviii. 11 ('And David avoided out of his presence twice').

491:22 **The evil spirits**   1 Sam. xviii. 10 ['the ... spirit'].

491:30 **It was not of myself.**   Brett mistyped as 'It was out of myself.' (TS, p. 61), and her reading was followed by PPI (p. 82). A hand, possibly that of DHL, altered 'It' to 'I' in TS; but apparently no one made this change in the carbon-copy typescript.

491:35 **the evil days**   Ecclesiastes xii. 1.

491:37 **man given over to trouble,**   Cf. Job v. 7 ('man is born unto trouble').

492:1 **And only then.**   DHL originally ended Scene 11 at this point, and added his usual indication 'curtain' at the bottom of the page (MS, p. 113), but he got no further than writing 'Scene XII' on the next page before deleting it, going back and adding a further two MS pages to the text of Scene 11.

492:6 **the Night ... publish it in Judah:**   See note on 439:30. Cf. Psalms xviii. 9 ('and darkness *was* under his feet') ... cf. 2 Sam. i. 20 ('Tell *it* not in Gath, publish *it* not in the streets of Askelon') and Jeremiah iv. 5 ('Declare ye in Judah, and publish in Jerusalem').

492:8 **the apple of their eyes,**   Regular *KJB* usage (e.g. Psalms xvii. 8, 'Keep me as the apple of the eye') for what is cherished: from the old supposition that the eye's pupil was a globular solid body.

492:27 **Hebron,**   City 22 miles s. of Jerusalem: capital of Judah under David (2 Sam. ii. 11).

492:29 **And behold ... to wife.**   Cf. 1 Sam. xviii. 17 ('Behold my elder daughter ... her will I give thee to wife').

492:31 **Who am ... the king?**   1 Sam. xviii. 18 ['... son in law...'].

492:33 **Only be ... Lord's battles!**   1 Sam. xviii. 17 ['... be thou valiant ... battles'].

492:34 **All my ... to serve.**   Although Brett's mistypings at 492:34 (see Textual apparatus) may have provoked DHL's alterations, it has been judged unwise to return to the MS reading of a sentence which he obviously considered carefully when revising.

493:3 *Two* HERDSMEN   A sensible emendation in PPII (p. 85). DHL specified 'Two shepherds' here and 'shepherd' at 493:5, but wrote stage directions throughout the scene for '1st Herdsman' and '2nd Herdsman' (MS, p. 116): a pencilled note '? herdsmen' (probably from the compositor) appears in the margin of PPI (p. 85). This edition also emends 'shepherd' at 493:5.

493:12 **How long, oh Herdsmen!**   Cf. Revelation vi. 10 ('How long, O Lord').

493:25 **feasted her week**   I.e. the marriage week: see Genesis xxix. 27–8 ('Fulfil her week . . .'). OT feasts commonly took a week: see Judges xiv. 12 ('the seven days of the feast').

493:30 **Adriel ... Merab ... to wife?**   Cf. 1 Sam. xviii. 19 ('But it came to pass at the time when Merab Saul's daughter should have been given to David, that she was given unto Adriel the Meholathite to wife'.) A Meholathite was an inhabitant of the city Abelmeholah in Issachar. DHL's accent on the 'o' presumably demonstrates his chosen pronunciation.

494:2 **butter-skin?**   A 'skin' in this sense is a container for liquids, etc., made from the hide of a small animal. DHL is imagining an archaic butter and cheese making process in which it replaces the churn; see 566:18.

494:23 **he fain would see**   Version of a construction appearing only twice in *KJB*: cf. Job xxvii. 22 ('he would fain flee out') and Luke xv. 16 ('he would fain have filled his belly with the husks that the swine did eat').

494:26 **clotted figs,**   Probably dried figs squashed together for easy carrying; cf. the 'cakes of figs' Abigail carries at 1 Sam. xxv. 18.

494:36 **Seemeth it ... lightly esteemed?**   1 Sam. xviii. 23 ['... *thing* to be a king's son in law . . .'].

494:38 **the king ... love thee.**   1 Sam. xviii. 22 ['the king hath delight in . . .']: Saul had 'commanded his servants' to 'Commune with David secretly' and tell him this.

495:2 **pricking**   Either 'piercing' ('with iron lance-points') or 'spurring a horse on' (cf. Edmund Spenser, *The Faerie Queene*, I. i. 1: 'A Gentle Knight was pricking on the plaine').

495:18 **heart of Israel ... a great tree.**   Cf. Isaiah xxvii. 6 ('He shall cause them that come of Jacob to take root: Israel shall blossom and bud, and fill the face of the world with fruit'). See also Numbers xvii. 8 ('the rod of Aaron ... was budded, and brought forth buds, and bloomed blossoms') and *Aaron's Rod*, ed. Kalnins, 108:10–16.

495:23 **[*Enter* SAUL *and* ADRIEL.]**   Adriel had left the stage at 495:7 'to bring him in' (and subsequently departs with Saul at 495:40, where DHL's original 'exeunt' had wrongly suggested that Saul and others left with him): Saul's entrance and Adriel's re-entrance here clearly precede David's greeting at 495:24.

495:29 **May the Lord bless thy house**   Cf. 2 Sam. vii. 29 and 1 Chronicles xvii. 27 ('let it please thee to bless the house').

495:31 **But my servants ... unto David.** Cf. 1 Sam. xviii. 20 ('And Michal Saul's daughter loved David: and they told Saul, and the thing pleased him').

495:34 **the new moon** Start of the lunar month, and considered holy, with sacrifices, worship and celebrations: see, e.g., 1 Sam. xx. 5, 18, 24.

495:35 **thou shalt ... the twain.** 1 Sam. xviii. 21 ['... son in law in *the one* ...'].

496:6 **take my stick ... the word of a king.** Presumably the 'driving-stick' of 495:16. The comic herdsman plays the role of the truth-telling fool in Shakespearean tragedy (cf. *King Lear*, I. iv. 99 – 'take my coxcomb') ... Ecclesiastes viii. 4 ['Where the word of a king *is, there is* power'].

496:15 **pills.** I.e. droppings: cf. 'Adolf', *England, My England*, ed. Steele, 204:19.

496:26 **entrails strain in me,** Cf. Genesis xliii. 30 ('his bowels did yearn upon his brother'). See note on 442:13.

496:27 **God of my salvation,** Cf. Psalms lxv. 5 ('God of our salvation'), etc.

496:30 **thy lightning ... my loins,** Cf. Job xl. 16 ('his strength *is* in his loins').

496:37 **fill thy jar.** A scene invented by DHL, but following the common biblical type-scene of the encounter with the future betrothed at a well: e.g. Abraham's encounter with Rebekah, and Jacob's encounter with Rachel (Genesis xxiv. 11–16, xxxix. 1–13). See Robert Alter, *The Art of Biblical Narrative* (New York, 1981), pp. 50–8.

497:34 **come in unto thee** Common *KJB* usage for sexual relations, e.g. 2 Sam. xii. 24, xvi. 21.

497:38 **not yea-and-nay!** 2 Corinthians i. 19 ['For the Son of God ... was not yea and nay, but in him was yea'].

498:6 **the body of God,** Cf. 'The Body of God', *The Complete Poems of D. H. Lawrence*, ed. Pinto and Roberts, p. 691.

498:9 **kindled of the Lord,** Cf. Isaiah x. 16 ('under his glory he shall kindle a burning'). 'Kindled' is common in *KJB*, especially for the destructive anger or wrath of God; the positive sense here directly contrasts with *KJB*.

498:12 **pomegranate tree [498:4] ... the fruits of the pomegranate** Language reminiscent of Song of Solomon iv–vi: cf. iv. 13 ('Thy plants *are* an orchard of pomegranates, with pleasant fruits').

498:29 **thou shalt lie in my bosom.** Cf. 1 Kings i. 2 ('let her lie in thy bosom'): an irony, given that 1 Kings describes the dying King David being given Abishag as a bedfellow.

498:36 **sealed her with his seal,** *KJB* usage is non-figurative, e.g. 1 Kings xxi. 8 ('she wrote letters ... and sealed *them* with his seal'). But cf. DHL's poem 'Seven Seals', l. 8 ('I will set a seal upon you from my lip'), *The Complete Poems of D. H. Lawrence*, ed. Pinto and Roberts, p. 153.

498:39 **the rose of Sharon** Song of Solomon ii. 1.

499:2 **keeper of David's nakedness.** 'Nakedness' in *KJB* sense means either 'genitals' (e.g. Exodus xxviii. 42) or 'sexual identity' (e.g. 1 Sam. xx. 30: 'to the confusion of thy mother's nakedness'): 'keeper' commonly means 'preserver' in

KJB (e.g. 1 Sam. xxviii. 2: 'I make thee keeper of mine head for ever'). DHL's reference may be the story of David's dance before the Lord and Michal's scorn (2 Sam. vi. 14–23); see Introduction, footnote 104.

499:3 **reive** The verb, like 'rieve' (which demonstrates its pronunciation), is a variant of 'reave', to steal, plunder, rob or pillage. DHL may however be (phonetically) misspelling 'rive', to separate or pull asunder.

499:22 **words like honey,** Cf. Psalms cxix. 103 ('How sweet are thy words unto my taste! *yea, sweeter* than honey to my mouth!').

499:32 **The king delighteth in thee** Cf. 1 Sam. xviii. 22 ('the king hath delight in thee').

499:39 **am I a poor man,** 1 Sam. xviii. 23 ['I *am* a …'].

500:2 **the king … any bride money,** 1 Sam. xviii. 25 ['The king … any dowry']. Cf. 500:28–9.

500:5 **But an … his enemies.** 1 Sam. xviii. 25 ['but an … Philistines, to be … of the king's enemies'].

500:13 **a ring** DHL's use of a stage convention (e.g. *Twelfth Night*, I. v. 305–6 and II. ii. 4–23): not in *KJB*.

500:25 **Ye would … the Philistine.** Cf. 1 Sam. xviii. 25 ('But Saul thought to make David fall by the hand of the Philistines').

501:3 *an image* 1 Sam. xix. 13: Hebrew 'teraphim', meaning household gods. In early times they appear to have been tolerated (though see Exodus xx. 4), but were later explicitly forbidden (see Hosea iii. 4). They were jealously guarded by families: e.g. the recovery by Rachel (wife of Jacob) of her father's 'images' (Genesis xxxi. 19, 34–5). Like *KJB*, DHL mistakenly uses 'teraphim' as a singular rather than as a plural: see 510:20–1, 512:17, 512:28 and 513:22–4.

501:17 **toward thy holy presence.** The reading of MS (p. 132). PPI (p. 96), probably following the carbon-copy typescript, reads 'toward thy holy temple' (the wording of Psalms v. 7). Someone – possibly DHL, but possibly a compositor – underlined the words 'toward' and 'temple' in PPI and added a ringed question mark in the margin. Since we cannot be sure who made the change to 'temple', and it may have been DHL who queried the reading in PPI, the reading of MS has been restored.

501:30 **Give ear** [501:4] *… a shield.* Psalms v. ['… Lord, consider … / … King, and my … / … O LORD; in … / … / … / … / … holy temple. / … righteousness because … enemies; make thy way … / … mouth; their … *is* an … sepulchre; they … / … transgressions; for … / … them: let … / … favour wilt … him as …'].

501:32 **thine anointed, and thy son.** Cf. Psalms cxxxii. 10 ('For thy servant David's sake turn not away the face of thine anointed').

501:35 **a son of God … the Lord is with me.** Cf. Genesis vi. 2, 4 ('the sons of God'), and see also *The Rainbow*, ed. Kinkead-Weekes, 257:6–38 … cf. 1 Sam. xvi. 18 ('the LORD *is* with him').

501:37 **the men … seek to destroy me.** Cf. 1 Sam. xix. 1, 11 ('And Saul spake … to all his servants, that they should kill David. / Saul also sent messengers unto

David's house ... to slay him in the morning'). Cf. too Zechariah xii. 9 ('seek to destroy all the nations').

502:4 **food** Deleted in MS (p. 134), 'pottage'. See Genesis xxv. 34, etc.

502:10 **hates me beyond measure.** Cf. Mark vi. 51 ('sore amazed in themselves beyond measure'), Mark vii. 37 ('beyond measure astonished') and Galatians i. 13 ('beyond measure I persecuted the church of God').

502:22 **death is near.** Cf. 1 Sam. xx. 3 ('*there is* a but a step between me and death').

502:25 **Jonathan loves David,** Cf. 1 Sam. xix. 2 ('Jonathan Saul's son delighted much in David ...').

502:27 **the king ... slay David.** Cf. 1 Sam. xix. 1 ('And Saul spake to Jonathan his son, and to all his servants, that they should kill David').

502:38 **my flesh wearies upon my bones.** Cf. Job xix. 20 ('My bone cleaveth to my skin and to my flesh') and Ecclesiastes xii. 12 ('much study *is* a weariness of the flesh').

503:8 **one day he will kill me.** Cf. 1 Sam. xxvii. 1 ('And David said in his heart, I shall now perish one day by the hand of Saul ...').

503:19 **he gave thee to me,** Cf. 1 Sam. xviii. 27 ('And Saul gave him Michal his daughter to wife').

503:25 **So Jonathan ... hid me.** Cf. 1 Sam. xix. 2–3 ('Jonathan told David, saying, Saul my father seeketh to kill thee ... abide in a secret *place*, and hide thyself: / And I will go out and stand beside my father in the field where thou *art* ...').

503:29 **loved thee again.** See 1 Sam. xix. 4–7.

503:34 **But Saul swore ... be slain.** 1 Sam. xix. 6 ['and Saul sware, *As* ... liveth, he ...'].

503:37 **And when ... go forth,** Cf. 2 Sam. xi. 1 ('And it came to pass, after the year was expired, at the time when kings go forth *to battle* ... ').

504:1 **people rejoiced, I saw** DHL inserted a full stop after 'rejoiced' and a 'But' before 'I' in TS (p. 78), in an attempt to repair the damage done by Brett when she omitted twenty words in the preceding three sentences in MS (p. 137) (see Textual apparatus). This edition has restored DHL's MS text and disregarded his subsequent revision.

504:12 **once more there was war** 1 Sam. xix. 8 ['And there was war again ...'].

504:18 **between thy breasts,** Cf. Song of Solomon i. 13 ('my wellbeloved ... shall lie all night betwixt my breasts').

504:25 **the men.** Dorothy Brett typed 'men' in place of 'the', and then typed 'the' over it (TS, p. 78), so that both words were obscured (■ ■ ■ in Textual apparatus). The compositors of PPI (p. 101) – using an even more obscure carbon-copy typescript – presumably believed 'the' was deleted and simply printed 'men'.

505:7 **It is ... in the night,** Revised in MS (p. 140) from 'Say not so. Thou art sweet to me, and all my desire.'

505:11 **sleep among the lilies.** Cf. Song of Solomon ii. 16 ('My beloved *is* mine and I *am* his: he feedeth among the lilies').

506:11 **Jonathan ... at the door.** DHL conflates Jonathan's advice to David at 1 Sam. xix. 2 ('abide in a secret *place*, and hide thyself') with Michal's advice to her husband to escape at 1 Sam. xix. 11. The Bible does not show Jonathan visiting David to give warning.

506:27 **Giver** The only appearance of the word in *KJB* is at 2 Corinthians ix. 7 ('God loveth a cheerful giver') but divine gifts are regularly described, e.g. Proverbs ii. 6 ('the LORD giveth wisdom').

507:16 **bid slay thee.** Cf. 1 Sam. xix. 11 ('Saul also sent messengers unto David's house, to watch him, and to slay him ...').

507:23 **slay him in the dawn.** 1 Sam. xix. 11 ['... the morning'].

507:30 **I am weary of my life,** Genesis xxvii. 46.

508:6 **blossoms like an almond tree,** Cf. Ecclesiastes xii. 5 ('and the almond tree shall flourish').

508:11 **This time ... thy life.** Cf. 1 Sam. xix. 11 ('If thou save not thy life to night, to morrow thou shalt be slain').

508:35 **Now must ... the fields.** See 1 Sam. xix. 12 ('So Michal let David down through a window: and he went, and fled, and escaped').

509:19 *She takes ... over it.)* Cf. 1 Sam. xix. 13 ('And Michal took an image, and laid *it* in the bed, and put a pillow of goat's *hair* for his bolster, and covered *it* with a cloth').

509:28 **sick and in his bed.** Cf. 1 Sam. xix. 14 ('And when Saul sent messengers to take David, she said, He *is* sick').

510:11 **in the secret place.** 1 Sam. xix. 2 ['in a ...'].

511:5 **naked at her bath,** Cf. 2 Sam. xi. 2, where David sees Bathsheba.

511:11 **The king ... upon the bed!** Cf. 1 Sam. xix. 15 ('And Saul sent the messengers *again* to see David, saying, Bring him up to me in the bed ...').

512:4 **1ST CAPTAIN** DHL originally wrote '1st Captain' here, and (in the next two speech headings) '2nd Captain' and '3rd Captain'. He then altered the latter two to '2nd Soldier' and '3rd Soldier', and also apparently attempted to delete '1st', but not clearly (MS, p. 154). Brett typed '1st Captain' (TS, p. 88), altered in PPII to 'CAPTAIN' (p. 111). This edition has, here and elsewhere, returned to the numbering of the Captains and has renumbered the soldiers.

512:15 **man of wood ... goat's hair bolster!** Cf. 1 Sam. xix. 16 ('*there was* an image in the bed, with a pillow of goats' *hair* for his bolster'). See also note on 501:3.

512:20 **SAUL** DHL introduces Saul into the scene, which the Bible does not.

512:32 **Why hast thou deceived me?** 1 Sam. xix. 17 ['... me so?'].

513:1 **He said ...** *me go;* 1 Sam. xix. 17 ['... me, Let ...'].

513:3 *why shouldst ... of men.* Cf. 1 Sam. xix. 17 ('why should I kill thee?').

513:5 **Why hast ... is escaped?** 1 Sam. xix. 17.

513:16 **my flesh ... rebel against me,** Cf. Isaiah i. 2 ('I have nourished and brought up children, and they have rebelled against me').

514:2 *Naioth* 1 Sam. xix. 19. DHL makes it a hill (see note on 517:3), but it was simply the place where Samuel supervised a 'company of the prophets prophesying' (1 Sam. xix. 20).

514:5 *Many* PROPHETS ... *psalteries, pipes and tabrets.* Cf. 1 Sam. x. 5 ('a company of prophets coming down from the high place with a psaltery, and a tabret, and a pipe ...'). Many editions of *KJB* give 'tambourine' as a marginal gloss for 'tabret' here and at xviii. 6. A tabret is either a small drum or a tambourine; see note on 435:6.

514:11 **Very God!** The source is not *KJB* but probably the Nicene Creed in the *Book of Common Prayer* ('Very God of very God').

514:26 **peace between ... and his.** Cf. 1 Sam. xx. 42 ('Go in peace ... The LORD be between me and thee, and between my seed and thy seed for ever') and 1 Sam. xxv. 6 ('Peace *be* both to thee, and peace *be* to thine house').

514:30 **Yea, verily—** Not a *KJB* phrase, though both words appear frequently.

514:36 **never see thy day.** Samuel would die (1 Sam. xxv. 1) before David became king.

515:2 **guiltless** Cf. 1 Sam. xxvi. 9 ('who can stretch forth his hand against the LORD's anointed, and be guiltless?').

515:36 **The God of Saul hath no face.** Cf. Exodus xxxiii. 20 ('Thou canst not see my face: for there shall no man see me, and live').

515:37 **Flee then, thou,** Brett mistyped MS's 'then' as 'thee' (TS, p. 94). This was revised in PPII, possibly by DHL (responsible for two significant subsequent changes on the same page: see TA entries for 516:3 and 516:5) to 'Flee thou, flee,'. But even if responsible for the change, he was correcting an oddity in his text rather than rethinking it. This edition returns to the reading of MS.

516:2 **I will bless thee!** Genesis xii. 2 ['... thee'].

516:22 **a flower thou shalt fade ... a burning bush,** Cf. Isaiah xl. 7, 8 ('the flower fadeth') ... see Exodus iii. 2–6.

516:28 **Bless me ... my Father!** Cf. Genesis xxvii. 34 ('Bless me, *even* me also, O my Father'].

516:30 **The Lord quicken thee!** Cf. Psalms cxix. 149, etc. ('O LORD, quicken me ...'). The form of Samuel's blessing recalls the tripartite blessing from the *Book of Common Prayer*: 'The Lord bless thee and keep thee. The Lord make his face to shine upon thee, and be gracious unto thee. The Lord lift up his countenance upon thee, and give thee peace ...'

516:30 **fall into no snare!—** Cf. Psalms xci. 3 ('Surely he shall deliver thee from the snare') and 1 Timothy vi. 9 ('they that will be rich fall into temptation and a snare ...').

516:38 **well of Shecu.** Almost certainly an erroneous reference to 1 Sam. xix. 22 ['a great well that is in Sechu']: a city in Benjamin, near Ramah.

517:3 **the Hill.** Cf. Psalms iii. 4 ('his holy hill').

517:13 **put yourselves in array ... the Name.** 1 Sam. iv. 2 ['the Philistines put themselves in array ...'] ... cf. Psalms xcix. 3 ('Let them praise thy great and terrible name; *for* it *is* holy'). See too note on 438:12.

517:18 **Armies there are ... our God!** Cf. 1 Sam. xvii. 26, etc. ('the armies of the living God').

517:22 **Ha-ha!** Job xxxix. 25 ['He saith among the trumpets, Ha, ha ...'].

517:23 **strong in the Lord!** Ephesians vi. 10 ['... Lord,'].

517:24 **unseen arrows of high heaven** Cf. DHL in September 1916: 'I want to crouch in the bushes and shoot them silently with invisible arrows of death' (*Letters*, ii. 650); cf. Psalms lxiv. 4, 7 ('... they may shoot in secret ... / But God shall shoot at them *with* an arrow; suddenly shall they be wounded'), and Psalms vii. 11, 13 ('... God is angry *with the wicked* every day. / He hath also prepared for him the instruments of death; he ordaineth his arrows against the persecutors').

517:36 **Peace be with you!** Traditional formal greeting, Genesis xliii. 23 ['... to you'], etc.

517:40 *beginning to ... the chant,* Cf. 1 Sam. xix. 23 ('and the Spirit of God was upon him also, and he went on, and prophesied ...'). Revised in MS (p. 165) from 'beginning to sway slightly to the chant'. In revision, DHL also cut a direction at 518:2 showing Saul speaking 'to the chant tune', while before revision the speech at 518:6–9 read: 'Gone! Gone! (to the chant) So he has gone from the fury of the Lord! Surely is he fled before the Lord. So shall he flee before the right! So shall he flee before the right!—(speaking) But gone? Whither gone?' (MS, p. 165).

518:2 **before the Lord ... Surely the ... this place!** Common in OT: 1 Sam. ii. 17, etc. ... Genesis xxviii. 16 ['... place; ...'].

518:4 **the great brightness ... among the prophets?** Cf. Hebrews i. 3 ('Who being the brightness of *his* glory ...') ... 1 Sam. x. 11–12.

518:6 **fled ... the high place!** 1 Sam. xx. 1 ... common in OT: 1 Sam. ix. 12, 13, 14, etc.

518:15 **Tarry** Linger, loiter: common *KJB* word – 1 Sam. i. 23, etc.

518:25 **Fire within fire** Cf. Ezekiel i. 4 ('a fire infolding itself').

518:32 **the son of Kish** 1 Sam. ix. 1–2.

518:37 *They untackle.)* OED2 2. 'unharness' (of horses) comes closest to what 'untackle' might mean. But DHL probably means they put down their tackle ('Implements of war, weapons; *esp.* arrows' – OED2 4.).

519:5 **Whiteness of wool ... Colours on thy coat** Cf. Isaiah i. 18 ('though your sins be as scarlet, they shall be as white as snow ... they shall be as wool'). DHL was also probably influenced by the popular hymn 'Though your sins be as scarlet / ... They shall be as wool' (words F. J. Crosby, music W. Doane): see *Sacred Songs and Solos*, ed. Ira D. Sankey (n.d.), no. 532 ... Cf. Joseph's coat of many colours (Genesis xxxvii).

519:18 **Blow a fierce flame on me,** Cf. Job xli. 21 ('a flame goeth out of his mouth').

519:21 *Throws down his coat,* Cf. 1 Sam. xix. 24 ('And he stripped off his clothes also, and prophesied before Samuel in like manner, and lay down naked all that day and all that night').

519:26 the flame is flame forever ... in my nostrils Cf. Ezekiel xx. 47 ('the flaming flame shall not be quenched'): see also note on 519:18 ... cf. Job xxvii. 3 ('the spirit of God *is* in my nostrils').

519:35 the glory of the Lord. Common *KJB* phrase: Exodus xvi. 7, etc.

520:2 the glory ... the high place! Cf. Ezekiel xi. 23 ('the glory of the LORD went up ... and stood upon the mountain').

520:5 the Lord inside a house, See 2 Sam. vii. 5–6: 'the word of the LORD' says to David, 'Shalt thou build me an house for me to dwell in? / ... I have not dwelt in *any* house since the time that I brought up the children of Israel out of Egypt ... but have walked in a tent and in a tabernacle.'

520:6 transfiguration! Christ was transfigured on the Mount of Olives: see Matthew xvii. 1–9, etc. For parallel figurative uses, see also *The Rainbow*, ed. Kinkead-Weekes, 91:3–7, 284:20, and 'The Horse-Dealer's Daughter', *England, My England*, ed. Steele, 148:20.

520:16 weasel ... from her mouth, Plutarch noted 'many people' who 'declare that the weasel ... brings forth its young by way of its mouth' (*De Iside et Osiride*, 381A). Aristotle attributed the idea to Anaxagoras and refuted it (*De Generatione Animalium*, iii. 756b 15), but mediaeval writers – perhaps noting, like Aristotle, the animal's habit of carrying its new-born in its mouth – continued to repeat it: see Florence McCullough, *Mediaeval Latin and French Bestiaries* (Chapel Hill, N.C., 1962), pp. 186–8.

520:19 lurking in holes of the earth, Cf. 1 Sam. xxiii. 23, where Saul is issuing orders for hunting down David ('take knowledge of all the lurking places where he hideth himself').

520:20 gods shall be pitiful, Cf. James v. 11 ('the Lord is very pitiful').

520:23 the sleep [520:8] ... the flame! A preliminary version of this speech mistakenly inscribed by DHL on the back of a leaf of MS already used for the opening of Scene 15 (see Introduction, p. lxix and Appendix v i) reads:

> sleep of sleeps descends. ⌈(casts himself down)⌉ Lord, I cast myself down before thee, night and day, as in the death, lie I naked before thy <terror and thy splendour.> ⌈nearness.⌉—Ah, what is life to me! Alas! that a man must live till death visiteth him, that he cannot walk away into the Lord! Alas! for my life! For my children and my children's children, alas! For the son of Jesse will wipe them out! Alas, for Israel! For the fox of cunning will trap the lion of Judah, and the weasel that skippeth and boundeth shall be at the throats of brave men. Yea! by cunning shall Israel prosper, after me, when I am dead, and by cunning, lurking in holes, shall the seed of Israel fill the earth. And the Lord of Glory will withdraw far off, and gods shall be pitiful.—But I, I feel my death upon me, even in the glory of the Lord. Yea! leave me in peace in the death, let me retreat with the flame! <(casts himself down)>
>
> (p. 170, leaf 136r)

521:3 whirlwind from the world. Cf. 2 Kings ii. 11 ('Elijah went up by a whirlwind into heaven') and Job xxxviii. 1 ('Then the LORD answered Job out of the whirlwind ...'). See also note on 442:3.

522:3 *Late afternoon ... the stone Ezel.* In *KJB*, specifically 'in the morning' of the third day (1 Sam. xx. 35), but DHL may be recalling David's suggestion that he should hide 'in the field unto the third *day* at even' (1 Sam. xx. 5). However, the indication at 522:5 that they meet on the 'fourth day' may result from a misreading of Jonathan's suggestion '*when* thou hast stayed three days, *then* thou shalt go down quickly ... and shalt remain by the stone Ezel' (1 Sam. xx. 19) ... the Hebrew word probably means 'a heap of stones'.

522:5 **seeketh my life.** 1 Sam. xx. 1.

522:7 **hinder mine enemies. Frustrate ... stumble,** Cf. Psalms xxvii. 2 ('mine enemies ... stumbled and fell'), Jeremiah xx. 11 ('my persecutors shall stumble') and Isaiah xliv. 24−5 ('the LORD ... That frustrateth').

522:7 **Oh my God!** 1 Chronicles xvii. 25, etc.

522:10 **not far from me ... hide and have hidden.** Cf. Psalms xxii. 11 ('Be not far from me'), etc. ... 1 Sam. xx. 5, 19, 24.

522:15 **his lad!** Cf. 1 Sam. xx. 21 ('I will send a lad ...').

522:17 **Oh Lord ... mine enemies ... compass me round.** Cf. Psalms xvii. 9 in the *Book of Common Prayer* ('mine enemies compass me round about ...') and Psalms vii. 1 ('O LORD my God ... save me from all them that persecute me').

522:17 **O Lord my God,** 1 Kings iii. 7, etc.

522:19 **in the secret place.** Cf. 1 Sam. xix. 2 ('abide in a secret *place*').

522:22 *Behold ... take them!* 1 Sam. xx. 21.

522:25 *The arrows are beyond thee* 1 Sam. xx. 22.

522:32 **a mark I have shot at,** Cf. 1 Sam. xx. 20 ('as though I shot at a mark').

523:2 **run thou, take up the arrows** Cf. 1 Sam. xx. 36 ('Run, find out now the arrows ...').

523:5 *as he goes ... over his head.* Cf. 1 Sam. xx. 36 ('as the lad ran, he shot an arrow beyond him').

523:6 **Is not ... beyond thee?** 1 Sam. xx. 37.

523:9 **Make speed! Haste! Stay not!** 1 Sam. xx. 38 ['... speed, haste, stay not'].

523:17 **Take thou ... go home.** Cf. 1 Sam. xx. 40 ('And Jonathan gave his artillery unto his lad, and said unto him, Go, carry *them* to the city').

523:26 DAVID *comes ... and weep.)* Cf. 1 Sam. xx. 41 ('David arose ... and fell on his face to the ground, and bowed himself three times: and they kissed one another, and wept one with another ...').

523:33 **what have I done!** 1 Sam. xx. 1 ['What ... done?'].

524:6 **Thou shalt not die.** 1 Sam. xx. 2.

524:15 **Slay me now!** Cf. 1 Sam. xx. 8 ('slay me thyself').

524:19 **go in peace ...** *for ever.* 1 Sam. xx. 42 ['Go ... saying, The ...'].

524:24 **the star-stone** Probably DHL's coinage for a meteorite. The gem Astrion, known to the ancients as Astroites ('Star-stone'), with asteriated crystals of sapphire and a six-sided star in the centre, is less likely.

524:26 **lies prudence.** At this point in Frieda's translation, DHL introduced two new sentences: 'Ehrsucht liegt dir im Innersten des Herzens, Ehrsucht und Eigenwille. Doch bist du mir vielleicht nicht ganz kalt, und das, was wir geschworen haben, wirst du nicht ganz vergessen' ['Ambition lies in your innermost heart, ambition and self-will. Yet you are, perhaps, not quite cold to me, and that which we have sworn you will not quite forget'] (GTSII, p. 104).

524:32 **flame, shall ... before thee,** In typing MS (p. 177), Brett made several errors (TS, pp. 107–8) (see Textual apparatus). PPI (p. 128) made some attempt to repair the damage, and in proof DHL made further adjustments. It would probably be unwise to conflate his changes with MS.

524:33 **whelp of the lion of Judah!** Cf. Genesis xlix. 9 ('Judah *is* a lion's whelp').

524:34 **tender, quick child.** At this point in Frieda's translation, DHL introduced the following: 'Denn du bist so mutig, and allein. Ja' ['For you are so brave, and alone. Yes'] (GTSII, p. 104).

524:36 **Yet go!** At this point in Frieda's translation, DHL introduced two new sentences: 'Auch du wirst nicht ganz und gar vergessen, du kannst es nicht, auch wenn du willst. Etwas aus mir soll in dir leben, und in deinem Samen bis an das Ende, und an den neuen Anfang. Ja geh!' ['You will not utterly forget either, you cannot, even if you wanted to. Something of me will live on in you and in your seed to the end, and on to the new beginning. Yes, go!'] (GTSII, p. 104).

525:3 **to the city** Cf. 1 Sam. xx. 42 ('and Jonathan went into the city') and 40.

Altitude

539:12 MARY [539:3] ... ELIZABETH 'Mary A.' on her first appearance (541:3): Mary Austin, née Hunter (1868–1934); American author who lived for many years in California and New Mexico: see her autobiography, *Earth Horizon* (Boston, 1932). She had defended DHL in print in the winter of 1920–1, but he thought her defence 'so boring' (*Letters*, iii. 654), and would remark early in 1929 that 'she only observed superficially, as if the Pueblo were some American village' (Nehls, iii. 287 and 707 n. 53). He almost certainly first met her at Taos, New Mexico, in the early summer of 1924; she regularly visited Mabel Luhan (see below).

Willard ('Spud') Johnson (1897–1968), American journalist and editor; editor and co-founder of the magazine *Laughing Horse*, 1922–39, to which DHL contributed. DHL first met him in Santa Fe in September 1922, when Johnson was acting as secretary to the poet Witter Bynner (see note on 549:20 below), but Johnson visited Taos on many occasions. DHL remarked on 14 May 1924 that he was 'really nice, in the last issue' (*Letters*, v. 42).

Clarence E. Thompson, Harvard graduate and later screen-writer, protégé of Alice Sprague (see below) who sent him to Taos and to Mabel Luhan. DHL first met him between 14 and 26 May 1924, when Thompson was staying at the Del Monte Ranch, Taos: 'I think he's a nice fellow – not weak really, at all ... a young New-Yorker staying here – nice boy' (*Letters*, v. 48, 59). See also Nehls, ii. 516 nn. 12 and 13, and Mabel Luhan's *Lorenzo in Taos* (New York, 1932), pp. 202–51. DHL referred to his 'rose coloured trousers' in a letter of November 1924 (*Letters*, v. 172).

688 *Explanatory notes*

Ida Rauh (1877–1970), American founder of Provincetown Players and outspoken feminist, actress and sculptress; m. 1911 Max Forrester Eastman (1883–1969), divorced 1922. She lived with Andrew Dasburg (see below) 1922–8; like others in their circle (for example Brynner and the linguist Jaime de Angulo), DHL thought she was married to him (see 553:14–15 and *Letters*, v. 28). See her obituary in *New York Times* (12 March 1970), 41, and Introduction, pp. lix–lx. DHL had met her by 7 April 1924, either at Santa Fe or at Taos.

Alice Louise Sprague, née Bragley; m. 1883 Carleton Sprague (1858–1916), editor. A New York friend of Mabel Luhan and of Clarence Thompson; see Nehls, ii. 516–17 n. 13. DHL met her around 19 June 1924 and found her 'a nice elderly woman' (*Letters*, v. 60); he and Frieda saw her again in New York in September 1925 (*Letters*, v. 302). Mabel Luhan describes how 'dear little Alice Sprague' came to stay at Taos in the 'early summer' of 1924: 'She went into the Pink House [one of the houses owned by Mabel Luhan] and every morning she walked across the alfalfa field in a full-skirted, white muslin dress, and with her graying hair parted and smoothed down, and her uptilted smile under her round brow, she looked like a drawing by Da Vinci. She was one of those who determinedly see only the best in anyone.' According to Mabel Luhan, she thought 'Lorenzo an avatar, and Clarence a potential genius'; DHL liked her because 'she did not molest him in any way' (*Lorenzo in Taos*, pp. 208, 211, 224). DHL used in the play the 'white muslin' and the problems she had with a banging door (ibid., pp. 227–8) (see 542:36, 549:25–32).

Mabel Dodge Sterne Luhan (as she spelled 'Lujan' to ensure its proper pronunciation), née Ganson (1879–1962), American patroness of the arts. Her encouragement originally brought DHL to Taos; he and Frieda arrived in September 1922, and lived in the Winter of 1922–3 in accommodation she provided at Taos and at the Del Monte Ranch, eighteen miles away. They returned in 1924 to live at the nearby Kiowa ranch (which she gave to Frieda). Her *Lorenzo in Taos* contains a good deal of description of the events of the summer of 1924 (pp. 164–279). See *Letters*, iv. 110 n. 4.

Antonio ('Tony') Lujan (d. 1963), a Taos Pueblo Indian; m. Mabel Dodge in 1923.

Elizabeth, Mabel Luhan's adopted daughter, was born *c.* 1906. Mabel had discovered her in an orphanage in 1914; she suffered from arrested development. DHL remarked in October 1924 that 'Eliz. was a good girl' (*Letters*, v. 151).

Johnson's 'Editorial Note' in Per remarked:

Although it is obvious that, contrary to custom, *none of the characters are fictitious*, it should be clearly understood that the 'Mary' of the play is by no means the late Mary Austin; that 'Mabel' is certainly not the author of *Lorenzo in Taos*; that 'Ida' is not, as you might suspect, Ida Rauh Eastman; that 'Clarence' is not also named Thompson; and that Lujan is not the patronymic of 'Tony.' 'Mrs Sprague,' although her first name is Alice, should not be confused with Mrs. Carleton Sprague of New York City; Elizabeth is not Mabel Luhan's adopted daughter; and of course you realize that the 'Spud' mentioned, is not the editor of this magazine. (p. 111)

Johnson also added a list of characters *Graciously described by the Editor*:

MARY: A Woman With Ideas, who can also cook.
SPUD: Referred to as a 'Young Intellectual,' but obviously not.

CLARENCE: A 'Young Aesthete,' addicted to rose-coloured trousers and jewels.
MILKMAN: Just that.
IDA: A Dramatic Actress, even at breakfast.
MRS. SPRAGUE: A benign wraith.
MABEL: A determined lady who always knows that she wants – and gets it.
INDIAN: Whose name is Joe.
TONY: An American Indian philosopher, Mabel's husband.
ELIZABETH: Younger and blonder than the others. (p. 112)

541:3 *at Taos.* Johnson altered to '. . . Mabel's house at TAOS' (TSC, p. 1): Mabel owned several houses in Taos but DHL means the 'Big House', Los Palomas.

541:4 *Om!* Hummed or chanted (pronounced 'a-u-m') to assist meditation: originally a sacred Hindu and Buddhist word of assent.

541:9 **this altitude,** Taos is at *c.* 8,000 ft.

541:23 **Emilia** Emilia (or Amelia') was Mabel Luhan's Mexican cook: DHL refers to her as 'Emilie' in his letters (*Letters*, v. 76 and 102).

541:31 **Mary ... Martha ... Magdalene?** Mary and Martha were sisters in a house visited by Christ; Mary 'sat at Jesus' feet, and heard his word' while Martha 'was cumbered about with much serving ... careful and troubled about many things' (Luke x. 38–42). 'Mary called Magdalene' (Luke viii. 2) was one of Christ's followers, to whom he appeared first after his resurrection (Mark xvi. 1–9); tradition links her with the woman (often thought of as a prostitute) whose sins Christ forgave (Luke vii. 47).

543:26 **a Chicago aesthetic.** I.e. an aesthete from Chicago, notorious for its violence, gangsters and slaughter-houses.

543:34 **ephemeral?** Revised in MS (p. 7) from 'trashy', here and at 543:35 (where DHL had underlined it).

544:31 **Professor Mack?** A reference to the distinguished botanist Professor Daniel Trembly MacDougal (1865–1958), who ran the Desert Laboratory at the University of Arizona at Tucson (see 544:31–3) and to whom Mary Austin was emotionally attached. She dedicated her 1924 book *The Land of Journey's Ending* to him; they corresponded (see 544:36) and occasionally travelled together. While not accepted into the text, the spelling 'Proffessor' in MS (p. 9) and 'dessicating' on the next line may indicate Ida's pronunciation, with an American stress on the first syllable. See, however, Textual apparatus at 38:35.

545:15 **the Plaza** Taos's main square, about 1 mile from Mabel Luhan's house.

547:4 **a guy** I.e. a fool (as at 547:33); DHL is experimenting with American slang.

547:19 **Andrew** Andrew Michael Dasburg (1887–1979), American painter, b. Paris; friend of Mabel Luhan and early modernist influence in Taos. Lived in Santa Fe 1922–8 with Ida Rauh. See Nehls, ii. 487–8 n. 40, obituary in *New York Times* (14 August 1979), p. 15, and Van Deren Coke, *Andrew Dasburg* (Albuquerque, 1979). DHL probably met him in the summer of 1924.

549:5 **Contentos.** A difficult horse owned by Mabel Luhan, and lent to DHL and Frieda in 1924; see DHL to Mabel Luhan, 4 June 1924: 'The horses were demons yesterday – I caught Contentos, and fastened him to a tree with a thick rope. You should have seen him. All the devils! He broke the rope ... We must hobble Contentos, or shoot him ... or shut him up' (*Letters*, v. 51; see too v. 41).

549:12 **The glory has departed.** I.e. 'Thus passes the glory of the world' (quoted in Latin at 552:3: 'Sic transit gloria mundi') – from the *De Imitatione Christi*, chap. III, by Thomas à Kempis (1380–1471).

549:16 **before the sun spoils them.** Per (p. 132) shows Johnson strengthening the domineering attitude of 'Mabel' and the subservient response of 'Spud' in this exchange, presumably in proof: see Textual apparatus 549:16, 17 (ii).

549:20 **Spud's queer ... queer, to** *me* **... is queer** Whereas Ida employs the old-fashioned meaning of the word, both Clarence and Mabel appear to be playing on the word's new (and very recent) meaning of 'homosexual'. *OED2*'s first citation (from writing) is from the USA in 1932; but the *New Dictionary of American Slang*, ed. R. L. Chapman (1986), p. 349, suggests that it was used from the 1920s. Johnson had been engaged in a homosexual relationship with Bynner, as both DHL and Mabel Luhan knew.

550:13 **moonshine** Illicitly distilled liquor: 1919–33 was the 'Prohibition' era in the USA, when (by a constitutional amendment) the manufacture, sale and distribution of intoxicating liquors was banned. See DHL's 1925 essay 'A Little Moonshine with Lemon', *Mornings in Mexico* (1927).

552:10 **Oh** The typist of TS first typed (p. 12) a capital 'A', then overtyped the 'A' with an 'O': the compositor of E1 read 'Ah'. At 552:32, when the typist first typed (p. 13) a capital 'T', then overtyped the 'T' with an 'A', the compositor of E1 produced 'Till' rather than 'All'.

552:28 **love's young dream** Cf. 'Love's Young Dream', poem and song in the *Irish Melodies* (1808–34) by Thomas Moore (1779–1852): 'No, there's nothing half so sweet in life / As love's young dream' (ll. 10–11).

553:27 **castor oil.** Glutinous oil, taken (or threatened) as a cathartic.

553:33 **to touch pitch** To become contaminated; proverbial, from Ecclesiasticus xiii. 1 ('He that toucheth pitch shall be defiled therewith').

Noah's Flood

557:11 [IST MAN ... [557:6] COSBY] This editorially supplied list of characters is followed by the one which DHL wrote into MSII. For Noah and his family, see Genesis v–ix. Noah was 'five hundred years old' when he 'begat Shem, Ham and Japheth' (Genesis v. 32); after God 'repented ... that he had made man on the earth' and determined to destroy him, Noah 'found grace in the eyes of the LORD'; on God's instructions, he built the Ark and survived the Flood (Genesis vi. 5–ix. 17). See too the character list in MSI below, where Noah also appears as 'Cronos. – Jathir': Cronos (or Chronos, or Kronos), originally a Canaanite deity, a fertility god and lord of heaven, was the youngest of the Titans of Greek mythology – son of Uranos (sky) and Gaea (earth), and brother of Iapetos (the Greek version of the Hebrew Japheth: see below) and Rhea (by whom he had six children). He ruled the earth and – warned that one of his children would supplant him – swallowed them as they were born. Rhea, however, hid Zeus and gave Cronos a stone to swallow; Zeus eventually deposed his father and threw him into Tartarus. 'Jathir' is unidentified: it is not a biblical name, though cf. 'Jathniel' and 'Japhia' (Joshua x. 3, etc.). DHL may be creating yet another variant of Japheth/Japhet.

Shem was the eldest son of Noah; Ham was the third son, and the father of Canaan. Their descendants are listed at Genesis x. 6–20 and 21–32. Japhet was the second son (*KJB* spelling 'Japheth'); his descendants are listed at Genesis x. 2–5; traditionally, the ancestor of a number of non-semitic races (e.g. the Hindus). In Greek myth, the Titan Iapetos, brother of Cronos, and father of Atlas and Prometheus: he helped Zeus overthrow Cronos.

The name Cosby is (in origin) Irish, and may link with Kate Leslie's experiences at the end of *The Plumed Serpent*: 'Kate was more Irish than anything, and the almost deathly mysticism of the aboriginal Celtic or Iberian peoples lay at the bottom of her soul. It was a residue of memory, something that lives on from the pre-Flood world ...' (*Plumed Serpent*, ed. Clark, 415:19–21). The description of Cosby as 'female-male' at 557:17 suggests Madame Blavatsky's description of the 'four-armed human creatures in those early days of the male-female hermaphrodites' in Atlantis (*The Secret Doctrine*, 1888, ii. 29). The word 'Kultur-träger' (557:17) – 'Culture-bearer' (German) – is also applied to Hermione in *WL* 16:20. It is remotely possible that DHL was thinking of Dudley Cosby (1862–1923), contributor of many articles to reviews and letters to the press: his pamphlet 'German Kultur: What Is It?' was published in *Towards Universal Peace* in 1915.

For Shem as 'Utterer' (557:12), 'Kanah' (557:12) and 'Shelah' (557:14) see below. The character list in MSI was as follows:

Shem + Kanah, Ham + Shelah, Japhet + Cosby

Shem—the utterer—the *I am. It is*
Kanah—the echoer—*It was. It shall be*
Ham—Heat
Shelah—Flux.
Japhit—Encompassing,—spreading—father of all: also *Destroyer*
father of fire—the injurer—the male-female
Cosby—the female-male—the Kultur-träger
Noah—Cronos.—Jathir

'Kanah' is perhaps a reference to 'Canaan' (or 'Kanaan' in German), the son of Ham; perhaps to the Greek word 'kanna', a measure of proportion, and root of the words 'canon' and 'cannon'. DHL originally wrote 'Phoebe', then 'Lilith', then 'Achsah' (MSI, p. 133). Phoebe was the Greek goddess Artemis in the guise of a moon goddess; Lilith was either (in Jewish folklore) a demon who attacks children or (in Talmudic literature) the first wife of Adam. Achsah Barlow Brewster (1878–1945) was the Jewish wife of the American Earl Brewster, both of whom DHL had known since April 1921; from the start of their friendship he had been struck by the oddity of her name: 'Might as well be Absalom for all I make of it' (iii. 719), 'Ach! ach Gott! – tiresome name to spell you've got' (iv. 101).

'Shelah' is, in *KJB*, a masculine name: third son of Judah (Genesis xxxviii. 5, etc.). The Celtic 'sheelah' (or 'sheelah-na-gigg'), the cult female figure portrayed with her legs wide apart, may also have influenced the name; as too may the Hebrew word 'Selah', a frequent verse ending in the Psalter, perhaps indicating a pause or rest. DHL originally wrote 'Rhea', then 'Lilith' (MSI, p. 133), suggesting that he had always thought of the character as female.

With regard to 'Shem': DHL is concerned elsewhere both with the 'utterer' (cf. the 'Foreword' to *Sons and Lovers*, ed. Baron and Baron, 467:15) and with '*I am*' (cf. 'The Crown', *Reflections on the Death of a Porcupine*, ed. Herbert, 266:18).

559:3 the Old One   I.e. Noah: see note on 557:11.

559:8 the sons of men ... the sons of God.   See Genesis vi. 1–2, 4:

> And it came to pass, when men began to multiply on the face of the earth, and daughters were born unto them, That the sons of God saw the daughters of men that they *were* fair; and they took them wives of all which they chose ... There were giants in the earth in those days; and also after that, when the sons of God came in unto the daughters of men, and they bare *children* to them, the same *became* mighty men which *were* of old, men of renown.

A favourite passage of DHL's: quoted and discussed in *The Rainbow*, ed. Kinkead-Weekes, 256:38–257:22; Ursula Brangwen also sees in her lover Anton Skrebensky 'one such as those Sons of God who saw the daughters of men, that they were fair' (271:16–18). See too DHL to Lady Ottoline Morrell in February 1915: 'We will be the Sons of God who walk here [...] on earth ... We will be aristocrats, and wise as the serpent in dealing with the mob' (ii. 273). It is difficult in both MSI and MSII (as in other DHL manuscripts) to be sure whether upper or lower case is being used for the initial 's' of 'sons'.

559:34 wittier   In dialect usage, 'cleverer, more intelligent': as an archaism, 'wiser'.

560:36 what Shem says?   DHL originally wrote 'what the Old One says' in MSI (p. 135) but then replaced 'Old One' with 'Shem' without removing the redundant 'the'. He did not transcribe it in MSII (p. 4).

561:2 the fern-seed fall brown; for bread.   Before its reproduction by means of minute spores was understood, the fern was often supposed to have invisible seed capable (for that reason) of making the possessor invisible. But DHL is probably thinking of antediluvian giant ferns, with giant spores, revealed in fossil plants and coal.

561:8 A bird ... the bush.   Proverbial.

561:11 the Great White Bird,   See note on 490:27.

562:5 heavy sky,   In MSI (p. 137), DHL first wrote 'heavy,', presumably intending to supply another adjective. He then squeezed in 'sky,' on to the right-hand edge of the paper but failed to delete the comma after 'heavy'. In MSII (p. 6) he omitted it.

563:19 the banks be gone beneath the flood.   It is just possible that – when transcribing MSI (p. 138) – DHL skipped a line and omitted six words from MSII (p. 8): see Textual apparatus at 563:18.

563:24 Your life ... water forever passing.   DHL had been profoundly influenced by John Burnet's *Early Greek Philosophy* (1892, repr. 1908), and derived much of his knowledge of Heraclitus (Greek philosopher, *fl. c.* 500 BC) and of Heraclitean flux from Burnet. See *Apocalypse and the Writings on Revelation*, ed.

Mara Kalnins (Cambridge, 1980), pp. 13–14, 211–14; *Twilight in Italy*, ed. Eggert, p. lv; *Reflections on the Death of a Porcupine*, ed. Herbert, pp. xxii–xxiii.

564:36 *A conch-shell* An archaic means of summoning people, which DHL may have heard at Hindu temples in Sri Lanka, March–April 1922.

566:20 **butter-skins ... the glass of earth into knives.** See note on 494:2 ... DHL's coinage, perhaps meaning 'metal'; cf. 'glass of lead' and 'glass of antimony' in old-fashioned science. However, he would certainly have seen antique ceremonial knives of the vitreous lava obsidian – volcanic glass – in museums in Mexico.

566:23 **you toil not, neither will you dance.** Cf. Matthew vi. 28 ('Consider the lilies of the field, how they grow; they toil not, neither do they spin').

567:3 **There is a time to give, and a time to withhold.** The formula 'A time to ... a time to' is used repeatedly in Ecclesiastes iii. 1–8.

The original ending to *David*

Note Annotation has not been supplied where the notes on *David* provide the requisite equivalent information.

577:4 **The Lord strengthen thee!** Psalms xx. 1–2 ('The LORD ... strengthen thee ...').

577:18 **As the Lord liveth?** Common phrase in 1 Sam. xiv. 39, 45, etc. See also 579:21.

577:26 **I fled from Naioth,** 1 Sam. xx. 1 ['And David fled ...'].

577:31 **he stripped himself ... before the Lord,** Cf. 1 Sam. xix. 24 ('he stripped off his clothes also, and prophesied before Samuel in like manner, and lay down naked all that day and all that night').

577:38 **my heart fails,** Cf. Psalms xl. 12 ('therefore my heart faileth me') and lxxiii. 26 ('My flesh and my heart faileth').

578:2 **I know not where to lay my head,** Cf. Matthew viii. 20 ('the Son of man hath not where to lay *his* head').

578:4 **This shall not be!** Psalms xxxvii. 10 ['the wicked *shall* ...'], etc.

578:6 **what have ... my life?** 1 Sam. xx. 1 ['What ... what ... and ...'].

578:10 **God forbid ... it is not so!** 1 Sam. xx. 2 ['... forbid: thou ... die: behold ... but that he ... me: and ... me? it ... *so*.'].

578:13 **sent the messengers, thrice ... and prophesied.** Cf. 1 Sam. xix. 21 ('And Saul sent messengers again the third time, and they prophesied also.').

578:20 *Let not* **... me and death.** 1 Sam. xx. 3 ['... grieved: but ... *as* the LORD liveth, and *as* thy soul liveth ... but a step ...'].

578:22 **Whatsoever thy ... for thee.** 1 Sam. xx. 4.

578:24 **Behold ... at meat,** 1 Sam. xx. 5 ['Behold, to morrow ...'].

578:35 **—But let me [578:25] ... thy father?** 1 Sam. xx. 5–8 ['but ... even. / If ... say, David ... for *there is* ... there for ... thus, *It is* well; thy ... peace: but ... by him. / Therefore thou shalt deal kindly ... servant; for ... with thee: notwithstanding, if ... be in me iniquity, slay ... thyself; for ...'].

578:38 **Far be it ... not tell thee?**   1 Sam. xx. 9 ['... thee: for ... would not I tell it thee?'].

579:2 **And who** [578:40] **... thee roughly,**   1 Sam. xx. 10 ['Who shall tell me? or what *if* thy father answer ...'].

579:3 **Come, let us go aside!**   Cf. 1 Sam. xx. 11 ('Come, and let us go out into the field.').

579:12 **Oh Lord** [579:4] **... in times past.**   1 Sam. xx. 12–13 ['O ... father about to morrow any time, *or* the third *day*, and, behold ... unto thee, and shew it thee; / The ... Jonathan: but ... will shew ... peace: and ... with thee, as he hath ... father.'].

579:13 **Samuel hath again ... of the Lord.**   There is no mention of this in *KJB*.

579:20 **shalt thou** [579:16] **... the earth.**   1 Sam. xx. 14–15 ['thou shalt not only while yet I live shew me the kindness of the LORD, that I die not: / But *also* thou shalt ... ever: no, ...'].

579:25 **Yet shalt thou swear it unto me.**   Cf. 1 Sam. xx. 17 ('And Jonathan caused David to swear again ...').

579:35 **and all David's house,**   Cf. 1 Sam. xx. 16 ('So Jonathan made *a covenant* with the house of David ...').

579:38 **Tomorrow is ... be empty.**   1 Sam. xx. 18 ['Tomorrow ... moon: and ...'].

580:4 **And when thou ... stone Ezel.**   Cf. 1 Sam. xx. 19 ('And *when* thou hast stayed three days, *then* thou shalt go down quickly, and come to the place where thou didst hide thyself when the business was *in hand*, and shalt remain by the stone Ezel.').

580:12 **And I will** [580:5] **... thee away.**   1 Sam. xx. 20–2 ['... side *thereof*, as though I ... / And, behold ... *saying*, Go ... lad, Behold ... them; then come thou: for ... hurt; *as* ... / ... man, Behold ... thee; go ...'].

580:19 **And touching ... for ever.**   1 Sam. xx. 23 ['And as touching ... have spoken of, behold, the ...'].

581:15 **a fire-pit**   Not in *OED2*, but DHL's meaning is clear; North American Indian practice probably suggested the idea.

581:22 **The place on Saul's left, facing Abner, is empty.**   Cf. 1 Sam. xx. 25 ('and Abner sat by Saul's side, and David's place was empty').

581:27 **In the Lord's name!**   Variant of common *KJB* phrase (see 1 Sam. xvii. 45, xx. 42, etc. – 'in the name of the Lord') – but here a grace before a meal.

581:29 **Phaltiel the son of Laish**   Phaltiel (2 Sam. iii. 15) or Phalti (1 Sam. xxv. 44) was the Benjamite to whom Saul gave his daughter Michal, David's wife; David asked Saul's son Ishbosheth to get her back, which he did (2 Sam. iii. 14–16).

582:6 **wherefore cometh ... today?**   1 Sam. xx. 27 ['Wherefore ... to day?'].

582:7 **Hath something ... not clean?**   I.e. free from ceremonial defilement, according to Mosaic Law. Cf. 1 Sam. xx. 26 ('he thought, Something hath befallen him, he *is* not clean; surely he *is* not clean.').

582:13 **David earnestly** [582:8] ... **king's table.** 1 Sam. xx. 28–9 ['... me *to* ... Bethlehem: / And he said, Let ... *there*: and ... not unto the ...'].

582:17 **Sayst thou so!** Cf. 1 Sam. xx. 30 ('Then Saul's anger was kindled against Jonathan ...').

582:33 **valiant against the king's enemies.** Cf. 1 Sam. xviii. 17 and 25 ('be thou valiant for me, and fight the LORD's battles ... to be avenged of the king's enemies').

583:2 **Thou son** [582:37] ... **surely die.** 1 Sam. xx. 30–1 ['... of the perverse... *woman*, do not I ... and unto the ... nakedness? / For ... kingdom. Wherefore...'].

583:3 **Wherefore shall ... he done?** 1 Sam. xx. 32 ['... what ...'].

583:5 **(hurls javelin at Jonathan)** Cf. 1 Sam. xx. 33 ('And Saul cast a javelin at him to smite him ...').

583:7 **in fierce anger** 1 Sam. xx. 34.

583:12 **The Lord reward it unto you.** 1 Sam. xxiv. 19 ('the LORD reward thee good ...').

583:22 **no man of war,** 1 Sam. xvi. 18 ['and a man ...'] and 2 Sam. xvii. 8 ['thy father *is* a man ...'].

583:35 **Yet he spoke to Moses.** See Exodus iii. 4 ('God called unto him out of the midst of the bush, and said, Moses, Moses'), etc.

584:6 **There is no commandment from God, save one,** Cf. Mark xii. 31 ('There is none other commandment greater than these') and Luke xviii. 19 ('save one').

584:14 **Is not the Lord with David?** Cf. 1 Sam. xvi. 18 ('and the LORD *is* with him') and 1 Sam. xviii. 12, 14 ('the LORD was with him').

584:25 **I am the bush ... burns not down.** Cf. Exodus iii. 2 ('the bush burned with fire, and the bush *was* not consumed').

586:15 **haste, stay not.** 1 Sam. xx. 38.

GLOSSARY OF DIALECT, REGIONAL, SLANG AND ARCHAIC WORDS

Note

The definitions supplied are those which apply best to the contexts of the plays in this volume. Words have been listed in lower-case forms even if their appearance in the text is in upper case. No distinction has been made between words of dialect origin and words pronounced with a regional accent; some non-dialect colloquialisms have been included. The following categories of words have not, in general, been included:

1 Standard English words with one letter altered, added or omitted (e.g. 'yis' for 'yes', 'cumpany' for 'company', 'childt' and 'chilt' for 'child', 'a'most' for 'almost'), and words with the last letter omitted or replaced by an apostrophe (e.g. 'livin'' for 'living', 'an'' for 'and'). Exceptions have been made for genuinely awkward examples (e.g. 'gi'e' for 'give', 'ha'e' for 'have').
2 Combinations of dialect words or pronunciations if they are easily recognisable (e.g. 'ivrythink' for 'everything').
3 Words in unusual but comprehensible grammatical forms (e.g. 'throwed' for 'threw', 'heered' for 'heard').
4 Dialect forms which have lost initial 'h' (e.g. ''ad' for 'had').
5 Words which because of hypercorrection or as an expression of strong emphasis have an 'h' prefixed (e.g. 'h'are' for 'are').

a', a	all; at; have; on
'a	have
abear	bear, tolerate
a-cause	because
addled	earned
'adna	had not
afore	before
after-damp	*see note on* 104:4
a-gait	going on
agen	against; next to
ah	I; yes
ah'n	I have
'alf	*see* not 'alf
allers	always
an, 'an	have
an' all, an' a', and all	indeed, really, truly; too, as well

anigh	near
'appen, 'appen so	*see* happen
'a'porth, 'ae'-porth	*see* ha'p'orth
a-purpose	on purpose
arena, are'na	aren't
art	are
as	who, which, what; that (*conj.*)
'asna, asna	hasn't
atop	on top
atween, a'tween	between
a-two	in two
ave'na, 'ave-na	haven't
a-whoam, awhoam	at home
ax, axin', axed	ask, asking, asked; 'to be asked in church' is to have your marriage banns published
ay, aye	yes
bacca	tobacco
back	bet (e.g., in support of an affirmation)
back-ards, back'ards	backwards
baffle	confuse, perplex, worry
baggage	term of reproach or abuse (applied mostly to women and children)
bally	euphemism for 'bloody'
bantle	batch
barm	yeast
batchy	silly, stupid, mad
baulkin'	getting in the way
become	suit
bed-latts	laths or slats to support mattress and bedding
begad	by God
begùm	by God, God Almighty
beguy	by God
be out, biout	without
Berty-Willie	a 'billycock' (bowler) hat
besom	woman with slovenly or loose habits
bested	arrived before
bin	been; are
bitted an' bobbed	bitten into and chewed
blackymoor	blackamoor, i.e. black man
blazes	hell, the flames of hell
blew	blue
blort than bustle, more	more talk than action
blortin' an' bletherin'	talking and babbling nonsense
bob	shilling; *see* p. 824

bobbied off	gone off
bobby	euphemism for 'bloody'
bobby-dazzler	something startlingly attractive
boiled my cabbage	repeated myself
boiling	the lot, the whole party (sometimes preceded by 'whole')
booth	tent; *see note on* 471:27
boozin'	drinking
böwks	books
b'r	but
brazen, brazened	impudent, shameless, impertinent
bregger	'brekker', breakfast
britches	breeches
brokken	broken
brown	*see* done brown
browt	brought
bug	conceited, vain, 'stuck up'
buggers	abusive term for men
bully raggin'	intimidating
bushel	large quantity
butty	*see notes on* 19:39 and 305:30
by	by the time that, before
cade	spoil, pet, fondle
calamniate	calumniate, slander
calf	*see note on* 463:6
can	drink
canna, canner	cannot, can't
canned	drunk
canst	can you
carney	wheedle, coax, flatter
carrying-on	bad behaviour
ca's	calls
'casions	occasions
catlick	a hasty wash
'cause	because
certing	certain
chair	cage for carrying coal, miners, etc., up and down the mine-shaft
chalked of a line	white as a sheet
chancy	choosy
chappil	chapel
checkweighman	man who (on behalf of the miners) checks the weight of mined coal at the surface
cheese it, cheeze it	stop it

chelp	quarrelsome chatter; impudence, cheek
chip	quarrel, fall out, disagree
chough	chatterer, prater
chuck	chicken, young bird, fowl, hen
chunter, chunterin'	grumbling
clamming, clammed	starving, starved, very hungry
clap	put
clat-fart, clat-farted	gossip, gossiped
claver	mouth; idle talk, chatter
clawk	snatch, seize greedily, covetously
clean as a whistle	perfectly
clenching	clutching
clodhopper	ill-bred or clumsy person, boor
close	tight-fisted
club-money	*see note on* 22:21
clunch	hard clay often found in the vicinity of coal
coal-slack	*see* slack
coddled, coddling	looked (looking) after with too much care
come again tomorrer	tell us another, come off it
comm	come, came
commin'	coming
commons	rations
con, conning	scan, peruse, pore over; learn by repetition
cop	get
cop out	die
corker	something or someone astonishing, stunning
cos, 'cos	because
coss	curse
cotter	entangle, mat together
couldna	could not
cöwd	cold
crambling	lame, shaky, tottering
crewel	cruel
crozzled up	shrivelled up with heat, burnt to a cinder
cry	a public announcement, as from a town crier
cump'ny	company
cunning	*see note on* 471:38
cut	temper
'd	would
dachess	duchess
dander	spirit
dark hour	evening, twilight
dart	*see note on* 491:10
day-man	miner employed on a daily wage

dead cert	absolutely certain, certainty
deep one, 'un, un	clever, cunning, crafty
didna	didn't
dodges	tricks
doesna, does'na	doesn't, do not
dog's nose	*see note on* 66:22
doited	silly (normally because of age)
done brown	made a fool of, outwitted
dost	you do; do you?
dosy-baked	stupid, dull, soft
dotty	dirty
doubt	fear; *see note on* 463:28
draggle-tail	feeble, ill-conditioned person; in particular a slovenly, untidy and dirty woman
dun	do; do not; don't
dunna	don't
dunno	don't know
durst	dare
dursn't, dursna	dare(s) not
eaten him ravishing	eaten him whole, with huge enjoyment
'eered	heard
'em	them
em'py	empty
enow	enough
'er, her	her, she
'ere	here
fa'	fall
face	mouth (as in 'stop thy face')
fad after	look after in a quiet way
fair	quite, completely, truly, really, actually
fall out	to quarrel
fat, fret your	*see* fret your fat
fawce	clever, sharp, shrewd, cunning, sly
feather-brain, a	light, giddy; *see note on* 455:19
ferrit, ferret	pry into, search out, find out about, rummage
fettle	clean, tidy up; attend to, look after
feyther	father
flat	person easily taken in, so not very 'sharp'
flig	pleased
flit, flitted	die, died
flummery	empty trifling
foisty	musty, mouldy
foolery	playing about

footle	toy with, spend time aimlessly, talk or act foolishly
force-put	a matter of compulsion or inevitability
fortnit	fortnight
fow	disagreeable, ill-tempered, angry
fra	from
fret your fat	worry
frit	frightened, scared
frowsty	mean, poor, lousy, shabby; musty, stale
fudged and haffled	evaded and prevaricated
fun, fun'	found
gab	talk
gabey, gaby	stupid, foolish person; simpleton, fool, idiot
gaffer	master, person in charge, foreman, overseer; head of household, husband
gallivant	go about in search of pleasure, gad about in showy fashion
game on, to have a	to be involved in some mischief or intrigue
gammy	lame
garn	nonsense; go on
gel	girl
gen	gave, given
ger, gerr, gerrin'	get, getting
gev	gave
gie, gi'e	give
gin	horse- or donkey-turned windlass of the old-fashioned gin pit
gleg	peep, pry, look furtively or slyly
gnawg	gnaw
good 'un	large one, long one, good one
go'n	going
grizzlin'	crying
gum, by gum	*see* begùm
gumption	quickness of understanding, common sense, shrewdness
guy, guyney	euphemism for 'God'
ha, ha', ha'e	have
hadna, 'adna	hadn't
haef, ha'ef	half
ha'en, ha'ein'	having
ha'ena	haven't
haffled	*see* fudged
han	have

hanna, 'anna	have you?; have not
Hanover	euphemism for 'hell', from 'go to Hanover!', i.e. go to hell!
ha'p'orth, ha'porth, hae'porth, haporth	half-penny worth, i.e. insignificant, negligible
happen	perhaps, possibly, maybe
hasna	hasn't
hast	have you
havna	haven't
hawksed	hauled
headstocks	visible structure of winding machinery at the pit-head
her	she, her
hersen	herself
hing	hang down
hitting things off	summing things up
hisself, hissèn, his'n	himself, his
hold thy gab	shut up
hole	dig out the space beneath an overhanging mass of coal
hole a stint	do a job of holing
holer	miner employed to hole
holl	throw, hurl
hoom	home
horkard	awkward
hoss	horse
hussy	pert girl; impudent, self-assertive, bossy woman
hutch up	move up
i'	in, into
ikey	haughty, proud, superior, cocky, putting on airs
injun	engine
innerds	inwards
inter	into
iron-men	coal-cutting machines; *see note on* 64:4
isna	isn't
'issen	himself, his
jackanapes	pert, impertinent person
jackin' up	ruining
jibber	horse which jibs (refuses)
jockey	fellow, cheat, swindler, impostor
johnny	man

jug-handle coiffure	hair-style with long curls shaped like jug-handles
kep	keep, kept
knivey	contemptible
lack, good lack	*see* lawk
la-di-da, lah-di-dah, lardy-da	pretentious in manner or speech
lanthorn	lantern
lawk, good lawk, laws, good laws	exclamation of astonishment, surprise or disgust; good Lord
leadin'	*see note on* 307:18
leasing, speak	tell lies
leave, as	as gladly, willingly: archaic form of 'lief'
leg, don't look so long in the	sit down
let in	trapped
like	used redundantly or to modify a statement, intensifying it, comparable to 'you see'; 'as it were'
linkin'	looking
livant	i.e. 'to levant': to abscond, to steal away
lodge	lie flat, go out (fire); place, lay
long	tall
look slippy	make haste, look sharp
look so long in the leg, don't	*see* leg
looney	fool
'lowance	allowance (of money or drink)
'lt	shalt (shall)
luik, luikin'	look, looking
lum	excellent, first rate (Lord love me)
lump	put together in one lump; beat, knock, thump violently, thresh
lump it	put up with it
lu'thee	look here
ma'e, ma'ein'	make, making
malapert	*see note on* 457:31
mar	damage; *see note on* 86:6
marded, mardin'	softened, softening
mardy, mard-soft	soft
maun, mun	must
mealy-mouthed	sanctimonious; not speaking directly or to the point; over-scrupulous
mek	make; type of manufacture
mester, master	husband, master, man, Mr

middling, middlin'	fairly well, tolerable(-ly); not too well
mob-cap, mopcap	woman's large cotton cap; a kind of Tam-o'-shanter
moleskin, moleskins	strong, heavy cotton cloth; working trousers made of moleskin
molly-coddle	take excessive care of; *see* coddle
moonshine	illicitly distilled alcohol; *see note on* 550:13
mope	wander about aimlessly, thoughtfully, remain apathetic, grope
morm, mormin' about	potter, trifle, wander about foolishly
mort	great deal
mosh	mash, pulp; crushed, soft
moudiwarp	mole
mug, pull a mug	face, to make a face
mulligrubs	stomach ache, fit of ill-temper or sulkiness, depression, low spirits
mun	must; certainly
munna	must not
munny	money
mushy	soft, decaying; mashed, pulpy, crumbly
mustache	old spelling of moustache (still possible early in twentieth century)
mysen	myself
'n	than'; 've (*have*)
naggles	niggles
nap	*see note on* 15:25
nation	euphemism for 'damnation'
near	mean
nedna, ne'dna, needna	needn't
nice	over-refined
nicker	neigh, whinny
niggled down	reduced down
nigh	nearly, possibly; near to
nip	squeeze
nobbut	only, nothing but
nob'dy, no'b'dy	nobody
noggin, noggins	mug, bowl
non, none	not; don't
nor	than (*after comparative*)
not 'alf, not half	much, very much
nowheer	nowhere
nowhow	how, how not
nowt, nöwt	nothing

occasions	needs, necessities
off'n	from, off, from off
Old Harry	the devil
old lad	cunning, sly devil
on	of, about
on't	of it
onter, ont'r	on to
ony	any
on'y	only
orming, ormin', 'ormin	silly, clumsy; tall, awkward; pretending, feigning
orts and slarts	leftovers (as from a meal)
o's	of his
oughtner	ought not
'out	without
outen's	out of his
outer	out of; about
öw	her, she; how
owd	old
ower	over
owt, wt	anything, something
palled … onter	passed on to, as a friend
panchion	large, shallow earthenware bowl
panoply	*see note on* 467:33
particler	particular
peck	heap
pennorth	a penny worth, as much as can be bought for a penny
pick-heft	pick handle
piece, a piece	term of contempt or abuse for a woman (e.g., a slow piece of goods)
piffler	a trifler
pills	droppings; *see note on* 496:15
pin, pinned	pin down, trap
pit bottle	tin container to be taken underground; filled with water or cold tea
pitch	*see* touch pitch
pop-shop	pawnshop
porin'	poring (over)
pretty, go	go gently
prithee	pray
proker	poker
proof	*see note on* 468:10
pulamiting	whining, whimpering

put's i's	puts it in his
queer	*see note on* 549:20
quiver-clothes-horse	frame of horizontal bars on which clothes are hung to dry or air
racket an' tacket	noise and destructiveness
racketty, rackety	noisy, fond of excitement
raight, raïght	right
rake	cover or bank up a fire with coal to make it burn slowly and stay alight
raker	large lump of coal (for raking)
ramp, ramped	burn vigorously, bright; blazing; heaped up
ravelled	confused, entangled
rayther	rather
reive	steal; *see note on* 499:3
rig	*see* run the rig
road	way, habit
roads	underground roadways and passages in the pit
ronk	rank, libidinous
room	right (e.g., to have room to talk: to have a right to speak)
rowdy	ruddy
ruddy	*see note on* 456:36
rum 'un	odd, strange (it's a rum 'un); good, excellent; thoroughly, completely
run the rig	have a wild time; *see note on* 209:16
rushes	leeks
's	his
samthing	something
sark	sarcasm, to be sarcastic
sarve	serve
saving	except
savvy	know, understand: from the French 'savoir'
sawny, sawney	fool, simpleton; stupid, foolish, weak person
sayn	saying
scandylos	scandalous
scawdrag	*see* scrawdrag
scraight, scraïght	cry, scream, weep
scrawdrag	scoundrel, worthless person
scroddy	mean, paltry, puny, meagre, rotten, tatty; *see note on* 243:24
scuffle	a bustle, hurry

scullery	the room off the kitchen for washing clothes and dishes, and where people often wash themselves
s'd, sh'd	should
seemly	apparently, seemingly
selvidge	*see note on* 67:27
sen	self (as in 'hissen')
shably	meanly, despicably (i.e. 'shabbily')
shanna, shanner	shan't
sharpshins	sharp-witted, clever person
sh'd	should
shift, to be made shift of	be moved about, to be used
shifting shirt	*see note on* 327:31
shilly-shally through	get through somehow
shindy, shine	row, brawl
sholl	shall
shonna	shan't
sides o' bacon	buttocks
sight	a great deal, a number, a quantity
sin, sin'	since
singlet	a thick flannel vest, sleeveless or with short sleeves, worn by miners
sinking, sinkin'	faint, ready to drop with fatigue, hunger, etc.
sithee	look here, you'll see
skedaddle off, skidaddle	run away, hurry off
skim	milk with the cream skimmed off
skirr	grating or rasping sound
slack	small or refuse coal
slarts	bits left over
slaver	drivel, talk nonsense
sleer, sleering	sneer, talk with sly offensiveness, talk or smile derisively
slink	loiter about, idle over one's work; slip by secretly
slither, slitherin'	waste, spend idly; untrustworthy, unsteady, slovenly
slive	sneak about, creep stealthily, do something slyly or secretly
sliving, slivin'	sly, deceitful, mean, sneaking, wicked
s'll	shall
slobber	kiss effusively, or in a loud, coarse manner; slaver; eat in a slovenly fashion
slorm, slormed, slormin'	crawl, slink away, go about with a hang-dog air; sullen, sly
slormy	slushy, sloppy

s'lt	shall (shalt)
sluther	slide, idle
slutherers	idlers
smockravel	puzzle, perplex
smug	put on a smug expression
snaggin' an' snarlin'	quarrelling and grumbling
snap	miner's food taken down the pit; *see too* snip
snap bag	miner's food bag (often of calico)
snap time	break and meal time
snappy	cross, ill-tempered, surly, irritable
snip	accept readily, esp. an offer of marriage (e.g., say snip to another's snap)
snip-snap-snorum	a round game of cards; take quickly and suddenly; secure a girl in marriage
sofey	sofa
softy	silly or weak person
sooth	true; *see note on* 467:15
sorry	term of address for man or boy; mate, friend, pal: *see note on* 324:20
sot, sotten	sat, has sat
squark	croaking, squawking
sta', stall	section of coal-face apportioned to a particular butty and team
statutes ground	*see note on* 343:21
staunch	strong, in good health
stint	day's task, work
stomach	pride
stool-arsed Jack's	*see note on* 348:11
stop, stoppages	deduct from pay; deduction from pay or allowances
stop thy face	shut up
strap	credit
stripling	*see note on* 450:31
stroke, of a	at once
stuff his mug	stop his mouth
sumb'dy	somebody
summat	something
sutler, a	*see note on* 439:6
swaller	swallow
swarf up, swarfed	make dirty with swarf (fine dirt of stone, metal, coal, etc.); mucky
swimmy	shaky, unsteady, weak; hesitating
't	it
t'	tha (you)

ta	you
tabs	ears
ta'e, ta'en	take, taken
tallygram	telegram
tallywag post	telegraph post
tan-tafflin	small tart, sweet delicacy
t'art	you are
tarry	linger, loiter; *see note on* 518:15
tater	potato
tat-ta, ta-ta	Goodbye
tear, in a tear	rage, passion; frantic rush, hurry
teenty	tiny; *see note on* 243:24
ter	you; to; too
ter'lt	you will (ter wilt)
tha	you
tha'd	you could, you would, you had
thaïgh, thäigh	you
tha'rt	you are
tha's	you have; there is
the'	there
thee	you
theer	there
the-etter	theatre
them	those (*demonstr.*)
thowt, thöwt	thought
thripenny	threepenny
throng	busy, hurried
throttle	throat, windpipe
th'rt	you are
thysen	yourself
tidy	fairly well, in tolerably good health; considerable
tip-callin'	playing games
'titled	entitled
tittivate, titivate	dress oneself up, smarten up, adorn
toff, toffed	dress up; very elaborately dressed (e.g., toffed up to the nines)
tomorrer	tomorrow; *see* come again tomorrer
touch pitch	become contaminated; *see note on* 553:33
töw	two
towil	towel
t'r	to (ter)
trapsein'	tramping, trudging (a long way)
trew, trewth	true, truth
trollop	idle, slovenly, slatternly woman; hussy

tun, tunn	barrel
tuppenny-ha'penny	something small or weak, worthless; contemptible
'twas	it was
twig	understand, realize
ud, 'ud	would
un, 'un	one
uncle	pawnbroker
union-pay	*see note on* 101:4
untackle	*see note on* 518:37
'ussy	hussy; idle, slovenly woman
vackum	vacuum
virtuise	*see note on* 398:22
wafflin', waffling	waving about, flapping in the wind, blown about
wakkened	wakened
wallit	wall-eyed, useless
wascoat	waistcoat
wasna	wasn't
wastrel	unhealthy
wellah	*see note on* 465:35
werritted	worried
wet-whiskers	man who dribbles in his beard
wezzel-brained	stupid (i.e. wizened-brained)
whackin' sight	great deal
wheer	where
whifft	whiff; hint; inkling; breath
whit-leather	white cured leather, not tanned
whittle	worry, fret, fidget
whoam	home
whoam-it	steady-on
wi, wi'	with
widder	widow
wik	week
winder	something that knocks the wind out of you, a knock-out blow
winders	windows
wi'out	without
wipe	blow
wiseling	*see note on* 457:16
witty	clever, intelligent; *see note on* 559:34
wor	was

work, all of a	in a state of fermentation
worn't, worna	wasn't, weren't
wouldna	wouldn't
wringer	crow-bar
wringin'	squeezing
wunna	will not, won't
yed	head
yer	you, your
yet	still
yi	yes
yo	you
yon	that, those; yonder
you'n	you have
yoursen	yourself

TEXTUAL APPARATUS

TEXTUAL APPARATUS

In the apparatus, whenever the reading of the base text is adopted (see Introduction, 'Texts'), it appears within the square bracket with no symbol. When a reading from a source later than the base-text has been preferred, it appears with its source-symbol within the square bracket; this is always followed by the reading of the base-text. Rejected readings follow the square bracket, in the sequence indicated for each text, with their first source denoted. In the absence of information to the contrary, the reader should assume that a variant recurs in all subsequent states. The following symbols are used editorially:

Ed. = Editor
~ = Substitution for a word in recording a punctuation or capitalisation variant
Om. = Omitted
■ = Overtyped letter
/ = Line or page break
C = Correction made by someone other than DHL (e.g. *TSC, MSC*)
R = Autograph corrections by DHL to a state of the text (i.e. the authorial corrections to the typescript for *David, TSR*)
[ ] = Editorial emendation or addition
{ } = Partial variant reading

When the symbol ~ is used in the Textual apparatus to record the repetition of a word including an apostrophe, it indicates that the word **including the apostrophe** has been correctly transmitted. Where an apostrophe has not been correctly transmitted, or where one has been inserted in a subsequent state of text, the swung dash is not employed.

Silent emendations

The apparatus records all textual variants between the base-texts and the texts here printed, except for silent emendations particular to each play, and for the following silent emendations:

1 Variants in layout, typography (including italics), speech headings (including the forms of characters' names, punctuation, repetition and omission), stage directions (including layout, the forms of characters' names, italics and punctuation) and scene numbering have not been recorded in the Textual apparatus. Where they form part of another variant, however, they are recorded in full.
2 The use of single and double quotation marks by DHL and his typists and compositors is not consistent; DHL's manuscript practice has normally been retained, and variants are not recorded unless they form part of another variant.

Incomplete or redundant quotation marks, omitted or misplaced apostrophes, and missing full stops at the end of sentences where no other punctuation exists, have been silently supplied or corrected. Lower-case letters at the beginning of sentences have been silently corrected to capital letters.

3 DHL frequently inscribed colloquial contractions without joining them up (e.g. 'did n't' and 'would n't'). Typists and compositors usually presented these as 'didn't' and 'wouldn't'; these normalisations have been adopted and are not recorded. DHL also sometimes used the ampersand '&' or the symbol '+': these have also been normalised as 'and', and are not recorded.

4 Variants in the lengths of spacing and of dashes in typescripts and printed texts (e.g. en, em or two-em dashes) have not been recorded in the Textual apparatus except where they form an integral part of another variant.

5 DHL usually wrote 'Mrs', 'Mr' and 'Dr' (and their fully capitalised forms) without a full stop; his typists and compositors often supplied one. DHL usually wrote words such as 'realise' and 'recognise' (and their derivative forms) with an 's'; typists and compositors changed these forms to 'realize', 'recognize', etc. DHL's practice has been preserved where appropriate manuscripts survive, but the habits of typists and compositors have not been recorded.

6 Obvious typists' and compositors' errors (e.g., 'wi' th' th' fellers' in *The Daughter-in-Law*, TCCI, p. 13: 310:4–5) have not in general been included in the Textual apparatus, but potentially significant errors in manuscript by DHL (e.g., 'that' for 'tha'' in *The Daughter-in-Law*, MS, p. 11) have been included (see Textual apparatus at 313:20); and typists' errors (e.g. 'peep,s' for 'peeps,' in *David*, TS, p. 58) have been included when they led to further textual corruption (see Textual apparatus at 489:9).

See too 'Conventions adopted for the printing of texts in this edition', pp. cxxv–cxxvi.

A Collier's Friday Night

MS = Autograph MS (Roberts E74a)
TCCI = Carbon copy TS (Roberts E74b)
TCCII = Carbon copy TS (no Roberts no.)
E1 = *A Collier's Friday Night* (Secker, 1934)

Silent emendations

1 DHL consistently wrote 'today', 'tonight' and 'goodnight'. *TCCI* consistently produced 'to-day', 'to-night' and 'good-night'; *TCCII* has 'today', 'to-night' and 'good-night' or 'good night'; *E1* consistently printed 'to-day', 'to-night' and 'good night'. These variants have not been recorded unless they are part of another variant.

2 DHL's spelling of 'aimiable' for 'amiable' has been silently corrected.

3 *TCCI* (and thus *TCCII* and *E1*) shortened the names of characters (e.g. 'Ernest' instead of 'Ernest Lambert'); DHL's practice has been preserved, and the variants are not recorded.

4 *E1* fairly often replaced *TCCII*'s dashes or three dots at the end of broken-off sentences with unspaced two-em dashes or three or four spaced dots; these readings are not recorded unless they form part of another variant.

5:2 Act 1. *Ed.*] *Om. MS* ACT I.
TCCI *ACT I E1*

5:14 *clothes TCCI*] cloth *MS*
clothes *MSC see note on* 5:14

5:21 *case TCCI*] case *MS chest*
TCCII

5:32 *mantel piece Ed.*] mantel piece
MS mantelpiece *TCCI*

5:33 *candle sticks Ed.*] candle sticks
MS candlesticks *TCCI*

6:8 *teapot Ed.*] teapot *MS teapot*
are TCCI

6:21 "Oh] NELLIE LAMBERT Oh!
TCCI

6:21 weary!"] ~! *TCCI* ~. *TCCII*

6:22 —You] ~ *TCCI*

6:22 late!] ~. *TCCI*

6:23 Kerton] Karton *TCCII*

6:29 –And] ~ *TCCI*

6:35 you.] ~! *TCCII*

6:38 Johnny or Sammy] ~, ~ ~,
TCCII

6:39 is is] ~, ~ *TCCII*

6:40 straight,] ~; *TCCII*

7:2 Pah,] ~! *TCCII*

7:2 up—!] ~! *TCCII*

7:9 it!] ~. *TCCI*

7:10 Why] ~, *TCCII*

7:13 apricots—.] ~ — *TCCI*
~ —— *E1*

7:15 Well] ~, *TCCII*

7:16 meat—!] ~! *TCCII*

7:17 *weariedly TCCI*] weariedly *MS*
wearily E1

7:19 some] ~, *TCCII*

8:1 teas] tea *TCCII*

8:3 *you*] you *TCCII*

8:4 Arms,] ~ *E1*

8:5 does] ~, *TCCII*

8:7 Ah] Oh *TCCII*

8:7 well—!] ~. *TCCI* ~! *TCCII*

8:13 tonight!] to-night! *TCCI*
to-night. *TCCII*

8:13 Oh] ~, *TCCI*

8:14 glad] ~, *TCCII*

8:17 No] ~, *TCCI*

8:18 night:] ~; *TCCII*

8:25 No] ~, *TCCI*

8:26 this] ~: *TCCI*

8:26 Oh] ~, *TCCI*

8:26 you.] ~? *TCCI*

8:32 week] ~, *TCCII*

8:36 —David] ~ *TCCI*

8:37 NELLIE LAMBERT . . . Johnny
Grocock. *Ed.*] Nellie Lambert
. . . Johnny Grocock. *MS Om.*
TCCI

8:39 GERTIE COOMBER *Ed.*] Gertie
Coomber *MS* NELLIE *TCCI see*
note on 8:38

8:39 likely!] ~. *TCCII*

9:4 fellow——] ~ — *TCCII*
~ —— *E1*

9:10 say] ~, *TCCII*

9:10 Yes] ~, *TCCII*

9:10 dear!] ~. *TCCI*

9:11 *yes*] ~, *TCCII*

9:11 certainly.] ~! *TCCII*

9:13 here] ~, *TCCI*

9:14 out] ~, *E1*

9:15 Oh] ~, *TCCI*

9:16 so ikey] sl ikey *TCCII* slikey
E1

9:17 my——] ~ — *TCCII* ~ ——
E1

9:19 —Oh] ~ *TCCI* ~, *TCCII*

9:19 glory,] ~! *TCCII*

9:19 Lambert!] ~. *TCCII*

9:29 *elbow Ed.*] elbow *MS elbows*
TCCI

9:30 *out Ed.*] out *MS Om. TCCII*

9:38 —'An] ~ *TCCI*

10:1 —It's] ~ *TCCII*

10:4 begin.] ~! *TCCI*

10:4 stopping] ~, *TCCII*

10:6 well] Well *TCCI* Well, *TCCII*

10:6 much] ~, *TCCII*

10:6 then: you'] ~. You *TCCI*

10:15 cloth!] ~. *TCCII*

10:17 *(dirty) TCCII*] (dirty) *MS, E1*

10:17 on] ~, *TCCII*

10:26 wascoat] wa's'coat *TCCII*

10:33 *Right Ed.*] Right *MS right*
TCCI

10:34 lazy] ~, *TCCII*

10:34 go.] ~! *TCCII*

11:2   bit,] ~ *E1*
11:10   *of the TCCI*] of the *MS of TCCII*
11:12   *Right Ed.*] Right *MS right TCCI*
11:14   *the TCCI*] the *MS his TCCII*
11:16   Lambert.] ~? *TCCI*
11:19   man, the] ~! The *TCCII*
11:21   Ah *(shortly) Ed.*] Ah (shortly) *MS* Ah, (shortly) *TCCI* (*shortly*) Ah, *TCCII* (*shortly*): Ah, *E1*
11:22   kid?] ~! *TCCII*
11:28   An'] And *TCCII*
11:29   'er 'arce] 'er 'arse *TCCII* 'er' arse *E1*
11:29   *crambling TCCI*] crambling *MS* scrambling *E1*
11:30   *Right Ed.*] Right *MS right TCCI*
11:30   *the TCCI*] the *MS his TCCII*
11:34   Gert] Gertie *TCCII*
12:2   *'mole-skin' TCCI*] 'mole-skin' *MS* moleskin *TCCII*
12:3   *Right Ed.*] Right *MS right TCCI*
12:6   it] ~, *TCCII*
12:6   pit,] ~ *E1*
12:12   on] ~, *TCCI*
12:13   *Her TCCI*] Her *MS* THE *TCCII* The *E1*
12:19   bitch,] ~; *TCCII*
12:22   wonder——.] ~ —— *TCCI* ~ — *TCCII* ~ —— *E1*
12:23   wonder,] ~ — *TCCII*
12:23   wonder——!] ~ ——— *TCCI* ~! *TCCII*
12:28   I.] ~? *TCCI*
12:30   up] ~, *TCCII*
12:31   expect.] ~? *TCCI*
12:32   —A] ~ *TCCI*
12:36   it,] ~ *E1*
12:40   a—.] ~ — *TCCI* ~ —— *E1*
12:40   it, it's] in. It's *TCCII*
12:40   blasted—!] ~ — *TCCI* ~ —— *E1*
13:7   *at TCCI*] at *MS on TCCII*
13:12   No,] ~; *TCCII*

13:14   nothing,] ~ *E1*
13:20   and——!] ~ — *TCCII* ~ —— *E1*
13:21   place] ~, *TCCII*
13:23   you'd 'a *Ed.*] you'd a *MS* you 'a *TCCII*
13:23   wanted——] ~ — *TCCII* ~ ——! *E1*
13:29   as *Ed.*] 'as *MS*
13:30   room———!] ~ —! *TCCII* ~ ——! *E1*
13:32   minute,] ~ *E1*
13:33   on: him] on; he's *TCCII*
13:34   college,] ~ *E1*
13:39   it.] ~, *TCCI* ~; *TCCII*
13:39   canner] canna *TCCI*
14:2   *Right Ed.*] Right *MS right TCCI*
14:9   *on TCCI*] on *MS Om. TCCII*
14:9   *Right Ed.*] Right *MS right TCCI*
14:10   Phww] Phew *TCCII*
14:11   here.] ~! *TCCII*
14:14   Oh] ~, *TCCII*
14:15   hippotamus] hippopotamus *TCCI see notes*
14:19   sickening!] ~? *TCCII*
14:20   Oh] ~, *TCCI*
14:23   No] ~, *TCCI*
14:25   Gie's . . . Sorry, gie's] Gi 'e 's . . . ~; gi 'e 's *TCCI*
14:27   tanyard] tan-yard *TCCI*
14:29   there] ~, *TCCI*
14:30   Coomber's] Coombers' *TCCI*
14:31   paper] ~, *TCCI*
14:33   nöwt . . . böwks] nowt . . . books *TCCII*
14:35   *He TCCI*] He *MS* FATHER *TCCII*
14:37   are,] ~; *TCCII*
14:38   weshed] washed *TCCII*
15:1   say Mater] ~, mater *TCCI*
15:1   seven and six] seven-and-six *TCCII*
15:2   sleeve.] ~? *TCCII*
15:3   term too.] ~, ~! *TCCII*
15:5   Piers the Ploughman] "Piers

the Ploughman" *TCCII Piers*
the Ploughman E1

15:6 Flaccius] Flaccus *TCCII*
15:10 for,] ~ — *TCCII*
15:11 liked.—] ~. *E1*
15:12 wild, seven and sixpence] ~.
Seven-and-sixpence *TCCII*
15:13 'em] tem, *TCCII*
15:13 nedna] needna *TCCI*
15:14 like——dunna] ~. Dunna
TCCII
15:14 'em] ~, *TCCII*
15:16 got] *Om. TCCII*
15:16 money,] ~ *E1*
15:18 nonsense, if] ~. If *TCCII*
15:21 Oh] ~, *TCCII*
15:21 Little] ~; *TCCII*
15:22 Mutterchen] Mütterchen
TCCII
15:23 be] ~, *TCCII*
15:25 nap:] ~; *TCCII*
15:27 collige] Collige *TCCI*
15:28 No] ~, *TCCII*
15:30 expect.] ~? *TCCI*
15:32 *brass tap TCCI*] brass tap *MS*
top TCCII
15:33 *singlet, or vest, TCCI*] singlet,
or vest, *MS singlet, TCCII*
singlet E1
15:39 what not] what-not *TCCII*
16:3 get] get an *TCCII*
16:4 Mater] mater *TCCII*
16:8 Aunt *TCCI*] aunt *MS*
16:13 Aunt Eunice *TCCI*] aunt ~
MS
16:15 Well] ~, *TCCI*
16:15 Mutter] Mütter *TCCII*
16:17 Oh] ~, *TCCII*
16:17 Ma] ma *TCCI*
16:20 crest] ~, *TCCII*
16:20 ever——] ~ ... *TCCII*
16:21 —It] ~ *TCCI*
16:22 pub——.] ~ —— *TCCI*
~ — *TCCII* ~. *E1*
16:23 Vernon:—] ~ — *TCCII*
16:24 tale.] ~! *TCCI*
16:29 dry!] ~? *TCCI*
16:32 *up TCCI*] up *MS Om. TCCII*

17:1 Substance: Oh Lord] ~! ~,
lord *TCCII*
17:2 —I] ~ *TCCI*
17:2 it. It] ~, it *TCCI* ~; it *TCCII*
17:2 me——!] ~! *TCCII*
17:3 thing—!] ~! *E1*
17:3 Savoy] ~, *TCCII*
17:4 was——] ~ — *TCCII*
17:7 Hello. Have] ~, have *TCCI* ~!
have *TCCII*
17:7 done.] ~? *TCCI*
17:8 *shouting from scullery Ed.*]
shouting from scullery *MS*
Shouting from scullery TCCII
from the scullery TCCII
17:8 doo-ar?] do-/ o-ar! *(shouting)*
TCCII doo-ar! (*Shouting.*) *E1*
17:11 you—] ~?— *TCCII*
17:15 *Her TCCII*] Her *MS* THE
TCCII The *E1*
17:18 Öw *TCCII*] öw *MS* Ow *TCCII*
17:18 (*she*) *TCCII*] (she) *MS*
17:19 *He rubs TCCI*] he rubs *MS*
Rubs TCCII
17:20 kid.] ~! *TCCII*
17:21 i'] in *TCCI*
17:23 i' cöwd] i' t'cöwd *TCCI* i'
t'cowd *TCCII*
17:25 back:] ~; *TCCII*
17:26 panchion onto] puncheon on to
TCCI
17:26 'arthstone] 'earthstone *TCCII*
17:27 an'—.] an— *TCCI* an'—
TCCII an'—— *E1*
17:30 wunna:] ~; *TCCII*
17:32 Who'd] Who's *E1*
17:33 Me!] ~. *TCCII*
17:37 lazy idle] ~, ~, *TCCII*
17:38 *table cloth Ed.*] table cloth *MS*
tablecloth TCCII
17:39 weshin'] washin' *TCCII*
18:1 Fancy,] ~! *TCCII*
18:2 dead!] ~. *TCCII*
18:5 Here] ~, *TCCI*
18:6 wesh!] wash. *TCCII*
18:9 OOO! Tha] Ooo! The *TCCII*
18:23 ERNEST LAMBERT'S VOICE *Ed.*]
Ernest Lambert's voice *MS*

ERNEST´S VOICE *TCCI* ERNEST
TCCII
18:23 Evening] evening *TCCI*
18:23 Barker!] ~. *TCCII*
18:24 Evenin'] evenin' *TCCI*
18:27 Evenin',] evenin', *TCCI*
18:27 Missis!] ~. *TCCII*
18:27 up stairs] upstairs *TCCI*
18:33 well] ~, *TCCII*
18:33 better!] ~. *TCCII*
18:34 again—.] ~. *TCCI*
18:35 Jakes,] ~; *TCCII*
18:36 nöwt] nowt *TCCII*
18:37 Mrs] Missis *TCCI* missis *E1*
18:38 Well—] ~, *TCCII*
18:39 back,] ~ *E1*
19:1 I'n] I'm *TCCII*
19:2 bag——.] ~—— *TCCI* ~.
　　　 TCCII
19:4 *She brings TCCI*] she brings
　　　 MS Brings. TCCII
19:6 wik: you] ~. You *TCCII*
19:10 evenin'] ~, *TCCII*
19:10 Missis!] ~. *TCCII*
19:12 *Enter*] *TCCI* enter *MS*
　　　 ENTER THE *TCCII Enter the*
　　　 E1
19:16 you'n arrived] you've ~,
　　　 TCCII
19:16 th'] the *TCCII*
19:16 Missis] missis *E1*
19:18 George *Ed.*] Walter *MS see note*
　　　 on 3:10
19:19 to] ~, *TCCII*
19:19 ger] get *TCCII*
19:24 things] ~, *TCCII*
19:24 fountain pens] fountain-pens
　　　 TCCII
19:26 mek] mak *TCCII*
19:28 Oh ah] Oh-ah *TCCII*
19:28 öw] 'ow *TCCII*
19:28 sayn] says *TCCII*
19:28 hold it] hold *TCCII*
19:29 vackum] vacum *TCCII*
19:30 this—] ~: *TCCII*
19:32 thing] ~, *E1*
19:33 a'! *Ed.*] 'a! *MS* a'. *TCCII*
19:36 bread] ~, *TCCI*

19:37 Mater] mater *TCCII*
20:2 right] ~, *TCCI*
20:3 —Yes] ~ *TCCI*
20:9 *(Curtain) Ed.*] End of Act I.
　　　 MS END OF ACT I. *TCCI*
21:3 *low TCCI*] low *MS Om.*
　　　 TCCII
21:3 *pocket TCCI*] pocket *MS*
　　　 pockets TCCII
21:5 shiftin'——.] ~—— *TCCI*
　　　 ~—*TCCII* ~. *E1*
21:10 Well] ~, *TCCI*
21:11 evening] ~, *TCCI*
21:12 Carlin:—just] ~—~ *TCCI* ~.
　　　 Just *TCCII*
21:12 off—?] ~? *TCCI*
21:14 öw's] 'ow's *TCCII*
21:15 Oh] ~, *TCCI*
21:16 thing! Oh] ~. ~, *TCCII*
21:17 on.] ~? *TCCI*
21:19 Ow's] Ow's *TCCII*
21:19 töw] tow *TCCII*
21:20 Hard] ~, *TCCI*
21:21 funny!] ~. *TCCII*
21:22 'eered] 'eared *TCCII*
21:23 Yes, do] ~. Do *TCCII*
21:24 it!] ~? *TCCI*
21:26 you!] ~? *TCCII*
21:27 An'] 'An *TCCII*
21:28 piece.] ~? *TCCII*
21:29 us.] ~? *TCCII*
21:29 minute—!] ~— *TCCII* ~.
　　　 E1
21:31 *to TCCI*] to *MS to the TCCII*
21:33 forward] ~, *TCCI*
22:5 Good night] Good-night *TCCI*
　　　 Good night, *TCCII*
22:5 then!] ~. *TCCII*
22:5 Goodnight] Good-night, *TCCI*
　　　 Good night, *TCCII*
22:15 *She counts TCCI*] She counts
　　　 MS Counts TCCII
22:19 pounds,] ~ *E1*
22:21 twenty eight!——]
　　　 twenty-eight!—— *TCCII*
　　　 Twenty-eight! ... *TCCII*
22:22 nothing———] ~ ... *TCCII*
　　　 ~ *E1*

22:23 will too— — —] ~, ~ ...
TCCII ~, ~ E1
22:24 though,] ~ — TCCII
22:25 Tunns— — —]
Tunns'— TCCII
22:25 six and six] six-and-six TCCII
22:28 air—!] ~? TCCI
22:29 Oh Mater] ~, mater TCCII
22:30 bother .... what's] ~! What's
TCCII
22:30 good ... if] ~? If TCCII
22:32 Oh] ~, TCCII
22:33 you— —] ~ — TCCII ~, E1
22:33 worry,] ~ E1
22:33 us,] ~ E1
22:34 know.] ~? TCCII
22:36 *Norfolk TCCI*] norfolk MS
22:37 'Åse's Ed.] "Åse's MS 'Ase's
TCCI
23:1 Barker ... Ed.] ~ .. MS ~.
TCCII
23:2 the 'Maiden's Prayer' Ed.] the
Maidens ~ MS 'The Maiden's
~' TCCI "The Maiden's ~"
TCCII
23:4 He He!!—] ~, he! TCCII
23:5 Pomp,] ~! TCCII
23:5 *She makes TCCI*] She makes
MS Makes TCCII
23:6 it] ~, TCCI
23:7 shindy!] ~. TCCII
23:10 go ... Ed.] ~ .. MS ~; TCCII
~ — E1
23:16 mother—] ~?— TCCII
23:17 —I] ~ TCCI
23:17 you] ~, TCCI
23:19 Mm] Um TCCI
23:33 Yes—ah'n] ~, ah's TCCII
23:24 tha 'asna] ~ ~, TCCII
23:28 down] ~, TCCI
23:28 top coat] top-/ coat TCCI
top-coat E1
23:28 an' then— —] an then—
TCCII
23:32 goodnight] good-night TCCI
good-night, TCCII good night,
E1
23:32 everybody:] ~; TCCII

23:32 goodnight] good-night, TCCI
good night, E1
23:32 Ernest:—] ~ — TCCII
23:33 yer Missis!] ~, ~. TCCII
23:35 will:] ~. TCCII
23:36 reasons] reason TCCII
23:36 shouldn't:] ~. TCCII
23:37 Goodnight] Good-night, TCCI
Good night, E1
23:38 *he TCCII*] he MS BARKER
TCCII
23:40 me] ~, TCCII
24:1 time ...] ~ E1
24:1 up ... the] ~! The TCCII
24:3 —It] ~ TCCI
24:3 it] ~, TCCII
24:6 it—] ~! TCCII
24:7 care, it] ~. It TCCII
24:9 *she TCCII*] she MS Om.
TCCII
24:11 Oh] ~, TCCI
24:14 —anything] Anything TCCII
24:15 No] ~, TCCII
24:15 cheese:] ~; TCCII
24:22 top:] ~; TCCII
24:22 half an hour:] half-an-/ hour;
TCCII half an hour; E1
24:24 them] ~, TCCII
24:25 —No] ~ TCCI
24:26 'no'. Ed.] 'no.' MS 'No'!
TCCII "No!" E1
24:33 French.— MS, TCCII] ~ —
TCCI ~. E1
24:34 Why?—.] ~?— TCCI ~?
TCCII
24:35 Nothing ... !] ~. TCCII
24:37 mud— — —] ~ ... TCCII ~
.... E1
24:38 brother, she'd] ~. She'd
TCCII
25:5 Oh] ~, TCCI
25:6 I!—you'd] ~?— ~ TCCI ~?
You'd TCCII
25:6 anybody— —] ~! TCCII
25:8 going.] ~? TCCII
25:11 raining] ~, TCCI
25:13 fine ...] ~! TCCII
25:14 fine:] ~; E1

25:17 anything] ~, *TCCI*
25:17 Mater] mater *TCCII*
25:19 on Gert!] ~, ~. *TCCII*
25:22 begin] be *TCCII*
25:23 —I] ~ *E1*
25:25 right:] ~; *TCCII* ~, *E1*
25:30 Well] ~, *TCCI*
26:2 you] ~, *TCCI*
26:3 down] ~, *TCCII*
26:3 —didn't] —Didn't *TCCII* Didn't *E1*
26:9 oh] ~, *TCCI*
26:9 besides] ~, *TCCII*
26:12 No:] ~; *TCCII*
26:13 night,] ~; *TCCII*
26:14 Yes,] ~; *TCCII*
26:16 sure . . . Ed.] ~ . . *MS* ~. *TCCII*
26:16 me,] ~; *TCCII*
26:18 I] ~, *TCCII*
26:19 bothering . . . Ed.] ~ . . *MS* ~. *TCCI*
26:19 to . . .] ~ *E1*
26:23 *She looks TCCI*] She looks *MS* Looks *TCCII*
26:25 Ah thanks—] ~, ~, *TCCII*
26:33 Ernest!] ~? *TCCII*
27:3 *kid TCCI*] kid *MS Om. TCCII*
27:20 mistaken— —.] ~. *TCCII*
27:21 coll.] Coll. *TCCI*
27:23 week.] ~? *TCCI*
27:24 it!] ~? *TCCI*
27:26 Oh—] ~, *TCCII*
27:26 college,—] ~ — *TCCII* College— *E1*
27:30 whereas] ~, *TCCII*
27:30 Oh, Coll's] oh, Coll.'s *E1*
27:33 me,] ~ *E1*
27:33 week— — —] ~ — *TCCII*
27:38 then— —?] ~ — —! *TCCI* ~ —! *TCCII* ~ — —! *E1*
27:39 — —how] How *TCCII*
28:2 Professors] professors *E1*
28:4 times,] ~; *TCCII*
28:10 Ay!—] ~! *E1*
28:13 place] places *TCCII*
28:13 great— —.] ~ — *TCCII* ~ — — *E1*

28:15 —And] —and *TCCII* — —and *E1*
28:16 bit— —] ~ — *TCCII* ~ — — *E1*
28:19 farce—?] ~? *TCCII*
28:22 disillusionised] disillusioned *E1*
28:23 everything,] ~ — *TCCII*
28:27 know?—] ~ — *TCCII*
28:32 *opens TCCI*] opens *MS goes to TCCII*
28:33 *dripping tin TCCI*] dripping tin *MS* dripping-pan *TCCII*
28:33 *knuckle TCCI*] knuckle *MS* knuckles *TCCII*
28:34 done— —] ~. *TCCII*
28:35 on Ed.] on *MS* in *TCCII*
28:37 doing!] ~? *TCCI* ~. *TCCII*
28:38 —I] ~ *TCCI*
28:40 —Verses] ~ *TCCI*
29:15 Well] ~, *TCCII*
29:18 much] ~, *TCCII*
29:28 —And] ~ *TCCI*
29:32 one,—] ~ *TCCI* ~, *TCCII*
29:32 History' 's— Ed.] History's'— *MS* History's' the *TCCI* History', 's the *TCCII* History," is the *E1*
30:2 best, yes] ~. Yes *TCCI*
30:10 Now] ~, *TCCII*
30:13 me— — —.] ~ . . . *TCCII*
30:14 side—.] ~ — *TCCI* ~. *TCCII*
30:18 me—.] ~. *TCCI*
30:20 I— —] ~ — *TCCII* ~ — — *E1*
30:22 —do I] Do I?— *TCCII* Do I— —? *E1*
30:24 —Yes] ~ *TCCI* ~, *TCCII*
30:30 are,] ~!— *TCCII*
30:31 issue!] ~. *TCCII*
30:31 woman—!] ~! *TCCII*
30:32 You] you *TCCI*
30:33 handles] hands *TCCII*
30:39 be] ~, *TCCII*
31:1 —Well—!] ~ — *TCCII* ~ — — *E1*
31:5 mistakes—] ~ . . . *TCCII*
31:10 *with the Ed.*] with the *MS* with *E1*

31:12 I——.] ~ ... *TCCII*
31:22 Now] ~, *TCCII*
31:22 oh] Oh *TCCI* Oh, *TCCII*
31:25 me.] ~! *TCCII*
31:28 No—o—o!] No-o-o! *TCCI*
         No-o-o. *TCCII*
31:32 —You] ~ *TCCI*
31:34 'Eurent.'] ~'. *TCCI* '~'?
         TCCII ~?" *E1*
31:36 *preterite*: the *preterite*, and] ~?
         The ~? And *TCCII* ~? The
         ~? And *E1*
31:38 *He—ominously TCCI*]
         He—ominously *MS Ominously*
         TCCII
32:2   être] *être TCCII*
32:3   well] Well *TCCII*
32:5   *awhile Ed.*] awhile *MS a while*
         TCCI
32:6   *He—softly TCCI*] He—softly
         MS Softly TCCII
32:8   MAGGIE PEARSON *Ed.*] She *MS*
         MAGGIE *TCCI*
32:14 serious—] ~; *TCCII*
32:15 free—.] ~. *TCCI*
32:17 —No] ~ *TCCII*
32:20 play-about] play about *TCCI*
32:20 'Shelley':] 'Shelley', *TCCII*
         Shelley, E1
32:21 know,] ~, — *TCCII* ~ — *E1*
32:21 boats——.] ~ ... *TCCII*
32:23 you] ~, *TCCII*
32:28 Ah] ~, *TCCII*
32:29 —I] ~ *TCCII*
32:30 mind,] ~ — *TCCII*
32:31 again] ~, *TCCII*
32:38 have?—] ~? *TCCII*
33:5   Why] ~, *TCCII*
33:5   him] ~, *TCCII*
33:8   Baudelaire,] ~ — *TCCII*
33:12 Should] should *TCCII*
33:14 go] ~, *TCCII*
33:14 like—.] ~ — *TCCI* ~. *TCCII*
33:17 There,] ~! *TCCII*
33:18 fine!] ~? *TCCII*
33:20 dark blue carpet,] dark-blue ~;
         TCCII
33:21 lighted] ~; *TCCII*

33:21 rich] ~, *TCCII*
33:25 *He begins TCCI*] he begins *MS*
         Begins TCCII
33:27 Damn!—] Damn! *TCCI*
         ERNEST Damn! *TCCII* ERNEST:
         Damn! *E1*
33:28 Hello] ~, *TCCI* Hell, *E1*
33:33 Hello] ~, *TCCI*
33:33 Ernie] Ernest *TCCII*
33:33 ter!] ~? *TCCII*
33:33 Hello] ~, *TCCI*
33:36 *while TCCI*] while *MS Om.*
         TCCII
34:2   What, does] ~! ~ *TCCII* ~!
         Does *E1*
34:3   the shop up] up shop *TCCII*
34:4   —Ay] ~ *TCCI*
34:5   eleven——] ~ — *TCCII*
         ~ —— *E1*
34:7   bad!—I'n't] bad? Isn't *TCCII*
34:8   Ma] He *TCCII*
34:12 Now] ~, *TCCII*
34:13 she] ~, *TCCI*
34:13 Ernie] Ernest *TCCII*
34:16 we] ~, *TCCI*
34:17 th'] the *TCCI*
34:21 we] ~, *TCCII*
34:21 out,] ~; *TCCII*
34:21 certs',] ~'— *TCCII* ~"— *E1*
34:22 we] ~, *TCCII*
34:27 *will*] ~, *TCCI* will, *TCCII*
34:27 Maggie!] ~. *TCCII*
34:31 Oh yes!] ~, ~. *TCCII*
34:33 wondered——.] ~ —— *TCCI*
         ~ — *TCCII* ~ —— *E1*
34:35 mouse traps and bird cages]
         mouse-traps and bird-cages
         TCCI
34:37 likely.] ~! *TCCII*
34:39 *Right!!*] ~! *TCCII*
35:1   surprise——.] ~ — *TCCI* ~.
         TCCII
35:3   No] ~, *TCCII*
35:3   Front!',] ~', *TCCII* ~," *E1*
35:5   lovly] lov'ly *TCCII*
35:5   f'r anyfing *TCCII*] fr' anyfing
         MS fr'anyfing *TCCI*
35:7   Ra-thèr!] Ra-ther *TCCII*

35:10 —I] ~ *TCCII*
35:11 Sunday...] ~. *TCCII*
35:13 *you*] you *TCCI*
35:18 Oh] ~, *TCCII*
35:18 us.] ~! *TCCII*
35:18 Was] Was it *TCCII*
35:19 athletics] Athletics *TCCI*
35:21 Oh... Oh] ~, ... ~, *TCCI*
35:23 *laughing Ed.*] laughing *MS*
　　　　Laughing TCCI Om. TCCII
35:24 goods—Women] ~ —women
　　　　TCCI ~, women *TCCII*
35:24 gently:] ~; *TCCII*
35:27 hat pins] hat-pins *TCCI*
35:28 Gypsy——] ~?— *TCCI*
35:29 'gipsy',] "gypsy" *TCCI* gypsy,
　　　　TCCII
35:31 No!] ~. *TCCII*
35:33 so] ~, *TCCI*
35:33 William.] ~! *TCCI*
35:33 *She sighs TCCI*] she sighs *MS*
　　　　Sighs TCCII
35:33 —'Sigh] '~ *TCCI* "~
　　　　TCCII
35:34 more] ~, *TCCI*
35:34 ladies.'] ~'. *TCCI* ~"—
　　　　TCCII
35:34 Oh] ~, *TCCI*
35:35 mutton bone] mutton-bone
　　　　TCCI
35:35 William,] ~?— *TCCII*
35:36 other.] ~? *TCCII*
35:37 bone,] ~ *TCCI*
35:37 for, *TCCII*] ~ *MS*
36:1 No,] ~; *TCCII*
36:1 have, *TCCI*] ~ *MS*
36:3 *will TCCII*] will *MS does*
　　　　TCCII
36:6 is!] ~? *TCCII*
36:7 to——] ~ — *TCCII* ~ ——
　　　　E1
36:7 words——] ~ — *TCCII*
36:9 Oh] ~, *TCCI*
36:14 Oh] ~, *TCCI*
36:14 done] ~, *TCCII*
36:17 on, either'll] ~. Either'll
　　　　TCCII
36:18 —a] A *TCCI*

36:18 Maggie,—olive coloured—]
　　　　~,—olive-coloured, *TCCII*
　　　　~ —olive-coloured, *E1*
36:20 and—] ~, *E1*
36:20 oh] ~, *TCCI*
36:20 know,] ~! *TCCII*
36:20 gestures':] ~'— *TCCII* ~"—
　　　　E1
36:23 lovly] lovely *TCCI*
36:23 f'r anyfing!—— *Ed.*] fr'
　　　　anyfing!—— *MS*
　　　　fr'anyfing?—— *TCCI*
　　　　f'r'anyfing?— *TCCII* f'r
　　　　anyfing?— *E1*
36:25 at] at a *TCCII*
36:25 up-hill'—] and up-/ hill'— ~
　　　　TCCI up-/ hill."—And
　　　　TCCII uphill."—And *E1*
36:26 Inter] ~. *TCCII*
36:26 Maths *E1*] maths *MS* Maths.
　　　　TCCII
36:27 college] ~, *TCCI*
36:28 —For] ~ *TCCI*
36:29 do!] ~. *TCCII*
36:31 anxious——.] ~ — *TCCII*
　　　　~ —— *E1*
36:32 are. And] ~, and *TCCII*
36:33 think 'Hm!] ~ —'~! *TCCI* ~:
　　　　"H'm. *TCCII*
36:34 ginger and white fellow,]
　　　　ginger-and-white ~; *TCCII*
36:38 Maggie,] ~; *TCCII*
36:39 bet] ~, *TCCI*
37:1 Beat,] ~! *TCCI*
37:1 devil;—] ~ —, *E1*
37:7 —What *TCCI*] —what *MS*
　　　　What *TCCII*
37:7 for—?] ~? *TCCII*
37:8 *flashing Ed.*] flashing *MS*
　　　　flushing TCCII
37:9 here,] ~; *TCCII*
37:11 ennui] *ennui TCCII*
37:16 *the TCCI*] the *MS Om.*
　　　　TCCII
37:22 *cellar TCCI*] *Om. MS* cellar
　　　　MSC
37:22 [*he is heard*] *Ed.*] *Om. MS*
37:27 Begùm] Begum *TCCII*

37:29	we—?—is it?—Oh—!] ∼ —? Is it— ∼! *TCCII* ∼ ——? Is it——? ∼! *E1*
37:33	Hel-lo] ∼, *TCCI*
37:33	Ernest,] ∼! *TCCII*
37:33	thick.] ∼! *TCCII*
38:7	—Ho—Ho—] ∼ — ∼ — *TCCI* No—no! *TCCII*
38:7	wild] ∼, *TCCI*
38:8	shame!—] ∼! *TCCII*
38:11	day] day and *TCCI*
38:22	*immediately TCCI*] immediately *MS Om. TCCII*
38:25	No!] ∼; *TCCII*
38:25	Hark] ∼! *TCCI*
38:26	cindery——] ∼. *TCCII*
38:31	Hm!] *Om. TCCI*
38:33	*He puts TCCI*] He puts *MS* Puts *TCCII*
38:34	*the other TCCI*] the other *MS* another *TCCII*
38:35	desiccated *TCCI*] dessicated *MS* desiccated, *TCCII*
38:36	—She'll] ∼ *TCCI*
38:36	Mag!] ∼. *TCCII*
38:39	him———] ∼ — *TCCII* ∼ —— *E1*
39:1	nutmeg grater] ∼ ∼, *TCCI* nutmeg-grater, *TCCII*
39:3	*he TCCI*] he *MS* ERNEST *TCCII* ERNEST *E1*
39:13	—But——!] ∼ — —! *TCCI* ∼ ... *TCCII*
39:15	doesn't——.'] ∼ — —' *TCCI* ∼ ..." *TCCII*
39:16	matter!] ∼? *TCCII*
39:21	*up it TCCI*] up it *MS it up* *TCCII*
39:23	Life——!] ∼ —! *TCCII* ∼ —— *E1*
39:25	Ah] ∼, *TCCII*
39:31	Ay—] ∼, *TCCII*
39:31	here,] ∼; *TCCII*
39:35	Chapel] chapel *TCCII*
40:3	mind,] ∼; *TCCII*
40:4	Lambert?] ∼. *TCCII*
40:4	'Adsum'!!] "∼!" *TCCII*
40:5	Ma's] Mas *E1*

40:7	Ma's, they] ∼! They *TCCII* Mas! They *E1*
40:9	out,] ∼! *TCCII*
40:10	pantry] ∼, *TCCI*
40:10	William!] ∼. *TCCII*
40:16	Hello] ∼, *TCCI* Hullo, *TCCII*
40:18	—have] —Have *TCCII* Have *E1*
40:26	Why] ∼, *TCCI*
40:36	going] ∼, *TCCII*
41:3	Road] ∼, *TCCII*
41:7	goodnight] good-night, *TCCI* good night, *E1*
41:7	everybody,] ∼. *TCCII*
41:10	Goodnight] Good-night, *TCCI* Good night, *E1*
41:10	Maggie,] ∼. *TCCII*
41:15	*side TCCI*] side *MS wide* *TCCII*
41:17	*flickering TCCI*] flickering *MS* flicking *TCCII*
41:18	beans!!] ∼! *TCCI*
41:21	you!] ∼? *TCCII*
41:22	Oh Lum] ∼, lum *TCCI*
41:23	warm——] ∼ — — — — — *TCCI* ∼! *TCCII*
41:24	*(Curtain) Ed.*] End of Act II. *MS* END OF ACT II. *TCCI* END OF ACT II *E1*
42:6	grin:] ∼! *E1*
42:7	him—!] ∼! *TCCII*
42:8	did!] ∼. *TCCII*
42:11	night] ∼, *TCCII*
42:11	Well'] ∼,' *TCCI* ∼," *TCCII*
42:11	said] ∼, *TCCII*
42:13	chips'] ∼,' *TCCI* ∼," *TCCII*
42:13	fool,] ∼; *TCCII*
42:15	her] ∼, *TCCI*
42:15	'Well] '∼, *TCCI* "∼, *TCCII*
42:15	fool.] ∼! *TCCI*
42:15	In] in *E1*
42:20	doesn't.] ∼! *E1*
42:22	said] told me *TCCI see notes*
42:24	—Oh] ∼ *TCCI*
42:26	like!—] ∼! *E1*
42:29	care] ∼, *TCCI*
42:35	Yes] ∼, *TCCI*
42:35	lady——] ∼!— *TCCII*

42:35 meat,—] ~ — *TCCI* ~, *TCCII*

42:36 Well] ~, *TCCI*

42:37 Duck] duck *TCCI*

42:37 down town,] ~ ~; *TCCII* downtown; *E1*

42:38 back] ~, *TCCII*

42:39 hug] lug *TCCI*

43:1 Well] ~, *TCCI*

43:2 —you] You *TCCII*

43:7 it] ~, *TCCI*

43:9 things!] ~. *TCCI*

43:11 *have*] have *TCCI*

43:11 said] ~: *TCCI*

43:11 Here Abel] ~, ~, *TCCI*

43:12 home?',] ~?' *TCCI* ~?" *TCCII*

43:21 looking,] ~; *TCCII*

43:22 something——.] ~ —— *TCCI* ~ — *TCCII* ~ —— *E1*

43:26 grape] ~, *TCCI*

43:27 Beatrice!] ~. *TCCII*

43:33 No] ~, *TCCI*

43:34 any] ~, *TCCI*

43:34 thanks *TCCI*] Thanks *MS*

44:3 [NELLIE LAMBERT *goes into the scullery.*] *Ed.*] *Om. MS*

44:6 three quarters] three-quarters *TCCII*

44:8 Well really,] ~, ~! *TCCII*

44:9 lot] bit *TCCII*

44:11 Pah—] ~!— *TCCII*

44:11 don't] doesn't *TCCII*

44:17 Old] old *TCCII*

44:17 Lad] Dad *TCCI see note on* 44:19

44:17 here] ~, *TCCII*

44:18 her,] ~; *TCCII*

44:23 —Now Beat—!] ~, ~! *TCCI*

44:24 No] ~, *TCCI*

44:25 —have some,] —Have ~, *TCCI* Have ~ — *TCCII*

44:25 *She speaks TCCI*] She speaks *MS Speaks TCCII*

44:28 No] ~, *TCCI*

44:33 Mother,] mother, *TCCI* mother; *TCCII* Mother; *E1*

44:37 woman, why] ~! Why *TCCII*

45:4 Hello,] ~! *TCCII*

45:6 Now Little Woman] ~, little woman *TCCI*

45:8 pine kernels] pine-kernels *E1*

45:10 Dacre's,] ~; *TCCII*

45:10 away,] ~; *TCCII*

45:11 all] ~, *TCCII*

45:15 Still—] ~, *TCCII*

45:15 nuts—!] ~. *TCCII*

45:15 one,] ~; *TCCII*

45:17 *an TCCI*] an *MS* the *TCCII*

45:20 I!] ~. *TCCII*

45:20 *She takes TCCI*] She takes *MS Takes TCCII*

45:21 away] ~, *TCCI*

45:21 Miss] miss *TCCII*

45:24 —There *Ed.*] —there *MS* There *TCCII*

45:29 *gelatine Ed.*] gelatine *MS* gela*t*ine *TCCI* gelatine *TCCII*

45:29 We like] He likes *TCCII*

45:30 corn-flour.—] cornflour. *TCCI*

45:31 pine kernels—] pine-kernels. *TCCII*

45:32 It] it *TCCII*

45:37 done?—] ~? *TCCI*

45:40 Lambert.] ~? *TCCI*

46:3 *(rising suddenly)*: Good Lack, it's *Ed.*] (rising suddenly) Good Lack, it's *MS* (*Rising suddenly*) Good lack, it's *TCCI* Good lack! (*Rising suddenly*) It's *TCCII* Good lack! (*Rising suddenly.*) It's *E1*

46:3 half past ten.] half-past ~! *TCCI*

46:4 rave?] ~! *TCCI*

46:5 Mother] mother *E1*

46:7 begins—but] ~. But *TCCII*

46:7 rate] ~, *TCCII*

46:8 wrath.] ~.— *TCCII*

46:13 Gracious] gracious *TCCI*

46:18 story!!] ~! *TCCII*

46:24 Hello] ~, *TCCI*

46:26 nuisance—] ~!— *TCCII*

46:30 *nonchalantly TCCI*] nonchalently *MS*

46:31 Gert,] ~; *TCCII*

46:33 Oh] ~, *TCCI*

46:34 moment] ~, *TCCII*
46:35 you?—] ~? *TCCI* ~! *TCCII*
46:36 cat.] ~! *TCCI*
46:37 Oh] ~, *TCCI*
46:38 you] ~, *TCCI*
47:1 he, with] ~? With *TCCII*
47:1 Pearson *MSC*] Coomber *MS*
47:3 hasn't!] ~. *TCCII*
47:10 Goodnight] Good-night, *TCCI*
Good night, *E1*
47:10 everybody—see] ~. See
TCCII
47:11 tomorrow] to-morrow, *TCCI*
47:17 am!] ~? *TCCII*
47:25 says] ~, *TCCI*
47:27 Ha,] ~! *TCCI*
47:30 think] ~, *TCCII*
47:31 'Oh] '~, *TCCI*
47:31 stop] stay *TCCII*
47:31 away.] ~! *TCCI*
47:32 Ah] ~, *TCCI*
47:36 hateful.] ~? *TCCI*
47:36 think] ~, *TCCII*
47:36 Oh] ~, *TCCI*
47:38 late!] ~? *TCCI*
47:40 way—] ~. *TCCII*
48:1 Nay—] ~, *TCCII*
48:4 loaves!] ~. *TCCII*
48:6 *She turns TCCI*] She turns *MS*
Turns TCCII
48:8 them] ~, *TCCII*
48:12 Oh] ~, *TCCI*
48:12 it!!] ~! *TCCII*
48:13 going,] ~ — *TCCII*
48:13 not!!] ~! *TCCII*
48:14 it,] ~? *TCCII*
48:15 going!] ~. *TCCII*
48:17 him] ~, *TCCII*
48:20 care,] ~. *TCCII*
48:21 Ram.] "~." *E1*
48:24 Well] ~, *TCCII*
48:24 then!!] ~! *TCCII*
48:28 Oh] ~, *TCCI*
48:28 him.] ~! *TCCII*
48:32 *in TCCI*] in *MS into TCCII*
48:33 thing.] ~! *TCCII*
48:37 thing—!] ~!— *TCCII*
48:38 there] ~, *TCCII*

48:39 *She goes TCCI*] She goes *MS*
Goes TCCII
49:1 comes!——] ~!— *TCCI*
49:3 thing,] ~ — *TCCII*
49:4 *rigid, TCCI*] rigidly *MS*
49:12 *he TCCI*] he *MS Om. TCCII*
49:13 *into TCCI*] into *MS to TCCII*
49:15 *her head away TCCI*] her head
away *MS away her head TCCII*
49:20 *awhile Ed.*] awhile *MS a while*
TCCI
49:26 it!!] ~! *TCCI*
49:27 'Somebody else!!'] ~ ~!
TCCI
49:27 else.] ~! *TCCI*
49:27 daft:] ~! *TCCI*
49:29 *The FATHER continues TCCI*]
The father continues *MS*
Continues TCCII
49:31 it,] ~! *TCCI*
49:31 it!!] ~! *TCCI*
49:32 Noo—!] No-o—! *TCCI* No-o.
TCCII
49:33 them—] ~, *TCCII*
49:38 share!] ~. *TCCII*
49:39 Yes, you do. *(Contemptuously.)*
Ed.] Yes, you do
(contemptuously). *MS*
(contemptuously) Yes, you do.
TCCII (contemptuously): Yes,
you do. *E1*
50:1 come] came *TCCII*
50:3 Somebody] Nobody *TCCII*
50:3 else,] ~. *TCCI*
50:4 else.] ~! *TCCII*
50:6 'os' ... 'as' *Ed.*] 'os' ... 'as' *MS*
O's ... A's TCCI
50:7 Nathing,] ~! *TCCII*
50:9 woman!] ~? *TCCI*
50:12 [*Sometime during the following,*
the FATHER sits down in a chair.]
Ed.] Om. *MS*
50:19 to.] ~! *TCCII*
50:20 well then—!] ~, ~! *TCCII*
50:22 it.] ~! *TCCII*
50:26 it,] ~. *TCCI* ~! *TCCII*
50:26 go,] ~ — *TCCII*
50:26 go!—!] ~!! *TCCI* ~! *TCCII*

50:28   What! What!] ~? ~? *TCCII*
50:29   all,] ~ *TCCII*
50:33   I,] ~?— *TCCII*
50:33   'em] ~, *TCCII*
50:33   then.] ~? *TCCI*
50:35   bitch.] ~! *TCCI*
50:35   you.] ~! *TCCI* ~? *TCCII*
50:37   yourself] ~, *TCCII*
50:40   he.] ~? *TCCI*
51:1   day.] ~! *TCCII*
51:5   liar.] ~! *TCCI*
51:9   liar.] ~ — *TCCI*
51:11   twenty two] twenty-two *TCCI*
51:12   him,] ~ — *TCCII*
51:14   don't,] ~. *TCCI*
51:14   everythink] everything *TCCII*
51:15   me.] ~? *TCCI*
51:16   dog.] ~! *TCCII*
51:18   slinking hussy.] stinking ~! *TCCI*
51:19   me:] ~. *TCCI*
51:20   me ... *TCCII*] ~ .. *MS*
51:24   you—] ~. *TCCI*
51:27   in.] ~! *TCCII*
51:28   sleering] sneering *TCCI*
51:28   devil] ~, *TCCI*
51:33   hound,] ~,— *TCCII* ~ — *E1*
51:33   little— —.] ~ — —! *TCCI*
        ~ — *TCCII* ~ —— *E1*
51:37   *will*!!] ~! *TCCII* ~! *E1*
52:3   fool— — —] ~! *TCCI*
52:4   *His TCCI*] his *MS* THE
        TCCII The *E1*
52:7   Ernest don't.] ~, ~! *TCCI*
52:8   *The* MOTHER *lamentable Ed.*]
        The mother lamentable *MS*
        Lamentable TCCI
52:9   —Let] ~ *TCCI*
52:9   likes——.] ~ — — — *TCCI*
        ~. *TCCII*
52:10   if——] ~ ... *TCCII*
52:23   house.] ~! *TCCII*
52:24   jocky] jockey *E1*
52:24   together.] ~! *TCCII*
52:25   daft,] ~ — *TCCII*
52:27   bitch.] ~! *TCCI*
52:28   *He turns TCCI*] He turns *MS*
        Turns *TCCII*

52:31   Ernest—!] ~! *TCCII*
52:35   it.] ~! *TCCI*
52:35   —I] ~ *TCCI*
52:36   it,] ~! *TCCII*
52:36   it.—] ~! *TCCII*
52:36   fool.] ~! *TCCII*
53:7   him] ~, *TCCII*
53:9   mustn't.] ~! *TCCII*
53:11   damned] ~, *TCCII*
53:11   fool.] ~! *TCCII*
53:17   is, *TCCI*] ~ *MS*
53:20   mother] Mother *TCCII*
53:21   nor] or *TCCII*
53:22   is,] ~ *TCCII*
53:23   Ernest.] ~? *TCCI*
53:27   shouting.] ~! *TCCII*
53:36   sure—!] ~! *TCCII*
53:37   say ...] ~! ... *TCCII*
53:38   cinder—] ~! *TCCII*
54:1   *She suddenly TCCI*] she
        suddenly *MS* Suddenly *TCCII*
54:2   son,] ~,— *TCCII* ~ — *E1*
54:6   difference—!] ~! *TCCII*
54:6   as] As *TCCI*
54:9   does!] ~. *TCCII*
54:10   doesn't—why] ~. Why
        TCCII
54:11   bread.] ~? *TCCI*
54:11   know] ~, *TCCI*
54:18   here,] ~: *TCCII*
54:19   poetry: should] ~. Should
        TCCII
54:21   Impressionism,] ~ — *TCCII*
54:23   that ...] ~ — *TCCII* ~ ——
        E1
54:26   Impressionism *TCCII*]
        impressionism *MS*
54:26   Pre-Raphaelitism——]
        pre-Raphaelitism—— *TCCI*
        pre-Raphaelitism. *TCCII*
        pre-Raphaelism. *E1*
54:28   And besides—] ~, ~, *TCCII*
54:32   I now.] ~, ~? *TCCI*
54:34   know——] ~ — *TCCII*
        ~ —— *E1*
54:36   boy——] ~,— *TCCII* ~ —
        E1
54:37   it——] ~. *TCCII*

54:38 —can I now?—can] Can ~
~?—can *TCCI* Can ~, ~? Can
TCCII

55:2 them— —] ~ ... *TCCII* ~
.... *EI*

55:5 —why] —Why *TCCI* Why
TCCII

55:6 her— —] ~ — *TCCII*

55:6 you] ~, *TCCII*

55:9 Well] ~, *TCCII*

55:10 there] ~, *TCCI*

55:13 well] ~, *TCCII*

55:16 you] ~, *TCCII*

55:24 sometimes— —] ~ — *TCCII*
~ — *EI*

55:28 to— —?] ~? *TCCII*

55:29 in:] ~; *TCCII*

55:30 reading,] ~ — *TCCI*

55:36 No,] ~; *TCCII*

56:2 it] ~, *TCCII*

56:6 Nellie—look] ~. Look *TCCII*

56:8 do!] ~. *TCCII*

56:13 Eddie:] ~, *TCCII*

56:13 forever] for ever *EI*

56:14 —and] And *TCCI*

56:17 would] ~, *TCCII*

56:18 night— —.] ~ — — *TCCI*
~ — *TCCII* ~ — *EI*

56:19 But] ~, *TCCI*

56:19 out—.] ~ — — *TCCI* ~.
TCCII

56:23 *anything*] any/ -thing *TCCII*
*any*thing *EI*

56:24 everything, ... everything,] ~;
... ~; *TCCII*

56:27 it:] ~. *TCCII*

56:30 her—] ~. *TCCII*

56:33 be] ~, *TCCII*

56:35 you—Only] ~.— ~ *TCCI*
~. ~, *TCCII*

56:35 well] ~, *TCCII*

56:36 it—but] ~. But *TCCII*

56:39 *shoulder and she Ed.*] shoulder
and she *MS* shoulder, and she
TCCI shoulder; She *TCCII*
shoulder. She *EI*

56:39 *and TCCI*] and *MS* and *gently*
TCCII

57:1 *him—and he*] him. He *TCCII*

57:3 There—] ~!— *TCCII*

57:3 in— —.] ~. *TCCII*

57:5 you] ~, *TCCI*

57:10 time.] ~! *TCCII*

57:11 scandalous.] ~! *TCCI*

57:16 her,] ~ — *TCCII*

57:16 baggage.] ~! *TCCII*

57:19 Hello] ~, *TCCI*

57:20 home.] ~? *TCCI*

57:21 Yes] ~, *TCCI*

57:21 Miss] miss *TCCII*

57:21 My Lady] my lady *TCCI*

57:23 night:] ~! *TCCI*

57:24 eleven.] ~? *TCCI*

57:25 likes: besides] ~. Besides
TCCI

57:29 night.] ~! *TCCII*

57:29 fool.] ~! *TCCII*

57:33 Oh] ~, *TCCI*

57:33 again, we've] ~! We've *TCCII*

57:39 carrying-on] carrying on *TCCI*

58:1 that.] ~? *TCCI*

58:2 nuisance:] ~. *TCCII*

58:4 Shame!!] ~! *TCCII*

58:6 Oh] ~, *TCCI*

58:7 home,] ~; *TCCII*

58:11 end.] ~? *TCCI*

58:12 No] ~, *TCCI*

58:12 didn't!—] ~.— *TCCII* ~. *EI*

58:15 said] ~, *TCCII*

58:24 you!—] ~? *TCCI*

58:25 Pa-in-law:—] father-in-law—
TCCII

58:30 Come] ~, *TCCI*

58:30 Ernest,] ~; *TCCII*

58:31 now,] ~! *TCCII*

58:35 flame, *TCCI*] ~ *MS*

58:37 it] *Om. TCCII*

58:38 Amen.] ~! *TCCI*

58:39 creature.] ~! *TCCII*

58:39 *She looks TCCI*] she looks *MS*
Looks *TCCII*

59:7 mother] Mother *TCCII*

59:19 bits—and] ~.—And *TCCII*

59:23 *and lights it, TCCI*] and lights
it, *MS Om. TCCII*

59:35 Goodnight!] Good-night!

	TCCI Good-night. *TCCII*			*(very softly)* Good-night.
	Good night. *E1*			*TCCII (very softly)*: Good
59:36	out.—] ∼,— *TCCI* ∼. *TCCII*			night. *E1*
59:37	Goodnight. *(Very softly.) Ed.*]	60:4		*(Curtain) Ed.*] End of Act III.
	Goodnight (very softly) *MS*			*MS* END OF ACT III. *TCCI* END
	Good-night. *(Very softly) TCCI*			OF ACT III *E1*

The Merry-go-Round

MS	=	Autograph MS (Roberts E237a)
TSI	=	Ribbon and carbon copy TS (Roberts E237d)
TSII	=	Ribbon TS (no Roberts no.)
Per	=	*Virginia Quarterly Review*, Christmas Number, xvii (1940–1), 1–44
E1	=	*Complete Plays* (Heinemann, 1965)

Silent emendations

1 Throughout, *E1* printed 'to-day', 'to-night', 'to-morrow'. DHL wrote these without hyphen; his practice has been preserved, and *E1*'s variants are not recorded in the Textual apparatus.

2 DHL's spelling of 'aimiable' for 'amiable' has been silently corrected.

3 British and American spelling variants (e.g. 'parlour' and 'parlor', 'whisky' and 'whiskey') are not recorded unless they are part of another variant.

4 Vowel-ligatures (e.g. 'æ' and 'œ') are printed as two letters in Latin words. Latin quotations in dialogue are italicised in *TSIIC*, *Per* and *E1*; the instances are not recorded unless they are part of another variant.

113:5	*with heaped up, Ed.*] with heaped up, *MS with a heaped up TSIIC with a heaped-up Per*	114:13		'ave-na] 'avena *TSIIC*
		114:13		nine] five *TSI see notes*
		114:19		mulligrubs] mulligrules *TSI*
113:5	*This Ed.*] This *MS* The *TSI* The *TSIIC*			mulligurles *TSII*
		114:19		non] not *TSIIC*
113:6	*contains TSIIC*] contains *MS* contains a *Per*	114:20		What,] ∼! *Per*
		114:20		Harry!] ∼? *TSII*
113:6	*wash-stand, and Ed.*] wash-stand, and *MS washtand, and TSIIC a washtand, and a Per*	114:21		he.] ∼? *TSI*
		114:22		'ad] 'as *TSII*
		114:23		back-ards] back'ards *TSIIC*
113:14	Eh] ∼, *TSIIC*	114:24		good-'un] good-un *TSI* good
113:16	Hemstock—?] ∼? *TSI*			'un *TSIIC*
113:18	anigh] nigh *TSIIC*	114:30		—But] ∼ *TSI*
113:19	forced.—] ∼. *TSI*	114:32		'Asn't *TSIIC*] As'n't *MS*
113:19	'im—] ∼ *TSI* ∼. *TSIIC*	114:34		*he*] he *TSI*
113:25	at] a' *TSIIC*	114:40		Hemstock—] ∼? *TSIIC*
113:32	gi'e] gi' *TSIIC*	115:6		Oh] ∼, *TSIIC*
113:32	cat-lick] catlick *TSIIC*	115:9		a] *Om. TSII*
114:2	there in] in there *TSIIC*	115:9		twelvemonth] twelve month
114:6	you.—] ∼. *TSI*			*TSIIC*
114:9	threatenin'.] threatenin! *TSI* threatnenin! *TSII* threatenin'! *TSIIC*	115:10		'er.—] ∼. *TSI*
		115:12		churlish—?] ∼? *TSIIC*
		115:13		sort] sor *TSII* sor' *TSIIC*

115:14 lad,—] ~, *TSIIC*
115:14 an' *Ed.*] an *MS* and *TSI*
115:14 'Mammy'] "Mammy" *Per* "mammy" *E1*
115:16 slormin'] stormin' *TSI*
115:22 'ead out o' th' door,] 'head out of' the 'door, *TSI* 'ead out of' the 'door *TSII* 'ead out of the door *TSIIC*
115:24 slidin'] ~, *TSIIC*
115:27 'ae'-porth] 'ae'-forth *TSI* 'un *TSIIC see notes*
115:29 Eh] ~, *TSIIC*
115:29 you, 'e'd] ~. 'e'd *TSII* ~. 'E'd *TSIIC*
115:31 money-box,] money box *TSIIC*
115:33 him.] ~! *TSIIC*
115:36 hark] harsh *TSI*
116:4 'aef *Ed.*] a'ef *MS* 'alf *TSIIC*
116:4 seen] see *TSI*
116:6 an' cocks shoutin'— *Ed.*] an' cocks shoutin— *MS* and cocks shoutin'. *TSI*
116:7 —tha's] Tha's *TSIIC*
116:7 tom-cat] tomcat *TSIIC*
116:7 breakfast—] ~. *TSIIC*
116:9 minutes.—] ~. *TSI*
116:10 bin] been *TSIIC*
116:10 pennorth *TSI*] pen north *MS* penn'orth *TSIIC*
116:13 'E's] He's *TSI*
116:15 bin] been *TSIIC*
116:23 there.] ~? *TSIIC*
116:26 a] *Om. TSII*
116:28 have—] ~, *TSIIC*
116:28 Harry *TSI*] ~, *MS*
116:32 barm-dumplings—] barm dumplings— *TSI* barm dumplings. *TSII*
116:34 Ma'e] Ha'e *TSI* Ha' *TSIIC*
116:34 crack—] ~. *TSI*
116:37 palavar] palaver *Per*
117:8 your] you *TSII* you' *TSIIC*
117:9 your] you *TSII* you' *TSIIC*
117:12 Oh] ~, *TSIIC*
117:13 'Oh'] "~" *TSIIC* "oh" *Per*
117:15 made.] ~? *TSIIC*
117:26 made—?] ~? *TSIIC*

117:27 —Does] ~ *TSI*
117:28 thaïgh] thaigh *TSI* tha *TSIIC*
117:29 —Now] ~ *TSI*
117:30 non want] want na *TSIIC*
117:37 stones] stone *Per*
117:39 th' bed] the bed *TSI*
117:40 bed-latts] bed slats *TSIIC*
118:1 What!—] ~! *TSIIC*
118:1 *stoops, dubious Ed.*] stoops dubious *MS* stoops *dubiously TSIIC*
118:3 it.] ~? *TSIIC*
118:4 Oh] ~, *TSI*
118:7 Oh yes—?] ~, ~ — *TSIIC*
118:11 Hemstock.] ~? *TSIIC*
118:12 up on] upon *TSI*
118:13 o' th'] o' the *TSI*
118:13 here] there *TSIIC*
118:21 Oh] ~, *TSIIC*
118:23 —How] ~ *TSI*
118:23 Nurse.] ~? *TSIIC*
118:26 collieries] colleries *TSIIC*
118:38 Oh] ~, *TSIIC*
118:39 I.—] ~. *TSI* ~? *Per*
118:40 Harry—Harry!—] ~. ~! *TSIIC*
119:2 *moustache E1*] moustache *MS* mustache *TSIIC*
119:6 'what's want',] 'What's ~', *TSI* 'What's ~' *TSII* "What's ~" *Per*
119:10 want—?] ~? *TSIIC*
119:11 what] why *TSIIC*
119:13 gi'e] gi' e *TSII* gi' *TSIIC*
119:16 —Perhaps] ~ *TSI*
119:18 Nurse. 'E's] ~, 'e's *Per*
119:19 baby.—] ~. *TSI*
119:19 yet.] ~? *TSIIC*
119:19 —'E] 'E *TSI*
119:20 Durst] durst *TSI*
119:21 eh?—] ~? *TSI*
119:26 thing—] ~. *TSI*
119:36 him *Ed.*] him *MS* him how *TSIIC*
119:37 tree-roots—] ~. *TSI*
120:6 you.] ~? *TSIIC*
120:8 now.] ~? *TSIIC*
120:17 man's fair smockravelled, an']

man's fair smock ravelled, an'
TSI man *TSIIC*

120:21 in *TSI*] in in *MS see notes*

120:22 vinegar.—] ~. *TSI*

120:26 abear] bear *Per*

120:27 —But] ~ *TSI*

120:28 go] do *TSI* die *TSIIC*

120:36 are.] ~! *TSIIC*

120:36 dried] dired *TSII* aired *TSIIC*

120:38 —not] —Not *TSII* Not *TSIIC*

120:39 father.—] ~. *TSI*

120:40 so 'ormin,] so; *TSI*

120:40 question.] ~? *TSI*

121:2 He] 'E *TSIIC*

121:3 Oh] ~, *TSIIC*

121:9 like] likes *TSI*

121:11 has] han *TSI*

121:13 sure—.] ~ — *TSI*

121:14 wage,—] ~, *TSI*

121:15 thee—what] ~. What *TSI*

121:17 know?] ~. *TSIIC*

121:19 I wish—I wish *TSI*] ~ ~/~ ~
MS see notes

121:20 and—.] ~ — *TSI*

121:21 Eh] ~, *TSIIC*

121:28 so.—] ~. *TSIIC*

122:5 —Ha] ~ *TSI*

122:6 —Can] ~ *TSI*

122:10 in] in the *Per*

122:10 doctor—] ~. *TSI*

122:11 he—?] ~? *TSIIC*

122:12 so—.] ~ — *TSI*

122:13 draggle-tail] draggletail *TSIIC*

122:13 —How] ~ *TSI*

122:16 Oh,—] ~, *TSI*

122:16 heart-brokken.—] ~. *TSI*
heartbroken. *TSII*

122:17 th'] the *TSI*

122:17 —His] ~ *TSI*

123:4 *Scene: TSI*] Scene: *MS Om.*
TSIIC

123:7 scraïghtin'] scraightin' *TSI*

123:14 not——] ~ — *TSIIC*

123:15 *old, withered clergyman Ed.*] old,
withered clergyman *MS*
withered, old clergyman, the
BARON, TSIIC

123:21 non] na *TSIIC*

123:23 arena] are na *TSI*

123:24 parish,] ~. *TSI*

123:24 von Ruge, *Ed.*] von Hube, *MS*
Von Hube. *TSII* von Ruge. *Per*
see notes

123:26 non ... non] na ... na *TSIIC*

123:28 Sir] sir *Per*

123:29 tell] ter *TSII* go to *TSIIC*

123:30 non] na *TSI*

123:31 *squarks Ed.*] squarks *MS*
squawks *TSIIC*

123:34 hollin'] haulin' *TSIIC*

123:39 go——] ~ — *TSIIC*

124:1 Ax] A sc *TSI* Ask *TSIIC*

124:1 An'] an' *TSI*

124:2 non] na *TSIIC*

124:2 goin'—.] ~ — *TSI*

124:6 country, *Ed.*] ~; *MS* ~ *TSIIC*

124:13 non] na *TSIIC*

124:14 Well] ~, *TSIIC*

124:15 minister.] ~? *TSIIC*

124:15 think——] ~ — *TSI*

124:16 THE BAKER *Ed.*] The Baker *MS*
THE BAKER *TSI Enter the*
BAKER *TSIIC*

124:16 *about forty: Ed.*] about forty:
MS of about forty. TSIIC

124:16 *dark moustache Ed.*] dark
moustache *MS Om. TSIIC*

124:21 strike's] strike is *Per*

124:24 un] 'un *TSIIC*

124:28 Oh,] *Om. TSIIC*

124:28 again.—] ~. *TSI*

124:31 your] you *TSII*

124:34 shably] shabbily *TSIIC*

124:37 job—.] ~ — *TSI*

124:40 Godfather] godfather *Per*

124:40 eh] ~, *TSIIC*

125:8 un] 'un *TSIIC*

125:10 —I've] ~ *TSI*

125:11 he—] ~? *TSIIC*

125:11 half a] half *TSII* a half *TSIIC*

125:12 ha'porth] ha-porth *TSII* ha-
p'orth *TSIIC*

125:15 —And] ~ *TSI*

125:16 eh] ~, *TSIIC*

125:16 what!] ~? *Per*

125:18 me—] ~. *TSI*

125:20 —One] ~ *TSI*
125:22 wasn't *TSI*] was n't *MS* wan't *TSII* wa'nt *TSIIC*
125:28 —A] ~ *TSI*
125:29 Ay—!—] ~!— *TSI* ~! *TSIIC*
125:31 —But] ~ *TSI*
125:33 manage—] ~ *TSIIC*
125:35 said——] ~ — *TSIIC*
125:35 *Enter* susy *Ed.*] Susy *MS* ENTER SUSY *TSI Enter* susy SMALLEY *TSIIC see notes*
125:40 'e. *TSI*] e. *MS* 'e? *TSIIC*
126:1 fun] foun' *Per*
126:1 I.] ~? *TSIIC*
126:3 garden—] ~. *TSI*
126:4 —You] ~ *TSI*
126:5 —That's] ~ *TSI*
126:6 ter] ther *TSII* thee *Per*
126:7 Ax] Asc *TSI* Ask *TSIIC*
126:8 thaïgh] thaigh *TSI* thee *TSIIC*
126:10 thee—!] ~! *TSI*
126:13 thaïgh] thaigh *TSI* tha *TSIIC*
126:14 more—] ~ *TSI* ~. *TSII*
126:15 Blazes] blazes *Per*
126:16 wasn't] wan't *TSII*
126:17 skulk] skilk *TSII*
126:17 'em—] em. *TSI* 'em. *TSIIC*
126:25 matched;—] ~; *TSI*
126:30 Oh shall you.] ~, ~ ~? *TSIIC*
126:31 childt] child *TSIIC*
126:36 a'—] ~. *TSI*
126:36 fowls!—] ~! *TSI*
126:39 HARRY: I'll— *Ed.*] Harry: I'll— *MS* HARRY: I'll *TSI Om. TSIIC*
126:39 *He Ed.*] He *MS* HARRY *TSIIC*
127:3 he.] ~? *Per*
127:3 slorm] storm *TSI*
127:6 it—!] ~ — *TSI*
127:7 —I] ~ *TSI*
127:8 —I] ~ *TSI*
127:8 —How] ~ *TSI*
127:12 SMALLEY *TSIIC*] Smalley *MS* SMALLEY *out E1*
127:17 th'] the *Per*
127:26 marries] married *TSII*
127:33 Goddards.] ~? *TSIIC* Goddard's? *Per*

127:34 —Well] ~ *TSI*
127:39 doctor. Just] ~ —just *TSI* ~,—just *TSII* ~, just *TSIIC* Doctor, just *Per*
127:39 shop—] ~. *TSIIC*
128:1 Oh] ~, *TSIIC*
128:1 doctor] Doctor *Per*
128:4 Good-morning] Good morning *TSI*
128:5 Broadbanks—!] ~! *TSIIC*
128:7 Well,] ~. *TSII*
128:7 am] am *Per*
128:7 ever——] ~ — *TSIIC*
128:8 —I] ~ *TSI*
128:12 do—.] ~ — *TSI*
128:17 Ah] ~, *TSIIC*
128:21 be——] ~ — *TSIIC*
128:22 praeterea *Ed.*] prœtera *MS* proetera *TSI* proetera *TSIIC* prœterea *Per*
128:31 impaired.'] ~'. *TSI* ~?" *TSIIC*
128:33 Cuique] *cuique TSIIC*
128:33 —You] ~ *TSI*
128:36 —You] ~ *TSII*
128:37 *Broadbanks MS*, *TSIIC*] Broadbanks *TSI* Broadbanks *Per*
128:38 Ha Ha] ha ha *TSIIC*
129:1 FOULES *(bowing)*: *Ed.*] Foules (bowing): *MS* FOULES: (bowing) *TSI* FOULES: *TSIIC*
129:1 Nurse—?] ~? *TSI*
129:6 tetigisti.—] ~. *TSI*
129:9 beg. Do] ~, Do *TSI* ~, do *TSIIC*
129:13 re.—] ~. *TSI*
129:18 Nurse—] ~. *TSIIC*
129:22 multa,] *multa Per*
129:23 *I*] I *TSI*
129:27 —yes] Yes *TSIIC*
129:28 you] ~ — *TSI*
129:35 Taedium vitae *Ed.*] Tœdium vitae *MS* Toedium vitae *TSI Toedium vitœ TSIIC Tœdium vitœ Per*
129:36 Weariness of Life] weariness ~ life *TSIIC*

129:37 *Life,*] Life? *Per*
129:37 *life*] life *TSII*
129:37 it?—] ~? *TSI*
130:3   experiences] experience *TSI*
130:5   it!] ~? *TSI*
130:6   us] ~, *TSIIC*
130:8   —And] ~ *TSI*
130:11 Goodmorning] Good morning *TSIIC*
130:17 I'm] I am *TSI*
130:20 it—!] ~! *TSIIC*
130:21 it.] ~? *TSIIC*
130:25 goloshes] galoshes *TSIIC*
130:25 Hemstock? *TSIIC*] ~/ *MS* ~. *TSI*
130:27 me.] ~! *TSIIC*
130:28 *They TSI*] They *MS* They all *TSII*
130:32 didna] dinna *Per*
130:35 I'm] I am *TSI*
130:36 —I] ~ *TSI*
130:38 Doctor.—] ~. *TSI*
130:38 Good-day] ~, *TSIIC* Good day, *E1*
130:39 [*Exit* NURSE.] *Ed.*] *Om. MS*
130:40 Goodday] Good-day *TSI* Good day *E1*
131:8   non] na *TSIIC*
131:11 —Wi'] ~ *TSI*
131:11 round,—] ~ — *TSIIC*
131:12 tha'd] tha's *TSII*
131:13 gen] gin *TSIIC*
131:15 *me*] me *Per*
131:15 'Er wouldna ... drink in *Ed.*] ~ ~ ... Mr Hemstock ... ~ ~ *MS* ~ ~ ... MR. HEMSTOCK ... ~ ~ *TSI Om. TSII*
131:18 thee, an' be lively—.] ~, ~ ~ ~ — *TSI Om. TSIIC*
131:20 Nurse.] ~! *TSIIC*
131:25 *flashing, Ed.*] flashing, *MS* flushing *TSII*
131:28 Oh,—] ~ — *TSIIC*
131:29 —there's] ~ *TSI* There's *TSII*
131:35 Poor] poor *TSI*
131:36 cuffs.—] ~. *TSI*
132:1   before—] ~. *TSIIC*

132:4   all right] alright *E1*
132:6   a] *Om. Per*
132:8   —But] ~ *TSI*
132:17 —Yes] ~ *TSI* ~, *TSIIC*
133:3   *Scene: The ... same evening. Ed.*] Scene: The Hemstock's kitchen; the lamp lighted/ Time: The same evening *MS Scene*: The Hemstock's kitchen: the lamp lighted./ *Time*: The same evening. *TSI The Hemstock's kitchen, with the lamp lighted. It is the same evening. TSIIC* The HEMSTOCKS' *kitchen, with the lamp lighted. It is the same evening. Per*
133:13 old.—] ~. *TSI*
133:16 A sight] S sight *TSII* Sight *TSIIC*
133:20 you?—] ~? *TSIIC*
133:23 th'] the *TSI*
133:23 kitchen? *TSIIC*] ~/ *MS* ~. *TSI*
133:24 'alf] 'half *TSI* half *TSIIC*
133:25 me—!] ~! *TSIIC*
133:30 —By] ~ *TSI*
133:30 she's] *she's TSI*
133:36 waitin'] saitin' *TSI* a saiting *TSII* a-waitin' *TSIIC*
134:2   hundred.] ~ .... *TSIIC*
134:4   Hm!—] ~! *TSI*
134:6   —But] ~ *TSIIC*
134:7   funny:] ~ — *TSI*
134:12 Hm!—] ~! *TSI*
134:13 Susy—?] ~? *TSIIC*
134:18 th' Vicarage] the vicarage *TSI*
134:19 —But] ~ *TSI*
134:21 here——] ~. *TSIIC*
134:25 What] Which *Per*
134:27 whistle,] ~ *TSI*
134:27 ferrited] ferreted *Per*
134:31 me—?] ~? *TSIIC*
134:35 *you.* To] ~, ~ *TSII* ~; to *Per*
134:37 sure—.] ~. *TSI*
134:40 down.—] ~. *TSI*
135:2   *are*] are *TSII*
135:3   accept!] ~? *TSI*

135:4   *pig*] pig *TSI*
135:6   —I'd] ~ *TSI*
135:16 one—?] ~? *TSIIC*
135:18 think.] ~? *TSIIC*
135:21 are—?] ~? *TSI* ~. *TSIIC*
135:22 —I] ~ *TSI*
135:23 —And] ~ *TSI*
135:27 would] wouldn't *Per*
135:28 now—?] ~? *TSI*
135:29 Dilly-Dilly!"] Dilly-Dilly"!
        TSI dilly-dilly"! *TSIIC*
135:30 —'Come] '~ *TSI* "~ *TSIIC*
135:33 must—] ~ *TSIIC*
135:38 about———] ~ — *TSIIC*
135:39 RACHEL *(a Ed.*] Rachel (a *MS*
        RACHEL: (a *TSI Enter*
        RACHEL, *a TSIIC*
135:40 *girl, Ed.*] girl, *MS* girl, *with*
        TSIIC
136:2   *softly): Ed.*] softly): *MS*
        softly)/ *TSI softly./* RACHEL:
        TSIIC
136:7   —No?—] ~? *TSI*
136:7   how's] How's *TSII*
136:12 me.—] ~. *TSI*
136:13 No] ~, *TSI*
136:16 all right] alright *E1*
136:16 —As] ~ *TSI*
136:17 —Thanks.—] ~. *TSI*
136:19 Yea—] Yes— *TSII* Yes, *TSIIC*
136:19 *am*] am *TSII*
136:21 go] ~, *TSIIC*
136:22 go] ~, *TSIIC*
136:28 —Oh] ~, *TSIIC*
136:29 whoa] Whow *TSI* whow,
        TSIIC
136:30 Oh] oh *TSIIC*
136:30 Ho." ' *Ed.*] ~.' *MS* ~! *TSI*
        ho!" *TSIIC* ho!' " *Per*
136:31 *He's*] He's *TSI* He's *TSII*
136:32 some time.] some times. *TSI*
        come times. *TSII* some times?
        TSIIC sometimes? *Per*
136:33 *we've*] we've *TSII*
136:33 corn—] ~. *TSIIC*
136:36 corn?—] ~? *TSIIC*
136:37 grains—no] ~. No *TSIIC*
136:38 What] What's *TSIIC*

137:2   When he's … But when]
        When He's as smooth as silk.
        But when *TSII* When *TSIIC*
137:5   Goodness.] ~! *TSIIC*
137:11 —An'] ~ *TSI*
137:11 are—.] ~ — *TSI* ~! *TSIIC*
137:13 yet—] ~. *TSIIC*
137:14 that—,] ~, *TSI*
137:14 pray—?] ~? *TSIIC*
137:16 me] ~. *TSIIC*
137:16 —Look] —look *TSII* Look
        TSIIC
137:18 Look] ~, *TSIIC*
137:20 —bring] ~ *TSI*
137:21 *low.*) I *Ed.*] low) ~ *MS* low)
        — ~ *TSI low),* ~ *TSIIC*
137:23 £250] two hundred and fifty
        pounds *Per*
137:24 THE BAKER … not yet! *Ed.*] The
        Baker … ~ ~! *MS* THE
        BAKER … ~ ~! *TSI* BAKER
        … ~ ~! *TSIIC Om. Per*
137:34 *to her TSIIC*] to her *MS Om.*
        Per
137:34 —And] ~ *TSIIC*
137:40 say.] ~? *TSIIC*
138:2   goin'] going *TSII*
138:2   awhile] a while *TSIIC*
138:3   see—] ~. *TSIIC*
138:5   business—] ~. *TSIIC*
138:6   up—?] ~? *TSIIC*
138:7   —I] ~ *TSI*
138:7   you,] ~; *TSIIC*
138:10 your] you *TSII*
138:12 hear?—] ~? *TSIIC*
138:13 Goodnight] God night *Per*
138:13 *Exit. TSIIC*] exit *MS* EXIT
        TSI Exit BAKER. *E1*
138:25 My word … it up.—] My work
        … ~ ~. *TSI Om. TSIIC*
138:27 —Are] ~ *TSI*
138:28 —Well] ~ *TSI*
138:30 —I] ~ *TSI*
138:31 —I] ~ *TSI*
138:31 —Do] ~ *TSI*
138:32 Gie's] Gi'e's *TSIIC*
138:33 you.—] ~. *TSI*
138:34 him.—] ~. *TSI*

138:34   *(Tears.) Ed.*] (tears) *MS*
         (Tears.) TSIIC (She cries.) E1
138:35   scraïght] scraight *TSI*
138:36   *(Sob): Ed.*] (Sob): *MS* (sob)
         TSI (Sob.) TSIIC (Sobs). E1
138:37   *(Tears). Ed.*] (tears). *MS*
         (Tears.) TSIIC (She cries.) E1
138:37   bad?—] ∼? *TSI*
138:38   half past] half-past *E1*
138:38   three—] ∼, *TSIIC*
138:38   and—] ∼ *TSI*
139:1   frightened for you. You]
         frightened for you *TSI*
         frightened, for you *TSII*
139:2   nowadays—] ∼. *TSIIC*
139:3   fun] foun' *TSIIC*
139:6   —What] ∼ *TSI*
139:6   done, tell] ∼? Tell *TSIIC*
139:8   spittoon] spitton *TSII*
139:15   'an'] ∼ *TSIIC*
139:15   so's'—] so'a— *TSII* so's—
         TSIIC
139:15   spittoon] spitton *TSII*
139:18   What—?] ∼? *TSIIC*
139:19   dummy—you've] ∼. You've
         TSIIC
139:19   you—] ∼. *TSI*
139:20   What—] ∼! *TSIIC*
139:20   what?] ∼! *TSI* What! *TSII*
139:21   —Sawdust] ∼ *TSI*
139:22   thee—] ∼. *TSII* ∼! *TSIIC*
139:24   it—] ∼! *TSIIC*
139:26   here!] ∼. *TSIIC*
139:27   Oh, what] ∼! ∼ *TSIIC* ∼!
         What *Per*
139:29   *leathern Ed.*] leathern *MS*
         leather *TSIIC*
139:31   me.—] ∼. *TSI* ∼! *TSIIC*
139:31   th'] the *Per*
139:36   HARRY: Did ... th' ... RACHEL:
         Yes. *Ed.*] Harry: Did ... th' ...
         Rachel: Yes. *MS* HARRY: Did
         ... the ... RACHEL: Yes. *TSI*
         Om. TSII
139:40   comin'] coming *TSI*
139:40   me—?] ∼? *TSIIC*
140:2   fright—?] ∼? *TSIIC*
140:3   Yes—] ∼. *TSI*

140:4   a'tween] atween *TSIIC*
140:5   worth—] ∼? *TSIIC*
140:6   —Yes] ∼ *TSI*
140:7   I—?] ∼? *TSIIC*
140:8   don't—] ∼. *TSIIC*
140:9   —An'] ∼ *TSI*
140:10   of—?] ∼? *TSIIC*
140:11   Oh] ∼, *TSIIC*
140:11   no—oh] ∼!—Oh, *TSIIC* ∼!
         Oh, *Per*
140:11   no—!] ∼! *TSI*
140:12   Yes—] ∼, *TSIIC*
140:13   Oh no, Harry.] oh ∼, ∼!
         TSIIC
140:14   Bowers—?] ∼? *TSI*
140:15   Oh—h—] Oh! *TSIIC*
140:16   again] again' *TSIIC*
140:16   chair back] chair-back *TSIIC*
140:18   dear, Oh dear, Oh dear] dear,
         Oh dear *TSII* dear, oh dear
         TSIIC
140:21   me.—] ∼. *TSI*
140:23   chelp] cheek *TSIIC*
140:24   *What!!*] *what? TSIIC* what? *Per*
140:31   lu'thee] lu' thee *TSIIC*
140:32   me.—Sithee!] ∼ — ∼! *TSI*
         ∼ —sithee? *TSIIC*
140:34   go.] ∼! *TSIIC*
140:35   sober:] sover: *TSII* sover.
         TSIIC
141:4   go—] ∼ *TSII*
141:6   on] o' *TSIIC*
141:7   —An'] ∼ *TSI*
141:8   *gently.) Ed.*] gently) *MS gently*
         now.) TSIIC
141:10   *(He takes ... will do. Ed.*] (He
         takes the sleepy bird in his
         arms) ... will do. *MS Om.*
         TSII
141:12   her,] ∼ *E1*
141:13   Pat—!] ∼! *TSIIC*
142:3   *Time: The same./ Scene: Ed.*]
         Time: The same./ Scene: *MS*
         Time: The same. Scene: TSIIC
         A few moments later. E1
142:11   me. Shut] ∼, shut *TSII* ∼;
         shut *TSIIC*
142:13   up—?] ∼? *TSI*

142:19   care, you] ~. You *E₁*
142:22   not] ~, *TSIIC*
142:22   it,] ~; *Per*
142:23   was.—] ~. *TSI*
142:24   money,—] ~— *TSI* ~, *TSIIC*
142:25   mouse-hole—] ~, *TSI* mouse
         hole, *TSIIC*
142:27   An'] an' *TSIIC*
142:27   bug] big *MSC see notes*
142:27   lord—] ~ *TSI*
142:28   wi'] with *TSI*
142:30   will—] ~. *TSIIC*
142:31   Well] ~, *TSIIC*
142:34   *me*] me *TSII*
142:36   know—?] ~? *TSI*
142:37   knows.] ~? *TSIIC*
142:38   Nurse—] ~, *TSIIC*
142:39   *His*] His *TSII*
143:2   All right] Alright *E₁*
143:2   *are*] are *TSII*
143:4   back—] ~. *TSIIC*
143:5   him—] ~. *TSIIC*
143:8   me—if] ~ —If *TSI* ~, if
         TSIIC
143:10   All right—] ~ ~, *TSIIC*
         Alright, *E₁*
143:11   Susy—] ~. *TSI*
143:12   ferrit] ferret *Per*
143:15   fish] fist *TSII*
143:18   *you*—so] ~, ~ *TSI* ~. so *TSII*
         ~. So *TSIIC*
143:19   ter] er *TSI* 'er *TSIIC*
143:19   —What] ~ *TSI*
143:21   *has*] has *TSII*
143:21   things—] ~, *TSIIC*
143:22   Bowers—] ~. *TSIIC*
143:23   Oh] ~, *TSIIC*
143:23   I?—] ~? *TSI*
143:25   lady—] ~. *TSI*
143:26   What—come] ~? Come *TSIIC*
143:27   out.] ~! *TSI*
143:28   *hiding—Ed.*] hiding— *MS*
         hiding as *TSII*
143:31   —Shut] ~ *TSI*
143:40   *entice*] entice *TSII*
144:1   honor] honour *E₁*
144:2   family—] ~? *TSIIC*
144:3   Baron—] ~, *TSIIC*

144:3   sin—] ~. *TSI*
144:8   ah] ~, *TSIIC*
144:8   insult.] ~! *TSIIC*
144:9   child—] ~. *TSII*
144:11   —That] ~ *TSI*
144:14   grave yard] graveyard *TSIIC*
144:15   those] ~, *TSIIC*
144:15   menfolk] men folk *TSI*
144:17   Hush—] ~, *TSIIC*
144:19   More—Ah] ~? ~, *TSIIC*
144:19   misery,—] ~, *TSI*
144:19   worms—! Where?—] ~! ~?
         TSI
144:21   gate-post] gate-/ post *Per*
         gatepost *E₁*
144:22   —Lovers] ~ *TSI*
144:22   there—] ~, *TSIIC*
144:23   man?—] ~? *TSI*
144:25   —Who] ~ *TSI*
144:25   you?—] ~? *TSI*
144:26   come] Come *TSII*
144:26   you—] ~. *TSI*
144:27   doing;—] ~; *TSI*
144:28   *titter.) Ed.*] titter) *MS titter is*
         heard.) TSIIC
144:29   man?—] ~? *TSI*
144:29   Sir] sir *TSII*
144:30   man.—] ~. *TSI*
144:31   mankind!] ~. *TSII*
144:32   girl—] ~. *TSI* ~? *TSIIC*
144:33   late—] ~. *TSI*
144:35   yourselves] youselves *TSII*
144:37   lust—.] ~. *TSI*
145:1   eye—] ~. *TSIIC*
145:1   *women Ed.*] women *MS woman*
         TSII
145:3   *flies away and TSIIC*] flies
         away and *MS Om. Per*
145:4   Oh—Come] oh, come *TSIIC*
145:4   away—] ~. *TSI* ~! *TSIIC*
145:5   Ha—Ha—] ~ — ~ *TSI*
         Ha—ha *TSII* ~! Ha! *TSIIC*
145:7   Ha—come] ~! Come *TSIIC*
145:7   on.] ~! *TSI*
145:9   me] ~, *TSIIC*
145:9   I— *TSIIC*] ~ *MS* ~ — —
         TSI
145:11   swine.] ~! *TSIIC*

145:15 *(head) Ed.*] (head) *MS Om.*
TSIIC

145:16 you.] ~! *TSIIC*

145:20 goin'] *Om. TSII*

145:21 old. If] ~, ~ *TSII* ~, if *Per*

145:23 They] Thy *TSII*

145:23 Help!—] ~! *TSIIC*

145:26 Baron—] ~! *TSIIC*

145:26 Oh—h——] Oh—h— *TSI*
oh—h— *TSII* Oh-h— *TSIIC*
Oh-h—— *E1*

145:28 *wrists TSIIC*] wrists *MS wrist*
Per

145:30 Ruge—my wife—] ~, ~ ~,
TSIIC

145:31 her—] ~. *TSI* ~! *TSIIC*

145:33 Little!—little] ~! Little *TSI* ~,
Little *TSII* ~, little *TSIIC*

145:34 one—] ~, *TSIIC*

145:34 thus—!] ~! *TSIIC*

145:36 Help Help Help!!!] ~, help,
help! *TSIIC*

145:38 goin'] going *TSII*

145:39 —What?—] ~? *TSI*

145:39 Oh—h!] Oh-h! *TSI* Oh-h—!
Per Oh-h——! *E1*

146:1 NURSE *Ed.*] Nurse *MS* NURSE
TSI Enter NURSE./ NURSE
TSIIC

146:1 —Who] ~ *TSI*

146:3 wife—] ~. *TSI* ~! *TSIIC*

146:3 wife—!] ~. *TSI* ~! *TSIIC*

146:5 Baroness!—] ~! *TSIIC*

146:5 Oh, how] oh, ~ *TSIIC*

146:11 hound. *TSI*] ~ *MS* ~? *TSIIC*

146:12 thaïgh] thaigh *TSI* tha *TSIIC*

146:14 certainly——] ~ — *TSIIC*

146:14 *(German.) Ed.*] (German) *MS
Om. TSIIC*

146:16 —Thief] ~ *TSI*

146:18 Tha] The *TSII*

146:23 —Help] —help *TSII*

146:23 Baron— *TSI*] ~ *MS*

146:26 all right] alright *E1*

146:27 golosher] galosher *TSIIC*

146:28 Oh] oh *TSIIC*

146:29 Ah] ~, *TSIIC*

146:29 Oh,] ~ *TSI* oh, *TSIIC*

146:30 have] haf *TSIIC*

146:30 ruffians.—] ~. *TSI*

146:31 Baron. You *Ed.*] ~; you *MS* ~:
You *TSI* ~, you *TSIIC*

146:33 have] haf *Per*

146:33 escaped—are] ~. Are *TSI*

146:35 golosh—?] golosh? *TSI* galosh?
TSIIC galosher? *Per*

146:38 ill—] ~. *TSI*

146:39 lanthorn] lantern *TSI*

146:40 goloshes] galoshes *Per*

147:1 *(Exeunt.) Ed.*] (exeunt) *MS*
(EXEUNT) *TSI* (*They leave.*)
TSIIC

147:2 snipe—!] ~! *TSIIC*

147:3 sarves] serves *TSII*

148:1 Act II. *Ed.*] *Om. MS*

148:2 3. *Ed.*] II. *MS* II *TSI* III
TSIIC

148:3 *Time: The same./ Scene: Ed.*]
*Time: the same./Scene: MS
Time: the same. Scene: TSIIC
Om. E1*

148:4 HEMSTOCK *TSIIC*] Hemstock
MS HEMSTOCK *is Per*

148:11 Hark] hark *TSIIC*

148:11 —Whatever—!] ~! *TSI*

148:13 —Whativer] Whativer *TSI*
Whatever *Per*

148:15 dreadful.—] ~. *TSI* ~! *TSIIC*

148:15 —What] ~ *TSI*

148:16 —I] ~ *TSI*

148:28 like.—] ~. *TSI*

148:30 tender: 'er] ~. 'Er *TSIIC*

148:37 burst.—] ~. *TSI*

148:37 Tha *has*] Tha has *TSII*

148:38 Nurse.—] ~. *TSI*

148:39 Oh] ~, *TSIIC*

149:1 —An'] ~ *TSI*

149:1 Dost] dost *TSIIC*

149:2 Nurse—?] ~? *TSI*

149:3 woman—] ~. *TSI*

149:4 work—.] ~ — *TSI*

149:6 scraïght] scraight *TSI*

149:9 *dunna*] dunna *Per*

149:9 Tha'rt a Nurse] thar't ~ nurse
TSIIC

149:10 ter—?] ~? *TSI*

149:11 Nurse] nurse *TSIIC*
149:12 —I] ~ *TSI*
149:14 am Nurse—] ~, ~, *TSIIC*
149:14 heart-sick] heartsick *TSIIC*
149:15 are. *Ed.*] ~ *MS* ~ — *TSI*
149:18 woman—!] ~. *TSI*
149:19 —What] ~ *TSI*
149:19 Nurse—?] ~? *TSI*
149:26 ax—. Is] ~ — ~ *TSI* ~ —is *TSIIC*
149:29 you—Don't] ~; don't *TSIIC*
149:30 —Then] ~ *TSI*
149:30 Hemstock—] ~, *TSI*
149:31 Baroness'] Baroness's *TSIIC*
149:32 —How] ~ *TSI*
149:33 Swimmy] Swimming *TSI*
149:33 like;—] ~:— *TSI* ~ — *TSIIC*
149:34 down.—There *Ed.*] ~.—there *MS* ~ —there *TSI*
149:39 awhile] a while *TSIIC*
150:2 Spoilin' 's] Spoilin's *TSI* Spoilin' is *TSIIC*
150:2 Nurse—] ~, *TSI*
150:3 Hemstock.] ~? *TSIIC*
151:3 *Time: The Ed.*] Time: the *MS* *Time: The TSI* Time: The *TSII* It is the *TSIIC* Time: it is the *Per* The *E1*
151:3 *succeeding TSIIC*] succeeding *MS after E1*
151:4 *Scene: TSIIC*] Scene: *MS Om. E1*
151:15 night—] ~. *TSIIC*
151:16 sleep—?] ~? *TSIIC*
151:17 *you*] you *TSI*
151:18 morning—?] ~? *TSI*
151:19 battle—] ~. *TSI*
151:21 I———I.—But] ~ ——— ~ ——. ~ *TSI* ~ ——— ~ ———. ~ *TSII* ~ — ~ —but *TSIIC*
151:22 cry 'Rudolf] ~, "~ *TSIIC*
151:23 Ruge'.] ~! *TSII* ~"! *TSIIC*
151:24 The] the *TSII*
151:27 obscurely,] ~. *TSII*
151:30 —Has] ~ *TSI*
151:34 things—] ~. *TSIIC*
151:35 golosh] galosh *TSIIC*

151:36 savation] salvation *TSIIC see notes*
151:38 hat,] ~ *Per*
151:38 15/- — *MS, E1*] 15/— *TSI*
152:1 goloshes] golloshes *TSII* galoshes *TSIIC*
152:1 —What] ~ *TSI*
152:1 Baron?—] ~? *TSI*
152:3 It] it *TSIIC*
152:3 twenty one] twenty-one *TSI*
152:4 penny—] ~. *TSIIC*
152:5 15/- *MS, E1*] 15/ *TSI*
152:5 —16] ~ *TSI*
152:5 18/6,] 18/6 *Per*
152:6 19, 20—] 19. 20— *TSI* 19.20— *TSII* 19.20 *TSIIC* 19,20. *Per* 19, 20. *E1*
152:6 *(Conning): Ed.*] (conning) *MS* (counting) *TSI (Counting.) TSIIC see notes*
152:6 —And] ~ *TSI*
152:6 Twenty one] Twenty-one *TSI*
152:8 Baroness *MSC*] Baron *MS see note on* 142:27
152:9 —Hark!—] ~! *TSI*
152:11 see—] ~. *TSIIC*
152:15 Goodmorning] Good morning *TSIIC*
152:17 golosh] galosh *TSIIC*
152:19 No] ~, *TSIIC*
152:21 brushing.—And] ~ — ~ *TSI* ~ —and *TSIIC*
152:22 golosh] galosh *Per*
152:22 hurt.—] ~. *TSI*
152:25 kitchen—] ~. *TSI*
152:25 heard] hear *TSII*
152:27 *Exit. TSIIC*] exit *MS* EXIT *TSI Exit* BARONESS *E1*
152:33 Baron—] ~, *TSIIC*
152:35 No] ~, *TSI*
152:37 father—] ~. *TSI*
152:39 them, to . . . mercy over] *Om. TSI*
153:1 —You] ~ *TSI*
153:5 pull] putt *TSII* put *TSIIC*
153:5 land—?] ~? *TSIIC*
153:6 stomach—.] ~. *TSI*

153:7 No] ~, *TSI*
153:9 Throttle-ha'penny'.] ~! *TSII*
　　　 ~!" *TSIIC*
153:10 Catch] "~ *TSIIC*
153:10 'Throttle-ha'penny'.—]
　　　 'Throttle-ha'penny'— *TSI*
　　　 Throttle-ha'penny"— *TSIIC*
　　　 Trottle-ha'penny"— *E1*
153:12 *so*] so *TSII*
153:16 Oh] ~, *TSIIC*
153:18 Baker—] ~, *TSIIC*
153:20 *shall*] shall *TSII*
153:21 dining-room *MS*, *E1*] dining
　　　 room *TSIIC*
153:24 —Good morning] ~ ~, *TSI*
153:26 Stand *there*] Stand there *TSII*
153:31 Sir] sir *TSIIC*
153:33 mine.'] ~!' *TSI* ~!" *TSIIC*
153:35 Baron—] ~, *TSII*
153:39 —On] ~ *TSI*
154:4 *Sir*] sir *TSIIC*
154:6 know——?] ~—? *TSIIC*
154:7 Ruge'—no] ~"? No *TSIIC*
154:15 her?] ~! *TSI*
154:19 Sir] sir *TSIIC*
154:23 Sir] sir *TSIIC*
154:23 maid.] ~? *TSIIC*
154:25 Sir] sir *TSIIC*
154:27 me—!!] ~! *TSIIC*
154:28 Baron!!!] ~! *TSIIC*
154:31 Oh] ~, *TSI*
154:31 Bowers—!] ~! *TSIIC*
154:33 Sir] sir *TSIIC*
154:35 untimely—] ~. *TSI*
154:40 kiss—?] ~? *TSI*
155:1 Then Sir] ~, sir *TSIIC*
155:3 surprising,—] ~ — *TSI*
155:5 —Ah] ~ *TSI*
155:6 man] men *TSII*
155:14 *you*] you *TSII*
155:14 —you] You *TSI*
155:15 are.] ~? *TSIIC*
155:19 chorister—?—] ~?— *TSI* ~?
　　　 TSIIC
155:21 But—] ~ *TSIIC*
155:21 —What] ~ *TSI*
155:21 maid—?] ~? *TSI*
155:22 care!—] ~! *TSI*

155:22 a married *TSIIC*] married a
　　　 MS
155:26 a—] ~ *TSI*
155:26 *will* ... *will*] will ... will *TSII*
155:26 'useless'] ~ *TSIIC*
155:27 Baron!!] ~! *TSIIC*
155:28 Sir,] sir, *TSIIC*
155:31 Nay] ~, *TSIIC*
155:32 Sir] sir *TSIIC*
155:32 failure:] ~, *TSI*
155:32 honor] honour *E1*
155:34 No] ~, *TSIIC*
155:35 No] ~, *TSIIC*
155:35 failed—] ~.— *TSII* ~.
　　　 TSIIC
155:36 Greenway—] ~. *TSIIC*
155:38 sentence—.] ~ —— *TSI* ~ —
　　　 TSIIC
155:40 Ah] ~, *TSIIC*
156:2 Rachel—] ~, *TSI*
156:5 *Will*] Will *TSII*
156:7 Sir] sir *TSIIC*
156:8 honor] honour *E1*
156:10 me—?] ~? *TSI*
156:11 morning] ~, *TSI*
156:11 Sir.—And *Ed.*] ~.—and *MS*
　　　 ~ —and *TSI* sir—and *TSIIC*
156:12 (*Exit—and* RACHEL.) *Ed.*]
　　　 (exit—and Rachel) *MS*
　　　 (EXIT—AND RACHEL) *TSI*
　　　 (*He and Rachel leave.*) *TSIIC*
　　　 (*He and* RACHEL *leave.*) *Per*
156:14 —Nurse] ~ *TSI*
156:15 racketty] rackety *E1*
156:16 Greenhills] Greenhill *TSIIC*
156:18 —she] she *TSI* She *TSIIC*
156:18 old.—] ~. *TSI* ~? *Per*
156:25 —Ah] ~ *TSI*
156:26 —I] ~ *TSI*
156:32 creatures—] ~. *TSI*
156:33 Ah] ~, *TSIIC*
156:34 Hemstock—.] ~. *TSI*
156:40 —You] ~ *TSI*
156:40 *should*] should *TSII*
157:1 There Baron,] ~ ~. *TSII* ~,
　　　 ~. *TSIIC*
157:15 Ah!—] ~! *TSI*
157:15 Sir] sir *TSIIC*

157:16 know no ruffian.] know, no. *TSI*
157:17 blow?—] ~? *TSI*
157:21 An' it] An't *TSII*
157:21 gen] gin *TSIIC*
157:22 Sir . . . Sir] sir . . . sir *TSIIC*
157:23 *make*] make *TSII*
157:28 such. Sir,] ~, Sir, *TSII* ~, sir; *TSIIC*
157:32 women.] ~? *TSIIC*
157:35 was] wan *TSII*
158:1 Sir] sir *TSIIC*
158:7 gizzard——] ~ — *TSI*
158:10 NURSE: I . . . *men*, Baron. *Ed.*] Nurse: ~ . . . ~, ~. *MS* NURSE: ~ . . . ~, ~. *TSI Om. TSII*
158:11 BARON: Baroness, speak. *Ed.*] Baron: ~, ~. *MS Om. TSI*
158:12 BARONESS *Ed.*] Baroness *MS* BARONESS *TSI* NURSE *TSII* NURSE *TSIIC*
158:12 *was*] was *TSII*
158:13 wasn't] wan't *TSII*
158:17 yourself] youself *TSII*
158:18 ower] over *TSII*
158:18 and] and it *Per*
158:25 —she] She *TSIIC*
158:32 *not*] not *TSII*
158:32 Sir] sir *TSIIC*
158:33 thing—] ~; *TSIIC*
158:39 wasn't] wan't *TSII*
158:40 attack—?] ~? *TSIIC*
159:3 see—] ~? *TSIIC*
159:7 wasn't it *you*] wan't it you *TSII*
159:7 an' our] and our *TSI*
159:8 you—?] ~? *TSIIC*
159:9 —Me] ~ *TSIIC*
159:9 Susy—!!] ~? *TSIIC*
159:13 liar—?—so] ~ —? ~ *TSI* ~ —? So *TSII* ~? So *TSIIC*
159:13 liar—?] ~? *TSI*
159:14 go—] ~. *TSIIC*
159:15 Broadbanks—?] ~? *TSIIC*
159:17 spots] pots *TSII* plots *TSIIC*
159:20 No] no *TSII*
159:22 Yes] ~, *TSIIC*

159:26 *(Exit.) Ed.*] (exit) *MS* (EXIT) *TSI* (RACHEL *leaves*.) *TSIIC*
159:32 have still] still have *TSI*
159:38 colliery—] ~. *TSI*
159:39 honor] honour *E1*
159:39 *Seating Ed.*] seating *MS Seats TSII*
159:40 *desk.) P* 'My *Ed.*] desk) *P* 'My *MS* desk)/'My *TSI desk.*)/ "My *TSIIC desk.*) "My *Per*
160:2 spoken *MS, E1*] sopked *TSII* spoked *TSIIC*
160:5 fulness] fullness *E1*
160:6 bounty. *P* Your] ~. Your *TSIIC*
160:7 hand,] ~. *TSII*
160:8 (signed)] *Om. TSIIC*
160:8 Ruge'/The] ~" The *TSIIC* ~."—The *Per*
161:1 Act III. *Ed.*] *Om. MS*
161:3 *Time: TSIIC*] Time: *MS, TSII* Time: *TSI Om. E1*
161:4 *Scene: TSIIC*] Scene: *MS* Scene: *TSI Om. E1*
161:9 wouldn't] shouldn't *TSIIC*
161:10 ungrateful] an ungrateful *TSIIC*
161:10 hussy.—] ~. *TSI*
161:13 year] years *Per*
161:14 drink.—] ~. *TSI*
161:15 today.] ~? *TSIIC* to-day? *E1*
161:17 out—] ~. *TSI*
161:22 *She*'d] She'd *TSI*
161:22 ate-n] aten *TSIIC*
161:27 drippin':] ~ — *Per*
161:30 *I*] I *TSII*
161:38 —Nay] ~ *TSI*
161:39 do] so *TSII*
162:2 treatment.] treatment, Nurse: *TSI* treatment, Nurse. *TSIIC*
162:8 chapel-going . . . church] Chapel-going . . . Church *Per*
162:19 all right] alright *E1*
162:22 Nurse?—] ~, *TSIIC*
162:29 not—good] ~ ~ *TSI*
162:29 nowt—] ~, *TSII*
162:32 Nurse—] ~, *TSIIC*
162:34 Nurse—] ~, *TSI*

162:39 Soloman] Solomon *TSIIC*
163:6 didn't—] ~. *TSI*
163:9 —Shall] ~ *TSI*
163:10 Nurse.] ~? *TSIIC*
163:12 Oh *MS, TSII*] ~, *TSI,*
    TSIIC
163:12 Nobis'. *Ed.*] ~.' *MS* ~!' *TSI*
    ~." *TSIIC*
163:17 *are Ed.*] are *MS Are TSIIC*
163:23 Music] ~, *TSIIC*
163:23 die/vibrates] ~, ~ *TSI*
163:28 Good-evenin'] Good-even' *TSI*
    Good even' *TSIIC*
163:31 —Will] ~ *TSI*
163:33 No] ~, *TSIIC*
163:37 *(Exit.) Ed.*] (exit) *MS* (EXIT)
    TSI (*He leaves.*) *TSIIC*
164:1 Brother] ~, *TSII*
164:2 singing—.'—] ~'— *TSI* ~"—
    TSIIC
164:2 man—!]. ~! *TSI*
164:5 sort—?] ~? *TSI*
164:6 understand—] ~. *TSI*
164:9 'Well ... yourself—'] ~ ... ~
    — *TSI*
164:10 criticism—?] ~? *TSI*
164:18 —I] ~ *TSI*
164:22 Pears] Pear's *Per* Pears' *E1*
164:22 Soap] Soapy *TSII*
164:22 baby:] ~ — *TSI*
164:23 it'—] ~', *TSI* ~," *TSIIC*
164:23 yourself] your self *E1*
164:30 flint—] ~. *TSIIC*
164:31 *may*] may *TSII*
164:37 soon.—] ~. *TSI*
165:4 —She] ~ *TSI*
165:7 Nurse—] ~. *TSIIC*
165:10 No] ~, *TSIIC*
165:12 —You] ~ *TSI*
165:13 —It] ~ *TSI*
165:18 be,] ~ *TSI*
165:20 amiable—.] ~ — *TSI*
165:21 particularly.—] ~. *TSI* ~?
    TSIIC
165:27 —I] ~ *TSIIC*
165:28 Wilcox—] ~. *TSI*
165:29 company—] ~. *TSIIC*
165:30 Arthur. You] ~, you *TSII*

165:32 I] I *TSII*
165:35 you—] ~. *TSI*
165:37 may.—] ~. *TSI*
166:1 —On] ~ *TSI*
166:6 I] I *TSII*
166:10 *You*] You *TSII*
166:13 7.0 and 9.0 *TSI*] 7·0 ~ 9·0 *MS*
    7 ~ 9 *TSIIC* seven ~ nine *Per*
166:13 p.m. *MS, E1*] P.M. *TSIIC*
    P. M. *Per*
166:16 *usual*] usual *TSII*
166:17 —This] ~ *TSI*
166:23 see.—] ~. *TSI*
166:23 Goodnight ... Goodnight]
    Good night ... Good night *Per*
166:25 life-long] lifelong *E1*
166:25 happiness—] ~. *TSI*
166:26 Goodnight] Good night *Per*
166:26 *Exit. TSIIC*] exit *MS* EXIT
    TSI Exit DR FOULES. *E1*
166:33 Th' owd] The 'owd *TSI*
166:39 work—] ~. *TSI*
167:5 Ha.] ~! *TSIIC*
167:6 it.] ~? *TSIIC*
167:14 —Do] ~ *TSI*
167:16 Ah] ah *TSIIC*
167:17 *so*] so *TSII*
167:20 life—] ~. *TSI*
167:27 no] not *TSII*
167:30 heart broken] heartbroken
    TSI
167:31 supper-time *MS, E1*] ~, *TSI*
    suppertime *TSIIC*
167:38 Women as] Woman is *TSIIC*
168:4 die—what] ~. What *TSIIC*
168:4 else.] ~? *TSIIC*
168:5 Oh] ~, *TSIIC*
168:6 *she*] she *TSII*
168:10 *he*] he *TSII*
168:10 anybody] everybody *TSIIC*
168:10 truth?—] ~? *TSI*
168:10 He wouldna—] *Om. TSIIC*
168:13 I?—] ~? *TSI*
168:13 dam] dam' *TSIIC*
168:15 Oh] ~, *TSIIC*
168:15 Hemstock—] ~. *TSI*
168:16 *is*] is *TSII*
168:20 Hell] hell *Per*

168:21 pigeon—] ~. *TSI*

168:26 All right] ~ ~, *TSIIC* Alright, *E1*

168:29 All right] ~ ~, *TSIIC* Alright, *E1*

168:32 has] had *TSII*

168:35 All right—say] ~ ~. Say *TSIIC* Alright. Say *E1*

168:36 more—] ~, *TSI*

168:39 All right,—] ~ ~ — *TSIIC* Alright— *E1*

169:3 occasions] occasion *TSIIC*

169:4 No] ~, *TSIIC*

170:1 IV. *Ed.*] IV. / Scene 1 *MS* IV / Scene 1 *TSI* IV / *Scene 1 Per* IV *E1*

170:2 *Time: TSIIC*] Time: *MS Om. E1*

170:2 *succeeding TSIIC*] succeeding *MS after E1*

170:2 *scene: third Ed.*] scene: third *MS scene. It is the third TSII*

170:3 *Scene: TSIIC*] Scene: *MS Om. E1*

170:7 very] away *Per*

170:8 *red eyed TSIIC*] red eyed *MS* red eyes *TSI red-eyed Per*

170:8 wasn't] wan't *TSII*

170:9 wasted.] ~? *TSIIC*

170:11 that: she] ~: She *TSII* ~. She *Per*

170:12 —But] ~ *TSI*

170:14 th'] the *TSI*

170:18 funny-tempered:] ~, *TSIIC*

170:19 roll] rool *TSII*

170:21 No—hated her—] ~, ~ ~; *TSIIC*

170:21 used] used her *TSIIC*

170:25 clothesline] ~, *TSI*

170:30 dreadful!—] ~! *TSI*

170:35 Don't you.] Don't, *TSIIC*

170:35 scar'd] scared *Per*

170:38 *starting Ed.*] starting *MS staring TSII*

171:2 Patty—!] ~! *TSI*

171:3 for] fer *TSII*

171:4 I.] ~? *TSIIC*

171:8 sin'—] ~, *TSI*

171:8 we,] ~ *Per*

171:8 Nurse.] ~? *TSIIC*

171:10 Nurse.] ~? *TSIIC*

171:16 frozzen] frozen *TSIIC*

171:16 mornin'.] ~ — *TSII*

171:18 *panchion TSIIC*] panchion *MS* pancheon *Per*

171:21 *panchion TSIIC*] panchion *MS* pancheon *Per*

171:26 —Best] ~ *TSI*

171:26 alone.—They] ~ — ~ *TSI* ~ —they *TSIIC*

171:31 Nurse.] ~? *TSIIC*

171:34 thaïgh] thaigh *TSI*

172:1 —muck] —much *TSI* Muck *TSIIC*

172:3 altered—] ~. *TSI*

172:4 in—] ~. *TSI*

172:6 *does*] does *TSII*

172:6 finicking] finicky *TSIIC*

172:7 time—] ~. *TSII*

172:10 *is*] is *TSII*

172:11 appalling—] ~. *TSIIC*

172:14 keep—.] ~ — *TSI* ~. *TSIIC*

172:15 —So] ~ *TSI*

172:16 that—if] ~. If *TSIIC*

172:20 me:] ~; *TSIIC*

172:23 —I] ~ *TSIIC*

172:25 one—not] ~. Not *TSIIC*

172:26 Ha.—] ~. *TSI*

172:26 —I] ~ *TSI*

172:27 still—she] ~. She *TSI*

172:30 —I] ~ *TSI*

172:32 bed-post] bed post *TSII* bedpost *TSIIC* bed-/ post *E1*

172:35 sometimes—poor] ~ —Poor *TSII* ~. Poor *TSIIC*

172:37 Oh] ~, *TSIIC*

173:4 up—] ~, *TSIIC*

173:6 Baroness—what] ~! What *TSIIC*

173:10 Baroness—] ~; *TSIIC*

172:13 —I] ~ *TSI*

173:13 there—] ~. *TSIIC*

173:14 father.] ~? *TSIIC*

173:15 and] *Om. TSIIC*

173:18 me.—] ~. *TSI*

173:20 time—] ~. *TSIIC*

173:20 go—] ~. *TSII*
173:21 'were ... delirious'] ~ ... ~ *TSIIC*
173:24 call—] ~. *TSIIC*
173:24 Goodnight] ~, *TSIIC* Good night, *Per*
173:24 *Exit. TSIIC*] exit *MS* EXIT *TSI Exit* NURSE. *E1*
173:28 Yes—] ~, *TSI*
173:30 work—?—] ~? *TSI*
173:31 —Things] ~ *TSI*
173:37 —You] ~ *TSI*
173:38 day.—] ~. *TSI*
174:3 *(Tears)*: *Ed.*] (tears): *MS (Tears.) TSIIC (She cries.) E1*
174:9 nedna] needna *TSII*
174:13 —Are] ~ *TSI*
174:15 know] knew *TSI*
174:16 you] *Om. TSII*
174:21 —Oh] ~ *TSI*
174:22 *(Tears.) Ed.*] (tears) *MS Om. TSIIC*
174:27 Harry—] ~. *TSIIC*
174:33 some day—] someday— *TSI* someday, *TSIIC*
174:33 shall:—] ~. *TSI*
174:35 —But] ~ *TSI*
174:36 —An'] ~ *TSI*
174:37 do—] ~. *TSI*
174:40 frozzen ... frozzen] frozen ... frozen *TSIIC*
175:1 Rachel—?] ~? *TSIIC*
175:2 What—?] ~? *TSIIC*
175:6 Yes—] ~ *Per* ~, *E1*
175:6 —Come] ~ *TSI*
175:7 *She weeps. Lighting a candle, she Ed.*] she weeps. Lighting a candle, she *MS* she weeps, lighting a candle, she *TSI She lights a candle, TSIIC*
175:9 *(Enter* MRS SMALLEY.*) Ed.*] *Om. MS Enter* SUSY. *TSIIC*
175:10 I s'd] Is'd *TSI* Ia'd *TSII* I'd *TSIIC*
175:10 never] *Om. TSIIC*
175:11 'ouse] 'house *TSI* house *E1*
175:11 em'py] empty *TSI*
175:11 —Oh] ~ *TSI*

175:11 Goodness!—] ~! *TSI* goodness! *TSIIC*
175:13 *red-eyed Ed.*] red-eyed *MS* red-/ eyes *TSI* red eyes *TSII with red eyes TSIIC*
175:14 —Oh] ~ *TSI*
175:15 Yes—did] ~. Did *TSIIC*
175:19 —Is] ~ *TSI*
175:20 —no,] —No, *TSI* No, *TSIIC*
175:20 grumpy—] ~, *TSIIC*
175:21 What—have] ~? Have *TSIIC*
175:23 it—what] ~ —What *TSI* ~. What *TSIIC*
175:23 Arthur—?] ~? *TSI*
175:26 but—] but *TSI* but what? *TSIIC*
175:27 —has] Has *TSIIC*
175:27 —our] Our *TSIIC*
175:29 Yes—] ~, *TSI*
175:33 fat, he's] ~. He's *TSIIC*
175:37 *Lady*] lady *TSII* lady *Per*
175:38 Well—] ~, *TSIIC*
176:5 whifft.—] snifft. *TSI* sniff. *TSIIC*
176:6 No—] ~, *TSIIC*
176:6 th'] the *TSII*
176:7 says.—] ~. *TSI*
176:12 Yes—] ~, *TSIIC*
176:15 Yes—] ~, *TSIIC*
176:15 me. *TSIIC*] ~ *MS* ~ — *TSI*
176:17 OO] Oh *TSIIC*
176:19 Look—] ~, *TSIIC*
176:19 table.—] ~. *TSI*
176:21 the] tha *Per*
176:23 *shrieks— Ed.*] shrieks— *MS* shrieks *TSII* more shrieks. *TSIIC*
176:27 Harry—] ~! *TSIIC*
176:28 up!] ~? *TSI*
176:29 it?—] ~? *TSI*
176:30 what] that *E1*
176:34 ter] ther *TSII*
176:36 what's] What's *TSI*
176:37 Rachel—!] ~! *TSIIC*
176:39 it?—] ~? *TSI*
176:39 it.] ~! *TSIIC*
177:2 you—] ~ —. *TSIIC* ~ —— *E1*

177:3 say.] ~? *TSIIC*
177:5 an'] and *TSI*
177:5 pounds—] ~ *TSIIC*
177:7 it] *Om. TSII*
177:10 you:—cats,] ~, ~ *TSIIC*
177:13 Indeed] ~, *TSIIC*
177:19 —But] ~ *TSI*
177:20 shanna] shan't *TSI*
177:21 Oh] ~, *TSIIC*
177:22 you. *TSI*] ~ *MS* ~? *TSIIC*
177:22 mistaken—it's] ~. It's *TSIIC*
177:24 Oh] ~, *TSIIC*
177:28 will: Couldna] ~, couldna *TSI*
177:32 clawk] claw *TSIIC*
177:34 will.] ~? *TSIIC*
177:35 here.—] ~. *TSI*
177:38 What!—] ~! *TSIIC*
177:38 Now] ~, *Per*
177:39 —Hast] ~ *TSIIC*
177:39 all?—] ~? *TSI*
178:5 If] *Om. TSIIC*
178:6 thaïgh] thaigh *TSI* tha *TSIIC*
178:6 'snap'. *TSI*] '~.' *MS* "~"?
    TSIIC
178:6 'Snap'] 'snap' *TSI* "snap"
    TSIIC
178:6 Nurse,—say] ~. Say *TSIIC*
178:7 'snap'.—] '~'— *TSI* "~."
    TSIIC
178:12 proper,—] ~ — *TSI*
178:12 lardy-da—oh] ~. Oh *TSI*
178:13 yes— —] Yes— *TSI* yes— *TSIIC*
178:16 all right] alright *EI*
178:18 No—] ~; *TSIIC*
178:22 pound] pounds *TSII*
178:23 is—] ~, *TSIIC*
178:25 *have*] have *TSII*
178:27 *shan't*] shan't *TSII*
178:27 Arthur:] ~; *TSIIC*
178:29 *your*] your *TSII*
178:34 brass] ~, *Per*
178:36 mandoline] mandolin *Per*
178:37 tickling—he] ~. He *TSIIC*
179:3 Cuckoo!—] ~! *TSI*
179:5 *(Curtain) Ed.*] *Om. MS*
    (CURTAIN) *TSI*
    (CURTAIN) TSIIC CURTAIN
    EI

180:2 Scene 1. *Ed.*] *Om. MS* SCENE
    I *EI*
180:3 *Time: TSIIC*] Time: *MS*
    Time: TSI Om. EI
180:4 *Place: TSIIC*] Place: *MS*
    Place: TSI Om. EI
180:4 *Porch Ed.*] Porch *MS porch*
    TSII the porch Per The porch
    EI
180:4 *Greenstone Ed.*] Greenstone *MS*
    Grunstom TSI
180:5 due] *Om. EI*
180:5 service. *Ed.*] service *MS* service.
    Mourners are leaving the church.
    TSIIC
180:10 2ND *Ed.*] 2*nd MS* 3RD *TSI* 3RD
    TSIIC 3rd *Per*
180:10 it.] ~? *TSIIC*
180:11 him,] ~ *TSII*
180:14 *(Exeunt.) Ed.*] (exeunt) *MS.*
    Exit 1ST and 2ND MOURNERS.
    EI
180:15 —No] ~ *TSI*
180:17 Sunday—they] ~. They
    TSIIC
180:20 *Exeunt. TSIIC*] exeunt *MS*
    Exit SUSY and 3RD MOURNER.
    EI
180:21 good—] ~. *TSIIC*
180:26 it—?] ~? *TSIIC*
180:27 axed] *Om. TSII*
180:27 Broadbanks—?] ~? *TSIIC*
180:29 it—what] ~. What *TSIIC*
180:31 dunno—the] ~. The *TSIIC*
180:34 *Exeunt. TSIIC*] exeunt *MS*
    Exit 4TH and 5TH MOURNERS.
    EI
180:35 'a] a *Per*
180:37 *wor*] wor *TSI*
181:3 thaïgh] thaigh *TSI* tha *TSIIC*
181:4 *(Exit.) Ed.*] (exit) *MS Exit*
    HARRY. *EI*
181:5 THE BAKER *Ed.*] Bowers *MS*
    BOWERS *TSI* BAKER *TSIIC*
181:5 morning] ~, *TSIIC*
181:7 for—] ~. *TSIIC*
181:8 Yes—] ~, *TSIIC*
181:10 of] for *TSI*

181:10 Why] ~, *Per*
181:11 mother-in-law *TSI*] mother in law *MS*
181:14 *frock coat Ed.*] frock coat *MS* frock Coat *TSII* frock-coated *TSIIC frock-coated Per*
181:18 Well] ~, *TSIIC*
181:18 *ham*] ham *TSI* am *TSIIC*
181:19 you—] ~. *TSI*
181:23 Hezekiah. You've] ~; you've *TSIIC*
181:24 Uncle] uncle *TSIIC*
181:24 that—] ~. *TSIIC*
181:26 thing—you know—] ~, ~ ~. *TSIIC*
181:28 Uncle ... Uncle] uncle ... uncle *TSIIC*
181:28 Pop-shop] pop-shop *TSIIC*
181:29 sell.—] ~. *TSI*
181:29 Goodmorning] Good morning *TSIIC*
181:30 Goodmorning.—] Goodmorning,— *TSI* Good morning. *TSIIC*
181:37 *in Ed.*] in *MS into the TSIIC*
181:37 —Oh] —oh *TSIIC*
181:38 you.] ~? *TSIIC*
181:39 BARONESS, *Ed.*] Baroness, *MS with* BARONESS *TSIIC*
182:3 Sir] sir *TSIIC*
182:4 promise—he] ~. He *TSI*
182:5 Rachel—] ~. *TSI*
182:6 Sir] sir *TSIIC*
182:6 word—!] ~ — *TSI* ~? *TSIIC*
182:12 Church—it] ~. ~ *TSIIC* ~. It *Per*
182:13 Church—] ~. *TSIIC*
182:16 My Lady] my lady *TSIIC*
182:17 Nurse?—] ~!— *TSI* ~! *TSIIC*
182:26 denyin'—] ~. *TSIIC*
182:26 had he Nurse?] *Om. TSIIC*
182:31 you Sir!] ~, sir! *TSIIC* ~ sir! *E1*
182:32 —Ah!—] ~! *TSIIC*
182:33 Go—Don't stir Sir] go—don't ~, sir *TSIIC*
182:36 die,] ~. *TSII*

182:38 church] Church *TSI*
182:39 —oh Uncle] —Oh Uncle *TSII* Oh uncle *TSIIC*
183:3 him,] ~ — *TSI*
183:4 on.—] ~ — *TSI* ~. *TSIIC*
183:6 —I] ~ *TSIIC*
183:7 Sir] sir *TSIIC*
183:9 money—though] ~. Though *TSII*
183:16 money.] ~? *TSIIC*
183:17 *some*] some *TSII*
183:20 Sir] sir *TSI*
184:1 Act V. *Ed.*] *Om. MS, TSIIC* ACT V *TSI*
184:2 *Time: The same. Ed.*] Time: The Same *MS* Time: The same. *TSI* Time: the same. *TSIIC Om. E1*
184:2 *Scene: TSIIC*] Scene: *MS Scene: TSI Om. E1*
184:6 yourself?—] ~? *TSI*
184:9 Hisn] His'n *TSI*
184:10 —Mine!—Why] ~! ~, *TSIIC*
184:15 What—?] ~? *TSIIC*
184:18 did—an' he agreed.—] ~, ~ he's ~. *TSIIC*
184:25 —An'] ~ *TSIIC*
184:27 on—?] ~? *TSIIC*
184:30 I'll] I'll *TSI*
184:32 *feyther*] feyther *TSI* father *TSII*
185:14 quiet—like] quiet-like *TSIIC*
185:14 by mysen] by unpen *TSI Om. TSIIC*
185:15 like a moudiwarp] like a mondiwarp *TSI Om. TSIIC*
185:18 make] mak *TSII* mak' *TSIIC*
185:19 dead-o-night] dead o'night *Per*
185:24 quiet—Rachel—?] ~, ~. *TSIIC*
185:25 mind;—] ~ — *TSIIC*
185:26 though—] ~, *TSIIC*
185:27 people—] ~. *TSIIC*
185:39 me—] ~, *TSIIC*
186:8 —I] ~ *TSII*
186:8 ha'] ha *TSI*
186:10 you.——] ~ — *TSIIC*
186:14 yesterday—] ~. *TSIIC*

186:16 it? *TSI*] ~ *MS*
186:21 ax] asc *TSI* ask *TSIIC*
186:21 *me*] me *TSI*
186:23 wonder.] ~? *TSIIC*
187:1 Act V. *Ed.*] *Om. MS, TSIIC*
ACT V *TSI*
187:3 *Time: The same. Ed.*] Time: the
Same. *MS Time*: The Same.
TSI Time: The same. *TSII*
Time: the same. TSIIC Om. E₁
187:4 *Scene: TSIIC*] Scene: *MS*
Scene: *TSI Om. E₁*
187:5 speak Sir] ~, sir *TSIIC*
187:7 I!] ~? *TSI*
187:8 not—] ~, *TSIIC*
187:11 done—?] ~? *TSIIC*
187:12 done—!!] ~! *TSIIC*
187:14 ever] never *TSII*
187:14 wasn't *Ed.*] was n't *MS* wan't
TSI
187:14 right—] ~. *TSIIC*
187:15 Sir—] sir, *TSIIC*
187:19 Rachel—?] ~? *TSIIC*
187:20 Yes] ~, *TSIIC*
187:21 me] see *TSII*
187:21 for—] ~ *TSI*
187:22 Nurse—?] ~? *TSIIC*
187:24 Scoundrel—Imposter] ~! ~
TSIIC ~! Impostor *Per*
187:26 likes] lives *TSII* loves *TSIIC*
187:31 Now] ~, *TSIIC*
187:33 back—] ~. *TSIIC*
187:34 look-out] lookout *TSI*
187:35 Rachel,—Ah] ~! ~, *TSIIC*
187:36 Now—] ~, *TSIIC*
187:37 —Of] ~ *TSIIC*
188:11 not—] ~. *TSIIC*
188:11 myself—] ~. *TSIIC*
188:11 me—] ~. *TSI*
188:14 you,—] ~ — *TSI*
188:15 sleep—'] ~ — *TSI* ~. *TSII*
~." *TSIIC*
188:16 What!—] ~! *TSI*
188:17 hear.] ~? *TSIIC*
188:19 hear—] ~ *TSIIC*
188:25 up—] ~. *TSI*
188:26 debateable] debatable *TSIIC*
188:26 tit-bit—!] ~! *TSI* ~. *TSIIC*

188:27 matter—speak] ~. Speak *TSI*
~. Speak, *TSIIC*
188:27 Nurse—] ~. *TSI*
188:29 raving—and] ~. And *TSI*
188:31 Oh but,] ~, ~ *TSIIC*
188:31 here—] ~. *TSI*
188:32 Silence] ~, *Per*
188:32 Sir] Sr *TSII* sir *TSIIC*
188:34 Well—] ~, *TSI*
188:38 Church] church *Per*
189:1 *are*] are *TSII*
189:3 Baroness.] ~? *TSIIC*
189:8 THE BAKER: Crozzled up. *Ed.*]
Bowers: Crozzled up. *MS*
BOWERS: Crozzled up. *TSI*
BOWERS: Grozzeld up. *TSII*
Om. TSIIC
189:9 Sir] sir *TSII*
189:11 *must*] must *TSII*
189:14 An'] And *TSII*
189:17 Enough—] ~, *TSIIC*
189:18 Sir] sir *TSIIC*
189:19 Von Hude—?] von Huge—?
TSI von Ruge? *TSIIC see*
notes
189:22 Sunday—] ~. *TSI*
189:23 consent—] ~. *TSIIC*
189:24 a] *Om. TSII*
189:24 refutation—] ~. *TSI*
189:28 done—] ~. *TSIIC*
189:37 Sunday? *TSIIC*] ~ *MS* ~.
TSI
189:40 we be axed in church] we be
axed in church with me *TSII*
you be axed in church with me
TSIIC
189:40 Sunday.] ~? *TSII*
190:1 enough.] ~! *TSIIC*
190:1 this.] ~! *TSIIC*
190:7 ladies—'Yes!'] ~ '~!' *TSI* ~,
"~"! *TSIIC*
190:8 'Yes!'] '~'. *TSI* "~"! *TSIIC*
190:13 Away—away—] ~! Away!
TSIIC
190:14 'As You Like It'. *Ed.*] '~ ~ ~
~' *MS* '~ ~ ~ ~'— *TSI* '~
you ~ it.' *TSII* "~ You ~ It."
TSIIC

190:15   it—] ~, *TSIIC*
190:15   not—] ~. *TSI*
190:18   father] Father *Per*
190:29   'As You Like It'. *Ed.*] '~ ~ ~

~' *MS* '~ you like it.' *TSII*
"~ You Like It." *TSIIC*
190:31   *(Curtain) Ed.*] *Om. MS*
         CURTAIN TSIIC

The Married Man

MS   = Autograph MS (Roberts E229a)
TSI = Ribbon and carbon copy TS (Roberts E229d)
TSII = Corrected ribbon and carbon copy TS (setting copy for periodical
         publication) (no Roberts no.)
Per = *Virginia Quarterly Review*, xvi (Autumn 1940), 523–47
E1   = *Complete Plays* (Heinemann, 1965)

Silent emendations

1 *E1* hyphenates words not hyphenated by DHL or in the other sources
('tomorrow', 'tonight', 'drawing room', 'dining room', 'smoke room', 'dressing
gown', 'goodbye'); 'all right' becomes 'alright' in *E1*. DHL's practice has been
preserved and these readings are not recorded unless they are part of another
variant.

2 British and American variants (e.g. 'behaviour' and 'behavior', 'humour' and
'humor', 'moustache' and 'mustache', etc.) are not recorded unless they form
part of another variant.

193:3   [*A bedroom in* MRS PLUM*'s
        cottage, shared by* DR GEORGE
        GRAINGER *and* WILLIAM
        BRENTNALL. *Both men are
        dressing.*] *Ed.*] *Om. MS*
        (SCENE: A bedroom shared by
        Grainger and Brentnall in the
        cottage of Mrs. Plum. Both
        men are dressing. Grainger
        goes to the door and calls to
        Mrs. Plum.) *TSI*
193:8   got.] ~? *TSI*
193:13 on] *Om. TSII*
193:18 it.] ~? *TSI*
193:19 cock-robin] cock robin *TSIIC*
193:21 Eee] Gee *TSI*
193:23 you] *Om. TSII*
193:23 *that*] that *TSI*
193:25 Eee] Gee *TSI*
193:28 Hee—hi—Hark] Hee-
        hee—hark *TSIIC*
193:29 Grainger.] ~? *TSI*
194:1   come, isn't] ~. isn't *TSII* ~.
        Isn't *TSIIC*

194:1   he] ~, *TSI*
194:6   Eee] Gee *TSI*
194:6   —But] ~ *TSII*
194:8   —Here] ~ *TSI*
194:11 *Exit. TSIIC*] exit *MS Exit* MRS
        PLUM. *E1*
194:12 yours, you] ~. You *TSI*
194:15 job.] ~? *TSI*
194:26 Well] ~, *TSIIC*
194:28 I] ~, *TSIIC*
194:35 emotion.] ~? *TSI*
195:1   just] first *TSI*
195:3   bachelor.] ~? *TSIIC*
195:13 Billy] Bill *TSII*
195:14 be.] ~? *TSI*
195:15 —come] —Come *TSI* Come
        TSII
195:19 you—] ~? *TSIIC*
195:21 Yes] Yis *TSIIC*
195:23 Sally's—] ~. *TSI*
195:29 I] ~, *TSIIC*
195:30 Oh] ~, *TSIIC*
195:30 goin'] going' *TSII* going
        TSIIC

195:31 tittivating] titivating *E1*
195:31 up.] ~? *TSIIC*
195:37 *fine*] fine *TSI see notes*
196:1 be] to be *TSI*
196:6 dam] damn *Per*
196:7 know—] ~. *TSI*
196:10 girls.] ~? *TSI*
196:16 Magneer. *TSIIC*] ~? *MS see notes*
196:17 no, nothing] ~. ~ *TSI* ~. Nothing *Per*
196:18 Oh] oh *TSIIC*
196:20 Thanks, *TSI*] ~; *MS*
196:26 do,] ~. *TSI*
196:30 jacket.] ~? *TSI*
196:31 God] ~, *E1*
196:34 *(Curtain) Ed.*] *Om. MS CURTAIN Per*
197:2 *A E1*] A *MS SCENE: A TSIIC*
197:6 *—in morning coat Ed.*] —in morning coat *MS, TSII Om. TSIIC*
197:18 often—] ~. *TSI*
197:22 It's] That's *TSIIC*
197:22 right—] ~. *TSI*
197:24 what is] what's *TSI*
197:25 Oh] oh *TSIIC*
197:31 London—!] ~! *TSI*
197:36 —that] That *TSIIC*
197:37 but—. Oh] ~ — ~ *TSI* ~ —oh *TSIIC*
198:23 gone.] ~? *TSI*
198:25 engaged—] ~. *TSI*
198:32 all.—] ~ — *TSI*
198:33 the 'George,] the '~," *TSII* "The ~," *TSIIC*
198:39 Tat-ta] Ta-ta *TSIIC*
198:40 *Exit. TSIIC*] exit *MS Exit* GRAINGER. *E1*
199:3 we] *me TSI*
199:7 *haughty Ed.*] haughty *MS* haughtily *TSIIC*
199:8 me?] ~. *TSIIC*
199:28 Oh] ~, *TSIIC*
199:28 fun.] ~! *TSIIC*
199:32 perhaps:] ~; *Per*
199:40 them.] ~? *TSI*

200:2 *Exit. TSIIC*] exit *MS Exit* ADA. *E1*
200:8 this] the *TSI*
200:9 flowers—] ~? *TSI*
200:20 say] say the *TSIIC*
200:27 yes!!] ~! *TSIIC*
200:32 yes!!] ~! *TSIIC*
200:37 chair!] ~. *E1*
200:39 Nay-nay-nay] Nay—nay—nay *TSI*
201:3 in—do—do] Om. *TSIIC*
201:5 here.] ~? *TSI*
201:10 *next Ed.*] next *MS next to TSII* next to *TSIIC*
201:19 Bless] bless *TSIIC*
201:22 Help Them] help them *TSIIC*
201:28 Ha!— ... Marriage] ~! ... marriage *TSIIC*
201:30 Grainger.] ~? *TSIIC*
201:35 marriage!] ~? *TSIIC*
201:36 there—when] ~ —When *TSI* ~. When *TSIIC*
202:6 Eh] eh *TSIIC*
202:10 Yes] Yis *Per*
202:11 Ada.] ~? *TSI*
202:18 *put Ed.*] put *MS put their TSIIC*
202:21 Your lips ... his seat): *Ed.*] ~ ~ ... Magneer (jumping in his seat): *MS Om. TSI*
202:23 Well] ~, *E1*
202:26 Excellent!—] ~! *TSI*
202:27 —you] —You *TSI You TSIIC*
202:28 Lucky] lucky *TSI*
202:31 dam] damn *TSIIC*
202:33 —no] —No *TSI No TSIIC*
202:35 Fine—how're] ~ —How're *TSII* ~. How're *TSIIC*
202:40 Grainger.] ~? *TSI*
203:1 Oh] ~, *Per*
203:1 Georgie's] George's *TSI*
203:4 be?] ~. *TSI*
203:14 Annie!] ~? *TSIIC*
203:18 thee—] ~ *TSI*
203:20 Settle] settle *TSIIC*
203:34 Oh] ~! *TSIIC*
203:34 do] Do *TSIIC*

203:40 don't.] ~! *TSIIC*
204:1 you—Sorry] ~ —sorry *TSI* ~?
Sorry *TSIIC*
204:2 hear!] ~? *TSIIC*
204:6 Who—where] ~? Where
TSIIC
204:7 cheeze] cheese *TSIIC*
204:10 No.] ~! *TSIIC*
204:11 —She] ~ *TSIIC*
204:12 that] ~, *TSIIC*
204:16 I am that! *(Bitterly.) Ed.*] I am
that! (bitterly) *MS* I am that!
(bitterly) *TSI* (*bitterly*): I am
that! *TSIIC*
204:27 Well] ~, *TSIIC*
204:32 me—] ~. *TSIIC*
204:32 will] Will *TSI*
204:33 room?—] ~? *TSIIC*
204:34 *Exit. TSIIC*] exit *MS* exit.
TSI Exit ADA. *E1*
204:35 you] ~, *TSIIC*
204:36 *Exit. TSIIC*] exit *MS* exit.
TSI Exit GRAINGER. *E1*
204:38 Brentnall.] ~? *TSIIC*
205:17 *are*] are *TSI*
205:18 big—?—] ~. *TSI*
205:27 Yes.] ~! *TSI*
205:28 Grainger—] ~, *TSI*
206:10 What] what *TSIIC*
206:16 and] And *TSI*
206:25 what is] What's *TSI* what's
TSIIC
206:34 Good-evening!— *Ed.*] ~ ┴
MS ~— *TSI* Good evening—
TSIIC
206:35 evening—] ~. *TSIIC*
206:38 —Nice] ~ *TSIIC*
207:3 any way] anyway *TSI*
207:9 *Exit. TSIIC*] exit *MS* Exit
SALLY. *E1*
207:19 Exit— *Ed.*] exit— *MS* Exit.
TSIIC Exit ANNIE. *E1*
207:20 Hell] hell *TSIIC*
207:21 Hell] hell *TSIIC*
207:22 Annie!] ~? *TSIIC*
207:31 Hell's] hell's *TSIIC*
207:38 Nothing] ~, *TSIIC*
207:40 can] ~, *TSIIC*

207:40 shanna] shanner *TSI*
208:12 *I've*] I've *TSII*
208:14 then.] ~? *TSI*
208:18 Well] ~, *TSI*
208:26 No] ~, *TSIIC*
208:31 Niver] Never *TSI*
208:32 *goodnight. Exit Ed.*] goodnight.
Exit *MS* good night, exit *TSII*
good night. Exeunt TSIIC
208:38 man] men *TSII*
209:9 living.] ~? *TSI*
209:13 No] ~, *TSIIC*
209:14 will.] ~: *TSIIC*
209:16 quick——' *Ed.*] ~———
MS ~— *TSIIC* ~—" *Per*
209:19 *(Curtain) Ed.*] End of Act II.
MS CURTAIN) *TSIIC*
CURTAIN Per CURTAIN *E1*
210:2 *The E1*] The *MS SCENE: The*
TSIIC
210:4 *NOT Ed.*] *not MS, TSIIC* not
TSII
210:4 *well-liking Ed.*] well-liking *MS*
well looking TSIIC
210:6 *leggings TSI, E1*] leggings *MS*
leggins *TSII* leggins *TSIIC*
210:8 *next TSI*] next *MS, TSII next*
to TSIIC
201:15 —Well] ~ *TSII*
210:17 *handkerchief. To Ed.*]
handkerchief to *MS*
handkerchief to TSIIC
210:20 London? Whativer] ~!
Whatever *TSI*
210:22 What] ~, *TSIIC*
210:26 yes.] ~! *TSIIC*
210:28 —Why] ~ *TSI*
210:35 you] ~, *TSI*
211:9 He . . . her. *(Laughs. Ed.*] He
. . . her (laughs) *MS* (*laughs.*):
He . . . her. *TSIIC*
211:16 Sally!] ~? *TSIIC*
211:21 *(Rhyme.) Ed.*] (rhyme) *MS*
Om. TSIIC
211:27 Charlie!] ~. *TSII*
211:29 love,] ~ *TSIIC*
211:32 down.] ~? *TSI*
211:38 Goodbye] ~, *TSIIC*

212:7 thumb!] ~. *TSIIC*
212:15 enough. But] ~, ~ *TSII* ~, but *TSIIC*
212:21 Oh] ~, *TSIIC*
212:36 —Are] ~ *TSI*
213:3 Whey-up] Whey—up *TSI*
213:5 Hark-ye] Hark—ye *TSI* Hark ye *TSIIC*
213:5 ye?—] ~! *TSIIC*
213:6 theer] there *TSIIC*
213:8 Billy!—by gosh—Billy!!] ~? By ~! ~! *TSIIC*
213:13 *suppressed Ed.*] suppressed *MS* *with suppressed TSIIC*
213:13 Oh—Oh, don't tickle.] ~, oh, ~ ~! *TSIIC*
213:14 *round Ed.*] round *MS around TSIIC*
213:15 Billy—] ~, *TSII*
213:15 gigglomania] gigglemania *TSII*
213:16 Gigglo-what] Giggolo—What *TSII* Giggolo—what *TSIIC*
213:17 Yes] ~, *TSI*
213:17 do.] ~! *TSIIC*
213:20 Don't—oh] ~! Oh *TSIIC*
213:26 for.] ~? *TSI*
213:33 lately.] ~? *TSI*
213:37 —Do] ~ *TSI*
213:39 No] ~, *TSIIC*
213:39 won't—fill] won't play any more. Fill *TSIIC*
213:39 up—] ~ *TSI*
214:1 Yes—yes—yes.] ~ ~ ~! *TSIIC* ~, ~, ~! *Per*
214:5 item!] ~. *TSI*
214:8 —Er] ~ *TSI*
214:11 ready.] ~? *TSI*
214:12 you] ~, *Per*
214:27 fond] go[?]d *TSII* good *TSIIC*
214:30 while.] ~? *TSI*
214:34 I.] ~? *TSI*
214:35 No] ~, *Per*
214:36 mean?—] ~? *TSIIC*
214:40 I?—] ~? *TSIIC*
215:10 Yes.—] ~ —— *TSI* ~ — *TSIIC*
215:31 work.] ~! *TSIIC*

215:31 off] ~, *TSI*
215:33 *they have ... and trousers. Ed.*] they have on white tennis shirts and trousers. *MS Om. TSIIC*
215:36 open—set] ~ —Set *TSI* ~? Set *TSIIC*
215:36 open] ~, *TSI*
216:1 valeta—] Valeta— *TSI* Valeta. *TSIIC*
216:8 Yes] ~, *TSIIC*
216:9 *One—two*] One—two *TSI* one—two *Per*
216:19 Well] ~, *Per*
216:31 me.] ~? *TSI*
216:35 *round TSIIC*] round *MS around Per*
216:36 Doctor] Dr. *TSIIC* Dr *E1*
216:40 me] ~, *TSIIC*
217:6 right.] ~, *TSII*
217:9 say.] ~? *TSI*
217:20 —Billy!!] — ~! *TSII* ~! *TSIIC*
217:21 *Leaves TSIIC*] leaves *MS He leaves E1*
217:24 *reels Ed.*] reels *MS reeling TSIIC*
217:24 —space] —Space *TSI* Space *TSIIC*
217:28 —how] How *TSIIC*
217:30 —no—no] No, ~ *TSIIC*
217:33 —no] —No *TSI* No *TSIIC*
217:34 than—] ~ *TSI*
217:37 you!] ~? *TSIIC*
218:4 —Can] ~ *TSIIC*
218:4 come.] come? *TSI* come in? *TSIIC*
218:12 *Exit. TSIIC*] exit *MS Exit* ELSA. *E1*
218:13 devil—!] ~ —? *TSIIC* ~ — *Per*
218:15 it.] ~! *TSIIC*
218:16 Well—*men*] ~! Men *TSIIC*
218:18 Men] *Men TSII*
218:19 OOO] Ooh *TSIIC*
218:20 *(Huge mirth.) Ed.*] (huge mirth) *MS Om. TSIIC*
218:21 —Well] ~ *TSI* ~, *Per*
218:21 *you*] you *Per*

218:22   —It's] ~ *TSII*
218:24   here] ~, *TSIIC*
218:26   Em'ler,] ~ *TSIIC*
218:31   all] ~, *TSIIC*
218:31   Grainger.] ~? *TSI*
218:34   No] ~, *TSIIC*
218:36   *and two married people, Ed.*] and two married people, *MS with a TSIIC*
218:37   —All] ~ *TSII*
218:37   Tom:] ~. *TSIIC*
218:37   that's] That's *TSII*
218:39   Ay—ay—] ~, ~, *TSIIC*
218:39   Billy!!] ~! *TSII*
219:1   tonight.] ~, *TSII*
219:7   alone.—] ~ — *Per*
219:9   charming—] ~. *TSI*
219:15   *cynical Ed.*] cynical *MS* Cynical *TSI* cynically *TSIIC*
219:36   Doctor] Dr *TSIIC*, *E1* Dr. *Per*
219:36   *holds out Ed.*] holds out *MS* holds *TSI* hold *TSII* hold *TSIIC* holds *E1*
220:6   *in TSIIC*] in *MS with Per*
221:2   *Scene: Ed.*] Scene: *MS* SCENE: *TSIIC Om. E1*
221:2   9.0 *Ed.*] 9·0 *MS* 9 *TSI* nine *TSIIC*
221:3   BRENTNALL *Ed.*] Brentnall *MS* BRENTNALL *are TSIIC*
221:5   Well ... damned,] ~, ... ~; *TSII*
221:6   strike—!] ~! *TSI*
221:11   hours—Oh—h] ~. Oh—h *TSIIC* ~. Oh-h *Per*
221:12   hours] ~, *TSIIC*
221:15   Don't] ~, *TSIIC*
221:17   blazes.] ~! *Per*
221:28   —Billy Brentnall.] ~ ~! *TSIIC*
221:35   family—] ~ *TSII* ~, *TSIIC*
221:38   says] say *TSII*
221:38   Sally:] ~, *TSI*
221:38   he's] He's *TSI*
221:38   man ... [222:3] I say] [*run on in TSIIC*]
221:39   he's] He's *TSIIC*
222:1   he] He *TSIIC*

222:3   you *Ed.*] You *MS*
222:17   bolt] belt *TSII*
222:20   bungler.—Has] ~ — ~ *TSI* ~—has *TSIIC*
222:24   *you're*] *you're TSI*
222:29   fails] failed *TSIIC*
222:30   *He's*] *He's TSI*
222:32   isn't *TSI*] is n't *MS* isn't, *TSIIC*
223:8   me!] ~? *TSIIC*
223:16   —Well] ~ *TSI* ~, *Per*
223:17   sure——] ~ — *TSIIC*
223:20   Don't] ~, *TSIIC*
223:23   you etc.] ~, etc., *TSIIC*
223:25   Well] ~, *TSIIC*
223:29   here.] ~? *TSI*
223:33   'em. *MS, TSII*] ~? *TSI*
223:39   lime light] limelight *TSIIC*
224:3   —Yes] ~ *TSI*
224:4   She's,—] ~ — *TSIIC* ~ *Per*
224:5   Jack.] ~? *TSI*
224:11   *He*] He *TSII*
224:18   *I'm*] *I'm TSI*
224:21   it's] It's *TSII*
224:22   Yes] ~, *TSIIC*
224:26   Yis—] ~. *TSI*
224:28   —and it] It *TSIIC*
224:29   Club] club *TSII*
224:32   marries] married *TSII*
224:36   Well] ~, *TSIIC*
224:38   Billy.—] ~. *TSIIC*
224:39   2.50 *TSI, E1*] 2·50 *MS* 2:50 *TSII*
225:5   —I'm] ~ *TSII*
225:5   Hall,] ~ *TSIIC*
225:5   Ashbourne,] ~ *TSI*
225:11   George-lad] George—lad *TSI*
225:15   *Exit. TSIIC*] exit *MS Exit* JACK. *E1*
225:16   —The] ~ *TSII*
225:21   yourself:] ~; *TSII*
225:21   goodnature] good nature *TSII*
225:36   ability—] ~. *TSI*
225:37   Well] ~, *Per*
225:37   a——] ~ — *TSI*
226:5   George!!] ~! *TSIIC*
226:6   George!!!] ~! *TSIIC*

226:7   blest] blessed *TSIIC*
226:10 angry!] ~? *TSIIC*
226:31 mother] Mother *TSI*
227:2   out—?] ~? *TSIIC*
227:3   go?—] ~? *TSIIC*
227:9   lot,—] ~— *TSIIC*
227:12 miserable.] ~? *TSI*
227:14 *but*] but *TSI*
227:17 get—] ~. *Per*
227:17 you ought.] *Om. Per*
227:18 No] ~, *TSIIC*
227:20 GRAINGER: When?/ ETHEL:
        TSIIC] Grainger: ~?/ Ethel:
        MS GRAINGER: ~?/
        ETHEL: *TSI Om. Per*
227:26 Why] ~, *TSIIC*
227:31 mean.] ~? *TSI*
227:32 me.] ~? *TSI*
227:33 No] ~, *TSIIC*
227:34 *fierce Ed.*] fierce *MS fiercely*
        TSIIC
227:40 me.] ~? *TSI*
228:1   him.] ~? *TSI*
228:7   smoke.] ~? *TSIIC*
228:3   BRENTNALL: That's ... ticket.
        (Aside.) Ed.] Brentnall: ~ ...
        ~. (aside) *MS* BRENTNALL:
        ~ ... ~. (aside) *TSI*
        BRENTNALL (*aside*): That's ...
        ticket. *TSIIC*
228:18 money] *money TSII money Per*
228:23 No] ~, *TSIIC*
228:25 job—?] ~.—? *TSI* ~? *TSIIC*
228:26 see.] ~— *TSIIC*
228:33 out.—] ~, *TSIIC*
228:36 *Exit TSIIC*] exit *MS Exit*
        ETHEL *E1*
229:2   to.] ~? *TSIIC*
229:4   honorably: say] ~! Say *TSII*
        honourably! Say *E1*
229:8   a——] ~— *TSIIC*
229:23 Sally?—~? *TSIIC*
229:28 you.] ~? *TSIIC*
229:29 do.] ~? *TSIIC*
229:31 Grainger?—] ~? *TSI*
229:36 happen] happened *E1*
229:38 quarrelling] quarreling
        TSIIC

229:39 half hour] half-hour *E1*
230:2   child.] ~? *TSIIC*
230:4   secret,] ~ *TSIIC*
230:5   into] in to be *Per*
230:10 me—?] ~? *TSIIC*
230:11 say—] ~ *TSIIC*
230:13 Oh] ~, *TSIIC*
230:14 about] *Om. TSI* of *TSIIC*
230:23 share.——] ~. *TSI*
230:24 daresn't, *Ed.*] dares n't, *MS*
        dare sn't *TSII* daren't *TSIIC*
230:25 —I] ~ *TSI*
230:27 minute.] ~? *TSIIC*
230:36 *danger*] danger *TSI*
230:39 you] ~, *TSI*
231:6   right] ~, *TSIIC*
231:12 Gott ... Ja!] *Gott sei dank, du*
        bist gekommen. Komm hinauf ...
        Ja! E1
231:15 Calladine——] ~— *TSI*
231:17 round—] ~. *TSI*
231:18 Magneer?—] ~— *TSIIC*
231:27 Oh—Oh] Oh-oh *TSI* Oh, oh
        Per
231:27 now. *Don't*] ~, *Don't TSII* ~,
        don't TSIIC ~ *don't Per*
231:28 white-wash] whitewash *TSIIC*
231:28 it.—] ~. *TSIIC*
231:30 others] ~. *TSIIC*
231:30 don't] Don't *Per*
231:31 baby.—] ~. *TSI*
231:35 motor-car *MS, E1*] motor car
        TSIIC
231:38 Ha!] "~!" *Per*
231:39 Ha!!] ~! *TSIIC*
232:1   ladies.—] ~. *TSI*
232:2   Sir] sir *TSIIC*
232:4   No—no—hear him!] ~, ~; ~
        ~. *TSIIC*
232:8   in] in the *TSI*
232:11 you—] ~ *TSI*
232:11 will!] ~? *TSIIC*
232:18 —not] Not *TSIIC*
232:22 Nay] ~, *TSIIC*
232:27 little. *Ed.*] ~ *MS* ~ — *TSI*
232:29 Yes] ~, *TSIIC*
232:34 think] ~, *TSIIC* ~: *E1*
232:34 extent.] ~? *TSIIC*

233:2   wife] ~ — *TSI*
233:6   Yes—] ~, *Per*
233:6   —If] ~ *TSI*
233:11   certainly—] ~ *TSI*
233:13   Ha!—ha!—] Ha-ha! *TSIIC*
233:14   *rather*] rather *TSI*
233:14   —But] ~ *TSI*
233:19   lunch.] ~? *TSIIC*
233:21   Goodbye . . . Grainger—] ~ . . .
         ~. *TSII* ~, . . . ~. *TSIIC*
233:22   Goodbye Sally—] ~, ~.
         TSIIC
233:22   Goodbye . . . Brentnall—] ~,
         . . . ~. *TSIIC*
233:29   *Exit. TSIIC*] exit *MS* EXIT
         TSII Exit ANNIE. *EI*
233:30   Goodbye] goodbye *TSIIC*
233:30   all.—] ~. *TSI*
233:32   No—no—no] ~ — ~. No
         TSIIC ~, ~. No *Per*
233:33   life. You] live. you *TSII* life;
         you *TSIIC*
233:35   Well] ~, *TSIIC*
233:36   Brentnall.] ~? *TSIIC*
233:38   come:] ~. *TSI*
233:38   *Exit. TSIIC*] exit *MS* EXIT
         TSII Exit SALLY. *EI*
234:1   world:] ~; *TSIIC*
234:2   in] is *TSII*
234:5   Goodbye] ~, *TSI*
234:7   downstairs.—By] ~ — ~ *TSI*
         ~ —by *TSIIC*

234:12   *Exit each of them. Ed.*] exit each
         of them *MS* EXIT each of
         them *TSII Exeunt* ELSA *and*
         BRENTNALL. *TSIIC*
234:13   *awhile TSIIC*] awhile *MS a
         while Per*
234:15   to.] ~? *TSIIC*
234:18   you.] ~? *TSIIC*
234:21   ETHEL: Well— *(Trying . . . cry).*
         —we'll *Ed.*] Ethel: Well—
         (trying not to cry) —we'll *MS*
         ETHEL: *(trying . . . cry)*
         —Well, we'll *TSI* ETHEL
         (trying not to cry) —Well, we'll
         TSII ETHEL: *(trying . . . cry)*:
         Well, we'll *TSIIC*
234:27   So,] ~ *TSI*
234:29   baby.] ~? *TSIIC*
235:1   for ever.] forever. *TSI* forever?
         TSIIC for ever? *EI*
235:2   for.] ~? *TSIIC*
235:4   *(Weeps.) Ed.*] (weeps) *MS* Om.
         TSI
235:5   shall.—] ~. *TSI*
235:7   lamb] land *TSII* lad *TSIIC*
235:8   him.] ~! *TSIIC*
235:9   GRAINGER *the baby Ed.*]
         Grainger the baby *MS* the
         baby to Grainger *TSI the baby
         to* GRAINGER *TSIIC*

The Fight for Barbara

MS   = Autograph MS (Roberts E130a)
Per = *Argosy*, December 1933, xiv, 68–90
EI   = *Complete Plays* (Heinemann, 1965)

Silent emendations

1 DHL's underlining of foreign words in dialogue was inconsistent at the
  beginning of *MS* and later ceased altogether. *Per* and *EI* introduced italics, but
  also inconsistently. In this edition, foreign words are not printed in italics;
  variants in *MS*, *Per* and *EI* are recorded.
2 Throughout, DHL wrote 'all right', 'tonight', 'tomorrow', 'goodnight'; *Per*
  printed 'all right', 'to-night', 'to-morrow', 'good night', and *EI* printed 'alright',
  'to-night', 'to-morrow', 'good night'. DHL's practice in *MS* has been followed,
  and these variants are not recorded unless they are part of another variant.

239:1 THE FIGHT FOR
BARBARA *Ed.*] The Fight for
Barbara/ A Comedy by D. H.
Lawrence *MS* D. H./
LAWRENCE'S/ Brilliant
Comedy/ "KEEPING/
BARBARA" *Per* The Fight for
Barbara/ A COMEDY IN
FOUR ACTS/ (1912) *E1 see
notes*

239:3 *Scene: Ed.*] Scene: *MS*
SCENE.—*Per 8.30 in the
morning. E1*

239:7 *Time: 8.30 in the morning. Ed.*]
Time: 8.30 in the morning. *MS*
TIME: 8-30 *in the morning. Per
Om. E1*

239:11 *Re-enter, Per*] Re-enter, *MS*
Re-enter WESSON, *E1*

239:15 Questa] *Questa E1*

239:17 Abondante misura *Per*]
Abondante misura MS, E1

239:18 that?—] ~? *Per*

239:18 Come *Ed.*] *Come MS*

239:19 Abondante misura—latte *Per*]
Abondante misura—latte MS
Abondante misura latte E1

239:20 Si *Per*] *Si MS, E1*

239:23 Come *Per*] Come *MS, E1*

239:24 Vous apprenez Anglais
—voi—inglese—! *Ed.*] *Vous
apprenez Anglais
—voi—inglese—! MS* Vous
apprenez anglais
—voi—inglese! *Per Vous
apprenez anglais—voi—inglese!
E1*

239:25 *(blushing) Ed.*] (blushing) *MS
Om. Per*

239:25 O] *O E1*

239:25 non—niente inglese *Per*]
non—niente inglese MS, E1

239:26 yes!—] ~! *Per*

239:26 Er] *Er E1*

239:26 fa tempo cattivo *Per*] *fa tempo
cattivo MS, E1*

239:27 Tempo cattivo *Per*] *Tempo
cattivo MS, E1*

239:27 si— *Ed.*] *si— MS* si. *Per si. E1*

239:29 Come *Ed.*] *Come MS*

239:31 Er *Per*] er *MS*

239:31 giorno—che giorno—?—]
giornoche giorno? *Per giorno
che giorno? E1*

239:32 Oggi?—domenica.] ~?
Domenica. *Per Oggi?
Domenica. E1*

239:33 WESSON: What ... [240:1]
Domenica! *Ed.*] Wesson: ~ ...
Francesca: *Domenica! MS Om.
Per*

240:2 Domenica!—dimanche—
Sonntag *Per*] *Domenica!—
dimanche—Sonntag MS
Domenica!—dimanche—
Sonntag E1*

240:3 Come *Ed.*] *Come MS*

240:4 Sunday *MS, E1*] Sonday *Per*

240:7 Buon giorno, Signore *Per*]
Buon giorno, Signore MS, E1

240:8 Buon giorno *Per*] *Buon giorno
MS, E1*

240:12 *26 Ed.*] 26 *MS twenty-six Per*

240:12 *rather Ed.*] rather *MS rather a
Per*

240:13 *in Ed.*] in *MS in the Per*

240:20 And pray] ~, ~, *Per*

240:20 as *dulcet!*] *as dulcet!—Per*

240:21 servant maid] servant-maid
Per

240:24 —these] These *Per*

240:26 —I] ~ *Per*

240:28 away. *Ed.*] ~ *MS* ~ — *Per*

240:29 —And] ~ *Per*

240:31 BARBARA: A ... actress. *Ed.*]
Barbara: ~ ... Wesson ... ~.
MS Om. Per

241:1 Remember] ~, *Per*

241:3 'Oh!',] "~!" *Per*

241:4 —and 'Oh' ... I know] *Om.
Per*

241:9 *the E1*] the *MS Om. Per*

241:9 Oh] ~, *Per*

241:10 —how adorable!— —] How ~!
Per

241:10 No] ~, *E1*

241:11 it's not right, and] *Om. Per*
241:13 No, *MS*, *E1*] ~; *Per*
241:13 servant maid] servant-maid *Per*
241:16 her . . . rate] ~, . . . ~, *Per*
241:20 Yes, *MS*, *E1*] ~; *Per*
241:21 hundred and twenty] hundred-and-twenty *Per*
241:26 dressing gown] dressing-gown *Per*
241:27 *our* domestic] our *Per*
241:31 it,] ~; *Per*
241:31 —This] ~ *Per*
241:32 *(He shakes . . . black tin.)*—*Ed.*] (he shakes onto it charcoal out of a big black tin)— *MS Om. Per*
241:34 What—?] ~? *Per*
241:35 'Oh!'] "~" *Per* "~!" *E1*
241:36 Well] ~, *Per*
241:36 out,] *Om. Per* out *E1*
241:38 it.] ~? *Per*
241:39 'Oh',] "~"; *Per* "~!"; *E1*
241:39 dear] ~, *Per*
242:4 ought—] ~. *Per*
242:4 is that charcoal burning?] *Om. Per*
242:6 This is . . . much as you.] *Om. Per*
242:10 oh] ~, *Per*
242:10 it!—and] ~? And *Per*
242:11 à l'italienne] l'Italienne *Per*
242:11 oh] ~, *Per*
242:12 am!] ~. *Per*
242:12 *a coffee mill Ed.*] a coffee mill *MS* the coffee-mill *Per*
242:19 WESSON *(sings)* . . . his own. *Ed.*] Wesson (sings) . . . ~ ~. *MS* [*Wesson sings it again*] *Per* WESSON *sings it again. E1*
242:24 Oh] ~, *Per*
242:27 me] me *Per*
242:29 —while] While *Per*
242:30 Oh] ~, *Per*
242:31 Belvedere *Per*] Belvêdere *MS*
242:32 tomorrer] to-morrer *Per*
242:35 know,] ~; *Per*
243:16 it.] ~? *Per*

243:18 Giacomo—] ~, *Per*
243:24 scroddy] seroddy *Per see notes*
243:30 *(Mocking.) Ed.*] (mocking) *MS Om. Per*
243:34 WESSON: Am . . . you *are!* *Ed.*] Wesson: ~ . . . Barbara . . . ~ ~! *MS Om. Per*
243:40 life—] ~! *Per*
244:1 WESSON: I . . . chocolate./ BARBARA: *Ed.*] Wesson: ~ . . . ~/ Barbara: *MS Om. Per*
244:5 How did . . . [244:13] any rate. *Ed.*] ~ ~ . . . Barbara . . . Wesson . . . Barbara . . . Wesson . . . ~ ~. *MS Om. Per*
244:14 failure] ~, *Per*
244:14 papa's] Papa's *Per*
244:21 —I'd] I'd *Per*
244:22 papa] Papa *E1*
244:24 Baronet] baronet *Per*
244:26 And Anna . . . [244:31] poor thing.— *Ed.*] ~ ~ ~ . . . Wesson . . . Barbara . . . Wesson . . . Barbara . . . ~ ~!— *MS Om. Per*
244:31 favorite] favourite *Per*
244:34 Tressider *Per*] Tressidder *MS see note on 237:9*
244:36 BARBARA: *Ed.*] Barbara: *MS Om. Per*
244:38 BARBARA: Only . . . a shame. *Ed.*] Barbara: ~ . . . Wesson . . . ~ ~. *MS Om. Per*
244:40 Oh] ~, *Per*
245:5 bedroom.] ~? *Per*
245:6 once, should] ~. Should *E1*
245:8 or] ~, *Per*
245:14 You'll have . . . [245:23] no watch. *Ed.*] ~ ~ ~ . . . Barbara . . . Wesson . . . Barbara . . . Wesson . . . Barbara . . . Wesson . . . ~ ~. *MS Om. Per*
245:24 Frederick!] ~. *Per*
245:25 WESSON *(sighing)* . . . come./ BARBARA: *Ed.*] Wesson (sighing) . . . ~./ Barbara: *MS Om. Per*
245:26 I left] I'd left *Per*
245:27 me.] ~? *Per*

245:29 Oh] ~, *Per*
245:29 out.] ~! *Per*
245:30 enough,] ~; *Per*
245:33 me.] ~? *Per*
245:35 his] this *E1*
245:37 Lucy used ... with him."] *Om. Per*
246:4 —*Why*] Why *Per*
246:5 —But] ~ *Per*
246:6 sensitive—!] ~ —— *Per*
246:9 Oh Giacomo,] ~, ~; *Per*
246:10 off.] ~? *Per*
246:11 shall] ~ — *Per*
246:14 But] ~, *Per*
246:16 Yes] ~, *Per*
246:22 you!] ~? *Per*
246:28 me.] ~ — *Per*
246:35 BARBARA: I'm ... [247:7] sake, no. *Ed.*] Barbara: ~ ... Wesson ... Barbara ... ~ ... Wesson ... Barbara ... [247:3] Wesson ... Barbara ... [247:7] Wesson ... ~, ~. *MS Om. Per*
247:11 stand up and] *Om. Per*
247:12 you,] ~ *Per*
247:16 Giacomo—] ~. *Per*
247:16 he *does* love me.] *Om. Per*
247:18 *want*] want *Per*
247:18 divorce,] ~ *Per*
247:20 —But] ~ *Per*
247:20 loop-hole] loop-/ hole *Per* loophole *E1*
247:21 —Ah] ~ *Per*
247:25 Convent] convent *Per*
247:29 true] ~, *Per*
247:30 I—] ~? *Per*
247:30 I *do* love you.] *Om. Per*
247:33 Frederick—] ~. *Per*
247:34 do—] ~. *Per*
248:1 me.—] ~. *Per*
248:2 sometimes Giacomo—now] ~, ~. Now *Per*
248:3 Sit down.] *Om. Per*
248:7 —I] ~ *Per*
248:9 drawing room] drawing-/ room *Per* drawing-room *E1*
248:16 then,] ~. *Per*
248:16 and leave me alone.] *Om. Per*

248:24 her,] ~. *Per*
248:24 and if ... head again.] *Om. Per*
248:27 *re-appear Ed.*] re-appear *MS* reappear *Per* re-enter *E1*
248:30 *young handsome Ed.*] young handsome *MS* handsome young *Per*
248:32 *He has ... is handsome. Ed.*] He has a cloak with a hood over his head—he is handsome *MS Om. Per*
248:33 buon] Buon *Per*
249:2 si] Si *Per*
249:4 Chilo] chilo *Per*
249:8 Oh] ~, *Per*
249:23 Well] ~, *Per*
249:23 much.] ~! *Per*
249:23 It is really too much.] *Om. Per*
249:30 false.] ~? *Per*
249:35 odds.] ~? *Per*
249:40 to] to it *E1*
250:8 Pooh,] ~! *Per*
250:9 —Can] ~ *Per*
250:20 I Giacometti.] ~, ~? *Per*
250:21 pecky] ~, *Per*
250:22 —say] Say *Per*
250:26 yes] ~, *Per*
250:34 Posta] *posta Per*
250:35 Oh] ~, *Per*
250:37 Posta] posta *Per*
250:38 The ... venom. *(Tearing ... envelope.) Ed.*] The ... venom (tearing open an envelope) *MS* The ... venom. [*Tearing ... envelope.*] *Per* (*tearing ... envelope*): The ... venom. *E1*
251:1 dear,] ~! *Per*
251:3 —If] ~ *Per*
251:7 And besides ... *letters.*)/ WESSON: *Ed.*] ~ ~ ... Barbara ... (She puts her hand on his. He sits glum. Then they both read their letters)/ Wesson: *MS Om. Per*
251:20 whiskey] whisky, *Per*
251:21 BARBARA: But ... [251:29] he won't. *Ed.*] Barbara: ~ ... Wesson ... Barbara ... [251:24]

Wesson ... Barbara ... [251:26]
Wesson ... Barbara ... [251:29]
Wesson ... ~ ~. *MS Om. Per*
251:30 Mama *Ed.*] mama *MS*
251:30 is.] ~, *Per*
251:32 —The] ~ *Per*
251:36 BARBARA: Don't ... he's not.
Ed.] Barbara: ~ ... Wesson ...
~ ~. *MS Om. Per*
251:39 24th *Per*] 24th *MS*
251:40 —do] Do *Per*
252:1 while] when *Per*
252:6 —Ugh!—how horrible!] *Om.*
Per
252:8 is] *is* vile *Per*
252:10 BARBARA: But ... think of. *Ed.*]
Barbara: ~ ... Wesson ... ~
~. *MS Om. Per*
252:13 to me] *Om. Per*
252:14 know] know that *Per*
252:16 WESSON: His ... that./
BARBARA:] Wesson: ~ ... ~./
Barbara: *MS Om. Per*
252:19 hate!] ~. *Per*
252:21 you!] ~? *Per*
252:23 BARBARA: But ... [252:30] All
right—] Barbara: ~ ... Wesson
... Barbara ... Wesson ...
Barbara ... Wesson: ~ ~ —
MS Om. Per
252:30 daggeroso] "daggerous" *Per*
252:31 —So] ~ *Per*
252:31 *(He looks fierce.) Ed.*] (he looks
fierce) *MS Om. Per*
252:33 Oh] ~, *Per*
252:33 *Laughing Ed.*] laughing *MS*
Laughs E1
252:34 Oh—] ~, *Per*
252:35 it] ~, *Per*
252:36 bleeding] *Om. Per*
253:1 Well] ~, *Per*
253:1 —Do] ~ *Per*
253:3 WESSON: He'll ... we do? *Ed.*]
Wesson: ~ ... Barbara ... ~
~? *MS Om. Per*
253:7 WESSON: Why ... don't know.
Ed.] Wesson: ~ ... Barbara ...
~ ~. *MS Om. Per*

253:11 said 'you] ~, "You *Per* ~:
"You *E1*
253:17 *never*] never *Per*
253:23 him!] ~? *Per*
253:24 him—] ~. *Per*
253:29 You perhaps] ~, ~, *Per*
253:29 good will] good-/ will *Per*
good-will *E1*
253:39 did it] did *Per*
254:1 BARBARA: Impatient ... [254:17]
getting desperate. *Ed.*] Barbara:
~ ... Wesson ... Barbara ...
[254:6] Wesson ... Barbara ...
[254:12] Wesson ... Barbara ...
[254:17]Wesson ... ~ ~. *MS*
Om. Per
254:18 back—] ~. *Per*
254:20 WESSON: Not ... thousand
promises. *Ed.*] Wesson: ~ ...
Barbara ... ~ ~. *MS Om. Per*
254:28 —there's] There's *Per*
254:30 yourself—*you*] ~. You *Per*
254:31 BARBARA: And ... [255:9] your
head. *Ed.*] Barbara: ~ ...
Wesson ... Barbara ... [254:38]
Wesson ... Barbara ... [255:1]
Wesson ... Barbara ... [255:4]
Wesson ... Barbara ... [255:9]
Wesson ... ~ ~. *MS Om. Per*
255:13 WESSON: No./ BARBARA: *Ed.*]
Wesson: No./ Barbara: *MS*
Om. Per
255:17 Giacometti—] ~, *Per*
255:19 unselfish,] ~ *Per*
255:27 WESSON *(clearing ... us./*
BARBARA: *Ed.*] Wesson (clearing
the breakfast table ... Barbara
(following him ... Wesson ...
~. Barbara: *MS Om. Per*
255:33 BARBARA *(laughing ... That's
why. Ed.*] Barbara (laughing ...
Wesson: ~ ~. *MS Om. Per*
255:39 —oh] Oh, *Per*
255:39 a rod—] as a rod. *Per*
256:5 nor] — ~ — *Per*
257:2 *Scene: Ed.*] Scene: *MS Om. Per*
Evening, several days after the
first act. E1 see entry for 257:8

257:4   *over a Per*] over *MS*

257:4   *very big . . . or back. Ed.*] very big and broad, without side or back. *MS Om. Per*

257:6   *with his . . . the table, Ed.*] with his collar and tie strewn on the table, *MS without his collar and tie, Per*

257:8   *Time: Evening . . . first act. Ed.*] Time: evening, several days after the first act. *MS Om. E1*

257:12   BARBARA: You . . . wasn't it? *Ed.*] Barbara: ~ . . . Wesson . . . ~ ~? *MS Om. Per*

257:18   in] into *Per*

257:22   stupid,] ~ *Per*

257:37   Oh——Oh] ~ —oh *Per*

257:38   he—] ~? *Per*

257:38   round-abouts] roundabouts *Per*

258:1   chicken—] ~. *Per*

258:4   WESSON: Will . . . *(Kisses him.) Ed.*] Wesson: ~ . . . Barbara . . . (kisses him) *MS Om. Per*

258:6   Barbara.] ~? *Per*

258:7   to.] ~? *Per*

258:9   WESSON: Through . . . thick hair! *Ed.*] Wesson: ~ . . . Barbara . . . ~! *MS Om. Per*

258:13   *(There is . . . his watch.) Ed.*] (There is a silence. He looks at his watch.) *MS Om. Per*

258:15   ten past six] ten-past-six *Per*

258:15   she was coming by?] *Om. Per*

258:16   five to six.] five-to-six? *Per*

258:17   she said] *Om. Per*

258:17   half past] half-past *Per*

258:18   Don't you . . . coming?] *Om. Per*

258:21   no *MS, E1*] No *Per*

258:25   *her—exit. She Per*] her—exit. She *MS her.)/Exit* WESSON. BARBARA *E1*

258:27   *He Per*] He *MS* WESSON *E1*

258:30   Yes—] *Om. E1*

258:30   Quick,] ~! *Per*

258:30   get ready . . . slippers on.] *Om. Per*

258:32   *(struggling) Ed.*] (struggling) *MS Om. Per*

258:33   *Their Ed.*] Their *MS Then Per*

258:35   VOICE OF BARBARA . . . [254:40] will think.' *Ed.*] Voice of Barbara . . . Voice of Wesson . . . Voice of Barbara . . . Voice of Wesson . . . ~ ~.' *MS Om. Per*

259:1   Mama.] ~! *Per*

259:5   It is such a rough road.] *Om. Per*

259:6   Wesson.] ~? *Per*

259:6   *(Her voice . . . protesting—enter Ed.*] (her voice . . . protesting—enter *MS [Enter Per Enter E1*

259:8   60 *Ed.*] 60 *MS sixty Per*

259:12   yes—] *Om. Per*

259:14   *(Takes off . . . [259:22] Re-enter . . . [259:23] desk.)/* LADY CHARLCOTE *Ed.*] (takes off . . . Wesson . . . Barbara [259:18] Lady Charlcote . . . Barbara [259:20] Lady Charlcote . . . Barbara . . . re-enter Wesson . . . desk)/ Lady Charlcote *MS Om. Per*

259:25   Barbara.] ~? *Per*

259:26   do!] ~. *Per*

259:31   it!] ~? *Per*

259:32   good,] ~ *Per*

259:33   Why do . . . her life——] *Om. Per*

259:35   But] ~, *Per*

259:35   I do I] ~ ~, ~ *Per*

259:35   *crocheting E1*] crochetting *MS crochetting Per*

259:39   How can . . . expect it!] *Om. Per*

260:1   Do you . . . a thing.] *Om. Per*

260:5   —And] ~ *Per*

260:6   life.] ~? *Per*

260:8   an *Per*] *Om. MS*

260:9   and be your mistress,] *Om. Per*

260:10   sister and . . . keep her.] friends? *Per*

260:17   Italians,] ~. *Per*

260:17   going under . . . [260:21] LADY CHARLCOTE *(continuing): Ed.*]

~ ~ ... Lady Charlcote
(continuing): *MS Om. Per*

260:23   pay—] ~. *Per*

260:23   and he ... keep her—] *Om. Per*

260:27   But] ~, *Per*

260:31   live.] ~? *Per*

260:31   Your father ... [260:37] of
you.] *Om. Per*

261:4   lives.] ~? *Per*

261:8   If *you* ... a position.] *Om. Per*

261:10   What] A woman—what *Per*

261:11   —And] ~ *Per*

261:12   *(Cries.) Ed.*] (cries) *MS Om.
Per*

261:20   ideas,] ~. *Per*

261:20   and your ... o'clock company.
Ed.] ~ ~ ... oclock company.
MS Om. Per

261:26   trouble,] ~ *Per*

261:30   You don't ... [261:36] forfeit
everything.] *Om. Per*

261:36   years' *E1*] years *MS*

261:37   time,] ~ *E1*

261:37   It is ... these things.] *Om. Per*

261:40   —Think of ... *is ducked.) Ed.*]
— ~ ~ ... She waits, he sits
twisting his fingers, his head is
ducked). *MS Om. Per*

262:4   you] ~, *Per*

262:8   What time ... seven./ LADY
CHARLCOTE: *Ed.*] ~ ~ ...
Wesson ... ~./ Lady
Charlcote: *MS Om. Per*

262:13   WESSON: If ... [262:17] thank
you. *Ed.*] Wesson: ~ ... Lady
Charlcote ... Wesson ... Lady
Charlcote ... ~ ~. *MS Om.
Per*

262:18   me. *(Exit.) Ed.*] me. (exit) *MS*
me [*Exit.*] *Per* me./ *Exit*
WESSON. *E1*

262:19   look, mama?] look? *Per*

262:20   *(she is ... pathetic) Ed.*] (she is
flustered, rather pathetic) *MS
Om. Per*

262:20   Oh poor fellow.] ~, ~ ~! *Per*

262:22   ill.] ~? *Per*

262:23   —he] He *Per*

262:24   you can] can you *Per*

262:25   that,] ~? *Per*

262:25   is more ... [262:40] late then.
Ed.] ~ ~ ... Barbara ... Lady
Charlcote ... [262:30] (she
cries) ... [262:32] Barbara ...
Lady Charlcote ... [262:37]
Barbara ... Lady Charlcote ...
~ ~. *MS Om. Per*

263:2   mine—] ~. *Per*

263:2   and his social peace.] *Om. Per*

263:4   you.] ~? *Per*

263:5   wanted—.] ~ — *Per*

263:5   he *Per*] I *MS*

263:14   BARBARA: Why ... Ah— *Ed.*]
Barbara: ~ ... Lady Charlcote
... ~ — *MS Om. Per*

263:18   du] de *Per*

263:21   No thank you,] ~, ~ ~. *Per*

263:21   I won't have any.] *Om. Per*

263:22   tea.] ~? *Per*

263:23   LADY CHARLCOTE: No ... at all?
Ed.] Lady Charlcote: ~ ...
Wesson ... ~ ~? *MS Om. Per*

263:26   I'll put ... *and hat.) Ed.*] ~ ~
... He goes out, fetches her
cloak and hat) *MS Om. Per*

263:28   Papa *MS, E1*] papa *Per*

263:30   *(To* WESSON *... her cloak): Ed.*]
(to Wesson, who helps her on
with her cloak) *MS Om. Per*

263:30   Oh thank you!—] ~, ~ ~ —
Per

263:31   mind.—] ~ — *Per*

263:35   BARBARA: Isn't ... *crocheting* ...
[264:3] her./ LADY CHARLCOTE:
Ed.] Barbara: ~ ... Lady
Charlcote ... Wesson ...
[263:40] Barbara (still
crochetting) ... Lady Charlcote
... Wesson ... ~./ Lady
Charlcote: *MS Om. Per*

264:3   Tressider *Ed.*] Tressidder *MS*

264:5   Yes—] ~. *Per*

264:5   Goodbye] Good-bye *Per*

264:6   Goodbye—] Good-bye. *Per*

264:6   —Oh] ~, *Per*

264:9   can't——] ~ — *Per*

264:13 *crocheting E1*] crochetting *MS*
crochetting *Per*

264:14 BARBARA: Well ... [264:22] to
her. *Ed.*] Barbara: ~ ...
Wesson ... Barbara (laughing)
It ... [264:19] Wesson ...
Barbara ... Wesson ... ~ ~.
MS Om. Per

264:23 common sense] commonsense
E1

264:24 you] *Om. Per*

264:25 —But] ~ *Per*

264:31 And as ... coal in—] *Om. Per*

264:34 carrying your slops] making
your bed *Per*

264:35 doing it] *Om. Per*

264:36 money—] ~, *Per*

265:3 BARBARA: No ... elegant—/
WESSON: *Ed.*] Barbara: ~ ...
~ —/ Wesson: *MS Om. Per*

265:13 had] *Om. Per*

265:16 I thought ... *him, crouching.)*
Ed.] ~ ~ ... imitates him,
crouching) *MS Om. Per*

265:22 —You] ~ *Per*

265:25 *(She sits ... her eyes.) Ed.*] (she
sits laughing helpless, wiping
her eyes) *MS Om. Per*

265:27 Well] ~, *Per*

265:27 do!] ~? *Per*

265:32 yap!'] ~" *Per*

265:33 little, *Per*] ~ *MS*

265:33 *(Laughs beyond speech.) Ed.*]
(laughs beyond speech) *MS
Om. Per*

265:37 up] ~, *Per*

265:39 —Mind] ~ *Per*

266:3 —Yap—Yap yap!—yap]
~—yapyap! Yap *Per*

266:5 *rouses Ed.*] rouses *MS* rises *Per*

266:5 Poor mama ... *(He giggles.)*
Ed.] ~ ~ ... (growling) ...
again (She puts her head on
her knees with laughter) ... (he
giggles) *MS Om. Per*

266:13 have *MS, E1*] had *Per*

266:13 had.] ~? *Per*

266:13 *(Laughing with ... yap—yap!*

Ed.] (laughing with little
shrieks ... ~ — ~! *MS Om.
Per*

266:18 —You] ~ *Per*

266:19 *(She screws ... in imitation.)*
Ed.] (she screws herself up in
imitation) *MS Om. Per*

266:20 Well] ~, *Per*

266:21 —Why] ~ *Per*

266:22 crow.] ~? *Per*

266:22 —It would ... a shock.] *Om.
Per*

266:25 —Or] ~ *Per*

266:27 *(She shows ... with laughter.)*
Ed.] (she shows him—collapses
onto the chair with laughter)
MS Om. Per

266:30 —What] ~ *Per*

266:32 —And] ~ *Per*

266:34 BARBARA: And ... bitten off.
Ed.] Barbara: ~ ... (laughing)
... Wesson (putting his hand
on the top of his head) ... ~
~. *MS Om. Per*

266:40 seriously.] ~, *Per*

267:1 BARBARA: Then why ...
WESSON: No, *Ed.*] Barbara:
They ~ ... Wesson: ~, *MS
Om. Per*

267:4 help,] ~ .... *Per*

267:4 and then ... again./ WESSON:
Ed.] ~ ~ ... Barbara ...
(laughing) ... ~./ Wesson: *MS
Om. Per*

267:19 —but] But *Per*

267:20 say] ~, *Per*

267:22 with their jaw] *Om. Per*

267:24 again.—] ~? *Per*

267:25 —Will] ~ *Per*

267:28 —*drinks wine. Ed.*] —drinks
wine) *MS Om. Per*

267:31 WESSON: Then ... I must. *Ed.*]
Wesson: ~ ... Barbara ... ~
~. *MS Om. Per*

267:33 *(A silence.) Ed.*] (a silence) *MS
Om. Per*

267:34 mad.] ~? *Per*

267:36 Well] ~, *Per*

267:37 to] to it *Per*
267:40 sense] ~, *Per*
268:2 *do*] ~, *Per*
268:10 sorrow, for that matter.] sorrow.
        Per
268:16 WESSON: You ... Tell me. *Ed.*]
        Wesson: ~ ... Barbara ... ~
        ~. *MS Om. Per*
268:19 me,] ~ *Per*
268:20 BARBARA *(making ... [268:36]*
        much better. *Ed.*] Barbara
        (making an explosive sound of
        derision) ... Wesson ...
        Barbara ... [268:23] (again
        exploding with laughter) ...
        Wesson ... Barbara ... [268:28]
        Wesson ... Barbara ... Wesson
        ... [268:33] Barbara ... Wesson
        ... ~ ~. *MS Om. Per*
268:39 me?—] ~? *Per*
269:3 *then!*] ~. *Per*
269:5 he] he want *Per*
269:6 then!] ~? *Per*
269:9 worshipped.] ~? *Per*
269:11 worshipped.] ~? *Per*
269:13 —you] You *Per*
269:13 *yourself.*] ~! *Per*
269:17 —Let] ~ *Per*
269:19 BARBARA: —Why ... choose to.
        Ed.] Barbara: —~ ... Wesson
        ... ~ ~. *MS Om. Per*
270:3 *Scene: The same. Ed.*] Scene:
        The same. *MS SCENE.—The
        same. Per Om. E1*
270:4 *Time: Ed.*] Time: *MS
        TIME.—Per Om. E1*
270:6 here.] ~? *Per*
270:11 come too—] ~, ~. *Per*
270:11 it would serve her right.] *Om.*
        Per
270:16 BARBARA: Oh ... she's late. *Ed.*]
        Barbara: ~ ... Wesson ...
        Barbara ... Wesson ... Barbara
        ... Wesson ... ~ ~. *MS Om.*
        Per
270:22 *you.*] ~? *Per*
270:23 impudence.—] ~ — *Per*
270:23 go.] ~! *Per*

270:25 to] do *Per*
270:28 go] go for *Per*
270:29 you.] ~? *Per*
270:32 —why should ... with it?] *Om.*
        Per
270:35 you.] ~? *Per*
270:37 myself] ~, *Per*
271:1 —And] ~ *Per*
271:9 —I will] ~ ~, *Per*
271:10 *from the window Ed.*] from the
        window *MS Om. Per*
271:12 two-pence ha'penny]
        twopence-ha'penny *Per*
271:12 'em] them *Per*
271:14 them.] ~! *Per*
271:16 flea.—] ~ — *Per*
271:19 me—] ~. *Per*
271:19 she is—she ... to me—] *Om.*
        Per
271:27 *moustache, has been handsome.)*
        Ed.] moustache, has been
        handsome, *MS moustache,. Per*
        moustache. E1
271:32 you, *Per*] ~ *MS*
272:1 under] under the *E1*
272:5 Your right ... belongs to.] *Om.*
        Per
272:8 base—] ~. *Per*
272:8 nothing more than robbery.]
        Om. Per
272:19 So?] ~! *Per*
272:23 WESSON: Yes./ SIR WILLIAM:
        Ed.] Wesson: Yes./ Sir
        William: *MS Om. Per*
272:27 state] State *Per*
272:28 daughter—] ~. *Per*
272:29 putting aside ... and relatives.]
        Om. Per
272:33 kicked out ... house, and] *Om.*
        Per
272:35 SIR WILLIAM: Yes ... [273:3]
        WESSON: So! *Ed.*] Sir William:
        ~ ... Wesson ... Sir William
        ... [272:40] Wesson ... Sir
        William ... Wesson ... Sir
        William ... Wesson: So! *MS*
        Om. Per
273:5 place,] ~ —— *Per*

273:5 leave no trace of yourself—]
Om. Per

273:8 paid.—] ~ — *Per*

273:8 But] but *E1*

273:15 SIR WILLIAM: I . . . WESSON: So!
Ed.] Sir William: ~ . . .
Wesson: So! *MS Om. Per*

273:19 house. *Ed.*] ~ *MS* ~ — *Per*

273:35 me,—] ~ — *Per*

273:36 dare] Dare *Per*

273:36 —A strumpet like you—!] *Om.*
Per

273:37 to] ~, *Per*

273:37 people.] ~! *Per*

273:39 and that is all—] *Om. Per*

273:40 SIR WILLIAM: I . . . more
decency. *Ed.*] Sir William: ~
. . . Barbara . . . ~ ~. *MS Om.*
Per

275:3 BARBARA: That . . . loss. *Ed.*]
Barbara: ~ . . . ~. *MS Om. Per*

274:11 Barbara,] ~. *Per*

274:11 and you . . . you get.] *Om. Per*

275:15 openly,] ~ *Per*

274:17 then] *Om. Per*

274:19 daughter] ~, *Per*

274:21 *(flashing) Ed.*] (flashing) *MS*
Om. Per

274:21 you.] ~? *Per*

274:22 worm!] ~? *Per*

274:22 *mad.*] ~! *Per* ~! *E1*

274:33 Oh] ~, *Per*

274:33 funker.] ~! *Per*

274:35 found] found him *Per*

274:35 —What] ~ *Per*

274:36 you.] ~? *Per*

274:40 No,] ~; *Per*

275:3 *(Plaintively.) Ed.*] (plaintively)
MS Om. Per

275:4 WESSON: But . . . hard,
Giacomo? *Ed.*] Wesson: ~ . . .
Barbara . . . ~, ~? *MS Om. Per*

275:6 If they . . . need we!] *Om. Per*

275:11 Yes] ~, *Per*

275:14 They'll come . . . in time.] *Om.*
Per

275:18 I feel . . . for me.] *Om. Per*

275:20 —I] ~ *Per*

275:22 —I] ~ *Per*

275:24 it Giacomo—] ~, ~?— *Per*

275:28 Then,] ~ *Per*

275:29 well—] ~, *Per*

276:9 mean] ~, *Per*

276:9 —Did] ~ *Per*

276:11 BARBARA *(laughing):* Poor . . . her
ear.) Ed.] Barbara (laughing): ~
Papa / Wesson . . . (he is kissing
her ear) *MS Om. Per*

276:14 Papa—] ~! *Per*

276:14 he'd have . . . a stool.] *Om. Per*

276:16 BARBARA: No . . . [276:31] will. /
WESSON: *Ed.*] Barbara: ~ . . .
Wesson . . . Barbara . . . dear
(kisses him) . . . [276:21]
Wesson (laughing shakily) . . .
Barbara . . . Wesson . . . [276:24]
Barbara (kissing him) . . .
Wesson . . . Barbara . . . Wesson
. . . Barbara . . . Wesson . . .
Barbara . . . ~. / Wesson: *MS*
Om. Per

276:33 No, *MS, E1*] ~; *Per*

276:33 —If] ~ *Per*

276:34 Why aren't . . . this life.] *Om.*
Per

276:36 they.] ~? *Per*

276:38 all] ~, *Per*

277:1 BARBARA: But . . . WESSON:
Refuse. *Ed.*] Barbara: ~ . . .
Wesson: ~. *MS Om. Per*

277:7 WESSON: Why . . . I couldn't.
Ed.] Wesson: ~ . . . Barbara . . .
~ ~. *MS Om. Per*

277:10 —would] Would *Per*

277:16 *Othello Ed.*] Othello *MS*

277:19 Yes!—] ~ — *Per*

277:20 you're *Ed.*] your *MS* you *Per*

277:24 Oh] O, *Per*

278:3 *Scene: The same— Ed.*] Scene:
The same— *MS SCENE.—*
The same. Per Om. E1

278:3 on the . . . *evening meal. Ed.*]
on the table are the dishes,
and copper saucepan, from
the evening meal. *MS Om.*
Per

278:5   *Time: Ed.*] Time: *MS*
        TIME.— Per Om. E1
278:7   *He does not look up. Ed.*] He
        does not look up. *MS Om. Per*
278:10 You've never ... like it? *Ed.*] ~
        ~ ... Wesson ... Barbara ... ~
        ~? *Om. Per*
278:15 nice.—] ~. *Per*
278:16 WESSON: I ... suit me? *Ed.*]
        Wesson: ~ ... Barbara ... ~
        ~? *MS Om. Per*
278:23 BARBARA *(laughing)* ... or
        not.— *Ed.*] Barbara (laughing)
        ... Wesson ... ~ ~.— *MS
        Om. Per*
278:29 —But] ~ *Per*
278:29 *you*'ve] you've *Per*
278:31 WESSON: I ... Barbara./
        BARBARA *Ed.*] Wesson: ~ ...
        ~./ Barbara *MS Om. Per*
278:35 *She sits Ed.*] She sits *MS Sits
        Per*
278:37 —It's] ~ *Per*
278:37 had,] ~. *Per*
278:37 and it ... [279:5] *sits
        pondering.) Ed.*] ~ ~ ...
        Wesson ... Barbara ... Wesson
        (pondering) ... Barbara
        (playing) ... (The Blue Danube
        Waltz continues—he sits
        pondering) *MS Om. Per*
279:6   off] ~, *Per*
279:11 Rubbish—where] ~!—Where
        Per
279:14 WESSON: No ... [279:19] have
        failed. *Ed.*] Wesson: ~./
        Barbara ... (sound of voices)
        ... Wesson ... Barbara ...
        Wesson ... ~ ~. *MS Om. Per*
279:21 BARBARA: Go ... [279:24] the
        good! *Ed.*] Barbara: ~ ...
        Wesson ... Barbara ... Wesson
        (standing stubborn) ... ~ ~!
        MS Om. Per
279:25 Quick!—] ~! *Per*
279:27 good—let] ~? Let *Per*
279:27 again!] ~. *Per*
279:29 Damn!!] ~! *Per*

279:33 *is dressed in homespun— Ed.*] is
        dressed in homespun— *MS
        Om. Per*
280:1   Hôtel] Hotel *Per*
280:1   half an hour *MS, E1*] half-an-
        hour *Per*
280:1   —she says ... be fair.] *Om. Per*
280:8   WESSON *(lingering)*: You— *Ed.*]
        Wesson (lingering): ~ — *MS
        Om. Per*
280:11 why—] ~ —— *Per*
280:12 you—?] ~? *Per*
280:13 *is*] is *Per*
280:15 you?—] ~? *Per*
280:23 FREDERICK: What ... *a pause.)
        Ed.*] Frederick: ~ ... (showing
        his teeth.)/(There is a pause)
        MS Om. Per
280:27 wife.] ~? *Per*
280:28 go] ~, *Per*
280:28 Mama will ... [280:32] to
        come. *Ed.*] ~ ~ ... Wesson ...
        Barbara ... Frederick ... ~ ~.
        MS Om. Per
280:39 *(There is a pause.) Ed.*] (there is
        a pause) *MS Om. Per*
281:4   *(There is a long silence.) Ed.*]
        (there is a long silence) *MS
        Om. Per*
281:7   Don't] ~, *Per*
281:10 BARBARA *(turning ... [281:29]*
        Thank you. *Ed.*] Barbara
        (turning impatiently to Lady
        Charlcote) ... [281:12] Lady
        Charlcote ... Barbara
        (faltering) ... Lady Charlcote
        ... [281:17] Barbara ... Lady
        Charlcote ... Barbara ...
        (another silence)/Lady
        Charlcote ... [281:21] Barbara
        (rising and going to the
        cupboard) ... (brings two
        decanters, and three glasses)/
        Lady Charlcote ... (Barbara
        pours her mother's drink, and
        drinks herself)/ Barbara ...
        Frederick ... Barbara ...
        Frederick: ~ ~. *MS Om. Per*

281:31 say,] ~ *Per*
281:37 FREDERICK: Of course . . . to me?
Ed.] Frederick: ~ ~ . . . ~ ~?
MS Om. Per
281:37 call. *Ed.*] ~? *MS see notes*
281:39 have.—] do. *Per*
281:39 It no doubt] ~, ~ ~, *Per*
282:2 —But] ~ *Per*
282:5 BARBARA; Then . . . [282:11] *is*
boring. *Ed.*] Barbara: ~ . . .
Frederick . . . Barbara . . .
[282:8] Lady Charlcote . . .
Frederick (turning to her) . . .
Lady Charlcote . . . ~ ~. *MS
Om. Per*
282:13 Barbara.] ~? *Per*
282:15 livant] gallivant *E1*
282:16 LADY CHARLCOTE . . . [282:22]
interesting chat. *Ed.*] Lady
Charlcote drinks again)/Lady
Charlcote . . . Barbara . . .
Frederick . . . ~ ~. *MS Om.
Per*
282:25 FREDERICK: Oh . . . [282:28]/
LADY CHARLCOTE: *Ed.*]
Frederick: ~ (bowing)/ Lady
Charlcote . . . (rising)/
Frederick . . . Lady Charlcote:
MS Om. Per
282:34 FREDERICK: Within . . . *is
silence.) Ed.*] Frederick: ~ . . .
Barbara . . . (there is silence)
MS Om. Per
282:37 BARBARA: What . . . I wonder.
Ed.] Barbara: ~ . . . Frederick:
~ ~. *MS Om. Per*
282:39 me Frederick—] ~, ~. *Per*
283:1 FREDERICK: You . . . and
sarcastic. *Ed.*] Frederick: ~ . . .
Barbara . . . ~ ~. *MS Om. Per*
283:4 *(showing his teeth) Ed.*]
(showing his teeth) *MS Om.
Per*
283:4 I try not] I'll try not to be. *E1*
283:5 full dress] full-dress *Per*
283:8 it— *Ed.*] ~,— *MS* ~. *Per*
283:10 Don't!] ~. *Per*
283:11 luck.—] ~. *Per*

283:11 suppose?] ~! *Per*
283:12 No—!] *Om. Per*
283:14 unjust.] ~! *Per*
283:15 Frederick!] ~. *Per*
283:16 FREDERICK: I . . . be said. *Ed.*]
Frederick: ~ (a silence)/
Barbara . . . ~ ~. *MS Om. Per*
283:19 BARBARA: About . . . go ahead.
Ed.] Barbara: ~ . . . Frederick
. . . ~ ~. *MS Om. Per*
283:25 Oh] ~, *Per*
283:26 —It] ~ *Per*
283:27 BARBARA: And . . . own work.
Ed.] Barbara: ~ . . . (begins to
cry)/ Frederick (with a sob) . . .
~ ~. *MS Om. Per*
283:30 don't!] *Om. Per*
283:31 must.] ~ —— *Per*
283:34 BARBARA *(rising . . . * FREDERICK:
Exactly. *Ed.*] Barbara (rising &
going back to her seat) . . .
Frederick: ~. *MS Om. Per*
283:37 There's] there's *Per*
283:39 of yours] to you *E1*
283:40 BARBARA: They . . . a wife. *Ed.*]
Barbara: ~ . . . Frederick . . . ~
~. *MS Om. Per*
284:4 you—] ~. *Per*
284:6 *(There is a silence.) Ed.*] (There
is a silence) *MS Om. Per*
284:9 FREDERICK: Ha . . . *adore* you—
Ed.] Frederick: ~ . . . Barbara
. . . ~ ~ — *MS Om. Per*
284:15 *(showing his teeth) Ed.*]
(showing his teeth) *MS Om.
Per*
284:15 daresay.—] dare say. *Per*
284:16 —I didn't appreciate you—]
Om. Per
284:23 You had . . . good husband.']
Om. Per
284:27 you—you didn't warm me—]
Om. Per
284:31 married.] ~ — *Per*
284:33 Lucerne.] ~? *Per*
284:35 —No] ~ *Per*
284:37 —And] ~ *Per*
284:38 —I sat . . . [285:7] it did. *Ed.*]

— ~ ~ ... Frederick ...
Barbara ... Frederick ...
Barbara ... ~ ~. *MS Om. Per*
285:9   It was hopeless.] *Om. Per*
285:11   tops?] ~! *Per*
285:13   How long ... deceiving me?]
         Om. Per
285:17   FREDERICK: And ... BARBARA:
         Never. *Ed.*] Frederick: ~ ...
         Barbara: ~. *MS Om. Per*
285:20   enquire] inquire *Per*
285:23   honor] honour *Per*
285:23   I?—] ~ — *Per*
285:26   FREDERICK: I ... *is silence.*) *Ed.*]
         Frederick: ~ ... There is
         silence) *MS Om. Per*
285:32   it—] ~? *Per*
285:37   FREDERICK: Though ... [286:1]
         leave you. *Ed.*] Frederick: ~ ...
         Barbara ... Frederick ...
         (another long silence) ...
         Barbara ... ~ ~. *MS Om. Per*
286:8   off.—] ~. *Per*
286:9   It may ... desperate one—]
         Om. Per
286:15   you.] ~? *Per*
286:16   you.] ~? *Per*
286:17   I have tried ... lightest wish.]
         Om. Per
286:21   you] ~, *E1*
286:21   me?—'] ~?"— *Per* ~?" *E1*
286:22   —why] Why *Per*
286:23   me—?] ~? *Per*
286:24   you. *(Crying.) Ed.*] ~ (crying)
         MS ~ [*crying*]; *Per* ~; *(crying)*
         E1
286:26   said] ~, *E1*
286:26   answer] ~, *Per*
286:27   —What] ~ *Per*
286:27   what was ... and falsity—] *Om.*
         Per
286:29   to you] ~ ~, *Per*
286:29   me—and] ~, ~ *Per*
286:32   Did you ... over it.] *Om. Per*
286:36   bit] piece *Per*
286:37   didn't— *Ed.*] did n't— *MS*
         didn't! *Per*
286:38   —You] ~ *Per*

286:40   away.—] ~ — *Per*
287:2   to.—] ~ — *Per*
287:3   I may ... [287:8] am done—]
         Om. Per
287:9   no,] ~ — *Per*
287:11   you've] you have *Per*
287:12   ruin.—] ~. *Per*
287:13   Something goes ... I keep
         sane—] *Om. Per*
287:15   sane—] ~. *Per*
287:18   no] ~, *Per*
287:18   no—no—] ~ — ~! *Per*
287:22   —I haven't ... [287:26] a
         squirrel—] *Om. Per*
287:31   When we were ... than you.—]
         Om. Per
287:34   paving-stone] paving stone *Per*
287:40   I didn't ... thought so—] *Om.*
         Per
288:4   time.] ~! *Per*
288:4   *(He shows ... eyes glitter.) Ed.*]
         (he shows his teeth—his dark
         eyes glitter) *MS Om. Per*
288:6   you.] ~! *Per*
288:7   you—] ~! *Per*
288:7   I could strangle you.] *Om. Per*
288:9   scream—] ~! *Per*
288:10   *suddenly Ed.*] suddenly *MS Om.*
         Per
288:12   devil.] ~! *Per*
288:13   hear—] ~?— *Per*
288:13   me—] ~? *Per*
288:15   Oh] oh *Per*
288:20   *(Another long silence.) Ed.*]
         (another long silence) *MS Om.*
         Per
288:25   me!—] ~! *Per*
288:26   falsity—?] ~? *Per*
288:35   No Frederick—why, *Ed.*] ~
         ~ — ~ *MS* ~, ~. Why, *Per*
288:37   FREDERICK: Why ... I was. *Ed.*]
         Frederick: ~ ... Barbara ... ~
         ~. *MS Om. Per*
289:5   there—] ~. *Per*
289:5   it would do me good.] *Om. Per*
289:8   —yes] Yes *Per*
289:8   you see] You ~ *Per*
289:10   I—] ~? *Per*

289:10 haven't I?—and ... you—*you*!]
  Om. Per
289:13 me,] ~ *Per*
289:14 it.] ~? *Per*
289:16 me—!] ~! *Per*
289:20 FREDERICK: And ... it did. *Ed.*]
  Frederick: ~ ... Barbara ... ~
  ~. *MS Om. Per*
289:25 waste paper] waste-/ paper *Per*
  waste-paper *E1*
289:27 sorry] ~, *Per*
289:27 can, I will] ~; ~ ~, *Per*
289:30 yes, you] ~! You *Per*
289:38 BARBARA: How ... [290:1]
  destroy me. *Ed.*] Barbara: ~ ...
  Frederick ... Barbara ...
  Frederick ... ~ ~. *MS Om.
  Per*
290:2 no] ~, *Per*
290:5 example.] ~? *Per*
290:8 FREDERICK: And ... don't
  know— *Ed.*] Frederick: ~ ...
  Barbara ... ~ ~ — *MS Om.
  Per*
290:14 months.] ~? *Per*
290:20 *(There is a silence.) Ed.*] (there
  is a silence) *MS Om. Per*
290:22 FREDERICK *(slowly)* ... [290:23]
  don't know. *Ed.*] Frederick
  (slowly) ... Barbara ... ~ ~.
  MS Om. Per
290:26 —But] ~ *Per*
290:26 know] ~, *Per*
290:29 Frederick—] ~. *Per*
290:29 I don't know *anything.*] *Om. Per*
290:30 come then] ~, ~, *Per*
290:33 tell.—] ~. *Per*
290:33 Frederick.] ~! *Per*
290:36 *cushion.* FREDERICK *suddenly ...
  and sobs—Ed.*] cushion.
  Frederick suddenly flings his
  arms on the table and sobs—
  MS cushion.]/ FREDERICK
  [*suddenly ... and sobs*]: *Per*
290:37 Oh Good] ~, good *Per*
290:38 it.] ~! *Per*
290:38 BARBARA *looks ... his shoulder.)
  Ed.*] Barbara looks at him, goes

and puts her hand on his
  shoulder) *MS* BARBARA [*looks
  ... his shoulder*]: *Per*
290:40 Don't] ~, *Per*
290:40 will.] ~! *Per*
291:1 it, Barbara.] it. *Per*
291:2 No] ~, *Per*
291:3 can—I ... *stops crying.) Ed.*]
  ~ — ~ ... (he stops crying)
  MS can. *Per*
291:5 me] ~, *Per*
291:6 No dear—no] ~, ~ ~, *Per*
291:9 know] ~, *Per*
291:11 —There's] ~ *Per*
291:22 BARBARA: He ... him in. *Ed.*]
  Barbara: ~ ... Lady Charlcote
  ... ~ ~. *MS Om. Per*
291:25 He'll probably ... to go.] *Om.
  Per*
291:28 Oh] ~, *Per*
291:28 it Mama.] ~, ~! *Per*
291:33 eleven—] ~. *Per*
291:36 Well—] ~, *Per*
292:3 one—] ~. *Per*
292:7 best] bed *Per*
292:7 —Goodnight!—Oh] Good
  night! ~, *Per*
292:8 Wesson—] ~, *Per*
292:12 *without taking ... of him Ed.*]
  without taking any notice of
  him *MS Om. Per*
292:14 you?—] ~? *Per*
292:15 do you want then] *do* you want
  Per
292:28 —tell] Tell *Per*
292:29 know—] ~. *Per*
292:29 I mean I don't know.] *Om. Per*
292:30 —I] ~ *Per*
292:31 merely] *Om. Per*
292:36 that.] ~? *Per*
292:37 not?—] ~? *Per*
292:39 here,] ~ *Per*
293:6 was it—] ~ ~? *Per*
293:8 that—at ... rate] ~. At ... ~,
  Per
293:10 so] *Om. Per*
293:15 —what] What *Per*
293:17 WESSON: It's ... of goods. *Ed.*]

Wesson: ~ ... Barbara ... ~
~. *MS Om. Per*

293:25 mighty *Per*] ~, *MS*
293:28 puppy dog] puppy-dog *Per*
293:31 him then] ~, ~, *Per*
293:32 him.] ~? *Per*
293:35 *house*] house *Per*
293:36 Pooh—what] ~! What *Per*
293:36 house—] ~? *Per*
293:36 poor little ... house
 contaminated!] *Om. Per*
294:1 his] this *E1*
294:4 to—] ~. *Per*
294:5 Oh] ~, *Per*
295:2 *Scene: The same. Ed.*] Scene:
 The same *MS SCENE.—The
 same. Per Om. E1*
295:3 *Time: Ed.*] Time: *MS
 TIME.— Per Om. E1*
295:5 am] ~, *Per*
295:7 Hôtel] Hotel *Per*
295:11 *not* going to Gardone] not ~ ~
 ~ *Per*
295:12 Hôtel *Ed.*] Hotel *MS*
295:13 WESSON: You ... Goodbye,
 monsieur. *Ed.*] Wesson: ~ ...
 Barbara ... ~, ~. *MS Om. Per*
295:19 I remember ... [295:31] all
 right. *Ed.*] ~ ~ ... Wesson ...
 Barbara ... Wesson ... Barbara
 ... ~ ~. *MS Om. Per*
295:32 hand-bag] handbag *Per*
295:34 WESSON: It's ... the Hôtel. *Ed.*]
 Wesson: ~ ... Barbara ... ~
 ~. *MS Om. Per*
295:36 hankys] hankies *Per*
296:6 to me] *Om. Per*
296:11 me,] ~ *Per*
296:11 upbringing] bringing-up *Per*
296:12 Oh] ~, *Per*
296:12 right.] ~! *Per* alright! *E1*
296:13 that] *Om. Per*
296:17 at all] *Om. Per*
296:18 Yes] ~, *Per*
296:19 No] ~, *Per*
296:22 Well] ~, *Per*
296:22 Lire] lire *Per*
296:25 *night*] night *Per*

296:26 *(A silence ensues.) Ed.*] (a
 silence ensues) *MS Om. Per*
296:27 well—] ~, *Per*
296:31 are.] ~! *Per*
296:34 WESSON: Now?/ BARBARA: Yes.
 Ed.] Wesson: ~?/ Barbara: ~.
 MS Om. Per
296:36 liar] Liar *Per*
297:1 *one pin, pulls off the hat, flings
 that Ed.*] one pin, pulls off the
 hat, flings that *MS hat, flings it
 Per*
297:4 fool.—] ~. *Per*
297:9 see—] ~! *Per*
297:11 to] ~, *Per*
297:16 you.] ~? *Per*
297:17 *backwards Ed.*] backwards *MS
 backward Per*
297:24 *speaks, faltering Ed.*] speaks
 faltering *MS speaks falteringly
 Per*
297:25 you Barbara.] ~, ~? *Per*
297:26 do,] ~ *Per*
297:27 *believe*] believe *Per*
297:27 there.] ~! *Per*
297:28 And you shan't—!] *Om. Per*
297:31 *You*] You *Per*
297:39 Giacomo,] ~. *Per*
297:39 I make him suffer so.] *Om. Per*
298:4 shall.] ~! *Per*
298:5 —You] ~ *Per*
298:6 choking] ~. *Per*
298:6 himself.—He'll ... the end.]
 Om. Per
298:8 *(Her head ... his shoulder.) Ed.*]
 (her head is on his shoulder)
 MS Om. Per
298:9 —You] ~ *Per*
298:14 BARBARA: But ... WESSON: Yes.
 Ed.] Barbara: ~ ... Wesson: ~.
 MS Om. Per
298:16 on] *Om. Per*
298:23 you] ~, *Per*
298:25 *Malheuresement*]
 Malheureusement *Per*
298:34 anyhow] anyway *Per*
298:39 —No] ~ *Per*
299:1 BARBARA: Sure?/ WESSON: Yes.

Ed.] Barbara: ~?/ Wesson: ~.
MS Om. Per

299:5 —And] ~ *Per*

299:5 Frederick] ~, *Per*
299:6 you.] ~? *Per*
299:12 —But] ~ *Per*

The Daughter-in-Law

MS = Autograph MS (Roberts E84a)
TCCI = Carbon copy TS (Roberts E84c)
TSII = Ribbon copy TS (Roberts E84b)
E1 = *Complete Plays* (Heinemann, 1965)

Silent emendations

1 'Gascoyne' – the spelling of *MS* – has been silently adopted throughout for the spelling 'Gascoigne' in *TCCI*, *TSII* and *E1*; the spelling 'Gascoigne' is indicated only when another variant is being recorded.

2 DHL gave single inverted commas for quotations within speeches and for names such as the 'Bell o' Brass' (311:15): *TCCI* and *TSII* often, and *E1* always, employ double inverted commas. DHL's practice has been adopted, but is not recorded except when another variant is being listed.

3 DHL frequently wrote ages and numbers without a hyphen, e.g. 'twenty two' and 'twenty one' (311:16), and almost always writes 'goodnight', 'goodbye', 'tonight', 'today', 'tomorrow' and 'tomorrer': his typists and printers frequently inserted hyphens or (in the case of 'goodnight') made two words out of one. In each case, DHL's practice has been adopted, and the typed and printed variants not recorded.

4 DHL usually wrote 'o'clock' without the apostrophe; the apostrophe has been silently inserted. At 356:14 a dialect variant ('aclock') in *MS* has been accepted and no apostrophe inserted. Other misplaced or missing apostrophes are recorded only if there is clear evidence of DHL preferring the misplacement (see, e.g., Textual apparatus and Explanatory notes for 354:11): errors such as 'Isnt' for 'Isn't' at 310:25 are not recorded.

5 DHL consistently wrote 'Missis' with a capital letter and 'mother' (as an address to Mrs Gascoyne and Mrs Purdy) with a small letter; *TSII* usually typed 'missis', and *E1* consistently printed 'missis' and 'Mother'. DHL's forms have been preferred, and such variants are not recorded except when another variant is being listed (as at 317:6 (ii)).

6 DHL consistently wrote 'All right' and 'all right': *E1* consistently emended to 'Alright' and 'alright': the readings of *E1* have not been recorded.

301:2 MRS GASCOYNE ... MINNIE GASCOYNE *Ed.*] *Om. MS* MRS GASCOIGNE / JOE / MRS PURDY / MINNIE *E1*

301:6 LUTHER GASCOYNE *Ed.*] *Om. MS* *The action of the play takes place in the kitchen of Luther Gascoigne's new home. E1*

301:7 CABMAN *Ed.*] *Om. MS*

303:3 *Scene: Ed.*] Scene: *MS Om. TCCI*

303:5 *Time: Ed.*] Time: *MS* TIME: *TCCI Om. E1*

303:6 *Personae: Ed.*] Personae: *MS* PERSONAE: *TCCI Om. E1*

303:9 *off his TCCI*] off his *MS* off *TSII off E1*

303:10 ha] ha' *TCCI*

303:11 *He Ed.*] He *MS JOE TCCI*
303:11 *the TCCI*] the *MS Om. TSII*
303:14 be-out] be out *TCCI*
303:19 an' hour] an hour *TCCI*
303:20 —why] Why, *TCCI*
303:21 brokken] broken *TSII*
303:22 ha'e] ha' *TSII*
303:24 gi'e] gie *TCCI*
303:26 *(He does Ed.)* (He does *MS*
        JOE: (*he does TCCI* JOE (does
        TSII JOE (*does E1*
303:26 *sulkily Ed.*] sulkily *MS sullenly*
        TCCI
303:28 when] where *TCCI*
303:28 I s'd] I'd *TCCI*
303:31 ma] me *TSII*
303:33 gammy arm] gammy-arm
        TCCI
303:35 rum-un] rum un *TCCI*
303:35 ha'ein'] ha'in' *TCCI*
303:36 *She gives TCCI*] She gives *MS*
        Gives *TSII* Gives *E1*
303:36 —An'] An' *TCCI*
303:37 wunna] winna *TCCI*
303:37 pay—another] ~. Another
        TCCI
303:39 *(blurts) Ed.*] (blurts) *MS Om.*
        TCCI
304:2 gi'e] gie *TCCI*
304:5 wouldna] wouldna' *TCCI*
304:6 thank yer] thank-yer *TCCI*
304:7 Well] ~, *TCCI*
304:7 raïght] raight *TCCI*
304:8 right] raight *TCCI*
304:9 *did*] did *TSII*
304:10 for pay for] fer pay fer *TSII*
304:11 'accident] accident *TCCI*
304:12 'titled] titled *TSII*
304:12 'e] he *TCCI*
304:17 pick-heft,] ~, — *TCCI* ~ —
        TSII
304:17 ta'e] ta's *TSII*
304:21 Yi] Ye' *TCCI*
304:23 gev] gen *TCCI*
304:24 accidint] accident *TCCI*
304:25 a-purpose] a'purpose *TCCI*
304:27 haccident] h'accident *TSII*
304:28 workin] workin' *TCCI*

304:30 that—] ~?— *TCCI*
304:34 enough] ~, *TCCI*
304:36 An'] An *E1*
304:36 bully raggin] bully-/ raggin'
        TCCI bully-raggin' *E1*
304:37 Bettesworth,] ~ *TCCI*
304:40 say] exactly say *TCCI*
304:40 Sir] sir *TCCI*
304:40 luikin'] linkin' *TCCI*
305:3 stall,] ~; *TCCI*
305:4 Well] ~, *TCCI*
305:6 cunjurin'] conjurin' *TSII*
305:6 pick heft] pick-heft *TCCI*
305:7 an' th'] an' the *TCCI*
305:8 know'.—] ~!" *TCCI*
305:8 twas] 'twas *TCCI*
305:9 done.'] ~. *TCCI*
305:10 Hm!] H'm. *TCCI* Hm. *E1*
305:11 clat-farted] clat-fasted *TCCI*
305:11 He says] He says, *TCCI*
305:12 me—Do] ~, 'Do *TCCI*
305:12 you know *TCCI*] you *MS*
305:13 haccident?] ~?' *TCCI*
305:13 —Take] '~ *TCCI*
305:14 mouth—' *Ed.*] ~ — *MS* ~.'"
        TCCI
305:15 out en's] outen's *TCCI*
305:15 ud do—] ~ ~. *TCCI* '~ ~. *E1*
305:18 comm] com *TCCI*
305:18 said 'Ow] ~: " 'Ow *TCCI*
305:19 said] ~, *TCCI*
305:19 on't' so] ~." So *TCCI*
305:19 says] ~, *TCCI*
305:20 on't—you] ~! You *TCCI*
305:20 —so] So *TCCI*
305:20 says] ~, *TCCI*
305:21 thripenny] thipenny *TSII*
305:21 No,' *Ed.*] ~.', *MS* ~,'. *TCCI*
        ~," *TSII*
305:21 —but] ~ *TCCI*
305:22 clunch'] ~," *TCCI*
305:22 wringin''] wringers," *TCCI*
305:23 says] ~, *TCCI*
305:23 you.] ~? *TCCI*
305:25 Why] ~, *TCCI*
305:27 ha] ha' *TCCI*
305:29 butty] ~, *TCCI*
305:30 rate.] ~? *TCCI*

305:30 yet—] ∼. *TCCI*
305:32 havin',] ∼; *TCCI*
305:33 afore yer] afore you *TCCI*
305:36 hanna—] ∼. *TCCI*
305:38 Ah] ∼, *TCCI*
305:38 sholl] shall *TCCI*
305:40 know, *TCCI*] ∼ *MS*
305:40 yer.] ∼? *TCCI*
306:1 ma] me *TSII*
306:2 mouse trap] mouse-trap *TCCI*
306:2 woman—you've *Ed.*] ∼/∼ *MS*
  ∼. You've *TCCI see note on*
  306:3
306:3 ter] to *TCCI*
306:4 better'nor] better nor *TCCI*
306:6 life—] ∼? *TCCI*
306:7 nowheer] nowhere *TCCI*
306:8 talk] ∼, *TCCI*
306:9 tongue—] ∼. *TCCI*
306:12 world.] ∼! *TCCI*
306:13 An' I'n] And I've *TCCI*
306:13 club money] club-money *TCCI*
306:15 nedna] needna *TCCI*
306:15 a] on *TCCI*
306:18 Now] ∼, *TCCI*
306:19 fortni't] fortnit *TCCI*
306:20 for,] ∼ — *TCCI*
306:20 as—] ∼ ... *TCCI*
306:21 *the TCCI*] the *MS Om. TSII*
306:23 *He rises—Ed.*] He rises— *MS*
  He rises; TCCI Rises, *TSII*
  Rises, *E1*
306:23 *the TCCI*] the *MS Om. TSII*
306:26 PURDY´S VOICE *Ed.*] Purdy's
  Voice *MS* PURDY *TCCI*
  PURDY *E1*
306:26 Well] ∼, *TCCI*
306:29 *in the TCCI*] in the *MS* in
  TSII in *E1*
306:31 PURDY´S VOICE *Ed.*] Purdy's
  Voice *MS* PURDY *TCCI*
  PURDY *E1*
306:33 PURDY *(appearing— Ed.*]
  Purdy's (appearing— *MS*
  PURDY *(appearing. TCCI*
  PURDY (appearing; *TSII*
  PURDY *enters. She is E1*
306:34 —I] ∼ *TCCI*

306:34 particler] partikler *TCCI*
  pertickler *TSII*
306:35 Oh] ∼, *TCCI*
306:39 my,] ∼! *TCCI*
307:3 an 's] an's *TCCI*
307:4 workin',] ∼; *TCCI*
307:5 know—!—] ∼! *TCCI*
307:6 th'] the *TCCI*
307:11 cumpany] company *TSII*
307:12 stall workin'] stall-/ workin'
  TSII stall-workin' *E1*
307:13 i's] in's *TSII*
307:16 Yis!] ∼. *TCCI*
307:18 four an' eight] four-an'-eight
  TCCI
307:19 nothink—] ∼. *TSII*
307:20 Frazer *Ed.*] Fraser *MS see notes*
307:26 his sen] hissen *TCCI*
307:27 batchelor] bachelor *TCCI*
307:34 Nethergreen.] ∼? *TCCI*
307:35 comfortable—it's] ∼. It's
  TCCI
307:36 th'] the *TCCI*
307:38 Yes!] ∼. *TCCI*
308:2 sickenin—well] sickenin'? Well
  TCCI
308:12 poorly] ∼, *TCCI*
308:13 comm] com *TSII*
308:15 sheet, *TCCI*] ∼ *MS*
308:15 mornin'] morning, *TCCI*
308:16 com'] com *TCCI*
308:17 as as] as 'as *TCCI* as *TSII*
308:17 myself.] ∼: *TCCI* ∼! *TSII*
308:20 a-cause] a'cause *TCCI*
308:21 a-Sat'day] a-Saturday, *TCCI* a'
  Saturday, *TSII*
308:21 wik days—an'] wik-days. An'
  TCCI
308:24 still—] ∼. *TCCI*
308:28 good natured] good-natured
  TCCI
308:29 myself] ∼, *TCCI*
308:31 trod.' *Ed.*] ∼. *MS* ∼." *TSII*
308:35 breath—] ∼. *E1*
308:35 —I'm] ∼ *TSII*
308:36 you] yer *TSII*
308:37 I.] ∼? *TCCI*
308:39 Nay—nay—] ∼, ∼, *TCCI*

308:39 niver] never *TCCI*
309:8   chilt] child *TSII*
309:12 Yea—yea] ~, ~, *TCCI*
309:14 Jim,] ~ *TSII*
309:14 palled] passed *E1*
309:15 Luther.—] ~. *TCCI*
309:16 th' 'Ram' *Ed.*] th' ~ *MS* "Th'
        ~" *E1*
309:22 man—] ~. *E1*
309:26 a] 'a *TCCI*
309:28 an'] and *TCCI*
309:29 lass.] ~? *TCCI*
309:30 niver] never *TCCI*
309:30 about—] ~. *E1*
309:31 th' fruit] the fruit *TCCI*
309:34 what—?] ~? *TCCI*
309:35 Well,—] ~ — *TCCI*
309:36 watters] wathers *TCCI*
309:36 like—] ~. *TSII*
309:37 ter] to *TCCI*
309:38 thowt] thought *TSII*
309:38 rether] rather *TCCI*
309:39 she'd] *she'd TSII*
309:39 know,] ~ — *TCCI*
310:3   piece—] ~ ... *TCCI*
310:4   th' 'Ram' *Ed.*] th' ~ *MS* "Th'
        ~" *E1*
310:4   wi'] wi *E1*
310:10 mysen] ~, *E1*
310:11 *he's] he's TCCI*
310:12 suffer.' *TCCI*] ~. *MS see notes*
310:14 An'] ~', *TSII*
310:15 mysen,] ~ *TSII*
310:20 ay,] *Om. TSII*
310:21 money.] ~! *TSII*
310:24 Nay] ~, *TCCI*
310:24 'er's] she's *TCCI*
310:25 she—oh] —?—~, *TCCI*
310:25 then.] ~? *TCCI*
310:27 fun'] fun *TCCI*
310:27 sale,] ~ *TCCI*
310:27 says 'well] ~, 'Well *TCCI*
310:29 come-day go-day] come-day-
        go-day *TSII*
310:32 can a] canna *E1*
310:33 much.] ~? *TCCI*
310:35 but—] ~ *TCCI*
310:35 an' he] an' she *E1*

310:37 tha'] thee *TCCI*
310:37 ower] over *TSII*
310:38 words—] ~. *TCCI*
310:38 Er] 'Er *TCCI*
311:2   'er—] ~. *TCCI*
311:8   nobody—] ~. *TCCI*
311:13 MRS GASCOYNE *Ed.*] Mrs
        Gascoyne *MS* MRS. GASC *TCCI*
        Om. TSII
311:15 uncle's] ~, *TCCI*
311:16 b'r] bu'r *TSII*
311:19 marry me] ~ ~, *TCCI*
311:19 mother'—] ~,' *TCCI* ~,"
        TSII Mother," *E1*
311:19 says] ~, *TCCI*
311:20 thinkin',] ~ *TCCI*
311:21 Howsoiver] Howsoever *TSII*
311:24 he—hadn't] ~? Hadn't *TCCI*
311:25 form.] ~? *TCCI*
311:26 see!] ~. *TCCI*
311:27 bidden.—] ~. *TCCI*
311:28 Hoity-toity] hoity-toity *TSII*
311:29 wasn't] wasna *TSII*
311:29 an] an' *TCCI*
311:30 myself 'she's] ~, she's *TCCI*
311:31 johnny in] johnny, *TCCI*
311:31 Berty-Willie] Bertie-Willie
        TCCI
311:31 cuffs.' *Ed.*] ~. *MS*
311:34 appen] 'appen *TCCI*
311:35 I'd] *I'd TCCI* I'd *TSII*
311:36 on't] o't *TCCI*
311:36 mormin'] mornin' *E1*
311:38 how do you do] ~-~-~ ~,
        TCCI ~-~-~-~, *TSII*
311:39 Gascoyne'] Gascoigne' *TCCI*
        Gascoigne", *E1*
311:39 walk,—] ~ — *TCCI* ~ ... *E1*
312:1   o'clock—*TCCI*] oclock— *MS*
        o'clock. *E1*
312:2   thank] Thank *E1*
312:3   Goodnight] Good night, *TCCI*
312:4   dies,] ~ *TCCI*
312:5   wi'] with *TCCI*
312:5   I'd] *I'd TCCI*
312:7   see her] see 'er *TSII*
312:7   ter th'] to the *TSII*
312:8   says] ~, *TCCI*

312:9 Luther',] ~,' *TCCI* ~, *E1*
312:9 shillin] shillin' *TCCI*
312:9 please—] ~." *E1*
312:10 'e] he *TCCI*
312:11 'im—] '~. *E1*
312:13 tail coat] tail-coat *TCCI*
312:13 pays.—Yes,] ~. "~," *E1*
312:14 that's] "~ *E1*
312:15 folk—] ~." *E1*
312:16 she.] ~? *TCCI*
312:17 except] cept *TCCI* 'cept *TSII*
312:20 'a been] bin *TCCI*
312:25 service.—] ~? *TCCI*
312:25 letter] ~: *TCCI*
312:26 thinkin'] thinking *TSII*
312:33 —Well] ~, *TCCI*
312:34 com'] com *TSII*
312:35 an'] and *TSII*
312:35 com'] com *TSII*
312:36 ha'ef] haef *TSII*
312:37 says] ~, *TCCI*
312:38 ha] ha' *TCCI*
312:39 says] ~, *TCCI*
312:39 put's i's] puts i's *TSII* puts 's *E1*
312:40 says] ~, *TCCI*
313:1 unlacin's] unlacin' 's *TCCI*
313:3 ter] to *TCCI*
313:3 do?' I … ter say?'] say?' *TCCI*
313:8 ha'ef] haef *TSII*
313:8 thinks 'that's] ~, 'That's *TCCI* ~: "That's *E1*
313:9 gev'] gen *TCCI*
313:10 read—] ~. *E1*
313:11 ter] to *TCCI*
313:11 says] ~, *TCCI*
313:13 money,] ~ *TSII*
313:14 ha'e] have *TCCI*
313:15 ter me] to me, *TCCI* to me: *E1*
313:16 a'right] ~? *TCCI*
313:16 —I says] ~ ~, *TCCI*
313:16 so,] ~; *TCCI*
313:19 A'nt's,] ~ *TCCI*
313:19 says What] ~: "~ *E1*
313:20 want?] ~?" *E1*
313:20 says 'thee] ~, 'Thee *TCCI* ~: "Thee *E1*
313:20 tha' *TCCI*] that *MS* tha *TSII*

313:21 says] ~, *TCCI* ~: *E1*
313:21 biout] bi-/ out *TSII* bi-out *E1*
313:22 owd fashioned] owd-fashioned *TCCI* old-fashioned *TSII*
313:23 says 'that's] ~, 'That's *TCCI* ~: "That's *E1*
313:23 Minnie'—she says] ~.' She ~, *TCCI* ~." She ~: *E1*
313:25 her.—] ~. *TCCI*
313:25 he] her *TCCI*
313:27 house—] ~. *TCCI*
313:30 Missis—] missis— *TSII* missis. *E1*
313:31 she *TCCI*] she *MS* who *TSII* who *E1*
313:35 it,] ~; *TCCI*
313:38 iver] ever *TCCI*
313:39 afore hand] aforehand *TCCI*
314:2 wi'thee] withee, *TCCI*
314:6 say—!] ~. *TCCI*
314:10 nights—] ~/ *TCCI* ~. *TSII*
314:11 Varley's,] ~ — *TCCI*
314:12 gallivantin'—] ~. *TCCI*
314:13 was.—] ~. *TCCI*
314:13 for] fer *TSII*
314:14 th'] the *TSII*
314:23 Well—] ~, *TCCI*
314:23 court—] ~. *TCCI*
314:23 thought 'His] ~, ~ *TCCI* ~, his *E1*
314:24 to—'] ~ — *TSII* ~ —— *E1*
314:34 Batford] Batsford *TCCI* see notes
314:35 An'] And *TCCI*
314:38 'inducement] inducement *TCCI*
314:38 for] ~, *TCCI*
315:3 man—] ~. *TCCI*
315:4 Missis,] ~; *TCCI* missis; *TSII*
315:6 want—thirty] ~? Thirty *TCCI*
315:6 pound] pounds *TSII*
315:7 Stapleton,] ~; *TCCI*
315:11 Well] ~, *TCCI*
315:13 th'] the *TCCI*
315:16 him.—Eh] ~? ~, *TCCI*
315:18 and] *Om. TCCI*
315:19 afront] a-/ front *TSII* a-front *E1*

315:20 ivrything's] iverything's *TCCI*
315:23 her.] ~? *TCCI*
315:31 in.] ~? *TCCI*
315:35 enough—] ~. *E1*
315:37 Why] ~, *TCCI*
315:39 her] 'er *TCCI*
316:1 it then,] ~, ~; *TCCI*
316:2 warm.] ~? *TCCI*
316:4 and My Sirs] ~, my sirs *TCCI*
316:4 sirs] ~, *TCCI*
316:4 it.] ~! *TCCI*
316:6 know.] ~? *TCCI*
316:8 lad,] ~; *TCCI*
316:8 thee] ~, *TSII*
316:11 it—isna it.] ~? — ~ ~? *TCCI*
316:12 'im—] ~. *TCCI*
316:14 it!] ~? *TCCI*
316:14 thysèn] thysen *TCCI*
316:15 today,] ~ *TCCI* terday *TSII*
316:16 been] bin *TCCI*
316:16 sets] sits *TCCI*
316:20 ter.] ~! *TCCI*
316:22 bletherin] bletherin' *TCCI*
316:23 thysèn] thysen *TCCI*
316:24 thee.] ~? *TCCI*
316:26 ud ... ud] 'ud ... 'ud *TCCI*
316:26 lad.—] ~. *E1*
316:27 it.—Er'd] ~? 'Er'd *TCCI* ~? 'Er's *TSII*
316:28 cause] 'cause *TCCI*
316:31 knowin'] knowing *TSII*
316:32 Well] ~, *TCCI*
316:32 shifty] shiftly *TSII*
316:35 better.—] ~. *E1*
316:36 yourn has,] yours ~; *TCCI*
316:37 all.—] ~. *E1*
316:39 scot free] scot-free *TCCI*
317:3 Street.] ~? *TCCI*
317:6 Gi'e] Gie *TSII*
317:6 mother,] ~; *TCCI* Mother; *E1*
317:7 wunna. *Ed.*] ~ *MS* ~! *TCCI*
317:8 ter] to *TSII*
317:11 'em] them *TSII*
317:11 themselves—it's] ~. It's *TCCI*
317:12 th'] the *TCCI*
317:15 An'] And *TCCI*
317:22 mine.—] ~. *E1*
317:22 Well—] ~, *TCCI*

317:24 An'] And *TSII*
317:29 Well—] ~, *TSII*
317:29 afternoon—] ~. *TCCI*
317:30 GASCOYNE *and* JOE *Ed.*]
  Gascoyne—Joe *MS* GASC
  TCCI GASCOIGNE *E1*
317:30 afternoon—good afternoon]
  afternoon./JOE { JOE *E1* }:
  Good afternoon *TCCI*
317:32 Well] ~, *TCCI*
317:33 wi' im] wi' 'm *TCCI* wi'm
  TSII
317:33 a'] all *TSII*
317:37 could.] ~! *TCCI*
317:38 *rage—Curtain Ed.*]
  rage—curtain *MS* rage *TCCI*
  rage *TSII* rage. *E1*
318:8 *the clock TCCI*] the clock *MS*
  clock *TSII* *clock E1*
318:8 *the lamp TCCI* the lamp *MS*
  lamp *TSII* *lamp E1*
318:9 him] ~, *TCCI*
318:9 half an' hour] half-an-hour
  TCCI
318:11 tick—] ~ ... *TCCI*
318:11 scratch,] ~; *TCCI* cratch; *TSII*
318:12 is.—] ~. *TCCI*
318:12 enough!—] ~! *TCCI*
318:19 *the TCCI*] the *MS Om. TSII*
318:23 finishin'] finishing *TSII*
318:23 com'] com *TSII*
318:24 bantle] batch *TSII*
318:29 *his Ed.*] his *MS* the *TCCI*
318:34 wesh] wash *TSII*
318:37 weshes] washes *TSII*
318:37 his-sèn] hissen *TCCI*
319:1 Eh] ~, *TCCI*
319:6 *going*] *go*ing *TCCI*
319:7 Ay] ~, *TCCI*
319:15 on] ~, *TCCI*
319:18 Oh] ~, *TCCI*
319:21 ter—] ~?— *TCCI*
319:23 bother,] ~ — *TCCI*
319:23 time,] ~ — *TCCI*
319:25 too] ter *TCCI*
319:26 o'] of *TSII*
319:26 failins] failin's *TCCI*
319:28 my] mu *TCCI*

319:28 cos] 'cos *TCCI*
319:28 ter] tha *TSII*
319:30 luck.—] ~. *E1*
319:32 been] bin *TSII*
319:35 —no] No *E1*
320:3 come.—] ~. *E1*
320:11 right—] ~.— *TCCI*
320:18 no-o!] ~. *TCCI*
320:19 *mustache Ed.*] mustache *MS*
    moustache TCCI
320:22 you,] ~; *TCCI*
320:24 Why,] ~ *TCCI*
320:26 rether] rather *TSII*
320:30 Hae!] ~ *TCCI* Hao *E1*
320:34 —you're] You're *TCCI*
321:6 laws—] ~!—*TCCI*
321:7 are] ~, *TCCI*
321:9 Nay] Bay, *TCCI* Nay, *TSII*
321:10 ivrywheer] ivrywhere *TCCI*
321:11 afford—] ~. *E1*
321:12 gre't] gret *TCCI*
321:14 year—] ~. *TCCI*
321:21 dunna] don't *TCCI*
321:22 get it.] do it? *TCCI*
321:22 thirty one—] thirty-one—
    TCCI thirty-one. *E1*
321:27 Why] ~, *TCCI*
321:27 doin'.] ~? *TCCI*
321:29 job:] ~; *TSII*
321:34 anything—] ~. *TCCI*
321:37 dayman] day-man *TCCI*
322:7 him] ~, *TCCI*
322:11 a tooth out] out a tooth *TSII*
322:21 ha'epenny] ha'penny *TCCI*
322:21 go.] ~? *TCCI*
322:22 No,] ~; *TCCI*
322:24 ha'epenny] ha'penny *TCCI*
322:25 Yis, thee] Yi. Thee *TCCI*
322:26 Why] ~, *TCCI*
322:29 Oh!—] ~! *E1*
322:33 me—it] ~? It *TCCI*
322:33 doin's?] ~. *TCCI*
322:35 for] ~, *TCCI*
322:36 you—are you—] ~! Are ~!
    TCCI
322:38 JOE *E1*] *Om. MS* JOE *TCCI*
322:38 commin' in] comin' in, *TCCI*
322:38 snarlin'. *TCCI*] ~) *MS*

322:39 in,] ~; *TCCI*
322:39 thee.] ~./ JOE { JOE *E1*} *enters.*
    TCCI
322:40 JOE *(entering):* Ed.] Joe
    (entering): *MS* JOE
    (ENTERING) *TCCI* JOE: *E1*
322:40 *yet*] yet *TCCI*
323:1 sins—] ~.— *TCCI* ~. *E1*
323:10 head.] ~? *TCCI*
323:14 spoon—shonna] ~. Shonna
    TCCI
323:17 th'] the *TCCI*
323:19 I.] ~? *TCCI*
323:19 floor 'break] ~, 'break *TCCI*
    ~: "Break *E1*
323:19 oh floor.] O floor! *TCCI*
323:21 right—] ~. *E1*
323:26 service. *Ed.*] ~ *MS* ~! *TCCI*
323:28 Er's] 'Er's *TCCI*
323:28 service,] ~/ *TCCI* ~ *TSII*
323:33 ha'ena] haena *TCCI*
323:36 But—] ~, *E1*
323:36 dearly beloved] dearly-beloved
    TCCI
323:37 brethren—] ~, *TCCI*
323:37 weep:] ~; *TSII*
323:38 dinner-plates.] ~ ... *TCCI*
323:38 Come] ~, *TCCI*
323:39 Minnie—] ~,— *TCCI* ~, *E1*
324:9 'er] her *TSII*
324:14 an'] and *TCCI*
324:16 *the TCCI*] the *MS Om. TSII*
324:20 gi'e 't] gi'e't *TCCI*
324:20 —But] ~—, *TCCI* ~, *E1*
324:20 Sorry] sorry *TCCI*
324:20 in] *Om. TSII*
324:20 it—] ~. *E1*
324:27 no—] *Om. TSII*
324:29 rule] ~, *TCCI*
324:31 does] dost *TCCI*
324:33 'er] her *TSII*
324:35 *A Ed.*] a *MS* A *TCCI Om.*
    TSII
324:37 commin'] com-/ in' *TCCI*
325:3 Ay—why] ~. Why *TCCI*
325:4 'er's] she's *TSII*
325:5 commin'] com-/ in' *TCCI*
325:6 Says *TCCI*] says *MS*

325:7 childt] child *TSII*
325:9 Oh] ~, *TCCI*
325:13 Harriet's *Ed.*] Harriets *MS*
Harriet *TCCI*
325:14 Oh] ~, *TCCI*
325:15 thought] ~, *TSII*
325:19 Goodness] goodness *TCCI*
325:20 pound—] ~. *E1*
325:22 Well] ~, *TCCI*
325:22 arena—] ~, *TCCI* arena', *TSII*
325:27 wishin] wishin' *TCCI*
325:28 God.] ~! *TCCI*
325:36 ha'ef an'hour] ha'ef an hour
TCCI haef an hour *TSII*
325:36 tha] than *E1*
325:37 hersen] thysen *TSII*
325:38 Er'll] 'Er'll *TSII*
325:38 an'] an *TCCI*
325:39 her.—] ~ ... *TCCI* 'er ...
TSII
325:39 meant—look] ~ —Look *TCCI*
~ ——Look *E1*
325:39 Joe—] ~, *TCCI*
325:40 now—!] ~! *TCCI*
326:2 minnit—nay] ~ —Nay *TCCI*
~. Nay *E1*
326:3 ha'—Joe—] ~ — ~ ... *TCCI*
~. ~ ... *E1*
326:6 Er never ne'd] 'Er niver ned
TCCI
326:7 Ah] ~, *TCCI*
326:7 though—] ~ ... *E1*
326:9 I'n] I've *TCCI*
326:10 Well—] ~, *TSII*
326:10 ha] ha' *TCCI*
326:11 it—] ~ ... *E1*
326:12 anyhow] ~, *TSII*
326:13 else.—] ~. *TCCI*
326:13 Arena] Arena' *TSII*
326:15 Er'll] 'Er'll *TCCI*
326:15 minnit—] ~. *TCCI*
326:18 somewheer] somewhere *TCCI*
326:20 thee. *TCCI*] ~ *MS* ~? *TSII*
326:27 know—sit] ~. Sit *TCCI*
326:28 says] sayd *TCCI* said *TSII*
326:28 What's] what's *E1*
326:30 righter] right *TCCI*
326:32 isn't] isna *TSII*

326:33 mester] Mester *TCCI*
326:37 that.—] ~ — *TSII* ~. *E1*
326:37 Eh] ~, *TCCI*
326:38 you'n] you've *TCCI*
326:39 Yes—] ~, *TCCI*
327:1 —So] ~ *TCCI*
327:1 it!] ~? *TCCI*
327:2 Ah—] ~, *TCCI*
327:2 it.] ~? *TCCI*
327:3 natty—very] ~. Very *TCCI*
327:5 *(Exit ... R.) Ed.*] (exit the two,
door R) *MS* EXEUNT the
two, door R. *TCCI* JOE *and* MRS
PURDY *exit R. E1*
327:7 mind.—] ~. *TCCI*
327:7 oldfashioned] old-fashioned
TCCI
327:8 like!—] ~! *E1*
327:9 JOE′S VOICE *Ed.*] Joe's Voice *MS*
JOE *TCCI* JOE *E1*
327:11 PURDY′S VOICE *Ed.*]
Purdy's Voice *MS*
PURDY *TCCI* PURDY *E1*
327:11 rether] rather *TSII*
327:12 JOE′S VOICE *Ed.*] Joe's Voice *MS*
JOE'S Voice *TCCI* JOE *TSII*
JOE *E1*
327:16 *dry Ed.*] dry *MS* Om. *TCCI*
327:19 well] ~, *TCCI*
327:19 it.—] ~. *TCCI*
327:21 theirselves] themselves *TCCI*
327:21 chairs] ~, *TSII*
327:25 to 'm] to'm *TCCI*
327:29 yes!] ~. *TCCI*
327:29 mysen,] ~ *TCCI*
327:30 my nose off] off my nose *TCCI*
327:35 yer.] ~? *TCCI*
327:37 I'n] I've *TCCI*
327:38 Yes] ~, *TCCI*
328:2 *singlet TCCI*] singlit *MS*
328:5 did!] ~. *TCCI*
328:7 luck—an'] ~. An' *TCCI*
328:7 goodnight] good-night, *TCCI*
good night, *E1*
328:12 Ah] Ay *TCCI*
328:16 Ah.] ~! *TCCI*, *E1* ~.! *TSII*
328:18 bu'] but *TSII*
328:18 is,—] ~ — *TSII*

328:20 *A Ed.*] a *MS Om. TSII*
328:20 Bertha] ~, *TCCI*
328:20 pay.] ~! *TCCI*
328:21 Eh] ~, *TSII*
328:22 says, 'Dunna] ~, 'dunna *TCCI*
328:23 him.] ~! *TCCI*
328:23 Right's] right's *EI*
328:24 thing] ~. *TCCI* ~, *TSII*
328:25 did!] ~. *EI*
328:28 nak'd] nek'd *TSII*
328:28 gre't] gra't *TSII*
328:29 gabey] gaby *TSII*
328:30 *can*] can *TCCI*
328:30 blessin'] blessing *TSII*
328:31 ma'] mau *TSII*
328:32 non i'] non in *TSII*
328:34 childt 'll] childt'll *TCCI*
328:37 commin'] comin' *TSII*
328:38 hours,] ~. *TSII*
328:38 her] 'er *TSII*
328:39 business] ~, *TSII*
329:1   *back TCCI*] back *MS* hard
        TSII hard *EI*
329:2   no] ~, *TCCI*
329:2   Er] 'Er *TSII*
329:2   her] 'er *TSII*
329:3   appen] 'appen *TSII*
329:6   'a] *Om. TSII*
329:10 your] yer *TSII*
329:13 sometime] some time *TCCI*
329:14 ne'dna] nedna *TSII*
329:17 Lucy *Ed.*] Lizzie *MS* Lizzy
        TSII see note on 315:8
329:20 I'n] I've *TCCI*
329:21 Yea] Yes *TSII*
329:21 well—] ~ ... *EI*
329:23 yer] you *TSII*
329:27 lad.] ~! *TSII*
329:31 th'] the *TSII*
329:34 yi.—] ~. *TCCI*
329:36 trustin'] trusting *TSII*
329:40 ivrythink] everything *TSII*
330:9   Er] 'Er *TSII*
330:9   nowhow] nohow *TSII*
330:10 it—] ~. *TCCI*
330:12 Bertha,] ~ *TCCI*
330:14 wrong] ~, *TCCI*
330:15 wrong—] ~. *EI*

330:18 *(entering) Ed.*] (entering) *MS*
        (Entering) TCCI
        (ENTERING) *TSII Om. EI*
330:18 No] ~, *TCCI*
330:20 Good-evening] Good evening
        TCCI
330:21 Good-evening] Good evening,
        TCCI Good evenin', *TSII*
330:21 goin'.—] ~ — *TCCI*
330:22 sayin',] ~ *TCCI*
330:22 th'ouse] th' ouse *TCCI* th 'ouse
        TSII th' 'ouse *EI*
330:23 so.] ~? *TCCI*
330:24 do] ~, *TCCI*
330:25 th'] the *TCCI*
330:25 you.] ~! *TCCI* ~? *TSII*
330:29 *can*] can *TSII*
330:31 No] ~, *TCCI*
330:31 no thanks—] ~, ~. *TCCI*
330:32 Goodnight] good-/ night
        TCCI good-night, *TSII* good
        night, *EI*
330:33 JOE *EI*] Harry *MS* HARRY
        TCCI JOE *TSII see notes*
330:33 her *Ed.*] her *MS Om. TCCI*
330:33 *door—exit.) Ed.*] door—exit)
        MS door—she exits) *TCCI*
        door—she EXIT) *TSII door*;
        MRS PURDY *goes out. EI*
330:34 *away*—LUTHER *Ed.*]
        away—Luther *MS*
        away—LUTHER *TCCI* away)
        / (LUTHER *TSII away as*
        LUTHER *EI*
330:34 *to her husband TCCI*] to her
        husband *MS* To her husband
        TSII Om. EI
330:37 about?] ~. *TSII*
330:40 ah.] ~! *TCCI*
331:4   away.] ~? *TSII*
331:5   th'] the *TSII*
331:7   no'b'dy] ~, *TCCI* nobody
        TSII
331:8   oh dear o'] oh, dearo' *TCCI*
331:9   cinematograph] Cinematograph
        EI
331:11 wi'] with *TSII*
331:19 Sisson.] ~? *TCCI*

331:28 plates.] ~? *TSII*
331:28 *the TCCI*] the *MS* a *TSII* a *EI*
331:29 *plate TCCI*] plates *MS see notes*
331:30 shine.—] ~. *EI*
332:1   him.—] ~— *TCCI* ~. *TSII*
332:3   ah.] ~! *TCCI*
332:8   to.—] ~. *TCCI*
332:11 This—] ~ ... *EI*
332:16 No] ~, *TCCI*
332:17 nobody—] ~ ... *EI*
332:18 he—] ~... *EI*
332:21 four] your *TCCI*
332:22 an] an' *TSII*
332:25 wi] wi' *TCCI*
333:2   *Scene:* LUTHER'S *house. Ed.*]
        Scene: Luther's house. *MS*
        SCENE: *Luther's house. TCCI*
        SCENE: Luther's house. *TSII*
        Om. *EI*
333:3   *Time: Ed.*] Time: *MS* TIME:
        TCCI Om. *EI*
333:3   *o'clock TCCI*] o'clock *MS,*
        TSII o'clock. LUTHER'S *house*
        EI
333:4   *Personae: Ed.*] Personae: *MS*
        PERSONAE: *TCCI* Om. *TSII*
333:11 wheer] where *TSII*
333:11 been!] ~? *TCCI*
333:13 have!] ~? *TSII*
333:16 half drunk] half-drunk *TCCI*
333:20 t' *TCCI*] 't *MS*
333:20 sofey. It's] sofa; it's *TSII*
333:23 't] it *TCCI*
333:27 Oh] ~, *TCCI*
333:32 *the table TCCI*] the table *MS*
        table *TSII*
333:32 *for the Ed.*] for the *MS for his*
        TCCI
333:35 a'] Om. *TSII*
333:39 dying,] ~; *TSII*
334:3   non] now *TCCI* Om. *TSII see*
        notes
334:5   back] ~, *TSII*
334:7   bin] ~, *TSII*
334:7   an'] and *TSII*
334:7   haven't] ~, *TSII*
334:9   the 'Ram'] "The Ram" *EI*

334:30 crawling—!] ~! *EI*
334:31 glad!—I'm glad!—] ~! ~ ~!—
        TCCI ~! ~ ~! *TSII*
334:31 ta'e 't] ta'e't *TCCI*
334:35 ha'] ha'a *TCCI* ha'e *TSII*
334:36 Pah—] ~!— *TSII*
334:39 no—no—] ~ — —~. *EI*
335:4   God!—] ~! *EI*
335:7   Joe's *TSII*] Harry's *MS see*
        note on 330:33
335:8   gi'e thee.] gie ~. *TSII*
335:12 I'n] I've *TCCI*
335:16 is.—] ~. *TCCI*
335:18 muck] suck *TSII*
335:18 ouse] 'ouse *TSII*
335:18 art.] ~? *TSII*
335:19 go] go *TCCI*
335:20 her:] ~; *TCCI*
335:22 Her—who] ~?—Who *TSII* ~?
        Who *EI*
335:24 glad!—] ~! *EI*
335:24 the] tha *TSII see notes*
335:25 not.] ~? *TSII*
335:26 I] I *TCCI*
335:28 yi—] ~. *EI*
335:40 me *TSII*] thee *MS see notes*
336:4   But—] ~ ... *EI*
336:5   I] I *TSII*
336:5   *but!*] ~ —! *TCCI* ~ ...! *EI*
336:13 me—who] ~. Who *TSII*
336:26 dreamp] dreamt *TCCI*
336:27 mother—] ~ ... *EI*
336:29 her] 'er *TSII*
336:33 Batford] Balford *TCCI see note*
        on 314:34
336:33 where—] ~. *EI*
337:1   Eh] ~, *TSII*
337:3   pound] pounds *TSII*
337:4   scot free] scot-free *TSII*
337:8   would—] ~, *TCCI*
337:8   gie't] gi e't *TCCI* gi'e't *TSII*
337:12 care—] ~. *TCCI*
337:13 to?] ~! *TSII*
337:14 I s'll] I'll *TCCI*
337:17 me—] ~, *TSII*
337:18 thee *TCCI*] the *MS*
337:29 women] woman *TSII*
337:30 dunno.—I might.—I

dunno.—] ~ — ~ ~ — ~ ~ —
TCCI ~ — ~ ~ — ~ ~. E*ı*

337:37 —So] ~ TCCI
337:38 Tha] Yha *TSII*
337:38 a-cause] a'cause *TSII*
338:3 you!] ~? TCCI
338:15 Cos] 'Cos *TSII*
338:18 dirt— *MS, TSII*] durt—
    TCCI dirt. E*ı*
338:25 can't—think—] ~. Think! E*ı*
338:31 —I] ~ TCCI
338:35 —We'n] We've TCCI
338:37 never] niver *TSII*
339:5 faults.] ~! *TSII*
339:11 A' right.—] A'right. TCCI
339:13 gev] giv TCCI
339:16 gi'e] give *TSII*
339:16 ta'e] ha'e TCCI
339:18 I'n] I've TCCI
339:18 wiks] weeks *TSII*
339:21 so.—] ~. *TSII*
339:24 I] I *TSII*
339:25 Nay—] ~, *TSII*
339:25 that.—] ~ — TCCI ~. E*ı*
339:33 down.] ~! *TSII*
340:8 ought.—] ~ — TCCI ~ ——
    E*ı*
340:13 scullery girl] scullery-girl
    TSII
340:18 you.—] ~. E*ı*
340:21 ah.] ~! TCCI
340:25 you—] ~ ... E*ı*
340:32 woman.] ~! *TSII*
340:32 children.] ~! *TSII*
340:34 it.] ~! *TSII*
340:37 you.—] ~. TCCI
341:9 man.] ~! *TSII*
341:11 lying,] ~ TCCI
341:12 me.] ~? *TSII*
341:13 they—] ~ ... E*ı*
341:17 *you'd*] you'd TCCI
341:29 you. I'm] ~!~ *TSII*
342:2 *Scene: ... house. Ed.*] Scene:
    The kitchen of Luther
    Gascoyne's house *MS*
    SCENE:— THE KITCHEN
    OF LUTHER GASCOYNE'S
    HOUSE. *TCCI* SCENE: The

kitchen of Luther Gascoyne's
house. *TSII Om.* E*ı*

342:3 *Time: ... afternoon. Ed.*] Time:
    A fortnight later—afternoon.
    MS TIME:— A fortnight
    later—afternoon. *TCCI* TIME:
    A fortnight later—afternoon.
    TSII A fortnight
    later—afternoon. The kitchen of
    LUTHER GASCOIGNE's *house.* E*ı*
342:4 *Personae: Ed.*] Personae: *MS*
    PERSONAE: *TCCI Om. TSII*
342:4 sen*ʳ Ed.*] sen*ʳ MS* SENIOR
    TCCI senior *TSII senior* E*ı*
342:7 Yes, didn't] ~. Didn't *TSII*
342:9 nowt. Though] ~, though
    TCCI
342:10 you—how] ~. How *TSII*
342:11 Ha'ef a crown] Ha'ef-a-crown
    TSII
342:12 Ha'ef a crown] Ha'ef-a-crown
    TSII
342:13 Why] ~, *TSII*
342:15 *(Exit.) Ed.*] (exit) *MS* (EXIT)
    TCCI The CABMAN *goes out.* E*ı*
342:23 ouse] 'ouse *TSII*
342:30 they'n] they'm *TSII*
342:32 boozin',] ~ TCCI boomin'
    TSII
342:32 count.—] ~. E*ı*
342:35 Ay!] ~. TCCI
342:36 ha] ha' *TSII*
342:38 awhoam] a-/ whoam *TSII*
    a-whoam E*ı*
343:1 Charley] Sharley TCCI
343:7 wife] ~, *TSII*
343:10 sure.—] ~. E*ı*
343:11 carryin's on] carryins on TCCI
    carryin's-on *TSII*
343:12 Why,] ~ — *TSII*
343:14 Frazer *Ed.*] Fraser *MS see note*
    on 307:20
343:20 colliers] colliers' *TSII*
343:21 red-coats] red coats *TSII*
343:22 Frazer's] Fraser's TCCI
343:22 i 's] i's TCCI in's *TSII*
343:24 laughin'] laughing TCCI
343:26 Nay. That] ~, that *TSII*

343:26 They'n] They've *TCCI*
343:26 th'] the *TCCI*
343:27 sayn] says *TSII*
343:28 ha'ein] ha'en *TCCI*
343:30 Riotin'.— *MS, TSII*] ~ — *TCCI* ~. *EI*
343:30 bobbied] bobbled *TSII*
343:32 Oh] ~, *TCCI*
343:33 goes.— *MS, TSII*] ~ — *TCCI* ~. *EI*
343:34 a'tween] atween *TCCI*
343:35 Oh] ~, *TCCI*
343:37 Tuesday] ~, *TCCI*
343:37 'e] 'e's *TSII*
344:4 Australey] Australay *TCCI*
344:5 You] you *EI*
344:5 thinkin] thinkin' *TCCI*
344:7 Hm] H'm *TSII*
344:9 world.—] ~. *EI*
344:15 it!] ~. *TCCI*
344:15 fun] fun' *TSII*
344:16 gen' him] gen 'im *TSII*
344:17 suffice.—] ~. *EI*
344:20 Oh] ~, *TCCI*
344:20 good.—] ~. *EI*
344:21 it] ~, *TSII*
344:22 Why] ~, *TSII*
344:22 where] wheer *TCCI*
344:34 An'] And *TSII*
344:36 Missis] ~, *TSII* missis, *EI*
344:37 His] his *TCCI*
344:39 Hm!—] H'm!— *TSII* H'm! *EI*
345:4 Hm!—] H'm!— *TSII* H'm! *EI*
345:8 Hello,] ~! *TSII*
345:9 Yes,] ~. *TSII*
345:11 Nay—] ~, *TSII*
345:17 stood!—] ~! *EI*
345:21 thee.— *MS, TSII*] ~ — *TCCI* ~. *EI*
345:22 days.] ~? *TCCI*
345:25 *she*'d] she'd *TCCI*
345:26 her.—] ~. *EI*
345:27 Walked!] ~. *TSII*
345:30 'ad] had *TSII*
345:30 chapel] Chapel *TCCI*
345:31 Haseldine] Heseldine *TSII*
345:31 th'] "Th' *EI*
345:31 'Badger *Ed.*] ~ *MS*

345:31 Box' *Ed.*] ~ *MS* ~" *EI*
345:34 Frazer's] Fraser's *TCCI*
345:35 roads,] ~ *TCCI*
346:3 Them] Then *TSII*
346:3 workins *Ed.*] workin's *MS*
346:12 smilin] smilin' *TCCI*
346:14 Then] ~, *TSII*
346:20 Now] ~, *TSII*
346:23 us.] ~? *TSII*
346:26 I'n] I've *TCCI*
346:26 th'] the *TCCI*
346:30 yi.] ~! *TCCI*
346:31 well.—] ~. *EI*
346:32 skidaddled] skedaddled *TSII*
346:34 com'n] come *TSII*
346:35 not,] ~; *TSII*
346:36 th'] the *TSII*
346:36 mesters 'll] mesters'll *TCCI*
346:39 fr' *TSII*] fr *MS*
346:39 Rooks] Rooke *TSII*
346:40 mornin] mornin' *TCCI*
347:2 to 'm] to'm *TSII*
347:3 us then,] ~, ~ *TCCI*
347:3 we'n] we've *TCCI*
347:7 says] ~, *TSII*
347:7 He *TCCI*] He's *MS*
347:8 strike.—] ~. *EI*
347:10 days. *TCCI*] days *MS* ~? *TSII*
347:11 fool.] ~! *TSII*
347:14 All right—she's] All right.—She's *TSII* Alright.—She's *EI*
347:15 ouse] 'ouse *TSII*
347:17 ter] yer *TSII*
347:19 I Luther] ~, ~ *TCCI*
347:21 I] ~, *TSII*
347:29 him] ~, *TSII*
347:30 wunna—] ~. *EI*
347:31 me!—] ~! *TCCI*
347:31 fool] ~, *TSII*
347:33 went.—] ~ — *TCCI* ~. *EI*
347:35 *knew*—] ~. *EI*
347:40 neither—] ~,— *TSII*
348:1 Well Minnie—] ~, ~ — *TCCI* ~, ~, *TSII*
348:7 Twice] ~, *TSII*
348:7 knowledge] ~, *TSII*

348:9 gramophone *TCCI*]
 gramaphone *MS see notes*
348:10 Oh] ~, *TCCI*
348:21 know.] ~? *TSII*
348:23 *You*] You *TCCI*
348:24 child. You] ~, you *TCCI*
348:29 I?—] ~? *TCCI*
348:30 *love*] love *TCCI*
348:31 Purdy.] ~? *TCCI*
348:37 have I] ~, ~ *TSII*
349:2 looks] look *TSII*
349:6 word]~, *TSII*
349:13 Ah] Ay *E1*
349:14 *you*] you *TCCI*
349:15 your sons] some *TCCI*
349:21 about,] ~ *TCCI*
349:33 her] ~, *TSII*
349:35 for. *Ed.*] ~ *MS* ~? *TCCI*
349:35 *(Exit—furious.) Ed.*]
 (exit—furious) *MS*
 (EXIT—FURIOUS) *TCCI* (EXIT,
 furious) *TSII* LUTHER *goes out,*
 furious. E1
349:37 *do*] do *TCCI*
349:40 do!—] ~! *E1*
349:40 marry] ~, *TSII*
350:5 mothers.] ~? *TSII*
350:6 Oh] ~, *TCCI*
350:6 you.] ~? *TCCI*
350:8 this] ~, *TSII*
350:11 never ought] ought never *TSII*
350:14 true] ~, *TCCI*
350:17 *him*] him *TSII*
350:27 Nay] ~, *TCCI*
350:27 mother—] ~, *TSII* Mother, *E1*
350:28 an' 'll] an'll *TCCI*
350:28 yi!] ~. *TSII*
350:30 An'] And *TSII*
350:33 ah!—] ~! *E1*
350:36 death,] ~ *TCCI*
350:37 road.—] ~. *TCCI*
350:37 wish, yi] ~ ~, *TCCI* ~, ~,
 TSII
351:2 me—.] ~. *TCCI*
351:3 Nay] ~, *TCCI*
351:5 t'r *TCCI*] tr *MS*
351:6 Australia.] ~! *TSII*
351:14 Tother] T'other *TCCI*

351:22 Ay—] ~, *TSII*
352:1 keep] ~, *TSII*
352:2 on.] ~? *TSII*
352:5 is] ~, *TSII*
352:5 —It] ~ *E1*
352:6 ne'd] ned *TSII*
352:7 wouldn't] wouldna *E1*
352:10 almost] *Om. E1*
352:11 of him to have it] him to *E1*
352:12 did.] ~! *TSII*
352:15 I] *Om. TSII*
352:23 Why] ~, *TSII*
352:31 ring] ~, *TSII*
352:34 *her hand out TCCI*] her hand
 out *MS* out her hand *TSII out*
 her hand E1
352:35 Look] ~, *TCCI*
352:36 Hm!] H'm! *TCCI* H'm. *TSII*
352:37 word] ~, *TCCI*
352:37 diamond] ~, *TSII*
353:2 buy.] ~? *TCCI*
353:13 Well] ~, *TCCI*
353:13 T-t-t-t. *Ed.*] T-t-t-t *MS* T-t-t-t!
 TCCI
353:14 never] niver *TSII*
353:15 Nay—] ~, *TSII*
353:16 T-t-t-t-t] T-t-t-t *TSII*
353:17 rether] rather *TCCI*
353:17 th'] the *TSII*
353:18 I] ~, *TSII*
353:20 Er] 'Er *TSII*
353:22 dealers'] dealer's *TCCI*
353:24 ter.] ~? *TCCI*
353:28 children—] ~. *TSII*
353:31 to] ter *TSII*
353:31 want.—] ~. *E1*
353:31 died—] ~ ... *E1*
353:38 'er] ~, *TCCI*
354:2 that] ~, *TCCI*
354:6 well.] ~ ... *E1*
354:7 soup tickets] soup-/ tickets
 TSII soup-tickets *E1*
354:8 life.] ~! *TSII*
354:11 men's *TSII*] mens' *MS see*
 notes
354:14 not.—] ~. *TCCI*
354:15 week,] ~ *TCCI*
354:18 one.—] ~. *E1*

354:19 must—] ~, *TCCI*
354:22 lass,] ~; *TSII*
354:28 Hell] hell *TSII*
354:29 Ah—] ~!— *TSII*
354:31 Come] ~, *TCCI*
354:31 go,] ~; *TCCI*
354:31 go] ~, *TCCI*
354:37 do—] ~. *TCCI* ~! *TSII*
354:38 I—what] ~!—what *E1*
354:38 I—] ~ ——! *E1*
355:1 Nay-nay] Nay—nay *TCCI*
355:1 oh nay-nay,] ~, nay—nay, *TCCI*
355:1 oh nay-nay!] ~, nay—nay! *TCCI*
355:2 Joe—come] ~. Come *TSII*
355:3 come] ~, *TCCI*
355:6 dear—] ~!— *TSII* ~! *E1*
355:10 thee.—] ~. *E1*
355:10 Come] ~, *TCCI*
355:11 *Exit TCCI*] exit *MS* EXIT *TSII* MRS GASCOIGNE *goes out E1*
356:2 *Scene: The same. Ed.*] Scene: The same *MS* SCENE:– *The Same TCCI* SCENE: The same *TSII Om. E1*
356:3 *Time: Ed.*] Time: *MS* TIME:– *TCCI* TIME: *TSII Om. E1*
356:4 *Personae: Ed.*] Personae: *MS* PERSONAE: *TCCI Om. TSII*
356:5 *re-enter TCCI*] re-enter *MS* re-enters *TSII re-enters E1*
356:10 be.] ~? *TCCI*
356:12 he.] ~? *TCCI*
356:14 aclock] o'clock *TCCI*
356:15 says] ~, *TSII* ~: *E1*
356:18 brokken] broken *TSII*
356:21 nowheer] nowhere *TSII*
356:26 down] doen, *TSII* down, *E1*
356:28 fools.] ~? *TSII*
356:31 said] ~, *TSII* ~: *E1*
356:31 lads.] ~! *TSII*
356:32 killed.] ~? *TSII*
356:33 only] *Om. TSII*
356:33 are.—] ~. *E1*
356:36 brokken] broken *E1*
356:38 I's] I'se *TSII*

357:3 think?] ~ —? *TSII* ~ ——? *E1*
357:5 Hark—!] ~ — *TCCI* ~! *TSII*
357:7 ingines!] ~? *TSII*
357:9 down.—] ~. *E1*
357:10 chuffin',] ~ *TCCI*
357:11 night.—] ~. *TCCI*
357:15 them] *Om. TSII*
357:17 at.] ~? *TCCI*
357:18 gun] ~, *TSII*
357:18 never] niver *TCCI*
357:21 —But] ~ *E1*
357:23 spite] spit *TCCI*
357:24 Oh] ~, *TCCI*
357:24 say—why] ~ — ~, *TCCI* ~!— Why, *TSII* ~! Why, *E1*
357:25 *accidents*] accidents *TCCI* accidents, *TSII*
357:27 theirselves] ~, *TCCI* ~: *E1*
357:28 sorry'—else] ~', ~ *TCCI* ~," ~ —, *TSII* ~," ~: *E1*
357:29 Oh] ~, *TCCI*
357:30 but] ~, *TSII*
357:37 they?] ~! *TSII*
357:37 Yi] ~, *TCCI*
358:4 plain as plain] ~ ~ ~, *TSII* ~ ~ ~: *E1*
358:4 Now then] Nowthen *TSII*
358:6 sons.—] ~ — *TCCI* ~ —— *E1*
358:7 o' men] ~ ~, *TCCI*
358:10 husband] husbands *TCCI*
358:16 see.—] ~. *E1*
358:17 an'] and *TSII*
358:20 afternoon—] ~. *E1*
358:23 have.—An'] ~ —An' *TCCI* ~ —an' *TSII*
358:24 'em —] em— *TSII* 'em. *E1*
358:25 Nay] ~, *TCCI*
358:26 yea] yes *TSII*
358:28 Nay—nay—] ~. Nay. *E1*
358:30 him—] ~. *E1*
358:33 'im] 'em *TCCI*
358:37 proker—] poker— *TSII* poker. *E1*
358:38 Oh] ~, *TCCI*
358:38 oh no—] ~, ~ — *TCCI* ~, ~. *E1*

358:39 other—] ~. *E1*
359:1 hurt] ~, *TSII*
359:3 together—an'] ~. An' *TSII*
359:3 first—] ~. *TSII*
359:10 Comin'?—] ~? *TCCI*
359:10 *She goes TCCI*] She goes *MS*
    Goes *TSII Goes E1*
359:13 boy—] ~!— *TSII* ~! *E1*
359:16 Joe—] ~?— *TSII*
359:18 whoam—] ~. *E1*
359:19 *clenching Ed.*] clenching *MS*
    Clenching TCCI clutching
    TSII clutching *E1*
359:20 wakkened—] ~. *E1*
359:22 enow!] ~. *TCCI*
359:22 *(Exit.) Ed.*] (exit) *MS* (EXIT)

TCCI MRS GASCOIGNE *goes out.*
E1
359:25 I—I] I—I— *TCCI* I—I— *E1*
359:27 whoam—] ~. *E1*
359:29 gen] gev *TCCI*
359:29 head ache] headache *TCCI*
359:32 —Minnie!] ~. *TCCI* ~ —
    TSII ~ —— *E1*
359:36 my love—] ~ ~! *E1*
359:37 true—] ~. *E1*
359:38 No] ~, *TCCI*
359:38 isn't—it isn't—] ~ — ~ ~.
    TCCI
360:3 No—] ~, *TSII*
360:6 go—] ~. *E1*
360:17 Oh] ~, *TCCI*

Preface to *Touch and Go*

MS   = Autograph MS (no Roberts no.)
E1   = *Touch and Go* (Daniel, 1920), pp. 5–12

363:1 Preface] PREFACE *E1*
363:7 People's *E1*] Peoples *MS*
363:31 now—.] ~.— *E1*
364:2 Pfui—] *Pfui E1*
364:9 People's ——.] ~ —— *E1*
364:14 *people* i.e. *Ed.*] *people* i.e *MS*
    people, *i.e. E1*
364:22 it's *E1*] its *MS*
364:30 being,] ~ *E1*
364:31 clock-work] clockwork *E1*
364:39 Mr.] ~ *E1*
365:2 ballot-paper. *P* It *Ed.*] ~ / It
    MS ~. It *E1 see note on* 365:3
365:8 jew-jaws] gewgaws *E1 see notes*
365:8 ever.] ~! *E1*
365:9 all: A People's *E1*] all: A
    Peoples *MS*
365:13 pick-cum shovel cum ballot]
    pick-cum-shovel-cum-ballot *E1*
365:17 —My] ~ *E1*
365:19 department!—] ~! *E1*
365:20 ten] *Om. E1*
365:20 a People's *Ed.*] a Peoples *MS* A
    People's *E1*

365:26 us] —no *E1 see notes*
365:28 men still] still men *E1*
365:28 v.] *v. E1*
365:34 goes through,] comes through,
    E1
365:39 problem,] ~ *E1*
366:1 problem,] ~ *E1*
366:4 versus] *versus E1*
366:8 versus] *versus E1*
366:34 bully] Bully *E1*
366:36 bully's] Bully's *E1*
366:37 bully] Bully *E1*
367:2 condition—!] ~! *E1*
367:5 Portias *E1*] Portia's *MS*
367:5 heads *E1*] head's *MS*
367:7 says] ~, *E1*
367:12 still,] ~ *E1*
367:25 silence—] ~. *E1*
367:36 comprehend,] ~ *E1*
368:13 Hermitage. June 1919]
    HERMITAGE, / *June* 1919.
    E1

Touch and Go

MS   = Autograph MS (Roberts E401.6)
TCC   = Carbon copy TS (no Roberts no.)
E1   = *Touch and Go* (Daniel, 1920)

Silent emendations

1 DHL's practice in *MS* was regularly to hyphenate compounds such as 'Good-evening' and 'Good-night'; to capitalise 'Sir' when used by his men to Gerald Barlow; to write 'and' in 'Barlow and Walsall'; and not to provide a comma at the ends of the lines of the songs and poems quoted. *E1* regularly printed the compounds without hyphens, spelled 'sir' with a lower-case 's', printed an ampersand in 'Barlow & Walsall' and added a comma at the end of the lines of songs and poems. DHL's *MS* practice has been followed and the variants of *E1* have not in these cases been recorded in the Textual apparatus.

2 *TCC* regularly misspelled 'Breffitt' as 'Brefitt' or 'Breffit' and often typed 'it's' for 'its', but failed to influence *E1*; its variants in these cases have not been recorded.

3 *TCC* frequently failed to record a dash after terminal punctuation, and *E1* sometimes did; these variants have not been recorded.

371:5 [WILLIE HOUGHTON] *Ed.*] *Om.* MS	373:22 it,] ~ *E1*
371:6 [*including* JOB ARTHUR FREER] *Ed.*] *Om.* MS	373:30 frock coat] frock-coat *E1*
	373:36 you] ~, *E1*
371:19 Missis] missis *E1*	374:4 mind—] ~. *E1*
371:20 life,] ~ *E1*	374:4 Arthur—.] ~. *TCC*
371:20 Walsalls] Walsall's *E1*	374:20 acknowledgements]
371:28 like,] ~ *E1*	acknowledgments *TCC*
371:29 Walsalls'll] Walsall's 'll *E1*	374:22 red rag] red-rag *E1*
372:13 tha] thee *TCC see notes*	374:23 government] Government *TCC*
372:18 Shakespeare—"Oh] ~: "~, *E1*	374:23 pits,] ~ *E1*
372:19 slaves—"] Slaves". *TCC*	374:28 cow,] ~ *E1*
slaves!" *E1*	374:35 masters,] ~ *E1*
372:24 Oh] ~, *E1*	375:1 pudding—] ~.— *TCC*
372:24 he!] ~? *E1*	375:2 motor-car] motor car *E1*
372:24 Well] ~, *TCC*	375:4 *office men*] office men *TCC*
372:26 Bible,] ~ *E1*	375:5 led— *TCC*] ~,— *MS*
372:27 slaves.] ~! *E1*	375:9 men,] ~ *E1*
372:35 ma'ein'] ma'lin' *TCC* makin' *E1*	375:29 —how] How *E1*
	376:2 Church] church *E1*
373:1 for!] ~? *TCC*	376:3 Church] church *E1*
373:2 men] ~, *E1*	376:7 on] ~, *E1*
373:4 lie] Lie *E1*	376:11 —Yes] ~ *TCC*
373:4 down,] ~ *E1*	376:14 happy.—] ~. *TCC*
373:9 it.] ~? *E1*	376:15 Yes—] ~,— *TCC* ~, *E1*
373:9 government] Government *TCC*	376:15 France,] ~ *E1*
373:17 seven-pence ha'penny:] sevenpence ~, *E1*	376:18 sickening.] ~! *E1*
	376:21 here, Goodbye] ~, goodbye *TCC* ~: good-bye *E1*

376:23 But] ~, *E1*
376:23 say.—Wait] ~ —wait *TCC* ~, wait *E1*
376:24 in to] into *E1*
376:26 Close—] ~. *TCC*
376:32 Why] why *TCC* why, *E1*
376:37 Well] ~, *E1*
376:37 well] ~, *E1*
376:37 be—. You] ~ —you *TCC*
377:2 servant,] ~ *E1*
377:4 not at all—] ~ ~ ~. *TCC*
377:5 yes] ~, *E1*
377:6 sick nurse] sick-nurse *E1*
377:9 models—] ~: *E1*
377:11 them—] ~. *TCC*
377:12 But] — ~ *E1*
377:19 threads—?] ~? *TCC*
377:26 you,] ~ *E1*
377:29 to. I] ~ —I *TCC*
377:30 again—] ~, *E1*
377:35 you—] ~, *E1*
378:3 Whatmore—] ~. *TCC*
378:13 —Anabel] ~ *TCC*
378:15 woman.—] ~. *TCC* ~! *E1*
379:7 Gerald] Jack *TCC see notes*
379:8 thrush,] ~ *E1*
379:11 that—.] ~ — *TCC* ~!— *E1*
379:18 true] ~, *E1*
379:21 loved:] ~ — *E1*
379:23 you.] ~! *E1*
379:27 lovely.] ~? *TCC*
379:28 Well—] ~, *E1*
379:30 fluff,—] ~ — *TCC*
379:31 all—] ~, *E1*
379:32 know—] ~ —? *E1*
379:33 them.] ~! *E1*
379:34 Well] ~, *E1*
379:36 Oh] ~, *E1*
379:36 Oh,] oh, *TCC*
380:4 glass,] ~ — *E1*
380:7 Clock] clock *TCC*
380:7 Father's room.—] Father's room. *TCC* father's room. *E1*
380:9 painting,] ~ — *E1*
380:20 business—he'll] ~. He'll *E1*
380:22 Oh] ~, *E1*
380:29 collieries—] ~ *TCC*
380:30 company] Company *TCC*

380:37 nature:] ~ — *E1*
381:5 me,] ~ *E1*
381:6 it,] ~ — *E1*
381:8 Ah yes—ah yes] ~, ~!— ~, ~! *E1*
381:11 Oh Oliver—] ~, ~. *TCC* ~, ~! *E1*
381:12 [*at the door*] *Ed.*] Om. *MS*
381:12 Hello Winnie.] ~, ~! *E1*
381:13 sanctum,] ~: *E1*
381:14 Oh] ~, *E1*
381:17 'sculptress',] ~? *TCC* ~, *E1 see notes*
381:19 Good.] ~! *E1*
381:21 *perfectly*] perfectly *TCC*
381:24 Win.—] ~ — *TCC* ~, *E1*
381:25 Yes Oliver—] ~, ~, *E1*
381:27 *vigni-vignons,*] *Vigni-vignons*— *E1*
381:38 it.—Do—] ~. ~ — *TCC* ~!~ *E1*
381:38 ma] Ma *E1*
381:38 a] *à E1*
382:1 —ready] Ready *E1*
382:4 Oh—tired] ~!— ~! *E1*
382:5 Oliver—oh Oliver] ~!— ~, ~! *E1*
382:6 Ah] Oh, *TCC*
382:9 morning room—] morning-room. *E1*
382:22 Ah.] ~! *E1*
382:23 now—] ~?— *E1*
382:25 it is] ~, ~ *E1*
382:33 together—?] ~? *E1*
382:35 No—] ~, *E1*
382:36 *awful*] awful *TCC*
383:3 know:] ~ — *E1*
383:6 Yes—] ~, *E1*
383:6 Norwegian,—] ~ — *E1*
383:12 Ha—ha—] ~, ~, *E1*
383:15 right—?] ~? *TCC*
383:16 No—no—] ~ — ~ *TCC* ~, ~, *E1*
383:17 Oliver,] ~ — *E1*
383:27 me,] ~ *E1*
383:34 No] ~, *E1*
383:38 mean.] ~? *E1*
383:40 *loves*—] ~. *E1*

384:1   me—] ~. *TCC* ~? *E1*
384:3   Gerald—] ~? *E1*
384:7   Ah.—] ~ — *TCC* ~! *E1*
384:8   No—] ~, *E1*
384:17 knows.—] ~. *TCC* ~! *E1*
384:30 never—/OLIVER *Ed.*] ~—/
       Oliver *MS* ~./OLIVER *E1*
384:32 hope—] ~,— *E1*
384:34 him—] ~; *E1*
384:36 happiness,] ~ — *E1*
384:37 hope,] ~ — *E1*
384:38 Yes—] ~, *E1*
384:39 Norway,] ~,— *E1*
384:40 it—] ~,— *E1*
385:1   ice—] ~, *E1*
385:2   knew,] ~ *E1*
385:3   Yes.] ~, *TCC*
385:7   No—] ~, *E1*
385:7   Father] father *E1*
385:12 it.—] ~. *TCC*
385:13 Wrath?—] ~? *E1*
385:14 world—] ~?— *E1*
385:23 it—] ~. *TCC*
385:36 much.] ~!— *E1*
385:38 wolf!] ~? *E1*
386:1   back-bone] backbone *E1*
386:4   stiff] ~, *E1*
386:5   wish.] ~! *E1*
386:9   Good Morning—Good-
       morning] Good-
       morning—good-morning *TCC*
       good morning—good morning
       E1
386:10 gathering.] ~! *E1*
386:12 little.—Thank] ~ —thank
       TCC
386:16 schemes] ~, *E1*
386:17 homely.—] ~. *TCC*
386:23 we Winifred] ~ ~, *TCC* ~, ~,
       E1
386:24 No Daddy. It's] ~ ~, it's *TCC*
       ~, daddy, it's *E1*
386:27 us:] ~ — *E1*
386:28 know,] ~; *E1*
386:29 it,] ~ — *E1*
386:31 Gerald] ~, *E1*
386:34 poor] ~, *E1*
386:35 No-no] ~, ~ *E1*

386:35 Gerald, no-no.] ~ — ~, ~! *E1*
386:36 —No-no—] ~, ~: *E1*
387:1   nonsense.] ~! *E1*
387:2   clerks,] ~ *E1*
387:4   feeling,] ~ — *E1*
387:14 am] ~, *TCC*
387:22 Gerald,] ~ — *E1*
387:23 fight.] ~! *E1*
387:26 their] your *E1*
387:26 woman!] ~? *E1*
387:30 peace—?] ~? *TCC*
387:39 war,] ~ — *E1*
387:40 children,] ~ — *E1*
388:8   stab it] ~ ~, *E1*
388:9   fight.] ~! *E1*
388:11 Yes] ~, *TCC*
388:12 Winifred. She] ~ —she *E1*
388:15 weak,] ~ *E1*
388:24 celibate!] ~? *TCC*
388:28 earth.] ~? *TCC*
388:31 blameless.—] ~ — *TCC*
388:33 Don't blame ... your pride.]
       Om. E1
388:39 it.] ~! *TCC*
389:3   goodness.—] ~. *TCC*
389:6   mother, no] ~ — ~ *E1*
389:8   mother—] ~, *E1*
389:12 hope—] ~. *TCC*
389:13 it,] ~ — *E1*
389:15 Daddy] daddy *E1*
390:9   then. My] ~, my *TCC* ~: my
       E1
390:11 [*Exit* WILLIAM.] *Ed.*] *Om. MS*
       see notes
390:23 the "Lincolnshire Poacher",
       Ed.] the ~ ~, *MS* "The ~ ~,"
       E1
390:24 darling—] ~, *E1*
390:24 chorus.] ~.— *E1*
390:30 Ah] ~, *E1*
390:31 know,] ~: *E1*
390:32 oh do—] ~, ~! *E1*
390:34 Any:] ~. *TCC*
390:35 mother.] ~? *E1*
390:36 —If] ~ *TCC*
391:7   No indeed, no] ~, ~ — ~, *E1*
391:7   you! *Ed.*] ~? *MS* ~. *E1 see*
       notes

391:16 Yes Sir] ~ sir *TCC* ~, sir *E1*
391:18 to.—] ~. *TCC*
391:19 connoisseur *TCC*] conoisseur *MS*
391:23 charming.] ~, *TCC*
391:23 Wrath—] ~:— *E1*
391:24 Anabel] *Anabel E1*
391:26 Anabel] ~, *E1*
391:28 genius—] ~!— *E1*
391:31 here—] ~. *E1*
391:32 Sir] sir *E1*
391:36 artists,] ~: *E1*
391:38 surely—.] ~ ... *TCC* ~ —— *E1*
392:3 father,] ~: *E1*
392:5 No] ~, *TCC*
392:8 —The] ~ *TCC*
392:12 child,] ~ *E1*
392:14 —It] ~ *TCC*
392:27 wrong— *TCC*] ~.— *MS*
392:32 rich—] ~?— *E1*
392:35 tug of war] tug-of-war *E1*
392:36 of possession] of possessions *TCC see notes*
393:6 Why] ~, *E1*
393:12 system,] ~ — *E1*
393:14 system,] ~; *E1*
393:16 system—] ~?— *E1*
393:20 himself,] ~ *E1*
393:26 unheard—] ~; *E1*
393:27 alleviated,] ~ *E1*
393:35 liberal,] ~; *E1*
393:39 Masters] Masters' *E1*
394:4 be,] ~ *E1*
394:5 But] ~, *E1*
394:8 summer time.—] summer-time. *E1*
394:9 suffering—] ~, *E1*
394:10 red-coats] redcoats *E1*
394:12 fellows—they] ~. They *E1*
394:14 immensely;] ~, *TCC* ~. *E1*
394:20 year,] ~ *E1*
394:21 radical,] ~ *E1*
394:29 individuals.—They] ~ —they *TCC*
394:34 Oh] ~, *E1*
394:35 badly—the] ~. The *E1*
394:37 down,] ~ *E1*

395:2 plants,] ~ *E1*
395:3 coal-cutters,] ~ — *E1*
395:3 iron-men] iron men, *E1*
395:4 them,] ~ — *E1*
395:5 done—] ~; *E1*
395:6 down,] ~ *E1*
395:9 worn, and gloomy,] ~ ~ ~; *E1*
395:14 unnatural,] ~; *E1*
395:16 it—] ~?— *E1*
395:21 Ah] ~, *E1*
395:22 different,] ~ *E1*
395:25 decent—] ~. *TCC*
395:26 Yes—indeed.] ~, ~.— *E1*
395:27 Oliver.—] ~ — *TCC* ~? *E1*
395:29 No] ~, *E1*
395:35 machine-excitement] machine excitement *E1*
395:37 Goodnight] goodnight *TCC* good-night *E1*
395:39 dear.] ~? *E1*
396:1 you—] ~. *E1*
396:2 Sir.] sir. *TCC* sir? *E1*
396:3 William—] ~. *TCC*
396:4 tired,] ~ *E1*
396:6 came over so tired] became so over-tired *E1*
396:6 Sir] sir *TCC*
396:10 over tired] over-tired *E1*
396:19 tragedy,] ~ — *E1*
396:21 couldn't] wouldn't *TCC*
396:24 However—] ~, *E1*
396:25 here—] ~, *E1*
396:26 comfortable—] ~. *E1*
396:33 window-curtains.] ~? *E1*
396:34 Yes—] ~, *E1*
396:35 slap bang] slap-bang *E1*
397:5 Father] father *E1*
397:6 tongue] face *E1*
397:26 angry,] ~ — *E1*
397:31 me] one *TCC see notes*
397:31 walls—] ~. *E1*
397:36 Labour,] ~ *E1*
398:1 myself.] ~ *TCC*
398:3 much.] ~? *TCC*
398:8 quieter,—] ~, *E1*
398:10 gentle—] ~. *E1*
398:12 Halifax Gentlemen] ~

gentlemen *TCC* ~, Gentleman,
    E1 see notes
398:18 No] ~, *TCC*
398:18 you,] ~ — *E1*
398:25 Oh] ~, *E1*
398:25 well.—] ~. *TCC*
398:27 Hello] ~, *E1*
398:28 Oh.] ~, *E1*
398:31 BARLOW *Ed.*] Barlow *MS*
    Barton *TCC* BARTON *E1*
398:32 you,] ~ *E1*
398:33 mother?] ~! *TCC*
398:34 do] ~, *E1*
398:38 Oh] ~, *E1*
399:8 heaven,] ~ *E1*
399:9 apart,] ~ *E1*
399:11 door,] ~ *E1*
399:14 Gerald,] ~ — *E1*
399:31 spy hole] spy-hole *E1*
399:35 no.] ~! *E1*
400:5 —and] And *TCC*
400:12 mother,] ~ — *E1*
400:17 Oh God.] ~, ~! *E1*
400:19 demure,] ~ *E1*
400:22 mother—] ~!— *E1*
400:27 anything!] ~? *E1*
400:28 family.] ~? *E1*
400:32 him—] ~. *TCC*
400:35 me.] ~? *TCC*
401:3 No,] ~ — *E1*
401:4 fight,] ~ — *E1*
401:5 must,] ~ — *E1*
401:5 alone,] ~: *E1*
401:8 place—] ~, *E1*
401:12 it] ~, *E1*
401:17 you,] ~ — *E1*
401:18 love.—] ~. *TCC*
401:18 Ah God, Ah God—] ~,
    ~ — ~ ~ — *TCC* ~, ~!— ~,
    ~! — *E1*
401:26 water.] ~? *E1*
401:26 softy.] ~! *E1*
401:29 Stop] ~, *E1*
401:29 off—] ~. *E1*
401:32 way] ~, *E1*
401:33 Anabel.] ~? *E1*
401:34 gently] *roughly E1 see note on*
    401:35

401:38 enough.] ~! *E1*
401:39 you.] ~! *E1*
402:2 out.] ~! *E1*
402:4 [*Exit* OLIVER *and* JOB ARTHUR.]
    Ed.] Om. *MS*
402:11 me—] ~!— *E1*
402:12 me.] ~! *E1*
402:16 Madam] madam *TCC*
402:22 Bah,] ~! *E1*
402:25 Yes] ~, *E1*
402:26 So—o—o:] So—o—o. *TCC*
402:28 —frightening] Om. *E1*
402:34 courage he] "~" ~ *E1*
402:36 for:] ~; *TCC*
403:4 —of— *TCC*] —~ *MS*
    —~ — *E1*
403:11 Cock-a-doodle-doo—!] ~!
    TCC
403:12 afraid,] ~; *E1*
403:15 rhyme] ~: *TCC*
403:16 gently] roughly *E1 see note on*
    401:35
403:17 sneezes—?] ~'—? *TCC* ~?
    E1
403:24 —What's] ~ *TCC*
403:27 Oh] ~, *E1*
403:34 Arthur.] ~? *TCC*
403:39 they!] ~? *TCC*
404:1 Yes,] ~; *E1*
404:7 office-clerks] office clerks *E1*
404:7 rush.] ~? *E1*
404:8 love—] ~; *E1*
404:15 Monday,] ~ *E1*
404:16 Yes. So] ~ —so *E1*
404:26 another—] ~. *E1*
404:27 stand—] ~? *E1*
404:29 weak,] ~ *E1*
404:30 office-men.—] ~. *TCC* office
    men. *E1*
404:30 sporting,] ~ *TCC*
404:31 you.] ~? *TCC*
404:36 Yes sir,] ~, ~, *TCC* ~, ~ —
    E1
404:38 it. *Ed.*] ~/ *MS* ~? *TCC see*
    notes
404:40 thing—] ~. *E1*
405:4 Oh] ~, *E1*
405:10 satisfied,] ~ *E1*

405:25 Ha,] ~! *E1*
405:33 office-men] office men *E1*
405:35 grievance,] ~ *TCC*
405:40 should *TCC*] ~, *MS*
406:1 sir,] ~; *E1*
406:11 fact] ~, *E1*
406:18 movement] ~, *E1*
406:25 see] ~, *E1*
406:25 understanding,] ~ *E1*
406:29 courage,] ~ *E1*
406:31 understanding,] ~; *E1*
406:33 know.—It] ~ —it *TCC*
406:37 can't,] ~ — *E1*
407:9 for] even for *E1*
407:10 slap dash,] slap-dash— *E1*
407:12 Yes] ~, *E1*
407:18 surprise—] ~. *TCC*
407:20 —But] ~ *TCC*
407:21 right.] ~? *E1*
407:22 Oh] ~, *E1*
407:24 we.] ~? *TCC*
407:28 that.] ~ — *E1*
407:31 pressing.—] ~. *TCC*
407:32 all.] ~! *E1*
407:36 they.] ~? *TCC*
407:40 you—] ~. *TCC*
408:1 good-night] good night *E1*
408:1 [*Exit* GERALD *and* JOB ARTHUR.]
        Ed.] (exeunt) *MS* EXEUNT.
        TCC (*Exeunt.*) *E1*
408:5 Miners] Miners' *E1*
408:14 Yes,] ~ — *E1*
408:14 sensitiveness—] ~ *TCC*
408:15 taste—] ~. *TCC*
408:18 manner—] ~. *E1*
409:12 But] ~, *E1*
409:16 whiskey] whisky *TCC*
409:20 No] ~, *E1*
409:22 times] ~, *TCC*
409:25 gods—do] ~.—Do *E1*
409:29 Good-night] goodnight *TCC*
        good night *E1*
409:34 Oh] ~, *E1*
409:36 Anabel.] ~! *E1*
409:38 Anabel.—] ~. *TCC* ~! *E1*
409:39 whiskey] whisky *TCC*
411:10 Wallsalls] Wallsalls' *E1*
411:12 ugliness—they] ~. They *E1*

411:18 offices—they] ~. They *TCC*
411:22 Yes—] ~, *E1*
411:27 we,] ~? *E1*
411:28 sad] ~, *E1*
411:30 Listen,] ~! *E1*
411:31 road,—] ~ — *E1*
411:33 we.] ~? *TCC*
412:1 And] ~, *E1*
412:2 Only] ~, *E1*
412:12 knows.] ~! *E1*
412:22 ask!] ~? *E1*
412:29 knows.] ~! *E1*
412:35 you.—And] ~ —and *TCC*
412:35 tonight] to-night *E1*
412:38 Yes] ~, *E1*
413:2 say] ~, *E1*
413:2 forgotten,"] ~"; *E1*
413:3 you] *you TCC*
413:7 be] be *TCC*
413:7 happy—as] ~. As *E1*
413:10 be both] both be *E1*
413:12 because] Because *E1*
413:14 so] ~, *E1*
413:17 But] Then *TCC*
413:24 now,—] ~ —— *E1*
413:35 am.—And] ~ —and *TCC*
414:11 aren't] are not *TCC*
414:12 Yes] ~, *E1*
414:12 am.—] ~ — *TCC*
414:16 sleeve—] ~. *TCC*
414:17 you—] ~. *TCC*
414:19 he loves] to love *TCC*
414:20 liar—] ~! *E1*
414:22 spies *E1*] spys *MS*
414:24 enemy—] ~. *TCC*
414:26 yourself.] ~? *E1*
414:26 your] your *TCC*
414:28 love—] ~? *E1*
414:31 Ha—] ~!— *E1*
414:33 right,] ~ — *E1*
414:35 unselfishly,] ~ — *E1*
414:35 do,] ~ — *E1*
414:36 you—] ~.— *TCC* ~. *E1*
414:39 do you!] Do you? *TCC*
414:39 you'd] You'd *E1*
414:40 if——] ~ —— *E1*
415:1 mind,] ~; *E1*
415:4 No.—] ~ — *TCC* ~. *E1*

415:4 CLERK *Ed.*] man *MS* man *TCC*

415:4 *another.) / GERALD: Ed.*]
another) / *Gerald: MS another)*
TCC another). E1

415:6 Sir] sir *TCC*

415:6 Good-evening] Good evening,
E1

415:13 *approach.) / GERALD: Ed.*]
approach) / *Gerald: MS*
approach) TCC approach.) E1

415:15 Good-night] Good night, *E1*

415:15 Sir] sir *TCC*

415:15 —Good-evening] Good
evening *E1*

415:16 Barlow—er] ∼. Er *E1*

415:16 Sir—?] sir? *E1*

415:18 Oh.] ∼! *E1*

415:20 No] ∼, *E1*

415:21 Goodnight] Good-night *TCC*
Good night, *E1*

415:23 Breffitt.] ∼? *TCC*

415:33 —Good-evening Sir—]
Good-evening Sir— *TCC*
Good evening, sir. *E1*

415:33 Good-evening Mr] Good
evening, ∼ *E1*

415:33 Barlow—er] ∼., er *TCC* ∼. Er
E1

415:34 Sir?—] sir? *E1*

415:36 Oh no] ∼, ∼, *E1*

415:38 office—] offic/ *TCC* office.
E1

416:1 Barlow,] ∼ — *E1*

416:1 as thinks] who think *TCC*

416:2 office-men] office men *E1*

416:5 Oh] ∼, *E1*

416:6 us—] ∼. *E1*

416:10 Yes.—Well] ∼ —well *TCC*

416:10 Good-night,] Goodnight *TCC*
good night, *E1*

416:12 Goodnight Sir.] Good night,
sir.— *E1*

416:14 lady,] ∼ *E1*

416:15 tomorrow.—] to-morrow. *E1*

416:16 think.] ∼? *TCC*

416:18 Good-night] Goodnight *TCC*
Good night, *E1*

416:18 Sir—] sir.— *E1*

416:18 Good-night] Goodnight *TCC*
Good night, *E1*

416:24 Ah] ah *TCC*

416:25 Office] office *TCC*

416:26 you.] ∼? *TCC*

416:27 No] ∼, *E1*

416:27 you.—] ∼ — *TCC*

416:31 office-men] office men *E1*

416:33 up] ∼, *E1*

416:35 hung,] ∼ — *E1*

416:39 you—] ∼?— *E1*

417:4 board] Board *E1*

417:5 at] on *E1*

417:6 Then] then *TCC*

417:11 out the] ∼, ∼ *E1*

417:15 staff,] ∼ *E1*

417:19 out,] ∼ *E1*

417:22 mean.] ∼ — *TCC*

417:28 mistake, I] ∼ — ∼ *E1*

417:31 for—] ∼. *E1*

417:33 is,] ∼ — *E1*

417:34 everything,] ∼ — *E1*

417:38 Sir,] sir— *E1*

418:2 would] ∼, *E1*

418:12 fine:—] ∼ — *TCC*

418:15 crass] ∼, *E1*

418:19 matter,] ∼ *TCC*

418:20 chaos.] ∼? *TCC*

418:27 *Lusting*] Dusting *TCC* —*Asking*
E1

418:27 strife.] ∼? *E1*

418:30 fashion—] ∼/ *TCC* ∼ *E1*

418:33 want.] ∼? *E1*

418:34 right—they're] ∼!—They're
E1

418:40 lovingkindness] lovingkindness *E1*

419:1 don't,] ∼ — *E1*

419:2 would] ∼, *E1*

419:11 No it isn't,] ∼, ∼ ∼: *E1*

419:14 you.] ∼? *TCC*

419:16 clerks.] ∼? *E1*

419:18 way.] ∼? *E1*

419:21 night …] ∼/ *TCC* ∼ —— *E1*
see notes

419:23 Sir.] sir? *E1*

419:34 Oh yes] ∼, ∼, *E1*

420:1 funny bone] funny-bone *E1*

420:5   see.] ~? *E1*
420:6   Ah] ~, *E1*
420:11   threat—] ~? *E1*
420:15   What] What do *E1*
420:15   say—] ~?— *E1*
420:15   see—] ~?— *E1*
420:16   see—you've] ~? You've *E1*
420:17   enough,] ~: *E1*
420:18   or you] or you'll *E1*
420:19   see— *TCC*] ~ *MS* ~? *E1*
420:21   Oh no—oh no—] ~, ~!— ~,
         ~! *E1*
420:26   Labour] labour *TCC*
420:27   [*getting up*] *Ed.*] *Om. MS see
         notes*
420:31   will,] ~ — *E1*
420:32   this—] ~. *E1*
420:33   begun—] ~?— *E1*
420:34   *you*—] ~. *E1*
420:38   vermin,] ~; *E1*
421:2   God.] ~! *E1*
421:3   vermin.] ~? *E1*
421:6   Yes. Vermin] ~, vermin *TCC*
421:12   it—] ~. *TCC* ~? *E1*
421:12   own,] ~ — *E1*
421:14   God,] ~! *E1*
421:18   Go—!] ~! *E1*
421:19   Go—!] ~! *TCC*
421:22   *go*—] ~! *E1*
421:24   What!] ~? *E1*
421:24   God,] ~! *E1*
421:28   away,] ~ — *TCC*
421:28   him.] ~ — *TCC* ~ —— *E1*
421:29   *floor TCC*] floor *MS* ground *E1*
421:33   you] ~, *E1*
421:33   Gerald—come] ~ —/ Come
         TCC ~. Come *E1*
421:37   God,] ~! *E1*
421:37   being—!] ~! *E1*
422:2   WILLIE *addressing Ed.*] *Willie
         Houghton MS Willie Houghton,
         TCC* HOUGHTON *addressing E1*
422:3   [*including* JOB ARTHUR] *Ed.*] *Om.
         MS*
422:5   week,] ~ *E1*
422:8   ideas] idea *TCC*
422:19   doing.—] ~ ... *TCC*
422:20   —and] And *TCC*

422:29   that] ~, *E1*
422:31   me.] ~? *TCC*
422:32   yi,] ~ — *TCC*
422:33   it. *TCC*] ~/ *MS* ~! *E1*
422:37   van men,] van men *TCC*
         vanmen *E1*
423:3   neighbour] neighbours *TCC*
423:6   style—] ~. *TCC* ~! *E1*
423:8   Keatings] Keating's *E1*
423:9   it.] ~! *E1*
423:9   up.] ~! *E1*
423:9   face.] ~! *E1*
423:9   gab.] ~! *E1*
423:16   stands] stand *E1*
423:17   precipice:] ~; *E1*
423:18   us:] ~; *E1*
423:22   fact—] ~. *TCC*
423:26   th'] the *TCC*
423:27   wi' 'em] wi' 'em—drop 'em
         down the shaft *TCC*
423:27   vermin—] ~? *E1*
423:31   right—shove] ~. Shove *TCC*
         ~! Shove *E1*
423:32   ay—] ~! *E1*
423:40   working-man] working-/ man
         TCC working man *E1*
424:1   he'll] he'd *TCC*
424:2   today—] ~.— *TCC* to-day.—
         E1
424:8   although] though *TCC*
424:9   this] the *TCC*
424:12   a little] a little tiny *TCC see
         notes*
424:15   beggar—] ~! *E1*
424:15   Hoi—] ~!— *E1*
424:15   hoi-ee—] ~!— *E1*
424:15   whoo—] ~!— *E1*
424:15   whoam-it,—] ~!— *E1*
424:16   bow-wow—] ~!— *E1*
424:16   wet-whiskers—] ~!— *E1*
424:18   cold, jeering *Ed.*] cold, jeering
         MS jeering, cold *TCC*
424:19   comin'—] comin'. *E1*
424:21   Barlow—See's] ~.—See 's *E1*
424:21   sithee?—] ~? *E1*
424:24   s'comin' *TCC*] s'comin *MS*
         's comin' *E1*
424:24   sorry] ~, *E1*

424:24 —who's] —Who's *TCC* Who's *E1*

424:25 that's] That's *E1*

424:25 behind,] ~/ *TCC* ~ *E1*

424:26 on, Sorry—] ~. ~!— *E1*

424:27 Lodnor?] Lodno/ *TCC* Loddo *E1*

424:32 'urry!] 'urry? *E1*

424:38 y'are] y' are *E1*

424:38 minute—] ~. *E1*

424:40 down Miss] ~ miss *TCC* ~, miss *E1*

425:2 down.—Lead] ~ —lead *TCC*

425:2 forrard. / VOICES: *Ed.*] forrard. / *Voices*: *MS* forrard. *TCC*

425:3 take 'em forrard—] ~ ~ ~. *E1*

425:4 road—] ~. *E1*

425:7 men—] ~. *TCC*

425:8 whoa!!] ~! *TCC*

425:9 pretty—] ~! *E1*

425:11 forrard. *TCC*] ~ *MS* ~! *E1*

425:13 step] ~, *E1*

425:14 Oh] ~, *E1*

425:14 you!] ~? *E1*

425:14 Tweet-tweet!—] Tweet—tweet!— *TCC* Tweet—tweet! *E1*

425:15 boys—] ~, *TCC*

425:15 space—] ~. *E1*

425:16 —Now] ~ *E1*

425:16 Now—Quiet] now—quiet *TCC*

425:18 gentlemen—] ~. *E1*

425:19 Shh-h-h] Sh-h-h *E1*

425:20 shh-h-h—] Shh-h-h— *TCC* Shh-h-h! *E1*

425:22 trouble—] ~. *TCC* ~? *E1*

425:24 Oh—Oh!] ~ —oh *TCC* ~!—oh! *E1*

425:24 Baa-lamb] baa-lamb *E1*

425:25 Baa-lamb] baa-lamb *E1*

425:26 you.—] ~. *TCC*

425:28 their] this *TCC*

425:30 employment—?] ~? *E1*

425:32 Oh—Oh] ~ —oh *TCC* ~!—oh! *E1*

425:32 do Barlow] ~, ~ *E1*

425:33 boy—naughty boy—] ~ — ~ ~! *E1*

425:37 answer—?] ~? *TCC*

425:38 foot—] ~. *E1*

425:39 La-di-da] da-di-da *TCC* Da-di-da *E1*

426:2 pardon—] ~! *E1*

426:3 clear—] ~! *E1*

426:5 him—] ~. *TCC* ~! *E1*

426:9 unnecessary—] ~. *E1*

426:10 knees.—] ~ — *TCC* ~! *E1*

426:13 Well] ~, *E1*

426:14 him—] ~! *E1*

426:15 kneel—] ~. *E1*

426:17 answer—] ~! *E1*

426:20 advance.] ~? *E1*

426:21 neck.] ~! *E1*

426:21 yelp.] ~! *E1*

426:23 men,] ~ *E1*

426:24 —Oh] —oh *TCC*

426:25 answer] ~, *E1*

426:26 bottle. *TCC*] ~ *MS* ~! *E1*

426:26 *force Ed.*] force *MS press TCC*

426:30 answer—] ~. *E1*

426:32 tick-tick] ~, *E1*

426:33 him—] ~! *E1*

426:34 quiet—] ~. *E1*

426:36 Squeeze] — ~ *E1*

426:36 him,] ~ — *E1*

426:36 him.] ~ — *E1*

426:37 Close] — ~ *E1*

426:38 whiskers—] ~! *E1*

426:40 There's a . . . a-winding *E1*] One—two—buckle my shoe—three *MS see notes*

427:2 knew] know *TCC*

427:4 yourself—] ~? *E1*

427:7 vermin—parish vermin—] ~ — ~ ~. *E1*

427:8 —And] ~ *TCC*

427:10 here.] ~? *E1*

427:12 this.] ~? *E1*

427:14 Gerald darling—Gerald] ~, ~ — ~, *E1*

427:14 oh] ~, *E1*

427:15 No . . . No] no . . . No *TCC* no, . . . no, *E1*

427:17 him 's] him's *TCC*

427:18 —ay . . . in it] *Om. TCC*

427:20 is] in *TCC*

427:20 no] ~, *E1*
427:21 down—] ~! *E1*
427:23 quiet—] ~.— *E1*
427:23 Now— *TCC*] ~ *MS* ~ ——
  E1
427:23 Barlow—] ~, *E1*
427:24 you?—] ~? *E1*
427:25 mind—] ~. *TCC*
427:28 beggar. *TCC*] ~ *MS* ~! *E1*
427:29 flatten him—] ~ ~! *E1*
427:31 *floor TCC*] floor *MS* ground *E1*
427:32 back—back—] ~ — ~! *E1*
427:34 heaven—] ~. *E1*
427:35 him. *TCC*] ~ *MS* ~! *E1*
428:1 —Now] ~ *TCC*
428:3 souls—] ~?— *E1*
428:4 foot—] ~?— *E1*
428:4 you. *Ed.*] ~ *MS* ~ — *TCC* ~?
  E1
428:9 vermin—] ~! *E1*
428:12 No-o-o! No-o! No-o!] No-o-o!
  No-o! *TCC* No-o-o-o! No-o!
  E1
428:13 enough, he's] ~ — ~ *E1*
428:16 OLIVER'S VOICE *Ed.*] *Oliver's
  voice MS* Oliver *TCC* OLIVER
  E1
428:28 go,—] ~.— *TCC* ~ — *E1*
428:29 up Gerald] ~, ~ *E1*
428:30 up,] ~ — *E1*
428:33 —You] ~ *E1*

428:34 their] this *TCC*
429:4 because] Because *E1*
429:6 will—] ~. *TCC*
429:7 side.] ~? *E1*
429:8 here] *Om. TCC*
429:15 have—] ~ *TCC*
429:16 —and] And *TCC*
429:17 wronged.] ~/ *TCC* ~? *E1*
429:19 *aren't*] aren't *TCC*
429:19 wrong,] ~ *E1*
429:27 continue?] ~. *E1*
429:32 haggling] struggling *TCC*
430:7 money,] ~ — *E1*
430:10 power—] ~. *E1*
430:25 them.] ~? *TCC*
430:28 Look] look *TCC*
430:29 way—] ~, — *E1*
430:35 do,] ~: *E1*
430:37 want,] ~ *E1*
430:37 see.] ~? *E1*
430:38 see.] ~? *E1*
430:39 going—] ~. *E1*
431:3 round,] ~ — *E1*
431:6 money—?] ~? *TCC*
431:11 way—] ~. *E1*
431:13 *(Curtain) Ed.*] (curtain) / The
  End. *MS* CURTAIN. /
  ****************** / *THE
  END.* / ****************** *TCC*
  (Curtain.) E1

David

MS = Autograph MS (Roberts E87a)
TS = TS (Roberts E87b)
TSR = DHL's revisions in *TS*
PPI = First page proofs (Roberts E87c)
PPIR = DHL's revisions in *PPI*
PPII = Second page proofs (no Roberts no.)
PPIIR = DHL's revisions in *PPII*
E1 = *David* (Secker, 1926)

Silent emendations

1 Simple mistakes in *MS* (e.g. 'on the the moon', p. 15), *TS* (e.g. 'haouse' for 'house', p. 21), *PPI* (e.g. 'risi' for 'rising', p. 62) and *PPII* (e.g. '*tgrea*' for '*great*', p. 23) have been not recorded unless they led to further textual corruption (see, e.g., 481:33), form part of another variant, or are significant in themselves.

Brett's typing errors in *TS* have only been recorded when they instituted corruptions in the transmission of the text (see, e.g., 470:32). She frequently left words incomplete on the right-hand edge of the page, where her typewriter's margin-setting refused to allow her to type further, and either she or DHL filled in the missing letters in ink: these ink additions have been regarded as part of the inscription of *TS*. Where either DHL or Brett, in *TS*, or DHL in *PPI* or *PPII*, or the compositors of *PPI* or *PPII*, succeeded in recovering the reading of *MS* – for example at 473:10, where DHL had written 'behold, my elder daughter Merab,' (*MS*, p. 70), Brett's *TS* produced 'behold my elder Merab' (p. 48), but DHL replaced the two missing commas and the missing 'daughter' in *TSR* – the errors of *TS* have not been recorded in the Textual apparatus.

2 The compositors of *PPI* habitually inserted '*SCENE.—*' in stage directions at the start of scenes, following the practice of *MS* in Scene 1. The practice was discontinued in *PPII* and *E1*. It has not been recorded here unless it forms part of another variant.

3 *TS* habitually typed 'King' and 'Kingdom' for DHL's *MS* 'king' and 'kingdom'; *PPI*, *PPII* and *E1* printed 'to-night' and 'to-morrow' for DHL's 'tonight' and 'tomorrow'; *TS* frequently altered DHL's exclamation 'oh' to 'Oh'; the compositors of *PPI* began the process of altering these to 'O', and *PPII* and *E1* completed the job, occasionally reverting to 'Oh'. *TS* and *PPI* also frequently altered DHL's 'nought' to 'naught' (see Explanatory note on 462:16). The practise of *MS* in all these cases has silently been adopted, and such variants recorded only where the alteration forms part of another variant.

4 In *MS*, DHL usually wrote 'he', 'him', 'himself', 'thou', 'thy' and 'thee' in references to OT God; he only used capital initial letters – and not consistently – for 'God' and 'Lord', where his *MS* usage is, however, frequently ambiguous. *TS* generally followed what it (sometimes erroneously) perceived as his usage. The compositors of *PPI*, however, began a process of normalisation completed in *E1*. The compositors sometimes (and *E1* always) also altered DHL's capitalised 'Lord' to 'lord' where a superior – but not God – was addressed. The practice of *MS* in all these cases has silently been adopted, except where the alteration forms part of another variant.

5 *TS* sometimes and *PPI* regularly omitted DHL's dash after a full-stop; the practice of *MS* in these cases has silently been followed, except where the alteration forms part of another variant.

6 Variations in lineation, capitalisation, italicisation, numbers presented in figures or in words, commas and full-stops between DHL's handwritten list of characters in *PPIR*, the printed lists in *PPII* and *E1*, and the list in this edition are not recorded; but DHL's handwritten list has been reproduced following that editorially established.

7 Lawrence was inconsistent in the naming and numbering of characters such as 'MAIDEN', '2ND MAIDEN', '1ST HERDSMAN', 'SOLDIER', 'SOLDIERS', '1ST SOLDIER', 'ANOTHER SOLDIER', '2ND SOLDIER', etc., in stage directions and speech-headings. This edition has regularised all these, and variations have not been recorded.

8 *PPI* regularly italicised punctuation following italic words: such italicised punctuation has not been recorded.

435:1   DAVID *PPI*] *David MS Saul MSR SAUL TS DAVID TSR see notes*

435:3   *Courtyard PPIR*] Scene: Courtyard *MS* SCENE.—*Courtyard PPI*

435:7   MICHAL *Ed.*] Michal *MS* Mi■ghal *TS* Merab *TSR* MERAB *PPI*

435:8   Amalekite!] ~. *PPI*

435:9   Amalekite.] ~! *TS*

435:10 Shur, *MS, PPIR*] ~ *PPI*

435:14 in] on *TS*

435:20 king.] King. *TS* King! *PPI*

435:23 heels] heel/ *TS* heel *PPI*

436:6   spears] their spears *TS*

436:9   heavy-footed? In *MS, TSR*] ~. In *TS* ~, in *PPI*

436:14 *War, and ... under heaven TSR*] War, and ... under heaven *MS*

436:28 Oh] ~, *PPI*

436:30 hand! *TSR*] ~. *MS*

436:36 Pharaoh's *PPI*] Pharoah's *MS*

436:37 yellow] and yellow *TS*

436:39 Ah! Ah! Ah! Ah!] Ah! Ah! Ah! *TS*

436:39 Agag,] ~; *PPI*

437:1   gold *TSR*] pearls *MS*

437:2   silver *TSR*] stones *MS*

437:3   Merab! Ay! *TSR*] ~. ~! *MS* ~. ~/ *TS*

437:6   *Noble Agag! ... of Givers!*—*TSR*] Noble Agag! ... of Givers! *MS Noble Agag! ... of Givers! PPI*

437:8   joys *TSR*] gold *MS*

437:10 maiden! *TSR*] ~. *MS*

437:12 thine] thy *TS*

437:21 find] finds *TS*

437:21 Treasure] treasure *TS*

437:23 Oh] ~, *E1*

437:24 me!—] ~! *TS*

437:24 Run!—] ~! *PPI*

437:25 caw! *TSR*] ~. *MS*

437:30 Samuel? *TSR*] ~! *MS*

437:31 quietly] quickly *TS*

437:31 Oh *TSR*] you *MS* O *PPI*

437:31 Agag! *PPIR*] ~. *MS*

437:33 MEN WITH SPEARS *Ed.*] men *MS* men *PPI*

438:2   field:] ~; *TS*

438:3   the] his *TS*

438:16 Lord! *TSR*] ~: *MS*

438:18 this] the *TS*

438:22 God.—But *Ed.*] ~.,—But *MS* ~, but *TS*

438:27 Deep *PPI*] Lord *MS*

438:28 voice] Voice *PPI*

438:29 Go] ~, *TS*

438:31 voice] Voice *PPI*

438:33 unclosing eyes] Unclosing Eyes *PPI*

438:34 voice] Voice *PPI*

438:36 prisoner *TSR*] *Om. MS*

438:37 of] *Om. TS*

439:1   offerings,] ~ *E1*

439:1   voice] Voice *PPI*

439:4   thy] *Om. TS*

439:7   —Lo] ~ *TS*

439:9   Living] living *TS*

439:11 servant] ~, *PPI*

439:11 is *TSR*] One is *MS*

439:12 this] the *TS*

439:12 compunction *TSR*] Compunction *MS*

439:13 their *TSR*] there *MS*

439:15 Lord *TSR*] One *MS*

439:15 fearedst] feardest *PPI* fearest *PPIIR see notes*

439:15 people, smaller than thyself. *TSR*] people. *MS*

439:16 cry] Cry *PPI*

439:17 people!— *TSR*] ~.— *MS* ~— *TS*

439:17 you] thee *PPI see notes*

439:26 king?] King! *TS*

439:31 world, *TSR*] ~ *MS, E1*

439:33 his] His *PPIIR*

439:34 barking] barkings *TS*

439:35 midmost] Midmost *E1*

439:38 thee *TSR*] thee again *MS*

440:1   commandment] commandments *TS*

440:7   Lord;] ~, *TS*

440:13 thou.—*(Pause.)* For *Ed.*]

thou.—(pause) For *MS*
thou;—(pause) and *TS* thou
(*pause*);—and *PPI*

440:13 moveth *TSR*] moveth behind
MS
440:14 man,] ~ *TS*
440:16 sinned.] ~, *TS*
440:17 thee!— *Ed.*] ~.— *MS* ~. *TS*
~! *TSR*
440:19 worship *PPI*] Worship *MS*
440:21 Sun *TSR*] Brightness *MS*
440:24 vision *TSR*] power *MS*
440:25 anointed,] ~ *TS*
440:28 father] ■ather *TS* Father *PPI*
440:29 thee! *TSR*] ~. *MS*
440:30 thee! *TSR*] ~. *MS*
440:31 Lord,] ~ *E1*
440:31 face! *TSR*] ~, *MS* ~: *PPI*
440:33 hips! *TSR*] ~. *MS*
440:34 feet! *TSR*] ~. *MS*
440:36 myself.] ~, *TS*
440:37 wings are *TSR*] might is *MS*
440:38 and] *Om. TS*
440:38 back! *TSR*] ~. *MS*
440:39 thy desire *TSR*] power *MS*
Thy desire *PPI*
441:1 awful *PPI*] unknown *MS Om.
TSR see notes*
441:2 heart *TSR*] cup *MS*
441:4 O Samuel! *TSR*] my Lord? *MS*
441:6 well.—] ~. *TS* ~! *PPI*
441:8 thou *TSR*] *Om. MS*
441:9 oh *TSR*] *Om. MS* O *PPI*
441:9 Abner. We] Abner, we *TS*
Abner, for we *TSR see notes*
441:14 Deep *PPI*] Lord *MS*
441:14 entreat, ah! *PPII*] entreat him
MS
441:23 *Enter* [JONATHAN, ABNER *and*]
1ST HERDSMAN *Ed.*] *Om. MS*
enter herdsman *TSR* Enter
HERDSMAN *PPI*
441:25 as] *Om. TS*
441:26 1ST *Ed.*] *Om. MS*
441:26 Amalekite,] ~ *TS*
441:29 1ST *Ed.*] *Om. MS*
441:31 High,] ~; *E1*
441:34 glad] gladden *MSC*

441:37 Might *PPII*] Lord *MS*
441:37 thee—] ~. *PPI*
442:2 *A room ... in prayer. E1*] *Om.
MS SCENE.—As before.
Night.* SAMUEL *in Prayer. PPI
SCENE.— Night.* SAMUEL *in
Prayer. PPIR As before. Night.*
SAMUEL *in prayer. PPII*
442:3 SAMUEL: *PPI*] Samuel (at night,
in prayer): *MS* Samuel: (at
night, in prayer) *TS*
442:3 whirlwind, *TSR*] ~ *MS*
442:7 flower,] ~. *PPI*
442:8 distance,] ~ *TS*
442:8 fanning of] fanning *TS*
442:15 Might.—] might.— *TS* might.
PPI
442:17 unseen almighty] Unseen
Almighty *TS see notes*
442:22 mover] Mover *PPI*
442:22 speak,] ~ *TS*
442:26 has] *Om. TS*
442:29 Oceans] oceans *PPI*
442:29 him up again] *Om. TS* him
TSR
442:30 thy self] thyself *TS* Thyself
PPII
442:32 for ever?—] for ever forever?—
TS for ever and forever?—
TSR for ever and for ever?
PPI
442:33 godless] Godless *TS*
442:34 god] God *TS*
442:35 —Bitter] ~ *PPI*
442:37 god] God *TS*
443:1 its] the *TS*
443:1 elements?—] ~? *TS*
443:6 *away,*] ~ *TS*
443:15 me,] ~ / *TS*
443:18 whisper] whispers *TS*
443:19 him *Ed.*] God *MS* Him *PPII*
443:21 head,] ~/ *TS*
443:30 place] place of *TS*
443:30 —So *PPII*] ~ *MS*
443:37 old—] ~. *TS*
444:3 [*Enter* JESSE *and* ELIAB.] *Ed.*]
Om. MS see notes
444:5 men in to] in to *TS*

444:6   in to *TSR*] in *MS* into *PPI*
444:13   curse us,] curses us *TS*
444:19   Bolt *PPII*] Lord *MS*
444:21   who] Who *PPII*
444:22   mouth—] ~. *PPI*
444:23   One *PPII*] God *MS*
444:27   us—] ~. *PPI*
444:28   father] Father *E1*
444:33   upon] on *TS*
444:39   in] *Om. TS*
445:4   out] *Om. TS*
445:7   One *PPII*] God *MS*
445:9   us to] us in to *TS* us into *E1*
445:15   crying: *Whither TS*] ~: *whither*
          MS
445:15   And though ... *Whither?*] *Om.*
          TS
445:17   whinneying] whinnying *E1*
445:21   who] Who *E1*
445:29   give] I give *MS see notes*
445:32   thee! *TSR*] ~. *MS*
445:33   people! *TSR*] ~. *MS*
445:36   yourselves,] yourselv / *TS*
          yourselves *TSR*
446:4   And it .. unto you. *TSR*] *Om.*
          MS
447:2   JESSE's *PPII*] Jesse's *MS*
          *SCENE.—*JESSE's *PPI*
447:2   *a small ... sun going down. PPI*]
          a cloth spread on the ground in
          a corner, for food; wooden
          trenchers {trenches *TS*} etc.
          Samuel before a small altar that
          is smoking — Jesse has
          sacrificed *MS* a small inner
          courtyard: a rude altar,
          smoking, and blood sprinkled
          round. Samuel before the altar,
          hands bloody. At another
          corner, a large fire, with a great
          pot seething, and pieces of
          meat on Spits. Jesse watches
          the spits. It is evening—sun
          going down *TSR*
447:7   feast *TSR*] meat *MS*
447:9   They are .... waiting. *PPI*]
          Om. MS They are waiting in
          the house. *TSR*

447:10   come forth! *TSR*] come, *MS*
          come *TS*
447:20   —And Eliab ... *Exit* ELIAB.*)*
          Ed.] *Om. MS* And Eliab ...
          exit Eliab) *TSR* And Eliab ...
          Exit ELIAB *PPI*
447:24   JESSE: Go thou,
          Abinadab!—*Ed.*] *Om. MS*
          Jesse: Go thou, Abinadab!—
          TSR JESSE: Go thou, Abinadab!
          PPI
447:24   Be all ... the house? *TSR*] *Om.*
          MS
447:26   ABINADAB: They ... sacrifice
          meat. *PPI*] *Om. MS*
          Abinadab: They ... sacrifice
          meat. *TSR*
447:31   JESSE: Go ... the fire, *Ed.*] *Om.*
          MS Jesse: Go ... the fire, *TSR*
          JESSE: Go ... the fire *PPI*
447:31   and turn ... spitted meat.
          TSR] *Om. MS*
447:33   SHAMMAH: Yea! ... not singe.
          PPI] *Om. MS* Shammah: Yea!
          ... not singe. *TSR*
447:34   forward! *TSR*] ~. *MS*
447:35   you! *TSR*] ~. *MS*
447:37   JESSE: Go ... a while. *PPI*] *Om.*
          MS Jesse: Go ... yet awhile.
          TSR
447:38   FOURTH SON: ... with me? *PPI*]
          Om. MS Fourth Son: ... with
          me? *TSR*
448:1   *(To him ... waits.)* Nay, *PPI*]
          Om. MS (to him ... waits)
          Nay, *TSR*
448:1   go or ... stand aside. *TSR*] *Om.*
          MS
448:2   *(He stands aside.) PPI*] *Om.*
          MS (4th son stays) / stands
          aside *TSR*
448:3   you. *MS, PPI*] you! *TSR*
448:4   JESSE: Turn ... be seen. *PPI*]
          Om. MS Jesse: Turn ... be
          seen. *TSR*
448:6   Thou art ... thou aside! *TSR*]
          Come! *MS* Thou art ... thou
          aside. *PPI*

448:7   *(Calling.)* Ho! *PPI*] *Om. MS*
(calling) Ho! *TSR*

448:7   *(To him PPI*] *Om. MS* (to him
TSR

448:7   *who waits.) . . .* brother. *(Enter
Ed.*] *Om. MS* who waits.) . . .
brother. (enter *TSR who waits.)*
. . . brother. / *Enter PPI*

448:8   SIXTH SON— *. . . the other . . .
after him.) Ed.*] *Om. MS* 6th
Son— . . . other . . . after him)
TSR SIXTH SON: *. . . the other . . .
after him.) PPI*

448:11   SIXTH SON . . . me, my father?
Ed.] *Om. MS* Sixth Son . . . me,
my father? *TSR* SIXTH SON . . .
me. My father? *PPI* SIXTH SON
. . . me, my Father? *PPII*

448:12   Samuel would . . . come
forward? *TSR*] Enter! Son! *MS*

448:15   I! Wilt thou me? *PPI*] The
Lord be with you. *MS* I!
Callest thou for me? *TSR*

448:16   JESSE: Nay . . . into the *PPI*]
Om. MS Jesse: Nay . . . into the
TSR

448:16   light, before . . . of God. *TSR*]
Om. MS light before . . . of
God. *PPI*

448:18   Nay, then . . . no more *TSR*]
There be no more without *MS*

448:20   Yea verily, there *TSR*] There
MS Yea, verily, there *E1*

448:24   JESSE: Go *PPI*] *Om. MS* Jesse:
Go *TSR*

448:24   thou Shammah . . . in now.—I
will see! *TSR*] *Om. MS* thou,
Shammah . . . in now. I will
see——! *PPI*

448:26   *also* SHAMMAH *PPI*] *Om. MS*
also Shammah *TSR*

448:27   ELIAB *PPI*] Eliab *MS* ELIAB
(coming forward from the fire)
TSR see notes

448:30   so] ~, *E1*

448:30   at] ot *TS* of *TSR*

448:31   Wonderful *TSR*] wonderful
MS

448:32   own. But] ~, but *PPI see notes*

448:32   the anointing be *TSR*] he
anoint this youth *MS*

448:33   for a *TSR*] to be a *MS*

448:35   to be king *TSR*] for his own
MS to be King *PPI*

448:39   this] the *TS*

448:40   mine] my *TS*

448:40   own.] ~; *PPI*

449:7   *and Ed.*] and *MS* with *TS with
PPI*

449:8   *(Enter* SHAMMAH.*) Ed.*] *Om.
MS* (enter Shammah) *TSR
Enter* SHAMMAH *PPI*

449:10   he. / SAMUEL *(aloud): Ed.*] he.
/ Samuel (aloud): *MS* he.
(Aloud:) PPI he. *(Aloud.) E1*

449:13   sun] Sun *PPII*

449:14   happenings among men.—
TSR] winds of fate.— *MS*
happenings among men. *PPI*

449:15   then. *MS, PPI*] ~! *TSR*

449:16   Deep *PPII*] beyond *MS* Lord
PPI

449:16   does the . . . thy soul *PPI*]
where the Wonder moves in
the whirlwind *MS* where the
wonder moves in the whirlwind
TS

449:17   Surely my . . . with God! *TSR*]
Om. MS

449:18   Glory *TSR, PPII*] glory *MS,
PPI*

449:18   himself *TSR*] itself *MS*
Himself *PPII*

449:19   Chooser *MS, TSR, E1*] Choser
TS, PPI

449:19   shalt be *TSR*] art *MS*

449:24   Deep's *PPII*] Lord's *MS*

449:25   thine] thy *TS*

449:26   Deep *PPII*] Lord *MS*

449:29   upon *TSR*] with *MS*

449:32   Ye shall *TSR*] We will *MS*

449:32   meat, and . . . sacrifice, this
night. *TSR*] meat. *MS* meat,
and . . . sacrifice this night. *PPI*

449:35   *They move . . . huge dish . . . cry,
lift down the pot. PPI*] They sit

449:39 Make it . . . Oh . . . this night!
TSR] *Om.* MS Make it . . . O
. . . this night! *PPI*

450:1 Unseen *TSR*] eagle *MS*

450:1 hands *PPII*] wings *MS*

450:3 ready from . . . is prepared
TSR] blest, and the sacrifice is
divided *MS*

450:4 you,] ~ *PPI*

450:4 of the feast, *TSR*] *Om.* MS

450:6 mischance *TSR*] worse *MS*

450:6 seek to . . . eat then *TSR*] rise
nor move. Eat *MS*

450:9 JESSE: The . . . go forth? *PPI*]
Om. MS Jesse: The . . . go
forth? *TSR*

450:12 eldest] oldest *PPI*

450:14 —Go . . . the feast. *TSR*] *Om.*
MS Go . . . the feast. *PPI*

450:15 [*Exit* ABINADAB.] *Ed.*] *Om.* MS

450:20 at] to *TS*

450:20 —Yea . . . that tasteth. *TSR*]
Om. MS Yea . . . that tasteth.
PPI

450:23 Today,] ~ *TS* To-day *PPI*

450:25 Bolt *PPII*] Lord *MS*

450:26 Voice] voice *TS*

450:28 thee] ~, *TS*

450:38 [*Enter* NEIGHBOURS.] *Ed.*] *Om.*
MS

450:39 enough! *TSR*] ~. *MS, PPI*

450:39 The guests . . . Oh . . . now . . .
women-folk . . . think thou
TSR] Return thou, David, to
thy sheep, and think no *MS*
The guests . . . Oh {O *E1*} . . .
out . . . womenfolk . . . think
thou *PPI see notes*

451:3 *(To the . . . [451:17] O Jesse!*
Ed.] *Om.* MS *(to the . . . O
Jesse! TSR see also following
entries to 451:16*

451:3 Yea *TSR*] Nay *PPI* Nay, *E1 see
notes*

451:3 and *TSR*] And *PPI*

451:3 meat! *PPI*] ~. *TSR*

451:7 forth! *TSR*] ~? *PPI*

451:7 Yea! Good *PPI*] ~, good *TSR*

451:7 oh *TSR*] O *PPI*

451:8 An heifer, *PPI*] Even an heifer
TSR

451:8 fat *PPI*] ~, *TSR*

451:8 Reach forth thy hand. *PPI*]
Om. TSR see note on 451:9

451:10 huge, *PPI*] huge *TSR*

451:13 day! / (Re-enter Ed.] day! /
Jesse: Reach forth thy hand.
TSR day! (Re-enter PPI see note
on 451:9*

451:15 silence.) / NEIGHBOUR: Verily
Ed.] silence) / Neighbour:
Verily *TSR silence.) Verily PPI*

451:16 this *PPI*] it *TSR*

452:4 3RD *Ed.*] 3rd *MS* 1st *TS* 1ST
PPI

452:10 it! *TSR*] ~. *MS*

452:17 neck—] ~. *TS*

452:23 wrong! *TSR*] ~. *MS*

452:23 answer! *TSR*] ~. *MS*

452:24 up? *TSR*] ~. *MS*

452:25 2ND *Ed.*] 2nd *MS* 3rd. *TS* 3RD
PPI

452:27 answer.] ~, *TS*

452:28 not? Say I, *TSR*] not? I'll
warrant *MS* not, say I? *PPI*

452:28 it's] It's *PPI*

452:31 Moo-oo! Moo-oo] Mooo-oo!
Moo-oo *TS*

452:31 home?] ~. *PPI*

452:38 *Loud Ed.*] loud *MS* much *TS*
Much PPI

452:39 Gilgal? *TSR*] ~ *MS* ~. *TS*

453:9 us] ~, *E1*

453:15 4TH *Ed.*] 4th *MS* 1st *TS* 1ST *PPI*

453:15 answer! / 1ST MAIDEN: *PPI*]
answer! / 1st Maiden: *MS*
answer! *E1*

453:18 anything!] ~. *TS*

453:21 say! *TSR*] ~. *MS*

453:22 are *PPI*] were *MS*

---

upon the ground, around the
trenchers, in silence *MS* They
move . . . huge bowl or dish . . .
cry, heave down the pot. *TSR*
*They move . . . huge dish . . . cry
lift down the pot. E1*

453:23 What,] ~ TS ~! TSR
453:24 morning.] ~? PPII
453:28 timely PPII] signal MS
453:32 Lord,] ~ TS
453:33 Oh,] ~! TS
453:34 Cursed above ... women-folk! TSI] Om. MS Cursed above ... women-folk! PPI
453:40 wondrous PPII] prophets MS
454:3 witchcraft! TSR] ~. MS
454:4 me! TSR] ~. MS
454:7 land.] ~, PPI
454:8 spirits and with TSR] witchcraft and MS
454:10 villages—] ~. PPI
454:11 But] ~, E1
454:11 Bolt PPII] Lord MS
454:12 spirits] Spirits TS
454:12 earth?] ~! TS
454:12 daughter.—Is] ~, is PPI
454:15 oh] Oh TS
454:18 witch! TSR] ~. MS
454:20 —The] ~ TS
454:22 Lord, TSR] ~ MS
454:22 Philistine] Philistines TS
454:24 Deep PPII] Lord MS
454:25 earth] the earth TS
454:27 Fire PPII] Lord MS
454:30 sky,] ~ TS
454:31 as good a TS] a good MS see notes
454:31 as when ... slew Agag, TSR] Om. MS
454:36 spirit TS] spirits MS see notes
454:36 gets TSR] steal MS steals TS
454:40 witch,] ~ PPI
455:1 sleepest.—] ~ — TS ~. PPI
455:4 slain! TSR] ~ MS
455:7 Oh King TSR] My Lord MS O King E1
455:9 Why] ~, E1
455:13 other seeresses] others seeresses TS others, seeresses, TSR
455:15 But yet, Oh King! thy servant has TSR] But my lord, I have MS But, my Lord, I have TS But yet, O King, thy servant has PPI

455:22 King TSR] Om. MS
455:25 Deep PPII] Lord MS
455:28 Yet Saul TSR] My Lord MS
455:29 deeds TSR] deeds MS
455:29 into] unto TS
455:30 Saul speaks TSR] He speaks MS
455:31 Spirit] spirit TS
455:32 the sight of all men TSR] deed MS
455:37 man's,] ~ — PPI
455:38 Oh King! TSR] my Lord. MS O King! PPI
455:40 Israel.] ~! PPII
456:7 Full PPII] Lord MS
456:12 anger.] ~? E1
456:21 man:] ~ — PPI
456:22 boy:] ~ — PPI
456:25 sheep-folds] sheepfolds E1
456:26 Gilgal!] ~,! TS ~? PPI
456:28 stars] the stars TS
456:34 run, MS, TSR] ~ TS, PPI
456:34 me?] ~. E1
456:36 boy] ~, E1
456:36 sun] ~, PPII
456:38 Surely,] ~ TS
456:39 night—] midnight. TS
457:1 more! TSR] ~. MS
457:9 me, at times,] ~ ~ ~ TS
457:14 heart?—] ~? PPI
457:16 Oh King TSR] my Lord MS O King PPI
457:23 Lord, who ... wet sand?—] Lord, Who ... wet sand? PPI see also following entry
457:24 this] the TS the PPI
457:25 say] says TS
457:26 sand:] sand: PPI sand; E1
457:26 forever] for ever PPI
457:27 in unto] into TS nigh unto TSR see notes
457:28 proper fire TSR] god-fire MS
457:32 be! TSR] ~. MS
457:37 had PPII] saw MS
457:39 yet TSR] now MS
458:2 takes] take PPI
458:9 the King TSR] my Lord MS
458:13 laughter of] laughter from TS

458:15 man, *MS, TSC*] ~ *TS, PPI*
458:16 daughters] daughter *TS*
458:17 anger—] ~. *TS*
458:22 You,] ~ *TS*
458:23 Dawn *PPII*] Lord *MS*
458:25 Lord?—] ~? *PPI*
458:32 Nameless,] ~. *TS* ~; *TSC*
458:35 tears] ~, *TS*
459:2   father, and Michal *TSR*] wife, my child *MS*
459:5   wife *MS, E1*] ~, *TS*
459:6   child, *MS, TSR, E1*] ~ *TS, PPI*
459:7   brother,] brother *PPI* brothers *E1*
459:10 is] is as *TS*
459:12 branches are hidden in blossom. *TSR*] brands burn in the one fire. *MS* brands burn in one fire. the *TS*
459:15 caught fire *TSR*] the flames mingle *MS*
459:16 Hope *PPII*] Lord *MS*
459:19 Fire *PPII*] Lord *MS*
459:28 then nothing,] nothing *TS*
459:29 much riches *TSR*] perfect riches *MS*
459:34 Myself,] *Om. TS*
460:3   Whirlwind *PPII*] whirlwind *MS*
460:5   moves *TSR*] moves in *MS* moves inn *TS*
460:5   Whirlwind *PPII*] whirlwind *MS*
460:6   well. But] ~, But *TS* ~, but *PPI*
460:6   Whirlwind *PPII*] whirlwind *MS*
460:14 it,] ~ *PPI*
460:20 man from the sheep *TSR*] shepherd youth *MS*
460:21 me,] ~ *PPI*
460:29 *in silence Ed.*] in silence *MS* silently *TS silently PPI*
461:4   sad.] ~, *TS*
461:5   sad?—] ~? *PPI*
461:6   gone out] are gone out *TS*
461:8   No-one] No one *PPI*

461:11 men! *TSR*] ~. *MS*
461:12 king! *PPI*] king. *MS* King. *TS* King! *TSR*
461:12 again! *TSR*] ~. *MS*
461:13 Saul *TSR*] him *MS*
461:14 Sheik] sheik *TS, PPII* shiek *PPI*
461:14 Anyhow] ~, *E1*
461:18 know?—] ~? *PPI*
461:19 and] ~, *E1*
461:26 sand,] ~ *TS*
461:30 I] I *TS*
461:30 else?—] ~? *PPI*
461:35 men; *TSR*] ~, *MS*
461:35 least,] ~ *TS*
461:36 Oh] O *E1 see notes*
461:38 anyhow?—] ~ *PPI*
462:1   be!—] ~. *TS*
462:2   woman! *TSR*] ~. *MS*
462:3   Philistines,] ~ *TS*
462:8   No, *MS, E1*] ~ *TS*
462:8   Lady] lady *PPI*
462:12 Oh] ~, *E1*
462:14 Nay!—] ~! *PPI* ~, *E1*
462:21 arrayed] arranged *TS*
462:22 hill,] ~ *PPI*
462:23 happens?] has happened! *TS* has happened? *E1*
462:23 Philistine] Philistines *TS*
462:26 Philistine *MS, TSC*] Philistines *TS, PPI*
462:31 father] ~, *PPI*
462:31 king] King *TS* King, *PPI*
462:33 huge,] ~: *E1*
462:33 one of those] one *TS* out *PPI*
463:1   Yea,] Yes, *TS* Yes; *E1*
463:1   him.] ~! *PPII*
463:6   praised,] ~ *TS*
463:6   calf.] ~! *E1*
463:7   shrew! *TSR*] shrew. Go call my wife. *MS*
463:13 huge,] ~ *TS*
463:15 say daily? *TSR*] say? *MS* say, daily? *PPII*
463:31 Philistine] Philistines *PPI*
464:1   on] in *TS*
464:1   no! *TSR*] ~. *MS*
464:5   his] the *TS*

464:8   thou! *TSR*] ~. *MS*
465:4   DAVID *entering ... a staff. PPI*]
         Om. MS David entering,
         carrying a staff) *TSR*
465:8   *armed PPI*] armed, forward
         MS armed) forward *TS* armed
         TSR
465:9   David!] ~? *E1*
465:9   Ho,] ~! *TS*
465:12   men-at-arms *TSR*] wolves *MS*
         wolvws *TS*
465:13   enquire] inquire *E1*
465:14   ten] the *TS*
465:15   the keeper *MS, E1*] keeper
         TS
465:23   fight?] ~. *PPII*
465:24   home? *TSR*] ~. *MS*
465:26   place] places *TS*
465:29   all *PPI*] *Om. MS see notes*
465:37   ill to live *TSR*] an ill sign *MS*
         in ill sign *TS*
466:5   Ho] He *TS* Ho, *PPII*
466:6   out] *Om. TS*
466:6   in] *Om. TS*
466:6   —am] am *TS* Am *PPI*
466:13   Ha-ha] Ha! ha *TS*
466:24   do,] ~ *PPI*
466:24   Philistine,] ~ / *TS*
466:25   Israel?—] ~? *PPI*
466:26   daughter, the] ~. The *TS, PPI*
         ~? The *TSR, E1*
466:33   so.] ~! *E1*
466:34   —The] ~ *TS*
466:39   SOLDIERS *Ed.*] Soldiers *MS*
         Soldier *TS* SOLDIER *PPI*
467:11   giant? *TSR*] ~. *MS*
467:13   3RD *Ed.*] Another *MS* ANOTHER
         PPI
467:13   Verily!—] ~, *TS*
467:13   thee] *Om. TS*
467:15   Verily! *TSR*] ~. *MS*
467:15   sooth,] ~ *TS*
467:17   SOLDIERS *Ed.*] Soldiers *MS*
         Soldier *TS* SOLDIER *PPI*
467:18   him?] ~. *E1*
467:21   man,] ~ *PPI*
467:23   this] the *TS*
467:24   go] go out *TS*

467:26   he] he is *TS*
467:32   brass,] ~ *TS*
467:36   this] the *TS*
467:38   bring] *Om. PPI*
468:5   Ashtaroth] Astaroth *TS see note
         on* 468:6
468:8   Yea *TSR*] Amen *MS*
468:8   proof *E1*] mail *MS see note on*
         468:10
468:10   SAUL *Ed.*] the king *MS* the
         King *TS the* KING *PPI*
468:14   array! *TSR*] ~. *MS*
468:19   —I] ~ *PPI*
468:24   DAVID: The ... not go. *Ed.*]
         David: The ... not go. *MS Om.
         TS*
468:29   blue *PPII*] dead *MS*
468:34   He *[takes] his staff—crosses Ed.*]
         crosses *MS* recrosses *TS* He
         picks up his staff—recrosses
         *TSR He picks up his staff, re-
         crosses PPI He picks up his staff,
         recrosses E1 see notes*
468:37   Goliath! *TSR*] ~. *MS* ~: *TS*
468:37   Philistine! *TSR*] ~. *MS*
469:12   throw! *TSR*] ~. *MS*
469:18   hosts] Hosts *TS*
469:28   *(Loud shouting of Israel.) Ed.*]
         (Loud shouting of Israel) *MS
         Om. TS*
469:32   carcases] carcass *TS*
470:2   give] *Om. TS* deliver *TSR*
470:5   thee—] ~ .... *PPI*
470:10   Ah!—Ah] ~! ~ *TS*
470:11   —Yea] ~ *TS*
470:13   Lord!—*Ed.*] Lord's doing!—
         MS Lord's doing! *TS* Lord' !
         TSR
470:13   thing? *TSR*] ~! *MS* ~/ *TS*
470:14   it!—] ~! *PPI*
470:17   giant!—] ~! *PPI*
470:19   him!—] ~! *PPI*
470:21   lip!—] ~! *PPI*
470:30   Israel!—] ~! *PPI*
470:31   *Wild Ed.*] wild *MS* loud *TS*
         Loud PPI
470:32   *past): Ed.*]): *MS*) *TS* past)
         TSR past). PPI

470:32 Philistine] Philistinex *TS*
    Philistines *PPI*

470:34 pursuit?—] ∼? *PPI*

470:39 see] can see *TS*

471:6 is he] he is *TS*

471:8 sweet-meats] sweetmeats *PPI*

471:15 hour!—] ∼.— *TS* ∼. *PPI*

471:16 where!—] ∼! *PPI*

471:19 is thy *PPII*] is the *MS*

471:20 sore *TSR*] cankered *MS*

471:22 I am not old.] *Om. TS*

471:27 Bethlehemite! *PPI*] ∼. *MS*
    Bethelehemite. *TS*
    Bethelehemite! *TSR*

471:28 coat *E1*] mail *MS see note on*
    468:10

471:33 hand, oh] ∼. Oh, *TS* ∼. Oh
    E1

471:33 victor! *TSR*] ∼. *MS*

471:37 —Oh,] — ∼ ■ *TS* ∼! *PPI*

472:7 hare *TSR*] rabbit *MS*

472:9 See! the *TSR*] ∼, the *MS* ∼!
    The *E1*

472:10 bone! *TSR*] ∼. *MS*

472:13 of death] *Om. TS*

472:20 willeth.—*Ed.*] willeth, Oh my
    Father.— *MS* willeth,.— *TSR*
    willeth. *PPI*

472:28 well!—] ∼. *PPI*

472:32 king! *Ed.*] king. *MS* King. *TS*
    King! *TSR*

472:32 Riches,] ∼ *PPI*

472:39 fall *TSR*] fall humbled *MS*

473:7 sheep-folds,] sheep-fold/ *TS*
    sheep-fold, *TSC* sheep-fold,
    TSC sheepfold, *E1*

473:14 Lord. / SAUL: Come ... my
    Lord *Ed.*] Lord. / Saul: Come
    ... my Lord *MS* Lord. / Saul:
    And my Lord *TS* Lord. And
    Saul *TSR*

474:6 army] armies *TS*

474:7 all the] all *TS*

474:15 CAPTAINS *Ed.*] Captains *MS*,
    TSR Captain *TS* CAPTAIN *PPI*

474:19 CAPTAINS *Ed.*] Captains *MS*,
    TSR Captain *TS* CAPTAIN *PPI*

474:19 *They strike their shields. PPI*]

    Om. MS They strike their
    shields *TSR*

474:20 SAUL: And ... Even so! *Ed.*]
    Saul: And ... Even So! *MS*
    Om. TS

474:23 son of ... is David,] *Om. TS*

474:27 *Striking shields. PPI*] *Om. MS*
    Striking shields *TSR*

474:31 Yea] ∼, *E1*

474:33 first] the first *TS*

474:37 *They clash ... martial noise.*
    PPI] *Om. MS* They clash
    shields with martial noise *TSR*

475:7 *The* CAPTAINS ... *him up. PPI*]
    Om. MS The captains rise,
    and lift locked shields before
    David, as if to raise him up
    TSR

475:12 captains] Captains *TS*

475:12 *He rises ... the* CAPTAINS. *PPI*]
    Om. MS He rises before the
    captains *TSR*

475:14 captains] Captains *TS*

475:15 inexperience,] ∼ *PPI*

475:16 Nay! *TSR*] ∼. *MS*

475:23 captains] Captains *TS*

475:25 *again PPI*] rise, and *MS* again
    TSR

475:25 *spear on shield, then PPI*] the
    spear as *MS* spear on shield,
    then *TSR*

475:35 us?—] ∼? *TS*

475:37 blood?—] ∼? *PPI*

476:6 all] *Om. TS*

476:14 man never before *TSR*] no man
    ever *MS*

476:16 me! *TSR*] ∼. *MS*

476:22 house,] ∼ *PPI*

476:26 oh] oh, *TS* O *PPI*

476:34 his *PPI*] his *MS Om. TS*

476:34 *long PPI*] long *MS Om. TS*

476:37 feathers,] ∼ *TS*

477:1 *leathern Ed.*] leathern *MS*
    leather *TS leather PPI*

477:5 upon *TSR*] thine upon *MS*

477:7 *leathern Ed.*] leathern *MS*
    leather *TS leather PPI*

477:12 now *Om. TS*

477:26 father! *TSR*] ∼. *MS* Father!
PPII

478:1 God.—] ∼. *PPI*

478:5 king-to-be *Ed.*] king *MS* King
TS King-to-be *TSR*

479:4 *distance—people waiting. Ed.*]
distance— *MS distance. PPI*
distance. People waiting. PPII

479:5 A-li-lu-lu-lu! Lu-a-li-lu] A-li-
lu-lu-l / lu-a-li-lu *TS* A-li-lu-
lu-lu-a-li-lu *PPI*

479:9 in.] ∼! *TS*

479:11 *(Repeat several times.) /* ALL:
Ed.] (repeat several times) /
All: *MS* ALL *(repeat several*
times): PPI

479:12 a! li! lu! lu! lu!] a! li! lu! lu! lu!
lu! *TS*

479:21 *(They repeat this continuously.)*
/ ALL: *Ed.*] (they repeat this
continuously) / All: *MS* (they
repeat continuously.) / All: *TS*
ALL *(repeat continuously): PPI*

479:22 Li-a-li-lu-lu-lu-lu!] Li-a-li-lu-
lu-lu! *TS* Li-a-li-lu-lu-lu? *PPI*

479:24 u! *TSR*] Lu! *MS*

479:28 ten!—] ∼! *PPI*

479:30 Lu-a-li-lu-lu-lu!] Lu-a-li-lu-lu-
lu-! *TS*

479:37 *and the refrain, Ed.*] and the
refrain, *MS* Om. *TS*

480:3 *gate, without response. PPI*]
gate, without response. *MS*
gate. *TSR*

480:7 *(Must . . . villagers.) Ed.*] (Must
be kept simple—plain—naïve
—villagers) *MS* Om. *PPI see*
notes

481:2 *people and PPII*] *Om. MS*

481:5 ye] we *TS*

481:9 Israel! *TSR*] ∼. *MS*

481:11 women?—] ∼? *PPI*

481:14 VOICE OF *Ed.*] *Om. MS*

481:15 VOICE OF *Ed.*] *Om. MS*

481:16 VOICES OF MAIDENS *Ed.*] *All*:
MS All: *TS* ALL: *PPI*

481:16 *A-li-lu-lu-a-li-lu!*] *A li-lu-lu-a-*
li-lu! PPI

481:23 Saul! *TSR*] ∼. *MS*

481:24 fancy *PPII*] see *MS*

481:30 SAUL *Ed.*] the king *MS* the
King *TS the* KING *PPI*

481:31 Lu-lu-lu-lu-a-li-lu]
Lu-li-lu-lu-a-li-lu *TS*

481:33 Saul *MS, TSR*] Saul t *TS* ∼,
PPI

481:34 Lu-lu-lu! / SAUL *Ed.*]
Lu-lu-lu! / Saul: *MS*]
Lu-lulu! / SAUL *E1*

481:37 two!—] ∼! *PPI*

482:3 Lu-lu-lu-a! / Here] Lu-lu-lu-!
a! Here *TS* Lu-lu-lul!—a! Here
PPI

482:4 come,] ∼ *TS*

482:6 oh] O *PPI*

482:8 Judah;] ∼, *TS*

482:13 shekels?] ∼ / *TS* ∼. *TSC*

482:15 Lord,] ∼ *TS*

482:15 Ramah;] ∼, *PPI*

482:17 Samuel?— *MS, TSR*] ∼? *TS,*
PPI

482:18 David?] ∼! *TS*

482:20 she.—] ∼ — *PPI* ∼. *E1*

482:21 oh] O *PPI*

482:25 said not] not said *TS*

482:25 Merab, look] ∼, Look *PPI* ∼!
Look *PPII*

482:28 Oh] ∼, *PPI*

482:29 black as a raven] raven black
TS

482:31 As yet he is not] He is not yet
TS

482:32 wouldest] wouldst *PPI*

482:34 daughter!] ∼. *TS*

482:39 fair, *MS, TSR*] ∼ *TS, PPI*

482:40 I!—] ∼! *PPI*

483:6: Ah] ∼, *E1*

483:9 father!—Why could] ∼.—Why
should *TS* ∼. Why should *PPI*

483:10 here?—] ∼. *PPI*

483:13 Ayee] Ayeee *TS*

483:13 us!—] ∼! *PPI*

483:15 Peace!—] ∼! *PPI*

483:18 —his] His *PPI*

483:18 Thou Jonathan!—] ∼,
Jonathan! *PPI*

483:19 oh] *Om. TS*
483:23 A-li-lu-ia] A-li-lu--a *TS*
        A-li-lu-a *PPI*
483:24 Empty handed] Empty-handed
        TS
483:26 —A-li-lu-lu!—Lu-lu-li-lu-a!]
        -A-li-lu-li! - Li-lu-li-lu-a! *TS*
        A-li-lu-li! Li-lu-li-lu-a! *PPI*
483:27 So,] ~ *TS*
483:28 so!—] ~! *PPI*
483:30 Saul!—] ~! *PPI*
483:40 Merab,] ~. *EI*
484:3   boy!—] ~! *PPI*
484:5   daughter!—] ~! *PPI*
484:5   Oh] ~, *EI*
484:5   quail!—] ~! *PPI*
484:7   caught!—] ~! *PPI*
484:8   boy! *TSR*] ~, *MS*
484:8   Oh] ~, *EI*
484:13 sayst] sayest *TS*
484:14 king! *Ed.*] king. *MS* King. *TS*
        King! *TSR*
484:22 Lu-li-lu-lu] Lu-li-lu-li *TS*
484:22 Lu-li-lu-lu-lu] Lu-li-lu-lu-li
        TS
485:5   he brings *TSR*] and brings *MS*
485:7   him!—] ~! *PPI*
485:11 Smooth faced] Smooth-faced
        PPI
485:18 King!—] ~! *PPI*
485:21 Judaea] Judea *PPI*
485:21 Judah?—] ~? *PPI*
485:31 upon *TSR*] against *MS*
485:33 David] ~, *TS*
485:34 him.—] ~— *TS* ~. *PPI*
485:34 up] *Om. TS*
485:39 supplanter?—] ~? *PPI*
486:1   thousand,] ~ *TS*
486:2   Saul,] ~ *EI*
486:2   Oh yes!—] ~, ~! *PPI* ~ ~! *EI*
486:4   *Lord's TSR*] *king's MS King's*
        TS
486:7   Philistines] Philistine *TS*
486:11 her!—] ~! *PPI*
486:13 Thunderer *PPII*] Lord *MS*
486:20 horn-anointed *PPII*] Lord's
        anointed *MS, TSR* Lord
        anointed *TS*

486:21 Judah!] ~? *EI*
486:24 Dark!— *Ed.*] Lord!— *MS*
        Lord! *PPI* Dark! *PPII*
486:26 Saul?—] ~? *PPI*
486:27 jealous worm *TSR*] envious
        canker *MS*
486:30 same:] ~; ~ — *PPI*
486:34 Morning Wind *PPII*] Lord thy
        God *MS*
486:35 of Days *PPII*] thy God *MS*
486:36 canst *TS*] can'st *MS*
486:36 heavens] Heavens *TS*
486:37 '*It*] ~ *TS*
486:37 *well!*'] ~!! *TS* ~!! *PPI* ~!?
        EI
486:39 sprout *PPII*] grow *MS*
487:2   the bright horn *PPII*] God
        MS
487:3   pass!—] ~! *PPI*
487:4   off?—] ~? *PPI*
487:5   Ashtaroth] Astaroth *EI*
487:8   hast *TSR*] hath *MS*
487:8   thunder *PPII*] voice *MS* Voice
        PPI
487:9   hast *TSR*] hath *MS*
487:9   Thunderer *PPII*] Presence
        MS
487:10 it ... it ... its] It ... It ... Its
        PPI
487:11 voices—!] ~! *PPI*
487:17 *how*] *How PPI*
487:17 *earth!*] ~. *TS*
487:19 Jonathan] ~, *PPI*
487:19 love] ~, *PPI*
487:22 *manly, from Psalm 8.) Ed.*]
        manly) / Psalm 8 *MS* manly)
        TS manly, from Psalm 8) *TSR*
        manly, from Psalm viii. PPI
487:24 VOICE OF SINGER: *Ed.*] *Om. MS*
        Voice of singer: PPII
487:24 "What] ~ *PPI*
487:25 him? *MS, TSR*] him? (Psalm
        8) *TS*
487:29 hands, thou] ~, /thou ~; /
        Thou *PPI*
487:29 feet;] ~: *PPI*
487:30 field; *PPI*] ~. *MS*
487:33 earth!" *Ed.*] earth!" / (tune the

church-bell tune of the Indians / [MUSIC] *MS* earth!"/tune the church bell of the Indians) [MUSIC] *TS* earth!" / [MUSIC] *TSR* earth! *PPI see notes*

487:38   dust!—] ~! *TS*

487:38   I naught! *TSR*] ~ ~, *MS* ~ ~; *PPI*

487:39   What,] ~ *TS*

487:39   not] *Om. TS*

487:40   ignorance.] ~? *E1*

488:1   —there] There *PPI*

488:1   desert,] ~ *PPI*

488:3   Ha] ~, *PPI*

488:9   end!—] ~! *PPI*

488:13   pillar] pillars *TS*

488:14   tall] a tall *E1*

488:17   god] God *TS*

488:18   blood.—Now] ~,—Now *TS* ~, now *PPI*

488:19   spring:] ~, *PPII*

488:19   locust-pillars] locust pillars *PPI*

488:22   Deep *PPII*] Lord, *MS* Lord *TSR*

488:24   —Yea] Yea, *PPI*

488:26   their *PPII*] even *MS*

488:28   in,] ~ — *PPI*

488:28   in the *TSR*] of the *MS*

488:29   godless] Godless *PPI*

488:29   god] God *PPI*

488:37   locusts,] ~ *TS*

488:39   ago,] ~ *TS*

489:1   locusts.—] ~. *PPI*

489:5   O David's *PPII*] The great *MS*

489:7   Ha-ha] Ha! Ha *TS*

489:8   Judah *PPII*] Israel *MS*

489:9   peeps,] peep■ *TS* peeps *PPI*

489:12   —Ha-ha!] —Ha! ha! *TS* Ha! Ha! *PPI*

489:15   his Lord, for his *Ed.*] the Lord, for the *MS* the Lord. for the *TS* the Lord. For the *TSR* his Lord. For his *PPI*

489:17   heart—] ~. *PPI*

489:19   visions!] ~. *TS*

489:23   spirits] spirit *TS*

489:26   breath of Might *PPII*] presence of God *MS*

489:26   first moved] first/ *TS* first got *TSR*

489:27   God] god *PPI*

489:33   pit] pit, down the pit *TS* pit—down the pit *PPI*

489:38   beetle of the beginning] Beetle ~ ~ Beginning *PPI*

489:38   yet] *Om. TS*

489:39   beetle] Beetle *PPI*

489:39   clamber *MS, TSC*] clambering *TS, PPI*

489:39   who] Who *E1*

489:40   Lord] the Lord *TS*

489:40   Hosts—] ~.— *TS* ~. *PPI*

490:1   e'en be *PPII*] I were *MS*

490:2   hour!] ~. *TS*

490:6   Peace! *TSR*] ~, *MS*

490:8   Serpent] serpent *TS*

490:8   forever] for ever *PPI*

490:13   Thus] thus *PPI*

490:14   —and] ~ *PPI*

490:14   thus—] ~ —— *PPI*

490:19   gods. *MS, PPI*] Gods. *TS* gods? *E1*

490:20   Great *MS, TSC*] great *TS, PPI*

490:20   forth—] ~. *PPI*

490:23   —If] ~ *PPI*

490:23   8. *Ed.*] 8, to the music above. *MS viii. PPI see note on* 487:33

490:28   goose,] ~ — *PPI*

490:29   gods] the Gods *TS* the gods *PPI*

490:30   great White] great white *TS* Great White *PPI*

490:33   Beetle—] ~.— *TS* ~. *PPI*

490:38   father] Father *PPII*

490:39   What, art thou] ~ ~ ~, *TS*

491:1   say!—] say / *TS* say *PPI*

491:3   prophecy!—] prophesy!— *TS* prophecy! *PPI*

491:4   "When] ~ *PPI*

491:4   the heavens] thy heavens *PPI*

491:5   ordained—"] ~. *PPI*

491:6   Art] art *TS*

491:13 *moody, silent Ed.*] moody,
silent *MS* moody silent, *TS*
moody silence, *TSR moody
silence, PPI*

491:16 heavens—] ~. *PPI*

491:20 David! *TSR*] ~. *MS*

491:20 hence! *TSR*] ~. *MS*

491:22 this,] ~. *PPI*

491:24 him? *TSR*] ~. *MS*

491:24 dead? *TS*] dead! *MS*

491:30 It was not] It was out *TS, PPI*
I was out *TSR see notes*

491:34 father!—] ~./ *TS* ~! *TSR*

491:34 Oh I] ~, I *PPI*

491:37 Lord!—] ~/ *TS* ~. *TSR*

491:38 winds!—] ~/ *TS* ~. *TSR*

491:39 men?] ~! *TS*

492:1 Ay!] *Om. TS*

492:3 very *TSR*] *Om. MS*

492:5 Night *PPII*] Lord *MS*

492:6 me!] *m/ TS* me. *TSR*

492:8 eyes,] ~ *PPII*

492:9 Judah, who *MS, PPII*] ~.
Who *TS, PPI* ~?—Who
TSR

492:10 Benjamin? *MS, PPII*] ~/ *TS*
~. *TSR*

492:15 Ah] ~, *E1*

492:17 David!] ~, *PPI*

492:19 shalt *TSR*] wilt *MS*

492:21 has the king ... against me
TSR] hath happened, Oh King
MS has the King ... against
me *PPI*

492:22 ill *TSR*] ill against thee *MS*

492:25 Ah] ~, *E1*

492:27 thy] the *TS*

492:30 I?] ~, *PPI*

492:32 heart. And] ~, And *TS* ~, and
PPI

492:33 battles!] ~. *TS*

492:34 the King's, *TSR*] in thy hand,
MS in thy hands *TS*

492:34 serve *TS*] serve thee *MS see
notes*

493:2 *in Ed.*] in *MS* at *TS* at *PPI*

493:3 HERDSMEN *PPII*] shepherds
MS shepherds PPI see notes

493:5 HERDSMAN *Ed.*] shepherd *MS
shepherd PPI see note on* 493:3

493:8 Oh-Oh-Oh-h-] Oh! Oh-Oh-h-
TS Oh! Oh-oh-h *PPI*

493:12 oh] Oh *TS* O *PPI*

493:12 Herdsmen] Herdman *PPI*
Herdsman *PPII*

493:14 —Ya] ~ *PPI*

493:16 Ho] ~, *PPI*

493:20 right!] ~? *E1*

493:26 Philistine.—] Philistines,— *TS*
Philistines. *PPI*

493:29 so?—] ~? *PPI*

493:30 Mehólathite] Meholathite *TS
see notes*

493:31 her?—] ~? *PPI*

494:5 —Oh herdsman] O herdsman
PPI O Herdsman *E1*

494:11 David!] ~? *E1*

494:13 [*Enter* ADRIEL.] *Ed.*] *Om. MS*

494:14 Ha] ~, *PPI*

494:30 it!—*TSR*] ~.— *MS* ~! *PPI*

494:31 chastenest *TSR*] chasteneth
MS

494:31 Philistine!—] Philitine!— *TS*
Philistine! *PPI*

494:33 thee!— *TSR*] ~.— *MS* ~!
PPI

494:33 Now therefore] ~, ~, *PPI*

495:2 lance-points, *TSR*] ~ *MS*

495:4 Lo! Here] lo! here *E1*

495:8 oh] Oh *TS* O *PPI*

495:12 menservants! But] ~, but *PPI*

495:13 Israel!—] ~! *PPI*

495:14 great *TSR*] haughty *MS* haugh
/ *TS*

495:17 Israel,—] ~. *PPI*

495:17 say,] ~: *PPI*

495:23 [*Enter* SAUL *and* ADRIEL.] *Ed.*]
Om. MS see notes

495:25 —Yea] Yea, *PPI*

495:31 me,] ~ *PPI*

495:33 oh] Oh *TS* O *PPI*

495:36 Let thy servant *TSR*] Ah, let
me *MS*

495:36 king! *Ed.*] king!{King *TS*}! Let
me be servant before Saul in all
things. *MS* King! *TSR*

495:37 and] an *E1*
495:39 serve, *TSR*] serve thee, *MS*
serve *PPI*
495:40 it! *TSR*] ~ *MS* ~. *TS*
495:40 *Exit, Ed.*] exeunt, *MS* exit *TS*
Exit PPII see note on 495:23
496:2 promises! *TSR*] ~. *MS* promis
/ *TS*
496:5 bargain?—] ~? *PPI*
496:5 take] Take *PPI*
496:6 stick!] ~. *TS*
496:6 worth the word *TSR*] as good
as the rod *MS*
496:12 Oh] ~, *PPI*
496:12 master *TSR*] my lord *MS* Lord
TS
496:16 oh man] Oh Man *TS* O Man
PPI
496:17 Oh] ~, *PPI*
496:17 master *PPI*] my Lord *MS* my
master *TSR*
496:19 Oh *Ed.*] Oh my lord *MS* Oh
my Lord *TS* Oh my *TSR* Oh,
PPI
496:20 Ay wellah!] ~, ~, *E1*
496:23 quickly,] ~ *TS*
496:25 Lord! *TSR*] ~, *MS* ~ *TS*
496:25 —My] ~ *TS*
496:27 salvation] Salvation *TS*
496:29 mark!— *TSR*] ~.— *MS* ~.
PPI
496:32 middle *TSR*] waist *MS*
496:32 life *TSR*] body *MS*
496:40 Oh] ~, *PPI*
497:4 —Her] ~ *TS*
497:10 waited *TSR*] waited for thee
MS
497:13 Oh] ~, *PPI*
497:15 shalt] shall *TS*
497:17 When] ■hen *TS* when *PPI*
497:18 of *TSR*] in *MS*
497:19 twain!] ~. *TS*
497:22 arouses *TSR*] springs up *MS*
497:24 to thy liking *TSR*] for thee *MS*
497:25 Ah no! Ah no! Ah no] Ah no!
Ah! Ah *TS* Ah, no! Ah! Ah
PPI
497:28 Oh] ~, *PPI* O *E1*

497:29 hillsides *TSR*] wind *MS*
497:31 thy] *Om. TS*
497:32 thy life *TSR*] thy body *MS*
497:32 life *TSR*] body *MS*
497:34 in] *Om. TS*
497:36 go?] ~. *PPI*
497:40 Oh] ~, *PPI*
498:1: oh] Oh *TS* O *PPI*
498:5 —Nay . . . and] and *TS* And
TSR
498:14 Wilt] Will *TS*
498:18 as] *Om. TS*
498:19 ship,] ~; *PPI*
498:20 onward] onwards *TS*
498:21 Oh] ~, *PPI*
498:23 marry *MS, PPII*] carry *TS*
498:28 a] *Om. TS*
498:29 shalt] shall *TS*
499:13 here—] ~. *TS*
499:14 Saul,] ~ *PPI*
499:19 Michal *TS*] Merab *MS*
499:20 Oh! *TSR*] ~ *MS*
499:20 new opened] new-opened *PPI*
499:22 Oh say,] ~, ~! *PPI*
499:23 oasis] Oasis *TS*
499:27 well.] ~? *PPI*
499:33 enemies, *MS, TSR*] ~ *TS*
499:33 David] ~, *PPI*
499:36 horns,] ~ *E1*
499:39 am I] I am *PPI*
500:2 bride money] bride-money *E1*
500:6 moon] ~, *E1*
500:7 cometh] ~, *PPI*
500:9 Michal his daughter] ~, ~ ~,
PPI
500:17 Michal my daughter] my
daughter michal *TS* my
daughter Michal *TSR*
500:18 must I] I must *TS*
500:19 moonless] ~, *E1*
500:26 man! *TSR*] ~. *MS* ~ / *TS*
500:27 Michal!] ~? *E1*
500:27 again] *Om. TS*
500:28 an *TSR*] a *MS*
500:28 enemy,] ~ *PPI*
500:30 Yea,] ~ *TS* ~! *TSR*
500:31 King's] kings' *PPI*
500:35 maidens] Maidens *E1*

501:2   *speaking PPI*] saying *MS*
      speaking *TSR*
501:3   *a PPI*] *Om. MS* a *TSR*
501:4   Lord;] ∼, *PPI*
501:5   my God] and my God *PPI*
501:7   Lord:] ∼; *TS*
501:17 presence] temple *PPI see notes*
501:19 enemies:] ∼; *PPI*
501:19 the] thy *PPI*
501:20 mouth:] ∼; *PPI*
501:21 as] *Om. PPI*
501:24 transgressions,] ∼; *PPI*
501:27 them;] ∼: *PPI*
501:29 favor] favour *E1*
501:32 Nay] ∼, *PPII*
501:32 thine] thy *TS* Thy *E1*
501:35 hath me ... Saul seek] seek *TS*
      seeks *TSR*
502:3   thyself] *Om. TS*
502:4   hours] hour/ *TS*
502:4   morning?—] ∼? *PPI*
502:11 I, I] I, *TS* I *PPI*
502:13 you,] ∼ *PPI*
502:13 wife,] ∼ *TS*
502:15 But] ∼, *E1*
502:18 Ah ... Ah] ∼, ... ∼, *PPI*
502:32 husband!] ∼, *PPI*
502:34 Yea verily! *TSR*] ∼ ∼. *MS* ∼,
      ∼! *PPI*
502:34 oh,] oh / *TS* O *PPI*
502:36 me,] ∼ *PPI*
502:39 thee?—] ∼? *PPI*
503:1   thee?—] ∼? *PPI*
503:9   sayst] sayest *TS*
503:16 anointed!—] ∼! *PPI*
503:18 him!] ∼. *TS*
503:18 verily!—] ∼! *PPI*
503:22 away,] ∼ *PPI*
503:26 finished,] ∼ *PPI*
503:30 as a man falling] man falling
      TS a man falling *TSR, E1* man
      a-falling *PPI*
503:35 passed,] ∼ *PPI*
503:38 and prevailed ... to Gilgal,]
      Om. TS
503:40 rejoiced,] rejoiced. But *TSR see*
      note on 504:1
504:2   hate!—] ∼! *PPI*

504:4   God *TSR*] the hand of God
      MS
504:8   him.—But] ∼ —But *TS*
      ∼ —But, *PPI* ∼ —but, *E1*
504:8   Oh,] O *PPI*
504:15 as *TSR*] like as *MS*
504:16 hawk] Hawk *TS*
504:18 even *PPII*] like *MS*
504:19 it—] ∼. *TS*
504:21 me,] ∼ *TS*
504:25 the] ■■■ *TS Om. PPI see*
      notes
504:30 Oh bitter! bitter] ∼, ∼! Bitter
      PPI
504:33 Oh] O *PPI* Oh, *E1*
504:36 Oh nay] ∼, ∼, *PPI*
504:38 joy.—Nay] ∼! ∼, *PPI*
504:39 Nay] ∼, *PPI*
505:4   thing. Thou] ∼, thou *PPI* ∼;
      thou *E1*
505:11 sleep *TSR*] browse *MS*
505:13 Ah ... Ah] ∼, ... ∼, *PPI*
505:14 Oh] O *PPI* Oh, *PPII*
505:19 Ah] ∼, *PPI*
505:19 gates] gate■ *TS* gate *PPI*
505:19 now] *Om. TS*
505:20 under,] ∼/ *TS*
506:2   *an hour or so later PPI*] an
      hour or so later *TSR Om. MS*
506:2   *but PPI*] only *MS*
506:3   *wooden PPI*] life-size *MS*
      wooden *TSR*
506:5   food!—] ∼! *PPI*
506:7   heart!—] ∼! *PPI*
506:12 again!—] ∼! *PPI*
506:16 *a Ed.*] a *MS Om. PPI*
506:20 sleep.—] ∼. *PPI*
506:22 Now *PPII*] God *MS*
506:26 Ah] ∼, *PPI*
506:27 Giver *PPII*] Lord God *MS*
      Lord *TS*
506:32 hath,] ∼ *TS*
506:37 hills *PPII*] Lord *MS*
506:38 dulled *TSR*] obscured *MS*
506:38 again. It] ∼, It *TS* ∼; it *PPI*
506:38 day, and ... is night. *PPII*]
      Lord, whose sun dies not. The
      clouds but pass. *MS*

507:6   Nay!—] ~! *PPI*
507:17 door!—] ~! *PPI*
507:17 flee!—] ~! *PPI*
507:18 door,] ~ *PPI*
507:18 *appears)*— *Ed.*] appears)— *MS*
       appears), *PPI*
507:19 men,] ~ *PPI*
507:25 Jonathan!—] ~! *PPI*
507:28 together, yea … are
       together!—] together!— *TS*
       together— *TSR*
507:30 wind] ~, *TS*
507:34 an'] an *TS*
507:35 Sayst] Sayest *TS*
507:35 Oh] ~, *PPII*
507:40 lie,] ~: *E1*
508:4   Verily,] Verilyb *TS* Verily *PPI*
508:5   spring-time] springtime *PPI*
508:6   almond tree] almond-tree *E1*
508:7   bud!—Oh] ~! ~, *PPI*
508:8   womb.] ~? *PPI*
508:10 an'] an *TS*
508:13 Ho! there] ~, ~ *E1*
508:14 water skin] water-skin *PPI*
508:15 bread. For] ~ —for *PPI*
508:21 thou shalt] shalt thou *PPI*
508:21 Oh] ~, *PPI*
508:25 ought] aught *PPI*
508:31 thou—] ~ —— *PPI*
508:32 *(re-entering) Ed.*] *Om. MS*
       (re-entering) PPII
508:33 men at arms] men-at-arms *TS*
508:34 Oh flee!] Oh flee! Oh *TS* Oh,
       flee! Oh, *PPI*
508:38 *end Ed.*] end *MS* ends *PPI*
508:40 —Go] ~ *TS*
509:2   unto *TSR*] into *MS*
509:3   Ha-a] Ha—a *PPI*
509:7   *the stake … window-space Ed.*]
       the stake … window-space *MS*
       space *TS* the stake *TSR the*
       stake PPI
509:10 oh] O *PPI*
509:10 spiteful *TSR*] evil *MS*
509:10 rope!] ~. *PPI*
509:15 will I] I will *TS*
509:18 *at PPI*] under *MS* at *TSR*
509:20 and my *MS, PPII*] and *TS*

509:23 old,] ~ — *TS* ~ *PPI*
509:23 BOY) *Ed.*] boy) *MS* BOY), *PPI*
509:28 and] an/ *TS Om. TSR*
509:32 oh] O *PPI*
509:34 now! *TSR*] ~ *MS* ~. *TS*
509:38 he] *Om. TS*
509:40 hush!] ~. *PPI*
510:5   1ST *PPII*] *Om. MS*
510:6   *Exeunt the* CAPTAINS *PPI*] exit
       MS exeunt the captains *TSR*
510:7   *short Ed.*] short *MS a short*
       PPI
510:18 Then will they] They will *TS*
510:20 oh] O *PPI*
510:20 God] god *TS*
510:23 Ho] ~, *PPI*
510:26 ye,] ~ *PPI*
510:33 sight *TSR*] name *MS*
510:35 An'] An *PPI*
510:36 Nay] ~, *PPI*
510:37 me! *TSR*] ~. *MS* ~? *PPI*
511:1   terrors nip] terror nip *TS*
       terror nips *TSR*
511:3   Oh] ~, *PPI*
511:5   bath *TSR*] ablutions *MS*
511:12 Oh] O *PPI* Oh, *E1*
511:13 enough!] ~? *PPI*
511:14 Oh] O *PPI* Oh, *E1*
511:18 escape] escapes *PPI*
511:18 us] me *TS*
511:20 Oh,] O *PPI*
511:21 hast *TSR*] hath *MS*
511:22 now thine ear! *TSR*] thine ear
       now! *MS* thine ear now/ *TS*
511:28 bed,] ~ *PPI*
511:30 Now,] ~ *TS*
511:34 say: yet] ~: Yet *TS* ~ —Yet
       PPI ~ ——Yet *E1*
511:34 will I] I will *TS*
511:38 daughter.] ~? *E1*
511:39 *followed by* [WOMAN-SERVANT
       and] soldiers *Ed.*] *Om. MS*
       followed by soldiers PPII
512:1   An'] An *PPI*
512:3   Now,] ~ *TS*
512:4   1ST CAPTAIN *PPI*] Captain *MS*
       1st Captain *TS* CAPTAIN *PPII*
       see notes

512:4 Ho] ~, *PPI*
512:10 Ho] ~, *PPI*
512:10 David!—] ~! *PPI*
512:15 goat's hair] goats hair *TS*
goats-hair *TSR* goat's-hair
PPII goats'-hair *E1*
512:16 this,] ~ *TS*
512:16 Michal's? *TSR*] ~! *MS*
512:20 *Pause—Voice of* SAUL *on the*
stair Ed.] pause—Voice of Saul
on the stair *MS* pause—voice
of . . . stair *TS Pause PPI*
512:21 SAUL *Ed.*] SAUL (*on the stair*)
PPI
512:22 *Enter* SAUL *Ed.*] enter Saul *MS*
Entering PPI Saul enters *PPII*
512:23 father] Father *PPII*
512:29 Oh God] ~ god *TS* ~, god
PPI
512:29 Oh alas . . . Oh] ~, ~ . . . ~,
PPI
512:30 Woe] woe *TS*
512:33 Oh, God] Oh, god *TS* O god
E1
512:36 slain,] ~! *PPI*
512:40 holpen *MS, TSR*] helpen *TS*,
PPI helped *PPII*
513:21 Jonathan,] ~; *PPI*
513:24 death. For] ~, For *TS* ~, for
PPI
513:24 liveth,] ~ *E1*
513:25 brothers] brother *TS*
513:27 father] Father *PPII*
513:27 him.] ~! *E1*
513:32 father] Father *PPII*
513:35 Ah . . . Ah] ~, . . . ~, *PPI*
514:1 15. *Ed.*] XIV *MS* XV *PPI*
514:4 *and lusty, Ed.*] and lusty, *MS*
an/ *TS* and *TSR and PPI*
514:4 *of Ed.*] of *MS* of the *TS of the*
PPI
514:7 1ST *Ed.*] a *MS* a *PPI*
514:10 Unseen *TSR*] unseen *MS*
514:10 Very] very *TS*
514:11 dares] dare *TS*
514:16 Father.] father? *PPI* Father?
PPI!
514:27 wife.] ~! *PPI*

514:30 verily—] ~ *TS* ~! *TSR*
514:31 *yea, verily!*—] Yea, ~? *PPI*
514:31 Hark] ~, *PPI*
514:32 shall] should *TS*
515:2 over,] ~/ *TS*
515:9 Father, *MS, PPII*] father *PPI*
515:10 not?—] ~? *PPI*
515:13 me!—] ~! *PPI*
515:14 Doth] Does *TS*
515:16 it?—] ~? *PPI*
515:17 thine] thine own *TS*
515:18 speak! *TSR*] ~. *MS*
515:25 and] Om. *TS*
515:25 sorrow,] ~ *PPI*
515:29 Wouldest] Wouldst *TS*
515:29 verily?—] ~? *PPI*
515:29 When the . . . wet rain? *TSR*]
Can the moon dance in the
arms of the sun? Will the hot
lion eat grass with the ram of
the flock? *MS*
515:31 —The] /~ *TS*
515:32 flame,] ~ *PPI*
515:33 in thine own likeness, *TSR*] as
a father *MS*
515:34 who fulfils thy desire.—*TSR*]
of great might.— *MS* who
fulfils thy desire. *PPI*
515:37 then, thou] thee, thou *TS* thou,
flee *PPII*
516:3 way of might, yea *PPII*] Lord's
way, with men *MS*
516:5 Strength *PPII*] God *MS*
516:6 thee! *TSR*] ~. *MS*
516:11 men!] ~? *E1*
516:11 father] Father *PPII*
516:17 stones,] ~■ *TS* ~ *PPI*
516:21 once as] once *TS*
516:23 men! *TSR*] ~. *MS*
516:26 I too] ~, ~, *PPI*
516:30 snare!—] ~! *PPI*
516:31 gone!—] ~. *PPI*
516:35 me—] ~ . . . *PPI*
517:1 place?—] ~? *PPI*
517:1 say] Say *TS*
517:2 him,] ~: *PPI*
517:3 Hill *PPII*] Lord *MS*
517:5 him,] ~: *E1*

517:11 *with flute—on the hill Ed.*] with
flute—on the hill *MS* with
flute—on ■■■ hill *TS* *on hill
with flute PPI*

517:12 Oh] O *PPI* Oh, *E₁*

517:12 God! *MS, E₁*] ~? *PPI*

517:12 Oh put] O put *PPI* Oh, put *E₁*

517:13 Name *PPII*] Lord *MS*

517:22 sayst] sayest *TS*

517:33 man,] ~. *TS*

517:34 Secretly,] ~ *TS*

517:37 king.] King. *TS* King! *PPII*

518:2 brightness!] ~ *PPI*

518:3 And] and *PPI*

518:7 Glory] ■lory *TS* glory *PPI*

518:7 So! He] ~ he *TS*

518:8 flame!—But] ~! But *PPI*

518:12 Yea! Come *PPII*] Why come
MS

518:13 go!—] ~!/ *TS*

518:14 hill! *TSR*] ~. *MS*

518:15 ARMED MEN *Ed.*] Men-at-arms
MS MEN-AT-ARMS *PPI*

518:22 Lord!] Oh Lord! *TS* O Lord!
PPI O Lord? *E₁*

518:26 *(Bis.) Ed.*] *Om. MS* (bis) *TSR*
Bis. PPI

518:29 sun] Sun *PPII*

518:32 cloud!] ~. *PPI* ~? *E₁*

518:34 ARMED MEN *PPII*] Soldiers *MS*
SOLDIERS *PPI*

518:35 King!] ~? *E₁*

518:36 an'] an *PPI*

518:38 Ha!—Ha!—] ~! - ~! - *TS* ~!
~! *PPI*

518:39 Ha!—] ~! *TS*

519:1 *woolen Ed.*] woolen *MS* woollen
PPI

519:1 1ST *PPII*] one *MS* *one PPI*

519:5 *(Bis.) Ed.*] *Om. MS* (bis) *TSR*
Bis. PPI

519:9 hearth? is *TSR*] ~, is *MS* ~?
Is *PPI*

519:9 thee? Kindler! It *Ed.*] thee, oh
Lord! It *MS* thee, Oh Lord! It
TS thee? Oh Lord! It *TSR*
thee? O Lord! it *PPI* thee?
Kindler! it *PPII*

519:11 unshadow itself *PPII*] shall call
to thee *MS*

519:11 mount *PPII*] call *MS*

519:12 Wave *PPI*] Lord *MS*

519:12 Brightness! *TSR*] brightness.
MS Brightness. *TS*

519:17 darkened,] ~ *PPI*

519:19 oh] Oh *TS*

519:19 flame!] ~. *PPI*

519:20 Oh] ~, *PPI*

519:20 the *PPII*] thy *MS*

519:29 away!] ~. *PPI*

519:32 flame of all glory! *TSR*] white
flame of glory. *MS*

519:33 body and *PPII*] gleaming *MS*

519:34 great *TSR*] great white *MS*

520:1 Oh . . . Oh] ~, . . . ~, *PPI*

520:2 up on] upon *TS*

520:3 close] enclose *TS*

520:6 transfiguration! *TSR*] ~. *MS*

520:6 Oh] ~, *PPI*

520:7 Oh] ~, *PPI*

520:10 day,] ~; *PPI*

520:11 Alas,] ~ *PPI*

520:12 Sun *PPII*] God *MS*

520:12 Alas!] ~ *E₁*

520:14 Alas!] ~ *E₁*

520:15 is a . . . her mouth, *TSR*]
skippeth and boundeth *MS*

520:17 Yea!] ~, *E₁*

520:18 cunning,] ~ *TS*

520:19 earth,] ~ *E₁*

520:22 Yea!] ~, *E₁*

520:25 7TH *Ed.*] Another *MS* ANOTHER
PPI

520:25 Yea!] ~, *E₁*

520:30 leaderless! Even] ~—even
PPI

520:31 6TH *Ed.*] Other *MS* OTHER *PPI*

  I T *PPII* 1ST *E₁*

520:36 God.] ~ *TS* ~, *PPI*

520:39 worm's *PPI*] worms *MS*

520:39 mouth] ~. *PPII*

521:1 hill] ~, *PPI*

521:2 flame, *TSR*] ~ *MS*

521:3 world.] ~ *TS* ~, *TSR*

521:4 grave . . . *TSR*] ~ *MS* ~ . . . .
PPI

522:1   16. *Ed.*] XV *MS* XVI *PPI*
522:2   in *Ed.*] in *MS* is *TS* is *PPI*
522:4   Now] ~, *PPI*
522:6   Lord! look] ~, Look *TS* ~, look *TSR*
522:6   me;] ~, *TS*
522:6   enemies.] ~ — *TS* ~!— *TSR* ~! *PPI*
522:7   God!—] ~! *PPI*
522:9   Yea] ~, *E1*
522:9   far away] away *TS* distant *TSR*
522:11   is] Is *PPI*
522:12   die!—] ~! *PPI*
522:13   fields!—] field!— *TS* field! *PPI*
522:13   Ah] ~, *PPI*
522:13   watch!—] ~! *PPI*
522:13   Jonathan?—] ~? *PPI*
522:14   men,] ~; *E1*
522:16   word!—] ~! *PPI*
522:22   *Behold!*] ~! *PPI* ~, *E1*
522:22   *them!*—] *them! PPI*
522:23   can I] I can *TS*
522:26   so!—] ~! *TS*
522:26   Yea!—] ~! *PPI*
522:29   LAD *PPII*] youth *MS* YOUTH *PPI*
522:32   now] ~, *E1*
522:33   *Balances Ed.*] balances *MS* balancing *TS Balancing PPI*
522:35   let] Let *E1*
522:35   Yea!] ~, *E1*
522:37   dead!—] ~! *PPI*
522:39   nose-tip.] ~! *TS*
522:39   —Now . . . *again.) Ed.*] —Now this time! (takes another arrow, shoots again) *MS Om. TS*
523:2   e'er] ere *E1*
523:7   —Here] ~, *PPI*
523:10   fourth—] ~ —— *PPI*
523:12   not!—] ~! *PPI*

523:12   a bush!—] a bush. *TS* bush. *PPI*
523:14   Behold,] ~ *TS*
523:14   still] *Om. TS*
523:16   all! Come] ~. ~ *TS* ~. ~, *E1*
523:18   a while] awhile *TS*
523:21   LAD *PPII*] boy *MS* BOY *PPI*
523:27   Saul.] ~° *TS* ~? *PPI*
523:29   Ah] ~, *PPI*
523:31   friend] a friend *TS*
523:37   Saul!—] ~! *PPI*
523:37   come. Till . . . comes the] come, and t / the *TS* come, and the *PPI*
524:3   Michal my wife] my wife *TS* Michal *PPII*
524:9   father's] father *TS*
524:18   saying,] ~: *TS*
524:20   Yea!] ~, *E1*
524:20   us.] ~! *E1*
524:23   thee!—] ~! *PPI*
524:28   wit] ~, *TS*
524:29   splendour and the] *Om. TS*
524:31   flame, shall . . . fall before *PPI*] flame of God, shall fall from *MS* flame, shall fall from / of God shall fall from *TS* flame, shall fall from God, shall fall from *PPI see note on* 524:32
524:32   shrewd whelp *TSR*] fox-whelp *MS* fox-faced whelp *TS*
524:33   Judah!—] ~! *PPI*
524:34   tender *TSR*] weird *MS*
524:39   Strength *PPII*] God *MS*
524:40   finish] ■■ finish *TS* ■■ finished *TSR* be finished *PPI*
525:2   dies!—] ~! *PPI*
525:3   city—] ~. *PPI*
525:5   *(Curtain) Ed.*] (Curtain) / The End. *MS* (Curtain) / THE END *TS* CURTAIN *PPI*

Altitude

MS   = Autograph MS (Roberts E13a)
TS   = Ribbon-copy TS (Roberts E13d)
Per = *Laughing Horse*, no. 20 (Summer 1938), pp. 113–35
E1   = *Complete Plays* (Heinemann, 1965), pp. 535–48

Whenever the *MS* reading is adopted, it appears within the square bracket with no symbol. Other variants appear in chronological order as given above. In the absence of information to the contrary, the reader should assume that a variant recurs in subsequent states.

When a reading from a source other than *MS* has been preferred or coincides with the adopted reading, it appears with its source-symbol within the square bracket; the *MS* reading follows the bracket along with further variants from later states.

Entries after 550:20 record only *MS*, *TS* and *E1*: *Per* prints no text after 550:20

The following symbols are used editorially:

C   = Autograph corrections by Willard Johnson in *TS*
Del. = Deleted by Willard Johnson in *TS*

541:1   *Altitude* / Scene 1.]
        ALTITUDE by D. H.
        Lawrence / Scene I *TS*
        ALTITUDE / the first scene
        of an unfinished play / by
        D. H. Lawrence *Per* SCENE I
        E1

541:3   MARY A. . . . *at Taos. Ed.*] Mary
        A. in kitchen doorway at Taos.
        MS The curtain rises revealing
        the kitchen of Mabel's house at
        TAOS / Mary A. stands in the
        sunny doorway *TSC [The {The
        E1} curtain rises, revealing the
        kitchen of* Mabel's {MABEL'S
        *E1} house at Taos. Mary {MARY
        E1} stands in the sunny doorway,
        Per*

541:4   *(chants to herself—says Om!
        resoundingly) Ed.*] —(chants
        {(chants *TS}* to herself—says
        Om! resoundingly.) *MS*
        (chanting to herself)—saying
        "Om!" resoundingly.) *TSC
        chanting to herself, saying "Om"
        {"Om" E1} resoundingly.]
        {resoundingly. E1} Per*

541:4   —This] ~ *Per*
541:6   waiting.] ~ . . . . *Per*
541:6   for? What for?] for? What for?
        / (Enter Spud, taking in the
        situation at a glance) *TSC* for?
        What for? / *[Enter* Spud,
        {*Enter* SPUD, *E1} taking in the*

        situation at a glance.] {*glance.
        E1} Per*
541:7   *(entering) Ed.*] (entering) *MS
        Del. TSC*
541:8   Goodmorning] Good morning
        Per
541:8   yet.—] ~ . . . . *Per*
541:13 fire, the] ~. The *TS*
541:16 Ah] Oh *TS*
541:18 *(MARY girds it on.) Ed.*] (Mary
        girds it on.) *MS Del. TSC*
541:19 To] (girding on the apron &
        busy at the stove) To *TSC
        [Girding {(girding E1} on the
        apron, and busy at the stove.]/
        To {stove): To E1} Per*
541:20 *(Busy at the stove.) Ed.*] (busy
        at the stove) *MS* (busy at the
        stove). *TS Del. TSC*
541:22 Oh Good-morning] ~
        good-morning *TS* ~,
        good-morning *Per* ~,
        good morning *E1*
541:22 Good morning]
        Good morning, *TS, E1*
        Good-morning, *Per*
541:24 neighbourhood.] ~? *Per*
541:25 Why] ~, *Per*
541:25 coming!] ~? *Per*
541:29 am] am the *Per*
541:32 rôle] role *TS*
542:3   wood.] wood. *[He goes out.]
        Per* wood. / *He goes out. E1*
542:7   Why] ~, *Per*

542:11 dreamer] Dreamer *Per*
542:13 muscle] muscles *Per*
542:14 commonsense] common-sense *Per*
542:18 MILKMAN *suddenly Ed.*]
Milkman suddenly *MS*
Milkman suddenly appears *TSC* The Milkman {MILKMAN *E1*} *suddenly appears Per*
542:20 Oh] ~, *TS*
542:20 yes, let's] yess, let's *TS* yess! Let's *TSC*
542:20 cream.] ~! *Per*
542:23 tomorrow... *wire door.*) *Ed.*]
tomorrow. (Milkman slams wire door) *MS* tomorrow. (Milkman slams wire door). *TS* tomorrow. *[Exit Milkman, slamming the screen door. Per* to-morrow. / *Exit* MILKMAN, *slamming the screen door. E1*
542:24 (CLARENCE ... *the gong.*) *Ed.*]
(Clarence goes out: loudly rings the gong) *MS* (Clarence follows him out: loudly rings the gong). *TSC* Clarence {CLARENCE *E1*} *follows him out and rings the gong loudly.] {loudly. E1} Per*
542:28 meanwhile—] ~. *TS*
542:29 rise] ~, *Per*
542:32 stable.] stable? / *[Enter Ida] Per* stable? / *Enter* IDA. *E1*
542:33 (*entering*): *Ed.*] (entering) *MS Om. Per*
542:36 *muslin—hovers—sits Ed.*]
muslin—hovers—sits *MS* muslin. *She hovers, then sits Per*
542:37 CLARENCE.) *Ed.*] Clarence) *MS* Clarence). *TSC* Clarence, *who re-enters at this moment.] Per* CLARENCE, *who re-enters at this moment. E1*
542:38 (*entering*) *Ed.*] (entering) *MS Om. Per*
542:38 er!] ~, *Per*
542:38 Goodmorning! Goodmorning] Good-morning! Good-

morning, *Per* Good morning! Good morning, *E1*
542:39 Sprague,] ~; *Per*
542:39 —Goodmorning] Good-morning, *Per* Good morning, *E1*
543:1 SPRAGUE: *Ed.*] S.: *MS* S: *TS* SPRAGUE *Per* SPRAGUE (*picks up a tumbler and wanders around with it*): *E1*
543:1 yes! (*Hunts ... with it.*) *Ed.*]
yes! (hunts round, finds a tumbler, and wanders round with it {it *TS*}) *MS* yes! *[Picks up a tumbler and wanders around with it.] / [Mabel pops in through the dining-room door.] Per* yes! / MABEL *pops in through the dining-room door. E1*
543:3 (*in doorway*) *Ed.*] (in doorway) *MS Om. Per*
543:5 I rang] *I* rang *TSC*
543:6 bed.] ~? *Per*
543:14 —Won't] ~ *TS*
543:15 it.] ~? *Per*
543:19 knife.] ~? *TS*
543:25 —My] ~ *TS*
543:25 God *MS, E1*] god *TS*
543:25 knife,] ~; *Per*
543:26 *bacon.*) *Ed.*] bacon.) *MS* bacon) *TS* bacon.] *Per* bacon.) / *Enter* INDIAN. *E1*
543:28 Hello] ~, *Per*
543:31 Joe.] Joe. *[Joe goes out with pail.] Per* Joe. / JOE *goes out with pail. E1*
543:35 Why] ~, *Per*
544:1 dead.] ~? *Per*
544:3 Well] ~, *Per*
544:4 *snorts Ed.*] snorts *MS* snorts again *TSC snorts again Per*
544:4 Indian.] ~! *Per*
544:9 (*Looks at his finger.*) *Ed.*] (looks at his finger) *MS Del. TSC*
544:10 Spud.] Spud. (Spud examines his finger, critically) *TSC* Spud. [Spud *examines his finger, critically.] Per* Spud. /

SPUD *examines his finger, critically. E1*

544:13 Anyway] ~, *Per*

544:15 But] ~, *Per*

544:17 Exactly. The] ~: The *TS* ~: the *E1*

544:18 signal!] ~. *TS*

544:21 it] ~, *TS*

544:22 it.] it. *[Joe re-enters with the pail.] Per* it. / JOE *re-enters with the pail. E1*

544:23 JOE *(entering):* Ed.] Joe (entering) *MS* Joe (entering): *TS* INDIAN *Per* INDIAN: *E1*

544:24 All right] Alright *E1*

544:25 *and* Ed.] and *MS Del. TSC*

544:25 *like.) Ed.*] like) *MS* like). *TS* like, but goes out.). *TSC like, but goes out.* Mabel {MABEL *E1*} *rushes at the stove] {stove. E1} Per*

544:26 MABEL *(rushing at the stove) Ed.*] Mabel (rushing at the stove) *MS Om. Per* MABEL *E1*

544:26 Mary!] ~. *TS*

544:31 Professor *TS*] Proffessor *MS see notes*

544:31 desiccating *TSC*] dessicating *MS see notes*

544:35 Why] ~, *TS*

544:39 Why how] Why, how *TS* How *Per*

545:2 MABEL *(ominously):* Well, Ed.] Mabel (ominously): Well, *MS* Mabel: (Ominously) Well, *TS* Well, *[ominously] Per* Well ... *(ominously) E1*

545:5 MRS SPRAGUE *E1*} Alice *MS* MRS. SPRAGUE *Per*

545:5 Why] ~, *TS*

545:11 Why] ~, *Per*

545:15 trousers!] ~? *TS*

545:16 Why] ~, *Per*

545:21 trousers.] ~? *Per*

545:23 No] ~, *Per*

545:25 own *MS, Per*] own true *TSC*

545:27 not.] ~? *Per*

545:31 all right] alright *E1*

545:34 or talk.] or talk— *TS* and talk— *Per*

546:3 you you] you *Per*

546:11 says.—] ~. *Per*

546:11 effort] efforts *TS*

546:15 Wait!] ~. *TS*

546:17 exhibitionist] ~, *TS*

546:19 aesthete] Aesthete *Per*

546:21 sink—yes!] ~. Yes: *TS*

546:22 *walks. Enter ... out vaguely.)* Ed.] walks. Enter Joe, who goes in & out vaguely.) *MS* walks. Enter Joe, who goes in and out). *TS* walks. Enter Joe,] *TSC walks. Enter Joe.] {*JOE. *E1}* Per

546:23 Hullo] Hello *TS* Hello, *Per*

546:23 hm!] ~? *Per*

546:24 JOE *Ed.*] Joe *MS* INDIAN *Per* INDIAN *E1*

546:33 Oh] ~, *Per*

546:35 CHORUS: *Ed.*] Chorus: *MS—TS* Ida:—*TSC* IDA *Per* IDA: *E1*

546:37 —Joe] ~ *TS*

546:38 Clarence's trousers.] his trousers? *Per*

546:39 JOE *Ed.*] Joe *MS* INDIAN *Per* INDIAN *E1*

547:1 Tony! Tony!] Tony, *Per*

547:2 down] *Om. Per*

547:3 it.] ~? *Per*

547:6 No,] ~. *TS*

547:7 Joe,] ~; *Per*

547:8 JOE *Ed.*] Joe *MS* INDIAN *Per* INDIAN *E1*

547:12 Don't] ~, *TS*

547:12 Oh] ~, *TS*

547:16 down] down to *TSC*

547:17 Ida!] Ida! *Per*

547:18 Mabel!] ~? *TS*

547:19 *talk!*] ~. *TS*

547:20 make] have *TSC*

547:22 colour. They] ~; They *TS* ~; they *Per*

547:24 *babyish MS, Per*] baleyish *TS* (babyish)? *TSC*

547:26 Do you] You *Per*

547:32 Well] ~, *Per*

547:32 him preventing] ~, ~ *TSC*
547:33 almost] *Om. TS*
547:35 The next time,] Next time *Per*
547:38 revelation.] ~? *TS*
547:40 And] *Del. TSC*
547:40 not.] not, for *Per*
548:7   Well] ~, *Per*
548:8   *(TONY gets up.) Ed.*] (Tony gets up.) *MS* (Tony gets up) *TS Del. TSC*
548:9   It is] It's *Per*
548:9   to you] you *Per*
548:15 for. To] ~: to *Per*
548:18 TONY *Ed.*] Tony *MS* Tony (at last getting up & approaching cupboard vaguely *TSC* TONY / *[Getting up at last and looking around vaguely] Per* TONY *(Getting up at last and looking around vaguely) E1*
548:22 don'] don't *TS*
548:22 breakfast.] ~! *Per*
548:24 Oh] ~, *Per*
548:24 dee—ar] dee-ar *TS*
548:32 perfect rhythm] ~ ~, *TS*
548:33 they are] they're *Per*
548:35 *Woman,*] ~ *TS*
548:36 think,] ~ *Per*
548:36 summer *MS, E1*] ~, *Per*
548:37 MABEL) *Ed.*] Mabel) *MS* Mabel/ *Per Mabel), E1*
549:4   MABEL: *Ed.*] Mabel: *MS Om. Per*
549:4   matter] matter, Elizabeth *Per*
549:11 *flannel trousers Ed.*] flannel trousers *MS flannels Per*
549:12 Oh] ~, *Per*
549:12 dear;—The] ~, the *TS*
549:16 them] them. Hurry, now *Per see notes*
549:17 Let] Well, let *Per*
549:17 *Drinks Ed.*] Drinks *MS Drinks hurriedly Per*
549:20 queer—] ~.— *Per*
549:20 is. Whether] ~; whether *Per*
549:22 sweet] swell *TS*
549:24 course,] ~ *Per*
549:34 Who?] ~, *Per*

549:34 he will] *Del. TSC*
549:35 safety-pin] safety pin *TS*
549:36 you] you can *TS*
549:37 same. What] same; but what *Per*
550:4   it.] ~? *Per*
550:6   Ye—es—! Maybe] Ye-es-! ~ *TS* Ye-es, maybe *Per*
550:10 Well—] ~, *Per*
550:10 Indians—] ~, *Per*
550:12 sun shine] sunshine *TS* sun *Per*
550:16 *telephone Ed.*] telephone *MS* the telephone *TSC the telephone Per*
550:16 *rings, and enter* SPUD *Ed.*] rings, and enter Spud *MS* rings; Spud enters *TSC rings;* Spud {SPUD *E1*} *enters Per*
550:16 *poppies and Ed.*] poppies & *MS* poppies and *TS* poppies, *TSC poppies, Per*
550:17 ELIZABETH *Ed.*] Elizabeth *MS* Elizabeth behind him *TSC* Elizabeth {ELIZABETH *E1*} *behind him Per*
550:17 *to telephone. Ed.*] to telephone. *MS* to telephone *TS* to telephone; *TSC to the telephone; Per*
550:18 *coffee. Ed.*] coffee. *MS* coffee. All speak at once *TSC coffee. All speak at once Per*
550:18 Hallo] Hello *TS*
550:20 beautiful!—*all at once.) Ed.*] beautiful!—all at once.) *MS* beautiful! all at once). *TS* beautiful! # End *TSC* beautiful! / *[CURTAIN] Per* beautiful! *E1*
550:21 You] ~, *E1*
550:21 Ida!—] ~! *TS*
550:21 *goes Ed.*] goes *MS goes to the telephone E1*
550:21 —Elizabeth] ~ *E1*
550:24 Why] ~, *E1*
551:1   Scene 2.] *Om. TS* SCENE II *E1*
551:2   SPUD *and* ELIZABETH *getting*

vases in next room *Ed.*] Spud
and Eliz. getting vases in next
room *MS Another room in the
house E1*

551:5   Busy what] What *TS*
551:10 Oh] ~, *E1*
551:10 don'] don't *TS*
551:11 Yes do!] ~ ~. *TS* ~, ~. *E1*
551:18 mean—] ~. *TS*
551:24 Well] ~, *E1*
551:24 to. That's] ~, that's *TS*
551:25 to you'd] ~, ~ *E1*
551:29 SPUD: Not ... the *fun. Ed.*]
        Spud: Not ... the *fun. MS Om.
        E1*
551:35 Why] ~, *E1*
551:35 *impossible*] impossible *E1*
552:5   we're not] we've not been *TS*
552:5   flirting—] ~. *TS*
552:8   Yes] ~, *E1*
552:10 Oh] Ah, *E1 see notes*
552:11 anyway Spud.] ~, ~? *E1*
552:13 don'] don't *TS*
552:15 SPUD: Well ... want to. *Ed.*]
        Spud: Well ... want to. *MS
        Om. E1*
552:19 *don'*] *don't TS*
552:21 reason.] ~? *E1*
552:23 Well *I*] ~, I *TS*
552:25 *meanness!*] ~. *TS*
552:28 love's] Love's *TS*

552:29 goodness] ~' *E1*
552:30 *want*] want *TS*
552:30 Elizabeth,] ~ *TS*
552:32 don't-wanter *Ed.*] dont-wanter
        MS don't wanter *TS*
552:32 All] Till *E1 see note on* 552:10
552:34 *fun!*] *fun. TS* fun. *E1*
552:38 then] ~, *E1*
552:39 *act*] act *E1*
552:39 don't-wanter *TS*] dont-wanter
        MS
553:3   *shouts Ed.*] shouts *MS* snorts
        TS snorts *E1*
553:4   *good*] good *TS*
553:6   *not going*] not going *TS*
553:10 *can*] can *E1*
553:10 *intend*] intend *TS*
553:11 married!] ~, *TS* ~. *E1*
553:14 twice:] ~; *TS*
553:15 *you've*] you've *TS*
553:18 *marriage*] marriage *E1*
553:24 young. Spud!] ~, ~. *E1*
553:25 Well] ~, *TS*
553:28 Lo-o-ve] L-o-o-ve *TS*
553:29 Well] ~, *E1*
553:35 —But] ~ *TS*
553:36 Spud.] ~? *TS*
553:37 I tell] I'll tell *TS*
553:37 you,] ~. *TS*
554:2   de—ar] de-ar *TS*
554:2   *doing!*] ~? *E1*

Noah's Flood

MSI   = First autograph MS (Roberts E273a)
MSII = Second autograph MS (Roberts E273b)
TCC   = Typed carbon-copy (Roberts E273d; E273e; E273c)
A1   = *Phoenix* (Viking Press, 1936)

From 557:3 to 564:25, whenever the *MSI* reading is adopted, it appears within the square bracket with no symbol. Other variants appear in chronological order as given above. In the absence of information to the contrary, the reader should assume that a variant recurs in subsequent states.

When a reading from a source other than *MSI* has been preferred or coincides with the adopted reading, it appears with its source-symbol within the square bracket; the *MSI* reading follows the bracket along with further variants from later states.

From 564:26 onwards, *MSI* is the only textual source; there is one editorial emendation, at 565:1. The apparatus is used to record authorial revisions in *MSI*. The entry to the left of the square bracket indicates the final reading: the entry to the right of the bracket indicates the reading before the author revised it.

557:3 [1ST MAN ... [557:11] COSBY] *Ed.*] *Om. MSI*

557:12 Noah. *MSII*] Shem + Kanah, Ham + Shelah, Japhet + Cosby *MSI* NOAH *TCC*

557:12 Shem the Utterer ... shall be *MSII*] Shem—the utterer—the *I am. It is* / Kanah—the echoer—*It was. It shall be MSI* SHEM (the Utterer) / I am, it is {is. *A1*} / and KANAH (the echoer {Echoer *A1*}) / it was, it shall be. *TCC*

557:14 Ham (Heat) ... (Flux) *MSII*] Ham—Heat / Shelah—Flux. *MSI* HAM (Heat) and SHELAH (Flux) *TCC*

557:15 Japhet (encompassing ... Kultur-träger) *MSII*] Japhit— Encompassing,—spreading— father of all: also *Destroyer* / —father of fire—the injurer —the male-female / Cosby —the female-male—the Kultur-träger / Noah—Cronos.— Jathir *MSI* JAPHET (encompassing, spreading, Father of All: also Destroyer) and / COSBY (female-male. Kultur-träger {Kulturträger *A1*}) *TCC*

559:1 *Noah's Flood Ed.*] *Om. MSI* Noah's Flood *MSII* NOAH'S FLOOD *TCC*

559:3 dark *MSII*] dusky *MSI*

559:5 Himself *MSII*] Himself he *MSI*

559:5 says the *MSII*] says that *MSI*

559:7 think you *MSII*] do you think *MSI*

559:8 than the sons] ~ ~ Sons *MSI*

559:8 God. *MSII*] ~? *MSI, TCC*

559:9 —The] ~ *TCC*

559:10 what *MSII*] who *MSI*

559:11 it ... Ask *MSII*] they are more stupid, it seems to me. Ask our *MSI*

559:12 demi-gods! *MSII*] ~. *MSI*

559:13 Sons *MSII*] sons *MSI, TCC*

559:15 snorts, ... wall. *MSII*] snorts. *MSI*

559:17 do we *MSII*] we will *MSI*

559:18 demi-gods, old ... Japhet. *MSII*] demi-gods: Noah, the Old One, and Shem, and Ham, and Japhet, the three sons of god. *MSI*

559:21 Bird *MSII*] bird *MSI*

559:23 name! *MSII*] ~. *MSI, TCC*

559:23 What *MSII*] But what *MSI*

559:23 who its *MSII*] who is its *MSI*

559:25 did *MSII*] would *MSI*

559:25 a *MSII*] the *MSI*

559:27 that ... Fire *MSII*] the bird that they call Fire, *MSI*

559:30 But his sons may *MSII*] Neither will his sons *MSI*

559:31 her] the *TCC*

559:32 ones *MSII*] one *MSI*

559:34 already are wittier *MSII*] are cleverer already *MSI*

559:34 god] God *TCC*

560:1 could *MSII*] would *MSI*

560:2 god] God *A1*

560:2 have *MSII*] take *MSI*

560:3 it should be *MSII*] we ought *MSI*

560:4 god] God *MSI, A1*

560:5 secret *MSII*] secrets *MSI*

560:5 save that *MSII*] except the secret *MSI*

560:6 god command and chide, but *MSII*] god, *MSI* God command ... but *A1*

560:7 Why are ... now be *MSII*] They live but by the trick of guarding the red bird, which is no more theirs than *MSI*

560:11 And *MSII*] —~ *MSI*

560:11 secret *MSII*] ~, *MSI*

560:11 power: merely *MSII*] ~! Merely *MSI*

560:14 beneath his ... mocked him. *MSII*] at him, and mocked his beard. *MSI*

560:15 Yet this ... dark bread. *MSII*] Om. *MSI*

560:16 swear *MSII*] take an oath, *MSI*

560:16 bird, *MSII*] ~ *MSI*

560:17 the demi-gods, *MSII*] these demi-gods *MSI*

560:20 Yes *MSI*] Yea *MSI* ~, *TCC*

560:21 Fire!] ~? *TCC*

560:21 the *MSII*] these *MSI*

560:21 demi-gods,] ~ *TCC*

560:22 catch the red bird, *MSII*] take this bird called Fire, we must *MSI*

560:23 us,] ~ *TCC*

560:24 like feathers of the sun, *MSII*] Om. *MSI*

560:24 hotter *MSII*] warmer *MSI*

560:27 heaven *MSII*] in the sky *MSI*

560:27 best *MSII*] brightest *MSI*

560:30 shivers seize us *MSII*] we shiver *MSI*

560:31 daytime] day-time *A1*

560:34 brightens *MSII*] warms *MSI*

560:35 fell *MSII*] turned *MSI*

560:36 Shem says? *MSII*] the Shem says. *MSI see notes*

560:37 bird *MSII*] bird that flutters *MSI*

560:37 demi-gods— *MSII*] ~. *MSI*

560:38 that *MSII*] this *MSI*

561:1 ferns *MSII*] leaven of ferns *MSI*

561:2 brown; *MSII*] ~, *MSI*, *TCC*

561:3 Ay, *MSII*] Yea, that is *MSI*

561:3 sun! But *MSII*] sun, and *MSI*

561:4 ray-feathers,] ~ *TCC*

561:4 through grey dust across *MSII*] in the dust of *MSI*

561:4 He is ... depended on *MSII*] We can't depend on him *MSI*

561:6 Ham *MSII*] that Ham *MSI*

561:6 we will forget the sick *MSII*] we'll dispense with the sickly *MSI*

561:7 in our *MSII*] down here, in our own *MSI*

561:9 Yet *MSII*] Yes, but *MSI*

561:11 that no ... ever seen *MSII*] the third one, that no man ever sees *MSI*

561:14 In the middle *MSII*] Deep at the centre *MSI*

561:14 a nest ... world. And *MSII*] the nest of the great white bird, and *MSI* a nest, and in ... world. And *TCC*

561:18 is a young one that *MSII*] Om. *MSI*

561:19 across *MSII*] Om. *MSI*

561:19 bough *MSII*] bough each day *MSI*

561:20 near us, each day, *MSII*] Om. *MSI*

561:20 feathers *MSII*] yellow feathers *MSI*

561:21 dust of space *MSII*] space-dust *MSI*

561:21 so *MSII*] so that *MSI*

561:21 him in the *MSII*] nought but *MSI*

561:21 flashing his *MSII*] and yellow flashing of *MSI*

561:22 —But] ~ *TCC*

561:22 fume of the *MSII*] puther of *MSI*

561:23 seeing, *MSII*] seeing, lives *MSI*

561:23 roosts *MSII*] Om. *MSI*

561:30 told *MSII*] has told *MSI*

561:31 Shem *MSII*] Shem! Shem *MSI*

561:31 fooling thee. *MSII*] clever at throwing dust in thy eyes.— *MSI*

561:31 thee the *MSII*] the the *MSI*

561:34 will he *MSII*] he will *MSI*

561:34 a great *MSII*] the Great *MSI* a Great *TCC*

561:34 Duck *MSII*] Bird *MSI*

561:35 will see. *MSII*] can see!— *MSI*

561:36 Nay!] ~, *TCC*

561:36 for *MSII*] For *MSI*

561:37 bough *MSII*] ~, *MSI*

561:37 western *MSII*] west *MSI*

561:38 air *MSII*] ~, *MSI*

561:39 heading *MSII*] headway *MSI*

562:1 air, dead *MSII*] air *MSI*

562:1 breast, save *MSII*] breasts of men, unless *MSI*

562:1 fresh *MSII*] Om. *MSI*

562:5 heavy sky, *MSII*] ~, ~, *MSI* *see notes*

562:5 send us . . . for us *MSII*] are folded, there is no joy *MSI*

562:6 so *MSII*] so it is that *MSI*

562:6 shiver, *MSII*] ~ *MSI*

562:7 upon us beforehand *MSII*] in our breast *MSI*

562:8 will no *MSII*] no more *MSI*

562:8 wave *MSII*] lifts *MSI*

562:8 gladly towards us *MSII*] for gladness *MSI*

562:9 should he be *MSII*] is he *MSI*

562:10 never *MSII*] no longer *MSI*

562:13 the sky . . . a voice *MSII*] an army calling aloud *MSI*

562:14 deep *MSII*] Om. *MSI*

562:15 wildness *MSII*] perfume *MSI*

562:16 sips *MSII*] breathes *MSI*

562:16 —But] ~ *TCC*

562:17 are answerless . . . universe. It . . . [562:21] us. So *MSII*] have turned away from the sun and the Bird beyond the sun. The hearts of men turn towards the beasts. Men have their backs to the Great White Bird, their hearts beat towards the beasts, towards the downward track, and the lust of degradation. So the bird lifts his wings no more to send his wind among us in the great freshness. And *MSI*

are answerless . . . Universe. It . . . going!—{going! *A1*} So . . . us. So *TCC*

562:22 and *MSII*] Om. *MSI*

562:22 towards deadness. We capture *MSII*] to the beasts, and to the vegetables, and to the metals which we worship, *MSI*

562:23 metal,] ~ *TCC*

562:23 and we . . . [562:29] fist. And *MSII*] which called the first answer to the Great White Bird, as the cock at dawn crows to the sun. We turn back to the old answerers, to the beast and the plant and the yellow-gold, and we give no answer of our own. We go down the slope of degradation, and *MSI* and we . . . answer.—{answer. *A1*} . . . fist. And *TCC*

562:30 1ST MAN: What . . . blue-brilliant . . . answerless.— . . . them, they . . . [562:40] their laughter. *Ed.*] 1st MAN: {1st. Man. *TCC* 1st Man: *A1*} What . . . blue-brilliant {blue, less brilliant *TCC*} . . . answerless.— {answerless. *TCC*} . . . them, they {them; they *TCC*} . . . their laughter. *MSII* Om. *MSI*

563:1 talker! *MSII*] ~. *MSI*

566:2 a *MSII*] Shem's *MSI*

566:2 decoy-duck, *MSII*] decoy duck, *MSI* decoy-duck *TCC*

563:2 decoy] drag *TCC*

563:3 cannot stoop . . . fern seed . . . of men.— *MSII*] have no meaning when men abandon them. *MSI* cannot stoop . . . fern-seed . . . of men.— *TCC* cannot stoop . . . fern seed . . . of men. *A1*

563:4 a fool *MSII*] the fool *MSI*

563:5 duck *MSII*] duck which is *MSI*

563:5 net.—] ~. *TCC*

563:6 And Japhet is *MSII*] Japhet is too *MSI*

563:6 Ah, *MSII*] ~ *MSI*

563:7 sons *MSII*] children *MSI*

563:7 your life . . . predicament. You *MSII*] you who *MSI*

563:7 warm and *MSII*] the warm and the *MSI*

563:8 cold, *MSII*] ~; *MSI, TCC*

563:8 care. If you fall into great *MSII*] care where you tread. If you fall among the *MSI*

563:9 down the crevices of *MSII*] over the edge of the *MSI*

563:10 vanished *MSII*] not *MSI*

563:11 are swept *MSII*] have passed *MSI*

563:11 heat nor . . . the waters *MSII*] heat, neither will the waters bear up your life *MSI*

563:13 must *MSII*] Om. *MSI*

563:14 for if *MSII*] but you know not whither the stream is going, nor whence it came. If *MSI*

563:14 but *MSII*] and *MSI*

563:15 likewise you *MSII*] you likewise *MSI*

563:15 of the . . . ask not *MSII*] Om. *MSI*

563:16 cometh nor *MSII*] cometh, and *MSI*

563:16 goeth. It *MSII*] goeth, the stream, you never ask. Though it *MSI*

563:16 forever] for ever *A1*

563:17 it *MSII*] and *MSI*

563:17 so *MSII*] Om. *MSI*

563:17 say:] ~. *TCC*

563:18 banks *MSII*] place of the stream be bare; watch lest the banks *MSI see note on* 563:19

563:19 the flood *MSII*] a flood *MSI*

563:19 wolves which are on the scent. And *MSII*] dogs that have slipped the leash of the frost, and *MSI*

563:20 on you *MSII*] to you from the sky *MSI*

563:21 from the sky, *MSII*] Om. *MSI*

563:22 are the wolves running for *MSII*] slipped the leash of the frost *MSI*

563:23 mid-heaven? . . . not. You *MSII*] mid-heaven, you know not and you *MSI*

563:24 a *MSII*] the *MSI*

563:24 forever] for ever *A1*

563:24 Ask then . . . Ask, and {Ask and *TCC*} . . . Oh wonderful {Oh, wonderful *TCC*} . . . serves.—So {serves. So *A1*} . . . [563:34] question. {questions. *TCC*} *MSII*] So says Japhet. *MSI*

563:35 It is so. *MSII*] Om. *MSI*

563:35 red bird in our hand *MSII*] bird called Fire *MSI*

563:36 force the . . . in obedience. So *MSII*] dispense with the sun and the Great White Bird, and *MSI*

563:38 sky, in . . . red bird. *MSII*] sky. All we need is this bird called Fire. This is all these demi-gods possess, which we do not possess. And with it, we are greater than they, for they are stupid and vague. *MSI*

564:1 true. That *MSII*] true, this *MSI*

564:1 need *MSII*] want *MSI*

564:2 take *MSII*] capture *MSI*

564:2 house, and . . . Men masters {Men, masters *A1*} . . . Sun shall {sun shall *A1*} . . . [564:11] his own. *MSII*] house. Let us be free. / 3rd Man: Ah Freedom! Let us be free! Free of these demi-gods. Men masters of Fire, and free on the face of the earth. / 1st Man: Men masters of fire, and free on the face of the earth! Ah hope! *MSI*

564:13 not? *MSII*] ~! *MSI, TCC*

564:13 heirs and successors of *MSII*]
later even than *MSI*
564:14 god *MSII*] God *MSI, A1*
564:15 fire: for it is a gift. *MSII*] fire.
MSI
564:15 to them, *MSII*] them *MSI*
564:16 god *MSII*] God *MSI, A1*
564:16 us *MSII*] us thou *MSI*
564:17 gift!— *MSII*] ~. *MSI* ~.—
TCC, A1
564:17 said: Nay! *MSII*] ~; ~, *MSI*
564:17 ye know not ... given you
MSII] your hearts are towards
the beast *MSI*
564:19 take. *MSII*] ~! *MSI*
564:20 Yes, we .. of them *MSII*] We
will take it, and be free *MSI*
564:21 sons of god *MSII*] the demi
gods *MSI* sons of God *A1*

564:21 We *MSII*] We will take our
own. We *MSI*
564:21 all. Let ... flutterer, and
{flutterer and *TCC*} ... said, it
{said: it *TCC*} ... a gift!
MSII] all the world. We have
right to everything. Let us take
it soon. / 1st Man: We will do
so. *MSI*
564:40 HAM {Ham *MSI*} *Ed.*] Shem
565:1 Kanah] Kir [...]
565:3 counsel] great counsel
565:12 between your eyes?] on your
brow?
565:29 here in] in
566:18 cheese] cheeses
566:30 Therefore] Wherefore
566:31 god] gold
567:12 Great] great

Of the compound words which are hyphenated at the end of a line in this edition,
only the following hyphenated forms should be retained in quotation:

5:29	*arm-chair*		397:36	low-down
12:2	*pit-breeches*		405:11	every-day-has-its-tomorrow
14:1	*dust-pan*		416:18	Good-night
15:34	*half-filled*		419:12	Good-evening
30:36	*terror-struck*		421:1	phrase-maker
38:29	*bread-charcoal*		424:15	whoam-it
59:9	*table-cloth*		438:12	blood-sacrifice
114:32	white-faced		449:5	well-nigh
161:27	whit-leather		467:37	ARMOUR-BEARER
174:16	dog-tired		479:30	Lu-a-li-lu-lu-lu
198:19	*self-possessed*		481:33	Lu-lu-lu-lu-al-li-lu-lu
239:11	*maid-servant*		481:37	Lu-lu-a-li-lu-lu-lu
239:13	*soup-tureen*		486:20	horn-anointed
245:14	table-cloths		489:7	Ha-ha
249:17	good-looking		498:39	men-at-arms
310:29	go-day		541:19	one-third
318:14	*pit-dirt*		541:28	go-between
322:3	apron-strings		543:8	coffee-pot
328:2	*pit-trousers*		545:29	rose-coloured
328:26	come-day		552:39	don't-wanter
356:5	*re-enter*		559:12	demi-gods
366:18	mechanico-material		559:25	demi-gods
368:4	cart-wheel		562:30	blue-brilliant
388:31	half-demented		563:39	half-answers
393:10	self-sacrifice		582:25	harp-strings
394:17	country-side			

A note on pounds, shillings and pence

Before decimalisation in 1971, the pound sterling (£) was the equivalent of 20 shillings (20/- or 20s). The shilling was the equivalent of 12 pence (12d). A price could therefore have three elements: pounds, shillings and pence (£, s, d). (The apparently anomalous 'd' is an abbreviation of the Latin *denarius*, but the other two terms were also originally Latin: the pound was *libra*; the shilling *solidus*.) Such a price might be written as £1 2s 6d or £1/2/6; this was spoken as 'one pound, two shillings and sixpence', or 'one pound two-and-six', or 'twenty-two and six'.

Prices below a pound were written (for example) 19s 6d, or 19/6, and spoken as 'nineteen shillings and sixpence' or 'nineteen and six'. Prices up to £5 were sometimes spoken in terms of shillings: so 'ninety-nine and six' was £4/19/6.

The penny was divided into two half-pence (pronounced 'ha'pence') and further divided into four farthings, but the farthing had minimal value and was mainly a tradesman's device for indicating a price fractionally below a shilling or pound. So 19/11¾ (nineteen and elevenpence three farthings) produced a farthing's change from a pound, this change often given as a tiny item of trade, such as a packet of pins.

The guinea was £1/1/- (one pound, one shilling) and was a professional man's unit for fees. A doctor would charge in guineas (so £5/5/- = 5 gns). Half a guinea was 10s 6d or 10/6 (ten and six).

The coins used were originally of silver (later cupro-nickel) and copper, though gold coins for £1 (a sovereign) and 10s (half-sovereign) were still in use in Lawrence's time. The largest silver coin in common use was the half-crown (two shillings and sixpence, or 2/6). A two-shilling piece was called a florin. Shillings, sixpences and threepences were the smaller sizes of silver coins. The copper coins were pennies, half-pence and farthings.

Common slang terms for money were 'quid' for a pound, 'half a crown', 'two bob' for a florin, 'bob' for a shilling (or shilling piece), 'tanner' for a sixpence (or sixpenny piece), 'threepenny-bit' (pronounced 'thripenny-bit'), and 'coppers' for pennies, half-pence or farthings; two pence would be pronounced 'tuppence'.

0 9 MAY 2018

Lightning Source UK Ltd.
Milton Keynes UK
UKOW02f0056151016

285209UK00004B/13/P